F·I·R·S·T C·A·N·A·D·I·A·N E·D·I·T·I·O·N

PRINCIPLES OF CORPORATE FINANCE

RICHARD BREALE
London Business School

◆

STEWART MYERS
Massachusetts Institute of Technology

◆

GORDON SICK
University of Alberta

◆

ROBERT WHALEY
University of Alberta

McGRAW-HILL RYERSON LIMITED
Toronto Montreal Auckland Bogotá Cairo Guatemala Hamburg
Lisbon London Madrid Mexico New Delhi Panama Paris San Juan São Paulo
Singapore Sydney Tokyo

PRINCIPLES OF CORPORATE FINANCE

FIRST CANADIAN EDITION

ISBN 0-07-548572-9

3 4 5 6 7 8 9 0 THB 5 4 3 2 1 0 9 8

Printed and bound in Canada

Canadian Cataloguing in Publication Data

Brealey, Richard A.
  Principles of corporate finance

Includes index.
ISBN 0-07-548572-9

1. Corporations – Finance. I. Myers, Stewart C. II. Sick, Gordon A., date –   III. Title.

HG4026.B684 1986   658.1'5   C85-099828-X

TO OUR PARENTS

CONTENTS

PART 4   PRACTICAL PROBLEMS IN CAPITAL BUDGETING

PART 6 DIVIDEND POLICY AND CAPITAL STRUCTURE

PART 10   MERGERS, INTERNATIONAL FINANCE, AND PENSIONS

PART 11   CONCLUSIONS

PREFACE

This book describes the theory and practice of corporate finance. We hardly need explain why financial managers should master the practical aspect of their job, but a word on the role of theory may be helpful.

Managers learn from experience how to cope with routine problems. But the best managers are also able to respond rationally to change. To do this you need more than time-honoured rules of thumb; you must understand *why* companies and financial managers behave the way they do. In other words, you need a *theory* of corporate finance.

Does that sound intimidating? It shouldn't. Good theory helps you understand what is going on in the world around you. It helps you ask the right questions when times change and new problems must be analyzed. It also tells you what things you do *not* need to worry about.

Throughout the book we show how to use financial theory to solve practical problems, and also to illuminate the facts and institutional material that students of corporate finance must absorb.

Of course the theory presented in this book is not perfect and complete—no theory is. There are some famous controversies in which financial economists cannot agree on what firms ought to do. We have not glossed over these controversies. We set out the main arguments for each side and tell you where we stand.

There are also a few cases where theory indicates that the practical rules of thumb employed by today's managers are leading to poor decisions. Where financial managers appear to be making mistakes, we say so, while admitting that there may be hidden reasons for their actions. In brief, we have tried to be fair but to pull no punches.

Once understood, good theory is common sense. Therefore we have tried to present it at a commonsense level. We have avoided abstract proofs and heavy mathematics. However, parts of the book may require a significant intellectual effort for those unused to economic reasoning. We have marked the most difficult sections and problems with asterisks, and suggest that you skim these sections on the first reading.

There are no ironclad prerequisites for reading this book except algebra and the English language. An elementary knowledge of accounting, statistics, and microeconomics is helpful, however. The study guide for this book (Charles A. D'Ambrosio, Stewart D. Hodges, Gordon A. Sick, and Robert E. Whaley, *Study Guide to Accompany Principles of Corporate Finance,* McGraw-Hill Ryerson, Toronto, 1986) includes chapter summaries, additional illustrations, solved problems, and other useful material.

Each chapter of this book closes with a summary, an annotated list of suggestions for further reading, a quick and easy quiz, and several more challenging questions and problems. Answers to the quiz questions may be found at the end of the book, along with present value tables and a glossary.

We should mention two matters of style now to prevent confusion later. First, you will notice that the most important financial terms are set in **boldface** type the first time they appear. Second, most algebraic symbols representing dollar values are set in capital letters. Other symbols are lowercase letters. Thus the symbol for a dividend payment is DIV; the symbol for a percentage of rate of return is r. We hope this will make our algebra easier to follow.

Readers of the previous world edition of this book may be interested to know what we have changed and added. We have added information about Canadian tax and corporate law as well as about Canadian financial institutions. Most of the corporate tax law appears in Chapter 6 and most of the personal tax law appears in Chapter 16. Bankruptcy law appears in Chapter 28. Information about Canadian money market instruments appears in Chapter 30. Other additions include a recognition of the problem of estimating systematic risk in the presence of infrequent stock trading (Chapter 9), a problem that is more significant in Canada than elsewhere. We have changed most of the real-life examples to relate to Canadian firms. However, we left some of the examples unchanged to reflect international flavour that was in the original text, particularly when the original example provided a cleaner or more straightforward illustration. The end-of-chapter quizzes and problems were expanded and altered to be consistent with the Canadian environment. The Appendix Tables were expanded and put into an easier-to-read format.

We have a long list of people to thank for their comments on our drafts and for their help with Canadian details: Laxmi Bhandari, Karen Farkas, Clyde Hurtig, Patricia Irwin, Henry Kennedy, Kevin Lewis, Rolf Mirus, Dave Mulder, Glen Mumey, Bill Rozeboom, Sondra Whaley, Bernard Yeung (all at the University of Alberta), Gail Frose, Ron Giammarino, John Jacobson, Alex Jeletzky (all of the University of British Columbia), Phelim Boyle, Ed Nosal, and Keith Sharp (of the University of Waterloo).

This list is almost surely incomplete. We know how much we owe to our colleagues and students. In many cases, the ideas that appear in this book are as much theirs as ours. Finally, we record the thanks we have personally conveyed to our wives, Diana, Maureen, Sondra, and Carmel, who for too long have found their lives disrupted by The Book.

Richard Brealey
London Business School

Stewart Myers
Sloan School of Business,
Massachusetts Institute of Technology

Gordon Sick
University of Alberta

Robert Whaley
University of Alberta

INTRODUCTION

PART 1

WHY FINANCE MATTERS

This book is about financial decisions by corporations. We should start by saying what these decisions are and why they are important.

To carry on business a modern company needs an almost endless variety of **real assets**. Many of them are tangible assets, such as machinery, factories, and offices; others are intangible, such as technical expertise, trademarks, and patents. All of them unfortunately need to be paid for. To obtain the necessary money the company sells pieces of paper called **financial assets**, or securities. These pieces of paper have value because they are claims on the firm's real assets. Financial assets include not only shares of stock but also bonds, bank loans, lease obligations, and so on.

The financial manager faces two basic problems. First, how much should the firm invest, and what specific assets should the firm invest in? Second, how should the cash required for investment be raised? The answer to the first question is the firm's **investment**, or **capital budgeting**, **decision**. The answer to the second is its **financing decision**. The financial manager attempts to find the specific answers that make the firm's shareholders as well off as possible.

Success is usually judged by value: shareholders are made better off by any decision that increases the value of their stake in the firm. Thus, you might say that a good investment decision is one that results in purchase of a real asset that is worth more than it costs—an asset that makes a net contribution to value. The secret of success in financial management is to increase value. That is a simple statement, but not a very helpful one. It is like advising an investor in the stock market to "buy low, sell high." The problem is how to do it.

1-1 WHY FINANCE IS CHALLENGING AND INTERESTING

There may be a few activities in which one can read a textbook and then "do it," but financial management is not one of them. That is why finance is worth studying. Who wants to work in a field where there is no room for experience, creativity, judgement, and a pinch of luck? Although this book cannot supply any of these items, it does present the concepts and information on which good financial decisions are based.

There are many reasons that the financial manager's job is challenging and interesting. Here are four important ones.

The Importance of Capital Markets

The first reason is that the financial manager must act as an intermediary, standing between the firm's operations and **capital markets**, where the firm's securities are traded. The financial manager's role is shown in Figure 1-1, which traces the flow of cash from investors to the firm and back to investors again. The flow starts when securities are issued to raise cash (arrow 1 in the figure). The cash is used to purchase real assets

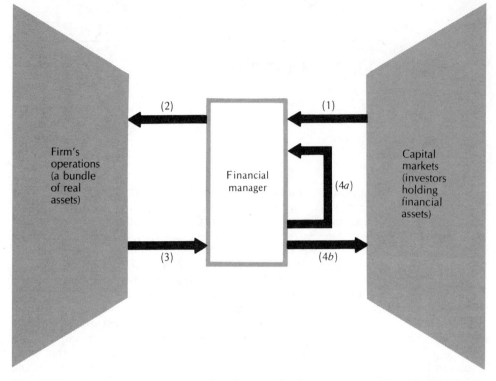

Figure 1-1 Flow of cash between capital markets and the firm's operations. Key: (1) cash raised by selling financial assets to investors; (2) cash invested in the firm's operations and used to purchase real assets; (3) cash generated by the firm's operations; (4a) cash reinvested; (4b) cash returned to investors.

Source: From *Modern Developments in Financial Management*, S.C. Myers, ed. Copyright © 1976 by Praeger Publishers, Inc., New York. Reprinted by permission of Holt, Rinehart and Winston.

used in the firm's operations (arrow 2). (You can think of the firm's operations as a bundle of real assets.) Later, if the firm does well, the real assets generate cash inflows, which more than repay the initial investment (arrow 3). Finally, the cash is either reinvested (arrow 4a) or returned to the investors who purchased the original security issue (arrow 4b). Of course the choice between arrows 4a and 4b is not a completely free one. For example, if a bank loans the firm money at stage 1, the bank has to be repaid this money plus interest at stage 4b.

Figure 1-1 shows that the financial manager has to deal with capital markets as well as the firm's operations. Therefore, the financial manager must understand how capital markets work.

The financing decision always reflects some theory about capital markets. For example, suppose a firm chooses to finance a major expansion program by issuing bonds. The financial manager must have considered the terms of the issue and concluded that it was fairly priced. That required a theory of how bonds are priced. The financial manager must also have asked whether the firm's stockholders would be made better or worse off by the extra debt standing between them and the firm's real assets. That required a theory of how corporate borrowing affects the well-being of stockholders.

The investment decision cannot be separated from capital markets either. A firm that acts in its stockholders' interest should accept those investments that increase the value of their stake in the firm. But that requires a theory of how common stocks are valued.

Understanding Value

Understanding how capital markets work amounts to understanding how financial assets are valued. This is a subject on which there has been remarkable progress over the past ten to twenty years. New theories have been developed to explain the prices of bonds and stocks. And, when put to the test, these theories have worked well. We therefore devote a large part of this book to explaining these ideas and their implications.

Time and Uncertainty

The financial manager cannot avoid coping with time and uncertainty. Firms often have the opportunity to invest in assets that cannot pay their way in the short run and that expose the firm and its stockholders to considerable risk. The investment, if undertaken, may have to be financed by debt that cannot be fully repaid for many years. The firm cannot walk away from such choices—someone has to decide whether the opportunity is worth more than it costs and whether the additional debt burden can be safely borne.

Understanding People

The financial manager needs the opinions and cooperation of many people. For instance, many new investment ideas come from plant managers. The financial manager wants these ideas to be presented fairly; therefore, the proposers should have no personal incentives to be either overconfident or overcautious. Take another example. In some firms the plant manager needs permission from the head office to buy a company car but not to lease it, and the line of least resistance may be to lease the car. In other firms the plant manager needs permission from the head office to buy or lease, and the line of least resistance may be to travel everywhere by cab. The financial manager has to be aware of these effects and has to devise procedures that will avoid as far as possible any conflicts of interest.

These are not the only reasons that financial management is interesting and challenging. We think that as you read this book you will find many others.

1-2 WHO IS THE FINANCIAL MANAGER?

In this book we will use the term *financial manager* to refer to anyone responsible for a significant corporate investment or financing decision. But except in the smallest firms, no *single* person is responsible for all the decisions discussed in this book. Responsibility is dispersed throughout the firm. Top management is of course continuously involved in financial decisions. But the engineer who designs a new production facility is also involved: the design determines the kind of real asset the firm will hold. The advertising manager may also make important investment decisions in the course of his or her work. A major advertising campaign is really an investment in an intangible asset. If potential customers are aware of your product and convinced they should buy it, you have an asset that will pay off in future sales and earnings.

Nevertheless, there are some managers who specialize in finance. The **treasurer** is usually the person most directly responsible for obtaining financing, managing the firm's cash account and its relationships with banks and other financial institutions, and making sure the firm meets its obligations to the investors holding its securities. Typical responsibilities of the treasurer are listed in the left-hand column of Table 1-1.

Table 1-1 Some typical responsibilities of the treasurer and controller.

Treasurer	Controller
Banking relationships	Accounting
Cash management	Preparation of financial statements
Obtaining financing	Internal auditing
Credit management	Payroll
Dividend disbursement	Custody of records
Insurance	Preparing budgets
Pensions management	Taxes

Note: This table is not an exhaustive list of tasks treasurers and controllers may undertake.

For small firms, the treasurer is likely to be the only financial executive. However, larger corporations usually also have a **controller**. The right-hand column of Table 1-1 lists the typical controller's responsibilities. Notice that there is a conceptual difference between the two jobs. The treasurer's function is primarily custodial—he or she obtains and manages the company's capital. By contrast, the controller's function is primarily one of inspecting to see that the money is used efficiently. The controller manages budgeting, accounting, and auditing.

The largest firms usually appoint a financial vice-president, who acts as the chief financial officer, overseeing both the treasurer's and the controller's work. In addition, the financial vice-president is deeply involved in financial policy making and corporate planning. Often he or she will have general managerial responsibilities beyond strictly financial issues.

Major capital investment projects are so closely tied to plans for product development, production, and marketing that managers from these areas are inevitably drawn into planning and analyzing the projects. If the firm has staff members specializing in corporate planning, they are naturally involved in capital budgeting too. Usually the treasurer, controller, or financial vice-president is responsible for organizing and supervising the capital budgeting process.

Because of the importance of many financial issues, ultimate decisions often rest by law or by custom with the board of directors.[1] For example, only the board has the legal power to declare a dividend or to sanction a public issue of securities. Boards usually delegate decision-making authority for small- or medium-sized investment outlays. But the authority to approve large investments is almost never delegated.

1-3 TOPICS COVERED IN THIS BOOK

This book covers investment decisions first, then financing decisions, and finally a series of topics in which investment and financing decisions interact and cannot be made separately.

In Parts 2, 3, and 4 we look at three different aspects of the investment decision. The first is the problem of how to value assets, the second is the link between risk and value, and the third is the management of the investment process. Our discussion of these topics occupies Chapters 2 to 12.

Eleven chapters devoted to the simple problem of "finding real assets that are worth more than they cost" may seem excessive, but that problem is not so simple in practice. Also, a conceptual base must be laid. So far, we have only asserted that increasing value is the appropriate financial objective for the firm. That assertion will have to be

---

[1]Often the firm's chief financial officer is also a member of its board of directors.

proved. We will also require a theory of how long-lived, risky assets are valued, and that requirement will lead us to basic questions about capital markets. For example:

- How are corporate bonds and stocks valued in capital markets?
- What risks are borne by investors in corporate securities? How can these risks be measured?
- What compensation do investors demand for bearing risk?
- What rate of return can investors in common stocks reasonably expect to receive?

Intelligent capital budgeting and financing decisions require answers to these and other questions about how capital markets work.

Financing decisions occupy Parts 5 through 7. We begin in Chapter 13 with another basic question about capital markets: "Do security prices reflect the fair value of the underlying assets?" The reason this question is so important is that the financial manager must know whether securities can be issued at a fair price. Exactly how and when securities should be issued are the subjects of the remaining chapters in Part 5.

Parts 6 and 7 continue the analysis of the financing decision, covering dividend policy, debt policy, and the alternative forms of debt. Literally dozens of different financing instruments are described and analyzed, including debentures, convertibles, term loans, leases, eurobonds, and many other exotic beasts. We will also describe what happens when firms find themselves in financial distress because of poor operating performance, excessive borrowing, or both. Furthermore, we will show how financing considerations sometimes affect capital budgeting decisions.

Part 8 covers financial planning. Decisions about investment, dividend policy, debt policy, and other financial issues cannot be reached independently. They have to add up to a sensible overall financial plan for the firm, one which increases the value of the shareholders' investment yet still retains enough flexibility for the firm to avoid financial distress and to pursue unexpected new opportunities.

Part 9 is devoted to decisions about the firm's short-term assets and liabilities. There are separate chapters on three topics: channels for short-term borrowing or investment, management of liquid assets (cash and marketable securities), and management of accounts receivable (money lent by the firm to its customers).

Part 10 covers three important problems that require decisions about both investment and financing. We first look at mergers and acquisitions. Then we consider international financial management. All the financial problems of doing business at home are present overseas, but the international financial manager faces the additional complication of dealing in more than one currency.

The final chapter in Part 10 describes how pension plans are created and financed by corporations. Pension plan management is not a traditional subject in corporate finance texts, but we think it should be. Pensions represent an enormous liability for corporations in the United States and Canada.

Part 11 is our conclusion. It also discusses some of the things we *don't* know about finance. If you can be the first to solve any of these puzzles, you will be justifiably famous.

1-4 SUMMARY

In Chapter 2 we will begin with the most basic concepts of asset valuation. However, let us first sum up the principal points made in this introductory chapter.

The overall task of financial management can be broken down into (1) the investment, or capital budgeting, decision and (2) the financing decision. In other words, the firm has to decide (1) how much to invest and what assets to invest in and (2) how to raise the necessary cash. The objective is to increase the value of the shareholders' stake in the firm.

The financial manager's job is a challenging and interesting one. He or she acts as an intermediary between the firm and the capital markets. Good financial managers understand how capital markets work and how long-lived, risky assets are valued. They also work to devise procedures and incentives that encourage others in the firm to act sensibly when financial problems arise.

In small companies there is often only one financial executive. However, the larger corporation usually has both a treasurer and a controller. The treasurer's job is to obtain and manage the company's financing. By contrast, the controller's job is one of inspecting to see that the money is used correctly. In large firms there may also be a financial vice-president who acts as the firm's chief financial officer.

Of course all managers, not just finance specialists, face financial problems. In this book we will use the term *financial manager* to refer to any person confronted with a corporate financing or investment decision.

QUIZ

1. Read the following passage: "Companies usually buy __(a)__ assets. These include both tangible assets such as __(b)__ and intangible assets such as __(c)__ . In order to pay for these assets, they sell __(d)__ assets such as __(e)__ . The decision regarding which assets to buy is usually termed the __(f)__ or __(g)__ decision. The decision regarding how to raise the money is usually termed the __(h)__ decision." Now fit each of the following terms into the most appropriate space: *financing, real, bonds, investment, executive airplanes, financial, capital budgeting, brand names.*

2. Which of the following statements more accurately describes the treasurer rather than the controller?
   (*a*) Likely to be the only financial executive in small firms
   (*b*) Monitors capital expenditures to make sure that they are not misappropriated
   (*c*) Responsible for investing the firm's spare cash
   (*d*) Responsible for arranging any issue of common stock
   (*e*) Responsible for the company's tax affairs

3. Which of the following are real assets, and which are financial?
   (*a*) A share of stock
   (*b*) A personal IOU
   (*c*) A trademark
   (*d*) A truck
   (*e*) Undeveloped land
   (*f*) The balance in the firm's chequing account
   (*g*) An experienced and hard working sales force
   (*h*) A corporate bond

VALUE

PART
·2·

THE CONCEPT OF NET PRESENT VALUE

Companies invest in a variety of real assets. These include tangible assets, such as plants and machinery, and intangible assets, such as management contracts and patents. The object of the investment, or capital budgeting, decision is to find real assets that are worth more than they cost. In this chapter we will show what this objective means in a country with extensive and well-functioning capital markets. At the same time we will take the first, most basic steps toward understanding how assets are valued. It turns out that if there is a good market for an asset, its value is exactly the same as the market price.

There are a few cases in which it is not that difficult to estimate asset values. In real estate, for example, you can hire a professional appraiser to do it for you. Suppose you own an apartment building. The odds are that your appraiser's estimate of its value will be within a few percent of what the building would actually sell for.[1] After all, there is continuous activity in the real estate market, and the appraiser's stock-in-trade is knowledge of the prices at which similar properties have recently changed hands.

Thus the problem of valuing real estate is simplified by the existence of an active market in which all kinds of properties are bought and sold. For many purposes no formal theory of value is needed. We can take the market's word for it.

But we have to go deeper than that. First, it is important to know how asset values are reached in an active market. Even if you can take the appraiser's word for it, it is important to understand *why* that apartment building is worth, say, $250,000 and not a higher or lower figure. Second, the market for most corporate assets is pretty thin. Look in the classified advertisements in *The Financial Post* or *The Wall Street Journal*: it is not often that you see a blast furnace for sale.

Companies are always searching for assets that are worth more to them than to others. That apartment house is worth more to you if you can manage it better than others. But in that case, looking at the price of similar buildings will not tell you what your apartment house is worth under your management. You need to know how asset prices are determined. In other words, you need a theory of value.

We start to build that theory in this chapter. We will stick to the simplest problems and examples to make basic ideas clear. Readers with a taste for more complication will find plenty to satisfy them in later chapters.

2-1 INTRODUCTION TO PRESENT VALUE

Later in this chapter we will prove why the concept of present value is useful. However, that concept will go down more easily if we first acquire an intuitive understanding of it.

---

[1] There are some kinds of properties that appraisers find really difficult to value—for example, nobody knows the potential selling price of the Taj Mahal or the Parthenon or the Eiffel Tower. But we assume that your apartment building is a standard property.

Suppose your apartment house burns down, leaving you with a vacant lot worth $50,000 and a cheque for $200,000 from the fire insurance company. You consider rebuilding, but your real estate adviser suggests putting up an office building instead. The construction cost would be $300,000, and there would also be the cost of the land, which might otherwise be sold for $50,000. On the other hand, your adviser foresees a shortage of office space and predicts that a year from now the new building would fetch $400,000 if you sold it. Thus you would be investing $350,000 now in the expectation of realizing $400,000 a year hence. You should go ahead if the **present value** of the expected $400,000 payoff is greater than the investment of $350,000. Therefore, you need to ask yourself, "What is the value today of $400,000 one year from now, and is that present value greater than $350,000?"

Calculating Present Value

The present value of $400,000 one year from now must be less than $400,000. The reason for this is summed up by the following principle: *a dollar today is worth more than a dollar tomorrow*, because the dollar today can be invested to start earning interest immediately.

Thus, the present value of a delayed payoff may be found by multiplying the payoff by a **discount factor** that is less than one. (If the discount factor were more than one, a dollar today would be worth *less* than a dollar tomorrow.) If C_1 denotes the expected payoff at time period 1 (one year hence), then

Present value (PV) = discount factor $\times$ C_1

This discount factor is expressed as the reciprocal of one plus a rate of return:

$$\text{Discount factor} = \frac{1}{1 + r}$$

The rate of return r is the reward investors demand for accepting delayed payment.

Let us consider the real estate investment, assuming for the moment that the $400,000 payoff is a sure thing. The office building is not the only way to obtain $400,000 a year from now. You could invest in federal government securities maturing in a year. Suppose these securities yield 7% interest. How much would you have to invest in them to receive $400,000 at the end of the year? That is an easy question. You would have to invest $400,000/1.07, which is $373,832. Therefore at an interest rate of 7%, the present value of $400,000 one year from now is $373,832.

Let's assume that, as soon as you've committed the land and begun construction on the building, you decide to sell your project. How much could you sell it for? That's another easy question. Since the property produces $400,000, investors would be willing to pay $373,832 for it. That's what it would cost them to get a $400,000 payoff from investing in government securities. Of course you could always sell your property for less, but why sell for less than the market will bear? The $373,832 present value is the only feasible price that satisfies both buyer and seller. Therefore, the present value of the property is also its market price.

To calculate present value, we discount expected future payoffs by the rate of return offered by comparable investment alternatives. This rate of return is often referred to as the **discount rate, hurdle rate,** or **opportunity cost of capital.** It is called the *opportunity cost* because it is the return forgone by investing in the project rather than investing in securities. In our example the opportunity cost was 7%. Present value was obtained by dividing $400,000 by 1.07:

$$PV = \text{discount factor} \times C_1 = \frac{1}{1 + r} C_1 = \frac{400{,}000}{1.07} = \$373{,}832$$

Net Present Value

The building is worth \$373,832, but this does not mean that you are \$373,832 better off. You committed \$350,000, and therefore your **net present value** is \$23,832. Net present value (**NPV**) is found by subtracting the required investment:

$$NPV = PV - \text{required investment} = 373{,}832 - 350{,}000 = \$23{,}832$$

In other words, your office development is worth more than it costs—it makes a *net* contribution to value. The formula for calculating NPV can be written as

$$NPV = C_0 + \frac{C_1}{1 + r}$$

remembering that C_0, the cash flow at time period 0 (that is, today) will usually be a negative number. In other words, C_0 is an investment and therefore a cash *outflow*. In our example, $C_0 = -\$350{,}000$.

A Comment on Risk and Present Value

We made one unrealistic assumption in our discussion of the office development: your real estate adviser cannot be *certain* about future values of office buildings. The \$400,000 figure represents the best *forecast*, but it is not a sure thing.

Therefore, our conclusion about how much investors would pay for the building is wrong. Since they could achieve \$400,000 with certainty by buying \$373,832 worth of federal government securities, they would not buy your building for that amount. You would have to cut your asking price to attract investors' interest.

Here we can invoke a second basic financial principle: *a safe dollar is worth more than a risky one.* Most investors avoid risk when they can do so without sacrificing return. However, the concepts of present value and the opportunity cost of capital still make sense for risky investments. It is still proper to discount the payoff by the rate of return offered by a comparable investment. But we have to think of *expected* payoffs and the *expected* rates of return on other investments.

Not all investments are equally risky. The office development is riskier than a government security but is probably less risky than drilling a wildcat oil well. Suppose you believe the project is as risky as investment in the stock market and that you forecast a 12% rate of return for stock market investments. Then 12% becomes the appropriate opportunity cost of capital. That is what you are giving up by not investing in comparable securities. You can now recompute NPV:

$$PV = \frac{400{,}000}{1.12} = \$357{,}143$$

$$NPV = PV - 350{,}000 = \$7{,}143$$

If other investors agree with your forecast of a \$400,000 payoff and with your assessment of a 12% opportunity cost of capital, then your property ought to be worth \$357,143 once construction is under way. If you tried to sell it for more than that, there would be no takers, because the property would then offer an expected rate of return lower than the 12% available in the stock market. The office building still makes a net contribution to value, but it is much smaller than our earlier calculations indicated.

In Chapter 1 we said that the financial manager must be concerned with time and uncertainty and their effects on value. This is clearly so in our example. The $400,000 payoff would be worth exactly that if it could be realized instantaneously. If the office building is as risk-free as government securities, the one-year delay reduces value to $373,832. If the office building is as risky as investment in the stock market, then uncertainty reduces value by a further $16,689 to $357,143.

Unfortunately, adjusting asset values for time and uncertainty is often more complicated than our example suggests. Therefore, we will take the two effects separately. For the most part, we will dodge the problem of risk in Chapters 2 through 6, either treating all payoffs as if they were known with certainty or talking about expected cash flows and expected rates of return without worrying how risk is defined or measured. Then in Chapter 7 we will turn to the problem of understanding how capital markets cope with risk.

Present Values and Rates of Return

We have decided that construction of the office building is a smart thing to do, since it is worth more than it costs—it has a positive net present value. To calculate how much it is worth, we worked out how much one would have to pay to achieve the same income by investing directly in securities. The project's present value is equal to its future income discounted at the rate of return offered by these securities.

We can re-express our criterion by saying that our property venture is worth undertaking because the return exceeds the cost of capital. The return on the capital invested is simply the profit as a proportion of the initial outlay:

$$\text{Return} = \frac{\text{profit}}{\text{investment}} = \frac{400,000 - 350,000}{350,000} = 14\%$$

The cost of capital invested is once again just the return forgone by *not* investing in securities. In our present case, if the office building is about as risky as investing in the stock market, the return forgone is 12%. Since the 14% return on the office building exceeds the 12% cost, we should start digging the foundations of the building.

Here then we have two equivalent decision rules for capital investment.

1. *Net present value rule*. Accept investments that have positive net present values.

2. *Rate-of-return rule*. Accept investments that offer rates of return in excess of their opportunity costs of capital.[2]

---

*2-2 FOUNDATIONS OF THE NET PRESENT VALUE RULE[3]

So far our discussion of net present value has been rather casual. Increasing NPV *sounds* like a sensible objective for a company, but it is more than just a rule of thumb. We

---

[2]You might check for yourself that these are equivalent rules. In other words, if the return 50,000/350,000 is greater than r, then the net present value $-350,000 + [400,000/(1 + r)]$ must be greater than zero. In Chapter 5 we shall see that when there are cash flows in more than one period, the rate-of-return rule is less easily applied.

[3]Sections marked with an asterisk contain more difficult material and may be skipped on a first reading.

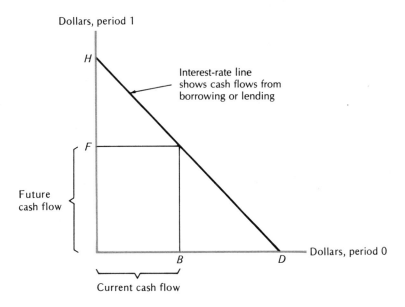

Dollars, period 1

H

Interest-rate line
shows cash flows from
borrowing or lending

F

Future
cash flow

B D Dollars, period 0

Current cash flow

Figure 2-1   Notice how borrowing and lending enlarge the individual's choice. By borrowing against future cash flow F, an individual can consume an extra BD today; by lending current cash flow B, the individual can consume an extra FH tomorrow.

need to understand why the NPV rule makes sense and why we look to the bond and stock markets to find the opportunity cost of capital.

Figure 2-1 illustrates the problem of choosing between spending today and spending in the future. Assume that you have a cash inflow of B today and F in a year's time. Unless you have some way of storing or anticipating income, you will be compelled to consume it as it arrives. This could be inconvenient or worse. If the bulk of your cash flow is received next year, the result could be hunger now and gluttony later. This is where the capital market comes in. It allows the transfer of wealth across time, so that you can eat moderately both this year and next.

The capital market is simply a market where people trade between dollars today and dollars in the future. The downward-sloping line in Figure 2-1 represents the rate of exchange in the capital market between today's dollars and next year's dollars; its slope is $1 + r$, where r denotes the one-year rate of interest. By lending all of your present cash flow, you could increase your *future* consumption by $(1 + r)B$ or FH. Alternatively, by borrowing against your future cash flow, you could increase your *present* consumption by $F/(1 + r)$ or BD.

Let us put some numbers into our example. Suppose that your prospects are as follows:

- Cash on hand: $B = \$20,000$
- Cash to be received one year from now: $F = \$25,000$

If you do not want to consume anything today, you can invest \$20,000 in the capital market at, say, 7%. The rate of exchange between dollars next year and dollars today is 1.07; this is the slope of the line in Figure 2-1. If you invest \$20,000 at 7%, you will obtain $\$20,000 \times 1.07 = \$21,400$. Of course, you also have \$25,000 coming in a year from now, so you will end up with \$46,400. This is point H in Figure 2-1.

What if you want to cash in the \$25,000 future payment and spend everything today on some ephemeral frolic? You can do so by borrowing in the capital market. The present value formula tells us how much investors would give you today in return for the promise of $25,000 next year:

$$PV = \frac{C_1}{1 + r} = \frac{25,000}{1.07} = \$23,364$$

This is the distance BD. The total present value of the current and future cash flows (point D in the figure) is found by adding this year's flow.

$$C_0 + \frac{C_1}{1 + r} = 20,000 + \frac{25,000}{1.07} = \$43,364$$

This is the formula that we used before to calculate net present value (except that in this case C_0 is positive).

What if you cash in but then change your mind and want to consume next year? Can you get back to point H? Of course—just invest the net present value at 7%.

Future value $= 43,364 \times 1.07 = \$46,400$

As a matter of fact, you can end up anywhere on the straight line connecting D and H depending on how much of the $43,364 current wealth you choose to invest. Figure 2-1 is actually a graphical representation of the link between present and future value.

*How the Capital Market Helps to Smooth Consumption Patterns

Few of us save all our current cash flow or borrow fully against our future cash flow. We try to achieve a balance between present and future consumption. But there is no reason to expect that the best balance for one person is best for another.

Suppose, for example, that you are of a prodigal disposition and favour present over future consumption. Your preferred pattern might be indicated by Figure 2-2. You choose to borrow BC against future cash flow and consume C today. Next year you are obliged to repay EF and, therefore, can consume only E. By contrast, if you have a more miserly streak, you might prefer the policy shown in Figure 2-3: you consume A today and lend the balance AB. In a year's time you receive a repayment of FG and are therefore able to indulge in consumption of G.[4]

Both the miser and the prodigal *can* choose to spend cash only as it is received, but in these examples both prefer to do otherwise. By opening up borrowing and lending opportunities, the capital market removes the obligation to match consumption and cash flow.

*In Which We Introduce Productive Opportunities

In practice individuals are not limited to investing in capital market securities: they may also acquire plant, machinery, and other real assets. Thus, in addition to plotting

---

[4]The exact balance between present and future consumption that each individual will choose depends on personal taste. Readers who are familiar with economic theory will recognize that the choice can be represented by superimposing an "indifference map" for each individual. The preferred combination is the point of tangency between the interest-rate line and the individual's indifference curve. In other words, each individual will borrow or lend until one plus the interest rate equals the marginal rate of time preference (i.e., the slope of the indifference curve).

the returns from buying securities, we can also plot an investment-opportunities line, which shows the returns from buying real assets. The return on the "best" project may well be substantially higher than returns in the capital market, so that the investment-opportunities line may be initially very steep. But, unless the individual is a bottomless pit of inspiration, the line will become progressively flatter. This is illustrated in Figure 2-4, where the first $10,000 of investment ranked in terms of return produces

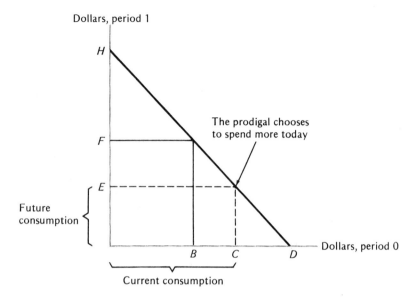

Figure 2-2   The prodigal chooses to borrow BC against tomorrow's cash flow, in order to consume C today and E tomorrow.

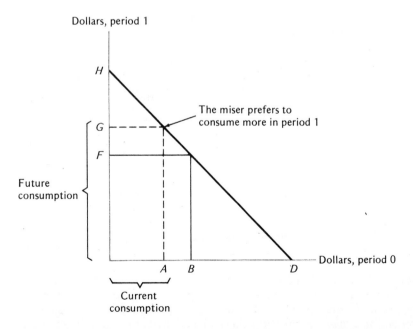

Figure 2-3   The miser chooses to lend AB, in order to consume A today and G tomorrow.

a subsequent cash flow of $20,000, whereas the next $10,000 offers a cash flow of only $15,000. In the jargon of economics, there is a declining marginal return on capital.

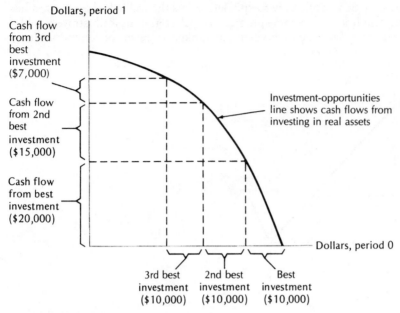

Dollars, period 1

Cash flow from 3rd best investment ($7,000)

Cash flow from 2nd best investment ($15,000)

Cash flow from best investment ($20,000)

Investment-opportunities line shows cash flows from investing in real assets

Dollars, period 0

3rd best investment ($10,000)   2nd best investment ($10,000)   Best investment ($10,000)

Figure 2-4   The effect of investment in real assets on cash flows in periods 0 and 1. Notice the diminishing returns on additional units of investment.

We can now return to our hypothetical example and inquire how your welfare would be affected by the possibility of investing in real assets. The solution is illustrated in Figure 2-5. To keep our diagram simple, we shall assume that you have maximum initial resources of D. Part of this may come from borrowing against future cash flow; but we do not have to worry about that, because, as we have seen, the amount D can always be deployed into future income. If you choose to invest any part of this sum in the capital market, you can attain any point along the line DH.

Now let us introduce investment in *real assets* by supposing that you retain J of your initial resources and invest the balance JD in plant and machinery. We can see from the curved investment-opportunities line that such an investment would produce a future cash flow of G. This is all very well, but maybe you do not want to consume J today and G tomorrow. Fortunately you can use the capital market to adjust your spending pattern as you choose. By investing the whole of J in the capital market, you can increase *future* income by GM. Alternatively, by borrowing against your entire future earnings of G, you can increase *present* income by JK. In other words, by *both* investing JD in *real* assets and borrowing or lending in the capital market, you can obtain any point along the line KM. Regardless of whether you are a prodigal or a miser, you have more to spend either today or next year than if you invest *only* in the capital market (that is, choose a point along the line DH). You also have more to spend either today or next year than if you invest *only* in real assets (that is, choose a point along the curve DL).

Let us look more closely at the investment in *real assets*. The maximum sum that could be realized today from the investment's future cash flow is JK. *This is the investment's present value*. Its cost is JD, and the difference between its present value and its cost is DK. *This is its net present value*. Net present value is the addition to your resources from investing in *real assets*.

Dollars, period 1

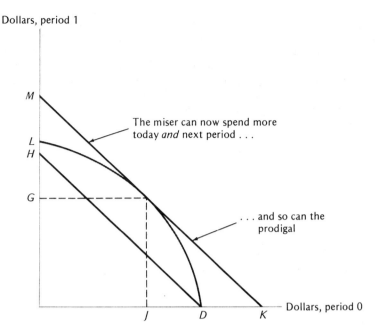

Figure 2-5   Both the prodigal and the miser have initial wealth of *D*. They are better off if they invest *JD* in real assets and then borrow or lend in the capital market. If they could invest *only* in the capital market, they would be obliged to choose a point along *DH*; if they could invest *only* in real assets, they would be obliged to choose a point along *DL*.

Investing the amount *JD* is a smart move—it makes you better off. In fact it is the smartest possible move. We can see why if we look at Figure 2-6. If you invest *JD* in real assets, the net present value is *DK*. If you invest, say, *ND* in real assets, the net present value declines to *DP*. In fact investing either more or less than *JD* in real assets *must* reduce net present value.

Dollars, period 1

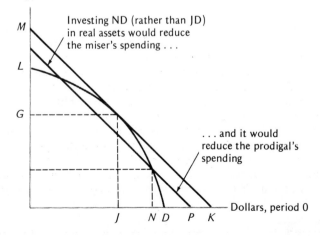

Figure 2-6   If the prodigal or the miser invests *ND* in real assets, the NPV of the investment would be only *DP*. The investor would have less to spend both today and tomorrow.

Notice also that by investing *JD*, you have invested up to the point at which the investment-opportunities line just touches and has the same slope as the interest-rate line. Now the slope of the investment-opportunities line represents the return on the marginal investment, so that *JD* is the point at which the return on the marginal investment is exactly equal to the rate of interest. In other words, you will maximize your wealth if you invest in *real* assets until the marginal return on investment falls to the rate of interest. Having done that, you will borrow or lend in the capital market until you have achieved the desired balance between consumption today and consumption tomorrow.

We now have a logical basis for the two equivalent rules that we proposed so casually at the end of Section 2-1. We can restate the rules as follows:

1. *Net present value rule.* Invest so as to maximize the net present value of the investment. This is the difference between the discounted, or present, value of the future income and the amount of the initial investment.

2. *Rate-of-return rule.* Invest up to the point at which the marginal return on the investment is equal to the rate of return on equivalent investments in the capital market. This is the point of tangency between the interest-rate line and the investment-opportunities line.

*A Crucial Assumption

In our examples, the miser and the prodigal placed an identical value on the firm's investment. This would not have been the case if they had not faced identical borrowing and lending opportunities. Whenever firms discount cash flows at capital market rates, they are implicitly making some assumptions about their shareholders' opportunities to borrow and lend. Strictly speaking, they are assuming:

1. that there are no barriers preventing access to the capital market and that no participant is sufficiently dominant as to have a significant effect on price;

2. that access to the capital market is costless and that there are no "frictions" preventing the free trading of securities;

3. that relevant information about the price and quality of each security is widely and freely available;

4. that there are no distorting taxes.

In sum, they are assuming a perfectly competitive capital market. Clearly, this is at best an approximation, but it may not be too bad a one. There are 1.5 million stockholders in Canada. Even a large institution like Royal Trust only controls about 3% of publicly traded Canadian stocks. Second, the costs of trading in securities are generally small, both in absolute terms and relative to the costs of trading in real assets like office buildings and blast furnaces. Finally, though there are obviously cases in which investors have possessed privileged information, the federal and provincial corporations acts and the provincial securities acts (as well as the United States Securities and Exchange Commission, if the securities are traded in the United States) ensure that potentially profitable information seldom remains the property of one individual for long.[5]

Even though our conditions are not fully satisfied, there is considerable evidence that security prices behave almost as if they were. This evidence is presented and discussed in Chapter 13.

---

[5]Avarice helps because any other individual who can obtain this information can use it to make trading profits.

---

*Imperfect Capital Markets

Suppose that we did not have such a well-functioning capital market. How would this damage our net present value rule?

As an example, Figure 2-7 shows what happens if the borrowing rate is substantially higher than the lending rate. This means that when you want to turn period 0 dollars into period 1 dollars (that is, lend), you move *up* a relatively flat line; when you want to turn period 1 dollars into period 0 dollars (that is, borrow), you move *down* a relatively steep line. You can see that would-be borrowers (who must move *down* the steep line) prefer the company to invest only *BD*. In contrast, would-be lenders (who must move *up* the relatively flat line) prefer the company to invest *AD*. In this case the two groups of shareholders want the manager to use different discount rates. The manager has no simple way to reconcile their differing objectives.

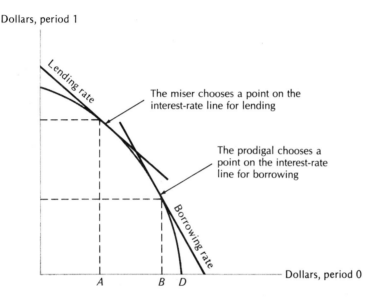

Figure 2-7   Here there are separate borrowing and lending rates. The steep line represents the interest rate for a borrower; the flatter line represents the rate for a lender. In this case the prodigal and the miser prefer different levels of capital investment.

No one believes that the competitive market assumption is fully satisfied. Later in this book we will discuss several cases in which differences in taxation, transaction costs, and other imperfections must be taken into account in financial decision making. However, we will also discuss research that indicates that, in general, capital markets function fairly well. That is one good reason for relying on net present value as a corporate objective. Another good reason is that net present value makes common sense; we will see that it gives obviously silly answers less frequently than its major competitors. But for now, having glimpsed the problems of imperfect markets, we shall, like an economist in a shipwreck, simply *assume* our life jacket and swim safely to shore.

2-3   A FUNDAMENTAL RESULT

The present value rule really dates back to the work of the great American economist Irving Fisher. What was so exciting about Fisher's analysis was his discovery, in 1930, that the capital investment criterion has nothing to do with the individual's preferences for current versus future consumption.[6] The prodigal and the miser are unanimous in the amount that they want to invest in real assets. Because they have the same investment criterion, they can co-operate in the same enterprise and can safely delegate the operation of that enterprise to a professional manager. Managers do not need to know anything about the personal tastes of their shareholders and should not consult their own tastes. Their task is to maximize net present value. If they succeed, they can rest assured that they have acted in the best interests of their shareholders.

Our justification of the net present value rule has been restricted to two periods and to certain cash flows. However, the rule also makes sense for cases in which the cash flows extend beyond the next period. The argument goes like this:

1. A financial manager should act in the interest of the firm's stockholders.
2. Each stockholder wants three things:
    (a) to be as rich as possible, that is, to maximize current wealth;
    (b) to transform that wealth into whatever time pattern of consumption he or she most desires;
    (c) to choose the risk characteristics of that consumption plan.
3. But stockholders do not need the financial manager's help to reach the best time pattern of consumption. They can do that on their own, providing they have free access to competitive capital markets. They can also choose the risk characteristics of their consumption plan by investing in more or less risky securities.
4. How then can the financial manager help the firm's stockholders? By increasing the market value of each stockholder's stake in the firm. The way to do that is to seize all investment opportunities that have a positive net present value.

This gives us the fundamental condition for the successful operation of a capitalist economy. Separation of ownership and management is a practical necessity for large organizations. Many corporations have hundreds of thousands of shareholders, no two with the same tastes, wealth, or personal opportunities. There is no way for all the firm's owners to be actively involved in management: it would be like running Metropolitan Toronto through a series of town meetings for all its citizens. Therefore, authority has to be delegated. The remarkable thing is that managers of firms can all be given one simple instruction: maximize net present value.

A Note on Other Corporate Goals

Some readers may be tempted to reject the net present value rule on the grounds that the concern of management should transcend the selfish interests of their shareholders. Of course, we do not know how energetically managers seek to maximize net present value, but we are reminded of a survey of businesspeople that inquired whether they attempted to maximize profits. They indignantly rejected the notion, protesting that they were responsible, God-fearing, and so on: their responsibilities went far beyond the narrow profit objective. But when the question was reformulated and they were asked whether they could increase profits by raising or lowering their selling price, they replied that neither policy would do so.[7] In a rather similar vein, we suspect that many

---

[6]I. Fisher, *The Theory of Interest*, Augustus M. Kelley, Publishers, New York, 1965 (reprinted from the 1930 edition). Our graphical illustration closely follows the exposition in E.F. Fama and M.H. Miller, *The Theory of Finance,* Holt, Rinehart and Winston, New York, 1972.

[7]Cited in G.J. Stigler, *The Theory of Price*, 3rd ed., The Macmillan Company, New York, 1966.

managers do not have an explicit objective of maximizing net present value and yet can think of no action that would do other than to reduce it.

Suppose, however, that we do believe that management should have these wider responsibilities. Management still must be able to analyze a decision from the shareholders' point of view if it is to strike a proper balance between their interests and those of consumers, employees, and society at large. The net present value calculation tells them how much a particular decision helps or hinders stockholders.

2-4 SUMMARY

In this chapter we have introduced the concept of present value as a way of valuing assets. Calculating present value is easy. Just discount future cash flow by an appropriate rate, usually called the *opportunity cost of capital*, or *hurdle rate*.

$$\text{Present value (PV)} = \frac{C_1}{1 + r}$$

Net present value is present value plus any immediate cash flow:

$$\text{Net present value (NPV)} = C_0 + \frac{C_1}{1 + r}$$

Remember that C_0 is negative if the immediate cash flow is an investment, that is, if it is a cash outflow.

The discount rate is determined by rates of return prevailing in capital markets. If the future cash flow is absolutely safe, then the discount rate is the interest rate on safe securities like federal government debt. If the size of the future cash flow is uncertain, then the expected cash flow should be discounted at the expected rate of return offered by equivalent-risk securities. We will talk more about this in Chapter 7.

Cash flows are discounted for two simple reasons: first, because a dollar today is worth more than a dollar tomorrow; and second, because a risky dollar is worth less than a safe one. Formulas for PV and NPV are numerical expressions of these ideas. We look to rates of return prevailing in capital markets to determine how much to discount for time and for risk. By calculating the present value of an asset, we are in effect estimating how much people will pay for it if they have the alternative of investing in the capital markets.

The concept of net present value allows efficient separation of ownership and management of the corporation. A manager who invests only in assets with positive net present values serves the best interests of each one of the firm's owners—regardless of differences in their wealth and tastes. This is made possible by the existence of the capital market, which allows each shareholder to construct a personal investment plan that is custom-tailored to his or her own needs. For example, there is no need for the firm to arrange its investment policy to obtain a sequence of cash flows that matches shareholders' preferred time patterns of consumption. The shareholders can shift funds forward or back over time perfectly well on their own, provided they have free access to competitive capital markets. In fact, their plan for consumption over time is constrained by only two things: their personal wealth (or lack of it) and the interest rate at which they can borrow and lend. The financial manager cannot affect the interest rate but can increase stockholders' wealth. The way to do so is to invest in assets having positive net present values.

FURTHER READING

The pioneering works on the net present value rule are:

I. Fisher, *The Theory of Interest*, Augustus M. Kelley, Publishers, New York, 1965. Reprinted from the 1930 edition.

J. Hirschleifer, "On the Theory of Optimal Investment Decision," *Journal of Political Economy*, **66**:329–352 (August 1958).

For a more rigorous textbook treatment of the subject, we suggest:

E.F. Fama and M.H. Miller, *The Theory of Finance*, Holt, Rinehart and Winston, New York, 1972.

QUIZ

1. C_0 is the initial cash flow on an investment, and C_1 is the cash flow at the end of one year. The symbol r is the discount rate.
   (*a*) Is C_0 usually positive or negative?
   (*b*) What is the formula for the present value of the investment?
   (*c*) What is the formula for the net present value?
   (*d*) The symbol r is often termed the *opportunity cost of capital*. Why?
   (*e*) If the investment is risk-free, what is the appropriate measure of r?

2. If the present value of $150 paid at the end of one year is $130, what is the one-year discount factor? What is the discount rate?

3. Calculate the one-year discount factor DF_1 for discount rates of (*a*) 10%, (*b*) 20%, and (*c*) 30%.

4. A merchant pays $100,000 for a load of grain and is certain that it can be resold at the end of one year for $132,000.
   (*a*) What is the return on this investment?
   (*b*) If this return is *lower* than the rate of interest, does the investment have a positive or a negative net present value?
   (*c*) If the rate of interest is 10%, what is the present value of the investment?
   (*d*) What is the net present value?

5. What is the net present value rule? What is the rate-of-return rule? Do the two rules give the same answer?

*6. In Figure 2-8, the sloping line represents the opportunities for investment in the capital market and the solid curved line represents the opportunities for investment in plant and machinery. The company's only asset at present is $2.6 million in cash.
   (*a*) What is the interest rate?
   (*b*) How much should the company invest in plant?
   (*c*) How much will this investment be worth next year?
   (*d*) What is the average rate of return on the investment in plant?
   (*e*) What is the marginal rate of return?
   (*f*) What is the present value of this investment?
   (*g*) What is the net present value of this investment?
   (*h*) What is the total present value of the company?
   (*i*) How much will the individual consume today?
   (*j*) How much will he or she consume tomorrow?

---

*Problems marked with an asterisk are more difficult.

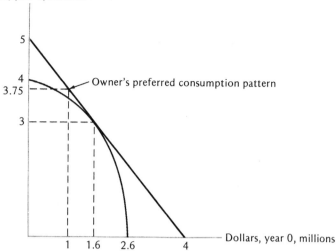

Figure 2-8   See Quiz, question 6.

7. We can imagine the financial manager doing several things on behalf of the firm's stockholders. For example, the manager might:
   (*a*) Make shareholders as wealthy as possible by investing in real assets with positive net present values.
   (*b*) Modify the firm's investment plan to help shareholders achieve a particular time pattern of consumption.
   (*c*) Choose high- or low-risk assets to match shareholders' risk preferences.
   (*d*) Help balance shareholders' cheque books.
   But in well-functioning capital markets, shareholders will vote for *only one* of these goals. Which one? Why?

QUESTIONS AND PROBLEMS

1. In Section 2-1, we analyzed the possible construction of an office building on a plot of land appraised at $50,000. We concluded that this investment had a positive NPV of $7,143.

   Suppose E. Coli Associates, the genetic consultants, offer to purchase the land for $60,000, $30,000 paid immediately and $30,000 after one year. Government securities maturing in one year yield 7%.
   (*a*) Assume E. Coli is sure to pay the second $30,000 instalment. Should you take their offer or start on the office building? Explain.
   (*b*) Suppose you are *not* sure E. Coli will pay. You observe that other investors demand a 10% return on their loans to E. Coli. Assume that the other investors have correctly assessed the risks that E. Coli will not be able to pay. Should you accept E. Coli's offer?

2. Write down the formulas for an investment's net present value and rate of return. Prove that NPV is positive *only* if the rate of return exceeds the opportunity cost of capital.

3. What is the net present value of a *firm's* investment in a government treasury security yielding 15% and maturing in one year? *Hint*: what is the opportunity cost of capital? Ignore taxes.

4. Calculate the NPV and rate of return for each of the following investments. The opportunity cost of capital is 20% for all four investments.

Investment	Initial Cash Flow, C_0	Cash Flow in Year 1, C_1
1	$-10,000$	$+20,000$
2	$-5,000$	$+12,000$
3	$-5,000$	$+5,500$
4	$-2,000$	$+5,000$

(a) Which investment is most valuable?

(b) Suppose each investment would require use of the same parcel of land. Therefore you can take only one. Which one? *Hint:* What is the firm's objective? To earn a high rate of return? Or to increase firm value?

*5. Redraw Figure 2-5 to scale to represent the following situation:

(a) A firm starts out with $10 million in cash.

(b) The rate of interest r is 10%.

(c) To maximize NPV the firm invests today $6 million in real assets ($C_0 = -6$ million). This leaves $4 million, which can be paid out to the shareholders.

(d) The NPV of the investment is $2 million.

When you have finished, answer the following questions:

(e) How much cash is the firm going to receive in year 1 from its investment?

(f) What is the marginal return from the firm's investment?

(g) What is the present value of the shareholders' investment after the firm has announced its investment plan?

(h) Suppose shareholders want to spend $6 million today. How can they do this?

(i) How much will they then have to spend next year? Show this on your drawing.

*6. Resketch Figure 2-5 to show how the firm's investment plan should be affected by a decline in the interest rate. Mark the NPV of the revised investment plan. Show whether the miser or the prodigal would be better off.

*7. Look again at Figure 2-5. Suppose the firm decides to invest *more* than *JD* in real assets. Redraw the interest-rate line to show the NPV of the revised investment plan. Show that both the miser *and* the prodigal are worse off.

*8. The interest-rate line in our diagrams always has a slope greater than one. Why?

9. "The discount rate is the rate at which the company will be able to reinvest its cash flows." Is that right? Discuss.

10. Respond to the following comment: "It's all very well telling companies to maximize net present value, but 'net present value' is just an abstract notion. What I tell my managers is that profits are what matters and it's profits that we're going to maximize."

11. Respond to the following comment: "It's no good just telling me to maximize my stock price. I can easily take a short view and maximize today's price. What I would prefer is to keep it on a gently rising trend."

12. Here's a harder question. It is sometimes argued that the net present value criterion is appropriate for corporations but not for governments. First, governments must consider the time preferences of the community as a whole rather than those of a few wealthy investors. Second, governments must have a longer horizon than individuals, for governments are the guardians of future generations. What do you think?

HOW TO CALCULATE PRESENT VALUES

In Chapter 2 we learned how to work out the value of an asset that produces cash exactly one year from now. But we did not explain how to value assets that produce cash two years from now or in several future years. That is the first thing that we must do in this chapter. We will then have a look at some short-cut methods for calculating present values and at some specialized present value formulas.

By then you will deserve some payoff for the mental investment you have made in learning about present values. In Chapter 4 we will try out the concept on common stocks, and after that we will tackle the firm's capital investment decisions at a practical level of detail.

3-1 VALUING LONG-LIVED ASSETS

Do you remember how to calculate the present value PV of an asset that produces a cash flow (C_1) one year from now?

$$PV = DF_1 \times C_1 = \frac{C_1}{1 + r_1}$$

The discount factor for year 1 cash flows is DF_1, and r_1 is the opportunity cost of investing your money for one year. Thus suppose you will receive a certain cash inflow of $100 next year ($C_1 = 100$) and the rate of interest on one-year Canadian Treasury bills is 7% ($r_1 = 0.07$). Then present value equals

$$PV = \frac{C_1}{1 + r_1} = \frac{100}{1.07} = \$93.46$$

The present value of a cash flow two years hence can be written in a similar way as

$$PV = DF_2 \times C_2 = \frac{C_2}{(1 + r_2)^2}$$

C_2 is the year 2 cash flow, DF_2 is the discount factor for year 2 cash flows, and r_2 is the annual rate of interest on money invested for two years. Continuing with our example, suppose you get another cash flow of $100 in year 2 ($C_2 = 100$). The rate of interest on two-year Treasury notes is 7.7% a year ($r_2 = 0.077$); this means that a dollar invested in two-year notes will grow to $1.077^2 = \$1.16$ by the end of two years. The present value of your year 2 cash flow equals

$$PV = \frac{C_2}{(1 + r_2)^2} = \frac{100}{(1.077)^2} = \$86.21$$

Valuing Cash Flows in Several Periods

One of the nice things about present values is that they are all expressed in current dollars—so that you can add them up. In other words, the present value of cash flow $A + B$ is equal to the present value of cash flow A plus the present value of cash flow B. This happy result has important implications for investments that produce cash flows in several periods.

We calculated above the value of an asset that produces a cash flow of C_1 in year 1, and we calculated the value of another asset that produces a cash flow of C_2 in year 2. Following our additivity rule, we can write down the value of an asset that produces cash flows in *each* year. It is simply

$$PV = \frac{C_1}{1 + r_1} + \frac{C_2}{(1 + r_2)^2}$$

We can obviously continue in this way and find the present value of an extended stream of cash flows:

$$PV = \frac{C_1}{1 + r_1} + \frac{C_2}{(1 + r_2)^2} + \frac{C_3}{(1 + r_3)^3} + \cdots$$

This is sometimes called the **discounted cash flow** (or **DCF**) formula. A shorthand way to write it is

$$PV = \sum \frac{C_t}{(1 + r_t)^t}$$

where Σ refers to the sum of the series. To find the *net* present value we add the (usually negative) initial cash flow just as in the period 1 case:

$$NPV = C_0 + PV = C_0 + \sum \frac{C_t}{(1 + r_t)^t}$$

*Why the Discount Factor Declines as Futurity Increases—And a Digression on Money Machines

If a dollar tomorrow is worth less than a dollar today, one might suspect that a dollar the day after tomorrow should be worth even less. In other words, the discount factor DF_2 should be less than the discount factor DF_1. But is this *necessarily* so, when there is a different interest rate r_t for each period?

Suppose r_1 is 20% and r_2 is 7%. Then

$$DF_1 = \frac{1}{1.20} = 0.83$$

$$DF_2 = \frac{1}{(1.07)^2} = 0.87$$

Apparently the dollar received the day after tomorrow is *not* necessarily worth less than the dollar received tomorrow.

But there is something wrong with this example. Anyone who could borrow and lend at these interest rates could become a millionaire overnight. Let us see how such a "money machine" would work. Suppose the first person to spot the opportunity is Hermione Kraft. Ms. Kraft first lends $1,000 for one year at 20%. That is an attractive enough return, but she notices that there is a way to earn an *immediate* profit on her investment and be ready to play the game again. She reasons as follows. Next year she will have $1,200, which can be reinvested for a further year. Although she does not know what interest rates will be at that time, she does know that she can always put the money in a chequing account and be sure of having $1,200 at the end of year 2. Her next step, therefore, is to go to her bank and borrow the present value of this $1,200. At 7% interest this present value is

$$PV = \frac{1,200}{(1.07)^2} = \$1,048$$

Thus Ms. Kraft invests $1,000, borrows back $1,048, and walks away with a profit of $48. If that does not sound like very much, remember that the game can be played again immediately, this time with $1,048. In fact it would take Ms. Kraft only 147 plays to become a millionaire (before taxes).[1]

Of course this story is completely fanciful. Such an opportunity would not last long in capital markets like ours. Any bank that would allow you to lend for one year at 20% and borrow for two years at 7% would soon be wiped out by a rush of small investors hoping to become millionaires and a rush of millionaires hoping to become billionaires. There are, however, two lessons to our story. The first is that a dollar tomorrow *cannot* be worth less than a dollar the day after tomorrow. In other words, the value of a dollar received at the end of one year (DF_1) must be greater than the value of a dollar received at the end of two years (DF_2). There must be some extra gain[2] from lending for two periods rather than one: $(1 + r_2)^2$ must be greater than $1 + r_1$.

Our second lesson is a more general one and can be summed up by the precept "There is no such thing as a money machine." In well-functioning capital markets, any potential money machine will be eliminated almost instantaneously by investors who try to take advantage of it. Therefore, beware of self-styled experts who offer you a chance to participate in a "sure thing."

Later in the book we will invoke the *absence* of money machines to prove several useful properties about security prices. That is, we will make statements like "The prices of securities X and Y must be in the following relationship—otherwise there would be a money machine and capital markets would not be in equilibrium."

---

[1] That is, $1,000 \times (1.04813)^{147} = \$1,002,000$.

[2] The extra return for lending two years rather than one is often referred to as a *forward rate of return*. Our rule says that the forward rate must be positive.

How Present Value Tables Help the Lazy

In principle there can be a different interest rate for each future period. This relationship between the interest rate and the maturity of the cash flow is called the **term structure of interest rates**. We are going to look at term structure in Chapter 21, but for now we will finesse the issue by assuming that the term structure is "flat"—in other words, the interest rate is the same regardless of the date of the cash flow. This means that we can replace the series of interest rates $r_1, r_2, \ldots, r_t$, and so on, with a single rate r and that we can write the present value formula as

$$PV = \frac{C_1}{1 + r} + \frac{C_2}{(1 + r)^2} + \cdots$$

So far all our examples can be worked out fairly easily by hand. Real problems are often much more complicated and require the use of an electronic calculator that is specifically programmed for present-value calculations or the use of present value tables. Here is a somewhat complex example that illustrates how such tables are used.

You have some bad news about your office building venture (the one described at the start of Chapter 2): the contractor says that construction will take two years instead of one and requests payment on the following schedule:

1. A $100,000 down payment now. (Note that the land, worth $50,000, must also be committed now.)

2. A $100,000 progress payment after one year.

3. A final payment of $100,000 when the building is ready for occupancy at the end of the second year.

Your real estate adviser maintains that despite the delay the building will be worth $400,000 when completed.

All this yields a new set of cash-flow forecasts:

Period	$t = 0$	$t = 1$	$t = 2$
Land	− 50,000		
Construction	− 100,000	− 100,000	− 100,000
Payoff			+ 400,000
Total	$C_0 = $ − 150,000	$C_1 = $ − 100,000	$C_2 = $ + 300,000

If the interest rate is 7%, then NPV is

$$NPV = C_0 + \frac{C_1}{1 + r} + \frac{C_2}{(1 + r)^2}$$

$$= -150,000 - \frac{100,000}{1.07} + \frac{300,000}{(1.07)^2}$$

Table 3-1 shows how to set up the calculations and how to get NPV. The discount factors can be found in Appendix Table 1 at the end of the book. Look at the first two entries in the column headed 7%. The top one is 0.935 and the second is 0.873. Thus you do not have to compute $1/1.07$ or $1/(1.07)^2$—you can pull the figures from the present-value table. (Notice that the other entries in the 7% column give discount factors out to 30 years and the other columns cover a range of discount rates from 1 to 30%.)

Table 3-1 Present value worksheet.

Period	Discount Factor	Cash Flow	Present Value
0	1.0	−150,000	−150,000
1	$\frac{1}{1.07} = 0.935$	−100,000	− 93,500
2	$\frac{1}{(1.07)^2} = 0.873$	+300,000	+261,900
			Total = NPV = $18,400

Fortunately the news about your office venture is not all bad. The contractor will accept a delayed payment so the PV of his fee is less than before. This partly offsets the delay in the payoff. Table 3-1 shows the NPV is $18,400—not a substantial decrease from the $23,800 calculated in Chapter 2. Since the NPV is positive, go ahead.

3-2 LOOKING FOR SHORTCUTS—PERPETUITIES AND ANNUITIES

Sometimes there are shortcuts that make it very easy to calculate the present value of an asset that pays off in different periods. Let us look at some examples.

Among the securities that have been issued by the British and Canadian governments are so-called **perpetuities**. These are bonds that the government is under no obligation to repay but that offer a fixed income for each year to perpetuity.[3] The rate of return on a perpetuity is equal to the promised annual payment divided by the present value:[4]

$$\text{Return} = \frac{\text{cash flow}}{\text{present value}}$$

$$r = \frac{C}{PV}$$

---

[3]In a fit of generosity, the Canadian government has indicated it will redeem its perpetuities in 1996 (they only have a 3% coupon payment).

[4]You can check this by writing down the present value formula.

$$PV = \frac{C}{1 + r} + \frac{C}{(1 + r)^2} + \frac{C}{(1 + r)^3} + \cdots$$

Now let $C/(1 + r) = a$ and $1/(1 + r) = x$. Then we have

$$PV = a(1 + x + x^2 + \cdots) \tag{1}$$

Multiplying both sides by x, we have

$$PVx = a(x + x^2 + \cdots) \tag{2}$$

Subtracting (2) from (1) gives us

$$PV(1 - x) = a$$

Therefore, substituting for a and x,

$$PV\left(1 - \frac{1}{1 + r}\right) = \frac{C}{1 + r}$$

Multiplying both sides by $(1 + r)$ and rearranging gives

$$r = \frac{C}{PV}$$

We can obviously twist this around and find the present value of a perpetuity given the discount rate r and the cash payment C. For example, suppose that some worthy person wishes to endow a chair in finance at a business school. If the rate of interest is 10% and if the aim is to provide $50,000 a year in perpetuity, the amount that must be set aside today is

$$\text{Present value of perpetuity} = \frac{C}{r} = \frac{50{,}000}{0.10} = \$500{,}000$$

How to Value Growing Perpetuities

Suppose now that our benefactor suddenly recollects that no allowance has been made for growth in salaries, which will probably average about 4% a year. Therefore, instead of providing $50,000 a year in perpetuity, the benefactor must provide $50,000 in year 1, 1.04 × $50,000 in year 2, and so on. If we call the growth rate in salaries g, we can write down the present value of this stream of cash flows as follows:

$$PV = \frac{C_1}{1+r} + \frac{C_2}{(1+r)^2} + \frac{C_3}{(1+r)^3} + \cdots$$

$$= \frac{C_1}{1+r} + \frac{C_1(1+g)}{(1+r)^2} + \frac{C_1(1+g)^2}{(1+r)^3} + \cdots$$

Fortunately, there is a simple formula for the sum of this geometric series.[5] If we assume that r is greater than g, our clumsy-looking calculation simplifies to

$$\text{Present value of growing perpetuity} = \frac{C_1}{r-g}$$

Therefore, if our benefactor wants to provide perpetually an annual sum that keeps pace with the growth rate in salaries, the amount that must be set aside today is

$$PV = \frac{C_1}{r-g} = \frac{50{,}000}{0.10 - 0.04} = \$833{,}333$$

How to Value Annuities

An **annuity** is an asset that pays a fixed sum each year for a specified number of years. The equal-payment house mortgage or instalment credit agreement are common examples of annuities. In each case the bank or trust company receives the series of payments, and so it *owns* the annuity. You promise to make the series of payments, and so you have *issued* the annuity.

---

[5]We need to calculate the sum of an infinite geometric series $PV = a(1 + x + x^2 + \cdots)$ where $a = C_1/(1+r)$ and $x = (1+g)/(1+r)$. In footnote 4, we showed that the sum of such a series is $a/(1-x)$. Substituting for a and x in this formula we find that

$$PV = \frac{C_1}{r-g}$$

Figure 3-1 illustrates a simple trick for valuing annuities. The first row represents a *perpetuity* that produces a cash flow of C in each year *beginning in year 1*. It has a present value of

$$PV = \frac{C}{r}$$

The second row represents a second *perpetuity* that produces a cash flow of C in each year *beginning in year t + 1*. It *will* have a present value of C/r in year t and it therefore has a present value today of

$$PV = \frac{C}{r}\left[\frac{1}{(1+r)^t}\right]$$

Both perpetuities provide a cash flow from year $t + 1$ onward. The only difference between the two perpetuities is that the first one *also* provides a cash flow in each of the years 1 through t. In other words, the difference between the two perpetuities is an annuity of C for t years. The present value of this annuity is, therefore, the difference between the values of the two perpetuities:

$$\text{Present value of annuity} = C\left[\frac{1}{r} - \frac{1}{r(1+r)^t}\right] = \frac{C}{r}\left[1 - \frac{1}{(1+r)^t}\right]$$

Note that two formulas for the present value of an annuity are given.[6] The first formula is provided to assist in the computation of present value when annuity tables are provided. The expression in brackets is the present value at discount rate r of an annuity of \$1 paid at the end of t periods and is tabulated for various pairs of r and t in Appendix Table 3. The second formula is provided to facilitate the interpretation of the present value of an annuity as the difference between the present values of two perpetuities and to ease the present value computation when annuity tables are not handily available.

---

[6]Again we can work this out from first principles. We need to calculate the sum of the finite geometric series

$$PV = a(1 + x + x^2 + \cdots + x^{t-1}) \tag{1}$$

where $a = C/(1 + r)$ and $x = 1/(1 + r)$. Multiplying both sides by x, we have

$$PVx = a(x + x^2 + \cdots + x^t) \tag{2}$$

Subtracting (2) from (1) gives us

$$PV(1 - x) = a(1 - x^t)$$

Therefore, substituting for a and x,

$$PV\left(1 - \frac{1}{1+r}\right) = C\left[\frac{1}{1+r} - \frac{1}{(1+r)^{t+1}}\right]$$

Multiplying both sides by $(1 + r)$ and rearranging gives

$$PV = C\left[\frac{1}{r} - \frac{1}{r(1+r)^t}\right] = \frac{C}{r}\left[1 - \frac{1}{(1+r)^t}\right]$$

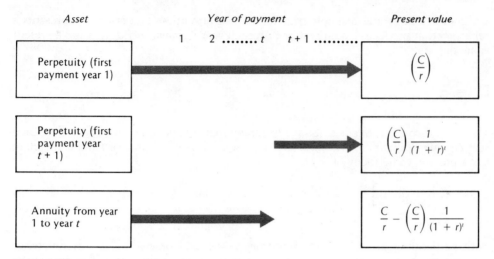

Figure 3-1 An annuity that makes payments in each of years 1 to t is equal to the difference between two perpetuities.

Suppose, for example, that our benefactor begins to vacillate and wonders what it would cost to endow the chair by providing $50,000 a year for only 20 years. The answer calculated from our formula is

$$PV = 50,000 \left[\frac{1}{0.10} - \frac{1}{0.10(1.10)^{20}} \right] = 50,000 \times 8.514 = \$425,700$$

Alternatively, we can simply look up the answer in the annuity table in the Appendix at the end of the book (Appendix Table 3). This table gives the present value of a dollar to be received in each of t periods. In our example $t = 20$ and the interest rate $r = 0.10$, and therefore we look at the twentieth number from the top in the 10% column. It is 8.514. Multiply 8.514 by $50,000, and we have our answer, $425,700.

You should always be on the lookout for ways in which you can use these formulas to make life easier. For example, we sometimes need to calculate how much a series of annual payments earning a fixed annual interest would amass to by the end of t periods. In this case it is easiest to calculate the *present* value and then multiply it by $(1 + r)^t$ to find the future value. Thus suppose our benefactor wished to know how much wealth $50,000 would produce if it were invested each year instead of being given to those no-good academics. The answer would be

Future value $= PV \times 1.10^{20} = \$425,700 \times 6.727 = \$2.86$ million

How did we know that 1.10^{20} was 6.727? Easy—we just looked it up in Appendix Table 2 at the end of the book: "Future Value of $1 at the End of t Periods."[7]

---

[7]For example, suppose you receive a cash flow of C in year 6. If you invest this cash flow at an interest rate of r, you will have by year 10 an investment worth $C(1 + r)^4$. You can get the same answer by calculating the *present value* of the cash flow $PV = C/(1 + r)^6$ and then working out how much you would have by year 10 if you invested this sum today.

Future value $= PV(1 + r)^{10} = \dfrac{C}{(1 + r)^6}(1 + r)^{10} = C(1 + r)^4$

3-3 COMPOUND INTEREST AND PRESENT VALUES

There is an important distinction between **compound interest** and **simple interest**. When money is invested at compound interest, each interest payment is reinvested to earn more interest in subsequent periods. In contrast, the opportunity to earn interest on interest is not provided by an investment that pays only simple interest.

Table 3-2   Value of $100 invested at 10% simple and compound interest.

	Simple Interest			Compound Interest			
Year	Starting Balance	+ Interest =	Ending Balance	Starting Balance	+	Interest	=	Ending Balance
1	100	+ 10 =	110	100	+	10	=	110
2	110	+ 10 =	120	110	+	11	=	121
3	120	+ 10 =	130	121	+	12.1	=	133.1
4	130	+ 10 =	140	133.1	+	13.3	=	146.4
10	190	+ 10 =	200	236	+	24	=	259
20	290	+ 10 =	300	612	+	61	=	673
50	590	+ 10 =	600	10,672	+	1,067	=	11,739
100	1,090	+ 10 =	1,100	1,252,783	+	125,278	=	1,378,061
200	2,090	+ 10 =	2,100	17,264,116,020	+	1,726,411,602	=	18,990,527,622

Table 3-2 compares the growth of $100 invested at compound versus simple interest. Notice that in the simple interest case, *the interest is paid only on the initial investment of $100.* Your wealth therefore increases by just $10 a year. In the compound interest case, you earn 10% on your initial investment in the first year, which gives you a balance at the end of the year of $100 \times 1.10 = $110. In year 2 you earn 10% on this $110, which gives you a balance at the end of the year 2 of $100 \times 1.10^2 = $121.

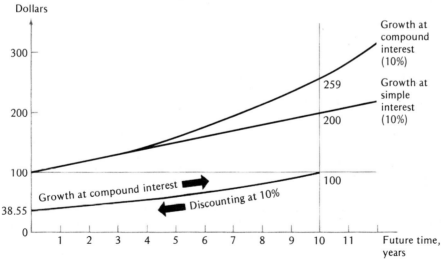

Figure 3-2   Compound interest versus simple interest. The top two ascending lines show the growth of $100 invested at simple and compound interest. The longer the funds are invested, the greater the advantage with compound interest. The bottom line shows that $38.55 must be invested now to obtain $100 after ten periods. Conversely, the present value of $100 to be received after ten years is $38.55.

Table 3-2 shows that the difference between simple and compound interest is nil for a one-period investment, trivial for a two-period investment, but overwhelming for an investment of 20 years or more. A sum of $100 invested at the time of Confederation and earning compound interest of 10% a year would now be worth over $6.3 million. Don't you wish your ancestors had shown rather more foresight?

The two top lines in Figure 3-2 compare the results of investing $100 at 10% simple interest and at 10% compound interest. It looks as if the rate of growth is constant under simple interest and accelerates under compound interest. However, this is an optical illusion. We know that under compound interest our wealth grows at a *constant* rate of 10%. Figure 3-3 is in fact a more useful presentation. Here the numbers are plotted on a semilogarithmic scale and the constant compound growth rates show up as straight lines.

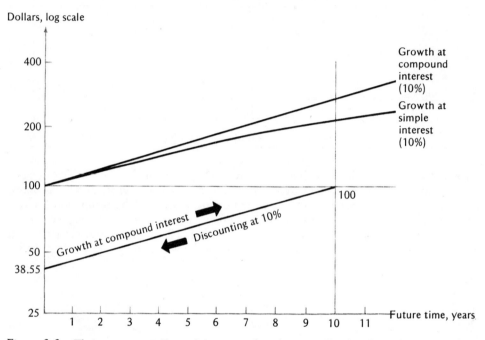

Figure 3-3   The same story as Figure 3-2, except that the vertical scale is logarithmic. A constant compound rate of growth means a straight ascending line. This graph makes clear that the growth rate of funds invested at simple interest actually *declines* as time passes.

Problems in finance generally involve compound interest rather than simple interest, and therefore financial people always assume that you are talking about compound interest unless you specify otherwise. Discounting is a process of compound interest. Some people find it intuitively helpful to replace the question "What is the present value of $100 to be received ten years from now, if the opportunity cost of capital is 10%?" with the question "How much would I have to invest now in order to receive $100 after ten years, given an interest rate of 10%?" The answer to the first question is

$$PV = \frac{100}{(1.10)^{10}} = \$38.55$$

And the answer to the second question is

Investment $\times (1.10)^{10} = 100$

$$\text{Investment} = \frac{100}{(1.10)^{10}} = \$38.55$$

The bottom lines in Figures 3-2 and 3-3 show the growth path of an initial investment of $38.55 to its terminal value of $100. One can think of discounting as traveling *back* along the bottom line, from future value to present value.

*A Note on Compounding Intervals

So far we have implicitly assumed that each cash flow occurs at the end of the year. This is sometimes the case. For example, in France and Germany most corporations pay interest on their bonds annually. However, in Canada, the United States and Britain, most pay interest semiannually. In these countries, the investor will be able to earn an additional six months' interest on the first payment, so that an investment of $100 in a bond that paid interest of 10% per annum compounded semiannually would amount to $105 after the first six months, and by the end of the year it would amount to $1.05^2 \times 100 = \$110.25$. In other words, 10% compounded semiannually is equivalent to 10.25% compounded annually. More generally, an investment of one dollar, at a rate of r per annum compounded m times a year, amounts by the end of the year to $\$[1 + (r/m)]^m$, and the equivalent annually compounded rate of interest is $[1 + (r/m)]^m - 1$.

The attractions to the investor of more frequent payments did not escape the attention of American savings and loan companies. Their rate of interest on deposits was traditionally stated as an annually compounded rate. The government, however, stipulated a maximum annual rate of interest that could be paid but made no mention of the compounding interval. When interest ceilings became effective, savings and loan companies changed progressively to semiannual and then to monthly compounding. Thus the equivalent annually compounded rate of interest increased first to $[1 + (r/2)]^2 - 1$ and then to $[1 + (r/12)]^{12} - 1$.

Eventually one company quoted a **continuously compounded rate**, so that payments were assumed to be spread evenly and continuously throughout the year. In terms of our formula, this is equivalent to letting m approach infinity.[8] This might seem like a lot of calculations for our savings and loan companies. Fortunately, however, someone remembered high school algebra and pointed out that as m approaches infinity $[1 + (r/m)]^m$ approaches $(2.718)^r$. The figure 2.718—or e, as it is called—is simply the base for natural logarithms.

The sum $1 invested at a continuously compounded rate of r will, therefore, grow to $e^r = (2.718)^r$ by the end of the first year. By the end of t years it will grow to $e^{rt} = (2.718)^{rt}$. Appendix Table 4 at the end of the book is a table of values of e^{rt}. Let us practice using it.

Example 1 Suppose you invest one dollar at a continuously compounded rate of 10% ($r = 0.10$) for one year ($t = 1$). The end-year value is simply $e^{0.10}$, which you can see

---

[8]When we talk about *continuous* payments, we are pretending that money can be dispensed in a continuous stream like a liquid. One can never quite do this. For example, instead of paying out $50,000 every year, our benefactor could pay out $100 every $17\frac{1}{2}$ hours or $1 every $10\frac{1}{2}$ minutes or 1¢ every $6\frac{1}{3}$ seconds but could not pay it out *continuously*. Financial managers *pretend* that payments are continuous rather than hourly, daily, or weekly because (1) it simplifies the calculations, and (2) it gives a *very* close approximation to the NPV of frequent payments.

from the second row of Appendix Table 4 is $1.105. In other words, investing at 10% a year *continuously* compounded is exactly the same as investing at 10.5% a year *annually* compounded.

Example 2 Now suppose you invest one dollar at a continuously compounded rate of 11% $(r = 0.11)$ for one year $(t = 1)$. The end-year value is now $e^{0.11}$, which you can see from the second row of Appendix Table 4 is $1.116. In other words, investing at 11% a year *continuously* compounded is exactly the same as investing at 11.6% a year *annually* compounded.

Example 3 Finally, suppose you invest one dollar at a continuously compounded rate of 11% $(r = 0.11)$ for two years $(t = 2)$. The final value of the investment is $e^{rt} = e^{0.22}$. You can see from the third row of Appendix Table 4 that $e^{0.22}$ is $1.246.

There is a particular value to continuous compounding in capital budgeting, where it may often be more reasonable to assume that a cash flow is spread evenly over the year than that it occurs at the year's end. It is very easy to adapt our previous formulas to handle this. For example, suppose that we wish to compute the present value of a perpetuity of C dollars a year. We already know that if the payment is made at the end of the year, we divide the payment by the *annually* compounded rate of r:

$$PV = \frac{C}{r}$$

If the same total payment is made in an even stream throughout the year, we use the same formula but substitute the *continuously* compounded rate.

For any other continuous payments, we can always use our formula for valuing annuities. For instance, suppose that our philanthropist has thought more seriously and decided to found a home for elderly donkeys, which will cost $50,000 a year, starting immediately, and spread evenly over 20 years. Previously, we used the annually compounded rate of 10%; now we must use the continuously compounded rate of $r = 9.53\%$ $(e^{0.0953} = 1.10)$. To cover such an expenditure, then, our philanthropist needs to set aside the following sum:[9]

$$PV = C\left(\frac{1}{r} - \frac{1}{r} \times \frac{1}{e^{rt}}\right)$$

$$= 50,000\left(\frac{1}{0.0953} - \frac{1}{0.0953} \times \frac{1}{6.727}\right) = 50,000 \times 8.932 = \$446,600$$

---

[9]To understand this formula it may help to remember that an annuity is simply the difference between a perpetuity received today and a perpetuity received in year t. A continuous stream of C dollars a year in perpetuity is worth C/r where r is the continuously compounded rate. Our annuity, then, is worth

$$PV = \frac{C}{r} - \text{present value of } \frac{C}{r} \text{ received in year } t$$

Since r is the continuously compounded rate, C/r received in year t is worth $(C/r) \times (1/e^{rt})$ today. Our annuity formula is therefore

$$PV = \frac{C}{r}\left[1 - \frac{1}{e^{rt}}\right]$$

Alternatively, we could have short-cut these calculations by using Appendix Table 5. This shows that, if the annually compounded return is 10%, then one dollar a year spread over 20 years is worth $8.932.

If you look back at our earlier discussion of annuities, you will notice that the present value of $50,000 paid at the *end* of each of the 20 years was $425,700. Therefore, it costs the philanthropist $21,900—or 5%—more to provide a continuous payment stream.

Often in finance we need only a ballpark estimate of present value. An error of 5% in a present value calculation may be perfectly acceptable. In such cases it doesn't usually matter whether we assume that cash flows occur at the end of the year or in a continuous stream. At other times precision matters, and we do need to worry about the exact frequency of the cash flows.

3-4 SUMMARY

The difficult thing in any present value exercise is to set up the problem correctly. Once you have done that, you must be able to do the calculations, but they are not difficult. Now that you have worked through this chapter, all you should need is a little practice.

The basic present value formula for an asset that pays off in several periods is the following obvious extension of our one-period formula:

$$PV = \frac{C_1}{1 + r_1} + \frac{C_2}{(1 + r_2)^2} + \cdots$$

You can always work out any present value using this formula, but when the interest rates are the same for each maturity, there may be some shortcuts that can reduce the tedium. We looked at three such cases. First, there was the case of an asset that pays C dollars a year in perpetuity. Its present value is simply

$$PV = \frac{C}{r}$$

Second, there was the case of an asset whose payments increase at a steady rate g in perpetuity. Its present value is

$$PV = \frac{C}{r - g}$$

Third, there was the case of an annuity that pays C dollars a year for t years. To find its present value we take the difference between the values of two perpetuities:

$$PV = \frac{C}{r}\left[1 - \frac{1}{(1 + r)^t}\right]$$

Our next step was to show that discounting is a process of compound interest. It is the amount that we would have to invest now at compound interest r in order to produce the cash flows C_1, C_2, and so on. When someone offers to lend us a dollar at an annual rate of r, we should always check how frequently the interest is to be compounded. If the compounding interval is annual, we will have to repay $(1 + r)^t$ dollars; on the other hand, if the compounding is continuous, we will have to repay

2.718^{rt} (or, as it is often called, e^{rt}) dollars. Very often in capital budgeting we are willing to assume that the cash flows occur at the end of each year, and therefore we discount them at an annually compounded rate of interest. Sometimes, however, it may be fairer to assume that they are spread evenly over the year; in this case we must make use of continuous compounding.

Present value tables will help us to perform many of these calculations. You have been introduced now to tables that show:

1. Present value of one dollar received at the end of year t;
2. Future value of one dollar by the end of year t;
3. Present value of one dollar received at the end of each year until year t;
4. Future value of one dollar invested at a continuously compounded rate of interest;
5. Present value of one dollar received continuously for t years when the annually compounded interest rate is r.

Finally, we introduced in this chapter two very important ideas that we will come across several times again. The first is that you can add present values: if your formula for the present value of $A + B$ is not the same as your formula for the present value of A plus the present value of B, you have made a mistake. The second is the notion that there is no such thing as a money machine: if you think you have found one, go back and check your calculations.

FURTHER READING

The material in this chapter should cover all you need to know about the mathematics of discounting; but if you wish to dig deeper, there are a number of books on the subject. Try, for example:

R. Osborn, *The Mathematics of Investment*, Harper & Row, Publishers, Incorporated, New York, 1957.
P. Zima and R.L. Brown, *Mathematics of Finance*, 2nd ed., McGraw-Hill Ryerson, Toronto, 1983.

QUIZ

1. At an interest rate of 12%, the six-year discount factor is 0.507. How many dollars is $.507 worth in six years if invested at 12%?

2. If the present value of $139 is $125, what is the discount factor?

3. If the eight-year discount factor if 0.285, what is the present value of $596 received in eight years?

4. If the cost of capital is 9%, what is the present value of $374 paid in year 9?

5. A project produces the following cash flows:

Year	Flow
1	432
2	137
3	797

If the cost of capital is 15%, what is the project's present value?

6. If you invest $100 at an interest rate of 15%, how much will you have at the end of eight years?

7. An investment of $232 will produce $312.18 in two years. What is the annual interest rate?

8. An investment costs $1,548 and pays $138 in perpetuity. If the interest rate is 9%, what is the net present value?

9. It costs $2,590 to insulate your home. Next year's fuel saving will be $220. If the interest rate is 12%, what percentage growth rate in fuel prices is needed to justify insulation? Assume fuel prices will grow in perpetuity at the rate g.

10. If you invest $502 at the end of each of the next nine years at an interest rate of 13%, how much will you have at the end?

11. Harold Filbert is 30 years of age and his salary next year will be $20,000. Harold forecasts that his salary will increase at a steady rate of 5% per annum until his retirement at age 60.
    (a) If the discount rate is 8%, what is the present value of these future salary payments?
    (b) If Harold saves 5% of his salary each year and invests these savings at an interest rate of 8%, how much will he have saved by age 60?
    (c) If Harold plans to spend these savings in even amounts over the subsequent 20 years, how much can he spend each year?

12. A factory costs $40,000. You reckon that it will produce an inflow after operating costs of $10,000 in year 1, $20,000 in year 2, and $30,000 in year 3. The opportunity cost of capital is 12%. Draw up a worksheet like that shown in Table 3-1 and use tables to calculate the net present value.

13. Do not use tables for these questions.. The interest rate is 10%.
    (a) What is the present value of an asset that pays one dollar a year in perpetuity?
    (b) The value of an asset that appreciates at 10% per annum approximately doubles in seven years. What is the approximate present value of an asset that pays one dollar a year in perpetuity beginning in year 8?
    (c) What is the approximate present value of an asset that pays one dollar a year for each of the next seven years?
    (d) A piece of land produces an income that grows by 5% per annum. If the first year's flow is $10,000, what is the value of the land?

* 14. Use the tables at the end of the book for each of the following calculations:
    (a) The cost of a new automobile is $10,000. If the interest rate is 5%, how much would you have to set aside now to provide this sum in five years?
    (b) You have to pay $12,000 a year in school fees at the end of each of the next six years. If the interest rate is 8%, how much do you need to set aside today to cover these bills?
    (c) You have invested $60,476 at 8%. After paying the above school fees, how much would remain at the end of the six years?
    (d) You have borrowed $1,000 and in return have agreed to pay back $1,762 in five years. What is the *annually* compounded rate of interest on the loan? What is the *continuously* compounded rate of interest?

QUESTIONS AND PROBLEMS

1. Use the discount factors shown in Appendix Table 1 at the end of the book to calculate the present value of $100 received in:
    (a) Year 10 (at a discount rate of 1%)
    (b) Year 10 (at a discount rate of 13%)
    (c) Year 15 (at a discount rate of 25%)
    (d) Each of years 1 through 3 (at a discount rate of 12%)

2. Use the *annuity factors* shown in Appendix Table 3 to calculate the present value of $100 in each of:
   (*a*) Years 1 through 20 (at a discount rate of 23%).
   (*b*) Years 1 through 5 (at a discount rate of 3%).
   (*c*) Years 3 through 12 (at a discount rate of 9%).

3. (*a*) If the one-year discount factor is 0.88, what is the one-year interest rate?
   (*b*) If the two-year interest rate of 10.5%, what is the two-year discount factor?
   (*c*) Given these one- and two-year discount factors, calculate the two-year annuity factor.
   (*d*) If the present value of $10 a year for three years is $24.49, what is the three-year annuity factor?
   (*e*) From your answers to (*c*) and (*d*), calculate the three-year discount factor.

4. A factory costs $800,000. You reckon that it will produce an inflow after operating costs of $170,000 a year for ten years. If the opportunity cost of capital is 14%, what is the net present value of the factory? What will the factory be worth at the end of five years?

5. Halcyon Lines is considering the purchase of a new bulk carrier for $8 million. The forecast revenues are $5 million a year and operating costs are $4 million. A major refit costing $2 million will be required after both the fifth and tenth years. After 15 years, the ship is expected to be sold for scrap at $1.5 million. If the discount rate is 8%, what is the ship's NPV?

6. As winner of a breakfast cereal competition, you can choose one of the following prizes:
   (*a*) $100,000 now;
   (*b*) $180,000 at the end of five years;
   (*c*) $11,400 a year forever;
   (*d*) $19,000 for each of ten years;
   (*e*) $6,500 next year and increasing thereafter by 5% a year forever.
   If the interest rate is 12%, which is the most valuable prize?

7. Refer back to the story of Ms. Kraft in Section 3-1.
   (*a*) If the one-year interest rate were 25%, how many plays would Ms. Kraft require to become a millionaire? (*Hint*: you may find it easier to use a calculator and a little trial and error.)
   (*b*) What does the story of Ms. Kraft imply about the relationship between the one-year discount factor, DF_1, and the two-year discount factor, DF_2?

8. Siegfried Basset is 65 years of age and has a life expectancy of 12 years. He wishes to invest $20,000 in an annuity that will make a level payment at the end of each year until his death. If the interest rate is 8%, what income can Mr. Basset expect to receive each year?

9. James and Helen Turnip are saving to buy a boat at the end of five years. If the boat costs $20,000 and they can earn 10% a year on their savings, how much do they need to put aside at the end of years one through five?

10. Kangaroo Autos is offering free credit on a new $10,000 car. You pay $1,000 down and then $300 a month for the next 30 months. Turtle Motors next door does not offer free credit but will give you $1,000 off the list price. If the rate of interest is 10% a year, which company is offering the better deal?

11. Recalculate the net present value of the office building venture in Section 3-1 at interest rates of 5%, 10%, and 15%. Plot the points on a graph with NPV on the vertical axis and the discount rates on the horizontal axis. At what discount rate (approximately) would the project have zero NPV? Check your answer.

12. (*a*) How much will an investment of $100 be worth at the end of ten years if invested at 15% a year simple interest?
    (*b*) How much will it be worth if invested at 15% a year compound interest?
    (*c*) How long will it take your investment to double its value at 15% compound interest?

*13. If the interest rate is 7%, what is the value of the following three investments?
    (*a*) an investment that offers you $100 a year in perpetuity with the payment at the *end* of each year;
    (*b*) a similar investment with the payment at the *beginning* of each year;
    (*c*) a similar investment with the payment spread evenly over each year.

*14. Refer back to Section 3-2. If the rate of interest is 8% rather than 10%, how much would our benefactor need to set aside to provide each of the following?
    (*a*) $50,000 at the end of each year in perpetuity;
    (*b*) a perpetuity that pays $50,000 at the end of the first year and that grows at 4% a year;
    (*c*) $50,000 at the end of each year for 20 years;
    (*d*) $50,000 a year spread evenly over 20 years.

*15. For an investment of $1,000 today, the Tiburon Finance Company is offering to pay you $1,600 at the end of eight years. What is the annually compounded rate of interest? What is the continuously compounded rate of interest?

*16. How much will you have at the end of 20 years if you invest $100 today at 15% *annually* compounded? How much will you have if you invest at 15% *continuously* compounded?

*17. You have just read an advertisement reading, "Pay us $100 a year for ten years and we will pay you $100 a year thereafter in perpetuity." If this is a fair deal, what is the rate of interest?

PRESENT VALUE OF BONDS AND STOCKS

We should warn you that being a financial expert has its occupational hazards. One is that you are liable to be cornered at cocktail parties by people who are eager to explain their system for investing in stocks and bonds. Fortunately, these bores go into temporary hibernation whenever the market goes down: during these times you can enjoy your parties.

We may exaggerate the perils of the trade. The point is that there is no easy way to ensure superior investment performance. Later in the book we will show that changes in security prices are fundamentally unpredictable and that this result is a natural consequence of well-functioning capital markets. Therefore, when we say that we propose in this chapter to *use* the concept of present value to price common stocks and bonds, we are not promising you a key to investment success; we simply believe that the idea can help you to understand why some investments are priced higher than others.

We begin the chapter with a brief review of how bonds are valued. It is brief because we shall be considering some of the refinements of bond valuation in Chapter 21. After our discussion of bonds we will look at the valuation of common stocks. We will explain the real difference between growth stocks and income stocks and the significance of earnings-per-share and price-earnings multiples.

A final word of caution. Everybody knows that common stocks are risky and that some are more risky than others. Investors, therefore, will not commit funds to stocks unless the expected rates of return are commensurate with the risks. The present value formulas we have discussed so far can take account of the effects of risk on value, but they do not tell us exactly *how* to do so. Recognize, therefore, that risk comes into the following discussion in a loose and intuitive way. A more careful treatment of risk starts in Chapter 7.

4-1 A QUICK LOOK AT HOW BONDS ARE VALUED

When you own a bond, you receive a fixed set of cash payoffs. Each year until the bond matures you get an interest payment and then at maturity you also get back the face value of the bond.

Suppose that at the end of 1982 you invest in a 12% 1987 Government of Canada bond, often called a "Canada 12 of 1987." The bond has a coupon rate of 12% and a face value of $1,000.[1] This means that each year until 1987 you receive an interest payment of $0.12 \times 1,000 = \$120$. The bond matures in 1987: in that year, the

---

[1]The face value of the bond is known as the *principal.* Therefore, when the bond matures, the government pays you principal and interest.

government pays you the final $120 interest, plus the $1,000 face value. The cash flows from owning the bond are therefore as follows:

	Cash Flows (dollars)			
1983	1984	1985	1986	1987
120	120	120	120	1,120

What is the market value in 1982 of this stream of cash flows? To determine that, we need to look at the return provided by similar bonds. Short-term Government of Canada bonds in late 1982 offered a return of about 10.7%. This is what investors were giving up when they bought the 12% bonds. Therefore, to value the 12% bonds of 1987, we need to discount the prospective stream of cash flows at 10.7%.

$$
\begin{aligned}
PV &= \sum_{t=1}^{5} \frac{C_t}{(1 + r)^t} \\
&= \frac{120}{1 + r} + \frac{120}{(1 + r)^2} + \frac{120}{(1 + r)^3} + \frac{120}{(1 + r)^4} + \frac{1,120}{(1 + r)^5} \\
&= \frac{120}{1.107} + \frac{120}{(1.107)^2} + \frac{120}{(1.107)^3} + \frac{120}{(1.107)^4} + \frac{1,120}{(1.107)^5} \\
&= \$1,048.41
\end{aligned}
$$

Bond prices are usually expressed as a percentage of face value. Thus, we can say that our 12% Canada bond is worth $1,048.41, or 104.84%.

We could have phrased our question the other way around and asked, "If the price of the bond is $1,048.41, what return do investors expect?" In that case, we would need to find the value of r that solves the following equation:

$$
1048.41 = \frac{120}{1 + r} + \frac{120}{(1 + r)^2} + \frac{120}{(1 + r)^3} + \frac{120}{(1 + r)^4} + \frac{1,120}{(1 + r)^5}
$$

The value of r is often called the bond's **yield to maturity** or **internal rate of return**. In our case, r is 10.7%. If you discount the cash flows at 10.7%, you arrive at the bond's price of $1,048.41. As we shall see in Chapter 5, the only *general* procedure for calculating r is by trial and error. But specially programmed electronic calculators can be used to calculate r, or you can use a book of bond tables that show values of r for different coupon levels and different maturities.

In calculating the value of the Canada 12s we made two approximations. First, we assumed that interest payments occur annually. In practice, most bonds make coupon payments *semiannually*. Therefore, instead of receiving $120 every year, an investor who held Canada 12s would receive $60 every *half* year. Second, we treated the 10.7% yield as an annually compounded rate. Bond yields are usually quoted as semiannually compounded rates.

You may have noticed that the formula we used for calculating the present value of Canada 12s was slightly different from the general present value formula that we developed in Section 3-1. In the latter case, we allowed for the fact that r_1, the rate of return offered by the capital market on one-year investments, may be different from

r_2, the rate of return offered on two-year investments. Later in Chapter 3 we finessed this problem by assuming that r_1 is the same as r_2. In this chapter we again assume that investors use the same rate to discount cash flows occurring in different years. That does not matter as long as short-term rates are approximately the same as long-term rates. But often when we value bonds we must discount each cash flow at a different rate. There will be more about that in Chapter 21.

4-2   HOW COMMON STOCKS ARE VALUED

Today's Price

The cash payoff to owners of common stocks comes in two forms: (1) cash dividends and (2) capital gains or losses. Usually investors expect to get some of each. Suppose that the current price of a share is P_0, that the expected price at the end of a year is P_1, and that the expected dividend per share is DIV_1. The rate of return investors expect from this share over the next year is defined as the expected dividend per share DIV_1 plus the expected price appreciation per share $P_1 - P_0$, all divided by the price at the start of the year P_0:

$$\text{Expected return} = r = \frac{DIV_1 + P_1 - P_0}{P_0}$$

This return expected by investors is often called the **market capitalization rate**.

Let us now see how our formula works. Suppose Fledgling Electronics stock is selling for $100 a share ($P_0 = 100$). Investors expect a $5 cash dividend over the next year ($DIV_1 = 5$). They also expect the stock to sell for $110 a year hence ($P_1 = 110$). Then the expected return to the stockholders is 15%:

$$r = \frac{5 + 110 - 100}{100} = 0.15, \text{ or } 15\%$$

Correspondingly, if you are given investors' forecasts of dividend and price and the expected return offered by other equally risky stocks, you can predict today's price:

$$\text{Price} = P_0 = \frac{DIV_1 + P_1}{1 + r}$$

For Fledgling Electronics $DIV_1 = 5$ and $P_1 = 110$. If r, the expected return on securities in the same "risk class" as Fledgling, is 15%, then today's price should be $100:

$$P_0 = \frac{5 + 110}{1.15} = \$100$$

How do we know that $100 is the right price? Because no other price could survive in competitive capital markets. What if P_0 were more than $100? Then Fledgling stock would offer an expected rate of return that was *lower* than other securities of equivalent risk. Investors would, therefore, shift their capital to the other securities and in the process would force down the price of Fledgling stock. If P_0 were less than $100, the process would reverse. Fledgling's stock would offer a *higher* rate of return than comparable securities. In that case, investors would rush to buy, forcing the price up to $100.

The general conclusion is that at each point in time *all securities in an equivalent risk class are priced to offer the same expected return.* This is a condition for equilibrium in well-functioning capital markets. It is also common sense.

But What Determines Next Year's Price?

We have managed to explain today's stock price P_0 in terms of the dividend DIV_1 and the expected price next year P_1. Future stock prices are not easy things to forecast directly. But think about what determines next year's price. If our price formula holds now, it ought to hold then as well:

$$P_1 = \frac{DIV_2 + P_2}{1 + r}$$

That is, a year from now investors will be looking out at dividends in year 2 and price at the end of year 2. Thus we can forecast P_1 by forecasting DIV_2 and P_2 and we can express P_0 in terms of DIV_1, DIV_2 and P_2:

$$P_0 = \frac{1}{1 + r}(DIV_1 + P_1) = \frac{1}{1 + r}\left(DIV_1 + \frac{DIV_2 + P_2}{1 + r}\right) = \frac{DIV_1}{1 + r} + \frac{DIV_2 + P_2}{(1 + r)^2}$$

Take Fledgling Electronics. A plausible way to explain why investors expect its stock price to rise by the end of the first year is that they expect higher dividends and still more capital gains in the second. For example, suppose that they are looking today for dividends of $5.50 in year 2 and a subsequent price of $121. That would imply a price at the end of year 1 of

$$P_1 = \frac{5.50 + 121}{1.15} = \$110$$

Today's price can then be computed either from our original formula

$$P_0 = \frac{DIV_1 + P_1}{1 + r} = \frac{5.00 + 110}{1.15} = \$100$$

or from our expanded formula

$$P_0 = \frac{DIV_1}{1 + r} + \frac{DIV_2 + P_2}{(1 + r)^2} = \frac{5.00}{1.15} + \frac{5.50 + 121}{(1.15)^2} = \$100$$

We have succeeded in relating today's price to the forecasted dividends for two years (DIV_1 and DIV_2) plus the forecasted price at the end of the *second* year (P_2). You will probably not be surprised to learn that we could go on to replace P_2 by ($DIV_3 + P_3$) /(1 + r) and relate today's price to the forecasted dividends for three years (DIV_1, DIV_2, and DIV_3) plus the forecasted price at the end of the *third* year (P_3). In fact we can look as far out into the future as we like, removing Ps as we go. Let us call this final period H. This gives us a general stock-price formula

$$P_0 = \frac{DIV_1}{1 + r} + \frac{DIV_2}{(1 + r)^2} + \cdots + \frac{DIV_H + P_H}{(1 + r)^H}$$

$$= \sum_{t=1}^{H} \frac{DIV_t}{(1 + r)^t} + \frac{P_H}{(1 + r)^H}$$

The expression $\sum_{t=1}^{H}$ simply means the sum of the discounted dividends from year 1 to year H.

Table 4-1 continued the Fledgling Electronics example for various time horizons, assuming that the dividends are expected to increase at a steady 10% compound rate. The expected price P_t increases at the same rate each year. Each line in the table represents an application of our general formula for a different value of H. Figure 4-1 provides a graphical representation of the table. Each column shows the present value of the dividends up to the time horizon and the present value of the price at the horizon. As the horizon recedes, the dividend stream accounts for an increasing proportion of present value, but the *total* present value of dividends plus terminal price always equals $100.

Table 4-1 Applying the stock valuation formula to Fledgling Electronics.

| | Expected Future Values | | Present Values | | |
Horizon Period (H)	Dividend (Div_t)	Price (P_t)	Cumulative Dividends	Future Price	Total
0	—	100	—	100.00	100
1	5.00	110	4.35	95.65	100
2	5.50	121	8.51	91.49	100
3	6.05	133.10	12.48	87.52	100
4	6.66	146.41	16.29	83.71	100
10	11.79	259.37	35.89	64.11	100
20	30.58	672.75	58.89	41.11	100
50	533.59	11,739.09	89.17	10.83	100
100	62,639.15	1,378,061.23	98.83	1.17	100

Assumptions:
1. Dividends increase at 10% per year, compounded.
2. Capitalization rate is 15%.

How far out could we look? In principle, the horizon period H could be infinitely distant. Common stocks do not expire of old age. Barring such corporate hazards as bankruptcy or acquisition, they are immortal. As H approaches infinity, the present value of the terminal price ought to approach zero, as it does in the final column of Figure 4-1. We can, therefore, forget about the terminal price entirely and express today's price as the present value of a perpetual stream of cash dividends. This is usually written as

$$P_0 = \sum_{t=1}^{\infty} \frac{DIV_t}{(1 + r)^t}$$

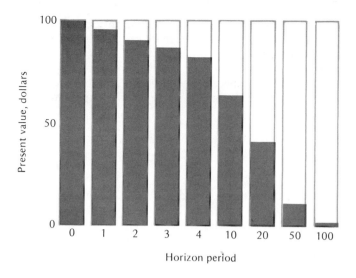

Figure 4-1 As your horizon recedes, the present value of the future price (shaded area) declines but the present value of the stream of dividends (unshaded area) increases. The *total* present value (future price and dividends) remains the same.

where the sign ∞ is used to indicate infinity. This discounted cash flow (DCF) formula for the present value of a stock is just the same as it is for the present value of any other asset. We just discount the cash flows—in this case the dividend stream—by the return that can be earned in the capital market on securities of comparable risk. Some find the DCF formula implausible because it seems to ignore capital gains. But we know the formula was *derived* from the assumption that price in any period is determined by expected dividends and capital gains over the next period.

Remembering our rule about adding present values, we might be tempted to conclude that the *total* value of a company's common stock must be equal to the discounted stream of *all* future dividends paid by the company. But we need to be a little careful here. We must only include the dividends that will be paid on *existing* stock. The company may at some future date decide to sell more stock and this will be entitled to its share of the subsequent dividend stream. The total value of a company's existing common stock is, therefore, equal to the discounted value of that *portion* of the total dividend stream that will be paid to the stock outstanding today. It sounds obvious but it is surprising how often people forget.

4-3 A SIMPLE WAY TO ESTIMATE THE CAPITALIZATION RATE

In Chapter 3 we encountered some simplified versions of the basic present value formula. Let us see whether they offer any insights into stock values. Suppose, for example, that we forecast a constant-growth trend in a company's dividends. This does not preclude year-to-year deviations from the trend: it means only that *expected* dividends grow at a constant rate. Such an investment would be just another example of the growing perpetuity that we helped our fickle philanthropist to evaluate in the last chapter. To find its present value we must divide the annual cash payment by the difference between the discount rate and the growth rate:

$$P_0 = \frac{DIV_1}{r - g}$$

Remember, however, that we can use this formula only when g, the anticipated growth rate, is less than r, the discount rate. As g approaches r, the stock price becomes infinite. Obviously r must be greater than g if growth really is perpetual.

Our growing perpetuity formula explains P_0 in terms of next year's expected dividend DIV_1, the projected growth trend g, and the expected rate of return on other securities of comparable risk r. Alternatively, the formula can be used to obtain an estimate of r from DIV_1, P_0, and g:

$$r = \frac{DIV_1}{P_0} + g$$

The market capitalization rate equals the **dividend yield** (DIV_1/P_0) plus the expected rate of growth in dividends (g).

These two formulas are much easier to work with than the general statement that "price equals the present value of expected future dividends."[2] For instance, imagine that we are analyzing Bell Canada Enterprises at the end of 1982 when its stock is selling for about $24.50 a share. Dividend payments for 1983 are expected to be $2.20 a share. Now we can calculate the first half of our formula:

$$\text{Dividend yield} = \frac{DIV_1}{P_0} = \frac{2.20}{24.50} = 0.09$$

The hard part is to estimate g. One line of reasoning starts with Bell Canada's **payout ratio**, the ratio of dividends to earnings per share (EPS). This has generally been around 65%. In other words, each year Bell Canada plows back into the business about 35% of earnings per share:

$$\text{Plowback ratio} = 1 - \text{payout ratio} = 1 - \frac{DIV_1}{EPS_1} = 1 - 0.65 = 0.35$$

Also, Bell's ratio of earnings per share to book equity per share is about 14%. This is its *return on equity* or ROE:

$$\text{Return on equity} = ROE = \frac{EPS_1}{\text{Book equity per share}} = 0.14$$

"Ma Bell" has always been a very stable company, and it may not be too unreasonable to assume that these relationships will continue to hold. If so, every year Bell will earn 14% of book equity and reinvest 35% of that, and therefore book equity will increase by $0.35 \times 0.14 = 0.05$. Since we assumed that the return on equity and the payout ratio are constant, earnings and dividends per share will also increase by 5%:

$$\begin{aligned} \text{Dividend growth rate} = g &= \text{plowback ratio} \times ROE \\ &= 0.35 \times 0.14 = 0.05 \end{aligned}$$

---

[2]These formulas were first developed in 1938 by J.B. Williams and were rediscovered by M.J. Gordon and E. Shapiro. See J.B. Williams, *The Theory of Investment Value*, Harvard University Press, Cambridge, Mass., 1938; and M.J. Gordon and E. Shapiro, "Capital Equipment Analysis: The Required Rate of Profit," *Management Science*, 3:102–110 (October 1956).

Now you have your estimate of the market capitalization rate (that is, the rate of return that investors use to discount Bell's future dividends):

$$r = \frac{DIV_1}{P_0} + g = 0.09 + 0.05 = 0.14 \text{ or } 14\%$$

Using the DCF Model to Set Electricity Prices

Although our estimate of the market capitalization rate for Bell stock seems reasonable enough, there are obvious dangers in analyzing any single firm's stock with such simple rules of thumb as the constant-growth DCF formula. First, the underlying assumption of regular future growth is at best an approximation. Second, even if it is an acceptable approximation, errors inevitably creep into the estimate of g. Remember, however, that r is not the personal property of Bell: in well-functioning markets, investors must capitalize the dividends of *all* securities in Bell's risk class at exactly the same rate. This means that we may do better to take a large sample of securities of equivalent risk, estimate r for each, and use the average of our estimates. Here is a practical example.

One task of the United States Federal Energy Regulatory Commission (FERC) is to set prices for interstate sales of electric power. These are almost always wholesale transactions. That is, an electric utility with surplus generating capacity will sell power to a utility in a neighbouring state. The buyer may have a shortage of capacity or it may not be able to produce electricity as cheaply as the seller.

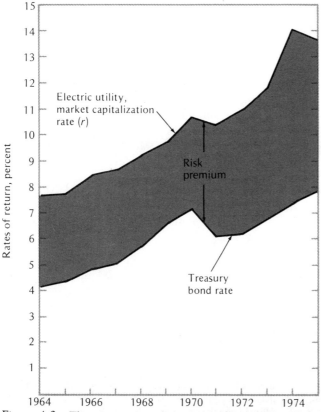

Figure 4-2   The average capitalization rate for electric utility common stocks was estimated with the constant-growth formula. Notice how r has increased roughly in line with increases in interest rates.

The sale price is supposed to cover all costs of producing and transporting the electricity, including interest and tax payments, *and* to provide a reasonable profit for the seller. What is "reasonable"? It is the profit that provides a fair rate of return to the seller on its equity investment in generating equipment, transmission lines, and so on. What is a "fair" rate of return? It is usually interpreted as r, the market capitalization rate for the selling firm's common stock. That is, the expected rate of return on investments made by electric utilities ought to be the same rate offered by securities having risks equivalent to the utility's common stock.

Thus FERC's problem of determining fair profits boils down to estimating r for the common stock of electric utilities. Accordingly FERC staff undertook to measure capitalization rates by the DCF formula.[3] The analysis included year-by-year estimates of r, using the constant-growth DCF formula, for each of 24 large electric utilities.[4] The average r for each year is plotted in Figure 4-2 for 1964–1975. Note that the utilities' market capitalization rate always lies above the interest rate on United States Treasury bonds. The difference between r and the federal government bond rate is generally called a *risk premium*: it is the extra return investors demanded for buying risky utility stocks rather than safe government bonds.

Some Warnings About Constant-Growth Formulas

These simple, constant-growth DCF formulas are extremely useful rules of thumb, but they are no more than that. Naive trust in the formulas has led many financial analysts to silly conclusions.

First, remember the difficulty of estimating r by analysis of one stock only. Try to work with a large sample of equivalent-risk securities. Even that may not work, but at least it gives the analyst a fighting chance, because the inevitable errors in estimating r for a single security tend to balance out across a broad sample.

Second, resist the temptation to apply the formula to firms having high current rates of growth. Such growth can rarely be sustained indefinitely, but the constant-growth DCF formula assumes it can. This erroneous assumption leads to an over-estimate of r.

Consider Growth-Tech, Inc., a firm with $DIV_1 = \$0.50$ and $P_0 = \$50$. That firm has plowed back 80% of earnings and has had a return on equity (ROE) of 25%. This means that *in the past*

Dividend growth rate = plowback ratio $\times$ ROE = $0.80 \times 0.25 = 0.20$

The temptation is to assume that the future long-term growth rate (g) also equals 0.20. This would imply

$$r = \frac{0.50}{50.00} + 0.20 = 0.21$$

But this is silly. No firm can continue growing at 20% per year forever, except possibly under extreme inflationary conditions. Eventually, profitability will fall and the firm will respond by investing less.

---

[3]The analysis was actually undertaken by the staff of FERC's predecessor, the Federal Power Commission. See Office of Economics, Federal Power Commission, "Standards for Determining a Fair Rate of Return on Equity Capital for Regulated Companies," September 1976.

[4]The growth rate g was estimated by fitting a trend line to past growth in the book value per share of the utilities. This was found to be a good proxy for the growth trend in dividends.

In real life the return on investment will decline *gradually* over time, but for simplicity let's assume it suddenly drops to 16% at year 3 and the firm responds by plowing back only 50% of earnings. Then g drops to $0.50(0.16) = 0.08$.

Table 4-2 Forecasted earnings and dividends for Growth-Tech. Note the changes in year 3: ROE and earnings drop, but payout ratio increases, causing a big jump in dividends. However, subsequent growth in earnings and dividends falls to 8% per year. Note that the increase in equity equals the earnings not paid out as dividends.

Year	1	2	3	4
Book equity	10.00	12.00	14.40	15.55
Earnings per share, EPS	2.50	3.00	2.30	2.49
Return on equity, ROE	0.25	0.25	0.16	0.16
Payout ratio	0.20	0.20	0.50	0.50
Dividends per share, DIV	0.50	0.60	1.15	1.24
Growth rate of dividends	—	0.20	0.92	0.08

Table 4-2 shows what's going on. Growth-Tech starts year 1 with assets of $10.00. It earns $2.50, pays out 50¢ as dividends, and plows back $2. Thus it starts year 2 with $10 + 2 = 12. After another year at the same ROE and payout, it starts year 3 with equity of $14.40. However ROE drops to 0.16 and the firm earns only $2.30. Dividends go up to $1.15, because the payout ratio increases, but the firm has only $1.15 to plow back. Therefore subsequent growth in earnings and dividends drops to 8%.

Now we can use our general DCF formula to find the capitalization rate r:

$$P_0 = \frac{DIV_1}{1 + r} + \frac{DIV_2}{(1 + r)^2} + \frac{DIV_3 + P_3}{(1 + r)^3}$$

Investors in year 3 will view Growth-Tech as offering 8% per year dividend growth. We will apply the constant-growth formula:

$$P_3 = \frac{DIV_4}{r - 0.08}$$

$$P_0 = \frac{DIV_1}{1 + r} + \frac{DIV_2}{(1 + r)^2} + \frac{DIV_3}{(1 + r)^3} + \frac{1}{(1 + r)^3} \frac{DIV_4}{(r - 0.08)}$$

$$= \frac{0.50}{1 + r} + \frac{0.60}{(1 + r)^2} + \frac{1.15}{(1 + r)^3} + \frac{1}{(1 + r)^3} \frac{1.24}{(r - 0.08)}$$

We have to use trial and error to find the value of r that makes P_0 equal $50. It turns out that the r implicit in these more realistic forecasts is approximately 0.099, quite a difference from our "constant-growth" estimate of 0.21.

A final warning. Do not use the simple constant-growth formula to test whether the market is correct in its assessment of a stock's value. If your estimate of the value is different from that of the market, it is probably because you have used poor dividend forecasts. Remember what we said at the beginning of this chapter about simple ways of making money on the stock market. There aren't any.

4-4 THE LINK BETWEEN STOCK PRICE AND EARNINGS PER SHARE

Investors often use the terms *growth stocks* and *income stocks*. They seem to buy growth stocks primarily for the expectation of capital gains, and they are interested in the future growth of earnings rather than in next year's dividends. On the other hand, they buy income stocks primarily for the cash dividends. Let us see whether these distinctions make sense.

Imagine first the case of a company that does not grow at all. It does not plow back any earnings and simply produces a constant stream of dividends. Its stock would be rather like the perpetual bond described in the last chapter. Remember that the return on a perpetuity is equal to the yearly cash flow divided by the present value. The expected return on our share would thus be equal to the yearly dividend divided by the share price (that is, the dividend yield). Since all the earnings are paid out as dividends, the expected return is also equal to the earnings per share divided by the share price (that is, the earnings-price ratio). For example, if the dividend is $10 a share and the stock price is $100, we have

$$\text{Expected return} = \text{dividend yield} = \text{earnings-price ratio}$$

$$= \frac{DIV_1}{P_0} \qquad = \frac{EPS_1}{P_0}$$

$$= \frac{10.00}{100} \qquad = 0.10$$

The price equals

$$P_0 = \frac{DIV_1}{r} = \frac{EPS_1}{r} = \frac{10.00}{0.10} = \$100$$

The expected return for growing firms can also equal the earnings-price ratio. The key is whether earnings are reinvested to provide a return greater or less than the market capitalization rate. For example, suppose our monotonous company suddenly hears of an opportunity to invest $10 a share next year. This would mean no dividend at $t = 1$. However, the company expects that in each subsequent year the project would earn $1 per share, so that the dividend could be increased to $11 a share.

Let us assume that this investment opportunity has about the same risk as the existing business. Then we can discount its cash flow at the 10% rate to find its net present value at year 1:

$$\text{Net present value per share at year 1} = -10 + \frac{1}{0.10} = 0$$

Thus the investment opportunity will make no contribution to the company's value; to put it another way, its prospective return is equal to the opportunity cost of capital.

What effect will the decision to undertake the project have on the company's share price? Clearly none. The reduction in value caused by the nil dividend in year 1 is exactly offset by the increase in value caused by the extra dividends in later years. Therefore, once again the market capitalization rate equals the earnings-price ratio:

$$r = \frac{EPS_1}{P_0} = \frac{10}{100} = 0.10$$

Table 4-3 repeats our example for different assumptions about the cash flow generated by the new project. Note that the earnings-price ratio, measured in terms of EPS_1, next year's expected earnings, equals the market capitalization rate (r) *only* when the new project's NPV = 0. This is an extremely important point—business people frequently make poor financial decisions because they confuse earnings-price ratios with the market capitalization rate.

Table 4-3   Effect on stock price of investing an additional $10 in year 1 at different rates of return. Notice that the earnings-price ratio overestimates r when the project has negative NPV and underestimates it when the project has positive NPV.

Project Rate of Return	Incremental Cash Flow, C	Project NPV in Year 1[a]	Project's Impact on Share Price in Year 0[b]	Share Price in Year 0, P_0	$\dfrac{EPS_1}{P_0}$	r
0.05	$ .50	−$5.00	−$4.55	$ 95.45	0.105	0.10
0.10	1.00	0	0	100.00	0.10	0.10
0.15	1.50	+5.00	+4.55	104.55	0.096	0.10
0.20	2.00	+10.00	+9.09	109.09	0.092	0.10
0.25	2.50	+15.00	+13.64	113.64	0.088	0.10

[a] Project costs $10.00 per share. NPV = $-10 + C/r$, where r = 0.10.
[b] NPV is calculated at year 1. To find the impact on P_0, discount for one year at r = 0.10.

In general, we can think of stock price as the capitalized value of average earnings under a no-growth policy, plus PVGO, the **present value of growth opportunities**:

$$P_0 = \frac{EPS_1}{r} + PVGO$$

The earnings-price ratio, therefore, equals

$$\frac{EPS_1}{P_0} = r\left(1 - \frac{PVGO}{P_0}\right)$$

It will underestimate r if PVGO is positive and overestimate it if PVGO is negative. (The latter case is less likely, since firms are rarely *forced* to take projects with negative net present values.)

*Calculating the Present Value of Growth Opportunities for Fledgling Electronics

Although in our last example both dividends and earnings were expected to grow, this growth made no net contribution to the share price. The stock was in this sense an "income stock." Now let us compare this case with that well-known "growth stock," Fledgling Electronics. You may remember that Fledgling's market capitalization rate,

r, is 15%. The company is expected to pay a dividend of $5 in the first year, and thereafter the dividend is predicted to increase indefinitely by 10% a year. We can, therefore, use the simplified constant-growth formula to work out Fledgling's price:

$$P_0 = \frac{DIV_1}{r - g} = \frac{5}{0.15 - 0.10} = \$100$$

Suppose that Fledgling has earnings per share of $8.33. Its payout ratio is then

$$\text{Payout ratio} = \frac{DIV_1}{EPS_1} = \frac{5.00}{8.33} = 0.6$$

In other words, the company is plowing back $1 - 0.6$, or 40% of earnings. Suppose also that Fledgling's ratio of earnings to book equity is $ROE = 0.25$. This explains the growth rate of 10%:

$$\text{Growth rate} = g = \text{plowback ratio} \times ROE = 0.4 \times 0.25 = 0.10$$

The capitalized value of Fledgling's earnings per share if it had a no-growth policy would be

$$\frac{EPS_1}{r} = \frac{8.33}{0.15} = \$55.56$$

But we know that the value of Fledgling stock is $100. The difference of $44.44 must be the amount that investors are paying for growth opportunities. Let's see if we can explain that figure.

Each year Fledgling plows back 40% of its earnings into new assets. In the first year Fledgling invests $3.33 at a permanent 25% return on equity. Thus the cash generated by this investment is $0.25 \times 3.33 = \$0.83$ per year starting at $t = 2$. The net present value of the investment as of $t = 1$ is

$$NPV_1 = -3.33 + \frac{0.83}{0.15} = \$2.22$$

Everything is the same in year 2 except that Fledgling will invest $3.67, 10% more than in year 1 (remember $g = 0.10$). Therefore at $t = 2$ an investment is made with a net present value of

$$NPV_2 = -3.33 \times 1.10 + \frac{0.83 \times 1.10}{0.15} = \$2.44$$

Thus the payoff to the owners of Fledgling Electronics stock can be represented as the sum of (1) a level stream of earnings, which could be paid out as cash dividends if the firm did not grow, and (2) a set of tickets, one for each future year, representing the opportunity to make investments having positive NPVs. We know that the first component of the value of the share is

$$\text{Present value of level stream of earnings} = \frac{EPS_1}{r} = \frac{8.33}{0.15} = \$55.56$$

The first ticket is worth $2.22 in $t = 1$; the second is worth $2.22 \times 1.10 = \$2.44$ in $t = 2$; the third is worth $\$2.44 \times 1.10 = \$2.69$ in $t = 3$. These are the forecasted cash values of the tickets. We know how to value a stream of future cash values that grows at 10% per year: use the simplified DCF formula, replacing the forecasted dividends with forecasted ticket values:

$$\text{Present value of growth opportunities} = \text{PVGO} = \frac{\text{NPV}_1}{r - g} = \frac{2.22}{0.15 - 0.10}$$

$$= \$44.44$$

Now everything checks:

$$
\begin{aligned}
\text{Share price} &= \text{present value of level stream of earnings} \\
&\quad + \text{present value of growth opportunities} \\
&= \frac{\text{EPS}_1}{r} + \text{PVGO} \\
&= \$55.56 + \$44.44 \\
&= \$100
\end{aligned}
$$

A General Expression Linking Dividends and Growth Opportunities

Zeus made a habit of appearing in unusual disguises to unsuspecting maidens. The general DCF formula for valuing stocks is rather like that: it keeps cropping up in different forms. Here is another useful version of the formula. Cash not retained and reinvested in the business is often known as **free cash flow**:

Free cash flow = revenue − costs − investment

But cash that is not reinvested in the business is paid out as dividends. So dividends per share are the same as free cash flow per share, and the general DCF formula can be written in terms of per share revenues, costs, and investment:

$$P_0 = \sum_{t = 1}^{\infty} \frac{(\text{Free cash flow per share})_t}{(1 + r)^t}$$

Notice that it is *not* correct to say that a share's value is equal to the discounted stream of its future earnings per share. That would recognize the *rewards* of investment (in the form of increased revenues) but not the *sacrifice* (in the form of investment). The correct formulation states that share value is equal to the discounted stream of free cash flow per share.

To summarize, we can think of a stock's value as representing either (1) the present value of the stream of expected future dividends, or (2) the present value of free cash flow, or (3) the present value of average future earnings under a no-growth policy plus the present value of growth opportunities.

Some companies have such extensive growth opportunities that they prefer to pay no dividends for long periods of time. Up to the time when this chapter was written, Digital Equipment Corporation (DEC) had never paid dividends, because any cash paid out to investors would have meant either slower growth or raising capital by some other means. Investors were evidently happy with management's decision to reinvest the earnings. How else can we explain DEC's $7 billion market value? Investors were willing to forgo cash dividends today in exchange for higher earnings and the expectation of high dividends sometime in the future. Thus DEC's common stock is not really a counterexample to the statement that stock price equals the present value of expected future dividends. DEC's dividends may continue to be zero for many years, but they are likely to be positive sooner or later. The company cannot continue to grow at 30% per year forever. Eventually growth must slow down, releasing funds that can be paid to the stockholders. It is that prospect that makes DEC shares valuable today.

The inevitable deceleration of rapid growth is illustrated by the history of IBM, the most famous growth stock of the period after World War Two. IBM has paid dividends since the 1930s, but most IBM stockholders bought the stock for growth, not dividends. Throughout the 1950s and 1960s the dividend yield (dividend per share as a percent of stock price) was very low—usually between 1 and 2%. Sales, earnings, and dividends grew at compound annual rates of roughly 20%.

That kind of growth cannot continue forever. By the mid-1970s IBM lacked investment opportunities attractive enough to justify continued growth at that rate. Yet its existing businesses remained healthy and profitable. Consequently, the firm accumulated cash at an embarrassing rate. It had $6.1 *billion* in cash and marketable securities at the end of 1976 and $5.4 billion at year-end 1977. It was therefore not surprising to find IBM paying more and more generous dividends: in 1978 it paid $2.88 per share on earnings per share of $5.32, a 54% payout ratio. (We noted earlier in this chapter that Bell Canada's payout ratio has averaged about 65%. Bell is the prototypical *income* stock.) Also, IBM spent about $1.4 billion in 1977 and 1978 to repurchase its own shares. That is, IBM distributed cash to its shareholders by buying shares from them. As Chapter 16 explains, this is essentially equivalent to paying a cash dividend.

What Do Price-Earnings Ratios Mean?

The **price-earnings ratio** is part of the everyday vocabulary of investors in the stock market. People casually refer to DEC stock as "selling at a high *P/E*." You can look up *P/E*s in stock quotations given in the newspaper. (However, the newspaper gives the ratio of current price to the more recent earnings. Investors are more concerned with price relative to *future* earnings.) Unfortunately, some financial analysts are confused about what price-earnings ratios really signify and often use the ratios in odd ways.

Should the financial manager celebrate if the firm's stock sells at a high *P/E*? The answer is usually yes. The high *P/E* shows that investors think that the firm has good growth opportunities (high PVGO), that its earnings are relatively safe and deserve a low capitalization rate (low *r*), or both. However, firms can have high price-earnings ratios not because price is high but because earnings are low. A firm that earns *nothing* (EPS = 0) in a particular period will have an *infinite P/E* as long as its shares retain any value at all.

Are relative *P/E*s helpful in evaluating stocks? Sometimes. Suppose you own stock in a family corporation whose shares are not actively traded. What are those shares worth? A decent estimate is possible if you can find a traded firm that has the same profitability, risks, and growth opportunities as those of your firm. Multiply your firm's earnings per share by the *P/E* of the counterpart firm.

Does a high *P/E* indicate a low market capitalization rate? No. There is *no* reliable association between a stock's price-earnings ratio and the capitalization rate *r*. The ratio of EPS to P_0 measures *r* only if PVGO = 0, and only if EPS is the average future earnings the firm could generate under a no-growth policy.

What Do Earnings Mean?

Another reason *P/Es* are hard to interpret is the difficulty of interpreting and comparing earnings per share, the denominator of the price-earnings ratio. What do earnings per share mean? They mean different things for different firms. For some firms they mean more than for others.

The problem is that the earnings that firms report are book, or accounting, figures, and as such reflect a series of more or less arbitrary choices of accounting methods. Almost any firm's reported earnings are changed substantially by the adoption of more or less "conservative" accounting procedures. A switch in the depreciation method used for reporting purposes directly affects EPS, for example. Yet it has *no* effect on cash flow, since depreciation is a noncash charge. (The depreciation method used for tax purposes, called **capital cost allowance**, *does* affect cash flow.) Other accounting choices that affect reported earnings are the valuation of inventory, the procedures by which the accounts of two merging firms are combined, the choice between expensing or capitalizing research and development, and the way the tax liabilities of the firm are reported. The list could go on and on.

We shall discuss the biases in accounting income and profitability measures in Chapter 12, after we have used present value concepts to develop measures of true, economic income. For the moment, we just want you to remember that accounting earnings are slippery animals.

4-5   SUMMARY

In this chapter we have used our new-found knowledge of present values to examine the market price of bonds and common stocks. In each case the value of the security is just like that of any other asset: it is equal to the stream of cash payments discounted at the rate of return that investors expect to receive on comparable securities.

The cash payments on a bond consist of the regular interest payments together with the final payment of the bond's face value. The rate of interest that makes the discounted value of these cash flows equal to the bond's market price is known as the bond's *yield to maturity* or *internal rate of return*.

Common stocks do not have a fixed maturity; their cash payments consist of an indefinite stream of dividends. Therefore, the present value of a common stock is

$$PV = \sum_{t=1}^{\infty} \frac{DIV_t}{(1 + r)^t}$$

However, we did not *derive* our DCF formula just by substituting DIV_t for C_t. We did not *assume* that the investors purchase common stocks solely for dividends. In fact, we began with the assumption that investors have relatively short horizons and invest for both dividends and capital gains. Our fundamental valuation formula is, therefore,

$$P_0 = \frac{DIV_1 + P_1}{1 + r}$$

This is a condition of market equilibrium: if it did not hold, the share would be overpriced or underpriced, and investors would rush to sell or buy it. The flood of sellers or buyers would force the price to adjust so that the fundamental valuation formula holds.

This formula will hold in each future period as well as the present. That allowed us to express next year's forecasted price in terms of the subsequent stream of dividends DIV_1, DIV_2, ...

We also made use of the formula for a growing perpetuity presented in Chapter 3. If dividends are expected to grow forever at a constant compound rate of g, then

$$P_0 = \frac{DIV_1}{r - g}$$

We showed how it is often helpful to twist this formula around and use it to estimate the capitalization rate r, given P_0 and estimates of DIV_1 and g.

Finally we transformed the general DCF formula into a statement about earnings and growth opportunities:

$$P_0 = \frac{EPS_1}{r} + PVGO$$

The ratio EPS_1/r is the capitalized value of the earnings per share that the firm would generate under a no-growth policy. PVGO is the net present value of the investments that the firm will make in order to grow. A "growth" stock is one for which PVGO is large relative to the capitalized value of EPS. Most growth stocks are stocks of rapidly expanding firms, but expansion alone does not create a high PVGO. What matters is the profitability of the new investments.

In earlier chapters, you should have acquired—we hope painlessly—a knowledge of the basic principles of valuing assets and a facility with the mechanics of discounting. Now you know something of how common stocks are valued and market capitalization rates estimated. In Chapter 5 we can begin to apply all this knowledge in a more specific analysis of capital-budgeting decisions.

FURTHER READING

There are a number of discussions of the valuation of common stocks in investment texts. We suggest:

W.F. Sharpe, *Investments*, 2nd ed., Prentice-Hall, Inc., Englewood Cliffs, N.J., 1981.
J.H. Lorie and M. Hamilton, *The Stock Market: Theories and Evidence*, Richard D. Irwin, Inc., Homewood, Ill., 1973.
R.A. Brealey, *An Introduction to Risk and Return for Common Stocks*, 2nd ed., The MIT Press, 1983.

J.B. Williams's original work remains very readable. See particularly Chapter V of:

J.B. Williams, *The Theory of Investment Value*, Harvard University Press, Cambridge, Mass., 1938.

The following articles provide important developments of Williams's early work. We suggest, however, that you leave the third article until you have read Chapter 16:

D. Durand, "Growth Stocks and the Petersburg Paradox," *Journal of Finance*, **12**:348–363 (September 1957).
M.J. Gordon and E. Shapiro, "Capital Equipment Analysis: The Required Rate of Profit," *Management Science*, **3**:102–110 (October 1956).
M.H. Miller and F. Modigliani, "Dividend Policy, Growth and the Valuation of Shares," *Journal of Business*, **34**:411–433 (October 1961).

There have also been many applications of the present value model. Two good examples are,

R.C. Higgins, "Growth, Dividend Policy and Capital Costs in the Electric Utility Industry," *Journal of Finance*, **29**:1189–1201 (September 1974).

B.G. Malkiel, "Equity Yields, Growth and the Structure of Share Prices," *American Economic Review*, **53**:467–494 (December 1963).

QUIZ

1. Company X is expected to pay an end-of-year dividend of $10 a share. After the dividend its stock is expected to sell at $210. If the market capitalization rate is 10%, what is the current stock price?

2. Company Y does not plow back any earnings and is expected to produce a level dividend stream of $5 a share. If the current stock price is $40, what is the market capitalization rate?

3. Company Z's dividends per share are expected to grow indefinitely by 5% a year. If next year's dividend is $10 and the market capitalization rate is 10%, what is the current stock price?

4. If company Z (see question 3) were to distribute all its earnings, it could maintain a level dividend stream of $15 a share. How much, therefore, is the market actually paying per share for growth opportunities?

5. Which of the following statements are correct?
   (*a*) The value of a share equals the discounted stream of future earnings per share.
   (*b*) The value of a share equals the present value of earnings per share assuming the firm does not grow, plus the net present value of future growth opportunities.
   (*c*) The value of a share equals the discounted stream of future dividends per share.

6. Calculate the present value of each of the following bonds, assuming a yield to maturity of 8%:

Bond	Annual Coupon, %	Maturity
A	5	1
B	5	2
C	5	6

7. Recalculate the present value of the bonds in question assuming the yield to maturity changes to 10%. Does a rise in the return that investors require have a larger effect on the price of long-term bonds or short-term bonds?

QUESTIONS AND PROBLEMS

1. Rework Table 4-1 assuming that the dividend on Fledgling Electronics is $10 next year and that it is expected to grow by 5% a year. The capitalization rate is 15%.

2. (*a*) Look in *The Financial Post*. Can you find the dividend yield on the Toronto Stock Exchange 300 Composite Index?
   (*b*) Assume that the expected return on common stocks is 8% higher than on short-term Government of Canada bonds. Use the constant growth model to estimate the expected dividend growth for the TSE 300.
   (*c*) Estimate the change in the TSE 300 Index if investors reduce their forecast of the dividend growth by 2%.

3. Look in a recent issue of *The Financial Post* at the section called "infoPost."
   (*a*) What is the latest price of Northern Telecom stock?

(*b*) What is the annual dividend payment and the dividend yield on Northern Telecom stock?

(*c*) What would the yield be if Northern raised its yearly dividend to $1.20?

(*d*) What is the *P/E* ratio on Northern Telecom stock?

(*e*) Use the *P/E* ratio to calculate Northern's earnings per share.

(*f*) Is Northern's *P/E* higher or lower than that of Imperial Oil?

(*g*) What are the possible reasons for the difference in *P/E*?

4. Look up Canadian Pacific's current stock price and yearly dividend payment. Assume that the payment is expected to grow at a constant rate g.

(*a*) What expected rate of return is indicated by (i) $g = 0.02$, (ii) $g = 0.05$, or (iii) $g = 0.10$?

(*b*) Make an estimate of g from the company's plowback rate and return on equity. What expected rate of return is indicated by your estimate?

5. You believe that next year the Dong Lumination Company will pay a dividend of $2 on its common stock. Thereafter you expect dividends to grow at a rate of 4% a year in perpetuity. If you require a return of 12% on your investment, how much should you be prepared to pay for the stock?

*6. Rework the analysis of the present value of the growth opportunities for Fledgling Electronics, assuming (i) that the dividend is $10 next year, (ii) that it is expected to grow by 5% a year, and (iii) that it plows back a constant 20% of earnings.

(*a*) What is next year's expected earnings per share (EPS_1)?

(*b*) What is the return on book equity (ROE)?

(*c*) What is PVGO?

7. What would happen to the value of the Canada 12s of 1987 (see Section 4-1) if the market rate of interest (*a*) fell to 9% and (*b*) rose to 12%? (Assume annual coupon payments.)

8. Calculate the value in 1982 of the following Government of Canada bonds, assuming that the rate of interest is 10%:

(*a*) $11^1/_4$%, 1989.

(*b*) $12^3/_4$%, 1992.

(*c*) $9^1/_4$%, 1997.

(In your calculations recognize the fact that coupon payments occur semiannually.)

9. Explain carefully why different stocks may have different *P/Es*. Show how the price-earnings ratio is related to growth, dividend payout, and the required return.

10. Suppose that there is a general increase in the rates of return that investors require. Show what effect this would have on the prices of short-term bonds (for example, one-year bonds), long-term bonds (for example, perpetuities), income stocks, and growth stocks.

11. Each of the following formulas for determining shareholders' required rate of return can be right or wrong depending on the circumstances:

(*a*) $r = \dfrac{DIV_1}{P_0} + g$

(*b*) $r = \dfrac{EPS_1}{P_0}$

For each formula construct a *simple* numerical example showing that the formula can give wrong answers and explain why the error occurs. Then construct another simple numerical example for which the formula gives the right answer.

12. A stock is selling at $50, with an expected dividend of $2. Short-term prospects are excellent: a 20% annual growth rate is expected for the next three years. After that, the growth rate is expected to drop to a more normal 6%. What is the expected long-run rate of return from buying the stock at $50? (*Hint*: you need to use a little trial and error to find r.)

13. Mr. T. Thumb is the president of Microtechnology, Inc., a very small private company. He expects revenues in the forthcoming year of $20 million and costs (including taxes) of $15 million. During the subsequent five years (that is, years two through six), Mr. Thumb forecasts that revenues and costs will grow by 25% a year, but he anticipates that all profits will need to be plowed back into the business. Thereafter he forecasts that growth will drop to 5% a year and that the company will need to plow back only 40% of profits. Mr. Thumb has recently been offered $75 million in cash for his company. Is this a fair offer if the opportunity cost of capital is 12%?

14. Consider a firm with existing assets that generate an EPS of $5. If the firm does not invest except to maintain existing assets, EPS is expected to remain constant at $5 a year. However, starting next year the firm has the chance to invest $3 per share a year in developing a newly discovered geothermal steam source for electricity generation. These investments are expected to generate a permanent 20% return. However, the source will be fully developed by the fifth year. What will be the stock price and earnings-price ratio assuming investors require a 12% rate of return? Show that the earnings-price ratio is 0.20 if the required rate of return is 20%.

15. Compost Science, Inc. (CSI) is in the business of converting Boston's sewage sludge into fertilizer. The business is not in itself very profitable. However, to induce CSI to remain in business, the Metropolitan District Commission (MDC) has agreed to pay whatever amount is necessary to yield CSI a 10% book return on equity. At the end of the year CSI is expected to pay a $4 dividend. It has been reinvesting 40% of earnings and growing at 4% a year.
    (*a*) Suppose CSI continues on this growth trend. What is the expected long-run rate of return from purchasing the stock at $100? What part of the $100 price is attributable to the present value of growth opportunities?
    (*b*) Now the MDC announces a plan for CSI to treat Cambridge sewage. CSI's plant will, therefore, be expanded gradually over five years. This means that CSI will have to reinvest 80% of its earnings for five years. Starting in year 6, however, it will again be able to pay out 60% of earnings. What will be CSI's stock price once this announcement is made and its consequences for CSI are known?

WHY NET PRESENT VALUE LEADS TO BETTER INVESTMENT DECISIONS THAN OTHER CRITERIA

In the first four chapters we have introduced, at times surreptitiously, most of the basic principles of the investment decision. In this chapter we consolidate that knowledge. We also take a critical look at other criteria that companies sometimes use to make investment decisions.

5-1 A REVIEW OF THE BASICS

Vegetron's financial manager is wondering how to analyze a proposed $1 million investment in a new venture called project X. He asks what you think.

Your response should be as follows: "First, forecast the cash flows generated by project X over its economic life. Second, determine the appropriate opportunity cost of capital. This should reflect both the time value of money and the risk involved in project X. Third, use this opportunity cost of capital to discount the future cash flows of project X. The sum of the discounted cash flows is called present value (PV). Fourth, calculate *net* present value (NPV) by subtracting the $1 million investment from PV. Invest in project X if its NPV is greater than zero."

However, Vegetron's financial manager is unmoved by your sagacity. He asks why NPV is so important.

Your reply: "Let us look at what is best for Vegetron stockholders. They want you to make their Vegetron shares as valuable as possible.

"Right now Vegetron's total market value (price per share times the number of shares outstanding) is $10 million. That includes $1 million cash we can invest in project X. The value of Vegetron's other assets and opportunities must therefore be $9 million. We have to decide whether it is better to keep the $1 million cash and reject project X or to spend the cash and accept project X. Let us call the value of the new project PV. Then the choice is as follows:

	Market Value (millions of dollars)	
Asset	Reject Project X	Accept Project X
Cash	1	0
Other assets	9	9
Project X	0	PV
	10	9 + PV

Clearly project X is worthwhile if its present value, PV, is greater than $1 million— that is, if net present value is positive."

Financial manager: "How do I know that the PV of project X will actually show up in Vegetron's market value?"

Your reply: "Suppose we set up a new, independent firm X, whose only asset is project X. What would be the market value of firm X?

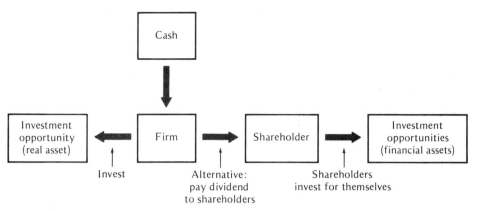

Figure 5-1 The firm can either keep and reinvest cash or return it to investors. (Arrows represent possible cash flows or transfers.) If cash is reinvested, the opportunity cost is the expected rate of return that shareholders could have obtained by investing in financial assets.

"Investors would forecast the dividends firm X would pay and discount those dividends by the expected rate of return of securities having risks comparable to firm X. We know that stock prices are equal to the present value of forecasted dividends.

"Since project X is firm X's only asset, the dividend payments we would expect firm X to pay are exactly the cash flows we have forecasted for project X. Moreover, the rate investors would use to discount firm X's dividends is exactly the rate we should use to discount project X's cash flows.

"I agree that firm X is entirely hypothetical. But if project X is accepted, investors holding Vegetron stock will really hold a portfolio of project X and the firm's other assets. We know the other assets are worth $9 million considered as a separate venture. Since asset values are additive we can easily figure out the portfolio value once we calculate the value of project X as a separate venture.

"By calculating the present value of project X, we are replicating the process by which the common stock of firm X would be valued in capital markets."

Financial manager: "I don't understand where the discount rate comes from."

Your reply: "I agree that the discount rate is difficult to measure precisely. But it is easy to see what we are *trying* to measure. The discount rate is the opportunity cost of investing in the project rather than in the capital market. In other words, instead of accepting a project, the firm can always give the cash to shareholders and let them invest it in financial assets.

"Figure 5-1 shows the trade-off. The opportunity cost of taking the project is the return shareholders could have earned had they invested the funds on their own. When we discount the project's cash flows by the expected rates of return on comparable financial assets, we are measuring how much investors would be prepared to pay for your project.

"But which financial asset? The fact that investors expect only 12% on Bell Canada Enterprises stock does not mean that a firm should purchase Fly-by-Night Electronics Company if it offers 13%. The opportunity-cost concept makes sense only if assets of equivalent risk are compared. In general, you should identify financial assets with risks equivalent to the project under consideration, estimate the expected rate of return on these assets, and use this rate as the opportunity cost."

5-2 COMPETITORS OF NET PRESENT VALUE

Let us hope the financial manager is by now convinced of the correctness of the net present value rule. But it is possible that the manager has also heard of some alternative investment criteria and would like to know why you do not recommend any of them. Just so that you are prepared, we will now look at the four most popular alternatives to the NPV rule. These are:

1. Payback
2. Average return on book value
3. Internal rate of return
4. Profitability index

As we look at these alternative criteria, it is worth keeping in mind the following key features of the net present value rule. First, the NPV rule recognizes that *a dollar today is worth more than a dollar tomorrow*, because the dollar today can be invested to start earning interest immediately. Any investment rule that does not recognize the time value of money cannot be sensible. Second, net present value depends solely on the *forecasted cash flows* from the project and the *opportunity cost of capital*. Any investment rule that is affected by the manager's tastes, the company's choice of accounting method, the profitability of the company's existing business, or the profitability of other independent projects will lead to inferior decisions. Third, *because present values are all measured in today's dollars, you can add them up*. Therefore, if you have two projects, A and B, the net present value of the combined investment is

$$NPV(A + B) = NPV(A) + NPV(B)$$

This additivity property has important implications. Suppose project B has a negative NPV. If you tack it onto project A, the joint project (A + B) will have a lower NPV than A on its own. Therefore, you are unlikely to be misled into accepting a poor project (B) just because it is packaged with a good one (A). As we shall see, the alternative measures do not have this additivity property. If you are not careful, you may be tricked into deciding that a package of a good and a bad project is better than the good project on its own.

5-3 PAYBACK

Companies frequently require that the initial outlay on any project should be recoverable within some specified cutoff period. The payback period of a project is found by counting the number of years it takes before cumulative forecasted cash flows equal the initial investment. Consider projects A and B:

	Cash Flows (dollars)					
Project	C_0	C_1	C_2	C_3	Payback Period (years)	NPV at 10%
A	−2,000	+2,000	0	0	1	− 182
B	−2,000	+1,000	+1,000	+5,000	2	+3,492

Project A involves an initial investment of $2,000 ($C_0 = -2,000$) followed by a single cash inflow of $2,000 in year 1. Suppose the opportunity cost of capital is 10%. Then project A has an NPV of −$182:

$$NPV(A) = -2,000 + \frac{2,000}{1.10} = -\$182$$

Project B also requires an initial investment of $2,000 but produces a cash inflow of $1,000 in years 1 and 2 and $5,000 in year 3. At a 10% opportunity cost of capital project B has an NPV of +$3,492:

$$NPV(B) = -2,000 + \frac{1,000}{1.10} + \frac{1,000}{(1.10)^2} + \frac{5,000}{(1.10)^3} = +\$3,492$$

Thus the net present value rule tells us to reject project A and accept project B.

The Payback Rule

Now let us look at how rapidly each project pays back its initial investment. With project A you take one year to recover your $2,000; with project B you take two years. If the firm used the **payback rule** with a cutoff period of one year, it would accept only project A; if it used the payback rule with a cutoff period of two or more years, it would accept both A and B. Therefore, regardless of the choice of cutoff period, the payback rule gives a different answer from the net present value rule.

The reason for the difference is that payback gives equal weight to all cash flows before the payback date and no weight at all to subsequent flows. For example, the following three projects all have a payback period of two years:

| | Cash Flow (dollars) | | | | | Payback |
Project	C_0	C_1	C_2	C_3	NPV at 10%	Period (years)
B	−2,000	+1,000	+1,000	+5,000	3,492	2
C	−2,000	0	+2,000	+5,000	3,409	2
D	−2,000	+1,000	+1,000	+100,000	74,867	2

The payback rule says that these projects are all equally attractive. But project B has a higher NPV than project C for any positive interest rate ($1,000 in each of years 1 and 2 is more valuable than $2,000 in year 2). And project D has a higher NPV than either B or C.

To use the payback rule a firm has to decide on an appropriate cutoff date. If it uses the same cutoff regardless of project life, it will tend to accept too many short-lived projects and too few long-lived ones. If, on average, the cutoff periods are too long, it will accept some projects with negative NPVs; if, on average, they are too short, it will reject some projects that have positive NPVs.

Many firms that use payback choose the cutoff period essentially by guesswork. It is possible to do better than that. If you know the typical pattern of cash flows, then you can find the cutoff period that would come closest to maximizing net present value.[1] However, this "optimal" cutoff point works only for those projects that have "typical" patterns of cash flows. So it is still better to use the net present value rule.

---

[1] If the inflows are, on average, spread evenly over the life of the project, the optimal cutoff for the payback rule is

$$\text{Optimal cutoff period} = \frac{1}{r} - \frac{1}{r(1 + r)^n}$$

where n denotes the project life. This expression for the optimal payback was first noted in M.J. Gordon, "The Pay-Off Period and the Rate of Profit," *Journal of Business*, 28:253–260 (October 1955). Note that this is just the formula for the present value of an annuity. Can you see why?

Discounted Payback

Some companies discount the cash flows before they compute the payback period. The **discounted payback rule** asks, "How many periods does the project have to last in order to make sense in terms of net present value?" This modification to the payback rule surmounts the objection that equal weight is given to all flows before the cutoff date. However, the discounted payback rule still takes no account of any cash flows after the cutoff date.

Suppose there are two mutually exclusive investments, A and B. Each requires a $20,000 investment and is expected to generate a level stream of cash flows starting in year 1. The annual cash flow for investment A is $6,500 and lasts for six years. The annual cash flow for B is $6,000 but lasts for ten years. The appropriate discount rate for each project is 10%. Investment B is clearly a better investment on the basis of net present value:

$$NPV(A) = -20,000 + \sum_{t=1}^{6} \frac{6,500}{(1.10)^t} = +\$8,309$$

$$NPV(B) = -20,000 + \sum_{t=1}^{10} \frac{6,000}{(1.10)^t} = +\$16,867$$

Yet A has higher cash receipts than B in each year of its life, and so obviously it has the shorter discounted payback. The discounted payback of A is a bit less than four years, since the present value of $6,500 at 10% for four years is $20,604. The discounted payback of B is a bit more than four years, since the present value of $6,000 for four years is $19,019.

Discounted payback is a whisker better than undiscounted payback. It recognizes that a dollar at the beginning of the payback period is worth more than a dollar at the end of the payback period. This helps, but it may not help much. The discounted payback rule still depends on the choice of an arbitrary cutoff date and it still ignores all cash flows after that date.

5-4 AVERAGE RETURN ON BOOK VALUE

Some companies judge an investment project by looking at its **book rate of return**. To calculate book rate of return it is necessary to divide the average forecasted profits of

---

Table 5-1a Computing the average book rate of return on an investment of $9,000 in project A.

	Cash Flow (dollars)		
Project A	Year 1	Year 2	Year 3
Revenue	12,000	10,000	8,000
Out-of-pocket cost	6,000	5,000	4,000
Cash flow	6,000	5,000	4,000
Depreciation	3,000	3,000	3,000
Net income	3,000	2,000	1,000

$$\text{Average book rate of return} = \frac{\text{average annual income}}{\text{average annual investment}} = \frac{2,000}{4,500} = 0.44$$

---

a project after depreciation and taxes by the average book value of the investment. This ratio is then measured against the book rate of return for the firm as a whole or against some external yardstick, such as the average book rate of return for the industry.

Table 5-1a shows projected income statements for project A over its three-year life. Its average net income is $2,000 per year (we assume for simplicity that there are no taxes). The required investment is $9,000 at $t = 0$. This amount is then depreciated at a constant rate of $3,000 per year. So the book value of the new investment will decline from $9,000 in year 0 to zero in year 3:

	Year 0	Year 1	Year 2	Year 3
Gross book value of investment	$9,000	$9,000	$9,000	$9,000
Accumulated depreciation	0	3,000	6,000	9,000
Net book value of investment	$9,000	$6,000	$3,000	$ 0
		Average net book value = $4,500		

The average net income is $2,000, and the average net investment is $4,500. Therefore, the average book rate of return is 2,000/4,500 = 0.44. Project A would be undertaken if the firm's target book rate of return is less than 44%.[2]

This criterion suffers from several serious defects. First, because it considers only the *average* return on book investment, there is no allowance for the fact that immediate receipts are more valuable than distant ones. Whereas payback gives no weight to the more distant flows, return on book gives them too much weight. Thus in Table 5-1b we can introduce two projects, B and C, which have the same average book investment, the same average book income, and the same average book profitability as project A. Yet A clearly has a higher NPV than B or C because a greater proportion of the cash flows for project A occur in the early years.

Table 5-1b   Projects A, B, and C all cost $9,000 and produce an average income of $2,000. Therefore, they all have a 44% book rate of return.

	Cash Flow (dollars)		
Project	Year 1	Year 2	Year 3
A Cash flow	6,000	5,000	4,000
Net income	3,000	2,000	1,000
B Cash flow	5,000	5,000	5,000
Net income	2,000	2,000	2,000
C Cash flow	4,000	5,000	6,000
Net income	1,000	2,000	3,000

Notice also that the average return on book depends on accounting income; it is not based on the cash flows of a project. Cash flows and accounting income are often very different. For example, the accountant labels some cash outflows *capital investment* and others *operating expenses*. The operating expenses are, of course, deducted immediately from each year's income. The capital expenditures are depreciated according to an arbitrary schedule chosen by the accountant. Then the depreciation charge is deducted from each year's income. Thus the average return on book depends on which items the accountant treats as capital investments and how rapidly they are depreciated.

---

[2]There are many variants on this rule. For example, some companies measure the *accounting return on cost*; that is, the ratio of average profits before depreciation but after tax to the initial cost of the asset.

However, the accountant's decisions have nothing to do with the cash flow[3] and therefore should not affect the decision to accept or reject.

A firm that uses average return on book has to decide on a yardstick for judging a project. This decision is also arbitrary. Sometimes the firm uses its current book return as a yardstick. In this case companies with high rates of return on their existing business may be led to reject good projects, and companies with low rates of return may be led to accept bad ones.

Payback is a bad rule. Average return on book is probably worse. It ignores the opportunity cost of money and is not based on the cash flows of a project, and the investment decision may be related to the profitability of the firm's existing business.

5-5 INTERNAL (OR DISCOUNTED CASH FLOW) RATE OF RETURN

Whereas payback and average return on book are ad hoc rules, internal rate of return has a much more respectable ancestry and is recommended in many finance texts. If, therefore, we dwell more on its deficiencies, it is not because they are more numerous but because they are less obvious.

In Chapter 2 we noted that net present value could also be expressed in terms of rate of return, which would lead to the following rule: "Accept investment opportunities offering rates of return in excess of their opportunity costs of capital." That statement, properly interpreted, is absolutely correct. However, interpretation is not always easy for long-lived investment projects.

There is no ambiguity in defining the true rate of return of an investment that generates a single payoff after one period:

$$\text{Rate of return} = \frac{\text{payoff}}{\text{investment}} - 1$$

Alternatively, we could write down the NPV of the investment and find that discount rate which makes NPV = 0.

$$\text{NPV} = C_0 + \frac{C_1}{1 + \text{Discount rate}} = 0$$

implies

$$\text{Discount rate} = \frac{C_1}{-C_0} - 1$$

Of course C_1 is the payoff and $-C_0$ the required investment, and so our two equations say exactly the same thing. *The discount rate that makes NPV = 0 is also the rate of return.*

Unfortunately, there is no wholly satisfactory way of defining the true rate of return of a long-lived asset. The best available concept is the so-called **discounted cash flow (DCF) rate of return** or **internal rate of return (IRR)**. The internal rate of return is used frequently in finance. It can be a handy measure, but, as we shall see, it can also

---

[3]Of course, the depreciation method used for tax purposes does have cash consequences that should be taken into account in calculating NPV.

---

be a misleading measure. You should, therefore, know how to calculate it and how to use it properly.

The internal rate of return is defined as the rate of discount that makes NPV = 0. This means that to find the IRR for an investment project lasting T years, we must solve for IRR in the following expression:

$$\text{NPV} = C_0 + \frac{C_1}{1 + \text{IRR}} + \frac{C_2}{(1 + \text{IRR})^2} + \cdots + \frac{C_T}{(1 + \text{IRR})^T} = 0$$

Actual calculation of IRR usually involves trial and error. For example, consider a project that produces the following flows:

Cash Flows (dollars)		
C_0	C_1	C_2
−4,000	+2,000	+4,000

The internal rate of return is IRR in the equation

$$\text{NPV} = 4,000 + \frac{2,000}{1 + \text{IRR}} + \frac{4,000}{(1 + \text{IRR})^2} = 0$$

Let us arbitrarily try a zero discount rate. In this case NPV is not zero but +$2,000:

$$\text{NPV} = -4,000 + \frac{2,000}{1.0} + \frac{4,000}{(1.0)^2} = +\$2,000$$

The NPV is positive; therefore the IRR must be greater than zero. The next step might be to try a discount rate of 50%. In this case net present value is −$889:

$$\text{NPV} = -4,000 + \frac{2,000}{1.50} + \frac{4,000}{(1.50)^2} = -\$889$$

The NPV is negative; therefore, the IRR must be less than 50%. In Figure 5-2 we have plotted the net present values implied by a range of discount rates. From this we can see that a discount rate of 28% gives the desired net present value of zero. Therefore IRR is 28%.

The easiest way to calculate IRR, if you have to do it by hand, is to plot three or four combinations of NPV and discount rate on a graph like Figure 5-2, connect the points with a smooth line, and read off the discount rate at which NPV = 0. It is of course quicker and more accurate to use a computer or a specially programmed calculator, and this is what most companies do.

Now, the *rule* for capital budgeting on the basis of internal rate of return is to accept an investment project if the opportunity cost of capital is less than the internal rate of return. You can see the reasoning behind this idea if you look again at Figure 5-2. If the opportunity cost of capital is less than the 28% IRR, then the project has a *positive* NPV when discounted at the opportunity cost of capital. If it is equal to the IRR, the project has a *zero* NPV. And if it is greater than the IRR, the project has a *negative* NPV. Therefore, when we compare the opportunity cost of capital with the IRR on our project, we are effectively asking whether our project has a positive NPV. This is true not only for our example. The rule will give the same answer as the net present value rule *whenever the NPV of a project is a smoothly declining function of the discount rate.*[4]

Many firms use internal rate of return as a criterion in preference to net present value. We think that this is a pity. Although, properly stated, the two criteria are formally equivalent, the internal rate of return rule contains several pitfalls.

Net present value, dollars

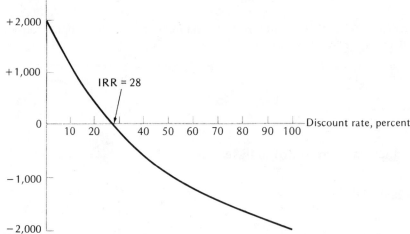

Figure 5-2   This project costs $4,000 and then produces cash inflows of $2,000 in year 1 and $4,000 in year 2. Its internal rate of return (IRR) is 28%, the discount rate at which NPV is zero.

Pitfall 1—Lending or Borrowing?

Not all cash-flow streams have the property that NPV declines as the discount rate increases. Consider the following projects A and B:

| Project | Cash Flows (dollars) | | IRR, % | NPV at 10% |
	C_0	C_1		
A	−1,000	+1,500	+50	+364
B	+1,000	−1,500	+50	−364

Each project has an IRR of 50%. (In other words, $-1,000 + 1,500/1.50 = 0$ and $+1,000 - 1,500/1.50 = 0$.)

Does this mean that they are equally attractive? Clearly not, for in the case of A, where we are initially paying out $1,000, we are *lending* money at 50%; in the case of B, where we are initially receiving $1,000, we are *borrowing* money at 50%. When we lend money, we want a *high* rate of return; when we borrow money, we want a *low* rate of return.

---

[4]Here is a word of caution. Some people confuse the internal rate of return and the opportunity cost of capital because both appear as discount rates in the NPV formula. The internal rate of return is a *profitability measure*, which depends solely on the amount and timing of the project cash flows. The opportunity cost of capital is a *standard of profitability* for the project, which we use to calculate how much the project is worth. The opportunity cost of capital is established in capital markets. It is the expected rate of return offered by other assets equivalent in risk to the project being evaluated.

If you plot a graph like Figure 5-2 for project B, you will find that NPV increases as the discount rate increases. Obviously the internal rate of return rule, as we stated it above, won't work in this case; we have to look for an IRR *less* than the opportunity cost of capital.

This is straightforward enough, but now look at project C:

| Project | Cash Flows (dollars) | | | | IRR, % | NPV at 10% |
	C_0	C_1	C_2	C_3		
C	+1,000	−3,600	+4,320	−1,728	+20	−0.75

It turns out that project C has zero NPV at a 20% discount rate. If the opportunity cost of capital is 10%, that means the project is a good one. Or does it? In part, project C is like borrowing money, because we receive money now and pay it out in the first period; it is also partly like lending money because we pay out money in period 1 and recover it in period 2. Should we accept or reject? The only way to find the answer is to look at the net present value. Figure 5-3 shows that the NPV of our project *increases* as the discount rate increases. If the opportunity cost of capital is 10% (that is, less than the IRR), the project has a very small negative NPV and we should reject.

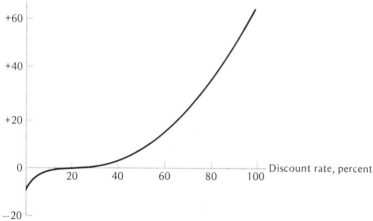

Figure 5-3   The net present value of project C increases as the discount rate increases.

Pitfall 2—Multiple Internal Rates of Return

Project C had a unique IRR, but this will not always be the case when there is more than one change in the sign of the cash flows. Consider, for example, project D. It costs $4,000 and brings you in $25,000 in the first year. Then in year 2 you have to pay out $25,000. (There are many projects that have terminal cash outflows. For example, if you strip-mine coal, you may have to invest substantial amounts to reclaim the land after the coal is mined.)

| Project | Cash Flows (dollars) | | | IRR, % | NPV at 10% |
	C_0	C_1	C_2		
D	−4,000	+25,000	−25,000	25 *and* 400	−1934

Note there are *two* discount rates that make NPV = 0. That is, *each* of the following statements holds:

$$NPV = -4,000 + \frac{25,000}{1.25} - \frac{25,000}{(1.25)^2} = 0$$

and

$$NPV = -4,000 + \frac{25,000}{5} - \frac{25,000}{(5)^2} = 0$$

In other words, the investment has IRRs of both 25 and 400%. Figure 5-4 shows how this comes about. As the discount rate increases, NPV initially rises and then declines. The reason for this is the double change in the sign of the cash-flow stream. There can be as many different internal rates of return for a project as there are changes in the sign of the cash flows.[5]

As if this is not difficult enough, there are also cases in which *no* IRR exists. For example, project E has a positive net present value at all discount rates.

| Project | Cash Flows (dollars) | | | IRR, % | NPV at 10% |
	C_0	C_1	C_2		
E	+1,000	−3,000	+2,500	none	+339

A number of adaptations of the IRR rule have been devised for such cases. Not only are they inadequate, they are unnecessary, for the simple solution is to use NPV.

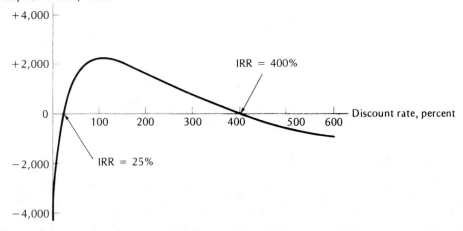

Figure 5-4 Project D has two internal rates of return. NPV = 0 at discount rates of 25% and 400%.

[5] By Descartes' "rule of signs" there can be as many different zeros (that is, zero values) to a polynomial as there are changes of sign and an internal rate of return is just a zero of a polynomial. For a discussion of the problem of multiple rates of return see J.H. Lorie and L.J. Savage, "Three Problems in Rationing Capital," *Journal of Business*, **28**:229–239 (October 1955); and E. Solomon, "The Arithmetic of Capital Budgeting," *Journal of Business*, **29**:124–129 (April 1956).

Pitfall 3—Mutually Exclusive Projects

Firms often have to choose from among several alternative ways of doing the same job or using the same facility. In other words, they need to choose from among **mutually exclusive projects**. Here too the IRR rule can be misleading.

Consider projects F and G:

Project	Cash Flows (dollars) C_0	C_1	IRR, %	NPV at 10%
F	−100	+200	100	82
G	−10,000	+15,000	50	3,636

Both are good projects, but G has the higher NPV and is, therefore, better. However, the IRR rule seems to indicate that if you have to choose, you should go for F since it has the higher IRR. If you follow the IRR rule, you have the satisfaction of earning a 100% rate of return; if you follow the NPV rule, you are $3,636 richer.

You can salvage the IRR rule in these cases by looking at the internal rate of return on the incremental flows. Here is how to do it. First, consider the smaller project (F in our example). It has an IRR of 100%, which is well in excess of the 10% opportunity cost of capital. You know, therefore, that F is acceptable. You now ask yourself whether it is worth making the additional $9,900 investment in G. The incremental flows from undertaking G rather than F are as follows:

Project	Cash Flows (dollars) C_0	C_1	IRR, %	NPV at 10%
G–F	−9,900	+14,800	49	3,554

The IRR on the incremental investment is 49%, which is also well in excess of the 10% opportunity cost of capital. So you should prefer project G to project F.[6]

Unless you look at the incremental expenditure, IRR is unreliable in ranking projects of different scale. It is also unreliable in ranking projects that offer different patterns of cash flow over time. For example, suppose the firm can take project H *or* project I (which generates cash flows in perpetuity) but not both (ignore J for the moment):

Project	Cash Flows (dollars) C_0	C_1	C_2	C_3	C_4	C_5	Etc.	IRR, %	NPV at 10%
H	−9,000	+6,000	+5,000	+4,000	0	0	...	33	3,592
I	−9,000	+1,800	+1,800	+1,800	+1,800	+1,800	...	20	9,000
J		−6,000	+1,200	+1,200	+1,200	+1,200	...	20	6,000

Project H has a higher IRR, but project I has the higher NPV. Figure 5-5 shows why the two rules give different answers. The solid line gives the net present value of project H at different rates of discount. Since a discount rate of 33% produces a net present

---

[6]You may, however, find that you have jumped out of the frying pan into the fire. The series of incremental cash flows may involve several changes in sign. In this case there are likely to be multiple IRRs and you will be forced to use the NPV rule after all.

value of zero, this is the internal rate of return for project H. Similarly, the dashed line shows the net present value of project I at different discount rates. The IRR of project I is 20%. (We assume project I's cash flows continue indefinitely.) Note that project I has a higher NPV so long as the opportunity cost of capital is less than 15.6%.

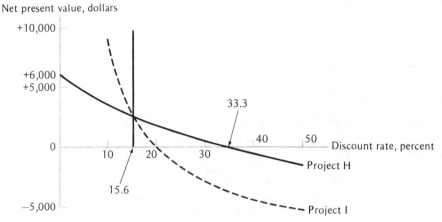

Figure 5-5   The IRR of project H exceeds that of project I, but the net present value of project I is higher *only* if the discount rate is less than 15.6%.

The reason IRR is misleading is that the total cash inflow of project I is larger but tends to occur later. Therefore, when the discount rate is low, I has the higher NPV; when the discount rate is high, H has the higher NPV. (You can see from Figure 5-5 that the two projects have the *same* NPV when the discount rate is 15.6%.) The internal rates of return on the two projects tell us that at a discount rate of 20% I has a zero NPV (IRR = 20%) and H has a positive NPV. Thus if the opportunity cost of capital were 20%, investors would place a higher value on the shorter-lived project H. But in our example the opportunity cost of capital is not 20% but 10%. Investors are prepared to pay relatively high prices for longer-lived securities, and so they will pay a relatively high price for the longer-lived project. At a 10% cost of capital, an investment in I has an NPV of $9,000 and an investment in H has an NPV of only $3,592.[7]

This is a favourite example of ours. We have gotten many businesspeople's reaction to it. When asked to choose between H and I, many choose H. The reason seems to be the rapid payback generated by project H. In other words, they believe that if they take H, they will also be able to take a later project like J (note that J can be financed using the cash flows from H), whereas if they take I, they won't have money enough for J. In other words they implicitly assume that it is a *shortage of capital* that forces the choice between H and I. When this implicit assumption is brought out, they usually admit that I is better if there is no capital shortage.

But the introduction of capital constraints raises two further questions. The first stems from the fact that most of the executives preferring H to I work for firms that would have no difficulty raising more capital. Why would a manager at GM, say, choose H

[7]It is often suggested that the choice between the net present value rule and the internal rate of return rule should depend on the probable reinvestment rate. This is wrong. The prospective return on another independent investment should *never* be allowed to influence the investment decision. For a discussion of the reinvestment assumption see A.A. Alchian, "The Rate of Interest, Fisher's Rate of Return over Cost and Keynes' Internal Rate of Return," *American Economic Review*, **45**:938–942 (December 1955).

on the grounds of limited capital? GM can raise plenty of capital and can take project J regardless of whether H or I is chosen; therefore J should not affect the choice between H and I. The answer seems to be that large firms usually impose capital budgets on divisions and subdivisions as a part of the firm's planning and control system. Since the system is complicated and cumbersome, the budgets are not easily altered, and so they are perceived as real constraints by middle management.

The second question is this. If there is a capital constraint, either real or self-imposed, should IRR be used to rank projects? The answer is no. The problem in this case is to find that package of investment projects that satisfies the capital constraint and has the largest net present value. The IRR rule will not identify this package. As we will show in Chapter 6, the only practical way to do so is to use the technique of linear programming.

When we have to choose between projects H and I, it is easiest to compare the net present values. But if your heart is set on the IRR rule, you can use it as long as you look at the internal rate of return on the incremental flows. The procedure is exactly the same as we showed above. First, you check that project H has a satisfactory IRR. Then you look at the return on the additional investment in I.

Project	Cash Flows (dollars)							IRR, %	NPV at 10%
	C_0	C_1	C_2	C_3	C_4	C_5	Etc.		
I–H	0	−4,200	−3,200	−2,200	+1,800	+1,800	...	15.6	+5,408

The IRR on the incremental investment in I is 15.6%. Since this is greater than the opportunity cost of capital, you should undertake I rather than H.

Pitfall 4—What Happens When We Can't Finesse the Term Structure of Interest Rates?

We have simplified our discussion of capital budgeting by assuming that the opportunity cost of capital is the same for all the cash flows, C_1, C_2, C_3, and so on. Now this is not the right place to discuss the term structure of interest rates, but we must point out certain problems with the IRR rule that crop up when short-term interest rates are different from long-term rates.

Remember our most general formula for calculating net present value:

$$NPV = C_0 + \frac{C_1}{1 + r_1} + \frac{C_2}{(1 + r_2)^2} + \cdots$$

In other words, we discount C_1 at the opportunity cost of capital for one year, C_2 at the opportunity cost of capital for two years, and so on. The IRR rule tells us to accept a project if the IRR is greater than the opportunity cost of capital. But what do we do when we have several opportunity costs? Do we compare IRR with r_1, r_2, r_3, . . . ? Actually we would have to compute a complex weighted average of these rates to obtain a number comparable to IRR.

What does this mean for capital budgeting? It means trouble for the IRR rule whenever the term structure of interest rates becomes important.[8] In a situation where it is

---

[8]The source of the difficulty is that the IRR is a derived figure without any simple economic interpretation. To define it, we can only say that it is the discount rate which, applied to all cash flows, makes NPV = 0. The IRR is a complex average of the separate interest rates. The problem here is not that the IRR is a nuisance to calculate but that it is not a very useful number to have.

important, we have to compare the project IRR with the expected IRR (yield to maturity) offered by a traded security that (1) is equivalent in risk to the project and (2) offers the same time pattern of cash flows as the project. Such a comparison is easier said than done. It is much better to forget about IRR and just calculate NPV.

Many firms use the IRR, thereby implicitly assuming that there is no difference between short-term and long-term rates of interest. They do this for the same reason that we have so far finessed the term structure: simplicity.[9]

The Verdict on IRR

We have given four examples of things that can go wrong with IRR. We gave only one example of what could go wrong with payback or return on book. Does this mean that IRR is four times worse than the other two rules? Quite the contrary. There is little point in dwelling on the deficiencies of payback or return on book. They are clearly ad hoc rules that often lead to silly conclusions. The IRR rule has a much more respectable ancestry. It is a less easy rule to use than NPV, but, used properly, it gives the same answer. Now that you know the pitfalls, you should be able to use it properly.

5-6 PROFITABILITY INDEX OR BENEFIT-COST RATIO

The **profitability index** (or **benefit-cost ratio**) is the present value of forecasted future cash flows divided by the initial investment:

$$\text{Profitability index} = \frac{PV}{-C_0}$$

The profitability-index *rule* tells us to accept all projects with an index greater than one. If the profitability index is greater than one, the present value PV is greater than the initial investment $-C_0$ and so the project must have a positive net present value. The profitability index, therefore, leads to exactly the same decisions as net present value.[10]

However, like internal rate of return, the profitability index can be misleading when we are obliged to choose between two mutually exclusive investments. Consider the following two projects:

| Project | Cash Flows (dollars) | | PV at 10% | Profitability Index | NPV at 10% |
	C_0	C_1			
K	−100	+200	182	1.82	82
L	−10,000	+15,000	13,636	1.36	3,636

Both are good projects, as the profitability index correctly indicates. But suppose the projects are mutually exclusive. We *should* take L, the project with the higher NPV. Yet the profitability index gives K the higher ranking.

---

[9]In Chapter 9, we will look at some special cases in which it would be misleading to use the same discount rate for both short-term and long-term cash flows.

[10]Some companies do not discount the benefits or costs before calculating the profitability index. The less said about these companies, the better.

As with internal rate of return, you can always solve such problems by looking at the profitability index on the *incremental* investment. In other words, you first check that project K is worthwhile; then you calculate the profitability index on the $9,900 additional investment in L.

| | Cash Flows (dollars) | | | Profitability | |
Project	C_1	C_0	PV at 10%	Index	NPV at 10%
L–K	−9,900	+14,800	13,454	1.36	3,554

The profitability index on the additional investment is greater than one, so you know that L is the better project.

Of our four rules, the profitability index most closely resembles net present value. In the next chapter we will encounter a rather special case in which the profitability index is the more useful rule. But for most purposes it is safer to work with net present values that add up, rather than with profitability indices that do not.

5-7 SUMMARY

If you are going to persuade your company to use the net present value rule, you must be prepared to explain why other rules do *not* give correct decisions. That is why we have devoted this chapter to four alternative investment criteria.

Some companies use the payback method to make investment decisions. In other words, they accept only those projects that recover their initial investment within some specified period. Payback is an ad hoc rule. It ignores the order in which cash flows come within the payback period, and it ignores subsequent cash flows entirely. It therefore takes no account of the opportunity cost of capital.

The simplicity of payback makes it an easy device for *describing* investment projects. Managers talk casually about "quick payback" projects in the same way that investors talk about "high *P/E*" common stocks. The fact that managers talk about the payback periods of projects does not mean that the payback rule governs their decisions. Some managers *do* use payback in judging capital investments. Why they rely on such a grossly oversimplified concept is a puzzle.

Some firms use average return on book value. In this case the company must decide which cash payments are capital expenditures and must pick appropriate depreciation schedules. It must then calculate the ratio of average income to the average book value of the investment and compare it with the company's target return. Average return on book is another ad hoc method. Since it ignores whether the income occurs next year or next century, it takes no account of the opportunity cost of money.

The internal rate of return (IRR) is defined as the rate of discount at which a project would have zero NPV. It is a handy measure and widely used in finance; you should therefore know how to calculate it. The IRR rule states that companies should accept any investment offering an IRR in excess of the opportunity cost of capital. The IRR rule is, like net present value, a technique based on discounted cash flows. It will, therefore, give the correct answer if properly used. The problem is that it is easily misapplied. There are four things to look out for:

1. *Lending or borrowing?* If a project offers positive cash flows followed by negative flows, NPV *rises* as the discount rate is increased. You should accept such projects if their IRR is *less* than the opportunity cost of capital.

2. *Multiple rates of return.* If there is more than one change in the sign of the cash flows, the project may have several IRRs or no IRR at all.

3. *Mutually exclusive projects.* Unlike NPVs, rates of return do not add up. If you tack a bad project onto a good project, the combined project may have a higher IRR than the good project on its own. You must make sure that you look at the IRR on each additional unit of investment. Also, the IRR rule may give the wrong ranking of mutually exclusive projects that differ in economic life or in scale of required investment.

4. *Short-term interest rates may be different from long-term rates.* The IRR rule requires you to compare the project's IRR with the opportunity cost of capital. But sometimes there is one opportunity cost of capital for one-year cash flows, a different cost of capital for two-year cash flows, and so on. In these cases there is no simple yardstick for evaluating the IRR of a project.

The fourth rule uses the profitability-index or benefit-cost ratio. It says that companies should accept projects only if the ratio of the discounted future cash flows to the initial investment is greater than one. This is just a roundabout way of saying that companies should accept projects with positive NPVs. The only drawback with using ratios is that you cannot add them up in the same way as you can add up values. Therefore you have to be careful when you are using this rule to choose between two projects.

This is a good point at which to stress political realities. Some people believe the earth is flat. It may be easier to persuade such people to accept the idea that the earth may be slightly curled at the corners than to convince them that it is completely round. You can therefore resolve that when you become president or treasurer, you will use net present value. But if the current management has an inalienable attachment to payback, you can still hope to make a substantial improvement by persuading them to use different cutoff periods for projects with different lives and to change to discounted payback.

If we are going to the expense of collecting forecasts, we might as well use them properly. Ad hoc criteria should therefore have no role in our firm's decisions, and the net present value rule should be employed in preference to other techniques using discounted cash flows. Having said that, we must be careful not to exaggerate the payoff of proper technique. Technique is important, but it is by no means the only determinant of the success of a capital-expenditure program. If the forecasts of cash flows are inadequate, even the most careful application of the net present value rule will fail.

FURTHER READING

Most capital budgeting texts contain a discussion of alternative budgeting criteria. See, for example:

H. Bierman, Jr. and S. Smidt, *The Capital Budgeting Decision*, 5th ed., The Macmillan Company, New York, 1980.

Classic articles on the internal rate of return rule include:

J.H. Lorie and L.J. Savage, "Three Problems in Rationing Capital," *Journal of Business*, **28**:229–239 (October 1955).
E. Solomon, "The Arithmetic of Capital Budgeting Decisions," *Journal of Business*, **29**:124–129 (April 1956).
A.A. Alchian, "The Rate of Interest, Fisher's Rate of Return over Cost and Keynes' Internal Rate of Return," *American Economic Review*, **45**:938–942 (December 1955).

For a discussion of the profitability index, see:

B. Schwab and P. Lusztig, "A Comparative Analysis of the Net Present Value and the Benefit-Cost Ratios as Measures of the Economic Desirability of Investment," *Journal of Finance*, **24**:507–516 (June 1969).

QUIZ

1. What is the opportunity cost of capital supposed to represent? Give a concise definition.

2. (a) What is the payback period on each of the following projects?

	Cash Flows (dollars)				
Project	C_0	C_1	C_2	C_3	C_4
A	−5,000	+1,000	+1,000	+3,000	0
B	−1,000	0	+1,000	+2,000	+3,000
C	−5,000	+1,000	+1,000	+3,000	+5,000

(b) *Given* that you wish to use the payback rule with a cutoff period of two years, which projects would you accept?
(c) If you use a cutoff period of three years, which projects would you accept?
(d) If the opportunity cost of capital is 10%, which projects have positive NPVs?
(e) "Payback gives too much weight to cash flows that occur after the cutoff date." True or false?
(f) "If a firm uses a single cutoff period for all projects, it is likely to accept too many short-lived projects." True or false?

3. A machine costs $8,000 and is expected to produce profit before depreciation of $2,500 in each of years 1 and 2 and $3,500 in each of years 3 and 4. Assuming that the machine is depreciated at a constant rate of $2,000 a year and that there are no taxes, what is the average return on book?

4. True or false? Why?
(a) "The average return on book rule gives too much weight to the later cash flows."
(b) "If companies use their existing return on book as a yardstick for new investments, successful companies will tend to undertake too much investment."

5. (a) Calculate the net present value of the following project for discount rates of 0%, 50%, and 100%.

Cash Flows (dollars)		
C_0	C_1	C_2
−6,750	+4,500	+18,000

(b) What is the IRR of the project?

6. Consider projects A and B:

	Cash Flows (dollars)			IRR,
Project	C_0	C_1	C_2	%
A	−4,000	+2,410	+2,930	21
B	−2,000	+1,310	+1,720	31

(a) The opportunity cost of capital is less than 10%. Use the IRR rule to determine which project or projects you should accept (i) if you can undertake both, and (ii) if you can undertake only one.
(b) Suppose that project A has an NPV of $690 and project B has an NPV of $657. What is the NPV of the $2,000 incremental investment in A?

7. Consider the following projects:

	Cash Flow (dollars)		
Project	C_0	C_1	C_2
A	−1,600	+1,200	+1,440
B	−2,100	+1,440	+1,728

(a) Calculate the profitability index for A and B assuming a 20% opportunity cost of capital.

(b) Use the profitability-index rule to determine which project(s) you should accept (i) if you could undertake both, and (ii) if you could undertake only one.

8. (a) Projects C and D both involve the same outlay and offer the same IRR, which exceeds the opportunity cost of capital. The cash flows generated by project C are larger than those of D but tend to occur later. Which project has the higher NPV?

(b) You have the chance to participate in a project that produces the following cash flows:

Cash Flows (dollars)		
C_0	C_1	C_2
+5,000	+4,000	−11,000

The internal rate of return is 13%. If the opportunity cost of capital is 10%, would you accept the offer?

QUESTIONS AND PROBLEMS

1. Consider the following projects:

	Cash Flows (dollars)					
Project	C_0	C_1	C_2	C_3	C_4	C_5
A	−1,000	+1,000	0	0	0	0
B	−2,000	+1,000	+1,000	+4,000	+1,000	+1,000
C	−3,000	+1,000	+1,000	0	+1,000	+1,000

(a) If the opportunity cost of capital is 10%, which projects have a positive NPV?

(b) Calculate the payback period for each project.

(c) Which projects would a firm using the payback rule accept if the cutoff period were three years?

2. Project A (shown in Table 5-1a) has undergone some revisions. The initial investment has been reduced to $6,000, and the firm proposes to depreciate this investment by $2,000 a year. Operating costs unfortunately have increased by $1,000 a year. If the opportunity cost of capital is 7%, how do these changes alter the NPV of the project? How do they affect the average return on book?

3. Consider a project with the following cash flows:

C_0	C_1	C_2
-100	$+200$	-75

(a) How many internal rates of return does this project have?
(b) The opportunity cost of capital is 20%. Is this an attractive project? Briefly explain.

4. Respond to the following comments:
   (a) "We like to use payback principally as a way of coping with risk."
   (b) "The great merit of the IRR rule is that one does not have to think about what is an appropriate discount rate."

5. The payback rule is still used by many firms despite its acknowledged theoretical shortcomings. Why do you think this is so?

6. Discounted payback ensures that you never accept a project with a negative NPV, but it doesn't stop you from *rejecting* projects with a positive NPV. Show why this is so.

7. Consider the following two projects:

	Cash Flows (dollars)			
Project	C_0	C_1	C_2	C_3
A	-100	$+40$	$+40$	$+32$
B	-100	$+30$	$+30$	$+69$

(a) Calculate the NPV of each project for discount rates of 0%, 10% and 20%. Plot these on a graph with NPV on the vertical axis and discount rate on the horizontal axis.
(b) What is the approximate IRR for each project?
(c) In what circumstances should the company accept project A?
(d) Calculate the NPV of the incremental investment (B-A) for discount rates of 0%, 10%, and 20%. Plot these on your graph. Show that the circumstances in which you would accept A over B are also those in which the IRR on the incremental investment is less than the opportunity cost of capital.

8. Mr. Cyrus Clops, the president of Giant Enterprises, has to make a choice between two possible investments:

	Cash Flows (thousands of dollars)			
Project	C_0	C_1	C_2	IRR, %
A	-400	$+241$	$+293$	21
B	-200	$+131$	$+172$	31

The opportunity cost of capital is 9%. Mr. Clops is tempted to take B, which has the higher IRR.
(a) Explain to Mr. Clops why this is not the correct procedure.
(b) Show him how to adapt the IRR rule to choose the best project.
(c) Show him that this project also has the higher NPV.

9. The Titanic Shipbuilding Company has a non-cancellable contract to build a small cargo vessel. Construction involves a cash outlay of $250,000 at the end of each of the next two years. At the end of the third year the company will receive

payment of $650,000. The company can speed up construction by working an extra shift. In this case there will be a cash outlay of $550,000 at the end of the first year followed by a cash payment of $650,000 at the end of the second year. Use the IRR rule to show the (approximate) range of opportunity costs of capital at which the company should work the extra shift.

10. Look again at projects A and B in Section 5-3. Assume that the projects are mutually exclusive and that the opportunity cost of capital is 20%.
   (*a*) Calculate the profitability index for each project.
   (*b*) Show how the profitability-index rule can be used to select the superior project.

MAKING INVESTMENT DECISIONS WITH THE NET PRESENT VALUE RULE

We hope that by now you are convinced that wise investment decisions are based on the net present value rule. In this chapter we can think about how to apply the rule to practical investment problems. Our task is threefold. The first issue is to decide what should be discounted. We know the answer in principle: discount cash flows. But useful forecasts of cash flows do not arrive on a silver platter. Often the financial manager has to make do with raw data supplied by specialists in product design, production, marketing, taxation and so on, and must check such information for relevance, completeness, consistency, and accuracy and then pull everything together into a usable forecast.

Our second task is to explain how the net present value rule should be used when there are project interactions. These occur when a decision about one project cannot be separated from a decision about another. Project interactions can be extremely complex. We will make no attempt to analyze every possible case. But we will work through most of the simple cases, as well as a few examples of medium complexity.

Our third task is to develop procedures for coping with capital rationing or other situations in which resources are strictly limited. There are two aspects to this problem. One is computational. Resource constraints often create problems of such complexity that a hunt-and-peck search for the right answer cannot cope with the vast number of alternatives. Linear programming can solve this problem and help the financial manager handle some project interactions at the same time. The other part of the problem is deciding whether capital rationing really exists and whether it invalidates net present value as a criterion for capital budgeting. Our discussion of these issues will take us back to the first principles outlined in Chapter 2.

6-1 WHAT TO DISCOUNT

Up to this point we have been concerned mainly with the mechanics of discounting and with the various methods of project appraisal. We have had almost nothing to say about the problem of *what* one should discount. When you are faced with this problem, you should always stick to three general rules:

1. Only cash flow is relevant.
2. Always estimate cash flows on an incremental basis.
3. Be consistent in your treatment of inflation.

We will discuss each of these rules in turn.

Only Cash Flow is Relevant

The first and most important point is that the net present value rule is stated in terms of cash flows. Cash flow is the simplest possible concept; it is just the difference between dollars received and dollars paid out. Many people nevertheless confuse cash flow with accounting profits.

Accountants *start* with "dollars in" and "dollars out," but to obtain accounting income they adjust these data in two important ways. First, they try to show profit as it is *earned* rather than when the company and the customer get around to paying their bills. Second, they sort cash outflows into two categories: current expenses and capital expenses. They deduct current expenses when calculating profit but do *not* deduct capital expenses. Instead they "depreciate" capital expenses over a number of years and deduct the annual depreciation charge from profits. As a result of these procedures, profits include some cash flows and exclude others, and are reduced by depreciation charges, which are not cash flows at all.

It is not always easy to translate the customary accounting data back into actual dollars—dollars you can buy beer with. If you are in doubt about what is a cash flow, simply count the dollars coming in and take away the dollars going out. Don't assume without checking that you can find cash flow by simple manipulation of accounting data.

You should always estimate cash flows on an after-tax basis. Some firms do not deduct tax payments. They try to offset this mistake by discounting the cash flows before taxes at a rate higher than the opportunity cost of capital. Unfortunately, there is no reliable formula for making such adjustments to the discount rate.

You should also make sure that cash flows are recorded *only when they occur* and not when the work is undertaken or the liability incurred. For example, taxes should be discounted from their actual payment date, not from the time when the tax liability is recorded in the firm's books.

Estimate Cash Flows on an Incremental Basis

The value of a project depends on *all* the additional cash flows that follow from project acceptance. Here are some things to watch for when you are deciding which cash flows should be included:

Do Not Confuse Average with Incremental Payoffs Most managers naturally hesitate to throw good money after bad. For example, they are reluctant to invest more money in a losing division. But occasionally you will encounter "turnaround" opportunities in which the *incremental* NPV on investment in a loser is strongly positive.

Conversely, it does not always make sense to throw good money after good. A division with an outstanding past profitability record may have run out of good opportunities. You would not pay a large sum for a 20-year-old horse, sentiment aside, regardless of how many races that horse had won or how many champions it had sired.

Here is another example illustrating the difference between average and incremental returns. Suppose that a railroad bridge is in urgent need of repair. With the bridge the railroad can continue to operate; without the bridge it can't. In this case the payoff from the repair work consists of all the benefits of operating the railroad. The incremental NPV of the investment may be enormous. Of course, these benefits should be net of all other costs and all subsequent repairs; otherwise the company may be misled into rebuilding an unprofitable railroad piece by piece.

Include All Incidental Effects It is important to include all incidental effects on the remainder of the business. For example, a branch line for a railroad may have a negative NPV when considered in isolation, but still be a worthwhile investment when one allows for the additional traffic that it brings to the main line.

Do Not Forget Working Capital Requirements   Net working capital (often referred to simply as *working capital*) is the difference between a company's short-term assets and liabilities. The principal short-term assets are cash, accounts receivable (customers' unpaid bills), and inventories of raw materials and finished goods. The principal short-term liabilities are accounts payable (bills that *you* have not paid). Most projects entail an additional investment in working capital. This investment should, therefore, be recognized in your cash-flow forecasts. By the same token, when the project comes to an end, you can usually recover some of the investment. This is treated as a cash inflow.

Forget Sunk Costs   Sunk costs are like spilt milk: they are past and irreversible outflows. Because sunk costs are bygones, they cannot be affected by the decision to accept or reject the project, and so they should be ignored.

This fact is often forgotten. For example, in 1971 Lockheed sought a United States government guarantee for a bank loan to continue development of the TriStar airplane. Lockheed and its supporters argued it would be foolish to abandon a project on which nearly $1 billion had already been spent. Some of Lockheed's critics countered that it would be equally foolish to continue with a project that offered no prospect of a satisfactory return on that $1 billion. Both groups were guilty of the so-called *sunk-cost fallacy*; the $1 billion was irrecoverable and, therefore, irrelevant.[1]

Include Opportunity Costs   The cost of a resource may be relevant to the investment decision even when no cash changes hands. For example, suppose a new manufacturing operation uses land that could otherwise be sold for $100,000. This resource is not free: it has an opportunity cost, which is the cash it could generate for the company if the project were rejected and the resource sold or put to some other productive use.

This example prompts us to warn you against judging projects on the basis of "before versus after." The proper comparison is "with or without." A manager comparing before versus after might not assign any value to the land because the firm owns it both before and after:

Before	Take Project	After	Cash Flow, Before versus After
Firm owns land	→	Firm still owns land	0

The proper comparison, which is with or without, is as follows:

Before	Take Project	After	Cash Flow, With Project
Firm owns land	→	Firm still owns land	0
	Do Not Take Project	After	Cash Flow, Without Project
	→	Firm sells land for $100,000	$100,000

Comparing the two possible "afters," we see that the firm gives up $100,000 by undertaking the project. This reasoning still holds if the land will not be sold but is worth $100,000 to the firm in some other use.

---

[1]U.E. Reinhardt provides an analysis of the values of the TriStar in 1971: "Break-even Analysis for Lockheed's TriStar: An Application of Financial Theory," *Journal of Finance*, **28**:821–838 (September 1973). (Reinhardt does not fall into the sunk-cost fallacy.)

Sometimes opportunity costs may be very difficult to estimate;[2] however, where the resource can be freely traded, its opportunity cost is simply equal to the market price. Why? It cannot be otherwise. If the value of a parcel of land to the firm is less than its market price, the firm will sell it. On the other hand the opportunity cost of using land in a particular project cannot exceed the cost of buying an equivalent parcel to replace it.

Beware of Allocated Overhead Costs   We have already mentioned that the accountant's objective in gathering data is not always the same as the investment analyst's. A case in point is the allocation of overhead costs. Overheads include such items as supervisory salaries, rent, heat, and light. These overheads may not be related to any particular project, but they have to be paid for somehow. Therefore, when the accountant assigns costs to the firm's projects, a charge for overhead is usually made. Now our principle of incremental cash flows says that in investment appraisal we should include only the *extra* expenses that would result from the project. A project may generate extra overhead expenses—and then again it may not. We should be cautious about assuming that the accountant's allocation of overheads represents the true extra expenses that would be incurred.

Be Consistent in Your Treatment of Inflation

Interest rates are usually quoted in *nominal* rather than *real* terms. In other words, if you buy a Treasury bill the government promises to pay you so many dollars. It makes no promises about what that money will buy. Investors take that into account when they decide what is a fair rate of interest.

For example, suppose that the rate of interest on a one-year Government of Canada Treasury bill is 8% and that next year's inflation is expected to be 6%. If you buy the bill, you get back principal and interest in period 1 dollars, which are worth 6% less than current dollars:

Invest Current Dollars		Receive Period 1 Dollars	Result
$1,000	→	$1,080	8% *nominal* rate of return

How much actual purchasing power is represented by the $1,080 return? Let us measure units of purchasing power in terms of current dollars. We convert period 1 dollars into current dollars by dividing by 1.06 (one plus the expected inflation rate):[3]

$$\text{Purchasing power of 1,080 period 1 dollars} = \begin{array}{c}\text{number of current} \\ \text{dollars having same} \\ \text{purchasing power}\end{array} = \frac{1,080}{1.06} = \$1,018.87$$

This is the *real* payoff to the bill holder:

---

[2]They may be so difficult to estimate that it is often preferable just to note their existence rather than attempt to quantify them.

[3]A 6% inflation rate means that $1.00 now has the same purchasing power as $1.06 next year. Thus, the real purchasing power of $1,080 next year is $1,080/1.06. Real purchasing power is measured in terms of today's dollars.

Invest Current Dollars		Expected Real Value of Period 1 Receipts	Result
			Expected real rate of return is
$1,000	$\rightarrow$	$1,018.87	0.0187, or about 2%

Thus we could say "The bill offers an 8% nominal rate of return" *or* "It offers a 1.87% expected real rate of return." Note that the nominal rate is certain but the real rate is only expected. The actual real rate cannot be calculated until period 1 arrives and the inflation rate is known.

If the discount rate is stated in nominal terms, then consistency requires that cash flows be estimated in nominal terms, taking account of trends in selling price, labour and materials cost, and so on. This calls for more than simply applying a single assumed inflation rate to all components of cash flow. Labour cost per hour of work, for example, normally increases at a faster rate than the consumer price index because of improvements in productivity and increasing real wages throughout the economy. Tax shields on depreciation (capital cost allowance) do not increase with inflation; they are calculated in nominal terms because tax law allows only the original cost of assets to be depreciated.

Of course, there is nothing wrong with discounting real cash flows at a real discount rate, although this is not commonly done. Here is a simple example showing the equivalence of the two methods.

Suppose your firm usually forecasts cash flows in nominal terms and discounts at a 15% nominal rate. In this particular case, however, you are given project cash flows estimated in real terms, that is, current dollars:

	Real Cash Flows (thousands of dollars)		
C_0	C_1	C_2	C_3
-100	$+35$	$+50$	$+30$

It would be inconsistent to discount these real cash flows at 15%. You have two alternatives: either restate the cash flows in nominal terms and discount at 15%, or restate the discount rate in real terms and use this to discount the real cash flows. We will now show you that both methods produce the same answer.

Assume that inflation is projected at 10% a year. Then the first cash flow for year 1, which is $35,000 in current dollars, will be $35,000 \times 1.10 = \$38,500$ in year 1 dollars. Similarly the cash flow for year 2 will be $50,000 \times (1.10)^2 = \$60,500$ in year 2 dollars, and so on. If we discount these nominal cash flows at the 15% nominal discount rate, we have

$$NPV = -100 + \frac{38.5}{1.15} + \frac{60.5}{(1.15)^2} + \frac{39.9}{(1.15)^3} = 5.5 \text{ or } \$5,500$$

Instead of converting the cash-flow forecasts into nominal terms, we could convert the discount rate into real terms by using the following relationship:

$$\text{Real discount rate} = \frac{1 + \text{nominal discount rate}}{1 + \text{inflation rate}} - 1$$

In our example this gives

$$\text{Real discount rate} = \frac{1.15}{1.10} - 1 = 0.045 \; or \; 4.5\%$$

If we now discount the real cash flows by the real discount rate, we have an NPV of $5,500, just as before:

$$\text{NPV} = -100 + \frac{35}{1.045} + \frac{50}{(1.045)^2} + \frac{30}{(1.045)^3} = 5.5 \; or \; \$5,500$$

Note that the real discount rate is approximately equal to the *difference* between the nominal discount rate of 15% and the inflation rate of 10%. Discounting at 5% would give NPV = $4,600—not exactly right, but close.

The message of all this is quite simple. Discount nominal cash flows at a nominal discount rate. Discount real cash flows at a real rate. Obvious as this rule is, it is sometimes violated. For example, in 1974 there was a political storm in Ireland over the government's acquisition of a stake in Bula Mines. The price paid by the government reflected an assessment of £40 million as the value of Bula Mines; however, one group of consultants thought that the company's value was only £8 million and others thought that it was as high as £104 million. Although these valuations used different cash-flow projections, a significant part of the difference in views seemed to reflect confusion about real and nominal discount rates.[4]

6-2 CORPORATE TAXES IN CANADA—THE BASICS

Businesses have many dealings with governments. They pay out money in the form of income taxes, property taxes, license fees, and stumpage charges, and they get some of it back as government grants and subsidies. The most important of these cash flows is the corporate income tax and you must know how it is calculated.

Income tax is paid at both the federal and provincial levels. Each province has its own tax laws. Since provincial laws are generally similar to the federal law, we will concentrate on federal law.[5]

Federal and provincial income taxes currently total about 46% of a company's taxable income.[6] However, when calculating taxable income, the firm is allowed to make a deduction for depreciation. In Canada this depreciation is called **capital cost allowance (CCA)**. Thus

Taxable income = revenues − expenses − CCA

Tax = 0.46 × Taxable income

Notice that CCA is not itself a cash flow, though it does affect the cash flow by reducing the tax paid by 0.46 × CCA. This tax saving is sometimes called the **CCA tax shield**

---

[4] In some cases it is unclear what procedure was used. At least one expert seems to have discounted nominal cash flows at a real rate. For a review of the Bula Mines controversy see E. Dimson, "Bula Mines: A Case Study," London Business School, 1978.

[5] The province of Quebec deviates the most sharply from the federal tax law.

[6] Appendix 6-1 discusses these tax rates in more detail. In particular, small companies pay tax at the lower rate of about 25%.

---

or **depreciation tax shield**. Also, CCA is not necessarily the same as the depreciation figure shown in the company's profit statement: Revenue Canada allows the company to keep one set of books for the tax collector and a different set for stockholders.

The Asset Class System

A few assets, such as land or securities, cannot be depreciated at all. The others are divided by Revenue Canada into different CCA **asset classes**. Some classes of assets can be depreciated much more rapidly than other classes.

Most industrial buildings fall into Class 3. Class 3 assets can be depreciated each year by 5% of the undepreciated balance. For example, suppose you start up a new business by investing $10 million in a new factory. In the first year you are entitled to a CCA deduction of 5% of this capital cost:

$$CCA = 0.05 \times 10 = \$0.5 \text{ million}$$

In the next year the undepreciated balance (known as the **undepreciated capital cost** or **UCC**) declines to $10 - 0.5 = \$9.5$ million. Therefore, in the second year you are entitled to a CCA deduction of $0.05 \times 9.5 = \$0.475$ million, and so on.

Most machinery falls into Class 8. Class 8 assets can be depreciated at a 20% rate. Thus, if you invested that $10 million in machinery, you would be entitled to a CCA deduction in the first year of $0.2 \times 10 = \$2$ million. In the second year the UCC would decline to $10 - 2 = \$8$ million and you would be entitled to a deduction of $0.2 \times 8 = \$1.6$ million, and so on.

All assets within a particular CCA class are depreciated as if they were one asset. For example, suppose that after the first year you acquire a second machine for $10 million. Your UCC of Class-8 assets would rise to $8 + 10 = \$18$ million, and the CCA deduction in the next year would be $0.2 \times 18 = \$3.6$ million.

The Disposition of Assets

The tax laws provide a complex set of rules that arise when an asset is sold. The procedure is as follows:

A. When a depreciable asset is sold, the lower of the sale price or the initial cost is deducted from the undepreciated capital cost of its asset class.

B. If Step A leaves a negative balance, this amount is called **recaptured depreciation** and is added to taxable income. The undepreciated capital cost of the asset class is then set to zero.

C. If Step A leaves a positive balance and *there are no other assets remaining* in the class, this remaining balance is called a **terminal loss**, and is deducted from taxable income. Also, the undepreciated capital cost is set to zero, so that the class ceases to generate CCA tax shields. But if Step A leaves a positive balance and *there are other assets remaining* in the class, this balance becomes the new UCC of the class and it continues to generate CCA tax shields.[7]

D. When an asset is sold for more than its initial cost, the difference between the sale price and initial cost is called a **capital gain**.[8] One-half of the capital gain is taxable and therefore is added to the year's taxable income.

---

[7] Many classes contain a large number of assets, so this CCA treatment of the sale of an asset is very common.

[8] Capital gains or losses also arise from the sale of non-depreciable assets such as land and financial securities. However, you never get a capital loss with a depreciable asset: Steps A, B, and C apply instead.

Example 1   Suppose you start a new business by purchasing a Class 8 machine for $10 million. After taking two years of CCA, the undepreciated capital cost of that machine is $6.4 million. At that point you sell the machine for $12 million. Because the sale price is higher than the asset cost, the machine has appreciated in value, not depreciated. Thus the tax authorities calculate that you have taken $10 - 6.4 = \$3.6$ million of depreciation to which you were (in an economic sense) not entitled. This $3.6 million of depreciation is, therefore "recaptured" and added to your income. In addition, you have also made a capital gain of $12 - 10 = \$2$ million. Half this gain is taxable, and is added to your taxable income.

Now, we have assumed that the machine is your only Class 8 asset. Suppose instead that there are other items in Class 8, and just before you dispose of the machine, Class 8 has a UCC greater than $10 million. Then there is no recaptured depreciation, but there is still the $2 million capital gain and a reduction of the UCC of Class 8 by $10 million.

Example 2   Again, suppose you buy a Class 8 machine for $10 million. But now suppose you sell the machine for $4 million after taking two years of CCA tax shields. If it is the only asset you have in Class 8, the UCC of the class is again $6.4 million at the time of sale, and you are allowed to deduct $6.4 - 4 = \$2.4$ million from your income as a terminal loss. In reality, the machine suffered economic depreciation to a value of $4 million, but the tax laws only allowed you to depreciate it to $6.4 million. The terminal loss can thus be regarded as an extra depreciation tax shield that brings the total tax depreciation into line with the economic depreciation.

You already know what happens in this example if there are other Class 8 assets: if the UCC of Class 8 exceeds $4 million at the time of sale, you simply deduct $4 million from the UCC and nothing else happens, but if the UCC is less than $4 million, you have recaptured depreciation.

Present Values of CCA Tax Shields

Our two examples illustrate a peculiar feature of the asset class system embodied in Canadian tax law: an asset can still generate CCA tax shields for the firm even after it is sold, provided there are other assets remaining in its class. To calculate the PV of a project, you must know how to calculate the PV of a perpetual CCA tax shield.

Suppose you start a new asset class by buying an asset. We'll use this notation to describe the asset and your firm:

C = capital cost of an asset acquired in year 0
d = CCA rate for the asset class
T_c = corporate tax rate
r = discount rate
UCC_t = undepreciated capital cost in year t after deducting CCA for the year

For simplicity, we'll assume you get your first CCA tax shield from the asset in year 1.[9] The UCC of the class starts out at $UCC_0 = C$, so the CCA you get for year 1 is $d \times UCC_0 = Cd$.

---

[9]This simplifies two aspects of Canadian tax law. First, there is the "half-year rule" which says that half of the asset cost C is added to the class in year 0 and the other half is added in year 1. Second, CCA is based on the UCC of the asset class at the tax year-end. Thus, you actually get half of the first year's CCA tax shield in year 0 and half in year 1. We'll get a simple formula that is not too far from the truth if we assume that all of the first year's CCA tax shield occurs in year 1. For a more precise formula, see Appendix 6-1.

After deducting the CCA, the UCC for year 1 becomes:

$$UCC_1 = UCC_0 - CCA$$
$$= C - Cd$$
$$= C(1 - d)$$

Similarly, the CCA taken for year 2 is

$$d \times UCC_1 = Cd(1 - d)$$

In year t, you will have taken $t-1$ previous CCA tax shields, so the UCC at the start of the year is $UCC_{t-1} = C(1-d)^{t-1}$. Thus, your CCA for year t will be

$$d \times UCC_{t-1} = Cd(1-d)^{t-1}$$

There are two ways you can handle CCA tax shields when computing the net present value of a project. On the one hand, you can compute the taxable income every year from the revenues, expenses, and CCA, and multiply by the tax rate to get the annual tax cash flow. Don't forget to include any recaptured depreciation or terminal loss when the project is salvaged. You must also account for any perpetual CCA tax shields left in the class after salvaging the project's assets. This approach is illustrated in Section 6-3. It is cumbersome unless you have access to an electronic spreadsheet program on a micro-computer.[10]

On the other hand, you can apply the tricks you learned in Chapter 3 to get simple formulas for the present value of the CCA tax shields themselves. Then you can add the PV of the CCA tax shields to the PV of the annual "after-tax" revenues and expenses to get the overall PV of the project. The after-tax revenues and expenses are simply revenues and expenses multiplied by $(1 - T_c)$. This approach gives the overall PV of the project because of the additivity property of present values discussed in Section 5-2. That is, if we let ATCF stand for the annual after-tax cash flow and Rev and Exp stand for revenues and expenses, respectively, then after-tax cash flow equals after-tax revenues net of expenses plus the CCA tax shield:

$$ATCF = (1 - T_c) \times (Rev - Exp) + T_c \times CCA$$

Because present values are additive, the PV of after-tax cash flows equals the PV of the after-tax revenues net of expenses plus the PV of the CCA tax shield:

$$PV\ (ATCF) = PV\ ((1 - T_c) \times (Rev - Exp)) + PV(T_c \times CCA)$$

Thus we have two equivalent approaches to calculating present values in the presence of taxes, and we shall use both in this text. They give the same answers.

Let's see how to calculate the PV of a CCA tax shield. First, let's suppose you never sell the asset. The project generates the following CCA tax shields.

---

[10]But you *must* use this approach if your firm is likely to have tax losses at some time in the future. These are carried back and forward against other years' income, as discussed in Appendix 6-1. This means that any benefit from CCA tax shields may be deferred until the firm has taxable income.

Year	1	2	3		t	$\cdots$
CCA tax shield	CdT_c	$CdT_c(1-d)$	$CdT_c(1-d)^2$	$\cdots$	$CdT_c(1-d)^{t-1}$	$\cdots$

This forms a perpetuity in the amount CdT_c that is growing (really declining) at the rate $-d$. From Section 3-2 we know that the present value of this is:[11]

$$\text{PV of perpetual CCA tax shield} = \frac{CdT_c}{r+d}$$

What happens if you sell the asset after using it for a few years? We use the same type of trick you saw in Section 3-2: we combine the present value of two declining perpetuities to calculate the present value of a declining annuity. Let's look at some examples showing how to combine tax principles and present value principles to get the PV of the tax shields. You can sharpen your understanding of these principles by doing some of the problems at the end of the chapter.

While going through these examples, remember that we always analyze the incremental cash flows created by the project in order to calculate its present value. In particular, we are looking for incremental changes in CCA and UCC that arise because of the purchase (or sale) of assets for the project. Fortunately the formula given above for the PV of a perpetual CCA tax shield still works if the firm already has other assets in the class to which the assets of the project are to be added. In this case the formula gives the PV of the incremental perpetual tax shields generated by the purchase of the asset for an amount C. This is exactly what we need in calculating the PV of the project.

Example 3 Suppose you buy $C = \$1$ million of pipeline assets in year 0 (Class 6, CCA rate $d = 0.10$). You will sell the assets in year 10 for $S = \$200,000$, at which time you will still have other assets in the class (which includes your fences and wharves) and a UCC in excess of $200,000. Your tax rate is 40% and your discount rate is 15%. You want to know the present value of the incremental tax shields generated by the ownership and sale of the asset. Since you have other assets in the class and a UCC in excess of the sale price, you will have neither recaptured depreciation nor a terminal loss. The only tax effect of the sale of the asset will arise from the reduction of the UCC of Class 6 by $200,000 in year 10. You have:[12]

---

[11]To see this, use the formula for a growing perpetuity with $C_t = CdT_c(1-d)^{t-1}$ and $g = -d$. Thus, $C_1 = CdT_c$.

We have

$$PV = \frac{C_1}{1+r} + \frac{C_1(1-d)}{(1+r)^2} + \frac{C_1(1-d)^2}{(1+r)^3} + \cdots$$

$$= \frac{C_1}{r-(-d)}$$

$$= \frac{CdT_c}{r+d}$$

[12]Here we assume, for simplicity, that the first CCA tax shield lost due to the sale occurs in year 11, or the year after the sale. The $SdT_c/(r+d)$ formula has already discounted the effect of the lost tax shields back to one year before the first lost tax shield, year 10, so you must discount it back another ten years. In reality, half of the first lost tax shield will be in year 10 and the other half will be in year 11, because the half-year rule effectively applies to asset dispositions as well. See Appendix 6-1.

PV of CCA tax shields

$$= \text{PV of perpetual tax shield on \$1 million in year 0}$$

$$- \text{ PV of perpetual tax shield on \$200,000 in year 10}$$

$$= \frac{CdT_c}{r + d} - \frac{1}{(1 + r)^{10}} \frac{SdT_c}{r + d}$$

$$= \frac{1{,}000{,}000 \times 0.1 \times 0.4}{0.15 + 0.1} - \frac{1}{(1.15)^{10}} \times \frac{200{,}000 \times 0.1 \times 0.4}{0.15 + 0.1}$$

$$= \$152{,}090$$

Note that the UCC generated by the pipeline after ten years of CCA tax shields is $\text{UCC}_{10} = (1 - 0.1)^{10} \times 1{,}000{,}000 = \$348{,}678$. Even *after* selling the pipeline assets in year 10, you will continue to depreciate $348{,}678 - 200{,}000 = \$148{,}678$ of them because of the special features in Canadian tax law.

The calculations in Example 3 are easy, since you do not need to know UCC_{10} to calculate an amount of recaptured depreciation or terminal loss. Most asset classes are very broadly defined and include many assets; the situation described in Example 3 is quite common. However, the Income Tax Regulations also specify many situations where an asset must be in a class by itself,[13] so the disposition of such an asset will always generate a terminal loss or recaptured depreciation.

Example 4   Suppose you have the same situation as in Example 3, except that the pipeline is the only Class 6 asset you have from years 0 through 10. You get a terminal loss of $\text{UCC}_{10} - S = \$148{,}678$, but you must also subtract UCC_{10} from the class balance, to close it out when the asset is sold. You have:

PV of ten years of CCA tax shields and terminal loss

$$= \text{PV of perpetual tax shield on \$1{,}000{,}000 in year 0}$$

$$+ \text{ PV of terminal loss tax shield on \$148{,}678 in year 10}$$

$$- \text{ PV of perpetual tax shield on \$348{,}678 in year 10}$$

$$= \frac{CdT_c}{r + d} + \frac{T_c}{(1 + r)^{10}} (\text{UCC}_{10} - S) - \frac{1}{(1 + r)^{10}} \frac{\text{UCC}_{10} dT_c}{r + d}$$

$$= \frac{1{,}000{,}000 \times 0.1 \times 0.4}{0.15 + 0.1} + \frac{0.4}{(1.15)^{10}} (348{,}678 - 200{,}000)$$

$$- \frac{1}{(1.15)^{10}} \frac{348{,}678 \times 0.1 \times 0.4}{0.15 + 0.1}$$

$$= \$160{,}910$$

Some Asset Classes Give Straight-Line Depreciation

Not all asset classes in Canada's tax system have the declining balance feature you have just seen. For example, a "two-year writeoff" (that is, straight line depreciation over

---

[13]Separate classes are required for rental properties worth more than $50,000, for many types of ships, for telecommunication spacecraft, and for assets associated with different "businesses."

two years) is allowed for some pollution control and energy conservation equipment. Also patents, franchises, and improvements to leasehold interests (for example, redecoration of a store you have leased) generate a straight-line capital cost allowance. The CCA tax shield is just an annuity in these cases.

The Investment Tax Credit

In addition to allowing a company to deduct CCA from taxable income, Canadian tax laws sometimes allow an investment tax credit. A **tax credit** is a reduction of taxes owing,[14] while an **allowance** (such as CCA) is only a reduction of taxable income. The size of the credit varies from 7% to 50% according to the nature of the investment, the region of the country, and the size of the business. For example, suppose you invest $10 million in an asset that is entitled to a 10% investment tax credit. Your tax bill that year is reduced by $0.1 \times 10 = \$1$ million. However, you are only allowed to claim CCA on a net capital cost of $9 million.

6-3 ANOTHER EXAMPLE—IM&C PROJECT

As the newly appointed financial manager of International Mulch and Compost Company (IM&C), you are about to analyze a proposal for marketing guano as a garden fertilizer. (IM&C's planned advertising campaign features a rustic gentleman who steps out of a vegetable patch singing, "All my troubles have guano way.")[15]

You are given the forecasts shown in Table 6-1. The project requires an investment of $10 million in plant and machinery (line 1), which is in Asset Class 10 (30%). This machinery can be dismantled and sold for net proceeds estimated at $1 million in period 7 (line 1, column 7). This amount is the plant's *salvage value*. IM&C always has many assets and a positive balance in Class 10.

Table 6-1 shows the incremental effects of accepting the project. For example, the undepreciated capital costs and the tax cash flows are incremental. Thus, a negative tax means a reduction in taxes paid by IM&C on its other projects. The raw data for a project are often presented in a "massaged form" like this to reflect the book value of the investment and estimated annual profits. Indeed, the pro forma depreciation figures that are usually given are those that would appear on annual financial statements. But we know they do not represent cash flows, so we have presented the capital cost allowances instead, which generate tax shields.[16]

Lines 5 to 11 in Table 6-1 show a simplified income statement for the guano project. This might be taken as a starting point for estimating cash flow. However, you discover that all figures submitted to you are based on costs and selling prices prevailing in year 0. IM&C's production managers realize there will be inflation, but they have assumed that prices can be raised to cover increasing costs. Thus they claim that inflation won't affect the real value of the project.

Though this line of argument sounds plausible, it will get you into trouble. First, opportunity costs of capital are usually expressed as *nominal* rates. You cannot use a nominal rate to discount real cash flows. Second, not all prices and costs increase at

---

[14]Naturally the credit cannot be claimed if there are no taxes owing. Moreover, the tax credit is limited to $7,500 + 0.5 \times$ (taxable income) in any one year. However, unused tax credits can be carried back up to three years and forward up to seven years.

[15]Sorry.

[16]This presents a problem if you are a financial analyst outside the firm. You may have access to audited financial statements for shareholders, but will not have access to the information on the tax return.

---

the same rate. For example, the tax savings provided by capital cost allowances are unaffected by inflation, since tax law allows you to depreciate only the original cost of the equipment, regardless of what happens to prices after the investment is made. On the other hand, wages generally increase faster than the inflation rate. Labour cost per tonne of guano will rise in real terms unless technological advances allow more efficient use of labour.

Assume that future inflation is forecasted at 10% a year. Table 6-2 restates Table 6-1 in nominal terms, assuming, just for simplicity, that sales, investment, operating costs, and required working capital appreciate at this general rate. You can see, however, that CCA is not affected by inflation.

Table 6-3 derives cash-flow forecasts from the investment and income data given in Table 6-2. Cash flow from operations is defined as sales less operating costs, other costs, and taxes.[17] The remaining cash flows include the changes in working capital, the initial capital investment, and the final recovery of salvage value. The salvage value exceeds the undepreciated capital cost of the assets at the time of disposal. Since IM&C has other assets in the same class, this will not result in recaptured depreciation. However, it will reduce the UCC of those other assets at the time of disposal. The item in line 7, column 7 reflects the loss of the present value of the associated tax shields.

IM&C estimates the nominal opportunity cost of capital for projects of this type as 20%. (We have already used this discount rate to calculate the PV of lost CCA on salvage.)[18] When all cash flows are added up and discounted, the guano project is seen to offer a net present value of $4.2 million:

$$NPV = -12,160 - \frac{528}{1.20} + \frac{3,012}{(1.20)^2} + \frac{5,756}{(1.20)^3} + \frac{9,405}{(1.20)^4} + \frac{9,383}{(1.20)^5} + \frac{6,072}{(1.20)^6}$$

$$+ \frac{3,802}{(1.20)^7} = 4,225 \text{ or } \$4,225,000$$

Separating Investment and Financing Decisions

Our analysis of the guano project takes no notice of how that project is financed. It may be that IM&C would decide to finance partly by debt, but, if it did, we would not subtract the debt proceeds from the required investment, nor would we recognize interest and principal payments as cash outflows. We would treat the project as if it were all equity-financed, treating all cash outflows as coming from stockholders and all cash inflows as going to them.

We approach the problem in this way so that we can separate the analysis of the investment decision from the financing decision. Then, when we have calculated NPV, we can undertake a separate analysis of financing. Financing decisions and their possible interaction with investment decisions are covered later in the book.

---

[17]Sales revenue may not represent actual cash inflow. Costs and taxes may not represent cash outflows. This is why change in working capital must be taken into account, as it is in Table 6-3. The "Further Note on Estimating Cash Flow" in this section discusses the relationship between operating cash flow and change in working capital in more detail.

[18]By discounting the depreciation tax shields at 20%, we implicitly assume that they are as risky as the other cash flows. Since they depend only on tax rates, depreciation method, and IM&C's ability to generate taxable income, they may well be less risky. Therefore, there are grounds for discounting the tax shields at a relatively low rate. There is more on this in Chapter 24.

Table 6-1 IM&C's guano project—Initial projections (figures in thousands of dollars).

Period	0	1	2	3	4	5	6	7
1. Capital investment	10,000							-1,000[a]
2. Undepreciated capital cost at year end	10,000	7,000	4,900	3,430	2,401	1,681	1,176	-177[b]
3. Working capital		500	1,065	2,450	3,340	2,225	1,130	0
4. Total book value[c] (2 + 3)	10,000	7,500	5,965	5,880	5,741	3,906	2,306	-177
5. Sales		475	10,650	24,500	33,400	22,250	11,130	
6. Operating costs		761	6,388	14,690	20,043	13,345	6,678	
7. Other costs	4,000	2,000						
8. Capital cost allowance (30% for Class 10)		3,000	2,100	1,470	1,029	720	504	353
9. Taxable income (5 – 6 – 7 – 8)	-4,000	-5,286	2,162	8,340	12,328	8,185	3,948	-353
10. Tax at 46%	-1,840	-2,432	995	3,836	5,671	3,765	1,816	-162
11. Profit after tax[c] (10 – 9)	-2,160	-2,854	1,167	4,504	6,657	4,420	2,132	-14[d]

[a] Salvage value.
[b] UCC of $823 in period 7 less salvage value. Since this is negative, it gives a reduction in future CCA tax shields on IM&C's other Class 10 assets.
[c] Based on depreciation charges being equal to CCA.
[d] This includes the profit on salvage: $-353 - (-162) + 177 = -14$.

Table 6-2 IM&C's guano project—Revised projections reflecting inflation (figures in thousands of dollars).

Period	0	1	2	3	4	5	6	7
1. Capital investment	10,000							-1,949[a]
2. Undepreciated capital cost at year end	10,000	7,000	4,900	3,430	2,401	1,681	1,176	-1,126[b]
3. Working capital		550	1,289	3,261	4,890	3,583	2,002	0
4. Sales		523	12,887	32,610	48,901	35,834	19,717	
5. Operating costs		837	7,729	19,552	29,345	21,492	11,830	
6. Other costs	4,000	2,200						
7. Capital cost allowances (30% for Class 10)		3,000	2,100	1,470	1,029	720	504	353
8. Taxable income (4 – 5 – 6 – 7)	-4,000	-5,514	3,058	11,588	18,527	13,622	7,383	-353
9. Tax at 46%	-1,840	-2,536	1,407	5,330	8,522	6,266	3,396	-162
10. Profit after tax (9 – 8)	-2,160	-2,978	1,651	6,258	10,005	7,356	3,987	-935[c]

[a] Salvage value.
[b] UCC of $823 in period 7 less salvage value.
[c] Includes $1,126 profit on salvage.

Table 6-3 IM&C's guano project—Cash flow analysis (figures in thousands of dollars).

Period	0	1	2	3	4	5	6	7
1. Sales		523	12,887	32,610	48,901	35,834	19,717	
2. Operating and other costs	4,000	3,037	7,729	19,552	29,345	21,492	11,830	
3. Tax on operations	−1,840	−2,536	1,407	5,330	8,522	6,266	3,396	−162
4. Cash flow from operations (1 − 2 − 3)	−2,160	22	3,751	7,728	11,034	8,076	4,491	162
5. Change in working capital		−550	−739	−1,972	−1,629	1,307	1,581	2,002
6. Capital investment and disposal	−10,000						1949	
7. PV of CCA tax shields lost on other projects							−311[a]	
8. Net cash flow and lost tax shield (4 + 5 + 6 + 7)	−12,160	−528	3,012	5,756	9,405	9,383	6,072	3,802
9. Present value at 20%	−12,160	−440	2,092	3,331	4,536	3,771	2,034	1,061

Net present value = $4,225

[a] Salvage value exceeds UCC (Table 6-2, line 2, column 7) by 1,126, so PV of lost CCA tax shields on other projects = $\dfrac{1,126 \times 0.3 \times 0.46}{0.2 + 0.3} = 311$

*A Further Note on Estimating Cash Flow

Now here is an important point. You can see from line 5 of Table 6-3 that working capital increases in the early and middle years of the project. Why is this? There are several possibilities.

1. Sales recorded on the income statement overstate actual cash receipts from guano shipments because customers are slow to pay their bills. Therefore, accounts receivable increase.

2. Projected operating costs understate cash outlays for raw materials and production. Therefore inventory increases.

3. An offsetting effect occurs if payments for materials and services used in guano production are delayed. In this case accounts payable will increase.

Thus a detailed cash-flow forecast for, say, year 3 might look like Table 6-4.

Instead of worrying about changes in working capital, you could estimate cash flow directly by counting up the dollars coming in and taking away the dollars going out. But you would still need to put together a projected income statement to estimate taxes.

Table 6-4 Details of cash-flow forecast for IM&C's guano project in year 3 (figures in thousands of dollars).

Cash Flows		Data From Forecasted Income Statement		Working Capital Changes
Cash inflow	=	Sales	−	Increase in accounts receivable
$31,110	=	32,610	−	1,500
Cash outflow	=	Operating costs and taxes	+	Increase in inventory net of increase in accounts payable
$25,354	=	(19,552 + 5,330)	+	(972 − 500)
Net cash flow	=	Cash inflow	−	Cash outflow
$5,756	=	31,110	−	25,534

A Final Comment on Project Analysis

Let's review. A few pages ago, you embarked on an analysis of IM&C's guano project. It appeared, at first, that you had all the facts you needed in Table 6-1, but many of those numbers had to be thrown away because they didn't reflect expected inflation. So you worked out revised projections and calculated project net present value.

You were lucky to get away with just one NPV calculation. In real situations, it often takes several tries to purge all inconsistencies and mistakes. Then there are "what if" questions. For example: what if inflation rages at 15% per year, rather than 10%? What if technical problems delay startup to year 2? What if gardeners prefer chemical fertilizers to your natural product?

You won't truly understand the guano project until these questions are answered. *Project analysis* is more than one or two NPV calculations, as we will see in Chapter 10.

However, before you become too deeply immersed in guano, we should now turn to the subject of project interactions.

6-4 PROJECT INTERACTIONS

Almost all decisions about capital expenditure involve either-or choices. The firm can build either a 90,000-square-metre warehouse or a 100,000-square-metre warehouse in one of several locations. It can heat it either by oil or by natural gas, and so on. These mutually exclusive options are simple examples of *project interactions*.

Project interactions can arise in countless ways. The literature of operations research and industrial engineering sometimes addresses cases of extreme complexity and difficulty. We will concentrate on five simple but important cases.

Case 1—Optimal Timing of Investment

The fact that a project has a positive NPV does not mean that it is best undertaken now. It might be even more valuable if undertaken in the future. Similarly, a project with a currently negative NPV might become a valuable opportunity if we wait a bit. Thus *any* project has two mutually exclusive alternatives: do it now, or wait and invest later.

The question of optimal timing of investment is not difficult under conditions of certainty. We first examine alternative dates (*t*) for making the investment and calculate its net *future* value as of each date. Then, to find which of the alternatives would add most to the firm's *current* value, we must work out

$$\frac{\text{Net future value as of date } t}{(1 + r)^t}$$

For example, suppose you own a large tract of inaccessible timber. To harvest it, you have to invest a substantial amount in access roads and other facilities. The longer you wait, the higher the investment required. On the other hand, lumber prices will rise as you wait, and the trees will keep growing, although at a gradually decreasing rate.

Let us suppose that the net value of the harvest at different future dates is as follows:

Year of Harvest	0	1	2	3	4	5
Net *future* value (thousands of dollars)	50	64.4	77.5	89.4	100	109.4
Change in value from previous year, %		+28.8	+20.3	+15.4	+11.9	+9.4

As you can see, the longer you defer cutting the timber, the more money you will make. However, your concern is with the date that maximizes the net *present* value of your investment. You therefore need to discount the net future value of the harvest back to the present. Suppose the appropriate discount rate is 10%. Then if you harvest the timber in year 1, it has a net *present value of* $58,500:

$$\text{NPV if harvested in year 1} = \frac{64.4}{1.10} = 58.5 \text{ or } \$58,500$$

The net present value (at $t = 0$) for other harvest dates is as follows:

Year of Harvest	0	1	2	3	4	5
Net present value (thousands of dollars)	50	58.5	64.0	67.2	68.3	67.9

The optimal point to harvest the timber is year 4 because this is the point that maximizes NPV.

Notice that before year 4 the net future value of the timber increases by more than 10% a year: the gain in value is greater than the cost of the capital that is tied up in the project. After year 4 the gain in value is still positive but less than the cost of capital. You maximize the net present value of your investment if you harvest your timber as soon as the rate of increase in value drops below the cost of capital.[19]

The problem of optimal timing of investment under uncertainty is, of course, much more complicated. An opportunity not taken at $t = 0$ might be either more or less attractive at $t = 1$; there is rarely any way of knowing for sure. Perhaps it is better to strike while the iron is hot even if there is a chance it will become hotter. On the other hand, if you wait a bit you might obtain more information and avoid a bad mistake.[20]

Case 2—Choosing Between Long- and Short-Lived Equipment

Suppose the firm is forced to choose between two machines, A and B. The two machines are designed differently, but have identical capacity and do exactly the same job. Machine A costs $15,000, and will last three years. It costs $4,000 per year to run. Machine B is an "economy" model costing only $10,000, but it will last only two years, and costs $6,000 per year to run.

Because the two machines produce exactly the same product, the only way to choose between them is on the basis of cost. Suppose we compute the present value of cost:

Machine	Costs (thousands of dollars)				Present Value at 10% (thousands of dollars)
	C_0	C_1	C_2	C_3	
A	+15	+4	+4	+4	24.95
B	+10	+6	+6		20.41

Should we take machine B, the one with the lower present value of costs? Not necessarily, because B will have to be replaced a year earlier than A. In other words, there is a future investment decision contingent on today's choice of A or B.

A commonly suggested solution is to assume that each machine is always replaced in the last year of its life with identical equipment. The cash flows from such a policy are:[21]

---

[19] Our timber-cutting example conveys the right idea about investment timing, but it misses an important practical point: the sooner you cut the first crop of trees, the sooner the second crop can start growing. Thus, the value of the second crop depends on when you cut the first. This more complex and realistic problem might be solved in one of two ways:
1. Find the cutting dates that maximize the present value of a series of harvests, taking account of the different growth rates of young and old trees.
2. Repeat our calculations, counting the future market value of cut-over land as part of the payoff to the first harvest. The value of cut-over land includes the present value of all subsequent harvests. The second solution is far simpler if you can figure out what cut-over land will be worth.

[20] H. Bierman and S. Smidt discuss the tree-cutting problem in *The Capital Budgeting Decision*, 5th ed., New York: The Macmillan Company, 1980, pp. 439–444.

[21] For example, in year 3 the owner of A pays $4,000 to operate the old machine and also pays out $15,000 to purchase the new machine. The net outflow is $19,000.

	Costs (thousands of dollars)						
	C_0	C_1	C_2	C_3	C_4	C_5	C_6
Chain of type A machines	+15	+4	+4	+19	+4	+4	+4
Chain of type B machines	+10	+6	+16	+6	+16	+6	+6

By year 6 A's owner wears out the second machine and B's owner wears out the third. Now the slate is clean. A replacement must be made in year 6 regardless of the initial choice of A or B. We can therefore compare the PVs of the costs of these two chains:

	Present Value of Costs at 10% (thousands of dollars)
Chain of type A machines	43.69
Chain of type B machines	51.22

Thus investing in a sequence of type A machines is better.

We can always handle the problem of differing lives by this method, but it can sometimes involve a lot of tedious calculation. Fortunately there is a simpler way. Look at the following two investments:

	Costs (thousands of dollars)				Present Value at 10% (thousands of dollars)
	C_0	C_1	C_2	C_3	
Machine A	+15	+4	+4	+4	24.95
Three-year annuity starting in period 1		+10.03	+10.03	+10.03	24.95

The first investment is machine A; the second is an annuity that has exactly the same life and present value as machine A. How did we know that the equivalent cash flow from the annuity is 10.03? It was easy! We set the NPV of the annuity equal to the present value of A and solved for the payment of the annuity:

PV of annuity = PV of cash outflows of A = 24.95

= annuity payment × three-year annuity factor

Therefore the annuity payment equals the present value divided by the annuity factor, which is 2.487 for three years and a 10% cost of capital.[22]

$$\text{Annuity payment} = \frac{24.95}{2.487} = 10.03$$

If we make a similar calculation for machine B, we get:

	Costs (thousands of dollars)			Present Value at 10% (thousands of dollars)
	C_0	C_1	C_2	
Machine B	+10	+6	+6	20.41
Equivalent two-year annuity		+11.76	+11.76	20.41

[22]This factor can be obtained from a PV table or from the annuity formula given in Section 3-2.

A chain of As is therefore exactly like a chain of cash outflows of $10,030 a year. A chain of Bs is exactly like a chain of cash outflows of $11,760 a year. Since a stream of $11,760 a year is worth more than one of $10,030 a year, a chain of Bs must have a higher present value of costs than a chain of As. Support, for example, that you persisted in replacing each machine with another of the same type. The cost of operating machine A *in perpetuity* would have a present value of $10,030/0.10 = $100,300, and the policy of operating machine B in perpetuity would have an NPV of 11,760/0.10 = $117,600. You would be $17,300 better off by always buying the more expensive machine.

Our rule for comparing assets of different lives is, therefore, as follows. Select the machine that has the lowest *equivalent annual cost*. The equivalent annual cost is simply the net present value of the cost divided by the annuity factor. If you would like to know the net present value of a policy of *always* replacing one machine with another of the same type, just divide the equivalent annual cost by the discount rate.

We must stress that these solutions are no more than second best.[23] If we know that we will replace machine A with machine C, or that replacement and operating costs will inflate, then we ought not to embrace second-best solutions for the sake of computational simplicity.

Finally, remember the reason chains are necessary. The reason is that A and B must be replaced at different future dates. The choice between them therefore affects future investment decisions. If subsequent decisions are not affected by the initial choice— for example, because neither machine will be replaced—then we do *not need to take future decisions into account.*[24]

Case 3—Deciding When to Replace an Existing Machine

The previous example took the life of each machine as fixed. In practice the point at which equipment is replaced reflects economic considerations rather than total physical collapse. *We* must decide when to replace. The machine will rarely decide for us.

Here is a common problem. You are operating an elderly machine that is expected to produce a net cash *inflow* of $4,000 in the coming year and $4,000 next year. After that it will give up the ghost. You can replace it now with a new machine, which costs $15,000 but is much more efficient and will provide a cash inflow of $8,000 a year for three years. You want to know whether you should replace your equipment now or wait a year. Notice that the earlier you get a new machine, the earlier it will need replacing. So the effective choice is between a *series* of new machines beginning either immediately or in one year. We can calculate the NPV of the new machine and also its equivalent annual cash flow, that is, the three-year annuity that has the same net present value:

	Cash Flows (thousands of dollars)				NPV at 10% (thousands of dollars)
	C_0	C_1	C_2	C_3	
New machine	−15	+8	+8	+8	4.895
Equivalent three-year annuity		+1.968	+1.968	+1.968	4.895

[23]The books listed under "Further Reading" at the end of this chapter describe more elaborate procedures.

[24]However, if neither machine will be replaced, then we would have to consider the extra revenue generated by machine A in its third year, when it will be operating but B will not.

In other words, a chain of new machines is equivalent to an annuity of $1,968 per year for the life of the chain. So we can equally well ask at what point we would want to replace our old machine with a series of "machines" that produce $1,968 a year. When the question is put this way, the answer is obvious. As long as your old machine can generate a cash flow of $4,000 a year, who wants to put in its place a series of "machines" that generate only $1,968 a year?

It is a simple matter to incorporate salvage values into this calculation. Suppose the current salvage value is $8,000 and next year's value is $7,000. Let's see where you come out next year if you wait and then sell. On the one hand you gain $7,000, but you lose today's salvage value *plus* a year's return on that money. That is, $8,000 × 1.1 = $8,800. Your net loss is $8,800 − $7,000 = $1,800, which only partly offsets the operating gain. You should not replace yet.

Remember: the logic of such comparisons requires that the possible line of new machines should be the best of the available alternatives. This means, among other things, that each machine in the chain should be replaced at the optimal point. Also remember that any calculation involving hypothetical series of identical machines rests on simplistic assumptions.

Case 4—Cost of Excess Capacity

Any firm with a computer encounters many proposals for using it. Recently installed computers tend to have excess capacity, and, since the immediate marginal cost of using such computers seems to be negligible, management often encourages new uses. Sooner or later, however, the load on the machine will increase to a point at which management must either terminate the uses they originally encouraged or invest in another computer several years earlier than they had planned. Such problems can be avoided if a proper charge is made for the use of spare capacity.

Suppose we have a new investment project that requires heavy use of the computer. The effect of adopting the project is to bring the purchase date of a new computer forward from year 4 to year 3. This new computer has a life of five years, and at a discount rate of 10% the present value of the cost of buying and operating it is $500,000.

We begin by converting the $500,000 present value of cost of the computer to an equivalent annual cost of $131,899 for each of five years.[25] Of course, when the new computer in turn wears out, we will replace it with another. So we face the prospect of computing expenses of $131,899 a year for an indefinite number of years. If we undertake the new project, the series of expenses begins in year 4; if we do not undertake it, the series begins in year 5. The new project, therefore, results in an *additional* computing cost of $131,899 in year 4. This has a present value of $131,899/(1.10)^4$, or $90,089. This cost is properly charged against the new project. When we recognize it, the NPV of the project may prove to be negative. If so, we still need to check whether it is worthwhile undertaking the project now and abandoning it later when the excess capacity of the present computer disappears.

Case 5—Fluctuating Load Factors

Although a $10 million warehouse may have a positive net present value, it should be built only if it has a higher NPV than a $9 million alternative. In other words, the NPV of the $1 million *marginal* investment required to buy the more expensive warehouse must be positive.

---

[25]The present value of $131,899 for five years discounted at 10% is $500,000.

One case in which this is easily forgotten occurs when equipment is needed to meet fluctuating demand. Consider the following problem. A widget manufacturer operates two machines, each of which has a capacity of 1,000 units a year. They have an indefinite life and no salvage value, and so the only costs are the operating expenses of $2 per widget. Widget manufacture, as everyone knows, is a seasonal business, and widgets are perishable. During the fall and winter, when demand is high, each machine produces at capacity. During the spring and summer, each machine works at 50% of capacity. If the discount rate is 10% and the machines are kept indefinitely, the present value of the costs is $30,000:

	Two Old Machines
Annual output per machine	750 units
Operating cost per machine	$2 \times 750 = \$1,500$
PV operating cost per machine	$1500/0.10 = \$15,000$
PV operating cost of two machines	$2 \times 15,000 = \$30,000$

The company is considering whether to replace these machines with newer equipment. The new machines have a similar capacity, and so two would still be needed to meet peak demand. Each new machine costs $6,000 and lasts indefinitely. Operating expenses are only one dollar per unit. On this basis the company calculates that the present value of the costs of two new machines would be $27,000:

	Two New Machines
Annual output per machine	750 units
Capital cost per machine	$6,000
Operating cost per machine	$1 \times 750 = \$750$
PV total cost per machine	$6,000 + 750/0.10 = \$13,500$
PV total cost of two machines	$2 \times 13,500 = \$27,000$

Therefore, it scraps both old machines and buys two new ones.

The company was quite right in thinking that two new machines are better than two old ones, but unfortunately it forgot to investigate a third alternative: to replace just one of the old machines. Since the new machine has low operating costs, it would pay to operate it at capacity all year. The remaining old machine could then be kept simply to meet peak demand. The present value of the costs under this strategy is $26,000:

	One Old Machine	One New Machine
Annual output per machine	500 units	1,000 units
Capital cost per machine	0	$6,000
Operating cost per machine	$2 \times 500 = \$1,000$	$1 \times 1000 = \$1000$
PV total cost per machine	$1,000/0.10 = \$10,000$	$6,000 + 1000/0.10 = \$16,000$
PV total cost of both machines	$26,000	

Replacing one machine saves $4,000; replacing two machines saves only $3,000. The net present value of the *marginal* investment in the second machine is $-\$1,000$.

6-5 CHOOSING THE CAPITAL EXPENDITURE PROGRAM WHEN RESOURCES ARE LIMITED

The entire discussion of methods of capital budgeting rests on the proposition that the wealth of a firm's shareholders is highest if the firm accepts *every* project that has a positive net present value. Suppose, however, that there are limitations on the investment program that prevent the company from undertaking all such projects. If this is the case, we need a method of selecting the package of projects that is within the company's resources yet gives the highest possible net present value.

Profitability Index Under Capital Rationing

Let us start with a very simple example. Suppose that there is a 10% opportunity cost of capital, that our company has total resources of $10 million, and that it has the following opportunities:

Project	Cash Flows (millions of dollars) C_0	C_1	C_2	NPV at 10% (millions of dollars)	Profitability Index
A	−10	+30	+5	21	3.1
B	−5	+5	+20	16	4.2
C	−5	+5	+15	12	3.4

The firm has sufficient resources to invest either in project A or in projects B and C. Although individually B and C have lower net present values than project A, when taken together they have the higher net present value. It is clear, therefore, that we cannot choose between projects solely on the basis of individual net present values. When funds are limited, we need to concentrate on getting the biggest bang for our buck. In other words, we much pick the projects that offer the highest ratio of present value to initial outlay. This ratio is simply the profitability index, or benefit-cost ratio, that we described in Chapter 5:

$$\text{Profitability index} = \frac{\text{present value}}{\text{investment}}$$

Of our three projects, B has the highest profitability index and C the next highest. Therefore, if our budget limit is $10 million, we should accept these two projects.

Unfortunately, there are some limitations to these simple ranking methods. One of the most serious is that they break down whenever more than one resource is rationed. For example, suppose that a $10 million budget limit applies to cash flows in *each* of years 0 and 1 and that our menu is expanded as follows:

Project	Cash Flows (millions of dollars) C_0	C_1	C_2	NPV at 10% (millions of dollars)	Profitability Index
A	−10	+30	+5	21	3.1
B	−5	+5	+20	16	4.2
C	−5	+5	+15	12	3.4
D	0	−40	+60	13	1.4

One strategy is to accept projects B and C; however, if we do this, we cannot also accept D, which costs more than our budget limit for period 1. An alternative is to accept project A in period 0. Although this has a lower net present value than the combination of B and C, it provides a $30 million positive cash flow in period 1. With that added to the $10 million budget we can also afford to undertake D. A and D have *lower* profitability indices than B and C, but they have a *higher* total net present value.

The reason that ranking on the profitability index fails in this example is that resources are constrained in each of two periods. In fact, this ranking method is inadequate whenever there is *any* other constraint on the choice of projects. This means that it cannot cope with cases in which two projects are mutually exclusive or in which one project is dependent on another.

*Some More Elaborate Capital Rationing Models

The simplicity of the profitability-index method may sometimes outweigh its limitations. For example, it may not pay to worry about expenditures in subsequent years if you have only a hazy notion of future capital availability or investment opportunities. But there are also circumstances in which the limitations of the profitability-index method are intolerable. For such occasions we need a more general method for solving the capital rationing problem.

We begin by restating the problem just described. Suppose that we were to accept proportion x_A of project A in our example. Then the net present value of our investment in the project would be $21x_A$. Similarly the net present value of our investment in project B can be expressed as $16x_B$, and so on. Our objective is to select the set of projects with the highest *total* net present value. In other words we wish to find the values of x that maximize

$$NPV = 21x_A + 16x_B + 12x_C + 13x_D$$

Our choice of projects is subject to several constraints. First, total cash outflow in period 0 must not be greater than $10 million. In other words,

$$10x_A + 5x_B + 5x_C + 0x_D \leq 10$$

Similarly, total outflow in period 1 must not be greater than $10 million.

$$-30x_A - 5x_B - 5x_C + 40x_D \leq 10$$

Finally, we cannot invest a negative amount in a project and we cannot purchase more than one of each. Therefore we have

$$0 \leq x_A \leq 1, 0 \leq x_B \leq 1, \ldots$$

Collecting all these conditions, we can summarize the problem as follows:

Maximize $21x_A + 16x_B + 12x_C + 13x_D$

Subject to

$$10x_A + 5x_B + 5x_C + 0x_D \leq 10$$

$$-30x_A - 5x_B - 5x_C + 40x_D \leq 10$$

$$0 \leq x_A \leq 1, 0 \leq x_B \leq 1, \ldots$$

One way to tackle such a problem is to keep selecting different values for $x_A, \ldots,$ x_D, noting which combination both satisfies the constraints and gives the highest net present value. But it's smarter to recognize that the equations above constitute a linear programming (LP) problem. It can be handed to a computer equipped to solve LPs.

The answer given by the LP method is somewhat different from the one we obtained earlier. Instead of investing in one unit of project A and one of project D, we are told to take half of project A, all of project B, and three-quarters of D. The reason is simple. The computer is a dumb, but obedient, pet, and since we did not tell it that $x_A, \ldots, x_D$ had to be whole numbers, it saw no reason to make them so. By accepting "fractional" projects, it is possible to increase NPV by $2.25 million. For many purposes this is quite appropriate. If project A represents an investment in 1,000 square metres of warehouse space or in 1,000 tonnes of steel plate, it might be feasible to accept 500 square metres or 500 tonnes, and quite reasonable to assume that cash flow would be reduced proportionately. If, however, project A is a single crane or oil well, such fractional investments make little sense.

When fractional projects are not feasible, we can use a form of linear programming known as *integer* (or *zero-one*) programming, which limits the variables to being integers. Unfortunately, integer programs are less common and more awkward to use.

Uses of Capital Rationing Models

Linear programming models seem tailor-made for solving capital budgeting problems when resources are limited. Why then are they not universally accepted either in theory or in practice? One reason is that these models are often not cheap to use. We know of an oil company that spent more than $4 million in one year on an investment planning model using integer programming. While linear programming is considerably cheaper in terms of computer time, it cannot be used when large, indivisible projects are involved.

Second, as with any sophisticated long-range planning tool, there is the general problem of getting good data. It is just not worth applying costly, sophisticated methods to poor data. Furthermore, these models are based on the assumption that all future investment opportunities are known. In reality, the discovery of investment ideas is an unfolding process.

Our most serious misgivings centre on the basic assumption that capital is limited. When we come to discuss company financing, we shall see that most firms do not face capital rationing and can raise very large sums of money on fair terms. Why then do many company presidents tell their subordinates that capital is limited? If they are right, the capital market is seriously imperfect. What then are they doing maximizing NPV?[26] We might be tempted to suppose that if capital is not rationed, they do not need to use the LP model and, if it is rationed, then surely they *ought* not to use it. But that would be too quick a judgement. Let us look at this problem more deliberately.

Soft Rationing   Many firms' capital constraints are "soft." They reflect no imperfections in capital markets. Instead they are provisional limits adopted by management as an aid to financial control.

Some ambitious divisional managers habitually overstate their investment opportunities. Rather than trying to distinguish which projects really are worthwhile, headquarters may find it simpler to impose an upper limit on divisional expenditures and thereby force the divisions to set their own priorities. In such instances budget limits are a rough but effective way of dealing with biased cash-flow forecasts. In other cases management may believe that very rapid corporate growth could impose intolerable strains on management and the organization. Since it is difficult to quantify such constraints explicitly, the budget limit may be used as a proxy.

---

[26]Don't forget that we had to assume perfect capital markets to derive the NPV rule.

Because such budget limits have nothing to do with any inefficiency in the capital market, there is no contradiction in using an LP model in the division to maximize net present value subject to the budget constraint. On the other hand, there is not much point in elaborate selection procedures if the cash-flow forecasts of the division are seriously biased.

Even if capital is not rationed, other resources may be. The availability of management time, skilled labour, or even other capital equipment often constitutes an important constraint on a company's growth. In Appendix 6-2 to this chapter we show you how the programming model we have described can be extended to incorporate such constraints. And we also show how they may be used to cope with project interactions.

Hard Rationing   Soft rationing should never cost the firm anything. If capital constraints become tight enough to hurt—in the sense that projects with significant positive NPVs are passed up—then the firm raises more money and loosens the constraint. But what if it *can't* raise more money—what if it faces *hard* rationing?

Hard rationing implies market imperfections, but that does not necessarily mean we have to throw away net present value as a criterion for capital budgeting. It depends on the nature of the imperfection.

Arizona Aquaculture, Inc. (AAI), borrows as much as the banks will lend it, yet it still has good investment opportunities. This is not hard rationing so long as AAI can issue stock. But perhaps it can't. Perhaps the founder and majority shareholder vetoes the idea from fear of losing control of the firm, or perhaps a stock issue would bring costly red tape or legal complications.[27]

This does not invalidate the NPV rule. AAI's *shareholders* can borrow or lend, sell their shares, or buy more. They have free access to security markets. The type of portfolio they hold is independent of AAI's financing or investment decisions. The only way AAI can help its shareholders is to make them richer. Thus AAI should invest its available cash in the package of projects having the largest aggregate net present value.

A barrier between the firm and capital markets does not undermine net present value so long as the barrier is the *only* market imperfection. The important thing is that the firm's *shareholders* have free access to well-functioning capital markets.

The method of net present value *is* undermined when imperfections restrict shareholders' portfolio choice. Suppose that Nevada Aquaculture, Inc. (NAI) is solely owned by its founder, Alexander Turbot. Mr. Turbot has no cash or credit remaining, but he is convinced that expansion of his operation is a high-NPV investment. He has tried to sell stock but has found that prospective investors, skeptical of prospects for fish farming in the desert, offer him much less than he thinks his firm is worth. For Mr. Turbot capital markets hardly exist. It makes little sense for him to discount the prospective cash flows at a market opportunity cost of capital.

6-6   SUMMARY

By now, present value calculations should be a matter of routine. However, forecasting cash flows will never be routine. It will always be a skilled, hazardous occupation. Mistakes can be minimized by following three rules.

1. Concentrate on cash flows after taxes. Be wary of accounting data masquerading as cash-flow data.

---

[27]A majority owner who is "locked in" and has much personal wealth tied up in AAI may be effectively cut off from capital markets. The NPV rule may not make sense to such an owner, though it will to the other shareholders.

2. Always judge investments on an incremental basis. Tirelessly track down all cash-flow consequences of your decision.

3. Treat inflation consistently. Discount nominal cash-flow forecasts at nominal rates and real forecasts at real rates.

We might add a fourth rule: recognize project interactions. Decisions involving only a choice of accepting or rejecting a project rarely exist, since capital projects can rarely be isolated from other projects or alternatives. The simplest decision normally encountered is accept or reject or delay. A project having a positive NPV if undertaken today may have a still higher NPV if undertaken tomorrow.

Another kind of project interaction stems from *capital rationing*. If capital is strictly limited, then acceptance of project A may preclude acceptance of B. If capital is limited in only one period, the objective of the firm shifts from maximizing NPV to maximizing NPV *per dollar of capital*. Projects can be ranked by their profitability index, and top-ranked projects chosen until funds are exhausted. This procedure fails when capital is rationed in more than one period or when there are other constraints on project choice. The only general solution is linear or integer programming.

"Hard" capital rationing always reflects a market imperfection—a barrier between the firm and capital markets. If that barrier also implies that the firm's shareholders lack free access to a well-functioning capital market, the very foundations of net present value crumble. Fortunately, hard rationing is rare for corporations in the United States and Canada. Many firms do use "soft" capital rationing, however. That is, they set up self-imposed limits as a means of financial planning and control.

This chapter is concerned with the mechanics of applying the net present value rule in practical situations. All our analysis boils down to two simple themes. First, be careful about the definition of alternative projects. Make sure you are comparing like with like. Second, make sure that your calculations include all incremental cash flows.

FURTHER READING

Canadian income tax law is consolidated in:

H.H. Stikeman, *Income Tax Act: Annotated*, 14th ed., Richard DeBoo, Don Mills, 1984.

A more readable but less comprehensive source of tax information is:

Canadian Master Tax Guide, 38th ed., CCH Canadian Limited, Don Mills, 1983.

The tax act and extensive editorial comment is provided in seven volumes, updated on a weekly subscription basis:

Canadian Tax Reporter, CCH Canadian Limited, Don Mills, 1982.

There are several good general texts on capital budgeting that cover project interactions. Two examples are:

E.L. Grant, W.G. Ireson, and R.S. Leavenworth, *Principles of Engineering Economy*, 6th ed., Ronald Press, New York, 1976.

H. Bierman and S. Smidt, *The Capital Budgeting Decision*, 5th ed., The Macmillan Company, New York, 1980.

Terborgh treats decisions involving machine replacement in detail.

G.W. Terborgh, *Business Investment Management*, Machinery and Allied Products Institute and Council for Technological Advancement, 1967.

The classic treatment of linear programming applied to capital budgeting is:

H.M. Weingartner, *Mathematical Programming and the Analysis of Capital Budgeting Problems*, Prentice-Hall, Inc., Englewood Cliffs, N.J., 1963.

There is a long scholarly controversy on whether capital constraints invalidate the NPV rule. Weingartner has reviewed this literature.

H.M. Weingartner, "Capital Rationing: *n* Authors in Search of a Plot," *Journal of Finance*, **32**:1403–1432 (December, 1977).

Reinhardt provides an interesting case study of a capital investment decision in:

U.E. Reinhardt, "Break-Even Analysis for Lockheed's TriStar: An Application of Financial Theory," *Journal of Finance*, **32**:821–838 (September 1973).

APPENDIX 6-1   CORPORATE INCOME TAXES IN CANADA

In this appendix we will discuss some more complicated issues in Canadian tax law, particularly as they relate to capital budgeting.

Corporate Tax Rates in Canada

The basic Canadian corporate tax rate is 46%, although this is reduced to 25% for small businesses by the *small business deduction*. A small business is basically a Canadian-controlled private corporation with cumulative before-tax earnings of less than $1 million. The reduced tax rate is available on the first $200,000 of taxable income each year.

The federal government allows a reduced tax rate for manufacturing and processing profits in the amount of 20% for small business and 40% for other business. From time to time, the federal government also imposes a surtax or allows an abatement to help implement short term fiscal policy. For 1983, the corporate surtax was 2.5% of federal tax paid for ordinary business.

The federal government reduces the corporate tax rate by 10% to allow for provincial corporate taxes. The provinces often use the federal definition of taxable income and charge provincial tax at their own rates. Most provinces charge a lower tax rate for small business. In 1983 the small business provincial rates varied from 0% to 12%, and the ordinary business rates from 5.5% to 16%.[28]

Some overall tax rates are illustrated in Table 6-5.

Loss Carry-Forward and Carry-Back

Recall that capital losses can only occur on the sale of non-depreciable assets, like land or securities. However, capital gains can occur on the sale of depreciable and non-depreciable assets. Taxpayers are allowed to:

1. deduct capital losses from capital gains in the same year;

2. **carry-back** capital losses for up to three years to be applied against previous capital gains; and

3. **carry-forward** capital losses against any future capital gains.

Ordinary losses (that is, non-capital losses) may be carried back up to three years or carried forward up to seven years, to be applied against taxable income.

---

[28]Ontario had a three-year tax holiday for eligible small businesses for taxation years ending between May 14, 1982 and May 14, 1985. Previously, Ontario had a 10% small-business tax rate.

Table 6-5   Calculation of corporate tax rates.

	Alberta		Ontario	
	Ordinary	Small Business	Ordinary	Small Business
Federal tax (manufacturing and processing)	40%	20%	40%	20%
Less: provincial tax credit	10%	10%	10%	10%
	30%	10%	30%	10%
Plus surtax (2.5% of federal tax for 1983)	0.75%	N/A	0.75%	N/A
	30.75%	10%	30.75%	10%
Plus provincial tax (1983)	11%	5%	14%	0%
Net income tax rate	41.75%	15%	44.75%	10%

Clearly you should carry losses back before you carry them forward, because you can benefit from their tax shields as they occur. However, the government only rebates excess taxes paid under a carry-back. It does not pay any interest on these taxes.

*The "Half-Year Rule" for Capital Cost Allowance and the Timing of Tax Payments

An amendment to the Canadian income tax laws (starting in 1982) has the effect of delaying the capital cost allowance tax shields on half of the asset's value by one year. This has been dubbed the "half-year rule." The half-year rule requires that, in the first year, only half of purchases net of sales are to be added to the asset class balance, and the other half is added for the next tax year. (If sales exceed purchases, the half year rule does not apply.) If we are going to incorporate the half-year rule, we should also be more precise in our analysis of the relative timing of the asset purchase and the receipt of CCA tax shields than we were in Section 6-2.

To get more precise PV formulas, let's use the same notation as in Section 6-2:

$$
\begin{aligned}
C &= \text{capital cost of asset (year 0)} \\
S &= \text{salvage value of asset (year n)} \\
d &= \text{CCA depreciation rate} \\
T_c &= \text{corporate tax rate} \\
r &= \text{discount rate} \\
UCC_t &= \text{undepreciated capital cost after deducting the CCA tax shield for year } t
\end{aligned}
$$

The incremental effect of purchasing the asset is to start depreciating half of it in year 0 and the other half in year 1, as follows:

Year	0	1	2	...	t	...
CCA on first half of asset	$Cd/2$	$Cd(1-d)/2$	$Cd(1-d)^2/2$	...	$Cd(1-d)^t/2$	...
CCA on second half of asset	0	$Cd/2$	$Cd(1-d)/2$	...	$Cd(1-d)^{t-1}/2$	...

We can multiply by T_c and discount these tax shields to get:[29]

PV of perpetual CCA tax shields

$$= \frac{1}{2}\left(CdT_c + \frac{CdT_c(1-d)}{1+r} + \frac{CdT_c(1-d)^2}{(1+r)^2} + \cdots\right)$$

$$+ \frac{1}{2}\left(\frac{CdT_c}{1+r} + \frac{CdT_c(1-d)}{(1+r)^2} + \cdots\right)$$

$$= \frac{1}{2}\frac{CdT_c}{r+d}(1+r) + \frac{1}{2}\frac{CdT_c}{r+d}$$

$$= \frac{CdT_c}{r+d}(1+r/2)$$

Compared to the formula in Section 6-2, this formula gives a PV of a perpetual CCA tax shield that is larger by a half-year of interest.[30] Clearly this is not a significant difference in many situations, but it could be important in evaluating projects (like leases) where competitive market forces drive the NPV of the project close to zero.

Now suppose the asset is in a class that has many other assets and a substantial UCC. We'll also assume that in the salvage year n other assets are added to the same class (for example, a replacement asset) with a cost greater than S. Since the half year rule works on acquisitions *net* of dispositions, the *incremental* effect of selling the asset for S in year n is to deduct $S/2$ from the UCC of the class in each of years n and $n+1$. Thus we have:

PV of incremental CCA tax shields

$$= \frac{CdT_c}{r+d}\left(1+\frac{r}{2}\right) - \frac{1}{(1+r)^n}\frac{SdT_c}{r+d}\left(1+\frac{r}{2}\right)$$

On the other hand, suppose the asset is always in a class by itself. Then

$$\text{UCC}_t = \frac{C}{2}\left((1-d)^{t+1} + (1-d)^t\right) = C(1-d)^t\left(1-\frac{d}{2}\right)$$

---

[29]To see this, you could grind out the sums of geometric series, as in Section 3-2, or simply note that the formula in Section 6-2 gives the PV of the tax shields (if they start in year 1) as $CdT_c/(r+d)$. If the tax shields start in year 0, there is one less year of discounting, so they would have a PV of $(1+r)CdT_c/(r+d)$.

[30]Some textbooks suggest that the PV of a perpetual CCA tax shield under the half-year rule is $\frac{CdT_c}{r+d}\frac{1+r/2}{1+r}$ because the tax shields on half of the asset start in year 1 and the tax shields on the other half don't start until year 2. This is analogous to taking tax shields in year 2 for cash expenses that occur in year 1, although these texts generally do not split the timing of expenses and their tax shields in this way. Even though there can be complicated schemes of tax-instalment payments under various circumstances, taking expenses and their tax shields in the same year gives the most accurate PV calculations. Thus, it is best to treat the CCA tax shields as starting in year 0, as we do here. See G.A. Sick, "The Effective Timing of Tax Flows," manuscript, University of Alberta, 1984.

A little algebra shows that the recapture and terminal loss cases can be combined to give:

PV of CCA tax shield and tax effect of recaptured depreciation or terminal loss

$$= \frac{CdT_c}{r + d}\left(1 + \frac{r}{2}\right) - \frac{1}{(1 + r)^n}\,UCC_n\,\frac{dT_c}{r + d} + \frac{T_c}{(1 + r)^n}\,(UCC_n - S)$$

*Project Interactions Arising From Recaptured Depreciation

Since Canadian tax law often groups the assets of many projects together in a single class, interactions can arise amongst projects regarding recaptured depreciation and terminal losses. For example, if you are about to face recaptured depreciation from the disposal of assets of an existing project, any project requiring new assets in the same class will effectively get a "fast write-off" of the new assets. On the other hand, if the existing project is about to get a terminal loss benefit, acquiring other assets in the same class will generate an onerous tax liability that should be avoided. Let's look at two examples of this. In both cases, we are evaluating a project that entails:

C = \$100,000 of assets
d = 0.1 (Class 6)
T_c = 0.4
r = 0.15
S = \$20,000, salvage in year 6

We'll ignore the half-year rule, and use the simple formulas of Section 6-2.

Example 1 Suppose your firm is planning to liquidate some assets in year 0, generating recaptured depreciation of \$150,000. By accepting the new project and putting \$100,000 back into Class 6 before the end of the tax year, your firm can avoid immediate recapture of \$100,000. In effect, all of the incremental CCA tax shield will be realized in year 0, as though there were a one-year tax write-off for the project. However, Class 6 will have a UCC of \$0 for years 1 to 5 and the salvage in year 6 will generate a recapture. The overall effect is:

PV of incremental CCA tax shield and recapture

$= T_c \times$ recapture avoided in year 0

$\quad - $ PV of $T_c \times$ recapture in year 6

$= 0.4 \times 100,000 - \dfrac{0.4}{(1.15)^6} \times 20,000$

$= \$36,541$

Example 2 Suppose your firm is planning to liquidate all of its Class 6 assets in year 0, generating a terminal loss of \$130,000. If you add the new assets to Class 6 before the tax year-end, you cannot close out the asset class and hence you will be ineligible for the terminal loss. Instead, the UCC of Class 6 will rise to \$230,000 (the original \$130,000 plus the new \$100,000). Salvage of the asset in year 6 will generate a terminal loss based on a UCC of $230,000\,(1 - 0.1)^6 = \$122,231$. In effect, the terminal loss on the old assets is deferred from year 0 to year 6, so we have

PV of deferred terminal loss and incremental CCA tax shields

$$= -0.4 \times 130,000 + \frac{230,000 \times 0.1 \times 0.4}{0.15 + 0.1} - \frac{1}{(1.15)^6} \frac{122,231 \times 0.1 \times 0.4}{0.15 + 0.1}$$

$$+ \frac{1}{(1.15)^6} \times 0.4 \times (122,231 - 20,000) = -\$5,976$$

Note that this is actually negative. You should try to avoid this situation by incorporating the project as a separate firm for tax purposes, by delaying the purchase of the asset until year 1, or by leasing the asset.

APPENDIX 6-2 SOME EMBELLISHMENTS TO THE CAPITAL RATIONING MODEL

In Section 6-5 we showed that when capital is rationed you can set up the investment decision as a linear programming problem. In this appendix we describe some embellishments to these models, and we show how you can use them to cope with other resource constraints and project interactions.

Cash Carry-Forward

A plant manager who is forced to return the unspent part of an annual capital allocation may be goaded into a substantial year-end investment in pink carpeting for the foundry floor or other equally silly assets. (How can you argue for a high budget next year if there's money left over this year?) Headquarters can alleviate this problem by permitting the manager to carry forward any unspent balance. (Then the manager could at least wait until January and get a better selection of carpet colours.) Let us take the sample problem that we described in Section 6-5. To incorporate the possibility of cash carry-forward, we simply need to add another term to our spending constraint. Let s denote funds transferred from year 0 to year 1 and let them earn interest at the rate of r. Then we can rewrite our constraint for year zero as

$$10x_A + 5x_B + 5x_C + 0x_D + s = 10$$

Similarly, the constraint for year 1 becomes

$$-30x_A - 5x_B - 5x_C + 40x_D \leq 10 + (1 + r)s$$

Since carrying forward a negative amount is equivalent to borrowing, we will probably wish to add the constraint $s \geq 0$.

Mutually Exclusive Projects

Suppose now that projects B and C are mutually exclusive. We can take care of this in an *integer* program by specifying that our *total* investment in the two projects cannot be greater than one.

$$x_B + x_C \leq 1, \; x_B, \; x_C = 0 \; or \; 1$$

In other words, if x_B is 1, x_C must be 0; if x_C is 1, x_B must be 0.

Contingent Projects

Suppose next that project D is an attachment to project A, and we cannot accept D *unless* we also accept A. In this case we need to add

$$x_D - x_A \leq 0, \; x_D, \; x_A = 0 \; or \; 1$$

In other words, if x_A is 1, x_D can be 0 or 1; but if x_A is 0, x_D must likewise be 0.

Constraints on Nonfinancial Resources

Money may not be the only scarce resource. Each of our projects may require services from a 12-person technical design department. If project A would employ three designers, project B two, and so on, we would need to add a constraint like

$$3x_A + 2x_B + 8x_C + 3x_D \leq 12$$

Constraints on Nonfinancial Output

Sometimes it is appropriate to place constraints on the total increase in physical capacity. Suppose that projects A and C produce four and three units, respectively, of the same product. If the company is unable to sell more than five units, it is necessary to add

$$4x_A + 3x_C \leq 5$$

We could go on—but you get the idea.

QUIZ

1. Which of the following should be treated as incremental cash flows when deciding whether to invest in a new manufacturing plant? The site is already owned by the company, but existing buildings would need to be demolished.
   (a) The market value of the site and existing buildings
   (b) Demolition costs and site clearance
   (c) The cost of a new access road put in last year
   (d) Lost earnings on other products due to executive time spent on the new facility
   (e) A proportion of the cost of leasing the president's jet airplane
   (f) Future depreciation of the new plant
   (g) The reduction in the corporation's tax bill resulting from the investment tax credit
   (h) The initial investment in inventories of raw materials
   (i) Money already spent on engineering design of the new plant

2. M. Loup Garou will be paid 100,000 French francs one year hence. This is a nominal flow, which he discounts at a 15% nominal discount rate:

$$PV = \frac{100,000}{1.15} = 86,957 \; francs$$

The inflation rate is 10%.
   Calculate the present value of M. Garou's payment using the equivalent *real* cash flow and *real* discount rate. (You should get exactly the same answer as he did.)

3. Machines A and B are mutually exclusive and are expected to produce the following cash flows:

| Machine | Cash Flows (thousands of dollars) | | | |
	C_0	C_1	C_2	C_3
A	−100	+110	+121	—
B	−120	+110	+121	+133

The opportunity cost of capital is 10%.
(a) Calculate the NPV of each machine.
(b) Use present value tables to calculate the equivalent annual cash flow from each machine.
(c) Calculate the NPV of a perpetual chain of each machine.
(d) Which machine should you buy?

4. Machine C was purchased five years ago for $200,000 and produces an annual cash flow of $80,000. It has no salvage value but is expected to last another five years. The company can replace machine C with machine B (see question 3, above) *either* now *or* at the end of five years. Which should it do?

5. Suppose you have the following investment opportunities, but only $100,000 available for investment. Which projects should you take?

Project	NPV	Investment
1	5,000	10,000
2	5,000	5,000
3	10,000	90,000
4	15,000	60,000
5	15,000	75,000
6	3,000	15,000

6. What is the difference between "hard" and "soft" capital rationing? Does soft rationing mean the manager should stop trying to maximize NPV? How about hard rationing?

7. You are considering whether to undertake a project that will generate revenues of $50,000 a year and expenses of $20,000 a year for eight years. To undertake the project you must invest $150,000 in machinery in Class 8 (20%). The corporate tax rate is 40% and your discount rate for the project is 12%. Calculate the NPV of the project under each of the following scenarios:
(a) You always have other assets and a positive UCC in Class 8, and you can salvage the machinery in nine years for:
   (i) $20,000
   (ii) $200,000
(b) The machine will always be in its own asset class and you can salvage the machinery in nine years for:
   (i) $20,000
   (ii) $30,000
   (iii) $200,000
(c) The machinery can be lumped in with other Class 8 assets, on which you are about to immediately realize recaptured depreciation of $100,000, and you can salvage the new machinery in nine years for $20,000. You do not plan any other purchases or sales of Class 8 assets for the next nine years.

8. You are planning to purchase a low-rise apartment building in Class 32 (10%) for $250,000 (net of the cost of land). Under Canadian tax law, this building must be in its own asset class, so you may have recaptured depreciation when you sell it. Indeed, you expect to sell the building in six years for $200,000, even though the UCC, after five years of CCA, would then be only $147,623. A friend has pointed out that the 10% CCA rate for Class 32 is only a *maximum* CCA rate, and you may take CCA at a lower rate if you wish. He recommends that you avoid recapture by taking CCA at a reduced rate so that the UCC in six years is exactly $200,000. What do you think?

QUESTIONS AND PROBLEMS

1. When appraising mutually exclusive projects, many companies calculate the value of an infinite chain of each item of equipment. In what circumstances do you think this procedure is likely to produce sensible decisions?

2. Calculate the NPV of some personal investment decision, such as buying a washing machine instead of using the laundromat, insulating the attic, or replacing the car. (It is probably wise to ignore the extra convenience of the new asset.)

3. Discuss the following statement: "We don't want individual plant managers to get involved in the firm's tax position. So instead of telling them to discount after-tax cash flows at 10%, we just tell them to take the pretax cash flows and discount at 20%."

4. Discuss the following statement: "We like to do all our capital budgeting calculations in real terms. It saves making any forecasts of the inflation rate."

5. A project requires use of spare computer capacity. If the project is not terminated, the company will need to buy an additional disk at the end of year 2. If it is terminated, the disk will not be filled until the end of year 4. If extra disks cost $10,000 and become filled in five years, and if the opportunity cost of capital is 10%, what is the present value of the cost of this extra usage if the project is terminated at the end of year 2? What if the project continues indefinitely?

6. Mrs. T. Potts, the treasurer of Ideal China, has a problem. The company has just ordered a new kiln for $400,000. Of this sum, $50,000 is described by the supplier as "installation cost." Mrs. Potts does not know whether Revenue Canada will permit the company to treat this cost as a current expense or as a capital investment. In the latter case, the company could claim a 7% investment tax credit on the $50,000 and put it in Class 8 (20%). If the tax rate is 46% and the opportunity cost of capital is 5%, what is the present value of the tax shield in either case?

7. You own 500 hectares of timberland, with young timber worth $40,000 if logged now. This represents 1,000 cords of wood worth $40 per cord net of costs of cutting and hauling. A paper company has offered to purchase your tract for $140,000. Should you accept the offer? You have the following information:

(a)

Years	Yearly Growth Rate of Cords Per Hectare
1–4	16%
5–8	11
9–13	4
14 and subsequent years	1

(b) You expect price per cord to increase at 4% per year indefinitely.

(*c*) The cost of capital is 9%. Ignore taxes.

(*d*) The market value of your land would be $100 per hectare if you cut and removed the timber this year. The value of cut-over land is also expected to grow at 4% per year indefinitely.

8. The Borstal Company has to choose between two machines that do the same job but have different lives. The two machines have the following costs:

Year	Machine A	Machine B
0	$40,000	$50,000
1	10,000	8,000
2	10,000	8,000
3	10,000 + replace	8,000
4		8,000 + replace

If the discount rate is 12%, which machine should Borstal buy?

9. Borghia Pharmaceuticals has $1 million allocated for capital expenditures. Which of the following projects should the company accept to stay within the $1 million budget? How much does the budget limit cost the company in terms of its market value? The opportunity cost of capital for each project is 11%.

Project	Investment (thousands of dollars)	NPV (thousands of dollars)	IRR, %
1	300	66	17.2
2	200	−4	10.7
3	250	43	16.6
4	100	14	12.1
5	100	7	11.8
6	350	63	18.0
7	400	48	13.5

10. The *Financial Analysts Journal* currently offers the following subscription options: one year, $36; two years, $63; three years, $81. These rates are expected to increase at the general rate of inflation. What is your optimal strategy, assuming you intend to be a permanent subscriber? Make other assumptions as appropriate.

11. The president's executive jet is not fully utilized. You judge that its use by other officers would increase direct operating costs by only $20,000 a year and would save $100,000 a year in airline bills. On the other hand, you believe that with the increased use the company will need to replace the jet at the end of three years rather than four. A new jet costs $1.1 million and (at current low rate of use) has a life of six years. Assume that the company does not pay taxes and that the opportunity cost of capital is 12%. Should you try to persuade the president to allow other officers to use the plane?

12. A project requires an initial investment of $100,000 and is expected to produce a cash inflow before tax of $26,000 per year for five years. Company A has substantial accumulated tax losses and is unlikely to pay taxes in the foreseeable future. Company B pays corporate taxes at a rate of 46% and can depreciate the investment for tax purposes in Class 8 (20%), which has many other assets and a substantial UCC. The asset will have no salvage value after five years.

Suppose the opportunity cost of capital is 8%. Is the project more attractive for the non-tax-paying company A, or for the tax-paying company B? Don't forget that company B is entitled to a 7% investment tax credit.

13. A widget manufacturer currently produces 200,000 units a year. It buys widget lids from an outside supplier at a price of $2 a lid. The plant manager believes that it would be cheaper to make these lids rather than buy them. Direct production costs are estimated to be only $1.50 a lid. The necessary machinery would cost $150,000. This investment would qualify for the 10% investment credit and would be placed in Class 10 (30%). The plant manager estimates that the operation would require additional working capital of $30,000 but argues that this sum can be ignored since it is recoverable at the end of the ten years. If the company pays tax at a rate of 46%, and the opportunity cost of capital is 15%, would you support the plant manager's proposal? State clearly any additional assumptions that you need to make.

Table 6-6   Cash flows and present value of Reliable Electric's proposed investment (see problem 14) (annual cash flows in thousands of dollars).

	1985	1986	1987	1988	1989–1995
1. Capital expenditure	−10,400				
2. Research and development	−2,000				
3. Working capital	−4,000				
4. Revenue		8,000	16,000	40,000	40,000
5. Operating costs		−4,000	−8,000	−20,000	−20,000
6. Overhead		−800	−1,600	−4,000	−4,000
7. Depreciation		−1,040	−1,040	−1,040	−1,040
8. Interest		−2,160	−2,160	−2,160	−2,160
9. Income	−2,000	0	3,200	12,800	12,800
10. Tax	0	0	552	5,888	5,888
11. Net cash flow	−16,400	0	2,648	6,912	6,912

Net present value = +9,055

Notes:
1. *Capital expenditure*: $8 million for new machinery and $2.4 million for a warehouse extension. The full cost of the extension has been charged to this project, although only about half of the space is currently needed. Since the new machinery will be housed in an existing factory building, no charge has been made for land and building.
2. *Research and development*: $1.82 million spent in 1984. This figure was corrected for 10% inflation from the time of expenditure to date. Thus 1.82 × 1.1 = $2 million.
3. *Working capital*: Initial investment in inventories.
4. *Revenue*: These figures assume sales of 2,000 motors in 1986, 4,000 in 1987, and 10,000 per year from 1988 through 1995. The initial unit price of $4,000 is forecasted to remain constant in real terms.
5. *Operating costs*: These include all direct and indirect costs. Indirect costs (heat, light, power, fringe benefits, and so on) are assumed to be 200% of direct labour costs. Operating costs per unit are forecasted to remain constant in real terms at $2,000.
6. *Overhead*: Marketing and administrative costs, assumed equal to 10% of revenue.
7. *Depreciation*: Straight-line for ten years.
8. *Interest*: Charged on capital expenditure and working capital at Reliable's current borrowing rate of 15%.
9. *Income*: Revenue less the sum of research and development, operating costs, overhead, depreciation, and interest.
10. *Tax*: 46% of income. However, income is negative in 1985. This loss is carried forward and deducted from taxable income in 1987.
11. *Net cash flow*: Assumed equal to income less tax.
12. *Net present value*: NPV of net cash flow at a 15% discount rate.

14. Reliable Electric is considering a proposal to manufacture a new type of industrial electric motor, which would replace most of its existing product line. A research breakthrough has given Reliable a two-year lead on its competitors. The project proposal is summarized in Table 6-6.

    (a) Read the notes to the table carefully. Which entries make sense? Which do not? Why or why not?

    (b) What additional information would you need to construct a version of Table 6-6 that makes sense?

    (c) Construct such a table and recalculate NPV. Make additional assumptions as necessary.

15. Suppose the IM&C guano project will be incorporated as a separate firm for income tax purposes, and the capital assets are eligible for a 7% investment tax credit. How does this change its NPV?

16. Your firm is planning to produce and sell a new type of widget, called a "midget" (a male widget). You already have a building on some land, but would require $5 million of Class 8 (20%) machinery. You paid $200,000 for the land five years ago and the building is in a class by itself—Class 3 (5%)—with an undepreciated capital cost of $150,000. Right now the land could be sold for $300,000 and the building for $100,000, but in 11 years they could be sold for $500,000 and $100,000 respectively. You can sell $2 million worth of midgets per year for ten years, with annual production costs of $1 million. The machinery can be salvaged in 11 years for $1.2 million. You always have many assets in Class 8, with a large UCC. There is no investment tax credit for this project. Your corporate tax rate is 40% and your opportunity cost of capital is 10%. What is the NPV of the project?

RISK

INTRODUCTION TO RISK AND RETURN IN CAPITAL BUDGETING

We have managed six chapters without directly addressing the problem of risk, but now the jig is up. We can no longer be satisfied with vague statements like, "The opportunity cost of capital depends on the risk of the project." We need to know how risk is defined and what the links are between risk and the opportunity cost of capital.

These topics will occupy the next three chapters. This chapter provides a general overview of the subject. We begin by looking at past returns from investments with different degrees of risk. We then discuss how risk is defined and measured, and finally we introduce an important theory linking risk and expected return.

If you are to use these ideas with any confidence, you need a better understanding of their foundations. Therefore, in Chapter 8 we shall review theory and evidence more carefully. You also need to be able to apply ideas in practical situations, so in Chapter 9 we describe in some detail how you can estimate the discount rate for an investment project.

7-1 FIFTY-SIX YEARS OF CAPITAL MARKET HISTORY IN ONE EASY LESSON

Studies by Ibbotson and Sinquefield and by Boyle, Panjer and Sharp

Financial analysts are blessed with an enormous quantity of data on American security prices and returns and a somewhat less bountiful quantity of data on Canadian security prices and returns. For example, University of Chicago's Center for Research in Security Prices (CRSP) has developed a file of prices and dividends for each month since 1926 for every stock that has been listed on the New York Stock Exchange (NYSE). Other American files give data for stocks that are traded on the American Stock Exchange and the over-the-counter market: data for bonds, for options and so on. The data files on Canadian securities generally provide little data on individual stock returns prior to 1963. *The Financial Post* has a file of weekly prices and returns for 307 Toronto Stock Exchange (TSE) stocks starting in 1965, and Université Laval has a file of monthly returns on 984 TSE stocks starting in 1963. There are also other files of Canadian security returns.

But this is supposed to be one easy lesson. We will, therefore, concentrate on an American study by Ibbotson and Sinquefield and a Canadian study by Boyle, Panjer and Sharp.[1] These studies measure, among other things, the historical performance of four American and four Canadian portfolios of securities:

1. A portfolio of Treasury bills—United States or Canadian government securities maturing in less than one year.[2]
2. A portfolio of long-term government bonds.
3. A portfolio of long-term corporate bonds.[3]
4. A stock market index—the Standard and Poor's Composite Index (S&P) in the United States and the Toronto Stock Exchange Composite Index (TSE) in Canada. These are portfolios of 500 and 300 common stocks, respectively.[4]

These portfolios offer different degrees of risk. Treasury bills are about as safe an investment as you can get. There is no risk of default and their short maturity means that the prices of Treasury bills are relatively stable. In fact, an investor who wishes to lend money for, say, six months can achieve a perfectly certain payoff by purchasing a Treasury bill maturing in six months. However, the investor cannot lock in a *real* rate of return: there is still uncertainty about inflation.

By switching to long-term government bonds, the investor acquires an asset whose price fluctuates as interest rates vary. (Bond prices fall when interest rates rise, and rise when interest rates fall.) An investor who switches from government to corporate bonds accepts an additional *default* risk. An investor who shifts from corporate bonds to common stocks has a direct share in the risks of the enterprise.

All these studies have calculated a rate of return for each of their portfolios for each year from 1926 to 1981. This rate of return reflects both cash receipts—dividends or interest—and the capital gain or loss realized during the year. Averages of the annual rates of return for each portfolio are shown in Table 7-1.[5] You can see that these returns coincide with our intuitive risk ranking. The safest Canadian investment, Treasury bills, also gave the lowest rate of return—3.6% a year in *nominal* terms and 0.5% in *real* terms.

---

[1]The studies are: R.G. Ibbotson and R.A. Sinquefield, *Stocks, Bonds, Bills and Inflation: The Past and the Future*, Financial Analysts Research Foundation, Charlottesville, V.A., 1982; and P.P. Boyle, H.H. Panjer, and K.P. Sharp, "Report on Canadian Economic Statistics 1924-1983," Canadian Institute of Actuaries, Ottawa, July 1984.

[2]Canada did not have Treasury bills prior to 1933, and Boyle, Panjer and Sharp use only Treasury bill data that start at 1946. Thus, to get a series for the whole period, we used the Ibbotson-Sinquefield Treasury bill for 1926-1933 and annual averages of three-month Canadian Treasury bill monthly auction rates, compounded annually for 1934-1981. The monthly Canadian treasury bill data are from the Statistics Canada CANSIM series B14007. CANSIM is a registered mark of Statistics Canada.

[3]The two bond portfolios were revised in each year to maintain a constant maturity.

[4]Actually, data for the TSE 300 Index in Canada are only available for periods starting in 1956, so the TSE Industrial Index was used for 1935-1956, and an index by Urquhart and Buckley for 1925-1934. (See Urquhart, M.C. and Buckley, K.A.H., *Historical Statistics of Canada*, Macmillan Company, Toronto, 1965.) Naturally, this raises questions as to whether these three indices are really comparable in terms of risk. Of course, the structure of the S & P Index has changed over time, as well.

[5]These are arithmetic averages. They are obtained by simply adding up the annual returns and dividing by the number of years. The arithmetic average return is higher than the compound annual return over the period. For example, suppose the market doubles in value one year and halves the next. Since you are back where you started, the compound annual return is zero. But the arithmetic average return is $(+100 - 50)/2 = +25\%$. When estimating discount rates, you are interested in the arithmetic average return.

Table 7-1 Average rates of return on common stocks, corporate bonds, government bonds, and treasury bills, 1926–1981 (figures in percent per year). (Canadian corporate bond data are for 1949–1981.)

Portfolio	Average annual rate of return (nominal)		Average annual rate of return (real)		Average risk premium (versus return from Treasury bills)	
	Canada	United States	Canada	United States	Canada	United States
Common stocks	11.7	11.4	8.3	8.3	8.1	8.3
Corporate bonds	4.1	3.7	−0.3	0.9	0.5	0.6
Government bonds	3.7	3.1	0.8	0.3	0.1	0
Treasury bills	3.6	3.1	0.5	0.1	0	0

Source: American data are from R.G. Ibbotson and R.A. Sinquefield, *Stocks, Bonds, Bills and Inflation: The Past and the Future*, Financial Analysts Research Foundation, Charlottesville, VA, 1982, Exhibit 29, p.71. Canadian results are from calculations based on the data reported in P.P. Boyle, H.H. Panjer, and K.P. Sharp, "Report on Canadian Economic Statistics 1924-1983," Canadian Institute of Actuaries, Ottawa, 1984, Tables 1A and 3B, and the Treasury bill data discussed in footnote 2.

In other words, the average rate of inflation over this period was about 3% per year. Long-term Canadian government bonds ("long Canadas") gave a slightly higher nominal return than Treasury bills, and corporate bonds gave still higher returns.[6] Common stocks were in a class by themselves. Investors who accepted the extra risk of common stocks received on average a premium of 8.1% a year (8.3% in the United States) more than Treasury bills.

You may ask why we look back more than a half-century to measure average rates of return. The reason is that annual rates of return for common stocks fluctuate so much that averages taken over short periods are meaningless. Our only hope of gaining insights from historical rates of return is to look at a very long period.

Using Historical Evidence to Evaluate Today's Cost of Capital

Suppose there is a capital-investment project which you know—don't ask how—has the same risk as the Toronto Stock Exchange Composite Index. We will say that it has the same degree of risk as the *market portfolio*, although this is speaking loosely, because the index does not include all risky securities. What rate should you use to discount this project's forecasted cash flows?

Clearly you should use the currently expected rate of return on the market portfolio: that is the return you would be forgoing. Let us call it r_m. One way to estimate r_m is to assume that the future will be like the past and that today investors expect to receive the same "normal" rates of return revealed by the averages shown in Table 7-1. In this case you would set r_m at 11.7%, the average of past market returns.

---

[6]Note, however, that *real* returns on Canadian corporate bonds were lower than real Treasury bill returns, so that there was a negative risk premium for corporate bonds. This is not statistically significant, because there were only 33 years of observations of Canadian corporate bonds. At first you might think it odd that corporate bonds had a higher nominal return, but a lower real return than Treasury bills. This results from the fact that nominal returns are the result of *compounding* (rather than adding) real returns with inflation rates as in Section 6-2, and the fact that real returns and inflation rates are correlated with each other.

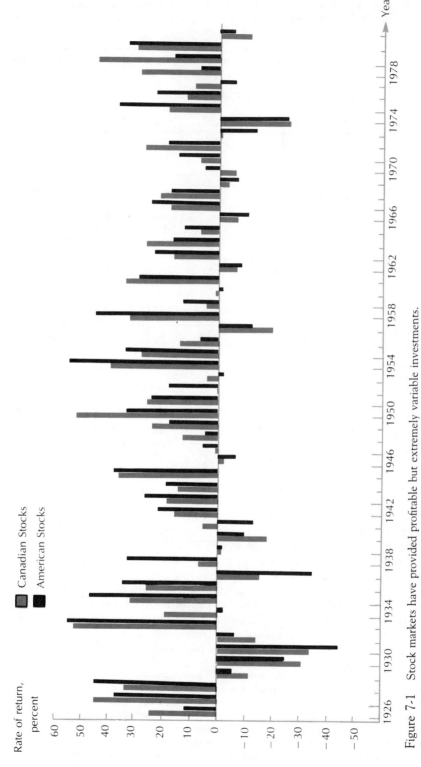

Figure 7-1 Stock markets have provided profitable but extremely variable investments.

Sources: R.G. Ibbotson and R.A. Sinquefield, *Stock, Bonds, Bills and Inflation: The Past and the Future,* Financial Analysts Research Foundation, Charlottesville, Virginia, 1982; P.P. Boyle, H.H. Panjer, and K.P. Sharp, "Report on Canadian Economic Statistics 1924–1983," Canadian Institute of Actuaries, Ottawa, July 1984.

Unfortunately, this is not the way to do it. The normal value of r_m is not likely to be stable over time. Remember that it is the sum of the risk-free interest rate r_f and a premium for risk. We know r_f varies over time. For example, as we write this chapter in September 1984, Treasury bills yield 12.1%, a long way above the 3.6% average return of our Treasury bill portfolio.

What if you were called upon to estimate r_m in 1984? Would you have said 11.7%? That would have made the risk premium negative! It is hard to believe that investors suddenly became less adverse to risk in 1984. A much more sensible procedure would have been to take the current interest rate on Treasury bills and add 8.1%, the average *risk premium* shown in Table 7-1. With a rate of 12.1% for Treasury bills, that would have given

$$r_m(1984) = r_f(1984) + \text{normal risk premium}$$
$$= 0.121 + 0.081 = 0.202 \text{ or } 20.2\%$$

The crucial assumption here is that there is a normal, stable risk premium on the market portfolio, so that the expected future risk premium can be measured by the average past risk premium. One could quarrel with this assumption, but at least it yields estimates of r_m that seem sensible.[7]

You now have a couple of benchmarks. You know the discount rate for safe projects and you know the rate for "average-risk" projects. But you don't know yet how to estimate discount rates for assets that do not fit these simple cases. In order to do that you have to learn (1) how to measure risk and (2) the relationship between risks borne and risk premiums demanded.

7-2   MEASURING PORTFOLIO RISK

Figure 7-1 shows the annual rates of return calculated by Ibbotson and Sinquefield and by Boyle, Panjer and Sharp for the American (S&P) and Canadian (TSE) stock market indices, respectively. The fluctuations in year-to-year returns are remarkably wide. The highest annual return on the TSE index was 51.6% in 1933 and 51.7% in 1950. On the other hand, there were losses exceeding 25% in three years, the worst being the −33.0% return in 1931.

Another way of presenting these data is by a histogram or frequency distribution. This is done in Figure 7-2, where the variability of year-to-year returns on the market portfolios shows up in the wide "spread" of outcomes.

Variance and Standard Deviation

The standard statistical measures of spread are **variance** and **standard deviation**. The variance of the market return is the expected squared deviation from the expected return. In other words,

Variance $(\tilde{r}_m)$ = the expected value of $(\tilde{r}_m - r_m)^2$

---

[7]It might be even better to assume a constant premium *per unit of risk* and to adjust for shifts in the risk of the market.

---

where $\tilde{r}_m$ is the actual return and r_m is the expected return.[8] The standard deviation is simply the square root of the variance:

$$\text{Standard deviation of } \tilde{r}_m = \sqrt{\text{variance } (\tilde{r}_m)}$$

Standard deviation is often denoted by σ and variance by σ^2.

Here is a very simple example showing how variance and standard deviation are calculated. Suppose you are offered the chance to play the following game. You start by investing \$100. Then two coins are flipped. For each head that comes up you get back your starting balance *plus* 20%, and for each tail that comes up you get back your starting balance *less* 10%. Clearly there are four equally likely outcomes:

- Head + head: you gain 40%
- Head + tail: you gain 10%
- Tail + head: you gain 10%
- Tail + tail: you lose 20%

There is a chance of one in four, or 0.25, that you will make 40%; a chance of two in four, or 0.5, that you will make 10%; and a chance of one in four, or 0.25, that you will lose 20%. The game's expected return is, therefore, a weighted average of the possible outcomes:

$$\text{Expected return} = (0.25 \times 40) + (0.5 \times 10) + (0.25 \times -20) = +10\%$$

Table 7-2 shows that the variance of percentage returns is 450. Standard deviation is the square root of 450, or 21. This figure is in the same units as the rate of return, so that we can say that the game's variability is 21%.

Table 7-2   The coin-tossing game: calculating variance and standard deviation.

(1) % Rate of Return $\tilde{r}$	(2) Deviation From Expected Return $\tilde{r} - r$	(3) Squared Deviation $(\tilde{r} - r)^2$	(4) Probability	(5) Probability x Squared Deviation
+40	+30	900	0.25	225
+10	0	0	0.5	0
−20	−30	900	0.25	225
		Variance = expected value of $(\tilde{r} - r)^2$ =		450
		Standard deviation = $\sqrt{\text{variance}}$ = $\sqrt{450}$ =		21

[8]Here is a technical point. When variance is estimated from a sample of observed returns, we add up the squared deviations and divide by $N - 1$, where N is the number of observations. We divide by $N - 1$, rather than N, to correct for what is called *the loss of a degree of freedom*. The formula is

$$\text{Variance } (\tilde{r}_m) = \frac{1}{N - 1} \sum_{t=1}^{N} (\tilde{r}_{mt} - r_m)^2$$

where

$\tilde{r}_{mt}$ = market return in period t

r_m = mean of the values of $\tilde{r}_{mt}$

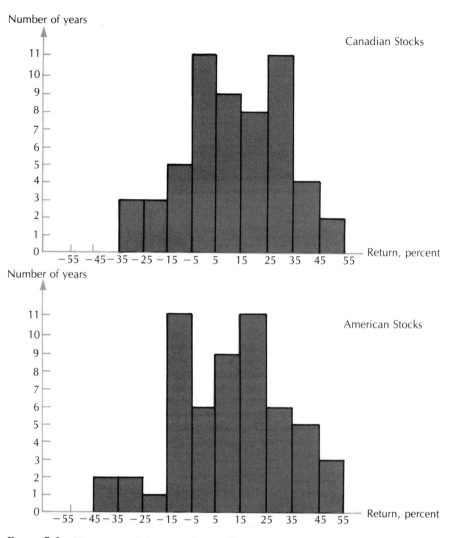

Figure 7-2   Histograms of the annual rates of return from stock markets in Canada and the United States, 1926-1981, showing the wide spreads of returns from investment in common stocks.
Sources: R.G. Ibbotson and R.A. Sinquefield, *Stocks, Bonds, Bills and Inflation: The Past and the Future*, Financial Analysts Research Foundation, Charlottesville, Virginia, 1982; P.P. Boyle, H.H. Panjer, and K.P. Sharp, "Report on Canadian Economic Statistics 1924–1983," Canadian Institute of Actuaries, Ottawa, July 1984.)

One way of defining uncertainty is to say that more things can happen than will happen. The risk of an asset can be completely expressed, as we first did for the coin-tossing game, by writing all possible outcomes and the probability of each one. For real assets this is cumbersome and often impossible. Therefore we use variance or standard deviation to summarize the spread of possible outcomes.[9]

---

[9]Which of the two we use is solely a matter of convenience. Since standard deviation is in the same units as the rate of return, it is generally more convenient to use standard deviation. However, when we are talking about the *proportion* of risk that is due to some factor, it is usually less confusing to work in terms of the variance.

These measures are natural indexes of risk.[10] If the outcome of the coin-tossing game had been certain, the standard deviation would have been zero. The actual standard deviation is positive because we *don't* know what will happen.

Or think of a second game, the same as the first except that each head means a 35% gain and each tail means a 25% loss. Again, there are four equally likely outcomes:

- Head + head: you gain 70%
- Head + tail: you gain 10%
- Tail + head: you gain 10%
- Tail + tail: you lose 50%

For this game the expected return is 10%, the same as the first game's. But its standard deviation is double that of the first game, 42 versus 21%. By this measure the second game is twice as risky as the first.

Measuring the Variability of Portfolios

In principle you could estimate the variability of any portfolio of stocks or bonds by the procedure we have just described. You would identify the possible outcomes, assign a probability to each outcome, and grind through the calculations. But where do the probabilities come from? You can't look them up in the newspaper; newspapers seem to go out of their way to avoid definite statements about prospects for securities. We once saw an article headlined "BOND PRICES POSSIBLY SET TO MOVE SHARPLY EITHER WAY." Stockbrokers are much the same. Yours may respond to your query about possible market outcomes with a statement like this:

> "The market currently appears to be undergoing a period of consolidation. For the intermediate term, we would take a constructive view provided economic recovery continues. The market could be up 20% a year from now, perhaps more if inflation moderates. On the other hand . . ."

The Delphic oracle gave advice, but no probabilities.

Most financial analysts start by observing past variability. Of course, there is no risk in hindsight, but it is reasonable to assume that portfolios with histories of high variability also have the least predictable future performance.

The annual standard deviations and variances observed for our four American and four Canadian portfolios were:[11]

Portfolio	Standard deviation σ		Variance σ^2	
	Canadian Market	American Market	Canadian Market	American Market
Treasury bills	3.7	3.1	13.8	9.6
Long-term government bonds	6.0	5.7	36.0	32.5
Corporate bonds	6.4	5.6	41.0	31.4
Common stocks	20.2	21.9	409.8	479.6

[10]As we explain in Chapter 8, standard deviation and variance are the correct measures of risk if the returns on stocks are normally distributed.

[11]Ibbotson and Sinquefield, *op. cit.*, exhibit 3, p. 15 and calculations based on Boyle, Panjer, and Sharp, *op. cit.*, Tables 1A, 3B and the Treasury-bill data discussed in footnote 2. Notice that when we are discussing the riskiness of *bonds* we must be careful to specify the time period. Long-term government bonds are risk-free to anyone who holds them to maturity.

You may find it interesting to compare the coin-tossing game and the stock market as alternative investments. If past is prologue, the Canadian stock market offers an expected annual return of 11.7%, with a standard deviation of 20.2%. The game offers 10% and 21%, respectively—slightly lower return, and about the same variability. Your gambling friends may have come up with a crude representation of the stock market. [12]

Of course there is no reason the market's variability should stay the same over a full 56-year period. For example, it is less now than in the boom-and-bust cycles of the last 1920s and early 1930s, but for the most part the degree of year-to-year variability has been reasonably stable at least since then. Here are standard deviations of the returns on Boyle, Panjer and Sharp's, and on Ibbotson and Sinquefield's, market portfolios, respectively:

Period	Market standard deviation σ_m	
	Canadian Market	American Market
1926 – 1935	31.1	33.5
1936 – 1945	17.1	23.9
1946 – 1955	18.4	18.1
1956 – 1965	17.0	16.5
1966 – 1975	16.6	19.7
1976 – 1981	19.4	16.0

How Diversification Reduces Risk

We can calculate our measures of variability just as well for individual securities as for portfolios of securities. Of course, 50-year averages are less interesting for specific companies than for the market portfolio—it is a rare company that faces the same business risks today as it did in 1926.

Table 7-3   Standard deviations for selected common stocks, 1978–1982 (figures in percent per year).

Stock	Standard Deviation	Stock	Standard Deviation
Bell Canada	15.1	B.C. Telephone	18.8
Interprovincial Pipeline	20.6	Pembina Pipeline	35.7
Alcan	32.6	Teck Corporation	54.6
Northern Telecom	32.5	Canadian Aviation Electronics	41.4
Imperial Oil	34.0	Dome Petroleum	52.8
Stelco	24.0	Interprovincial Pipe and Steel	35.6

Derived from monthly returns reported on the Université Laval stock data file.

[12]Past is probably not prologue. As we explained, recent risk-free rates of interest have been much higher than average rates over the entire 1926–1981 period. The expected return on the market portfolio should likewise be higher than its past average. This does not change the point made by our comparison.

Table 7-3 presents estimated standard deviations for 12 well-known common stocks for a recent five-year period.[13] The stocks in the left-hand column are "blue-chips," issued by big, established companies; those in the right-hand column are for smaller firms in the same industries.

Do the standard deviations given in Table 7-3 look "high" to you? They should. Remember that the market portfolio's standard deviation was 20.2 during the 1926–1981 period. Of our individual stocks, only Bell Canada (now Bell Canada Enterprises) and B.C. Telephone had lower standard deviations than the market portfolio. Most stocks are substantially more variable than the market portfolio and only a handful are less variable.

This raises an important question: "The market portfolio is made up of individual stocks, so why doesn't its variability reflect the average variability of its components?" The answer is that *diversification reduces variability*.

Wagner and Lau conducted an experiment which illustrates how even a little diversification can provide a substantial reduction in variability. They formed portfolios of differing size from a sample of stocks and then calculated the standard deviation of returns from each of these portfolios. You can see from Figure 7-3 that diversification can almost half the variability of returns. But you can get most of this benefit with relatively few stocks: the improvement is slight when the number of securities is increased beyond, say ten.

Diversification works because prices of different stocks do not move exactly together. Statisticians make the same point when they say that stock price changes are imperfectly correlated. Look, for example, at Figure 7-4. You can see that an investment in *either*

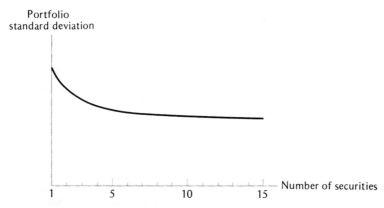

Figure 7-3   General results of Wagner and Lau's experiment. Diversification reduces risk (standard deviation) rapidly at first, then more slowly.

Source: W.H. Wagner and S.C. Lau, "The Effect of Diversification on Risk," *Financial Analysts Journal*, **26**:7–13 (November–December 1971).

---

[13]These estimates are derived from *monthly* rates of return. Five annual observations are insufficient for estimating variability. We converted the monthly variance into an annual variance by multiplying by 12. That is, the variance of the monthly return is about one-twelfth of the annual variance. The longer you hold a security or portfolio, the more risk you have to bear.

This conversion assumes that successive monthly returns are statistically independent. This is, in fact, a good assumption, as we will show in Chapter 13.

Because variance is approximately proportional to the length of time interval during which a security or portfolio return is measured, standard deviation is about proportional to the square root of the interval.

Return, percent

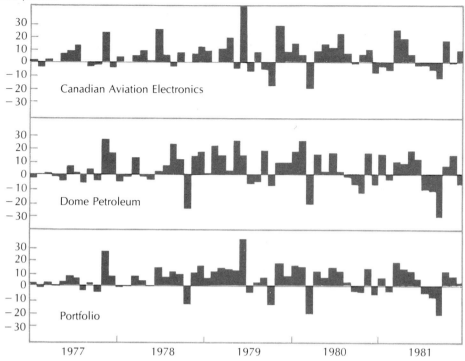

Figure 7-4 A portfolio with equal holdings in Canadian Aviation Electronics and Dome Petroleum would have been less variable than an investment in either stock alone.

Canadian Aviation Electronics (CAE) *or* Dome Petroleum would have been very variable. But there were many occasions on which a decline in the value of one stock was canceled out by a rise in the price of the other.[14] Therefore there was an opportunity to reduce your risk by diversification. Figure 7-4 shows that if you had divided your funds evenly between the two stocks, your portfolio would have been substantially less variable than an investment in either one alone.[15]

The risk that can potentially be eliminated by diversification is called **unique risk**.[16] Unique risk stems from the fact that many of the perils that surround an individual company are peculiar to that company and perhaps its immediate competitors. But there is also some risk that you can't avoid however much you diversify. This risk is generally known as **market risk**.[17] Market risk stems from the fact that there are other economy-wide perils that threaten all businesses. That is why stocks have a tendency to "move together." And that is why investors are exposed to "market uncertainties" no matter how many stocks they hold.

In Figure 7-5 we have redrawn Wagner and Lau's diagram but we have divided the risk into its two parts—unique risk and market risk. If you only have a single stock,

---

[14]The coefficient of correlation between the returns on the two stocks was low (0.36).

[15]For the period 1977–1981, the standard deviations of CAE and Dome were 41% and 44%, respectively. The standard deviation of a portfolio half invested in each was about 35%.

[16]Unique risk is often called *unsystematic risk, residual risk*, or *specific risk*.

[17]Market risk is often called *systematic risk*.

unique risk is very important, but once you have a portfolio of ten or more stocks, diversification has done the bulk of its work. For a reasonably well-diversified portfolio, only market risk matters. Therefore, the predominant source of uncertainty for a diversified investor is that the market will rise or plummet, carrying the investor's portfolio with it.

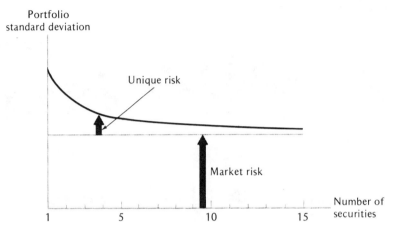

Figure 7-5   Diversification eliminates unique risk. But there is some risk that diversification *cannot* eliminate. This is called *market risk*.

7-3   HOW INDIVIDUAL SECURITIES AFFECT PORTFOLIO RISK

In the last section we presented some data on the variability of 12 individual securities. Teck Corporation had the highest standard deviation and Bell the lowest. If you had held Teck on its own, the spread of possible returns would have been almost four times greater than if you had held Bell on its own. But that is not a very interesting fact. Wise investors don't put all their eggs into just one basket: they reduce their risk by diversification. They are therefore interested in the effect each stock will have on the risk of their portfolio. This brings us to one of the principal themes of this chapter: **The risk of a well-diversified portfolio depends on the market risk of the securities included in the portfolio.** Tattoo that statement on your forehead if you can't remember it any other way. It is one of the most important ideas in this book.

Market Risk is Measured by Beta

If you want to know the contribution of an individual security to the risk of a well-diversified portfolio, it is no good thinking about how risky that security is if held in isolation—you need to measure its *market* risk, and that boils down to measuring how sensitive it is to market movements. This sensitivity of an investment's return to market movements is usually called its *beta* (β).

The steeply sloping line in Figure 7-6(a) shows how the outlook for stock A is affected by market movements. Each extra 1% rise in the market results in a further 2% rise in the price of stock A. Thus A has a beta of 2.0.

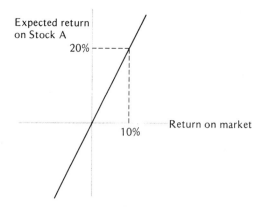

Figure 7-6(*a*) The expected return on stock A changes by 2% for each extra 1% return on the market. Its beta is therefore 2.0.

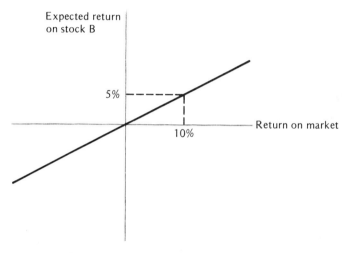

Figure 7-6(*b*) The expected return on stock B changes by 0.5% for each extra 1% return on the market. Its beta is therefore 0.5.

The gently sloping line in Figure 7-6(*b*) shows that the return on stock B is not so sensitive to the market. Each extra 1% rise in the market produces only an extra 0.5% rise in the price of B. Thus B has a beta of 0.5.[18]

A diversified portfolio of high beta stocks is more risky than a diversified portfolio of low beta stocks. For example, Figure 7-7 shows the performance of two mutual funds—Keystone S-1 Fund and Keystone S-4 Fund. Both funds were well-diversified and therefore had little unique risk. Yet the S-4 fund was about twice as variable as the S-1 fund. The reason is that the stocks in the S-4 fund were very sensitive to market changes: they had, on average, a beta of 1.6. The standard deviation of a well-diversified portfolio of stocks with a beta of 1.6 would be 1.6 times that of the market portfolio. The stocks in the S-1 fund were less affected by market movements: they had, on average, a beta of 0.9. The standard deviation of a well-diversified portfolio of stocks

---

[18]Beta is measured by the slope of the lines in Figure 7-6(*a*) and (*b*). For simplicity, we have drawn these lines so that they pass through the intercept; that is, both stocks are expected to give a zero return when the market gives a zero return. This is not generally true, as we will explain in Chapter 8.

with a beta of 0.9 is 0.9 times the standard deviation of the market portfolio.[19] Of course, on average, stocks have a beta of 1.0. A well-diversified portfolio of such stocks would therefore have the same standard deviation as the market portfolio.

We repeat the general point: *the risk of a well-diversified portfolio depends on the average beta of the securities included in the portfolio.* Thus a security's contribution to portfolio risk depends on the security's beta.

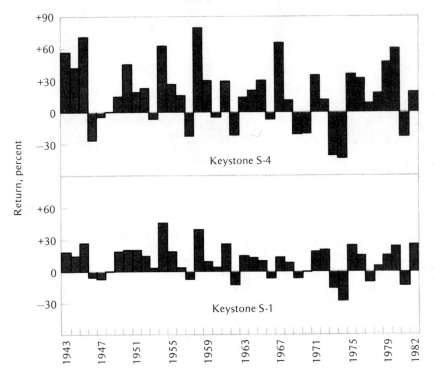

Figure 7-7 These two mutual funds are both well-diversified, but the S-4 fund is about twice as variable as S-1. This is because it is more sensitive to market movements.

The practical problems of estimating and using betas are taken up in Chapter 9. However, you may find it interesting to look at Table 7-4, which shows how past market movements have affected the 12 stocks we discussed earlier. Bell had the lowest beta; its stock price was about one third as sensitive as the average stock to market movements. Dome Petroleum was at the other extreme; its price was more than 1.7 times as sensitive as the average stock to market movements.

7-4 RELATIONSHIP BETWEEN RISK AND RETURN

At the beginning of this chapter, we looked at the returns on selected investments. The least risky investment was Treasury bills. Since the return on Treasury bills is fixed,

---

[19]This statement is exactly true if the "well-diversified" portfolio is *perfectly* correlated with the market—that is, if the correlation coefficient between the portfolio and the market returns is +1.0. The statement is only approximately for the Keystone Funds because their returns were not perfectly correlated with the market. The correlation coefficients were 0.96 and 0.89 for the S-1 and S-4 funds, respectively. We are indebted to Keystone Custodian Funds, Inc., for supplying the returns of these funds.

Table 7-4 Betas for selected common stocks: 1975 to 1982.

Stock	Beta β	Stock	Beta β
Bell Canada	0.32	B.C. Telephone	0.44
Interprovincial Pipeline	0.37	Pembina Pipeline	0.90
Alcan	1.04	Teck Corporation	1.69
Northern Telecom	0.64	Canadian Aviation Electronics	1.02
Imperial Oil	1.20	Dome Petroleum	1.29
Stelco	0.75	Interprovincial Pipe and Steel	0.97

Derived from monthly returns reported on the Université Laval stock data file and data on the TSE 300 Total Return Index reported in the Toronto Stock Exchange Fact Book, various annual issues.

it is unaffected by what happens to the market. Thus the beta of Treasury bills is zero. The *most* risky investment we considered was the market portfolio of common stocks. This has average market risk: its beta is 1.0.

Wise investors don't run risks just for fun. They are playing with real money. Therefore they require a higher return from the market portfolio than from Treasury bills. The difference between the return on the market and the interest rate is termed the *market risk premium*. Over the past 56 years the average market risk premium ($r_m - r_f$) has been 8.1% per year.

In Figure 7-8 we have plotted the risk and expected return from Treasury bills and the market portfolio. You can see that Treasury bills have a beta of zero and a risk premium of zero.[20] The market portfolio has a beta of 1.0 and an expected risk premium of $r_m - r_f$. This gives us two benchmarks for the expected risk premium. But what is the expected risk premium when beta is not zero or one?

In the mid-1960s three economists—Jack Treynor, William Sharpe, and John Lintner—produced an answer to this question.[21] Their answer is known as the *capital asset pricing model*. The model's message is both startling and simple. In a competitive market, the expected risk premium varies in direct proportion to beta. This means that in Figure 7-8, all investments must plot along the sloping line, known as the *security market line*. The expected risk premium on an investment with a beta of 0.5 is, therefore, *half* the expected risk premium on the market; and the expected risk premium on an investment with a beta of 2.0 is *twice* the expected risk premium on the market. We can write this relationship as:

Expected risk premium on stock = beta × expected risk premium on market

$$r - r_f = \beta(r_m - r_f)$$

We have given you a bald statement of the capital asset pricing model. We will now give you a glimpse of where that formula came from and how it can be used to estimate the cost of capital. Then in the next two chapters we will examine both topics in more detail.

---

[20]The return on Treasury bills is fixed regardless of how much the market rises or falls. Therefore, the bills have a beta of zero. Remember also that the risk premium is the difference between the investment's expected return and the risk-free rate. For Treasury bills, the difference is zero.

[21]See W.F. Sharpe, "Capital Asset Prices: A Theory of Market Equilibrium Under Conditions of Risk," *Journal of Finance*, **19**:425–442 (September 1964); J. Lintner, "The Valuation of Risk Assets and the Selection of Risky Investments in Stock Portfolios and Capital Budgets," *Review of Economics and Statistics*, **47**:13–37 (February 1965); Treynor's article has not been published.

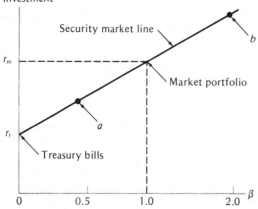

Expected return
on investment

Security market line

r_m

Market portfolio

a

r_f

Treasury bills

b

0   0.5   1.0   2.0 β

Figure 7-8   The capital asset pricing model states that in well-functioning capital markets the expected risk premium on each investment is proportional to its beta. This means that each investment should lie on the sloping security market line connecting Treasury bills and the market portfolio.

One investment strategy is to first decide what proportion of your money you are prepared to put at risk, and then invest this sum in the market portfolio. If you have any money left over, you can *lend* it at a fixed rate of interest; if you don't have enough money, you can *borrow* the balance at a fixed rate of interest.

For example, suppose that you invest 50% of your money in the market portfolio and lend the balance. Then the beta of your investment would be midway between the beta of the market ($\beta_m = 1.0$) and the beta of the loan ($\beta_f = 0.0$):

$$\text{Beta of investment} = \left(\begin{array}{c}\text{proportion} \\ \text{in market}\end{array} \times \begin{array}{c}\text{beta of} \\ \text{market}\end{array}\right) + \left(\begin{array}{c}\text{proportion} \\ \text{in loan}\end{array} \times \begin{array}{c}\text{beta of} \\ \text{loan}\end{array}\right)$$

$$\beta = (0.5 \times 1.0) + (0.5 \times 0.0)$$

$$= 0.5$$

The expected risk premium on your investment would also be midway between the expected risk premium on the market ($r_m - r_f$) and the expected risk premium on the loan (zero):

$$\text{Expected risk premium on investment} = \left(\begin{array}{c}\text{proportion} \\ \text{in} \\ \text{market}\end{array} \times \begin{array}{c}\text{expected} \\ \text{risk} \\ \text{premium} \\ \text{on market}\end{array}\right)$$

$$+ \left(\begin{array}{c}\text{proportion} \\ \text{in loan}\end{array} \times \begin{array}{c}\text{expected} \\ \text{risk} \\ \text{premium} \\ \text{on loan}\end{array}\right)$$

$$r - r_f = (0.5 \times (r_m - r_f)) + (0.5 \times 0.0)$$

$$= 0.5(r_m - r_f)$$

In Figure 7-8, we have marked this investment strategy with the letter *a*.

If you are more audacious, you might choose to invest all your own money and an equal amount of borrowed money in the market portfolio. In this case, the beta of your investment would be twice the beta of the market.[22]

$$\begin{matrix} \text{Beta of} \\ \text{investment} \end{matrix} = \left(\begin{matrix} \text{proportion} \\ \text{in market} \end{matrix} \times \begin{matrix} \text{beta of} \\ \text{market} \end{matrix} \right) + \left(\begin{matrix} \text{proportion} \\ \text{in loan} \end{matrix} \times \begin{matrix} \text{beta of} \\ \text{loan} \end{matrix} \right)$$

$$\beta = (2.0 \times 1.0) + (-1.0 \times 0.0)$$
$$= 2.0$$

The expected risk premium on your investment would also be twice the expected risk premium on the market:

$$\begin{matrix} \text{Expected risk premium} \\ \text{on investment} \end{matrix} = \left(\begin{matrix} \text{proportion} \\ \text{in} \\ \text{market} \end{matrix} \times \begin{matrix} \text{expected} \\ \text{risk} \\ \text{premium} \\ \text{on market} \end{matrix} \right)$$

$$+ \left(\begin{matrix} \text{proportion} \\ \text{in loan} \end{matrix} \times \begin{matrix} \text{expected} \\ \text{risk} \\ \text{premium} \\ \text{on loan} \end{matrix} \right)$$

$$r - r_f = (2.0 \times (r_m - r_f)) + (-1.0 \times 0.0)$$
$$= 2.0(r_m - r_f)$$

In Figure 7-8, we have marked this investment strategy with the letter *b*.

These two examples show that you can obtain *any* position along the security market line simply by investing part of your money in the market portfolio and borrowing or lending the balance. The portfolios along the line set a standard of your other investments: you will be willing to hold them only if they offer equally good prospects.[23] Thus the required risk premium for any investment is given by the security market line:

$$r - r_f = \beta(r_m - r_f)$$

Using the Capital Asset Pricing Model to Calculate Expected Returns

In Chapter 4, we explained that the price of a common stock is equal to the discounted value of the expected dividend and end-of-period price:

$$P_o = \frac{DIV_1 + P_1}{1 + r}$$

---

[22]Notice that the "proportion in loan" is negative. Borrowing money is equivalent to lending a negative amount.

[23]Suppose you could find a stock with a negative beta. Its expected risk premium would be negative; that is, it would offer a *lower* expected return than Treasury bills. There is a good reason for this. A stock with a negative beta would be very desirable. If you invested in both the stock and the market portfolio in the proper proportions, you could reduce risk dramatically.

We defined the discount rate r as the expected return offered by other equally risky stocks. The capital asset pricing model allows us to be more specific about this discount rate.

To figure out the returns investors are expecting from particular stocks, we need three numbers—r_f, $(r_m - r_f)$ and β. In September 1984 the interest rate on Treasury bills (r_f) was 12.1%. From past evidence, we would judge that $r_m - r_f$ is about 8.1%. Finally, in Table 7-4, we gave you estimates of the betas of 12 stocks. Table 7-5 puts these numbers together to give an estimate of the expected return from each stock. Let's take Imperial Oil as an example:

Table 7-5 These estimates of the returns *expected* by investors in the fall of 1984 were based on the capital asset pricing model. We assumed that the interest rate, $r_f = 12.1\%$, and the expected market risk premium, $r_m - r_f = 8.1\%$.

Stock	Beta β	Expected return $r_f + \beta (r_m - r_f)$
Bell Canada	0.32	14.7
Interprovincial Pipeline	0.37	15.1
Alcan	1.04	20.5
Northern Telecom	0.64	17.3
Imperial Oil	1.20	21.8
Stelco	0.75	18.2
B.C. Telephone	0.44	15.7
Pembina Pipeline	0.90	19.4
Teck Corporation	1.69	25.8
Canadian Aviation Electronics	1.02	20.4
Dome Petroleum	1.29	22.5
Interprovincial Pipe and Steel	0.97	20.0

$$\text{Expected rate of return} = r = r_f + \beta(r_m - r_f)$$
$$= 0.121 + 1.20\,(0.081)$$
$$= 0.218 \text{ or } 21.8\%$$

You can also use the capital asset pricing model to find the discount rate for a new capital investment. For example, suppose that you are analyzing a proposal by Northern Telecom to expand its capacity. At what rate should you discount the forecasted cash flows? According to Table 7-5, investors are looking for a return of 17.3% from businesses with the risk of Northern. So the cost of capital for a further investment in the same business is 17.3%.[24]

In practice, choosing a discount rate is seldom so easy. (After all, you can't expect to be paid a fat salary just for plugging numbers into a formula.) For example, you must learn how to adjust for the extra risk caused by company borrowing and how to estimate the discount rate for projects that do not have the same risk as the company's existing business. But these refinements can wait until Chapter 9.

---

[24]Remember that instead of investing in plant and machinery, the firm could return the money to the shareholder. The opportunity cost of investing is the return that shareholders could expect to earn by buying financial assets. This expected return depends on the market risk of the assets, not on their unique risk.

7-5 DIVERSIFICATION AND VALUE ADDITIVITY

We have seen that diversification reduces risk and, therefore, makes sense for individual investors. But does it also make sense for the firm? Is a diversified firm more attractive to investors than an undiversified one? If it is, we have an *extremely* disturbing result. If diversification is an appropriate corporate objective, the financial manager faces a problem of horrendous complexity, for each project would need to be analyzed as a potential addition to the firm's portfolio of projects. The value of the diversified package would be greater than the sum of the parts. Present values would no longer add.

Diversification is undoubtedly a good thing, but that does not mean that firms should practice it. If investors were *not* able to hold a large number of securities, then they might want firms to diversify for them. But investors *can* diversify.[25] In many ways they can do so more easily than firms. Individuals can invest in the steel industry this week and pull out the next week. A firm cannot do that. To be sure, the individual would have to pay brokerage fees on the purchase and sale of steel company shares, but think of the time and expense for a firm to acquire a steel company or to start up a new steel-making operation.

You can probably see where we are heading. If investors can diversify on their own account, they will not pay any *extra* for firms that diversify. And if they have a sufficiently wide choice of securities, they will not pay *less* because they are unable to invest separately in each factory. Therefore, in countries like the United States and Canada, which have large and competitive capital markets, diversification does not add to a firm's value or subtract from it. The total value is the sum of its parts.

This conclusion is important for corporate finance, because it justifies adding present values. The concept of value additivity is so important that we will give a formal definition of it. If the capital market establishes a value PV(A) for asset A and PV(B) for B, the market value of a firm that holds only these two assets is:

$$PV(AB) = PV(A) + PV(B)$$

A three-asset firm combining assets A, B, and C would be worth PV(ABC) = PV(A) + PV(B) + PV(C), and so on for any number of assets.

We have relied on intuitive arguments for value additivity. But the concept is a general one that can be proved formally by several different routes.[26] The concept of value additivity seems to be widely accepted, for thousands of managers add thousands of present values daily, usually without thinking about it.

Value Additivity and the Capital Asset Pricing Model

The capital asset pricing model states that investors do not demand extra expected return just to cover a firm's *unique* risk. The only risk investors care about is the risk that they *cannot* diversify away—that is, the *market* risk. But the firm can't diversify away market risk either. Therefore, diversification by the firm has no impact on the opportunity cost of capital.

Here's a simple example that illustrates how value additivity works in the context of betas and the capital asset pricing model. Suppose we have two projects, A and B.

---

[25]One of the simplest ways for an individual to diversify is to buy shares in a mutual fund that holds a diversified portfolio.

[26]You may wish to refer to the Appendix to Chapter 31, which discusses diversification and value additivity in the context of mergers.

Each offers a $100 cash flow at year 1, and zero cash flow in all subsequent years. The beta for project A is $\beta_A = 1.0$. The beta for project B is $\beta_B = 2.0$. We will assume a risk-free rate of $r_f = 10\%$ and a market risk premium of $r_m - r_f = 8\%$. The capital asset pricing model gives the following opportunity costs of capital for the two projects:

$$r = r_f + \beta(r_m - r_f)$$

$$r_A = 0.10 + 1.0(0.08) = 0.18$$

$$r_B = 0.10 + 2.0(0.8) = 0.26$$

The present values of the two projects are therefore:

$$PV_A = \frac{100}{1 + r_A} = \frac{100}{1.18} = 84.75$$

$$PV_B = \frac{100}{1 + r_B} = \frac{100}{1.26} = 79.36$$

We can also consider a project AB formed by combining A and B. Here is what we know so far:

Project	Cash Flow	Beta	Opportunity Cost of Capital	Present Value
A	100	1.0	0.18	84.75
B	100	2.0	0.26	79.37
AB	200	?	?	?

Value additivity tells us that PV(AB) = PV(A) + PV(B). That implies

$$PV(AB) = 84.75 + 79.37 = 164.12$$

We'll *assume* that's right,[27] and now show that the capital asset pricing model gives the same answer.

First, calculate the beta of project AB. It's a weighted average of β_A and β_B, with weights determined by the present values of the two projects.

$$\beta_{AB} = \beta_A \frac{PV(A)}{PV(AB)} + \beta_B \frac{PV(B)}{PV(AB)}$$

$$= 1.0 \frac{84.75}{164.12} + 2.0 \frac{79.37}{164.12}$$

$$= 1.4836$$

Calculate the opportunity cost of capital for AB.

---

[27]We're not using this example to prove value additivity; we're merely showing that the capital asset pricing model is consistent with value additivity.

$$r_{AB} = r_f + \beta_{AB}(r_m - r_f)$$
$$= 0.10 + 1.4836(0.08)$$
$$= 0.2187$$

Calculate the present value of AB:

$$PV_{AB} = \frac{200}{1 + r_{AB}} = \frac{200}{1.2187} = 164.12$$

Thus everything works out. If we had started with beta (1.4836) for a project AB, without knowing the present values of A and B as spearate assets, we would have valued AB correctly.

Of course, in practice, you aren't handed any of the betas. You have to estimate them. We will discuss how betas are estimated in Chapter 9.

7-6 SUMMARY

Our review of capital market history showed that the returns received by investors have varied according to the risks they have borne. At one extreme, very safe securities like Treasury bills have provided an average return over half a century of only 3.6% a year. The riskiest securities that we looked at were common stocks. They have provided an average return of 11.7%, a premium of more than 8% over the safe rate of interest.

This gives us two benchmarks for the opportunity cost of capital. If we are evaluating a safe project, we discount at the current risk-free rate of interest. If we are evaluating a project of average risk, we discount at the expected return on the average common stock, which historical evidence suggests is about 8% above the risk-free rate. That still leaves us with a lot of assets that don't fit these simple cases. Before we can deal with them, we need to learn how to measure risk.

Risk is best judged in a portfolio context. Most investors do not put all their eggs in one basket: they diversify. Thus the effective risk of any security cannot be judged by an examination of that security alone. Part of the uncertainty about the security's return is diversified away when the security is grouped with others in a portfolio.

Risk in investment means that future returns are unpredictable. This spread of possible outcomes is usually measured by standard deviation. The standard deviation of the *market portfolio*—generally represented by the Toronto Stock Exchange 300 Composite Index—is around 20% a year.

Most individual stocks have higher standard deviations than this, but much of their variability represents *unique* risk that can be eliminated through diversification. Diversification cannot eliminate *market* risk. Diversified portfolios are exposed to variations in the general level of the market.

A security's contribution to the risk of a well-diversified portfolio depends on how far the security is liable to be affected by a general market decline. This sensitivity to market movements is known as *beta* (β). Beta measures the amount that investors expect the stock price to change for each additional 1% change in the market. The average beta of all stocks is 1.0. A stock with a beta greater than one is unusually sensitive to market movements; a stock with a beta less than one is unusually insensitive to market movements. The standard deviation of a well-diversified portfolio is proportional to its beta. Thus a diversified portfolio invested in stocks with a beta of 2.0 will have twice the risk of a diversified portfolio invested in stocks with a beta of 1.0.

We looked at the relationship between risk and return in a well-functioning capital market, and presented a model of risk and return known as the *capital asset pricing model.*

Its message is simple: if investors can invest some fraction of their money in the market portfolio and borrow or lend the balance, they can obtain any point on the security market line, as shown in Figure 7-8. In that case, an investor should be willing to hold a security with a particular beta only if it offers an equally good return. Therefore, all securities should plot along this line. Another way to say the same thing is that the expected risk premium should increase in proportion to the security's beta:

Expected risk premium = beta × (expected market risk premium)

$$r - r_f = \beta(r_m - r_f)$$

One theme of this chapter is that diversification is a good thing *for the investor*. This does not imply that *firms* should diversify. Corporate diversification is redundant if investors can diversify on their own account, though it does not hurt if it does not noticeably reduce the range of choices open to investors. Since diversification does not affect the firm's value, present values add even when risk is explicitly considered. *Value additivity* lets us avoid fundamental rethinking of the net present value rule for capital budgeting.

FURTHER READING

There are several records of the performance of North American securities since 1926.

R.G. Ibbotson and R.A. Sinquefield, *Stocks, Bonds, Bills and Inflation: The Past and the Future*, Financial Analysts Research Foundation, Charlottesville, VA., 1982.

L. Fisher and J.H. Lorie, *A Half Century of Returns on Stocks and Bonds*, University of Chicago, Graduate School of Business, Chicago, 1977.

P.P. Boyle, H.H. Panjer, and K.P. Sharp, "Report on Canadian Economic Statistics 1924–1983," Canadian Institute of Actuaries, Ottawa (July 1984).

Merton discusses the problems encountered in measuring average returns from historical data:

R.C. Merton, "On Estimating the Expected Return on the Market: An Exploratory Investigation," *Journal of Financial Economics*, 8:323–361 (December 1980).

Most investment texts devote a chapter or two to the distinction between market and unique risk and to the effect of diversification on risk. See, for example:

J.H. Lorie and M. Hamilton, *The Stock Market: Theories and Evidence*, Richard D. Irwin, Inc., Homewood, Ill., 1973.

W.F. Sharpe, *Investments*, 2nd ed., Prentice-Hall, Inc., Englewood Cliffs, N.J., 1981.

An important analysis of the degree to which stocks move together is:

B.F. King, "Market and Industry Factors in Stock Price Behavior," *Journal of Business*, Security Prices: A Supplementary, 39:179–190 (January 1966).

There have been several studies of the way standard deviation is reduced by diversification. Our diagrams are based on:

W.H. Wagner and S.C. Lau, "The Effect of Diversification on Risk," *Financial Analysts Journal*, 27:48–53 (November–December 1971).

Formal proofs of the value additivity principle can be found in:

S.C. Myers, "Procedures for Capital Budgeting under Uncertainty," *Industrial Management Review*, 9:1–20 (Spring 1968).

L.D. Schall, "Asset Valuation, Firm Investment and Firm Diversification," *Journal of Business*, 45:11–28 (January 1972).

QUIZ

1. (a) What was the average annual return on Canadian common stocks from 1926 to 1981 (approximately)?
   (b) What was the average difference between this return and the return on Treasury bills?
   (c) What was the average return on Treasury bills in real terms?
   (d) What was the standard deviation of annual returns on the market index?
   (e) Was this market standard deviation more or less than that on most individual stocks?

2. Fill in the missing words:
   Risk is usually measured by the variance of returns or the _____, which is simply the square root of the variance. As long as the stock price changes are not perfectly _____, the risk of a diversified portfolio is _____ than the risk of the individual stocks.
   The risk that can be eliminated by diversification is known as _____ risk. But diversification cannot remove all risk; the risk that it cannot eliminate is known as _____ risk.
   The theory linking risk and expected return is known as the _____ model. It states that all stocks lie along the _____ line. A risk-free stock has a beta of ___ and, therefore, its expected return is equal to the _____: a stock that contributes an average amount of risk has a beta of _____ and, therefore, its expected return is equal to the expected return on the _____.

3. True or false?
   (a) Investors prefer diversified companies because they are less risky.
   (b) The capital asset pricing model implies that, if you could find an investment with a negative beta, its expected return would be less than the interest rate.
   (c) The expected return on an investment with a beta of 2.0 is twice as high as the expected return on the market.
   (d) If stocks were perfectly positively correlated, diversification would not reduce risk.
   (e) The contribution of a stock to the risk of a well-diversified portfolio depends on its market risk.
   (f) If a stock lies below the security market line, it is undervalued.
   (g) A well-diversified portfolio with a beta of 2.0 is twice as risky as the market portfolio.
   (h) An undiversified portfolio with a beta of 2.0 is less than twice as risky as the market portfolio.

4. What is the beta of each of the stocks shown in Table 7-6?

Table 7-6   See quiz, question 4.

Stock	Expected Stock Return if Market Return is -10%	Expected Stock Return if Market Return is $+10\%$
A	0	+20
B	−20	+20
C	−30	0
D	+15	+15
E	+10	−10

5. A portfolio contains equal investments in ten stocks. Five have a beta of 1.2; the remainder have a beta of 1.4. The portfolio beta is which of the following?
   (a) 1.3
   (b) Greater than 1.3 because the portfolio is not completely diversified
   (c) Less than 1.3 because diversification reduces beta

6. During the past five years, the stock of General American Fish (GAF) has moved as follows:

Year	1	2	3	4	5
Price change, %	+20	−10	−30	+5	+15

   (a) Calculate the variance and standard deviation on the returns of GAF.
   (b) Is this standard deviation higher or lower than that of the market?

7. Suppose that the Treasury bill rate is 4% and the expected return on the market is 10%. Using the information in Table 7-4:
   (a) Calculate the expected return from Stelco.
   (b) Find the highest expected return that is offered by one of these stocks.
   (c) Find the lowest expected return that is offered by one of these stocks.
   (d) Would Dome Petroleum offer a higher or lower expected return if the interest rate were 6% rather than 4%? Assume the expected market return stays at 10%.
   (e) Would Bell Canada offer a higher or lower expected return if the interest rate were 6%?

8. The capital asset pricing model states that a stock has the same market risk and expected return as:
   (a) A portfolio with proportion β invested in Treasury bills and $1 - \beta$ in the market.
   (b) A portfolio with β invested in the market and $1 - \beta$ in Treasury bills
   (c) A portfolio evenly divided between the market and Treasury bills
   Which is the correct answer?

9. Here is another question on the capital asset pricing model. Stock A has a beta of 0.5 and investors expect it to return 7%. Stock B has a beta of 1.5 and investors expect it to return 15%. What is the expected return on the market and the risk premium on the market?

QUESTIONS AND PROBLEMS

1. The Treasury bill rate is 4% and the expected return on the market portfolio is 12%. On the basis of the capital asset pricing model:
   (a) Draw a graph similar to Figure 7-8 showing how expected return varies with beta.
   (b) What is the risk premium on the market?
   (c) What is the required return on an investment with a β of 1.5?
   (d) If an investment with a β of 0.8 offers an expected return of 9.8%, does it have a positive NPV?
   (e) If the market expects a return of 11.2% from stock X, what is its beta?

2. Estimate the returns expected by investors *today* for the 12 stocks in Table 7-4. Plot the expected returns against beta as in Figure 7-8.

3. A company is deciding whether to make a stock issue to raise money for an investment project that has the same risk as the market and an expected return of 20%. If the risk-free rate is 10% and the expected return on the market is 15%, the company should go ahead
   (a) Unless the company's beta is greater than 2.0
   (b) Unless the company's beta is less than 2.0
   (c) Whatever the company's beta
   Which answer is correct? Say briefly why.

4. The stock of United Merchants has a beta of 1.0 and very high unique risk. If the expected return on the market is 20%, the expected return on United will be
   (a) 10% if the interest rate is 10%
   (b) 20%
   (c) More than 20% because of the high unique risk
   (d) Indeterminate unless you also know the interest rate
   Which is the right answer: Say *briefly* why.

5. The expected return on a stock is frequently written as $r = \alpha + \beta r_m$, where r_m is the expected return on the market. The capital asset pricing model says that in equilibrium
   (a) $\alpha = 0$
   (b) $\alpha = r_f$ (the risk-free rate of interest)
   (c) $\alpha = (1 - \beta)r_f$
   (d) $\alpha = (1 - r_f)\beta$
   Which is correct?

6. Estimate the expected return from the stock market in Canada over the next year. Subtract the current dividend yield to give you a rough estimate of the expected capital appreciation.

7. "The job of financial managers is to select a portfolio of projects offering the maximum return for the minimum risk. In principle, this means that they have to think about how the returns on each pair of projects are correlated." Explain why this is or is not true.

MORE ABOUT THE RELATIONSHIP BETWEEN RISK AND RETURN

In Chapter 7, we began to come to grips with the relationship between risk and expected return. Here is the story so far.

What makes an investment in the stock market risky is that there is a spread of possible outcomes. The usual measure of this spread is the standard deviation or variance.

The risk of any stock can be broken into two parts. There is the *unique* risk that is peculiar to the stock, and there is the *market* risk that stems from market-wide variations. Investors can eliminate unique risk by holding a well-diversified portfolio, but they cannot eliminate market risk. *All* the risk of a fully diversified portfolio is market risk.

A stock's contribution to the risk of a fully diversified portfolio depends on its sensitivity to market changes. This sensitivity is generally known as *beta*. A security with a beta of 1.0 has average market risk—a well-diversified portfolio of such securites has the same standard deviation as the market index. A security with a beta of 0.5 has below-average market risk—a well-diversified portfolio of these securities tends to move half as far as the market moves and has half the market's standard deviation.

Since investors can diversify away unique risk, they will not demand a higher return from stocks that have above-average unique risk. But they *will* demand higher return from stocks with above-average *market* risk. The capital asset pricing model states that the expected risk premium from any investment should vary in direct proportion to its market risk.

In this chapter, we shall see how this relationship between risk and return stems from the efforts of each investor to choose a sensible portfolio.

8-1 HARRY MARKOWITZ AND THE BIRTH OF PORTFOLIO THEORY

Most of the ideas in Chapter 7 date back to an article written in 1952 by Harry Markowitz.[1] Markowitz drew attention to the common practice of portfolio diversification and showed exactly how an investor can reduce the standard deviation of portfolio returns by choosing stocks that do not move exactly together. But Markowitz did not stop there—he went on to work out the basic principles of portfolio construction. These principles are the foundation for most of what we can say about the relationship between risk and return.

Let us begin with Figure 8-1 which shows a histogram of the daily returns on Canadian Pacific stock from 1980 to 1982. On this histogram we have superimposed a bell-shaped **normal distribution**. Strikingly similar, are they not? And we have not cheated in our

---

[1] H.M. Markowitz, "Portfolio Selection," *Journal of Finance*, **7**:77–91 (March 1952).

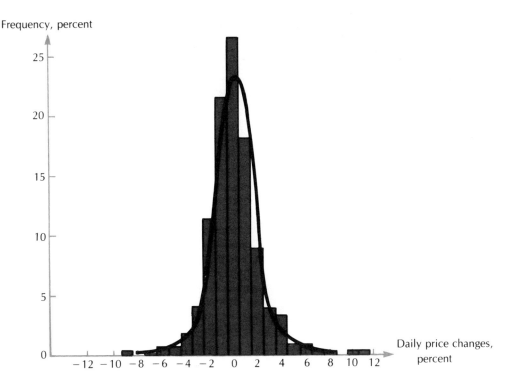

Figure 8-1 Daily price changes of Canadian Pacific stock from 1980 to 1982 are approximately normally distributed.

choice of stock. When measured over short intervals, the past rates of return on almost any stock conform closely to a normal distribution.[2]

One important feature of a normal distribution is that it can be completely defined by two numbers. One is the average or "expected" return; the other is the variance or standard deviation. Now you can see why, in Chapter 7, we discussed the calculation of expected return and standard deviation. They are not just arbitrary measures: if returns are normally distributed, they are the *only* two measures that an investor need consider.

Figure 8-2 pictures the distribution of possible returns from two investments. Both offer an expected return of 10%, but A has much the wider spread of possible outcomes. Its standard deviation is 30%; the standard deviation of B is 15%. Most investors dislike uncertainty and would therefore prefer B to A.

Figure 8-3 pictures the distribution of returns from other investments. This time both have the *same* standard deviation but the expected return is 20% from stock C and only 10% from stock D. Most investors like high expected returns and would therefore prefer C to D.

Combining Stock into Portfolios

Suppose that you are wondering whether to invest in the shares of Canadian Aviation Electronics (CAE) or Stelco. You decide that CAE offers an expected return of 21% and Stelco an expected return of 16%. After looking back at the past variability of the

---

[2]There is, however, one qualification. If you were to measure returns over *long* intervals, the distribution would be skewed. You would encounter returns greater than 100% but none less than −100%.

two stocks, you also decide that the standard deviation of returns is 40% for CAE and 20% for Stelco. Figure 8-4 illustrates the choice that you confront. CAE offers the higher expected return but it is considerably more risky.

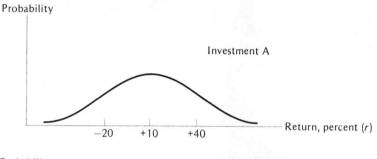

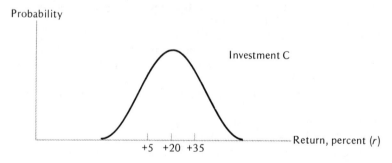

Figure 8-2   These two investments both have an *expected* return of 10% but because investment A has the greater spread of *possible* returns, it is more risky than B. We can measure this spread by the standard deviation. Investment A has a standard deviation of 30%, B, 15%. Most investors would prefer B to A.

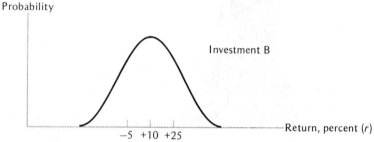

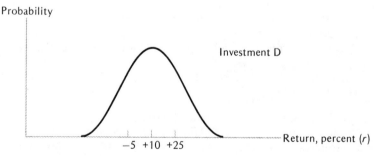

Figure 8-3   The standard deviation of possible returns is 15% for both these investments, but the expected return from C is 20% compared with an expected return from D of only 10%. Most investors would prefer C to D.

There is no reason you should restrict yourself to holding only one stock. For example, you might consider investing 33% of your portfolio in the shares of CAE and the remainder in Stelco. The expected return on this portfolio is simply a weighted average of the expected returns on the individual stocks:

Expected portfolio return $= (0.33 \times 21) + (0.67 \times 16) = 17.7\%$

Calculating the expected portfolio return is easy. The hard part is to work out the risk of your portfolio. Your first inclination may be to assume that it is a weighted average of the standard deviations of the individual holdings—that is, $(0.33 \times 40) + (0.67 \times 20) = 26.7\%$. But that would be correct only if the prices of the two stocks moved in perfect lockstep. In any other circumstances, diversification would reduce the risk below 26.7%.

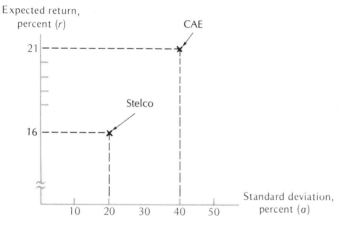

Figure 8-4 Here is a plot of the expected returns and standard deviations for just two stocks. CAE has an expected return of 21% and a standard deviation of 40%. Stelco has an expected return of 16% and a standard deviation of 20%.

The exact procedure for calculating the variance of a two-stock portfolio is given in Figure 8-5. You need to fill in four boxes. To complete the top left box, you weight the variance of the returns on stock 1 (σ_1^2) by the *square* of the proportion invested in it (x_1^2). Similarly, to complete the bottom right box, you weight the variance of the returns on stock 2 (σ_2^2) by the *square* of the proportion invested in stock 2 (x_2^2).

	Stock 1	Stock 2
Stock 1	$x_1^2 \sigma_1^2$	$x_1 x_2 \sigma_{12}$ $= x_1 x_2 \rho_{12} \sigma_1 \sigma_2$
Stock 2	$x_1 x_2 \sigma_{12}$ $= x_1 x_2 \rho_{12} \sigma_1 \sigma_2$	$x_2^2 \sigma_2^2$

Figure 8-5 The variance of a two-stock portfolio is the sum of these four boxes. x_i = proportion invested in stock j; σ_i^2 = variance of return on stock i; σ_{ij} = covariance of returns on stock i and j ($\rho_{ij}\sigma_i\sigma_j$); ρ_{ij} = correlation between returns on stocks i and j.

The entries in these diagonal boxes depend on the *variances* of stocks 1 and 2; the entries in the other two boxes depend on their covariance. As you might guess, the covariance is a measure of the degree to which the two stocks "covary." The covariance is equal to the product of the correlation coefficient ρ_{12} and the two standard deviations:

Covariance between stocks 1 and 2 $= \sigma_{12} = \rho_{12}\sigma_1\sigma_2$

For the most part stocks tend to move together. In this case the correlation coefficient ρ_{12} is positive and therefore the covariance σ_{12} is also positive. If the prospects of the stocks were wholly unrelated, both the correlation coefficient and the covariance would be zero; and if the stocks tended to move in opposite directions, the correlation coefficient and the covariance would be negative. Just as you weighted the variances by the square of the proportion invested, so you must weight the covariance by the *product* of the two proportionate holdings x_1 and x_2. Once you have completed these four boxes, you simply add up the entries in order to obtain the portfolio variance:

Portfolio variance $= (x_1^2\sigma_1^2) + (x_2^2\sigma_2^2) + 2(x_1x_2\rho_{12}\sigma_1\sigma_2)$

The portfolio standard deviation is of course the square root of the variance.

Now you can try putting in some figures for CAE and Stelco. We said earlier that if the two stocks were perfectly correlated, the standard deviation of the portfolio would lie 33% of the way between the standard deviations of the two stocks. Let us check that out by filling in the boxes with $\rho_{12} = +1$.

	CAE	Stelco
CAE	$x_1^2\sigma_1^2 = (0.33)^2 \times 1,600$	$x_1x_2\rho_{12}\sigma_1\sigma_2 = 0.33 \times 0.67 \times 1 \times 40 \times 20$
Stelco	$x_1x_2\rho_{12}\sigma_1\sigma_2 = 0.33 \times 0.67 \times 1 \times 40 \times 20$	$x_2^2\sigma_2^2 = (0.67)^2 \times 400$

The variance of your portfolio would be the sum of these entries:

Portfolio variance $= [(0.33)^2 \times 1,600] + [(0.67)^2 \times 400]$

$+ 2[0.33 \times 0.67 \times 1 \times 40 \times 20]$

$= 707.6$

The standard deviation would be $\sqrt{707.6} = 26.6\%$, one third of the way between 20 and 40.

Diversification reduces risk only when the correlation is less than one. The greatest diversification payoff comes when the two stocks are *negatively* correlated. Unfortunately, this almost never occurs with real stocks, but just for illustration, let us assume it for CAE and Stelco. As long as we are being unrealistic, we might as well go whole hog and assume perfect negative correlation ($\rho_{12} = -1$). In this case:

Portfolio variance $= [(0.33)^2 \times 1,600] + [(0.67)^2 \times 400]$

$+ 2[0.33 \times 0.67 \times (-1) \times 40 \times 20]$

$= 0$

When there is perfect negative correlation, there is always a portfolio strategy (represented by a particular set of portfolio weights) that will completely eliminate risk.[3]

In practice, CAE and Stelco neither move in perfect lockstep nor do they move in opposite directions. If the past experience is any guide, the correlation between the two stocks is about 0.3. If we go through the same exercise again with $\rho_{12} = +0.3$, we find:

$$\text{Portfolio variance} = [(0.33)^2 \times 1,600] \times [(0.67)^2 \times 400]$$
$$+ 2[0.33 \times 0.67 \times 0.3 \times 40 \times 20]$$
$$= 460$$

The standard deviation is $\sqrt{460} = 21\%$. The risk is now *less* than 33% of the way between 20 and 40—in fact, only a trifle more than investing in Stelco alone.

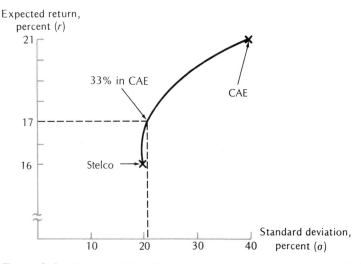

Figure 8-6   The curved line illustrates how expected return and standard deviation change as you hold different combinations of two stocks. For example, if you invest 33% of your money in CAE and the remainder in Stelco, your expected return is 17%, which is 33% of the way between the expected returns on the two stocks. The standard deviation is 21%, which is *much less* than 33% of the way between the standard deviations on the two stocks. This is because diversification reduces risk.

We can also use these formulas to calculate the expected return and risk of other combinations of CAE and Stelco. In Figure 8-6, we have assumed a correlation of 0.3 and we have plotted the expected return and risk that you could achieve by different combinations of these two stocks.

Which of these combinations is best? That depends partly on your stomach. If you want to stake all on getting rich quickly, you would do best to put all your funds in CAE. If you want a more peaceful life, you should invest part of your money in Stelco—to minimize risk you should keep your investment in CAE small.

---

[3]Since the standard deviation of CAE is twice that of Stelco, you need to invest twice as much in Stelco to eliminate risk in this two-stock portfolio.

Choosing Portfolios from Many Stocks

These methods for calculating expected portfolio return and risk can easily be extended to portfolios containing three or more securities. The expected return is always just a weighted average of the expected returns on the individual stocks. To calculate the variance of the portfolio, we just have to fill in more boxes. Each of those along the diagonal—the shaded boxes in Figure 8-7—contains the variance of the stock weighted by the square of the proportion invested in the stock. Each of the other boxes contains the covariance between that pair of securities, weighted by the product of the proportions invested. The portfolio variance is the sum of all these boxes.

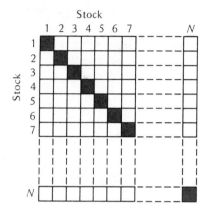

Figure 8-7   To find the variance of any N-stock portfolio we must add up a matrix like this. The diagonal boxes contain variance terms $(x_i^2\sigma_i^2)$ and the off-diagonal boxes contain covariance terms $(x_ix_j\sigma_{ij})$.

Figure 8-8 shows how your choice is enlarged when you have a larger selection of securities. Each cross represents the combination of risk and return offered by a different individual security. By mixing these securities in different proportions, you can reduce your risk and obtain an even wider selection of risk and expected return. For example, the range of attainable combinations might look something like the broken-egg-shaped area in Figure 8-8. Since you wish to increase expected return and reduce standard

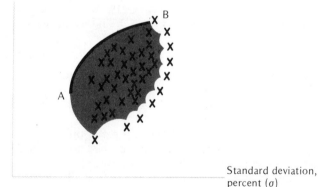

Figure 8-8   Each cross shows the expected return and standard deviation from investing in a single stock. The broken-egg-shaped area shows the possible combinations of expected return and standard deviation if you invest in a *mixture* of stocks. If you like high expected returns and dislike high standard deviations, you will prefer portfolios along the heavy line. These are *efficient* portfolios.

deviation, you will be interested only in those portfolios that lie along the heavy solid line. Markowitz called them *efficient portfolios*. Whether you want to choose the minimum risk portfolio (portfolio A) or the maximum expected return portfolio (portfolio B) or some other efficient portfolio depends on how much you dislike taking risk.

The problem of finding these efficient portfolios is similar to a problem that we encountered in Chapter 6. There we wanted to deploy a limited amount of capital in a mixture of projects to give the highest total NPV. Here we want to deploy a limited amount of capital to give the highest expected return for a given standard deviation. In principle both problems can be solved by a hunt-and-peck procedure—but only in principle. To solve the capital-rationing problem in practice, we can employ linear programming techniques; to solve the portfolio problem, we can employ a variant of linear programming known as *quadratic programming*. If we estimate the expected return and standard deviation for each stock in Figure 8-8, and also the correlation between each pair of stocks, then we can use a standard computer program to calculate the set of efficient portfolios.

Limits to Diversification

When we showed you in Figure 8-7 how to calculate the risk of a portfolio, did you notice how much more important the covariances become as we add securities to the portfolio? When there are just two securities, there is an equal number of variance boxes and covariance boxes. When there are many securities, the number of covariances is much larger than the number of variances. Thus the variability of a well-diversified portfolio reflects mainly the covariances.

Suppose we are dealing with portfolios in which equal investments are made in each of N stocks. The proportion invested in each stock is, therefore, $1/N$. So in each variance box we have $(1/N)^2$ times the variance and in each covariance box we have $(1/N)^2$ times the covariance. There are N variance boxes and $N^2 - N$ covariance boxes. Therefore

$$\text{Portfolio variance} = N\left(\frac{1}{N}\right)^2 \times \text{average variance}$$

$$+ (N^2 - N)\left(\frac{1}{N}\right)^2 \times \text{average covariance}$$

$$= \frac{1}{N} \times \text{average variance} + \left(1 - \frac{1}{N}\right) \times \text{average covariance}$$

Notice that as N increases, the portfolio variance steadily approaches the average covariance. If the average covariance were zero, it would be possible to eliminate *all* risk by holding sufficient securities. Unfortunately common stocks move together, not independently. Thus most of the stocks the investor can actually buy are tied together in a web of positive covariances, which set the limit to the benefits of diversification. In Chapter 7, we referred to the risk that cannot be diversified away as *market risk*. Now you can understand the precise meaning of that term. Market risk is the average covariance of all securities. This is the bedrock risk remaining after diversification has done its work.

Contribution to Portfolio Risk

If we want to know the contribution of an individual security to the risk of a portfolio, it is no good thinking about the risk of that security if it is held in isolation. We need to take account of how it covaries with the other stocks in the portfolio.

Look again at Figure 8-7. The sum of all the boxes in the first row shows the contribution of stock 1 to portfolio risk; the sum of the boxes in the second row shows the contribution of stock 2; and so on. This means that contribution of stock 1 to portfolio risk depends on its market value (x_1) and its average covariance with all the stocks in the portfolio ($\sum\limits_{j=1}^{N} x_j\sigma_{1j}$). To put it another way, the risk stock 1 contributes to the portfolio depends on its relative market value (x_1) and its covariance with the portfolio (σ_{1p}):

$$\text{Contribution to risk} = x_1\sigma_{1p}$$

If you want to measure the *proportion* of the risk contributed by stock 1, you can express these measures as a proportion of the portfolio risk (σ_p^2):

$$\begin{array}{c}\textit{Proportionate} \text{ contribution} \\ \text{to portfolio risk}\end{array} = \frac{x_1\sigma_{1p}}{\sigma_p^2}$$

Obviously the *total* proportion of risk accounted for by all stocks in the portfolio must equal 1.0.

The ratio σ_{1p}/σ_p^2 is the sensitivity of stock 1 to changes in the value of the portfolio. If this ratio is greater than one, then stock 1 is usually sensitive to changes in portfolio value. A marginal increase in your holding would, therefore, increase portfolio risk. If the ratio is less than one, then stock 1 is relatively insensitive to changes in portfolio value. In this case, a marginal increase in your holding would reduce portfolio risk.

Suppose that the portfolio is the market portfolio. Then the ratio σ_{1p}/σ_p^2 is the stock's *beta*, which we discussed, but never properly defined, in Chapter 7. Beta is simply a measure of the stock's marginal contribution to the risk of the market portfolio. Stocks with betas greater than one have an above-average impact on the market's risk; stocks with betas less than one have a below-average impact.

Borrowing and Lending

We have talked about efficient common stock portfolios but we must also take account of the possibility that you can lend and borrow money at some risk-free rate of interest r_f. If you invest part of your money in Treasury bills (that is, lend money) and place the remainder in common stock portfolio S, you can obtain any combination of expected return and risk along the straight line joining r_f and S in Figure 8-9.[4] Since borrowing is merely negative lending, you can extend the range of possibilities to the right of S by borrowing funds at an interest rate of r_f and investing them as well as your own money in portfolio S.

Let us put some numbers on this. Suppose that portfolio S has an expected return of 15% and a standard deviation of 16%. Treasury bills offer an interest rate (r_f) of 5% and are risk-free (that is, their standard deviation is zero). If you invest half your money in portfolio S and lend the remainder at 5%, the expected return on your investment is halfway between the expected return on S and the expected return on Treasury bills:

---

[4]If you want to check this, write down the formula for the standard deviation of a two-stock portfolio:

$$\text{Standard deviation} = \sqrt{x_1^2\sigma_1^2 + x_2^2\sigma_2^2 + 2x_1x_2\rho_{12}\sigma_1\sigma_2}$$

Now see what happens when security 2 is riskless—that is, $\sigma_2 = 0$.

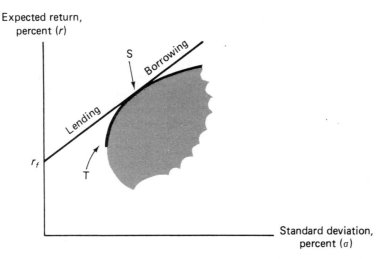

Figure 8-9 Lending and borrowing extend the range of investment possibilities. If you invest in portfolio S and lend or borrow at the risk-free interest rate, r_f, you can achieve any point along the straight line from r_f through S. This gives you a higher expected return for any level of risk than if you just invest in common stocks.

$r = (\frac{1}{2} \times \text{expected return on S}) + (\frac{1}{2} \times \text{interest rate}) = 10\%$

And the standard deviation is halfway between the standard deviation of S and the standard deviation of Treasury bills:

$\sigma = (\frac{1}{2} \times \text{standard deviation of S}) + (\frac{1}{2} \times \text{standard deviation of bills}) = 8\%$

Or suppose you decide to go for the big time: you borrow at the Treasury bill rate an amount equal to your initial wealth and invest everything in portfolio S. You have twice your own money invested in S but you have to *pay* interest on the loan. Therefore your expected return is:

$r = (2 \times \text{expected return on S}) - (1 \times \text{interest rate}) = 25\%$

And the standard deviation of your investment is:

$\sigma = (2 \times \text{standard deviation of S}) - (1 \times \text{standard deviation of bills}) = 32\%$

You can see from Figure 8-9 that when you lend a portion of your money you end up partway between r_f and S; if you can borrow money at the risk-free rate you can extend your possibilities beyond S. You can also see that, regardless of what level of risk you choose, you can get the highest expected return by a mixture of portfolio S and borrowing or lending. There is no reason ever to hold, say, portfolio T.

This means that we can separate the investor's job into two stages. First, the "best" portfolio of common stocks must be selected—S in our example.[5] Second, this portfolio must be blended with borrowing or lending to obtain an exposure to risk that suits the

_____

[5]Portfolio S is the point of tangency to the set of efficient portfolios. It offers the highest expected risk premium $(r - r_f)$ per unit of standard deviation (σ).

investor's particular tastes. Each investor, therefore, should put money into just two benchmark investments—a risky portfolio S and a risk-free loan (borrowing or lending).[6]

What does portfolio S look like? If you have better information than your rivals, you will want it to include relatively large investments in the stocks you think are undervalued. But in a competitive market you are unlikely to have a monopoly on good ideas. In that case there is no reason to hold a different portfolio of common stocks from anybody else. In other words, the market portfolio would be the most efficient portfolio for you. That is why many professional investors invest in a market-index portfolio and why most others hold well-diversified portfolios.

8-2 THE RELATIONSHIP BETWEEN RISK AND RETURN

We have now suggested four basic principles of portfolio selection:

1. Investors like high expected return and low standard deviation. Common stock portfolios that offer the highest expected return for a given standard deviation are known as *efficient portfolios*.

2. If you want to know the marginal impact of a stock on the risk of a portfolio, you must look not at the risk of that stock in isolation, but at its contribution to portfolio risk. That contribution depends on the stock's sensitivity to changes in the value of the portfolio.

3. A stock's sensitivity to changes in the value of the *market* portfolio is known as *beta*. Beta, therefore, measures the marginal contribution of a stock to the risk of the market portfolio.

4. If investors can borrow and lend at the risk-free rate of interest, then they should always hold a mixture of the risk-free investment and one particular common stock portfolio. The composition of this stock portfolio depends only on investors' assessment of the prospects for each stock and not on their attitude to risk. If they have no superior information, they should hold the same stock portfolio as everybody else—in other words, they should hold the market portfolio.

We now need to consider the implications of these ideas for the way securities are priced. We discussed this topic briefly in Chapter 7 when we described the capital asset pricing model. This model states that in competitive markets, the expected returns on each stock must plot along the security market line, as shown in Figure 8-10.

To see why stocks should lie along the security market line, imagine that you are choosing a portfolio. Some stocks will add to the risk of the portfolio and you will, therefore, buy them only if they also increase the expected return. Others will reduce portfolio risk and you may, therefore, be prepared to buy them even if they also reduce the portfolio's expected return. If the portfolio you have chosen is efficient, each of your investments must work equally hard for you. So, if one stock has a greater marginal effect on the risk of the portfolio than another stock, it must also have proportionately greater expected return. This means that if you plot each stock's expected return against its marginal contribution to the risk of your efficient portfolio, you will find that the stocks lie along a straight line, as in Figure 8-11. This is *always* the case: if a portfolio is efficient, there must be a straight-line relationship between each stock's expected return and its marginal contribution to portfolio risk. The converse is also true: if there is not a straight-line relationship, the portfolio is not efficient.

---

[6]This so-called *separation theorem* was first pointed out by J. Tobin, in "Liquidity Preference as Behavior Toward Risk," *Review of Economic Studies*, **25**:65–86 (February 1958).

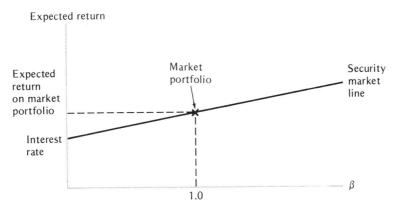

Figure 8-10   The capital asset pricing model states that the security market line describes the relationship between a stock's expected return and its beta. *Note*: The beta of the market portfolio is the average beta of all stocks, that is, 1.0.

Now you can see that Figures 8-10 and 8-11 are identical *if* the efficient portfolio in Figure 8-11 is the market portfolio. (Remember that the beta of a stock measures its marginal contribution to the risk of the market portfolio.) So the capital asset pricing model boils down to the statement that the market portfolio is efficient. As we have already seen, this will be so if each investor has the same information and faces the same opportunities as everyone else. In these circumstances, each investor should hold the same portfolio as everyone else—in other words, each should hold the market portfolio.

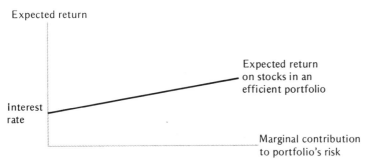

Figure 8-11   If a portfolio is efficient, each stock should lie along a straight line linking the stock's expected return with its marginal contribution to the portfolio's risk.

What Would Happen if a Stock Did Not Lie on the Market Line?

In Chapter 7 we sketched what would happen if a particular stock did not lie on the market line. Let us now look more carefully at this case. Figure 8-12 depicts the consequences of four possible investment policies:

Policy 1   Suppose you just hold the market portfolio. Then the diagonal line in Figure 8-12 shows the relationship between the risk premium on your investment and the risk premium on the market. Not surprisingly, the risk premium on your investment ($r - r_f$) is always equal to the market risk premium ($r_m - r_f$). (Note that Figure 8-12 shows a range of possible outcomes for the market. The vertical scale shows expected risk premiums *given* particular outcomes for the market.)

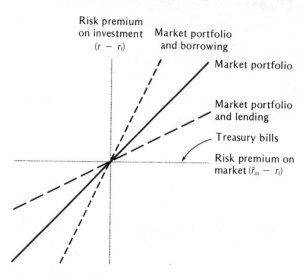

Figure 8-12 These lines show how the expected risk premium on your investment is related to the actual risk premium on the market. If you borrow and invest in the market portfolio, the line will be steep; if you lend and invest in the market portfolio, it will be relatively flat.

Policy 2 Now suppose instead that you invest all your money in risk-free bills. Regardless of what happens to the market, you will just earn the rate of interest r_f. The risk premium on your investment is always zero. It is, therefore, represented by the horizontal axis in Figure 8-12.

Policy 3 Another possibility is to divide your money evenly between the market portfolio and risk-free bills. In that case, your risk premium will always be midway between the market risk premium and the rate of interest.

Policy 4 If you are more daring, you might choose to borrow funds at the risk-free interest rate and invest these and an equal amount of your own money in the market portfolio. In this case the risk premium on your investment will be twice as high as on the market portfolio.

Of course these are not the only possible policies. By holding an appropriate mixture of the market portfolio and borrowing or lending, an investor can achieve *any* of the positions that can be represented by a straight line passing through the origin in Figure 8-12. If the portfolio involves borrowing, it has above-average risk and the slope of the line is *greater* than 1.0. If the portfolio involves lending, it has below-average risk and the slope of the line is *less* than 1.0.

Now look at Figure 8-13(*a*). The lighter line is known as a **characteristic line**. It shows the relationship between the expected risk premium on a security and the market risk premium. You can see that this security is unaffected by the market. Therefore it has a beta of zero. It also has a negative expected risk premium. What would you do if such a stock were offered to you? We hope you would not buy it—if you want an investment with a beta of zero. Treasury bills are better. If everybody shares your view of the stock's prospects, the price of security A will have to fall.

Suppose now that someone offers you the stock shown by the lighter characteristic line in Figure 8-13(*b*). It has a beta of 1.0. But, if that is the risk you want, you would do better with the market portfolio that offers a higher expected risk premium whatever the market does. Once again the price will have to fall.

Our third hypothetical stock is represented by the lighter characteristic line in Figure 8-13(*c*). It has a beta of 0.5. But you can expect to do better in all circumstances by

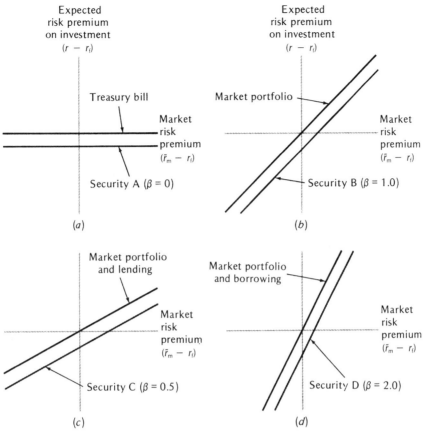

Figure 8-13   (a) Nobody loves security A: the Treasury bill gives a higher expected return regardless of what happens to the market. (b) Nobody loves security B: the market portfolio gives a higher expected return regardless of what happens to the market. (c) Nobody loves security C: a mixture of the market portfolio and lending gives a higher expected return regardless of what happens to the market. (d) Nobody loves security D: a mixture of the market portfolio and borrowing gives a higher expected return regardless of what happens to the market.

investing half your funds in Treasury bills and half in the market portfolio. So nobody is going to want to buy the stock. Finally, Figure 8-13(d) shows a stock with a beta of 2.0. This time you could expect to do better in all circumstances by borrowing at the interest rate r_f and investing in the market portfolio.

We think we have made our point. An investor can always obtain an expected risk premium of $\beta(r_m - r_f)$ by holding a mixture of the market portfolio and a risk-free loan. So in well-functioning markets nobody will hold a stock that offers an expected risk premium of *less* than $\beta(r_m - r_f)$. But what about the other possibility? Are there stocks that offer a higher expected risk premium? If we take all stocks together, we have the market portfolio. Its beta is 1.0 and its expected risk premium is:

Expected market risk premium $= \beta(r_m - r_f) = r_m - r_f$

Since the stocks *on average* offer an expected risk premium of $\beta(r_m - r_f)$ and since none offers a *lower* expected risk premium, then there can't be any that offer a *higher* premium. The expected risk premium on each and every stock is:

$$r - r_f = \beta(r_m - r_f)$$

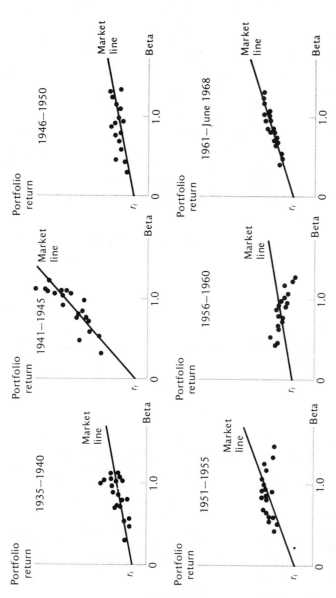

Figure 8-14 The capital asset pricing model states that the *expected* return from any investment should lie on the market line. The dots show the *actual* returns from portfolios with different betas.

Source: Results supplied by E.F. Fama and J.D. MacBeth. See their paper, "Risk, Return and Equilibrium: Empirical Tests," *Journal of Political Economy,* **81**:607–636 (May 1973).

8-3 VALIDITY AND ROLE OF THE CAPITAL ASSET PRICING MODEL

Any economic model is a simplified statement of reality. We need to simplify in order to interpret what is going on around us. But we also need to know how much faith we can place in our model.

Let us begin with some matters on which there is broad agreement. First, few people quarrel with the idea that investors require some extra return for taking on risk. That is why common stocks have given on average a higher return than Treasury bills. Who would want to invest in risky common stocks if they offered only the *same* expected return as bills? We wouldn't, and we suspect you wouldn't either.

Second, investors do appear to be concerned principally with those risks that they cannot eliminate by diversification. If this were not so, we should find that stock prices increase whenever two companies merge to spread their risks. And we should find that investment companies that invest in the shares of other firms are more highly valued than the shares they hold. But we don't observe either phenomenon. Diversifying mergers don't increase stock prices and investment companies are no more highly valued than the shares they hold.

The capital asset pricing model captures these ideas in a simple way. That is why many financial managers find it the most convenient tool for coming to grips with the slippery notion of risk. And it is why economists often use the capital asset pricing model to demonstrate important ideas in finance even when there are other ways to prove these ideas. In years to come, economists will develop better models of risk and return, but it is doubtful whether they will ever develop a simpler and more intuitively appealing model.

Tests of the Capital Asset Pricing Model

The ultimate test of any model is whether it fits the facts. Unfortunately there are two problems in testing the capital asset pricing model. First, it is concerned with *expected* returns, whereas we can observe only *actual* returns. Second, the market portfolio should include all risky investments, whereas most market indices contain only a sample of common stocks.[7]

No study has properly tackled the second problem, but a paper by Fama and MacBeth avoids the main pitfalls that come from having to work with actual rather than expected returns. Fama and MacBeth grouped all New York Stock Exchange stocks into 20 portfolios. They then plotted the estimated beta of each portfolio in one ten-year period against the portfolio's average return over a subsequent five-year period.[8] Figure 8-14 shows what they found. You can see that the estimated beta of each portfolio told investors quite a lot about its future return.

If the capital asset pricing model is correct, investors would not have expected any of these portfolios to perform better or worse than a comparable package of Treasury bills and the market portfolio. Therefore, the expected return on each portfolio, given the market return, should plot along the sloping lines of Figure 8-14. Notice that the

---

[7]See, for example, R. Roll, "A Critique of the Asset Pricing Theory's Tests; Part 1: On Past and Potential Testability of the Theory," *Journal of Financial Economics*, 4:129–176 (March 1977).

[8]Fama and MacBeth first estimated the beta of each stock by using the returns in each odd month. They then formed portfolios on the basis of the odd-month betas. Finally, they re-estimated the beta of each portfolio by using only the returns in each even month. This rather ingenious trick insured that the estimated betas for each portfolio were largely unbiased and free from error. E.F. Fama and J.D. MacBeth, "Risk, Return and Equilibrium: Empirical Tests," *Journal of Political Economy*, **81**:607–636 (May 1973).

---

actual returns on Fama and MacBeth's portfolios do plot *roughly* along these lines. That is encouraging, but we should like to know why the portfolios don't plot *exactly* along the lines. Is it because the capital asset pricing model is only a rough approximation to real markets? Or is it because the tests are not appropriate? (Remember that Fama and MacBeth are looking at *actual* returns, whereas the capital asset pricing model is concerned with expectations; also, Fama and MacBeth did not include *all* risky assets in their market index.) Unfortunately, nobody knows which explanation is correct. Betas that are calculated using a stock market index seem to tell us something about expected return, but we can't be sure what we would find if we were able to calculate betas using the full market portfolio of *all* risky assets.

What Market Index Should be Used in Canada?

We have stressed the notion that the market index must include *all* risky assets. Does that mean we should use an international index that is weighted more heavily towards American stocks than Canadian stocks, simply because the American market is so much larger than the Canadian market? Or should we use the observation that Canadians, on the whole, own more Canadian stocks than American stocks,[9] and take an index that is more heavily weighted with Canadian stocks? Or does it matter which index we use?

Certainly the American and Canadian market indices are highly correlated with each other. But they are not *perfectly* correlated, and Roll has shown that this can be enough to create substantially different estimates of expected return, depending on which index is used to calculate beta.[10]

Brennan and Schwartz approached the problem from an empirical perspective, by asking whether some combination of American and Canadian stock market indices provided a better fit for a security market line than the Canadian index alone.[11] In effect, they estimated a security market line, as in Figure 8-14, which related portfolio returns to Canadian betas (that is, betas calculated using a Canadian stock market index).[12] Then they checked to see whether the deviation of the portfolios from the market line could be explained by the American betas of the portfolio (that is, betas calculated using an American stock market index). They found no evidence to suggest a need to use the American betas. This suggests that, in Canada, it is appropriate to use a Canadian market index (like the TSE 300 Composite Index) to calculate betas that are to be used in the capital asset pricing model.

Assumptions Behind the Capital Asset Pricing Model

In getting to the capital asset pricing model we made a number of assumptions that we did not fully spell out. For example, we assumed that investment in Treasury bills is risk-free. It is true that there is little chance of default with Treasury bills, but they don't guarantee a *real* return. There is still the risk of inflation. Another assumption

---

[9]One reason Canadians concentrate on domestic stocks is that Canadian stocks expose Canadian investors to lower personal taxes (see Chapter 16). Another reason may be that Canadians find it more awkward to transact in American security markets than in Canadian security markets.

[10]See R. Roll, *op cit.*

[11]See M.J. Brennan and E.S. Schwartz, "Asset Pricing in a Small Economy: A Test of the Omitted Assets Model," undated manuscript, University of British Columbia.

[12]Many Canadian stocks are traded infrequently, and this causes some problems in estimating betas. Brennan and Schwartz used the Dimson approach to estimating beta to adjust for this. See Chapter 9.

was that investors can *borrow* money at the same rate of interest as they can lend. Generally, borrowing rates are higher than lending rates.

It turns out that many of these assumptions are not crucial and with a little pushing and pulling it is possible to modify the capital asset pricing model to handle them. The really important assumption behind the model is that investors are content to invest their money in a limited number of benchmark portfolios such as Treasury bills and the market portfolio. As long as that is the case, we can express a security's expected return in terms of the expected return on these portfolios.[13]

Arbitrage Pricing Theory

The capital asset pricing model may reign today, but no one regards it as Ultimate Truth. A new model will take the throne sooner or later, but we can't say now which model that will be. It may be one of the existing extensions or generalizations of the simple capital asset pricing model,[14] or it may be something completely new.

Most existing theories have a clear family resemblance. However, one new theory, Stephen Ross's *arbitrage pricing theory*,[15] comes from a different family. We will briefly sketch Ross's approach.

The capital asset pricing model follows from an analysis of how investors can construct efficient portfolios. Arbitrage pricing theory skips this step and starts instead by *assuming* that each stock's return depends on several independent influences or "factors." Moreover, the return *must* obey the following simple relationship:

$$\begin{matrix} \text{Expected return} \\ \text{on stock} \end{matrix} = a + b_1(\text{factor 1}) + b_2(\text{factor 2}) + b_3(\text{factor 3}) + \cdots$$

The theory doesn't say what the factors are: there could be an oil price factor, an interest rate factor, and so on. The return on the market portfolio *might* serve as one factor, but then again it might not.

Some stocks will be more sensitive to a particular factor than others. Dome Petroleum would be more sensitive to an oil factor than, say, Stelco. If factor 1 picks up unexpected changes in oil prices, b_1 would be higher for Dome.[16]

Now think of a portfolio whose expected return depended on factor 1 *only*. Buying this portfolio is like buying the factor; think of the return on this "pure play" portfolio as the return on the factor itself. Each of the other factors has its own pure play portfolio and thus its own return.

---

[13]See, for example, M.C. Jensen (ed.), *Studies in the Theory of Capital Markets*, Frederick A. Praeger, Inc., New York, 1972. In the introduction to his book, Jensen provides a very useful summary of some of these variations on the capital asset pricing model. In each case, the definition of market risk or of the two benchmark portfolios changes, but the general form of the model does not change. For practical purposes, none of these alternative forms is as widely used as the standard model.

[14]Two prominent contenders are R.C. Merton, "An Intertemporal Capital Asset Pricing Model," *Econometrica*, **41**:867–887 (September 1973), and D.T. Breeden, "An Intertemporal Asset Pricing Model with Stochastic Consumption and Investment Opportunities," *Journal of Financial Economics*, 7:265–296 (September 1979).

[15]S.A. Ross, "The Arbitrage Theory of Capital Asset Pricing," *Journal of Economic Theory*, **13**:341–360 (December 1976).

[16]Indeed, to the extent that high oil prices hurt Stelco (through higher transportation and manufacturing costs for its products and less demand for the steel in large cars), we might expect that b_1 would be *negative* for Stelco.

The arbitrage pricing model states that each stock's risk premium depends on two things: first, the risk premiums associated with each factor, and, second, the stock's sensitivity to each of the factors (that is, the stock's b_1, b_2, b_3, and so on). The formula is:

$$\text{Risk premium on stock} = r - r_f = b_1 \left(r_{\text{factor 1}} - r_f\right) + b_2\left(r_{\text{factor 2}} - r_f\right) + \cdots$$

What would happen if the expected risk premium on a stock were lower than this? In that case, Ross argues, there would be a money machine. Investors would sell the stock and buy a package of other fairly priced stocks with the same average sensitivity to each factor. The new portfolio would be equally exposed to changes in oil prices, interest rates, and so on, but it would offer a higher expected return.

What if the expected risk premium were higher? Then smart investors would sell other stocks and rush to buy this one. The pressure of their demand would force up the price and force down the return and risk premium, until Ross's equation held.

Will the arbitrage pricing theory provide a better handle on expected returns? That depends partly on whether it is possible to (1) identify the factors affecting stock returns and (2) measure the expected return on each of these factors as well as the sensitivity of stocks to them. Research on these issues is at a very early stage.[17] Until these practical problems are solved, the capital asset pricing model, or another model drawn from its family, is likely to remain the dominant theory of risk and return.

8-4 SUMMARY

In the first part of this chapter, we described some basic principles of portfolio selection. We suggested that most investors would like to increase the expected return on their portfolios and to reduce the standard deviation of the return. A portfolio that gives the highest expected return for a given standard deviation, or the lowest standard deviation for a given expected return, is known as an efficient portfolio. Working out the expected return on a portfolio is easy; simply take a weighted average of the expected returns on the individual stocks. The standard deviation of the portfolio return is more complicated to calculate because it depends on the standard deviation of each stock and the correlation between each pair of stocks.

Investors who are restricted to holding common stocks should choose an efficient portfolio that suites their attitude to risk. But investors who can also borrow and lend at the risk-free rate of interest should choose the "best" common stock portfolio *regardless* of their attitude to risk. Having done that, they can then set the risk of their overall portfolio by deciding what proportion of their money they are willing to invest in stocks. For an investor who has only the same opportunities and information as everybody else, the best stock portfolio is the same as the best stock portfolio for other investors. In other words, he or she should invest in a mixture of the market portfolio and a risk-free loan (that is, borrowing or lending.)

A stock's marginal contribution to portfolio risk is measured by its sensitivity to changes in the value of the portfolio. If a portfolio is efficient, there will be a straight-line relationship between each stock's expected return and its marginal contribution to the risk of the portfolio. The marginal contribution of a stock to the risk of the

---

[17]See R. Roll and S.A. Ross, "An Empirical Investigation of the Arbitrage Pricing Theory," *Journal of Finance*, 35:1073–1103 (December 1980).

market portfolio is measured by *beta*. So if the market portfolio is efficient, there will be a straight-line relationship between the expected return and beta of each stock. That is the fundamental idea behind the capital asset pricing model.

The capital asset pricing model is the best-known model of risk and return. A number of modifications have been proposed to cope with such complexities as different borrowing and lending rates. The arbitrage pricing model offers an alternative theory of risk and return. All financial economists, however, agree on two basic ideas: (1) investors require extra expected return for taking on risk, and (2) they appear to be concerned predominantly with the risk that they cannot eliminate by diversification.

FURTHER READING

The pioneering article on portfolio selection is:

H.M. Markowitz, "Portfolio Selection," *Journal of Finance*, **7**:77–91 (March 1952).

There are a number of textbooks on portfolio selection that explain both Markowitz's original theory and some ingenious simplified versions. We like:

W.F. Sharpe, *Portfolio Theory and Capital Markets*, McGraw-Hill Book Company, New York, 1971.

Of the three pioneering articles on the capital asset pricing model, Jack Treynor's has never been published. The other two articles are:

W.F. Sharpe, "Capital Asset Prices: A Theory of Market Equilibrium under Conditions of Risk," *Journal of Finance*, **19**:425–442 (September 1964).
J. Lintner, "The Valuation of Risk Assets and the Selection of Risky Investments in Stock Portfolios and Capital Budgets," *Review of Economics and Statistics*, **47**:13–37 (February 1965).

The subsequent literature on the capital-asset pricing model is enormous. The following book provides a collection of some of the more important articles plus a very useful survey by Jensen:

M.C. Jensen (ed.), *Studies in the Theory of Capital Markets*, Frederick A. Praeger, Inc., New York, 1972.

Another very good survey article is:

F. Modigliani and G.A. Pogue, "An Introduction to Risk and Return," *Financial Analysts Journal*, **30**:68–80 (March–April 1974); 69–88 (May–June 1974).

There have been a number of tests of the capital asset pricing model. Some of the more important tests are:

E.F. Fama and J.D. MacBeth, "Risk, Return and Equilibrium: Empirical Tests," *Journal of Political Economy*, **81**:607–636 (May 1973).
F. Black, M.C. Jensen, and M. Scholes, "The Capital Asset Pricing Model: Some Empirical Tests," in M.C. Jensen (ed.), *Studies in the Theory of Capital Markets*, Frederick A. Praeger, Inc., New York, 1972.
M.R. Gibbons, "Multivariate Tests of Financial Models," *Journal of Financial Economics*, **10**:3–27 (March 1982).

Three tests of asset pricing models in a Canadian context are:

M.J. Brennan and E.S. Schwartz, "Asset Pricing in a Small Economy: A Test of the Omitted Assets Model," undated manuscript, University of British Columbia.
P. Hughes, "A Test of the Arbitrage Pricing Model," *Proceedings of the Annual Conference of the Finance Division of the Administrative Sciences Association of Canada*, **3**:1–10 (1982).

R.A. Morin, "Market Line Theory and the Canadian Equity Market," *Journal of Business Administration*, **12**:57–76 (Fall 1980).

For a critique of empirical tests of the model, see:

R. Roll, "A Critique of the Asset Pricing Theory's Tests; Part 1: On Past and Potential Testability of the Theory," *Journal of Financial Economics*, **4**:129–1976 (March 1977).

Two alternative models of asset prices are described in:

D.T. Breeden, "An Intertemporal Asset Pricing Model with Stochastic Consumption and Investment Opportunities," *Journal of Financial Economics*, **7**:265–296 (September 1979).
S.A. Ross, "The Arbitrage Theory of Capital Asset Pricing," *Journal of Economic Theory*, **13**:341–360 (December 1976).

QUIZ

1. Figures 8-15 and 8-16 purport to show the range of attainable combinations of expected return and standard deviation.
   (*a*) Which diagram is incorrectly drawn and why?
   (*b*) Which is the efficient set of portfolios?
   (*c*) If r_f is the rate of interest, mark with an X the optimal stock portfolio.

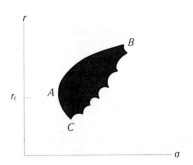

Figure 8-15   See Quiz, question 1.

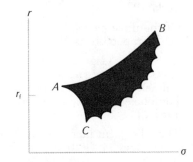

Figure 8-16   See Quiz, question 1.

2. For each of the following pairs of investments, state which would always be preferred by a rational investor (assuming that these are the *only* investments that are available to the investor):

   (*a*) Portfolio A $r = 18\%$ $\sigma = 20\%$
         Portfolio B $r = 14\%$ $\sigma = 20\%$
   (*b*) Portfolio C $r = 15\%$ $\sigma = 18\%$
         Portfolio D $r = 13\%$ $\sigma = 8\%$
   (*c*) Portfolio E $r = 14\%$ $\sigma = 16\%$
         Portfolio F $r = 14\%$ $\sigma = 10\%$

3. To calculate the variance of a three-stock portfolio you need to add nine boxes:

Use the same symbols that we used in this chapter; that is, x_1 = proportion invested in stock 1 and σ_{12} = covariance between stocks 1 and 2. Now complete the nine boxes.

4. Consider the following four portfolios:
   (a) 50% in Treasury bills, 50% in share W
   (b) 50% in share W, 50% in share X, where the returns on W and X are perfectly positively correlated
   (c) 50% in share X, 50% in share Y, where the returns are uncorrelated
   (d) 50% in share Y, 50% in share Z, where the returns are perfectly negatively correlated
   In which of these cases would the standard deviation of the portfolio lie exactly midway between that of the two securities?

5. In which of the following situations would you get the largest reduction in risk by spreading your investment across two stocks:
   (a) When the two shares are perfectly correlated
   (b) When there is no correlation
   (c) When there is modest negative correlation
   (d) When there is perfect negative correlation.

6. (a) Plot the following risky portfolios on a graph:

Portfolio	A	B	C	D	E	F	G	H
Expected return, r, %	10	12.5	15	16	17	18	18	20
Standard deviation, σ, %	23	21	25	29	29	32	35	45

   (b) Five of these portfolios are efficient and three are not. Which are inefficient ones?
   (c) Suppose you can also borrow and lend at an interest rate of 12%. Which of the above portfolios is best?
   (d) Suppose you are prepared to tolerate a standard deviation of 25%. What is the maximum expected return that you can achieve if you cannot borrow or lend?
   (e) What is your optimal strategy, if you can borrow or lend at 12% and are prepared to tolerate a standard deviation of 25%? What is the maximum expected return that you can achieve?

7. The standard deviation of the market return is about 20%.
   (a) What is the standard deviation of returns on a well-diversified portfolio with a beta of 1.5?
   (b) What is the standard deviation of returns on a well-diversified portfolio with a beta of 0?
   (c) A well-diversified portfolio has a standard deviation of 15%. What is its beta?
   (d) A poorly diversified portfolio has a standard deviation of 20%. What can you say about its beta?

QUESTIONS AND PROBLEMS

1. (a) List four common stocks that are likely to have very high standard deviations and four stocks that are likely to have very low standard deviations.
   (b) List four pairs of securities that are likely to be highly correlated and four pairs that are likely to be relatively uncorrelated.

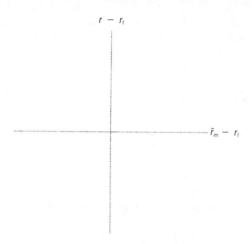

$r - r_f$

$\bar{r}_m - r_f$

Figure 8-17   See Questions and Problems, 2.

2. Enter in Figure 8-17 the characteristic line for (i) a portfolio that is evenly divided between Treasury bills and the market index, and (ii) a portfolio that is financed half by borrowing and is entirely invested in the market index.

3. Last week Prudence Puffin analyzed three common stock portfolios. She remembers that portfolio X offered an expected return of 10% and standard deviation of 10%, and that portfolio Y offered an expected return of 14% and standard deviation of 20%. Unfortunately all that she can remember about portfolio Z is that it is the best of the three portfolios as long as the interest rate is between 5% and 9%. Otherwise she would do better to invest in one of the other two portfolios and borrow or lend the balance of her money.

     What are the expected return and standard deviation of portfolio Z?
     When should Ms. Puffin invest in portfolio X and portfolio Y?

4. "There's upside risk and downside risk. Standard deviation doesn't distinguish between them." Do you think the speaker has a fair point?

5. Respond to the following comments:
    (a) "Risk is not variability. If I know a stock is going to fluctuate between $10 and $20, I can make myself a bundle."
    (b) "There are all sorts of risk in addition to beta risk. There's the risk that we'll have all downturn in demand, there's the risk that my best plant manager will drop dead, there's the risk of a hike in steel prices. You've got to take all things into consideration."
    (c) "Risk to me is the probability of loss."
    (d) "Those guys who suggest beta is a measure of risk make the big assumption that betas don't change."

6. "There may be some truth in the capital asset pricing model, but over the past year many stocks gave a substantially higher return than the capital asset pricing model predicted and many others gave a substantially lower return." Is this a valid criticism of the model?

7. Sketch the efficient set of common stock portfolios. Show the combinations of expected return and risk that you could achieve if you could borrow and lend at the same risk-free rate of interest. Now show the combinations of expected return and risk that you could achieve if the rate of interest is higher for borrowing than for lending.

8. Look back at the calculation for CAE and Stelco in Section 8-1. Recalculate the expected portfolio return and standard deviation for different values of x_1 and x_2 assuming $\rho_{12} = 0$. Plot the efficient frontier as in Figure 8-6.
   Repeat the exercise for $\rho_{12} = +1$ and for $\rho_{12} = -1$.

9. Here are some historical data on the risk characteristics of Northern Telecom and CAE:

	Northern	CAE
β (beta)	0.54	1.21
Yearly standard deviation of return	29.4	40.7

   The standard deviation of the return on the market was 20%.
   (a) The correlation coefficient of Northern's return versus CAE's was 0.35. What is the standard deviation of a portfolio half invested in CAE and half in Northern?
   (b) What is the standard deviation of a portfolio one-third invested in Northern, one-third in CAE and one-third in Treasury bills?
   (c) What is the standard deviation if the portfolio is split equally between Northern and CAE, and financed at 50% margin—that is, the investor puts up only 50% of the total amount and borrows the balance from the broker?
   (d) What is the *approximate* standard deviation of a portfolio composed of 100 stocks with β's of 0.54, like Northern? How about 100 stocks, like CAE? (*Hint*: Part (d) should not require anything but the simplest arithmetic to answer.)

10. Mark Harrywitz proposed to invest in two shares, X and Y. He expects a return of 12% from X and 8% from Y. The standard deviation of the returns is 8% for X and 5% for Y. The correlation coefficient between the returns is 0.2.
    (a) Compute the expected return and standard deviation of the following portfolios:

Portfolio	% in X	% in Y
1	50	50
2	25	75
3	75	25

    (b) Sketch the set of portfolios composed of X and Y.
    (c) Suppose that Mr. Harrywitz can also borrow or lend at an interest rate of 5%. Show on your sketch how this alters his opportunities. Given that he can borrow or lend, what proportions of the common stock portfolio should be invested in X and Y?

11. You believe that there is a 40% chance that stock A will decline by 10% and a 60% chance that it will rise by 20%. Correspondingly, there is a 30% chance that stock B will decline by 10% and a 70% chance that it will rise by 20%. The correlation coefficient between the two stocks is 0.7. Calculate the expected return, the variance, and the standard deviation for each stock. Then calculate the co-variance between their returns.

12. Hilda Hornbill has invested 60% of her money in share A and the remainder in share B. She assesses their prospects as follows:

	A	B
Expected return, %	15	20
Standard deviation, %	20	22
Correlation between returns		0.5

(*a*) What is the expected return and standard deviation of returns on her portfolio?

(*b*) How would your answer be changed if the correlation coefficient were 0 or −0.5?

(*c*) Is Ms. Hornbill's portfolio better or worse than one invested entirely in share A, or is it not possible to say?

13. An individual invests 60% of his funds in stock I and the balance in stock J. The standard deviation of returns on I is 10% and on J it is 20%. Calculate the variance of portfolio returns assuming
(*a*) The correlation between the returns is 1.0
(*b*) The correlation is 0.5
(*c*) The correlation is 0.0

14. (*a*) How many variance terms and how many covariance terms do you need to sum to calculate the risk of a 100 share portfolio?
(*b*) Suppose all stocks had a standard deviation of 30% and a correlation with each other of 0.4. What is the standard deviation of the returns on a portfolio that has equal holdings in 100 stocks?
(*c*) What is the standard deviation of a fully diversified portfolio of such stocks?

15. During the 1960s the standard deviation σ of returns from a typical share was about 0.25 (or 25%) a year. The correlation ρ between the returns of a typical pair of shares was about 0.3. Calculate the variance and standard deviation of the returns on a portfolio that had equal investments in two shares, three shares, and so on up to ten shares.

Use your estimates to draw two graphs like Figure 7-5. How large is the underlying market risk that cannot be diversified away?

16. The market portfolio has a standard deviation of 20% and the covariance between the returns on the market and those on stock Z is 800.
(*a*) What is the beta of stock Z?
(*b*) What would be the standard deviation of a fully diversified portfolio of such stocks?
(*c*) What is the average beta of all stocks?
(*d*) If the market portfolio gave a 5% higher return than you expected, by how much is the return on portfolio Z likely to exceed your expectations?

17. It is often useful to know how well your portfolio is diversified. Two measures have been suggested:
(*a*) The variance of the returns of a fully diversified portfolio as a proportion of the variance of the returns on *your* portfolio.
(*b*) The number of shares in a portfolio that (i) has the same risk as yours, (ii) is invested in "typical" shares, and (iii) has equal amounts invested in each share.

Suppose that you hold eight stocks. All are fairly typical—they have a standard deviation σ of 0.40 a year and the correlation ρ between each pair is 0.3. Of your fund, 20% is invested in one stock, 20% in a second, and the remaining 60% is spread evenly over a further six stocks.

Calculate each of the above two measures of portfolio diversification.

CAPITAL BUDGETING AND THE CAPITAL ASSET PRICING MODEL

Long before the development of capital asset pricing theory, smart financial managers adjusted for risk in capital budgeting. They realized intuitively that, if other things are equal, risky projects are less desirable than safe ones. Therefore they demanded a higher rate of return from risky projects or they based their decisions on conservative estimates of the cash flows.

Various rules of thumb are often used to make these risk adjustments. For example, many companies estimate the rate of return required by investors in its securities and use this **company cost of capital** to discount the cash flows on all new projects. Since investors require a higher rate of return from a very risky company, such a firm will have a higher company cost of capital and will set a higher discount rate for its new investment opportunities.

You can use the capital asset pricing model as a rule of thumb for estimating the company cost of capital. For instance, the stock of Digital Equipment Corporation (DEC) had a beta of 1.38 at the end of 1982. The corresponding expected rate of return was 0.193, or about 20%.[1] Therefore, according to the company cost of capital rule, DEC should have been using a 20% discount rate to compute project net present values.[2]

This is a step in the right direction. Even though we can't measure betas or the market risk premium with absolute precision, it is still reasonable to assert that DEC faced more risk than the average firm and, therefore, should have demanded a higher rate of return from its capital investments.

But the company cost of capital rule can also get a firm into trouble if the new projects are more or less risky than its existing business. Each project should be evaluated at *its own* opportunity cost of capital. This is a clear implication of the value-additivity principle introduced in Chapter 7. For a firm composed of assets A and B, firm value is

Firm value = PV(AB) = PV(A) + PV(B) = sum of separate asset values

Here PV(A) and PV(B) are valued just as if they were mini-firms in which stockholders could invest directly. Note: investors would value A by discounting its forecasted cash flows at a rate reflecting the risk of A. They would value B by discounting at a rate reflecting the risk of B. The two discount rates will, in general, be different.

---

[1] Since DEC is an American stock, its beta was calculated against an American stock index. The risk-free rate in the United States at the end of 1982 was 7.8%, and the expected market risk premium from Table 7-1 is 8.3%.

[2] We chose DEC because it did not use any significant amount of debt financing—most Canadian stocks have a higher proportion of debt. Thus, DEC's cost of capital is the rate of return investors expect on its common stock. The complications caused by debt are discussed later in this chapter.

If the firm considers investing in a third project C, it should also value C as if it were a mini-firm. That is, it should discount the cash flows of C at the expected rate of return investors would demand to make a separate investment in C. *The true cost of capital depends on the use to which the capital is put.*

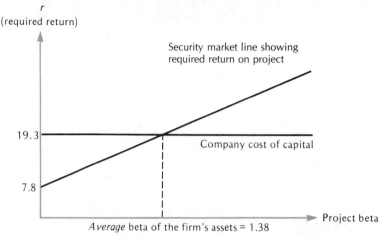

Figure 9-1   A comparison between the company cost of capital rule and the required return under the capital asset pricing model. DEC's company cost of capital is about 20%. This is the correct discount rate only if the project beta is 1.38. In general, the correct discount rate increases as project beta increases. DEC should accept projects with rates of return above the security market line relating required return to beta.

Capital asset pricing theory tells us to invest in any project offering a return that more than compensates for the *project's beta.* This means that DEC should have accepted any project above the upward-sloping market line in Figure 9-1. If the project had a high beta, DEC needed a higher prospective return than if the project had a low beta. Now contrast this with the company cost of capital rule which is to accept any project *regardless of its beta* as long as it offers a higher return than the *company's* cost of capital. In terms of Figure 9-1 it tells DEC to accept any project above the horizontal cost of capital line—that is, any project offering a return of more than 20%.

It is clearly silly to suggest that DEC should demand the same rate of return from a very safe project as from a very risky one. If DEC used the company cost of capital rule, it would reject many good low-risk projects and accept poor high-risk projects. It is also silly to suggest that, just because Bell Canada has a low company cost of capital, it is justified in accepting projects that DEC would reject. If you followed such a rule to its seemingly logical conclusion, you would think it possible to enlarge the company's opportunities by investing a large sum in Treasury bills. That would make the common stock safe and create a low company cost of capital.[3]

The notion that each company has some individual discount rate or cost of capital is widespread, but far from universal. Many firms require different returns from different categories of investment. Discount rates might be set, for example:

Category	Discount Rate, %
Speculative ventures	30
New product	20
Expansion of existing business	15 (company cost of capital)
Cost improvement, known technology	10

[3]If the present value of an asset depended on the identity of the company that bought it, present values would not be additive. Remember that a good project is a good project is a good project.

Our object in this chapter is to show you how to use beta and the capital asset pricing model to help cope with risk in practical capital-budgeting situations. The main problem is to estimate the discount rate:

$$r = r_f + (\text{project beta})(r_m - r_f)$$

And in order to do that you have to figure out the project beta. It is a difficult problem: so much so that many people hope it will go away if they ignore it. They may go away but unfortunately the problem won't—any investment decision that is made contains an *implicit* assumption about project risk.

We will start by reconsidering the problems you would encounter in using beta to estimate a company's cost of capital. It turns out that beta is difficult to measure accurately for an individual firm: much greater accuracy can be achieved by looking at an average of similar companies. But then we have to define *similar*. Among other things we will find that a firm's borrowing policy affects its stock's beta. It would be misleading, for example, to average the betas of Dome Petroleum, which is a heavy borrower, and Alberta Energy, which is not.

The company cost of capital is the correct discount rate for projects that have the same risk as the company's existing business, but *not* for those that are safer or riskier than the company's average. The problem is to judge the relative risks of the projects available to the firm. To handle that problem, we will need to dig a little deeper and look at what features make some investments riskier than others. After you know *why* Bell Canada stock has less market risk than, say, MacMillan Bloedel, you will be in a better position to judge the relative risks of capital investment opportunities.

There is still another complication: project betas can shift over time. Some projects are safer in youth than in old age; others are riskier. In this case, what do we mean by *the* project beta? There may be a separate beta for each year of the project's life. To put it another way, can we jump from the capital asset pricing model, which looks out one period into the future, to the discounted-cash-flow formula that we developed in Chapters 2 to 6 for valuing long-lived assets? Most of the time it is safe to do so, but you should be able to recognize and deal with exceptions.

As you have no doubt guessed, capital asset pricing theory supplies no mechanical formula for measuring and adjusting for risk in capital budgeting. These tasks of financial management will be among the last to be automated. The best a financial manager can do is to combine an understanding of the theory with good judgement and a good nose for hidden clues. Therefore don't be discouraged if we dwell on the problems of using the theory. Do you want to be a dilettante who is interested solely in the theory, or a professional who looks to theory for help but not always a final answer? If it's the latter, then press on.

9-1 MEASURING BETAS

Suppose you were considering an across-the-board expansion by your firm. Such an investment would have about the same degree of risk as the existing business. Therefore you should discount the projected flows at the company cost of capital. To estimate that, you could begin by estimating the beta of the company's stock.

An obvious way to measure the beta of a stock is to look at how its price has responded in the past to market movements. For example, in Figures 9-2(a) and 9-2(b) we have plotted monthly rates of return from Bell and MacMillan Bloedel against market returns for the same months. In each case we have fitted a line through the points. Beta is the slope of the line. It varied from one period to the other, but there is little doubt that MacMillan Bloedel's beta was greater than Bell's. If you had used the past beta of either stock to predict its future beta, you would, in most cases, not have been too far off.

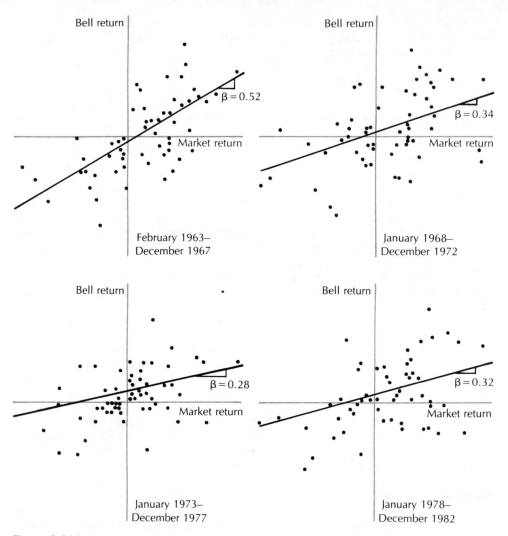

Bell return

β=0.52

Market return

February 1963–
December 1967

Bell return

β=0.34

Market return

January 1968–
December 1972

Bell return

β=0.28

Market return

January 1973–
December 1977

Bell return

β=0.32

Market return

January 1978–
December 1982

Figure 9-2(a)   We can use data on past prices to obtain an estimate of Bell Canada's beta. Notice that it is consistently less than one.

Stability of Betas over Time

Of course, evidence from two (carefully selected) stocks is not worth much, but betas appear to be reasonably stable. An extensive study of stability was provided by Sharpe and Cooper.[4] They divided stocks into ten classes according to the estimated beta in that period. Each class contained one-tenth of the stocks in the sample. The stocks with the lowest betas went into class 1. Class 2 contained stocks with slightly higher betas, and so on. They then looked at the frequency with which stocks jumped from one class to another. The more jumps, the less stability. You can see from Table 9-1 that there is a marked tendency for stocks with very high or very low betas to stay that way. If you are willing to stretch the definition of *stable* to include a jump to an adjacent

[4]W.F. Sharpe, and G.M. Cooper, "Risk-Return Classes of New York Stock Exchange Common Stocks, 1931–1967," *Financial Analysts Journal*, **28**:46–54, 81 (March–April 1972).

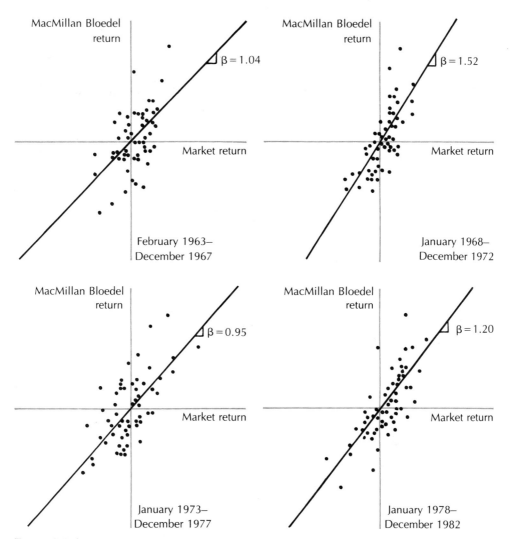

Figure 9-2(*b*) Here is a similar exercise for MacMillan Bloedel. Notice that its estimated beta is consistently greater than Bell's.

risk class, then from 40% to 70% of the betas were stable over the subsequent five years.

One reason these estimates of beta are only imperfect guides to the future is that the stocks may genuinely change their market risk. However, a more important reason is that the betas in any one period are just estimates based on a limited number of observations. If good company news coincides by chance with high market returns, the stock's beta will appear higher than if the news coincides with low market returns. We can twist this the other way around. If a stock appears to have a high beta, it may be because it genuinely does have a high beta, or it may be because we have overestimated it.

This explains some of the fluctuation in betas observed by Sharpe and Cooper. Suppose a company's true beta really is stable. Its apparent (estimated) beta will fluctuate from period to period due to random measurement errors. So the stability of true betas is probably better than Sharpe and Cooper's results seem to imply.

Table 9-2 A page from Merrill Lynch's "beta book."

M L P F & S , I N C . - - - M A R K E T   S E N S I T I V I T Y   S T A T I S T I C S

TKR SYMB	SECURITY NAME	09/82 CLOSE PRICE	BETA	ALPHA	R-SQR	RESID STD DEV-N	---STD.ERR.--- OF BETA	OF ALPHA	ADJUSTED BETA	NUMBER OF OBSERV
DJW	DESIGNCRAFT JEWEL INDS INC	4.375	2.23	2.60	.24	17.24	.50	2.24	1.82	60
DSO	DESOTO INC	17.750	.86	-.11	.20	7.39	.22	.96	.91	60
DESP	DESPATCH INDS INC	10.000	.40	.59	.13	5.02	.13	.65	.60	60
DCI1	DETREX CHEM IND	32.500	1.35	1.34	.34	8.25	.24	1.07	1.23	60
DTL'	DETROIT & CDA TUNL CORP	10.750	.07	-.28	.01	3.82	.11	.50	.38	60
DTE	DETROIT EDISON CO	12.000	.46	-.63	.13	5.04	.15	.65	.64	60
DTE1	DETROIT EDISON CO PFD CONV	64.500	.37	-.17	.08	5.01	.15	.65	.58	60
DVP	DEVELOPMENT CORP AMER	13.500	1.96	2.41	.35	11.66	.34	1.51	1.64	60
GEV	DEVON GROUP INC	24.813	.86	2.74	.05	14.85	.43	1.93	.90	60
DNY	DEWEY ELECTRS CORP	4.750	.15	3.95	.02	16.82	.49	2.18	.44	60
DEX	DEXTER CORP	28.375	1.02	.65	.29	6.96	.20	.90	1.01	60
DIA9	DI AN CTLS INC	2.000	1.42	2.20	.07	20.60	.63	2.66	1.28	60
DIG	DI GIORGIO CORP	9.500	.82	.20	.14	8.55	.25	1.11	.88	60
DIG9	DI GIORGIO CORP PFD CONV	15.750	1.04	.02	.21	8.74	.26	1.13	1.03	60
DINO	DIAGNOSTIC CORP	4.750	.60	2.29	.01	25.21	.89	3.72	.73	46
DNH	DIAGNOSTIC DATA INC	3.500	2.24	-.45	.25	16.27	.50	2.11	1.82	60
DFC	DIAL CORP	.000	.58	2.63	.02	12.84	.38	1.67	.72	60
DMD	DIAMOND CRYSTAL SALT CO	24.750	.87	.78	.15	8.71	.25	1.13	.92	60
DN	DIAMOND INTL CORP	41.500	.98	.31	.22	7.99	.23	1.04	.98	60
DIA	DIAMOND SHAMROCK CORP	19.125	1.63	-1.07	.58	6.16	.18	.80	1.42	60
DBRL	DIBRELL BROS INC	17.500	.48	1.26	.07	7.10	.21	.92	.65	60
DBD	DIEBOLD INC	54.500	.86	3.35	.16	8.31	.24	1.08	.90	60
DIGI	DIGICON INC	9.500	2.16	2.88	.22	17.43	.51	2.26	1.77	60
DILO	DIGILOG INC	10.000	.42	3.58	.01	18.09	.53	2.35	.62	60
DEC	DIGITAL EQUIP CORP	78.875	1.38	.51	.57	5.30	.16	.69	1.25	60
DDS	DILLARD DEPT STORES CL A	39.875	1.10	2.07	.01	8.48	.25	1.10	.40	60
DHM	DILLINGHAM CORP	13.500	1.08	1.88	.08	14.89	.44	1.93	1.06	60
DHM1	DILLINGHAM CORP	13.000	.52	1.56	.05	9.00	.26	1.17	.68	60
DLL	DILLON COS INC	25.375	.52	.65	.08	7.05	.21	.92	.68	60
DINB	DINNER BELL FOODS INC	8.500	.52	.09	.05	9.05	.26	1.18	.68	60

BASED ON S&P 500 INDEX, USING STRAIGHT REGRESSION   PAGE 38

Source: Merrill Lynch, Pierce, Fenner and Smith, Inc., "Security Risk Evaluation," September 1982.

Table 9-1	Sharpe and Cooper divided stocks into risk classes according to their betas in one five-year period (class 10 contains high betas, class 1 contains low betas). They then looked at how many of these stocks were in the same risk class five years later.

Risk Class	% in Same Risk Class Five Years Later	% Within One Risk Class Five Years Later
10	35	69
9	18	54
8	16	45
7	13	41
6	14	39
5	14	42
4	13	40
3	16	45
2	21	61
1	40	62

Using a Beta Book

Because of the investment community's interest in market risk, beta estimates of varying quality are regularly published by a number of brokerage and advisory services. Table 9-2 shows an extract from one of the better known American services. Look more closely at Digital Equipment Corporation (DEC), one of the stocks in Table 9-2. Merrill Lynch recorded the change in the price of DEC stock and in the level of the market (represented by Standard and Poor's Composite Index) in each month during a five-year period. That made 60 monthly observations. DEC's beta of 1.38 was estimated by "straight" regression; that is, by using a standard least squares regression program to find the line of "best fit."[5]

The other information in Table 9-2 is also interesting.

Alpha   Figure 9-3 shows the line Merrill Lynch's regression program fitted to the plot of price changes on DEC and the market. Beta is then the slope of the line and alpha (α) is the intercept. DEC's alpha was 0.51.

Alpha is a rate of price appreciation. Its units are percent per period (in this case percent per month, since the line was fitted to monthly data). The alpha of 0.51 is approximately equal to 12 × 0.51 or 6% per year. From Figure 9-3 we see that alpha was the average rate of price appreciation earned by DEC stockholders when investors in the market as a whole earned nothing. Investors in some of the other stocks listed in Table 9-2 were not so lucky. What about the future? Will DEC continue to offer such high rates of appreciation? Possibly, but you should not bet on it. The most likely outcome is that the return (price appreciation plus dividend yield) will simply compensate for the market risk.

---

[5]Although it is easy in principle to find a line of best fit, there are some tricks to finding the best time span over which to measure returns, to dealing with stocks that only trade infrequently, and so on. The infrequent trading problem is particularly important in Canada, and is discussed in Section 9-2. Some "beta services" are much more careful than others. In particular, past experience suggests approaching Canadian beta services with caution. For example, some lists show almost all betas to be less than 1.0, even though the average or market beta must be 1.0. This may be be due to missing or "misaligned" data (that is, stock returns are from a different month than the corresponding market index returns).

Perhaps this book will help to stimulate sufficient demand for "beta books" that they will become more available in Canada. Until then, you may find it better to calculate your own betas. Fortunately, the raw data are readily available in, for example, the *Toronto Stock Exchange Review*.

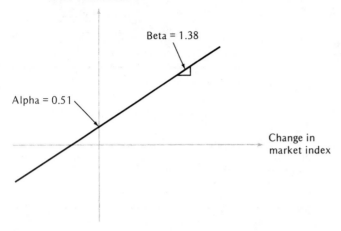

Figure 9-3   Results of regressing DEC's price changes on the market changes for 60 months ending in September 1982. The slope of the fitted line is beta. The intercept is alpha.

R-Squared and Residual Standard Deviation   The column headed *R-SQR* shows the proportion of the total variance of DEC stock price changes that can be explained by market movements. That is, 57% of its risk is market risk, and 43% is unique risk.

The next column is the amount of unique or diversifiable risk, measured as a standard deviation: 5.30% per month for DEC, equivalent to 18% per year. This is the standard deviation of the unique price change, that part of the actual change that was not explained by the change in the market index.[6]

Standard Errors of Alpha and Beta   Merrill Lynch's betas are simply *estimates* based on 60 particular months. Therefore, we would like to have an idea of the extent of possible error in these estimates. The column labeled *STD. ERR. OF BETA* provides this information. Statisticians set up a *confidence interval* of the estimated value plus or minus two standard errors. Thus the confidence interval for DEC's beta is between 1.38 plus or minus (2 × 0.16). If you state that the *true* beta for DEC was between 1.06 and 1.70, you have a 95% chance of being right.

Similarly, the standard error of alpha tells us to be cautious about inferring anything as to DEC's "true" or "normal" alpha.[7] All we can say is that DEC stockholders did very well in this particular period.

Adjusted Beta   Merrill Lynch uses an adjustment formula that gives better predictions than the unadjusted figures listed under *BETA*. The formula pushes high betas down toward 1.0 and low betas up toward 1.0. DEC's adjusted beta is 1.25.

Adjusted betas are tricky to work with, and the Bayesian statistics needed to understand them are beyond the scope of this book. Thus we will stick to "raw" betas.

---

[6]From these two columns we can figure out the *total* risk of DEC stock. The unique variance is the square of the unique standard deviation: $(5.30)^2 = 28.1$ per month. We know this amounts to 43% of the total variance, and so total variance must be 28.1/0.43, or 65.3 per month. The total variance per *year* is therefore $65.3 \times 12 = 784$ and the standard deviation per year is $\sqrt{784} = 28.0\%$.

[7]Therefore, the fact that DEC's alpha is well above any number that would be predicted by the capital asset pricing model is not evidence against the model. A fair test must examine the performance of many stocks over a long time period.

Industry Betas and the Divisional Cost of Capital

That concludes our lesson on how to estimate and predict betas for individual stocks. You should now understand the basic idea of how to estimate a stock's beta by fitting a line to past data, and you should be able to read and understand a publication like Merrill Lynch's "beta book." Bear in mind that such estimates should enable you to pick up major differences in market risk, but they do not allow you to draw fine distinctions. The reason is that you are exposed to potentially large estimation errors when you estimate betas of individual stocks from a limited sample of data. Fortunately these errors tend to cancel out when you estimate betas of *portfolios*. Suppose that you were to compute the average of the betas of 100 common stocks. The standard error of the average would be about one-tenth of the average standard error of the 100 individual betas.[8] That is why it is often easier to estimate *industry betas* than betas for individual firms.

If DEC is contemplating an across-the-board expansion, it would be reasonable to discount the cash flows at the company cost of capital. To estimate this company cost of capital, DEC could use its stock beta or, better still, the average beta of several similar minicomputer manufacturers.[9] Suppose, however, that DEC proposed instead to invest in the production of computer-controlled machine tools. The company cost of capital is not likely to be the right discount rate for its new machine tool division. For such a venture the company needs an estimate of the division's cost of capital. This is where the notion of an industry beta comes into its own. Probably the best way to

Table 9-3   Industry betas.

Industry	Beta
Electronic components	1.49
Crude petroleum and natural gas	1.07
Retail department stores	0.95
Petroleum refining	0.95
Motor vehicle parts	0.89
Chemicals	0.88
Metal mining	0.87
Food	0.84
Trucking	0.83
Textile mill products	0.82
Paper and allied products	0.82
Retail grocery stores	0.76
Airlines	0.75
Steel	0.66
Railroads	0.61
Natural gas transmission	0.52
Telephone companies	0.50
Electric utilities	0.46

Note: These are *asset* betas. The effect of financial leverage on beta has been removed.

Source: U.S. Federal Energy Regulatory Commission, Testimony of Gerald A. Pogue, Williams Pipe Line Co., Docket Nos. OR79-1, et al., p. 74.

---

[8] If the observations are independent, the standard error of the estimated mean declines in proportion to the square root of the number of observations.

[9] But we would have to adjust the observed betas for differences in the debt policies of the firms. This is explained in Section 9-3.

estimate the discount rate for such an expansion is to use the beta of a portfolio of firms in the machine tool industry.

Thus we can think of *divisional* costs of capital as a way station between company and project costs of capital. Company costs of capital are nearly useless for diversified firms. If DEC's machine tool venture becomes at all significant, DEC's beta will not measure the risk of *either* the machine tool *or* the minicomputer businesses. It will just measure the average risk of the two divisions. A company cost of capital based on DEC's beta will almost inevitably be too high for one division and too low for another.

In Table 9-3 we set out some estimates of industry betas. They range from a high of 1.49 for electronic components to a low of 0.46 for electric utilities. You can see why diversified companies should set different discount rates for their different activities.

9-2 INFREQUENT TRADING AND BETA ESTIMATION

A problem occurs when we estimate the betas of infrequently or thinly traded stock. We say a stock is infrequently traded if there are so few investors interested in buying or selling the stock that long time intervals may pass between trades on the stock exchange. This is more of a problem when rates of return are calculated over short time periods. Widely followed stocks, like Dome Petroleum and Canadian Pacific, have many trades in any given day, so infrequent trading is not a problem with these stocks when rates of return are calculated over time periods of one day or longer. However, many stocks in Canada and the United States do not trade every day, and this causes a serious problem even if we estimate betas from monthly rates of return.

Fowler, Rorke, and Jog[10] examined the 634 securities listed continuously on the Toronto Stock Exchange from 1970 to 1979, and found that only 38, or 6% of them, had a trade on the last day of every month, a further 328, or 51.7% of them, traded every month, but not always on the last day, and 268, or 42.3% of them, failed to have any trade during some months of the study.

To see how this can affect beta estimates, suppose you use monthly rates of return on the stock and the securities in the market index to estimate beta. *Information* about these securities that is important to investors arrives on a regular basis, and this causes their prices to rise and fall when they are traded. (In Figure 8-1 we saw that the price of Canadian Pacific stock changes on most days, so that, for practical purposes, information about CP and many other firms arrives in the market continuously.)

The problem occurs when there are no stock trades recorded to reflect the impact of the most up-to-date information on the stock. This is illustrated in Figure 9-4. Suppose the last trade for the stock in May occurs on May 20 and the last trade in June occurs on June 15, because the stock is infrequently traded. These trades give the prices upon which the rate of return for June is calculated. This rate of return will be based partly on information that arrives in May and will ignore some information that arrives in June. For simplicity, let us assume all the stocks in the market index trade on May 31 and June 30, so the index rate of return for June is based precisely on all the information that arrives in June.

When we regress monthly stock returns on market index returns to measure betas we are trying to measure the extent to which the information about market index securities that arrives in June (for example) also affects the stock value. That is, we want to relate June information about the market index to June information about the stock. But the rates of return we use for the stock will miss some of the June stock information and substitute May stock information in its place. As a result, the regression

---

[10]See D.J. Fowler, C.H. Rorke, and V.M. Jog, "Thin Trading and Beta Estimation Problems on the Toronto Stock Exchange," *Journal of Business Administration*, **12**:77–90 (Fall 1980).

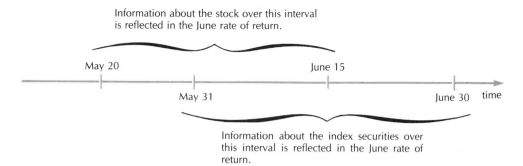

Information about the stock over this interval is reflected in the June rate of return.

May 20

May 31

June 15

June 30   time

Information about the index securities over this interval is reflected in the June rate of return.

Figure 9-4   Infrequent trading of a stock causes its return to be calculated over a different time interval than the return for the market index.

understates the strength of the joint relationship between the stock and the index. That is, *the use of standard regression techniques results in underestimation of the betas of infrequently traded stocks.*[11] This problem is often called a *Fisher effect*, after Lawrence Fisher, of the University of Chicago, who first called attention to it.

*Can We Improve Canadian Beta Estimates?

Several statistical techniques have been proposed to reduce or eliminate the "bias" or tendency to underestimate the betas of infrequently traded stocks. The techniques fall into two basic categories.

The first category includes techniques proposed by Scholes and Williams, by Dimson, and by Fowler, Rorke, and Jog.[12] The basic idea is to measure the covariances of the stock return with the contemporary index return as well as with the index returns before and after the stock return since the information involved in the reported stock return is associated with the information in the index returns in the months before (if the stock is subject to infrequent trading) and also the index returns in the months after (if the index is subject to infrequent trading). These covariances are all combined in an appropriate way to get an improved estimate of beta.

The advantage of these techniques is that they tend to eliminate all of the bias in the estimate of beta that results from infrequent trading. The problem is that they introduce a lot of new statistical "noise," or random variability, in the estimate of beta, so that the standard error of the estimates tends to be high. The extra noise arises because three noisy covariance estimates are used rather than one, as in the standard regression approach.

Fowler, Rorke, and Jog studied the question of which of the two evils (*bias* and *noise*) is worse by examining the (mean squared) estimation errors of all the techniques in this first category. They conclude that:

It is quite clear from the results presented that for most circumstances OLS [that is, standard regression technique] provides the best overall estimates. Only for some

---

[11]In the extreme case of a stock that never trades, its reported rate of return will always be zero, which appears to be riskless. The measured beta of such a stock will be zero.

[12]See M. Scholes and J. Williams, "Estimating Betas from Nonsynchronous Data," *Journal of Financial Economics*, 5:309–327 (December 1977), E. Dimson, "Risk Measurement when Shares are Subject to Infrequent Trading," *Journal of Financial Economics*, 7:197–226 (June 1979), and Fowler, Rorke, and Jog, op. cit.

extreme cases does the SW [Scholes-Williams] technique yield better estimates and its use in normal circumstances is unnecessary.[13]

In fact, an examination of their results indicates that in the cases where the complicated Scholes-Williams technique is better, the standard (OLS) regression approach is not far behind. Moreover, if you use the standard regression approach you know the direction of your potential error (underestimate), but with the Scholes-Williams approach the direction is random.

The second category of techniques to remove the bias towards underestimation of the betas of infrequently traded stocks involves estimating the bias of the standard (OLS) regression and then multiplying the estimated beta by a factor to eliminate the bias. This was proposed by Fowler, Rorke, and Jog.[14] The only problems with their technique are that it is computationally cumbersome and that it requires a lot of data. The data that are needed are the probabilities of the last trade of the month for a given stock occurring on the various days of the month. That is, they need to know the amount of overlap of the intervals over which stock return and the index return are calculated, as illustrated in Figure 9-4.

9-3   HOW TO ESTIMATE PHILADELPHIA ELECTRIC'S COST OF CAPITAL—AN EXAMPLE

In Chapter 4 we showed you how to use the constant-growth DCF formula to estimate market capitalization rates for common stocks.[15] That is essentially the same problem we are discussing here: the market capitalization rate for DEC's stock is also its company cost of capital. The constant-growth formula and the capital asset pricing model are two different ways of getting a handle on the same problem.[16]

Remember that we faced many of the same difficulties there as we do here. In particular, the constant-growth DCF formula is less reliable for an individual firm than for a sample of comparable-risk firms. We therefore suggested that the financial analyst might "take a large sample of equivalent risk securities, measure r for each, and average." We gave an example in which the constant-growth DCF formula was applied to a sample of large electric utilities.

Table 9-4 shows estimates of beta and the standard errors of these estimates for the common stocks of each of the utilities.[17] Most of the standard errors are less than that of DEC, but they are still large enough to preclude a precise estimate of any particular utility's beta (look at the standard error for Pennsylvania Power & Light). But our confidence about the beta of a portfolio of the utilities is much better: its standard error is only about 0.03.

Are these utility stocks really equivalent-risk securities? Judging from Table 9-4 that appears to be a reasonable assumption. Much of the spread of estimated betas could be attributed to random measurement errors. It would be hard to reject the hypothesis

---

[13]Fowler, Rorke, and Jog, op. cit., p. 88.

[14]See D.J. Fowler, C.H. Rorke, and V.M. Jog, "A Bias Correcting Procedure for Beta Estimation in the Presence of Thin Trading," Administrative Sciences Association of Canada, *Proceedings of 1981 Conference*, Halifax, 95–105.

[15]See Section 4-3.

[16]In Chapter 4 we pointed out that the constant-growth formula will not give you very good estimates of the required rate of return for stocks with rapid or unstable growth. But in other cases, the constant-growth formula could give you a useful check on the estimate of r that you get from the capital asset pricing formula.

[17]We were unable to obtain the data necessary to compute a beta for Teco Energy.

Table 9-4   Betas for Moody's 24 electric utilities, 1978–1982.

Firm	Beta	Standard Error
Baltimore Gas & Electric	0.41	0.16
Boston Edison	0.30	0.14
Carolina Power & Light	0.31	0.17
Central Hudson Gas & Electric	0.33	0.14
Central Main Power	0.40	0.15
Cincinnati Gas & Electric	0.40	0.17
Cleveland Electric	0.43	0.17
Commonwealth Edison	0.45	0.14
Consolidated Edison	0.32	0.15
Dayton Power & Light	0.35	0.14
Delmarva Power & Light	0.33	0.16
Detroit Edison	0.46	0.15
Florida Progress	0.35	0.12
Houston Industries	0.50	0.15
Idaho Power	0.35	0.12
Indianapolis Power & Light	0.47	0.15
Northeast Utilities	0.33	0.13
Pacific Gas & Electric	0.20	0.13
Pennsylvania Power & Light	0.45	0.20
Philadelphia Electric	0.36	0.14
Public Service Corporation of Colorado	0.61	0.15
Southern California Edison	0.45	0.12
Teco Energy	—	—
Utah Power & Light	0.39	0.13
Portfolio beta:	0.39	0.03

Source: Merrill Lynch, Pierce, Fenner and Smith, Inc., "Security Risk Evaluation," October 1982. The portfolio was constructed by assuming equal investment in each of the companies.

that the "true" beta was the same for each of the firms. It seems that the authors of the study quoted in Chapter 4 were not off-base in working with this sample for their DCF analysis.

Let us consider how a financial manager at, say, Philadelphia Electric might have used the information in Table 9-4 to figure out the firm's cost of capital. There are two clues to the true beta of this stock; the direct estimate of 0.36 and the average estimate for the industry of 0.39. Fortunately, these two pieces of evidence are in broad agreement, so let us suppose for the moment that our financial manager takes the easy way out and elects to use the figure of 0.36. At the end of 1982 the American risk-free rate of interest r_f was 7.8%. Therefore if the financial manager had accepted our estimate of 8.3% for the risk premium on the market, the conclusion would be that the expected rate of return on Philadelphia Electric stock was 10.8%:

$$r = r_f + \beta(r_m - r_f)$$
$$= 0.078 + 0.36(0.083) = 0.108, \text{ or } 10.8\%$$

Is that the company cost of capital? Unfortunately not. There is one more step.

The cost of capital is a hurdle rate for capital-budgeting decisions. It depends on the *business risk* of the firm's investment opportunities. The risk of a common stock reflects the business risk of the real assets held by the firm. But shareholders also bear *financial risk* to the extent that the firm issues debt to finance its real investments. The more a firm relies on debt financing, the riskier its common stock is.

We did not have to worry about this in DEC's case, because DEC had no debt. But electric utilities use a great deal: their outstanding debt is typically worth more than their outstanding equity.

The act of borrowing is said to create *financial leverage* or *gearing*. Financial leverage pushes the firm's common stock or *equity beta* above its *asset beta*. Which beta should we use?

Asset Betas and Equity Betas

Think again of what the *company* cost of capital is and what it is used for. We *define* it as the opportunity cost of capital for the firm's existing assets; we *use* it to value new assets that have the same risk as the old ones. The right beta for calculating the company cost of capital is the beta of the firm's existing assets, its *asset beta*.

Think of a simple balance sheet with assets on the left and debt and equity on the right.

Asset value	Debt value	(D)
	Equity value	(E)
Asset value	Firm value	(V)

Note that the values of debt and equity add up to firm value ($D + E = V$), and that firm value equals asset value.

Stockholders own the firm's equity but they can't claim all of the asset value; they have to share it with debtholders. The debtholders receive part of the cash flows generated by the firm's assets, and they may bear part of the asset's risks. (For example, if the assets turn out to be worthless, there will be no cash to pay stockholders *or* debtholders.) But debtholders of big firms such as Philadelphia Electric bear much less risk than stockholders. Debt betas are typically close to zero—close enough that for large blue-chip companies many financial analysts just assume $\beta_{debt} = 0$. But we want the asset beta, β_{asset}. How do we get it?

Suppose you buy *all* the firm's securities—100% of the debt and 100% of the equity. You would own the assets lock, stock, and barrel. You wouldn't have to share the firm's asset value with anyone; every dollar of cash the firm pays out would be paid out to you. You wouldn't share the risks with anyone else, either; you bear them all. Thus the beta of your debt plus equity portfolio would equal the firm's asset beta.

The beta of this hypothetical portfolio is just a weighted average of the debt and equity betas.[18]

$$\beta_{asset} = \beta_{portfolio} = \beta_{debt}\frac{debt}{debt + equity} + \beta_{equity}\frac{equity}{debt + equity}$$

Calculating Philadelphia Electric's Asset Beta and Company Cost of Capital

Now that we know how to derive the beta of a firm's assets from the beta of its stock, we can return to the problem of figuring out Philadelphia Electric's company cost of

---

[18]Here we ignore certain tax complications. If debt interest generates valuable tax savings, then the formula for β_{asset} changes somewhat.

capital. We have already estimated its common stock beta at 0.36. In 1982 common stock accounted for about 35% of the market value of Philadelphia Electric's securities. The remaining 65% consisted of debt and preferred stock. To keep matters simple we will just lump the preferred stock in with the debt and assume both are risk-free.[19] This gives us the following estimates for the beta of Philadelphia Electric assets:

$$\beta_{asset} = \beta_{debt}\frac{debt}{debt + equity} + \beta_{equity}\frac{equity}{debt + equity}$$

$$= 0(0.65) + 0.36(0.35) = 0.13$$

Of course this is a very low number. The reason it is so low is that Philadelphia Electric's stock beta is low (only 0.36) despite its heavy use of debt and correspondingly high financial risk. When the financial risk is removed, we find the remaining business risk to be small.

With a risk-free rate of 7.8% and an expected market risk premium of 8.3% Philadelphia Electric's cost of capital is

$$r = r_f + \beta_{asset}(r_m - r_f)$$

$$= 0.078 + 0.13(0.083) = 0.089, \text{ or } 8.9\%$$

This estimate is probably low, because we arbitrarily assumed Philadelphia Electric's debt was totally risk-free. If we had used $\beta_{debt} = 0.15$,

$$\beta_{asset} = \beta_{debt}\frac{debt}{debt + equity} + \beta_{equity}\frac{equity}{debt + equity}$$

$$= 0.15(0.65) + 0.36(0.35)$$

$$= 0.22$$

$$r = r_f + \beta_{asset}(r_m - r_f)$$

$$= 0.078 + 0.22(0.083) = 0.097, \text{ or } 9.7\%$$

Business and Financial Risk

A firm's asset beta reflects its *business risk*. The *difference* between its equity and asset beta reflects *financial risk*. More debt means more financial risk.

What would happen if Philadephia Electric decided to use more debt and correspondingly less equity? It would not affect the firm's *business* risk. There would be no change in the firm's asset beta, and no change in the beta of a portfolio of *all* the firm's debt and equity security. The *equity* beta would change, however.

Let's go back to our formula for β_{asset},

$$\beta_{asset} = \beta_{debt}\frac{debt}{debt + equity} + \beta_{equity}\frac{equity}{debt + equity}$$

---

[19]We will discuss preferred stock in Chapter 14. For now all you need to know is that it is less risky than common stock but more risky than debt.

and solve the formula for β_{equity}:

$$\beta_{equity} = \beta_{asset} + (\beta_{asset} - \beta_{debt})\frac{debt}{equity}$$

If we assume Philadelphia Electric's debt is risk-free, we have

$$\beta_{equity} = 0.13 + (0.13 - 0)\frac{0.65}{0.35} = 0.36$$

But if the company switched to 75% debt, β_{equity} would go up to 0.52. We would expect to find this number in a future edition of Merrill Lynch's beta book. On the other hand, if Philadelphia Electric paid off all its debt, we would expect to find:

$$\beta_{equity} = \beta_{asset} + (\beta_{asset} - \beta_{debt})\frac{D}{E}$$

$$= 0.13 + (0.13 - 0)\frac{0}{1.0}$$

$$= 0.13$$

With no debt, the firm's asset and equity betas would be exactly the same.

In general, the observed equity beta depends on the firm's asset beta, β_{asset}, the spread between the asset and debt betas, $\beta_{asset} - \beta_{debt}$, and the ratio of debt to equity. Figure 9-5 plots the relationship assuming risk-free debt ($\beta_{debt} = 0$).

In many ways we have given an oversimplified version of how financial leverage affects equity risks and returns. We have said nothing about taxes, for example. The

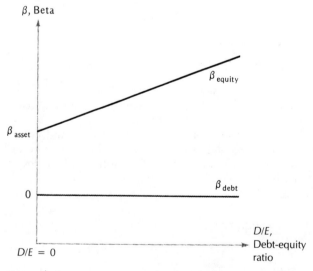

Figure 9-5   Effect of financial leverage on β_{equity}, the beta of the firm's common stock. The higher the debt-equity ratio, the higher β_{equity}. When the firm uses no debt ($D/E = 0$), $\beta_{equity} = \beta_{asset}$; β_{asset} measures the business risk of the firm's assets. Note that this figure is drawn assuming risk-free debt ($\beta_{debt} = 0$).

finer points can wait. For now, there are really just two points to remember. First, *financial leverage creates financial risk*. The beta of the firm's stock increases in proportion to the amount borrowed. Second, *asset betas can always be calculated as a weighted average of the betas of the various debt and equity securities issued by the firm*. Of course, it is the asset beta that is relevant in capital-budgeting decisions, not the beta of the firm's stock.[20]

9-4 WHAT DETERMINES ASSET BETAS?

Stock or industry betas provide a rough guide to the risk typically encountered in various lines of business. But an asset beta for, say, the steel industry can take us only so far. Not all investments made in the steel industry are "typical." What other kinds of evidence about business risk might a financial manager examine?

In some cases the asset is publicly traded. If so, we can simply estimate its beta from past price data. For example, suppose a firm wants to analyze the risks of holding a large inventory of copper. Because copper is a standardized, widely traded commodity, it is possible to calculate rates of return from holding copper and to calculate a copper beta.[21]

What should we do if our asset has no such convenient price record? Our advice is to search for characteristics of the asset that are associated with high or low betas. We wish we had a fundamental scientific understanding of what these characteristics are. We see business risks surfacing in capital markets, but as yet there is no completely satisfactory theory describing how those risks are generated. Nevertheless, some things are known.

Cyclicality

Many people intuitively associate risk with the variability of book or accounting earnings. But much of this variability reflects diversifiable or unique risk. Lone prospectors in search of gold look forward to extremely uncertain future earnings, but whether they strike it rich is unlikely to depend on the performance of the market portfolio. Even if they do find gold, they do not bear much market risk. Therefore, an investment in gold has a high standard deviation but a relatively low beta.

What really counts is the strength of the relationship between the firm's earnings and the aggregate earnings on all real assets. We can measure this either by the *accounting beta* or by the *cash-flow beta*. These are just like a real beta except that changes in book earnings or cash flow are used in place of rates of return on securities. We would predict that firms with high accounting or cash-flow betas should also have high stock betas— and the prediction is correct.[22]

This means that cyclical firms—firms whose revenues and earnings are strongly dependent on the state of the business cycle—tend to be high-beta firms. Thus you should demand a higher rate of return from investments whose performance is strongly tied to the performance of the economy.

---

[20]Incidentally, financial risk has been removed from the figures shown in Table 9-3; they are estimated industry asset betas.

[21]Because trading in copper is less active than in the stock market, you may encounter the "Fisher effect" discussed in Section 9-2. Your estimate of beta will likely be lower than the true beta.

[22]For example, see W.H. Beaver and J. Manegold, "The Association Between Market-Determined and Accounting-Determined Measures of Systematic Risk: Some Further Evidence," *Journal of Financial and Quantitative Analysis*, **10**:231–284 (June 1975).

*Operating Leverage

We have already seen that financial leverage—in other words, the commitment to fixed debt charges—increases the beta of an investor's portfolio. In just the same way, operating leverage—in other words, the commitment to fixed *production* charges—must add to the beta of a capital project. Let's see how this works.

The cash flows generated by any productive asset can be broken down into revenue, fixed costs, and variable costs

$$\text{Cash flow} = \text{revenue} - \text{fixed cost} - \text{variable cost}$$

Costs are variable if they depend on the rate of output. Examples are raw materials, sales commissions, and some labour and maintenance costs. Fixed costs are cash outflows that occur regardless of whether the asset is active or idle—property taxes, for example, or the wages of workers under contract.

We can break down the asset's present value in the same way:

$$\text{PV(asset)} = \text{PV(revenue)} - \text{PV(fixed cost)} - \text{PV(variable cost)}$$

Or equivalently:

$$\text{PV(revenue)} = \text{PV(fixed cost)} + \text{PV(variable cost)} + \text{PV(asset)}$$

Those who *receive* the fixed costs are like debtholders in the project. Those who receive the net cash flows from the asset are like holders of levered equity in PV(revenue).

We can now figure out how the asset's beta is related to the betas of the values of revenue and costs. We just use our previous formula with the betas relabeled:

$$\beta_{revenue} = \beta_{fixed\ cost} \frac{\text{PV(fixed cost)}}{\text{PV(revenue)}} + \beta_{variable\ cost} \frac{\text{PV(variable cost)}}{\text{PV(revenue)}}$$

$$+ \beta_{asset} \frac{\text{PV(asset)}}{\text{PV(revenue)}}$$

In other words, the beta of the value of the revenues is simply a weighted average of the beta of its component parts. Now the fixed-cost beta is zero by definition: whoever receives the fixed costs holds a safe asset. The betas of the revenues and variable costs should be approximately the same, because they respond to the same underlying variable, the rate of output. Therefore, we can substitute $\beta_{revenue}$ for $\beta_{variable\ cost}$ and solve for the asset beta. Remember that $\beta_{fixed\ cost} = 0$.

$$\beta_{asset} = \beta_{revenue} \frac{\text{PV(revenue)} - \text{PV(variable cost)}}{\text{PV(asset)}}$$

$$= \beta_{revenue} \left[1 + \frac{\text{PV(fixed cost)}}{\text{PV(asset)}} \right]$$

Thus, given the cyclicality of revenues (reflected in $\beta_{revenue}$), asset beta is proportional to the ratio of the present value of fixed costs to the present value of the project.

Now you have a rule of thumb for judging the relative risks of alternative designs or technologies for producing the same product. Other things being equal, the alternative with the higher ratio of fixed costs to project value will have the higher project beta.

Firms or assets whose costs are mostly fixed are said to have high *operating leverage*. As we have seen, the analogy between financial and operating leverage is almost exact. The beta of the stock increases in proportion to the ratio of debt to equity, and the beta of the asset increases in proportion to the ratio of the value of the fixed costs to the value of the asset. Empirical tests confirm that companies with high operating leverage actually do have high betas.[23]

Searching for Clues

Recent research suggests a variety of other factors that affect an asset's beta.[24] But going through a long list of these possible determinants would take us too far afield.

You cannot hope to estimate the relative risk of assets with any precision, but good managers examine any project from a variety of angles and look for clues as to its riskiness. They know that high market risk is a characteristic of cyclical ventures and of projects with high fixed costs. They think about the major uncertainties affecting the economy and consider how projects are affected by these uncertainties.[25]

---

*9-5 ANOTHER LOOK AT DISCOUNTED CASH FLOW

We have spent the bulk of this chapter discussing how you might estimate the risk and required return on a project. We now have to worry a little about what happens as risk changes over the life of a project.

We have implied that an expected rate of return calculated from the capital asset pricing model

$$r = r_f + \beta(r_m - r_f)$$

could be plugged into the standard discounted cash flow formula as

$$PV = \sum_{t=1}^{T} \frac{C_t}{(1 + r)^t} = \sum_{t=1}^{T} \frac{C_t}{[1 + r_f + \beta(r_m - r_f)]^t}$$

You should not take that step without thinking about it first. In capital budgeting we must usually value cash flows extending over several future periods. The discounted cash flow formula does this in one step, but the capital asset pricing model looks at rates of return and prices over one period at a time.

---

[23]See B. Lev. "On the Association between Operating Leverage and Risk," *Journal of Financial and Quantitative Analysis*, 9:627–642 (September 1974).

[24]This work is reviewed in G. Foster, *Financial Statement Analysis*, Prentice-Hall, Inc., Englewood Cliffs, N.J., 1978, Chapter 9.

[25]Sharpe's article on a "multi-beta" interpretation of market risk offers a useful way of thinking about these uncertainties and tracing out their impact on a firm's or project's risk. W.F. Sharpe, "The Capital Asset Pricing Model: A 'Multi-Beta' Interpretation," in H. Levy and M. Sarnat (eds.), *Financial Decision Making Under Uncertainty*, New York, Academic Press, 1977.

One-period projects pose no problems:

$$PV = \frac{C_1}{1 + r} + \frac{C_1}{1 + r_f + \beta(r_m - r_f)}$$

Longer-lived assets likewise pose no problem if you have an estimate of PV_1, future value one period hence

$$PV_0 = \frac{C_1 + PV_1}{1 + r} = \frac{C_1 + PV_1}{1 + r_f + \beta(r_m - r_f)}$$

But suppose that your company is evaluating the construction of a nuclear power station and asks your advice on how to calculate its present value. Would you tell it not to bother about anything other than the cash flow in the first period and the end-of-period value? Of course not. The end-of-period value depends on the cash flow in later periods. You would want a formula that explicitly took this into account.

When this problem arose in Chapter 3 we solved it by expressing PV_1 as $(C_2 + PV_2)/(1 + r)$, and substituting until all future PVs were eliminated and PV_0 was tied only to the asset's cash flow stream. This is formally correct only if we *know* the discount rates that will prevail in future periods will be the same as this year's. Among other things,[26] this requires the asset's beta to be constant over the asset's entire future life. Only under that crucial assumption is it strictly proper to write down the discounted cash flow formula with a single discount rate for all future cash flows.

What does that assumption mean in practical terms? To answer that question we must develop alternative formulas for calculating present value when beta and r *do* vary.

*Certainty Equivalents

Let us start again with a single future cash flow C_1. If C_1 is certain, its present value is found by discounting at the risk-free rate r_f:

$$PV = \frac{C_1}{1 + r_f}$$

If the cash flow is risky, the normal procedure is to discount its forecasted (expected) value at a *risk-adjusted discount rate r*, which is greater than r_f.[27]

Another approach is to ask, "What is the smallest *certain* return for which I would exchange the risky cash flow $\tilde{C}_1$?" This is called the *certainty equivalent of* $\tilde{C}_1$, denoted by CEQ_1.

Suppose that the forecasted value of the risky cash flow is $1,000 but that you would be willing to trade it for a safe cash flow of as little as $800. Then $800 is the certainty equivalent of the risky cash flow. You are indifferent between an $800 *safe* return and an *expected*, but risky, cash flow of $1,000.

---

[26]See E.F. Fama, "Risk-Adjusted Discount Rates and Capital Budgeting under Uncertainty," *Journal of Financial Economics*, 5:3–24 (August 1977); or S.C. Myers and S.M. Turnbull, "Capital Budgeting and the Capital Asset Pricing Model: Good News and Bad News," *Journal of Finance*, 32:321–332 (May 1977).

[27]The quantity r can be less than r_f for assets with negative betas. But the betas of the assets corporations hold are almost always positive.

What is the present value of the $1,000 forecasted cash flow? It must be the same as the present value of a certain $800, because by definition you are indifferent between the two flows. Suppose the risk-free rate of interest is $r_f = 0.08$. Then

$$\text{PV of forecasted \$1,000 cash flow} = \frac{CEQ_1}{1 + r_f} = \frac{800}{1.08} = \$740.74$$

You could have gotten the same answer by discounting $1,000 at a risk-adjusted rate. We can figure out what the proper discount rate is. If

$$PV = \frac{1,000}{1 + r} = \$740.74$$

then $r = 0.35$, or 35%.

Now we have two equivalent expressions for PV.[28]

$$PV = \frac{C_1}{1 + r} = \frac{CEQ_1}{1 + r_f}$$

As long as you look only one period into the future, the two formulas are exactly the same. But there are important differences when the concept of certainty equivalents is applied to cash flows generated by long-lived assets.[29]

*Relationship of the Certainty Equivalent and Risk-Adjusted Discount Rate Formulas for Long-Lived Assets

We can easily extend the concept of certainty equivalents to long-lived assets:

$$PV = \sum_{t=1}^{T} \frac{CEQ_t}{(1 + r_f)^t} = \sum_{t=1}^{T} \frac{a_t C_t}{(1 + r_f)^t}$$

where a_t is the ratio of the certainty equivalent of a cash flow to its expected value $(a_t = CEQ_t/C_t)$. Normally a_t will be positive, but less than 1.0.[30]

When we discount at a constant risk-adjusted rate r, we are implicitly making a special assumption about the coefficients a_t. Consider an asset offering cash flows in

---

[28]CEQ_1 can be calculated directly from the capital asset pricing model. The formula is:

$$CEQ_1 = C_1 - \lambda \, cov \, (\tilde{C}_1, \tilde{r}_m)$$

where cov $(\tilde{C}_1, \tilde{r}_m)$ is the covariance between the dollar cash flow $(\tilde{C}_1)$ and the return on the market portfolio $(\tilde{r}_m)$, and

$$\lambda = \frac{r_m - r_f}{\sigma_m^2}$$

Here $r_m - r_f$ is the expected risk premium on the market portfolio; σ_m^2 is the variance of the market return. The quantity λ is often referred to as the *market price of risk*. In the appendix to this chapter we show you where this formula for CEQ_1 comes from.

[29]The risk-adjusted discount rate formula can always be applied to long-lived assets if a different discount rate is used for each period. But that approach does not help explain the assumption required for use of a constant risk-adjusted rate.

[30]The quantity a_t would be greater than 1.0 for negative-beta assets.

Table 9-5 Example showing certainty equivalents implied by use of constant risk-adjusted discount rate.

Period	Expected Cash Flow $= C_t$	Present Value Using 10% Risk-Adjusted Discount Rate, $PV = C_t/(1.10)^t$	Certainty Equivalent CEQ_t Implied By Use of 10% Discount Rate, $CEQ_t = C_t \left(\dfrac{1+r_f}{1+r}\right)^t$	a_t, Ratio of CEQ_t to C_t	Present Value of CEQs at 4% Risk-Free Rate
0	−350	−350	−350	1.00	−350
1	100	91	95	0.945	91
2	100	83	89	0.894	83
3	100	75	85	0.845	75
4	100	68	80	0.799	68
5	100	62	76	0.755	62
Net present value =		29			29

Note: By using a constant risk-adjusted discount rate of 10% the financial manager is implicitly making larger deductions for risk from the later cash flows. Notice that discounting the cash flows at 10% *or* the certainty equivalents at 4% would give NPV = 29.

two periods. If the certainty equivalent and risk-adjusted discount rate formulas are really equivalent, they should give the same present value for each cash flow:

$$\frac{C_1}{1 + r} = \frac{a_1 C_1}{1 + r_f} \quad \text{and} \quad \frac{C_2}{(1 + r)^2} = \frac{a_2 C_2}{(1 + r_f)^2}$$

But this implies that

$$a_1 = \frac{1 + r_f}{1 + r} \quad \text{and} \quad a_2 = \left(\frac{1 + r_f}{1 + r}\right)^2 = (a_1)^2$$

In general, you are justified in using a constant risk-adjusted discount rate r to value the cash flow for each period only if the value of a_t *decreases* over time at a constant rate. The formula is

$$a_t = \left(\frac{1 + r_f}{1 + r}\right)^t = (a_1)^t$$

*Using Risk-Adjusted Discount Rates—An Example

Consider a project requiring $350 today ($t = 0$) and offering expected cash flows of $100 per year for five years. The risk-free rate is 4%, the market risk premium is 9%, and the estimated beta is 0.67; therefore the financial manager settles on a discount rate of

$$r = r_f + \beta(r_m - r_f)$$
$$= 0.04 + 0.67(0.09) = 0.10, \text{ or } 10\%$$

The project's net present value is calculated as

$$\text{NPV} = \text{PV} - 350 = \sum_{t=1}^{5} \frac{100}{(1.10)^t} - 350 = \$29$$

What is the financial manager implicitly assuming about the values of a_t? The answer is given by Table 9-5. By using a constant discount rate the financial manager is effectively making a much larger deduction for risk from the later cash flows. The larger deduction is reflected in lower values for a_t. Notice also that a_t decreases at a constant compound rate of about 5.5% per year.

It is usually reasonable to assume that risk increases at a constant rate. For example, if you are willing to assume that beta is constant in each future period, then the risk borne *per period* will be constant but cumulative risk will grow steadily as you look further into the future.

*When You *Cannot* Use a Single Risk-Adjusted Discount Rate for Long-Lived Assets

Here is a disguised, simplified, and somewhat exaggerated version of an actual project proposal that one of the authors was asked to analyze. The scientists at Vegetron have come up with an electric mop, and the firm is ready to go ahead with pilot production and test marketing. The preliminary phase will take a year and cost $125,000. Management feels that there is only a 50% chance that pilot production and market tests will be successful. If they are, then Vegetron will build a $1 million plant, which would generate an expected annual cash flow in perpetuity of $250,000 a year after taxes. If they are not successful, the project will have to be dropped.

The expected cash flows (in thousands of dollars) are

$C_0 = -125$

$C_1 = 50\%$ chance of $-1,000$ and 50% chance of 0

$\quad = 0.5(-1,000) + 0.5(0) = -500$

C_t, for $t = 2, 3, \ldots$

$\quad = 50\%$ chance of 250 and 50% chance of 0

$\quad = +0.5(250) + 0.5(0) = 125$

Management has little experience with consumer products and considers this a project of extremely high risk.[31] Therefore, they discount the cash flow at 25%, rather than Vegetron's normal 10% standard:

$$\text{NPV} = -125 - \frac{500}{1.25} + \sum_{t=2}^{\infty} \frac{125}{(1.25)^t} = -125 \text{ or } -\$125,000$$

This seems to show that the project is not worthwhile.

Management's analysis is open to criticism if the first year's experiment resolves a high proportion of the risk. If the test phase is a failure, then there's no risk at all—the project is *certain* to be worthless. If it is a success, there could well be only normal risk from there on. That means there is a 50% chance that in one year Vegetron will have the opportunity to invest in a project of *normal* risk, for which the *normal* discount rate of 10% would be appropriate. Thus they have a 50% chance to invest $1 million in a project with a net present value of $1.5 million:

$$\text{Success} \to \text{NPV} = -1,000 + \frac{250}{0.10} = +1,500 \text{ (50\% chance)}$$

Pilot production and market tests

$$\text{Failure} \to \text{NPV} = 0 \text{ (50\% chance)}$$

Thus, we could view the project as offering an expected payoff of $0.5(1,500) + 0.5(0) = 750$ or $750,000 at $t = 1$ on a $125,000 investment at $t = 0$. Of course, the certainty equivalent of the payoff is less than $750,000 but a_1 would have to be very small to justify rejecting the project. For example, if the CEQ is half the expected value ($a_1 = 0.5$), and the risk-free rate is 7%, the project is worth $225,500:

---

[31] We will assume they mean high *market* risk.

$$NPV = C_0 + \frac{a_1 C_1}{1 + r_f}$$

$$= -125 + \frac{0.5(750)}{1.07} = 225.5, \text{ or } \$225,500$$

Not bad for a $125,000 investment—and quite a change from the negative NPV that management got by discounting all future cash flows at 25%.

*A Common Mistake

You sometimes hear people say that because distant cash flows are "riskier," they should be discounted at a higher rate than earlier cash flows. That's quite wrong: *any* risk-adjusted discount rate automatically recognizes the fact that more distant cash flows have more risk. The reason is that the discount rate compensates for the risk borne *per period*. The more distant the cash flows, the greater the number of periods and the larger the *total* risk adjustment.

9-6 SUMMARY

In Chapter 8 we set out some basic principles for valuing risky assets. In this chapter we have tried to show you how to apply these principles to practical situations.

The problem is easiest when you believe that the project has the same market risk as the company's existing assets. In this case, the required return would be equal to the required return on the company's securities. This is often called the *company's cost of capital*. Capital asset pricing theory states that the required return on any asset depends on its beta:

$$r = r_f + \beta(r_m - r_f)$$

Therefore to figure out the company's cost of capital you need to find the beta of its assets.

A good place to start is with the beta of the company's stock. The most common way to estimate the beta of a stock is to figure out how the stock price has responded to market changes in the past. Of course this will only give you an estimate of the stock's true beta. You may get a more reliable figure if you take an average of the estimated betas for a group of similar companies.

Suppose that you now have an estimate of the stock's beta. Can you plug that into the capital asset pricing formula to find the company cost of capital? No, the stock beta may reflect both business and financial risk. Whenever a company borrows money, it increases the beta (and the expected return) of it stock. Therefore, to calculate the company cost of capital, you must first adjust the beta of the stock to remove the effect of this financial risk.

The company cost of capital is the correct discount rate for projects that have the same risk as the company's existing business. Many firms, however, use the company cost of capital to discount the forecasted cash flows on all new projects. This is a dangerous procedure. It is *project risk* that counts.

We cannot give you a neat formula that will allow you to estimate project betas, but we can give you some clues. For instance, you should try to figure out how far the cash flows are affected by the overall performance of the economy: cyclical investments are generally high-beta investments. Another thing you should look at is the project's operating leverage: fixed production charges work like fixed debt charges; that is, they increase beta.

There is one more fence to jump. The capital asset pricing model values only the cash flow for the first period (C_1). But most projects go on producing cash flows for several years. It would be very convenient if you could use the capital asset pricing model risk-adjusted rate r to discount each of these cash flows:

$$ PV = \sum_{t=1}^{T} \frac{C_t}{(1 + r)^t} = \sum_{t=1}^{T} \frac{C_t}{[1 + r_f + \beta(r_m - r_f)]^t} $$

If you do this, you are implicitly assuming that cumulative risk *increases* at a constant rate as you look further out into the future. That assumption is usually reasonable. The assumption is precisely true when the project's future beta will be constant, that is, when risk *per period* will be constant.

It is the exceptions that prove the rule. You should therefore be on the alert for projects where risk very clearly does *not* increase steadily. In these cases, you should break the project into segments within which the same discount rate can be reasonably used. Or you should use the certainty-equivalent version of the DCF model which allows you to make separate risk adjustments to each period's cash flow.

As we pointed out in Chapter 8, the capital asset pricing model is probably not the ultimate truth about risk and return in capital markets. New, and presumably better theories will emerge as research continues. But the capital asset pricing model is a useful rule of thumb, and a good vehicle for presenting basic concepts. That is why we have devoted this chapter to its application to capital-budgeting problems.

Finally, remember that the most fundamental principle presented in this chapter does not depend on the capital asset pricing model. The principle is:

> Each project should be evaluated at its own opportunity cost of capital; the true cost of capital depends on the use to which the capital is put.

This follows from value additivity. The capital asset pricing model implies value additivity, but value additivity holds as well under other theories of asset valuation.

FURTHER READING

There is a good review article by Rubinstein on the application of the capital-asset pricing model to capital investment decisions:

M.E. Rubinstein, "A Mean-Variance Synthesis of Corporate Financial Theory," *Journal of Finance*, **28**:167–182 (March 1973).

For evidence on the stability of betas estimated from past stock price data, see:

M.E. Blume, "On the Assessment of Risk," *Journal of Finance*, **26**:1–10 (March 1971).
W.F. Sharpe and G.M. Cooper, "Risk-Return Classes of New York Stock Exchange Common Stocks, 1931–1967," *Financial Analysts Journal*, **28**:46–54, 81 (March–April 1972).

There have been a number of studies of the relationship between accounting data and beta. Many of these are reviewed in:

G. Foster, *Financial Statement Analysis*, Prentice-Hall, Inc., Englewood Cliffs, N.J., 1978.

For some ideas on how one might break down the problem of estimating beta, see:

W.F. Sharpe, "The Capital Asset Pricing Model: A 'Multi-Beta' Interpretation," in H. Levy and M. Sarnat (eds.), *Financial Decision Making Under Uncertainty*, New York, Academic Press, 1977.

The assumptions required for use of risk-adjusted discount rates are discussed in:

E.F. Fama, "Risk-Adjusted Discount Rates and Capital Budgeting under Uncertainty," *Journal of Financial Economics*, **5**:3–24 (August 1977).

S.C. Myers and S.M. Turnbull, "Capital Budgeting and the Capital Asset Pricing Model: Good News and Bad News," *Journal of Finance*, **32**:321–332 (May 1977).

The relationship between the certainty equivalent and risk-adjusted discount rate valuation formulas was first discussed by:

A.A. Robichek and S.C. Myers, "Conceptual Problems in the Use of Risk-Adjusted Discount Rates," *Journal of Finance*, **21**:727–730 (December 1966).

APPENDIX 9-1 USING THE CAPITAL ASSET PRICING MODEL TO CALCULATE CERTAINTY EQUIVALENTS

When calculating present value you can take account of risk in either of two ways. You can discount the expected cash flow C_1 by the risk-adjusted discount rate r:

$$PV = \frac{C_1}{1 + r}$$

Alternatively, you can discount the certainty equivalent cash flow CEQ_1 by the risk-free rate of interest r_f:

$$PV = \frac{CEQ_1}{1 + r_f}$$

In this appendix we show how you can derive CEQ_1 from the capital asset pricing model.

We know from our present value formula that $1 + r$ equals the expected dollar payoff on the asset divided by its present value:

$$1 + r = \frac{C_1}{PV}$$

The capital asset pricing model also tells us that $1 + r$ equals

$$1 + r = 1 + r_f + \beta(r_m - r_f)$$

Therefore,

$$\frac{C_1}{PV} = 1 + r_f + \beta(r_m - r_f)$$

To find beta, we calculate the covariance between the asset return and the market return and divide by the market variance:

$$\beta = \frac{\text{cov}\,(\tilde{r}, \tilde{r}_m)}{\sigma_m^2} = \frac{\text{cov}\,[(\tilde{C}_1/PV - 1, \tilde{r}_m)]}{\sigma_m^2}$$

The quantity $\tilde{C}_1$ is the future cash flow and is, therefore, uncertain. But PV is the asset's present value: it is *not* unknown, and therefore, does not "covary" with $\tilde{r}_m$. Therefore, we can rewrite the expression for beta as

$$\beta = \frac{\text{cov}\,(\tilde{C}_1, \tilde{r}_m)}{\text{PV}\,\sigma_m^2}$$

Substituting this expression back into our equation for C_1/PV gives

$$\frac{C_1}{\text{PV}} = 1 + r_f + \frac{\text{cov}\,(\tilde{C}_1, \tilde{r}_m)}{\text{PV}} \times \frac{r_m - r_f}{\sigma_m^2}$$

The expression $(r_m - r_f)/\sigma_m^2$ is the expected risk premium on the market per unit of variance. It is often known as the *market price of risk* and is written as λ (lambda). Thus

$$\frac{C_1}{\text{PV}} = 1 + r_f + \frac{\lambda\,\text{cov}\,(\tilde{C}_1, \tilde{r}_m)}{\text{PV}}$$

Multiplying through by PV and rearranging, gives

$$\text{PV} = \frac{C_1 - \lambda\,\text{cov}\,(\tilde{C}_1, \tilde{r}_m)}{1 + r_f}$$

This is the certainty-equivalent form of the capital-asset pricing model. It tells us that, if the asset is risk-free, cov $(\tilde{C}_1, \tilde{r}_m)$ is zero and we simply discount C_1 by the risk-free rate. But, if the asset is risky, we must discount the certainty equivalent of C_1. The deduction that we make from C_1 depends on the market price of risk and on the covariance between the cash flows on the project and the return on the market.

QUIZ

1. Suppose a firm uses its company cost of capital to evaluate all capital projects. What kinds of mistakes will it make?

2. A project costs $100,000 and offers a single $150,000 cash flow one year hence. The project beta is 2.0 and the market risk premium $(r_m - r_f)$ is 8%. Look up current risk-free interest rates in *The Globe and Mail* or another newspaper. Use the capital asset pricing model to find the opportunity cost of capital and the present value of the project.

3. Look again at Table 9-2 and the row of statistics shown for Diamond Shamrock Corp. Define and interpret each of these statistics.

4. A company is financed 40% by risk-free debt. The interest rate is 10%, the expected market return is 20%, and the stock's beta is 0.5. What is the company cost of capital?

5. The total market value of the common stock of the Okenfenokee Real Estate Company is $6 million, and the total value of its debt is $4 million. The treasurer estimates that the beta of the stock is currently 1.5 and that the expected risk premium on the market is 10%. The Treasury bill rate is 8%.

(a) What is the required return on Okenfenokee stock?

(b) What is the beta of the company's existing portfolio of assets?

(c) Estimate the company's cost of capital.

(d) Estimate the discount rate for an expansion of the company's present business.

(e) Suppose the company wants to diversify into the manufacture of rose-coloured spectacles. The beta of unleveraged optical manufacturers is 1.2. Estimate the required return on Okenfenokee's new venture.

*6. Which of these four companies is likely to have the higher company cost of capital?

(a) A's sales force is paid a fixed annual rate; B's is paid on a commission basis.

(b) B produces machine tools; D produces breakfast cereal.

*7. Select the appropriate phrase from within each pair of brackets: "In calculating PV there are two ways to adjust for risk. One is to make a deduction from the expected cash flows. This is known as *the certainty-equivalent method.* It is usually written as $PV = [CEQ_t/(1 + r_f)^t; CEQ_t/(1 + r_m)^t]$. The certainty-equivalent cash flow, CEQ_t, can be written as $a_t C_t$, where a_t is [greater than one; less than one]. Another way to allow for risk is to discount the expected cash flows at a rate of r. If we use the capital asset pricing model to calculate r, r is $[r_f + \beta r_m; r_f + \beta(r_m - r_f); r_m + \beta(r_m - r_f)]$. This method is *exact* for a one-period project. It is exact for a long-lived project only if the values of a_t [increase at a constant rate; are constant; decrease at a constant rate]. For the majority of projects, the use of a single discount rate, r, is probably a perfectly acceptable approximation."

*8. A project has a forecasted cash flow of $110 in year 1 and $121 in year 2. The interest rate is 5%, the estimated risk premium on the market is 10%, and the project has a beta of 0.5. If you use a constant risk-adjusted discount rate, what would be

(a) The present value of the project?

(b) The certainty-equivalent cash flows in years 1 and 2?

(c) The ratio (a_t) of the certainty-equivalent cash flows to the expected cash flows in years 1 and 2?

QUESTIONS AND PROBLEMS

1. Look at Table 9-2.

(a) How much did Digiloc's price tend to change in an unchanged market?

(b) Which stock had price changes that were most closely related with the market? What proportion of the stock's risk was market risk, and what proportion was unique risk?

(c) What is the confidence interval on Digiloc's beta?

(d) Why is the adjusted beta for Dibrell higher than the unadjusted beta?

(e) What is the total risk of Diebold, Inc., *per year?*

2. Explain the estimate of alpha for Diebold, Inc., in Table 9-2. Why is this not a good guide to the stock's future alpha? What is your best forecast of alpha?

3. (a) Nero Violins has the following capital structure:

Security	Beta	Total Market Value (thousands of dollars)
Debt	0	100
Preferred stock	0.20	40
Common stock	1.20	200

What is the firm's asset beta (that is, the beta of its stock if it were all equity financed)?

(b) Assume the capital asset pricing model is correct. What discount rate should Nero set for investments that expand the scale of its operations without changing its asset beta? Assume any new investment is all-equity financed. Plug in numbers that are reasonable today. Specify two discount rates, one real and one nominal.

4. Amalgamated Products has three operating divisions:

Division	% of Firm Value
Food	50
Electronics	30
Chemicals	20

To estimate the cost of capital for each division, Amalgamated has identified the following three principal competitors:

	Estimated Equity Beta	Debt/(Debt + Equity)
United Foods	0.8	0.3
General Electronics	1.6	0.2
Associated Chemicals	1.2	0.4

(a) Assuming that the debt of these firms is risk-free, estimate the asset beta for each of Amalgamated's divisions.

(b) Amalgamated's debt to debt plus equity ratio is 0.4. If your estimates of divisional betas are right, what is Amalgamated's equity beta?

(c) Assume that the risk-free interest rate is 7% and the expected return on the market index is 15%. Estimate the cost of capital for each of Amalgamated's divisions.

(d) How much would your estimates of each division's cost of capital change if you assumed that each company's debt had a beta of 0.2?

5. Calculate the financial leverage for any three companies in Table 9-2 (other than DEC), and estimate the opportunity cost of capital for a "typical" investment by each firm.

6. Look back at the IM&C guano project in Section 6-3. Estimate the opportunity cost of capital of this project today, assuming it has a beta of 1.7, and re-estimate the project's NPV. Assume that r_m is 18% and r_f is 10%.

7. "The errors in estimating beta are so great that you might just as well assume that all betas are one." Do you agree?

*8. A project has the following forecasted cash flows:

Cash Flows (thousands of dollars)			
C_0	C_1	C_2	C_3
−100	+40	+60	+50

The estimated project beta is 1.5. The market return r_m is 16%, and the risk-free rate r_f is 7%.

(a) Estimate the opportunity cost of capital and the project's present value (using the same rate to discount each cash flow).

(b) What are the certainty-equivalent cash flows in each year?

(c) What is the ratio (a_t) of the certainty-equivalent cash flow to the expected cash flow in each year?

(d) Explain why this ratio declines.

9. Recalculate Table 9-5 assuming that:

(a) Expected cash flow is $150 per year for five years

(b) The risk-free rate of interest is 5%

(c) The market risk premium is 9%

(d) The estimated beta is 1.2

* 10. The McGregor Whiskey Company is proposing to market diet scotch. The product will first be test marketed for two years in Southern Ontario at an initial cost of $500,000. This test launch is not expected to produce any profits but should reveal consumer preferences. There is a 60% chance that demand will be satisfactory. In this case, McGregor will spend $5 million to launch the scotch nationwide and will receive an expected annual profit of $700,000 in perpetuity. If demand is not satisfactory, diet scotch will be withdrawn.

Once consumer preferences are known, the product will be subject to an average degree of risk, and therefore, McGregor requires a return of 12% on its investment. However, the initial test-market phase is viewed as much riskier, and McGregor demands a return of 40% on this initial expenditure.

What is the NPV of the diet scotch project?

11. "For a high beta project, you should use a high discount rate to value positive cash flows and a low discount rate to value negative cash flows." Is this statement correct? Should the sign of the cash flow affect the appropriate discount rate?

12. The president of Amalgamated Blue Sky Resources, Ltd., a small mining company, says, "We will never use the capital asset pricing model to estimate our cost of capital because our beta is only 0.6 and we feel this is too low to reflect the true risk of our company." Discuss.

* 13. Find a monthly copy of the *Toronto Stock Exchange Review* in your library. In it, locate the following information:

(a) The value of the TSE 300 Composite Total Return Index. This is the TSE 300 Composite Index with dividends reinvested.

(b) The values of Total Return Indices representing the performance of: oil and gas producers, forest products companies, steel producers, and gold mines.

(c) The closing stock prices of Northern Telecom, Stelco, and Canadian Pacific Ltd.

Now, collect a sequence of 25 issues of the *TSE Review* and calculate 24 monthly rates of return for each of these stocks and indices. Since the *TSE Review* does not record dividend payment or ex dividend dates, you'll have to ignore dividends in calculating the stock rates of return. This will not affect beta estimates very much. (You can also find these data in a loose-leaf manual called the *Toronto Stock Exchange 300 Stock Price Index System*.) What are the betas of these stocks and indices? You'll need a computer or calculator to perform the regressions.

PRACTICAL PROBLEMS IN CAPITAL BUDGETING

PART 4

A PROJECT IS NOT A BLACK BOX

A *black box* is something that we accept and use but do not understand. For most of us a computer is a black box. We may know what it is supposed to do, but we do not understand how it works and, if something breaks, we cannot repair it.

We have been treating capital projects as black boxes. In other words, we have talked as if managers are handed unbiased cash-flow forecasts and their only task is to assess risk, choose the right discount rate, and crank out net present value. Actual financial managers won't rest until they understand what makes the project tick and what could go wrong with it. Remember Murphy's law, "If anything can go wrong, it will," and O'Reilly's corollary, "at the worst possible time."

Even if the project's risk is wholly diversifiable, you still need to understand why the venture could fail. Once you know that, you can decide whether it is worth trying to resolve the uncertainty. Maybe further expenditure on market research would clear up these doubts about acceptance by consumers, maybe another drill hole would give you a better idea of the size of the ore body, and maybe some further work on the test bed would confirm the durability of those welds. If the project really has a negative NPV, the sooner you can identify it, the better. And even if you decide that it is worth going ahead on the basis of present information, you do not want to be caught by surprise if things subsequently go wrong. You want to know the danger signals and the actions you might take.

In short, managers avoid black boxes whenever they can, and they reward whoever can help them look inside. Consequently, consultants and academics have developed procedures for what we will call *project analysis.* We will discuss several of the procedures in this chapter, mainly sensitivity analysis, break-even analysis, Monte Carlo simulation, and decision trees. There is no magic in these techniques, just computer-assisted common sense. You don't need a license to use them.

Some analysts have proposed these techniques not only for project analysis but also as a supplement or replacement for net present value. You can imagine our reaction to that. Their proposals seem to reflect a belief that net present value cannot cope with risk. But we have seen that it can cope.

10-1 SENSITIVITY ANALYSIS

Uncertainty means that more things can happen than will happen. Therefore, whenever you are confronted with a cash-flow forecast, you should try to discover what else can happen.

Put yourself in the well-heeled shoes of the treasurer of the Jalopy Motor Company. You are considering the introduction of a small electrically powered car for city use.

Your staff members have prepared the cash-flow forecasts shown in Table 10-1. Since NPV is positive at 10% opportunity cost of capital, it appears to be worth going ahead.

$$NPV = -150 + \sum_{t=1}^{10} \frac{30}{(1.10)^t} = \$34.3 \text{ million}$$

Before you decide, you want to delve into these forecasts[1] and identify the key variables that determine whether the project succeeds or fails. It turns out that the marketing department has estimated revenue as follows:

Unit sales = new product's share of market × size of car market

= 0.01 × 10 million = 100,000 cars

Revenue = unit sales × price per unit

= 100,000 × 3,750 = \$375 million

The production department has estimated variable costs per unit as \$3,000. Since projected volume is 100,000 cars per year, *total* variable cost is \$300 million. Fixed costs are \$30 million per year. The initial investment can be depreciated on a straight-line basis over the ten year period, and profits are taxed at a rate of 50%.

Table 10-1 Preliminary cash-flow forecasts in millions of dollars for Jalopy Motor's electric car project.

	Year 0	Years 1 to 10
Investment	150	
1. Revenue		375
2. Variable cost		300
3. Fixed cost		30
4. Depreciation for tax purposes		15
5. Pretax profit (1 − 2 − 3 − 4)		30
6. Tax		15
7. Net profit (5 − 6)		15
8. Operating cash flow (4 + 7)		30
Net cash flow	−\$150	\$30

Assumptions:
Investment is depreciated over ten years straight line.
Income is taxed at a rate of 50%.

These seem to be the important things you need to know, but look out for unidentified variables. Perhaps there are patent problems, or perhaps you will need to invest in service stations that will recharge the car batteries. The greatest dangers often lie in these *unknown* unknowns, or "unk-unks," as scientists call them.

---

[1]Bear in mind, when you are working with cash-flow forecasts, the distinction between the expected value and the most likely (or modal) value. Present values are concerned with *expected* cash flows— that is, the weighted average of the possible cash flows. If the distribution of possible outcomes is skewed, the expected cash flow will not be the same as the most likely cash flow.

Having found no unk-unks (no doubt you'll find them later), you conduct a **sensitivity analysis** with respect to market size, market share, and so on. To do this, the marketing and production staffs are asked to give optimistic and pessimistic estimates for the underlying variables. These are set out in the left-hand columns of Table 10-2. The right-hand side shows what happens to the project's net present value if the variables are set *one at a time* to their optimistic and pessimistic values. Your project appears to be by no means a sure thing. The most dangerous variables appear to be market share and unit variable cost. If market share is only 0.004 (and all other variables are as expected), then the project has an NPV of −$104 million. If unit variable cost is $3,600 (and all other variables are as expected), then the project has an NPV of −$150 million.

Table 10-2 To undertake a sensitivity analysis of the electric car project, we set each variable *in turn* at its most pessimistic or optimistic value and recalculate the net present value of the project.

| Variable | Range | | | Net Present Value (millions of dollars) | | |
	Pessimistic	Expected	Optimistic	Pessimistic	Expected	Optimistic
Market size	9 million	10 million	11 million	+11	+34	+57
Market share	0.004	0.01	0.016	−104	+34	+173
Unit price	$3,500	3,750	3,800	−42	+34	+50
Unit variable cost	$3,600	3,000	2,750	−150	+34	+111
Fixed cost	$40 million	30 million	20 million	+4	+34	+65

Value of Information

Now you can check whether an investment of time or money could resolve some of the uncertainty *before* your company parts with the $150 million investment. Suppose that the pessimistic value for unit variable cost partly reflects the production department's worry that a particular machine will not work as designed and that the operation will have to be performed by other methods at an extra cost of $200 per unit. The chance that this will occur is only one in ten. But, if it did occur, the extra $200 unit cost would reduce after-tax cash flow by

Unit sales × additional unit cost × (1 − tax rate)

$$= 100,000 \times 200 \times 0.50 = \$10 \text{ million}$$

It would reduce the net present value of your project by

$$\sum_{t=1}^{10} \frac{10}{(1.10)^t} = \$61.4 \text{ million}$$

Suppose further that a $100,000 pretest of the machine will reveal whether it will work and allow you to clear up the problem. It clearly pays to invest $100,000 to avoid a 10% probability of $61.4 million loss. You are ahead by −100,000 + 0.10 × 61,400,000 = 6,040,000.

On the other hand, the value of additional information about market size is small. Because the project is acceptable even under pessimistic assumptions about market size, you are unlikely to be in trouble if you have misestimated that variable.[2]

Limits to Sensitivity Analysis

Sensitivity analysis boils down to expressing cash flows in terms of unknown variables and then calculating the consequences of misestimating the variables. It forces the manager to identify the underlying variables, indicates where additional information would be most useful, and helps to expose confused or inappropriate forecasts.

One drawback to sensitivity analysis is that it always gives somewhat ambiguous results. For example, what exactly does *optimistic* or *pessimistic* mean? The marketing department may be interpreting the terms in a different way from the production department. Ten years from now, after hundreds of projects, hindsight may show that the marketing department's pessimistic limit was exceeded twice as often as the production department's; but what you may discover ten years hence is no help now. One solution is to ask the two departments for a *complete* description of the various odds. However, it is far from easy to extract a forecaster's subjective notion of the complete probability distribution of possible outcomes.[3]

Another problem with sensitivity analysis is that the underlying variables are likely to be interrelated. What sense does it make to look at the effect in isolation of an increase in market size? If market size exceeds expectations, it is likely that demand will be stronger than you anticipated and unit prices will be higher. And why look in isolation at the effect of an increase in price? If inflation pushes prices to the upper end of our range, it is quite probable that costs will also be inflated. And so on.

Sometimes the analyst can get around the problem by defining underlying variables so that they are roughly independent. But you cannot push *one-at-a-time* sensitivity analysis too far. It is impossible to obtain expected, optimistic, and pessimistic values for total *project* cash flows from the information in Table 10-2.

Examining the Project under Different Scenarios

If the variables are interrelated, it may help to consider some alternative plausible combinations. For example, perhaps the company economist is worried about the possibility of another sharp rise in world oil prices. The direct effect of this would be to encourage the use of electrically powered cars. The popularity of "compacts" after the oil price increases in the 1970s leads you to estimate that an immediate 20% price rise in oil would enable you to capture an extra 0.3% of the automobile market. On the other hand, the economist also believes that higher oil prices would prompt a world recession and at the same time stimulate inflation. In that case, market size might be in the region of 8 million cars and both prices and costs might be 15% higher than your initial estimates. Table 10-3 shows that this scenario of higher oil prices and

---

[2]Of course, these are very simple examples. The derivation of optimal rules for investing in information is a well-developed part of Bayesian statistics. See H. Raiffa, *Decision Analysis: Introductory Lectures on Choices under Uncertainty*, Addison-Wesley Publishing Company, Inc., Reading, Mass., 1968; and H. Raiffa and R. Schlaifer, *Applied Statistical Decision Theory*, Division of Research, Graduate School of Business Administration, Harvard University, Boston, 1961.

[3]If you doubt this, try some simple experiments. Ask the person who repairs your television to state a numerical probability that your set will work for at least one more year. Or construct your own subjective probability distribution of the number of telephone calls you will receive next week. That ought to be easy. Try it.

Table 10-3 How the net present value of the electric car project would be affected by higher oil prices and a world recession.

	Cash Flows Years 1 to 10 (millions of dollars)	
	Base Case	High Oil Prices and Recession Case
1. Revenue	375	449
2. Variable cost	300	359
3. Fixed cost	30	35
4. Depreciation for tax return	15	15
5. Pretax profit (1 − 2 − 3 − 4)	30	40
6. Tax	15	20
7. Net profit (5 − 6)	15	20
8. Net cash flow (4 + 7)	+30	35
Present value of cash flows	+184	+215
Net present value	+34	+65

	Assumptions	
	Base Case	High Oil Prices and Recession Case
Market size	10 million	8 million
Market share	0.01	0.013
Unit price	$3,750	$4,313
Unit variable cost	$3,000	$3,450
Fixed cost	$30 million	$35 million

recession would on balance help your new venture. Its net present value would increase to $65 million.

Managers often find it helpful to look at how their product would fare under different scenarios. It allows them to look at different but *consistent* combinations of variables. Forecasters generally prefer to give an estimate of revenues or costs under a particular scenario than to give some absolute optimistic or pessimistic value.

Break-Even Analysis

When we undertake a sensitivity analysis of a project or when we look at alternative scenarios, we are asking how serious it would be if sales or costs turn out to be worse than we forecasted. Managers sometimes prefer to rephrase this question and ask how bad sales can get before the project begins to lose money. This exercise is known as **break-even analysis**.

In the left-hand portion of Table 10-4 we set out the revenues and costs of the electric car project under different assumptions about annual sales.[4] In the right-hand portion of the table we discount these revenues and costs to give us the *present value* of the inflows and the *present value* of the outflows. *Net* present value is of course the difference between these numbers.

You can see that NPV is strongly negative if the company does not produce a single car. It is just positive if (as expected) the company sells 100,000 cars and is strongly positive if it sells 200,000 cars. Clearly the *zero*-NPV point occurs a little under 100,000 cars.

---

[4]Notice that if the project makes a loss, this loss can be used to reduce the tax bill on the rest of the company's business. In this case the project produces a tax saving—the tax outflow is negative.

Table 10-4 NPV in millions of dollars of electric car project under different assumptions about unit sales.

Unit Sales (thousands of cars)	Inflows Revenue Years 1 to 10	Year 0 Investment	Years 1 to 10 Variable Costs	Fixed Costs	Taxes	PV Inflows	PV Outflows	NPV
0	0	150	0	30	−22.5	0	196	−196
100	375	150	300	30	15	2,304	2,270	34
200	750	150	600	30	52.5	4,608	4,344	264

In Figure 10-1 we have plotted the present value of the inflows and outflows under different assumptions about annual sales. The two lines cross when sales are 85,000 cars. This is the point at which the project has zero NPV. As long as sales are greater than 85,000, the project has a positive NPV.

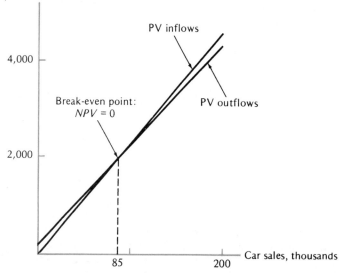

Figure 10-1 A break-even chart showing the present value of Jalopy's cash inflows and outflows under different assumptions about unit sales. NPV is zero when sales are 85,000.

Instead of working with the present values of the inflows and outflows, we could work equally well with the equivalent annual revenues and costs. The annual cost of the project includes the recurring costs (variable costs, fixed costs, and taxes) *plus* the equivalent annual cost of the $150 million initial investment. To calculate the equivalent annual cost of the initial investment we divide the investment by the ten-year annuity factor:

$$\text{Equivalent annual cost of investment} = \frac{\text{Investment}}{\text{10-year annuity factor}}$$

$$= \frac{150}{6.145} = \$24.4 \text{ million}$$

In Table 10-5 we show the equivalent annual revenues and costs under our three assumptions about unit sales. The final column of this table shows the difference between the annual revenues and costs. As long as this is positive, the project has a positive NPV.

Table 10-5   Equivalent annual cash flow from the electric car project under different assumptions about unit sales (millions of dollars).

| Unit Sales (thousands of cars) | Inflows | Equivalent Annual Outflow | | | | | Net Equivalent Annual Flow |
	Revenues	Initial Investment	Variable Costs	Fixed Costs	Taxes	Total	
0	0	24.4	0	30	−22.5	31.9	−31.9
100	375	24.4	300	30	15	369.4	5.6
200	750	24.4	600	30	52.5	706.9	43.1

In Figure 10-2 we have plotted the equivalent annual revenues and costs against different levels of sales. As you would expect, it tells exactly the same story as Figure 10-1. The two lines cross when sales are 85,000 cars. At this point, equivalent annual revenues equal equivalent annual costs and the project has zero NPV.

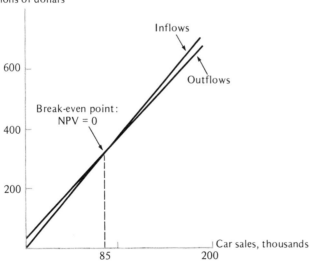

Figure 10-2   We can redraw our break-even chart in terms of Jalopy's equivalent annual revenues and costs. The net equivalent annual outflow is zero when sales are 85,000.

It really makes no difference whether we work with present values or equivalent annual revenues and costs. The two methods give identical answers. Very frequently, however, managers do not use either method: instead, they calculate the break-even points in terms of accounting profits. Table 10-6 shows the effect on Jalopy's after-tax profit of differences in electric car sales. Once again, in Figure 10-3 we have plotted revenues and costs against unit sales. But the story this time is different. Figure 10-3, which is based on accounting profits, shows a break-even point of 60,000 cars; Figures 10-1 and 10-2, which are based on present values and equivalent annual flows, both show a break-even point of 85,000 cars. Why the difference?

Table 10-6   Effect of the electric car project on accounting profit under different assumptions about unit sales (millions of dollars).

Unit Sales (thousands of cars)	Revenue	Variable Costs	Fixed Costs	Depreciation	Taxes	Total Costs	Profit After Tax
0	0	0	30	15	−22.5	22.5	−22.5
100	375	300	30	15	15	360	15
200	750	600	30	15	52.5	697.5	52.5

When we work in terms of accounting profit, we deduct depreciation of $15 million each year to cover the cost of the initial investment. If Jalopy sells 60,000 cars a year, revenues will be sufficient both to pay operating costs and to recover the initial outlay of $150 million. But they will *not* be sufficient to repay the *opportunity cost* of that $150 million. If we allow for the fact that the $150 million could have been invested elsewhere to earn 10%, the annual cost of the investment is not $15 million but $24.4 million.

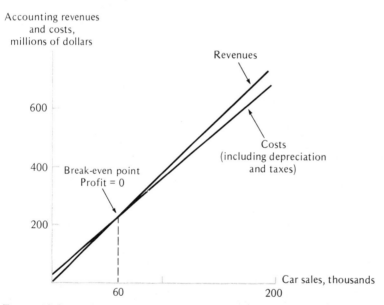

Figure 10-3   Sometimes break-even charts are constructed in terms of accounting numbers. After-tax profit is zero when sales are 60,000.

Companies that break even on an accounting basis are really making a loss—they are losing the opportunity cost of their investment. Reinhardt has described a dramatic example of this mistake.[5] In 1971 Lockheed managers found themselves having to give evidence to the United States Congress on the viability of the company's L-1011 TriStar

---

[5]U.E. Reinhardt, "Break-Even for Lockheed's TriStar: An Application of Financial Theory," *Journal of Finance*, **28**:821–838 (September 1973).

program. They argued that the program appeared to be "commercially attractive" and that TriStar sales would eventually exceed the break-even point of about 200 aircraft. But in calculating this break-even point, Lockheed appears to have ignored the opportunity cost of the huge $1 billion capital investment on this project. Had it allowed for this cost, the break-even point would probably have been nearer to 500 aircraft.

10-2   MONTE CARLO SIMULATION

Sensitivity analysis allows you to consider the effect of changing one variable at a time. By looking at the project under alternative scenarios, you can consider the effect of a *limited number* of plausible combinations of variables. **Monte Carlo simulation** is a tool for considering *all* possible combinations. It therefore enables you to inspect the entire distribution of project outcomes. Its use in capital budgeting is principally associated with David Hertz[6] and McKinsey and Company, the management consultants. As we shall see, it is a controversial method.

Imagine that you are a gambler at Monte Carlo. You know nothing about the laws of probability (few gamblers do), but a friend has suggested to you a complicated strategy for playing roulette. Your friend has not actually tested the strategy but is confident that it will *on the average* give you a $2\frac{1}{2}$% return for every 50 spins of the wheel. Your friend's optimistic estimate for any series of 50 spins is a profit of 55%; your friend's pessimistic estimate is a loss of 50%. How can you find out whether these really are the odds? An easy but possibly expensive way is to start playing and record the outcome at the end of each series of 50 spins. After, say, 100 series of 50 spins each, plot a frequency distribution of the outcomes and calculate the average and upper and lower limits. If things look good, you can then get down to some serious gambling.

An alternative is to tell a computer to simulate the roulette wheel and the strategy. In other words, you could instruct the computer to draw numbers out of its hat to determine the outcome of each spin of the wheel and then to calculate how much you would make or lose from the particular gambling strategy.

That would be an example of Monte Carlo simulation. In capital budgeting we replace the gambling strategy with a model of the project, and the roulette wheel with a model of the world in which the project operates. Let's see how this might work with our project for an electrically powered car.

Simulating the Electric Car Project

Step 1: Modeling the Project   The first step in any simulation is to give the computer a precise model of the project. For example, the sensitivity analysis of the car project was based on the following implicit model of cash flow:

Cash flow   = (revenues − costs − depreciation) × (1 − tax rate)

+ depreciation

Revenues   = market size × market share × unit price

Costs   = (market size × market share × variable unit cost) + fixed cost

---

[6]See D.B. Hertz, "Investment Policies That Pay Off," *Harvard Business Review*, **46**:96–108 (January–February 1968).

This model of the project was all you needed for the simple-minded sensitivity analysis we described above. But if you wish to simulate the whole project, you need to think about how the variables are interrelated.

For example, consider the first variable—market size. The marketing department has estimated a market size of 10 million cars in the first year of the project's life, but of course you do not *know* how things will work out. Actual market size will exceed or fall short of expectations by the amount of the department's error in the forecast:

$$\text{Market size, year 1} = \text{expected market size, year 1} \times \left(1 + \begin{array}{c} \text{proportionate} \\ \text{forecast error,} \\ \text{year 1} \end{array} \right)$$

You *expect* the forecast error to be zero but it could turn out to be positive or negative. You can write the market size in the second year in exactly the same way:

$$\text{Market size, year 2} = \text{expected market size, year 2} \times \left(1 + \begin{array}{c} \text{proportionate} \\ \text{forecast error,} \\ \text{year 2} \end{array} \right)$$

But at this point you must consider how the expected market size in year 2 is affected by what happens in year 1. If car sales are below expectations in year 1, it is likely that they will continue to be below in subsequent years. Suppose that a shortfall in sales in year 1 would lead you to revise down your forecast of sales in year 2 by a like amount. Then

Expected market size, year 2 = actual market size, year 1

Now you can rewrite the market size in year 2 in terms of the actual market size in the previous year plus a forecast error:

$$\text{Market size, year 2} = \text{market size, year 1} \times \left(1 + \begin{array}{c} \text{proportionate} \\ \text{forecast error,} \\ \text{year 2} \end{array} \right)$$

In the same way you can describe the expected market size in year 3 in terms of market size in year 2 and so on.

This set of equations illustrates how you can describe interdependence between different *periods*. But you also need to allow for interdependence between different *variables*. For example, the price of electrically powered cars is likely to increase with general inflation and with market size. Suppose that these are the only uncertainties and that a 10% shortfall in market size would lead you to predict a 3% reduction in price. Then you could model the first year's price as follows:

$$\text{Price, year 1} = \text{expected price, year 1} \times \left(1 + \begin{array}{c} \text{error in} \\ \text{inflation} \\ \text{forecast,} \\ \text{year 1} \end{array} + \begin{array}{c} 0.3 \times \text{error in} \\ \text{market size} \\ \text{forecast,} \\ \text{year 1} \end{array} \right)$$

Then, if these variations in the inflation rate and market size exert a permanent effect on price, you can define the second year's price as

$$\text{Price, year 2} = \text{expected price, year 2} \times \left(1 + \begin{array}{c} \text{error in} \\ \text{inflation} \\ \text{forecast,} \\ \text{year 2} \end{array} + \begin{array}{c} 0.3 \times \text{error in} \\ \text{market size} \\ \text{forecast,} \\ \text{year 2} \end{array} \right)$$

$$= \text{actual price, year 1} \times \left(1 + \begin{array}{c} \text{error in} \\ \text{inflation} \\ \text{forecast,} \\ \text{year 2} \end{array} + \begin{array}{c} 0.3 \times \text{error in} \\ \text{market size} \\ \text{forecast,} \\ \text{year 2} \end{array} \right)$$

The complete model of your project would include a set of equations for each of the variables—market size, price, market share, unit variable cost, and fixed cost. You can imagine that even if you allow for only a few interdependencies between variables and across time, the result would be quite a complex list of equations.[7] Perhaps that is not a bad thing if it forces you to understand what the project is all about. Model building is like spinach: you may not like the taste, but it is good for you.

Step 2: Specifying Probabilities   Remember the procedure for simulating the gambling strategy? The first step was to specify the strategy, the second was to specify the numbers on the roulette wheel, and the third was to tell the computer to select these numbers at random and calculate the results of the strategy:

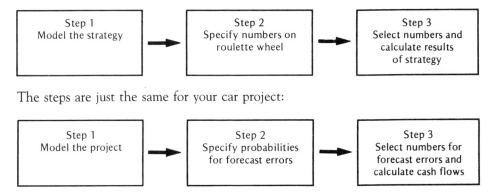

The steps are just the same for your car project:

Figure 10-4 illustrates how you might go about specifying your possible errors in forecasting market size. You *expect* market size to be 10 million cars. You obviously don't think that you are underestimating or overestimating market size; therefore your expected forecast error is zero. On the other hand, the marketing department has given you a range of possible estimates. Market size could be as low as 9 million cars or as high as 11 million cars. Thus the forecast error has an expected value of zero and a range of plus or minus 10%.

You need to draw up similar patterns of the possible forecast errors for each of the other variables that are in your model.[8]

---

[7]Specifying the interdependencies is the hardest and most important part of a simulation. If all components of project cash flows were unrelated, simulation would rarely be necessary.

[8]Figure 10-4 asserts that you are less likely to have made a large forecast error than a small forecast error. More precisely, it says that the probability of a possible error declines in proportion to the absolute size of the error. But forecast errors do not always fit this pattern. For example, the marketing department may feel that it is equally likely that market size will fall anywhere within the 9 million to 11 million car range.

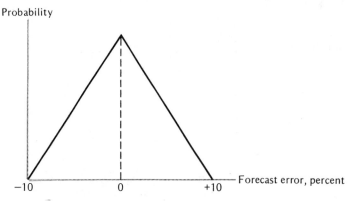

Probability

−10   0   +10   Forecast error, percent

Figure 10-4   Distribution of errors in forecasting market size. The expected error is zero, but the error could be as large as plus or minus 10%.

Step 3: Simulate the Cash Flows   The computer now *samples* from the distribution of the forecast errors, calculates the resulting cash flows for each period, and records them. After many iterations you begin to get accurate estimates of the probability distributions of the project cash flows.[9]

Figure 10-5 shows the output of some actual simulations of the Jalopy Motor Company project. You can see that in the first year the expected cash flow is about $31 million and that there is a 95% chance that the cash flow will fall within the range $4 million to $57 million.

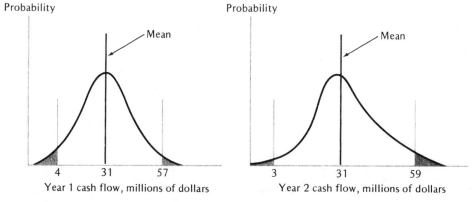

Probability   Probability

Mean   Mean

4   31   57   3   31   59
Year 1 cash flow, millions of dollars   Year 2 cash flow, millions of dollars

Figure 10-5   An example of the simulation output for the first two years of the electric car project. It provides cash-flow forecasts (that is, the means of the simulated distributions) as well as some idea of the predictability. The outer pairs of vertical lines include 95% of the simulated cash flows.

Have you noticed one slightly curious feature of this result? Our simulations tell us that the expected cash flow in each year is about $31 million, but the new products group told you that the expected cash flow was $30 million. They evidently arrived at this figure by taking the expected sales, multiplying by the expected profit per unit, and deducting the expected fixed cost and tax:

[9]Accurate only to the extent that your model and the probability distributions of the forecast errors are accurate. Remember the GIGO principle: "Garbage in, garbage out."

$$\text{Expected sales (units)} \times \left(\text{expected unit price} - \begin{array}{c} \text{expected} \\ \text{variable} \\ \text{unit cost} \end{array} \right)$$

$$- \text{ expected fixed costs} - \text{expected tax}$$

$$100{,}000 \, (3{,}750 - 3{,}000) - 30 \text{ million} - 15 \text{ million} = \$30 \text{ million}$$

Unfortunately, there was an error in the logic of the new products group. The expected revenues are *not* equal to the expected unit sales times the expected unit price unless sales and price are unrelated. If that sounds odd to you, consider the following example. Suppose a firm is equally likely to sell 100 items at a price of \$1 each or 300 items at a price of \$3 each. Its expected unit sales are $(100 + 300)/2 = 200$, and the expected price is $(1 + 3)/2 = \$2$. The expected unit sales times the expected price is, therefore, $200 \times 2 = \$400$. But the expected *revenue* is $[(100 \times 1) + (300 \times 3)]/2 = \$500$.

Similarly in the case of Jalopy Motors, price tends to go up and down with sales volume. Therefore the calculations of the new products group have *underestimated* the expected cash flow. Simulation therefore has given us one useful piece of information: project NPV is

$$- 150 + \sum_{t = 1}^{10} \frac{31}{(1.10)^t} = \$40 \text{ million}$$

Assessing Simulation: You Pay for What You Get

Simulation, though costly and complicated, has the obvious merit of compelling the forecaster and the decision maker to face up to uncertainty and to interdependencies.

Once you have constructed your model, it is simple to analyze what would happen if you were able to narrow down the range of uncertainty about any of the variables. You may also be able to use it to explore the effect of modifications to the project.

All this makes simulation sound like a panacea for the world's ills. But, as usual, you pay for what you get. In fact you sometimes pay for *more* than you get.

It is not just a matter of the time and money spent in building the model. It is extremely difficult to estimate interrelationships between variables and the underlying probability distributions, even when you are trying to be honest. But in capital budgeting, forecasters are seldom impartial and the probability distributions on which the simulation is based can be highly biased.

In practice, a simulation that attempts to be realistic will also be very complex. That usually means the decision maker delegates the task of constructing the model to management scientists or consultants. The danger here is that, even if the builders understand their creation, the decision maker cannot and therefore does not rely on it. This is a common but ironic experience: the model that was intended to open up black boxes ends up creating another one.

Misusing Simulation

The financial manager, like a detective, must use every clue. Simulation should be regarded as one of several ways to obtain information about expected cash flows and risk. But the final investment decision involves only one number, net present value.

Some of the early champions of simulation made much greater claims for the method. They started with the premise that net present value cannot in itself reflect risk properly and, therefore, they bypassed that last crucial step.

In this alternative approach the financial manager is given distributions not of cash flows but of NPVs or internal rates of return. Now that may sound attractive—isn't a whole distribution of NPVs better than a single number? But we shall see that this "more is better" reasoning leads the financial manager into a trap.

First, we should explain what is meant by a distribution of NPVs. The cash flows for each iteration of the simulation model are translated into a net present value *by discounting at the risk-free rate*. Why are they not discounted at the opportunity cost of capital? Because, if you know what that is, you don't need a simulation model, except perhaps to help forecast cash flows. The risk-free rate is used to avoid prejudging risk.

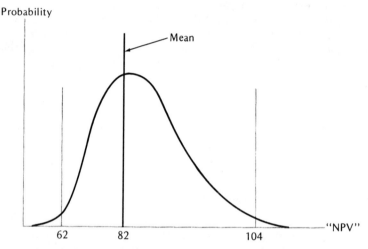

Figure 10-6   Some advocates of simulation propose that the financial manager should be presented with a distribution of "NPVs" like this one of the electric car project.

Look at Figure 10-6, which shows the distribution of NPVs for the Jalopy Motor project. The "expected NPV" includes no allowance for risk. Risk is reflected in the dispersion of the NPV distribution. Thus the term *net present value* takes on a very different meaning from the usual one. If an asset has a number of possible "present values," it makes little sense to associate PV with *the* price the asset would sell at in a competitive capital market.[10]

The "risk" of this distribution ignores the investors' opportunity to diversify. Moreover, it is sensitive to the definition of the project. If two unrelated projects are combined, the "risk" of the NPV of the combined projects will be less than the average "risk" of the NPVs of the two separate projects. That not only offends the value additivity principle, but it also encourages sponsors of marginal projects to beat the system by submitting joint proposals.

---

[10]The only interpretation we can put on these bastard NPVs is the following: suppose all uncertainty about the project's ultimate cash flows were resolved the day after the project is undertaken. On that day the project's opportunity cost of capital would fall to the risk-free rate. The distribution of NPVs represents the distribution of possible project values on that second day of the project's life.

Finally, it is very difficult to interpret a distribution of NPVs. Since the risk-free rate is not the opportunity cost of capital, there is no economic rationale for the discounting process. Because the whole edifice is arbitrary, managers can only be told to stare at the distribution until inspiration dawns. No one can tell them how to decide or what to do if inspiration never dawns.

Some of these difficulties can be dodged by presenting a distribution of internal rates of return. This avoids the arbitrary discount rate at the cost of introducing all the problems associated with the internal rate of return. Moreover, the manager is again left staring at the distribution with no guidance concerning the acceptable balance of expected return and variance of return.[11]

10-3 DECISION TREES AND SUBSEQUENT DECISIONS

If financial managers treat projects as black boxes, they may be tempted to think only of the first accept–reject decision and to ignore the subsequent investment decisions that may be tied to it. But if subsequent investment decisions depend on those made today, then today's decision may depend on what you plan to do tomorrow.

An Example: Vegetron

We have already solved in the last chapter a simple sequential decision problem, Vegetron's electric mop project. The problem was the following one:

> The scientists at Vegetron have come up with an electric mop and the firm is ready to go ahead with pilot production and test marketing. The preliminary phase will take a year and cost $125,000. Management feels that there is only a 50/50 chance that the pilot production and market tests will be successful. If they are, then Vegetron will build a $1 million plant, which will generate an expected annual cash flow in perpetuity of $250,000 a year after taxes. If they are not successful, Vegetron will not continue with the project.

Of course, Vegetron *could* go ahead even if the tests fail. Let's suppose that in that case the $1 million investment would generate only $75,000 per year.

Financial managers often use **decision trees** for analyzing projects involving sequential decisions. Figure 10-7 displays the electric mop problem as a decision tree. You can think of it as a game between Vegetron and fate. Each square represents a separate decision point for Vegetron; each circle represents a decision point for fate. Vegetron starts the play at the left-hand box. If Vegetron decides to test, then fate casts the enchanted dice and decides the result of the tests. If the tests are successful—there is a probability of $1/2$ that they will be—then the firm faces a second decision: invest $1 million in a project offering a $1.5 million net present value or stop. If the tests fail, Vegetron has a similar choice but the investment yields a net present value of $-$250,000.

It is obvious what the second-stage decisions will be: invest if the tests are successful and stop if they fail. The net present value of stopping is zero, so the decision tree boils down to a simple problem: should Vegetron invest $125,000 now to obtain a 50% chance of $1.5 million a year later?

---

[11]He or she might use the standard deviation of the IRR as a proxy for the relative risk of projects in the same line of business, however.

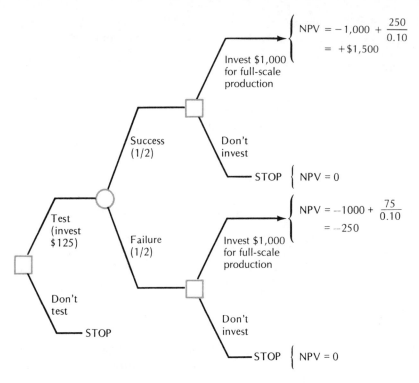

$$NPV = -1,000 + \frac{250}{0.10}$$
$$= +\$1,500$$

Invest $1,000 for full-scale production

Success (1/2)

Don't invest

STOP $\Big\{$ NPV = 0

$$NPV = -1000 + \frac{75}{0.10}$$
$$= -250$$

Test (invest $125)

Failure (1/2)

Invest $1,000 for full-scale production

Don't test

STOP

Don't invest

STOP $\Big\{$ NPV = 0

Figure 10-7 The electric mop example from Chapter 9 expressed as a decision tree. This is a project involving sequential decisions. The investment in testing generates the opportunity to invest in full-scale production. (All figures are in thousands; probabilities are in parentheses.)

*A Tougher Example: Magna Charter

Magna Charter is a new corporation formed by Agnes Magna to provide an executive flying service for the Windsor–Québec City corridor. The founder thinks there will be a ready demand from businesses that cannot justify a full-time company plane but nevertheless need one from time to time. However, the venture is not a sure thing. There is a 40% chance that demand in the first year will be low. If it is low, there is a 70% chance that it will remain low in subsequent years. On the other hand, if the initial demand is high, there is an 80% chance that it will stay high.

The immediate problem is to decide what kind of plane to buy. A brand-new turboprop costs $400,000. A used piston-engine plane costs only $200,000 but has less capacity and customer appeal. Moreover, the piston-engine plane is an old design and likely to depreciate rapidly. Ms. Magna thinks that next year secondhand piston aircraft will be available for only $100,000.

That gives Ms. Magna an idea: why not start out with one piston plane and buy another if demand is still high? It will cost only $100,000 to expand. If demand is low, Magna Charter can sit tight with one small, relatively inexpensive aircraft.

Figure 10-8 displays these choices. The square on the left marks the company's initial decision to purchase a turboprop for $400,000 or a piston aircraft for $200,000. After the company has made its decision, fate decides on the first year's demand. You can see in parentheses the probability that demand will be high or low, and you can see the expected cash flow for each combination of aircraft and demand level. At the end of the year the company has a second decision to make if it has a piston-engine aircraft: it can either expand or sit tight. This decision point is marked by the second square.

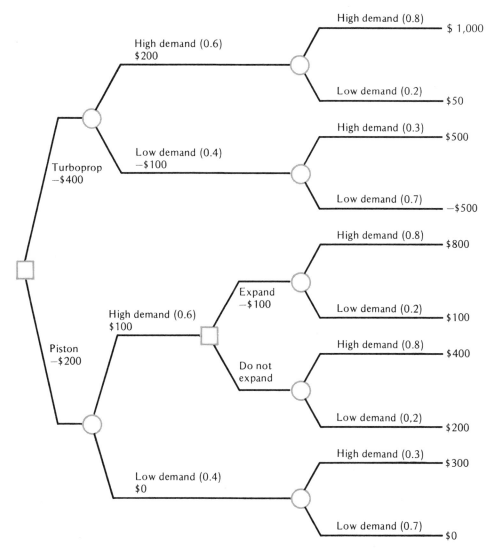

Figure 10-8   Decision tree for Magna Charter. Should it buy a new turboprop or a smaller, secondhand piston-engine plane? A second piston plane can be purchased in year 1 if demand turns out to be high. (All figures are in thousands.)

Finally fate takes over again and selects the level of demand for year 2. Again you can see in parentheses the probability of high or low demand. Notice that the probabilities for the second year depend on the first-period outcomes. For example, if demand is high in the first period, then there is an 80% chance that it will also be high in the second. The chance of high demand in *both* the first and second periods is 0.6×0.8 = 0.48. After the parentheses we again show the profitability of the project for each combination of aircraft and demand level. You can interpret each of these figures as the present value at the end of year 2 of the cash flows for that and all subsequent years.

The problem for Ms. Magna is to decide what to do today. We solve that problem by thinking first what she would do next year. This means that we start at the right side of the tree and work backward to the beginning on the left.

The only decision that Ms. Magna needs to make next year is whether to expand if purchase of a piston-engine plane is succeeded by high demand. If she expands, she invests $100,000 and receives a payoff of $800,000 if demand continues to be high and $100,000 if demand falls. So her *expected* payoff is

(Probability high demand × payoff with high demand)

$$+ \text{ (probability low demand}$$

$$\times \text{ payoff with low demand)}$$

$$= (0.8 \times 800) + (0.2 \times 100) = \$660,000$$

If the opportunity cost of capital for this venture is 10%,[12] then the net present value of expanding, computed as of year 1, is

$$\text{NPV} = -100 + \frac{660}{1.10} = +500 \text{ or } \$500,000$$

If Ms. Magna does *not* expand, the expected payoff is

(Probability high demand × payoff with high demand)

$$+ \text{ (probability low demand}$$

$$\times \text{ payoff with low demand)}$$

$$= (0.8 \times 400) + (0.2 \times 200) = \$360,000$$

The net present value of *not* expanding, computed as of year 1, is

$$\text{NPV} = 0 + \frac{360}{1.10} = +327 \text{ or } \$327,000$$

Expansion obviously pays if market demand is high.

Now that we know what Magna Charter ought to do if faced with the expansion decision, we can "roll back" to today's decision. If the first piston-engine plane is bought, Magna can expect to receive cash worth $600,000 in year 1 if demand is high and cash worth $82,000 if it is low:

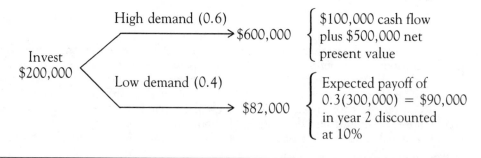

---

[12]We are guilty here of assuming away one of the most difficult questions. Just as in the Vegetron mop case, the most risky part of Ms. Magna's venture is likely to be the initial prototype project. Perhaps we should use a lower discount rate for the second piston-engine plane than for the first.

The net present value of the investment in the piston-engine plane is therefore $157,000:

$$NPV = -200 + \frac{0.6(600) + 0.4(82)}{1.10} = +\$157,000$$

If Magna buys the turboprop, there are no future decisions to analyze, and so there is no need to roll back. We just calculate expected cash flows and discount:

$$NPV = -400 + \frac{0.6(200) + 0.4(-100)}{1.10}$$

$$+ \frac{0.6[0.8(1,000) + 0.2(50)] + 0.4[0.3(500) + 0.7(-500)]}{(1.10)^2}$$

$$= -400 + \frac{80}{1.10} + \frac{406}{(1.10)^2} = +8, \text{ or } \$8,000$$

Thus, the investment in the piston-engine plane has an NPV of $157,000; the investment in the turboprop has an NPV of $8,000. The piston-engine plane is the better bet. Note, however, that the choice would seem much closer if we forgot to take account of the option to expand. In that case the NPV of the piston-engine plane would drop from $157,000 to $63,000:

$$NPV = 200 + \frac{0.6(100) + 0.4(0)}{1.10}$$

$$+ \frac{0.6[0.8(400) + 0.2(200)] + 0.4[0.3(300) + 0.7(0)]}{(1.10)^2}$$

$$= +63 \text{ or } \$63,000$$

The value of the *option to expand* is, therefore,

$$157 - 63 = +94, \text{ or } \$94,000$$

*Bailing Out

If the option to expand has value, how about the option to *contract* or to abandon the venture entirely?

We have assumed that Magna Charter can buy a secondhand piston-engine plane for $100,000 in year 1. We can also assume that it could sell one for the same amount. That is exactly what it should do if it buys the piston-engine plane and encounters low demand: $100,000 cash received from the sale of the plane now is obviously better than a 30% chance of a recovery in demand and $300,000 a year later.

Let's suppose that the turboprop could be sold for $300,000 in year 1. Again, it obviously makes sense to sell if demand is low.

But now we must think again about the decision to buy the piston-engine plane. If Magna Charter can "bail out" of either investment, why not take the turboprop and shoot for the big payoff?

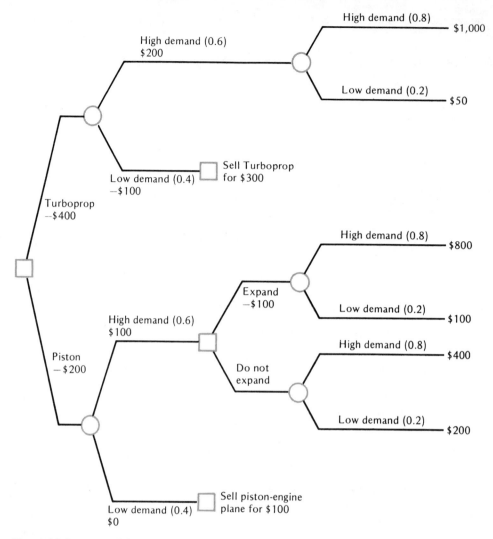

Figure 10-9   Revised decision tree for Magna Charter, taking account of the possibility of abandoning the business if demand turns out to be low. (All figures are in thousands.)

Figure 10-9 represents Magna Charter's decision problem with the abandonment options included. First, we figure out the net present value of buying the turboprop. This reduces to a simple one-period problem:

$$\text{Invest } \$400,000 \begin{cases} \text{High demand (0.6)} \rightarrow \$936,000 \quad \begin{cases} \$200,000 \text{ cash flow} \\ \text{plus } \$736,000 \text{ net} \\ \text{present value} \end{cases} \\ \text{Low demand (0.4)} \rightarrow \$200,000 \quad \begin{cases} -\$100,000 \text{ cash flow} \\ \text{plus } \$300,000 \text{ from} \\ \text{sale of plane} \end{cases} \end{cases}$$

$$\text{NPV} = -400 + \frac{0.6(936) + 0.4(200)}{1.10} = +183, \text{ or } \$183,000$$

Thus, when we allow for the possibility of abandonment, the net present value of the turboprop investment increases from $8,000 to $183,000. The value of the *option to abandon* is

$$\text{Value of abandonment option} = \text{NPV with abandonment} - \begin{array}{c}\text{NPV without}\\\text{abandonment}\end{array}$$

$$= 183 - 8$$

$$= 175, \text{ or } \$175,000$$

Now we figure out the net present value of buying the piston-engine plane with the abandonment option included. The payoffs for this plane are as follows:

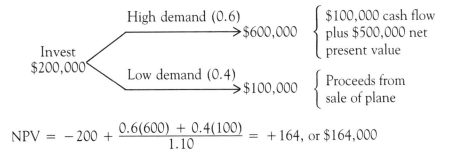

$$\text{NPV} = -200 + \frac{0.6(600) + 0.4(100)}{1.10} = +164, \text{ or } \$164,000$$

With the abandonment option the piston-engine plane is worth $164,000; without it, the plane is worth $157,000. Therefore the value of the abandonment option is

$$164 - 157 = 7, \text{ or } \$7,000$$

It is a good thing we remembered the possibility of reselling the aircraft. When we include the value of the abandonment option, the turboprop has an NPV of $183,000 and the piston-engine plane has an NPV of only $164,000.

Abandonment Value and Capital Budgeting

Abandonment value—the value of the option to bail out of a project—is a simple idea that has surprisingly broad practical implications. In a way it is just common sense; disaster, like a cat, is always waiting to pounce, and so you must always be prepared to cut and run.

Some assets are easier to bail out of than others. Tangible assets are usually easier to sell than intangible ones.[13] It helps to have active secondhand markets, which really only exist for standardized, widely used items. Real estate, airplanes, trucks, and certain machine tools are likely to be relatively easy to sell. The knowledge accumulated by Vegetron's research and development program, on the other hand, is a specialized intangible asset and probably would not have a significant abandonment value.

In the worst case a firm's stockholders can bail out by going bankrupt. It may sound strange to say that an investor is helped by the possibility of bankruptcy, but it is true.

---

[13]This is of course not always the case. Some tangible assets you have to pay to get rid of—worn out refrigerators, for instance.

Investors in corporations have *limited liability*: they risk only the money they invest. From their point of view there is a limit to the money the firm can lose; they always have the option of walking away from the firm and leaving its problems in the hands of the creditors and the bankruptcy courts.[14]

Expansion value can be just as important as abandonment value. When things turn out well, the quicker and easier the business can be expanded, the better. The best of all possible worlds occurs when good luck strikes and you find that you can expand quickly *but your competitors cannot.*

Pro and Con Decision Trees

Our examples of abandonment and expansion are extreme simplifications of the sequential decision problems that financial managers face. But they make an important general point. If today's decisions affect what you can do tomorrow, then tomorrow's decisions have to be analyzed before you can act rationally today.

Any cash-flow forecast rests on some assumption about the firm's future investment and operating strategy. Often that assumption is implicit. Decision trees force the underlying strategy into the open. By displaying the links between today's and tomorrow's decisions, they help the financial manager to find the strategy with the highest net present value.[15]

The trouble with decision trees is that they get so _____ complex so _____ quickly (insert your own expletives). What will Magna Charter do if demand is neither high nor low but just middling? In that event Ms. Magna might sell the turboprop and buy a piston-engine plane, or she might defer expansion and abandonment decisions until year 2. Perhaps middling demand requires a decision about a price cut or an intensified sales campaign.

There are other possibilities. Perhaps there is uncertainty about future prices of secondhand aircraft. If so, abandonment will depend not just on the level of demand but also on the level of secondhand prices. What is more, secondhand prices are likely to be depressed if demand is low and buoyant if demand is high.

We could draw a new decision tree covering this expanded set of events and decisions. Try it if you like: you'll see how fast the circles, squares, and branches accumulate.

Life is complex, and there is very little we can do about it. It is therefore unfair to criticize decision trees because they can become complex. Our criticism is reserved for analysts who let the complexity become overwhelming. The point of decision trees is to allow explicit analysis of possible future events and decisions. They should be judged not on their comprehensiveness but on whether they show the most important links between today's and tomorrow's decisions. Decision trees used in real life will be more complex than Figures 10-8 and 10-9, but they will nevertheless display only a small fraction of possible future events and decisions. Decision trees are like grapevines: they are productive only if they are vigorously pruned.

Our analysis of the Magna Charter project begged an important question. The option to expand enlarged the spread of possible outcomes and therefore increased the risk of investing in a piston aircraft. Conversely, the option to bail out narrowed the spread of possible outcomes. So it reduced the risk of investment. We should have used different

---

[14]We will discuss bankruptcy in Chapters 18 and 28.

[15]Some analysts go further than that. Like the early advocates of simulation models, they start with the premise that net present value cannot take account of risk. They therefore propose that the decision tree should be used to calculate a *distribution* of "NPVs" or internal rates of return for each possible sequence of company decisions. That may sound like a gingerbread house, but you should know by now that there is a witch inside.

discount rates to recognize these changes in risk, but decision trees do not tell us how to do this. In fact, decision trees don't tell us how to value options at all; they are just a convenient way to summarize cash-flow consequences. But the situation is not hopeless. Modern techniques of option valuation are beginning to help value these investment options. We will describe these techniques in Chapter 20.

Decision Trees and Monte Carlo Simulation

We have said that any cash-flow forecast rests on assumptions about future investment and operating strategy. Think back to the Monte Carlo simulation model that we constructed for the Jalopy Motor Company. What strategy was that based on? We don't know. Inevitably Jalopy will face decisions about pricing, production, expansion, and abandonment, but the model builder's assumptions about these decisions are buried in the model's equations. At some point the model builder may have explicitly identified a future strategy for Jalopy, but it is clearly not the optimal one. There will be some runs of the model when nearly everything goes wrong and when in real life Jalopy would abandon to cut its losses. Yet the model goes on period after period, heedless of the drain on Jalopy's cash resources. The most unfavourable outcomes reported by the simulation model would never be encountered in real life.

On the other hand, the simulation model probably understates the project's potential value if nearly everything goes right: there is no provision for expanding to take advantage of good luck.

Most simulation models incorporate a "business as usual" strategy, which is fine as long as there are no major surprises. The greater the divergence from expected levels of market growth, market share, cost, and so on, the less realistic is the simulation. Therefore the extreme high and low simulated values—the "tails" of the simulated distributions—should be treated with extreme caution. Don't take the area under the tails as realistic probabilities of disaster or bonanza.

10-4 SUMMARY

There is more to capital budgeting than grinding out calculations of net present value. If you can identify the major uncertainties, you may find that it is worth undertaking some additional preliminary research that will *confirm* whether the project is worthwhile. And even if you decide that you have done all you can to resolve the uncertainties, you still want to be aware of the potential problems. You do not want to be caught by surprise if things go wrong: you want to be ready to take corrective action.

There are three ways in which companies try to identify the principal threats to a project's success. The simplest is to undertake a sensitivity analysis. In this case the manager considers in turn each of the determinants of the project's success and estimates how far the present value of the project would be altered by taking a very optimistic view or a very pessimistic view of that variable.

Sensitivity analysis of this kind is easy, but it is not always helpful. Variables do not usually change one at a time. If costs are higher than you expect, it is a good bet that prices will be higher also. And if prices are higher, it is a good bet that sales volume will be lower. If you don't allow for the dependencies between the swings and the merry-go-rounds, you may get a false idea of the hazards of the fairground business. Many companies try to cope with this problem by examining the effect on the project of alternative plausible combinations of variables. In other words, they will estimate the net present value of the project under different scenarios and compare this estimate with the base case.

In a sensitivity analysis you change variables one at a time: when you analyze scenarios, you look at a limited number of alternative combinations of variables. If you want to go whole hog and look at *all* possible combinations of variables, then you will probably need to use Monte Carlo simulation to cope with the complexity. In that case you must construct a complete model of the project and specify the probability distribution of each of the determinants of cash flow. You can then ask the computer to select a random number for each of these determinants and work out the cash flows that would result. After the computer has repeated this process a hundred or so times, you should have a fair idea of the expected cash flow in each year and the spread of possible cash flows.

Simulation can be a very useful tool. The discipline of building a model of the project can in itself lead you to a deeper understanding of the project. And once you have constructed your model, it is a simple matter to see how the outcomes would be affected by altering the scope of the project or the distribution of any of the variables. There are of course limits to what you can learn from simulations. A marine engineer uses a tank to simulate the performance of alternative hull designs but knows that it is impossible to fully replicate the conditions the ship will encounter. In the same way, the financial manager can learn a lot from "laboratory" tests but cannot hope to build a model that accurately captures all the uncertainties and interdependencies that really surround a project.

Books about capital budgeting sometimes create the impression that, once the manager has made an investment decision, there is nothing to do but sit back and watch the cash flows unfold. In practice, companies are constantly modifying their operations. If cash flows are better than anticipated, the project may be expanded; if they are worse, it may be contracted or abandoned altogether. Good managers take account of these options when they value a project. One convenient way to analyze them is by means of a decision tree. You identify the principal things that could happen to the project and the main counteractions that you might take. Then, working back from the future to the present, you can calculate which action you *should* take in each case. Once you know that, it is easy to work out how much the value of the project is increased by these opportunities to react to changing circumstances.

Many of the early articles on simulation and decision trees were written before we knew how to introduce risk into calculations of net present value. Their authors believed that these techniques might allow the manager to make investment decisions without estimating the opportunity cost of capital and calculating net present value. Today we know that simulation and decision analysis cannot save you from having to calculate net present value. The value of these techniques is to help the manager go behind the cash-flow forecast; they help the manager to understand what could go wrong and what opportunities are available to modify the project. That is why we described them as tools to open up black boxes.

FURTHER READING

For an excellent case study of break-even analysis, see:

U.E. Reinhardt, "Break-Even Analysis for Lockheed's TriStar: An Application of Financial Theory," *Journal of Finance*, **28**:821–838 (September 1973).

The principal exponent of simulation in investment appraisal is David Hertz. See:

D.B. Hertz, "Investment Policies that Pay Off," *Harvard Business Review*, **46**:96–108 (January–February 1968).

D.B. Hertz, "Risk Analysis in Capital Investment," *Harvard Business Review*, **42**:95–106 (January–February 1964).

Lewellen and Long are generally against simulation. See, however, Myers's "Postscript."

W.G. Lewellen and M.S. Long, "Simulation vs. Single-Value Estimates in Capital Expenditure Analysis," *Decision Sciences*, **3**:(1972).

S.C. Myers, "Postscript: Using Simulation for Risk Analysis," in S.C. Myers, ed., *Modern Developments in Financial Management,* Praeger Publishers, Inc., New York, 1976.

The use of decision trees in investment appraisal is discussed in:

J. Magee, "How to Use Decision Trees in Capital Investment," *Harvard Business Review,* **42:**79–96 (September–October 1964.)

R.F. Hespos and P.A. Strassmann, "Stochastic Decision Trees for the Analysis of Investment Decisions," *Management Science,* **11:**244–259 (August 1965).

Hax and Wiig discuss how Monte Carlo simulation and decision trees were used in an actual capital budgeting decision:

A.C. Hax and K.M. Wiig, "The Use of Decision Analysis in Capital Investment Problems," *Sloan Management Review,* **17:**19–48 (Winter 1976).

The abandonment option in capital budgeting was first analyzed by:

A.A. Robichek and J.C. Van Horne, "Abandonment Value in Capital Budgeting," *Journal of Finance,* **22:**577–590 (December 1967).

QUIZ

1. Define and briefly explain each of the following terms or procedures:
   (*a*) Project analysis
   (*b*) Sensitivity analysis
   (*c*) Break-even analysis
   (*d*) Monte Carlo simulation
   (*e*) Decision tree
   (*f*) Abandonment value
   (*g*) Expansion value

2. What is the NPV of the electric car project under the following *scenario?*

Market size	11 million
Market share	0.01
Unit price	$4,000
Unit variable cost	$3,600
Fixed cost	$20 million

3. Jalopy Motor is considering an alternative production method for its electric car. It would require an additional investment of $150 million but would reduce variable costs by $40 million a year.
   (*a*) What is the NPV of this alternative scheme?
   (*b*) Draw break-even charts for this alternative scheme along the lines of Figures 10-1 and 10-3.
   (*c*) Explain how you would interpret the break-even figures.

4. Summarize the problems a manager would encounter in interpreting a standard sensitivity analysis, such as the one shown in Table 10-2. Which of these problems are alleviated by examining the project under alternative scenarios?

5. True or false?
   (*a*) Project analysis is unnecessary for projects with asset betas that are equal to zero.
   (*b*) Sensitivity analysis can be used to identify the variables most crucial to a project's success.
   (*c*) Sensitivity analysis gives "optimistic" and "pessimistic" values for project cash flow and NPV.

(*d*) The break-even sales level of a project is higher when a *break-even* is defined in terms of NPV rather than accounting income.

(*e*) Monte Carlo simulation can be used to help forecast cash flows.

(*f*) Monte Carlo simulation eliminates the need to estimate a project's opportunity cost of capital.

(*g*) Decision trees are useful when future decisions may depend on today's decision.

(*h*) High abandonment value increases NPV, other things being equal.

6. Suppose a manager has already estimated a project's cash flows, calculated its NPV, and done a sensitivity analysis like the one shown in Table 10-2. List the additional steps required to carry out a Monte Carlo simulation of project cash flows.

7. Use a decision tree to show that it pays Jalopy Motor to conduct a pretest of the suspect machine (see Section 10-1).

8. Big Oil is wondering whether to drill for oil in West Pembina. The prospects are as follows:

Depth of Well (feet)	Total Cost (millions of dollars)	Cumulative Probability of Finding Oil	PV of Oil (if found) (millions of dollars)
10,000	2	0.5	5
15,000	2.5	0.6	4.5
20,000	3	0.7	4

Draw a decision tree showing the successive drilling decisions to be made by Big Oil. How deep should it be prepared to drill?

QUESTIONS AND PROBLEMS

1. Your staff has come up with the following revised estimates for the electric car project:

	Pessimistic	Expected	Optimistic
Market size	8 million	10 million	12 million
Market share	0.004	0.01	0.016
Unit price	$3,000	$3,750	$4,000
Unit variable cost	$3,500	$3,000	$2,750
Fixed cost	$50 million	$30 million	$10 million

Conduct a sensitivity analysis. What are the principal uncertainties in the project?

2. Amalgamated Boot is proposing to replace its old shoe-making machinery with more modern equipment. The new equipment costs $10 million and the company expects to sell its old equipment for $1 million. The attraction of the new machinery is that it is expected to cut manufacturing costs from their current level of $8 a pair to $4. However, as the following table shows, there is some uncertainty both about future sales and about the performance of the new machinery:

	Pessimistic	Expected	Optimistic
Sales (millions of pairs)	0.4	0.5	0.7
Manufacturing cost with new machinery (dollars per pair)	6	4	3
Economic life of new machinery (years)	7	10	13

Conduct a sensitivity analysis of the replacement decision assuming (a) a discount rate of 12%, and (b) that Amalgamated does not pay taxes.

3. Use Visicalc (or a similar computer spread sheet) to perform a sensitivity analysis of the IM&C guano project in Section 6-2. Examine the effect of differences in:
    (a) the inflation rate
    (b) the project life
    (c) working capital requirements
    (d) sales
    (e) operating costs
    (f) the discount rate

*4. Agnes Magna has found some errors in her data (see Section 10-3). The corrected figures are as follows:

Price of turbo, year 0 = $350,000
Price of piston, year 0 = $180,000
Price of turbo, year 1 = $300,000
Price of piston, year 1 = $150,000
Discount rate = 8%

Redraw the decision tree with the changed data. Calculate the value of the option to expand. Recalculate the value of the abandonment option. Which plane should Ms. Magna buy?

*5. Ms. Magna has thought of another idea. Perhaps she should buy a piston-engine plane now. Then, if demand is high in the first year, she can sell it and buy a turboprop. Redraw Figure 10-8 to incorporate this possibility. What should Ms. Magna do?

6. For what kinds of capital investment projects do you think Monte Carlo simulation would be most useful? For example, can you think of some industries in which this technique would be particularly attractive? Would it be more useful for large-scale investments than small ones? Discuss.

7. You own an unused gold mine that will cost $100,000 to reopen. If you open the mine, you expect to be able to extract 1,000 ounces of gold a year for each of three years. After that, the deposit will be exhausted. The gold price is currently $500 an ounce, and each year the price is equally likely to rise or fall by $50 from its level at the start of the year. The extraction cost $460 an ounce and the discount rate is 10%.
    (a) Should you open the mine now or delay in the hope of a rise in the gold price?
    (b) What difference would it make to your decision if you could costlessly (but irreversibly) shut down the mine at any stage?

8. Read and criticize the Hax–Wiig article mentioned in the "Further Reading" for this chapter. Are all of their recommendations consistent with finance theory?

9. You are considering a new consulting service. There is a 60% chance that demand will be high in the first year. If it is high, there is an 80% chance that it will continue high indefinitely. If demand is low in the first year, there is a 60% chance that it will continue low indefinitely.
    If demand is high, forecasted revenue is $90,000 a year; if demand is low, forecasted revenue is $70,000 a year. You can cease to offer the service at any point, in which case, of course, revenues are zero. Costs other than computing are forecasted at $50,000 a year regardless of demand. These costs also can be terminated at any point. You have a choice on computing costs. One possibility is to buy your

own minicomputer. This involves an initial outlay of $200,000 and no subsequent expenditure. It has an economic life of ten years and no salvage value. The alternative is to rent computer time as you need it. In this case computer costs are 40% of revenues.

Assume that the computing decision cannot be reversed (that is, if you buy a computer, you cannot resell it; if you do *not* buy it today, you cannot do so later). There are no taxes and the opportunity cost of capital is 10%.

Draw a decision tree showing the alternatives. Is it better to buy a computer or rent? State clearly any additional assumptions that you need to make.

WHERE POSITIVE NET PRESENT VALUES COME FROM

We have now spent several chapters explaining exactly how to calculate net present values but we have had little to say about the forecasts that are the basis of every investment decision. But good investment decisions require good cash flow forecasts. If financial managers are to get the kind of forecasts that they need, they must understand how those forecasts are produced. What can financial managers do to ensure that everybody is acting consistently? It is impossible to make rational investment choices if each forecaster is employing different assumptions about the prospects for the economy. How also should financial managers cope with biased or exaggerated forecasts? It's easy if the biases can be identified before the fact, but that is rarely possible. Perhaps crude rules of thumb, like payback, can protect against forecasting disasters. Is there any way to distinguish NPVs that are truly positive from those that merely reflect overoptimism? We suggest that managers should ask some probing questions about the possible source of economic gains.

11-1 INCONSISTENT ATTITUDES AND ASSUMPTIONS

Inconsistent recommendations and forecasts can crop up in various ways. For example, some managers are more averse to risk than others and they may let their attitudes toward risk interfere with their judgement of what is a good project. Managers of divisions that have assured good performance are more likely to propose high risk projects than managers of faltering divisions with an uncertain future. Also a large division is more likely than a small division to risk a $1 million loss. Such a loss might merely dent the profits of the larger division, but it could throw the managers of the small division out of work.

A manager's attitude to risk will partly depend on the way his or her performance is measured and rewarded. A good measurement and reward system should have some tolerance for mistakes and should be able to discriminate between good decisions and lucky ones. Ideally, managers would be rewarded for good decisions thwarted by bad luck and penalized for bad decisions rescued by good luck.

Another danger is that investment proposals may be based on inconsistent assumptions. For example, suppose the manager of your furniture division is bullish on housing starts but the manager of your appliance division is bearish. This inconsistency makes the projects of the furniture division look better than those of the appliance division. Senior management ought to negotiate a consensus estimate and make sure that all NPVs are recomputed using that joint estimate. Then a rational decision can be made.

This is why many firms begin the capital budgeting process by establishing forecasts of economic indicators like inflation and the growth in national income, as well as forecasts of particular items that are important to the firm's business, such as housing starts or the price of raw materials. These forecasts can then be used as the basis for all project analyses.[1]

11-2   THE PROBLEMS OF BIAS AND ERRORS

Overoptimism and exaggeration appear to be very common in financial forecasts. For example, a study by one company of 50 projects showed that the actual present value of "cost reduction" projects was 10% above the forecast, whereas for "sales expansion" projects the actual present value was 40% *below* the forecast, and for "new products" it was 90% *below*.[2] Perhaps these results were not typical, but it looks as if management was receiving grossly biased forecasts on any project that involved expansion.

You will probably never be able to eliminate bias completely, but if you are aware of why bias occurs, you are at least part of the way there. Project sponsors are likely to overstate their case deliberately only if you, the financial manager, encourage them to do so. For example, if they believe that success depends on having the largest division rather than the most profitable one, they will propose large expansion projects that they do not truly believe have positive NPVs. Or, if they believe you won't listen to them unless they paint a rosy picture, you will be presented with many rosy pictures. Or if you invite each division to compete for limited resources, you will find that each attempts to outbid the other for those resources. The fault in such cases is your own— it is only because you are holding up the hoop that others try to jump through it.

Our development of the net present value rule assumed implicitly that you are supplied with unbiased cash-flow forecasts. If the forecasts are biased, the net present value rule may lead to wrong decisions. If you are aware that a forecaster always doubles the original figures, you can correct for this bias. But what do you do when you do not know forecasters' idiosyncracies or when they play games with you? In that case, you may find that ad hoc procedures sometimes provide better protection against the effects of bias than the net present value rule.

Suppose, for example, that a divisional manager is congenitally overoptimistic. Simple application of the net present value rule would lead to too much investment by that division: the company may, therefore, do better to pretend that capital is limited and confine the division's spending to some arbitrary amount. That *forces* the divisional manager to define priorities.[3] Or suppose that forecasters' biases are stronger for more distant cash flows—it's much easier to put on the rose coloured glasses if you're forecasting 10 or 15 years into the future. The net present value rule will then give long term forecasts more weight than they deserve. The financial manager might do better to use a payback criterion that places *no* weight on them.

These two examples illustrate that, unless the forecasts are corrected for bias, the ad hoc criterion can *sometimes* give the better result. The converse is also true: a company

---

[1] If consistency between forecasts is a good thing *within* companies, how about *among* companies? A diversified investor has a stake in many firms. It is the money of the investors that these companies are committing to projects. Is it in investors' interest for different companies to judge projects on the basis of different views of the economic outlook? If companies do follow their own muse, some projects with *high* returns are liable to be rejected because one firm's management is unduly pessimistic about the economic outlook. And other projects with *low* returns are liable to be accepted because another firm's management is unduly optimistic about the economic outlook. Investors might be better off if each firm gave up trying to outguess the other on the economic outlook and stuck to a consensus forecast.

[2] Cited in J.L. Bower, *Managing the Resource Allocation Process,* Division of Research, Graduate School of Business Administration, Harvard University, Boston, 1970.

[3] Of course, it may also encourage divisions to compete even more strongly to get a large allocation of funds to invest.

that uses an ad hoc criterion may *sometimes* find that it pays to use biased forecasts.[4] Two wrongs do not make a right, but they may come closer than a right and a wrong combined.

We should stress that we are *not* recommending the use of ad hoc criteria. The essential point is that improvements in one aspect of the decision-making process must take account of deficiencies in other areas.

Errors in Forecasting

Let us suppose that you have persuaded all your project sponsors to give honest forecasts. You have eliminated the problem of bias but the forecasts will still contain errors. Some errors will be positive and some negative; the average error will be zero. But that is little consolation because you only want to accept projects with *truly* superior profitability.

Think, for example, of what would happen if you were to jot down your estimates of the cash flows from operating various items of equipment. You would probably find that about half *appeared* to have positive net present values. This is not because you personally possess any superior skill in operating jumbo jets or running a chain of laundromats but because you have introduced a large amount of error into your estimates of the cash flows. The more projects you contemplate, the more likely you are to uncover projects that *appear* to be extremely worthwhile. Indeed, if you were to extend your activities to making cash-flow estimates of other companies, you would also find a number of *apparently* attractive merger candidates. In some of these cases you may have genuine information and the proposed investment really may have a positive NPV. But in many other cases the investment only looks good because you have made a forecasting error.

11-3   LOOK FIRST AT MARKET VALUES

What can you do to prevent forecast errors from swamping genuine information? We suggest that you begin by looking at market values.

The following parable should help to illustrate what we mean by this. Your local Cadillac dealer is announcing a special offer. For $20,001 you not only get a brand new Cadillac, you also get the chance to shake hands with your favourite movie star. You wonder how much you are paying for that handshake. There are two possible approaches to the problem. You could evaluate the worth of the Cadillac's power steering, disappearing windshield wipers, and other features and conclude that the Cadillac is worth $21,000. This would seem to suggest that the dealership is willing to pay $999 to have a movie star shake hands with you. Alternatively, you might note that the market price for Cadillacs is $20,000, so that you are paying a dollar for the handshake. As long as there is a competitive market for Cadillacs, the latter approach is more appropriate.

Whenever security analysts value a company's stock, they are also faced with the task of valuing a package. They must evaluate all the information that is known to the market about a company *and* they must evaluate the information that is known only to them. The information that is known to the market is the Cadillac; the private information is the handshake with a movie star. Investors have already evaluated the

---

[4]We stress the word *sometimes*. In very many circumstances use of an ad hoc criterion makes matters worse. For a discussion of the interactions between criterion, forecasting ability, and bias, see P. Marsh and R.A. Brealey, "The Use of Imperfect Forecasts in Capital Investment Decisions," *Proceedings of the European Finance Association, 1975*, North Holland, Amsterdam, 1975.

information that is generally known. Security analysts do not need to evaluate this information again. They can *start* with the market price of the stock and concentrate on valuing their private information.

While lesser mortals would instinctively accept the Cadillac's market value of $20,000, the financial manager is trained to enumerate and value all the costs and benefits from an investment, and is therefore tempted to substitute his or her own opinion for the market's. Unfortunately this approach increases the chance of error. Many capital assets are traded in a competitive market and so it makes sense to *start* with the market price and then ask why these assets should earn more in your hands than in those of your rivals.

For example, we encountered a department store chain that estimated the present value of the expected cash flows from each proposed store, including the price at which it could eventually sell the store. Although the firm took considerable care with these estimates, it was disturbed to find that the conclusions were heavily influenced by the forecasted selling price of each store. Thus, despite the fact that the firm disclaimed any particular real estate expertise, it discovered that its investment decisions were unintentionally dominated by its assumptions about future real estate prices. Thereafter, whenever he was faced with a proposal to open a new store, the financial manager always checked the decision by asking the following question: "Let us assume that the property is fairly priced. What is the evidence that it is best suited to one of our department stores rather than to some other use?"

Here is another example of how market prices can help you make better decisions. Kingsley Solomon is considering a proposal to open a new gold mine. He estimates that the mine will cost $200 million to develop and that in each of the next ten years it will produce 0.1 million ounces of gold at a cost, after mining and refining, of $200 an ounce. Although the extraction costs can be predicted with reasonable accuracy, Mr. Solomon is much less confident about future gold prices. His best guess is that the price will rise by 5% per year from its current level of $400 an ounce. At a discount rate of 10%, this gives the mine an NPV of $-$10 million.

$$\text{NPV} = -200 + \frac{0.1(420 - 200)}{1.10} + \frac{0.1(441 - 200)}{1.10^2} + \cdots + \frac{0.1(652 - 200)}{1.10^{10}}$$

$$= -\$10 \text{ million}$$

Therefore the gold mine project is rejected.

Unfortunately, Mr. Solomon did not look at what the market was telling him. What is the present value of an ounce of gold? Clearly, if the gold market is functioning properly, it is the current price—$400 an ounce. Gold does not produce any income, so $400 is the discounted value of the expected future gold price.[5] Since the mine is expected to produce a total of 1 million ounces (0.1 million ounces per year for ten

---

[5]Investing in an ounce of gold is like investing in a stock that pays no dividends: the investor's return comes entirely as capital gains. Look back at Section 4-2, where we showed that P_0, the price of a stock today, depends on DIV_1 and P_1, the expected dividend and price for next year, and the opportunity cost of capital r:

$$P_0 = \frac{\text{DIV}_1 + P_1}{1 + r}$$

But for gold $\text{DIV}_1 = 0$, so

$$P_0 = \frac{P_1}{1 + r}$$

years), the present value of the revenue stream is $1 \times 400 = \$400$ million.[6] We assume that 10% is an appropriate discount rate for the relatively certain extraction costs. Thus

NPV = − initial investment + PV revenues − PV costs

$$= -200 + 400 - \sum_{t=1}^{10} \frac{0.1 \times 200}{1.10^t} = \$77 \text{ million}$$

It looks as if Kingsley Solomon's mine is not such a bad bet after all.

Mr. Solomon's gold was just like anyone else's gold. So there was no point in trying to value it separately. By taking the present value of the gold sales as given, Mr. Solomon was able to focus on the crucial issue: were the extraction costs sufficiently low to make the venture worthwhile?

Our example is somewhat special. Unlike gold, most commodities are not kept solely for investment purposes, and therefore you cannot automatically assume that today's price is equal to the present value of the future price. But when you do have the market value of an asset, *use it*, at least as a starting point for your analysis.

One more example. Suppose that an oil company is contemplating an additional investment in tankers. Tankers are freely traded in a competitive market. Therefore the present value of a tanker to the oil company is equal to the tanker's market price *plus* any extra gains that are likely to come from having the oil company, rather than another owner, operate the vessel.

11-4 FORECASTING ECONOMIC RENTS

We recommend that financial managers ask themselves whether an asset is more valuable in their hands than another's. A bit of classical microeconomics can help to answer that question. When an industry settles into long run competitive equilibrium, all its assets are expected to earn their opportunity costs of capital—no more and no less. If they earned more, firms in the industry would expand, or firms outside the industry would try to enter it.

In words, *today's price is the present value of next year's price.* Therefore we don't have to know either P_1 or r to find the present value. *Today's price is also the present value of the year 2 price.* Since DIV$_2$ = 0,

$$P_1 = \frac{P_2}{1+r}$$

and we can express P_0 as

$$P_0 = \frac{P_1}{1+r} = \frac{1}{1+r}\left(\frac{P_2}{1+r}\right) = \frac{P_2}{(1+r)^2}$$

In general,

$$P_0 = \frac{P_t}{(1+r)^t}$$

This holds for any asset that pays no dividends, is traded in a competitive market, and costs nothing to store. Storage costs for gold or common stock are very small compared to asset value.

Storage costs would have to be treated as negative dividends. The owner of a warehouse full of butter would have to *pay* cash for use of the warehouse, refrigeration, and so on.

[6]We assume that the extraction rate does not vary with the gold price. If it does, you would need to read Chapter 20 before you could value the mine.

Profits that *more* than cover the opportunity cost of capital are known as *economic rents*. These rents may be either temporary[7] (in the case of an industry that is not in long-run equilibrium) or persistent (in the case of a firm with some degree of monopoly or market power). The NPV of an investment is simply the discounted value of the economic rents it will produce. Therefore when you are presented with a project that appears to have a positive NPV, don't just accept the calculations at face value. They may reflect simple estimate errors in forecasting cash flows. Probe behind the cash flow estimates and try to identify the economic model on which the cash flow projections were based. Good managers already do this. They try to identify and exploit areas in which their firm has a special advantage.

*11-5   EXAMPLE—MARVIN ENTERPRISES DECIDES TO EXPLOIT A NEW TECHNOLOGY

To illustrate some of the problems involved in predicting economic rents, let us leap forward to the 1990s and look at the decision by Marvin Enterprises to exploit a new technology.[8]

One of the most unexpected developments of the 1990s was the remarkable growth of a completely new industry. By 1998, annual sales of gargle blasters totaled $1.68 billion or 240 million units. Although it controlled only 10% of the market, Marvin Enterprises was among the most exciting growth companies of the decade. Marvin had come late into the business, but it had pioneered the use of integrated microcircuits to control the genetic engineering processes used to manufacture gargle blasters. This development had enabled producers to cut the price of gargle blasters from $9 to $7 and had thereby contributed to the dramatic increase in the size of the market. The estimated demand curve in Figure 11-1 shows just how responsive demand is to such price reductions.

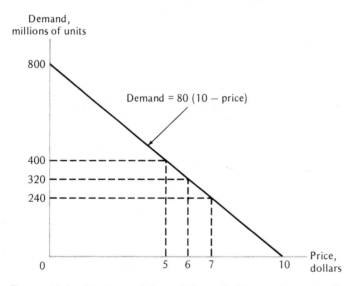

Figure 11-1   The demand "curve" for gargle blasters shows that for each $1 cut in price there is an increase in demand of 80 million units.

---

[7]Temporary rents are often called *quasi rents*.

[8]We thank Stewart Hodges for permission to adapt this example from a case prepared by him, and the BBC for permission to use the term *gargle blasters*.

Table 11-1 Size and cost structure of the gargle blaster industry before Marvin announced its expansion plans.

Technology	Capacity (millions of units) Industry	Marvin	Capital Cost per Unit (dollars)	Manufacturing Cost per Unit (dollars)	Salvage Value per Unit (dollars)
First generation (1992)	120	...	17.50	5.50	2.50
Second generation (1996)	120	24	17.50	3.50	2.50

Note: Selling price is $7 per unit. One "unit" means one gargle blaster.

Table 11-1 summarizes the cost structure of the old and new technologies. While companies with the new technology were earning 20% on their initial investment, those with first generation equipment had been hit by the successive price cuts. Since all of Marvin's investment was in the 1996 technology, it had been particularly well placed during this period.

Rumours of new developments at Marvin had been circulating for some time and the total market value of Marvin's stock had risen to $460 million by January 1999. At that point Marvin called a press conference to announce another technological breakthrough. Management claimed that their new third generation process involving mutant neurons enabled the firm to reduce capital costs to $10 and manufacturing costs to $3 a unit. Marvin proposed to capitalize on this invention by embarking on a huge $1 billion expansion program that would add 100 million units to capacity. The company expected to be in full operation within 12 months.

Before deciding to go ahead with this development, Marvin had undertaken extensive calculations on the effect of the new investment. The basic assumptions were as follows:

1. The cost of capital was 20%.

2. The production facilities had an indefinite physical life.

3. The demand curve and the costs of each technology would not change.

4. There was no chance of a fourth-generation technology in the foreseeable future.

5. The corporate income tax, which had been abolished in 1990, was not likely to be reintroduced.

Marvin's competitors greeted the news with varying degrees of concern. There was general agreement it would be five years before any of them would have access to the new technology. On the other hand, many consoled themselves with the reflection that Marvin's new plant could not compete with fully depreciated existing plant.

Suppose that you were Marvin's financial manager. Would you have agreed with the decision to expand? Do you think it would have been better to go for a larger or smaller expansion? How do you think Marvin's announcement is likely to affect the price of its stock?

You have a choice. You can go on *immediately* to read *our* solution to these questions. But you will learn much more if you stop and work out your own answer first. Try it.

*Forecasting Prices of Gargle Blasters

Up to this point in any capital budgeting problem we have always given you the set of cash flow forecasts. In the present case you have to *derive* those forecasts.

The first problem is to decide what is going to happen to the price of gargle blasters. Marvin's new venture will increase industry capacity to 340 million units. From the demand curve in Figure 11-1, you can see that the industry can sell this number of gargle blasters only if the price declines to $5.75:

$$\text{Demand} = 80(10 - \text{price})$$
$$= 80(10 - 5.75) = 340 \text{ million units}$$

If the price falls to $5.75, what will happen to companies with the 1992 technology? They also have to make an investment decision—should they stay in business or should they sell their equipment for its salvage value of $2.50 per unit? With a 20% opportunity cost of capital, the NPV of staying in business is

$$\text{NPV} = -\text{investment} + \text{PV}(\text{price} - \text{manufacturing cost})$$
$$= -2.50 + \frac{5.75 - 5.50}{0.20} = -\$1.25 \text{ per unit}$$

Smart companies with 1992 equipment will, therefore, see that it is better to sell off capacity. No matter what their equipment originally cost or how far it is depreciated, it is more profitable to sell the equipment for $2.50 per unit than to operate it and lose $1.25 per unit.

As capacity is sold off, the supply of gargle blasters will decline and the price will rise. An equilibrium is reached when the price gets to $6. At this point 1992 equipment has a zero NPV:

$$\text{NPV} = -2.50 + \frac{6.00 - 5.50}{0.20} = \$0 \text{ per unit}$$

How much capacity will have to be sold off before the price reaches $6? You can check that by going back to the demand curve:

$$\text{Demand} = 80(10 - \text{price})$$
$$= 80(10 - 6) = 320 \text{ million units}$$

Therefore Marvin's expansion will cause the price to settle down at $6 a unit and will induce first-generation producers to withdraw 20 million units of capacity.

But after five years Marvin's competitors will also be in a position to build third-generation plants. As long as these plants have positive NPVs, companies will increase their capacity and force prices down once again. A new equilibrium will be reached when the price reaches $5. At this point, the NPV of new third-generation plants is zero and there is no incentive for companies to expand further:

$$\text{NPV} = -10 + \frac{5.00 - 3.00}{0.20} = \$0 \text{ per unit}$$

Looking back once more at our demand curve, you can see that with a price of $5 the industry can sell a total of 400 million gargle blasters:

$$\text{Demand} = 80(10 - \text{price}) = 80(10 - 5) = 400 \text{ million units}$$

The effect of the third-generation technology is, therefore, to cause industry sales to expand from 240 million units in 1998 to 400 million five years later. But this rapid growth is no protection against failure. By the end of five years any company that has only first-generation equipment will no longer be able to cover its manufacturing costs and will be *forced* out of business.

*The Value of Marvin's New Expansion

We have shown that the introduction of third-generation technology is likely to cause gargle blaster prices to decline to $6 for the next five years and to $5 thereafter. We can now set down the expected cash flows from Marvin's new plant:

	Year 0 (Investment)	Years 1 to 5 (Revenue − Manufacturing Cost)	Years 6, 7, 8, ... (Revenue − Manufacturing Cost)
Cash flow, per unit (dollars)	− 10	6 − 3 = 3	5 − 3 = 2
Cash flow, 100 million units (millions of dollars)	−1,000	600 − 300 = 300	500 − 300 = 200

Discounting these cash flows at 20% gives us

$$\text{NPV} = -1,000 + \sum_{t=1}^{5} \frac{300}{(1.20)^t} + \frac{1}{(1.20)^5}\left(\frac{200}{0.20}\right) = \$299 \text{ million}$$

It looks as if Marvin's decision to go ahead was correct. But there is something we have forgotten. When we evaluate an investment, we must consider *all* incremental cash flows. One effect of Marvin's decision to expand is to reduce the value of its existing 1996 plant. If Marvin decided not to go ahead with the new technology, the $7 price of gargle blasters would hold until Marvin's competitors start to cut prices in five years' time. Marvin's decision, therefore, leads to an immediate $1 cut in price. This reduces the present value of its 1996 equipment by

$$24 \text{ million} \times \sum_{t=1}^{5} \frac{1.00}{(1.20)^t} = \$72 \text{ million}$$

Considered in isolation, Marvin's decision has an NPV of $299 million. But it also reduces the value of existing plant by $72 million. The net present value of Marvin's venture is, therefore, 299 − 72 = $227 million.

*Alternative Expansion Plans

Marvin's expansion has a positive NPV, but perhaps Marvin could do better to build a larger or smaller plant. You can check that by going through the same calculations as above. First you need to estimate how the additional capacity will affect gargle blaster prices. Then you can calculate the net present value of the new plant and the change in the present value of the existing plant. The total NPV of Marvin's expansion plan is

Total NPV = NPV of new plant + change in PV of existing plant

We have undertaken these calculations and plotted the results in Figure 11-2. You can see how total NPV would be affected by a smaller or larger expansion.

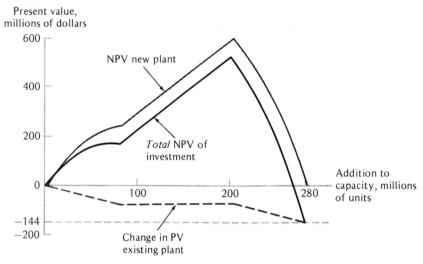

Figure 11-2   Effect on net present value of alternative expansion plans. Marvin's 100-million-unit expansion has a total NPV of $227 million (total NPV = NPV new plant + change in PV existing plant = 299 − 72 = 227). Total NPV is maximized if Marvin builds 200 million units of new capacity. If Marvin builds 280 million units of new capacity, total NPV is −$144 million.

When the new technology becomes generally available in 2004, firms will construct a total of 280 million units of new capacity.[9] But Figure 11-2 shows that it would be foolish for Marvin to go that far. If Marvin added 280 million units of new capacity in 1999, the discounted value of the cash flows from the new plant would be zero *and* the company would have reduced the value of its old plant by $144 million. To maximize NPV Marvin should construct 200 million units of new capacity and set the price just below $6 to drive out the 1992 manufacturers. Output is, therefore, less and price is higher than either would be under free competition.[10]

---

[9]Total industry capacity in 2004 will be 400 million units. Of this, 120 million units is second-generation capacity, and the remaining 280 million units is third-generation capacity.

[10]Notice that we are assuming all customers have to pay the same price for their gargle blasters. If Marvin could charge each customer the maximum price that customer was willing to pay, output would be the same as under free competition. Such direct price discrimination is illegal and in any case difficult to enforce. But firms do search for indirect ways to differentiate between customers. For example, stores often offer free delivery, which is equivalent to a price discount for customers who live at an inconvenient distance. Publishers differentiate their product by selling hardback copies to libraries and paperbacks to impecunious students. In the early years of electronic calculators, manufacturers put a high price on their product. Although buyers knew that the price would be reduced in a year or two, the additional outlay was more than compensated by the convenience of having the machines for the extra time.

*The Value of Marvin Stock

Let us think about the effect of Marvin's announcement on the value of its common stock. Marvin has 24 million units of second-generation capacity. In the absence of any third generation technology, gargle blaster prices would hold at $7 and Marvin's existing plant would be worth

$$PV = 24 \text{ million} \times \frac{7.00 - 3.50}{0.20}$$

$$= \$420 \text{ million}$$

Marvin's new technology reduces the price of gargle blasters initially to $6 and after five years to $5. Therefore the value of existing plant declines to

$$PV = 24 \text{ million} \times \left[\sum_{t=1}^{5} \frac{6.00 - 3.50}{(1.20)^t} + \frac{5.00 - 3.50}{0.20 \times 1.20^5} \right]$$

$$= \$252 \text{ million}$$

But the *new* plant makes a net addition to shareholders' wealth of $299 million. So after Marvin's announcement its stock will be worth[11]

$$252 + 299 = \$551 \text{ million}$$

Now here is an illustration of something we talked about in Chapter 4. Before the announcement, Marvin's stock was valued in the market at $460 million. The difference between this figure and the value of the existing plant represented the present value of Marvin's growth opportunities (PVGO). The market valued Marvin's ability to stay ahead of the game at $40 million even before the announcement. After the announcement PVGO rises to $299 million.[12]

The Lessons of Marvin Enterprises

Marvin Enterprises may be just a piece of science fiction, but the problems it confronts are very real. Whenever IBM considers a new generation of computers or Imperial Oil evaluates a new method of producing heavy oil or Polaroid thinks about developing a new camera, these firms must face up to exactly the same issues as Marvin. We have tried to illustrate the *kind* of questions you should be asking when presented with a set of cash flow forecasts. Of course no economic model is going to predict the future with accuracy. Perhaps Marvin can hold the price above $6. Perhaps competitors will not appreciate the rich pickings to be had in the year 2004. In that case, Marvin's expansion

---

[11]To finance the expansion Marvin is going to have to see $1,000 million of new stock. Therefore the *total* value of Marvin's stock will rise to $1,551 million. But investors who put up the new money will receive shares worth $1,000 million. The value of Marvin's old shares after the announcement is therefore $551 million.

[12]Notice that the market value of Marvin stock will be greater than $551 million if investors expect the company to expand again within the five-year period. In other words, PVGO after the expansion may still be positive. Investors may expect Marvin to *stay* one step ahead of its competitors, or to successfully apply its special technology in other areas.

would be even more profitable. But would you want to *bet* $1 billion on such possibilities? We don't think so.

Investments often turn out to earn far more than the cost of capital because of a favourable surprise. This surprise may, in turn, create a temporary opportunity for further investments earning more than the cost of capital. But anticipated and more prolonged rents are less common. Unless there are substantial economies of scale, prospective rents will naturally lead to the entry of rival producers. That is why you should be suspicious of any investment proposal that predicts a stream of economic rents into the indefinite future. Try to estimate *when* competition will drive the NPV of new plants down to zero and think what that implies for the price of your product.

Many companies try to identify the major growth areas in the economy and then concentrate their investment in these areas. But the sad fate of first generation gargle blaster manufacturers illustrates how rapidly existing plants can be made obsolete by changes in technology. It is fun being in a growth industry when you are at the forefront of the new technology, but a growth industry has no mercy on technological laggards.

You can expect to earn economic rents only if you have some superior resource such as management, sales force, design team, or production facilities. Therefore, rather than trying to move into growth areas, you would do better to identify your firm's comparative advantages and try to capitalize on them. Unfortunately, superior profits will still not accrue to the firm unless it can also avoid paying for them. For example, the Boeing 757 is a much more efficient plane to operate than older aircraft. But that does not mean the airlines that operate the 757 can expect to earn supernormal profits. The greater efficiency is likely to be reflected in the price Boeing charges for the 757. An airline will earn superior profits (that is, economic rents) only if the 757 is more valuable to it than to other operators.[13]

We do not wish to imply that good investment opportunities don't exist. For example, such opportunities frequently arise because the firm has invested money in the past that gives it the option to expand cheaply in the future. Perhaps the firm can increase its output just by adding an extra production line, whereas its rivals would need to construct an entire new factory. In such cases, you must take into account not only *whether* it is profitable to exercise your option, but also *when* it is best to do so.

Marvin also reminded us of project interactions, which we first discussed in Chapter 6. When you estimate the incremental cash flows from a project, you must remember to include the project's impact on the rest of the business. By introducing the new technology immediately, Marvin reduced the value of its existing plant by $72 million. Sometimes the losses on existing plants may completely offset the gains from a new technology. That is why we sometimes see established, technologically advanced companies deliberately slowing down the rate at which they introduce new products.

Notice that Marvin's economic rents were equal to the difference between its costs and those of the marginal producer. The costs of the marginal 1992 generation plant consisted of the manufacturing costs plus the opportunity cost of not selling the equipment. Therefore, if the salvage value of the 1992 equipment were higher, Marvin's competitors would incur higher costs and Marvin could earn larger rents. We took the salvage value as given, but it in turn depends on the cost savings from substituting outdated gargle blaster equipment for some other asset. In a well-functioning economy, assets will be used so as to minimize the *total* cost of producing the chosen set of outputs. The economic rents earned by any asset are equal to the total extra costs that would be incurred if that asset were withdrawn.

---

[13]The rent you earn because equipment worth more to you than to your rivals is known as "consumer surplus." If Boeing were able to charge each customer the maximum price it were prepared to pay, no airline could expect to earn a consumer surplus from operating the 757 and Boeing would capture all the benefits.

When Marvin announced its expansion plans, many owners of first generation equipment took comfort in the belief that Marvin could not compete with their fully depreciated plant. Their comfort was misplaced. Regardless of past depreciation policy, it paid to scrap first generation equipment rather than to keep it in production. Do not expect that numbers in your balance sheet can protect you from harsh economic reality.

11-6 SUMMARY

It helps to use net present value when making investment decisions, but that is not the whole story. Good investment decisions depend both on a sensible criterion and on sensible forecasts. In this chapter, we have looked at some of the things financial managers can do to get the forecasts they need.

One source of trouble is inconsistency in the macroeconomic assumptions that underlie the forecasts. If cash-flow forecasts for one project assume no inflation and those for another project are based on a 5% inflation rate, meaningful comparisons between these projects are impossible. The financial manager must therefore ensure that all forecasts within the company are based on a consistent view.

The net present value criterion is concerned with *expected* cash flows. But many of the cash flow forecasts the financial manager receives are likely to be biased. Companies employ a variety of ad hoc ways for limiting the worst effects of bias. For example, if the head office believes that each division is submitting overoptimistic forecasts, it can force the divisions to be more critical by imposing capital rationing. A financial manager who does away with these ad hoc rules without tackling the underlying problem may well bring about worse investment decisions. That is why the manager must think about how project sponsors can be encouraged to give fair and honest forecasts and how cases of overoptimism or exaggeration can be identified.

Projects may look attractive for two reasons: (1) there may be some errors in the sponsor's forecasts; (2) the company can genuinely expect to earn excess profit from the project. Good managers, therefore, try to ensure that the odds are stacked in their favour by expanding in areas in which the company has a comparative advantage. We like to put this another way by saying that good managers try to identify projects which will generate "economic rents."

Our story of Marvin Enterprises illustrates the origin of rents and how they determine a project's cash flows and net present value.

Any present value calculation, including our calculation for Marvin Enterprises, is subject to error. That's life: there's no other sensible way to value most capital investment projects. But some assets, such as gold, real estate, crude oil, ships, airplanes, and financial assets such as stocks and bonds, are traded in reasonably competitive markets. When you have the market value of such an asset, *use it*, at least as a starting point for your analysis.

FURTHER READING

For a discussion of some of the consequences of poor or biased cash-flow forecasts, see:

P. Marsh and R.A. Brealey, "The Use of Imperfect Forecasts in Capital Investment Decisions," in *Proceedings of the European Finance Association, 1975,* North Holland, Amsterdam, 1975.

Most microeconomics texts contain a discussion of the determinants of economic rents. See, for example,

R.L. Miller, *Intermediate Microeconomics,* McGraw-Hill Book Company, New York, 1978.

For an interesting analysis of the likely effect of a new technology on the present value of existing assets, see

S.P. Sobotka and C. Schnabel, "Linear Programming as a Device for Predicting Market Value: Prices of Used Commerical Aircraft, 1969–65," *Journal of Business*, **34**:10–30 (January 1961).

QUIZ

1. You have inherited 250 hectares of prime Saskatchewan farmland. There is an active market in land of this type, and similar properties are selling for $2,000 per hectare. Net cash returns per hectare are $150 per year. These cash returns are expected to remain constant in real terms. How much is the land worth? A local banker has advised you to use a 12% discount rate.

2. Which of the following statements are true?
   (*a*) A firm that earns the opportunity cost of capital is earning economic rents.
   (*b*) A firm that invests in positive NPV ventures expects to earn economic rent.
   (*c*) Financial managers should try to identify areas where their firm can earn economic rents, because it's there that positive NPV projects are likely to be found.
   (*d*) Economic rent is the equivalent annual cost of operating capital equipment.

3. Demand for concave utility meters is expanding rapidly, but the industry is highly competitive. A utility meter plant costs $50 million to set up and it has an annual capacity of 500,000 meters. The production cost is $5 per meter, and this cost is not expected to change. If the machines have an indefinite physical life and the cost of capital is 10%, what is the price of a utility meter?
   (*a*) $5
   (*b*) $10
   (*c*) $15

4. The following comment appeared in *Aviation Week and Space Technology*, July 25, 1966: "Alitalia has decided against ordering an advanced technology jet transport. The carrier's analysis, in common with some other airlines, indicates that it can operate fully depreciated Douglas DC-8s at fare levels competitive with a Boeing 747. This is because seat or ton-mile costs of a fully depreciated current generation subsonic jet may not differ greatly from the advanced technology jet." Discuss whether the low depreciation charge on a DC-8 justifies the continued use of that plane. Under what circumstances would it pay to operate 747s?

5. If a capital equipment producer brings out a new, more efficient product, who is likely to get the benefits? In what circumstances would purchase of the new equipment be a positive NPV investment?

QUESTIONS AND PROBLEMS

1. Suppose you are considering investing in an asset for which there is a reasonably good secondary market. Specifically, you're Pacific Western Airlines and the asset is a Boeing 737—a very widely used airplane. How does the presence of a secondary market simplify your problem in principle? Do you think these simplifications could be realized in practice? Explain.

2. Photographic laboratories recover and recycle the silver used in photographic film. Stikine River Photo is considering purchase of improved equipment for their lab at Telegraph Creek. Here is the information they have:

(*a*) The equipment costs $100,000.

(*b*) It will cost $80,000 per year to run.

(*c*) It has an economic life of ten years and would be in Asset Class 8 with a 20% CCA rate (see Section 6-2).

(*d*) It will recover an additional 5,000 ounces of silver per year.

(*e*) Silver is selling for $20 per ounce. Over the past ten years, the price of silver has appreciated by 4.5% per year in real terms. Silver is traded in an active, competitive market.

(*f*) Stikine's marginal tax rate is 40%.

(*g*) Stikine's company cost of capital is 8% in real terms.

What is the NPV of the new equipment? Make additional assumptions as necessary.

3. Does it make any difference whether a capital equipment producer sells equipment or rents it out? Does it affect the producer's willingness to bring out new products?

4. The manufacture of polysyllabic acid is a competitive industry. Most plants have an annual output of 100,000 tonnes. Operating costs are 90 cents a tonne and the sales price is $1 a tonne. A 100,000-tonne plant costs $100,000, has an indefinite life, and a scrap value of $60,000.

Phlogiston, Inc., proposes to invest $100,000 in a plant that employs a new low cost process to manufacture polysyllabic acid. The plant has the same capacity as existing units, but operating costs are 85 cents a tonne. Phlogiston estimates that it has two years' lead over each of its rivals in use of the process but is unable to build any further plants itself before year 2. Also it believes that demand over the next two years is likely to be sluggish and that its new plant will therefore cause temporary overcapacity.

You can assume that there are no taxes, and that the cost of capital is 10%.

(*a*) By the end of year 2 the prospective increase in acid demand will require the construction of several new plants using the Phlogiston process. What is the likely NPV of such plants?

(*b*) What would be the present value of each of these new plants?

(*c*) What does that imply for the price of polysyllabic acid in year 3 and beyond?

(*d*) Would you expect existing plant to be scrapped in year 2? How would your answer differ if scrap value were $40,000 or $80,000?

(*e*) The acid plants of United Alchemists, Inc. have been fully depreciated. Can it operate them profitably after year 2?

(*f*) Acidosis, Inc. purchased a new plant last year for $100,000 and is writing it down by $10,000 a year. Should it scrap this plant in year 2?

(*g*) What would be the present value of Phlogiston's venture?

5. The Cambridge Opera Association has come up with a unique door prize for its December (1986) fund-raising ball: 20 door prizes will be distributed, each one a ticket entitling the bearer to receive a cash award from the Association on December 30, 1987. The cash award is to be determined by calculating the ratio of the level of the Toronto Stock Exchange 300 Composite Stock Price Index[14] on December 30, 1987, to its level on June 30, 1987, and multiplying by $100. Thus, if the index turns out to be 125 on June 30, 1987, and 150 on December 30, 1987, the payoff will be $100 \times (150/125) = \$120$.

After the ball, a black market springs up in which the tickets are traded. What will the tickets sell for on January 1, 1987? On June 30, 1987? Assume the risk free interest rate is 10% per year. Also, assume the Cambridge Opera Association will

---

[14]To be more precise, they will use the TSE 300 Total Return Index, which has dividends reinvested.

be solvent at year end 1987 and will in fact pay off on the tickets. Make other assumptions as necessary.

Would ticket values be different if the tickets' payoffs depended on the TSE Oil and Gas Producer Index rather than the TSE 300 Composite?

6. You are asked to value a large building in northern Ontario. The valuation is needed for a railroad bankruptcy settlement. Here are the facts:
   (a) The settlement *requires* that the building's value equal the present value of the *net cash proceeds* the railroad would receive if it cleared the building and sold it for its highest and best nonrailroad use, which is as a warehouse.
   (b) The building has been appraised at $1 million. This figure is based on actual recent selling prices of a sample of similar northern Ontario buildings used as, or available for use as, warehouses.
   (c) If rented out today as a warehouse, the building could generate $60,000 per year. This cash flow is calculated *after* out-of-pocket operating expenses, and *after* real estate taxes of $50,000 per year:

Gross rents	$160,000
Operating expenses	50,000
Real estate taxes	50,000
Net	$ 60,000

   Gross rents, operating expenses, and real estate taxes are uncertain but are expected to grow with inflation.
   (d) However, it would take one year and $200,000 to clear out the railroad equipment and prepare the building for use as a warehouse. This expenditure would be spread evenly over the next year.
   (e) The property will be put on the market when ready for use as a warehouse. Your real estate advisor says that properties of this type take, on average, one year to sell after they are put on the market. However, the railroad could rent out the building as a warehouse while waiting for it to sell.
   (f) The opportunity cost of capital for investment in real estate is 8% in *real* terms.
   (g) Your real estate advisor notes that selling prices of comparable buildings in northern Ontario have declined, in real terms, at an average rate of 2% per year over the last ten years.
   (h) A 5% sales commission would be paid by the railroad at the time of the sale.
   (i) The railroad pays no income taxes. It would have to pay property taxes.

7. The world airline system is composed of the routes X and Y, each of which requires ten aircraft. These routes can be serviced by three types of aircraft—A, B, and C. There are five A-type aircraft available, ten B-type, and ten C-type. These aircraft are identical except for their operating costs which are as follows:

Aircraft Type	Annual Operating Cost (thousands of dollars)	
	Route X	Route Y
A	15	15
B	25	20
C	45	35

   The aircraft have a useful life of five years and a salvage value of $10,000.
   The aircraft owners do not operate the aircraft themselves but rent them out to the operators. Owners act competitively to maximize their rental income, and

operators attempt to minimize their operating costs. Air fares are also competitively determined.

Assume the cost of capital is 10%.

(a) Which aircraft would be used on which route and how much would each aircraft be worth?

(b) What would happen to usage and prices of each aircraft if the number of A-type aircraft increased to ten?

(c) What would happen if the number of As increased to 15?

(d) What would happen if the number of As increased to 20?

State any additional assumptions you need to make.

ORGANIZING CAPITAL EXPENDITURE AND EVALUATING PERFORMANCE AFTERWARDS

CHAPTER

·**12**·

Our task up to this point has been to show how a firm *should* set its capital budget. In this chapter we discuss how this is done in practice. We give particular attention to how capital budgeting is organized and to the administrative problems that inevitably crop up.

A good capital budgeting system does more than just make accept–reject decisions on individual projects. It must tie into the firm's long-range planning process—the process that decides what lines of business the firm concentrates in and sets out plans for financing, production, marketing, research and development, and so on. It must also tie into a procedure for measurement of performance. Otherwise the firm has no way of knowing how its decisions about capital expenditure finally turn out. Measurement of performance occupies a substantial part of this chapter. The pitfalls in measuring profitability are serious but not as widely recognized as they should be.

12-1 CAPITAL BUDGETS AND PROJECT AUTHORIZATIONS

For most sizable firms the first step in the investment process is the preparation of an annual **capital budget**, which is a list of planned investment projects and a breakdown of planned investment outlays by plant and division. (In this chapter we will think of plants as building blocks for divisions, and divisions as building blocks for firms. That is arbitrary: there may be more than two layers. Also, divisions are often organized by product line, region, or some other business unit.) In principle, the capital budget should be a list of all positive NPV opportunities open to the firm.

Most firms let project proposals bubble up from plants for review by division management, and from divisions for review by senior management. The administrative process typically works as follows.

Plant managers identify "interesting" opportunities, analyze them, and decide which ones are really worthwhile. Proposed expenditures for these projects are then submitted to division managers for further review. Some of the proposals by the plants do not "make the cut" at the divisional level. But divisional management may add its own ideas, usually new, larger ventures, like manufacturing a new product, that plant managers could not be expected to initiate. The lists of the divisions are forwarded to the corporate controller, who prunes and consolidates them into a proposed company budget. For very large diversified firms there may be several intermediate review stages.

The resulting budget is a list of proposed new projects for the coming year and of any projects from former years that are incomplete. Supporting information is usually provided on standard forms, supplemented by descriptive memoranda for larger projects. Since approval of the budget rarely confers authority to spend money, backup information is not as detailed at this stage as it is later. Projects below a specified size are typically not even listed separately, but simply included under a blanket approval for a given division or plant. In many companies the budget also contains rough estimates of likely expenditures over a five-year period.

The suggested budget is then reviewed by senior management and staff specializing in planning and financial analysis. It may be considered initially by a committee that includes the president, treasurer, and controller. Usually there are negotiations between the firm's senior management and its divisional management, and perhaps there will also be special analyses of major outlays or ventures into new areas, before the budget is submitted to the board for approval. Once approved, the budget generally remains the basis for planning over the ensuing year. In a few firms, however, it is updated each quarter.

Because each proposal in the budget requires subsequent specific authorization, the use of a budget involves some duplication of effort. But it allows information exchange up and down the management hierarchy before attitudes have hardened and personal commitments have been made. The danger with the whole procedure is loss of flexibility. There is a tendency for most projects to appear for the first time in the annual budget, and in some companies it is difficult to initiate project ideas at any other time of year.

Project Authorizations

The approval of a capital budget rarely confers authority to undertake the expenditures listed in the budget. Most companies stipulate that formal **appropriation requests** should be prepared for each proposal. The requests are accompanied by more or less elaborate backup, depending on the project's size, novelty, and strategic importance. Also, the type of backup information required depends on project category. Some firms use a fourfold breakdown:

1. Safety or environmental outlays required by law or company policy—for example, for pollution control equipment
2. Maintenance or cost reduction—for example, machine replacement
3. Capacity expansion in existing businesses
4. Investment for new products or ventures

The information requirements for projects differ across these categories:

1. Pollution control does not have to pay its own way. The main issue is whether standards are met at minimum present value of cost. The decision is likely to hinge on engineering analyses of alternative technologies.
2. Engineering analysis is also important in machine replacement, but new machines have to pay their own way. In category 2 above, the firm faces the classical capital budgeting problems described in Chapter 6.
3. Projects in category 3 are less straightforward capital budgeting problems; these decisions may hinge on forecasts of demand, of possible shifts in technology, and of competitors' strategies.
4. Projects in category 4 are most likely to depend on intangibles. The first projects in a new area may not have positive NPVs if they are considered in isolation, yet the firm may go ahead in order to establish a position in a market and pave the way for profitable future projects. The first projects are not taken for their own sake, but because they give the firm a valuable *option* to undertake follow-on projects. Thus, for projects in category 4, cash-flow forecasts may be less important than the issue of whether the firm enjoys some technological or other advantage that promises to generate economic rents for the firm. That issue becomes the main focus of project analysis.

Most large companies have manuals providing check lists to make sure that all relevant costs and alternatives are considered. The manual may contain instructions showing how to forecast cash flows and how to compute NPV, internal rate of return, or other measures of project value. Sometimes the manual also specifies the opportunity cost of capital.

Though appropriation requests may be prepared by the project originator, the plant manager is usually responsible for submitting them. These requests come up through the ranks of operating management for approval at each succeeding level. If the project is large, the request may be checked at some stage by staff accountants, engineers, and economists. The number of hurdles the proposal must pass depends on the magnitude of the expenditure involved.

Because the investment decision is central to the development of the firm, authorization tends to be reserved for senior management. Almost all companies set ceilings on the size of capital projects that divisional managers can authorize without specific approval from their superiors. Moreover, the ceilings are surprisingly low. Scapens and Sale surveyed 203 larger firms, with average capital budgets of $130 million per year, and found that the average ceiling for individual projects was only $136,000.[1] When you consider that a large company may generate thousands of authorization requests each year, the limited extent of delegation is striking.

Bottom-Up versus Top-Down

We have pictured the capital investment process as if all proposals bubbled up from the bottom of the organization. That is never the whole story. The managers of plants A and B cannot be expected to see the potential economies of scale of closing their plants and consolidating production at a new plant C. We expect divisional management to propose plant C. Similarly, divisions 1 and 2 may not be eager to give up their own data processing operations to a large, central computer. That proposal would come from senior management.

The final capital budget must also reflect strategic choices made by senior management. Strategic planning attempts to identify the businesses in which the firm has a real competitive advantage. It also attempts to identify businesses to sell or liquidate as well as declining businesses that should be allowed to run down. Strategic planning is really capital budgeting on a grand scale.

In many firms, strategic plans impose a strong top-down input to capital-budgeting decisions. Projects that appear to have negative NPVs may be accepted if they help to establish the firm in a business with good long-run potential. Similarly, projects that appear to have positive NPVs may be rejected if the firm plans to run down this part of its business. Of course, if a "declining" business continually generates high NPV projects, the strategic planners ought to think again—perhaps the business isn't declining.

The Decision Criteria Firms Actually Use

We know that companies use a number of different criteria for project selection. Table 12-1 shows the results of a survey by Schall, Sundem, and Geijsbeek of the relative popularity of different techniques. Notice the popularity of theoretically inappropriate techniques like payback and book rate of return, usually in combination with IRR,

---

[1] R.W. Scapens and J.T. Sale, "Performance Measurement and Formal Capital Expenditure Controls in Divisionalized Companies," *Journal of Business Finance and Accounting*, 8:389–420 (Autumn 1981).

Table 12-1 This survey of capital investment procedures shows that many firms use more than one investment criterion and that they frequently employ theoretically inappropriate criteria.

Payback	Return on Book	IRR	NPV	% of Firms Using Each Combination of Criteria
x	x	x	x	17
x	x	x		14
x	x		x	9
x		x	x	9
	x	x	x	2
x	x			8
x		x		8
x			x	7
		x	x	7
	x		x	4
	x	x		2
		x		6
	x			4
			x	2
x				2

Source: L.D. Schall, G.L. Sundem, and W.R. Geijsbeek, "Survey and Analysis of Capital Budgeting Methods," *Journal of Finance*, **33**:281–287 (March 1978), table 1, p. 282.

NPV, or both. But comparison of this study with earlier ones confirms that the sophisticated techniques are gaining.[2]

Of course, the use of intelligent techniques does not guarantee intelligent decisions. You can have good techniques and poor judgement, or vice versa. Often operating managers display considerable conceptual confusion on financial issues. One encounters such statements as, "We do all three (book rate of return, payback, and internal rate of return) and may decide that one is more relevant than the other," or "We don't use present value because it can't handle uncertainty." Even when companies do impose theoretically justifiable criteria, their application is often imperfect. For example, a British survey noted that almost half of the companies producing cash-flow estimates treated depreciation as a cash outflow.[3] Many companies think they can ignore inflation in cash-flow forecasts because "on the average revenues increase to cover inflated costs."

There is ignorance in the world. But before we get too smug, let's stop and think of other explanations. There are, in fact, several.

The Role of Judgement Businesspeople often act smarter than they talk. (For students and scholars it is the other way around.) They may make correct decisions but they may not be able to explain them in the language of finance and economics. Many decisions are fundamentally intuitive. If *intuitive* sounds capricious, replace the word with *informed judgement*. As we argued in Chapter 11: if a firm enjoys an advantage

---

[2]An earlier survey of large Canadian firms produced similar results: while 35% of respondents used some method of discounted cash flow analysis in 1962, 79% did so in 1972. See C.G. Hoskins and M.J. Dunn, "The Evaluation of Capital Expenditure Proposals under Uncertainty: The Practice of Large Corporations in Canada," *Journal of Business Administration*, **6**:45–55, Fall 1974.

[3]See L.E. Rockley, *Investment for Profitability: An Analysis of the Policies and Practices of UK and International Companies*, Business Books Ltd., London, 1973.

that promises to generate economic rents in a stable or growing business, it probably should press on regardless of calculated payback or present value. Experience helps in identifying such opportunities.

Of course, this is not a complete answer. Few decisions are totally judgemental. In principle, if *any* quantitative measure of project value affects a decision, it should be present value, not payback or return on book.

Communication Payback is the easiest way to *communicate* an idea of project profitability. It is important to have one measure everyone can understand, because capital budgeting is a process of discussion and negotiation involving people from all parts of the firm. Insisting that everyone commenting on a project do so in terms of NPV may cut off those who don't understand NPV, but who nevertheless can contribute useful information.

There is a law at work here that we can also observe working in television, publishing, and many other areas: a wider audience demands simpler concepts and language. Perhaps we could have sold more copies of this book by making it easier.

Rewards to Managers Plant and divisional managers are concerned for their own futures. Sometimes their interests conflict with stockholders'. New plant managers, for example, naturally want to demonstrate good performance right away in order to move up the corporate ladder. Perhaps they will propose quick-payback projects even if NPV is sacrificed. If their performance is judged on book earnings, they will be attracted by projects whose accounting results look good. Even if managers propose the right (NPV-maximizing) projects, we can understand their concern for payback and book return.

The problem lies in the way many firms measure performance and reward managers. Don't expect them to concentrate only on NPV if you always demand quick results or if you will reward them later on the basis of book return. More on this later in the chapter.

12-2 PROBLEMS AND SOME SOLUTIONS

Problems of Cooperation

Valuing capital investment opportunities is hard enough when you can do the entire job yourself. In real life it is a cooperative effort. Although cooperation brings more knowledge and intelligence to bear, it brings its own problems. Some are unavoidable— just another cost of doing business. Some can be alleviated by adding checks and balances to the capital investment process.

Many of the problems stem from sponsors' eagerness to obtain approval for their favourite projects. As the proposal proceeds up the organization, alliances are formed. Preparation of the request inevitably involves discussions and compromises, which limit subsequent freedom of action. Thus once a division has screened its plants' proposals, the plants unite in competing against "outsiders."

This competition among divisions can be put to good use if it forces division managers to develop better justifications for what they want to do. But the competition has its costs as well. Several thousand appropriation requests may reach the senior management level each year, all of them essentially sales documents presented by united fronts and designed to persuade. Alternative schemes have been filtered out at an earlier stage. The danger is that senior management cannot obtain (let alone absorb) the information to evaluate each project rationally.

The dangers are illustrated by the following practical question. "Should we establish a definite opportunity cost of capital for computing the NPV of projects in our furniture division?" The answer in theory is a clear yes, providing that the projects of the division are all in the same risk class. Remember that most project analysis is done at the plant or divisional level. Only a small proportion of project ideas analyzed survives for submission to top management. Plant and division managers cannot judge projects correctly unless they know the true opportunity cost of capital.

Suppose senior management settles on 12%. That helps plant managers make rational decisions. But it also tells them exactly how optimistic they have to be to get their pet project accepted. BMSW's second law states that the proportion of proposed projects having a positive estimated NPV is independent of top management's estimate of the opportunity cost of capital.[4] If the law is true, top management is better off concealing its estimates of the cost of capital, asking instead for NPVs calculated for a range of different discount rates, and applying the right rate when the final decision is made.

A firm that accepts poor information at the top faces two consequences. First, senior management cannot evaluate individual projects. In a study by Bower of a large multidivisional company, projects that had the approval of a division general manager were seldom turned down by his or her group of divisions, and those reaching the executive committee were almost never rejected. Second, the only effective control available to management is to impose expenditure limits on individual plants or divisions. The effect is to force the subunits to choose among projects and to encourage the divisions to compete for funds. The firm ends up using capital rationing as a way of decentralizing decisions.

Of course, capital rationing is not the only solution. Firms can improve the quality of information flowing to the top by setting up corporate capital budgeting staffs to enforce consistency, uncover specified assumptions, and undertake sophisticated analyses of major projects.

These analysts may also have to ferret out local managers who are evading the controls in the capital investment process. For example, managers may be permitted to approve projects only up to a certain value. But this authority may become infinite if each project can be broken down into a large number of small parts. The following story illustrates this problem:

> Our [top managers] like to make all the major capital decisions. They think they do, but I've just seen one case where a division beat them.
> I received for editing a capital request from the division for a large chimney. I couldn't see what anyone could do with just a chimney so I flew out for a visit. They've built and equipped a whole plant on plant expense orders. The chimney is the only indivisible item that exceeded the $50,000 limit we put on the expense orders. Apparently they learned informally that a new plant wouldn't be favourably received, and since they thought the business needed it, and the return would justify it, they built the damn thing.[5]

This embarrassment might have been avoided if the firm had imposed a limit on individual discretionary expenditures and *also* on the total amount of such expenditures by each manager in any one year.

A similar difficulty stems from the imprecise concept of a capital expenditure. It may not be material whether a firm purchases or leases a piece of equipment: the subsequent effect on operating cash flows is similar. Clearly management's interest is in controlling the acquisition of any important asset, whether it be leased or purchased. It also wants

---

[4]There is no first law. We thought "second law" sounded better. There *is* a third law, but that is for another chapter.

[5]Cited in J.L. Bower, *Managing the Resource Allocation Process: A Study of Corporate Planning and Investment*, Division of Research, Graduate School of Business Administration, Harvard University, Boston, 1970, p. 15.

to control acquisition not only of tangible assets, but also of intangible ones such as a patent or a long-term contract. Authorization procedures should be broadly construed and should not encourage the inefficient substitution of one kind of asset for another.

Another problem is to ensure that the authorization request draws attention to all likely contingent expenditures. Too often, seemingly small and innocuous investments are the first step in a chain of economically dependent investments. Management should be aware of the full consequences of letting a plant or division get its foot in the door.

Some Partial Solutions

We risk overemphasizing the problems and underemphasizing the ability of organizations to cope with them. They cope because people are sensible and because informal communication and negotiation reinforce formal procedures. There are also formal solutions, most of them mentioned in passing as we discussed the problems. Now we will present them in a more organized way.

Corporate Staff Corporate staff can be assigned to enforce consistency in project analyses, check the assumptions behind cash-flow forecasts, and undertake special analyses. Large corporations often have special staff departments devoted to these tasks.

Budgeting and Planning The capital budget is a part of a broader budgeting and planning cycle. The firm has to set operating budgets for plants and divisions and also plan marketing, research, financing, and long-term growth. Capital investments have to make sense in terms of these other plans.

Strategic Choices We referred to strategic planning as *capital budgeting on a grand scale*. It attempts to identify the businesses that offer the best long-run opportunities and to develop a plan for achieving success in those businesses.

Strategic planning deals in intangibles. Present values are rarely calculated explicitly. But the goal is clear: to identify areas where the firm has a competitive advantage. Firms that emphasize strategic planning are doing just what we recommended in Chapter 11: looking for the sources of economic rents as a check against bias and exaggeration in cash-flow forecasts.

A firm's capital investment choices should reflect both "bottom-up" and "top-down" processes—capital budgeting and strategic planning, respectively. The two processes should complement one another. Plant and division managers, who do most of the work in bottom-up capital budgeting, may not see the forest for the trees. Strategic planners may have a mistaken view of the forest because they do not look at the trees one by one.

Strategic planning is more important in some industries than in others. It is not important for oil exploration companies, which have to analyze prospects one by one. It is important in industries where tomorrow's opportunities are created by today's investments and where success depends on intangible assets like technology, product design, and reputation, or on elaborate marketing and distribution systems. Intangible assets are hard to evaluate in a purely bottom-up process.

Decentralization Most decisions on significant capital outlays are reserved for top management. At least that is the formal process. The real decisions may be made further down in the organization. Senior management may have limited effective control over project-by-project decisions because of lack of information at the top.

When this happens capital investment decisions are effectively decentralized regardless of what formal procedures specify. Many firms force divisions to set their own priorities by setting rigid constraints on the capital expenditures of the divisions. Other firms are less rigid: they accept decentralization; they relax and enjoy it, keeping control by budgeting, planning, and monitoring the overall operations of the divisions.

But decentralization can only work if plant and division managers are rewarded for doing the right things. The way performance is measured and rewarded affects the kinds of projects that are proposed. Capital tends to flow more easily to divisions that seem to perform well.

Therefore any discussion of the capital expenditure process has to consider what happens *after* the project is accepted. That is our next topic.

12-3 EVALUATING PERFORMANCE

Most firms have formal procedures for evaluating the performance of their capital investments. There are three aspects to performance measurement. First, companies need to monitor projects under construction to ensure that there are no serious delays or cost overruns. Second, companies generally conduct a post-mortem on major projects shortly after they have begun to operate. These investigations are known as **postaudits**. They help to identify problems that need repairing, to check the accuracy of forecasts, and to suggest questions that should have been asked before the project was undertaken. Postaudits pay off mainly by helping managers do a better job when they come to analyze the next round of investment proposals. Finally, there is ongoing performance measurement, which is done through the firm's accounting and control system. We will explain how that system should work to support the capital investment process and why it sometimes fails.

Controlling Projects in Progress

Control over projects is an essential follow-up to a decision to authorize expenditure. The authorization usually specifies how much money may be spent and when. Control is established by accounting procedures for recording expenditures as they occur. Typically, companies will permit up to 10% expenditure overruns, but beyond that the sponsor is required to submit a supplemental appropriation request. To ensure that the money is not diverted to other uses, the sponsor is also required to submit a revised appropriation request if there is any significant change in the nature of the project.

To avoid delays, a few companies attempt to set limits to the length of time before construction begins. Almost all firms require the sponsor to submit a formal notice of completion, so that the accumulated costs can be transferred to the permanent accounts and any unspent cash can be recovered rather than kept in a hidden kitty for miscellaneous uses.

These procedures are necessary aspects of control. More general information on progress is usually contained in monthly or quarterly status reports.

Postaudits

Postaudits of capital expenditures are now undertaken in most large firms. Not all projects are audited, and those that are are usually audited only once. A few firms require further audits for "problem" projects. The most common time for audit is one year after construction or installation is completed.

The audit is usually the responsibility of the corporation's controller and is handled by the internal audit department. Because this department may be ill-equipped to assess technical issues, the task is sometimes jointly assigned to accounting and engineering departments. Sometimes the audit is delegated to plants, and not infrequently it is assigned to the project originator. The scope for conflicts of interest in such cases is obvious.

It is a sensible precaution to check on the progress of recent investments. Otherwise problems may go undetected and uncorrected. Postaudits can also provide useful insights to the next round of decision making on capital investments. After a postaudit the controller may say, "We should have anticipated the extra working capital needed to support the project." Next time working capital will get the attention it deserves.

The postaudit is sometimes also used to monitor the quality of forecasts made by project proposers. However, it is worth sounding a note of caution here. The audit is usually taken far too soon after installation to provide any clear assessment of the project's success. And, since the forecasters rarely specify the economic assumptions behind their forecasts, it is hard to measure if they really got it right or if they were bailed out by a buoyant economy. Finally, the number of audited projects is so small and their authorship so imprecise that it is difficult to associate forecasting ability with a particular type of project or proposer.

Of course, the mere threat of postaudit may spur the forecaster to greater accuracy. But it can work the other way around. Many managers make conservative forecasts in the belief that what matters is to beat one's forecasts. In other cases the threat of audit may cause risky projects to be suppressed altogether.

Problems in Measuring Incremental Cash Flows after the Fact

Often postaudits cannot measure all cash flows generated by a project. It may be impossible to split the project away from the rest of the business.

Suppose you have just taken over a trucking firm that operates a package delivery service for local stores. You decide to try to revitalize the business by cutting costs and improving service. This requires three investment projects:

1. Buy five new trucks
2. Construct two additional dispatching centres
3. Buy a small computer to keep track of packages and schedule trucks

A year later you try a postaudit of the computer. You verify that it is working properly and check actual costs of purchase, installation and training against projections. But how do you identify the incremental cash *inflows* generated by the computer? No one has kept records of the extra gas that *would have* been used, or the number of packages that *would* have been lost, had the computer not been installed. You may be able to verify that service is better, but how much of the improvement comes from the new trucks, how much from the dispatching centres, and how much from the computer? It is impossible to say. The only meaningful way to judge the success or failure of your revitalization program is to examine the delivery business as a whole.

Evaluating Operating Performance

Think again of your package delivery business. We could measure its performance in two ways:

1. *Actual versus projected.* We could compare actual operating earnings or cash flow with what you predicted.
2. *Actual profitability versus an absolute standard of profitability.* We could also compare actual profitability against an absolute standard of profitability. Ideally we would like to know the present value of that business's future cash flow relative to the parent firm's current investment in it. The current investment is the value of the assets now committed to the business if they were put to the best alternative use.

The first measure is easy to understand and implement. The second is full of pitfalls, as we will now see.

Accounting Rate of Return as a Performance Measure

Let us think for a moment about how profitability should be measured in principle. It is easy enough to compute the true or "economic" rate of return for a common stock that is continuously traded. We just record cash receipts (dividends) for the year, add the change in price over the year, and divide by the beginning price:

$$\text{Rate of return} = \frac{\text{cash receipts} + \text{change in price}}{\text{beginning price}} = \frac{C_1 + (P_1 - P_0)}{P_0}$$

The numerator of the expression for rate of return (cash flow plus change in value) is called **economic income**:

Economic income = cash flow + change in present value

Any reduction in present value represents **economic depreciation**; any increase in present value represents *negative* economic depreciation. Therefore

Economic depreciation = reduction in present value

and

Economic income = cash flow − economic depreciation

The concept works for any asset. Rate of return equals cash flow plus change in value divided by starting value. The return on the package delivery service for 1984 is

$$\text{Rate of return} = \frac{C_{1984} + (PV_{1984} - PV_{1983})}{PV_{1983}}$$

where PV_{1983} and PV_{1984} indicate the present values of the business at the ends of 1983 and 1984.

The only hard part in measuring economic income and return is calculating present value. You can observe market value if shares in the asset are actively traded, but few plants, divisions, or capital projects have *their own* shares traded in the stock market. You can observe the present market value of *all* the firm's assets but not of any one of them taken separately.

Accountants rarely even attempt to measure present value. Instead they give us net book value (BV), which is original cost less depreciation computed according to some arbitrary schedule. Many companies use the book value to calculate the book return on investment (ROI):

Book income = cash flow − book depreciation
$$= C_1 + (BV_1 - BV_0)$$

Therefore

$$\text{Book ROI} = \frac{C_1 + (BV_1 - BV_0)}{BV_0}$$

If book depreciation and economic depreciation are different (they are rarely the same), then the book profitability measures will be wrong; that is, they will not measure true profitability. (In fact, it is not clear that accountants should even *try* to measure true profitability. They could not do so without heavy reliance on subjective estimates of value. Perhaps they should stick to supplying objective information, and leave the estimation of value to managers and investors.)

12-4 EXAMPLE—MEASURING THE PROFITABILITY OF THE NODHEAD SUPERMARKET

Supermarket chains invest heavily in building and equipping new stores. The regional manager of a chain is about to propose investing $1 million in a new store in Nodhead. Projected cash flows are:

Year	1	2	3	4	5	6	After Year 6
Cash flow (thousands of dollars)	100	200	250	298	298	298	0

Of course real supermarkets last more than six years. But these numbers are realistic in one important sense: it may take two or three years for a new store to catch on— that is, to build up a substantial, habitual clientele. Thus cash flow is low for the first few years even in the best locations.

We will assume the opportunity cost of capital is 10%. The Nodhead store's NPV at 10% is zero. It is an acceptable project, but not an unusually good one:

$$NPV = -1,000 + \frac{100}{1.10} + \frac{200}{(1.10)^2} + \frac{250}{(1.10)^3} + \frac{298}{(1.10)^4} + \frac{298}{(1.10)^5} + \frac{298}{(1.10)^6} = 0$$

It is not hard to forecast economic income and the rate of return. Table 12-2 shows the calculations. From the cash-flow forecasts we can forecast present value at the start of periods 1 to 6. Cash flow plus *change* in present value equals economic income. Rate of return equals economic income divided by start-of-period value.

Of course, these are forecasts. Actual future cash flows and values will be higher or lower. Table 12-2 shows that investors *expect* to earn 10% in each year of the store's six-year life. In other words, investors expect to earn the opportunity cost of capital each year from holding this asset.[6]

Table 12-3 shows the store's forecasted *book* profitability assuming straight-line depreciation over its six-year life. The book ROI is lower than the true return for the first two years and higher afterwards.[7] The error can be traced to the use of straight-line depreciation, which overstates economic depreciation at first and understates it later on. Note that any kind of accelerated depreciation would make the errors worse. Economic depreciation is *decelerated* in this case.

---

[6]This is a general result. Forecasted profitability always equals the discount rate used to calculate the estimated future present values.

[7]The errors in book ROI always catch up with you in the end. If the firm chooses a depreciation schedule that overstates a project's return in some years, it must also understate the return in other years. In fact, you can think of a project's IRR as a kind of average of the book returns. It is not a simple average, however. The weights are the project's book values discounted at the IRR. See J.A. Kay, "Accountants, Too, Could Be Happy in a Golden Age: The Accountant's Rate of Profit and the Internal Rate of Return," *Oxford Economic Papers*, 28:447–460 (1976).

Table 12-2 Forecasted economic income and rate of return for the proposed Nodhead store. Economic income equals cash flow plus change in present value. Rate of return equals economic income divided by value at start of year.

	Year					
	1	2	3	4	5	6
Cash flow	100	200	250	298	298	298
Present value, at *start* of year, 10% discount rate	1,000	1,000	901	741	517	271
Present value at *end* of year, 10% discount rate	1,000	901	741	517	271	0
Change in value during year	0	−99	−160	−224	−246	−271
Economic income	100	101	90	74	52	27
Rate of return	0.10	0.10	0.10	0.10	0.10	0.10
Economic depreciation	0	99	160	224	246	271

Note: There are minor rounding errors in some annual figures.

Table 12-3 Forecasted book income and ROI for the proposed Nodhead store. Book ROI is lower than the economic rate of return for the first two years and higher thereafter.

	Year					
	1	2	3	4	5	6
Cash flow	100	200	250	298	298	298
Book value at *start* of year, straight-line depreciation	1,000	833	667	500	333	167
Book value at *end* of year, straight-line depreciation	833	667	500	333	167	0
Change in book value during year	−167	−167	−167	−167	−167	−167
Book income	−67	+33	+83	+131	+131	+131
Book ROI	−0.067	+0.04	+0.124	+0.262	+0.393	+0.784
Book depreciation	167	167	167	167	167	167

Book Earnings versus True Earnings

At this point the regional manager steps up on stage for the following soliloquy:

"The Nodhead store's a decent investment. I really should propose it. But if we go ahead, I won't look very good at next year's performance review. And what if I also go ahead with the new stores in Russet, Gravenstein, and Sheepnose? Their cash-flow patterns are pretty much the same. I could actually appear to lose money next year. The stores I've got won't earn enough to cover the initial losses on four new ones.

"Of course, everyone knows new supermarkets lose money at first. The loss would be in the budget. My boss will understand—I think. But what about her boss? What if the board of directors starts asking pointed questions about profitability in my region? I'm under a lot of pressure to generate better earnings. Pamela Quince, the upstate manager, got a bonus for generating a 40% increase in book ROI. *She* didn't spend much on expansion. . . . "

The regional manager is getting conflicting signals. On the one hand he is told to find and propose good investment projects. *Good* is defined by discounted cash flow.

On the other hand, he is also urged to increase book earnings. But the two goals conflict because book earnings do not measure true earnings. The greater the pressure for immediate book profits, the more the regional manager is tempted to forgo good investments or to favour quick-payback projects over longer-lived projects, even if the latter have higher NPVs.

Does ROI Give the Right Answer in the Long Run?

Some people downplay the problem we have just described. Is a temporary dip in book profits a major problem? Don't the errors wash out in the long run, when the region settles down to a steady state with an even mix of old and new stores?

It turns out that the errors diminish but do *not* exactly offset. The simplest steady-state condition occurs when the firm does not grow, but reinvests just enough each year to maintain earnings and asset values. Table 12-4 shows steady-state book ROIs for a regional division that opens one store a year. For simplicity we assume the division starts from scratch and that each store's cash flows are carbon copies of the Nodhead store. The true rate of return on each store is, therefore, 10%. But, as Table 12-4 demonstrates, steady-state book ROI, at 12.6%, overstates the true rate of return. Therefore, you cannot assume that the errors in book ROI will wash out in the long run.

Table 12-4   Book ROI for a group of stores like the Nodhead store. The steady-state book ROI overstates the 10% *economic* rate of return.

	Year					
	1	2	3	4	5	6
Book income for store						
1	−67	+33	+83	+131	+131	+131
2		−67	+33	+83	+131	+131
3			−67	+33	+83	+131
4				−67	+33	+83
5					−67	+33
6						−67
Total Book Income	−67	−34	+49	180	311	442
Book value for store						
1	1,000	833	667	500	333	167
2		1,000	833	667	500	333
3			1,000	833	667	500
4				1,000	833	667
5					1,000	833
6						1,000
Total Book Value	1,000	1,833	2,500	3,000	3,333	3,500
Book ROI for all stores = $\frac{\text{total book income}}{\text{total book value}}$	−0.067	−0.019	+0.02	+0.06	+0.093	+0.126[a]

[a] Steady-state book ROI.
Note: Book income = cash flow + change in book value during year.

Thus we still have a problem even in the long run. The extent of error depends on how fast the business grows. We have just considered one steady state with a zero growth rate. Think of another firm with a 5% steady-state growth rate. Such a firm would invest $1,000 the first year, $1,050 the second, $1,102.50 the third, and so on. Clearly the faster growth means more new projects relative to old ones. The greater weight given to young projects, which have low book ROIs, the lower the business's apparent profitability. Figure 12-1 shows how this works out for a business composed of projects like the Nodhead store. Book ROI will either overestimate or underestimate the true rate of return unless the amount that the firm invests each year grows at the same rate as the true rate of return.[8]

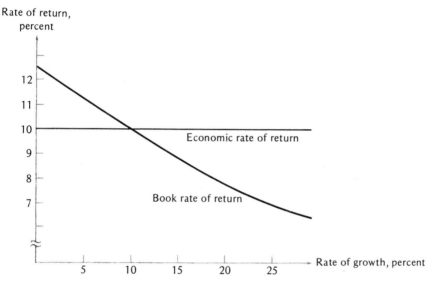

Figure 12-1   The faster a firm grows, the lower its book rate of return, providing true profitability is constant. This graph is drawn for a firm composed of identical projects all like the Nodhead store (Table 12-2), but growing at a constant compund rate.

Book measures of profitability can be wrong or misleading because:

1. Errors occur at different stages of project life. Book measures are likely to understate true profitability for new projects and overstate it for old ones.

2. Errors also occur when firms or divisions have a balanced mix of old and new projects. Our "steady-state" analysis shows this.

3. Errors occur because of inflation, basically because inflation shows up in revenue faster than it shows up in costs. For example, a firm owning a plant built in 1960 will, under standard accounting procedures, calculate depreciation in terms of the plant's original cost in 1960 dollars. The plant's output is sold for current dollars. This is why the United States Securities and Exchange Commission and the Canadian Institute of Chartered Accountants now require large corporations to report what their profits would be under replacement cost accounting. This procedure bases

---

[8]This also is a general result. Biases in steady-state book ROIs disappear when the growth rate equals the true rate of return. This was discovered by E. Solomon and J. Laya, "Measurement of Company Profitability: Some Systematic Errors in Accounting Rate of Return," in A.A. Robichek (ed.), *Financial Research and Management Decisions*, John Wiley & Sons, Inc., New York, 1967, pp. 152–183.

depreciation, not on the original cost of the firm's assets, but on what it would cost to replace its assets at current prices.

4. Book measures are often confused by "creative accounting." Some firms pick and choose among available accounting procedures, or even invent new ones, in order to make their income statements and balance sheets look good. This was done with particular imagination in the "go-go years" of the mid-1960s.

Investors and financial managers, having been burned by inflation and creative accounting, have learned not to take accounting profitability at face value. Yet many people do not realize the depth of the problem. They think that if firms adopted inflation accounting and eschewed creative accounting, everything would be all right except perhaps for temporary problems with very old or very young projects. In other words, they worry about reasons 3 and 4, and a little about reason 1, but not at all about 2. We think reason 2 deserves more attention.

12-5 WHAT CAN WE DO ABOUT BIASES IN ACCOUNTING PROFITABILITY MEASURES?

The dangers in judging profitability by accounting measures are clear from this chapter's discussion and examples. To be forewarned is to be forearmed. But we can say something beyond just "be careful."

It is natural for firms to set an absolute standard of profitability for plants or divisions. Ideally that standard should be the opportunity cost of capital for investment in the plant or division. But if performance is measured by book ROI, then the standard should be adjusted to reflect accounting biases.

This is easier said than done, because accounting biases are notoriously hard to measure in complex practical situations. Thus, many firms end up asking not, "Did the widget division earn more than its cost of capital last year?" but, "Was the widget division's book ROI typical of a successful firm in the widget industry?" The underlying assumptions are (1) similar accounting procedures are used by other widget manufacturers and (2) successful widget companies earn their cost of capital.

There are some simple accounting changes that could reduce biases in book ROI. Remember that the biases all stem from *not* using economic depreciation. Therefore why not switch to economic depreciation? The main reason is that each asset's present value would have to be re-estimated every year. Imagine the confusion if this were attempted. You can understand why accountants set up a depreciation schedule when an investment is made and then stick to it apart from exceptional circumstances. But why restrict the choice of depreciation schedules to the old standbys, straight-line, double-declining balance, and sum-of-the-years' digits? Why not specify a depreciation pattern that at least matches *expected* economic depreciation? For example, the Nodhead store could be depreciated according to the expected economic depreciation schedule shown in Table 12-2. This would avoid any systematic biases.[9] It would break no law or accounting standard. This step seems so simple and effective that we are at a loss to explain why firms have not adopted it.[10]

Much of the pressure for good book earnings comes from the top management. Chief executives have good reasons to shoot for good short-run earnings. Probably their bonuses depend on it. The market watches current earnings per share (partly because

---

[9]Using expected economic depreciation will not generate book ROIs that are exactly right unless realized cash flows exactly match forecasted flows. But we expect forecasts to be right on average.

[10]This procedure has been suggested by several authors, most recently by Zvi Bodie in "Compound Interest Depreciation in Capital Investment," *Harvard Business Review*, **60**:58–60 (May–June 1982).

---

it isn't allowed to look over top management's shoulder at the five-year plan). Is it surprising that top management does not always jump happily into high-NPV projects that will depress next year's earnings per share?

We do not mean to imply that chief executives typically sacrifice long-run value for immediate earnings. But they at least *worry* about earnings, and their worries affect attitudes and decisions down the line.

We think managers worry too much. They are uptight about book earnings. They often picture investors as mindless creatures who respond only to the latest earnings announcement. Investors are more sophisticated than that. Polaroid Corporation provides a good example. Its earnings dropped sharply in the early 1970s because of heavy development expenditures on the SX-70 instant camera, which was successfully introduced in 1973. If investors looked only at the latest earnings announcement they would have concluded that Polaroid was in big trouble in 1972. In fact they understood *why* earnings were low and acted accordingly.

Financial managers can help investors do better by *not* playing the earnings game. That is, they should not hire creative accountants or emphasize book earnings while downplaying more fundamental information about their firm's performance. The firm that brags only about its book earnings will be judged on its book earnings.

12-6 SUMMARY

We began this chapter by describing how capital budgeting is organized and ended by exposing serious biases in accounting measures of financial performance. Inevitably such discussions stress the mechanics of organization, control, and accounting. It is harder to talk about the informal procedures that reinforce the formal ones. But remember that it takes informal communication and personal initiative to make capital budgeting work. Also, the accounting biases are partly or wholly alleviated because managers and stockholders are smart enough to look behind reported book earnings.

Formal capital-budgeting systems usually have four stages:

1. Preparation of a *capital budget* for the firm. This is a plan for capital expenditure by plant, division, or other business unit.
2. *Project authorizations* give authority to go ahead with specific projects.
3. Procedures for *control of projects under construction* warn if projects are behind schedule or costing more than planned.
4. *Postaudits* check on the progress of recent investments.

The formal criteria used in project evaluation are a mixture of modern rules like net present value and internal rate of return, and old-fashioned rules like payback and average return on book. The old rules survive partly because everyone understands them; they provide a common language for discussing the project. They also survive because of the way performance is evaluated and rewarded. If managers are expected to generate quick results, and results are measured as contribution to book earnings, then management is naturally interested in payback and book return.

Most specific project proposals originate at the plant of division level. If the project doesn't cost much, it may be approved by middle management. But the final say on major capital outlays belongs to top management. The desire of top management to retain control of capital budgeting is understandable. But the chief executive cannot undertake a detailed analysis of every project he or she approves. Information at the top is often limited; project proposals may be designed more to persuade than inform.

Top management copes by relying on staff financial analysts, by making capital budgeting part of a broader budgeting and planning process, and by keeping the capital budgeting process flexible and open to informal communication.

Capital budgeting is not entirely a bottom-up process. Strategic planners practice "capital budgeting on a grand scale" by attempting to identify those businesses in which the firm has a special advantage. Project proposals that support the firm's accepted overall strategy are much more likely to have clear sailing as they come up through the organization.

Usually the plant or division proposing a capital investment will be responsible for making the project work. A project's sponsors are naturally concerned that the project performs well, and also that it *appears* to perform well. Thus the way the firm evaluates operating performance can affect the kinds of projects that middle managers are willing to propose.

There are two approaches to performance measurement. The first and easier is to compare actual cash flow with projected cash flow. The second is to compare actual profitability with the opportunity cost of capital. Both approaches are needed.

The second approach is the difficult and dangerous one. Most firms measure performance in terms of accounting or book profitability. Unfortunately book income and ROI are often seriously biased measures of true profitability and thus should not be directly compared to the opportunity cost of capital.

In principle, true or economic income is easy to calculate: you just subtract economic depreciation from the asset's cash flow for the period you are interested in. Economic depreciation is simply the decrease in the asset's present value during the period. (If the asset's value increases, then economic depreciation is negative.)

Unfortunately we can't ask accountants to recalculate each asset's present value every time income is calculated. But it does seem fair to ask why they don't try at least to match book depreciation schedules to typical patterns of economic depreciation.

FURTHER READING

The most extensive study of the capital budgeting process is:

J.L. Bower, *Managing the Resource Allocation Process,* Division of Research, Graduate School of Business Administration, Harvard University, Boston, 1970.

Scapens and Sale's article is a more up-to-date survey of current practice.

R.W. Scapens and J.T. Sale, "Performance Measurement and Formal Capital Expenditure Controls in Divisionalized Companies," *Journal of Business Finance and Accounting*, 8:389–420 (Autumn 1981).

There are many surveys of the application of capital budgeting criteria, including:

C.G. Hoskins and M.J. Dunn, "The Evaluation of Capital Expenditure Proposals under Uncertainty: The Practice of Large Corporations in Canada," *Journal of Business Administration*, 6:45–55 (Fall 1974).

L.D. Schall, G.L. Sundem, and W.R. Geijsbeek, "Survey and Analysis of Capital Budgeting Methods," *Journal of Finance*, 33:281–287 (March 1978).

T. Klammer, "Empirical Evidence of the Adoption of Sophisticated Capital Budgeting Techniques," *Journal of Business*, 45:387–397 (July 1972).

Swalm and Weingartner discuss some of the incentive problems arising in corporations:

R.O. Swalm, "Utility Theory: Insights into Risk-taking," *Harvard Business Review*, 44:123–136 (November–December 1966).

H.M. Weingartner, "Some New Views on the Payback Period and Capital Budgeting," *Management Science*, 15:B594–607 (August 1969).

Biases in book ROI and procedures for reducing the biases are discussed by:

E. Solomon and J. Laya, "Measurement of Company Profitability: Some Systematic Errors in the Accounting Rate of Return," in A.A. Robichek (ed.), *Financial Research and Management Decisions,* John Wiley & Sons, Inc., New York, 1967, pp. 152–183.

F.M. Fisher and J.I. McGowan, "On the Misuse of Accounting Rates of Return to Infer Monopoly Profits," *American Economic Review,* **73**:82–97 (March 1983).

J.A. Kay, "Accountants, Too, Could Be Happy in a Golden Age: The Accountant's Rate of Profit and the Internal Rate of Return," *Oxford Economic Papers,* **28**:447–460 (1976).

Z. Bodie, "Compound Interest Depreciation in Capital Investment," *Harvard Business Review,* **60**:58–60 (May–June 1982).

QUIZ

1. True or false?
   (a) The approval of a capital budget allows managers to go ahead with any projects included in the budget.
   (b) In most companies the controller authorizes all appropriation requests for capital expenditures.
   (c) Typically, companies will permit up to 10% expenditure overruns, but beyond that the sponsor is required to submit a supplemental appropriation request.
   (d) Most firms use several criteria for project selection.
   (e) Postaudits are usually undertaken about five years after project completion.
   (f) Setting capital budgets and project authorizations is a bottom-up process. Strategic planning, insofar as it affects capital investment decisions, is a top-down process.

2. Fill in the blanks:
   A project's economic income for a given year equals the project's ____ less its ____ depreciation. Book income is typically ____ than economic income early in the project's life and ____ than economic income later in its life.

3. Consider the following project:

Period	0	1	2	3
New cash flow	−100	0	78.55	78.55

   The internal rate of return is 20%. The NPV, assuming a 20% opportunity cost of capital, is exactly zero. Calculate the expected *economic* income and economic depreciation in each year.

4. True or false?
   (a) Book profitability measures are biased measures of true profitablity for individual assets. However, these biases "wash out" when firms hold a balanced mix of old and new assets.
   (b) Accountants do not allow firms to pick and choose among accounting procedures to make their income statements look good.
   (c) The Canadian Institute of Chartered Accountants now requires large corporations to report what their profits would be under replacement cost accounting.
   (d) Systematic biases in book profitability would be avoided if companies used depreciation schedules which matched expected economic depreciation. However, few, if any, firms have done this.

QUESTIONS AND PROBLEMS

1. Discuss the value of postaudits. Who should conduct them? When? Should they consider solely financial performance? Should they be confined to the larger projects?

2. Rework Table 12-4 assuming that the firm's investment expands by 10% per year; that is, it invests $1 million in year 0, $1.10 million in year 1, and so on. Then rework the table assuming a 20% annual expansion. How does the bias in the steady-state book ROI vary with the rate of expansion?

3. Suppose that the cash flows from Nodhead's new supermarket are as follows:

Year	0	1	2	3	4	5	6
Cash flows thousands of dollars	−1,000	+298	+298	+298	+138	+138	+138

(a) Recalculate economic depreciation. Is it accelerated or decelerated?
(b) Rework Tables 12-2 and 12-3 to show the relationship between the "true" rate of return and book ROI in each year of the project's life.
(c) Redraw Figure 12-1 to show how the bias in steady-state ROI varies with the rate of firm growth.

Year	0	1	2	3
Cash flows (millions of dollars)	−12	+5.20	+4.80	+4.40

4. Consider an asset with the following cash flows:
The firm uses straight-line book depreciation. Thus, for this project, it writes off $4 million per year in years 1, 2, and 3. The discount rate is 10%.
(a) Show that economic depreciation equals book depreciation.
(b) Show that the book rate of return is the same in each year.
(c) Show that the project's book profitability is its true profitability.
Notice that you've just illustrated an interesting theorem: if the book rate of return is the same in each year of a project's life, the book rate of return equals the IRR.

5. For internal accounting purposes, many firms charge each subsidiary or division for the cost of the capital that it uses. Income after deduction of this charge is usually known as *residual income.*
   What do you think are the advantages and disadvantages of such a system? How would you measure residual income?

6. Many accountants believe that instead of showing the written-down book value of the company's assets, the balance sheet should show the "written-down replacement cost." What is meant by this statement? Do you agree?

7. A project is expected to produce the following cash flows:

C_0	C_1	C_2	C_3
−900	+300	+400	+500

(a) Find the IRR of the project.
(b) Calculate the accounting return in each year assuming straight-line depreciation.
(c) In footnote 7, we stated that the IRR is a weighted average of the accounting returns where the weights are equal to the book values (at start of year) discounted by the IRR. Show that this is true for the above project.

8. Here is a harder question. It is often said that book income is overstated when there is rapid inflation because book depreciation understates true depreciation.

What definition of *true depreciation* is implicit in this statement? Does *true depreciation* equal *economic depreciation* as we have defined the latter term?

9. Instead of looking at past market returns for a guide to the cost of capital, some financial managers look at past accounting returns. What do you think are the advantages of doing this?

10. The following are extracts from two newsletters sent to a stockbroker's clients:

Investment Letter—March 1986

Kipper Parlours was founded earlier this year by its president, Mr. Albert Herring. It plans to open a chain of kipper parlours where young people can get together over a kipper and a glass of wine in a pleasant, intimate atmosphere. In addition to the traditional grilled kipper, the parlours serve such delicacies as Kipper Schnitzel, Kipper Grandemere, and (for dessert) Kipper Sorbet.

The economics of the business are simple. Each new parlour requires an initial investment in fixtures and fittings of $200,000 (the property itself is rented). These fixtures and fittings have an estimated life of five years and are depreciated straight-line over that period. Each new parlour involves significant start-up costs and is not expected to reach full profitability until its fifth year. Profits per parlour are estimated as follows:

	Year After Opening				
	1	2	3	4	5
Profit	0	40	80	120	170
Depreciation	40	40	40	40	40
Profit after depreciation	−40	0	40	80	130
Book value at start of year	200	160	120	80	40
Return on investment, %	−20	0	33	100	325

Kipper has just opened its first parlour and plans to open one new parlour each year. Despite the likely initial losses (which simply reflect start-up costs), our calculations show a dramatic profit growth and a long-term return on investment that is substantially higher than Kipper's 20% cost of capital.

The total market value of Kipper stock is currently only $250,000. In our opinion, this does not fully reflect the exciting growth prospects and we strongly recommend clients to buy.

Investment Letter—April 1986

Albert Herring, president of Kipper parlours, yesterday announced an ambitious new building plan. Kipper plans to open two new parlours next year, three the year after, and so on.

We have calculated the implications of this for Kipper's earnings per share and return on investment. The results are extremely disturbing and under the new plan, there seems to be no prospect of Kipper *ever* earning a satisfactory return on capital.

Since March, the value of Kipper's stock has fallen by 40%. Any investor who did not heed our earlier warnings should take the opportunity to sell the stock now.

Compare Kipper's accounting and economic income under the two expansion plans. How does the change in plan affect the company's return on investment? What is the present value of Kipper stock? Ignore taxes in your calculations.

FINANCING DECISIONS AND MARKET EFFICIENCY

CORPORATE FINANCING AND THE SIX LESSONS OF MARKET EFFICIENCY

Up to this point we have concentrated almost exclusively on the left-hand side of the balance sheet—the firm's capital expenditure decision. Now we move to the right-hand side and to the problems involved in providing finance for the capital expenditures. To put it crudely, you've learned how to spend money—now learn how to raise it.

Of course, we haven't totally ignored financing in our discussion of capital budgeting. But we made the simplest possible assumption: all-equity financing. That means we assumed that the firm raises its money by selling stock and then invests the proceeds in real assets. Later, when those assets generate cash flows, the cash is either returned to stockholders or invested in a second generation of real assets. Stockholders supply all of the firm's capital, bear all the business risks, and receive all the rewards.

Now we are turning the problem around. We take the firm's present portfolio of real assets and its future investment strategy as given, and then determine what the best financing strategy is. We will analyze trade-offs between different financing alternatives. For example,

- Should the firm reinvest most of its earnings in the business or should it pay them out as dividends?
- If the firm needs more money, should it issue more stock or should it borrow?
- Should it borrow short-term or long-term?
- Should it borrow by issuing a normal long-term bond or a convertible bond (that is, a bond that can be exchanged by the bondholders for common stock of the firm)?

There are countless other financing trade-offs, as you will see.

The purpose of holding the firm's capital budgeting decision constant is to separate those decisions from the financing decision. Strictly speaking, this assumes that capital budgeting and financing decisions are *independent*. In many circumstances this is a quite reasonable assumption. The firm is generally free to change its capital structure by repurchasing one security and issuing another. In that case there is no need to associate a particular investment project with a particular source of cash. The firm can think first about what projects to accept and second about how they should be financed.

Sometimes decisions about capital structure depend on project choice or vice versa, and in those cases the investment and financing decisions have to be considered jointly. However, we defer discussion of such interactions of financing and investment decisions until later in the book.

13-1 WE ALWAYS COME BACK TO NPV

Although it is helpful to separate investment and financing decisions, there are basic similarities in the criteria for making them. The decisions to purchase a machine tool or to sell a bond each involve valuation of a risky asset. The fact that one asset is real and the other financial doesn't matter. In both cases we end up computing net present value.

The phrase *net present value of borrowing* may seem odd to you. But the following example should help to explain what we mean. As part of its policy of encouraging small business, the government offers to lend your firm $100,000 for ten years at an interest rate of 3%. This means that the firm is liable for interest payments of $3,000 in each of the years 1 through 10 and that it is responsible for repaying the $100,000 in the final year. Should you accept the offer?

We can compute the NPV of the loan agreement in the usual way. The one difference is that the first cash flow is *positive* and the subsequent flows *negative*:

NPV = amount borrowed − present value of interest payments

$\qquad$ − present value of loan repayment

$$= +100,000 - \left[\sum_{t=1}^{10} \frac{3,000}{(1+r)^t} \right] - \frac{100,000}{(1+r)^{10}}$$

The only missing variable is r, the opportunity cost of capital. You need that to value the liability created by the loan. We reason this way. The government's loan to you is a financial asset: a piece of paper representing your promise to pay $3,000 per year plus the final repayment of $100,000. How much would that paper sell for if freely traded in capital markets? It would sell for the present value of those cash flows, discounted at r, the rate of return offered by other securities of equivalent risk. Now, the class of equivalent-risk securities includes other bonds issued by your firm, so that all you have to do to determine r is to answer this question: "What interest rate would my firm have to pay to borrow money directly from the capital markets rather than from the government?"

Suppose that this rate is 10%. Then

$$\text{NPV} = +100,000 - \left[\sum_{t=1}^{10} \frac{3,000}{(1.10)^t} \right] - \frac{100,000}{(1.10)^{10}}$$
$$= +100,000 - 56,988 = +\$43,012$$

Of course, you don't need any arithmetic to tell you that borrowing at 3% is a good deal when the fair rate is 10%. But the NPV calculation tells you just how much that opportunity is worth ($43,012). It also brings out the essential similarity of investment and financing decisions.

Differences between Investment and Financing Decisions

In some ways investment decisions are simpler than financing decisions. The number of different financing instruments (that is, securities) is continually expanding. You will have to learn the major families, genera, and species. You should also be aware of the major financial institutions that provide financing for business firms. Finally, the vocabulary of financing has to be acquired. You will learn about *tombstones, red herrings, balloons, sinking funds,* and many other exotic beasts—behind each of these terms lies an interesting story.

There are also ways in which financing decisions are much easier than investment decisions. First, financing decisions do not have the same degree of finality as investment decisions. They are easier to reverse. In other words, their abandonment value is higher.

Second, it's harder to make or lose money by smart or stupid financing strategies. In other words, it is difficult to find financing schemes with NPVs significantly different from zero. That reflects the nature of the competition.

When the firm looks at capital investment decisions, it does *not* assume that it is facing perfect, competitive markets. It may have only a few competitors that specialize in the same line of business in the same geographical area. And it may own some unique assets that give it an edge over its competitors. Often these assets are intangible items, like patents, expertise, reputation, or market position. All this opens up the opportunity of making superior profits and of finding projects with positive NPVs. It also makes it difficult to tell whether any specific project has a positive NPV.

In financial markets your competition is all other corporations seeking funds, to say nothing of the provincial, local, and federal governments, financial institutions, individuals, and foreign firms and governments that also come to Bay Street for financing. The investors who supply financing are comparably numerous, and they are smart: money attracts brains. The financial amateur often views capital markets as *segmented*, that is, broken down into distinct sectors. But money moves between those sectors, and it moves fast.

Remember that a good financing decision generates a positive NPV. It is one in which the amount of cash raised exceeds the value of the liability created. But turn that statement around. If selling a security generates a positive NPV for you, it must generate a negative NPV for the buyer. Thus, the loan we discussed was a good deal for your firm, but a negative NPV investment from the government's point of view. By lending at 3% it offered a $43,012 subsidy.

What are the chances that your firm could consistently trick or persuade investors into purchasing securities with negative NPVs to them? Pretty low. In general, firms should assume that the securities they issue are fairly priced and therefore have NPV equal to zero.

Efficient Capital Markets

We are leading up to the fundamental financial concept of **efficient capital markets**. *If capital markets are efficient, then purchase or sale of any security at the prevailing market price is a zero-NPV transaction.*

Does that sound like a sweeping statement? It is. That is why we have devoted all of the rest of this chapter to the history, logic, and tests of the efficient-market hypothesis.

You may ask why we start our discussion of financing issues with this conceptual point, before you have even the most basic knowledge about securities, issue procedures, and financial institutions. We do it this way because financing decisions seem overwhelmingly complex if you don't learn to ask the right questions. We are afraid you might flee from confusion to the myths that often dominate popular discussion of corporate financing.

You need to understand the efficient-market hypothesis, not because it is *universally* true and relevant, but because it leads you to ask the right questions.

13-2 WHAT IS AN EFFICIENT MARKET?

When economists say that the security market is efficient, they are not talking about whether the filing is up-to-date or whether desk tops are tidy. They mean that information is widely and cheaply available to investors and that all relevant and ascertainable information is already reflected in security prices. That is why purchases or sales in an efficient security market are zero-NPV transactions.

A Startling Discovery: Price Changes are Random

As is so often the case with important ideas, this concept of efficient markets was a by-product of a chance discovery. In 1953, the Royal Statistical Society met in London to discuss a rather unusual paper.[1] Its author, Maurice Kendall, was a distinguished statistician and its subject was the behaviour of stock and commodity prices. Kendall's purpose had been to separate out regular price cycles, but to his surprise he could not find any such cycles. Each series appeared to be "a 'wandering' one, almost as if once a week the Demon of Chance drew a random number . . . and added it to the current price to determine the next week's price." In other words, prices seemed to follow a *random walk.*

If you are not sure what we mean by "random walk," you might like to think of the following example. You are given $100 to play a game. At the end of a month a coin is tossed. If it comes up heads, you win 3% of your investment; if it is tails, you lose 1%. Therefore your capital at the end of the first month is worth $103 or $99. At the end of the second month the coin is tossed again. Now the possible outcomes are:

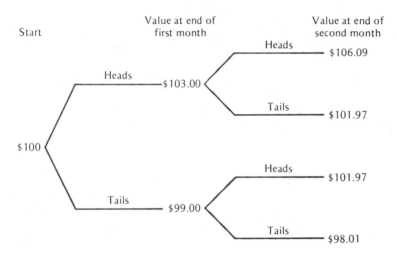

This process is a random walk with a positive drift of 1% per month.[2] It is a random walk because successive changes in value are independent. That is, the odds each month of winning are 50%, regardless of the value at the start of the month or of the pattern of heads and tails in the previous months.

Figure 13-1 shows the outcome from playing the game for one 60-month period. It is easy to imagine cycles in the value of the investment, but you know it was randomly generated.

When Maurice Kendall suggested that stock prices follow a random walk, he was implying that the price changes are as independent of one another as the gains and losses in our game. To most economists this was a startling and bizarre idea. In fact the idea was *not* completely novel. It had been proposed in an almost forgotten doctoral

---

[1] See M.G. Kendall, "The Analysis of Economic Time-Series, Part 1. Prices." *Journal of the Royal Statistical Society,* **96**:11–25 (1953).

[2] The drift is equal to the expected outcome:

$$\frac{1}{2}(3) + \frac{1}{2}(-1) = 1\%$$

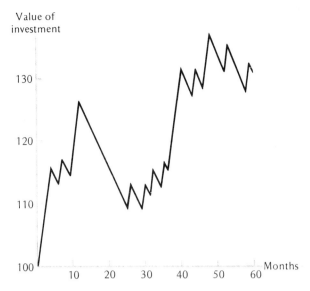

Figure 13-1 Here is one example of what could happen if you played our coin-tossing game for 60 months.

thesis written 53 years earlier by a Frenchman, Louis Bachelier.[3] Bachelier's suggestion was original enough, but his accompanying development of the mathematical theory of random processes anticipated by five years Einstein's famous work on the random motion of gas molecules in collision.

Kendall's work did not suffer the neglect of Bachelier's. As computers and data became more readily available, economists and statisticians rapidly amassed a large volume of supporting evidence. Let us look very briefly at the kinds of tests they have used.

Suppose you wished to assess whether there is any tendency for price changes to persist from one day to the next. You might begin by drawing a scatter diagram of changes on successive days. Figure 13-2 is an example of such a diagram. Each cross shows the change in the price of Dome Petroleum stock on successive days. Suppose the percentage price change is +9.2% from Monday to Tuesday and +5.4% from Tuesday to Wednesday. This gives the circled point in the northeast quadrant of Figure 13-2. If there was a systematic tendency for a positive price change to be followed by another positive one, there would be many points in the northeast quadrant and few in the southeast quadrant. It is obvious from a glance that there is very little pattern in these price movements, but we can test this more precisely by calculating the coefficient of correlation between each day's price change and the next. If price movements persisted, the correlation would be strongly positive; if there were no relationship, it would be 0. In our example, the correlation was 0.04—there was a very faint tendency for a price rise to be followed by another price rise.

Figure 13-2 showed the behaviour of only one stock but our finding is typical. Researchers have looked at daily changes, weekly changes, monthly changes; they have

[3]See L. Bachelier, *Théorie de la Spéculation*, Gauthier-Villars, Paris, 1900. Reprinted in English (A.J. Boness, trans.) in P.H. Cootner (ed.), *The Random Character of Stock Market Prices*, M.I.T. Press, Cambridge, Mass., 1964, pp. 17–78. During the 1930s the food economist Holbrook Working had also noticed the random behaviour of commodity prices. See H. Working, "A Random Difference Series for Use in the Analysis of Time Series," *Journal of the American Statistical Association*, **29**:11–24 (March 1934).

looked at many different stocks in many different countries and for many different periods; they have calculated the coefficient of correlation between these price changes; they have looked for runs of positive or negative price changes; they have examined some of the so-called *technical rules* that have been used by some investors to exploit the "patterns" they claim to see in past stock prices. With remarkable unanimity researchers have concluded that there is no useful information in the sequence of past changes in stock price. As a result, many of the researchers have become famous. None has become rich.

Price change day t + 1

Price change day t

Figure 13-2   Each point shows a pair of returns for Dome Petroleum stock on two successive days during 1979, 1980, or 1981. For example, the circled point records a return of 9.2% on one day and a 5.4% return the following day. This scatter diagram shows no relationship between successive days.

A Theory to Fit the Facts

We have mentioned that the initial reaction to the random walk finding was surprise. It was in fact several years before economists appreciated that this price behaviour is exactly what one should expect in any competitive market.

Suppose, for example, that you wish to sell an antique painting at an auction but you have no idea of its value. Can you be sure of receiving a fair price? The answer is that you can if the auction is sufficiently competitive. In other words, you need to satisfy yourself that it is to be fairly conducted,[4] that there is no substantial cost involved in submitting a bid, and that the auction is attended by a reasonable number of skilled potential bidders, each of whom has access to the available information. In this case, no matter how ignorant *you* may be, competition among experts will ensure that the price you realize fully reflects the value of the painting.

In just the same way, competition among investment analysts will lead to a stock market in which prices at all times reflect true value. But what do we mean by *true*

---

[4]That includes no collusion among bidders.

value? It is potentially a slippery phrase. True value does not mean ultimate *future value*—we do not expect investors to be fortunetellers. It means an equilibrium price that incorporates *all* the information available to investors at that point in time. That was our definition of an efficient market.

Now you can begin to see why price changes in an efficient market are random. If prices always reflect all relevant information, then they will change only when new information arrives. But new information *by definition* cannot be predicted ahead of time (otherwise it would not be new information). Therefore price changes cannot be predicted ahead of time. To put it another way, if stock prices already reflect all that is predictable, then stock price *changes* must reflect only the unpredictable. The series of price changes must be random.[5]

Figure 13-3 Cycles self-destruct as soon as they are recognized by investors. The stock price instantaneously jumps to the present value of the expected future price.

Suppose, however, that competition among research analysts were not so strong and that there were predictable cycles in stock prices. Investors could then make superior profits by trading on the basis of these cycles. Figure 13-3, for example, shows a two-month upswing for Establishment Industries (EI). The upswing started last month, when EI's stock price was $40, and it is expected to carry the stock price to $60 next month. What will happen when investors perceive this bonanza? It will self-destruct. Since EI stock is a bargain at $50, investors will rush to buy. They will stop buying only when the stock offers a normal rate of return. Therefore, as soon as a cycle becomes apparent to investors, they immediately eliminate it by their trading.

Two types of investment analyst help to make price changes random. Many analysts study the company's business and try to uncover information about its profitability that will shed new light on the value of the stock. These analysts are often called *fundamental analysts*. Competition in fundamental research will tend to ensure that prices reflect *all*

---

[5]When economists speak of stock prices as following a random walk, they are being a little imprecise. A statistician reserves the term *random walk* to describe a series that has a constant expected change each period and a constant degree of variability. But market efficiency does not imply that risks and expected returns cannot shift over time. The correct term for a wandering series with *shifting* expected changes and variability is a *submartingale*.

relevant information and that price changes are unpredictable. The other analysts study the past price record and look for cycles. These analysts are called *technical analysts*. Competition in technical research will tend to ensure that current prices reflect all information in the past sequence of prices and that future price changes cannot be predicted from past prices.

Three Forms of the Efficient-Market Theory

Harry Roberts has defined three levels of market efficiency.[6] The first is the case in which prices reflect all the information contained in the record of past prices. Roberts called this a *weak* form of efficiency. The random-walk research shows that the market is at *least* efficient in this weak sense.

The second level of efficiency is the case in which prices reflect not only past prices but all other published information. Roberts called this a *semistrong* form of efficiency. Researchers have tested this by looking at specific items of news, such as announcements of earnings and dividends, forecasts of company earnings, changes in accounting practices, and mergers.[7] Most of this information was rapidly and accurately impounded in the price of the stock.

Finally, Harry Roberts envisaged a *strong* form of efficiency in which prices reflect not just public information but *all* the information that can be acquired by painstaking fundamental analysis of the company and economy. In such a case, the stock market would be like our ideal auction house: prices would *always* be fair and *no* investor would be able to make consistently superior forecasts of stock prices. Most tests of this view have involved an analysis of the performance of professionally managed portfolios. These studies have concluded that, after taking account of differences in risk, no group of institutions has been able to outperform the market consistently and that even the differences between the performance of individual funds are no greater than you would expect from chance.[8]

Although few simple economic ideas are as well supported by the evidence as the efficient-market theory, it would be wrong to pretend that there are no puzzles or apparent exceptions. For instance, New York Stock Exchange specialists seem to have made consistently superior profits; so do company managers when they deal in their own company's stock.[9] These are two cases that don't seem to square well with the strong form of the efficient-market theory.

---

[6]See H.V. Roberts, "Statistical Versus Clinical Prediction of the Stock Market." Unpublished paper presented to the Seminar on the Analysis of Security Prices, University of Chicago, May 1967.

[7]See, for example, R. Ball and P. Brown, "An Empirical Evaluation of Accounting Income Numbers," *Journal of Accounting Research*, **6**:159–178 (Autumn 1968); R.R. Pettit, "Dividend Announcements, Security Performance, and Capital Market Efficiency," *Journal of Finance,* **27**:993–1007 (December 1972); G. Foster, "Stock Market Reaction to Estimates of Earnings Per Share by Company Officials," *Journal of Accounting Research*, **11**:25–37 (Spring 1973); R.S. Kaplan and R. Roll, "Investor Evaluation of Accounting Information: Some Empirical Evidence," *Journal of Business*, **45**:225–257 (April 1972); G. Mandelker, "Risk and Return: The Case of Merging Firms," *Journal of Financial Economics,* **1**:303–335 (December 1974); and G. Charest, "Returns to Dividend Splitting Stocks on the Toronto Stock Exchange," *Journal of Business Administration*, **12**:1–18 (Fall 1980).

[8]M. Jensen, "The Performance of Mutual Funds in the Period 1945–64," *Journal of Finance,* **23**:389–416 (May 1968); and D. Grant, "Investment Performance of Canadian Mutual Funds: 1960–1974," *Journal of Business Administration*, **8**:1–10 (Fall 1976).

[9]See V. Niederhoffer and M.F.M. Osborne, "Market Making and Reversal on the Stock Exchange," *Journal of the American Statistical Association*, **61**:897–916 (December 1966) and S.P. Pratt and C.W.

We believe that there is now widespread agreement that capital markets function well. So nowadays when economists come across instances where this apparently isn't true, they don't throw the efficient-market hypothesis onto the economic garbage heap. Instead they ask whether there isn't some missing ingredient that their theories ignore. For example, in the past few years a good deal of evidence has accumulated that the stocks of small companies have had higher average returns than the stocks of large companies with similar risk.[10] To our knowledge no economist has been tempted as a consequence to make a massive investment in small companies. Instead they have assumed that investors aren't stupid and have looked at whether the small-company stocks suffer from some other defect, such as a lack of easy marketability, that is not allowed for in our theories or tests.

Some Misconceptions

The efficient-market hypothesis is frequently misinterpreted. One common error is to think that it implies perfect forecasting ability. In fact it implies only that prices reflect all available information. In the same vein, some have suggested that prices cannot represent fair value because they go up and down. The answer, however, is that they would not represent fair value *unless* they went up and down. It is because the future is so uncertain and people are so often surprised that prices fluctuate. (Of course, when we look *back*, nothing seems quite so surprising: it is easy to convince ourselves that we really knew all along how prices were going to change.) A rather different temptation is to believe that the inability of institutions to achieve superior portfolio performance is an indication that portfolio managers are incompetent. This is incorrect. Market efficiency exists only because competition is keen and portfolio managers are doing their job.

Another error is to think that the random behaviour of stock prices implies that the market is irrational. *Randomness* and *irrationality* are not synonymous. Stock price changes are random because investors are rational and competitive. There is an important corollary to this. If the price of any risky asset does *not* vary randomly, then its price *cannot* represent competitive market value.

When we talk about an efficient market, we mean that the market is functioning well and the prices are fair. For the financial manager the concept of market efficiency entails six main lessons. Let us consider them in turn and at the same time introduce briefly some of the issues with which we shall be concerned in subsequent chapters.

DeVere, "Relationship Between Insider Trading and Rates of Return for NYSE Common Stocks," in J.H. Lorie and R.A. Brealey (eds.), *Modern Developments in Investment Management*, 2nd ed., Frederick A. Praeger, Inc., New York, 1978.

Canadian stock exchanges have market makers or registered traders, but no specialists. Both stand ready to make a market as buy and sell orders come in from investors. However, each NYSE stock has only one specialist, while each Canadian stock may have several market makers. Thus, a specialist has monopolistic access to information about any imbalance between buy and sell orders, which may be used to earn superior profits.

[10]See, for example, R.W. Banz, "The Relationship Between Return and Market Value of Common Stocks," *Journal of Financial Economics*, 9:3–18 (March 1981); M.R. Reinganum, "Misspecification of Capital Asset Pricing: Empirical Anomalies Based on Earnings Yields and Market Values," *Journal of Financial Economics*, 9:19–46 (March 1981); and I.G. Morgan, A.L. MacBeth, and D.J. Novak, "The Relationship between Equity Value and Abnormal Returns in the Canadian Stock Market," Working Paper 81–12, Queen's University (April 1983).

13-3 THE FIRST LESSON OF MARKET EFFICIENCY: MARKETS HAVE NO MEMORY

The weak form of the efficient-market hypothesis states that the sequence of past price changes contains no information about future changes. Economists express the same idea more concisely when they say that the market has no memory. Sometimes financial managers *seem* to act as if this were not the case. For example, they are often reluctant to issue stock after a fall in price. They are inclined to wait for a rebound. Similarly, managers favour equity rather than debt financing after an abnormal price rise. The idea is to "catch the market while it is high." But we know that the market has no memory and the cycles that financial managers seem to rely on do not exist.

Sometimes a financial manager will have inside information indicating that the firm's stock is overpriced or underpriced. Suppose, for example, that there is some good news the market does not know but you do. The stock price will rise sharply when the news is revealed. Therefore, if the company sold shares at the current price, it would be offering a bargain to new investors at the expense of present stockholders. But inside information has nothing to do with the history of the stock price. Your firm's stock could be selling now at half its price of a year ago and yet you could have special information suggesting that it is *still* grossly overvalued. Or it may be undervalued at twice last year's price.

13-4 THE SECOND LESSON OF MARKET EFFICIENCY: TRUST MARKET PRICES

In an efficient market you can trust prices. They impound all available information about the value of each security.

This means that in an efficient market there is no way for most investors to achieve consistently superior rates of return. That is important for the financial manager who is responsible for the firm's pension fund. If this is organized or funded on the assumption that the portfolio manager's acumen is likely to add another percent or two to the fund's annual return, the company is destined to disappointment. The return on the pension fund will be affected relatively little by the manager's ability to "pick stocks." It will depend much more on the degree of risk assumed, on the extent to which large brokerage fees are incurred by excessive trading, and on the manager's judgement in selecting securities that are appropriate for a fund that does not pay taxes.

The operations of the company may also be directly affected by management's faith in its investment skills. For example, one company will often purchase another simply because its management thinks that the stock is undervalued. On approximately half the occasions the stock of the acquired firm really will be undervalued. But on the other half it will be overvalued. On average the value will be correct, so that the acquiring company is playing a fair game except for the costs of the acquisition.

Example: Northwestern Bell's Bond Repurchase Offer

Here is another instance in which the financial manager should trust market prices. In early 1977 four American Telephone and Telegraph, Inc. (AT&T) subsidiaries offered to repurchase outstanding bonds that had been issued in 1974 at a time of high interest rates. The bonds of one issue by Northwestern Bell carried a *coupon rate* of 10% and had a *maturity* of 40 years. In other words, Northwestern Bell had promised to pay the bondholder $100 a year for every $1,000 borrowed. These interest payments were to continue for 40 years, until 2014, at which time the original amount borrowed was to be repaid.

The bonds had a zero NPV *at the time of issue*. The fair interest rate at that time was 10%:

$$\text{NPV at time of issue} = + 1,000, - \sum_{t=1}^{40} \frac{100}{(1.10)^t} - \frac{1,000}{(1.10)^{40}} = 0$$

$$= \text{amount borrowed} - \text{present value of interest payments}$$
$$- \text{present value of loan repayment}$$

By January 1977 interest rates on newly issued bonds had dropped to approximately 8.2%. As a result, the market value of the Northwestern Bell bonds on January 20 had risen to $1,130. Northwestern Bell would clearly have gained by handing back to each bondholder the original amount borrowed ($1,000 a bond) and cancelling the debt issue. But the company had no right to do so, at least not in 1977. The firm did have the option to repurchase or "call" the bonds in 1979 at a price of $1,085.70, but that option was no help in 1977.[11]

Northwestern Bell offered to repurchase the bonds for $1,160, in effect offering bondholders a bonus of $30 per bond for agreeing to retire the issue. Bondholders were naturally happy to accept the unexpected $30 bonus, and 80% of the issue was retired.

Why did Northwestern Bell do it? The stated reason was to reduce interest charges. These interest charges amounted to $15 million a year on the old bonds. Notice that the company could have financed the repurchase by issuing 1,160/1,000 × $150 million or $174 million of fresh debt at an interest rate of 8.2%. Therefore instead of paying out $15 million as interest, it would have had to pay out only 0.082 × 174 = $14.3 million, a saving of $700,000 per year.

But what was the NPV of this venture? The company was investing $1,160 per bond to eliminate a liability with a market value of $1,130. In an efficient market the price of the bonds must represent their true value. Therefore the NPV of the transaction was −$30 per bond.

Northwestern Bell was right. The bond repurchase did reduce interest charges. But our analysis shows that this was no justification for the transaction in an efficient market. Why didn't the firm wait and call the bonds in 1979 at the lower price of $1,085.70 stated in the bond contract? Northwestern Bell's managers are not stupid. Thus we suspect that there was some other reason for the repurchase.[12] Our point is that the *stated* reason was clearly wrong in an efficient bond market.

13-5 THE THIRD LESSON OF MARKET EFFICIENCY: THERE ARE NO FINANCIAL ILLUSIONS

In an efficient market there are no financial illusions. Investors are unromantically concerned with the firm's cash flows and the portion of those cash flows to which they are entitled.

---

[11]But the call option explains why the bonds sold at only $1,130 and not at the present value of $100 per year for 37 years followed by a final payment of $1,000. Investors anticipated that the bonds would be retired before maturity.

[12]Taxes are one possibility. If Northwestern Bell could claim the difference between $1,160 cost of repurchase and the $1,000 face value of each bond as a loss for tax purposes, the firm's income taxes for 1977 were reduced by 48% of $160. If so the effective repurchase cost was $1,083.20, not $1,160.

Stock Splits and Dividends

We can illustrate our third lesson by looking at the effect of stock splits and stock dividends. Every year many companies increase the number of shares in issue either by subdividing the stock that is already outstanding or by distributing more shares of stock as dividends. For a large company, the administrative costs of such action may exceed a million dollars. Yet it does not affect in any other way the company's cash flows nor the proportion of these cash flows attributable to each shareholder. You may think that you are better off, but that is an illusion.

Suppose the stock of Chaste Manhattan Finance Company is selling for $210 per share. A 3-for-1 split would replace each outstanding share with three new shares.[13] Chaste would probably arrange this by printing two new shares for each original share and distributing the new shares to its stockholders as a "free gift." After the split we would expect each share to sell for $210/3 = $70. Dividends per share, earnings per share, and all other "per share" variables would be one-third their previous levels.

A variety of justifications have been proposed for splits and stock dividends. One endorsement came from the president of a large American corporation, who observed that stock dividends "give shareholders a reasonable hedge against inflation and let them participate in the increase in book value. On the other hand," he warned, "it would be silly to declare [them] if not earned because that would just lower the book value." A further argument was proposed by the chairman of another company, who suggested that paying a stock dividend would provide investors with "a greater return while at the same time conserving cash to finance the company's anticipated growth."[14] A third and disarmingly simple explanation was offered by a textbook, which observed that stockholders like stock splits because they expect them to be followed by more stock splits. Claims such as these contrast strongly with the efficient-market notion that investors are concerned solely with their share of the company's cash flows.

Of course extremely high stock prices are inconvenient for small investors. In October 1983 one share in the Swiss drug firm Hoffman La Roche was priced at 90,000 Swiss francs or about $42,000. That is a nuisance if you only have $1,000 to invest. A stock split by Hoffman La Roche could therefore have significant convenience value. But convenience value does not justify the many companies that split their shares when they are selling for less than $100.

We can check whether investors are fooled by stock splits by looking at whether there were any abnormal changes in the stock price at the time of the split. First, however, we must explain how you can use some of the ideas in Chapter 9 to identify these abnormal price movements. In Chapter 9 we introduced you to Merrill Lynch's "beta book." This contains two measures of each stock's performance. Alpha (α) describes how much on average the stock price moved when the market was unchanged. Beta (β) describes the average additional return for each 1% change in the market index. For example, Table 9-2 showed that DEC's stock price rose on average by 0.51% per month when the market was unchanged ($\alpha = 0.51$), and it rose a further 1.38% for each 1% change in the market index ($\beta = 1.38$). Now suppose you were interested in the performance of DEC's stock in January 1983, when the market rose 2.8%. On past evidence you would judge that the expected change in the stock price that month was

---

[13]There are some confusing transatlantic differences in terminology. In the United Kingdom such increases usually take the form of a "scrip issue." A 2-for-1 scrip issue (that is, two new shares in addition to one old) is equivalent to a 3-for-1 stock split.

[14]Cited in J.E. Walter, *Dividend Policy and Enterprise Valuation,* Wadsworth Publishing Company, Inc., Belmont, Calif., 1967.

Expected price change $= \alpha + (\beta \times \text{market change})$

$$= 0.51 + (1.38 \times 2.8) = 4.4\%^{[15]}$$

In fact DEC's stock price rose by 22.5% in January 1983. Its abnormal price change was, therefore,

Abnormal price change $=$ actual change $-$ expected change

$$= 22.5 - 4.4 = 18.1\%$$

This 18.1% rise in DEC's stock price was over and above the normal rise in such market conditions.[16]

Now we can look at the abnormal price movements that generally take place around the time of a stock split. Figure 13-4 summarizes the results of an important study of splits during the period 1926–1960.[17] It shows the abnormal performance of stocks around the time of the split after adjusting for the increase in the number of shares.[18] Notice the rise in price before the split. The announcement of the split would have occurred in the last month or two of this period. That means the decision to split is both the consequence of a rise in price and the cause of a further rise. It looks as if shareholders are not as hard-headed as we have been making out: they do seem to care about form as well as substance. However during the subsequent year, two-thirds of the splitting companies announced above-average increases in cash dividends. Usually such an announcement would cause an unusual rise in the stock price, but in the case of the splitting companies there was no such occurrence at any time after the split.[19] Indeed, the stocks of those companies that did *not* increase their dividends by an above-average amount declined in value to levels prevailing well before the split. The apparent explanation is that the split was accompanied by an explicit or implicit promise of a subsequent dividend increase, and the rise in price at the time of the split had nothing

---

[15]It is important when estimating α and β that you choose a period in which you believe the stock behaved normally. If its performance was abnormal, then estimates of α and β cannot be used to measure the return investors expected.

[16]You can also use the capital asset pricing model to measure abnormal returns. This states that the expected return for DEC stock is

Expected return $= r_f + \beta(r_m - r_f)$

The market return (r_m) in January 1983 was equal to the 2.8% change in the index plus the 0.4% monthly dividend yield. The interest rate (r_f) was 9.5% a year or about 0.75% a month. Therefore,

Expected return $= 0.75 + 1.38(3.2 - 0.75) = 4.1\%$

Abnormal return $=$ actual return $-$ expected return

$$= 22.5 - 4.1 = 18.4\%$$

The two methods in this case give nearly identical answers.

[17]See E.F. Fama, L. Fisher, M. Jensen, and R. Roll, "The Adjustment of Stock Prices to New Information," *International Economic Review*, 10:1–21 (February 1969).

[18]By this we mean that the study looked at the change in the shareholder's wealth. A decline in the price of Chaste Manhattan stock from $210 to $70 at the time of the split would not affect shareholder's wealth.

[19]This does not imply that investors like high-dividend payouts for their own sake. It could be that dividend increases are valued only because they are a sign of company prosperity. We will discuss this point in Chapter 16.

to do with a predilection for splits as such but with the information that it was thought to convey. A stock split seems an expensive way to send the message, however.[20]

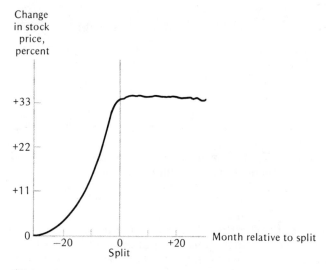

Figure 13-4 Changes in stock price at the time of a stock split. The changes are adjusted for both general market movements and the increase in the number of shares. Notice the rise before the split and the absence of abnormal changes after the split.

Source: E. Fama, L. Fisher, M. Jensen, and R. Roll, "The Adjustment of Stock Prices to New Information," *International Economic Review*, 10 (February 1969), fig. 2b, p. 13.

Accounting Changes

There are other occasions on which managers seem to assume that investors suffer from financial illusion. For example, some firms devote enormous ingenuity to the task of manipulating earnings reported to stockholders. This is done by "creative accounting"—that is, by choosing accounting methods that stabilize and increase reported earnings. Presumably firms go to this trouble because management believes that stockholders take the figures at face value. Leonard Spacek, one of America's leading accountants, echoes this belief in the following complaint.

> Let us assume that you sincerely want to report the profits in the way you feel fairly presents the true results of your company's business. . . . This is an admirable and objective motive; but when you do this, you find that your competitor shows a relatively more favourable profit result than you do. This creates a demand for his stock, while yours lags behind. You put your analyst to work, and you find that if your competitor followed the same accounting practices you do, your results would be better than his. . . . You show this analysis to your complaining stockholders. Naturally they ask, "If this is true, and if your competitor's accounting practices are generally accepted, too, why not change your accounting practices and thus improve your profits?" At that point you try to explain why your accounting is much more factual and reliable

---

[20]Guy Charest, in "Returns to Splitting Stocks on the Toronto Stock Exchange," *Journal of Business Administration*, **12**:19–40 (Fall 1980), studied 177 Canadian stock splits that occurred between 1963 and 1975. He found that prices tend to *fall* significantly in the 24 months following a split, which suggests that investors may have ignored negative information associated with the split announcement. However, these anomalous results may be unreliable because of the small sample size.

---

than your competitor's. Your stockholders listen, but nothing you can say will convince them that they should give up a 20%, 50%, or 100% possible increase in the market values just because you like certain accounting practices better than others.[21]

Is Spacek right? Can the firm increase its market value by creative accounting? Or are the firm's shares traded in an efficient, well-functioning market, in which investors can see through such financial illusions?

A number of researchers have tried to resolve this question by looking at how the market reacts when companies change their accounting methods. For example, Kaplan and Roll have studied what happens to stock prices when companies boost their reported profits by switching from accelerated depreciation to straight-line depreciation.[22] This switch is purely cosmetic. It reduces the reported depreciation charge but it does not affect the company's tax bill—the tax authorities allow firms to use accelerated depreciation for tax purposes but straight-line depreciation for reporting purposes.

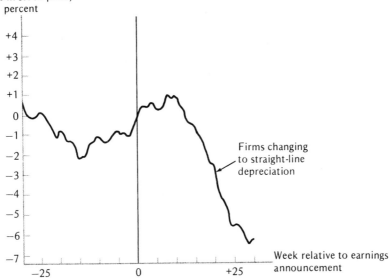

Figure 13-5   Kaplan and Roll's study shows that investors are not misled by accounting changes that are designed to inflate earnings. (Changes in price of the firms' stock are adjusted for general market movements.)

Source: R.S. Kaplan and R. Roll, "Investor Evaluation of Accounting Information: Some Empirical Evidence," *Journal of Business*, 45 (April 1972), fig. 1c, p. 239. © 1972 by the University of Chicago. All rights reserved.

Figure 13-5 shows the results of Kaplan and Roll's study. The preliminary announcement of increased earnings seems to prompt a slight abnormal rise in the stock price but this could simply be because investors were not informed at that stage of the accounting change. Within three months of the earnings announcement investors appear to have concluded that the accounting cosmetics were a sign of weakness rather than strength.

---

[21]See L. Spacek, "Business Success Requires an Understanding of Unsolved Problems of Accounting and Financial Reporting." Address before the Financial Accounting Class, Graduate School of Business Administration, Harvard University, September 25, 1959.

[22]See R.S. Kaplan and R. Roll, "Investor Evaluation of Accounting Information: Some Empirical Evidence," *Journal of Business*, 45:225–257 (April 1972).

This result not only suggests the futility of earnings manipulation. It also raises some more basic questions about the role of accounting conventions. Jack Treynor illustrates the problem with the fable of nail soup:

There was once a band of itinerant soldiers who, when they had difficulty persuading townsmen to feed them, hit upon the following solution. They set a large pot of water to boiling and then, when all the townsmen were watching curiously, dropped in a nail and announced with much licking of lips that they were making nail soup. The townsmen were assured that there would be enough soup for everybody. When one of the soldiers allowed that a few carrots actually improved the flavour of nail soup, a townsman dashed off to fetch some carrots. When it was observed that tomatoes made a wonderful garnish for nail soup, another townsman quickly produced some tomatoes. Soon the nail soup contained beef stock, turnips, and onions. Before the soup was served, the nail was removed. But the townsmen continued to regard the soup as nail soup.

Nail soup was nourishing, but not because of the nail. Earnings have information content, but not because of the ingredients that have been the main concern of the FASB and the AcSC.[23] Accountants painstakingly put the nail into the soup; analysts painstakingly take it out, all the while believing they are really supping on nail soup. The overall process may seem unnecessarily complicated since the same result could have been obtained without the nail.[24]

13-6 THE FOURTH LESSON OF MARKET EFFICIENCY: THE DO-IT-YOURSELF ALTERNATIVE

In an efficient market investors will not pay others for what they can do equally well themselves. As we shall see, many of the controversies in corporate financing centre on how well individuals can replicate corporate financial decisions. For example, companies often justify mergers on the grounds that they produce a more diversified and hence more stable firm. But if investors can hold the stocks of both companies, why should they thank the companies for diversifying? It is much easier and cheaper for them to diversify than it is for the firm.

The financial manager needs to ask the same question when considering whether it is better to issue debt or common stock. If the firm issues debt, it will create financial leverage. As a result, the stock will be more risky and it will offer a higher expected return. But stockholders can obtain financial leverage without the firm's issuing debt. They can issue debt on their own account. The problem for the financial manager is, therefore, to decide whether it is cheaper for the company to issue debt than for the individual shareholder.

13-7 THE FIFTH LESSON OF MARKET EFFICIENCY: SEEN ONE STOCK, SEEN THEM ALL

The elasticity of demand for any article measures the percentage change in the quantity demanded for each percentage addition to the price. If the article has close substitutes, the elasticity will be strongly negative; if not, it will be near zero. For example, coffee,

---

[23]FASB is the Financial Accounting Standards Board in the United States; AcSC is the Accounting Standards Committee of the Canadian Institute of Chartered Accountants.

[24]See J.L. Treynor, "Discussion: Changes in Accounting Techniques and Stock Prices," *Empirical Research in Accounting: Selected Studies*, 1972, Institute for Professional Accounting, Graduate School of Business, University of Chicago, Chicago, 1972, p. 43.

which is a staple commodity, has a demand elasticity of about -0.2. This means that a 5% increase in the price of coffee changes sales by $-0.2 \times 0.05 = 0.01$; in other words, it reduces demand by only 1%. Consumers are likely to regard different *brands* of coffee as much closer substitutes for each other. Therefore the demand elasticity for a particular brand could be in the region of, say, -2.0. A 5% increase in the price of Maxwell House relative to that of Nescafé would in this case reduce demand by 10%.

Investors don't buy a stock for its unique qualities; they buy it because it offers the prospect of a fair return for its risk. This means that stocks should be like very similar brands of coffee, almost perfect substitutes for each other. Therefore, the demand for one company's stock should be very elastic. If its prospective risk premium is lower relative to its risk than other stocks, *nobody* will want to hold that stock. If it is higher, *everybody* will want to hold it.

Suppose that you want to sell a large block of stock. Since demand is elastic, you naturally conclude that you need only cut the offering price very slightly to attract buyers. Unfortunately that doesn't necessarily follow. When you come to sell your stock, other investors may suspect that you want to get rid of it because you know something they don't. Therefore they will revise their assessment of the stock's value downward. Demand is still elastic but the whole demand curve moves down. Elastic demand does *not* imply that stock prices never change: it *does* imply that you can sell large blocks of stock at close to the market price *as long as you can convince other investors that you have no private information.*

Here is one case that supports this view. In June 1977 the Bank of England offered its holding of BP shares for sale at 845 pence each. The bank owned nearly 67 million shares of BP, so that the total value of the holding was £564 million, or about $970 million. It was a huge sum to ask the public to find, and the sale was by far the largest of its kind in history.

Anyone who wished to apply for BP stock had nearly two weeks within which to do so. Just before the bank's announcement the price of BP stock was 912 pence. Over the next two weeks the price drifted down to 898 pence, largely in line with the British equity market. Therefore by the final application date, the discount being offered by the bank was only 6%. In return for this discount, any applicant had to raise the necessary cash, taking the risk that the price of BP would decline before the result of the application was known, and had to pass over to the Bank of England the next dividend on BP.

If Maxwell House coffee is offered at a discount of 6%, the demand is unlikely to be overwhelming. But the discount on BP stock was enough to bring in applications for $4,600 million worth of stock,[25] 4.7 times the amount on offer.

We admit that this case was unusual in some respects, but an important study by Myron Scholes of a large sample of secondary offerings confirmed the ability of the market to absorb blocks of stock.[26] The average effect of the offerings was to reduce the stock price slightly, but the decline was almost independent of the amount offered. Scholes' estimate of the demand elasticity for a company's stock was $-3,000$. Of course this figure was not meant to be precise, but you can see the point he was making.

Here again we encounter an apparent contradiction with practice. Many corporations seem to believe that the demand elasticity is not only low, but that it varies with the stock price, so that when the price is relatively low new stock can only be sold at a substantial discount. American state and federal regulatory commissions, which set the

---

[25]However, applicants were required to put up only £3 per share on application and the remainder at a later date.

[26]See M. Scholes, "The Market for Securities: Substitution versus Price Pressure and the Effects of Information on Share Prices," *Journal of Business*, **45**:179–211 (April 1972). A secondary distribution is a large block of stock sold off the floor of the exchange.

prices charged by telephone companies, electric companies, and other utilities, often allow 10% higher earnings to compensate the firm for price "pressure." This pressure is the decline in the firm's stock price that is supposed to occur when new shares are offered to investors. Yet Denis Logue and Robert Jarrow, who searched for evidence of pressure, found that new stock issues by utilities resulted in a *temporary* decline in price of only about 2%.[27] We will come back to the subject of pressure when we discuss stock issues in Chapter 15.

13-8 THE SIXTH LESSON OF MARKET EFFICIENCY: READING THE ENTRAILS

If the market is efficient, prices impound all available information. Therefore, if only we can learn to read the entrails, security prices can tell us a lot about the future. For example, in Chapter 25 we will show how information in the company's accounts can help the financial manager to estimate the probability of bankruptcy. But of course these accounts are only one of many sources of information available to investors. The return offered by the company's bonds and the performance of its common stock are, therefore, just as good indicators of bankruptcy as accounting data.[28]

Here is another example. Statistics Canada and the United States National Bureau of Economic Research have identified series of leading indicators of economic activity.[29] Since stock prices are heavily influenced by economic prospects, it is not surprising that they earn relatively high marks as leading indicators. In other words, the TSE 300 Index represents an informed consensus about Canada's economic prospects.

Suppose that investors are confident that interest rates are going to rise over the next year. In that case, they will prefer to wait before they enter into long-term loans. Any firm that wants to borrow long-term money today will have to offer the inducement of a higher rate of interest. In other words, the long-term rate of interest will have to be higher than the one-year rate. Differences between the long-term interest rate and the short-term rate tell you something about what investors expect to happen to short-term rates in the future.[30]

13-9 SUMMARY

The patron saint of the Bolsa (stock exchange) in Barcelona, Spain, is Nuestra Señora de la Esperanza—Our Lady of Hope. She is the perfect patron, for we all hope for superior returns when we invest. But competition between investors will tend to produce an efficient market. In such a market, prices will rapidly impound any new information, and it will be very difficult to make consistently superior returns. We may indeed *hope*, but all we can rationally *expect* in an efficient market is that we shall obtain a return that is just sufficient to compensate us for the time value of money and for the risks we bear.

---

[27]See D.E. Logue and R.A. Jarrow, "Negotiation vs. Competitive Bidding in the Sale of Securities by Public Utilities," *Financial Management*, 7:31–39 (Autumn 1978).

[28]See W.H. Beaver, "Market Prices, Financial Ratios and the Prediction of Failure," *Journal of Accounting Research*, 6:179–192 (Autumn 1968).

[29]See G.H. Moore and J. Shiskin, *Indicators of Business Expansions and Contractions*, National Bureau of Economic Research, New York, 1967.

[30]We will discuss the relationship between short-term and long-term interest rates in Chapter 21. Notice, however, that in an efficient market the difference between the prices of *any* short-term and long-term contracts always says something about how participants expect prices to move.

The efficient-market hypothesis comes in three different flavours. The weak form of the hypothesis states that prices efficiently reflect all the information contained in the past series of stock prices. In this case it is impossible to earn superior returns simply by looking for patterns in stock prices—in other words, price changes are random. The semistrong form of the hypothesis states that prices reflect all published information. That means it is impossible to make consistently superior returns just by reading the newspaper, looking at the company's annual accounts, and so on. The strong form of the hypothesis states that stock prices effectively impound all available information. It tells us that inside information is hard to find because in pursuing it you are in competition with thousands, perhaps millions, of active, intelligent, and greedy investors. The best you can do in this case is to assume that securities are fairly priced and to hope that one day Nuestra Señora will reward your humility.

The concept of an efficient market is astonishingly simple and remarkably well-supported by the facts. Less than 20 years ago any suggestion that security investment is a fair game was generally regarded as bizarre. Today it is not only widely accepted in business schools, but it also permeates investment practice and government policy toward the security markets.

For the corporate treasurer who is concerned with issuing or purchasing securities the efficient-market theory has obvious implications. In one sense, however, it raises more questions than it answers. The existence of efficient markets does not mean that the financial manager can let financing "take care of itself." It only provides a starting point for analysis. It is time to get down to details about securities, issue procedures, and financial institutions. We start in Chapter 14.

FURTHER READING

Most modern investment texts contain a chapter on market efficiency from the viewpoint of the investment manager. See, for example:

R.A. Brealey, *An Introduction to Risk and Return from Common Stocks,* 2nd ed., M.I.T. Press, Cambridge, Mass., 1983.
J.H. Lorie and M. Hamilton, *The Stock Market: Theories and Evidence,* Richard D. Irwin, Inc., Homewood, Ill., 1973.
W.F. Sharpe, *Investments,* 2nd ed., Prentice-Hall, Inc., Englewood Cliffs, N.J., 1981.

A good review article on market efficiency is:

E.F. Fama, "Efficient Capital Markets: A Review of Theory and Empirical Work," *Journal of Finance,* **25**:383–417 (May 1970).

There are several books of readings that contain a selection of the more important original articles on the subject. See, for example:

P.H. Cootner (ed.), *The Random Character of Stock Market Prices,* M.I.T. Press, Cambridge, Mass., 1964.
J.H. Lorie and R.A. Brealey (eds.), *Modern Developments in Investment Management,* 2nd ed., Frederick A. Praeger, Inc., New York, 1978.

The efficiency of Canadian stock markets has been studied in:

C.H. Rorke, I. Willis, R.L. Hagerman, and R.D. Richmond, "The Random Walk Hypothesis in the Canadian Equity Market," *Journal of Business Administration,* **8**:23–41 (Fall 1976).
G. Charest, "Returns to Dividend Changing Stocks on the Toronto Stock Exchange," *Journal of Business Administration,* **12**:1–18 (Fall 1980).
G. Charest, "Returns to Splitting Stocks on the Toronto Stock Exchange," *Journal of Business Administration,* **12**:19–40 (Fall 1980).
W.M. Lawson, "Market Efficiency: the Trading of Professionals on the Toronto Stock Exchange," *Journal of Business Administration,* **12**:41–56 (Fall 1980).

QUIZ

1. Stock prices appear to behave as though successive values

   (*a*) Are random numbers
   (*b*) Follow regular cycles
   (*c*) Differ by a random number
   Which (if any) of these statements are true?

2. Supply the missing words: "There are three forms of the efficient-market hypothesis. Tests of randomness in stock prices provide evidence for the _____ form of the hypothesis. Tests of stock price reaction to well-publicized news provide evidence for the _____ form and tests of the performance of professionally managed funds provide evidence for the _____ form. Market efficiency results from competition between investors. Many investors search for new results from competition between investors. Many investors search for new information about the company's business that would help them to value the stock more accurately. This is known as _____ research. Such research helps to ensure that prices reflect all available information: in other words, it helps to keep the market efficient in the _____ form. Other investors study past stock prices for recurrent patterns that would allow them to make superior profits. This is known as _____ research. Such research helps to ensure that prices reflect all the information contained in past stock prices: in other words, it helps to keep the market efficient in the _____ form.

3. Which of the following statements (if any) are true? The efficient-market hypothesis assumes:

   (*a*) That there are no taxes
   (*b*) That there is perfect foresight
   (*c*) That successive price changes are independent
   (*d*) That investors are irrational
   (*e*) That there are no transaction costs
   (*f*) That forecasts are unbiased

4. The stock of United Boot is priced at $400 and offers a dividend yield of 2%. The company has a 2-for-1 stock split.

   (*a*) Other things equal, what would you expect to happen to the stock price?
   (*b*) Other things equal, what would you expect to happen to the dividend yield?
   (*c*) In practice, would you expect the stock price to fall by more or less than this amount?
   (*d*) Suppose a few months later United Boot announces a rise in dividends that is exactly in line with that of other companies. Would you expect the announcement to lead to a slight abnormal rise in the stock price, a slight abnormal fall, or no change?

5. True or false?

   (*a*) Financing decisions are less easily reversed than investment decisions.
   (*b*) Financing decisions don't affect the total size of the cash flows; they just affect who receives the flows.
   (*c*) Tests have shown that there is almost perfect negative correlation between successive price changes.
   (*d*) The semistrong form of the efficient-market hypothesis states that prices reflect all publicly available information.
   (*e*) In efficient markets the expected return on each stock is the same.
   (*f*) Myron Schole's study of the effect of secondary distributions provided evidence that the demand for a single company's shares is highly elastic.

QUESTIONS AND PROBLEMS

1. How would you respond to the following comments?
   (a) "Efficient market, my eye! I know of lots of investors who do crazy things."
   (b) "Efficient market? Balderdash! I know at least a dozen people who have made a bundle in the stock market."
   (c) "The trouble with the efficient-market theory is that it ignores investors' psychology."
   (d) "Despite all the limitations, the best guide to a company's value is its written-down book value. It is much more stable than market value, which depends on temporary fashions."

2. Respond to the following comments:
   (a) "The random-walk theory with its implication that investing in stocks is like playing roulette is a powerful indictment of our capital markets."
   (b) "If everyone believes you can make money by charting stock prices, then price changes won't be random."
   (c) "The random-walk theory implies that events are random but many events are not random—if it rains today, there's a fair bet that it will rain again tomorrow."

3. Which of the following observations *appear* to indicate market inefficiency? Explain whether the inefficiency is weak, semistrong, or strong. (*Note*: if the market is not weak-form-efficient, it is said to be *weak-form-inefficient*; if it is not semistrong-form-efficient, it is *semistrong-form-inefficient*, and so on.)
   (a) American tax-exempt municipal bonds offer lower pretax returns than taxable government bonds.
   (b) Managers make superior returns on their purchases of their company's stock.
   (c) There is a positive relationship between the return on the market in one quarter and the change in aggregate corporate profits in the next quarter.
   (d) There is disputed evidence that stocks that have appreciated unusually in the recent past continue to do so in the future.
   (e) The stock of an acquired firm tends to appreciate in the period before the merger announcement.
   (f) Stocks of companies with unexpectedly high earnings *appear* to offer high returns for several months after the earnings announcement.
   (g) Very risky stocks on the average give higher returns than safe stocks.

4. Look again at Figure 13-4.
   (a) Is the steady rise in the stock price before the split evidence of market inefficiency?
   (b) How do you think those stocks performed that did *not* increase their dividends by an above-average amount?

5. Stock splits are important because they convey information. Can you suggest some other financial decisions that convey information?

6. Estimate the *abnormal* return in each of the past three months for one of the stocks shown in Table 9-2.

7. Select a small sample of mutual funds and estimate whether they have been able to achieve consistently abnormal returns. (*Hint*: funds may have different degrees of risk.)

8. It is sometimes suggested that low price-earnings stock are generally underpriced. Describe a possible test of this view. Be as precise as possible.

9. "If a project provides an unusually high rate of return in one year, it will probably do so again in the next year." Does this statement make sense if you use the definition of economic rate of return that we gave in Chapter 12?

10. "Long-term interest rates are at record highs. Most companies, therefore, find it cheaper to finance with common stock or relatively inexpensive short-term bank loans." Discuss.

11. "If the efficient-market hypothesis is true, then it makes no difference what securities a company issues. All are fairly priced." Does this follow?

12. "If the efficient-market hypothesis is true, the pension fund manager might as well select a portfolio with a pin." Explain why this is not so.

13. Bond dealers buy and sell bonds at very low spreads. Used car dealers buy and sell cars at very wide spreads. What has this got to do with the strong form of the efficient-market hypothesis?

AN OVERVIEW OF CORPORATE FINANCING

This chapter begins our analysis of long-term financing decisions—a task we will not complete until Chapter 24. We will devote considerable space in these chapters to the classic finance problems of dividend policy and the use of debt versus equity financing. Yet to concentrate on these problems alone would miss the enormous *variety* of financing instruments that are used by companies today.

Look, for example, at Table 14-1. It shows the many long-term securities issued by Canadian Pacific. Yet CP has not come close to exhausting the different kinds of securities that exist.

This chapter introduces you to the principal families of securities, and it explains how they are used by corporations. We also draw attention to some interesting aspects of the behaviour of the firms issuing these securities.

14-1 COMMON STOCK

Definitions

Table 14-2 shows the common equity of Canadian Pacific as it was reported in the company's books at the end of 1982.

The maximum number of shares that can be issued is known as the *authorized share capital*—for CP, it is 100 million shares. This maximum is specified in the firm's articles of incorporation and can be increased only with the permission of the stockholders. CP has already issued 71,662,280 shares, and so it can issue slightly more than 28 million more without the stockholders' approval.

The issued shares are entered in the company's books at their par value. Each share has a par value of $5. Thus, the total book value of the issued shares is 71,662,280 × $5 = $358,311,400.

Par value has little economic significance. Many companies issue shares with no par value.[1] In this case, the stock is listed in the accounts at an arbitrarily determined figure.

The price of new shares sold to the public almost always exceeds the par value. The difference is entered in the company's accounts as additional paid-in capital or capital surplus. Thus if CP sold an additional 100,000 shares at $50 a share, the common stock account would be increased by 100,000 × $5 = $500,000, and the additional paid-in capital account by 100,000 × ($50 − $5) = $4,500,000.

If shares are reacquired by the company from its investors, they can be **cancelled** by reversing the above procedure or held as **treasury shares** and written into the books

---

[1]In fact, the new Canada Business Corporations Act and most of the new provincial acts of incorporation no longer allow shares with par value. When CP continues its corporate existence under the new act, it will have to convert its shares to ones of no par value.

as an offset to common equity. If the firm is incorporated under the Canada Business Corporations Act, however, it cannot have treasury shares.

Usually CP pays out less than half its earnings as dividends. The remainder is retained in the business and used to finance new investment. The cumulative amount of retained earnings is $3,259,648,000.

Table 14-1   Large firms often use many different kinds of securities. Look at the long-term securities that have been issued by Canadian Pacific Limited and its subsidiaries. Note that there are several issues of most of these security types.

Stock:
  Ordinary (common) stock
  Cumulative redeemable preferred shares
Long-term debt:
  Collateral trust bonds
  Equipment trust certificates
  Bank loans
  Mortgages
  Notes
  Guaranteed notes
  Sinking fund bonds
  First mortgage sinking fund bonds
  Sinking fund debentures
  Floating-rate income debentures
Other liabilities:
  Perpetual 4% consolidated debenture stock (denominated in pounds sterling, U.S. dollars and Canadian dollars)

Table 14-2   Book value of common stockholders' equity of Canadian Pacific, December 31, 1982 (figures in thousands).

Common shares ($5 par value per share)	358,311
Premium on stock and other paid-in surplus	343,921
Retained income	3,259,648
	$3,961,880

Note:
Shares	
Authorized shares	100,000,000
Issued shares	71,662,280

Source: Canadian Pacific Limited 1982 Annual Report.

Stockholders' Rights

The common stockholders are the owners of the corporation. They therefore have a general *pre-emptive right* to anything of value that the company may wish to distribute. They also have the ultimate control of the company's affairs. In practice this control is limited to a right to vote, either in person or by proxy, on appointments to the board of directors and a number of other matters.

If the corporation's articles specify a *majority voting system*, each director is voted upon separately and stockholders can cast one vote for each share they own. If the articles permit *cumulative voting*, the directors are voted upon jointly and the stockholders can, if they want, allot all their votes to just one candidate.[2] Cumulative voting makes it easier for a minority group among the stockholders to elect directors representing the group's interests. That is why minority groups devote so much of their efforts to campaigning for cumulative voting.

The issues on which stockholders are asked to vote are rarely contested, particularly in the case of large, publicly traded firms. Occasionally there are proxy contests in which the firm's existing management and directors compete with outsiders for control of the corporation. But the odds are stacked against the outsiders, for the insiders can get the firm to pay all the costs of presenting their case and obtaining votes.

Most companies issue just one class of common stock. Occasionally, however, a firm may have two classes outstanding, which differ in their right to vote and receive dividends. Suppose a firm needs fresh equity capital but its present stockholders do not want to relinquish their control of the firm. The existing shares could be labeled class A and class B shares issued to outside investors. The class B shares could have limited voting privileges, although they might sell for less as a result.

14-2   A FIRST LOOK AT CORPORATE DEBT

When they borrow money, companies promise to make regular interest payments and to repay the principal (that is, the original amount borrowed) according to an agreed schedule. However, this liability is limited. Stockholders have the right to default on any debt obligation, handing over the corporation's assets to the lenders. Clearly they will choose to do this only if the value of the assets is less than the amount of the debt.

Because lenders are not regarded as proprietors of the firm, they do not normally have any voting power. The company's payments of interest are regarded as a cost and are deducted from taxable income. Thus interest is paid from *before-tax* income. In contrast, dividends on common stock are paid out of *after-tax* income. Therefore the government provides a tax subsidy on the use of debt that it does not provide on equity.

Debt Comes in Many Forms

Some orderly scheme of classification is essential to cope with the almost infinite variety of corporate debt claims. We will spend several chapters examining the various features of corporate debt. But here is a preliminary guide to the major distinguishing characteristics.

Maturity   Long-term debt is an obligation repayable more than one year from the date of issue. Debt due in less than one year is carried on the balance sheet as a current liability. Clearly, however, it is artificial to call a 364-day note short-term and a 366-day note long-term (except on leap years).

There are corporate bonds of nearly every conceivable maturity. Canadian Pacific's **perpetuities** have no specified maturity. They may survive forever. At the other extreme, we find firms borrowing literally overnight. We describe how this is done in Chapter 30.

Repayment Provision   Long-term loans are commonly repaid in a steady, regular way, perhaps after an initial grace period. For publicly traded bonds this is done by means of a **sinking fund**. Each year the firm pays a sum of cash into a sinking fund which is then used to repurchase the bonds.

---

[2]For example, suppose there are five directors to be elected and you own 100 shares. You therefore have a total of $5 \times 100 = 500$ votes. Under the majority voting system, you can cast a maximum of 100 votes for any one candidate. Under a cumulative voting system you can cast all 500 votes for your favourite candidate.

Most firms issuing debt to the public reserve the right to **call** the debt—that is, to repay and retire all the bonds in a given issue before the final maturity date. Call prices are specified when the debt is originally issued. Usually lenders are given at least five years of call protection. During this period the firm cannot call the bonds.

Seniority Some debt instruments are **subordinated**. In the event of default the subordinated lender gets in line behind the firm's general creditors. The subordinated lender holds a junior claim and is paid after all senior creditors are satisfied.

When you lend money to a firm you can assume that you hold a senior claim unless the debt agreement says otherwise. However, this does not always put you at the front of the line, for the firm may have set aside some of its assets specifically for the protection of other creditors. That brings us to our next classification.

Security We have used the word *bond* to refer to all kinds of corporate debt, but in some contexts it means **secured** debt; often bonds are secured by mortgages on plant and equipment, and unsecured long-term claims are usually called *debentures.*[3] In the event of default, the bondholders have a general claim on the mortgaged assets; investors holding debentures have a general claim on the unmortgaged assets but only a junior claim on the mortgaged assets.

Floating versus Fixed Rates The interest payment or *coupon* on most long-term debt is fixed at the time of issue. If a $1,000 bond is issued when long-term interest rates are 10%, the firm continues to pay $100 per year regardless of how interest rates fluctuate.

Loan agreements negotiated with banks usually incorporate a **floating rate**. For example, your firm may be offered a loan at "1% above prime." The **prime rate**, which is the interest rate the bank charges on loans to its most creditworthy customers, is adjusted up or down as interest rates on traded securities change.[4] Therefore when the prime rate changes, the interest on your floating rate loan also changes.

Country and Currency Many large firms, particularly those having significant overseas operations, borrow abroad. If such a firm wants long-term debt, it will probably borrow by an issue of **eurobonds** sold simultaneously in several countries; if it wants short-term debt, it will probably obtain a **eurodollar** loan from a bank.

Corporations sometimes issue bonds denominated in foreign currencies. Often their overseas subsidiaries borrow directly from banks in the countries in which the subsidiaries are operating.

A Debt by Any Other Name

The word *debt* sounds straightforward, but companies enter into a number of financial arrangements that look suspiciously like debt but are treated differently in the accounts. Some of these obligations are easily identifiable. For example, accounts payable are simply obligations to pay for goods that have already been delivered. Other arrangements are not so easily detected. For example, instead of borrowing money to buy equipment, many companies **lease** or rent it on a long-term basis. As we will show in Chapter 24, such arrangements are economically equivalent to secured long-term debt.

---

[3]The terminology can be confusing. A *debenture* in the United States and Canada signifies unsecured debt; in Great Britain it usually refers to *secured* debt.

[4]Canadian Schedule A banks (that is the large banks) generally quote loans relative to a prime rate, but the smaller Schedule B banks (often subsidiaries of foreign financial institutions) usually quote loans as a premium over their cost of funds, because they generally issue paper (accept deposits) matched in size and currency to specific loans. When Schedule A banks make loans denominated in foreign currency, they follow a similar procedure.

14-3 PREFERRED STOCK

In the chapters that follow, we shall have much more to say about common stock and debt. **Preferred stock** will occupy less of our time later on. However, we shall see that it sometimes has tax advantages compared to debt and that it is a useful method of financing in mergers and certain other special situations.

Preferred stock is legally an equity security. Despite the fact that it offers a fixed dividend like debt, payment of the dividend is almost invariably within the complete discretion of the directors. The only stipulation is that no dividends may be paid on the common until after the preferred dividend has been paid. For some older issues the firm could pay common dividends *without* making up preferred dividends that had been skipped in previous years. This gave an opportunity for considerable abuse. Therefore, almost all new issues specifically provide that the obligation should be **cumulative** so that the firm must pay *all* past preferred dividends before common stockholders get a cent.

Like common stock, preferred stock does not have a final repayment date. However, roughly half the issues make some provision for periodic retirement and in many cases companies have an option to **redeem** or call preferred stock at a specified price. If the company goes out of business, the claim of the preferred stock is junior to that of any debt but senior to that of common stock.

The contract that sets out the terms of the preferred stock also imposes restrictions on the company, including some limits on payments to common stockholders either as dividends or through repurchase of the common stock. These restrictions may also stipulate that the company cannot make any payments to common stockholders unless it is able to maintain a minimum level of common equity and a minimum ratio of working capital to debt and preferred. Other clauses typically require that further issues of securities must have the consent of two-thirds of the preferred shareholders unless the ratio of equity to all debt and preferred stock exceeds a specified minimum.

Preferred stock rarely confers full voting privileges. However, almost always the consent of two-thirds of the preferred holders must be obtained on all matters affecting the seniority of their claim. Most issues also provide the holder with some voting power if the preferred dividend is skipped.

Unlike interest payments on debt, dividends are not an allowable deduction from taxable corporate income. Thus, the dividend is paid from after-tax income. However, dividend income is generally not taxed when received by Canadian corporations, and is taxed at reduced or even negative rates when received by individuals. (This is discussed more fully in Chapter 16.) Thus, preferred shares are a popular method of financing when the tax benefits in the hands of the investors are worth more than the tax burden imposed on the issuer.

For example, suppose a bank will lend at an interest rate of 10%. After paying tax on the interest at 46%, the bank will receive a net return of $(1 - 0.46) \times 10 = 5.4\%$. Alternatively, the bank can recover an equally high return by buying a preferred stock with a tax-free yield of 5.4%. On the other hand, if a corporation pays no taxes, for example, it is better off paying a 5.4% yield on preferred stock than 10% interest on a loan. Fearing an erosion of its tax base, Parliament made it harder for banks to buy preferred stock from other corporations with section 258 of the Income Tax Act in 1979.

Moreover, the dividend tax credit also makes preferred shares a popular financing vehicle in Canada. In the United States, preferred shares are relatively rare, since they are taxed at full personal rates. They are sometimes purchased by corporations, since corporations only have to count 15% of a dividend as taxable income. Also, regulated American public utilities, which can take tax payments into account when negotiating the rates they charge customers, can effectively pass the tax disadvantage of preferred stock on to the consumer. As a result, a large fraction of the dollar value of new American offerings of nonconvertible preferred stock consists of issues by utilities.

14-4 CONVERTIBLE SECURITIES

Corporations often issue securities with terms that can be altered subsequently at the option of the firm, the holder of the security, or both. We have already seen one example, the call option on corporate bonds, which allows the firm to retire a bond issue before its maturity date.

Options often have a substantial effect on value. The most dramatic example is provided by a **warrant** which is *nothing but* an option issued by a corporation. The owner of a warrant can purchase a set number of common shares at a set price on or before a set date. For example, in June 1983 you could have purchased a Canada Trustco Mortgage Co. warrant for $17.75. That security gave the right to purchase one share of class A common stock for $21.26 per share at any time up to and including December 15, 1983. Warrants are often sold as part of a package of other securities. Thus, the firm might make a "combination offer" of bonds and warrants.

A **convertible bond** is like a package of corporate bond and a warrant. There is one principal difference. When the owners of a convertible wish to exercise their option to buy shares, they do not pay cash—they just give up the bond. The bond is *converted* into a specific number of shares.[5]

These examples do not exhaust the options encountered by the financial manager. Far from it: we will see in Chapter 20 that *all* corporate securities can be analyzed in terms of options. In fact, once you read that chapter and learn how to analyze options, you will find that they are all around you.

14-5 VARIETY'S THE VERY SPICE OF LIFE

We have indicated several dimensions along which corporate securities can be classified. The financial manager has at least that many alternatives in designing corporate securities. As long as you can convince investors of its attractions, you can issue a convertible, callable, subordinated, floating-rate bond denominated in Deutschemarks. Rather than combining features of existing securities, you may create an entirely new one. Firms and countries that produce commodities like silver and oil have issued "commodity-linked" bonds, which pay off in either money or in the underlying commodity. For example, in 1980, the Sunshine Mining Company, operator of the largest American silver mine, issued $50 million bonds backed by silver. Each $1,000 bond pays a coupon rate of $8\frac{1}{2}\%$, and at maturity Sunshine Mining promises to pay either the $1,000 face value or the market value of 50 ounces of silver, whichever is greater.[6]

Variety is intrinsically good. People have different tastes, levels of wealth, rates of tax and so on. Why not offer them a choice? Of course the problem is that it may be expensive for the firm to design new securities. But if you can think of a new security that will appeal to investors, you may be able to increase the value of your company.

That completes our tour of corporate securities. You may feel like the tourist who has just emerged from 12 cathedrals in five days. But there will be plenty of time in later chapters for reflection and analysis.

---

[5]Convertible preferred is also issued, often to finance mergers.

[6]This example is cited in Eduardo Schwartz, "The Pricing of Commodity-Linked Bonds," *Journal of Finance*, **37**:525–539 (May 1982). Schwartz also describes how to determine the market value of such bonds using the Black-Scholes option pricing methodology of Chapter 20.

14-6 PATTERNS OF CORPORATE FINANCING

Let us now turn to Table 14-3, which summarizes the relative importance of alternative sources of capital for corporations in Canada. The most striking aspect of this table is the dominance of internally generated cash (line 7), defined as cash flow from operations less cash dividends paid to stockholders.[7] Internally generated cash normally covers a majority of firms' capital requirements: it fell below half of total expenditures in only five years.

Do Firms Rely too Heavily on Internal Funds?

As we have already noted, retained earnings are additional capital invested by shareholders—they represent, in effect, a compulsory issue of shares. A firm which retains $1 million could have paid out the cash as dividends and then sold new common shares to raise additional capital. In the same way, any reinvestment of dollars labeled "depreciation" amounts to investing dollars that could have been paid to investors. The opportunity cost of capital ought not to depend on whether the project is financed by depreciation, retained earnings, or a new stock issue.

Some people have been distressed by the heavy reliance on internal funds. Gordon Donaldson, in a field survey of corporate debt policies, encountered several firms which acknowledged "that it was their long-term object to hold to a rate of growth which was consistent with their capacity to generate funds internally." A number of other firms appeared to apply more stringent criteria to expenditure proposals that might require outside finance. Donaldson pointed out that depending on retained earnings is the line of least resistance for most companies; it allows them to avoid "the glare of publicity and shareholder attention" which accompanies a public issue. His concern may well be justified, but there may be other, less sinister explanations.[8]

William Baumol has expressed a slightly different concern about the use of retained earnings. He argued as follows:

> . . . A very substantial proportion of American business firms manage to avoid the *direct* disciplining influences of the securities market, or at least to evade the type of discipline which can be imposed by the provision of funds to inefficient firms only on extremely unfavourable terms. A company which makes no direct use of the stock market as a source of capital can, apparently, proceed to make its decisions confident in its immunity from this type of punishment by the impersonal mechanism of the stock exchange.[9]

---

[7]In Table 14-3, internally generated cash was calculated by adding CCA (or depreciation) and depletion to retained earnings for the year. CCA and depletion are noncash expenses. Thus retained earnings for the year understates the cash flow available for reinvestment.

[8]See G. Donaldson, *Corporate Debt Capacity*, Division of Research, Graduate School of Business Administration, Harvard University, Boston, 1961, chap. 3, especially pp. 51–56. One less sinister explanation would be the following: as we suggested in Chapter 11, if management has to invest on the basis of severely biased cash-flow forecasts, it may well use such simple capital-rationing schemes as a crude guide to an appropriate rate of expansion.

[9]Reprinted by permission of the publisher from *The Stock Market and Economic Efficiency* by W.J. Baumol (New York, Fordham University Press, 1965), copyright © 1965 by Fordham University Press, p. 70. Another related concern is commonly expressed by left-wing politicians in Great Britain. They argue that since retained earnings provide the bulk of industry's capital needs, the securities markets serve little function. Of course, the individual shareholders are happy for the firm to plow back their money *only* because the securities markets allow them to sell their stock if they need liquidity.

Table 14-3   Sources and uses of funds in nonfinancial corporations.

	Sources and Uses (% of total)[a]										
	1962	1963	1964	1965	1966	1967	1968	1969	1970	1971	1972
Uses:											
1. Capital expenditures	61	63	61	59	65	73	68	74	80	70	74
2. Investment in inventories	7	6	9	12	9	0[b]	4	7	3	4	5
3. Investment in liquid assets	3	1	3	0[b]	1	5	5	2	0	3	2
4. Investment in accounts receivable	14	13	12	15	11	10	9	8	10	12	9
5. Other	15	17	14	14	14	11	13	10	7	11	10
6. Total expenditures	100	100	100	100	100	100	100	100	100	100	100
Sources:											
7. Internally generated cash[c]	66	66	60	53	52	63	62	60	63	53	55
8. Financial deficit (6−7)	34	34	40	47	48	37	38	40	37	47	45
= required external financing											
Financial deficit covered by:											
9. Net stock issues	9	9	8	7	6	7	8	12	7	5	3
10. Net increase in long-term debt	23	18	21	24	29	23	24	16	25	22	13
11. Net increase in short-term debt	7	3	4	6	6	9	5	11	1	12	10
12. Increase in accounts payable	7	11	7	12	8	4	2	5	3	9	11
13. Discrepancy[d]	11	8	0[b]	2	2	5	2	4	(1)	1	(8)
	Expenditure and Deficit (millions of dollars)										
Total expenditures	5,990	6,424	8,320	10,097	10,913	9,563	10,421	11,335	11,380	14,290	15,301
Financial deficit	2,056	2,165	3,304	4,779	5,205	3,568	3,926	4,530	4,211	6,675	6,821

Sources and Uses (% of total)[a]

	1973	1974	1975	1976	1977	1978	1979	1980	1981	1982
Uses:										
1. Capital expenditures	63	57	76	77	73	56	56	64	60	97
2. Investment in inventories	7	12	(4)	3	1	(1)	6	(3)	0[b]	(28)
3. Investment in liquid assets	5	1	3	5	4	6	2	4	(1)	2
4. Investment in accounts receivable	15	18	17	9	13	19	14	12	11	4
5. Other	9	12	8	6	9	19	22	23	31	25
6. Total expenditures	100	100	100	100	100	100	100	100	100	100
Sources:										
7. Internally generated cash	50	42	57	64	57	43	45	48	36	64
8. Financial deficit (6−7)	50	58	43	36	43	57	55	52	64	36
= required external financing										
Financial deficit covered by:										
9. Net stock issues	5	3	5	4	9	11	10	10	10	10
10. Net increase in long-term debt	15	20	20	21	21	20	19	21	26	31
11. Net increase in short-term debt	12	16	12	13	3	10	12	12	27	1
12. Increase in accounts payable	11	17	11	4	7	13	12	12	9	(2)
13. Discrepancy	(7)	(1)	5	6	(3)	1	1	2	8	4

Expenditure and Deficit (millions of dollars)

	1973	1974	1975	1976	1977	1978	1979	1980	1981	1982
Total expenditures	21,254	28,577	22,984	26,158	29,619	42,267	51,890	55,241	69,050	36,928
Financial deficit	10,523	16,458	9,777	9,321	12,647	23,896	28,481	28,968	44,130	13,384

[a]Columns may not add to 100% because of rounding.
[b]Less than 0.5%.
[c]Net income plus capital cost allowance and depletion less cash dividends paid to stockholders.
[d]As reported by Statistics Canada; the excess of external financing over the financial deficit.

Derived from: Statistics Canada, *Financial Flow Accounts, 1961–1979*, pp. 242–243, and Matrix 702 from CANSIM, which is the registered trademark for Statistics Canada's machine-readable data base.

In this passage, Baumol echoes a widespread belief that internal funds are allocated by management, whereas external funds are somehow allocated by investors. It is not obvious that this is true. For example, if the authorized capital is sufficient, a company can *always* raise money by the sale of shares as long as it sets the price sufficiently low. Any discipline, therefore, must exist solely in the mind of the manager.

The subject is not one on which we can take a strong stand. Donaldson's diagnosis of management's motives is by no means implausible, but equally we have no good reason to suppose that managers would invest more wisely if they were forced to use the capital market more frequently.[10]

When Do Firms Need External Finance?

Line 8 of Table 14-3 shows that corporations have incurred a financial deficit in every year since 1962. Thus they have been persistent sellers of financial assets.

The financial deficit is linked to the general level of economic activity. Figure 14-1 illustrates this. In general, the deficit is lowest when the economy is pulling out of a recession. At this point companies are operating well below capacity, and so even a small increase in sales can produce a sharp improvement in profits and retained earnings. But the *need* for funds does not increase so sharply. As long as companies have significant spare capacity, management is unlikely to authorize major investment in new plant. Furthermore, the pickup in sales may reduce inventories, which releases cash.

The financial deficit is usually largest when economic activity begins to turn down. The decline in sales brings about a fall in retained earnings but the high level of investment in plant and inventory continues until firms have managed to adjust their spending to the gathering recession.

It is natural to associate bad times with a shortage of funds. But for corporations as a whole the opposite relationship holds.

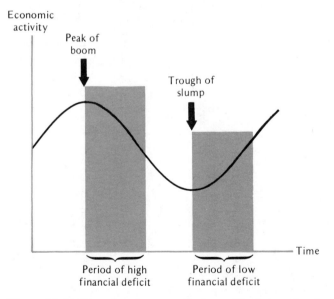

Figure 14-1 Companies are generally short of funds just after the peak of a boom. They need new funds least just after the bottom of a slump.

---

[10]Even if Donaldson is right, how do we know whether managers impose too high a standard for external capital or too low a one for retained earnings?

Timing Debt and Equity Issues

A further interesting aspect of Table 14-3 is the extent of the year-to-year variation in stock issues. Compare 1969 with 1972 (an extreme example but it illustrates the point):

Stock Issues	1969	1972
As % of total corporate sources of funds	12	3
As % of financial deficit	30	7
Absolute amount, in millions	$1,378	$454

In 1969 issues of equity amounted to $1,378 million. In 1972, just three years later, only $454 million was issued.

There is no simple explanation for this behaviour. Several things appear to be happening simultaneously. Firms do have target ratios of debt to equity. If debt weighs too heavily in their capital structure, they acquire equity by retaining earnings or issuing stock. If the debt ratio is too low, they favour debt over equity. But firms are never precisely on target. They are continually buffeted by changing business conditions. They always move toward the targets but they hardly ever get there. Because the adjustment process is slow, it does not preclude substantial short-term fluctuations in capital structure and in external financing by corporations.

Some of the fluctuations in stock issues can be explained by managers' attempts to time these issues. Studies by Taggart and others in the United States and by Marsh in Great Britain show that stock is more likely to be issued after stock prices have risen.[11] The rational explanation for this is that an increase in the stock price signals expanded investment opportunities, and the need to finance these investments really prompts the stock issues. Unfortunately the rational explanation doesn't explain all the facts. It tells us why firms raise more money in *total* when stock prices are historically high but it does not tell us why they only issue more equity and not more debt. If anything, a company should be even more ready to issue debt at such times, because the company's higher market value and enhanced prospects increase its "debt capacity." Yet Marsh finds exactly the opposite behaviour: debt issues do *not* respond to high stock prices, other things being equal. Firms in effect substitute equity for debt issues at precisely the time they should find it easier to borrow more.

Why should managers act in this way? Do they believe that equity is cheap when stock prices are historically high? As we pointed out in Chapter 13, in an efficient market buying or selling stock is a zero-NPV transaction regardless of whether the price is historically high or historically low. We don't know why managers prefer to issue equity rather than debt after a rise in the stock price, but it is difficult not to conclude that a lot of misplaced effort goes into timing stock issues.

Has Capital Structure Changed?

In 1974 *Business Week* devoted a special edition to "The Debt Economy," which described a United States in which everybody appeared to be a borrower and there was not a lender in sight. Prominent among these borrowers were American corporations, which, it was pointed out, had tripled their debt in the previous 15 years. With typical understatement, *Business Week* concluded that this debt imposed "an ominously heavy

---

[11]R.A. Taggart, "A Model of Corporate Financing Decisions," *Journal of Finance,* **32**:1467–1484 (December 1977); P. Marsh, "The Choice between Equity and Debt: An Empirical Study," *Journal of Finance*, Vol. 37, pp. 121–144, March 1982.

burden with the world as it is today—ravaged by inflation, threatened with economic depression, torn apart by the massive redistribution . . . "[12]

Is there really a trend to heavier reliance on debt financing? This is a hard question to answer in general, because financing policy varies so much from industry to industry and firm to firm. But a few statistics will do no harm as long as you keep these difficulties in mind.

Table 14-4 shows the aggregate balance sheets of all manufacturing corporations in Canada and the United States at the end of 1982. If all Canadian or American manufacturing corporations were merged into one gigantic firm, Table 14-4 would be their balance sheets.

Table 14-4 Aggregate balance sheets for manufacturing corporations in Canada[a] and the United States, 1982 (figures in billions of domestic dollars).

	Canada	U.S.		Canada	U.S.
Current assets[b]	59.4	657.8	Current liabilities	36.0	407.8
Fixed assets (net)[c]	60.2	643.4	Long-term debt	30.7	292.9
Other long-term assets	19.2	311.7	Other long-term liabilities[c]	10.9	129.9
			Total long-term liabilities	41.5	422.8
			Stockholders' equity	61.3	782.3
Total assets	138.8	1,612.9	Total liabilities and stockholders' equity	138.8	1,612.9

[a]Canadian data for firms having $10 million or more in total assets, only.
[b]Include land, mineral rights, and construction in progress, as well as plant and equipment.
[c]Includes deferred taxes and several miscellaneous categories.
Source: Statistics Canada, *Industrial Corporations, Financial Statistics*, Fourth Quarter, 1982, pp. 22–25. United States Department of Commerce, Bureau of the Census, *Quarterly Financial Report for Manufacturing, Mining, and Trade Corporations*, Fourth Quarter, 1982, p. 56.

The table shows that Canadian manufacturing corporations had total book assets of $138.8 million. On the right-hand side of the balance sheet, we find total long-term liabilities of $41.5 million and stockholders' equity of $61.3 million.

What was the debt ratio of manufacturing corporations in Canada[13] in 1982? It depends on what you mean by "debt." If all liabilities are counted as debt, the debt ratio is 0.56:

$$\frac{\text{Debt}}{\text{Total assets}} = \frac{36.0 + 41.5}{138.8} = 0.56$$

This measure of debt includes both current liabilities and long-term obligations. Sometimes financial analysts look at the proportions of debt and equity in long-term financing. The proportion of debt in long-term financing is

---

[12]Reprinted from the October 12, 1974, issue of *Business Week*, p. 45, by special permission; © 1974 by McGraw-Hill, Inc., New York, N.Y. 10020. All rights reserved.

[13]For the American corporations the ratio of debt to total assets is 0.51 and the ratio of long-term debt to long-term financing is 0.35.

$$\frac{\text{Long-term liabilities}}{\text{Long-term liabilities} + \text{stockholders' equity}} = \frac{41.5}{41.5 + 61.3} = 0.40$$

Figure 14-2 plots these two ratios from 1962 to 1982. There is a clear upward shift from the 1950s to the 1980s. By these measures corporations are "using more debt." We do not know whether the shift to more debt is permanent or why it has occurred. However, it is worth noting that the rate of inflation began to accelerate in the late 1960s, and remained high through the 1970s. Rapid inflation means that the *book* value of corporate assets falls behind the actual value of those assets. If corporations are borrowing against *actual* value, it would not be surprising to observe rising ratios of debt to book asset values.

To illustrate, suppose that you bought a house ten years ago for $30,000. You financed the purchase in part with a $15,000 mortgage, 50% of the purchase price. Today the house is worth $60,000. Suppose you repay the remaining balance of your original mortgage and take out a new mortgage for $30,000, which is again 50% of current market value. Your *book* debt ratio would be 100%. The reason is that the book value of the house is its *original* cost of $30,000 (we assume no depreciation). An analyst having only book values to work with would conclude that you had decided to "use more debt"—ten years ago your book debt ratio was only 50%. But you have no more debt relative to the actual value of your house.

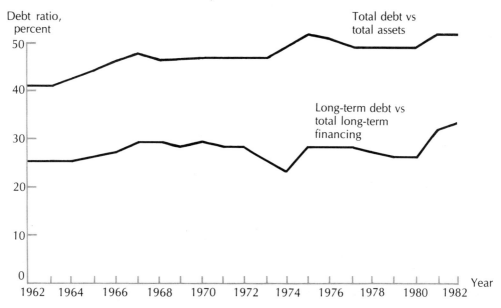

Figure 14-2   Average debt ratios for manufacturing corporations in Canada have increased in the postwar period. However, note that these ratios compare debt with the book value of total assets and total long-term financing. The actual value of corporate assets is higher as a result of inflation. (Derived from: Statistics Canada, *Corporation Financial Statistics*, various issues, and CANSIM, Matrix 006639. CANSIM is the registered Trade Mark for Statistics Canada's machine-readable data base.)

14-7 SUMMARY

Financing is principally a marketing problem. The company tries to split the cash flows generated by its assets into different streams that will appeal to investors with different tastes, wealth, and tax rates. In this chapter we have introduced you to the principal sources of finance and outlined their relative importance.

The simplest and most important source of finance is shareholders' equity, raised either by stock issues or retained earnings.

The next most important source of finance is debt. Debtholders are entitled to a fixed regular payment of interest and the final repayment of principal. But the company's liability is not unlimited. If it cannot pay its debts, it can file for bankruptcy. The usual result is that the debtholders then take over and operate the company's assets.

Note that the tax authorities treat interest payments as a cost. That means the company can deduct interest when calculating its taxable income. Interest is paid from pretax income.

The third source of finance is preferred stock. Preferred is like debt in that it promises a fixed dividend payment, but payment of this dividend is within the discretion of the directors. They must, however, pay the dividend on the preferred before they are allowed to pay a dividend on the common stock. Lawyers and tax experts treat preferred as part of the company's equity. That means preferred dividends must be paid out of after-tax income. This is one reason that preferred is less popular than debt. The principal attraction of preferred stock is the softened tax treatment of dividends in the hands of Canadian investors.

The fourth source of finance consists of options. These are not recorded separately in the company's balance sheet. The simplest option is the warrant that gives its holder the right to buy a share at a set price by a set date. Warrants are often sold in combination with other securities and are merely recorded in a note to the accounts. Convertible bonds are securities that give their holder the right to convert the bond into shares. They are therefore like a mixture of straight debt and a warrant.

Table 14-3 summarized the ways in which companies raise and spend money. Have another look at it and try to get some feel for the numbers. Notice that:

1. Internally generated cash is the principal source of funds. Some people worry about that: they think that if management does not have to go to the trouble of raising the money, it won't think so hard when it comes to spending it.

2. Internally generated cash does not provide all the money companies need. The deficit is particularly large after a period of buoyant sales: this is the time when companies tend to come to the capital markets for more money.

3. There are cycles in company financing. Sometimes companies prefer to issue debt, sometimes equity. In part this reflects their attempt to keep to a target debt-equity ratio. But it also looks as if companies try to make equity issues after a market rise. Nobody knows why they do this. There does not seem any reason to do so in an efficient market. An equity issue is a zero-NPV transaction regardless of whether the stock price has just risen or fallen.

Table 14-4 shows the net effect of this fund raising aggregate balance sheet of manufacturing corporations in the United States and Canada.

FURTHER READING

Donaldson describes a survey of corporate attitudes to different sources of finance in:

C. Donaldson, *Corporate Debt Capacity*, Division of Research, Graduate School of Business Administration, Harvard University, Boston, 1961.

Some common concerns about the role of the capital market in providing funds for industry are set out in:

W.J. Baumol, *The Stock Market and Economic Efficiency*, Fordham University Press, New York, 1965.

Taggart and Marsh provide some evidence on why and when companies use different sources of finance:

R.A. Taggart, "A Model of Corporate Financing Decisions," *Journal of Finance*, **32**:1467–1484 (December 1977).

P. Marsh, "The Choice between Equity and Debt: An Empirical Study," *Journal of Finance*, **37**:121–144 (March 1982).

QUIZ

1. The authorized share capital of the Alfred Cake Company is 100,000 shares. The equity is currently down in the company's books as follows:

Common stock ($0.50 par value)	$40,000
Additional paid-in capital	10,000
Retained earnings	30,000
Common equity	80,000
Treasury stock (2,000 shares)	5,000
Net common equity	$75,000

   (*a*) How many shares are issued?
   (*b*) How many are outstanding?
   (*c*) Explain the difference between your answers to (*a*) and (*b*).
   (*d*) How many more shares can be issued without the approval of shareholders?
   (*e*) Suppose that the company issues 10,000 shares at $2 a share. Which of the above figures would be changed?

2. If there are ten directors to be elected and a shareholder owns 80 shares, indicate the maximum number of votes that he or she can cast for a favourite candidate under:
   (*a*) Majority voting
   (*b*) Cumulative voting

3. Choose from the terms below the one that best fits the blanks.
   (*a*) Debt maturing in more than one year is often called _____ debt.
   (*b*) An issue of bonds that is sold simultaneously in several countries is called a _____ .
   (*c*) If a lender ranks behind the firm's general creditors in the event of default, his or her loan is said to be _____ .
   (*d*) Unsecured bonds are usually termed _____ bonds.
   (*e*) In many cases, a firm is obliged to make regular contributions to a _____ , which is then used to repurchase bonds.
   (*f*) Most bonds give the firm the right to repurchase or _____ the bonds at specified prices.
   (*g*) The rate that banks charge to their most creditworthy customers is generally termed the _____ .
   (*h*) The interest rate on bank loans is often tied to short-term interest rates. These loans are usually called _____ loans.
   (*i*) A long-term, noncancellable rental agreement is called a _____ .

   lease, funded, floating rate, eurobond, commercial paper, term loan, subordinated, call, sinking fund, prime rate, debentures, mortgage bond, senior, unfunded, eurodollar rate.

4. The figures in the following table are in the wrong order. Can you place them in their correct order?

	% of Total Sources in 1982
Internally generated cash	10
Financial deficit	31
New share issues	1
Long-term debt issues	64
Short-term debt issues	34

QUESTIONS AND PROBLEMS

1. "It is frequently held that the cost of funds on the security market falls whenever stock prices rise, just as the yield of a bond varies inversely with its price. One would think that it pays management to turn to the market for funds whenever the cost of stock market capital, thus interpreted, falls sufficiently."[14] Discuss.

2. It is sometimes suggested that since retained earnings provide the bulk of industry's capital needs, the securities markets are largely redundant. Do you agree?

3. Can you think of any new kinds of security that might appeal to investors? Why do you think they have not been issued?

4. Look back at Table 14-2.
   (a) Suppose that Canadian Pacific issues 15,000 shares at $40 a share. Rework Table 14-2 to show the company's equity after the issue.
   (b) Suppose CP subsequently repurchases and cancels 10,000 shares at $45 a share. Rework Table 14-2 to show the effect of the further change.

5. The shareholders of the Pickwick Paper Company need to elect five directors. There are 100,000 shares outstanding. How many shares do you need to own to *ensure* that you can elect at least one director if:
   (a) The company has majority voting.
   (b) It has cumulative voting.

6. Compare the yields on preferred stocks with those on corporate bonds. Can you explain the difference?

7. Who are the main holders and issuers of preferred stock? Explain why.

---

[14]W.J. Baumol, op. cit., p. 71.

HOW CORPORATIONS ISSUE SECURITIES

In Chapter 14 we saw that corporations face a persistent financial deficit, which they meet by selling securities. There are a number of ways in which they can do this. Here are some of the principal alternatives:

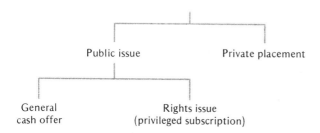

Many issues are sold publicly and are then traded on the securities markets. Before a firm can make a public offering, it has to satisfy the appropriate securities commissions that investors have been given the important facts about the issue. In the first part of this chapter we will look at what that involves.

A public issue can be offered either to investors at large or directly to the firm's existing stockholders. The first method is called a **general cash offer**; the second is called a **privileged subscription** or **rights issue**. After we have looked at the features that are common to all public issues, we will describe in turn the idiosyncracies of the general cash offer and the rights issue. We will also describe a recent American innovation called **shelf registration**, which allows large, creditworthy companies to avoid much of the delay and paperwork of traditional procedures.

Sometimes investors intend to hold on to their securities and are not worried about whether they can sell them. In this case there is little advantage to a public issue, and the firm may prefer to make a **private placement** of the securities directly with one or two financial institutions. At the end of this chapter we will tell you how this is done.

Much of this chapter is concerned with the basic mechanics of security issues;[1] but these lead us to several important and difficult questions. Here are four of these questions:

1. A firm wanting to issue securities can invite competitive bids by underwriters for each issue or maintain a stable, long-term relationship with a single underwriter. (As we will explain, underwriters are financial midwives who bring the infant issue into the capital markets.) Does the competition reduce transaction costs or allow the firm to sell the securities on more favourable terms? We shall look at some recent evidence.

---

[1]We concentrate here primarily on long-term financing. The issue of short-term debt is discussed in Chapter 30.

2. Do large stock issues depress the stock prices of the issuing firms? Many financial executives believe they do.

3. Is there anything wrong in issuing stock at prices below book value per share? Many financial executives believe this depresses stock price.

4. Corporations in the United States have been increasingly reluctant to issue rights to their existing stockholders. Why?

One comment before we proceed: most of this chapter is concerned with how companies "go public" and how they raise money subsequently. But when a firm goes public, it does not rise like Venus from the sea; most firms going public have been in business for some time, and occasionally they are very large companies indeed. When Gulfstream Aerospace made its first public stock issue, it already had annual sales of about $500 million.

Equity investment in private companies is generally known as *venture capital*. Venture capital may be provided by investment institutions or by wealthy individuals who are prepared to back an untried company in exchange for a piece of the action. There are also specialist venture capital companies. For example, American Research and Development (ARD) backed Digital Equipment Corp. long before it became a household name. ARD made handsome capital gains when Digital subsequently went public.

Of course, private companies also borrow, chiefly from banks and insurance companies. Sometimes venture capitalists will buy a young firm's debt as well as its equity.

Now let's return to this chapter's main topic: how corporations issue securities.

15-1 THE PUBLIC ISSUE

Securities Commission Jurisdictions

In Canada, securities law is primarily a provincial matter, but in the United States, it is largely a federal matter. Each jurisdiction has its own securities commission to regulate the sale of securities within its boundaries. In the United States, there is the Securities and Exchange Commission (SEC); in Ontario, there is the Ontario Securities Commission (OSC); and so on. Much of the legislation for these various jurisdictions is similar, partly because of leadership roles assumed by the SEC and the OSC.[2] However, a firm seeking a broadly based distribution of its securities in all ten provinces as well as the United States must obtain approval from 11 different securities commissions.[3] We will point out important idiosyncracies of the various jurisdictions, but most of what we will say will apply to all jurisdictions.

---

[2]Since there are a lot of fixed costs associated with operating a securities commission, some of the smaller provinces are reluctant to pass legislation that is as comprehensive as that passed by Ontario or the United States.

The laws governing the sale of securities derive principally from laws passed following the 1929 stock market crash.

[3]There are also so-called "blue-sky" laws in each American state that regulate security sales. For example, in December 1980, when Apple Computer Inc. made its first public issue, the Massachusetts state government decided the offering was too risky for its residents and therefore barred sale of the shares to individual investors in the state. The state relented later on, after the issue was out and the price had risen. Needless to say, this action was not acclaimed by Massachusetts investors.

The states do not usually reject security issues by honest firms through established underwriters. We cite this example simply to illustrate the potential power of state securities laws.

General Procedures

Certain general procedures must be followed in *any* public issue regardless of the type of security involved. The first formal step is approval of the issue by the board of directors. Sometimes an issue of stock requires an increase in the firm's authorized capital, and in that case a special meeting of the stockholders must be called to obtain consent to the increase.

Then a preliminary **prospectus**[4] is filed with the appropriate securities commissions. It is also distributed to potential investors in the security and is often called a *red herring* because of the statement printed in red ink denying that the company is trying to sell securities before the issue is approved. The preliminary prospectus contains financial statements as well as information about the proposed financing and the firm's history, existing business and plans for the future, but does not contain some details such as the offering price of the issue. With the preliminary prospectus, the underwriters may attempt to "pre-sell" the issue or accept "indications of interest" from potential buyers.

After the securities commissions have studied the preliminary prospectus, they notify the company of any deficiencies and request additions and changes. An amended prospectus is then filed, and so on, until the issue is approved.[5] The final prospectus must be sent to all purchasers of the securities. At the same time the company publishes a "tombstone" advertisement, listing the names of the underwriters from whom the prospectus may be obtained. In Figure 15-1, we reproduce an example of a tombstone advertisement for a large issue that involved many of the leading underwriters.

It would be impractical to reproduce a complete prospectus in this book. We therefore do the next best two things. First, we exhort the reader to acquire and examine a prospectus. Second, we reproduce in the appendix to this chapter a condensed example, which should give an impression of the mixture of valuable information and redundant qualifications that characterizes these documents. The securities commissions take particular care to ensure that investors' eyes are opened to the danger of purchase. Some investors have joked that, if they read prospectuses carefully, they would never dare buy any new issue.

The company may have other tasks during the process of issuing a security. Unless it is very small, the company will need to appoint a **registrar** and perhaps some co-registrars to record any issues of stock and to prevent any unauthorized issue. It will probably have to appoint a **transfer agent**, and possibly several regional co-agents, to look after the transfer of the newly issued securities.

---

[4]Canadian resource companies or companies that are issuing more shares of a security that is already publicly traded can sometimes file a relatively simple **statement of material facts** instead of a full prospectus. In other circumstances, a firm can issue a **short form prospectus** that can incorporate by reference information filed with the securities commission, but not included in the prospectus.

If the issue is to be sold in the United States, the preliminary prospectus forms a part of a larger file called the **registration statement**, which is submitted to the SEC. The registration statement is not needed for loans maturing within nine months or issues involving less than $300,000. The latter are known as *Regulation A* issues, and for these the SEC needs only a simple notification and an example of the offering circular that is to be sent to prospective buyers.

[5]In Canada, the securities can legally be sold as soon as each of the securities commissions issues a **receipt** for the final prospectus. The time between issuing receipts for the preliminary and final prospectuses must be at least ten days. In the United States, the registration statement becomes effective 20 days after it is accepted by the SEC, and then the securities can legally be sold. The securities commissions are concerned solely with disclosure, and they have no power to prevent an issue as long as there has been proper disclosure.

This advertisement is not to be construed as a public offering in any province of Canada of the securities mentioned herein. Such offering will be made only by means of a prospectus in those provinces where such prospectus has been accepted for filing by a securities commission or similar authority in such province.

New Issue

$125,000,000

Bell Canada

12.65% Debentures, Series DN

To be dated November 15, 1984 — To mature November 15, 2003

Price: 100

The Debentures are offered pursuant to a prospectus dated November 1, 1984, copies of which may be obtained from such of the undernamed and other dealers who may lawfully offer these securities.

Dominion Securities Pitfield Limited	**Wood Gundy Inc.**
Richardson Greenshields of Canada Limited	**Lévesque, Beaubien Inc.**

Merrill Lynch Canada Inc.	**McLeod Young Weir** Limited	**Nesbitt Thomson Bongard** Inc.
Burns Fry Limited	**Midland Doherty** Limited	**Walwyn Stodgell Cochran Murray** Limited
Pemberton Houston Willoughby Incorporated	**Bell Gouinlock** Limited	**Geoffrion, Leclerc** Inc.
Molson Rousseau Inc.	**Bache Securities** Inc.	**Tassé & Associates,** Limited
Odlum Brown Limited	**Brault, Guy, O'Brien** Inc.	**Casgrain & Company** Limited
Gordon Capital Corporation	**McNeil, Mantha,** Inc.	**Andras, Hatch & Hetherington** Ltd.
Burgess Graham Securities Limited	**F.H. Deacon, Hodgson** Inc.	**John Graham & Company** Limited
MacDougall, MacDougall & MacTier Inc.	**Maison Placements Canada** Inc.	**McLean McCarthy** Limited
Osler, Wills, Bickle Limited		**Scotia Bond Company** Limited

November 1984

Figure 15-1 "Tombstone" advertisements such as this list the underwriters to a new issue. Used by permission of Bell Canada.

Costs of a Public Issue

A public issue creates substantial administrative costs. The registration procedure itself, which involves management, counsel, and accountants as well as the underwriters and their advisers, may cost from about $50,000 to more than $100,000. In addition, the firm must pay fees for registering the new securities, printing and mailing costs, and so on.

Table 15-1   Issue costs as a percent of proceeds for registered issues of common stock during 1971–1975.

Size of Issue (millions of dollars)	General Underwritten Cash Offers			Underwritten Rights Issues		
	Underwriters' Compensation, %	Other Expenses, %	Total Cost, %	Underwriters' Compensation, %	Other Expenses, %	Total Cost, %
0.50 to 0.99	7.0	6.8	13.7	3.4	4.8	8.2
1.00 to 1.99	10.4	4.9	15.3	6.4	4.2	10.5
2.00 to 4.99	6.6	2.9	9.5	5.2	2.9	8.1
5.00 to 9.99	5.5	1.5	7.0	3.9	2.2	6.1
10.00 to 19.99	4.8	0.7	5.6	4.1	1.2	5.4
20.00 to 49.99	4.3	0.4	4.7	3.8	0.9	4.7
50.00 to 99.99	4.0	0.2	4.2	4.0	0.7	4.7
100.00 to 500.00	3.8	0.1	4.0	3.5	0.5	4.0
Average	5.0	1.2	6.2	4.3	1.7	6.1

Source: C.W. Smith, "Alternative Methods for Raising Capital: Rights versus Underwritten Offerings," *Journal of Financial Economics*, **5**:273–307 (December 1977), table 1, p. 277.

The other major explicit cost of a public issue is underwriting. Underwriters play a triple role—providing advice to the company, then buying the issue, and finally reselling it to the public. In a cash offer they are paid a *spread*—that is, they are allowed to buy the shares for less than the *offering price* at which the securities are finally bought by investors. In the case of a rights offer they are paid *standby* and *take-up* fees. We will define these two terms later.

Tables 15-1 and 15-2 show the average underwriting and administrative costs for stock issues and debt issues, respectively. Two aspects of the data are of immediate interest.

First, it is more expensive to issue stock than the same amount of debt. This partly reflects the greater administrative costs of stock issues,[6] but it is chiefly because underwriters require compensation for the greater risks they bear in buying and reselling stock.

Table 15-2   Average underwriting and administrative costs for underwritten public issues of bonds 1960–1969 classified by size of issue.

Size of Issue (millions of dollars)	Underwriters' Compensation, %	Other Expenses, %
Under 0.50	13.6	6.2
0.50 to 0.99	7.7	5.2
1.00 to 1.99	6.4	3.0
2.00 to 4.99	4.6	1.7
5.00 to 9.99	1.6	0.9
10.00 to 19.99	1.2	0.6
20.00 to 49.99	1.1	0.4
50.00 and above	0.8	0.3

Source: R. Hillstrom and R. King (eds.), *1960–69: A Decade of Corporate and International Finance*, Investment Dealers Digest, Inc., New York, p. 18.

---

[6]The figures do not capture *all* administrative costs. For example, they do not include management time spent on the issue.

Second, a large part of the issue cost is fixed. Therefore there are economies of scale in issuing securities: issue costs may absorb 15% of a $1 million underwritten stock issue but only 4% of a $500 million issue. A $500 million debt issue would face issue costs of less than 1%.

Security issues can be costly in yet another way. If the offering price is *less* than the true value of the issued securities, then investors who buy the issue get a bargain at the expense of the firm's existing stockholders. The costs of *underpricing* are hidden but nevertheless real, and in some cases they may exceed the other issue costs. We will have more to say about this later.

15-2   THE GENERAL CASH OFFER

At the beginning of this chapter we subdivided public issues into two categories:

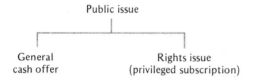

General cash offers are sold to investors at large; rights issues are sold directly to the firm's existing stockholders. Virtually all debt is sold by general cash offer. Equity securities may or may not be.

The first public issue by a company is known as an **unseasoned** issue. A company making an unseasoned issue usually has no alternative but to make a general cash offer. If the firm's existing owners were willing to buy the new issue, the company would not need to "go public." Later, when the company makes additional, seasoned stock issues, it can offer them to its existing shareholders on a rights issue basis. We start by examining the general cash offer and then move on to the rights issue.

The Role of the Underwriter in a General Cash Offer

Most cash offers are underwritten. The underwriter offers financial and procedural advice and handles the actual sale of the issue. Usually the underwriter buys the security for less than the offering price and accepts the risk of not being able to resell it. This spread between the underwriters' buying price and the offering price represents payment both for their advice and for their role in marketing the issue. In the more risky cases the underwriter usually receives some extra noncash compensation, such as warrants to buy additional stock. Occasionally, where a new issue of common stock is regarded as particularly risky, the underwriter may be unwilling to enter into a fixed commitment and will handle the issue only on a "best efforts" or an "all-or-none" basis. *Best efforts* means that the underwriter promises to sell as much of the issue as possible but does not guarantee the sale of the entire issue. *All or none* means that if the entire issue cannot be sold at the offering price, the deal is called off, and the issuing company receives nothing.

Many companies have a well-established relationship with a particular underwriter, who underwrites the firm's security issues and provides other financial services. The underwriting fee is then negotiated with that firm. But sometimes companies ask for competitive bids from underwriters for each new security issue. In fact, American utility holding companies are required to select their underwriters on the basis of competitive bids.

When the issue is large, a group of underwriters will get together to form a **syndicate** or **banking group** to handle the sale. In this case one firm becomes the **lead underwriter** and acts as syndicate manager. For this job, it keeps about 20% of the spread. A further 20% to 30% of the spread is used to pay the syndicate that buys the issue or provides assurance that it will be sold. The remaining 50% to 60% goes to the larger number of firms in the **selling group**; these firms are liable only for the purchase of the securities they order from the banking group.

If the market price falls below the stated offering price, the principal underwriter may be allowed by the underwriting agreement to support the market by repurchasing shares at the market price.[7] We have no information about the effects of such stabilization. But, if capital markets are efficient, then transactions affect prices only insofar as they are thought to convey information. In that case, the underwriters' efforts at stabilization cannot have a lasting effect on prices and cannot be in the true interests of the selling group.

In any case, if the issue obstinately remains unsold and the market price falls substantially below the offering price, the underwriters have no alternative but to break the syndicate. The members then dispose of their commitments individually, as best they can.

Most companies raise new capital only occasionally, but underwriters are in the business all the time. Established underwriters are, therefore, worried about their reputation and will not handle a new issue unless they believe the facts have been presented fairly to investors. Thus, in addition to handling the sale of an issue, the underwriters in effect give a "Good Housekeeping Seal of Approval" to it. This implied endorsement may be worth quite a bit to the issuing company.

Who are the Underwriters?

Since underwriters play such a crucial role in the general offer, we should look at who they are.[8] The market is dominated by a few firms that enjoy great prestige, experience, and financial resources. Table 15-3 lists some of the largest underwriting firms in Canada and the United States. Note that, since Canadian firms raise a lot of their capital in the United States, American firms like Morgan Stanley can make it into the top seven in Canada.

Table 15-3   Principal underwriters listed in order of total value of issues underwritten in 1982.

Canada	United States
Wood Gundy	Morgan Stanley
Dominion Securities Ames	Merrill Lynch White Weld
Pitfield Mackay Ross	Salomon Brothers
McLeod Young Weir	Goldman Sachs
Merrill Lynch	First Boston
Morgan Stanley	Lehman Brothers, Kuhn Loeb
Richardson Greenshields	Blyth Eastman Paine Webber

Source: *The Financial Post*, July 14, 1984, p. 12; *The Wall Street Journal*, Jan. 11, 1983, p. 43. Reprinted by permission of *The Wall Street Journal*, © Dow Jones & Company, Inc. 1983. All rights reserved.

---

[7]In such cases, syndicate members could escape their obligation by selling their shares in the market to the principal underwriter. To prevent this, a record is kept so that syndicate members whose shares end up in the hands of the principal underwriter lose that portion of their selling concession.

[8]In the United States, underwriters are usually called **investment bankers**, although they are usually called underwriters in Canada. In either case, they are security dealers or brokers.

Underwriting is characterized by a well-established hierarchy, which is reflected in the ordering of the names on the tombstone advertisement in Figure 15-1. The lead underwriters are listed in alphabetical order at the top of the list. Then comes the banking group, and finally the selling group.

Firms guard their rankings with an extraordinary possessiveness that is somewhat reminiscent of the attempts of a dynasty to perpetuate itself. Morgan Stanley, for example, has refused to allow its name to appear on the tombstone unless it is at the head of the list. Firms that struggle to attain a particular ranking often have to consent to being listed "out of order." But the old regime does change. The 1984 merger of Dominion Securities Ames and Pitfield Mackay Ross will undoubtedly push them higher up the ladder. Gordon Capital Corp. has aggressively used innovations such as the **bought deal**,[9] which have increased its share of the market. In the United States, firms like Merrill Lynch White Weld have used their strong sales forces to increase their participation and rankings, while large, traditional houses like Morgan Stanley have formed loose networks with regional firms to increase their distribution capacity.

Setting the Price in a General Cash Offer

We have already discussed the direct costs of a cash offer. There is also a potential indirect cost, for if the issue is sold below its true worth, there must be a loss to the company's existing stockholders. How efficient is the system at pricing issues?

Pricing is most difficult for issues of unseasoned stock. In these cases the underwriter has very little guidance as to the market value of the security. A number of researchers have tried to measure how well underwriters have managed to gauge the value of unseasoned securities. With remarkable unanimity they have found that on the average investors who buy at the issue price realize very high returns over the following weeks. For example, a study by Roger Ibbotson of 120 new issues indicated an abnormal return of 13% in the first month and 8% in the second. Thus it appears that underwriters pitch the issue price below the stock's true market value.

This underpricing does not imply that any investor can expect to become wealthy by purchasing unseasoned stock from the underwriters, for if the issue is attractive, the underwriters will not have enough stock to go around. In order to get stock at the issue price investors would probably have to be prepared to pay indirectly through allocating more brokerage business to the underwriter than they otherwise would. Therefore underpricing helps underwriters. It gains them the gratitude of investors who buy the issue, and it reduces the risk of underwriting. Does that mean the underwriter earns excessive profits? Possibly, but not necessarily. If the business is sufficiently competitive, underwriters will take all these hidden benefits into account when they negotiate the spread.

Many investment bankers and institutional investors argue that underpricing is in the interests of the issuing firm. They say that a low offering price on the initial offer raises the price of the stock when it is subsequently traded in the market and enhances the firm's ability to raise further capital. At least one industrialist has accepted this argument, for writing some time after his company went public, the president of Manpower described the pricing decision as follows:

> Our underwriting group suggested a price of $15. The general market was strong . . .
> when our registration statement was filed and we felt that the public might well pay

---

[9]The agreements between the firm issuing the securities and the underwriter often include some protection for the underwriter in the form of a **market-out clause**. If the underwriter is having trouble selling the issue because of, say, a rise in interest rates, such a clause will often allow the underwriter to back out of the deal. With a bought deal, such a clause does not exist, and the underwriter must suffer any losses that may occur while the issue is being marketed.

$17 or $18 for our stock rather than $15. Our underwriters were strong in their desire to have the issue sold at $15 a share on the basis that this was a proper price for the stock. They pointed out that the after-market was important and that the price could decline if the stock was overpriced. Having practised law for many years prior to entering the Manpower program, it was always my opinion that clients should not second-guess their counsellors. I had to follow the same rules in accepting the advice of our investment bankers. And how right our underwriting group was! Within six months our stock rose from $15 a share to $50. Would the stock have had this dramatic increase if the initial price had been $17 or $18? There may have been some who felt that it was overpriced initially and would not have been in the market for our stock. Suffice it to say that the overall result was extremely good. It points out the importance of working with competent investment bankers who guide you in these matters.[10]

Contentment at selling an article for one-third of its ultimate worth is a rare quality.

Competitive Bidding

American public utility holding companies are generally required to choose underwriters by competitive bids (although sometimes, when a holding company faces "unsettled market conditions," the SEC relents and allows negotiation). Utilities that are not organized as holding companies can do as they like.

The competition is real. Utilities almost always get at least two bids. For smaller issues, where fewer firms are needed to form a syndicate, four or five bids may be made. But does the competition make a difference?

It does reduce the spreads charged by underwriters. For example, a study by Logue and Jarrow of 122 utility stock issues between 1963 and 1974 found average spreads of 4.2% for negotiated issues and 3.0% for competitive ones.[11] Yet negotiated underwriting is used by almost all firms that have a choice. Why?

Underwriters argue that negotiated offerings allow them to allocate more time to marketing the issue—identifying large buyers, recruiting salespeople in brokers' local offices, and so on. This marketing is most effective if done well before the issue date. Under competitive bidding, a syndicate does not put the same effort into marketing because the investment is wasted if the syndicate does not win. Therefore it has to attract buyers by underpricing the issue rather than by salesmanship.

If the underwriters are right, we ought to observe that competitive offerings cause a larger temporary price decline around the offering date. Logue and Jarrow looked for this effect. Figure 15-2 shows what they found. Apparently there is, on the average, some pressure with both types of issue.[12] But it is roughly 1% greater for competitive offerings, just about enough to offset the greater spread charged in negotiated issues.

---

[10]From E.L. Winter, *A Complete Guide to Making a Public Offering.* © 1962, published by Prentice-Hall, Inc., Englewood Cliffs, N.J., 07632.

[11]D.E. Logue and R.A. Jarrow, "Negotiation vs. Competitive Bidding in the Sale of Securities by Public Utilities," *Financial Management,* **7**:31–39 (Autumn 1978).

[12]There seems to be a small drop in price any time a sale of common stock is announced. This is probably an "information effect." That is, the very willingness of the seller to sell conveys a little bit of bad news about the true worth of the shares. Potential buyers realize that a sale is more likely when the seller thinks the shares are overpriced than when he or she thinks they are underpriced; the buyers adjust their bids accordingly. This information effect was first noted by Myron Scholes, in a study we reviewed in Section 13-7. See M. Scholes, "The Market for Securities: Substitution vs. Price Pressure and the Effect of Information on Share Prices," *Journal of Business*, **45**:179–211 (April 1972).

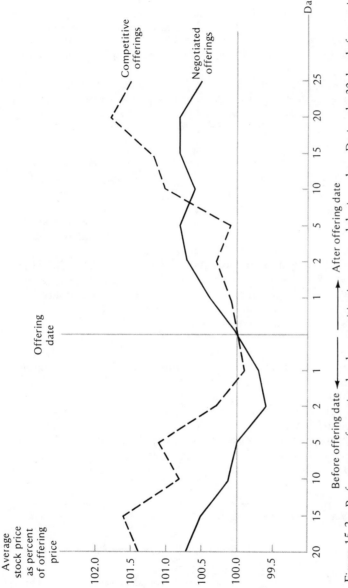

Figure 15-2 Performance of negotiated and competitive issues around the issue date. During the 20 days before an issue of utility stock, price pressure appears to be greater when the stock is sold by competitive bidding. This additional price pressure offsets the lower underwriting spread.

Source: D.E. Logue and R.A. Jarrow, "Negotiation vs. Competitive Bidding in the Sale of Securities by Public Utilities," *Financial Management*, 7:31–39 (Autumn 1978), exhibits 5 and 6, p. 37.

This is a controversial issue and we suspect that Logue and Jarrow's study may not be the final word on it. But their results indicate that the choice between negotiated and competitive underwriting is a toss-up and that on average nothing is lost if firms give underwriting business to the investment bankers they work with on other matters. Small or obscure firms, whose securities stand to benefit most from careful marketing, are best advised to avoid the formal, competitive bidding system. Of course, nothing prevents them from shopping around among potential underwriters.

Pricing General Cash Offers Outside Canada and the United States

It is interesting to look at other methods for pricing general cash offers. In Great Britain issues of unseasoned stock are usually made by an "offer for sale." Orders for the stock at the issue price are publicly invited and, if they exceed the total amount on offer, the allotments are scaled down proportionately. For example, if one million shares are issued at 50 pence per share, but applications are received for two million shares, the issue would be "two times subscribed." Each bidder would be allotted 50% of the number of shares he or she offered to buy. Since there is also some possibility that the issue may be undersubscribed, the company will pay a small fee to a group of institutions who in return guarantee to buy any unsold stock.

One drawback with the Canadian and American systems is that underwriters have a conflict of interest. They would like to get the company the best deal they can but they would also like to price the issue low and sell it to their clients. Under the British system underwriters do not decide who gets the stock; this reduces the conflict of interest. However, the risk of mispricing is passed on to the subscriber in a magnified form. Investors who believe the issue is cheap will also expect it to be oversubscribed. Therefore they will apply for more stock than they really want. But that is a dangerous game, because, if they are wrong in their estimate of the stock's value, they are also likely to be wrong in their estimate of the oversubscription. Therefore, they will receive a large allocation of the unattractive issues and a small allocation of the attractive ones. If they are smart, they will not play the game unless there is substantial underpricing on the average.

If you don't know what price to charge for an article, one solution is to put it up for auction. In France unseasoned stock is generally sold in this way.[13] The shares are sold at a price slightly *below* the bid that would clear the issue. That makes it impossible to satisfy all those who have bid at or above that price. Therefore investors who put in the highest bids receive less stock than they asked for. This system is rather like a survey of investors' opinions about the value of the stock, with a reward in the form of slightly underpriced shares for those who produce the most useful estimates.

The American and Canadian governments sell their weekly issues of Treasury bills by auction. Also, Exxon auctioned off bond issues in 1976, 1977, and 1982, raising a total of $440 million. But auctions make most sense when there is a lot of uncertainty about the value of the security. The system seems to work well in France for unseasoned common stock.[14] Perhaps it should be used here, as well.

---

[13]See J.G. McDonald and B.C. Jacquillat, "Pricing of Initial Equity Issues: The French Sealed-Bid Auction," *Journal of Business*, **47**:37–47 (January 1974).

[14]An auction system was also used in Great Britain in the mid-1960s for issues of unseasoned common stock. It has been used from time to time since. For an evaluation of the British issue methods see E. Dimson, "The Efficiency of the British New Issue Market for Ordinary Shares," Ph.D. dissertation, London Business School, 1979.

15-3   THE PRIVILEGED SUBSCRIPTION OR RIGHTS ISSUE

We have examined what happens when firms sell their securities to the public at large: now we must look at what happens when they restrict the offer to existing stockholders.

Firms' articles of incorporation often state that shareholders have a **pre-emptive right** to subscribe to new offerings. Such a provision simply reinforces the fact that shareholders, as owners of the business, are entitled under common law to anything of value that the company may distribute, including the potentially valuable opportunity to buy new issues of securities. A strict interpretation of pre-emptive rights would place intolerable restrictions on management's freedom of action, and so it is not surprising that these rights have been interpreted in a limited way. First, they usually apply to issues of common stock, to convertible securities, and to voting preferred stock, but not to issues of debt. Second, they do not apply to common stock that is issued as payment for a merger, nor do they apply to issues of stock to employees, nor to stock which has been repurchased from shareholders and then held in the company treasury for subsequent resale.[15] The last exemption will seem strange to those who believe that the life history of a particular share is an irrelevant bygone.

How Rights Issues Work

It is important to understand the mechanics of offering securities to existing shareholders. Let us look at an example. In January 1984, the Toronto-Dominion Bank issued over $240,000,000 of common stock by a rights issue. The preliminary stages of the issue were similar to those for any other public issue, although in this case, since a lot of information about T-D is publicly available, the bank merely had to issue an "offering letter" to buyers, rather than a full prospectus. The offering letter did not contain any financial statements, although these were filed with the appropriate securities commissions. The major difference lay in selling procedures. Shareholders of record (that is, those listed on the company's books as share owners) on December 5, 1983 were sent "rights certificates"[16] showing that they owned one "right" for each share they held. Seven of these rights entitled a shareholder to buy one additional share at a subscription or issue price of $14.625 at any time before January 10, 1984. To take advantage of the offer, the shareholder simply had to **exercise** the right by completing the subscription form on the rights certificate and forwarding it with payment[17] to the bank's subscription agent, the Royal Trust Company.

Shareholders could either sell, exercise, or throw away these rights. The rights were listed for trading on Canadian stock exchanges. The remaining shareholders should have postponed any exercise decision until the expiry date. At that point, they should have taken advantage of the opportunity to buy stock at $14.625 if, and only if, the stock price was higher than $14.625.

To guard against the danger that the price might end up below the subscription price, T-D arranged for the issue to be underwritten.[18] Instead of actually buying the issue as

---

[15]This is largely academic now in Canada, since most firms no longer have treasury stock. See Section 14-1.

[16]Sometimes the rights certificate is called a **warrant**.

[17]The bank also offered to accept nine monthly instalment payments of $1.46, starting on January 10, 1984, and a tenth instalment of $1.49 on October 10, 1984. The buyer would not receive dividend payments on the shares, except to the extent that shares were fully paid up. The Bank Act formerly required banks to offer this time-payment method for shares. Although this is not currently required of banks, T-D chose to allow this method of payment.

[18]Most rights issued are underwritten.

in the cash offer, the underwriters were paid a **standby fee** of $2,000,000.[19] In return, they stood ready to buy up to 6,837,607 unsubscribed or "residual" shares for at least the subscription price, less a **take-up fee** of $0.3291 per share purchased. The underwriters were protected by a market-out clause, allowing them out of the standby arrangement if there were various types of significant adverse changes in market conditions.

As it turned out, T-D shares closed at $17\frac{1}{8}$ on the January 10 expiry date. Even though this was above the $14\frac{5}{8}$ subscription price, there were about 300,000 shares that were unsubscribed, because the shareholders failed to exercise or sell their rights. (These shareholders were likely either on vacation or simply not well informed.) The resulting residual shares were sold in Europe by the underwriters.[20] As an alternative, T-D could have provided (but did not provide) an **oversubscription privilege** to its shareholders, allowing them to buy the residual shares at the subscription price.

How a Rights Issue Affects the Stock Price

The left-hand portion of Table 15-4 shows the case of a stockholder who owned seven shares of T-D stock just prior to the rights issue. The price of the stock at that time was about $16.00, and so this stockholder's holding was worth 16 × 7 or $112. The T-D offer gave the opportunity to purchase one additional share for $14.625. Put yourself in the stockholder's shoes. If you buy the new share immediately, your holding increases to eight shares and, other things being equal, the value of the eight shares is 112 + 14.625 = $126.625. The price per share after the issue would no longer be $16, but 126.625/8 = $15.83.

Table 15-4   Issue price in a rights offering does not affect the shareholder's wealth.

Details	Terms	
	1 for 7 at $14.625	1 for 3½ at $7.3125
Prior to issue		
Number of shares held	7	7
Share price (cum-rights)	$16.00	$16.00
Value of holding	$112.00	$112.00
After issue		
Number of new shares	1	2
Amount of new investment	$14.625	2 × $7.3125 = $14.625
Total value of holding	$126.625	$126.625
Total number of shares	8	9
New share price (ex-rights)	$126.625/8 = $15.83	$126.625/9 = $14.07
Value of a right	$16 − 15.83 = $0.17	$16 − 14.07 = $1.93

[19]We will talk a little more about standby fees and how to value them in Chapter 20. The standby fee was over and above fees paid to the investment dealers who merely facilitated the sale of rights (by maintaining an "orderly market") as well as the exercise of rights. That is, in addition to the standby fee of $2,000,000, a fee of $374,175 was paid to a managing group of four dealers. The managing group formed a larger "sponsoring dealer group," and this latter group received an additional $1,170,752. Moreover, a still larger "facilitating dealer group" received $0.1887 per share for facilitating the exercise of rights (with a minimum of $20 and a maximum of $2,500 for each client that exercised).

[20]T-D wanted to expand its European shareholder base, and the underwriting group included several European investment dealers. T-D did not register the issue in the United States, so United States shareholders could not subscribe and had to sell their rights. We are grateful to the T-D bank for providing some of these details.

The only difference between the old $16 shares and the new $15.83 shares was that the former carried the rights to subscribe to the issue. Therefore the old shares are generally termed cum-rights or rights-on shares and the new shares are termed ex-rights shares. The 17 cent difference in price between the two shares represented the price of one right. We can confirm that this is the correct price of the right by imagining a second investor who had no stock in T-D, but wished to acquire some. One way to do this would be to buy seven rights at 17 cents and then exercise them at a further cost of $14.625. The total cost of this investor's share would be $7 \times \$0.17 + \$14.625 = \$15.82$, which, save for rounding error, is the same outlay required to buy one of the new shares directly.

Formulas for Computing Rights Values

We showed that the value of a right is equal to the difference between the cum-rights (rights-on) price and the ex-rights price:

Value of right = cum-rights price − ex-rights price

It is sometimes helpful to twist this formula around and derive the value of a right directly from the cum-rights price. Suppose that investors are offered the opportunity to buy one new share for every N old shares that they hold. If you buy N cum-rights shares and then exercise your rights to buy one new share, you will end up with $N + 1$ ex-rights shares. That tells us the correct relationship between the cum-rights price and the ex-rights price, given the issue or subscription price:

$N \times$ cum-rights price + issue price = $(N + 1) \times$ ex-rights price

Substituting this relationship in our formula for the value of a right, we have

$$\text{Value of right} = \text{cum-rights price} - \frac{N \times \text{cum-rights price} + \text{issue price}}{N + 1}$$

$$= \frac{\text{cum-rights price} - \text{issue price}}{N + 1}$$

In our example,

$$\text{Value of right} = \frac{16 - 14.625}{7 + 1} = \$0.17$$

Alternatively, if you want to work in terms of the ex-rights price:

$$\text{Value of right} = \frac{(N + 1) \times \text{ex-rights price} - \text{issue price}}{N} - \text{ex-rights price}$$

$$= \frac{\text{ex-rights price} - \text{issue price}}{N}$$

$$= \frac{15.83 - 14.625}{7} = \$0.17$$

Issue Price is Irrelevant as Long as the Rights are Exercised

It should be clear on reflection that T-D could have raised the same amount of money on a variety of terms. For example, instead of a 1-for-7 at \$14.625, it could have made a 1-for-$3\frac{1}{2}$ at \$7.3125.[21] In this case it would have sold twice as many shares at half the price. If we now work through the arithmetic again in the right-hand portion of Table 15-4, we can see that the alternative terms would not have affected the total value of our shareholder's investment, although it would have altered the number of shares held and also the price per share.

It is not surprising that the issue price is irrelevant in a rights offering. After all, it cannot affect the real plant and equipment owned by the company or the proportion of these assets to which each shareholder is entitled. Therefore the only thing a firm ought to worry about in setting the terms of a rights issue is the possibility that the stock price will fall below the issue price. If that happens, shareholders will not take up their rights and the whole issue will be torpedoed. You can avoid the danger by arranging a standby agreement with the underwriter. But standby agreements tend to be expensive. It may be cheaper just to set the issue price low enough to foreclose the possibility of failure.

A Word on Dilution

Many financial managers disagree with our statement that the issue price in a rights offering is largely irrelevant. They believe that the cost of an issue is inversely proportional to the issue price. One reason managers are reluctant to sell shares at a low price is that they are worried about earnings "dilution." The greater the issue discount, the more shares that have to be sold to raise a given amount of money. That "dilutes" earnings per share. But we know that this is not the relevant variable. Any reduction in earnings per share is exactly offset by an increase in the number of shares held by each shareholder. The issue price does not affect the *total* profits earned on investments. You don't make a pie smaller just by cutting it into smaller pieces and you don't make a firm any less valuable by allocating its profits to a larger number of shares.

Managers also do not like to issue shares if it means selling them below book value. The imagined dangers of this are dramatized by the sad tale of Quangle Hats. Quangle's profitability is as follows:

Book net worth	\$100,000
Number of shares	1,000
Book value per share	\$100,000/1,000 = \$100
Net earnings	\$8,000
Earnings per share	\$8,000/1,000 = \$8.00
Price-earnings ratio	10
Stock price	10 × \$8.00 = \$80.00
Total market value	\$80,000

The total amount of money that has been put up by Quangle's stockholders is \$100,000—\$100 per share. But that investment is earning only \$8 per share—an 8% book return. Investors evidently regard this return as inadequate, for they are only willing to pay \$80 per share for Quangle stock.

Now suppose that Quangle raises \$10,000 by issuing 125 additional shares at the market price of \$80 per share—suppose also that the \$10,000 is invested to earn a

---

[21]Or, equivalently, a 2-for-7 at \$7.3125.

return of 8%. In that case, we would expect investors to continue to pay $10 for each $1 of Quangle's earnings. Now we have:

	Before the Issue	After the Issue
Book net worth	$100,000	$110,000
Number of shares	1,000	1,125
Book value per share	$100,000/1,000 = $100	$110,000/1,125 = $97.78
Net earnings	$8,000	8% of book net worth = $8,800
Earnings per share	$8,000/1,000 = $8.00	$8,800/1,125 = $7.82
Price-earnings ratio	10	10
Stock price	10 × $8.00 = $80.00	10 × $7.82 = $78.20
Total market value	$80,000	$88,000

We note that selling stock below book *does* decrease book value per share and stock price as well.

But there are two things wrong with our example. First, we assumed investors could be tricked into paying $80 for shares shortly destined to be worth $78.20. Actually, if Quangle wishes to raise $10,000, it will have to offer shares *worth* $10,000. And since we know that aggregate market value after the stock issue is $88,000 the *original* 1,000 shares must end up with an aggregate value of $78,000. The price per share will therefore be $78,000/1,000 = $78 and the firm will have to issue $10,000/78 = 128 shares to raise the capital it requires.

Many financial analysts would stop at this point, satisfied that they had "proved" the folly of selling stock for less than book value. But there is a second thing wrong with our example: we never questioned Quangle's decision to expand. It is raising $10,000 and getting only $8,000 in additional market value. In other words, the market's verdict is that expansion has an NPV of −$2,000. Note that this is exactly the loss suffered by the original shareholders.

What if the investment earned a 10% return? In that case the issue of shares would cause the firm's market value to increase by $10,000 to $90,000, and the earnings per share and stock price would be unchanged. Quangle could therefore raise $10,000 by selling only $10,000/80 = 125 new shares.[22]

The point is simple. There is no harm whatsoever in selling stock at prices below book value per share, as long as investors know that you can earn an adequate rate of return on the new money. If the firm has good projects and needs equity capital to finance them, then "dilution" should not bar it from going to the market.

Market Reaction to Rights Issues

Because rights issues throw a large additional supply of shares onto the market, it is widely believed that they must depress the stock price. If the proposed issue is very large, the price pressure may, it is thought, be so severe as to make it almost impossible to raise new money. If so, the firm effectively faces capital rationing.

Of course, the stock price falls in every rights issue when the stock changes from cum-rights to ex-rights. But that drop is compensated by the value of the right. Here we are referring to a possible further drop in price—a drop that would actually reduce stockholders' wealth.

---

[22]Of course the announcement of a stock issue by a company whose price is already selling well below book might be poorly received by investors if the low stock price reflects pessimism about the firm's future prospects. But the same investment program financed any other way would have the same impact on stockholders' wealth.

This belief in price pressure implies an opportunity to buy newly issued shares for less than their true value. It is, therefore, inconsistent with market efficiency. The alternative view stresses that investors buy stocks because they offer a fair reward for their risk. If the stock price fell solely because of increased supply, then that stock would offer a reward that was *more* than commensurate with the risk and investors would be attracted to it as donkeys to a thistle. If *this* belief is correct, rights issues would cause a significant fall in price only if investors thought that the money was likely to be misspent. In any other circumstances, the company should be able to sell large amounts of stock with only a minor impact on price.

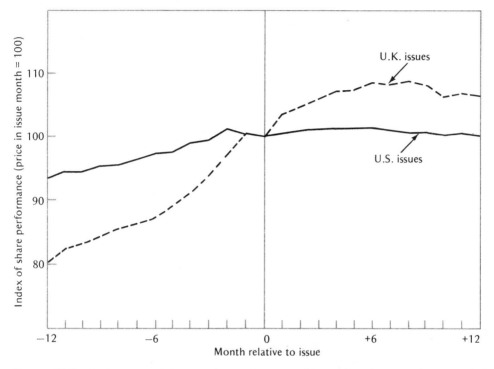

Figure 15-3   Performance of shares making rights issues. Notice that there is only a very slight decline in price at the time of the issue. The analysis is based on 854 rights issues in the United States, 1925–1975, and 254 issues in the United Kingdom, 1962–1972.

In Chapter 13 we referred to Myron Scholes's impressive study of what happens when investors sell large amounts of stock. He found that demand was very responsive to minor changes in price. Now look at Figure 15-3. It shows the results of two studies— one by Clifford Smith of American rights issues, the other by Paul Marsh of British rights issues.[23] There is not much evidence here of those stock price declines that keep investment bankers awake at night. Smith found an average decline of 1.4% in the months immediately surrounding the issue.[24] In the case of Marsh's data you need a

---

[23]C.W. Smith, "Alternative Methods for Raising Capital: Rights versus Underwritten Offerings," *Journal of Financial Economics*, **5**:273–307 (December 1977); P.R. Marsh, "Equity Rights Issues and the Efficiency of the U.K. Stock Market," *Journal of Finance*, **34**:839–862 (September 1979).

[24]This result is also consistent with the study by Logue and Jarrow of utilities in the United States, op. cit. You will remember that they found pressure of about 1% for stock issued by negotiated underwriting.

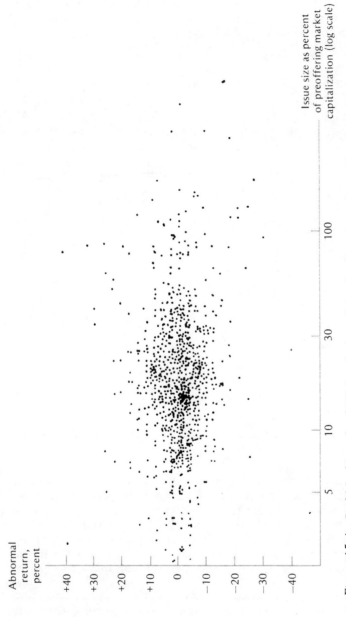

Abnormal
return,
percent

Issue size as percent
of preoffering market
capitalization (log scale)

Figure 15-4 Paul Marsh's study of 997 British issues shows that there is no detectable relationship between the size of a rights issue and the performance of the share in the ex-rights week.
Source: P.R. Marsh, "Equity Rights Issues and the Efficiency of the U.K. Stock Market," *Journal of Finance*, **34**:839–862 (September 1979), p. 859.

magnifying glass to find any price pressure. The stock price fell on the average by only 0.5% in the months surrounding the issue.

Figure 15-3 was based on a mixture of small and large issues. Perhaps we should find greater price pressure if we looked just at large issues. Paul Marsh has another diagram that helps answer that question. Figure 15-4 shows the price decline during the ex-rights week plotted against the relative size of the issue. You can readily see that the degree of pressure was unrelated to the size of the issue, which is exactly what Scholes found when he looked at sales of large blocks of shares by American investors.

It seems fairly clear that price pressure is largely a myth: as long as firms have worthwhile projects, they can normally issue stock at the market price. But what about some of those other popular beliefs about rights issues? How true are they? For example, we mentioned in Chapter 13 that many financial managers believe it is better to make a rights issue after a rise in the stock price. Figure 15-3 shows how strongly that belief is held: in both the United States and Great Britain rights issues were timed to follow a buoyant market for the stock. But Paul Marsh's study shows that investors don't seem to care about this. A rights issue is just as well received after a market fall as after a market rise.[25]

Dilution is another subject that we have discussed. We have argued that the issue price is irrelevant, but many financial managers think that it is wrong to dilute earnings per share by selling stock at a substantial discount. Paul Marsh's data seem to bear us out. The size of the discount has no effect on the market reaction to the rights issue.[26]

The Choice between the Cash Offer and the Rights Issue

We have now reviewed the two principal forms of public issue—the cash offer to all investors and the rights issue to existing shareholders. The former method is used for almost all debt issues and unseasoned stock issues and for many seasoned stock issues. The latter is used mainly for seasoned stock issues.

One essential difference between the two methods is that in a rights offering the issue price is largely irrelevant. Shareholders can sell either their new stock or their rights in a free market. Therefore, they can expect to receive a fair price. In a cash offer, however, the issue price may be important. If the company sells stock for less than the market would bear, the buyer has made a profit at the expense of existing shareholders. Although this danger creates a natural presumption in favour of the rights issue, it can be argued that underpricing is only a serious problem in the case of the unseasoned issue of stock where a rights issue is not a feasible alternative.

In practice, most companies avoid rights issues. Some firms whose stockholders have enjoyed pre-emptive rights have cajoled their stockholders into giving them up. For example, consider the following appeal made in 1976 by Consolidated Edison to its stockholders:

> Expenses involved in a pre-emptive Common Stock rights offering are significantly greater than expenses involved in a direct offering of Common Stock to the public due to additional printing and mailing costs, expenses associated with the handling of rights and the processing of subscriptions, higher underwriters' commissions and the longer time required for consummation of the financing. Thus, if the amendment is adopted, the Company will be able to obtain the amount of capital needed through

---

[25]To be precise, Marsh estimated that the performance of the overall market in preceding weeks explained 0.2% of the variation in postissue performance.

[26]It explained 0.1% of the variation in postissue performance.

the issuance of fewer shares. Over a period of time this will result in slightly less dilution, higher equity value per share, and better earnings per share.[27]

What are the major points in this argument?

1. *Higher expenses?* Take another look at Table 15-1. Rights issues seem no more expensive than general cash offers. Note also that underwriters' compensation is a major part of the costs of rights issues, and that rights issues don't have to be underwritten. *Nonunderwritten* rights issues might be significantly *cheaper* than general cash offers.[28]

2. *Longer time required?* Perhaps an extra month—not an important consideration.

3. *Fewer shares issued?* You should know the argument against that one by now.

In short, the arguments that firms make for avoiding rights issues just don't make sense. We don't know why they use cash offers. Perhaps there are hidden reasons but until they are uncovered we recommend right issues.

15-4 SHELF REGISTRATION

In February 1982 the SEC in the United States issued its Rule 415, which allows large companies to file a single registration statement covering financing plans for up to two years into the future. The actual issue, or issues, can be done with scant additional paperwork, whenever the firm needs the cash or thinks it can issue securities at an attractive price. This is called shelf registration—the registration statement is "put on the shelf," to be taken down and used as needed.

The SEC initially approved shelf registration on a trial basis only, but the new issue procedure was an immediate hit: it accounted for about $20 billion of new securities in the first ten months it was in force. Permanent approval for shelf registration was given in November 1983.

Think of how a financial manager might use shelf registration. As financial manager of Establishment Industries, you anticipate a need for up to $200 million of new long-term debt during the next year or so. You file a shelf registration for that amount. We will assume that Establishment Industries qualifies for shelf registration and that the SEC approves the filing.

Establishment now has prior approval to issue up to $200 million of debt, but it isn't obligated to issue a penny. Nor is it required to work through any particular underwriters—the registration statement may name one or more underwriters the firm thinks it may work with, but others can be added later.

Now you can sit back and issue debt as needed, in bits and pieces if you like. Suppose Merrill Lynch comes across an insurance company with $10 million ready to invest in blue-chip corporate bonds. Your phone rings. It's Merrill Lynch offering to buy $10 million of your bonds, priced to yield, say, $12\frac{1}{2}\%$. If you think that's a good price, you say "OK" and the deal is done, subject to only a little additional paperwork. Merrill

---

[27]We are indebted to Clifford Smith for finding the quotation from Consolidated Edison.

[28]Clifford Smith, who prepared Table 15-1, also calculated costs for a small sample of nonunderwritten rights issues, and found average issue costs of only 2.5%. However, Hansen and Pinkerton have questioned the relevance of this sample—for example, it included several rights issues by AT&T subsidiaries, in which most of the newly issued shares were purchased directly by AT&T. These were really intracompany deals, so it is no surprise to find that issue costs were low. Apparently there are not enough bona fide, nonunderwritten rights issues to justify firm conclusions about their average cost. See C.W. Smith, op. cit., p. 277, and R.S. Hansen and J.M. Pinkerton, "Direct Equity Financing: A Resolution of a Paradox," *Journal of Finance*, 37:651–666 (June 1982).

Lynch then resells the bonds to the insurance company, it hopes at a slightly higher price than it paid for them, thus earning a middleman's profit.

Here is another possible deal. Suppose you don't know, or don't believe, that capital markets are efficient, and you think you see a window of opportunity in which interest rates are "temporarily low." You invite bids for $100 million of bonds. Some bids may come from large investment bankers acting alone, others from ad hoc syndicates. But that's not your problem: if the price is right, you just take the best deal offered.

Thus shelf registration gives firms several different things that they did not have previously:

1. Securities can be issued in dribs and drabs without incurring excessive transaction costs.

2. Securities can be issued on short notice.

3. Security issues can be timed to take advantage of "market conditions" (although any financial manager who can *reliably* identify favourable market conditions could make a lot more money by quitting and becoming a bond or stock trader instead).

4. The issuing firm can make sure that underwriters compete for its business. It can, in effect, auction off securities.

Underwriters do compete. Although several large investment banking houses lobbied hard against Rule 415 when the SEC was considering it, once the rule was approved, they played the new game with gusto. As an attorney who works with them observed, "If the SEC passed a rule saying you had to do underwriting in Watertown, N.Y., in the snow stark naked, these guys would take the first plane up."[29]

Not all companies eligible for shelf registration actually use it for all their public issues. Sometimes they believe they can get a better deal by making one large issue through traditional channels, especially when the security to be issued has some unusual feature or when the firm believes it needs the investment banker's counsel or stamp of approval on the issue. Shelf registration is thus less common for issues of common stock or convertible securities than for garden variety corporate bonds.

15-5 THE PRIVATE PLACEMENT

Whenever a company makes a public offering, it is required to obtain approval from the securities commissions for the jurisdictions in which it sells the issue. It can avoid this costly process if it is willing to sell the security privately. In Canada, this can be done if the purchasers are "exempt institutions," such as banks, trust companies, or insurance companies. A private placement can also be made to senior officers of the firm making the offering, or their close relatives, or to fewer than 25 sophisticated investors.

One of the disadvantages of a private placement is that the investor cannot easily resell the security. For the common stock investor this drawback looms large, so **letter stock**, as it is called,[30] is rarely issued except by small, closely held companies.

Liquidity is less important to institutions like life insurance companies, which invest huge amounts of money in corporate debt for the "long haul." Consequently, an active private placement mechanism has evolved for corporate debt. The size of this market is illustrated by Table 15-5, which shows the numbers of public and private offerings and the aggregate amounts raised through each channel from 1976 to 1980. You can

---

[29]Quoted in Tim Carrington, "New Ball Game: Investment Bankers Enter a New Era," *Wall Street Journal*, June 21, 1982, p. 10.

[30]So-called because it requires a letter from the buyer confirming that the stock is not bought for resale, or will not be sold within a specified period of time.

see that private placements outnumbered public issues, although the public issues were generally larger. Also note that private placements were used more by industrial firms than by utilities.

Table 15-5   A comparison of debt financing in public and private markets, 1976–1980. In some years, the total amount of private placements nearly matches the amount raised by public issues (figures in billions, numbers of issues in parentheses).

	Utilities		Industrials		Total[a]	
	Private	Public	Private	Public	Private	Public
1976	$2.2	8.2	10.6	8.4	20.5	31.9
	(109)	(128)	(540)	(99)	(963)	(454)
1977	1.9	8.3	13.8	4.9	23.7	27.6
	(97)	(113)	(810)	(88)	(1,290)	(448)
1978	2.0	7.7	12.3	4.1	21.7	23.4
	(123)	(92)	(731)	(106)	(1,323)	(364)
1979	3.8	9.2	7.9	6.5	19.5	28.9
	(127)	(98)	(661)	(109)	(1,209)	(343)
1980	1.7	13.1	6.9	15.2	14.5	41.6
	(76)	(138)	(494)	(212)	(933)	(517)

[a] Includes issues by transportation, finance, and other companies in addition to issues by utilities and industrials.

Source: Compiled from issues listed in the *Investment Dealers Digest*, by G.D. Hawkins, "Essays on Non-Publicly Issued Debt: Revolving Credit Agreements and the Pricing of Privately Placed Debt," unpublished Ph.D. dissertation, MIT, 1982, table I, p. 57.

About a third of the privately placed debt is negotiated directly between the company and the lender. If the issue is too large to be absorbed by one institution, the company generally employs an investment banker to act as agent. This agent helps to draw up an offering memorandum, which is the private placement counterpart of the prospectus. If the issue is straightforward, the agent may send the memorandum to several prospective buyers simultaneously. Otherwise the agent may attempt to gain the support of a respected institutional investor to act as a bell cow in attracting other institutions.

As you would expect, the costs of issuing private placements are less than for public issues. Unfortunately, we have no up-to-date statistics on issue costs for private placements, but we do know that underwriting costs are substantially lower than, say, the figures shown for public debt issues in Table 15-2. This is a particular advantage for companies making smaller issues.

Another advantage of the private placement is that the debt contract can be custom-tailored for firms with special problems or opportunities. The relationship between borrower and lender is much more intimate. Imagine a $20 million debt issue privately placed with an insurance company and compare it with an equivalent public issue held by 200 anonymous investors. The insurance company can justify a more thorough investigation of the company's prospects and therefore may be more willing to accept unusual terms or conditions.[31] Renegotiating the debt contract in response to unexpected developments is also extremely cumbersome for a public issue but relatively easy for a private placement.

[31] Of course debt with the same terms could be offered publicly but then 200 separate investigations would be required—a much more expensive proposition.

Therefore, it is not surprising that private placements occupy a particular niche in the corporate debt market, namely loans to small-sized and medium-sized firms. These are the firms that face the highest issue costs in public issues, that require the most detailed investigation, and that may require specialized, flexible loan arrangements.[32]

Of course these advantages are not free. Lenders in private placements have to be compensated for the risks they face and for the costs of research and negotiation. They also have to be compensated for holding an illiquid asset. All of these factors are rolled into the interest rate paid by the firm. It is difficult to generalize about the differences in interest rates between private placements and public issues, but a typical differential is on the order of 50 basis points or 0.50 percentage points.

15-6 SUMMARY

In this chapter we have summarized the various procedures for issuing corporate securities. In particular, we have looked at two forms of public issue, the cash offer and the rights offer, and we have looked at the private placement. It is always difficult to summarize a summary. Instead we will attempt to state the most important implications for the financial manager who must decide how to raise capital:

1. *Larger is cheaper.* There are always economies of scale in issuing securities. It is cheaper to go to the market once for $10 million than to make two trips for $5 million each. Consequently firms "bunch" security issues. That may often mean relying on short-term financing until a large issue is justified. Or it may mean issuing more than is needed at the moment in order to avoid another issue later.

2. *There are no issue costs for retained earnings.* There are significant costs associated with any stock issue. But stock issues can be avoided to the extent that the firm can plow back its earnings. Why then do we observe firms paying generous cash dividends *and* issuing stock from time to time? Why don't they cut the dividend, reduce new issues, and avoid paying underwriters, lawyers, and accountants? This is a question to which we will return in Chapter 16.

3. *Rights are no more expensive than cash offers.* If you do issue stock, a rights issue may be the cheapest way to do it. Of course a rights issue is infeasible if you are selling stock to the public for the first time.

4. *Private placements for the small, risky, and unusual.* We do not mean that large, safe, and conventional firms should rule out private placements. Enormous amounts of capital are sometimes raised by this method. For example, AT&T once borrowed $500 million in a single private placement. But the special advantages of private placement stem from avoiding registration expenses and a more direct relationship with the lender. These are not worth as much to blue-chip borrowers.

5. *Watch out for underpricing.* In a rights issue underpricing does not matter. But in any other case it is a hidden cost to the existing shareholders. Fortunately, it is usually serious only for companies who are selling stock to the public for the first time. There is hardly any underpricing of public debt issues. Cash offers of seasoned stock may encounter underpricing of perhaps 1%. There is evidence of slightly greater underpricing when underwriters are selected by competitive bid, but the spread in these cases is correspondingly lower.

---

[32]However, many large companies use private placements too. Gregory Hawkins examined a sample of large firms listed in the 1977 *Moody's Industrial Manual.* Eight percent of the firms that had made public debt issues had *also* borrowed privately. See G.D. Hawkins, "Essays on Non-Publicly Issued Debt: Revolving Credit Agreements and the Pricing of Privately Placed Debt," unpublished Ph.D. dissertation, MIT, 1982, table II, p. 62.

6. *Don't be too concerned about pressure.* The securities markets are large compared with any single firm. If you can convince investors that you can earn a fair rate of return on their money, you should be able to raise substantial sums without significantly affecting the market price.

7. *Shelf registration may be the wave of the future.* It seems best suited for debt issues, and for stock issues by well-known companies. It seems least suited for issues by small or obscure companies, or for issues of unusually risky or complex securities.

FURTHER READING

Two useful works on investment banking and the new issue market are:

I. Friend et al., *Investment Banking and the New Issues Market*, The World Publishing Company, Cleveland, 1967.

S.L. Hayes, A.M. Spence, and D.V.P. Marks, *Competition in the Investment Banking Industry*, Harvard University Press, Cambridge, Mass., 1983.

There have been a number of studies of the efficiency of the market for unseasoned issues of common stock. Two good articles to start with are:

R.G. Ibbotson, "Price Performance of Common Stock New Issues," *Journal of Financial Economics*, 2:235–272 (September 1975).

D.E. Logue, "On the Pricing of Unseasoned Equity Issues: 1965–1969," *Journal of Financial and Quantitative Analysis*, 8:91–104 (January 1973).

Smith in the United States and Marsh in Great Britain have looked at the efficiency of the market for rights issues. See:

P.R. Marsh, "Equity Rights Issues and the Efficiency of the U.K. Stock Market," *Journal of Finance*, 34:839–862 (September 1979).

C.W. Smith, "Alternative Methods for Raising Capital: Rights versus Underwritten Offerings," *Journal of Financial Economics*, 5:273–307 (December 1977).

Smith, in the article cited just above, argues that nonunderwritten rights issues are the cheapest way to issue stock. Hansen and Pinkerton disagree. See:

R.S. Hansen and J.M. Pinkerton, "Direct Equity Financing: A Resolution of a Paradox," *Journal of Finance*, 37:651–666 (June 1982).

A good analysis of the relative merits of negotiated underwriting and competitive bidding is given in:

D.E. Logue and R.A. Jarrow, "Negotiation vs. Competitive Bidding in the Sale of Securities by Public Utilities," *Financial Management*, 7:31–39 (Autumn 1978).

For an analysis of the role of private placements see:

E. Shapiro and C.R. Wolf, *The Role of Private Placements in Corporate Finance*, Division of Research, Graduate School of Business Administration, Harvard University, Boston, 1972.

APPENDIX 15-1   EXAMPLE OF A NEW PROSPECTUS

On January 7, 1985, ULS Capital Corporation offered for sale $60,000,000 of fixed/floating rate preferred shares. We reproduce on the following pages the first four of the prospectus's 31 pages. Page four gives a table of contents for the whole prospectus. The prospectus includes 12 pages of financial statements.

Cumulative redeemable retractable preferred share offerings have been popular in Canada for many years. The idea of allowing the dividend rate to float according to changes in short-term interest rates became popular in the 1980s.

NEW ISSUE   January 7, 1985

$60,000,000
(2,400,000 shares)

ULS CAPITAL CORPORATION
a subsidiary of Leitch Transport Ltd

$2.25 Cumulative Redeemable Retractable Fixed/Floating Rate First Preferred Shares, Series A

The holders of the shares offered hereunder (the "Senior Preferred Shares") will be entitled to quarterly fixed cumulative preferential cash dividends at the rate of $2.25 per share per annum from the date of issue, commencing on April 15, 1985 and ending on January 15, 1991. Thereafter, the holders will receive quarterly cumulative preferential cash dividends at a rate equal to one-quarter of 70% of the average of the Prime Rate of a specified Canadian chartered bank for stated periods, subject to a minimum annual rate of 7½% and a maximum annual rate of 15%. See "Details of the Offering".

Retraction Privilege

The Senior Preferred Shares are retractable at the option of the holder on January 15, 1995 at $25 per share plus all accrued and unpaid dividends.

Deposit Agreement

On the date of issue of the Senior Preferred Shares there will be deposited with Canada Permanent Trust Company (the "Trustee") from a Canadian chartered bank with assets in excess of $68 billion an irrevocable letter of credit in an amount equal to the aggregate issue price of, and the redemption premium and two quarterly dividends on, such shares. If ULS Capital fails to make any dividend or other payment required to be made on the shares prior to the retraction date, or fails to redeem the shares on the retraction date to the extent required, holders of such shares may deposit them with the Trustee who will draw on the letter of credit to pay to holders the issue price plus accrued dividends and any applicable premium. See "Deposit Agreement".

The Toronto Stock Exchange has conditionally approved the listing of the Senior Preferred Shares, subject to ULS Capital fulfilling the requirements of such Exchange on or before April 3, 1985, including distribution of the Senior Preferred Shares to a minimum number of public shareholders.

In the opinion of counsel, the Senior Preferred Shares will be eligible for investment under certain statutes. See "Eligibility for Investment".

ULS Capital had insufficient earnings in the 12 months ended September 30, 1984 to cover the dividend requirements on the Senior Preferred Shares.

Price: $25 per share to yield initially 9% per annum

	Price to public	Underwriter's fee(1)	Net proceeds (2)
Per share	$25.00	$0.25	$24.75
....	$25.00	$0.75	$24.25
Total.......................	$60,000,000	$1,500,000	$58,500,000

(1) The Underwriter's fee per Senior Preferred Share is $0.25 with respect to any such shares sold to certain specified financial institutions and $0.75 on all other sales subject to a maximum total fee of $1,500,000. The total fee is expected to be approximately $1,500,000.

(2) Before deducting expenses of issue estimated at $300,000.

(3) The Underwriter's fee and the other expenses of issue will be paid as described under "Use of Proceeds".

We, as principals, conditionally offer the Senior Preferred Shares subject to prior sale if, as and when issued by ULS Capital and delivered to us in accordance with the conditions contained in the agreement referred to under "Plan of Distribution" and subject to the approval of certain legal matters on behalf of ULS Capital and Upper Lakes Shipping Ltd. by Campbell, Godfrey & Lewtas and on our behalf by Smith, Lyons, Torrance, Stevenson & Mayer.

Subscriptions will be received subject to rejection or allotment in whole or in part and the right is reserved to close the subscription books at any time without notice. It is expected that definitive certificates will be available for delivery on the date of closing, anticipated to be on or about January 22, 1985.

Dominion Securities Pitfield Limited

TORONTO	MONTREAL	VANCOUVER	CALGARY	WINNIPEG	VICTORIA	NANAIMO	SALMON ARM	VERNON
EDMONTON	LETHBRIDGE	RED DEER	SASKATOON	BARRIE	BELLEVILLE	BRAMPTON	BRANTFORD	CAMBRIDGE
CHATHAM	COLLINGWOOD	CORNWALL	EXETER	GUELPH	HAMILTON	KINGSTON	KITCHENER	LONDON
NORTH BAY	ORILLIA	OSHAWA	OTTAWA	OWEN SOUND	PETERBOROUGH	ST. CATHARINES	SARNIA	SAULT STE. MARIE
SUDBURY	THUNDER BAY	TIMMINS	WALLACEBURG	WELLAND	WINDSOR	WOODSTOCK	LAVAL	
POINTE CLAIRE	QUEBEC CITY	SHERBROOKE	MONCTON	SAINT JOHN	CHARLOTTETOWN	HALIFAX	ST. JOHN'S	
	NEW YORK	LONDON	PARIS	LAUSANNE	GENEVA	HONG KONG		

Permission granted by ULS Capital Corporation.

PROSPECTUS SUMMARY

Issuer: ULS Capital Corporation ("ULS Capital"), a wholly-owned subsidiary of Leitch Transport Ltd.

Issue: $60,000,000 of $2.25 Cumulative Redeemable Retractable Fixed/Floating Rate First Preferred Shares, Series A – 2,400,000 shares at $25 per share.

Dividends: Fixed cumulative preferential cash dividends of $2.25 per share per annum, payable quarterly on the 15th day of January, April, July and October in each year commencing on April 15, 1985, and ending on January 15, 1991. Assuming an issue date of January 22, 1985, an initial dividend of $0.5188 per share will be payable on April 15, 1985.

Commencing on April 15, 1991, quarterly cumulative preferential cash dividends at a rate equal to one-quarter of 70% of the average of the Prime Rate of a specified Canadian chartered bank in effect on each day during the three month period ending on the 25th day of the month preceding the dividend payment date for which the determination is being made, subject to a minimum annual rate of 7½% and a maximum annual rate of 15%.

Retraction Privilege: Retractable at the option of the holder on January 15, 1995, at $25 per share plus all accrued and unpaid dividends.

Deposit Agreement: At the date of the issue of the Senior Preferred Shares there will be deposited with Canada Permanent Trust Company from a Canadian chartered bank with assets in excess of $68 billion an irrevocable letter of credit in an amount equal to the aggregate issue price of, and the redemption premium and two quarterly dividends on, the Senior Preferred Shares. As the Senior Preferred Shares are retired or the aggregate redemption premium is reduced, the amount of the letter of credit will be reduced accordingly. If, prior to the retraction date, ULS Capital fails to make any dividend or other payment required to be made on the Senior Preferred Shares, or fails to redeem the Senior Preferred Shares on the retraction date to the extent required, holders of such shares may deposit them with the Trustee who will draw on the letter of credit to pay to holders the issue price plus accrued dividends plus any applicable premium.

Redemption: Not redeemable on or before January 15, 1989, but redeemable thereafter at the option of ULS Capital at prices declining from $25.50 per share to $25 per share after January 15, 1991, plus, in each case, all accrued and unpaid dividends.

Purchase Fund: ULS Capital will use all reasonable efforts to purchase for cancellation in the open market or by invitation for tenders 4% of the Senior Preferred Shares outstanding on January 16, 1995 in each successive 12 month period, the first such period commencing January 16, 1995, at prices not exceeding $25 per share plus an amount equal to all dividends, if any, accrued and unpaid thereon plus costs of purchase.

Priority: The Senior Preferred Shares will rank on a parity with all other series of First Preferred Shares and rank prior to the Second Preferred Shares and the Common Shares with respect to the payment of dividends and the distribution of assets on a liquidation, dissolution or winding-up.

Income Tax Considerations: Dividends on Senior Preferred Shares will be treated for Canadian income tax purposes as taxable Canadian dividends for Canadian shareholders who are individuals. Specified financial institutions will be entitled to deduct dividends on the Senior Preferred Shares in computing their taxable income provided that certain conditions are met; other corporations will not be entitled to deduct such dividends.

Use of Proceeds: The $60,000,000 proceeds to be received by ULS Capital from the sale of the Senior Preferred Shares will be used concurrently to purchase shares of Upper Lakes Shipping Ltd. ("Upper Lakes") having substantially similar attributes (the "Series 1 Preferred Shares"). Upper Lakes will use such proceeds to reduce its outstanding bank debt. Upper Lakes will pay ULS Capital a financial structuring fee of $1,915,000, out of which ULS Capital will pay the expenses of issue, including Underwriter's fee.

2

Asset Coverage ULS Capital:	Based on the pro forma balance sheet of ULS Capital as at December 5, 1984 and after giving effect to this issue, the net tangible assets of ULS Capital were $60,051,300, which is 1.0 times the aggregate issue price of the Senior Preferred Shares.
Asset Coverage Upper Lakes:	Based on the balance sheet of Upper Lakes as at September 30, 1984, and after giving effect to the issue of the Series 1 Preferred Shares and the use of proceeds

Asset Coverage ULS Capital: Based on the pro forma balance sheet of ULS Capital as at December 5, 1984 and after giving effect to this issue, the net tangible assets of ULS Capital were $60,051,300, which is 1.0 times the aggregate issue price of the Senior Preferred Shares.

Asset Coverage Upper Lakes: Based on the balance sheet of Upper Lakes as at September 30, 1984, and after giving effect to the issue of the Series 1 Preferred Shares and the use of proceeds

- adjusted consolidated net tangible assets before and after deduction of deferred income taxes were $158,527,000 and $116,029,000, respectively, which amounts to 2.64 times and 1.93 times, respectively, the aggregate issue price of the Senior Preferred Shares

- adjusted consolidated net tangible assets before deduction of long term debt and before and after deduction of deferred income taxes were 1.72 times and 1.41 times, respectively, the sum of the long term debt and the aggregate issue price of the Senior Preferred Shares.

Dividend Coverage ULS Capital: For the 12 months ended December 5, 1984, the earnings of ULS Capital were insufficient to meet the annual dividend requirements on the Senior Preferred Shares.

Dividend and Interest Coverage Upper Lakes: For the 12 months ended September 30, 1984, after giving effect to the issue of the Series 1 Preferred Shares and the use of proceeds, the pre-tax income of Upper Lakes before deduction of interest expense on total debt was

- 1.19 times the sum of the annual interest expense on total debt outstanding as at September 30, 1984 and the annual dividend requirements on the Senior Preferred Shares

- 0.89 times the sum of the annual interest expense on total debt outstanding as at September 30, 1984 and the annual grossed-up dividend requirements on the Senior Preferred Shares.

UPPER LAKES SHIPPING LTD.

Upper Lakes and its subsidiaries are engaged in the shipping business and in related businesses including shipbuilding and ship repairing, the operation of a grain elevator, grain trading and a participation in a semi-submersible drilling rig.

SELECTED CONSOLIDATED INFORMATION
OF UPPER LAKES SHIPPING LTD.
(in thousands of dollars)

	Nine months ended September 30		Fiscal year ended				
			December 31	March 31			
	1984	1983	1983	1983	1982	1981	1980
	(unaudited)						
Revenue	$99,718	$101,673	$133,434	$189,392	$148,707	$135,904	$115,363
Net income (loss) for the period	(641)	(3,084)	(4,866)	(7,031)	1,399	5,569	6,840
Working capital from operations	12,988	10,611	16,738	10,638	14,033	19,262	23,714
Capital expenditures	3,268	23,069	16,349	24,544	33,580	42,610	39,345

	As at		
	September 30 1984	December 31 1983	March 31 1983
	(unaudited)		
Total assets	$303,641	$301,560	$296,099
Long term debt	136,861	142,592	138,057
Shareholders' equity	56,946	58,517	64,240

This is a summary only and should be read in conjunction with the more detailed information and financial statements appearing elsewhere in this prospectus.

3

TABLE OF CONTENTS

ELIGIBILITY FOR INVESTMENT

In the opinion of Campbell, Godfrey & Lewtas and of Smith, Lyons, Torrance, Stevenson & Mayer, the Senior Preferred Shares, at the date of original issue, will be eligible investments without resort to the so-called "basket" provisions but subject to the general investment criteria set out in the applicable statutes for:

(i) insurance companies registered under the Canadian and British Insurance Companies Act (Canada) or the Foreign Insurance Companies Act (Canada) and insurance companies licensed under the Insurance Act (Ontario) and insurance companies governed by the Insurance Act (British Columbia);

(ii) loan companies licensed under the Loan Companies Act (Canada), trust companies licensed under the Trust Companies Act (Canada) and loan corporations and trust companies registered under the Loan and Trust Corporations Act (Ontario); and

(iii) pension funds registered under the Pension Benefits Standards Act (Canada), the Pension Benefits Act (Ontario), the Pension Benefits Act (Alberta) or an Act respecting supplemental pension plans (Quebec).

In the opinion of counsel the Senior Preferred Shares, when listed on a prescribed stock exchange, will be eligible investments under the Income Tax Act (Canada) for trusts governed by registered retirement savings plans, registered retirement income funds, deferred profit sharing plans and registered home ownership savings plans.

QUIZ

1. Beside each of the following issue methods we have listed two issues. Choose the one most likely to employ that method.
   (a) Public auction (bond issue by utility holding company/issue of Treasury bills)
   (b) Negotiated general cash offer (issue of unseasoned stock/issue of Treasury bills)
   (c) Privileged subscription (issue of seasoned stock/issue of unseasoned stock)
   (d) Competitive general cash offer (bond issue by industrial company/bond issue by utility holding company)
   (e) Private placement (issue of seasoned stock/bond issue by industrial company)
   (f) Shelf registration (issue of unseasoned stock/bond issue by a large industrial company)

2. Each of the following terms is associated with one of the events beneath. Can you match them up?
   (a) Company registrar
   (b) Best efforts
   (c) Tombstone
   (d) Red herring
   (e) Shelf registration
   (f) Letter stock
   (g) Regulation A
   > (A) The company issues a preliminary prospectus.
   > (B) Small issues are placed in a special classification and exempted from registration.
   > (C) Some issues are privately placed and exempted from issuing a prospectus.
   > (D) An advertisement is published in the financial press listing members of the underwriting syndicate.
   > (E) A trust company is appointed to ensure that no unauthorized shares are issued.
   > (F) The underwriter accepts responsibility only to try to sell the issue.
   > (G) Several issues of the same security may be made under one registration.

3. All issues involve some administrative costs. In addition issues *may* involve the following explicit or hidden costs:
   (a) Filing expenses
   (b) Underwriter's spread
   (c) Standby and take-up fees
   (d) Underpricing
   (e) Discount for nonmarketability
   Indicate which of these costs are usually associated with each of the following issues:
   (A) A rights issue
   (B) A general cash offer of unseasoned stock
   (C) A directly negotiated private placement

4. State for each of the following pairs of issues which you would expect to involve the lower proportionate underwriting and administrative costs, other things equal:
   (a) A large issue/a small issue
   (b) A bond issue/a common stock issue
   (c) A large negotiated bond issue/a large competitive bond issue
   (d) A nonunderwritten rights issue/a general cash offer
   (e) A small private placement of bonds/a small general cash offer of bonds

5. The Electric Teaspoon Company has outstanding 100 shares currently priced at $40 a share. The company proposes to make a rights issue of one new share for each

two shares held, at $10. Assuming that the money is invested to earn a fair return, give values for the following:

(a) Number of rights needed to purchase one share
(b) Number of new shares
(c) Amount of new investment
(d) Total value of company after issue
(e) Total number of shares after issue
(f) Cum-rights price
(g) Ex-rights price
(h) Price of a right

Is it cheaper to buy the share ex-rights or to buy and exercise the rights?

6. Without looking at the text, show the relationship between the value of the right and the cum-rights price.

QUESTIONS AND PROBLEMS

1. Assess the system for making new issues of unseasoned stock in Canada. What do you think would be the most effective alternative method? Be as precise as possible.

2. "For underwritten rights issues of less than $1 million, the costs of flotation amount to about 10% of proceeds. This means that the opportunity cost of external equity capital is about ten percentage points higher than that of retained earnings." Does this follow?

3. Discuss the following comment: "Firms whose stock is selling at low P/E ratios find it unwise to raise capital by issuing new common stock. They should raise capital through other channels."

4. Here is recent financial data on Pisa Construction, Inc.

Stock price = $40
Number shares = 10,000
Book net worth = $500,000
Market value of firm = $400,000
Earnings per share = $4
Return on investment = 8%

Pisa has not performed spectacularly to date. However, it wishes to issue new shares to obtain $80,000 to finance expansion into a promising market. Pisa's financial advisers think a stock issue is a poor choice because, among other reasons, "sale of stock at a price below book value per share can only depress the stock price and decrease shareholders' wealth." To prove the point they construct the following example: "Suppose 2,000 new shares are issued at $40 and the proceeds invested. (Neglect issue costs.) Suppose return on investment doesn't change. Then

Book net worth = $580,000

Total earnings = 0.08 (580,000) = $46,400

$$\text{Earnings per share} = \frac{46,400}{12,000} = 3.87$$

Thus, EPS declines, book value per share declines, and share price will decline proportionately to $38.70."

Evaluate this argument with particular attention to the assumptions implicit in the numerical example.

5. In 1984 Pandora, Inc. makes a rights issue at $5 a share of one new share for every four shares held. Before the issue there were 10 million shares outstanding and the share price was $6.
   (a) What is the total amount of new money raised?
   (b) How many rights are needed to buy one new share?
   (c) What is the value of one right?
   (d) What is the prospective ex-rights price?
   (e) How far could the total value of the company fall before shareholders would be unwilling to take up their rights?

6. Problem 5 contains details of a rights offering by Pandora, Inc. Suppose that the company had decided to issue new stock at $4. How many shares would it have needed to issue to raise the same sum of money? Recalculate the answers to questions (b) to (e) in problem 5. Show that Pandora's shareholders are just as well off if it issues the shares at $4 per share rather than the $5 price asumed in question 5.

7. Construct a simple numerical example to show the following:
   (a) Existing stockholders are made worse off when a company makes a cash offer of new stock below the market price.
   (b) Existing stockholders are *not* made worse off when a company makes a rights issue of new stock below the market price even if the stockholders do not wish to take up their rights.

DIVIDEND POLICY AND CAPITAL STRUCTURE

PART

◆6◆

THE DIVIDEND CONTROVERSY

In this chapter we explain how companies set their dividend payments and we discuss the controversial question of how dividend policy affects value.

Why should you care about the answer to this question? Of course, if you are responsible for deciding on your company's dividend payment, you will want to know how it affects value. But there is a more general reason than that. We have up to this point assumed that the company's investment decision is independent of its financing policy. In that case a good project is a good project is a good project, no matter who undertakes it or how it is ultimately financed. If dividend policy does not affect value, that is still true. But perhaps it *does* affect value. In that case the attractiveness of a new project may depend on where the money is coming from. For example, if investors prefer companies with high payouts, companies might be reluctant to take on investments financed by retained earnings.

The first step toward understanding dividend policy is to recognize that the phrase means different things to different people. Therefore we must start by defining what we mean by it.

A firm's decisions about dividends are often mixed up with other financing and investment decisions. Some firms pay low dividends because management is optimistic about the firm's future and wishes to retain earnings for expansion. In this case the dividend is a by-product of the firm's capital budgeting decision. Suppose, however, that the future opportunities evaporate, that a dividend increase is announced, and that the stock price falls. How do we separate the impact of the dividend increase from the impact of investors' disappointment at the lost growth opportunities?

Another firm might finance capital expenditures largely by borrowing. This releases cash for dividends. In this case the firm's dividend is a by-product of the borrowing decision.

We must isolate dividend policy from other problems of financial management. The precise question we should ask is: "What is the effect of a change in cash dividends paid, *given the firm's capital budgeting and borrowing decisions?*" Of course the cash used to finance a dividend increase has to come from somewhere. If we fix the firm's investment outlays and borrowing, there is only one possible source—an issue of stock. Thus we define *dividend policy* as the trade-off between retaining earnings on the one hand and paying out cash and issuing new shares on the other.

This trade-off may seem artificial at first, for we do not observe firms scheduling a stock issue with every dividend payment. But there are many firms that pay dividends and also issue stock from time to time. They could avoid the stock issues by paying lower dividends. Many other firms restrict dividends so that they *do not* have to issue shares. They could issue stock occasionally and increase the dividend. Both groups of firms are facing the dividend policy trade-off.

16-1 HOW DIVIDENDS ARE PAID

The dividend is set or "declared" by the firm's board of directors. They make an announcement that the payment will be made to all those stockholders who are registered on a particular "record date," which is usually about one to four weeks after the date of the announcement. Dividend cheques are mailed to stockholders about two to four weeks after the record date.

Shares are normally bought and sold "with dividend" or "cum dividend" until four days before the record date. But investors who buy with dividend do not have to worry if their shares are not registered in time. The dividend must be paid over to them by the seller. Similarly, investors who buy a share "ex dividend" are obliged to return the dividend if they receive it.

Some Legal Limitations on Dividends

Suppose that an unscrupulous board decided to sell all the firm's assets and distribute the money as dividends. That would not leave anything in the kitty to pay the company's debts. Therefore, bondholders usually guard against this danger by placing a limit on dividend payments.

Federal and provincial law also helps to protect the company's creditors against excessive dividend payments. For example, for federally incorporated companies, the Canada Business Corporations Act prohibits payment of a dividend if there are "reasonable grounds for believing" that, after payment of the dividend, either, (a) the corporation would be "unable to pay its liabilities as they become due," or (b) "the realizable value of the corporation's assets would . . . be less than . . . its liabilities and stated capital . . ."[1] A company's stated capital is the total amount of stock issued. In effect, dividends must come of the retained earnings and must not push the firm too close to insolvency.

If a firm decides to wholly or partially liquidate, it may repurchase its shares on the open market or by a tender offer, or pay a "liquidating dividend," but this may reduce the realizable value of its assets below its liabilities plus stated capital. In that case, the firm must, by a special resolution of the shareholders, reduce its stated capital.[2]

These laws give most corporations a large degree of flexibility in deciding what to pay out. Nevertheless, they do help prevent unscrupulous firms from escaping their creditors.

Par value of stock has little economic significance. It was often set arbitrarily at $1 per share. Now Canadian corporations issue stock with no par value.

Dividends Come in Many Forms

Most dividends are paid in the form of cash. *Regular cash dividends* are usually paid quarterly, but a few companies declare them monthly, semiannually, or annually.[3] The term *regular* merely indicates that the company expects that it will be able to maintain the payment in the future. If the company does not want to give that kind of assurance,

---

[1]Section 40 of the Canada Business Corporations Act [1975].

[2]Canada Business Corporations Act, Section 36.

[3]Many companies have automatic dividend reinvestment plans. The usual procedure is for the corporation to send the dividends of the participating stockholders directly to a trust company, which then purchases stock on behalf of shareholders in the open market. However, some firms issue new shares directly to stockholders who wish to reinvest dividends. Often the new shares are issued at a 5% discount from market price; the firm offers this sweetener because it saves the underwriting costs of a regular share issue. Sometimes 10% or more of total dividends will be reinvested under such plans.

---

it usually declares both a regular and an *extra dividend*. Investors understand that the extra dividend may not be repeated. Finally, the term *special dividend* tends to be reserved specifically for payments that are unlikely to be repeated.

Paying a dividend reduces the amount of retained earnings shown on the firm's balance sheet. However, if all retained earnings are "used up," and if funds are not needed for the protection of creditors, the company may be permitted to pay a *liquidating dividend*. Because such payments are regarded as a return of capital, they are not taxed as income.

Dividends are not always paid in the form of cash. Frequently companies declare *stock dividends*. For example, in the United States, General Tire has paid a yearly stock dividend of 2% for more than a decade. That means it sends each shareholder two extra shares for every 100 shares that he or she currently owns. In Canada, many firms have allowed shareholders the option of receiving cash or stock dividends. A stock dividend is very much like a stock split. Both increase the number of shares, and both reduce value per share, other things equal. If the stock dividend or stock split is distributed among all shareholders, nobody is made better off. But if some shareholders can receive stock dividends and some can receive cash dividends, they may all be able to act to minimize personal taxes, as discussed in Section 16-5.

There are also other types of noncash dividends. For example, companies sometimes send shareholders a sample of their product. The British company Dominion International (formerly Dundee Crematorium) offers its more substantial shareholders a discount cremation. Needless to say, you are not *required* to receive this dividend.

Share Repurchase

When a firm wants to pay cash to its shareholders, it usually declares a cash dividend. But an alternative and increasingly popular method is to repurchase its own stock. In the period 1973–1974, the United States government imposed a limit on dividends but it forgot to impose a limit on share repurchase. Many firms discovered share repurchase for the first time, and the total value of repurchases swelled to about a fifth of the value of dividend payments. IBM was one of the firms to repurchase its stock in 1974. As IBM's rapid expansion of the 1960s slowed down, the company found itself with more cash than it needed. Therefore in 1974 IBM gave back $1.4 billion to its stockholders by repurchasing shares.

There are three principal methods of repurchase: (1) Shares are often acquired in the open market. (2) Shares can be acquired by a general tender offer either to all shareholders or just to small shareholders.[4] In this case the firm usually engages an investment banker to manage the tender and pays a special commission to brokers who persuade shareholders to accept the offer. (3) Finally, repurchase may take place by direct negotiation with a major shareholder.

The most important distinction between repurchase and dividends lies in their tax treatments. This is discussed in Section 16-5.

16-2   HOW DO COMPANIES DECIDE ON DIVIDEND PAYMENTS?

Lintner's Model

In the mid-1950s John Lintner conducted a classic series of interviews with corporate managers about their dividend policies.[5] Most of them thought of the problem in terms

---

[4] The costs of printing and mailing annual reports, dividend cheques, and so on, are the same for small stockholders as for large ones. Firms often try to reduce these costs by buying out small holdings.

[5] J. Lintner, "Distribution of Incomes of Corporations among Dividends, Retained Earnings, and Taxes," *American Economic Review*, **46**:97–113 (May 1956).

of the proportion of earnings that should be paid out rather than in terms of the proportion that should be kept back to finance expansion. They felt that stockholders were entitled to a fair share of the firm's earnings and that the firm should have some long-term target payout ratio.

Suppose that a firm always stuck to its target payout ratio. Then the dividend payment in the coming year (DIV_1) would equal a constant proportion of earnings per share (EPS_1):

$$DIV_1 = \text{target dividend}$$
$$= \text{target ratio} \times EPS_1$$

The dividend *change* would equal

$$DIV_1 - DIV_0 = \text{target change}$$
$$= \text{target ratio} \times EPS_1 - DIV_0$$

A firm that always stuck to its payout ratio would have to change its dividend whenever earnings changed. But the managers in Lintner's survey were reluctant to do this. They believed that shareholders prefer a steady progression in dividends. Therefore even if circumstances appeared to warrant a large increase in their company's dividend, they would move only partway toward their target payment. Their dividend changes therefore seemed to conform to the following model:

$$DIV_1 - DIV_0 = \text{adjustment rate} \times \text{target change}$$
$$= \text{adjustment rate} \times (\text{target ratio} \times EPS_1 - DIV_0)$$

The more conservative the company, the more slowly it would move toward its target and, therefore, the *lower* would be its adjustment rate.

Lintner's simple model suggests that the dividend depends in part on the firm's current earnings and in part on the dividend for the previous year, which in turn depends on that year's earnings and the dividend in the year before. Therefore if Lintner is correct, we should be able to describe dividends in terms of a weighted average of past earnings.[6] The probability of an increase in the dividend rate should be greatest when *current* earnings have increased; it should be somewhat less when only the earnings from the previous year have increased, and so on. Table 16-1 sets out the results of a study by Fama and Babiak of dividend payments by 392 companies in the United States between 1946 and 1964. The results bear out Lintner's model—the likelihood of a dividend

---

[6]This can be demonstrated as follows: Dividends per share in time t are

$$DIV_t = aT(EPS_t) + (1 - a)DIV_{t-1} \qquad (1)$$

where a is the adjustment rate and T the target payout ratio. But the same relationship holds in $t - 1$:

$$DIV_{t-1} = aT(EPS_{t-1}) + (1 - a)DIV_{t-2} \qquad (2)$$

Substitute for DIV_{t-1} in (1):

$$DIV_t = aT(EPS_t) + aT(1 - a)(EPS_{t-1}) + (1 - a)^2 DIV_{t-2}$$

We can make similar substitutions for DIV_{t-2}, DIV_{t-3}, and so on, thereby obtaining

$$DIV_t = aT(EPS_t) + aT(1 - a)(EPS_{t-1}) + aT(1 - a)^2(EPS_{t-2}) + \cdots + aT(1 - a)^n(EPS_{t-n})$$

Table 16-1 Fama and Babiak's study shows that the probability of a dividend increase depends on how recently earnings have increased.

Direction of Recent Earnings Changes			Proportion of Companies		
Current Year	Previous Year	Two Years Earlier	Increasing Dividend, %	Maintaining Dividend, %	Reducing Dividend, %
+	+	+	81	8	11
+	+	−	67	15	18
+	−	+	58	17	25
−	+	+	54	15	32
+	−	−	49	18	34
−	+	−	45	19	36
−	−	+	35	17	48
−	−	−	25	25	50

Source: E.F. Fama and H. Babiak, "Dividend Policy: An Empirical Analysis," *Journal of the American Statistical Association*, **63**:1132–1161 (December 1968), p. 1134.

increase depends both on the number of occasions on which earnings have risen and on how recently they have risen.

Fama and Babiak went on to estimate the target ratio and the adjustment rate for each company. They found that on average firms aimed to distribute nearly half of their net income and to move about a third of the way toward this objective in any one year.

Effects of Information

We have suggested above that the dividend payment depends on both last year's dividend and this year's earnings. This simple model seems to provide a fairly good explanation of how companies decide on the dividend rate, but it is unlikely to be the whole story. For example, we would also expect managers to take future prospects into account when setting the payment. And that is what we find. When companies pay dividends lower than our simple model suggests, earnings on the average subsequently decline. When they pay dividends higher than the model suggests, earnings on the average subsequently rise by an abnormal amount.[7]

Do you remember from Chapter 13 that stock splits lead to a rise in the value of the company's shares? That is not because the market likes stock splits but because it realizes that they signal future prosperity. It may be the same with dividends. Dividend increases result in a rise in share prices. But we must not jump to the conclusion that this is because investors like high rates of payout. It could simply be due to the information dividends convey about future profits.

16-3   THE CONTROVERSY OVER DIVIDEND POLICY

Now we turn to the controversial question of how dividend policy affects value. One endearing feature of economics is that it can always accommodate not just two, but three opposing points of view. And so it is with the controversy about dividend policy. On the right there is a conservative group, which believes that an increase in dividend

---

[7]See, for example, R. Watts, "The Information Content of Dividends," *Journal of Business*, **46**: 191–211 (April 1973), for an analysis of information effects in the United States.

payout increases firm value. On the left, there is a radical group, which believes that an increase in payout reduces value. And in the centre there is a middle-of-the-road party, which claims that dividend policy makes no difference.

The middle-of-the-road party was founded in 1961 by Miller and Modigliani (always referred to as "MM" or "M and M"), when they published a theoretical paper showing the irrelevance of dividend policy in a world without taxes, transaction costs, or other market imperfections.[8] By the standards of 1961, MM were leftist radicals, because at that time most people believed that even under idealized assumptions increased dividends made shareholders better off.[9] But now MM's proof is generally accepted as correct, and the argument has shifted to whether taxes or other market imperfections alter the situation. In the process MM have been pushed toward the centre by a new leftist party, which argues for *low* dividends, particularly in the United States. The leftists' position is based on MM's argument modified to take account of taxes and costs of issuing securities. The conservatives are still with us, relying on essentially the same arguments as in 1961.

We begin our discussion of dividend policy with a presentation of MM's original argument. Then we will undertake a critical appraisal of the positions of the three parties. Perhaps we should warn you before we start that our own position is slightly to the left of centre for American dividends, and slightly to the right of centre for Canadian dividends.

Dividend Policy is Irrelevant in Perfect Capital Markets

In their classic 1961 article, MM argued as follows: suppose your firm has settled on its investment program. You have worked out how much of this program can be financed from borrowing, and you plan to meet the remaining funds requirement from retained earnings. Any surplus money is to be paid out as dividends.

Now think what happens if you want to increase the dividend payment without changing the investment and borrowing policy. The extra money must come from somewhere. If the firm fixes its borrowing, the only way it can finance the extra dividend is to print some more shares and sell them. The new stockholders are going to part with their money only if you can offer them shares that are worth as much as they cost. But how can the firm do this when its assets, earnings, investment opportunities and, therefore, market value are all unchanged? The answer is that there must be a *transfer of value* from the old to the new shareholders. The new ones get the newly printed shares, each one worth less than before the dividend change was announced, and the old ones suffer a capital loss on their shares. The capital loss borne by the old shareholders just offsets the extra cash dividend they receive.

Figure 16-1 shows how this transfer of value occurs. Our hypothetical company pays out a third of its total value as a dividend and it raises the money to do so by selling new shares. The capital loss suffered by the old stockholders is represented by the reduction in the size of the shaded boxes. But that capital loss is exactly offset by the fact that the new money raised (the white boxes) is paid over to them as dividends.

Does it make any difference to the old stockholders that they receive an extra dividend payment plus an offsetting capital loss? It might if that were the only way they could

---

[8]M.H. Miller and F. Modigliani, "Dividend Policy, Growth and the Valuation of Shares," *Journal of Business*, 34:411–433 (October 1961).

[9]Not *everybody* believed dividends make shareholders better off. MM's arguments were anticipated in 1938 in J.B. Williams, *The Theory of Investment Value*, Harvard University Press, Cambridge, Mass., 1938. Also, a proof very similar to MM's was developed by J. Lintner in "Dividends, Earnings, Leverage, Stock Prices and the Supply of Capital to Corporations," *Review of Economics and Statistics*, 44:243–269 (August 1962).

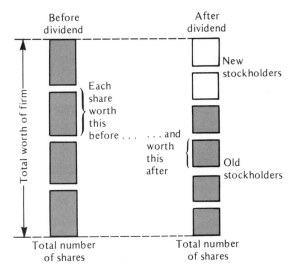

Figure 16-1 This firm pays out a third of its worth as a dividend and raises the money by selling new shares. The transfer of value to the new stockholders is equal to the dividend payment.

get their hands on cash. But as long as there are efficient capital markets, they can raise the cash by selling shares. Thus the old shareholders can "cash in" either by persuading the management to pay a higher dividend or by taking a "home-made dividend," by selling some of their shares. In either case there will be a transfer of value from old to new shareholders. The only difference is that in the former case this transfer is caused by a dilution in the value of each of the firm's shares, and in the latter case it is caused by a reduction in the number of shares held by the old shareholders. The two alternatives are compared in Figure 16-2.

Because investors do not need dividends to get their hands on cash, they will not pay higher prices for the shares of firms with high payouts. Therefore firms ought not to worry about dividend policy. They could let dividends fluctuate as a by-product of their investment and financing decisions.

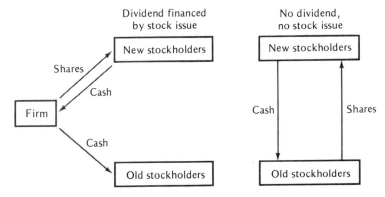

Figure 16-2 Two ways of raising cash for the firm's original shareholders. In each case the cash received is offset by a decline in the value of the old stockholders' claim on the firm. If the firm pays a dividend, each share is worth less because more shares have to be issued against the firm's assets. If the old stockholders sell some of their shares, each share is worth the same but the old stockholders have fewer shares.

Dividend Irrelevance—An Illustration

Consider the case of Rational Demiconductor, which at this moment has the following balance sheet:

Rational Demiconductor's balance sheet (market values).

Cash ($1,000 held for investment)	$1,000	$0	Debt
Fixed assets	$9,000	$10,000 + NPV	Equity
Investment opportunity ($1,000 investment required)	NPV		
Total asset value	$10,000 + NPV	$10,000 + NPV	Value of firm

Rational Demiconductor has $1,000 cash earmarked for a project requiring $1,000 investment. We do not know how attractive the project is, and so we enter it at NPV; after the project is undertaken it will be worth $1,000 + NPV. Note that the balance sheet is constructed with market values; equity equals the market value of the firm's outstanding shares (price per share times number of shares outstanding). It is not necessarily equal to book net worth.

Now Rational Demiconductor uses the cash to pay a $1,000 dividend to its stockholders. The benefit to them is obvious: $1,000 of spendable cash. It is also obvious that there must be a cost. The cash is not free.

Where does the money for the dividend come from? Of course, the immediate source of funds is Rational Demiconductor's cash account. But this cash was earmarked for the investment project. Since we want to isolate the effects of dividend policy on shareholders' wealth, we assume that the company *continues* with the investment project. That means that $1,000 cash must be raised by new financing. This could consist of an issue of either debt or stock. Again, we just want to look at dividend policy for now, and we defer discussion of the debt–equity choice until Chapters 17 and 18. Thus Rational Demiconductor ends up financing the dividend with a $1,000 stock issue.

Now we examine the balance sheet after the dividend is paid, the new stock sold, and the investment undertaken. Because Rational Demiconductor's investment and borrowing policies are unaffected by the dividend payment, its *overall* market value must be unchanged at $10,000 + NPV.[10] We know also that if the new stockholders pay a fair price, their stock is worth $1,000. That leaves us with only one missing number—the value of the stock held by the original stockholders. It is easy to see that this must be

$$\text{Value of original stock} = \text{value of company} - \text{value of new stock}$$
$$= (10,000 + \text{NPV}) - 1,000$$
$$= \$9,000 + \text{NPV}$$

The old shareholders have received a $1,000 cash dividend and incurred a $1,000 capital loss. Dividend policy doesn't matter.

By paying out $1,000 with one hand and taking it back with the other, Rational Demiconductor is recycling cash. To suggest that this makes shareholders better off is like advising a cook to cool the kitchen by leaving the refrigerator door open.

Of course, our proof ignores taxes, issue costs, and a variety of other complications. We will turn to those items in a moment. The really crucial assumption in our proof

---

[10]All other factors that might affect Rational Demiconductor's value are assumed constant. This is not a necessary assumption, but it simplifies the proof of MM's theory.

is that the new shares are sold at a fair price. The shares sold to raise $1,000 must actually be *worth* $1,000.[11] In other words, we have assumed efficient capital markets.

Calculating Share Price

We have assumed that Rational Demiconductor's new shares can be sold at a fair price, but what is that price and how many new shares are issued?

Suppose that before this dividend payout the company had 1,000 shares outstanding and that the project had an NPV of $2,000. Then the old stock was worth in total $10,000 + NPV = $12,000, which works out at $12,000/1,000 = $12 per share. After the company has paid the dividend and completed the financing, this old stock is worth $9,000 + NPV = $11,000. That works out at $11,000/1,000 = $11 per share. In other words, the price of the old stock falls by the amount of the $1-per-share dividend payment.

Now let us look at the new stock. Clearly, after the issue this must sell at the same price as the rest of the stock. In other words, it must be valued at $11. If the new stockholders get fair value, the company must issue $1,000/$11 or 91 new shares in order to raise the $1,000 that it needs.

Share Repurchase

We have seen that any increased cash dividend payment must be offset by a stock issue if the firm's investment and borrowing policies are held constant. In effect the stockholders finance the extra dividend by selling off part of their ownership of the firm. Consequently, the stock price falls by just enough to offset the extra dividend.

This process can also be run backwards. With investment and borrowing policy given, any *reduction* in dividends must be balanced by a reduction in the number of shares issued or by repurchase of previously outstanding stock. But if the process has no effect on stockholders' wealth when run forward, it must likewise have no effect when run in reverse. We will confirm this by another numerical example.

Suppose that a technical discovery reveals that Rational Demiconductor's new project is not a positive NPV venture, but a sure loser. Management announces that the project is to be discarded, and that the $1,000 earmarked for it will be paid out as an extra dividend of $1 per share. After the dividend payout, the balance sheet is:

Rational Demiconductor's balance sheet (market value).

Cash	$0	$0	Debt
Existing		$9,000	Equity
fixed assets	$9,000		
New project	$0		
Total asset value	$9,000	$9,000	Total firm value

Since there are 1,000 shares outstanding, the stock price is $10,000/1,000 = $10 before the dividend payment and $9,000/1,000 = $9 *after* the payment.

What if Rational Demiconductor uses the $1,000 to repurchase stock instead? As long as the company pays a fair price for the stock, the $1,000 buys $1,000/$10 = 100 shares. That leaves 900 shares worth 900 × $10 = $9,000.

As expected, we find that switching from cash dividends to share repurchase has no effect on shareholders' wealth. They forgo a $1 cash dividend but end up holding shares worth $10 instead of $9.

---

[11]The "old" shareholders get all the benefit of the positive NPV project. The "new" shareholders require only a fair rate of return. They are making a zero NPV investment.

Note that when shares are repurchased the transfer of value is in favour of those stockholders who do not sell. They forgo any cash dividend but end up owning a larger slice of the firm. In effect they are using their share of Rational Demiconductor's $1,000 distribution to buy out some of their fellow shareholders.

16-4 THE RIGHTISTS

Much of traditional finance literature has advocated high-payout ratios. Here, for example, is a statement of the rightist position made by Graham and Dodd in 1951:

> . . . the considered and continuous verdict of the stock market is overwhelmingly in favor of liberal dividends as against niggardly ones. The common stock investor must take this judgment into account in the valuation of stock for purchase. It is now becoming standard practice to evaluate common stock by applying one multiplier to that portion of the earnings paid out in dividends and a much smaller multiplier to the undistributed balance.[12]

Another author has written a book urging the government to enforce full distribution of earnings on the grounds that it "would almost certainly double or treble (within a short period) the market value of equities."[13]

This belief in the importance of dividend policy is common in the business and investment communities. Stockholders and investment advisers continually pressure corporate treasurers for increased dividends. When we had wage–price controls in the United States in 1974 and in Canada in 1975–1978, it was deemed necessary to have dividend controls as well. As far as we know, no labour union objected that "dividend policy is irrelevant." After all, if wages are reduced, the employee is worse off. Dividends are the shareholders' wages, and so if the payout ratio is reduced the shareholder is worse off. Therefore fair play requires that wage controls be matched by dividend controls. Right?

Wrong! You should be able to see through that kind of argument by now. But let us turn to some of the more serious arguments for a high-payout policy.

Do MM Ignore Risk?

One of the most common and immediate objections to MM's argument about the irrelevance of dividends is that dividends are cash in hand while capital gains are at best in the bush. It may be true that the recipient of an extra cash dividend forgoes an equal capital gain, but if the dividend is safe and the capital gain is risky, isn't the stockholder ahead?

It is true that dividends are more predictable than capital gains. Managers can stabilize dividends but they cannot control stock price. From this it seems a small step to conclude that increased dividends make the firm less risky.[14] But the important point is, once again, that as long as investment policy and borrowing are held constant, a firm's *overall*

---

[12]These authors later qualified this statement, recognizing the willingness of investors to pay high price-earnings multiples for growth stocks. But otherwise they have stuck to their position. We quoted their 1951 statement because of its historical importance. Compare B. Graham and D.L. Dodd, *Security Analysis: Principles and Techniques*, 3rd ed., McGraw-Hill Book Company, New York, 1951, p. 432, with B. Graham, D.L. Dodd, and S. Cottle, *Security Analysis: Principles and Techniques*, 4th ed., McGraw-Hill Book Company, New York, 1962, p. 480.

[13]See A. Rubner, *The Ensnared Shareholder*, Macmillan International Ltd., London, 1965, p. 139.

[14]By analogy one could presumably argue that interest payments are even more predictable, so that a company's risk would be diminished by increasing the proportion of receipts paid out as interest.

cash flows are the same regardless of payout policy. The risks borne by *all* the firm's stockholders are likewise fixed by its investment and borrowing policies, and unaffected by dividend policy.[15]

A dividend increase creates a transfer of ownership between "old" and "new" stockholders. The old stockholders—those who receive the extra dividend and do not buy their part of the stock issue undertaken to finance the dividend—find their stake in the firm reduced. They have indeed traded a safe receipt for an uncertain future gain. But the reason their money is safe is not because it is special "dividend money," but because it is in the bank. If the dividend had not been increased, the stockholders could have achieved an equally safe position just by selling shares and putting the money in the bank.

If we really believed that old stockholders are better off by trading a risky asset for cash, then we would also have to argue that the new stockholders—those who trade cash for the newly issued shares—are worse off. But this doesn't make sense: the new stockholders are bearing risk, but they are getting paid for it. They are willing to buy because the new shares are priced to offer a return adequate to cover the risk.

MM's argument for the irrelevance of dividend policy does not assume a world of certainty: it assumes an efficient capital market. Market efficiency means that the transfers of value created by shifts in dividend policy are carried out on fair terms. And since the *overall* value of (old and new) stockholders' equity is unaffected, nobody gains or loses.

Market Imperfections

We believe—and it is widely believed—that MM's conclusions follow from their assumption of perfect and efficient capital markets. Nobody claims their model is an exact description of the so-called "real-world." Thus the dividend controversy finally boils down to arguments about imperfections or inefficiencies.

There is a natural clientele for high-payout stocks. For example, some financial institutions are legally restricted from holding stocks lacking established dividend records. Trusts and endowment funds may prefer high-dividend stocks because dividends are regarded as spendable "income," whereas capital gains are "additions to principal," which cannot be spent.[16]

There is also a natural clientele of investors who look to their stock portfolios for a steady source of cash to live on. In principle this cash could be easily generated from stocks paying no dividends at all; the investor could just sell off a small fraction of his or her holdings from time to time. But it is simpler and cheaper for Canadian Pacific to send a quarterly cheque than for its stockholders to sell, say, one share every three months. Canadian Pacific's regular dividends relieve many of its shareholders of transaction costs and considerable inconvenience.

Those advocating generous dividends might go on to argue that a regular cash dividend relieves stockholders of the risk of having to sell shares at "temporarily depressed" prices. Of course, the firm will have to issue shares eventually to finance the dividend,

---

[15]There are a number of variations of the "bird-in-the-hand" argument. Perhaps the most persuasive is found in M.J. Gordon, "Dividends, Earnings and Stock Prices," *Review of Economics and Statistics*, **41**:99–105 (May 1959). He reasoned that investors run less risk if the firm pays them cash now rather than retaining and reinvesting it in the hope of paying higher future dividends. But careful analysis of Gordon's argument—see M.J. Brennan, "A Note on Dividend Irrelevance and the Gordon Valuation Model," *Journal of Finance*, **26**:1115–1122 (December 1971), for example—shows that he was really talking about changes in investment policy, not dividend policy.

[16]Most colleges and universities are legally free to spend capital gains from their endowments, but this is rarely done.

but (the argument goes) the firm can pick the *right time* to sell. If firms really try to do this and if they are successful—two big *ifs*—then stockholders of high payout firms do indeed get something for nothing.

There is another line of argument that you can use to justify high payouts. Think of a market in which investors receive very little reliable information about a firm's earnings. Such markets exist in some European countries where a passion for secrecy and a tendency to construct many-layered corporate organizations produce asset and earnings figures that are next to meaningless. Some people say that, thanks to creative accounting, the situation is little better in Canada and the United States. How does an investor in such a world separate marginally profitable firms from the real money makers? One clue is dividends. A firm that reports good earnings and pays a generous dividend is putting its money where its mouth is.[17] We can understand why investors would favour firms with established dividend records. We can also see how the information content of dividends would come about. Investors would refuse to believe a firm's reported earnings announcements unless they were backed up by an appropriate dividend policy.

MM regard the informational content of dividends as a temporary thing. A dividend increase signals management's optimism about future earnings, but investors will be able to see *for themselves* whether the optimism is justified. The jump in stock price that accompanies an unexpected dividend increase *would have happened anyway* as information about future earnings comes out through other channels. Therefore, MM expect to find changes in dividends associated with stock price movements, but no permanent relationship between stock price and the firm's long-run target payout ratio. MM believe management should be concerned with dividend *changes*, but not with the average *level* of payout.

16-5   THE TAXATION OF INVESTMENT INCOME

Dividend, capital gain, and interest income are taxed at different rates. Individual Canadian investors can receive up to $1,000 of Canadian investment income (interest and taxable dividends) tax-free. Aside from this, interest income is taxed as ordinary income when received either by an individual or by a corporation. That is, interest income is taxed at the same rate as wage and salary income for individuals, and at the same rate as income from operations for corporations.

In Canada, major changes in the tax treatment of capital gains occurred in 1972 and 1985. Capital gains were not taxed prior to 1972 and, usually, only *half* of capital gains derived after that have been added to taxable income.[18] Generally, capital gains are taxed only when they are *realized* (i.e., when the asset is sold). This treatment applies to individual as well as corporate investors. A 1985 federal law will ultimately allow individuals (not corporations) a lifetime exemption of tax on their first $500,000 of capital gains (that is, $250,000 of taxable capital gains). Even gains derived between

---

[17]Of course, firms can cheat in the short run by overstating earnings and scraping up cash to pay a generous dividend. But it is hard to cheat in the long run, for a firm that is not making money will not have the cash flow to pay out. Financing dividends by issuing stock is self-defeating, for it ultimately reduces dividends per share and thereby reveals that the initial dividend was not supported by earnings.

[18]That is, capital gains are normally taxed at half the rate for ordinary income, and, generally speaking, private individuals may elect to have this treatment for all their investment gains. However, a stock trader or dealer must take capital gains as ordinary income. There is no minimum holding period for the preferential treatment, as the United States had prior to its 1987 tax reform.

1972 and 1985 are eligible for the exemption, as long as the asset is sold in 1985 or later. The effect is to make most individual Canadian investors untaxed on capital gains, just as they were prior to 1972.

Dividends are not taxed when received by a public corporation, such as one that is traded on a Canadian stock exchange. On the other hand, the **dividend tax credit** (DTC) system applies to the taxation of Canadian dividends in the hands of Canadian investors who are individuals (not corporations). It reduces the burden of the *double taxation* of shareholder income that occurs when cash flows that produce dividends are taxed at the corporate level as well as at the personal level. The dividend tax credit system results in a negative tax on dividends for investors in low tax brackets. This system has generally become more generous from 1972 to 1986, but has become less generous since then. Its rationale is discussed in Appendix 16-1.

The Personal Taxation of Dividends and Capital Gains

Since corporations are not allowed to deduct the dividends they pay from taxable income, corporate cash flows that generate either dividends or retained earnings are taxed in the same manner at the corporate level. The only difference is the personal taxation in the hands of investors. Starting in 1987, if an individual receives a dividend from a Canadian corporation, its value is "grossed-up" by $33^1/_3$% to yield a "taxable dividend" which is taxed as ordinary personal income. This is offset by a dividend tax credit of $16^2/_3$% of the grossed-up dividend, which is deducted from federal tax payable. Provincial tax is then computed as a proportion of the net federal tax payable.

From 1982–86, the situation was the same, except that dividends were grossed-up by 50% and the federal portion of the dividend tax credit was $22^2/_3$% of the grossed-up dividend. (Provincial tax rates for 1983 varied from 38.5% to 60%, except in Quebec, which has a separate tax system.) Table 16-2 illustrates the 1982–86 taxation of a $100 dividend for three different marginal federal tax rates: the minimum 6%, the 25% rate corresponding to the $22,284–$34,664 taxable income bracket for 1984, and the maximum 34%. The net marginal tax rates on the dividend received are −35.9%, 5.0%

Table 16-2   Personal taxation of dividends and capital gains for a provincial tax rate of 43.5%. Here we assume that the $1,000 exemption for Canadian investment income and any exemption for capital gains have been all used up.

	Marginal Federal Tax Rate		
	6%	25%	34%
Dividend	$100.00	$100.00	$100.00
Taxable or grossed-up dividend	150.00	150.00	150.00
Tax on grossed-up dividend	9.00	37.50	51.00
less $22^2/_3$% DTC	− 34.00	− 34.00	− 34.00
Net federal tax on dividend	− 25.00	3.50	17.00
Net provincial tax (43.5% of federal tax)	− 10.88	1.52	7.40
Total personal tax on dividend	− $35.88	$5.02	$24.40
Capital gain	$100.00	$100.00	$100.00
Taxable capital gain	50.00	50.00	50.00
Federal tax on capital gain	3.00	12.50	17.00
Provincial tax (43.5% of federal tax)	1.31	5.44	7.40
Total personal tax on capital gain	$4.31	$17.94	$24.40

and 24.4%, respectively, in those three cases, when the provincial tax is 43.5% of the federal tax.

Note that the dividend tax credit can yield a *negative* marginal tax rate (and the DTC is received even if the grossed-up dividends are not subject to tax under the $1,000 Canadian investment income deduction). In contrast, if the $100 had been retained in the firm and the investor sold the shares immediately to realize an incremental $100 capital gain, which was subject to tax, the marginal personal tax rates on the capital gain would have been 4.3%, 17.9% and 24.4%, respectively, in Table 16-2. Thus, from a tax perspective, all investors would have preferred dividends to immediately realized taxable capital gains (or, at worst, will be indifferent between the two).

On the other hand, the 1985 budget eliminated the tax on an individual investor's first $500,000 of capital gains. Moreover, many investors are in a position to defer some or all of their taxable capital gains because they need not sell their stock. Even those who desire a regular annual income from their investments can defer much of their capital gain on "home-made dividends" because they don't have to sell off all of their investment at once. For example, suppose someone buys $10,000 of non-dividend-paying stock and sells 10% of that stock a year later as a home-made dividend when the stock price has increased by $1,200 or 12% to $11,200. The investor receives $1,120 for shares that cost $1,000, and thus realizes a capital gain of $120 which is only 1.2% of the $10,000 investment. The remaining $1,000 of the home-made dividend is not taxed, and tax on the remaining $1,080 of the gain is deferred. The deferral reduces the present value of any capital gains tax. If the capital gains are deferred far enough into the future, the present value of the capital gains tax is negligible.

For all these investors who paid little or no tax on capital gains, it would be more appropriate to compare the net tax on dividends in Table 16-2 to a zero capital gains tax rate. In this case, only investors below the $22^2/_3$% federal tax bracket would have preferred dividends to capital gains.

Stock Repurchase and Stock Dividends

Stock repurchases by Canadian corporations generally get one of two tax treatments. If the shares are purchased on the open market, the seller receives a capital gains treatment, since it cannot be determined whether the buyer is a general member of the public or the corporation.[19] If the shares are not repurchased on the open market (for example, the shares are tendered directly to the corporation), the tax situation is more complex. In many cases, for example when the shareholder is a Canadian dealing at "arm's length" with the corporation, the sale is also treated as a capital gain. In other cases, the share repurchase is treated as a combination of a "deemed dividend," a capital gain, and a return of "paid-up capital" (similar to stated capital), which is not taxed.[20]

Prior to 1985, stock dividends were not taxed on receipt of the dividend, but were treated as an acquisition of shares at a zero cost. In effect, the stock dividend was taxed as a capital gain when the shares were ultimately sold. Since the 1985 budget eliminated the tax on most capital gains, it also eliminated the capital gains treatment of stock dividends. Stock dividends are now taxed just like ordinary cash dividends, and have lost their special capital gains treatment.

---

[19]Income Tax Act, subsection 84(6).

[20]In the Income Tax Act, subsection 84(8) provides for the capital gains treatment. Provision for the deemed dividend is in subsection 84(3), and the capital gains associated with it arise in subparagraph 54(h)(x).

Tax Treatment in the United States

Investment income is taxed differently in the United States than it is in Canada. There are two reasons American tax laws are important in Canadian finance. First, many Canadian firms are listed on American stock exchanges and their managers should be aware of the tax implications of the investment income they pass to their American shareholders. Second, the difference in the tax regimes affords us an opportunity to study whether the firms and investors in the two countries make different decisions regarding the dividend/capital gains trade-off.

Prior to 1987, the Internal Revenue Service (IRS) allowed American individuals to receive up to $100 of American cash dividends tax-free, and then taxed the remainder as regular income. If a capital gain was derived over a period of less than 12 months, all of it was added to an individual's income and taxed, but if the capital gain was derived over a longer period, it was called a long-term gain and only 40% of the gain was added to income and taxed. Starting in 1987, capital gains and dividends are both taxed as regular income. Prior to 1987, American corporations had to include 15% of the dividends they received in their taxable income and pay a 30% tax on realized capital gains. In 1987, these figures changed to 20% and 34%, respectively.

Stock repurchases in the United States receive a capital gains treatment, like open market repurchases in Canada. Interest income received by individuals or corporations is taxed as ordinary income, just like salary income or operating income.

Canadian dividends and interest paid to foreign investors are generally subject to a 10%–15% tax, withheld at the source and remitted to the Canadian government. American residents are subject to tax on their world investment income. However, in accordance with the Canada-U.S. tax treaty, American residents can use the Canadian withholding tax to generate a foreign tax credit against their American taxes. Thus, from the viewpoint of American recipients, Canadian investment income is generally taxed in the same manner as American investment income.

Canadians receiving American dividends and interest also generally face a 15% withholding tax and are allowed a foreign tax credit of that amount against their Canadian tax. However, American dividends do not generate a dividend tax credit in Canada. From the viewpoint of a Canadian recipient, Canadian interest and salary income and American interest and dividend income are all treated in the same manner, except that American income does not qualify for the $1,000 investment income deduction in Canada.

16-6 RESPONSES TO TAXES: A SWINGING PENDULUM

So far we have seen that some investors will pay lower taxes on dividends and some will pay lower taxes on capital gains. One group, which we will call "clientele D," includes Canadian investors in low tax brackets as well as investors who trade stocks often and cannot avail themselves of any exemption from taxation of capital gains. They will prefer dividends to capital gains. The other group, which we will call "clientele G," includes investors in high tax brackets, who either do not trade their stocks often or are in a position to be able to use the $500,000 exemption from taxation of capital gains. They will prefer capital gains to dividends. Since Canadian public corporations pay no tax on dividends they receive from other taxable Canadian corporations, and do not get an exemption from the taxation of capital gains, they are in clientele D. The Canadian system has swung from no taxes on capital gains and high taxes on dividends to moderately high taxes on capital gains and low taxes on dividends. With the May 1985 federal budget, Canada has reduced and almost eliminated taxes on capital gains. Thus, the Canadian population has shifted from clientele G to clientele D during the period from 1970 to 1985, although there will be a slight reversal from clientele D back to clientele G starting in 1985.

In contrast, the American public and many American companies are in clientele G, with respect to receipt of both American and Canadian stock income, because dividends are generally taxed more heavily than capital gains in the United States.

How Taxes Affect Values

Corporations can transmute dividends into capital gains by shifting their dividend policies. Clientele D investors would prefer stocks with high-dividend yields and should be willing to pay more for stocks with high-dividend yields. In other words, they should be willing to accept a lower *pretax* rate of return from securities offering returns in the form of dividends rather than taxable capital gains.

Table 16-3   Effects of a shift in dividend policy when capital gains are taxed more heavily than dividends. The low payout stock (firm A) must sell at a lower price in order to provide the same after-tax return because capital gains are taxed more heavily than dividends. The net tax rates on dividends and capital gains correspond to the 25% marginal federal tax bracket and a 43.5% provincial tax rate, as in Table 16-2. We assume that the investor has used up all tax exemptions for dividend and capital gains income.

	Firm A (no dividend)	Firm B (high dividend)
Today's stock price	$100.00	$101.41
Next year's price	$112.19	$102.19
Capital gain	$12.19	$0.78
Dividend	$0.00	$10.00
Next year's price plus dividend	$112.19	$112.19
Before-tax rate of return	$\frac{12.19}{100} \times 100 = 12.2\%$	$\frac{10.78}{101.41} \times 100 = 10.6\%$
Net tax on dividend at 5.02%	$0.00	$0.0502 \times 10 = \$0.50$
Tax on capital gain at 17.94%	$0.1794 \times 12.19 = \$2.19$	$0.1794 \times 0.78 = \$0.14$
Total after-tax income (dividends plus capital gains)	$(0 + 12.19) - 2.19 = \$10.00$	$(10.00 + 0.78) - (0.50 + 0.14) = \$10.14$
After-tax rate of return	$\frac{10}{100} \times 100 = 10.0\%$	$\frac{10.14}{101.41} \times 100 = 10.0\%$

Table 16-3 illustrates this. The shares of firms A and B are equally risky. Investors expect A to be worth $112.19 per share next year. The share price of B is expected to be only $102.19, but a $10 dividend is also forecast, and so the total pretax payoff is the same, $112.19. Yet we find that clientele D investors should be willing to pay more for a share of stock B than of stock A, and hence get a lower pretax rate of return from B. The reason is obvious: clientele D investors are taxed less heavily on dividends and B's return is mainly in the form of dividends. Table 16-3 shows that A and B are exactly equivalent investments to investors who are in the 25% marginal federal tax bracket, pay 43.5% provincial tax, and pay tax on capital gains annually. Each offers a 10% return after all taxes. The difference between the stock prices of A and B is exactly the present value of the extra taxes such investors face if they buy A.

Exactly the opposite is true for clientele G investors, who are taxed more heavily on dividends than capital gains. They would pay more for stocks with low dividend yields. The question is which effect is stronger: will high dividend yield stocks sell for more or less than low dividend yield stocks on the basis of taxes?

Michael Brennan is one of those who believe that the world is like Table 16-3. He looked at what happens when you introduce taxes into an otherwise perfect market and found that the capital asset pricing model continues to hold, but on an *after-tax* basis.[21] Thus, if A and B have the same beta, they should offer the same after-tax rate of return. The spread between pretax and posttax returns is determined by all investors' tax rates on dividends and capital gains. A risky stock must earn a premium for risk as measured by beta, and a premium for its dividend yield. The dividend yield premium is positive if clientele G predominates and negative if clientele D predominates.

Tax-Based Clientele Effects

These tax effects will generally cause clientele D investors to buy high dividend yield stocks, and clientele G investors to generally buy low dividend yield stocks. However, we would not expect strict demarcation lines for these clienteles, since clientele D investors will often purchase *some* low dividend yield stocks in order to diversify away unique or unsystematic risk. They will search for an optimal trade-off between losses due to the heavier taxation of high capital gain stocks, versus the higher risk that would occur if they were not well-diversified. Similarly, clientele G investors will tend to buy *some* high dividend yield stocks.

To help dissolve these tax-based clienteles, Canadian firms developed programs to allow investors the option of receiving either cash dividends (taxed as a dividend) or stock dividends (taxed as a capital gain). This was done either by allowing the investor to elect the method in which the dividends are to be paid, or by creating two inter-convertible classes of shares, on one of which a cash dividend was paid and on the other of which a stock dividend was paid. By 1982, at least 78 firms had such programs. Unfortunately, the 1985 federal budget introduced a tax on stock dividends just like cash dividends. Thus, there will be no more merit (at least on a tax basis) in allowing investors the option of receiving either stock or cash dividends.

The desire by investors for diversification and flexibility in choosing between high and low dividend policy firms can also be satisfied if the various firms in any particular industry each choose a distinct high or low dividend payout. This will allow an investor to buy stocks with desirable dividend payouts, and still be diversified across many different industries. Unfortunately, in practice, there is little variation in dividend policy, within particular industries in Canada.

Another Response by Firms to Clientele Effects

We have seen that, depending on the relative numbers of clientele D and clientele G investors, high dividend yield stocks can sell at a higher or lower price than low dividend yield stocks of the same risk. For example, suppose there is a predominance of clientele D investors who are taxed more heavily on capital gains than dividends. Then firms could increase their share prices if they increase their dividend payouts, because this would

---

[21]M.J. Brennan, "Taxes, Market Valuation and Corporate Financial Policy," *National Tax Journal*, 23:417–427 (December 1970).

make them more attractive to clientele D investors. Under general circumstances,[22] the resulting increase in dividends would satisfy some of the overall demand of investors for high dividend stocks. Thus they would require less of a pretax return premium per unit of dividend yield to compensate them for the higher tax on *any* low dividend paying stocks. If enough firms were to convert to a high dividend yield, the premium would vanish and low dividend firms would have the same pretax return (and price) as high dividend firms of the same risk. Exactly the opposite would happen if there is a preponderance of clientele G investors—aggregate dividend yields would fall in response to the higher demand for capital gains as opposed to dividends.

Overall, we would expect to see firms shifting, in aggregate, to an optimal dividend policy at which there is no positive or negative premium required of high dividend stocks. At this point, dividend policy would be irrelevant for each firm, even from a tax viewpoint. However, firms as a *whole* will have an optimal dividend policy.[23]

If this line of reasoning is correct, the following two hypotheses should hold:

1. Canadian firms, on the whole, should have increased their dividend yields throughout the 1970s as capital gains were taxed more heavily and dividends less heavily. After 1985, the overall dividend yields in Canada should fall somewhat, in response to the partial capital gains tax exemption and the increased tax on dividends.

2. Canadian firms should generally have higher dividend yields than American firms because the United States tax system favours capital gains over dividends more than the Canadian system.

Let's see whether Canadian firms have responded to the changing tax incentives and have really made hypotheses 1 and 2 valid. A reasonable measure of the dividends paid out in Canada is the amount of dividends paid out on the Toronto Stock Exchange 300 Composite Index (TSE). It can be compared with the Standard and Poor's 500 Composite Index (S&P) in United States. Figure 16-3 shows the annual dividend yields on these two indices from 1956 to 1983. From 1956 to 1973, the yields on these two indices were close to each other. Both dividend yields rose sharply in 1974 (mainly because Canadian and American stock prices fell in 1974). After that, however, the TSE dividend yield fell overall, while the S&P dividend yield was generally steady. The evidence in Figure 16-3 seems to be at odds with both hypotheses 1 and 2. Canadian dividend yields fell relative to American dividend yields in the 1970s, just when the Canadian tax system swung more heavily in favour of dividends. Also, Canadian dividend yields have never been systematically higher than American dividend yields.

However, we may have overstated the case against hypothesis 1, because we looked at dividend *yields* rather than dividend *payments*. Figure 16-4 shows the annual rates of change in dividend payments to the TSE 300 and S&P 500 indices. The indices had similar rates of dividend change from 1957 to 1972. But from 1973 to 1975 and from

---

[22]This actually requires a technical variation on the model developed by Brennan. In his model, the return premium required to compensate for taxes on a unit of dividend yield does not depend on how many firms have high and low dividend yields, nor on the dividend yield of the firm in question: the relationship between the premium and dividend yield is a straight line. Litzenberger and Ramaswamy ("Dividends, Short Selling Restrictions, Tax-Induced Investor Clienteles and Market Equilibrium," *Journal of Finance*, **35**:469–482 [May 1980]) have incorporated restrictions on short sales of stock in a model like Brennan's and they show that the return premium on a high dividend yield stock will be largely determined by the marginal tax rates of the clientele attracted to it. In this general setting, a change in dividend policy will change the clientele faced by the firm, and hence change the tax-based return premium for a unit of dividend yield.

[23]This line of reasoning is analogous to an argument by Merton Miller with regard to taxation and capital structure, which is discussed in Chapter 18. It is also related to an argument by Black and Scholes about American dividends, which we will discuss later.

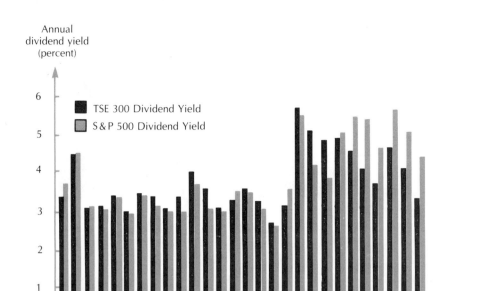

Annual dividend yield (percent)

■ TSE 300 Dividend Yield
□ S&P 500 Dividend Yield

1956   1960   1964   1968   1972   1976   1980   Year

Figure 16-3   Dividend yields in Canada and the United States, 1956–1983.

Source: Year-end data from *The Toronto Stock Exchange 300 Stock Price Indexes Manual*, 1979, plus *Annual Updates* to 1983. Used by permission of the Toronto Stock Exchange, Index Department. Fourth quarter data from *Standard and Poor's Statistical Service Security Price Index Record*, New York, 1984.

1978 to 1980, the TSE rate of dividend increase greatly outpaced the S&P rate of dividend increase. This could very well have been the result of the two major changes in Canada's dividend and capital gains tax laws, which took effect in 1972 and 1978.[24] To reconcile the difference between the evidence in Figures 16-3 and 16-4, note that while the TSE dividend payments were increasing faster than the S&P dividend payments, the value of the TSE 300 Index was increasing at an even greater rate, relative to the value of the S&P 500 Index. As a result, the TSE dividend yield fell below the S&P dividend yield.[25]

Thus, we have some support for hypothesis 1. On the other hand, hypothesis 2 is an open question. Canadian tax laws seem to favour dividends over capital gains more than American tax laws do, but it is not clear that Canadian corporations have relatively higher dividend payouts in response to this. Perhaps Canadian firms have responded to the demand for dividends with preferred share offerings. Since preferred shares are not included in either the TSE 300 nor the S&P 500 indices, these indices may not,

[24]The S&P dividend payment to the index appears to be the dividends paid prior to the end of the year, while the TSE dividend payment to the index is a prospective annual rate of dividend payment, based on the most current "indicated" dividends. Thus, the timing of the two dividend payment measures is not identical, although it is not clear that this creates serious problems in interpreting Figure 16-4. For example, the rates of change for the dividends of the two indices are very similar during the 1957–1972 period, when tax laws were stable.

[25]Khouri and Smith ("Dividend Policy and the Capital Gains Tax in Canada," *Journal of Business Administration*, 8:19–38 [Spring 1977]) studied a related pair of hypotheses by comparing the dividend policies of 145 Canadian firms with those of 130 similar American firms, for the 1963–1973 period. Their conclusions were similar. Note, however, that their time period is shorter and they did not attempt to look at the aggregate effect of all firms' behaviour.

in fact, be a good measure of total dividends paid to investors. Further research is needed before we can come to a definitive conclusion on the question.

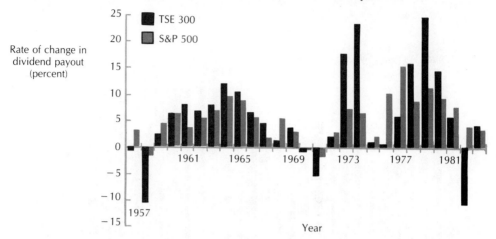

Figure 16-4 Rates of change in dividend payouts in Canada and the United States, 1957–1983. *Source*: Year-end data from *The Toronto Stock Exchange 300 Stock Price Indexes Manual*, 1979, plus *Annual Updates* to 1983. Used by permission of the Toronto Stock Exchange, Index Department. Fourth quarter data from *Standard and Poor's Statistical Service Security Price Index Record*, New York, 1984.

American Tax-Based Clienteles and the Left-Wing View

You will recall that most private American investors are in clientele G. This implies that American firms should be able to increase their share prices simply by announcing that they will eliminate their dividends and instead distribute cash to their shareholders by a share repurchase program. This can be regarded as a left-wing view, in contrast to the right-wing view favouring high dividend payouts we discussed earlier.

Few leftists would go quite that far. A firm that eliminates dividends and starts repurchasing stock on a regular basis may find that the Internal Revenue Service would recognize the repurchase program for what it really is and would tax the payments accordingly. That is why financial managers never announce that they are repurchasing shares to save stockholders taxes; they give some other reason.[26]

The low-payout party nevertheless maintains that the market rewards firms with low-payout policies. And they hold that firms that pay cash dividends and as a result must issue shares from time to time make a serious mistake. Any such firm is essentially financing its dividends by issuing stock; it should cut its dividends to the point at which stock issues are unnecessary. This not only saves taxes for shareholders, it avoids the transaction costs of the stock issues.[27]

If investors are influenced by taxes, American stocks should also attract special tax clienteles. Low-payout stocks should be owned principally by investors with high marginal tax rates and high-payout stocks should be owned principally by investors with low marginal tax rates. A survey of the portfolios of individual investors by Lewellen

---

[26]They might say, "Our stock is a good investment," or, "We want to have the shares available to finance acquisitions of other companies." What do you think of these rationales?

[27]These costs can be substantial. Refer back to Chapter 15, especially Table 15-1.

Table 16-4 A survey of the portfolios of individual investors by Lewellen and others provides some indirect evidence that investors are influenced by taxes. The authors grouped shares by their dividend yield and then estimated the marginal tax rate of the shareholders. Low-yield shares were on the average held by investors with the highest marginal tax rates.

Group	Yield, %	Marginal Tax Rate, %
1	7.9	36
2	5.4	35
3	4.4	38
4	3.5	39
5	2.7	38
6	1.8	41
7	0.6	40
8	0.0	41
9	0.0	42
10	0.0	41

Source: W.G. Lewellen, K.L. Stanley, R.C. Lease, and G.G. Schlarbaum, "Some Direct Evidence on the Dividend Clientele Phenomenon," *Journal of Finance*, **33**:1385–1399 (December 1978).

and others seems to bear this out. Table 16-4 shows that the stocks with the lowest yields were on the average held by investors with the highest marginal tax rates.[28]

It is hard to deny that taxes are important to investors. You can see that in the bond market. Interest on municipal bonds is not taxed in the United States, and so municipals sell at low pretax yields. Interest on federal government bonds is taxed, and so these bonds sell at higher pretax yields.

The real estate market is another case where investors take extreme care to distinguish prospective capital gains from ordinary income. It does not seem likely that investors in bonds and real estate just forget about taxes when they enter the stock market.

16-7 ANOTHER MIDDLE-OF-THE-ROAD APPROACH

We have just seen some strong tax-based arguments favouring low dividends in the United States (as well as some arguments favouring higher dividends in Canada, which were somewhat more equivocal). There is still a case to be made for a middle-of-the-road approach, even in the American tax setting. First, we'll look at this approach as it applies in the United States (where it was born), and then examine the extent to which it applies in Canada.

Black and Scholes

The middle-of-the-road party, which is principally represented by Black and Scholes, maintains that a company's value is not affected by its dividend policy.[29] We have already seen that this would be the case if there were no impediments such as transaction

[28]See W.G. Lewellen, K.L. Stanley, R.C. Lease, and G.G. Schlarbaum, "Some Direct Evidence on the Dividend Clientele Phenomenon," *Journal of Finance*, **33**:1385–1399 (December 1978). These findings are supported by a study of stockownership by Blume and others. See M.E. Blume, J. Crockett and I. Friend, "Stockownership in the United States: Characteristics and Trends," *Survey of Current Business*, **54**:16–40 (November 1974).

[29]F. Black and M.S. Scholes, "The Effects of Dividend Yield and Dividend Policy on Common Stock Prices and Returns," *Journal of Financial Economics*, 1:1–22 (May 1974).

costs or taxes. Black and Scholes, however, are aware of these phenomena and argue their case from a different viewpoint. They concede that, if the supply of dividends were fixed, low-payout stocks could be more highly valued and offer lower pretax rates of return. On the other hand, if companies could increase their share price by distributing less, they would surely have done so. In this case, we should assume that dividends are where they are because no company believes that it could increase its stock price simply by changing its dividend policy.

This "supply effect" is not inconsistent with the existence of clientele G investors in high-tax brackets who demand low-payout stocks. Firms recognized that clientele long ago. Enough firms may have switched to low-payout policies to satisfy fully the clientele's demand. If so, there is no incentive for *additional* firms to switch to low-payout policies.

Black and Scholes similarly recognize a "high-payout clientele" (clientele D), but argue that this clientele is satisfied also. If all clienteles are satisfied, it doesn't matter which one a particular firm chooses to appeal to. If Black and Scholes are right, we should not expect to observe any general association between dividend policy and market values, and the value of any individual company would be independent of its choice of dividend policy.

How to Avoid Taxes on Dividends in the United States

The weakest point of the Black-and-Scholes argument is its failure to explain why there would be any Americans in clientele D. Miller and Scholes have put forward one explanation.[30] They point to the fact that the tax laws allow plenty of opportunity for the investor to postpone the tax on dividends or to transform dividends into capital gains. For example, suppose that you have invested $10,000 in a stock offering a dividend yield of 5% and a capital gain of 5%. At the end of the year your tax return shows:

Ordinary Income	Capital Gains
Dividends = 0.05 × 10,000 = $500	Gain = 0.05 × 10,000 = $500

Now someone points out that you can offset interest on borrowing against your investment income. Therefore you borrow $20,000 at, say, $7^{1}/_{2}$% and invest this additional sum in the common stock, for a total investment of $30,000. At the end of the year your tax return looks like this:

Ordinary Income		Capital Gains
Dividends = 0.05 × 30,000 = $1,500		Gain = 0.05 × 30,000 = $1,500
Less interest = 0.075 × 20,000 = $1,500		
Net ordinary income	$0	

You don't need to pay any tax now on your dividends but your borrowing has increased the risk of your investment. If this increased risk is not to your taste, you may have an alternative. Suppose that you can find a financial institution that will manage your money and that is not taxed on investment income. In that case you borrow $6,667 rather than $20,000 and hand it over to the institution that promises to repay your money with interest at some agreed date. You now have a risk-free asset worth $6,667 (your investment with the financial institution), and this exactly offsets your risk-free

---

[30]M.H. Miller and M.S. Scholes, "Dividends and Taxes," *Journal of Financial Economics*, 6:333–364 (December 1978).

liability of $6,667 (your loan). You have, therefore, neutralized the risk that resulted from borrowing. Let us look at how the transaction affects your tax liability. The interest on this loan is $0.075 \times \$6,667 = \$500$, which can be deducted from your dividend income of $500, leaving you with no tax to pay on your dividends. The financial institution uses your $6,667 to invest in risk-free bonds, but, unlike you, it does not pay tax on its investment income. When you eventually get your money back from this institution, you may be taxed on any gain that you have made, but that is many years away.

In practice, the government does not allow you to avoid taxes so easily. You cannot simply ask a financial institution to manage your money free of tax; for example, if you invest through a mutual fund, you are taxed on investment income just as if you invest directly. On the other hand, Miller and Scholes point out that you can get most of the benefits we have described if you buy a whole life insurance policy or increase your contribution to a pension scheme. Because life insurance companies and pension funds are not taxed on their investment income, it pays wealthy people to save through these institutions. If they borrow to pay their insurance premium or pension contribution, they can use the interest on this loan to offset the dividend income on their common stock investments. Therefore the government's favourable tax treatment of life insurance and pension plans provides an opportunity for investors to postpone taxes on investment income.[31]

In our view, the important contribution of the middle-of-the-road school is their insistence on the following point: you cannot maintain that companies could increase their value by changing their dividend policy unless you can simultaneously explain why they have not already done so. On the other hand, although there are tax incentives to purchase insurance or make additional pension contributions, we are not fully convinced by Miller and Scholes's argument that investors should totally ignore the firm's dividend policy in making their portfolio choices.

Does This Work in Canada?

We have already used the Black-Scholes type of argument that says there will be a "supply effect" whereby firms adjust their aggregate dividend policy to match the tax brackets of the various investing clienteles, until dividend policy becomes irrelevant for individual firms. In fact, the argument applies more strongly in Canada because of the presence of a significant clientele that prefers dividends.

The Miller-Scholes technique for eliminating taxes on dividends does not work in exactly the same manner for Canadians, but it can lead to similar results. In Canada, the interest expense on loans used to purchase securities is tax deductible if it is used to provide investment income, and it is not limited to the amount of dividend income that is received, as it is in the United States. Thus, the Miller-Scholes technique should apply to eliminating taxes on dividend as well as capital gain income in Canada.

In Canada, whole life insurance policies are not a good vehicle for accruing interest income without tax. However, registered retirement savings plans (RRSPs), pension plans, and deferred profit sharing plans (DPSPs) are all popular vehicles for avoiding tax on investment income.[32] All of these allow pretax personal income to be invested

---

[31]Miller and Scholes's argument leaves some unanswered questions. Do investors in the United States use the same devices to eliminate taxes on interest? Until recently, investors could also have shielded taxes on earned income in the same way, but presumably they didn't. Why?

[32]However, there are limitations to their use. For example, in 1984, annual RRSP contributions had to be less than $5,500 as well as less than 20% of the taxpayer's earned income. Moreover, if any contributions were made to the taxpayer's pension plan, RRSP contributions also had to be less than $3,500 minus the taxpayer's pension contributions. The May 1985 federal budget proposes to alter these limits to allow larger contributions, in general.

in a manner that results in no personal tax on the investment income. When the plans are cashed in, personal tax is paid on all proceeds. However, Miller and Scholes have pointed out that paying tax on these plans upon withdrawal has the same effect as investing posttax personal income in a whole life insurance policy, and not having it taxed upon withdrawal (provided the investor has the same marginal tax rates at the time of contribution and withdrawal).

Certainly, if most investors actually were to follow the Miller-Scholes strategy, dividend policy would be irrelevant from a tax standpoint for firms as a whole, as well as for individual firms.

16-8   THE EMPIRICAL EVIDENCE

The obvious way to solve the dividend quandary is to look at the evidence and test whether high-yielding stocks do offer different expected returns. Unfortunately, there are difficulties in measuring these effects.

Suppose that stock A is priced at $100 and is expected to pay a $5 dividend. The *expected* yield is, therefore, 5/100 = 0.05 or 5%. The company now announces bumper earnings and a $10 dividend. Thus with the benefit of hindsight, A's *actual* dividend yield is 10/100 = 0.10 or 10%. If the unexpected increase in earnings causes a rise in A's stock price, we will observe that a high actual yield is accompanied by a high actual return. But that would not tell us anything about whether a high *expected* yield was accompanied by a high *expected* return. In order to measure the effect of dividend policy, we need to estimate the dividends that investors expected.

A second problem is that nobody is quite sure what is meant by a high-dividend yield. For example, utility stocks are generally regarded as offering a high yield. But do they have a high yield all the year or only in months or on days that dividends are paid? Perhaps for most of the year they have zero yield and are perfect holdings for the highly taxed individual.[33] Of course the high taxpayer would not want to hold a utility stock on the days dividends are paid, but he or she could sell the stock temporarily to a security dealer. The dealer is taxed equally on dividends and capital gains, and therefore should not demand any different return for holding stocks over the dividend period. If shareholders can pass stocks freely between each other at the time of the dividend payment, we should not observe any tax effects at all.

A third problem is that most empirical studies have looked for a straight-line relationship between yield and return. But if there are any asymmetries in the tax system, the relationship might be more complicated.[34]

Given these difficulties in measuring the relationship between expected yield and return, it is not surprising that different researchers have come up with different results. Table 16-5 summarizes some of the findings in United States and Canadian markets. In all of the American tests, the estimated tax rate is positive. In other words, high-yielding American stocks appear to have lower prices and offer higher returns. But while the dividends-are-bad school can claim that the weight of evidence is on its side, the contest is by no means over. Many respected scholars in the United States, including Merton Miller and Myron Scholes, still believe that dividend policy doesn't matter. They stress the difficulty of measuring dividend yield properly and proving the link between dividend yield and expected return.

---

[33]Suppose there are 250 trading days in a year. Think of a stock paying quarterly dividends. We could say that the stock offers a high dividend yield on four days, but a zero dividend yield on the remaining 246 days.

[34]A restriction on short sales of stock is one such asymmetry, because it prevents tax savings on payments made to cover dividends while an investor is short from being made at the same rate as tax costs on dividends received while an investor is long. See footnote 22.

The Canadian market study by Morgan is particularly interesting because it is broken into two periods, which are divided by the date (December 1971) when capital gains taxes were introduced in Canada. The implied "tax rate" in Table 16-5 is more correctly interpreted as (a weighted average across investors of)

$$T = \frac{T_d - T_g}{1 - T_g}$$

where T = "implied tax rate"

T_d = tax rate on dividend income

T_g = tax rate on capital gains income

Table 16-5   Some tests of the effect of yield on returns.

Test	Test Period	Interval	Implied "Tax Rate," %	Standard Error of Tax Rate
American Market				
Brennan	1946–1965	Monthly	34	12
Black & Scholes (1974)	1936–1966	Monthly	22	24
Litzenberger & Ramaswamy (1979)	1936–1977	Monthly	24	3
Litzenberger & Ramaswamy (1982)	1940–1980	Monthly	14–23	2–3
Rosenberg & Marathe (1979)	1931–1966	Monthly	40	21
Bradford & Gordon (1980)	1926–1978	Monthly	18	2
Blume (1980)	1936–1976	Quarterly	52	25
Miller & Scholes (1982)	1940–1978	Monthly	4	3
Stone & Bartter (1979)	1947–1970	Monthly	56	28
Morgan (1982)	1946–1977	Monthly	21	2
Canadian Market				
Morgan (1980)	1968–1971	Monthly	59	17
	1972–1977	Monthly	−10	8

Sources: M.J. Brennan, "Dividends and Valuation in Imperfect Markets: Some Empirical Tests," unpublished paper, not dated.

F. Black and M. Scholes, "The Effects of Dividend Yield and Dividend Policy on Common Stock Prices and Returns," *Journal of Financial Economics*, 1:1–22 (May 1974).

R.H. Litzenberger and K. Ramaswamy, "The Effect of Personal Taxes and Dividends on Capital Asset Prices: Theory and Empirical Evidence," *Journal of Financial Economics*, 7:163–195 (June 1979).

R.H. Litzenberger and K. Ramaswamy, "The Effects of Dividends on Common Stock Prices: Tax Effects or Information Effects," *Journal of Finance*, 37:429–443 (May 1982).

B. Rosenberg and V. Marathe, "Tests of Capital Asset Pricing Model Hypotheses," in H. Levy (ed.), *Research in Finance I*, Greenwich, Conn.: JAI Press (1979).

D.F. Bradford and R.H. Gordon, "Taxation and the Stock Market Valuation of Capital Gains and Dividends," *Journal of Public Economics*, 14:109–136 (1980).

M.E. Blume, "Stock Returns and Dividend Yields: Some More Evidence," *Review of Economics and Statistics*, 567–577 (November 1980).

M.H. Miller and M. Scholes, "Dividends and Taxes: Some Empirical Evidence," *Journal of Political Economy,* 90:1118–1141 (1982).

B.K. Stone and B.J. Bartter, "The Effect of Dividend Yield on Stock Returns: Empirical Evidence on the Relevance of Dividends," W.P.E.-76-78, Georgia Institute of Technology, Atlanta, Ga.

I.G. Morgan, "Dividends and Capital Asset Prices," *Journal of Finance*, 37:1071–1086 (September 1982).

I.G. Morgan, "Dividends and Stock Price Behaviour in Canada," *Journal of Business Administration*, 12:91–106 (Fall 1980).

If $T_g = 0$, then $T = T_d$ is just the tax rate on dividends. Morgan estimated this as 59% for the period prior to the introduction of the capital gains tax. If the tax rate on capital gains for most investors exceeds that on dividends, the implied tax rate, T, is actually negative. This is consistent with the $T = -10\%$ (which is actually insignificantly different from zero) that Morgan reports for the 1972–1977 period. In other words, Morgan's evidence suggests that the dividends-are-bad school was correct in Canada prior to 1972, but not after 1972. In fact, the empirical evidence for 1972–1977 suggests that there was no particular reason to support high or low dividends. The dividend tax credit became more generous after 1977, so it may be that future empirical tests in Canada will favour the dividends-are-good school.

16-9 SUMMARY

Dividends come in many forms. The most common is the regular cash dividend, but sometimes companies pay an extra or special cash dividend, and sometimes they pay a dividend in the form of stock. A firm is not free to pay whatever dividends it likes. It may have promised its bondholders that it would not declare large dividends, and it is also prevented by law from paying dividends if it is insolvent or if it has insufficient surplus.

The company's dividends policy does not affect its own tax payments but it can affect the taxes paid by its shareholders. The taxation of dividends is softened by the dividend tax credit system, which yields negative taxes on dividends to low income investors. Capital gains are sometimes taxed at half the rate or ordinary personal income and sometimes not taxed at all. From a tax standpoint, only high income investors will prefer capital gains to dividends.

As an alternative to dividend payments, the company can repurchase its own stock. Although this has the same effect of distributing cash to shareholders, the shareholders are generally taxed only on the capital gains that they may realize as a result of the repurchase.

When managers decide on the dividend, their primary concern seems to be to give shareholders a "fair" level of dividends: if that does not leave enough money to finance expansion, the company pays the dividend and makes an issue of shares. Most managers have a conscious or subconscious long-term target payout rate. If firms simply applied the target payout rate to each year's earnings, dividends would fluctuate wildly. Managers, therefore, try to smooth dividend payments by moving only partway toward the target payout in each year. Also they don't just look at past earnings performance: they try to look into the future when they set the payment. Investors are aware of this and they know that a large dividend increase is often a sign of optimism on the part of management.

If we hold the company's investment policy constant, then dividend policy is a trade-off between cash dividends and the issue or repurchase of common stock. Should firms retain whatever earnings are necessary to finance growth and pay out any residual as cash dividends? Or should they increase dividends and then (sooner or later) issue stock to make up the shortfall of equity capital? Or should they reduce dividends below the "residual" level and use the released cash to repurchase stock?

If we lived in an ideally simple and perfect world, there would be no problem, for the choice would have no effect on market value. The controversy centres on the effects of dividend policy in our flawed world. A common—though by no means universal—view in the investment community is that high payout enhances share price. There are natural clienteles for high-payout stocks. But we find it difficult to explain a *general* preference for dividends other than in terms of an irrational prejudice. The case for "liberal dividends" depends largely on a wealth of tradition.

The most obvious and serious market imperfection is the different tax treatment of dividends and capital gains. This creates two investor clienteles: one that prefers low dividends and one that prefers high dividends. This suggests that firms should adjust their dividend policies so that some firms satisfy one clientele and other firms satisfy the other. If this occurs, dividend policy does not matter for an individual firm, but it is important for firms as a whole.

These theories are too incomplete and the evidence is too sensitive to minor changes in specification to warrant any dogmatism. Our sympathies, however, lie with those who stress the tax consequences of dividend policy, and our recommendations to companies would emphasize the following points. First, there is little doubt that sudden shifts in dividend policy can cause abrupt changes in stock price. The principal reason is the information that investors read into the company's actions, although some casual evidence suggests that there may be other less rational explanations.[35] Given such problems, there is a clear case for defining the firm's target payout and making relatively slow adjustments toward it. If it is necessary to make a sharp change in the dividend rate, the company should provide as much forewarning as possible and take considerable care to ensure that the action is not misinterpreted.

Subject to these strictures, we believe that many Canadian firms should continue to increase their dividend payout rates, in response to the evolution of Canadian tax law to favour dividends more than capital gains. If a firm has many American shareholders, the benefits of dividends for some Canadian shareholders must be weighed against the costs of dividends for the American shareholders, and such firms may find it best to opt for the low dividend clientele. Even though there is empirical evidence suggesting that there was no tax-based premium or discount for high dividend payout Canadian stocks in 1972–1977, Canadian tax law has come to favour dividends more highly since then and it is not clear that enough Canadian firms have responded by increasing their dividend payouts. Our enthusiasm for dividends has been tempered somewhat by the 1985 and 1986 tax law changes which eliminate taxes on capital gains for most investors and tax dividends more heavily.

Finally, remember that your view on dividend policy may affect your choice of discount rate for capital investments. If you believe dividend policy makes no difference, then your choice of investment projects is logically separate from your choice of dividend. But if you believe that dividend policy does change the required return, then the investment decision is not independent of the financing decision. The discount rate in that case must recognize the payout rate.

FURTHER READING

Lintner's classic analysis of how companies set their dividend payments is provided in:

J. Lintner, "Distribution of Incomes of Corporations among Dividends, Retained Earnings, and Taxes," *American Economic Review*, **46**:97–113 (May 1956).

There have been a number of tests of how well Lintner's model describes dividend changes. One of the best known is:

E.F. Fama and H. Babiak, "Dividend Policy: An Empirical Analysis," *Journal of the American Statistical Association*, **63**:1132–1161 (December 1968).

---

[35]For example, in an article in *Fortune* Carol Loomis tells the story of General Public Utilities ("A Case for Dropping Dividends," *Fortune*, June 15, 1968, pp. 181 ff.). In 1968 its management decided to reduce its cash dividend to avoid a stock issue. Despite the company's assurances, it encountered considerable opposition. Individual shareholders advised the president to see a psychiatrist, institutional holders threatened to sell their stock, the share price fell nearly 10%, and eventually GPU capitulated.

The pioneering article on dividend policy in the context of a perfect capital market is:

M.H. Miller and F. Modigliani, "Dividend Policy, Growth and the Valuation of Shares," *Journal of Business*, **34**:411–433 (October 1961).

The most powerful advocacy of the "dividends are good" case is:

M.J. Gordon, "Dividends, Earnings and Stock Prices," *Review of Economics and Statistics*, **41**:99–105 (May 1959).

The source of the difference between MM and Gordon is discussed in:

M.J. Brennan, "A Note on Dividend Irrelevance and the Gordon Valuation Model," *Journal of Finance*, **26**:1115–1122 (December 1971).

The effect of differential rates of tax on dividends and capital gains is analyzed rigorously in the context of the capital asset pricing model in:

M.J. Brennan, "Taxes, Market Valuation and Corporate Financial Policy," *National Tax Journal*, **23**:417–427 (December 1970).

The tax implications are also the basis for the following readable article:

C.J. Loomis, "A Case for Dropping Dividends," *Fortune*, June 15, 1968, pp. 181 ff.

The argument that dividend policy is irrelevant even in the presence of taxes is presented in:

F. Black and M.S. Scholes, "The Effects of Dividend Yield and Dividend Policy on Common Stock Prices and Returns," *Journal of Financial Economics*, **1**:1–22 (May 1974).
M.H. Miller and M.S. Scholes, "Dividends and Taxes," *Journal of Financial Economics*, **6**:333–364 (December 1978).

A brief review on some of the empirical evidence is contained in:

R.H. Litzenberger and K. Ramaswamy, "The Effects of Dividends on Common Stock Prices: Tax Effects or Information Effects," *Journal of Finance*, **37**:429–443 (May 1982).

An empirical analysis of the effect of differential taxation of dividends and capital gains in Canada is in:

I.G. Morgan, "Dividends and Stock Price Behaviour in Canada," *Journal of Business Administration*, **12**:91–106 (Fall 1980).

An alternative approach to empirically estimating the differential impact of dividend and capital gains taxation involves examining the price drop of shares as they go ex-dividend. With American data, this is done by Elton and Gruber; with Canadian data this is done by Lakonishok and Vermaelen, and by Booth and Johnston:

E. Elton and M. Gruber, "Marginal Stockholder Tax Rates and the Clientele Effect," *Review of Economics and Statistics*, **52**:68–70 (February 1970).
J. Lakonishok and T. Vermaelen, "Tax Reform and Ex-Dividend Day Behavior," *Journal of Finance*, **38**:1157–1179 (September 1983).
L.D. Booth and D.J. Johnston, "The Ex-Dividend Day Behavior of Canadian Stock Prices: Tax Changes and Clientele Effects," *Journal of Finance*, **39**:457–476 (June 1984).

APPENDIX 16-1   THE DIVIDEND TAX CREDIT AND THE ELIMINATION OF DOUBLE TAXATION

Canadian legislators have made a significant effort to eliminate the double taxation of dividends at the corporate and at the personal level by means of the dividend tax credit (DTC). We will start by discussing the *theory* of the DTC, and conclude by relating it to Canada's tax laws.

The basic idea of the DTC is that the government will pay a tax credit to the shareholder for the corporate tax paid on the pretax cash flow used to generate a dividend, and then tax the shareholder on the total amount received: the dividend *and* the tax credit. In this way, dividends are effectively taxed at the personal level, but not the corporate level.

Let

DIV = dividend paid by a firm

T_c = corporate tax rate

T_p = marginal personal tax rate on ordinary salary and interest income

C = pretax corporate cash flow required to support the dividend

Since dividends are paid out of after-tax cash flows, we have $C(1 - T_c) = $ DIV or $C = $ DIV$/(1 - T_c)$. The cash flow, C, is often called the "grossed-up dividend." The government then permits the shareholder a dividend tax credit equal to the amount of the corporate tax paid. That is,

$$\text{DTC} = T_c C$$

$$= \frac{T_c \, \text{DIV}}{1 - T_c}$$

The system actually used in Canada is complicated by two facts: first, personal tax is assessed at the federal and provincial level, and second, there are two basic corporate tax rates—one for small business and one for ordinary business.

Let

T_{pfed} = marginal personal federal tax rate

T_{prov} = provincial tax as a proportion of federal tax

Then, the overall marginal personal tax rate is $T_p = T_{\text{pfed}}(1 + T_{\text{prov}})$. (All provinces but Quebec calculate personal taxes in this manner.) Similarly, the dividend tax credit is partly generated by the federal and partly by the provincial governments, so that

$$\text{DTC} = \text{DTC}_{\text{fed}}(1 + T_{\text{prov}})$$

where DTC_{fed} is the dividend tax credit on the federal tax return.

From 1982 to 1986, the grossed-up dividend was 150% of the dividend actually paid, so that $T_c = 33^{1}/_3\%$ was the corporate tax rate implied by the dividend tax credit system, since $1.5 = 1/(1 - 0.3333)$. The federal dividend tax credit was $22^{2}/_3\%$ of the grossed-up dividend. From

$$\text{DTC} = \text{DTC}_{\text{fed}}(1 + T_{\text{prov}}) \text{ and DTC} = T_c C$$

we have

$$T_c C = 0.2267 \, C(1 + T_{\text{prov}})$$

so that

$$T_{\text{prov}} = 47\%$$

Thus, if the corporate tax rate was $33^1/_3\%$ and the provincial personal tax was 47% of the federal tax, the dividend tax credit works perfectly to eliminate the double taxation of dividends.[36] In actual fact, in 1982, provincial personal taxes varied from 38.5% to 59% of federal tax.

Note that small business basically pays tax at 25% and ordinary business basically pays tax at 46%.[37] The 1982–86 system over-compensated for the double taxation of small business (and only partially eliminated the double taxation of ordinary business). To compensate for the excess generosity, the 1983–86 tax laws included a $12^1/_2\%$ "dividend distribution tax" for small business that effectively raised their overall corporate tax rate to $33^1/_3\%$. To see how this worked, note that the grossed-up dividend C equalled 1.5 DIV so that the desired corporate tax (at $T_c = 33^1/_3\%$) was 0.5 DIV. The corporate tax actually paid was $0.25\ C = 0.25 \times 1.5$ DIV $= 0.375$ DIV. The difference, 0.125 DIV, was collected as the distribution tax.

Starting in 1987, the grossed-up dividend was reduced to 133% of the dividend and the dividend tax credit was reduced to $16^2/_3\%$ of the grossed-up dividend. This corresponds to a 25% corporate tax rate and provincial taxes at 50% of personal federal taxes, so the dividend distribution tax has been eliminated.

Overall, the dividend tax credit system works toward the elimination of double taxation by making the total corporate and personal taxes on corporate equity cash flows equal to what would have resulted from *no corporate taxes*, and personal taxes at the same rates as applied to ordinary personal income. This effect is called the **integration** of the corporate and personal tax systems and was supported by the Carter Royal Commission on Taxation.[38] Full integration has been achieved with wages, salaries, and interest income, because these cash outflows are tax-deductible for the corporation and taxable only in the hands of the recipient. From the calculations above, we can see that full integration is achieved for the dividends of small firms, but not for large firms. A natural question to ask is, "Why should corporations pay any tax at all if the integration concept is appropriate?" The answer is that it prevents the corporate structure from being used to defer taxes (via retention of earnings), thereby reducing their present value. Under full integration, taxes on corporate equity income are merely prepayments of personal taxes.

QUIZ

1. In 1983, Imperial Oil paid a regular quarterly dividend of $0.35 a share.
   (*a*) Match each of the following sets of dates:

(A) Monday, February 21		(a) Record date	
(B) Tuesday, February 22		(b) Payment date	
(C) Wednesday, February 23		(c) Ex-dividend date	
(D) Tuesday, March 1		(d) Last with-dividend date	
(E) Thursday, March 31		(e) Declaration date	

---

[36]This analysis also provides investors with a popular rule of thumb regarding equivalent bond and preferred share yields. The DTC system works in such a way that dividends from preferred shares are equivalent, after personal taxes, to a pretax interest or salary cash flow equal to the grossed-up dividend. Thus, a dividend yield of r was equivalent to a grossed-up bond yield of $1.5r$. For example, an investor should be indifferent between an 8% preferred share and a 12% bond, provided the two securities have the same risk and term to maturity, and the provincial tax is close to 47% of federal tax. After 1986, the same preferred share is only equivalent to a $1.33 \times 8 = 10.6\%$ bond yield.

[37]For more detail, see Appendix 6-1.

[38]*Report of the Royal Commission on Taxation*, Ottawa, Queen's Printer, 1966.

(*b*) On one of these dates the stock price is likely to fall by about the value of the dividend. Which date and why?

(*c*) The stock price in early January was $30. What was the prospective dividend yield?

(*d*) The earnings per share for 1983 were forecast at around $3.00. What was the percentage payout rate?

(*e*) Suppose that in 1983 the company paid a 10% stock dividend. What would be the expected fall in the stock price?

2. Indicate which of the following statements are false:

(*a*) A company may not generally pay a dividend out of paid-up capital.

(*b*) A company may not generally pay a dividend if it is insolvent.

(*c*) Realized capital gains are taxed at the marginal rate of income tax.

(*d*) Corporations are taxed on dividends received.

(*e*) The stock dividend is taxed as income.

3. Between 1964 and 1982 one could explain 80% of the variation in GM's dividend changes by the following equation:

$$DIV_t - DIV_{t-1} = 1.66 + 0.77 \, (0.35 \, EPS_t - DIV_{t-1})$$

What do you think was

(*a*) GM's target payout ratio?

(*b*) The rate at which dividends adjusted toward the target?

4. Refer to the first balance sheet presented for Rational Demiconductor in Section 16-3. Again it uses its cash to pay a $1,000 cash dividend, planning to issue stock to recover the cash required for investment. But this time catastrophe hits before the stock can be issued. A new pollution control regulation increases manufacturing costs to the extent that the value of Rational Demiconductor's existing business is cut in half, to $4,500. The NPV of the new investment opportunity is unaffected, however. Show that dividend policy is still irrelevant.

5. Suppose all investments offered the same expected return *before* tax. Consider two equally risky Canadian shares, Hi and Lo. Hi shares pay a generous dividend and offer low expected capital gains. Lo shares pay low dividends and offer high expected capital gains. Which of the following investors would prefer the Lo shares? Which would prefer the Hi shares? Which wouldn't care? Explain.

(*a*) An individual in a high tax bracket who rarely trades stocks, and who is
   (i) an American resident
   (ii) a Canadian resident.

(*b*) An individual in a low tax bracket who is
   (i) an American resident
   (ii) a Canadian resident.

(*c*) A Canadian pension fund.

(*d*) A Canadian security dealer that is a public corporation.

6. Company X pays a dividend of $10 a share. How much would you expect the price to fall on the ex-dividend date in each of the following cases?

(*a*) The capital market is perfectly competitive and there are no taxes.

(*b*) Each investor is subject to a 10% tax on dividends.

(*c*) Each investor is subject to a 10% tax on dividends and 15% on capital gains, which are realized every year.

7. Prior to 1977, Revenue Canada grossed-up dividends by one-third and had a (federal) dividend tax credit of 20% of grossed-up dividends. What corporate and provincial tax rates is this consistent with?

QUESTIONS AND PROBLEMS

1. Look in a recent issue of *The Financial Post* at "Dividend Notices" and "infoPost" and choose a company reporting a regular dividend.
   (a) How frequently does the company pay a regular dividend?
   (b) What is the amount of the dividend?
   (c) By what date must your stock be registered for you to receive the dividend?
   (d) How many weeks later is the dividend paid?
   (e) Look up the stock price and calculate the annual yield on the stock.

2. Respond to the following comment: "It's all very well saying that I can sell shares to cover cash needs, but that may mean selling at the bottom of the market. If the company pays a regular dividend, investors avoid that risk."

3. "Dividends are the shareholder's wages. Therefore, if a government adopts an income policy that restricts increases in wages, it should in all logic restrict increases in dividends." Does this make sense?

4. How would a government-imposed dividend freeze affect
   (a) Stock prices?
   (b) The volume of capital investment?

5. "Risky companies tend to have lower target payout ratios and more gradual adjustment rates." Explain what is meant by this statement. Why do you think it is so?

6. Consider the following two statements: "Dividend policy is irrelevant." "Stock price is the present value of expected future dividends" (see Chapter 4). They *sound* contradictory. This question is designed to show that they are fully consistent.

   The current price of the shares of Charles River Mining Corporation is $50. Next year's earnings and dividends per share are $4 and $2, respectively. Investors expect perpetual growth at 8% per year. The expected rate of return demanded by investors is $r = 12\%$.

   We can use the perpetual-growth model

   $$P_0 = \frac{DIV_1}{r - g} = \frac{2}{0.12 - 0.08} = 50$$

   Suppose that Charles River Mining announces that it will switch to a 100% payout policy, issuing shares as necessary to finance growth. Use the perpetual-growth model to show that current stock price is unchanged.

7. A shareholder receives $100 in dividends from a Canadian corporation in 1983. Suppose her provincial tax is 38.5% of federal tax. What is the net tax on dividends if her marginal federal tax rate is
   (a) 16%?
   (b) 43%?

8. The expected pretax return on three stocks is divided between dividends and capital gains in the following way:

Stock	Expected Dividend	Expected Capital Gain
A	$0	$10
B	5	5
C	10	0

(*a*) If each stock is priced at $100, what are the expected net returns on each stock to the following investors:

Investor Characteristics	Federal Tax Bracket	Provincial Tax as a Proportion of Federal Tax	Time to Realization of Capital Gain
(i) Pension fund			
(ii) Individual	18%	48%	Indefinite deferral
(iii) Individual	30%	48%	Indefinite deferral
(iv) Individual	30%	48%	One year
(v) American individual	30%		Indefinite deferral

(*b*) Recalculate the expected net returns assuming stock A is priced at $115, B at $100, and C at $90. Other things equal, which stock would be most attractive?

9. How should a pension fund's investment policy be affected by the manager's view of the dividend controversy? Why don't pension fund managers invest only in the very highest yielding stocks? *Note*: The investment returns on pension funds are not taxed.

10. "The stock market, which once valued Texaco at a premium over the other international oils, now assigns it the same multiple it assigns to Exxon. And even that, probably, has more to do with Texaco's high dividend (the yield is currently 7.7%) than it does with Texaco's prospects." (*Forbes*, April 17, 1978.) Is this explanation from *Forbes* plausible?

11. An article on stock repurchase in the *Los Angeles Times* noted that "An increasing number of companies are finding that the best investment they can make these days is in themselves." Discuss this view. How is the desirability of repurchase affected by company prospects and the price of its stock?

12. Adherents of the "dividends-are-good" school have sometimes pointed to the fact that stocks with high yields tend to have above-average price-earnings multiples. Is this evidence convincing? Discuss.

13. For each of the following four groups of companies, state whether you would expect them to distribute a relatively high or low proportion of current earnings and whether you would expect them to have a relatively high or low price-earnings ratio.
(*a*) High-risk companies
(*b*) Companies that have recently experienced an unexpected decline in profits
(*c*) Companies that expect to experience a decline in profits
(*d*) "Growth" companies with valuable future investment opportunities

14. "Many companies use stock repurchase to increase earnings per share. For example, suppose that a company is in the following position:

Net profit	$10 million
Number of shares before repurchase	1 million
Earnings per share	$10
Price-earnings ratio	20
Share price	$200

The company now repurchases 200,000 shares at $200 a share. The number of shares declines to 800,000 shares and the earnings per share increase to $12.50. Assuming the price-earnings ratio stays at 20, the share price must rise to $250.00." Discuss.

15. (a) The Horner Pie Company pays a quarterly dividend of $1. Suppose that the stock price is expected to fall on the ex-dividend date by 90 cents. Would you prefer to buy on the with-dividend date or the ex-dividend date if you were (1) a tax-free investor, (2) an investor with a marginal tax rate of 40% on income (and 16% on capital gains)?

  (b) In a study of ex-dividend behaviour in the United States, Elton and Gruber estimated that the stock price fell on the average by 85% of the dividend. Assuming that the tax rate on capital gains is 40% of the rate on income tax, what does Elton and Gruber's result imply about investors' marginal rate of income tax?

  (c) Elton and Gruber also observed that the ex-dividend price fall was different for high-payout stocks and for low-payout stocks. Which group would you expect to show the larger price fall?

  (d) Would the fact that investors can trade stocks freely around the ex-dividend date alter your interpretation of Elton and Gruber's study?

16. Booth and Johnston studied ex-dividend behaviour of Canadian stocks from 1970 to 1980.

  (a) Their data show that the average price drop in 1972–1976 was 47% of the dividend. In that period, dividends were grossed-up by one-third to get taxable dividends, and the federal dividend tax credit was 20% of the grossed-up dividend. Capital gains were taxed at 50% of the ordinary personal tax rate. Assume that they are realized annually. Suppose the typical investor was in Ontario, where provincial tax was 30.5% of federal tax during 1972–1976. What marginal federal personal tax rate is implied by these data?

  (b) Booth's and Johnston's data showed that, in the 1978–1980 period, the average price drop was 62% of the dividend. In that period, dividends were grossed-up by 50% and the federal dividend tax credit was 25% of the grossed-up dividend. Capital gains were still taxed at 50% of the ordinary income rate, but Ontario tax had risen to 44% of federal tax. What marginal federal personal tax rate is implied by these data?

17. Suppose Canadian lawmakers decided to eliminate all of the 46% corporate tax paid on income used to generate dividends for ordinary firms.

  (a) If provincial personal tax is 47% of federal personal tax, by how much must dividends be grossed-up and what would be the appropriate federal dividend tax credit?

  (b) Given your answer to (a), what would be the appropriate dividend distribution tax if the government wishes to exactly eliminate double taxation for small businesses with a tax rate of 25%?

18. Your firm has declared a cash dividend of $1.00 per share. Some shareholders have elected to receive a stock dividend instead of the cash dividend, and this is to be based on a stock price of $55, which is the average stock price for the five days preceding the payment date. If a shareholder holds 100 shares, how many shares should he or she receive as a stock dividend? (Include fractions of shares.)

19. In setting a stock price to convert cash dividends to stock dividends, some firms use an average stock price from some time interval prior to the ex-dividend date and some use an average stock price from some time interval after the ex-dividend date. Which method treats all shareholders equally from a pretax standpoint? Why?

20. You and your cousins have recently inherited a substantial sum of money and your cousins have come to you for advice regarding how to invest their share. They want to know whether to invest in five-year bonds or high-grade preferred shares. The shares will pay an 8% dividend for each of the next five years, and then will

be redeemed for their initial purchase price. You feel that the risks of the two securities are the same, and that the decision should be made on the basis of tax considerations. Your cousins face the following taxes:

	Federal Tax Bracket	Provincial Tax
Bert	34%	52%
Ernie	16%	52%
Hilda	34%	45%
Elsie	16%	45%

Which bond yields are equivalent to the 8% dividend yield, for each of your four cousins?

DOES DEBT POLICY MATTER?

A firm's basic resource is the stream of cash flows produced by its assets. When the firm is financed entirely by common stock, all those cash flows belong to the stockholders. When it issues both debt and equity securities, it undertakes to split up the cash flows into two streams, a relatively safe stream that goes to the debt holders and a more risky one that goes to the stockholders.

The firm's mix of different securities is known as its **capital structure**. The choice of capital structure is fundamentally a marketing problem. The firm can issue dozens of distinct securities in countless combinations but it attempts to find the particular combination that maximizes its overall market value.

Are these attempts worthwhile? We must consider the possibility that *no* combination has any greater appeal than any other. Perhaps the really important decisions concern the company's assets, and decisions about capital structure are mere details—matters to be attended to but not worried about.

Modigliani and Miller (MM), who showed that dividend policy doesn't matter in perfect capital markets, also showed that financing decisions don't matter in perfect markets.[1] Their famous "Proposition I" states that a firm cannot change the *total* value of its securities just by splitting its cash flows into different streams: the firm's value is determined by its real assets, not by the securities it issues. Thus capital structure is irrelevant as long as the firm's investment decisions are taken as given.

MM's Proposition I allows complete separation of investment and financing decisions. It implies that any firm could use the capital budgeting procedures presented in Chapters 2 to 12. In those chapters we never worried about where the money for capital expenditures comes from. We assumed all-equity financing without really thinking about it. If Proposition I holds, that is exactly the right approach.

We believe that in practice capital structure *does* matter, but we nevertheless devote all of this chapter to MM's argument. If you don't fully understand the conditions under which MM's theory holds, you won't fully understand why one capital structure is better than another. The financial manager needs to know what kinds of market imperfection to look for.

In Chapter 18 we will undertake a detailed analysis of the imperfections that are most likely to make a difference: taxes, the costs of bankruptcy, and the costs of writing

---

[1]MM's paper (F. Modigliani and M.H. Miller, "The Cost of Capital, Corporation Finance and the Theory of Investment," *American Economic Review*, 48:261–297 (June 1958)) was published in 1958, but their basic argument was anticipated in 1938 by J.B. Williams and to some extent by David Durand. See J.B. Williams, *The Theory of Investment Value*, Harvard University Press, Cambridge, Mass., 1938, and D. Durand, "Cost of Debt and Equity Funds for Business: Trends and Problems of Measurement," in *Conference on Research in Business Finance*, National Bureau of Economic Research, New York, 1952. For a simple, straightforward presentation of the theory, see F. Modigliani and M.H. Miller, "Reply to Heins and Sprenkle," *American Economic Review*, 59:592–595 (September 1969).

and enforcing complicated debt contracts. We will also argue that it is naive to suppose that investment and financing decisions can be completely separated.

But in this chapter we isolate the decision about capital structure by holding the decision about investment fixed. We also assume that dividend policy is irrelevant.

17-1 THE EFFECT OF LEVERAGE IN A COMPETITIVE TAX-FREE ECONOMY

We have referred to the firm's choice of capital structure as a *marketing problem*. The financial manager's problem is to find the combination of securities that has the greatest overall appeal to investors—the combination that maximizes the market value of the firm. Before tackling this problem, we ought to make sure that a policy that maximizes firm value also maximizes the wealth of the shareholders.

Let D and E denote the market values of the outstanding debt and equity of the Wapshot Mining Company. Wapshot's 1,000 shares sell for $50 apiece. Thus

$$E = 1,000 \times 50 = \$50,000$$

Wapshot has also borrowed $25,000, and so V, the aggregate market value of all Wapshot's outstanding securities, is

$$V = D + E = \$75,000$$

Wapshot's stock is known as *levered equity*. Its stockholders face the benefits and costs of *financial leverage* or *gearing*. Suppose that Wapshot "levers up" still further by borrowing an additional $10,000 and paying the proceeds out to shareholders as a special dividend of $10 per share. This substitutes debt for equity capital with no impact on Wapshot's assets.

What will Wapshot's equity be worth after the special dividend is paid? We have two unknowns, E and V:

Old debt	$25,000 ⎫	
New debt	$10,000 ⎭ $35,000 = D	
Equity	?	= E
Firm value	?	= V

If V is $75,000 as before, then E must be $V - D = 75,000 - 35,000 = \$40,000$. Stockholders have suffered a capital loss that exactly offsets the $10,000 special dividend. But if V increases to, say, $80,000 as a result of the change in capital structure, then $E = \$45,000$ and the stockholders are $5,000 ahead. In general, any increase or decrease in V caused by a shift in capital structure accrues to the firm's stockholders. We conclude that a policy that maximizes the market value of the firm is also best for the firm's stockholders.

This conclusion rests on two important assumptions: first, that Wapshot can ignore dividend policy and, second, that after the change in capital structure the old and new debt is *worth* $35,000.

Dividend policy is probably relevant but there is no need to repeat the discussion of Chapter 16. We need only note that shifts in capital structure sometimes force important decisions about dividend policy. Perhaps Wapshot's cash dividend has costs that should be weighed against any benefits achieved by its increased financial leverage.

Our second assumption that old and new debt ends up worth $35,000 seems innocuous. But it could be wrong. Perhaps the new borrowing has increased the risk of the old bonds. If the holders of old bonds cannot demand a higher rate of interest to compensate for the increased risk, the value of their investment is reduced. In this case Wapshot's stockholders gain at the expense of the holders of old bonds even though the overall value of the debt and equity is unchanged.

But this anticipates issues better left to Chapter 18. In this chapter we will assume that any issue of debt has no effect on the market value of existing debt.[2]

Enter Modigliani and Miller

Let us accept the notion that the financial manager would like to find the combination of securities that maximizes the value of the firm. How is this done? MM's answer is that the financial manager should stop worrying: in a perfect market any combination of securities is as good as another. The value of the firm is unaffected by its choice of capital structure.

You can see this by imagining two firms that generate the same stream of operating income and differ only in their capital structure. Firm U is unlevered. Therefore the total value of its equity E_U is the same as the total value of the firm V_U. Firm L, on the other hand, is levered. The value of its stock is, therefore, equal to the value of the firm less the value of the debt: $E_L = V_L - D_L$.

Now think which of these firms you would prefer to invest in. If you don't want to take much risk, you can buy common stock in the unlevered firm U. For example, if you buy 1% of firm U's shares, your investment is $0.01\ V_U$ and you are entitled to 1% of the gross profits:

Dollar Investment	Dollar Return
$0.01\ V_U$	0.01 Profits

Now compare this with an alternative strategy. This is to purchase the same fraction of both the debt and the equity of firm L. Your investment and return would then be as follows:

	Dollar Investment	Dollar Return
Debt	$0.01\ D_L$	0.01 Interest
Equity	$0.01\ E_L$	0.01 (Profits − interest)
Total	$0.01\ (D_L + E_L)$ $= 0.01\ V_L$	0.01 Profits

Both strategies offer the same payoff: 1% of the firm's profits. In well-functioning markets two investments that offer the same payoff must have the same cost. Therefore 0.01 V_U must equal 0.01 V_L: the value of the unlevered firm must equal the value of the levered firm.

Suppose that you are willing to run a little more risk. You decide to buy 1% of the outstanding shares in the *levered* firm. Your investment and return are now as follows:

---

[2]See E.F. Fama, "The Effects of a Firm's Investment and Financing Decisions," *American Economic Review*, **68**:272–284 (June 1978), for a rigorous analysis of the conditions under which a policy of maximizing the value of the firm is also best for the stockholders.

Dollar Investment	Dollar Return
$0.01\ E_L$ $= 0.01\ (V_L - D_L)$	$0.01\ (\text{Profits} - \text{interest})$

But there is an alternative strategy. This is to borrow $0.01\ D_L$ on your own account and purchase 1% of the stock of the *unlevered* firm. In this case, your borrowing gives you an immediate cash *inflow* of $0.01\ D_L$, but you have to pay interest on your loan equal to 1% of the interest that is paid by firm L. Your total investment and return are, therefore, as follows:

	Dollar Investment	Dollar Return
Borrowing	$-0.01\ D_L$	-0.01 Interest
Equity	$0.01\ V_U$	0.01 Profits
Total	$0.01\ (V_U - D_L)$	$0.01\ (\text{Profits} - \text{interest})$

Again both strategies offer the same payoff: 1% of profits, after interest. Therefore, both investments must have the same cost. The quantity $0.01\ (V_U - D_L)$ must equal $0.01\ (V_L - D_L)$ and V_U must equal V_L.

It does not matter whether the world is full of cautious investors, incautious investors, or a mixture of each. All would agree that the value of the unlevered firm U must be equal to the value of the levered firm L. As long as investors can borrow or lend on their own account on the same terms as the firm, they can "undo" the effect of any changes in the firm's capital structure. This is the basis for MM's famous Proposition I: "The market value of any firm is independent of its capital structure."

The Law of the Conservation of Value

MM's argument that debt policy is irrelevant is an application of an astonishingly simple idea. If we have two streams of cash flow, A and B, then the present value of $A + B$ is equal to the present value of A plus the present value of B. We met this principal of *value additivity* in our discussion of capital budgeting, where we saw that in perfect capital markets the present value of two assets combined is equal to the sum of their present values considered separately.

In the present context we are not combining assets, but splitting them up. But value additivity works just as well in reverse. We can slice a cash flow into as many parts as we like; the values of the parts will always sum back to the value of the unsliced stream. (Of course, we have to make sure that none of the stream is lost in the slicing. We cannot say, "The value of a pie is independent of how it is sliced," if the slicer is also a nibbler.)

This is really a *law of conservation of value*. The value of an asset is preserved regardless of the nature of the claims against it. Thus Proposition I: firm value is determined on the *left-hand* side of its balance sheet by real assets—not by the proportions of debt and equity securities issued by the firm.

The simplest ideas often have the widest application. For example, we could apply the law of conservation of value to the choice between issuing preferred stock, common stock, or some combination. The law implies that the choice is irrelevant, assuming perfect capital markets and providing that the choice does not affect the firm's investment, borrowing, and operating policies. If the total value of the equity "pie" (preferred and common combined) is fixed, the firm's owners (its common stockholders) do not care how this pie is sliced.

The law also applies to the *mix* of debt securities issued by the firm. The choices of long-term versus short-term, secured versus unsecured, senior versus subordinated, and convertible versus non-convertible debt all should have no effect on the overall value of the firm.

Combining assets and splitting them up will not affect values as long as they do not affect an investor's choice. When we showed that capital structure does not affect choice, we implicitly assumed that both companies and individuals can borrow and lend at the same risk-free rate of interest. As long as this is so, individuals can "undo" the effect of any changes in the firm's capital structure.

In practice, corporate debt is not risk-free and firms cannot escape with rates of interest appropriate to a government security. Some people's initial reaction is that this alone invalidates MM's proposition. It is a natural mistake, but capital structure can be irrelevant even when debt is risky.

If a company borrows money, it does not *guarantee* repayment: it repays the debt in full only if its assets are worth more than the debt obligation. The shareholders in the company, therefore, have limited liability.

Many individuals would like to borrow with limited liability. They might, therefore, be prepared to pay a small premium for levered shares *if the supply of levered shares was insufficient to meet their needs.*[3] But there are literally thousands of common stocks of companies that borrow. Therefore it is unlikely that an issue of debt would induce them to pay a premium for *your* shares.[4]

An Example of Proposition I

Macbeth Spot Removers is reviewing its capital structure. Table 17-1 shows its current position. The company has no leverage and all the operating income is paid as dividends to the common stockholders (we assume still that there are no taxes). The expected earnings and dividends per share are $1.50, but this figure is by no means certain—it

Table 17-1 Macbeth Spot Removers is entirely equity-financed. Although it *expects* to have an income of $1,500 a year in perpetuity, this income is not certain. This table shows the return to the stockholder under different assumptions about operating incomes. We assume no taxes.

Data				
Number of shares	1,000			
Price per share	$10			
Market value of shares	$10,000			

Outcomes				
Operating income, dollars	500	1,000	**1,500**	2,000
Earnings per share, dollars	0.50	1.00	**1.50**	2.00
Return on shares, %	5	10	**15**	20
			Expected outcome	

[3]Of course individuals could *create* limited liability if they chose. In other words, the lender could agree that borrowers need repay their debt in full only if the assets of company X are worth more than a certain amount. Presumably individuals don't enter into such arrangements because they can obtain limited liability more simply by investing in the stocks of levered companies.

[4]Capital structure is also irrelevant if each investor holds a fully diversified portfolio. In that case he or she owns all the risky securities offered by a company (both debt and equity). But anybody who owns *all* the risky securities doesn't care about how the cash flows are divided between different securities.

could turn out to be more or less than $1.50. The price of each share is $10. Since the firm expects to produce a level stream of earnings in perpetuity, the expected return on the share is equal to the earnings-price ratio, $1.50/10.00 = 15\%$.[5]

Ms. Macbeth, the firm's president, has come to the conclusion that shareholders would be better off if the company had equal proportions of debt and equity. She therefore proposes to issue $5,000 of debt at an interest rate of 10% and use the proceeds to repurchase 500 shares. To support her proposal, Ms. Macbeth has analysed the situation under different assumptions about operating income. The results of her calculations are shown in Table 17-2.

Table 17-2   Macbeth Spot Removers is wondering whether to issue $5,000 of debt at an interest rate of 10% and repurchase 500 shares. This table shows the return to the shareholder under different assumptions about operating income.

Data				
Number of shares	500			
Price per share	$10			
Market value of shares	$5,000			
Market value of debt	$5,000			

Outcomes				
Operating income, dollars	500	1,000	1,500	2,000
Interest, dollars	500	500	500	500
Equity earnings, dollars	0	500	1,000	1,500
Earnings per share, dollars	0	1	2	3
Return on shares, %	0	10	20	30
Return on debt, %	10	10	10	10
			Expected outcome	

In order to see more clearly how leverage would affect earnings per share, Ms. Macbeth has also produced Figure 17-1. The solid line shows how earnings per share would vary with operating income under the firm's current all-equity financing. It is, therefore, simply a plot of the data in Table 17-1. The dotted line shows how earnings per share would vary given equal proportions of debt and equity. It is, therefore, a plot of the data in Table 17-2.

Ms. Macbeth reasons as follows: "It is clear that the effect of leverage depends on the company's income. If income is greater than $1,000, the return to the equity holder is *increased* by leverage. If it is less than $1,000, the return is *reduced* by leverage. The return is unaffected when operating income is exactly $1,000. At this point the return on the market value of the assets is 10%, which is exactly equal to the interest rate on the debt. Our capital structure decision, therefore, boils down to what we think about income prospects. Since we expect operating income to be above the $1,000 break-even point, I believe we can best help our shareholders by going ahead with the $5,000 debt issue."

As financial manager of Macbeth Spot Removers, you reply as follows: "I agree that leverage will help the shareholder as long as our income is greater than $1,000. But your argument ignores the fact that Macbeth's shareholders have the alternative of borrowing on their own account. For example, suppose that a person borrows $10 and then invests $20 in two unlevered Macbeth shares. This person has to put up only $10

---

[5]See Chapter 4, Section 3.

of his or her own money. The payoff on the investment varies with Macbeth's operating income, as shown in Table 17-3. This is exactly the same set of payoffs as the investor would get by buying one share in the levered company. Therefore a share in the levered company must also sell for $10. If Macbeth goes ahead and borrows, it will not allow investors to do anything that they could not do already, and so it will not increase value."

The argument that you are using is exactly the same as MM used to prove Proposition I.

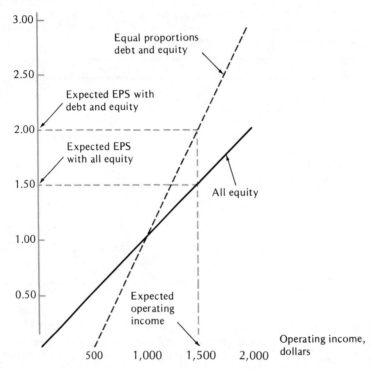

Figure 17-1 Borrowing increases Macbeth's EPS (earnings per share) when operating income is greater than $1,000 and reduces EPS when operating income is less than $1,000. Expected EPS rise from $1.50 to $2.

Table 17-3 Individual investors can replicate Macbeth's leverage.

	Operating Income, Dollars			
	˒500	1,000	1,500	2,000
Earnings on two shares, dollars	1	2	3	4
Less interest at 10%, dollars	1	1	1	1
Net earnings on investment, dollars	0	1	2	3
Return on $10 investment, %	0	10	20	30
			Expected outcome	

17-2 HOW LEVERAGE AFFECTS RETURNS

Implications of Proposition I

Consider now the implications of Proposition I for the expected returns on Macbeth stock:

	Current Structure: All Equity	Proposed Structure: Equal Debt and Equity
Expected earnings per share	$1.50	$2.00
Price per share	$10.00	$10.00
Expected return on share, %	15	20

Leverage increases the expected stream of earnings per share, but *not* the share price. The reason is that the change in the expected earnings stream is exactly offset by a change in the rate at which the earnings are capitalized. The expected return on the share (which for a perpetuity is equal to the earnings-price ratio) increases from 15% to 20%. We now show how this comes about.

The expected return on a firm's assets r_A is equal to the expected operating income divided by the total market value of the firm's securities:

$$\text{Expected return on assets} = r_A = \frac{\text{expected operating income}}{\text{market value of all securities}}$$

We have seen that in perfect capital markets the company's borrowing decision does not affect *either* the firm's operating income *or* the total market value of its securities. Therefore the borrowing decision also does not affect the expected return on the firm's assets r_A.

Suppose that an investor holds all of a company's debt and all its equity. This investor would be entitled to all the firm's operating income; therefore, the expected return on the portfolio would be equal to r_A.

The expected return on a portfolio is equal to a weighted average of the expected returns on the individual holdings. Therefore the expected return on a portfolio consisting of *all* the firm's securities is

$$\begin{pmatrix}\text{Expected return} \\ \text{on assets}\end{pmatrix} = \left(\begin{matrix}\text{proportion} \\ \text{in debt}\end{matrix} \times \begin{matrix}\text{expected} \\ \text{return on} \\ \text{debt}\end{matrix}\right) + \left(\begin{matrix}\text{proportion} \\ \text{in equity}\end{matrix} \times \begin{matrix}\text{expected} \\ \text{return on} \\ \text{equity}\end{matrix}\right)$$

$$r_A = \left(\frac{D}{D+E} \times r_D\right) + \left(\frac{E}{D+E} \times r_E\right)$$

We can rearrange this equation to obtain an expression for r_E, the expected return on the equity of a levered firm:

$$\begin{matrix}\text{Expected return} \\ \text{on equity}\end{matrix} = \begin{matrix}\text{expected} \\ \text{return on} \\ \text{assets}\end{matrix} + \begin{matrix}\text{debt-} \\ \text{equity} \\ \text{ratio}\end{matrix} \times \left(\begin{matrix}\text{expected} \\ \text{return on} \\ \text{assets}\end{matrix} - \begin{matrix}\text{expected} \\ \text{return on} \\ \text{debt}\end{matrix}\right)$$

$$r_E = r_A + \frac{D}{E}(r_A - r_D)$$

Proposition II

This is MM's Proposition II: the expected rate of return on the common stock of a levered firm increases in proportion to the debt-equity ratio (D/E), expressed in market values; the rate of increase depends on the spread between r_A, the expected rate of return on a portfolio of all the firm's securities, and r_D, the expected return on the debt. Note that $r_E = r_A$ if the firm has no debt.

We can check out this formula for Macbeth Spot Removers. Before the decision to borrow

$$r_E = r_A = \frac{\text{expected operating income}}{\text{market value of all securities}}$$

$$= \frac{1,500}{10,000} = 0.15, \text{ or } 15\%$$

If the firm goes ahead with its plan to borrow, the expected return on assets r_A is still 15%. The expected return on equity is

$$r_E = r_A + \frac{D}{E}(r_A - r_D)$$

$$= 0.15 + \frac{5,000}{5,000}(0.15 - 0.10)$$

$$= 0.20, \text{ or } 20\%$$

The general implications of MM's Proposition II are shown in Figure 17-2. The figure assumes that the firm's bonds are essentially risk-free at low debt levels. Thus r_D is independent of D/E and r_E increases linearly as D/E increases. As the firm borrows more, the risk of default increases and the firm is required to pay higher rates of interest. Proposition II predicts that when this occurs the rate of increase in r_E slows down. This

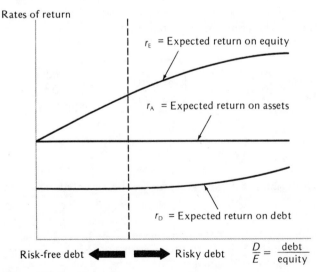

Figure 17-2 MM's Proposition II. The expected return on equity r_E increases linearly with the debt-equity ratio so long as debt is risk-free. But if leverage increases the risk of the debt, debt holders demand a higher return on the debt. This causes the rate of increase in r_E to slow down.

is also shown in Figure 17-2. The more debt the firm has, the less sensitive r_E is to further borrowing.

Why does this happen? Essentially because holders of risky debt bear some of the firm's business risk. As the firm borrows more, more of that risk is transferred from stockholders to bondholders.

The Risk-Return Trade-off

Proposition I says that financial leverage has no effect on shareholders' wealth. Proposition II says that the rate of return they can expect to receive on their shares increases as the firm's debt-equity ratio increases. How can shareholders be indifferent to increased leverage when it increases expected return? Any increase in expected return is exactly offset by an increase in risk and therefore in shareholders' *required* rate of return.

Look at what happens to the risk of Macbeth shares if it moves to equal debt-equity proportions. Table 17-4 shows how a shortfall in operating income affects the payoff to the shareholders.

Table 17-4 Leverage increases the risk of Macbeth shares.

		Operating Income	
		$500	$1,500
All equity:	Earnings per share, dollars	0.50	1.50
	Return on shares, %	5	15
50% debt:	Earnings per share, dollars	0	2.00
	Return on shares, %	0	20

You can see that the debt-equity proportion does not affect the *dollar* risk borne by equity holders. Suppose operating income drops from $1,500 to $500. Under all-equity financing, equity earnings drop by $1 per share. There are 1,000 outstanding shares, and so *total* equity earnings fall by $1 × 1,000 = $1,000. With 50% debt, the same drop in operating income reduces earnings per share by $2. But there are only 500 shares outstanding, and so total equity income drops by $2 × 500 = $1,000, just as in the all-equity case.

However, the debt-equity choice does amplify the spread of *percentage* returns. If the firm is all-equity-financed, a decline of $1,000 in the operating income reduces the return on the shares by 10%. If the firm issues risk-free debt with a fixed interest payment of $500 a year, then a decline of $1,000 in the operating income reduces the return on the shares by 20%. In other words, the effect of leverage is to double the amplitude of the swings in Macbeth's shares. Whatever the beta of the firm's shares before the refinancing, it would be 'twice as high afterwards.

Just as the expected return on the firm's assets is a weighted average of the expected return on the individual securities, so likewise is the beta of the firm's assets a weighted average of the betas of the individual securities.[6]

$$\text{Beta of atlas} = \left(\begin{array}{c} \text{proportion} \\ \text{of debt} \end{array} \times \begin{array}{c} \text{beta of} \\ \text{debt} \end{array} \right) + \left(\begin{array}{c} \text{proportion} \\ \text{of equity} \end{array} \times \begin{array}{c} \text{beta of} \\ \text{equity} \end{array} \right)$$

$$\beta_A = \left(\frac{D}{D + E} \times \beta_D \right) + \left(\frac{E}{D + E} \times \beta_E \right)$$

---

[6]This equation should look familiar. We used it in Section 9-3 to work out how a change in leverage would affect the beta of Philadelphia Electric stock.

We can rearrange this equation to obtain an expression for β_E, the expected return on the equity of a levered firm:

$$\text{Beta of equity} = \frac{\text{beta of}}{\text{assets}} + \frac{\text{debt-equity}}{\text{ratio}} \times \left(\frac{\text{beta of}}{\text{assets}} - \frac{\text{beta of}}{\text{debt}} \right)$$

$$\beta_E = \beta_A + \frac{D}{E}(\beta_A - \beta_D)$$

Now you can see why investors require higher returns on levered equity. The required return simply rises to match the increased risk.

In Figure 17-3 we have plotted the expected returns and the risk of Macbeth's securities, assuming that the interest on the debt is risk-free.[7]

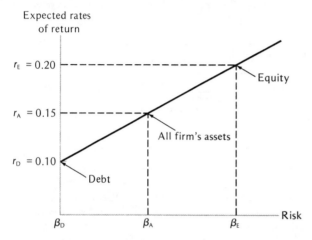

Figure 17-3   If Macbeth is unlevered, the expected return on its equity equals the expected return on its assets. Leverage increases both the expected return on equity (r_E) and the risk of equity (β_E).

17-3   THE TRADITIONAL POSITION

What did financial experts think about debt policy before MM? It is not easy to say because with hindsight we see that they did not think too clearly.[8] However, a "traditional" position has emerged in response to MM. In order to understand it, we have to discuss the **weighted average cost of capital**.

The expected return on a portfolio of all the company's securities is often referred to as the *weighted average cost of capital*:[9]

$$\text{Weighted average cost of capital} = r_A = \left(\frac{D}{V} \times r_D \right) + \left(\frac{E}{V} \times r_E \right)$$

---

[7] In this case $\beta_D = 0$ and $\beta_E = \beta_A + (D/E)\beta_A$.

[8] Financial economists in the year 2000 may remark on BMSW's blind spots and clumsy reasoning. On the other hand, they may not remember us at all.

[9] Remember that in this chapter we ignore taxes. In Chapter 19, we shall see that the weighted average cost of capital formula needs to be amended when debt interest can be deducted from taxable profits.

The weighted average cost of capital is used in capital budgeting decisions to find the net present value of projects that would not change the business risk of the firm.

For example, suppose that a firm has $2 million of outstanding debt and 100,000 outstanding shares selling at $30 per share. Its current borrowing rate is 8% and the financial manager thinks that the stock is priced to offer a 15% return, therefore $r_E = 0.15$. (The hard part is estimating r_E, of course.) This is all we need to calculate the weighted average cost of capital:

D = $2 million
E = 100,000 shares $\times$ $30 per share = $3 million

$$\text{Weighted average cost of capital} = \left(\frac{D}{V} \times r_D\right) + \left(\frac{E}{V} \times r_E\right)$$

$$\left(\frac{2}{5} \times 0.08\right) + \left(\frac{3}{5} \times 0.15\right)$$

$$= 0.122, \text{ or } 12.2\%$$

Note that we are still assuming that Proposition I holds. If it doesn't, we can't use this simple weighted average as the discount rate even for projects that do not change the firm's business "risk class." As we will see in Chapter 19, the weighted average cost of capital is at best a starting point for setting discount rates.

Two Warnings

Sometimes the objective in financing decisions is stated not as "maximize overall market value" but as "minimize the weighted average cost of capital." These are equivalent objectives under the simplifying assumptions we have made so far. If MM's Proposition I does *not* hold, then the capital structure that maximizes the value of the firm also minimizes the weighted average cost of capital, *provided* that operating income is independent of capital structure. Remember that the weighted average cost of capital equals the expected operating income divided by the market value of all securities. Anything that increases the value of the firm reduces the weighted average cost of capital if operating income is constant. But if operating income is varying too, all bets are off.

In Chapter 18 we will show that financial leverage can affect operating income in several ways. Therefore maximizing the value of the firm is *not* always equivalent to minimizing the weighted average cost of capital.

Warning 1 Shareholders want management to increase the firm's value. They are more interested in being rich than in owning a firm with a low weighted average cost of capital.

Warning 2 Trying to minimize the weighted average cost of capital seems to encourage logical short circuits like the following. Suppose that someone says: "Shareholders demand—and deserve—higher expected rates of return than bondholders do. Therefore debt is the cheaper capital source. We can reduce the weighted average cost of capital by borrowing more." But this doesn't follow if the extra borrowing leads stockholders to demand a still higher expected rate of return. According to MM's Proposition II, the "cost of equity capital" r_E increases by just enough to keep the weighted average cost of capital constant.

This is not the only logical short circuit you are likely to encounter. We have cited two more in question 5 at the end of this chapter.

Rates of Return on Levered Equity—The Traditional Position

You may ask why we have even mentioned the weighted average cost of capital at this point if it is often wrong or confusing as a financial objective. We had to because the traditionalists accept this objective and argue their case in terms of it.

The logical short circuit we just described rested on the assumption that r_E, the expected rate of return demanded by stockholders, does not rise as the firm borrows more. Suppose, just for the sake of argument, that this is true. Then r_A, the weighted average cost of capital, must decline as the debt-equity ratio rises.

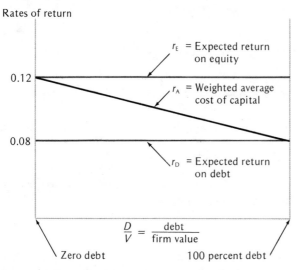

Figure 17-4 If the expected rate of return demanded by stockholders r_E is unaffected by financial leverage, then the weighted average cost of capital r_A declines as the firm borrows more. At 100% debt r_A equals the borrowing rate r_D. Of course this is an absurd and totally unrealistic case.

Take Figure 17-4, for example, which is drawn on the assumption that shareholders demand 12% no matter how much debt the firm has, and that bondholders always want 8%. The weighted average cost of capital starts at 12% and ends up at eight. Suppose that this firm's operating income is a level, perpetual stream of $100,000 a year. Then firm value starts at

$$V = \frac{100,000}{0.12} = \$833,333$$

and ends up at

$$V = \frac{100,000}{0.08} = \$1,250,000$$

The gain of $416,667 falls into the stockholders' pockets.[10]

---

[10]Note that Figure 17-4 relates r_E and r_D to D/V, the ratio of debt to firm value, rather than to the debt-equity ratio D/E. In this figure we wanted to show what happens when the firm is 100% debt-financed. At that point $E = 0$ and D/E is infinite.

Of course this is absurd: a firm that reaches 100% debt *has to be bankrupt*. If there is *any* chance that the firm could remain solvent, then the equity retains some value, and the firm cannot be 100% debt-financed. (Remember that we are working with the *market* values of debt and equity.)

But if the firm is bankrupt and its original shares are worthless pieces of paper, then its lenders *are* its new shareholders. The firm is back to all-equity financing! We assumed that the original stockholders demanded 12%—why should the new ones demand any less? They have to bear all of the firm's business risk. [11]

The situation described in Figure 17-4 is just impossible. [12] However, it is possible to stake out a position somewhere *between* Figures 17-3 and 17-4. That is exactly what the traditionalists have done. Their hypothesis is shown in Figure 17-5. They hold that a moderate degree of financial leverage may increase the expected equity return r_E although not to the degree predicted by MM's Proposition II. But irresponsible firms that borrow *excessively* find r_E shooting up faster than MM predict. Consequently, the weighted average cost of capital r_A declines at first, then rises. Its minimum point is the point of optimal capital structure. Remember than minimizing r_A is equivalent to maximizing overall firm value if, as the traditionalists assume, operating income is unaffected by borrowing.

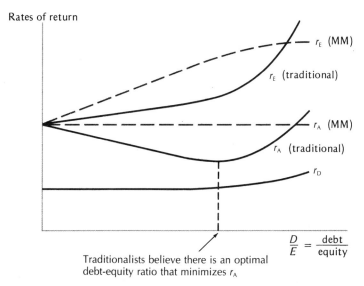

Figure 17-5   The dashed lines show MM's view of the effect of leverage on the expected return on equity r_E and the weighted average cost of capital r_A. The solid lines show the traditional view. Traditionalists say that borrowing at first increases r_E more slowly than MM predict but that r_E shoots up with excessive borrowing. If so, the weighted average cost of capital can be minimized if you use just the right amount of debt.

---

[11]We ignore the costs, delays, and other complications of bankruptcy. They are discussed in Chapter 18.

[12]This case is often termed the *net-income* (NI) approach because investors are assumed to capitalize income *after* interest at the same rate regardless of financial leverage. In contrast, MM's approach is a net-operating-income (NOI) approach, because the value of the firm is fundamentally determined by operating income, the total dollar return to *both* bondholders and stockholders. This distinction was emphasized by Durand in his important, pre-MM paper (op. cit.).

Two arguments might be advanced in support of the traditional position. First, it could be that investors don't notice or appreciate the financial risk created by "moderate" borrowing, although they wake up when debt is "excessive." If so, investors in moderately leveraged firms may accept a lower rate of return than they really should.

That seems naive.[13] The second argument is better. It accepts MM's reasoning as applied to perfect capital markets, but holds that actual markets are imperfect. Imperfections may allow firms that borrow to provide a valuable service for investors. If so, levered shares might trade at premium prices compared to their theoretical values in perfect markets.

Suppose that corporations can borrow more cheaply than individuals. Then it would pay investors who want to borrow to do so indirectly by holding the stock of levered firms. They would be willing to live with expected rates of return that do not fully compensate them for the business and financial risk they bear.

Is corporate borrowing really cheaper? It's hard to say. Interest rates on home mortgages are not too different from rates on high-grade corporate bonds.[14] Rates on margin debt (borrowing from a stockbroker with the investor's shares tendered as security) are not too different from the rates firms pay banks for short-term loans.

There are some individuals who face relatively high interest rates, largely because of the costs lenders incur in making and servicing small loans. There are economies of scale in borrowing. A group of small investors could do better by borrowing via a corporation, in effect pooling their loans and saving transaction costs.[15]

But suppose that this class of investors is large, both in number and in the aggregate wealth it brings to capital markets. Shouldn't the investors' needs be fully satisfied by the thousands of levered firms already existing? Is there really an unsatisfied clientele of small investors standing ready to pay a premium for one more firm that borrows?

Maybe the market for corporate leverage is like the market for automobiles. Americans need millions of automobiles and are willing to pay thousands of dollars apiece for them. But that doesn't mean that you could strike it rich by going into the automobile business. You're at least 50 years too late.

Where to Look for Violations of MM's Propositions

MM's propositions depend on perfect capital markets. Here we are using the phrase *perfect capital markets* a bit loosely, for scholars have argued about the *degree* of perfection necessary for Proposition I. (We remember an off-the-cuff comment made many years ago by Ezra Solomon: "A perfect capital market should be *defined* as one in which the MM theory holds.")

We believe capital markets are generally well-functioning, but they are not 100% perfect 100% of the time. Therefore, MM must be wrong some times in some places. The financial manager's problem is to figure out when and where.

That is not easy. Just finding market imperfections is insufficient.

---

[13]The first argument may reflect a confusion between financial risk and the risk of default. Default is not a serious threat when borrowing is moderate; stockholders worry about it only when the firm goes "too far." But stockholders bear financial risk—in the form of increased volatility of rate of return and higher beta—even when the chance of default is nil. We demonstrated this in Figure 17-3.

[14]One of the authors once obtained a home mortgage at a rate one-half percentage point *less* than the contemporaneous yield on long-term AT&T bonds.

[15]Even here there are alternatives to borrowing on personal account. Investors can draw down their savings accounts or sell a portion of their invesment in bonds. The impact of reductions in lending on the investor's balance sheet and risk position is exactly the same as increases in borrowing.

Consider the traditionalists' claim that imperfections make borrowing costly and inconvenient for many individuals. That creates a clientele for whom corporate borrowing is better than personal borrowing. That clientele would, in principle, be willing to pay a premium for the shares of a levered firm.

But maybe they don't *have* to pay a premium. Perhaps smart financial managers long ago recognized this clientele and shifted the capital structures of their firms to meet its needs. The shifts would not have been difficult or costly to make. But if the clientele is now satisfied it is no longer willing to pay a premium for levered shares. Only the financial managers who *first* recognized the clientele extracted any advantage from it.

Today's Unsatisfied Clienteles are Probably Interested in Exotic Securities

So far we have made little progress in identifying cases where firm value might plausibly depend on financing. But our examples illustrate what smart financial managers look for. They look for an *unsatisfied* clientele, investors who want a particular kind of financial instrument but because of market imperfections can't get it or can't get it cheaply.

MM's Proposition I is violated when the firm, by imaginative design of its capital structure, can offer some *financial service* that meets the needs of such a clientele. Either the service must be new and unique, or the firm must find a way to provide some old service more cheaply than other firms or financial intermediaries can.

Now, is there an unsatisfied clientele for garden-variety debt or levered equity? We doubt it. But perhaps you can invent an exotic security and uncover a latent demand for it.

AT&T's Stillborn Savings Bonds

On October 9, 1970, a front-page article appeared in *The Wall Street Journal* with the headline "AT&T Mulls Offering Ma Bell Savings Bonds Similar to Treasury's." The reporter quoted "sources" at AT&T who described the terms of the possible issue. The bonds would be sold directly to investors in $100 denominations through 2,000 AT&T business offices. They would yield at least 6.5%. Investors would not receive cash interest payments. Instead, the value of the bonds would appreciate over time, in the same way that a savings deposit grows when you leave the interest to accumulate. Thus, at a 6.5% yield you might purchase a ten-year bond for $100 and ten years later cash it in for

$$\text{Future value} = \$100(1.065)^{10} = \$187.71$$

This was an almost exact copy of a United States savings bond, except that the interest rate was higher. At the time, United States savings bonds offered only 5%, or 5.5% if held for a full ten years.[16]

AT&T's motives were clear. It borrows billions of dollars yearly, and at that time its newly issued bonds were yielding about 8.6%. Borrowing at 6.5% would have been a big improvement.

---

[16]In this respect, United States savings bonds differ from Canada Savings Bonds, for owners of CSBs can allow their interest to compound as in the United States or can receive regular coupon payments. Bonds that do not pay regular coupons are called **discount bonds**. Some investment dealers in the United States and Canada now buy government bonds, clip off the coupons, and repackage the parts as **strip bonds**, which are mini-bonds that make cash payments at their maturity only. These discount bonds are discussed in Section 21-2.

And there was a natural market for AT&T savings bonds, an unsatisfied clientele of investors who found it difficult to take advantage of the high yields offered in the bond market. Even the most conservative investor could obtain a 7.3% yield in seven-year United States notes: corporate bonds yielded 8% and up.

Yet there were billions of dollars on deposit in bank savings accounts and savings and loan associations. The *maximum* rate offered on these accounts was 6% on deposits committed for a two-year period. Most of the deposits yielded only about 5%.

Why didn't depositors cash in and invest in bonds? Many of them did.[17] But many did not, partly from inertia and unfamiliarity with the bond market, and partly because buying bonds is inconvenient if you only have a few hundred or a few thousand dollars to invest. The minimum denomination for a corporate bond is $1,000. Ten thousand dollars is more common.

AT&T savings bonds would have offered such investors an easy, convenient way to earn 6.5% or more. At the same time it would have saved AT&T a lot of money. It was a great idea.

What created this opportunity? What explained the spread between bond rates and yields on savings accounts? The most important cause was restrictions imposed by the United States government on interest rates offered to small investors.[18] The government was trying to protect savings institutions by limiting competition for their depositors' money. The fear was that depositors would run off in search for higher yields, causing a cash drain that savings institutions would not be able to meet, cutting off the supply of funds from those institutions for new real estate mortgages, and knocking the housing market for a loop. The savings institutions could not compete by offering higher interest rates on deposits—even if the government had allowed them to—because most of their past deposits had been locked up in fixed-rate mortgages issued when interest rates were lower.

These regulations helped the savings institutions, and may have helped the housing market, but they were grossly unjust to small investors, who lost billions in interest income. We have never been able to understand why there was no political pressure to compensate small investors for the cost of these restrictions, or why consumer advocates never took up the small investor's cause.

Anyway, it was no surprise to find both savings institutions and the federal government arrayed against AT&T's plan. AT&T capitulated and its idea died a quiet death.

But if we believe the idea would have worked, then we have found a counter-example to MM's Proposition I. AT&T could have increased its overall market value by issuing savings bonds rather than garden-variety debt and equity.

The most serious market imperfections often are those created and protected by government. Yet even the restrictions on savings accounts yields have weakened over time. More and more investors have switched into corporate and government bonds. United States banks and savings institutions have gradually raised rates offered to investors willing to salt their money away for a few years. They compete for regular deposits by offering extra services in lieu of higher interest rates, and offer so-called NOW accounts, which are essentially interest-bearing chequing accounts. Some savings banks offer "free gifts"—toasters, radios, hair dryers—to new depositors.

In the 1970s "money market funds" were invented. They are mutual funds invested in Treasury bills, commercial paper, and other high-grade, short-term debt instruments.

---

[17]This is called *disintermediation* (probably the longest word in this book). The investor who withdraws funds from a savings account and invests directly in securities is reducing the role of financial intermediation. The intermediary (the savings institution) is no longer used as a vehicle for investment.

[18]In the United States, this was called Regulation Q. Canada also had ceilings on the interest rates that banks could pay small depositors, but dropped them several years before the erosion of Regulation Q in the United States.

Any saver with a few thousand dollars to invest can gain access to these instruments through a money fund, yet the investor can withdraw funds anytime by writing a cheque against his or her money-fund balance. These money market funds have become enormously popular. By mid-1983, their assets had increased to about $170 billion in the United States. (Money market funds are not needed in Canada, because banks and other savings institutions can offer money market rates of interest to their depositors.)

In short, there are many more options open to the small investor now than there were in 1970. AT&T's savings bonds might work today, but the clientele who would want them has eroded. If *you* ever find an unsatisfied clientele, do something about it right away, or capital markets will evolve and steal it from you.

17-4 SUMMARY

At the start of this chapter we characterized the firm's financing decision as a marketing problem. Think of the financial manager as taking all of the firm's real assets and selling them to investors as a package of securities. Some financial managers choose the simplest package possible: all-equity financing. Some end up issuing dozens of debt and equity securities. The problem is to find the particular combination that maximizes the market value of the firm.

Modigliani and Miller's (MM's) famous Proposition I states that no combination is better than any other—that the firm's overall market value (the value of all its securities) is independent of capital structure. Firms that borrow do offer investors a more complex menu of securities, but investors yawn in response. The menu is redundant. Any shift in capital structure can be duplicated or "undone" by investors. Why should they pay extra for borrowing indirectly (by holding shares in a levered firm) when they can borrow just as easily and cheaply on their own accounts?

MM agree that borrowing increases the expected rate of return on shareholders' investment. But it also increases the risk of the firm's shares. MM show that the risk increase exactly offsets the increase in expected return, leaving stockholders no better or worse off.

Proposition I is an extremely general result. It applies not just to the debt-equity trade-off but to *any* choice of financing instruments. For example, MM would say that the choice between long-term and short-term debt has no effect on firm value.

The formal proofs of Proposition I all depend on the assumption of perfect capital markets.[19] MM's opponents, the "traditionalists," argue that market imperfections make personal borrowing excessively costly, risky, and inconvenient for some investors. This creates a natural clientele willing to pay a premium for shares of levered firms. The traditionalists say that firms should borrow to realize the premium.

But this argument is incomplete. There may be a clientele for levered equity, but that is not enough; the clientele has to be *unsatisfied*. There are already thousands of levered firms available for investment. Is there still an unsatiated clientele for garden-variety debt and equity? We doubt it.

Proposition I is violated when financial managers find an untapped demand and satisfy it by issuing something new and different. The argument between MM and the traditionalists finally boils down to whether this is difficult or easy. We lean toward MM's view: finding unsatisfied clienteles and designing exotic securities to meet their needs is a game that's fun to play but hard to win.

---

[19]Proposition I can be proved umpteen different ways. The references at the end of this chapter include several more abstract and general proofs. Our formal proofs have been limited to MM's own arguments and (in the appendix) a proof based on the capital asset pricing model.

FURTHER READING

The pioneering work on the theory of capital structure is:

F. Modigliani and M.H. Miller, "The Cost of Capital, Corporation Finance and the Theory of Investment," *American Economic Review*, **48**:261–297 (June 1958).

However, Durand deserves credit for setting out the issues that MM later solved:

D. Durand, "Cost of Debt and Equity Funds for Business: Trends and Problems in Measurement," in *Conference on Research in Business Finance*, National Bureau of Economic Research, New York, 1952, pp. 215–247.

A somewhat difficult article that analyzes capital structure in the context of capital asset pricing theory is:

R.S. Hamada, "Portfolio Analysis, Market Equilibrium and Corporation Finance," *Journal of Finance*, **24**:13–31 (March 1969).

More abstract and general theoretical treatments can be found in:

J.E. Stiglitz, "On the Irrelevance of Corporate Financial Policy," *American Economic Review*, **64**:851–866 (December 1974).
E.F. Fama, "The Effects of a Firm's Investment and Financing Decisions," *American Economic Review*, **68**:272–284 (June 1978).

APPENDIX 17-1   MM AND THE CAPITAL ASSET PRICING MODEL

We showed in Section 17-2 that, as the firm increases its leverage, the expected equity return goes up in lockstep with the beta of the equity. Given this, it should be no surprise to find that we can use the capital asset pricing model to derive MM's Proposition I. The following demonstration has been simplified by assuming that the firm can issue risk-free debt.

The firm is initially all-equity financed. Its expected end-of-period value is V_1, which we take to include any operating income for the initial period. We now draw on the certainty-equivalent form of the capital asset pricing model, which we derived in Appendix 9-1. This states that the present value of the firm is

$$V = E = \frac{V_1 - \lambda \text{Cov} (\tilde{V}_1, \tilde{r}_m)}{1 + r_f}$$

where λ is the market price of risk $(r_m - r_f)/(\sigma_m^2)$.

Now suppose that that the firm borrows D at the risk-free rate of interest and distributes the proceeds to stockholders. They get D dollars now but next year they will have to repay the debt with interest. Therefore instead of receiving V_1 at the end of the year, they can expect to receive only $V_1 - (1 + r_f)D$. The present value of their levered equity is therefore

$$E = \frac{V_1 - (1 + r_f)D - \lambda \text{Cov} [\tilde{V}_1 - (1 + r_f)D, \tilde{r}_m]}{1 + r_f}$$

But since $(1 + r_f)D$ is known, it has no effect on the covariance. When debt is risk-free, stockholders have to bear *all* the risk associated with $\tilde{V}_1$. Therefore, we substitute Cov $(\tilde{V}_1, \tilde{r}_m)$ for Cov $[\tilde{V}_1 - (1 + r_f)D, \tilde{r}_m]$. This gives us

$$E = \frac{V_1 - (1 + r_f)D - \lambda \, \text{Cov} \, (\tilde{V}_1, \tilde{r}_m)}{1 + r_f}$$

$$= \frac{V_1 - \lambda \, \text{Cov} \, (\tilde{V}_1, \tilde{r}_m)}{1 + r_f} - D$$

To calculate the value of the *firm* we add the value of the debt D. This gives

$$V = \frac{V_1 - \lambda \, \text{Cov} \, (\tilde{V}_1, \tilde{r}_m)}{1 + r_f}$$

The value of the levered firm is identical to the value of the unlevered firm.

QUIZ

1. Assume a perfectly competitive market with no corporate or personal taxes. Companies A and B each earn gross profits of P and differ only in their capital structure—A is wholly equity-financed and B has debt outstanding on which it pays a certain $100 of interest each year. Investor X purchases 10% of the equity of A.
   (*a*) What profits does X obtain?
   (*b*) What alternative strategy would provide the same result?
   (*c*) Suppose investor Y purchases 10% of the equity of B. What profits does Y obtain?
   (*d*) What alternative strategy would provide the same result?

2. Ms. Kraft owns 50,000 shares of the common stock of Copperhead Corporation with a market value of $2 per share, or $100,000 overall. The company is currently financed as follows:

	Book Value
Common stock (8 million shares)	$2,000,000
Short-term loans	$2,000,000

   Copperhead now announces that it is replacing $1 million of short-term debt with an issue of common stock. What action can Ms. Kraft take to ensure that she is entitled to exactly the same proportion of profits as before? (Ignore taxes.)

3. The common stock and debt of Northern Sludge are valued at $50 million and $30 million, respectively. Investors currently require a 16% return on the common stock and an 8% return on the debt. If Northern Sludge issues an additional $10 million of common stock and uses this money to retire debt, what happens to the expected return on the stock? Assume that the change in capital structure does not affect the risk of the debt and that there are no taxes. If the risk of the debt did change, would your answer underestimate or overestimate the expected return on the stock?

4. Company C is financed entirely by common stock and has a β of 1.0. The stock has a price-earnings multiple of ten and is priced to offer a 10% expected return. The company decides to repurchase half the common stock and substitute an equal value of debt. If the debt yields a risk-free 5%,
   (*a*) Give:
      (i) The beta of the common stock after the refinancing
      (ii) The beta of the debt
      (iii) The beta of the company (that is, stock and debt combined)

(b) Give:
    (i) The required return on the common stock before the refinancing
    (ii) The required return on the common stock after the refinancing
    (iii) The required return on the debt
    (iv) The required return on the company (that is, stock and debt combined) after the refinancing
(c) Assume that the operating profit of firm C is expected to remain constant. Give:
    (i) The percentage increase in earnings per share
    (ii) The new price-earnings multiple

5. Suppose that Macbeth Spot Removers issues $2,500 of debt and uses the proceeds to repurchase 250 shares.
    (a) Rework Table 17-2 to show how earnings per share and share return now vary with operating income.
    (b) If the beta of Macbeth's assets is 0.8 and its debt is risk-free, what would be the beta of the equity after the increased borrowing?

6. True or false? Explain briefly.
    (a) Stockholders always benefit from an increase in company value.
    (b) MM's Proposition I assumes that actions that maximize firm value also maximize shareholder wealth.
    (c) The reason that borrowing increases equity risk is because it increases the probability of bankruptcy.
    (d) If firms did not have limited liability, the risk of their assets would be increased.
    (e) If firms did not have limited liability, the risk of their equity would be increased.
    (f) Borrowing does not affect the return on equity if the return on the firm's assets is equal to the interest rate.
    (g) As long as the firm is certain that the return on assets will be higher than the interest rate, an issue of debt makes the shareholders better off.
    (h) MM's Proposition I implies that an issue of debt increases expected earnings per share and leads to an offsetting fall in the price-earnings ratio.
    (i) MM's Proposition II assumes increased borrowing does not affect the interest rate on the firm's debt.
    (j) Borrowing increases firm value if there is a clientele of investors with a reason to prefer debt.

7. Note the two blank graphs in Figure 17-6. On graph (a), assume MM are right, and plot the relationship between financial leverage and (i) the rates of return on

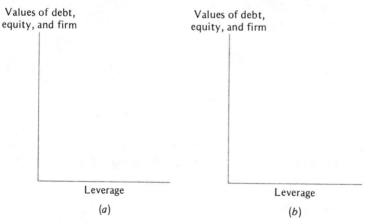

Figure 17-6   See quiz question 7.

debt and equity and (ii) the weighted average cost of capital. Then fill in graph (*b*) assuming the traditionalists are right.

QUESTIONS AND PROBLEMS

1. Companies A and B differ only in their capital structure. A is financed by 30% debt and 70% equity; B is financed by 10% debt and 90% equity. The debt of both companies is risk-free.
   (*a*) Mr. X owns 1% of the common stock of A. What other investment package would produce identical cash flows for Mr. X?
   (*b*) Mrs. Y owns 2% of the common stock of B. What other investment package would produce identical cash flows for Mrs. Y?
   (*c*) Show that neither Mr. X nor Mrs. Y would invest in the common stock of B, if the *total* value of company A were less than that of B.

2. Hubbard's Pet Foods is financed 80% by common stock and 20% by bonds. The expected return on the common stock is 12% and the rate of interest on the bonds is 6%. Assuming that the bonds are default-free, draw a graph that shows the expected return of Hubbard's common stock r_E and the expected return on the package of common stock and bonds r_A for different debt-equity ratios.

3. Here is a limerick:

   > There once was a man named Carruthers,
   > Who kept cows with miraculous udders.
   > He said, "Isn't this neat?
   > They give cream from one teat,
   > And skim milk from each of the others!"

   What is the analogy between Mr. Carruthers's cows and firms' financing decisions? What would MM's Proposition I, suitably adapted, say about the value of Mr. Carruthers's cows? Explain.

4. "MM totally ignore the fact that as you borrow more, you have to pay higher rates of interest." Explain carefully whether this is a valid objection.

5. Indicate what's wrong with the following arguments:
   (*a*) "As the firm borrows more and debt becomes risky, both stock- and bondholders demand higher rates of return. Thus by *reducing* the debt ratio we can reduce *both* the cost of debt and the cost of equity, making everybody better off."
   (*b*) "Moderate borrowing doesn't significantly affect the probability of financial distress or bankruptcy. Consequently moderate borrowing won't increase the expected rate of return demanded by stockholders."

6. Each of the following statements is false or at least misleading. Explain why in each case.
   (*a*) "A capital investment opportunity offering a 10% DCF rate of return is an attractive project if it can be 100% debt-financed at an 8% interest rate."
   (*b*) "The more debt the firm issues, the higher the interest rate it must pay. That is one important reason why firms should operate at conservative debt levels."

7. Can you invent any new kinds of debt that might be attractive to investors? Why do you think they have not been issued?

8. It has been suggested that one disadvantage of common stock financing is that share prices tend to decline in recessions, thereby increasing the cost of capital and deterring investment. Discuss this view. Is it an argument for greater use of debt financing?

HOW MUCH SHOULD A FIRM BORROW?

CHAPTER

·18·

In Chapter 17 we found that debt policy rarely matters in well-functioning capital markets. Few financial managers would accept that conclusion as a practical guideline. If debt policy doesn't matter, then they shouldn't worry about it—financing decisions should be delegated to underlings. Yet financial managers do worry about debt policy. This chapter explains why.

If debt policy were *completely* irrelevant, then actual debt ratios should vary randomly from firm to firm and industry to industry. Yet almost all airlines, utilities, and real estate development companies rely heavily on debt. And so do most firms in capital-intensive industries like steel, aluminum, chemicals, and mining. On the other hand, it is rare to find a drug company or advertising agency that is not predominantly equity-financed. Glamorous "growth" companies like Polaroid, Northern Telecom, Hewlett-Packard, and Digital Equipment Corporation rarely use much debt despite rapid expansion and often heavy requirements for capital.

The explanation of these patterns lies partly in the things we left out of the last chapter. We ignored taxes. We assumed bankruptcy was cheap, quick, and painless. It isn't, and there are costs associated with financial distress even if legal bankruptcy is ultimately avoided. We ignored potential conflicts of interest between the firm's security holders. For example, we did not consider what happens to the firm's "old" creditors when new debt is issued or when a shift in investment strategy takes the firm into a riskier business. We ignored the possible *interactions* of investment and financing decisions.

Now we will put all these things back in: taxes first, then the costs of bankruptcy and financial distress. This will lead us to conflicts of interest and to possible interactions of financing and investment decisons. In the end we will have to admit that debt policy *does* matter.

However, we will *not* throw away the MM theory we developed so carefully in Chapter 17. We're shooting for a theory combining MM's insights *plus* the effects of taxes, costs of bankruptcy and financial distress, and various other complications. We're not dropping back to the traditional view based on imperfections in the capital market. Instead, we want to see how well-functioning capital markets *respond* to taxes and the other things covered in this chapter.

18-1 CORPORATE TAXES

Debt financing has one important advantage under the corporate income tax system in Canada and the United States. The interest that the company pays is a tax-deductible expense. Dividends and retained earnings are not. Thus the return to bondholders escapes taxation at the corporate level.

Table 18-1 shows simple income statements for firm U, which has no debt, and firm L, which has borrowed $1,000 at 8%. The tax bill of L is $36.80 less than that of U. This is the *tax shield* provided by the debt of L. In effect the government pays 46% of the interest expense of L. The total income that L can pay out to its bondholders and stockholders increases by that amount.

Table 18-1 The tax-deductibility of interest increases the total income that can be paid out to bondholders and stockholders.

	Income Statement of Firm U	Income Statement of Firm L
Earnings before interest and taxes	$1,000	$1,000,00
Interest paid to bondholders	0	80.00
Pretax income	1,000	920.00
Tax at 46%	460	423.20
Net income to stockholders	$ 540	$ 496.80
Total income to both bondholders and stockholders	$0 + 540 = $540	$80 + 496.80 = $576.80
Interest tax shield (0.46 × interest)	$0	$36.80

Tax shields are valuable assets. Suppose that the debt of L is permanent. (That is, it plans to refinance its present debt obligations when they mature and to keep "rolling over" its debt obligations indefinitely.) It looks forward to a permanent stream of cash flows, $36.80 per year. The risk of these flows is likely to be less than the risk of the operating assets of L. The tax shields depend only on the corporate tax rate[1] and on the ability of L to earn enough to cover interest payments. Now the corporate tax rate does not vary much over time. And the ability of L to earn its interest payments must be reasonably sure—otherwise it could not have borrowed at 8%.[2] Therefore we should discount the interest tax shields at a relatively low rate.

But what rate? The most common assumption is that the risk of the tax shields is the same as that of the interest payments generating them. Thus we discount at 8%, the expected rate of return demanded by investors who are holding the firm's debt:

$$\text{PV tax shield} = \frac{36.80}{0.08} = \$460$$

In effect the government itself assumes 46% of the $1,000 debt obligation of L.

Under these assumptions, the present value of the tax shield is independent of the return on the debt r_D. It equals the corporate tax rate T_c times the amount borrowed D:

$$\text{Interest payment} = \text{return on debt} \times \text{amount borrowed}$$
$$= r_D \times D$$

$$\text{PV tax shield} = \frac{\text{corporate tax rate} \times \text{expected interest payment}}{\text{expected return on debt}}$$

$$= \frac{T_c\,(r_D D)}{r_D} = T_c D$$

---

[1]Always use the marginal corporate tax rate, not the average rate. For large corporations earning taxable income in Canada and the United States, the marginal tax rate is about 46%. Average rates are often much less than this because of the investment tax credit, the small business deduction, and various other adjustments.

[2]If the income of L does not cover interest in some future year, the tax shield is not necessarily lost. L will have a tax loss for the year, which can be used to reduce taxable income in other years. The loss carry-back and carry-forward rules are discussed in Appendix 6-1.

Of course PV tax shield is less if the firm does not plan to borrow permanently, or if it may not be able to use the tax shields in the future.

How Do Interest Tax Shields Contribute to the Value of Stockholders' Equity?

Northern Telecom is a large, successful Canadian firm that uses very little long-term debt. Table 18-2(a) shows simplified book and market value balance sheets for Northern as of the 1982 year-end.

Suppose that you had been Northern's financial manager in 1982, with complete responsibility for its capital structure. You decide to borrow an additional $196.4 million on a permanent basis and use the proceeds to repurchase shares.

Table 18-2(b) shows the new balance sheets. The book version simply has $196.4 million more long-term debt and $196.4 million less equity. But we know that Northern's assets must be worth more, for its tax bill has been reduced by 46% of the interest on the new debt. In other words, Northern has a new asset, PV tax shield, which is worth $T_c D = 0.46 \times 196.4 = \$90.3$ million. If the MM theory holds *except* for taxes, firm value must increase by $90.3 million to $3,876.6 million. Northern's equity ends up worth $2,920.5 million.

Now you have repurchased $196.4 million worth of shares but Northern's equity value has dropped by only $106.1 million. Therefore Northern's stockholders must be $90.3 million ahead. Not a bad day's work.[3]

Table 18-2(a)   Simplified balance sheets for Northern Telecom December 31, 1982 (figures in millions).

Book values			
Net working capital	$ 636.9	$ 244.6	Long-term debt
Long-term assets	1,127.0	515.1	Other long-term liabilities
		1,004.2	Equity
Total assets	$1,763.9	$1,763.9	Total liabilities

Market values			
Net working capital	$ 636.9	$ 244.6	Long-term debt
Market value of long-term assets	3,149.4	515.1	Other long-term liabilities
		3,026.6	Equity
Total assets	$3,786.3	$3,786.3	Market value of firm

Notes
1. The $636.9 million of net working capital is computed as the reported short-term assets of $1,315.0 million, net of reported short-term liabilities of $678.1 million. Thus the total assets and the total liabilities shown above are actually $678.1 million less than those reported in Northern's 1982 balance sheet. The $515.1 million for "other long-term liabilities" is a residual figure and, for simplicity, is assumed to include all liabilities that do not create interest tax shields.
2. Market value is assumed to equal book value for net working capital, long-term debt, and other long-term liabilities. Equity is entered at actual market value: number of shares times closing price on December 31, 1982. The difference between the market and book values of long-term assets is equal to the difference between the market and book values of equity.
3. The market value of long-term assets includes the tax shield on the existing debt. This tax shield is assumed to be worth $0.46 \times 244.6 = \$112.5$ million.

---

[3]Notice that as long as the bonds are sold at a fair price, all the benefits from the tax shield go to the shareholders.

Table 18-2(b) Balance sheets for Northern Telecom with an additional $196.4 million of long-term debt substituted for stockholder's equity (figures in millions).

Book values			
Net working capital	$ 636.9	$ 441.0	Long-term debt
Long-term assets	1,127.0	515.1	Other long-term liabilities
		807.8	Equity
Total assets	$1,763.9	$1,763.9	Total liabilities

Market values			
Net working capital	$ 636.9	$ 441.0	Long-term debt
Market value of long-term assets	3,149.4	515.1	Other long-term liabilities
		2,920.5	Equity
Present value of additional tax shields	90.3		
Total assets	$3,876.6	$3,876.6	Market value of firm

Notes:
1. The figures in Table 18-2(b) for net working capital, long-term assets and other long-term liabilities are identical to those in Figure 18-2(a).
2. Present value of tax shields assumed equal to corporate tax rate (46%) times amount of additional debt obligation.

MM and Taxes

We have just developed a version of MM's Proposition I as "corrected" by them to reflect corporate income taxes.[4] The new proposition is

Value of firm = value if all-equity-financed + PV tax shield

In the special case of permanent debt,

Value of firm = value if all-equity-financed + $T_c D$

Our imaginary financial surgery on Northern Telecom provides the perfect illustration of the problems inherent in this "corrected" theory. That $90.3 million windfall came too easily; it seems to violate the law that "There is no such thing as a money machine." And if Northern's stockholders would be richer with $441.0 million of corporate debt, why not $882 or $1,763.9 million?[5] Our formula implies that firm value and stockholders' wealth continue to go up as D increases. The implied optimal debt policy is embarrassingly extreme: all firms should be 100% debt-financed.

MM were not that fanatical about it. For one thing, no one would expect the formula to apply at extreme debt ratios. But that does not explain why firms like Northern

---

[4]MM's original article (F. Modigliani and M.H. Miller, "The Cost of Capital, Corporation Finance and the Theory of Investment," *American Economic Review*, **48**:261–297 (June 1958)) recognized interest tax shields, but did not value them properly. They put things right in their 1963 article "Corporate Income Taxes and the Cost of Capital: A Correction," *American Economic Review*, **53**:433–443 (June 1963).

[5]The last figure would correspond to a 100% *book* debt ratio. But Northern's *market* value would be $4,485.2 million according to our formula for firm value. Northern's common shares would have an aggregate value of $2,206.2 million.

thrive with so little debt. Some American firms like Kodak and Hewlett-Packard have even lower debt-equity ratios than Northern. It is hard to believe that the managers of all these firms are simply missing the boat.

Moreover, there are no dramatic differences between corporate debt ratios now and ratios before World War II when the corporate income tax was negligible or nonexistent. How do we explain this if the tax advantages of corporate borrowing are so compelling?

Therefore we have argued ourselves into a corner. There are just two ways out:

1. Perhaps a fuller examination of the system of corporate *and personal* taxation will uncover a tax disadvantage of corporate borrowing, offsetting the present value of the corporate tax shield.

2. Perhaps firms that borrow incur other costs—bankruptcy costs, for example—offsetting the present value of the tax shield.

We will now explore these two escape routes.

18-2 CORPORATE AND PERSONAL TAXES

The existence of personal taxes does not reduce the tax advantages of corporate borrowing *provided* that all kinds of personal income are taxed at the same rate.

Look back at the example in Table 18-1. Firm U is unlevered; firm L has borrowed $1,000 at 8%. The annual corporate tax shield produced by L's borrowing is $0.46 \times 80 = \$36.80$ a year. Therefore, the total income to investors is increased by that $36.80.

In Table 18-3 we have added *personal* taxes to Table 18-1 on the assumption that the income of both bondholders and stockholders is taxed at a rate of 30%. Notice that investors in firm L have to pay personal tax on their extra income of $36.80. Therefore their *after-tax* income is increased by $36.80 (1 − 0.30) = $25.76.

Table 18-3   Personal income taxes reduce, but do not eliminate, the tax shield generated by corporate borrowing.[a]

	Firm U	Firm L
Total income to both bondholders and stockholders (before personal tax; see Table 18-1)	0 + $540 = $540	$80 + 496.80 = $576.80
Tax shield generated by interest on corporate debt	0	$ 36.80
Tax paid by bondholders (30% marginal rate)	0	0.30 × 80 = $ 24.00
Tax paid by stockholders (30% marginal rate)	0.30 × 540 = $162	0.30 × 496.80 = $149.04
Total personal tax paid	$162	$173.04
Total after-tax income to both bondholders and stockholders	540 − 162 = $378	576.80 − 173.04 = $403.76
Tax shield remaining after personal taxes		$403.76 − 378 = $ 25.76

[a] An important assumption is that equity and interest income are subject to the same personal income tax rate.

We assumed that the debt of L is permanent. What is the present value of $25.76 per annum in perpetuity? Since this cash flow is computed *after personal taxes*, we have to discount at an opportunity cost of capital *likewise computed after personal taxes.* The stockholders of L can obtain 8% before tax, but only $8(1 - 0.3) = 5.6\%$ after tax. Thus

$$\text{PV tax shield (after personal tax)} = \frac{25.76}{0.056} = \$460$$

But this is the same answer we got before we ignored personal taxes entirely. The cash flow due to the corporate income tax shield is 30% less when personal taxes are recognized, but so is the opportunity cost of capital.

In general, if investors are willing to lend at a prospective return *before* personal taxes of r_D, then they must also be willing to accept a return *after* personal taxes of $r_D(1 - T_p)$, T_p is the marginal rate of personal tax. Thus we can compute the value after personal taxes of the tax shield on permanent debt:

PV tax shield =

$$\frac{\text{corporate tax rate} \times \text{expected interest payment} \times (1 - \text{personal tax rate})}{\text{after-tax expected return on debt}}$$

$$= \frac{T_c \times (r_D D) \times (1 - T_p)}{r_D \times (1 - T_p)}$$

$$= T_c D$$

This brings us back to our previous formula for firm value:

Value of firm = value if all-equity financed + $T_c D$

Many scholars and business people stop here, confirmed in their conclusions that (1) there is a tax advantage to corporate debt, and (2) you can ignore personal taxes in computing the present value of that advantage. Unfortunately, our system of personal taxation is not as simple as we have just painted it. We will now attempt to go a bit deeper, although that takes us into a complex and controversial area.

But Debt Attracts Higher Personal Tax than Equity

In Chapter 16 we saw that, in Canada, capital gains and dividends are taxed at reduced rates. In fact, capital gains are often untaxed and the net personal tax on dividends is negative below the 22.67% federal tax bracket and positive above that. Thus, the effective personal tax on equity income is often close to zero. On the other hand, interest income is taxed at the same rate as wage and salary personal income. Thus, in many cases, equity income is taxed at the corporate level but only lightly at the personal level, while interest income is taxed at the personal level but not at the corporate level.

If personal tax is higher on bond interest than corporate tax on equity income, corporate borrowing may end up reducing the firm's market value. It all depends on the marginal tax rate of bondholders. Table 18-4 provides an illustration in which the personal tax on interest income is so high that it is unwise for the firm to borrow. Total income to L's bondholders and stockholders is less than to U's stockholders. Therefore the value of firm L must be less than that of firm U.

Table 18-4 Corporate borrowing can reduce firm value when bondholders face high personal tax rates and equity income escapes taxation.

	Firm U	Firm L
Total income to both bondholders and stockholders (before personal tax; see Table 18-1)	0 + $540 = $540	$80 + 496.80 = $576.80
Tax shield generated by interest on corporate debt	0	$ 36.80
Tax paid by bondholders (50% marginal rate)	0	0.50 × 80 = $ 40.00
Tax paid by stockholders (not taxed)	0	0
Total personal tax paid	$ 0	$ 40.00
Total after-tax income to both bondholders and stockholders	$540	576.80 − 40 = $536.80
Tax shield remaining after personal taxes		$536.80 − 540 = −$ 3.20

A Generalization

Up to this point we have relied almost entirely on numerical examples. We must try to generalize.

We continue to assume that, except for taxes, MM are right to say that capital structure is irrelevant. When personal taxes are introduced, the firm's objective is no longer to minimize the *corporate* tax bill; the firm should try to minimize the present value of *all* taxes paid on corporate income. "All taxes" include corporate *and* personal taxes paid by bondholders as well as stockholders.

Figure 18-1 illustrates how corporate and personal taxes are affected by leverage. Depending on the firm's capital structure, a dollar of operating income will accrue to investors either as debt interest or equity income (dividends or capital gains). That is, the dollar can go down either branch of Figure 18-1.

Notice that Figure 18-1 distinguishes between T_p, the personal tax rate on interest, and T_{pE}, the effective personal rate on equity income. The quantity T_{pE} is a weighted average of the personal tax rate on dividends and the present value of the personal tax rate on capital gains. The weights depend on the proportions of equity income received as dividends and as capital gains. The quantity T_{pE} is less than T_p and it may even be negative.[6]

The firm's objective should be to arrange its capital structure so as to maximize after-tax income. You can see from Figure 18-1 that corporate borrowing is better if

---

[6]Using the notation of Appendix 16-1, we have

$T_p = T_{pfed} \times (1 + T_{prov})$ (tax rate on interest)

$T_d = 1.5 \times (T_{pfed} - 0.2267) \times (1 + T_{prov})$ (tax rate on dividends)

$T_g = \begin{cases} 0, \text{ or} & \text{(no tax if capital gains are exempt)} \\ 0.5 \times T_{pfed} \times (1 + T_{prov}) \times \text{PV factor} & \text{(tax rate on deferred capital gains)} \end{cases}$

By manipulating these expressions and noting that the highest federal tax rate is $T_{pfed} = 0.34$, one can see that $T_d < T_p$ and $T_g < T_p$. Of course, T_{pE} is a weighted average of T_d and T_g so $T_{pE} < T_p$, as well.

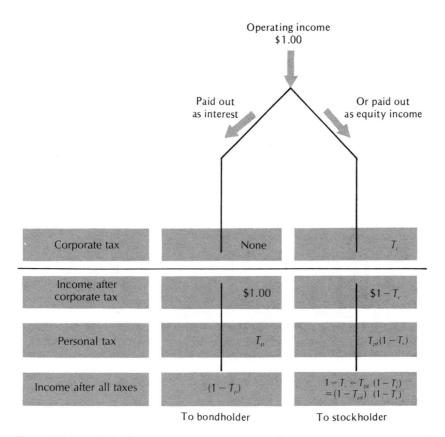

Figure 18-1   The firm's capital structure determines whether operating income is paid out as interest or equity income. Interest is taxed only at the personal level. Equity income is taxed at both the corporate and the personal levels. However, T_{pE}, the personal tax rate on equity income, is less than T_p because of the dividend tax credit and because equity income is received partly as capital gains.

$(1 - T_p)$ is more than $(1 - T_{pE}) \times (1 - T_c)$; otherwise it is worse. Corporate debt policy is irrelevant if

$$(1 - T_p) = (1 - T_{pE}) \times (1 - T_c)$$

We seem to have a simple, practical decision rule. Arrange the firm's capital structure to shunt operating income down that branch of Figure 18-1 where the tax is least. But it isn't that easy. Put yourself in the financial manager's shoes: what's T_{pE}? The shareholder roster of a large corporation may include low-income people (such as retirees), as well as millionaires. All possible tax brackets will be mixed together. And it's the same with T_p, the personal tax rate on interest. The large corporation's "typical" bondholder might be a tax-exempt pension fund, but many taxpaying investors also hold corporate debt. Our simple rule cannot cope with a variety of personal tax rates.

There are two ways of simplifying the analysis: recalling the concept of tax integration in Canada, and employing a model by Merton Miller. We will discuss both of these in turn.

Tax Integration and Capital Structure

The dividend tax credit system in Canada is intended to "integrate" the personal and corporate tax systems and reduce or eliminate the double taxation of equity income at the personal and corporate level. That is, if the system works perfectly, the "bottom line" income after all taxes should be the same for both branches of Figure 18-1. Let's see what actually happens. First, consider the case of a firm that pays tax at $33^1/_3\%$ and passes all equity income to shareholders in the form of dividends. In Appendix 16-1, we showed how the dividend tax credit system has the effect of making an owner indifferent between taking ordinary (interest or salary) income out of such a firm and dividend income out of the same firm. That is, if T_d is the personal tax rate on dividend income,

$$1 - T_p = (1 - T_d) \times (1 - 0.3333)$$

If the shareholders receive dividend income rather than capital gains, $T_{pE} = T_d$, so that corporate debt policy would be irrelevant.

But the income of large firms faces a higher tax rate of $T_c = 46\%$, so the double taxation of dividend income for their owners is slightly more onerous than the taxation of interest income.[7] Thus, the Canadian tax system is not perfectly integrated and large firms would be *slightly* better off shunting their operating income down the debt branch of Figure 18-1, rather than the equity branch (if they always pay out equity income in the form of dividends).

What if some or all of the equity income is paid out in the form of capital gains? Unfortunately, Canadian legislators have made no attempt to integrate the tax system for equity income that is in the form of capital gains. If the equity income branch of Figure 18-1 is in the form of capital gains, low tax bracket investors would prefer that operating income be passed down the debt branch, and high tax bracket investors would prefer that it be passed down the equity branch.

Certainly the dividend tax credit system has blunted the bald preference for debt implied by the "corrected" MM theory, but there still may be a preference for debt or for equity in Canada, because equity investors receive a mixture of dividends and capital gains, and because all investors face a variety of personal tax rates. Moreover, there is nothing like the dividend tax credit system in the United States, yet many American firms have *lower* debt to equity ratios than similar Canadian firms. We will turn to another theory that may help resolve these issues.

Merton Miller's "Debt and Taxes"

To discuss these issues, we turn to "Debt and Taxes," Merton Miller's 1976 Presidential Address to the American Finance Association.[8] Miller's model is both insightful and controversial.

Consider a simple world in which all equity income comes as unrealized capital gains. In that case nobody pays any tax on equity income; T_{pE} is zero for all investors. But the rate of tax on bond interest depends on the investor's tax bracket. Tax-exempt institutions do not pay any tax on interest; for them T_p is zero. At the other extreme, millionaires pay tax at a rate of about 50% on bond interest: for them T_p is 0.50. Most investors fall somewhere between these two extremes.

---

[7] That is, for an individual Canadian investor, and $T_c = 0.46$,

$$1 - T_p = (1 - T_d) \times (1 - 0.3333) > (1 - T_d) \times (1 - T_c)$$

[8] M.H. Miller, "Debt and Taxes," *Journal of Finance*, **32**: 261–276 (May 1977). Some of the issues and ideas in Miller's paper were also discussed in D. Farrar and L.L. Selwyn, "Taxes, Corporate Financial Policy and the Returns to Investors," *National Tax Journal*, **20**: 144–154 (December 1967) and in some unpublished papers by Fischer Black.

Suppose that companies are initially financed entirely by equity. If financial managers are on their toes, this cannot represent a stable situation. Think of it in terms of Figure 18-1. If every dollar goes down the equity branch, there are no taxes paid at the personal level (remember $T_{pE} = 0$). Thus the financial manager need consider only corporate taxes, which we know create a strong incentive for corporate borrowing.

As companies begin to borrow, some investors have to be persuaded to hold corporate debt rather than common stock. There should be no problem in persuading tax-exempt investors to hold debt. They do not pay any personal taxes regardless of whether they hold bonds or stocks. Thus, the initial impact of borrowing is to save corporate taxes and to leave personal taxes unchanged.

But, as companies borrow more, they need to persuade taxpaying investors to migrate from stocks to bonds. Therefore they have to offer a bribe in the form of a higher interest rate on their bonds. Companies can afford to bribe investors to migrate as long as the corporate tax saving *is greater than* the personal tax loss. But there is no way that companies can bribe millionaires to hold their bonds. The corporate tax saving cannot compensate for the extra personal tax that those millionaires would need to pay. Thus the migrations stop when the corporate tax saving *equals* the personal tax loss. This point occurs when T_p, the personal tax rate of the migrating investor, equals the corporate tax rate T_c.

Let us put some numbers on this. The corporate tax rate T_c is 46%. We continue to assume that T_{pE}, the effective rate of tax on equity income, is zero for all investors. In this case, companies will bribe investors with tax rates below 46% to hold bonds. But there is nothing to be gained (or lost) by persuading investors with tax rates *equal* to 46% to hold bonds. In the case of these investors $1 of operating income will produce income after all taxes of $0.54, regardless of whether the dollar is interest or equity income:

	Income Remaining after All Taxes
Income paid out as interest	$1 - T_p = 1 - 0.46 = \$0.54$
Income paid out as equity income	$(1 - T_{pE})(1 - T_c) = (1 - 0)(1 - 0.46) = \$0.54$

Implications of Miller's Model

Miller's model has several important implications. First, there is an optimal debt-equity ratio for corporations as a whole. It is determined by the corporate tax rate and the funds available to individual investors in the various tax brackets. If the corporate tax rate is increased, migration starts again, leading to a higher debt-equity ratio for companies as a whole. If personal tax rates are increased, the migration reverses, leading to a lower debt-equity ratio. If *both* personal and corporate tax rates are increased by the same amount—ten percentage points, say—there is no migration and no change. That explains why there was no substantial increase in the debt-equity ratio when the corporate income tax rose drastically at the start of World War II. Personal tax rates were simultaneously increased by about the same amount.

Second, the companies in our example that first sold bonds to tax-exempt investors may have gained an advantage. But once the "low" taxpayers have invested in bonds and the migrations have stopped, no single firm can gain an advantage by borrowing more or suffer any penalty by borrowing less. Therefore there is no such thing as an optimal debt-equity ratio *for any single firm*. The market is interested only in the *total* amount of debt. No single firm can influence that.

*Comments and Questions

It is hard not to like Miller's model; it explains so much, so neatly. But on some levels it raises more questions than it answers.

If we take Miller's argument literally, tax-exempt institutions such as pension funds ought to invest only in bonds and highly taxed individuals ought to invest only in equities. But we don't observe any obvious clienteles of this kind.

Also, firms *do* pay dividends and investors *do* sell their shares from time to time, and so pay capital gains taxes. Thus T_{pE}, the effective personal tax rate on equity income, is not generally zero. We saw in Chapter 16 that Miller has joined the middle-of-the-road party, which holds that investors have ways of avoiding taxes on equity income and that dividend policy is thus irrelevant despite taxes. But not all of Miller's fellow party members would be further willing to assume that $T_{pE} = 0$.

However, Miller did extend his "Debt and Taxes" model to reflect personal taxes on equity income. Suppose that $T_{pE} = 0.20$. Then the total tax on the right-hand branch of Figure 18-1 is 46% of equity income plus 20% of whatever is left over—in all, $0.46 + 0.20 \times (1 - 0.46) = 0.57$ or 57%. The story of shifting clienteles we just told could be repeated under this new assumption. Migration would continue until taxpayers in the 57% tax bracket were just indifferent between corporate bonds and equity.[9]

Miller's model ignores another way to save taxes. Consider a wealthy taxpayer in the 46% tax bracket. In Miller's world the taxpayer would be willing to hold corporate bonds, but without enthusiasm. He or she would see no payoff to switching from corporate bonds to common stocks. But there would be a big payoff to switching from *direct* investment in corporate bonds to *indirect* investment by way of a pension fund, Registered Retirement Savings Plan, or other tax-sheltered institution. In that way, he or she would escape tax on interest.

Thus Miller's final clientele may not be the last stop after all. There should be further migration as all tax-paying individuals sell their direct holdings of corporate bonds and invest via institutions instead. In principle, the migration would continue until all taxable debt is held by tax-exempt institutions. That would take us back to the point where there is once again a clear tax advantage to corporate borrowing.[10]

Municipal Bonds in the United States

So far we have assumed that there are only two types of security—common stocks and corporate bonds. Let us think what happens when we introduce municipal bonds. The unusual feature about American municipal bonds is that the interest on them is not subject to income tax. This means that investors are willing to hold corporate bonds only if the *after-tax* yield on corporates is at least as high as the *pretax* yield on tax-exempt municipals.[11] Now we know that Miller's model implies that investors with tax rates of 46% are prepared to hold corporate bonds. For each dollar of pretax interest on corporate bonds these investors receive only 54 cents after tax. Therefore the pretax

---

[9]The maximum personal tax rate is currently less than this. Therefore, all investors with equity tax rates, T_{pE}, of 20% (or more) would prefer debt. This would leave few, if any, investors to hold equity. In other words, if the tax rate on equity income is sufficiently high, we are forced back to an MM world where there is a tax advantage to borrowing.

[10]In essence, such an investor is using the Miller-Scholes technique of Chapter 16 to eliminate the tax on interest income (instead of dividend income). If the investor also uses the Miller-Scholes technique to eliminate taxes on dividends and defers capital gains, he or she has $T_{pE} = T_p = 0$. If all investors do this, debt would always be preferred to equity, unless we also have $T_c = 0$, because irrelevance requires $(1 - T_p) = (1 - T_{pE}) \times (1 - T_c)$. That is, it is difficult to reconcile steadfast beliefs in both the Miller-Scholes argument for dividend irrelevance and the Miller argument for debt irrelevance.

[11]Since interest on municipals is not subject to tax, their after-tax yield is the same as their pretax yield.

---

yield on tax-exempt bonds cannot be more than 54% of the pretax yield on taxable bonds. This suggests another test of Miller's theory: find a tax-exempt bond and a taxable bond that are identical in all other respects and check whether the yield on the tax-exempt bond is 54% of the yield on the taxable bond.

For example, companies in the United States occasionally arrange to finance an investment by a simultaneous issue of taxable debentures and tax-exempt industrial revenue bonds. Industrial revenue bonds are an unusual hybrid. They are not issued by the company itself but a municipality that wishes to encourage local investment. The interest on industrial revenue bonds is tax-exempt; on the other hand, all payments on the bonds are the responsibility of the company. So, apart from their tax-exempt status, industrial revenue bonds are similar to corporate debentures.[12]

In 1978 five companies issued taxable debentures and at the same time arranged a comparable issue of tax-exempt revenue bonds. Table 18-5 shows that on average the yield on the tax-exempt issue was 78% of the yield on the taxable issue. If these bonds are exactly comparable, Miller's model is wrong and there is a net tax advantage to corporate borrowing.[13]

Table 18-5   Yields on simultaneous issues of taxable and tax-exempt bonds, 1978.

	Yield on Taxable Bond, %	Yield on Tax-Exempt Bond, %	Ratio
Exel Ind	9.25	7.13	0.77
Carolina Fruit Carriers Corp	9.88	7.50	0.76
Haverty Furniture	10.00	7.75	0.78
Lucherby Furniture	9.75	7.75	0.80
Perini Corp	9.50	7.38	0.78

Source: R.H. Gordon and B.G. Malkiel, "Corporation Finance," in H.J. Aaron and J.A. Pechman (eds.), *How Taxes Affect Economic Behavior*, The Brookings Institution, Washington, D.C., 1981.

*Taxes, Debt Policy, and Dividend Policy

Under various choices of dividend and debt policies, the corporation can convert its operating cash flows into any of three types of flows:

1. Dividend equity flows,
2. Capital gain equity flows,
3. Interest flows on debt.

In Canada, the dividend tax credit makes the dividend and interest flows equivalent on a total tax basis if the corporate tax rate is $33\frac{1}{3}$%.[14] But if large firms face a tax

---

[12]If companies had the choice, they would always prefer an issue of tax-exempt industrial revenue bonds. However, the U.S. Treasury limits the amount that can be issued.

[13]The bonds in Table 18-5 are long-term bonds. There is evidence that the yield differentials on short-term bonds are much closer to Miller's model. For a discussion of this point, see M. Mussa and R. Kormendi, "The Taxation of Municipal Bonds," American Enterprise Institute, Washington, D.C., 1979; C. Trczinka, "The Pricing of Tax-Exempt Bonds and The Miller Hypothesis," *Journal of Finance*, **37**:907–924 (September 1982); and J. Skelton, "Banks, Firms and the Relative Pricing of Tax-Exempt and Taxable Bonds," unpublished paper, University of California, Berkeley, August 1982.

[14]They are also equivalent for a small firm paying taxes at 25% because of the dividend distribution tax. Recall Appendix 16-1.

rate of 46%, interest flows should be preferred to equity flows. Their only important decision should be between capital gains and interest flows.

This is nice in theory, but it flies in the face of actual corporate and investor practice. For example, many large Canadian corporations have preferred shares that provide cash flows mainly in the form of dividends—and they are very popular with individual investors. Also, prior to 1985 many Canadian corporations allowed their shareholders the option of a taxable dividend or capital gains treatment on their dividend flows, and their shareholders often opted for the dividend flow.

Dividends are so popular that we must have doubts that the tax situation is as simple as we have stated to this point. Perhaps the *marginal* corporate tax rate is closer to $33^1/_3\%$ than to 46% for the firms that issue preferred shares. In the next section, we will see how the "risk" of tax losses in the future can drive down the effective marginal tax rate for highly levered corporations.

*A Compromise Theory

The majority of financial managers and economists believe our tax system favours corporate borrowing. Before Miller's paper, they had fallen into the habit of calculating the tax advantage of financial leverage as T_cD, the PV of the tax shields generated by a perpetual stream of corporate interest payments. When pressed they admitted that this is a first approximation only, and they professed a willingness to consider personal taxes too, if only they had a sensible model showing them how to do it.

Enter Miller's model, which recognizes that investors have different personal tax rates, but which says financial managers ought to forget about taxes entirely in choosing between debt and equity. Yet the model is clearly oversimplified: if accepted, it upsets the majority's apple cart without picking up all the apples. How does the majority react? Cautiously. They stick to their old beliefs, but profess them with less vigour than before.

Figure 18-2 summarizes the dilemma. Both MM and Miller agree that there is a corporate tax shield on debt that is equal to 46% of the interest payments. The corporate tax shield is shown by the solid horizontal line in Figure 18-2. It pays companies to

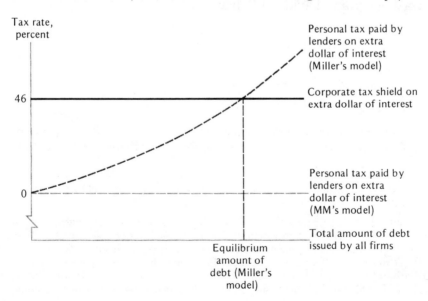

Figure 18-2   It pays companies to borrow as long as the corporate tax saving exceeds the extra personal tax paid by the marginal lender. MM and Miller disagree only about how the extra personal tax varies with total company borrowing.

issue more debt as long as this corporate tax shield exceeds the personal tax cost to the marginal lender.

The disagreement between MM and Miller centres on the tax position of the marginal lender. MM implicitly assume that personal taxes are zero (the dotted *horizontal* line in Figure 18-2). In this case the corporate tax shield *always* exceeds the tax rate of the marginal lender and companies should borrow to the hilt.

Miller assumes that investors are subject to different tax rates. Therefore, as the total amount of corporate debt increases, investors with higher tax rates must be bribed to hold debt. In this case the tax rate of the marginal lender is shown by the broken *upward-sloping* line in Figure 18-2.[15] The equilibrium amount of debt in Miller's model is reached when the corporate tax benefit to the borrower equals the personal tax cost to the marginal lender. As long as all companies pay the same rate of tax, it is immaterial which firms supply this debt.

Figure 18-2 also provides a clue as to where we might look for a compromise theory. Consider the assumption that the corporate tax shield on debt is a constant 46% regardless of the amount borrowed. In practice few firms can be *sure* they will show a taxable profit in the future. If a firm shows a loss and cannot carry the loss back against past taxes, its interest tax shield must be carried forward with the hope of using it later. The firm loses the time value of money while it waits. If its difficulties are deep enough, the wait may be permanent and the interest tax shield lost forever.

Notice also that borrowing is not the only way to shield income against tax. Firms have accelerated write-offs for plant and equipment. They have the investment tax credit. Investment in many intangible assets can be expensed immediately. So can contributions to the firm's pension fund. The more that firms shield income in these other ways, the lower the expected tax shield from borrowing.[16]

If there is a chance that firms will make a loss, the *expected* corporate tax shield is less than 46%. The more a firm borrows, the higher the probability of loss and therefore the lower the expected tax shield.[17] In Figure 18-3 we have redrawn the corporate tax

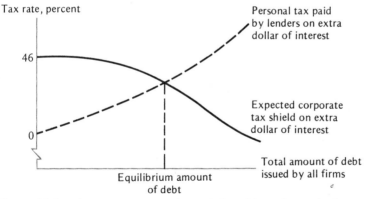

Figure 18-3   If companies cannot be sure of taxable profits in the future, the expected corporate tax saving will be less, and less debt will be issued.

---

[15]We have arbitrarily shown this as a smooth curve. In practice there would be a series of steep sections and plateaus.

[16]For a discussion of the effect of these other tax shields on company borrowing see H. DeAngelo and R. Masulis, "Optimal Capital Structure Under Corporate and Personal Taxation," *Journal of Financial Economics*, **8**:5–29 (March 1980).

[17]For some evidence on the average marginal tax rate of United States firms see J.J. Cordes and S.M. Sheffrin, "Taxation and the Sectoral Allocation of Capital in the U.S.," *National Tax Journal*, **34**: 419–432 (1981).

shield line to recognize this. The expected tax shield for the marginal borrower starts close to 46% but it declines as more debt is issued. We continue to represent the personal tax payments on debt interest by an upward-sloping line. The total amount of debt that will be issued is again given by the point at which the tax benefit to the marginal borrower equals the tax payment by the marginal lender, but this equilibrium differs from Miller's model in three ways.

First, if companies cannot be sure they can take full advantage of the corporate tax shield, the total amount of debt issued will be less than in Miller's model. (The intersection in Figure 18-3 is further left than in Figure 18-2.)

Second, since companies cannot be sure of benefiting from the corporate tax shield, they will not be prepared to pay such a high rate of interest on the debt. (The intersection in Figure 18-3 is lower than in Figure 18-2.)[18]

Third, since companies have different expected tax rates, the corporate tax shields are worth more to some firms than to others. For example, look at Figure 18-4. The lower line depicts the expected corporate tax saving from an additional dollar of interest payments for the Drop Forge and Basic Slag Company. Drop Forge has large accumulated tax loss carry-forwards and uncertain prospects. So there is little chance that it will be able to use any corporate tax shield. Since the expected tax saving is less than the expected personal tax payment by the marginal lender, borrowing has a negative net present value for Drop Forge. By contrast the upper line shows the expected corporate tax saving from an additional dollar of interest payment for Con Gas, a company whose income is relatively high and stable. Since the expected corporate tax saving exceeds the lender's expected personal tax payment, borrowing is a positive-NPV activity for Con Gas. But the more Con Gas borrows, the greater the chance that it will incur future losses. This places a limit on the amount of borrowing the company should undertake.

To maximize value, Con Gas should borrow until the expected tax saving on its last dollar of interest is equal to the expected personal tax payment by the lender. The shaded area in Figure 18-4 shows the total net benefit each year to Con Gas.

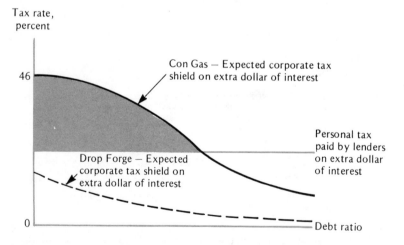

Figure 18-4 Drop Forge is unlikely to earn taxable profits and therefore should not borrow. Con Gas should borrow until the expected corporate tax saved on extra borrowing equals the personal tax paid by the lender. (Note: the personal tax paid by lenders is unaffected by the debt ratio of an individual company.)

---

[18]This would explain why the difference between the yield on tax-exempt American municipal and taxable corporate bonds is less than Miller's model predicts.

We don't pretend that this is the whole story. Our point is that there may be an intermediate position if you are not prepared to go out on a limb for either MM or Miller. Our own view is that there is a moderate tax advantage to corporate borrowing, at least for companies that are reasonably sure they can use the corporate tax shields. For companies that do not expect to be able to use the corporate tax shields we believe there is a moderate tax disadvantage.

18-3   COSTS OF FINANCIAL DISTRESS

Suppose that you accept the majority view. The majority believes there is a tax advantage to corporate borrowing, which is consistent with the view of MM before one of the M's (Miller) deserted it.[19] That view is

Value of firm = value if all-equity-financed + PV tax shield

We have already noted why this is unacceptable: it implies that all firms should be 100% debt-financed. If you believe the value of the tax shield is significantly positive, but don't believe that firms should borrow up to the hilt, then you must look for some offsetting disadvantage to corporate debt.

The majority argues as follows. A firm that borrows more increases the odds of financial distress. Financial distress occurs when promises to creditors are broken, or honoured with difficulty. Sometimes financial distress leads to bankruptcy. Sometimes it means only that the firm skates on thin ice.

Market value

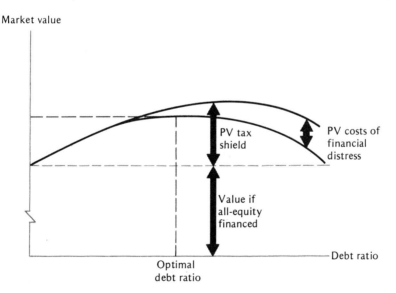

Figure 18-5   The value of the firm is equal to its value if all-equity financed plus PV tax shield minus PV costs of financial distress. The manager should choose the debt ratio that maximizes firm value.

---

[19]We don't mean to imply that all of the majority would agree with MM in the absence of taxes. But Proposition I is not the issue here, and so we will assume it holds.

As we will see, financial distress is costly. Investors know that levered firms may fall into financial distress, and they worry about it. That worry is reflected in the current market value of the levered firm's securities. Thus, the value of the firm is

$$\text{Value of firm} = \text{value if all-equity-financed} + \text{PV tax shield} - \text{PV costs of financial distress}$$

The costs of financial distress depend on the probability of distress and the magnitude of costs encountered if distress occurs.

Figure 18-5 shows how the trade-off between the tax benefits and the costs of distress determines optimal capital structure. PV tax shield initially increases as the firm borrows more. At moderate debt levels the probability of financial distress is trivial, and so PV cost of financial distress is small and tax advantages dominate. But at some point the probability of financial distress increases rapidly with additional borrowing; the costs of distress begin to take a substantial bite out of firm value. Also, if the firm can't be sure of profiting from the corporate tax shield, the tax advantage of debt is likely to dwindle and eventually disappear. The theoretical optimum is reached when the present value of tax savings due to additional borrowing is just offset by increases in the present value of costs of distress.[20]

Costs of financial distress covers several specific items. Now we identify these costs and try to understand what causes them and why they cannot be avoided.

Bankruptcy Costs

You rarely hear anything nice said about corporate bankruptcy. But there is some good in almost everything. Corporate bankruptcies occur when stockholders exercise their *right to default*. That right is valuable: when a firm gets into trouble, limited liability allows stockholders simply to walk away from it, leaving all its troubles to its creditors. The former creditors become the new stockholders, and the old stockholders are left with nothing.

In our legal system all stockholders automatically enjoy limited liability. But suppose that this were not so. Suppose that there were two firms with identical assets and operations. Each firm has debt outstanding and each has promised to repay $1,000 (principal and interest) next year. But only one of the firms, Ace Limited, enjoys limited liability. The other firm, Ace Unlimited, does not; its stockholders are personally liable for its debt.

Figure 18-6 compares next year's possible payoffs to the creditors and stockholders of these two firms. The only differences occur when next year's asset value turns out to be less than $1,000. Suppose that next year the assets of each company are worth only $500. In this case Ace Limited defaults. Its stockholders walk away; their payoff is zero. Bondholders get the assets worth $500. But Ace Unlimited's stockholders can't walk away. They have to cough up $500, the difference between asset value and the bondholders' claim. The debt is paid whatever happens.

Suppose that Ace Limited does go bankrupt. Of course, its stockholders are disappointed that their firm is worth so little, but that is an operating problem having nothing to do with financing. Given poor operating performance, the right to go bankrupt—the right to default—is a valuable privilege. As Figure 18-6 shows, Ace Limited's stockholders are in better shape than Unlimited's are.

---

[20]Nothing in Miller's theory rules out costs of financial distress. Miller would redraw Figure 18-5, but with PV tax shield = 0.

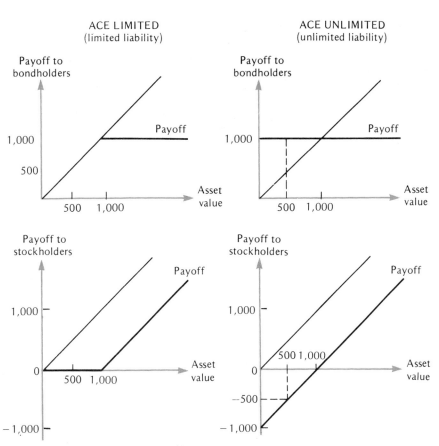

Figure 18-6 Comparison of limited and unlimited liability for two otherwise identical firms. If the two firms' asset values are less than $1,000, Ace Limited stockholders default and its bondholders take over the assets. Ace Unlimited stockholders keep the assets, but they must reach into their own pockets to pay off its bondholders. The total payoff to both stockholders and bondholders is the same for the two firms.

The example illuminates a mistake people often make in thinking about the costs of bankruptcy. Bankruptcies are thought of as corporate funerals. The mourners (creditors and especially shareholders) look at their firm's present sad state. They think of how valuable their securities used to be and how little is left. Moreover, they think of the lost value as a cost of bankruptcy. That is the mistake. The decline in the value of assets is what the mourning is really about. That has no necessary connection with financing. The bankruptcy is merely a legal mechanism for allowing creditors to take over when the decline in the value of assets triggers a default. Bankruptcy is not the *cause* of the decline in value. It is the result.

Be careful not to get cause and effect reversed. When a person dies, we do not cite the implementation of his or her will as the cause of death.

We said that bankruptcy is a legal mechanism allowing creditors to take over when a firm defaults. Bankruptcy costs are the costs of using this mechanism. There are no bankruptcy costs at all shown in Figure 18-6. Note that only Ace Limited can default and go bankrupt. But, regardless of what happens to asset value, the *combined* payoff to the bondholders and stockholders of Ace Limited is always the same as the *combined* payoff to the bondholders and stockholders of Ace Unlimited. Thus the overall market values of the two firms now (this year) must be identical. Of course, Ace Limited's *stock* is worth more than Ace Unlimited's stock because of Ace Limited's right to default. Ace Limited's *debt* is worth correspondingly less.

Our example was not intended to be strictly realistic. Anything involving courts and lawyers cannot be free. Suppose that court and legal fees are $200 if Ace Limited defaults. The fees are paid out of the remaining value of Ace's assets. Thus if asset value turns out to be $500, creditors end up with only $300. Figure 18-7 shows next year's *total* payoff to bondholders and stockholders net of this bankruptcy cost. Ace Limited, by issuing risky debt, has given lawyers and the court system a claim on the firm if it defaults. The present market value of the firm is reduced by the present value of this claim.

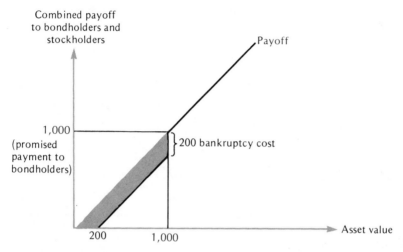

Figure 18-7 Total payoff to Ace Limited security holders. There is a $200 bankruptcy cost in the event of default (shaded area).

It is easy to see how increased leverage affects the present value of the costs of financial distress. If Ace borrows more, it must promise more to bondholders. This increases the probability of default and the value of the lawyers' claim. It increases PV costs of financial distress and reduces Ace's present market value.

The costs of bankruptcy come out of stockholders' pockets. Creditors foresee the costs and foresee that *they* will pay them if default occurs. For this they demand compensation in advance in the form of higher payoffs when the firm does *not* default. That is, they demand a higher promised interest rate. This reduces the possible payoffs to stockholders and reduces the present market value of their shares.

Evidence on Bankruptcy Costs

Warner has reported legal and administrative costs of 11 United States railroad bankruptcies. The average cost was about $2 million spread over many years. (On average, it took 13 years before the railroads were reorganized and released from the bankruptcy courts. For one railroad it took 23 years.)

Two million dollars is not small change. But, on average, the costs were only 5.3% of the overall market value of the railroads' debt and equity securities, estimated just before bankruptcy. The costs declined to 1.4% of overall market value estimated five years prior to bankruptcy, when the railroads were in better health. That is a small number. Suppose that you are the financial manager of a railroad facing a 20% chance of bankruptcy in five years.[21] Using Warner's results, you guesstimate the present value of bankruptcy costs as follows:

$$\begin{array}{lll} \text{Expected} \\ \text{cost} \end{array} = \begin{array}{l} \text{probability} \\ \text{of bankruptcy} \end{array} \times \begin{array}{l} \text{cost of bankruptcy as proportion} \\ \text{of firm's current market value} \end{array}$$

$$= 0.2 \times 0.014 \text{ (value of firm)} = 0.0028 \text{ (value of firm)}$$

Discount back five years at, say, 8%:

$$\text{PV costs of bankruptcy} = \frac{0.0028}{(1.08)^5} \text{ (value of firm)} = 0.0019 \text{ (value of firm)}$$

Trivial. Of course, Warner's data apply only to railroads. But legal and administrative costs should be no larger proportion of firm value for, say, a sample of large manufacturing firms.[22] Railroad bankruptcies are notoriously complex and protracted.

Direct versus Indirect Costs of Bankruptcy

So far we have discussed the *direct* (that is, legal and administrative) costs of bankruptcy. There are indirect costs too, which are nearly impossible to measure. But we have circumstantial evidence indicating their importance.

The indirect costs reflect the difficulties of running a railroad—or any company—while it is going through bankruptcy. Management's efforts to prevent further deterioration in the firm's business are often undermined by the delays and legal tangles that go with bankruptcy as a legal process.

The Penn Central railroad has the distinction of being the largest bankruptcy in the United States so far. It went under in June 1970. Four years later, with bankruptcy proceedings nowhere near completion, *Business Week* published an article called "Why the Penn Central is Falling Apart." Here are some excerpts.

> As its creditors hound it—some of them want to shut it down to get back their money—the railroad must continue operations at a time when it can barely keep running without pouring in huge sums to rebuild its facilities. Those sums, however, will not be available until the railroad shows that it can be reorganized.

Penn Central could have raised money by selling off some of its assets, but its creditors naturally opposed this:

> . . . Scores of other problems arise from a lack of money. Agonizing for everyone on the Penn Central, there is a tremendous source of capital that cannot be touched. For example, just about every abandoned mine branch in the Allegheny Mountains is chock full of old Penn Central cars destined for scrap. With today's scrap prices, they are a potential gold mine. But the creditors will not allow this asset to be turned into cash that will be reinvested in the estate, since that estate is eroding day by day.

The creditor's interest also got in the way of sensible maintenance:

> And the creditor problems do not stop there. Between Indianapolis and Terre Haute, the former Pennsylvania and New York Central RRs had double-track, high-speed

---

[21]Investors weren't able to predict the railroad bankruptcies five years before they happened. We are assuming that railroads like the ones that Warner examined had a 20% chance of going bankrupt in five years. That is one guess, but any other guess will do for present purposes.

[22]Bankruptcy costs are likely to be larger for *small* firms: there are economies of scale in going bankrupt, as in many other economic endeavours.

---

main lines rarely more than three miles apart. After the merger, most traffic was routed over the old New York Central route and the Pennsy line's second track was picked up. There are still 11 mi. of double track on the old Pennsy, though, and the 132-lb. rail is in excellent shape. It is desperately needed on the old New York Central line where double traffic and deferred maintenance have left much of that stretch with 10 mph speed limits.

The obvious thing is to use the old rail on the Penn Central line. Unfortunately,

> . . . the rail belongs to a Pennsy subsidiary, itself in reorganization, and the creditors will not permit the asset to be moved to a subsidiary of the New York Central except for "cash on the barrel," which, of course, is unavailable. [23]

We do not know what the sum of direct and indirect costs of bankruptcy amounts to. We suspect it is a significant number, particularly for large firms for which proceedings would be lengthy and complex. Perhaps the best evidence is the reluctance of creditors to force bankruptcy. In principle, they would be better off to end the agony and seize the assets as soon as possible. Instead creditors often overlook defaults in the hope of nursing the firm over a difficult period. They do this in part to avoid costs of bankruptcy. [24] There is an old financial saying, "Borrow $1,000 and you've got a banker. Borrow $1,000,000 and you've got a partner."

*Financial Distress without Bankruptcy

Not every firm that gets into trouble goes bankrupt. As long as the firm can scrape up enough cash to pay the interest on its debt, it may be able to postpone bankruptcy for many years. Eventually the firm may recover, pay off its debt, and escape bankruptcy altogether.

When a firm is in trouble, both bondholders and stockholders want it to recover. But in other respects their interests may be in conflict. In times of financial distress the security holders are like many political parties—united on generalities but threatened by squabbling on any specific issue.

Financial distress is costly when these conflicts of interest get in the way of proper operating, investment, and financing decisions. Stockholders are tempted to forsake the usual objective of maximizing the overall market value of the firm and to pursue narrower self-interest instead. They are tempted to play games at the expense of their creditors. We will now illustrate how such games can lead to costs of financial distress.

Here is the Circular File Company's present book balance sheet:

Circular File Company (Book Values)			
Net working capital	$ 20	$ 50	Bonds outstanding
Fixed assets	80	50	Common stock
Total assets	$100	$100	Total liabilities

We will assume there is only one share and one bond outstanding. The stockholder is also the manager. The bondholder is somebody else.

---

[23]Reprinted from the October 12, 1974, issue of *Business Week* by special permission, © 1974 by McGraw-Hill, Inc., New York, N.Y. 10020. All rights reserved.

[24]There is another reason. Creditors are not always given absolute priority in bankruptcy. Absolute priority means that creditors must be paid in full before stockholders receive a cent. Sometimes reorganizations are negotiated which provide "something for everyone," even though creditors are *not* paid in full. Thus creditors can never be sure how they will fare in bankruptcy.

Here is its balance sheet in market values—a clear case of financial distress, since the face value of Circular's debt ($50) exceeds the firm's market value ($30):

Circular File Company (Market Values)			
Net working capital	$20	$25	Bonds outstanding
Fixed assets	10	5	Common stock
Total assets	$30	$30	Total liabilities

If the debt matured today, Circular's owner would default, leaving the firm bankrupt. But suppose that the bond actually matures one year hence, that there is enough cash for Circular to limp along for one year, and that the bondholder cannot "call the question" and force bankruptcy before then.

The one-year grace period explains why the Circular share still has value. Its owner is betting on a stroke of luck that will rescue the firm, allowing it to pay off the debt with something left over. The bet is a long shot—the owner wins only if firm value increases from $30 to more than $50.[25] But the owner has a secret weapon: he controls investment and operating strategy.

*Risk Shifting: The First Game

Suppose that Circular has $10 cash. The following investment opportunity comes up:

Now	Possible Payoffs Next Year
	$120 (10% probability)
Invest	
$10	
	$0 (90% probability)

This is a wild gamble and probably a lousy project. But you can see why the owner would be tempted to take it anyway. Why not go for broke? Circular will probably go under anyway, and so the owner is essentially betting with the bondholder's money. But the owner gets most of the loot if the project pays off.

Suppose that the project's NPV is −$2 but that it is undertaken anyway, thus depressing firm value by $2. Circular's new balance sheet might look like this:

Circular File Company (Market Values)			
Net working capital	$10	$20	Bonds outstanding
Fixed assets	18	8	Common stock
Total assets	$28	$28	Total liabilities

Firm value falls by $2, but the owner is $3 ahead because the bond's value has fallen by $5. The $10 cash that used to stand behind the bond has been replaced by a very risky asset worth only $8.

Thus a game has been played at the expense of Circular's bondholder. The game illustrates the following general point. Stockholders of levered firms gain when business risk increases. Financial managers who act strictly in their shareholders' interests (and *against* the interests of creditors) will favour risky projects over safe ones. They may even take risky projects with negative NPVs.

---

[25]We are not concerned here with how to work out whether $5 is a fair price for stockholders to pay for the bet. We will come to that in Chapter 20 when we discuss the valuation of options.

This warped strategy for capital budgeting clearly is costly to the firm and to the economy as a whole. Why do we associate the costs with financial distress? Because the temptation to play is strongest when the odds of default are high. General Motors would never invest in our negative-NPV gamble. Its creditors are not vulnerable to this type of game.

*Refusing to Contribute Equity Capital: The Second Game

We have seen how stockholders, acting in their immediate, narrow self-interest, may take projects that reduce the overall market value of their firm. These are errors of commission. Conflicts of interest may also lead to errors of omission.

Assume that Circular cannot scrape up any cash, and therefore cannot take that wild gamble. Instead a *good* opportunity comes up: a relatively safe asset costing $10 with a present value of $15 and NPV $= +$5$.

This project will not in itself rescue Circular, but it is a step in the right direction. We might therefore expect Circular to issue $10 of new stock and to go ahead with the investment. Suppose that a second share is issued to the original owner for $10 cash. The project is taken. The new balance sheet might look like this:

Circular File Company (Market Values)			
Net working capital	$20	$33	Bonds outstanding
Fixed assets	25	12	Common stock
Total assets	$45	$45	Total liabilities

The total value of the firm goes up by $15 ($10 of new capital and $5 NPV). Notice that the Circular bond is no longer worth $25, but $33. The bondholder receives a capital gain of $8 because the firm's assets include a new, safe asset worth $15. The probability of default is less and the payoff to the bondholder if default occurs is larger.

The stockholder loses what the bondholder gains. Equity value goes up not by $15, but by $15 − $8 = $7. The owner puts in $10 of fresh equity capital but gains only $7 in market value. Going ahead is in the firm's interest, but not the owner's.

Again, our example illustrates a general point. If we hold business risk constant, any increase in firm value is shared among bondholders and stockholders. The value of any investment opportunity *to the firm's stockholders* is reduced because project benefits must be shared with bondholders. Thus it may not be in the stockholders' self-interest to contribute fresh equity capital even if that means forgoing positive-NPV investment opportunities.

This problem theoretically affects all levered firms, but it is most serious when firms land in financial distress. The greater the probability of default, the more bondholders have to gain from investments that increase firm value.

*And Three More Games, Briefly

As with other games, the temptation to play is particularly strong in financial distress.

1. Cash in and Run Stockholders may be reluctant to put money into a firm in financial distress, but they are happy to take the money out—in the form of a cash dividend, for example. The market value of the firm's stock goes down by less than the amount of the dividend paid, because the decline in *firm* value is shared with creditors. This game is just "refusing to contribute equity capital" run in reverse.

2. Playing for Time When the firm is in financial distress, creditors would like to salvage what they can by forcing the firm to settle up. Naturally, stockholders want to delay this as long as they can. There are various devious ways of doing this, for example through accounting changes designed to conceal the true extent of trouble, by encouraging false hopes of spontaneous recovery, or by cutting corners on maintenance, research and development, and so on, in order to make this year's operating performance look better.

3. Bait and Switch This game is not always played in financial distress, but it is a quick way to get *into* distress. You start with a conservative policy, issuing a limited amount of relatively safe debt. Then you suddenly switch and issue a lot more. That makes all your debt risky, imposing a capital loss on the "old" bondholders. Their capital loss is the stockholders' gain.

*What the Games Cost

Why should anyone object to these games so long as they are played by consenting adults? Because playing them means poor decisions about investments and operations.

The more the firm borrows, the greater the temptation to play the games (assuming the financial manager acts in the stockholders' interest). The increased odds of poor decisions in the future prompt investors to mark down the present market value of the firm. The fall in value comes out of stockholders' pockets. Potential lenders, realizing that games may be played at their expense, protect themselves by demanding better terms.

Therefore it is ultimately in the stockholders' interest to avoid temptation. The easiest way to do this is to limit borrowing to levels at which the firm's debt is safe or close to it.

But suppose that the tax advantages of debt spur the firm on to a high debt ratio and a significant probability of default or financial distress. Is there any way to convince potential lenders that games will not be played? The obvious answer is to give lenders veto power over potentially dangerous decisions.

There we have the ultimate economic rationale for all that fine print backing up corporate debt. Debt contracts almost always limit dividends or equivalent transfers of wealth to stockholders; the firm may not be allowed to pay out more than it earns, for example. Additional borrowing is almost always limited. For example, many companies are prevented by existing bond indentures from issuing any additional long-term debt unless their ratio of earnings to interest charges exceeds 2.0.

Sometimes firms are restricted from selling assets or making major investment outlays except with the lenders' consent. The risks of "playing for time" are reduced by specifying accounting procedures and by giving lenders access to the firm's books and its financial forecasts.

Of course fine print cannot be a complete solution for firms that insist on issuing risky debt. The fine print has its own costs; you have to spend money to save money. Obviously a complex debt contract costs more to negotiate than a simple one. Afterwards it costs the lender more to monitor the firm's performance. Lenders anticipate monitoring costs and demand compensation in the form of higher interest rates; thus the monitoring costs are ultimately paid by stockholders.

Perhaps the most severe costs of the fine print stem from the constraints it places on operating and investment decisions. For example, an attempt to prevent the "risk shifting" game may also prevent the firm from pursuing *good* investment opportunities. At the minimum there are delays in clearing major investments with lenders. In some cases lenders may veto high-risk investments even if net present value is positive. Lenders can lose from risk shifting even when the firm's overall market value increases. In fact, the lenders may try to play a game of their own, forcing the firm to stay in cash or low-risk assets even if good projects are forgone.

Thus, debt contracts cannot cover every possible manifestation of the games we have just discussed. Any attempt to do so would be hopelessly expensive and doomed to failure in any event. Human imagination is insufficient to conceive of all the possible things that could go wrong. We will always find surprises coming at us on dimensions we never thought to think about.

We hope we have not left the impression that managers and stockholders always succumb to temptation unless restrained. Usually they refrain voluntarily, not only from a sense of fair play, but also on pragmatic grounds: a firm or individual that makes a killing today at the expense of a creditor will be coldly received when the time comes to borrow again. Aggressive game playing is done only by out-and-out crooks and by firms in extreme financial distress. Firms limit borrowing precisely because they don't wish to land in distress.

Costs of Distress Vary with Type of Asset

Suppose your firm's only asset is a large downtown hotel, mortgaged to the hilt. The recession hits, occupancy rates fall, and the mortgage payments cannot be met. The lender takes over and sells the hotel to a new owner and operator. You use your firm's stock certificates for wallpaper.

What is the cost of bankruptcy? In this example, probably very little. The value of the hotel is, of course, much less than you hoped, but that is due to the lack of guests, not to the bankruptcy. The direct bankruptcy costs of Heartbreak Hotel are restricted to items such as legal and court fees, real estate commissions, and the time of the lender in sorting things out.

Suppose we repeat the story of Heartbreak Hotel for Fledgling Electronics. Everything is the same, except for the underlying real assets—not real estate but a high-tech going concern, a growth company whose most valuable assets are technology, investment opportunities, and its employees' human capital.

If Fledgling gets into trouble, the stockholders may be reluctant to put up money to cash in on its growth opportunities. Failure to invest is likely to be much more serious for Fledgling than for a company like Heartbreak Hotel.

If Fledgling finally defaults on its debt, the lender would find it much more difficult to cash in by selling off the assets. Many of them are intangibles, which have value only as a part of a going concern.

Could Fledgling be kept as a going concern through default and reorganization? Maybe, but there are a number of difficulties. First the odds of defections by key employees are higher than if the firm had never gotten into financial trouble. Special guarantees may have to be given to customers who are doubtful whether the firm will be around to service its products. Aggressive investment in new products and technology will be difficult; each class of creditors will have to be convinced that it is in their interest for the firm to invest new money in risky ventures.

Our examples of the hotel and electronics firm illustrate that the values of some assets can pass through bankruptcy and reorganization largely unscathed; the values of other assets are likely to be considerably diminished. The losses are greatest for the intangible assets that are linked to the health of the firm as a going concern—for example, technology, human capital, and brand image. That may be why debt ratios are low in the pharmaceutical industry, where value depends on continued success in research and development, and in many service industries where value depends on human capital. We can also understand why highly profitable growth companies, such as Northern Telecom or Digital Equipment Corporation, use mostly equity finance.[26]

---

[26]Recent empirical research confirms that firms holding largely intangible assets borrow less. See M. Long and I. Malitz, "Investment Patterns and Financial Leverage," National Bureau of Economic Research, Working Paper, January 1983; and S. Williamson, "The Moral Hazard Theory of Corporate Capital Structure: Empirical Tests," unpublished Ph.D. dissertation, MIT, November 1981.

The moral of these examples is: *Do not think only about the probability that borrowing will bring trouble. Think also of the value that may be lost if trouble comes.*

18-4 CHOOSING THE FIRM'S DEBT-EQUITY RATIO

A Checklist

It should be clear that there are no simple answers to the capital structure decision. For example, we can't say that more debt is always better. Debt may be better than equity in some cases, worse in others. We suggest, however, that you use a three-dimensional checklist when thinking about capital structure. These dimensions are taxes, risk, and asset type.

1. Taxes If your company is in a taxpaying position, an increase in leverage reduces the income tax paid by the company and increases the tax paid by investors. If the company has large accumulated losses, an increase in leverage cannot reduce corporate taxes but does increase personal taxes.

Of course you are not just interested in whether the company is currently paying taxes but whether it will do so throughout the life of the debt. Firms with high and stable income streams are more likely to remain in a taxpaying position, but even they may be unable to take full advantage of the interest tax shields if they borrow too much; hence our recommendation that there is a tax advantage to borrowing for companies that are reasonably sure that they can use the interest tax shields and a disadvantage for those that are unlikely to use them.

Remember also that borrowing is not the only way to shield income. For example, investment tax credits, capital cost allowances, and depletion allowances (in resource industries) can be used to reduce corporate taxes.

2. Risk With or without bankruptcy, financial distress is costly. Other things equal, distress is more likely for firms with high business risk. That is why such firms generally issue less debt.

3. Asset Type The costs of distress are likely to be greater for firms whose value depends on growth opportunities or intangible assets. These firms are more likely to forgo profitable investment opportunities and, if default occurs, their assets may be less saleable. Hence firms whose assets are weighted toward intangible assets should borrow significantly less, on average, than firms holding assets you can kick.

Planning Ahead

When you issue debt, you need to persuade the lenders that you will be able to repay their loan. Therefore it is usual to draw up a set of *pro forma* income statements and balance sheets. These are simply your best forecasts of the firm's profits, assets, and liabilities.

You may find when you do this that the firm is unlikely to generate sufficient cash internally to repay the loan. That is not in itself a cause for alarm—remember that most growing firms run a financial deficit and are, therefore, repeatedly raising new capital. But such a result should prompt you to ask two questions. First, "Can the maturity of the proposed loan be extended so that the firm can repay the loan out of income?" Second, "Is the firm likely to be *able* to raise the additional debt or equity that it will need to repay the proposed loan?"

Most managers are not only interested in the expected outcome: they also want to know what could happen if things go wrong. The techniques that we used in Chapter 10 for examining a single project can also be used to examine the firm as a whole.

For example, before their firm issues a large amount of debt, many financial managers conduct a break-even analysis. In other words, they look at how far sales or profits could decline without imperiling the firm's ability to service the loan. Or they look at how well the firm would fare under alternative plausible scenarios. Or they use Monte Carlo simulation to estimate the whole distribution of financial consequences.

The capital structure decision cannot be made in a vacuum. It has to form part of a sensible financial plan that takes into account future investment opportunities, the firm's dividend policy, and so on. That is why the financial manager needs to think about the effects of an issue of debt or equity on future income and balance sheets.

Pro forma income statements and balance sheets will indicate future financing needs. But they won't tell you much about whether you will be able to raise the necessary money. In other words, they won't tell you when you are bankrupt. Remember that bankruptcy occurs when the market value of the firm is less than the payments that have to be made on the debt. When this happens, the shares are worthless and the shareholders have no incentive to put up any further capital. If you want to estimate the risk of bankruptcy, you need to estimate the distribution of future company values. Here again you may find it useful to use simulation to estimate the odds that the market value of the company will be less than the payments that need to be made on the debt.

18-5   SUMMARY

Our goal in this chapter was to build a theory of optimal capital structure combining MM's insights with an analysis of taxes and financial distress.

The value of the firm equals

Value if all-equity-financed + PV tax shield − PV costs of financial distress

The cost of financial distress can be broken down as follows:

1. Bankruptcy costs
   (*a*) Direct costs such as court fees
   (*b*) Indirect costs reflecting the difficulty of managing a company undergoing reorganization

2. Costs of financial distress short of bankruptcy
   (*a*) Conflicts of interest between bondholders and stockholders of firms in financial distress may lead to poor operating performance and investment decisions. Stockholders acting in their narrow self-interest can gain at the expense of creditors by playing "games" that reduce the overall value of the firm.
   (*b*) The fine print in debt contracts is designed to prevent these games. But fine print increases the costs of writing, monitoring, and enforcing the debt contract.

The value of the tax shield is more controversial. Let us define the net tax shield as T^* times the interest payment on the debt $r_D D$. To calculate present value, this tax shield is usually discounted at the borrowing rate r_D. In the special case of permanent debt

$$\text{PV tax shield} = \frac{T^*(r_D D)}{r_D} = T^* D$$

The problem is to identify T^*.

Most economists have become accustomed to thinking only of the corporate tax advantages of debt. Because firms do not pay corporate tax on any profits that are paid out as interest, interest payments provide a corporate tax shield. If this is the only tax consequence of debt, then for a taxpaying company the net tax saving T^* is simply the marginal corporate tax rate.

The principal difficulty with this view is that many firms seem to thrive with no debt at all despite the strong inducement to borrow. Miller has presented an alternative theory that may explain this. He argues that the net tax saving T^* is really zero when personal taxes as well as corporate taxes are considered. Interest income is not taxed at the corporate level but is taxed at the personal level. Equity income is taxed at the corporate level but largely escapes personal taxes.

Some investors such as pension funds are not liable to tax; therefore they do not mind whether they hold debt or equity. It clearly pays companies to persuade these investors to hold debt—the corporate tax saved is greater than the personal tax lost. Other investors are subject to very high rates of personal tax. There is no way that companies can afford to persuade these investors to hold debt—the corporate tax saved would be less than the personal tax lost.

Thus companies can afford to bribe investors to switch from equity into debt as long as the corporate tax rate is greater than the personal tax rate of the migrating investor. This establishes an optimal debt ratio for the aggregate of corporations. But, if the total supply of debt suits investors' needs, any single taxpaying firm must find that debt policy does not matter.

We suggest that the truth lies somewhere between these two theories. Borrowing may make sense for some firms but not for others. If a firm can be fairly sure of earning a profit, there is likely to be a moderate net tax saving from borrowing. In these cases T^* is greater than zero but less than 0.46. However for firms that are unlikely to earn sufficient profits to benefit from the corporate tax shield, there is probably a net tax disadvantage to borrowing. For these firms T^* could be negative.

There is no neat formula that you can plug in to find the optimal capital structure. But we recommend that you employ a three-dimensional checklist of taxes, risk, and asset type. This provides a framework for making sensible borrowing decisions.

FURTHER READING

Modigliani and Miller's analysis of the present value of interest tax shields at the corporate level is in:

F. Modigliani and M.H. Miller, "Corporate Income Taxes and the Cost of Capital: A Correction," *American Economic Review*, **53**:433–443 (June 1963).

F. Modigliani and M.H. Miller, "Some Estimates of the Cost of Capital to the Electric Utility Industry, 1954–57," *American Economic Review*, **56**:333–391 (June 1966).

The following articles consider personal as well as corporate taxes:

D. Farrar and L.L. Selwyn, "Taxes, Corporate Financial Policy and the Returns to Investors," *National Tax Journal*, **20**:144–154 (December 1967).

M.H. Miller, "Debt and Taxes," *Journal of Finance*, **32**:261–276 (May 1977).

Miller's theory is extended to include depreciation and other tax shields in:

H. DeAngelo and R. Masulis, "Optimal Capital Structure Under Corporate Taxation," *Journal of Financial Economics*, **8**:5–29 (March 1980).

Estimates of bankruptcy costs are presented in:

J.B. Warner, "Bankruptcy Costs: Some Evidence," *Journal of Finance*, **32**:337–348 (May 1977).

The following four articles analyze the conflicts of interest between bondholders and stockholders, and their implications for financing policy. (Do not read the fourth article until you have read Chapter 20.)

M.J. Gordon, "Towards a Theory of Financial Distress," *Journal of Finance*, **26**:347–356 (May 1971).

M.C. Jensen and W.H. Meckling, "Theory of the Firm: Managerial Behavior, Agency Costs and Ownership Structure," *Journal of Financial Economics*, **3**:305–360 (October 1976).

S.C. Myers, "Determinants of Corporate Borrowing," *Journal of Financial Economics*, **5**: 146–175 (1977).

D. Galai and R.W. Masulis, "The Option Pricing Model and the Risk Factor of Stock," *Journal of Financial Economics*, **3**:53–82 (January–March 1976).

For an interesting survey of the capital structure controversy, see:

R.H. Gordon and B.G. Malkiel, "Corporation Finance," in H.J. Aaron and J.A. Pechman (eds.), *How Taxes Affect Economic Behavior*, The Brookings Institution, Washington, D.C., 1981.

Donaldson has described how corporations set their borrowing targets. He also suggests how these targets can be set more intelligently.

G. Donaldson, *Corporate Debt Capacity: A Study of Corporate Debt Policy and the Determination of Corporate Debt Capacity*, Divison of Research, Graduate School of Business Administration, Harvard University, Boston, 1962.

G. Donaldson, *Strategy for Financial Mobility*, Division of Research, Graduate School of Business Administration, Harvard University, Boston, 1969.

QUIZ

1. Compute the present value of interest tax shields generated by these three debt issues. Consider corporate taxes only. The marginal tax rate is $T_c = 0.46$.
   (*a*) A $1,000, one-year loan at 8%.
   (*b*) A five-year loan of $1,000 at 8%. Assume no principal is repaid until maturity.
   (*c*) A $1,000 perpetuity at 7%.

2. Here are book and market value balance sheets of the United Frypan Company: tax credit of 25% of taxable dividends. Provincial personal tax is 50% of federal tax.

Book				Market			
Net working capital	20	Debt	40	Net working capital	20	Debt	40
Long-term assets	80	Equity	60	Long-term assets	140	Equity	120
	100		100		160		160

Assume that MM's theory holds with taxes. There is no growth and the $40 of debt is expected to be permanent. Assume a 40% corporate tax rate.
   (*a*) How much of the firm's value is accounted for by the debt-generated tax shield?
   (*b*) How much better off will UF's shareholders be if the firm borrows $20 more and uses it to repurchase stock?
   (*c*) Now suppose that a law is passed eliminating the deductibility of interest for tax purposes after a grace period of five years. What will be the new value of the firm, other things equal? (Assume an 8% borrowing rate.)

3. Suppose that the rate of corporate income tax is reduced to 40%. What would Miller predict about corporate debt policy?

4. Compute the total corporate plus personal taxes paid on debt and equity income for each of the following cases. In each case, specify whether the tax advantage lies with debt or equity. Assume the corporate tax rate is $T_c = 0.40$. Capital gains when realized are taxed at one-half the rate on debt, which is the ordinary personal tax rate. Taxable dividends are 150% of dividends, but there is a federal dividend

tax credit of 25% of taxable dividends. Provincial personal tax is 50% of federal tax.

Case	Investor's Federal Tax Bracket	Form of Equity Income
a	0.	All dividends
b	0.25	All dividends
c	0.25	All capital gains, never realized
d	0.35	All capital gains, never realized
e	0.35	All dividends
f	0.45	All dividends

* 5. "The firm can't use interest tax shields unless it has (taxable) income to shield." What does this statement imply for the debt policy? Explain briefly.

* 6. Let us go back to Circular File's market value balance sheet:

Net working capital	$20	$25	Bonds outstanding
Fixed assets	10	5	Common stock
Total assets	$30	$30	Total liabilities

Who gains and who loses from the following manoeuvres?
(a) Circular scrapes up $5 in cash and pays a cash dividend.
(b) Circular halts operations, sells its fixed assets, and converts net working capital into $20 cash. Unfortunately the fixed assets fetch only $6 on the second-hand market. The $26 cash is invested in Treasury bills.
(c) Circular encounters an acceptable investment opportunity, NPV = 0, requiring an investment of $10. The firm borrows to finance the project. The new debt has the same security, seniority, and so on as the old.
(d) Suppose that the new project has NPV = +$2 and is financed by an issue of preferred stock.
(e) The lenders agree to extend the maturity of their loan from one year to two years in order to give Circular a chance to recover.

7. What types of firms would be likely to incur heavy costs in the event of bankruptcy or financial distress? What types would incur relatively light costs? Give a few examples of each type.

QUESTIONS AND PROBLEMS

1. Montmorency Inc. has assets of $100 million and these are expected to remain unchanged in real terms. Assume that the real interest rate is 5%, the corporate tax rate is 46%, and debt interest is paid at the end of each year. If debt is a constant 30% of the value of the assets, what is PV tax shield
   (a) If there is no expected inflation?
   (b) If expected inflation is 10% a year?

2. "The trouble with MM's argument is that it ignores the fact that individuals can deduct interest for personal income tax." Show why this is not an objection. What difference would it make if individuals were not allowed to deduct interest for personal tax?

3. Look back at the Northern Telecom example in Section 18-1. Suppose that Northern moves to a 40% book debt ratio by issuing debt and using the proceeds to

repurchase shares. Assume that MM's theory holds except for taxes. Now reconstruct Table 18-2(*b*) to reflect the new capital structure. Before it changes its capital
structure, Northern has 35.45 million shares outstanding. What is the stock price
before and after the change?

4. Calculate the tax shield for an actual company assuming
   (*a*) Debt is permanent.
   (*b*) MM are right.
   How would the stock price change if the company announced tomorrow that it
   intended to replace all its debt with equity?

* 5. Explain the implications of Miller's 1976 presidential address for the debt policy
   of:
   (*a*) A company that pays corporate income tax.
   (*b*) A company that is not in a taxpaying position.
   (*c*) A company that is paying taxes now, but is unsure that it will have taxable
   income in the future.

* 6. Recalculate Miller's equilibrium assuming that equity returns are taxed at half the
   rate of personal income tax on interest receipts.

7. Look at some real companies with different types of assets. What operating problems
   would each encounter in the event of financial distress? How well would the assets
   keep their value?

8. Imagine the following very simple world. There are three groups of investors with
   the following tax rates:

Group	Tax Rate, %
A	60
B	40
C	0

They can choose from perpetual American municipal bonds, perpetual corporate
bonds, and common stock. Municipals and common stock attract no personal tax.
Interest from corporate bonds attracts personal tax but is deductible for corporate
tax. The corporate tax rate is 50%. Interest payments on municipals total $20
million. Cash flow (before interest and taxes) from corporations totals $300 million.
Each group starts with the same amount of money. Regardless of what changes are
made in capital structure, the three groups always invest the same amount as each
other, and they require a minimum return of 10% after taxes on any security.
   (*a*) Suppose that companies are financed initially by common stock. Company X
   now decides to allocate $1 million of its pretax cash flows to interest payments
   on debt. Which group or groups of investors will buy this debt? What will be
   the rate of interest? What will be the effect on the value of Company X?
   (*b*) Other companies have followed the example of X and interest payments now
   total $150 million. At this point Company Y decides to allocate $1 million
   to interest payments on debt. Which group or groups will buy this debt? What
   will be the rate of interest? What will be the effect on the value of company Y?
   (*c*) Total interest payments have somehow risen to $250 million. Now com-
   pany Z substitutes common stock for debt, thereby *reducing* interest payments
   by $1 million. Which group or groups will sell their debt to Z? At what rate
   of interest can Z repurchase the debt? What will be the effect on Z's value?
   (*d*) What is the equilibrium capital structure? Which groups will hold which
   securities? What is the rate of interest? What is the total value of all companies?

Show that in equilibrium even an unlevered company has no incentive to issue debt. Similarly show that even a company with above-average leverage has no incentive to reduce its debt.

* 9. Here is a difficult problem. What difference does capital cost allowance make to Miller's equilibrium? Try recalculating the equilibrium in problem 8, assuming that companies can deduct CCA of:
   (a) $100 million, perpetually.
   (b) $50 million, perpetually.

*10. The expected return on (risk-free) equity is 14% and the interest rate is 20%.
   (a) What is the implied personal tax rate of the marginal lender? (Assume that equity income is free of personal tax.)
   (b) Company A has large CCA tax shields and uncertain income. As a result, A's expected marginal rate of corporate tax is 40% if it finances solely with equity. For every 5% increase in A's debt ratio, A's marginal tax rate is expected to decline by 2%. How much should A borrow?

11. A Canadian corporation has a pretax cash flow of $1,000. The cash can either go to create interest for a bondholder or a dividend for a stockholder. The investor has a 20% marginal federal tax rate and lives in a province where provincial tax is 47% of personal federal tax. Dividends are grossed up by 50% for tax purposes and there is a federal dividend tax credit of $22^2/_3$% of grossed-up dividends. How much cash would go to the bondholder or the stockholder, after all taxes, in the following cases:
   (a) The corporate tax rate is 25% and there is a $12^1/_2$% distribution tax paid on dividends.
   (b) The corporate tax rate is $33^1/_3$% and there is no distribution tax on dividends.
   (c) The corporate tax rate is 46% and there is no distribution tax on dividends.
   Are these answers consistent with what you learned in Section 18-2?

*12. The Salad Oil Storage Company (SOS) has financed a large part of its facilities with long-term debt. There is a significant risk of default, but the company is not on the ropes yet. Explain:
   (a) Why SOS stockholders could lose by investing in a positive-NPV project financed by an equity issue.
   (b) Why SOS stockholders could gain by investing in a negative-NPV project financed by an equity issue.
   (c) Why SOS stockholders could gain from paying out a large cash dividend.
   How might the firm's adherence to a target debt ratio mitigate some or all of the problems noted above?

*13. (a) Who benefits from the "fine print" in bond contracts when the firm gets into financial trouble? Give a one-sentence answer.
   (b) Who benefits from the fine print when the bonds are issued? Suppose the firm is offered the choice of issuing (1) a bond with standard restrictions on dividend payout, additional borrowing, and so on, and (2) a bond with minimal restrictions, but a much higher interest rate? Suppose the interest rates on both (1) and (2) are fair from the viewpoint of lenders. Which bond would you expect the firm to issue? Why?

INTERACTIONS OF INVESTMENT AND FINANCING DECISIONS

We first addressed problems of capital budgeting in Chapter 2. At that point we had said hardly a word about financing decisions; we proceeded under the simplest possible assumption about financing, namely, all-equity financing. We were really assuming an idealized Modigliani-Miller (MM) world in which all financing decisions are irrelevant. In a strict MM world, firms can analyse real investments as if they are to be all-equity-financed; the actual financing plan is a mere detail to be worked out later.

Under MM assumptions, decisions to spend money can be separated from decisions to raise money. In this chapter we reconsider the capital budgeting decision when investment and financing decisions *interact* and cannot be separated.

In the early chapters you learned how to value a capital investment opportunity by a four-step procedure:

1. Forecast the project's incremental after-tax cash flow.

2. Assess the project's risk.

3. Estimate the opportunity cost of capital, that is, the expected rate of return offered to investors by the equivalent-risk investments traded in capital markets.

4. Calculate NPV using the discounted-cash-flow formula.

In effect, we were thinking of each project as a mini-firm, and asking, "How much would that mini-firm be worth if we spun it off as a separate, all-equity-financed enterprise? How much would investors be willing to pay for shares in the project?"

Of course, this procedure rests on the concept of *value additivity*. In well-functioning capital markets the market value of the firm is the sum of the present value of all the assets held by the firm[1]—the whole equals the sum of the parts. If value additivity did *not* hold, then the value of the firm with the project could be more or less than the sum of the separate value of the project and the value of the firm without the project. We could not determine the project's contribution to firm value by evaluating it as a separate mini-firm.

In this chapter we stick with the value-additivity principle, but extend it to include value contributed by financing decisions as well as value contributed by investment decisions. That leads us to a simple and straightforward approach to analyzing the interactions of financing and investment decisions. The idea is to start by estimating the project's "base-case" value as an all-equity-financed mini-firm, and then to adjust this project's base-case NPV to account for the project's impact on the firm's capital structure. Thus

---

[1]*All assets* means intangible as well as tangible assets. For example, a going concern is usually worth more than a haphazard pile of tangible assets. Thus, the aggregate value of a firm's tangible assets often falls short of its market value. The difference is accounted for by going-concern value or by other intangible assets such as accumulated technical expertise, an experienced sales force, or valuable growth opportunities.

Adjusted NPV (ANPV, or just APV for short) = base-case NPV

+ NPV of financing decisions caused by project acceptance

Once you identify and value the side effects of financing a project, calculating its APV (adjusted net present value) is no more than addition or subtraction.

There is another way to capture financing side effects. This alternative procedure is more widely used than APV, and it *looks* simpler: you just change the discount rate for the project's cash flows. We will discuss the pros and cons of the adjusted discount rate after you master APV.

19-1 THE ADJUSTED-PRESENT-VALUE RULE

The adjusted-present-value rule is easiest to understand in the context of simple numerical examples. We start by analyzing a project under base-case assumptions, and then consider possible financing side effects of accepting the project.

The Base Case

The APV method begins by valuing the project as if it were a mini-firm financed solely by equity. Consider a project requiring $10 million investment and offering a level after-tax cash flow of $1.8 million per year for ten years. The project's opportunity cost of capital is 12%, which reflects the project's business risk. Investors would demand a 12% expected return to invest in the mini-firm's shares.

Thus the mini-firm's base-case NPV is

$$\text{NPV} = -10 + \sum_{t=1}^{10} \frac{1.8}{(1.12)^t} = +\$0.17 \text{ million or } \$170,000$$

Considering the project's size, this figure is not significantly greater than zero. In a pure MM world where no financing decision matters, the financial manager would lean toward taking the project but would not be heartbroken if the project were discarded.

Issue Costs

But suppose that the firm actually has to finance the $10 million investment by issuing stock (it will not have to issue stock if it rejects the project) and that issue costs soak up 5% of the gross proceeds of the issue. That means the firm has to issue $10,526,000 in order to obtain $10,000,000 cash. The $526,000 difference goes to underwriters, lawyers, and others involved in the issue process.[2]

The project's APV is calculated by subtracting the issue cost from base-case NPV:

APV = base-case NPV − issue cost = +170,000 − 526,000 = −$356,000

The firm would reject the project because APV is negative.

Subsidized Financing

Consider a different financing scenario. The firm has $5 million cash available for investment. Suppose that the investment project we have been discussing is a plan to

---

[2]Some of these costs may be tax-deductible expenses for the firm. If so, the after-tax transaction costs will be less than $526,000.

produce solar water heaters for single-family homes. The government, eager to encourage solar energy, offers to help finance the project by lending $5 million at a subsidized rate of 5%. The loan calls for the firm to pay the government $647,500 annually for ten years (this amount includes both principal and interest).

What is the value of being able to borrow from the government at 5%? It depends on the interest rate the firm would have to pay on an unsubsidized loan. If that rate is 8%, and we ignore taxes,[3] the net present value of the government loan is

$$\text{NPV of subsidized loan} = 5,000,000 - \sum_{t=1}^{10} \frac{647,500}{(1.08)^t}$$
$$= 5,000,000 - 4,345,000 = +\$655,000$$

Because the firm cannot get the subsidized loan without taking on the solar water heater project, the loan's value should be added to the base-case NPV. The project becomes much more attractive:

APV = base-case NPV + NPV of subsidized loan

= +170,000 + 655,000 = $825,000

What if the firm did not have $5 million in cash and had to sell that amount of stock to go ahead? Then APV would reflect two adjustments: addition of the NPV of the government loan and subtraction of the issue costs of the new stock. Suppose that issue costs are 5% of gross proceeds. The firm has to issue $5,263,000 of stock to get $5 million. Then

APV = base-case NPV + NPV of subsidized loan − issue cost

= +170,000 + 655,000 − 263,000

= +$562,000

APV is still positive. Therefore, go ahead with the project.

Additions to the Firm's Debt Capacity

Consider still another case. Suppose that the firm has a 50% target debt ratio. Its policy is to limit debt to 50% of the book value of its assets. Thus, if it invests more, it borrows more; in this sense investment adds to the firm's debt capacity.[4]

Is debt capacity worth anything? The most widely accepted answer is "yes" because of the tax shields generated by interest payments on corporate borrowing. (You may wish to look back to our discussion of debt and taxes in Chapter 18.) For example, MM's original theory states that the value of the firm is independent of its capital structure *except* for the present value of interest tax shields:

Firm value = value with all-equity financing + PV tax shield

---

[3]The tax advantage to corporate borrowing is the next topic in our discussion of APV.

[4]*Debt capacity* is potentially misleading because it seems to imply an absolute limit to the amount the firm is *able to* borrow. That is not what we mean. The firm limits borrowing to 50% of assets because it believes that to be the best policy. It could borrow more if it wanted to.

Table 19-1 Calculating the present value of interest tax shields on debt supported by the solar heater project (figures in thousands).

Year	Debt Outstanding at Start of Year	Interest	Interest Tax Shield	Present Value of Tax Shield
1	$5,000	$400	$184	$170
2	4,500	360	166	142
3	4,000	320	147	117
4	3,500	280	129	95
5	3,000	240	110	75
6	2,500	200	92	58
7	2,000	160	74	43
8	1,500	120	55	30
9	1,000	80	37	18
10	500	40	18	9
				Total $757

Assumptions:
1. Marginal tax rate = 0.46; tax shield = 0.46 × interest.
2. Debt principal repaid at end of year in ten $500,000 instalments.
3. Interest rate on debt is 8%.
4. Present value calculated at the 8% borrowing rate. The assumption here is that the tax shields are just as risky as the interest payments generating them.

This theory tells us to compute the value of the firm in two steps: first compute its base-case value under all-equity financing, and then add the present value of taxes saved due to a departure from all-equity financing. This procedure is like an APV calculation for the firm as a whole.

We can repeat the calculation for a particular project. For example, suppose that the solar heater project increases the firm's assets by $10 million and therefore prompts it to borrow $5 million more. To keep things simple, we assume that this $5 million loan is repaid in equal instalments, so that the amount borrowed declines with the depreciating book value of the solar heater project. We also assume that the loan is *not* subsidized and therefore carries an interest rate of 8%. Table 19-1 shows how the value of the interest tax shields is calculated. This is the value of the additional debt capacity contributed to the firm by the project. We obtain APV by adding this amount to the project's NPV:

$$APV = \text{base-case NPV} + \text{PV tax shield}$$
$$= +170,000 + 757,000 = \$927,000$$

The Value of Interest Tax Shields

In Table 19-1, we boldly assumed that the firm could fully capture interest tax shields of 46 cents on the dollar discounted back to the present. The true value of the tax shield is almost surely less:

1. You can't use tax shields unless you pay taxes, and you don't pay taxes unless you make money. Few firms can be *sure* that future probability will be sufficient to use up the interest tax shields.
2. The government takes two bites out of corporate income: the corporate tax and the tax on bondholders' and stockholders' personal income. The corporate tax favours debt; the personal tax favours equity.

In Chapter 18, we argued that the effective tax shield on interest was not 46% ($T_c = 0.46$), but some lower figure T^*. We were unable to pin down an exact figure for T^* (some respected scholars believe $T^* = 0$).

Suppose for example, that we believe $T^* = 0.30$. We can easily recalculate the APV of the solar heater project. Just multiply the present value of the interest tax shields by 30/46. The bottom line of Table 19-1 drops from $757,000 to 757,000 (30/46) = $494,000. APV drops to:

$$\text{APV} = \text{base case NPV} + \text{PV tax shield}$$
$$= +170,000 + 494,000 = \$664,000$$

Review of the Adjusted-Present-Value Approach

If the decision to invest in a capital project has important side effects on other financial decisions made by the firm, those side effects should be taken into account when the project is evaluated.

The idea behind APV is "divide and conquer." The approach does not attempt to capture all the side effects in a single calculation. A series of present value calculations is made instead. The first establishes a base-case value for the project: its value as a separate, all-equity-financed mini-firm. Then each side effect is traced out and the present value of its cost or benefit to the firm is calculated. Finally, all the present values are added together to estimate the project's total contribution to the value of the firm. Thus, in general,

$$\text{Project APV} = \text{base-case NPV} + \frac{\text{sum of the present value of the side}}{\text{effects of accepting the project}}$$

19-2 ADJUSTED DISCOUNT RATES—AN ALTERNATIVE TO ADJUSTED PRESENT VALUE

Calculating APV is not mathematically difficult, but tracing out and evaluating a project's financial side effects takes financial sophistication. Many firms use a simpler procedure. They adjust the discount rate rather than adjusting present value. This allows them to calculate net present value only once, rather than the two or more times required by APV. They set the discount rate for project acceptance equal to an *adjusted cost of capital* which reflects the opportunity cost of capital *and* the project's financing side effects.

Example: The Geothermal Project

We will explain the adjusted-cost-of-capital approach with an even simpler numerical example. The project calls for tapping geothermal energy to supply heat and air conditioning for a shopping centre. The investment required is $1 million. Once installed the project will save $220,000 per year after taxes. To keep the arithmetic simple, we will assume the saving continues indefinitely. The business risk of the venture requires a 20% discount rate—this is r, the opportunity cost of capital. Thus the project's base-case NPV is just positive:

$$\text{Base-case NPV} = -1,000,000 + \frac{220,000}{0.20}$$

$$= +\$100,000$$

We assume that the project has one financing side effect. It expands the firm's borrowing power by \$400,000. The project lasts indefinitely, and so we treat it as supporting perpetual debt. In other words, the firm is assumed to borrow \$400,000 against the project, and to maintain that borrowing come hell or high water. If the borrowing rate is 14% and the net tax shield per dollar of interest is $T^* = 0.30$, the project supports debt that generates interest tax shields of $0.3 \times 0.14 \times 400,000 = \$16,800$ per year forever. The present value of these tax shields is $16,800/0.14 = \$120,000$. Thus the geothermal project's APV is:

$$\text{APV} = \text{base-case NPV} + \text{PV tax shield}$$

$$= +100,000 + 120,000 = +\$220,000$$

The geothermal project looks even better when its contribution to corporate debt capacity is recognized.

The present value of the interest tax shield is $+\$120,000$. Therefore the geothermal project would still be acceptable even if base-case NPV were as low as $-\$120,000$. What does that imply for the minimum acceptable *income* from the project? To answer that question, we set base-case NPV at $-\$120,000$ and solve for the project's annual income:

$$\begin{array}{c}\text{Minimum acceptable} \\ \text{base-case NPV}\end{array} = -1,000,000 + \frac{\text{annual income}}{0.20}$$

$$= -120,000$$

$$\text{Annual income} = 0.2(1,000,000 - 120,000) = \$176,000$$

Thus, the minimum acceptable income from the project is \$176,000 a year and the minimum acceptable IRR is $176,000/1,000,000 = 0.176$ or 17.6%.[5] This is the lowest return that the firm would be willing to accept from projects like this one; it is the IRR at which APV is zero.

Suppose that we encounter another perpetuity. Its opportunity cost of capital is also $r = 0.20$, and it also expands the firm's borrowing power by 40% of the investment. We know that if such a project offers an IRR greater than 17.6%, it will have a positive APV. Therefore, we could shorten the analysis by just discounting the project's cash inflows at 17.6%.[6] This discount rate is often called the adjusted cost of capital. It reflects both the project's business risk and its contribution to the firm's debt capacity.

We will denote the adjusted cost of capital by r^*. To calculate r^*, we find the minimum acceptable internal rate of return—the IRR at which APV = 0. The rule is

Accept projects which have a positive NPV at the adjusted cost of capital r^*.

---

[5]Since the project produces a level stream of cash flows in perpetuity, IRR = cash flow divided by investment.

[6]Remember that forecasted project cash flows do *not* reflect the tax shields generated by any debt the project may support.

A General Definition of the Adjusted Cost of Capital*

We now have two concepts of the cost of capital:

Concept 1: The Opportunity Cost of Capital (r)   The expected rate of return offered in capital markets by equivalent-risk assets. This depends on the risk of the project's cash flows.

Concept 2: The Adjusted Cost of Capital (r^*)   An adjusted opportunity cost or hurdle rate that reflects the financing side effects of an investment project.

Some people just say "cost of capital." Sometimes their meaning is clear in context. At other times, they don't know which concept they are referring to and that can sow widespread confusion.

When financing side effects are important, you should accept projects with positive APVs. But if you know the adjusted discount rate, you don't have to calculate APV; you just calculate NPV at the adjusted rate. If we could find a simple, universally correct method for calculating r^*, we would be all set. Unfortunately, there is no such method. There are some reasonably adequate rules of thumb, however.

MM's Formula   One formula for calculating r^* was suggested by Modigliani and Miller (MM).[7] MM's formula is

$$r^* = r(1 - T^*L)$$

where r is the opportunity cost of capital and L is the project's marginal contribution to the firm's debt capacity as a proportion of the project's present value. The value of L may be higher than the firm's overall debt ratio or lower than the firm's overall debt ratio. Remember, T^* reflects the net tax saving attached to a dollar of future interest payments.

Example of MM's Formula   The contribution of the geothermal project to the firm's debt capacity is $400,000. Therefore $L = 0.40$. The project's opportunity cost of capital is $r = 0.20$ and we continue to assume that $T^* = 0.30$. We worked out earlier that the project's adjusted cost of capital was $r^* = 0.176$. That is precisely what we get using the MM formula:

$$r^* = r(1 - T^*L)$$
$$= 0.20(1 - 0.3(0.4)) = 0.176 \text{ or } 17.6\%$$

How Reliable is MM's Formula?   The MM formula works for the geothermal project or for any other project that is expected to (1) generate a level, perpetual cash flow and (2) support permanent debt. The formula is exactly right only if these two assumptions are met. Assets offering perpetual cash-flow streams are like abominable snowmen: often referred to but seldom seen. But MM's formula still works reasonably well for projects with limited lives or irregular cash-flow streams. Using the formula to calculate the present value of these projects will typically result in an error of 2% to 6%.[8] This is not too bad when you consider that a biased cash-flow forecast could put project value off the mark by plus or minus 20%.

---

[7]The formula first appeared in F. Modigliani and M.H. Miller, "Corporate Income Taxes and the Cost of Capital: A Correction," *American Economic Review*, **53**:433–443 (June 1963). It is explained more fully in M.H. Miller and F. Modigliani, "Some Estimates of the Cost of Capital to the Electric Utility Industry: 1954–1957," *American Economic Review*, **56**:333–391 (June 1966). In these articles, MM assumed that T^* equals the corporate tax rate T_c.

[8]See S.C. Myers, "Interactions of Corporate Financing and Investment Decisions—Implications for Capital Budgeting," *Journal of Finance*, **29**:1–25 (March 1974).

What Happens when Future Debt Levels are Uncertain

We wish we could stop at this point and go on to something easier. But conscience won't allow it. Any capital budgeting procedure that assumes debt levels are fixed when a project is undertaken is grossly oversimplified. For example, we assumed that the geothermal project contributed $400,000 to the firm's debt capacity—not just when the project is undertaken, but "from here to eternity." That amounts to saying that the future value and risk of the project will not change—a strong assumption indeed. Suppose the price of oil shoots up unexpectedly a year after the project is undertaken; since the geothermal project saves oil, its cash flow and value shoot up too. Suppose the project's value doubles. In that case, won't its contribution to debt capacity also double, to $800,000? It works the other way too: if the oil price falls out of bed, the contribution to debt capacity tumbles.

Suppose the firm's rule is not "Always borrow $400,000," but "Always borrow 40% of the geothermal project's value." Then if project value increases, the firm borrows more. If it decreases, it borrows less. Under this policy, you can no longer discount future interest tax shields at the borrowing rate because the shields are no longer certain. Their size depends on the amount actually borrowed and, therefore, on the actual future value of the project.

When the firm adjusts its borrowing to keep a constant debt proportion, it can often be a wearisome task to calculate the project's APV. Fortunately, James Miles and Russell Ezzell have derived an adjusted discount rate formula for this problem:[9]

$$r^* = r - Lr_DT^* \left(\frac{1 + r}{1 + r_D} \right)$$

where r_D is the borrowing rate. For the geothermal project, we would calculate an adjusted cost of capital of:

$$r^* = 0.20 - 0.4(0.14)(0.3) \left(\frac{1.2}{1.14} \right) = 0.1823 \text{ or } 18.23\%$$

Discounting the project's cash flows at 18.23% gives a net present value of

$$NPV = -1,000,000 + \frac{220,000}{0.1823}$$

$$= +\$207,000$$

The Miles-Ezzell formula works only for firms that maintain a constant debt proportion, but in these cases, it is exact for any cash-flow pattern or project life.[10] It is also much easier to use than the adjusted-present-value method.

How Useful are Adjusted-Cost-of-Capital Formulas?

We now have two adjusted-cost-of-capital formulas. The major *conceptual* difference between the two formulas lies in their assumptions about the amount of debt the firm

---

[9]J. Miles and R. Ezzell, "The Weighted Average Cost of Capital, Perfect Capital Markets, and Project Life: A Clarification," *Journal of Financial and Quantitative Analysis*, **15**:719–730 (September 1980).

[10]Remember that the MM formula was exact, given its assumption about debt policy, only for perpetuities.

can or will issue against the project. MM assume this amount is fixed. Miles and Ezzell assume it will vary with the project's future value. Miles and Ezzell's assumption is more attractive theoretically, but on the other hand, we have to admit that firms' debt policies are sticky: we don't see firms issuing or retiring debt every time their stock price goes up or down. So the truth may be somewhere in between.

Truth's exact location may not be so important. The geothermal and solar heater projects were attractive, regardless of which method or formula we used. This is one illustration of BMSW's third law: *You can make a lot more money by good investment decisions than by good financing decisions.*

Nevertheless, it's important to understand the assumptions underlying the formulas and their relationship to the more general APV rule. Both formulas assume that financing affects firm value only through interest tax shields. This is a bold simplification. Most financial scholars and practitioners agree that the tax shields have value—although even this is controversial, as we saw in Chapter 18. But practically no one believes that interest tax shields are the *only* thing governing the financing decision. The decision to accept a project may lead to a stock issue and to issue costs. It may force the firm to shift its dividend policy, or it may enable the firm to make use of an advantageous financial lease or government-subsidized financing. The adjusted-cost-of-capital formulas assume that side effects like these do not exist, or, if they do exist, that they do not matter.

Of course firms can, if they wish, derive more complicated formulas for calculating the adjusted cost of capital in cases where these kinds of financing side effects do matter. But such effects are rarely worth the trouble. It is much simpler to calculate the net present value of side effects separately and then work out the adjusted present value.[11]

19-3 THE WEIGHTED-AVERAGE-COST-OF-CAPITAL FORMULA

Formulas are like cheese: too large a helping may cause insomnia. Fortunately, you need learn only one other formula for calculating adjusted present values. This is the *weighted-average cost of capital.* Sometimes we call it the *textbook formula,* since many other textbooks have put heavy emphasis on it. The formula is:[12]

$$r^* = r_D(1 - T_c)\frac{D}{V} + r_E\frac{E}{V}$$

where r^* = the adjusted cost of capital

r_D = the firm's current borrowing rate

T_c = the marginal *corporate* income tax rate—not the effective rate T^* used in Sections 19-1 and 19-2

---

[11]Of course you can still use the MM formula or the Miles and Ezzell formula to take account of the interest tax shields and then add on the present value of any other financing side effects.

[12]If $T_c = 0$, the weighted-average cost of capital simplifies to

$$r_D\frac{D}{V} + r_E\frac{E}{V}$$

This is exactly the formula that we introduced in Chapter 17, where we assumed that there are no corporate taxes.

r_E = the expected rate of return on the firm's stock (a function of the firm's business risk *and* its debt ratio)

D, E = the market values of currently outstanding debt and equity

$V = D + E$ = the total market value of the firm

The first thing to notice about the weighted-average formula is that all variables in it refer to the firm as a whole. As a result the formula gives the right discount rate only for projects that are just like the firm undertaking them. The formula works for the "average" project. It is incorrect for projects that are safer or riskier than the average of the firm's existing assets. It is incorrect for projects whose acceptance would lead to an increase or decrease in the firm's debt ratio.

The idea behind the weighted-average formula is simple and intuitively appealing. If the new project is profitable enough to pay the (after-tax) interest on the debt used to finance it, and also to generate a superior expected rate of return on the equity invested in it, then it must be a good project. What is a "superior" equity return? One that exceeds r_E, the expected rate of return required by investors in the firm's shares. Let us see how this idea leads to the weighted-average formula.

Suppose that the firm invests in a new project that is expected to produce the same yearly income in perpetuity. If the firm maintains the same debt ratio, the amount of debt used to finance the project is

$$\text{Firm's debt ratio} \times \text{investment} = \frac{D}{V} \times \text{investment}$$

Similarly, the equity used to finance the project is

$$\text{Firm's equity ratio} \times \text{investment} = \frac{E}{V} \times \text{investment}$$

If the project is worthwhile, the income must cover after-tax interest charges and provide an acceptable return to equityholders. The after-tax interest costs on the additional debt are equal to

$$\text{After-tax interest rate} \times \text{value of debt} = r_D(1 - T_c) \times \frac{D}{V} \times \text{investment}$$

The minimum acceptable income to equityholders is

$$\text{Expected return on equity} \times \text{value of equity} = r_E \times \frac{E}{V} \times \text{investment}$$

Therefore, for the project to be acceptable, its income *must exceed*:

$$r_D(1 - T_c) \times \frac{D}{V} \times \text{investment} + r_E \times \frac{E}{V} \times \text{investment}$$

This brings us back to the weighted-average formula. Just divide through by the initial investment:

$$\frac{\text{Income}}{\text{Investment}} \quad \textit{must exceed} \quad r_D(1 - T_c)\frac{D}{V} + r_E\frac{E}{V}$$

Note that the ratio of the project's annual income to investment is just the project's return. Therefore our formula gives the minimum acceptable rate of return from the project.

We have derived the textbook formula only for firms and projects offering perpetual cash flows. But Miles and Ezzell have shown that the formula works for any cash-flow pattern if the firm adjusts its borrowing to maintain a constant debt ratio D/V regardless of whether things turn out well or poorly. When the firm departs from this policy, the textbook formula is only approximately correct.

Now We Apply the Textbook Formula to the Geothermal Project

Imagine the geothermal project set up as an independent, one-asset firm, which we'll call Geothermal, Inc. Once the project is built, Geothermal's market value will be worth the initial investment of $1,000,000 plus the project's APV.

In Section 19-2, we calculated that if Geothermal maintains a constant debt ratio of 40%, the APV is $207,000. Thus Geothermal's balance sheet should turn out as follows:

	Geothermal, Inc. (Market Values)		
Assets (initial investment + APV)	1,207,000	482,800	Debt (D) (40% of firm value)
		724,000	Equity (E) (60% of firm value)
	1,207,000	1,207,000	

Each year the equity holders expect to receive the cash flow from the investment, (C) *less* the interest payment on debt ($r_D D$), *plus* the interest tax shield ($T_c r_D D$):

$$\text{Expected equity income} = C - r_D D + T_c r_D D$$
$$= 220,000 - 0.14(482,800) + 0.46(0.14)(482,800)$$
$$= 183,500$$

The expected rate of return on equity is equal to the expected equity income divided by the equity value:

$$\text{Expected equity return} = r_E = \frac{\text{Expected equity income}}{\text{Equity value}}$$
$$= \frac{183,500}{724,200} = 0.253 \text{ or } 25.3\%$$

Now suppose Geothermal unexpectedly encounters another investment opportunity. The second is a clone of the first in all dimensions save profitability: it has the same business risk and the same time pattern of cash flows. Geothermal therefore plans to borrow 40% of the project's value.

If management has forgotten the calculations we did in Section 19-2, it can use the textbook formula to find the appropriate adjusted discount rate.

$$r^* = r_D(1 - T_c)\frac{D}{V} + r_E \frac{E}{V}$$

$$= 0.14(1 - 0.46)(0.4) + 0.253(0.6)$$

$$= 0.1823 \text{ or } 18.23\%$$

That's exactly the same figure that we got earlier using the Miles and Ezzell formula.

Using the Textbook Formula: An Application to the Railroad Industry

One of the handy features of the textbook formula is that you can often use stock market data to get an estimate of r_D and r_E. The chief drawback of the formula is that it works only for projects that do not change the firm's business risk or financing. Here's a case where that drawback didn't matter.

In mid-1974 the assets of the Penn Central Railroad were taken over by Conrail, a new, federally sponsored corporation in the United States. Since Penn Central had declared bankruptcy in 1971, the assets taken by Conrail really belonged to the railroad's creditors. Congress set up a special court to determine fair compensation.

Although the Penn Central system was generating hair-curling losses overall, some of its freight lines were potentially profitable. In 1978 one of the authors was asked to estimate a discount rate for valuing the cash flows these lines would have produced, had Conrail not taken them over. He was asked to assume that these freight lines would have had the same business risk and financing as the railroad industry generally. That sounded like a job for the textbook formula. An extensive investigation boiled down to the following calculation:

$$r^*(\text{in mid-1974}) = r_D(1 - T_c)D/V + r_E E/V$$

$$= 0.087(1 - 0.5)(0.45) + 0.16(0.55)$$

$$= 0.1076 \text{ or about } 10\,\tfrac{3}{4}\%$$

The formula's components were derived as follows:

$r_D = 0.087$, a weighted average of bond yields for ten major railroads in mid-1974

$T_c = 0.50$. The corporate income tax rate in mid-1974 was 48%. Two percentage points were added to cover state income taxes.

$D/V = 0.45$. The estimated average market debt-to-value ratio for ten major railroads. Thus $E/V = 0.55$.

$r_E = 0.16$. Railroad stocks on average appeared to have about the same risk as the market portfolio. Their betas averaged out close to 1.0. Thus $r_E = r_M$. The 16% market return equals the sum of the Treasury bill yield in mid-1974 plus the historical risk premium on the market portfolio.

Of course each of these numbers was to some extent controversial. Other expert witnesses used the same textbook formula to arrive at substantially different answers. Anyone brave enough to estimate a discount rate in public can expect controversy.

Mistakes People Make in Using the Weighted-Average Formula

The real danger with the weighted-average formula is that it tempts people to make logical errors. For example, manager Q, who is campaigning for a pet project, might look at the formula

$$r^* = r_D(1 - T_c) \frac{D}{V} + r_E \frac{E}{V}$$

and think, "Aha! My firm has a good credit rating. It could borrow, say, 90% of the project's cost if it likes. That means $D/V = 0.9$ and $E/V = 0.1$. My firm's borrowing rate r_D is 8% and the required return on equity r_E is 15%. Therefore

$$r^* = 0.08(1 - 0.46)(0.9) + 0.15(0.1) = 0.054 \text{ or } 5.4\%$$

When I discount at that rate, my project looks great."

Q is wrong on several counts. First, the weighted-average formula only works for projects that are carbon copies of the firm. The firm isn't 90% debt-financed.

Second, the immediate source of funds for a project has no necessary connection with the hurdle rate for the project. What matters is the project's overall contribution to the firm's borrowing power. A dollar invested in Q's pet project will not increase the firm's debt capacity by 90 cents. It if borrows 90% of the project's cost, it is really borrowing in part against its *existing* assets. Any advantage from financing the new project with more debt than normal should be attributed to the old projects, not to the new one.

Third, even if the firm were willing and able to lever up to 90% debt, its cost of capital would not decline to 5.4% (as Q's naive calculation predicts). You cannot increase the debt ratio without creating financial risk for stockholders and thereby increasing r_E, the expected rate of return they demand from the firm's common stock. Going to 90% debt would certainly increase the borrowing rate too.

19-4 SUMMARY

Investment decisions always have side effects on financing: every dollar spent has to be raised somehow. Sometimes the side effects are irrelevant or at least unimportant. In an ideal world with no taxes, transaction costs, or other market imperfections, only investment decisions would affect firm value. In such a world firms could analyze all investment opportunities as if they were all-equity-financed. Firms would decide which assets to buy and then worry about getting the money to pay for them. No one would worry about where the money might come from, because debt policy, dividend policy, and all other financing choices would have no impact on stockholder's wealth.

The side effects cannot be ignored in practice. Therefore in this chapter we showed you how they should be taken into account.

The technique is simple. We first calculate the present value of the project as if there are no important side effects. Then we adjust present value to calculate the project's total impact on firm value. The rule is to accept the project if adjusted net present value (APV) is positive:

Accept project if APV = base-case NPV + present value of financing side effects > 0

The base-case NPV is the project's NPV computed assuming all-equity financing and perfect capital markets. Think of it as the project's value if it were set up as a separate mini-firm. You would compute the mini-firm's value by forecasting its cash flows and discounting at the opportunity cost of capital for the project. The cash flows should be net of the taxes that an all-equity-financed mini-firm would pay.

Financing side effects are evaluated one by one and their present values added to or subtracted from base-case NPV. We looked at several cases:

1. *Issue costs.* If accepting the project forces the firm to issue securities, then the present value of issue costs should be subtracted from base-case NPV.

2. *Special financing.* Sometimes special financing opportunities are tied to project acceptance. For example, the government might offer subsidized financing for socially desirable projects. You simply compute the present value of the financing opportunity and add it to base-case NPV.

3. *Interest tax shields.* Debt interest is a tax-deductible expense. Most people believe that interest tax shields contribute to firm value. Thus a project that prompts the firm to borrow more generates additional value. The project's APV is increased by the present value of interest tax shields on debt the project supports.

Remember not to confuse *contribution to corporate debt capacity* with the immediate source of funds for investment. For example, a firm might, as a matter of convenience, borrow $1 million for a $1 million research program. But the research would be unlikely to contribute $1 million in debt capacity; a large part of the $1 million new debt would be supported by the firm's other assets.

Also remember that *debt capacity* is not meant to imply an absolute limit on how much the firm *can* borrow. The phrase refers to how much it *chooses* to borrow. Normally the firm's optimal debt level increases as its assets expand; that is why we say that a new project contributes to corporate debt capacity.

Calculating APV may require several steps: one step for base-case NPV, and one for each financing side effect. Many firms try to calculate APV in a single calculation. They do so by the following procedure. After-tax cash flows are forecasted in the usual way—that is, as if the project is all-equity-financed. But the discount rate is adjusted to reflect the financing side effects. If the discount rate is adjusted correctly, the result is APV:

$$\begin{matrix} \text{NPV at adjusted} \\ \text{discount rate} \end{matrix} = \text{APV} = \begin{matrix} \text{NPV at opportunity} \\ \text{cost of capital} \end{matrix} + \begin{matrix} \text{present value of} \\ \text{financing side effects} \end{matrix}$$

Unfortunately, there is no formula for adjusting the discount rate that is simple and generally correct. However, there are two useful rules of thumb. The first is the Modigliani-Miller (MM) formula:

$$r^* = r(1 - T^*L)$$

Here r is the opportunity cost of capital and r^* is adjusted cost of capital. The quantity T^* is the net tax saving per dollar of interest paid, and L is the proportional contribution made by the project to corporate borrowing power.

MM's formula is strictly correct only for projects offering level, perpetual cash-flow streams and supporting permanent debt. But the errors from applying it to other types of projects are not serious.

Miles and Ezzell have developed another formula

$$r^* = r - Lr_D T^* \left(\frac{1 + r}{1 + r_D} \right)$$

This formula assumes the firm will adjust its borrowing to follow every fluctuation in future project value. If this assumption is right, the formula works for projects of any maturity or cash-flow pattern.

The Miles-Ezzell formula typically gives adjusted discount rates slightly higher than MM's. The truth is probably somewhere in between. However, both formulas share a serious limitation: they assume that the present value of additional interest tax shields is the *only* side effect of accepting the project.

To apply the MM and Miles-Ezzell formulas, you need to know r, the cost of capital for an all-equity-financed project. If you don't know r, you may be able to calculate the adjusted cost of capital using the weighted-average or textbook formula:

$$r^* = r_D(1 - T_c)\frac{D}{V} + r_E\frac{E}{V}$$

Here r_D and r_E are the expected rates of return demanded by investors in the firm's bonds and stock, respectively. The quantities D and E are the current *market values* of debt and equity, while the quantity V is the total market value of the firm ($V = D + E$).

Unfortunately this formula only works for projects that are carbon copies of the existing firm—projects with the same business risk that will be financed to maintain the firm's current, market debt ratio.

Remember that all these formulas are rules of thumb. And remember the assumptions underlying them. When you encounter a project that seriously violates these assumptions, you should go back to APV.

FURTHER READING

For a discussion of adjusted present value, see Myers's article and the subsequent comments:

S.C. Myers, "Interactions of Corporate Financing and Investment Decisions—Implications for Capital Budgeting," *Journal of Finance*, **29**:1–25 (March 1974).

S. Bar-Yosef, "Interactions of Corporate Financing and Investment Decisions—Implications for Capital Budgeting: Comment," *Journal of Finance*, **32**:211–217 (March 1977), followed by Myers's "Reply."

D. Ashton and D. Atkins, "Interactions of Corporate Financing and Investment Decisions—Implications for Capital Budgeting: A Further Comment," *Journal of Finance*, **33**:1447–1453 (December 1978).

Formulas for the adjusted discount rate are explained in:

F. Modigliani and M.H. Miller, "Corporate Income Taxes and the Cost of Capital: A Correction," *American Economic Review*, **53**:433–443 (June 1963).

M.H. Miller and F. Modigliani, "Some Estimates of the Cost of Capital to the Electric Utility Industry: 1954–1957," *American Economic Review*, **56**:333–391 (June 1966).

J. Miles and R. Ezzell, "The Weighted Average Cost of Capital, Perfect Capital Markets and Project Life: A Clarification," *Journal of Financial and Quantitative Analysis*, **15**:719–730 (September 1980).

There have been dozens of articles on the weighted-average cost of capital and other issues discussed in this chapter. Here are three representative ones:

F.D. Arditti, "The Weighted-Average Cost of Capital: Some Questions on Its Definition, Interpretation and Use," *Journal of Finance*, **28**:1001–1007 (September 1973).

M.J. Brennan, "A New Look at the Weighted-Average Cost of Capital," *Journal of Business Finance*, **5**:24–30 (1973).

D.R. Chambers, R.S. Harris, and J.J. Pringle, "Treatment of Financing Mix in Analyzing Investment Opportunities," *Financial Management*, **11**:24–41 (Summer 1982).

QUIZ

1. A project costs $1 million and has a base-case NPV of exactly zero (NPV $= 0$). What is the project's APV in the following cases?
   (a) If the firm invests, it has to raise $500,000 by stock issue. Issue costs are 15% of net proceeds.
   (b) The firm has ample cash on hand. But if it invests, it will have access to $500,000 of debt financing at a subsidized interest rate. The present value of the subsidy is $175,000.
   (c) If the firm invests, its debt capacity increases by $500,000. The present value of interest tax shields on this debt is $76,000.
   (d) If the firm invests, it issues equity, as in (a), and borrows, as in (c).

2. Consider the APV of the solar heater project, as calculated in Table 19-1. How would the APV change if the net tax shield per dollar of interest is not $T_c = 0.46$, but $T^* = 0.40$? What if $T^* = 0.10$?

3. Consider a project lasting one year only. The initial outlay is $1,000 and the expected inflow is $1,200. The opportunity cost of capital is $r = 0.20$. The borrowing rate is $r_D = 0.10$, the net tax shield per dollar of interest is $T^* = 0.20$, and the firm plans to borrow 30% of project value.
   (a) What is the project's base-case NPV?
   (b) What is its APV?

4. Calculate the adjusted cost of capital for the one-period project discussed in Quiz question 3, just above.
   (a) First, use the MM formula.
   (b) Then use the Miles-Ezzell formula.
   (c) Calculate the project's NPV using the discount rates you calculated in (a) and (b). Which gives the right answer? (Compare your answer to Quiz question 3.)

5. Calculate the weighted-average cost of capital for Federated Junkyards, using the following information.

   - Debt: $75,000,000 outstanding, at book value. The debt is trading at 90% of par. The yield to maturity is 16%.
   - Equity: 2,500,000 shares selling at $42 per share. Assume the expected rate of return on Federated's stock is 25%.
   - Taxes: Federated's marginal tax rate is $T_c = 0.23$.

6. What is the *opportunity cost of capital* for one of Federated's junkyards? Assume the junkyard is average risk. Use your answer to Quiz question 5 and the Miles-Ezzell formula.

7. The textbook formula seems to imply that debt is "cheaper" than equity—that is, that a firm with more debt could use a lower discount rate r^*. Does this make sense? Explain briefly.

QUESTIONS AND PROBLEMS

1. Consider another perpetual project like the geothermal project in Section 19-2. Its initial investment is $1,000,000 and the expected cash inflow is $85,000 a year in perpetuity. The opportunity cost of capital with all-equity financing is 10%, and the project allows the firm to borrow an additional $40,000 at 7%. Assume the net

tax advantage to borrowing is 30 cents per dollar of interest paid ($T^* = 0.30$). What is the project's APV?

2. Suppose the project described in problem 1 is to be undertaken by a university. Funds for the project will be withdrawn from the university's endowment, which is invested in a widely diversified portfolio of stocks and bonds. However, the university can also borrow at 7%.

   Suppose the university treasurer proposes to finance the project by issuing $400,000 of perpetual bonds at 7%, and by selling $600,000 worth of common stocks from the endowment. The expected return on the common stocks is 10%. He therefore proposes to evaluate the project by discounting at a weighted-average cost of capital, calculated as:

$$r^* = r_D \frac{D}{V} + r_E \frac{E}{V}$$

$$= 0.07 \left(\frac{400,000}{1,000,000} \right) + 0.10 \left(\frac{600,000}{1,000,000} \right)$$

$$= 0.088 \text{ or } 8.8\%$$

   What's right or wrong with the treasurer's approach? Should the university invest? Should it borrow?

3. Digital Organics has the opportunity to invest $1 million now ($t = 0$) and expects after-tax returns of $600,000 in $t = 1$ and $700,000 in $t = 2$. The project will last for two years only. The appropriate cost of capital is 12% with all-equity financing, the borrowing rate is 8%, and DO's target debt ratio for a project of this type is 0.3. Assume debt tax shields have a net value of 30 cents per dollar of interest paid. Calculate the project's APV using each of the following methods.
   (*a*) Use the procedure followed in Table 19-1, where debt ratios were assumed fixed in terms of book values.
   (*b*) Discount project cash flows at an adjusted rate derived from the Miles-Ezzell formula.
   (*c*) Use an adjusted rate derived from the MM formula.

4. The Bunsen Chemical Company is currently at its target debt ratio of 40%. It is contemplating a $1 million expansion of its existing business. This expansion is expected to produce a cash inflow of $130,000 a year in perpetuity.
   The company is uncertain whether to undertake this expansion and how to finance it. The two options are a $1 million issue of common stock or a $1 million issue of 20-year debt. The flotation costs of a stock issue would be around 5% of the amount raised and the flotation costs of a debt issue would be around $1\frac{1}{2}\%$.
   Bunsen's financial manager, Ms. Polly Ethylene, estimates that the required return on the company's equity is 14%, but she argues that the flotation costs increase the cost of new equity to 19%. On this basis, the project does not appear viable.
   On the other hand, she points out that the company can raise new debt on a 7% yield that would make the cost of new debt $8\frac{1}{2}\%$. She therefore recommends that Bunsen should go ahead with the project and finance it with an issue of long-term debt.
   Is Ms. Ethylene right? How would you evaluate the project?

5. Can you explain why we use the marginal corporate tax rate (T_c) in the textbook formula, but the *net* tax shield per dollar of interest (T^*) in the MM and Miles-Ezzell formulas?

6. List the assumptions underlying the MM adjusted discount rate formula. Derive the formula algebraically for a perpetual project. Then try to derive it for a one-period project like the one described in Quiz question 3. Keep MM's other assumptions intact. *Hint*: You will end up with the Miles-Ezzell formula. In other words, their formula works for one-period projects; MM's does not.

7. Suppose you wanted to figure out the *opportunity* cost of capital (r) for the United States railroad industry in mid-1974. You have an estimate of r^*, the adjusted discount rate: $10^3/_4\%$ as reported in Section 19-3. *Hint*: We presented two formulas linking r and r^*.

8. Suppose the firm issued not just debt and equity, but preferred stock also. How would this change the weighted-average cost of capital formula? How would it change the MM and Miles-Ezzell formulas?

VALUING THE DIFFERENT KINDS OF DEBT

CORPORATE LIABILITIES AND THE VALUATION OF OPTIONS

The world's largest securities market in terms of the dollar value of securities traded is the New York Stock Exchange. Which do you think is the second largest—the American Exchange, London, Tokyo? The answer is none of these—it is the Chicago Board Options Exchange (CBOE). The CBOE is a success story in finance. It was founded in 1973. Within five years investors were trading options to buy or sell more than 10 million shares daily.

In Canada, organized option trading began in December 1975. Today, stock options trade on the Toronto Stock Exchange (TSE), the Montreal Exchange (ME), and the Vancouver Stock Exchange (VSE), with the TSE accounting for more than two-thirds of the trading volume in 1984.

Option trading is a specialized business and its devotees speak a language of their own. They talk of calls, puts, straddles, butterflies, deep-in-the-money options, and naked options. We will not tell you the meaning of *all* these terms but by the time you have finished this chapter you should know the principal kinds of options and how to value them.

Why should a financial manager of an industrial company be interested in such matters? The reason is that financial managers spend a large part of their time evaluating options—not options traded on the CBOE, but corporate investment and financing problems that have options embedded in them.

Many capital investment proposals include an option to buy additional equipment at some future date. For instance, the company may invest in a patent that allows it to exploit a new technology or it may purchase adjoining land that gives it an opportunity to expand. In each case the firm is paying money today for the option to make a further investment. To put it another way, it is acquiring *growth opportunities*. We discussed these options in Chapter 4 and in Chapter 10 we showed how you can use decision trees to analyze Magna Charter's options to expand a project or to abandon it. We return to Magna Charter in Appendix 20-2 to this chapter, which shows how to calculate the value of the abandonment option using option pricing theory.

Here is another example of an investment decision that involves a disguised option. You are considering the purchase of a tract of land in the Northwest Territories that is known to contain gold deposits. Unfortunately, the cost of extraction is higher than the price for which you could currently sell the gold. Does that mean the land is almost worthless? Not at all. You are not obliged to mine the gold, but the land gives you the option to do so. Of course, if you know that the gold price will remain below the extraction cost, then the option is worthless. But if there is uncertainty about future gold prices, you could be lucky and make a killing.

In Chapters 14 and 15 we discussed a variety of options associated with new financing. For example:

1. Warrants and convertible securities give their holders an option to exchange their securities for common stock.

2. Rights issues give the existing shareholders an option to buy the new issue.

3. A standby arrangement gives the company the option to sell the rights issue to its investment banker if the new shares are not purchased by existing stockholders.

4. A call option on a bond gives the company the right to repurchase the bond before maturity.

In fact, *every* issue of a corporate security creates options. We will demonstrate this in Section 20-1. Then in the following sections we will describe the options traded on the TSE and show how investors use options to change the risk of their portfolios. Later in the chapter a formal model for valuing options will be presented.

Our primary goal in this chapter is to convey an understanding of options, their properties, and how they are valued. We are asking you to invest to acquire several important concepts. The return to this investment comes primarily in later chapters, where these concepts are applied to a variety of corporate financial problems. But we also present some simple applications in this chapter.

20-1 EVERY ISSUE OF A CORPORATE SECURITY CREATES OPTIONS

In Chapter 18 we discussed the plight of Circular File Company, which borrowed $50 per share against assets with a book value of $100. But the firm was unsuccessful, and the *market* value of its assets fell to $30. Circular's bond and stock prices fell to $25 and $5, respectively. Circular's *market* value balance sheet is now:

Circular File Company (market values)			
Asset value	$30	$25	Bonds
		5	Stock
	$30	$30	Firm value

If Circular's debt were due and payable now, the firm could not repay the $50 it originally borrowed. It would default, bondholders receiving assets worth $30 and stockholders receiving nothing. The reason Circular stock is worth $5 is that the debt is *not* due now but rather is due a year from now. A stroke of good fortune could increase firm value enough to pay off the bondholders in full, with something left over to give stockholders a capital gain as well. For example, if firm value doubles to $60, its common stock will be worth $60 − $50 = $10, and Circular's stockholders will receive a $5 capital gain.

Of course this is a long shot. On the other hand, the most Circular's stockholders can lose is $5. They are betting a relatively small amount of money in exchange for a small probability of a big payoff.

Figure 20-1 shows an illustrative probability distribution for the future value of Circular's assets. There is a 70% chance that they will be worth $50 or less, so that Circular's stockholders will receive nothing. But there is a 30% chance that they will be able to pay off the $50 debt obligation with something left over. If asset value turns out to be greater than $50, every additional dollar of value goes directly into the stockholders' pockets.

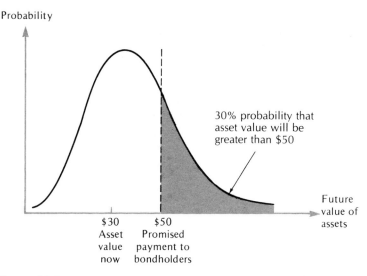

Probability

30% probability that
asset value will be
greater than $50

$30
Asset
value
now

$50
Promised
payment to
bondholders

Future
value of
assets

Figure 20-1 Circular File Company will default when its debt comes due if the value of its assets turns out to be less than the $50 promised to bondholders. The value of its assets is now $30; but there is a 30% chance that the value will be greater than $50 when the debt matures.

Circular File's common stock is really a **call option** written on the firm's assets, with an **exercise price** of $50, the amount the firm has promised to repay to bondholders. In general, *all* common stocks of firms that borrow can be regarded as call options.[1]

Let us explain. A call option gives its owner the right to buy stock at a specified exercise or "striking" price on or before a specified expiration date. For example, consider a one-year call option written on one share of the stock of the Rectangular File Company. The option has an exercise price of $50. Suppose that Rectangular's assets and prospects are *exactly* the same as Circular's except that Rectangular has no debt. Thus Rectangular's stock is worth $30 per share.

Rectangular File Company (market values)			
Asset value	$30	$ 0	Bonds
		30	Stock
	$30	$30	Firm value

The left-hand side of Table 20-1 shows the possible payoffs to the owner of the one-year call option on Rectangular stock. If the firm's assets and stock are worth $50 or less next year, the option will have no value; it will expire unexercised. No one would put up the $50 exercise price to acquire stock worth only $45. On the other hand, if Rectangular stock turns out to be worth $60, the call option will pay off $10, which is the profit from buying stock worth $60 for the exercise price of $50.

Now compare these payoffs with the payoffs to Circular stockholders, which are shown in the right-hand column of Table 20-1. You can see that the payoffs are identical for any given future value of the assets of Circular and Rectangular. If we were to plot the payoffs to the Rectangular call option, the resulting figure would look *exactly* like Figure 20-1. Remember that we have assumed that Circular's and Rectangular's assets are identical.

---

[1] This relationship was first recognized by Fischer Black and Myron Scholes, in "The Pricing of Options and Corporate Liabilities," *Journal of Political Economy*, 81:637–654 (May–June 1973).

Thus the common stock of a levered firm is a call option written on the firm's assets. This is an extremely important insight. It means that anything we can learn about traded call options applies to common stocks also. But in order to exploit this insight, we have to examine traded options in more detail.

Table 20-1 Comparison of possible payoffs to Circular File Company stockholders and to owners of a call option on the stock of Rectangular File Company.

Rectangular File Company			Circular File Company	
Asset Value	Stock Value	Payoff to Call Option ($50 Exercise Price)	Asset Value	Payoff to Stockholders ($50 Debt Due and Payable)
$ 20	$ 20	$ 0	$ 20	$ 0
40	40	0	40	0
50	50	0	50	0
60	60	10	60	10
80	80	30	80	30
100	100	50	100	50

Note: If asset value is $50 or less, it does not pay to exercise the call option on Rectangular stock. The option is worthless. If asset value is $50 or less, Circular defaults on its debt and its stock is worthless.

20-2 CALLS, PUTS, AND SHARES

In Chapter 13 we met Louis Bachelier, who in 1900 first suggested that security prices follow a random walk. Bachelier also devised a very convenient shorthand to illustrate the effects of investing in options.[2] Let us use this shorthand to compare three possible investments—buying a call option, buying a put option, and buying the share itself.

A call option gives its owner the right to buy stock at a specified "exercise" or "striking" price. In some cases, the option can be exercised only on one particular day and it is then conventionally known as a *European* call; in other cases, it can be exercised on or before that day and it is then known as an *American* call. All call options traded in the United States and Canada are American. Although we shall initially concentrate on the conceptually simpler European option, almost all our remarks apply equally well to its American cousin. Figure 20-2(*a*) shows the possible values just before expiration of a call option that is exercisable at $100. If the share price at that time turns out to be *less* than this figure, nobody will pay $100 to obtain the share via the call option. Our call option will in that case be valueless and we will throw it away. On the other hand, if the share price turns out to be greater than $100, it will pay us to exercise our option to buy the share. In this case the option will be worth the market value of the share *minus* the $100 that we must pay to acquire it.

Now let us look at a European **put option** with the same exercise price. Whereas the call gives us the right to *buy* a share for $100, the comparable put gives us the right to *sell* it for $100. Therefore the circumstances under which the put will be valuable are just the opposite of those under which the call will be valuable. We can see this from Figure 20-2(*b*). If the share price immediately before expiration turns out to be *greater* than $100, nobody will want to sell the share at that price. Our put option will be worthless. Conversely, if the share price turns out to be *less* than $100, it will pay to buy the share and then take advantage of the option to sell it for $100. In this case,

---

[2]L. Bachelier, *Théorie de la Spéculation*, Gauthier-Villars, Paris, 1900. Reprinted in English in P.H. Cootner (ed.), *The Random Character of Stock Market Prices*, M.I.T. Press, Cambridge, Mass., 1964.

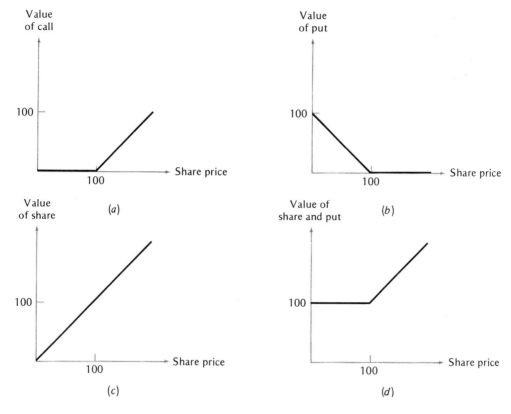

Figure 20-2   Payoffs to owners of calls, puts, and shares (shown by the heavy lines) depend on the share price. (*a*) Result of buying call exercisable at $100. (*b*) Result of buying put exercisable at $100. (*c*) Result of buying share. (*d*) Result of buying share and put option exercisable at $100; this is equivalent to owning a call and having $100 in the bank.

the value of put option at expiration is the difference between the $100 proceeds of the sale and the market price of the share. For example, if the share is worth $60, the put is worth $40:

Value of put option at expiration = exercise price

$$- \text{market price of the share}$$

$$= \$100 - \$60 = \$40$$

Our third investment consists of the share itself. Figure 20-2(*c*) betrays few secrets when it shows that the value of this investment is always exactly equal to the market value of the share.

Selling Calls, Puts, and Shares

Let us now look at the position of an investor who *sells* these investments. The individual who sells, or "writes," a call promises to deliver shares if asked to do so by the call buyer. In other words, the buyer's *asset* is the *seller's* liability. If at expiration the share price is below the exercise price, the buyer will not exercise the call and the seller's liability will be zero. If it rises above the exercise price, the buyer will exercise and the seller will give up the shares. The seller loses the difference between the share price and the exercise price received from the buyer.

Suppose that the exercise price is $100 and the stock price turns out to be $150. The call option will be exercised. The seller is forced to sell stock worth $150 for only $100 and therefore loses $50. Of course the buyer gains $50.

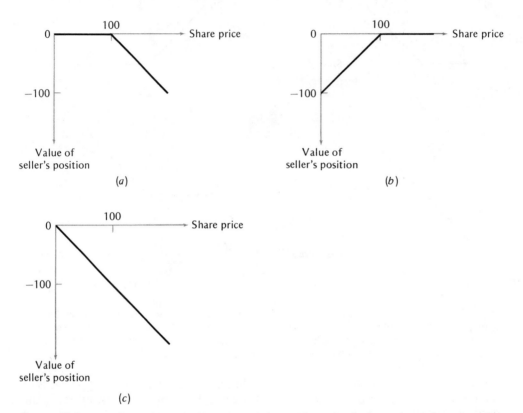

Figure 20-3 Payoffs to sellers of calls, puts, and shares (shown by the heavy lines) depend on the share price. (*a*) Result of selling call exercisable at $100. (*b*) Result of selling put exercisable at $100. (*c*) Result of selling share short.

In general the seller's loss is the buyer's gain, and vice versa. Figure 20-3(*a*) shows the payoffs to the seller. Note that Figure 20-3(*a*) is just Figure 20-2(*a*) drawn upside down.

In just the same way we can depict the position of an investor who sells or "writes" a put by standing Figure 20-2(*b*) on its head. The seller of the put has agreed to pay $100 for the share if the put buyer should request it. Clearly the seller will be safe as long as the share price remains above $100 but will lose money if the share price falls below this figure. The worst thing that can happen is for the stock to be worthless. The seller would then be obliged to pay $100 for a stock worth $0. The "value" of the option position would be −$100.

Finally Figure 20-3(*c*) shows the position of someone who sells the stock short. Short sellers sell stock they do not yet own. There is a saying on Wall Street:

He who sells what isn't his'n
Buys it back or goes to prison.

Eventually, therefore, the short seller will have to buy the stock back. The short seller will make a profit if it has fallen in price and a loss if it has risen. You can see that Figure 20-3(c) is simply an upside-down Figure 20-2(c).[3]

*Holding Calls, Puts, and Shares in Combination

We now return to the option buyer and see what happens when we add two investments together. Suppose, for example, that our portfolio contains *both* the share and an option to sell (put) it for $100. We can read off the value of each of these holdings from Figures 20-2(b) and 20-2(c). Notice that if the share price rises above $100, the put option will be worthless and the value of our portfolio will be equal to that of the share. Conversely, if the share price falls below $100, the decline in the value of the share will be exactly offset by the rise in that of the put. In Figure 20-2(d) we have plotted the total value of these two holdings.

This diagram tells us something about the relationship between a call option and a put option. We can see why if we compare it with Figure 20-2(a). Regardless of the share price, the final value of our combined investment in the share and the put is exactly $100 greater than that of a simple investment in the call. In other words, if you (1) buy the call and (2) put aside enough money to pay the $100 exercise price on the expiration date, you have an investment identical to someone who buys the share and also an option to sell it for $100. At the expiration date both strategies give the investor the choice between $100 cash or owning the share. Since the two packages give *identical* payoffs, they should at all times sell for the same price. This gives us a fundamental relationship for European options

Value of call + present value of exercise price[4] = value of put + share price

To repeat, this relationship holds because the payoff of

{Buy call, invest present value of exercise price in safe asset}
                                            is identical to the payoff of {buy put, buy share}

Here is a slightly different example. Suppose that you want to invest in a particular stock but you have no cash on hand. However, you know you will receive $100 three months hence. Therefore you borrow the present value of $100 from your bank and invest that amount in the stock. We assume that is enough to buy one share. At the end of three months your payoff is the share price less the $100 owed the bank. Now compare this with an alternative strategy, which is to *buy* a three-month call option with an exercise price of $100 and to *sell* a three-month put option with an exercise price of $100. The final value of such a package would be equal to the sum of Figures 20-2(a) and 20-3(b). Figure 20-4 shows that this sum is always equal to the market price of the share less $100. It is not difficult to see why. If the share price rises we would exercise our call and pay $100 to obtain the share; if it goes down, the other person would exercise it and sell us a share for $100. In either case, we would pay $100

---

[3]Selling short is not as simple as we have described it. For example, a short seller usually has to put up margin, that is, deposit cash or securities with the broker. This assures the broker that the short seller will be able to repurchase the stock when the time comes to do so.

[4]This present value is calculated at the *risk-free rate of interest*. It is the amount you would have to invest today in Treasury bills to realize the exercise price on the option's expiration date.

and acquire the share. Since our two investment strategies have exactly the same consequences, they should have exactly the same value. In other words, we have the following rearrangement of our earlier equation:

Value of call − value of put = share price − present value of exercise price

which holds because

{Buy call, sell put} is identical to
{Buy share, borrow present value of exercise price[5]}

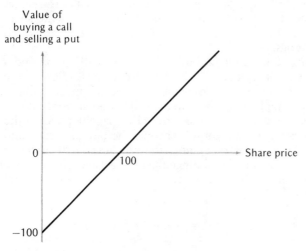

Value of buying a call and selling a put

0

100

Share price

−100

Figure 20-4 Result of buying a call and selling a put, each exercisable at $100. Whatever happens to the share price, you end up paying $100 and acquiring the share at the expiration date of the option. You could achieve the same outcome by buying the share and borrowing the present value of $100, to be repaid on the expiration date.

Of course there are many ways to express the basic relationship between share price, call and put values, and the present value of the exercise price. Each expression implies two investment strategies that give identical results.

One more example. Solve the basic relationship for the value of a put:

Value of put = value of call − value of share + present value of exercise price

From this expression you can deduce that

{Buy put} is identical to
{buy call, sell share, invest present value of exercise price}

In other words, if puts were not available you could create them by selling shares, buying calls, and lending.

---

[5]Present value is computed at the risk-free rate of interest. In other words, the comparison assumes that you are certain to pay off the loan.

Manoeuvres such as these are called *option conversions*. Calls can be converted into puts, or vice versa, by taking the appropriate position in the share and borrowing or lending. As a result, we *do not need* calls, puts, shares, *and* borrowing or lending in this world (and we hope not in the next). Given any three of these investment opportunities we can always construct the fourth.

*Bondholders Own the Firm but Have Sold a Call on It

Whenever a firm borrows, the lender effectively acquires the company and the shareholders obtain the option to buy it back by paying off the debt. The stockholders have in effect purchased a call option from bondholders. For example, Circular File's balance sheet might be expressed this way:

Circular File Company (market values)			
Asset value	$30	$25 = asset value − value of call = bond value	
		5 = value of call = stock value	
	$30	$30 = asset value = firm value	

In other words,

{Buy bonds} is identical to {Buy assets, sell call} is identical to
{Lend present value of promised payment, sell put}

We can sum up by presenting Circular's balance sheet in terms of asset value, put value, and the present value of a sure $50 payment:

Circular File Company (market values per share)		
Asset value	$30	$25 = present value of promised payment − value of put = bond value
		5 = asset value − present value of promised payment + value of put = stock value
	$30	$30 = asset value = value of firm

Now look again at the basic valuation relationship between calls and puts:

Value of call + present value of exercise price = value of put + share price

To apply this to Circular File, we have to interpret "share price" as "asset value," because Circular File's common stock is a call option written on the firm's assets. Also, "present value of exercise price" is the present value of receiving $50 (the promised payment to bondholders) *for sure* next year. Thus

Value of call + present value of promised payment to bondholders
= value of put + asset value

Now we can solve for the value of Circular stock, which equals the value of a call on Circular's assets:

Value of stock = asset value

− present value of promised payment to bondholders

+ value of put

Circular's stockholders have, in effect, (1) bought the firm's assets, (2) borrowed the present value of $50, with the obligation to repay regardless of what happens, but also (3) bought a put on the firm's assets with an exercise price of $50. Having the put allows stockholders to escape the consequences of their promise to repay $50 to bond-holders. If firm value turns out to be less than $50, stockholders exercise their put for the $50 exercise price. Of course stockholders do not receive $50 in cash. Instead, by giving up the firm's assets to its bondholders, they are relieved of the $50 debt obligation.

What if Circular's stockholders did not have limited liability? Then, if Circular's assets turn out to be worth less than $50, this amount will have to be paid out of their own pockets. They will have no put to exercise. Therefore, the value of limited lia-bility—the option to default—is the value of a put on the firm's assets with an exercise price equal to the promised payment to bondholders.

Of course the option to default is extremely valuable to Circular's stockholders because default is likely to occur. At the other extreme, the value of Bell Canada Enterprises stockholders' option to default is trivial compared to the value of Bell Canada assets. Default on Bell Canada bonds is possible but extremely unlikely. Option traders would say that the put of Circular's stockholders is "deep in-the-money" because today's asset value ($30) is well below the exercise price ($50). The put of Bell Canada stockholders is well "out-of-the-money" because the value of Bell Canada's assets substantially exceeds the value of Bell Canada debt.

We know that owning Circular's bonds is equivalent to owning the assets, but selling a call against them. It is also equal to the present value of the $50 promised payment (calculated on the assumption of no default) less the value of stockholders' option to default:

Value of bonds = asset value − value of call

= present value of promised payment to bondholders

− value of put

20-3 TWO SIMPLE PROBLEMS IN OPTIONS AND CORPORATE FINANCING

Before we turn to option valuation, it may be useful to illustrate how an understanding of options can help to disentangle some popular fallacies in corporate finance. We will give two examples.

The Case for Standby Agreements

In Chapter 15 we discussed rights issues of common stock. Remember that when a company makes a rights issue, about three weeks elapse between the offering and the final acceptance date. If the stock price on the acceptance date is lower than the subscription (exercise) price, the shareholders will not subscribe to the issue. The company frequently avoids the risk of a failed issue by engaging an underwriter. In this case the firm pays a standby fee and in exchange the underwriter agrees to purchase any unsold stock. It is sometimes argued that this is a wholly wasted expense. The company can reduce the risk of a failed issue to negligible proportions *and* avoid the necessity for the standby agreement if it sets the subscription price far enough below the current market price.[6] "Far enough below" means low enough to essentially eliminate

[6] Of course, the lower the subscription price, the larger the number of shares that must be issued to raise a given amount of funds.

the possibility that stock price will fall below the subscription price during the three-week subscription period.

But suppose that the firm does *not* follow this strategy. It sets a relatively high subscription price (but still below the current stock price) and arranges a standby agreement. Now, an underwriter who bears risk because of a standby agreement must be serving a useful function. Notice that the issuing firm never sells stock directly. Instead the stockholders issue themselves rights, which are just short-term call options to buy stock. The standby agreement in effect assures the firm that these call options will be exercised.

Look at it from the underwriter's viewpoint. In a standby the underwriter agrees to buy stock at the subscription price if the rights are not exercised. When will this happen? When the stock price falls below the subscription price. For example, suppose that the subscription price is $20 per share and 1 million rights are issued. Suppose also that the stock price falls from $25 per share to $15 at the end of the subscription period. Naturally the rights expire unexercised, and the underwriter must accept 1 million shares and pay $20 for each of them. Since the shares are worth only $15, the underwriter loses $(20 - 15) \times (1 \text{ million}) = \$5$ million.

The underwriter has sold a put on 1 million shares to the firm, with an exercise price of $20 per share. The cost of the put to the firm is the standby fee paid to the underwriter. In our example, the underwriter lost because stock price fell and the firm exercised the put. That was bad luck for the underwriter; but if the stock price had held above $20, the rights would have been exercised and the underwriter would have just pocketed the standby fee.

But do the stockholders lose anything if the company decides not to underwrite the issue and to pitch the price so low that it cannot possibly fail? Yes—they lose the handy put option to sell stock to the underwriter in the event of a price decline. A put option is always worth having if it does not cost too much. The trouble with standby arrangements is not that they are *in principle* bad but that they are usually overpriced. For example, one study estimated that the value of the put option was about 0.1% of the amount issued, compared with an average fee of 1.1%.[7] That suggests that companies should as a general rule avoid standby agreements.

The Case for Issuing Warrants

Many companies issue warrants. These are exactly like long-term call options. Their owners are entitled to purchase from the company a set number of common shares at a set price on or before a set date. Their use has been advocated on the following grounds:[8]

> A company that wishes to sell common stock must usually offer the new stock at 10% to 20% below the market price in order for the flotation to be a success.[9] However, if warrants are sold for cash, exercisable at 20% to 50% above the market price off the common, the result will be equivalent to selling common stock at a premium rather than a discount; and if the warrants are never exercised, the proceeds from their sale will become a clear profit to the company.

---

[7]These estimates are based on the Black-Scholes option pricing model, which we describe later in this chapter. See P.R. Marsh, "An Analysis of Equity Rights Issues on the London Stock Exchange," unpublished Ph.D. dissertation, London Business School, 1977, pp. 333–335.

[8]See S.T. Kassouf: *Evaluation of Convertible Securities*, Analytical Investors, New York, 1966, p. 6. We hasten to add that Kassouf's lapse is *not* characteristic of him. He is a respected scholar who has made important contributions to finance.

[9]This is an overestimate of the discount associated with seasoned issues. See Section 15-2.

In corporate finance, as in most of economics, you should always suspect arguments of the "heads I win, tails you lose" variety. If the shareholder inevitably wins, the warrant holder must inevitably lose. But that does not sound right. Surely there must be some price at which it makes sense to buy warrants.

Suppose that your company's stock is priced at $100 and that you are considering an issue of warrants exercisable at $120. You believe that you can sell these warrants at $10. If the stock price subsequently fails to reach $120, the warrants will not be exercised. You will have sold warrants for $10 each, which with the benefit of hindsight proved to be worthless to the buyer. If the stock price reaches $130, say, the warrants will be exercised. Your firm will have received the initial payment of $10 *plus* the exercise price of $120. On the other hand, it will have issued to the warrant holders stock worth $130 per share. The net result is a standoff. You have received a payment of $130 in exchange for a liability worth $130.

Think now what happens if the stock price rises *above* $130. Perhaps it goes to $200. In this case the warrant issue will end up producing a loss of $70. This is not a cash outflow but an opportunity loss. The firm receives $130, but in this case it could have sold stock for $200. On the other hand, the warrant holders gain $70: they invest $130 in cash to acquire stock that they can sell, if they like, for $200.

Our example is oversimplified—for instance, we have kept quiet about the time value of money and risk—but we hope it has made the basic point. When you sell warrants, you are selling options and getting cash in exchange. Options are valuable securities. If they are properly priced this is a fair trade—in other words, it is a zero net present value transaction.

You can see why the quotation is misleading. When it refers to "selling stock at a premium," the implicit comparison is to the market value of the stock today. The relevant comparison is to what it may be worth tomorrow.

20-4 WHAT DETERMINES OPTION VALUES?

So far we have said nothing about how the market value of options is determined. We do know what an option is worth when it matures, however. Consider, for example, our earlier case of an option to buy stock at $100. If the stock price is below $100 at

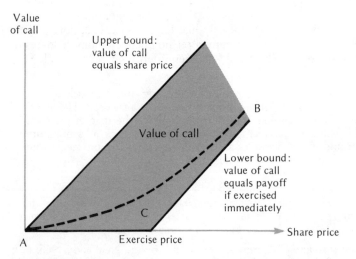

Figure 20-5   Value of a call before its expiration date (dashed line). The value depends on the stock price. It is always worth more than its value if exercised now (heavy line). It is never worth more than the stock price itself.

the expiration date, the call will be worthless; if the stock price is above $100, the call will be worth $100 less than the value of the stock. In terms of Bachelier's diagram we have the relationship depicted by the heavy line in Figure 20-5.

Even before maturity the price of the option can never remain *below* the heavy line in Figure 20-5. For example, if our option were priced at $50 and the stock at $200, it would pay any investor to buy the option, exercise it for an additional $100, and then sell the stock. That would give a money machine with a profit of $50. The demand for options from investors using the money machine would quickly force the option price up at least to the heavy line in the figure. For options that still have some time to run, the heavy line is therefore a *lower* limit on the market price of the option.

The diagonal line in Figure 20-5 is the *upper* limit to the option price. Why? Because the stock gives a higher ultimate payoff whatever happens. If at the option's expiration the stock price ends up above the exercise price, the option is worth the stock price *less* the exercise price. If the stock price ends up below the exercise price, the option is worthless, but the stock's owner still has a valuable security. Let *P* be the stock price at the option's expiration date and assume the option's exercise price is $100. Then the extra dollar returns realized by stockholders are:

	Stock Payoff	Option Payoff	Extra Payoff from Holding Stock Instead of Option
Option exercised (*P* greater than $100)	*P*	*P* − 100	$100
Option expires unexercised (*P* less than or equal to $100)	*P*	0	*P*

If the stock and the option sold at the same price everyone would rush to sell the option and buy the stock. Therefore, the option price must be somewhere in the shaded region of Figure 20-5. In fact, it will lie on a curved, upward-sloping line like the dashed curve shown in the figure. This line begins its travels where the upper and lower bounds meet (at zero). Then it rises, gradually becoming parallel to the upward-sloping part of the lower bound. This line tells us an important fact about option values: *The value of an option increases as stock price increases*, if the exercise price is held constant.

That should be no surprise. Owners of call options clearly hope for the stock price to rise, and are happy when it does. But let us look more carefully at the shape and location of the dashed line. Three points, *A, B,* and *C* are marked on the dashed line. As we explain each point you will see why the option price has to behave as the dashed line predicts.

Point A: *When the stock is worthless the option is worthless.*

A stock price of zero means that there is no possibility the stock will ever have any future value.[10] If so, the option is sure to expire unexercised and worthless, and it is worthless today.

Point B: *When the stock price becomes large, the option price approaches the stock price less the present value of the exercise price.* Notice that the dashed line representing the option price in Figure 20-5 eventually becomes parallel to the ascending heavy line representing the lower bound on the option price. The reason is as follows: the higher the stock price, the higher the probability that the option will eventually be exercised. If the stock price is high enough, exercise becomes a virtual certainty; the probability that the stock price will fall below the exercise price before the option expires becomes trivially small.

---

[10]If a stock *can* be worth something in the future, then investors will pay *something* for it today, although possibly a very small amount.

If you own an option that you *know* will be exchanged for a share of stock, you effectively own the stock now. The only difference is that you don't have to *pay* for the stock (by handing over the exercise price) until later, when formal exercise occurs. Buying the call is equivalent to buying the stock, but financing part of the purchase by borrowing. The amount implicitly borrowed is the present value of the exercise price. The value of the call is therefore equal to the stock price less the present value of the exercise price.

This brings us to another important point about options. Investors who acquire stock by way of a call option are buying on instalment credit. They pay the purchase price of the option today, but they do not pay the exercise price until they actually take up the option. This delayed payment is particularly valuable if interest rates are high and the option has a long maturity. With an interest rate r_f and the time to maturity t, then we would expect the value of the option to depend on the *product*[11] of r_f and t: *The value of an option increases with both the rate of interest and the time to maturity.*

Point C: *The option price always exceeds its minimum value* (except when stock price is zero). We have seen that the dashed and heavy lines in Figure 20-5 coincide when stock price is zero (point A), but elsewhere the lines diverge; that is, the option price must exceed the minimum value given by the heavy line. The reason for this can be understood by examining point C.

At point C, the stock price exactly equals the exercise price. The option is therefore worthless if exercised today. However, suppose that the option will not expire until three months hence. Of course we do not know what the stock price will be at the expiration date. There is roughly a 50% chance that it will be higher than the exercise price, and a 50% chance that it will be lower. The possible payoffs to the option are therefore:

Outcome	Payoff
Stock price rises (50% probability)	Stock price less exercise price (option is exercised)
Stock price falls (50% probability)	Zero (option expires worthless)

If there is a positive probability of a positive payoff, and if the worst payoff is zero, then the option must be valuable. That means the option price at point C exceeds its lower bound, which at point C is zero. In general, the option prices will exceed their lower bound values as long as there is time left before expiration.

One of the most important determinants of the *height* of the dashed curve (that is, of the difference between actual and lower-bound value) is the likelihood of substantial movements in the stock price. An option on a stock whose price is unlikely to change by more than 1% or 2% is not worth much; an option on a stock whose price may halve or double is very valuable.

Figures 20-6(*a*) and 20-6(*b*) illustrate this point. The figures compare the payoffs at expiration of two options with the same exercise price and the same stock price. The figures assume that stock price equals exercise price (like point C in Figure 20-5), although this is not a necessary assumption. The only difference is that the price of stock Y at its option's expiration date (Figure 20-6(*b*)) is much harder to predict than the price of stock X at its option's expiration date. You can see this from the probability distributions superimposed on the figures.

---

[11]Using continuous compounding, the present value of the exercise price is exercise price $\times$ $e^{-r_f t}$. The discount factor $e^{-r_f t}$ depends on the product of r_f and t.

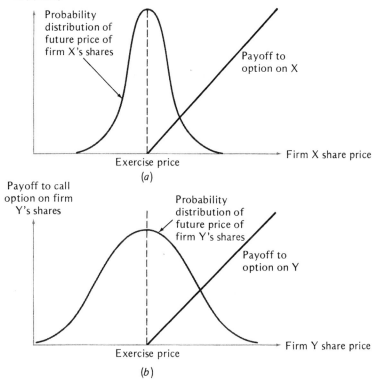

Figure 20-6 Call options are written against the shares of (a) firm X and (b) firm Y. In each case, the current share price equals the exercise price, so that each option has a 50% chance of ending up worthless (if the share price falls) and a 50% chance of ending up "in the money" (if the share price rises). However, the chance of a *large* payoff is greater for the option on firm Y's share, because Y's stock price is more volatile and therefore has more "upside potential."

In both cases there is roughly a 50% chance that stock price will decline and make the options worthless; but if the prices of stocks X and Y rise, the odds are that Y will rise more than X. Thus there is a larger chance of a big payoff from the option on Y. Since the chance of a zero payoff is the same, the option on Y is worth more than the option on X. Figure 20-7 illustrates this: the higher curved line belongs to the option on Y.

The probability of large stock price changes during the remaining life of an option depends on two things: (1) the variance (that is, volatility) of the stock price *per period* and (2) the number of periods until the option expires. If there are t remaining periods, and the variance per period is σ^2, the value of the option should depend on cumulative variability $\sigma^2 t$.[12] Other things equal, you would like to hold an option on a volatile

---

[12]Here is an intuitive explanation. If the stock price follows a random walk (see Section 13-2), successive price changes are statistically independent. The cumulative price change before expiration is the sum of t independent random variables. The variance of a sum of independent random variables is the sum of the variances of those variables. Thus, if σ^2 is the variance of the daily price change, and there are t days until expiration, the variance of the cumulative price change is $\sigma^2 t$.

stock (high σ^2). Given volatility, you would like to hold an option with a long life ahead of it (large t). Thus the value of an option increases *with both the variability of the share and the time to maturity.*

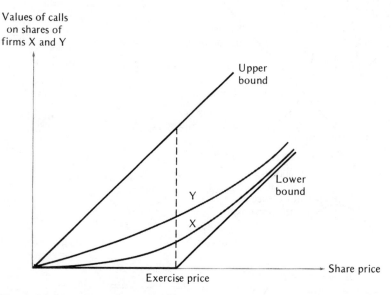

Figure 20-7 Values of calls on shares of firm X and shares of firm Y. The call on Y's shares is worth more because Y's shares are more volatile (see Figure 20-6). The higher curved line describes the value of a call on Y's shares; the lower curved line describes the value of a call on X's shares.

It's a rare person who can keep all these properties straight at first reading. Therefore, we have summed them up in Table 20-2.

Table 20-2 What the price of a call option depends on.

---

1. If the following variables *increase*	the changes in the call option price are:
Stock price (P)	positive
Exercise price (EX)	negative
Interest rate (r_f)	positive
Time to expiration (t)	positive
Volatility of stock price (σ)	positive

2. Other properties:
   a. Upper bound. The option price is always less than the stock price.
   b. Lower bound. The option price never falls below the payoff to immediate exercise ($P - $ EX or zero, whichever is larger).
   c. If the stock is worthless, the option is worthless.
   d. As the stock price becomes very large, the option price approaches the stock price less the present value of the exercise price.

20-5 AN OPTION-VALUATION MODEL

We would now like to replace the qualitative statements of Table 20-2 with an exact option-valuation model—a formula we can plug numbers into and get a definite answer.

The search for that formula went on for years before Fischer Black and Myron Scholes finally found it. Before we show you what they found, we should say a few words to explain why the search was so difficult.

Why Discounted Cash Flow Won't Work for Options

Our standard operating procedure of (1) forecasting expected cash flow and (2) discounting at the opportunity cost of capital is not helpful for options. The first step is messy but feasible.[13] Finding *the* opportunity cost of capital is impossible, because the risk of an option changes every time the stock price moves,[14] and we know it *will* move along a random walk through the option's lifetime.

When you buy a call you are *taking a position* in the stock but putting up less of your own money than if you had bought the stock directly. Thus an option is always riskier than the underlying stock. It has a higher beta and a higher standard deviation of return.

How much riskier the option is depends on the stock price relative to the exercise price. An option that is in the money (stock price greater than exercise price) is safer than one that is out of the money (stock price less than exercise price). Thus a stock price increase raises the option's price and reduces its risk. When the stock price falls, the option's price falls *and* its risk increases. That is why the expected rate of return investors demand from an option changes day by day, or hour by hour, every time the stock price moves.

We repeat the general rule: the higher the stock price relative to the exercise price, the safer the option, although the option is always riskier than the stock. The option's risk changes every time the stock price changes.

Constructing Option Equivalents from Common Stocks and Borrowing

If you've digested what we've said so far, you can appreciate why options are hard to value by standard discounted cash-flow formulas, and why a rigorous option valuation technique eluded economists for many years. The breakthrough came when Black and Scholes exclaimed "Eureka! We have found it![15] The trick is to set up an *option equivalent* by combining common stock investment and borrowing. The net cost of buying the option equivalent must equal the value of the option."

We will show you how this works by a simple numerical example. We will work out the value of a one-year option to buy the stock of Wombat Corporation at an exercise price of $160. To keep matters simple, we will assume that Wombat stock can do only two things over the coming year—either the price will fall to $110 from its current level of $140 or it will rise to $210. We will also assume that the one-year rate of interest is 10%.

If Wombat's stock price falls to $110, the call option will be worthless, but if the price rises to $210, the option will be worth $210 - 160 = \$50$. The possible payoffs to the option are therefore:

	Stock Price = $110	Stock Price = $210
1 call option	$0	$50

[13]You have to work with a *truncated* probability distribution of outcomes, for example the shaded area of Figure 20-1.

[14]It also changes over time even with the stock price constant.

[15]We do not know whether Black and Scholes, like Archimedes, were sitting in bathtubs at the time.

Now compare these payoffs with those that you would get if you bought one share of stock and borrowed $100 from the bank:

	Stock Price = $110	Stock Price = $210
1 share of stock	$110	$210
Repayment of loan + interest	−110	−110
Total payoff	$0	$100

Notice that the payoffs from the levered investment in the stock are identical to the payoffs from *two* call options. Therefore, both investments must have the same value:

Value of 2 calls = value of share − $100 bank loan

$$= 140 - 100 = \$40$$

Value of 1 call = $20

Presto! You've valued a call option.

Unfortunately, our example is fanciful in one important respect: there will be far more than two possible prices for Wombat's stock at the end of the year; normally there is a continuum of prices.

We could make the problem slightly more realistic by assuming that there were two possible changes in the stock price in each six-month period. That would produce four possible prices by the end of the year. It would still be possible to construct a series of levered investments in the stock giving exactly the same prospects as the option.

There is no reason that we should stop at six-month periods. We could go on to take shorter and shorter intervals, in each of which there were two possible changes in Wombat's stock price. Eventually we would reach a situation in which Wombat's stock price was changing continuously and generating a continuum of possible year-end prices. We could still replicate the call option by a levered investment in the stock, but we would need to adjust the degree of leverage continuously as the year went by.

It may sound a tedious business to calculate the value of this levered investment, but Black and Scholes derived the formula that does the trick. This seemingly unpleasant-looking formula[16] is:

Present value of call option $= PN(d_1) - EXe^{-r_f t}N(d_2)$

where $d_1 = \dfrac{\ln(P/EX) + r_f t + \sigma^2 t/2}{\sigma\sqrt{t}}$

$d_2 = d_1 - \sigma\sqrt{t}$

---

[16]In a risk-neutral world, the call option formula may be thought of as:

Present value of call option $= e^{-r_f t}\,[E(P_t|P_t > EX) - EX]\,\text{Prob}(P_t > EX)$

where $E(\bullet)$ is the expected value operator and P_t is the stock price at the option's expiration. The terms in the Black-Scholes formula, therefore, may be interpreted as: (a) $N(d_2)$, the probability that the call option will be in-the-money at expiration, (b) $PN(d_1)$, the present value of the expected terminal stock price conditional upon the call option being in-the-money at expiration times the probability that the call will be in-the-money at expiration, and (c) $EXe^{-r_f t}N(d_2)$, the present value of the cost of exercising the option at expiration times the probability that the call will be in-the-money at expiration. This insight into the Black-Scholes formula was first suggested by J.C. Cox and S.A. Ross, "The Valuation of Options for Alternative Stochastic Processes," *Journal of Financial Economics,* 3:145–166.

$N(d)$ = cumulative normal probability density function[17]

EX = exercise price of option

t = time to exercise date

P = price of stock now

σ^2 = variance per period of (continuously compounded) rate of return on the stock

r_f = (continuously compounded) risk-free rate of interest

For our purposes the precise formula is less important than the terms that appear in it. Notice that the willingness of individuals to bear risk does not affect value, nor does the expected return on the stock.[18] The value of the option increases with the level of the stock price relative to the exercise price (P/EX), the time to expiration times the interest rate ($r_f t$), and the time to expiration times the stock's variability ($\sigma^2 t$).

Using the Black-Scholes Formula

Earlier in this chapter we distinguished between a European option, which can only be exercised on one date, and an American option, which can be exercised on or before the final date. Since in the absence of dividends a rational investor will never exercise a call option before maturity,[19] the Black-Scholes formula applies to both European and American calls.

If we wish to calculate the value of a European put, we simply have to subtract the stock price from the value of the call and add the present value of the exercise price. (See Section 20-3.)[20]

So far, we have implicitly assumed that the common stock on which the option is written does not pay dividends. If it does, the value of the call option diminishes. The reason is that dividend payments reduce future share price, thereby reducing the possible payoff to the option. When dividends are paid you can still use the simple Black-Scholes model to give a *rough* approximation to the option value. Before using the model, you must first estimate the present value of dividend payments over the option's life, and

---

[17]That is, $N(d)$ is the probability that a unit normally distributed random variable x will be less than or equal to d. Such probabilities are tabulated in Appendix Tables 8(*a*) and 8(*b*).

[18]Although the expected return affects the price of the stock, it does not affect the option value relative to the stock value.

[19]If the call option holder exercises early, he or she incurs the cost EX. On the other hand, if he or she waits to the expiration of the option to exercise, the present value of the exercise cost is $\text{EX}e^{-r_f t}$. Thus, other things being equal, the American call option holder will choose to hold his or her option to expiration.

[20]That is, the formula for the value of a European put is:

$$\text{Present value of put option} = \text{EX}e^{-r_f t}N(-d_2) - PN(-d_1)$$

where all notation is the same as it was for the call. Unfortunately, this modification is not appropriate for an American put, since it can sometimes pay to exercise such an option before maturity in order to reinvest the exercise price. For example, suppose that immediately after acquiring an American put the stock price falls to zero. In this case there is no advantage to holding on to the option. Such an option would be worth more "dead" than "alive." See R.C. Merton, "Theory of Rational Option Pricing," *Bell Journal of Economics and Management Science,* 4:141–183 (Spring 1973), pp. 156–160. Therefore, an American put is worth more than a European put. The difference is greatest when you are sure that you will want to exercise the option. In that case, the American put is worth the value of a European put *plus* the extra interest that you could earn on your money by exercising the option now.

deduct this amount from the price of the stock. You then use this adjusted stock price in the option formula.[21]

We have seen how you can use the Black-Scholes model to evaluate simple options. Unfortunately the options that a financial manager has to evaluate are rarely simple. Also, the simplifying assumptions underlying the Black-Scholes model are often violated. Sometimes the Black-Scholes model is a reasonable approximation. However, economists have also begun to develop more elaborate versions of the Black-Scholes model that can handle more complicated problems. Option valuation is a growth business and you ought to keep your eyes open for new developments.

In Appendix 20-1, we show how option tables make it easy to apply the Black-Scholes formula.

20-6 SUMMARY

In Chapter 10 we showed you how important it is in capital budgeting decisions to evaluate the option to expand the project at a later date or to abandon it. In this chapter you have come across a number of other financial options. For example, you now know common stock can be thought of as a call option written on the assets of the firm.

There are two basic types of option. An American call is an option to buy an asset at a specified exercise price on or before a specified exercise date. Similarly, an American put is an option to sell the asset at a specified price on or before a specified date. European calls and puts are exactly the same except that they *cannot* be exercised before the specified exercise date.

What determines the value of a call option? Common sense tells us that it ought to depend on three things:

1. In order to exercise an option you have to pay the exercise price. Other things being equal, the less you are obliged to pay, the better. Therefore, the value of an option increases with the ratio of the asset price to the exercise price.

2. You do not have to pay the exercise price until you decide to exercise the option. Therefore, an option gives you a free loan. The higher the rate of interest and the longer the time to maturity, the more this free loan is worth. Therefore the value of an option increases with the interest rate multiplied by the time to maturity.

3. If the price of the asset falls short of the exercise price, you won't exercise the option. You will, therefore, lose 100% of your investment in the option no matter how far the asset depreciates below the exercise price. On the other hand, the more the price rises *above* the exercise price, the more profit you will make. Therefore the option holder does not lose from increased variability if things go wrong, but gains if they go right. The value of an option increases with the variance per period of the stock return multiplied by the number of periods to maturity.

These qualitative relationships have been extended by Black and Scholes in a formal option-valuation formula. Appendix 20-1 shows you how to use this formula. We suggested that you look out for ways in which it can be adapted to solve the many option problems that beset the financial manager.

We will use the concepts presented in this chapter to analyze important issues arising later in this book. In this chapter we used option concepts to:

1. Show that underwriters who provide standby agreements in rights offerings provide a valuable service. (We also commented that they seem to overcharge for the service.)

---

[21]The present value of dividends should be calculated at the risk-free rate r_f.

---

2. Analyze the case for issuing warrants. (Warrants are essentially call options issued by the firm.)

Also, Appendix 20-2 shows how to use option pricing concepts to calculate the salvage or abandonment value of an asset.

FURTHER READING

The classic articles on option valuation are:

F. Black and M. Scholes, "The Pricing of Options and Corporate Liabilities," *Journal of Political Economy*, **81**:637–654 (May–June 1973).
R.C. Merton, "Theory of Rational Option Pricing," *Bell Journal of Economics and Management Science*, **4**:141–183 (Spring 1973).

Recent advances in option valuation include the pricing of American call options written on dividend-paying stocks and the pricing of American put options. See:

R. Geske, "A Note on an Analytical Valuation Formula for Unprotected American Call Options on Stocks with Known Dividends," *Journal of Financial Economics*, **7**:375–380 (December 1979).
R. Geske and H.E. Johnson, "The American Put Option Valued Analytically," *Journal of Finance*, **39**:1511–1524 (December 1984).
L.W. MacMillan, "Analytic Approximation for the American Put Option," *Advances in Futures and Options Research*, **1** (1985).
R. Roll, "An Analytic Valuation Formula for Unprotected American Call Options on Stocks with Known Dividends," *Journal of Financial Economics*, **5**:251–258 (November 1977).
R.E. Whaley, "On the Valuation of American Call Options on Stocks with Known Dividends," *Journal of Financial Economics*, **9**:207–211 (June 1981).

Empirical tests of option pricing models include:

F. Black and M. Scholes, "The Valuation of Option Contracts and A Test of Option Market Efficiency," *Journal of Finance*, **27**:399–418 (May 1972).
R.E. Whaley, "Valuation of American Call Options on Dividend-Paying Stocks," *Journal of Financial Economics*, **10**:29–58 (March 1982).

Black's article provides an easy-to-read discussion of options and their uses:

F. Black, "Fact and Fantasy in the Use of Options," *Financial Analysts Journal*, **31**:36–41, 61–72 (July–August 1975).

APPENDIX 20-1   USING OPTION-VALUATION MODELS

Does the Black-Scholes option-valuation formula seem a little removed from the real world? It should not. Every day, dealers on the Toronto Stock Exchange use this formula to make huge trades. These dealers are not, for the most part, trained in the formula's mathematical derivation; they just use a specially programmed calculator or a set of tables to find the value of the option.

Appendix Tables 6 and 7 allow you to use the Black-Scholes formula to value a variety of simple options.[22] In order to use the tables, follow these three steps:

- Step 1: Multiply the standard deviation of the proportionate changes in the asset's value by the square root of time to the option's expiration. For example, suppose that you wish to value a four-year option on the stock of Wombat

---

[22]These tables are grouped with the present value tables at the back of the book.

Corporation and that the standard deviation of the stock price changes is 40% per year.

$$\text{Standard deviation} \times \sqrt{\text{time}} = 0.40 \times \sqrt{4} = 0.80$$

- Step 2: Calculate the ratio of the asset value to the present value of the option's exercise price. For example, suppose that Wombat's stock price is currently $140, that the option's exercise price is $160, and that the interest rate is 12%. Then

$$\text{Asset value} \div \frac{160}{(1.12)^4} = 1.4$$

- Step 3: Depending on whether the option is a call or a put, turn to Table 6 or 7 and look up the entry corresponding to the numbers that you calculated in Steps 1 and 2. For example, Table 6 shows that a four-year call option on Wombat stock would be worth 43.1% of the stock price or about $60. Table 7 shows that a four-year put option would be worth 14.53% of the stock price or about $20.

Example: Valuing a Put Option

James Bagwash is considering the sale of his company, United Bagwash, to World Enterprises (WE). To facilitate this sale, he is prepared to guarantee profits of at least $10 million in each of the next four years. How much are these guarantees worth?

Notice that the guarantees are like a series of put options. Each year WE has the option to give Bagwash the actual profits in exchange for $10 million. If profits exceed $10 million, WE will keep the profits; if they are less than $10 million, WE will receive the guaranteed amount of $10 million.

When you value an option on a share, you need to know how much that share is currently worth. In the present case you wish to value four options, one for each year's profits. So your first task is to estimate the present value of each year's profits. Let us suppose that you forecast the profits as follows and then calculate their present value at a discount rate of 20%:

Year	Forecast Profits (millions)	PV (Profits) at $r = 0.20$ (millions)
1	$ 8.5	$7.1
2	11.5	8.0
3	14.7	8.5
4	19.7	9.5

There are two other items of information that you need to value each option. The first is the standard deviation of the proportionate annual profit changes, which we shall suppose is 30% per year.[23] The second is the short-term interest rate, which we shall take to be 12%.

You are now in a position to value the guarantee for year 1. The first step is to multiply the standard deviation by the square root of time:

---

[23] The Black-Scholes model assumes that changes in the value of the asset are lognormally distributed. In the present case that would imply that Bagwash's profits cannot be negative—perhaps a dangerous assumption.

Standard deviation × square root of time = $0.30 \times \sqrt{1.0} = 0.30$

The second step is to calculate the ratio of the asset's value to the present value of the exercise price:

$$\text{Asset value} \div \frac{10}{1.12} = 0.80$$

You can now look up the value of the put option in Table 7. Find the entry corresponding to the column for 0.30 and the row for 0.80. It shows that the value of the option is 29.42% of the value of the asset. Thus James Bagwash's guarantee of the first year's profits is worth $0.2942 \times 7.1 = \$2.1$ million.

You should now be able to work out the value of the guarantee for the other years. The answers are as follows:

Year	Standard Deviation × √Time	Asset Value ÷ PV(Exercise Price)	Value of Put Option (millions)
1	0.30	0.8	0.2942 × 7.1 = 2.1
2	0.42	1.0	0.1620 × 8.0 = 1.3
3	0.52	1.2	0.1160 × 8.5 = 1.0
4	0.60	1.5	0.0711 × 9.5 = 0.7
			$5.1

It appears that World Enterprises should be prepared to pay an extra $5 million for the profit guarantees.

APPENDIX 20-2 CALCULATING ABANDONMENT VALUE USING OPTION PRICING THEORY

Now that you've solved Mr. Bagwash's problem (in Appendix 20-1), it should be a snap to apply option-pricing concepts to the calculation of abandonment value. Turn back to Section 10-3, where that airborne pioneer Agnes Magna was shown trying to decide whether or not to buy a $400,000 turboprop for Magna Charter. The possible cash returns to this investment are shown in Figure 20-8.

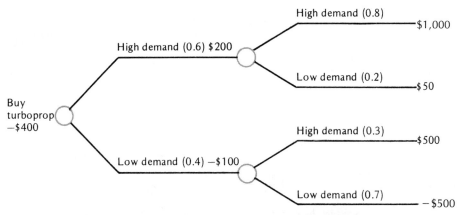

Figure 20-8   Possible cash returns from purchasing a $400,000 turboprop. See Figure 10-8. Note that payoffs to possible future abandonment are *not* shown. (All dollar figures are in thousands. Probabilities are in parentheses.)

Note that these cash returns do *not* incorporate abandonment value. Ms. Magna will actually sell the turboprop for $300,000 if demand in year 1 turns out to be low. We showed in Chapter 10 that the option to sell increases the NPV of investing in the turboprop from $8,000 to $183,000. In other words, the option to abandon was worth $175,000.[24]

$$\begin{array}{ccc} \text{NPV with} \\ \text{abandonment} \end{array} = \begin{array}{ccc} \text{NPV without} \\ \text{abandonment} \end{array} + \begin{array}{ccc} \text{value of} \\ \text{abandonment option} \end{array}$$

$$\$183,000 \quad = \quad \$8,000 \quad + \quad \$175,000$$

Since the turboprop costs $400,000, its *gross* present value is

$$\begin{array}{ccc} \text{PV with} \\ \text{abandonment} \end{array} = \begin{array}{ccc} \text{PV without} \\ \text{abandonment} \end{array} + \begin{array}{ccc} \text{value of} \\ \text{abandonment option} \end{array}$$

$$\$583,000 \quad = \quad \$408,000 \quad + \quad \$175,000$$

Owning the turboprop is like owning an asset worth $408,000; *in addition* it is like owning a put option on that asset with a maturity of one year and an exercise price of $300,000. Thus, you can apply what you know about valuing puts to valuing abandonment options.

You start by calculating project present value *without* abandonment—that is, assuming that you have to stick with the project even if it turns out sour. This is a standard discounted cash-flow calculation. Then you assemble the other information required to value a put. Let's try these numbers:

- Asset value[25]   = $335,000
- Exercise price   = $300,000
- Maturity   =   1 year
- Interest rate   =   5%
- Standard deviation assuming no abandonment   =   50%

---

[24]We also calculated the value of abandonment option for a smaller piston-engined plane, but for present purposes, we will worry just about the turboprop.

[25]Why $335,000, when we just quoted PV without abandonment of $408,000? The reason is that we want to exclude the present value of the cash flows received at year 1. We assume Ms. Magna can sell the turboprop only *after* receiving these flows. Thus, the present value of these flows should be excluded from the year 0 present value used in the option valuation formula.

Let's work this out. If Ms. Magna buys the turboprop and demand is high, she gets an immediate $200 cash flow plus the present value of cash flows in year 2. If we exclude the immediate cash flow,

$$\text{PV (year 1)} = \frac{0.8 \times 1,000 + 0.2 \times 50}{1.1} = 736$$

If demand is low, she pays out $100 and also incurs a $182 liability. Excluding the payout,

$$\text{PV (year 1)} = \frac{0.3 \times 500 + 0.07 \times -500}{1.1} = -182$$

Now weigh these outcomes by their probabilities and discount to year 0.

$$\text{PV} = \frac{0.6 \times 736 + 0.4 \times (-182)}{1.1} = 335 \text{ or } \$335,000$$

These give us

$$\text{Standard deviation} \times \text{square root of time to maturity} = 0.50 \times \sqrt{1} = 0.50$$

$$\text{Asset value} \div \frac{300,000}{1.05} = 1.17, \text{ or about } 1.15$$

Appendix Table 7 tells us that the option to bail out of the turboprop at year 1 is worth 12.63% of asset value, or $0.1263 \times 335,000 = \$42,310$.

This value is about \$133,000 lower than the abandonment value we obtained by decision-tree analysis in Chapter 10. The difference can be traced to the implicit assumptions of the Black-Scholes option-valuation formula. Figure 20-9 shows the major difference. In Chapter 10, we assumed only two things could happen in year 1: high demand (60% chance) or low demand (40% chance). High demand led to a present value in year 1 of \$735,000. Low demand led to a year-1 present value, with no abandonment, of \$182,000.[26] These two outcomes are shown in the top panel of Figure 20-9.

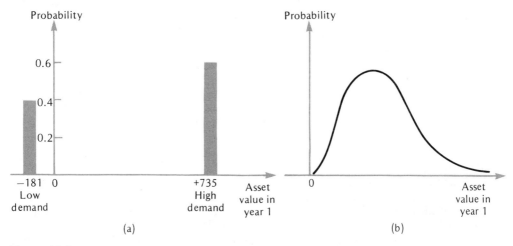

Figure 20-9 In histogram (*a*), we assume only two things can happen to Ms. Magna's venture: high demand or low demand. The histogram shows the asset values at year 1 for the two cases. Graph (*b*) shows a lognormal probability distribution of possible asset values. The lognormal distribution is more realistic because it recognizes a continuum of possible values. However, note that it assigns zero probability to negative asset values.

However, "high demand" and "low demand" almost never exhaust possible future outcomes. Demand could be overwhelming, zero, or at any intermediate level. This range of possible future demands implies a range of future values. The Black-Scholes formula assumes that these future values fall into the lognormal probability distribution shown at the bottom of Figure 20-9. Even with a very high standard deviation (50% per year), Ms. Magna's "downside risks," assuming no abandonment, are much less than we assumed in Chapter 10.[27] Therefore, the abandonment option is also worth less.

---

[26]These numbers are calculated in footnote 24.

[27]In fact, the −\$182,000 value in the low-demand outcome is impossible in a lognormal distribution, because lognormally distributed variables can't fall below zero.

We are not saying that future asset values are always lognormally distributed. But when that is not a bad assumption, you may be able to use the Black-Scholes option-pricing formula to calculate abandonment value.

Some Extensions

The option to abandon a project is a put option. But there are different kinds of put options. We assumed Ms. Magna held a *European* put, exercisable only at its maturity in year 1. We also assumed that the put's exercise price—the turboprop's second-hand value—was known in advance at year 0.

However, what if demand is high in year 1, but lousy afterward? Ms. Magna might abandon in year 2, 3, or at any time during the turboprop's service life. The plane's future second-hand value will be its present value in its best alternative use. This value will not generally be known in advance.

In general, the option to abandon a project is equivalent to an *American* put option on a *dividend-paying* stock, in which both the dividend payments and the exercise price are uncertain. The exercise price is the salvage value of the project. The cash flows to the project are equivalent to the dividend payments on the stock. The project can be abandoned at any time in the future.

You can't solve the general-abandonment-value problem with the simple Black-Scholes formula. However, considerable progress is being made in developing numerical solution procedures.[28]

Abandonment Value in Disguise

Here's another case that turns out to be an abandonment-value problem in disguise. Suppose you expect to need a new plant ready to produce turbo-encabulators in 36 months. If design A is chosen, construction must begin immediately. Design B is more expensive, but you can wait 12 months before breaking ground. Figure 20-10 shows the cumulative present value of construction costs for the two designs up to the 36-month deadline. Assume that the designs, once built, are equally efficient and have equal production capacity.

A standard discounted-cash-flow analysis would probably rank design A ahead of design B. But suppose the demand for turbo-encabulators falls and the new factory is not needed; then, as Figure 20-10 shows, the firm would be better off wth design B provided the project is abandoned before month 24.[29]

This is also an abandonment-value problem. The underlying asset is the present value of the turbo-encabulator project, assuming that the firm is committed to complete plant construction. Think of putting the present value of required construction expenditure in an escrow account. The account would of course be larger for design B than for design A. If either design is abandoned before month 36, however, its "salvage value" is the *unspent* balance in the escrow account. This is the exercise price at which the firm can "put" the turbo-encabulator project between month 0 and month 36.

We are back to standard abandonment option, where future exercise prices are determined by the pattern of cumulative investment in the design being valued. Project net present value is equal to (1) project present value assuming a commitment to complete construction[30] *less* (2) the present value of construction costs assuming this

---

[28]See S.C. Myers and S. Majd, "Calculating Abandonment Value Using Option Pricing Theory," Working Paper, Sloan School of Management, MIT, 1983.

[29]We assume for simplicity that construction outlays are totally lost if the project is abandoned before construction is complete. Our story is easily adapted if some of the outlays can be recovered.

[30]This present value would include the present value of abandoning the completed plant *after* month 36.

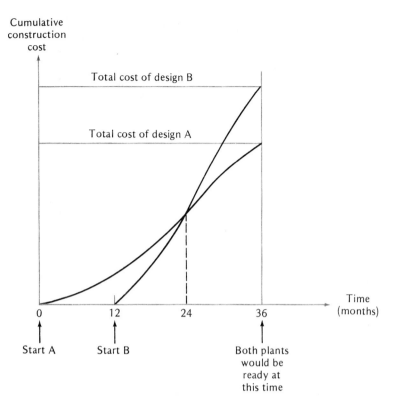

Cumulative
construction
cost

Total cost of design B

Total cost of design A

Time
(months)

0   12   24   36

Start A   Start B   Both plants
would be
ready at
this time

Figure 20-10 Cumulative construction cost of the two plant designs. Plant A takes 36 months to build, plant B only 24. But plan B costs more.

commitment, *plus* (3) the present value of the option to abandon before construction is completed. The value of (3) reflects the option to recover part of the construction costs comprising (2).

Design B could be more valuable than design A, if design B's abandonment value outweighed its higher cost.

QUIZ

1. Complete the following passage: A _____ option gives its owner the opportunity to buy stock at a specific price that is generally called the _____ price. A _____ option gives its owner the opportunity to sell stock at a specified _____ price.

   Options that can be exercised only at maturity are called _____ options. _____ options can be exercised at any time before they expire.

   The common stock of firms that borrow is a _____ option. Stockholders effectively sell the firm's _____ to _____, but retain the option to buy the _____ back. The exercise price is the _____.

2. Fill in the blanks:
   (*a*) A firm that issues warrants is selling a _____ option.
   (*b*) A firm that enters a standby agreement acquires a _____ option.
   (*c*) Rights are _____ options on the issuing firm's stock.

(d) An oil company acquires mining rights to a silver deposit. It is not obligated to mine the silver, however. The company has effectively acquired a _____ option, where the exercise price is the cost of opening the mine.

(e) Some preferred shareholders have the right to redeem their shares at par value after a specified date. (If they hand over their shares, the firm sends them a cheque equal to the shares' par value.) These shareholders have a _____ option.

(f) An executive who qualifies for a stock option plan acquires a _____ option.

(g) An investor who buys stock in a levered firm acquires a _____ option on the firm's assets.

(h) A firm buys a standard machine with a ready secondhand market. The second-hand market gives the firm a _____ option.

3. Note Figure 20-11(a) and 20-11(b). Match each figure with one of the following option positions:
   (a) Call buyer.
   (b) Call seller.
   (c) Put buyer.
   (d) Put seller.

4. Suppose that you hold a share of stock and a put option on that share. What is the payoff when the option expires if
   (a) The stock price is below the exercise price?
   (b) The stock price is above the exercise price?

*5. There is another strategy involving calls and borrowing and lending that gives the same payoffs as the strategy described in question 4. What is the alternative strategy?

6. What is the lower bound to the price of a call option? What is the upper bound?

7. Indicate what a call option is worth if:
   (a) The stock price is zero.
   (b) The stock price is extremely high relative to the exercise price.

8. How does the price of a call option respond to the following changes, other things equal? Does the call price go up or down?
   (a) Stock price increases.
   (b) Exercise price is increased.
   (c) Risk-free interest rate increases.

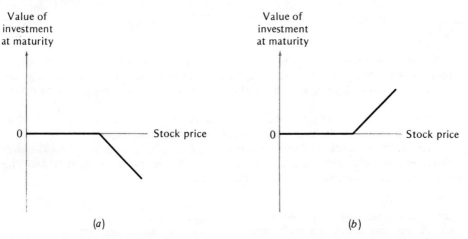

Value of investment at maturity — Stock price

(a)

Value of investment at maturity — Stock price

(b)

Figure 20-11   See Quiz, question 3.

(*d*) Expiration date of the option is extended.

(*e*) Volatility of the stock price falls.

(*f*) Time passes, so the option's expiration date comes closer.

9. "An option is always riskier than the stock it is written on." True or false? How does the risk of an option change when the stock price changes?

10. Use Appendix Tables 6 and 7 to value the following options.

(*a*) A call option written on a stock selling for $60 per share. The stock's standard deviation is 6% per month. The option has a $60 exercise price and matures in three months. The risk-free interest rate is 1% per month.

(*b*) A put option written on the same stock at the same time, with the same exercise price and expiration date.

11. Use the Black-Scholes formula for a European call and Appendix Tables 8(*a*) and 8(*b*) to value the call option described in Quiz question 10(*a*). Interpret the terms of the Black-Scholes formula as they are described in footnote 16 of this chapter.

12. Use the Black-Scholes formula for a European put from footnote 20 and Appendix Tables 8(*a*) and 8(*b*) to value the put option described in Quiz question 10(*b*). Interpret the terms of the Black-Scholes formula as you did for the call option in Quiz question 11.

QUESTIONS AND PROBLEMS

1. Look up the terms of actual call and put options traded on the TSE. Plot their payoffs at maturity using diagrams like those in Figures 20-2 and 20-3.

2. Explain why the value of a call depends on each of the following:

(*a*) The *product* of volatility per period and time to maturity.

(*b*) The *product* of the risk-free interest rate and time to maturity.

3. Look at actual trading prices of call options to check whether they behave as the theory presented in this chapter predicts. For example:

(*a*) Follow several options as they approach maturity. How would you expect their prices to behave? Do they actually behave that way?

(*b*) Compare two call options written on the same stock with the same maturity but different exercise prices.

(*c*) Compare two call options written on the same stock with the same exercise price but different maturities.

4. Indicate how the value of Circular File common stock (see Section 20-1) would change if:

(*a*) The value of the firm's assets increases.

(*b*) The maturity of its debt is extended.

(*c*) The assets become safer (less volatile).

(*d*) The risk-free rate of interest increases (hold the value of the firm's assets constant).

5. Your firm issued five-year warrants in 1980 when its stock price was $75 per share. The warrants had an exercise price of $125. In 1985 the firm's stock price is $175 and all the warrants are exercised. *Using hindsight*, was the 1980 decision to issue warrants a wise one? Explain.

6. The Rank and File Company is considering a rights issue to raise $50 million. An underwriter offers to "stand by" (that is, to guarantee the success of the offering) for a $2 million fee.

(*a*) What kind of an option does Rank and File acquire if it accepts the underwriter's offer?

(*b*) What determines the value of the option?

(*c*) How would you calculate whether the underwriter's offer is a fair deal?

7. Why does the value of a call depend on the dividend yield of the stock the call is written on? Why are warrant values more sensitive to dividend yield than values of call options traded on the TSE?

*8. Indicate which *one* of the following statements is correct:

(*a*) Value of put + present value of exercise price = value of call + share price

(*b*) Value of put + share price = value of call + present value of exercise price

(*c*) Value of put − share price = present value of exercise price − value of call

(*d*) Value of put + value of call = share price − present value of exercise price

The correct statement equates the value of two investment strategies. Plot the payoffs to each strategy as a function of the stock price. Show that the two strategies give identical payoffs.

9. The price of Backwoods Chemical Company stock on January 20 is $90 per share. Three call options are trading on the stock, one maturing on April 20, one on July 20, and one on October 20. All three options have the same $100 exercise price. The standard deviation of Backwoods stock is 42% per year. The risk-free interest rate is 11% per year. What are the three call options worth?

*10. The common stock of Triangular File Company is selling at $90. A 26-week call option written on Triangular File's stock is selling for $8. The call's exercise price is $100. The risk-free interest rate is 10% per year.

(*a*) Suppose that puts on Triangular stock are not traded, but you want to buy one. How would you do it?

(*b*) Suppose that puts *are* traded. What should a 26-week put with an exercise price of $100 sell for?

(*c*) Test the option conversion formula you used to answer (*a*) and (*b*) by using it to explain the relative prices of traded puts and calls.

11. Refer again to the Circular File balance sheet given in Section 20-1. Suppose that the Canadian government suddenly offers to guarantee the $50 principal payment due bondholders next year and also to guarantee the interest payment due next year. (In other words, if firm value falls short of the promised interest and principal payment, the government will make up the difference.) This offer is a complete surprise to everyone. The government asks nothing in return, and so its offer is cheerfully accepted.

(*a*) Suppose that the promised interest rate on Circular's debt is 10%. The rate on one-year Canadian government notes is 8%. How will the guarantee affect bond value?

(*b*) The guarantee does *not* affect the value of Circular stock. Why? (*Note*: There could be some effect if the guarantee allows Circular to avoid costs of financial distress or bankruptcy. See Section 18-3.)

(*c*) How will the value of the firm (debt plus equity) change?

Now suppose that the government offers the same guarantee for *new* debt issued by Rectangular File Company. Remember that Rectangular's assets are identical to Circular's, but Rectangular has no existing debt. Rectangular accepts the offer and uses the proceeds of a $50 debt issue to repurchase or retire stock.

Will Rectangular stockholders gain from the opportunity to issue the guaranteed debt? By how much, approximately? (Ignore taxes.)

12. How would you use Appendix Tables 6 and 7 to estimate the volatility of a common stock on which call options are written and actively traded?

VALUING RISKY DEBT

How do you estimate the present value of a company's bonds? The answer is simple. You take the cash flows and discount them at the opportunity cost of capital. Therefore if a bond produces cash flows of C dollars per year for N years and is then repaid at its face value ($1,000), the present value is

$$PV = \frac{C}{1 + r_1} + \frac{C}{(1 + r_2)^2} + \cdots + \frac{C}{(1 + r_N)^N} + \frac{\$1,000}{(1 + r_N)^N}$$

where $r_1, r_2, \ldots, r_N$ are the appropriate discount rates for the cash flows to be received by the bond's owner in years $1, 2, \ldots, N$.

That is correct as far as it goes but it does not tell us anything about what *determines* the discount rate. For example:

1. In 1948 Canadian Treasury bills offered an average return of 0.4%: in 1983 they offered a return of 9.4%. Why does the same security offer radically different yields at different points in time?

2. In 1983 the Government of Canada could borrow for one to three years at an average interest rate of 9.4%, but it had to pay an average rate of 11.8% for loans of ten years and longer. Why do bonds maturing at different dates offer different rates of interest? In other words, why is there a *term structure* of interest rates?

3. In 1983 the Canadian government could issue bonds with more than ten years to maturity at a rate of 11.8%. You could not have borrowed at that rate. Why not? What explains the premium you have to pay?

These questions lead to deep issues that will keep economists simmering for years. But we can give general answers and at the same time present some fundamental ideas.

Why should the financial manager care about these ideas? Who needs to know how bonds are priced as long as the bond market is active and efficient? Efficient markets protect the ignorant trader. If it is necessary to check whether the price is right for a proposed bond issue, you can check the prices of similar bonds. There is no need to worry about the historical behaviour of interest rates, about the term structure, or about the other issues discussed in this chapter.

We do not believe that ignorance is desirable even when it is harmless. At least you ought to be able to read *The Globe and Mail* and talk to investment bankers. More important, you will encounter many problems of bond pricing where there are no similar instruments already traded. How do you evaluate a private placement with a custom-tailored repayment schedule? How about financial leases? In Chapter 24 we will see that they are essentially debt contracts, but often extremely complicated ones, for which traded bonds are not close substitutes. You will find that the terms, concepts, and facts presented in this chapter are essential to the analysis of these and other practical problems in financing covered in Chapters 22 through 24.

We begin therefore, with our first question: "Why does the general level of interest rates change over time?"

21-1 THE CLASSICAL THEORY OF INTEREST

Real Interest Rates

Suppose that everyone knows that there is not going to be any inflation. If so, all interest rates are *real* rates—they include no premium for anticipated inflation. What are the essential determinants of the rate of interest in such a world? The classical economist's answer to this question is summed up in the title of Irving Fisher's great book: *The Theory of Interest: As Determined by Impatience to Spend Income and Opportunity to Invest It.*[1] The real interest rate, according to Fisher, is the price that equates the supply and demand for capital. The supply depends on people's willingness to save— that is, to postpone consumption. The demand depends on the opportunities for productive investment. We introduced this concept in Chapter 2, when we depicted the savings and investment choices of individual consumers and producers. Savings and investment determine, and are determined by, the interest rate. Figures 21-1, 21-2, and 21-3 show how this happens.

Each firm faces a menu of investment opportunities. We represent the menu by the downward-sloping line in Figure 21-1. As the firm invests more, it exhausts opportunities for high rates of return and is forced to take projects with lower and lower rates of return. It will stop investing when it runs out of projects offering rates of return greater than the opportunity cost of capital, which is just the interest rate (we are ignoring

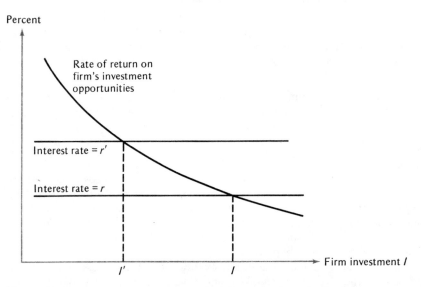

Figure 21-1 Investment opportunity schedule for the firm. As the firm invests more, it is forced to undertake projects with lower and lower rates of return. It stops when the return on a project equals the interest rate. Thus an increase in the interest rate from r to r' would reduce investment from I to I'.

---

[1]Augustus M. Kelley, Publishers, New York, 1965; originally published 1930.

risk here). For example, if the interest rate is r, the firm will invest l; if it is r', the firm will invest l'.

The firm's investment-opportunity schedule describes its *demand for capital* as a function of the interest rate it faces. The *total* demand for capital in the economy is the sum of all firms' investment-opportunity schedules. This total demand is the downward-sloping line in Figure 21-2.

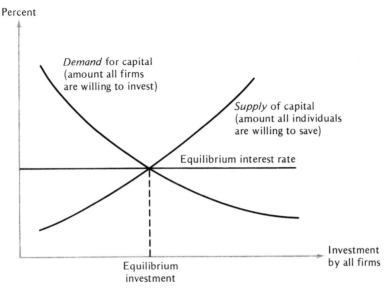

Figure 21-2   Interest rate is determined by the supply of and demand for capital. The market settles on the interest rate that matches the amount firms are willing to invest with the amount individuals are willing to save.

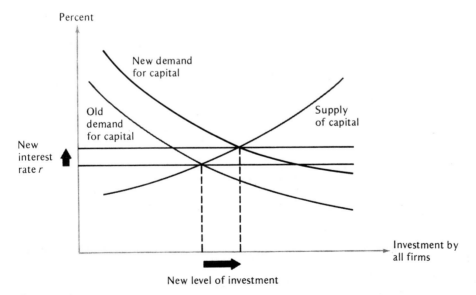

Figure 21-3   Interest rate changes in response to shifts in the curves describing the supply of and demand for capital. In this case, firms' investment opportunities become more favourable, and so firms are willing to invest more at any given interest rate. The result is an increase in both the interest rate and the amount invested.

The total *supply* of capital ultimately depends on the amount individuals are willing to save.[2] This amount is also a function of the interest rate. We have drawn the supply of capital (saving) as the upward-sloping line in Figure 21-2.[3] The equilibrium interest rate is determined by the condition that saving has to equal investment for the economy as a whole. In other words, capital markets settle on the interest rate that balances firms' willingness to invest with individuals' willingness to save.[4] This occurs at the intersection of the investment and saving curves in Figure 21-2.

The interest rate changes when one or both of these curves change. For example, suppose that investment prospects generally improve. Firms have more good projects, and so are willing to invest more at any interest rate. This is shown in Figure 21-3 by an outward shift in the investment-opportunity schedule. As a result the interest rate has to rise to induce individuals to save the additional amount that firms want to invest. The new equilibrium occurs at the intersection of the new investment-opportunities curve and the old curve describing the supply of capital.

Fisher's theory emphasizes that the real rate of interest depends on real phenomena. A high aggregate willingness to save may be associated with such factors as high aggregate wealth (because wealthy people usually save more), an uneven distribution of wealth (an even distribution would mean few rich people, who do most of the saving), and a high proportion of middle-aged people (the young don't need to save and the old don't want to—"You can't take it with you").

Correspondingly, a high aggregate propensity to invest (that is, a steep investment-opportunity line) may be associated with a high level of industrial activity or major technological advances. One would suspect that most of these influences would shift slowly and orderly, particularly on a worldwide basis. It is not surprising, therefore, that as far as one can tell, the real short-term rate of interest appears to have remained fairly stable at around 0% in most major industrial countries.[5]

Inflation and Interest Rates

Now let us see what Irving Fisher had to say about the effect of inflation on interest rates. Suppose that consumers are equally happy with 100 apples today or 105 apples in a year's time. Then the real or "apple" rate of interest is 5%. Suppose also that I know the price of apples will increase over the year by 10%. Then I will part with $100 today if I am repaid $115 at the end of the year. That $115 is needed to buy me 5% more apples than I can get for my $100 today. In other words, the nominal or "money" rate of interest must equal the real or "apple" rate plus the prospective rate of inflation. A change of one percentage point in the expected inflation rate produces a change of one percentage point in the nominal interest rate.[6] That is Fisher's theory:

---

[2]Some of this saving is done indirectly. For example, if you hold 100 shares of CP stock, and CP retains earnings of $1 per share, CP is saving $100 on your behalf.

[3]It could be downward-sloping, so that a higher interest rate means *less* saving. Here is an example of why this might happen. Suppose that you need $10,000 20 years hence for your children's university expenses. How much will you have to set aside today to cover this obligation? The answer is the present value of $10,000 after 20 years, or $10,000/(1 + r)^{20}$. The higher r, the lower the present value and the less you have to set aside.

[4]Notice what would happen if, say, the interest rate were higher than the equilibrium rate. Individuals would want to save more and companies would want to invest less. The excess supply of savings would force the interest rate back to the equilibrium level.

[5]For example, Table 7-1 shows that the average real interest rate earned by investing in Treasury bills was 0.5% in Canada and 0.1% in the United States from 1926–1981.

[6]The apple example was taken from R. Roll, "Interest Rates on Monetary Assets and Commodity Price Index Changes," *Journal of Finance*, 27:251–278 (May 1972).

---

a change in the expected rate of inflation will cause the same change in the nominal interest rate.

In principle, there is no upper limit to the real rate of interest. But is there any lower limit? For example, is it possible for the money rate of interest to be 5% and the expected rate of inflation to be 10%, thus giving a negative real interest rate? If this happens, you may be able to make money in the following way. You borrow $100 at an interest rate of 5% and you use the money to buy apples. You store the apples and sell them at the end of the year for $110, which leaves you enough to pay off your loan plus $5 for yourself.

Since easy ways to make money are rare, we can conclude that, if it doesn't cost anything to store goods, the money rate of interest is unlikely to be less than the expected rise in prices. But many goods are even more expensive to store than apples, and others cannot be stored at all (you can't store haircuts, for example). For these goods, the money interest rate can be less than the expected price rise.

Comment If you look back to our discussion of inflation and discount rates in Section 6-1, you will see that our apple example is a bit oversimplified. If apples cost $1.00 apiece today and $1.10 next year, you need $1.10 \times 105 = \$115.50$ next year to buy 105 apples. The money interest rate is 15.5%, not 15.

The exact formula relating real and money rates is

$$1 + r_{money} = (1 + r_{real})(1 + i)$$

where i is the expected inflation rate. Thus

$$r_{money} = r_{real} + i + i(r_{real})$$

In our example, the money rate should be

$$r_{money} = 0.05 + 0.10 + 0.10(0.05) = 0.155$$

When we said the money rate should be 15%, we ignored the "cross-product" term $i(r_{real})$. This is a common rule of thumb, because the cross-product is usually small. But there are countries where i is large (sometimes 100% per year or more). In such cases it pays to use the full formula.

Back to Fisher's Theory Critics of Fisher's theory of the effect of inflation on interest rates have usually fastened on the assumption that the real rate of interest is not changed by the inflation rate. For example, if changes in prices are associated with changes in the level of industrial activity, then in inflationary conditions I might want more or less than 105 apples in a year's time to compensate me for the loss of 100 today.

We wish we could show you the past behaviour of interest rates and *expected* inflation. Instead, we have done the next best thing and plotted in Figure 21-4 the return on Canadian Treasury bills against *actual* inflation. Notice, first, that since 1948 the return on Treasury bills has been below the inflation rate almost as often as it has been above. Hence our earlier argument that the *real* interest rate has averaged about 0%.

Fisher's theory states that changes in anticipated inflation produce corresponding changes in the rate of interest. But there is very little evidence of this in the early years shown in Figure 21-4. During this period, the return on Treasury bills scarcely changed even though inflation fluctuated sharply. Either these changes in inflation were unanticipated or Fisher's theory was wrong. Since 1954, there appears to have been a closer relationship between interest rates and inflation in Canada.[7] Therefore, it is worth looking more carefully at how well Fisher's theory has worked in these recent years.

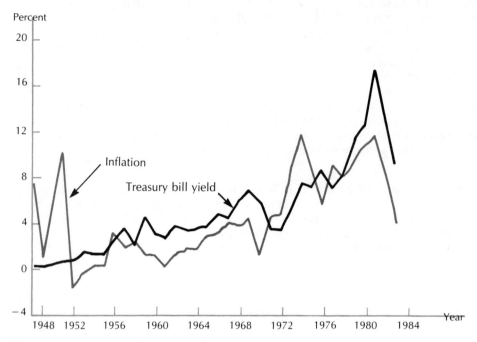

Figure 21-4   The yield on Canadian Treasury bills and the rate of inflation 1948–1983.
Source: Report on Canadian Economic Statistics 1924–1983. Canadian Institute of Actuaries, July 1984.

Eugene Fama has suggested that one way to test Fisher's theory is to twist it around and measure whether the inflation rate can be forecasted by subtracting a constant real rate from the observed nominal interest rate. That is, if Fisher is right,

$$\text{Nominal interest rate} = \text{real interest rate} + \text{inflation rate forecasted by investors}$$

or

$$\text{Inflation rate forecasted by investors} = \text{nominal interest rate} - \text{real interest rate}$$

Of course, investors cannot predict the actual inflation rate perfectly—there will be a random forecast error. But in an efficient market, we expect them to be right on the average. Thus, the forecast error should be zero on the average.

---

[7]Until 1954, Treasury bills were not an important source of financing for the Government of Canada. Trading in Treasury bills was largely confined to chartered banks and the Bank of Canada. In an attempt to develop an organized money market, the Canadian government introduced a weekly Treasury bill auction market in early 1953 and then later in the same year allowed and encouraged money market dealers to trade Treasury bills. With the more active and liquid market came a more competitive interest rate.

Suppose that each quarter we observe the nominal return on Treasury bills and the *actual* rate of inflation. We fit the following equation to these data:

$$\begin{matrix} \text{Actual} \\ \text{inflation rate} \end{matrix} = a + b(\text{nominal interest rate}) + \text{random forecasting error}$$

If Fisher is correct, the coefficient b should be close to 1.0 and the constant term a should be equal to minus the real interest rate.

We estimated b on United States data for 1953 to 1982 as 0.96 and on Canadian data for the period 1953 to 1983 as 0.68.[8] Thus, nominal interest rates appear to have been reasonably good predictors of inflation rates in both countries, with the nominal interest rates in Canada slightly overstating the corresponding rates of inflation. Nevertheless, if you want to predict the rate of inflation over the next year, it appears that a good place to start is by observing the one-year government bond yield and subtracting the historical average real rate of return. On the other hand, if you want to work out what the Treasury bill rate will be next year, you should start thinking about what rate of inflation economists will be predicting for next year.

Before leaving this topic, we must add two qualifications. First, the real interest rate is really an *expected* rate. When you buy a Treasury bill and hold it to maturity, you know what the dollar payoff will be, but the *real* payoff is uncertain because future inflation is not wholly predictable. Thus, to be perfectly precise, we should define the real interest rate as follows:

Real interest rate = *expected* real rate of return from investment in Treasury bills

= nominal rate of return on Treasury bills

− *expected* rate of inflation

Second, Nelson and Schwert, and Hess and Bicksler have pointed out that the (expected) real interest rate *does* vary over time.[9] If that is so, Fama's test may be inappropriate.

Until these problems have been resolved, we recommend that you look on Fisher's theory simply as a useful rule of thumb. Thus, if the expected inflation rate changes, your best bet is that there will be a corresponding change in the interest rate.

21-2 TERM STRUCTURE AND YIELDS TO MATURITY

We turn now to the relationship between short-term and long-term rates of interest. Suppose that we have a simple loan which pays $1 at time 1. The present value of this loan is

$$PV = \frac{1}{1 + r_1}$$

---

[8]Fama fitted his equation to U.S. data for the period 1953 to 1971. His estimate of b was 0.98, which is almost identical to our figure. See E.F. Fama, "Short-Term Interest Rates as Predictors of Inflation," *American Economic Review*, **65**:269–282 (June 1975).

[9]C.R. Nelson and G. Schwert, "Short-Term Interest Rates as Predictors of Inflation: On Testing the Hypothesis that the Real Rate of Interest is Constant," *American Economic Review*, **67**: 478–486 (June 1977); P. Hess and J. Bicksler, "Capital Asset Prices versus Time Series Models as Predictors of Inflation," *Journal of Financial Economics*, **2**:341–360 (December 1975).

Thus we discount the cash flow at r_1, the rate appropriate for a one-period loan. This rate is fixed today; it is often called today's one-period **spot rate**.

If we have a loan that pays $1 at both times 1 and 2, present value is

$$PV = \frac{1}{1 + r_1} + \frac{1}{(1 + r_2)^2}$$

Thus the first period's cash flow is discounted at today's one-period spot rate and the second period's flow is discounted at today's two-period spot rate. The series of spot rates r_1, r_2, and so on is one way of expressing the **term structure** of interest rates.

Measuring Yield to Maturity

Rather than discounting each of the payments at a different rate of interest, we could find a single rate of discount that would produce the same present value. Such a rate

---

Table 21-1 Each page of this mini-book of bond tables shows bond prices for a different coupon level.

Coupon = 5%   Page 1

Yield	Years				
	6	8	10	12	14
6.0%	95.02	93.72	92.56	91.53	90.62
8.0	85.92	82.52	79.61	77.13	75.01
10.0	77.84	72.91	68.84	65.50	62.75
12.0	70.66	64.63	59.86	56.07	53.08
14.0	64.26	57.49	52.33	48.39	45.38

Coupon = 6%   Page 2

Yield	Years				
	6	8	10	12	14
6.0%	100.00	100.00	100.00	100.00	100.00
8.0	90.61	88.35	86.41	84.75	83.34
10.0	82.27	78.32	75.08	72.40	70.20
12.0	74.85	69.68	65.59	62.35	59.78
14.0	68.23	62.21	57.62	54.12	51.45

Coupon = 7%   Page 3

Yield	Years				
	6	8	10	12	14
6.0%	104.98	106.28	107.44	108.47	109.38
8.0	95.31	94.17	93.20	92.38	91.67
10.0	86.71	83.74	81.31	79.30	77.65
12.0	79.04	74.74	71.33	68.62	66.48
14.0	72.20	66.94	62.92	59.86	57.52

Coupon = 8%   Page 4

Yield	Years				
	6	8	10	12	14
6.0%	109.95	112.56	114.88	116.94	118.76
8.0	100.00	100.00	100.00	100.00	100.00
10.0	91.14	89.16	87.54	86.20	85.10
12.0	83.23	79.79	77.06	74.90	73.19
14.0	76.17	71.66	68.22	65.59	63.59

is known as the **yield to maturity**, though it is in fact no more than our old acquaintance, the internal rate of return (IRR), masquerading under another name. If we call the yield to maturity y, we can write the present value as

$$PV = \frac{1}{1 + y} + \frac{1}{(1 + y)^2}$$

All you need to calculate y is the price of a bond, its annual payment, and its maturity. You can then rapidly work out the yield with the aid of a preprogrammed calculator or you can find it in a set of bond tables.

Look at Table 21-1, which contains eight pages from a mini-book of bond tables. Each page shows yields for bonds with a particular coupon. For example, suppose that you have an 8% bond maturing in ten years and priced at 85. (Bond prices are quoted as percentages of the bonds' face value.) Look at page 4, which shows yields for bonds with an 8% coupon, and run your eye down the column for ten years. A bond priced at 87.54 yields 10% and a bond priced at 77.06 yields 12%. Obviously the yield on your bond lies somewhere in between, about 10.5%.

Table 21-1   (*Continued*)

Coupon = 9%						Page 5
			Years			
Yield	6	8	10	12	14	
6.0%	114.93	118.84	122.32	125.40	128.15	
8.0	104.69	105.83	106.80	107.62	108.33	
10.0	95.57	94.58	93.77	93.10	92.55	
12.0	87.42	84.84	82.80	81.17	79.89	
14.0	80.14	76.38	73.51	71.33	69.66	

Coupon = 10%						Page 6
			Years			
Yield	6	8	10	12	14	
6.0%	119.91	125.12	129.75	133.87	137.53	
8.0	109.39	111.65	113.59	115.25	116.66	
10.0	100.00	100.00	100.00	100.00	100.00	
12.0	91.62	89.89	88.53	87.45	86.59	
14.0	84.11	81.11	78.81	77.06	75.73	

Coupon = 11%						Page 7
			Years			
Yield	6	8	10	12	14	
6.0%	124.89	131.40	137.19	142.34	146.91	
8.0	114.08	117.48	120.39	122.87	124.99	
10.0	104.43	105.42	106.23	106.90	107.45	
12.0	95.81	94.95	94.27	93.72	93.30	
14.0	88.09	85.83	84.11	82.80	81.79	

Coupon = 12%						Page 8
			Years			
Yield	6	8	10	12	14	
6.0%	129.86	137.68	144.63	150.81	156.29	
8.0	118.77	123.30	127.18	130.49	133.33	
10.0	108.86	110.84	112.46	113.80	114.90	
12.0	100.00	100.00	100.00	100.00	100.00	
14.0	92.06	90.55	89.41	88.53	87.86	

Real books of bond tables contain several hundred pages, each crammed with bond prices for different combinations of coupon, yield and maturity, but in all other respects, they are the same as our mini-book of Table 21-1.

An Example   The yield to maturity is unambiguous and easy to calculate. It is the stock in trade of any bond dealer. By now, however, you should have learned to treat any internal rate of return with suspicion.[10] The more closely we examine the yield to maturity, the less informative it is seen to be. Here is an example.

It is 1990. You are contemplating an investment in Government of Canada bonds. You come across the following quotations for two bonds:

Bond	Price	Yield to Maturity, % (IRR)
5s of '95	85.21	8.78
10s of '95	105.43	8.62

The phrase "5s of '95" means a bond maturing in 1995 paying annual interest amounting to 5% of the bond's face value. The interest payment is called a *coupon* payment. Bond investors would say that these bonds have a 5% coupon. Face value plus interest are paid back at maturity, 1995. The price of each bond is quoted as a percent of face value. Therefore, if face value is $1,000, you would have to pay $852.10 to buy the bond and your yield would be 8.78%. Letting 1990 be $t = 0$, 1991 be $t = 1$, and so on,[11] we have the following discounted cash-flow calculation.

	Cash Flows						Yield in %
Bond	C_0	C_1	C_2	C_3	C_4	C_5	
5s of '95	−852.10	+50	+50	+50	+50	+1,050	8.78
10s of '95	−1,054.30	+100	+100	+100	+100	+1,100	8.62

Although the two bonds mature at the same date, they presumably were issued at different times, the 5s when interest rates were low, and the 10s when interest rates were high.

Are the 5s of '95 a better buy? Is the market making a mistake by pricing these two issues at different yields? The only way you will know for sure is to calculate the bond's present values using spot rates of interest, r_1 for 1991, r_2 for 1992, and so on. This is done in Table 21-2.

The important assumption in Table 21-2 is that long-term interest rates are higher than short-term interest rates. We have assumed that the one-year interest rate is $r_1 = 0.05$, the two-year rate is $r_2 = 0.06$, and so on. When each year's cash flow is discounted at the rate appropriate to that year, we see that each bond's present value is exactly equal to the quoted price. Thus each bond is *fairly priced*.

Why do the 5s have a higher yield? Because for each dollar that you invest in the 5s you receive relatively little cash inflow in the first four years and a relatively high cash inflow in the final year. Therefore, although the two bonds have identical maturity dates, the 5s provide a greater proportion of their cash flows in 1995. In this sense the 5s are a longer-term investment than the 10s. Their higher yield to maturity just reflects the fact that long-term interest rates are higher than short-term rates.

---

[10]See Section 5-4.

[11]Coupon payments are actually made semiannually—the owners of the 5s of '95 would receive $25 every six months. Thus our calculations are a little bit off what you would get from using bond tables like Table 21-1.

Table 21-2 Calculating present value of two bonds when long-term interest rates are higher than short-term rates.

Period	Interest Rate	Present Value Calculations			
		5s of '95		10s of '95	
		C_1	PV at r_t	C_t	PV at r_t
$t = 1$	$r_1 = 0.05$	$ 50	$ 47.62	$ 100	$ 95.24
$t = 2$	$r_2 = 0.06$	50	44.50	100	89.00
$t = 3$	$r_3 = 0.07$	50	40.81	100	81.63
$t = 4$	$r_4 = 0.08$	50	36.75	100	73.50
$t = 5$	$r_5 = 0.09$	1,050	682.43	1,100	714.92
	Totals	$1,250	$852.11	$1,500	$1,054.29

Problems with Yield to Maturity

With this example in mind, we can sum up the problems with the yield to maturity.

First, when a bond's yield to maturity is calculated, the *same* rate is used to discount *all* payments to the bondholder. The bondholder may actually demand different rates of return (r_1, r_2, and so on) for different periods. Unless two bonds offer exactly the same pattern of cash flow over time, they are likely to have different yields to maturity. Therefore the yield to maturity on one bond can offer only a rough guide to the appropriate yield on another.

Second, yields to maturity do not determine bond prices. It is the other way around. The demand by companies for capital and the supply of savings by individuals combine to determine the spot rates r_1, r_2, and so on. These rates then determine the value of any package of future cash flows. Finally, *given* the value, we can compute the yield to maturity. We cannot, however, derive the appropriate yield to maturity *without* first knowing the value. We cannot, for example, assume that the yield should be the same for two bonds with the same maturity unless they also happen to have the same coupon.

The yield to maturity is a complicated average of spot rates of interest. Suppose that r_2 is greater than r_1. Then the yield on a two-year coupon bond must lie between r_1 and r_2. In this case, the yield on the two-year bond provides an underestimate of the two-year spot rate. Of course, if r_2 is less than r_1, it would be the other way around— the yield on the two-year bond would overestimate the two-year spot rate. Sometimes these differences can be dramatic. For example, in Britain in 1977 the 20-year spot rate of interest r_{20} was nearly 20%. But the *yield* on high-coupon bonds maturing in 20 years was only about 13%. The reason was that short-term spot rates of interest were much lower than 20%. The yield on 20-year bonds was an average of short-term and long-term rates.[12]

Thus it is dangerous to rely on the yield to maturity—like most averages, it hides much of the interesting information.

*Measuring the Term Structure

If you just want a quick, summary measure of the return offered on a bond, look at the yield to maturity. But if you want to understand why different bonds sell at different

---

[12]For a good analysis of the relationship between the yield to maturity and spot interest rates, see S.M. Schaefer, "The Problem of Redemption Yields," *Financial Analysts Journal*, **33**:59–67 (July–August 1977).

prices, you are going to have to dig deeper to estimate spot rates of interest. That is not something that most bond analysts do at the moment. Here's your chance to be ahead of the game.

Look back at Table 21-2, which shows how investors value the 5% bonds of '95. Each bond is like a package of five mini-bonds. The package contains one mini-bond paying $50 at $t = 1$, another paying $50 at $t = 2$, and so on up to the fifth mini-bond, which pays $1,050 at $t = 5$.

To calculate the spot rates of interest, we must first work out the price of each mini-bond. For example, in 1990, you could buy the following packages:

1. Invest $1,704.22 to buy *two* 5s of '95.

2. Invest $1,054.30 to buy *one* 10 of '95.

Each package provides a $100 cash flow for four years. But in year 5, when the bonds mature, the first package gives 2 × 1,050 = $2,100, and the second package gives 1 × $1100 = $1,100. Thus, the only cash-flow advantage of package 1 occurs in year 5. It costs $649.92 more to buy package 1 ($1,704.22 − $1,054.30 = $649.92), but you gain $1,000 in year 5 ($2,100 − $1,100 = $1,000).

Investors must be indifferent between the two packages—if they were not, they would dump one bond and buy the other, and the bond prices would change. Thus an extra $1,000 received in year 5 must be worth $649.92 now:

PV($1,000 in year 5) = $649.92

But this present value depends on the five-year spot rate r_5:

$$PV = \frac{1,000}{(1 + r_5)^5} = 649.92$$

Solving for r_5, we find that it equals 0.09 or 9%.

In this example, we had two bonds with the same five-year maturity, but different coupons. This allowed us to work out the price of a mini-bond that made a payment only in year 5 and this in turn gave us the five-year spot rate. In order to work out the exact prices of mini-bonds and spot rates for all other periods, we would need a complete series of matching bonds. In practice, we are never so fortunate, but as long as we have a fair spread of coupons and maturities, we can get quite satisfactory estimates of the spot rates.[13] For example, the solid line in Figure 21-5 shows some estimates by Barr Rosenberg of spot interest rates in December 1982.

In Canada the more common name for mini-bonds is **strip bonds**. The name arose because a typical government bond issue consists of two parts. The first is a certificate bearing a face value ranging from $1,000 to $1 million and is redeemable 20 to 30 years from the issue date, and the second is a detachable "strippable" sheet of 40 to 60 interest coupons, which are redeemable on specified dates during the bond's life. The term *strip bond* then refers to the first part of the bond, that is, the bond stripped of its coupons.

Recently, a number of financial institutions in Canada and the United States have purchased long-term government bond issues and have reissued them as strip bonds,

---

[13]You may also have to adjust for the fact that low-coupon bonds, because they sell at a discount, get a tax break relative to high-coupon bonds. Part of the low-coupon bonds' expected return comes as capital gains, because the discount diminishes over time. Also, bonds may have differing call provisions (see Section 22-3).

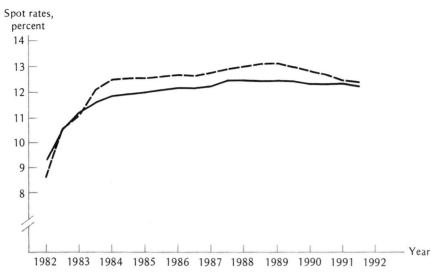

Figure 21-5 Estimated spot interest rates on United States Treasury Securities, August 24, 1982. The solid line gives estimates made by Barr Rosenberg Associates. The broken line shows rates on Salomon Brothers mini-bonds. The first maturity date is November 1982.

each of which makes only one payment at maturity.[14] These strip bonds are popular with individual investors who want to provide themselves with a future nest-egg to combine with their retirement savings plans. The price of a $100,000, 20-year strip bond today is as little as 10% of the face value (that is, the bond has a promised yield of 12.2% annually).

The strip bond or mini-bond yields provide another way to measure spot interest rates. Simply look at the interest rates on each of these bonds. For example, the broken line in Figure 21-5 shows the rates of interest on the Salomon Brothers mini-bonds in December 1982.

*Duration and Volatility

Table 21-3 shows for the 5s of '95 the present value of each year's cash flow as a proportion of the bond's total value. Notice that the cash flow in year 5 accounts for only 80.9% of value. Nearly 20% of value comes from earlier cash flows. It is somewhat misleading, therefore, to describe the bond as a five-year bond; the *average* time to each cash flow is less than five years.

Bond analysts often use the term *duration* to describe the average time to each payment. If we call the total value of the bond V, then duration is calculated as follows:

$$\text{Duration} = \frac{\text{PV}(C_1)}{V} \times 1 + \frac{\text{PV}(C_2)}{V} \times 2 + \frac{\text{PV}(C_3)}{V} \times 3 + \cdots$$

---

[14]These strip bonds have a variety of exotic names. In Canada, for example, Guaranty Trust issues are known as *Cougar Residuals* and North West Trust issues as *The Nugget*. In the United States, Merrill Lynch labels their mini-bond issues TIGRs (Treasury Investment Growth Receipts) and at Salomon Brothers they are known as CATS (Certificates of Accrual on Treasury Securities).

For the 5s of '95,

$$\text{Duration} = (0.054 \times 1) + (0.050 \times 2) + (0.046 \times 3) + \cdots$$
$$= 4.505 \text{ years}$$

Table 21-3 The first four columns show that the final cash flow accounts for only 80.9% of the present value of the 5s of '95. The final column shows how to calculate a weighted average of the time to each flow. This average is termed the bond's "duration."

Year	C_t	$PV(C_t)$ at 8.78%	Proportion of Total Value $(PV(C_t)/V)$	Proportion of Total Value × Time
1	$ 50	$ 45.96	0.054	0.054
2	50	42.26	0.050	0.100
3	50	38.85	0.046	0.138
4	50	35.71	0.042	0.168
5	1,050	689.42	0.809	4.045
		$V = 852.20$	1.000	Duration = 4.505 years

The 10s of '95 have the same maturity as the 5s, but the first four years' coupon payments account for a greater fraction of the bond's value. In this sense, the 10s are a shorter bond than the 5s. The duration of the 10s is only 4.193 years.

Let us look now at what happens to the prices of our two bonds as interest rates change:

	5s of '95		10s of '95	
	New Price	% Change	New Price	% Change
Yield falls 0.5%	$87.00	+2.10	$107.48	+1.95
Yield rises 0.5%	83.47	−2.04	103.41	−1.91
Difference	3.53	4.14	4.07	3.86

Thus, a 1% variation in yield causes the price of the 5s to change by 3.53 or 4.14%. We can say that the 5s have a *volatility* of 4.14%.

Notice that the 5% bonds have the greater volatility and they also have the longer duration. In fact, a bond's volatility is directly related to its duration:

$$\frac{\text{Volatility}}{\text{(percent)}} = \frac{\text{duration}}{1 + \text{yield}}$$

In the case of the 5s,

$$\frac{\text{Volatility}}{\text{(percent)}} = \frac{4.505}{1.0878} = 4.14$$

Volatility is a useful summary measure of the likely effect of a change in interest rates on a debt portfolio.

Example Potterton Leasing has just arranged a large lease that will provide additional rental income of $2 million a year for eight years. At an interest rate of 12%, these rentals have a present value of $9.94 million. (We will forget about taxes in this example.)

Potterton has acquired a new financial asset worth $9.94 million; at least that is its value today—it may have a different value tomorrow if interest rates change.

Now Potterton issues $1.91 million of one-year debt and $8.03 million of six-year debt, each with a 12% coupon. Think of its new asset and new liabilities as a package: Does Potterton stand to gain or lose from a change in interest rates?

We can answer this question by calculating the duration of Potterton's new asset (the lease) and its new liability (the package of one- and six-year debt). It turns out that both have a duration of 3.9 years. Thus, both are equally affected by a change in interest rates. If interest rates rise, the present value of Potterton's new lease income will decline, but the value of its debt obligation will also decline by an equal amount. Conversely, if interest rates fall, both the value of the lease income and the debt payments will rise by the same amount. By equalizing the duration of its assets and liabilities, Potterton has *immunized* itself against any change in interest rates.

Notice two things about this example. As interest rates change and time passes, the duration of Potterton's assets may no longer be the same as that of its liabilities. If Potterton wishes to remain immunized against interest rate changes, it must be prepared to adjust the duration of its debt.

Second, Potterton is protected only against an across-the-board change in interest rates. But perhaps short-term interest rates and long-term rates do not move exactly together. In this case, to immunize itself against interest rate movements, Potterton would need to consider two volatility measures. It would need to ensure that its assets and liabilities were equally affected by changes in the short-term rate, and that they were equally affected by changes in the long rate as well.

21-3   EXPLAINING THE TERM STRUCTURE

The term structure in Figure 21-5 is upward-sloping. In other words, long rates of interest are higher than short rates. This is the more common pattern but sometimes it is the other way around, with short rates higher than long rates. Why do we get these shifts in term structure?

Ms. Long's Problem

Let us look at a simple example. Ms. Long wants to invest $1,000 for two years. Two strategies open to her are described in Table 21-4. Strategy L1 is to put the money in a one-year bond at an interest rate of r_1. At the end of the year she must then take her money and find another one-year bond. Let us call the rate of interest on this second bond $_1r_2$—that is, the spot rate of interest at time 1 on a loan maturing at time 2.[15] As Table 21-4 shows, the final payoff to this strategy is $1,000(1 + r_1)(1 + {_1r_2})$.

Of course Ms. Long cannot know for sure what the one-period spot rate of interest $_1r_2$ will be next year. Suppose that she *expects* it to be 11%. That is, $E(_1r_2) = 0.11$. The current one-period spot rate is 10%. The expected final payoff is

$$1,000(1 + r_1)[1 + E(_1r_2)] = 1,000(1.10)(1.11) = \$1,221$$

Instead of making two separate investments of one year each, Ms. Long could invest her money today in a bond that pays off in year 2 (strategy L2 in Table 21-3). That

---

[15] Be careful to distinguish $_1r_2$ from r_2, the spot interest rate on a *two-year* bond held from time 0 to time 2. The quantity $_1r_2$ is a *one-year* spot rate established at time 1.

is, she would invest at the *two-year* spot rate r_2, and receive a final payoff of $1,000$ $(1 + r_2)^2$. If $r_2 = 0.105$, the payoff is $1,000(1.105)^2 = \$1,221$.

Table 21-4   Two investment strategies for Ms. Long, who wants to invest $1,000 for two years.

Strategy	Now	Year 1	Year 2 (Final Payoff)
L1 invest in 2 one-year bonds	$1,000	→ Invest in first bond yielding r_1 $1,000(1 + r_1)$	→ Invest in second bond yielding r_2 $1,000(1 + r_1)(1 + {}_1r_2)$
L2 invest in 1 two-year bond	$1,000	—————————————→ Invest in bond yielding r_2	$1,000(1 + r_2)^2$
Strategy L2 can be expressed as	$1,000	→ Invest for one year at r_1 $1,000(1 + r_1)$	→ Invest for second year at implicit forward rate f_2 $1,000(1 + r_1)(1 + f_2)$

Now, look below the dashed line in Table 21-4. The table shows that strategy L2 can be reinterpreted as investing for one year at the spot rate r_1 and for the second year at a **forward rate** f_2. The forward rate is *implicit* in the two-year spot rate r_2. It is also *guaranteed*: by buying the two-year bond, Ms. Long can "lock in" an interest rate of f_2 for the second year she invests.

Suppose that the two-year spot rate is 10.5% as before. Then the forward rate f_2 must be 11%. By definition, the forward rate for $t = 2$ is the implicit interest rate in the second year of the two-year loan:

$$(1 + r_2)^2 = (1 + r_1)(1 + f_2)$$

$$(1.105)^2 = (1.10)(1 + f_2)$$

$$f_2 = \frac{(1.105)^2}{1.10} - 1 = 0.11$$

or 11%.[16] The two-year spot rate of 10.5% is an average of the 10% one-year spot rate and the 11% forward rate.

What should Ms. Long do? One possible answer is that she should follow the strategy that gives the highest *expected* payoff. That is, she should compare:

Expected Payoff to Strategy L1	To	(Certain) Payoff to Strategy L2
$1,000(1 + r_1)[1 + E({}_1r_2)]$	to or to	$1,000(1 + r_2)^2$ $1,000(1 + r_1)(1 + f_2)$

Strategy L1 gives the higher expected return if $E({}_1r_2)$, the expected future spot rate, exceeds the forward rate f_2 implicit in the two-year spot rate r_2. In our numerical example, with $r_1 = 0.10$, $r_2 = 0.105$, and $E({}_1r_2) = 0.11$, the two strategies give the same expected return:

---

[16]Actually 11.002%. We rounded.

	Payoff
Strategy L1	$1,000(1.10)(1.11) = \$1,221$ (expected)
Strategy L2	$1,000(1.105)^2 = \$1,221$ (certain)

Mr. Short's Problem

Now let us look at the decision faced by Mr. Short. He also has $1,000 to invest, but he wants it back in one year. An obvious strategy is to invest in a one-year bond. In this case, his payoff is $1,000(1 + r_1)$—see strategy S1 in Table 21-5. A second strategy (S2 in the table) is to buy a two-year bond and sell it after one year. The sale price will be the bond's present value in year 1. At that time, the bond will have one year to maturity. Its present value will be equal to its year-2 payoff $1,000(1 + r_2)^2$ discounted at $_1r_2$, the one-period spot rate prevailing in year 1:

$$\text{PV of two-year bond at year 1} = \frac{1,000(1 + r_2)^2}{1 + {}_1r_2}$$

We know from Ms. Long's problem that the two-period rate r_2 can be expressed in terms of the one-period spot rate r_1 and the forward rate f_2. Thus

$$\text{PV of two-year bond at year 1} = \frac{1,000(1 + r_1)(1 + f_2)}{1 + {}_1r_2}$$

Of course Mr. Short cannot predict the future spot rate, and therefore he cannot predict the price at year 1 of the two-year bond. But if $r_2 = 0.105$, and he expects the spot rate to be $_1r_2 = 0.11$, then the expected price is

$$\frac{1,000(1.105)^2}{1.11} = \frac{1,221}{1.11} = \$1,100$$

What should Mr. Short do? Suppose that he prefers the strategy that gives the highest expected payoff. Then he should compare:[17]

---

[17]Here we are making an approximation because the expected payoff of S2 in $t = 1$ is not exactly equal to $[1,000(1 + r_2)^2]/[1 + E(_1r_2)]$. We should calculate the expected price of the two-year bond at $t = 1$. Call this $\tilde{P}$. By definition

$$\tilde{P} = \frac{1,000(1 + r_2)^2}{1 + {}_1r_2}$$

and

$$E(\tilde{P}) = E\left[\frac{1,000(1 + r_2)^2}{1 + {}_1r_2}\right]$$

But

$$E\left[\frac{1,000(1 + r_2)^2}{1 + {}_1r_2}\right] \text{ is only approximately equal to } \frac{1,000(1 + r_2)^2}{1 + E(_1r_2)}$$

In general, for any positive random variable $\tilde{x}$, $E(1/\tilde{x})$ is greater than $1/E(\tilde{x})$. This is an example of *Jensen's inequality*. Ignoring Jensen's inequality can be dangerous if the variance of $\tilde{x}$ is large.

Table 21-5 Two investment strategies for Mr. Short, who wants to invest $1,000 for one year.

Strategy	Now		Year 1 (Final Payoff)
S1 invest in one-year bond	$1,000	$\xrightarrow{\text{Invest in } r_1}$	$1,000(1 + r_1)$
S2 invest in two-year bond, but sell in year 1	$1,000	$\xrightarrow[\text{year 1}]{\text{Invest, sell for PV at}}$	$\dfrac{1,000(1 + r_2)^2}{1 + {}_1r_2}$

(Certain) Payoff to Strategy S1	To	Expected Payoff to Strategy S2
$1,000(1 + r_1)$	to	$\dfrac{1,000(1 + r_2)^2}{1 + E({}_1r_2)}$
	or to	$\dfrac{1,000(1 + r_1)(1 + f_2)}{1 + E({}_1r_2)}$

Strategy S2 is better if the forward rate f_2 exceeds the expected future spot rate $E({}_1r_2)$. If Mr. Short faces the same interest rates as Ms. Long [$r_1 = 0.10$, $r_2 = 0.105$, $E({}_1r_2) = 0.11$, $f_2 = 0.11$], the two strategies give the same expected return:

	Payoff
Strategy S1	$1,000(1.10) = \$1,100$ (certain)
Strategy S2	$\dfrac{1,000(1.105)^2}{1.11} = \dfrac{1,000(1.10)(1.11)}{1.11} = \$1,100$ (expected)

The Expectations Hypothesis

You can see that if the world is made up of people like Ms. Long and Mr. Short, all trying to maximize their expected return, then the one-year and two-year bonds can exist side by side only if

$$f_2 = E({}_1r_2)$$

This condition was satisfied in our numerical example—both f_2 and $E({}_1r_2)$ equaled 11%. But what happens if the forward rate exceeds the expected future spot rate? Then both Long and Short prefer investing in two-year bonds. If the world were entirely made up of expected-return maximizers, and f_2 exceeds $E({}_1r_2)$, no one would be willing to hold one-year bonds. On the other hand, if the forward rate were less than the expected future spot rate, no one would be willing to hold two-year bonds. Since investors *do* hold both one-year and two-year bonds, it follows that forward rates of interest must equal expected future spot rates (providing that investors are only interested in expected return).

This is the **expectations hypothesis** of the term structure.[18] It says that the *only* reason for an upward-sloping term structure is that investors expect future spot rates to be higher than current spot rates; the *only* reason for a declining term structure is that

---

[18]The expectations hypothesis is usually attributed to Lutz and Lutz. See F.A. Lutz and V.C. Lutz, *The Theory of Investment in the Firm*, Princeton University Press, Princeton, N.J., 1951.

investors expect spot rates to fall below current levels. The expectations hypothesis also implies that investing in short-term bonds (as in strategies L1 and S1) gives exactly the same expected return as investing in long-term bonds (as in strategies L2 and S2).

The Liquidity-Preference Theory

One problem with the expectations theory is that it says nothing about risk. Look back for a moment at our two simple cases. Ms. Long wants to invest for two years. If she buys a two-year bond, she can nail down her final payoff today. If she buys a one-year bond, she knows her return for the first year but she does not know at what rate she will be able to reinvest her money. If she does not like this uncertainty, she will tend to prefer the two-year bond, and she will hold one-year bonds only if

$E(_1r_2)$ is greater than f_2

What about Mr. Short? He wants to invest for one year. If he invests in a one-year bond, he can nail down his payoff today. If he buys the two-year bond, he will have to sell it next year at an unknown price. If he does not like this uncertainty, he will prefer the one-year investment, and he will hold two-year bonds only if

$E(_1r_2)$ is less than f_2

Here we have the basis for the **liquidity-preference** theory of term structure.[19] Other things being equal, Ms. Long will prefer to invest in two-year bonds and Mr. Short in one-year bonds. If more companies want to issue two-year bonds than there are Ms. Longs to hold them, they will need to offer a bonus to tempt some of the Mr. Shorts to hold them. Conversely, if more companies want to issue one-year bonds than there are Mr. Shorts to hold them, they will need to offer a bonus to tempt some of the Ms. Longs to hold them.

Any bonus shows up as a difference between forward rates and expected future spot rates. This difference is usually called the **liquidity premium**.

Suppose that there is a shortage of people like Ms. Long. Then the liquidity premium will be positive—that is, the forward rate will exceed the expected spot rate. Advocates of the liquidity-preference theory believe that for the most part, investors want to lend short and companies want to borrow long, so that liquidity premiums are positive.

If the liquidity-preference theory is right, the term structure should be upward-sloping more often than not. A positive liquidity premium rewards investors for lending long. This reward shows up in higher long-term rates of interest. Of course, if future spot rates are expected to fall, the term structure could be downward-sloping and *still* reward investors for lending long. But the liquidity-preference hypothesis would predict a less dramatic downward slope than the expectations hypothesis would.

Introducing Inflation

We argued above that Ms. Long could nail down her return by investing in two-year bonds. What do we mean by that? If the bonds are issued by the U.S. Treasury, she

---

[19]The liquidity-preference hypothesis is usually attributed to Hicks. See J.R. Hicks, *Value and Capital: An Inquiry into Some Fundamental Principles of Economic Theory*, 2d ed., Oxford University Press, Oxford 1946. For a theoretical development, see R. Roll, *The Behavior of Interest Rates: An Application of the Efficient Market Model to U.S. Treasury Bills*, Basic Books, Inc., Publishers, New York, 1970.

can be virtually certain that she will be paid the promised number of dollars. But she cannot be certain what that money will buy. The expectations theory and the liquidity-preference theory of term structure implicitly assume that future inflation rates are known. Let us consider the opposite case in which the *only* uncertainty about interest rates stems from uncertainty about inflation.[20]

Suppose that Irving Fisher is right and short rates of interest always incorporate fully the market's latest views about inflation. Suppose also that the market learns more as time passes about the likely inflation rate in a particular year. Perhaps today it has only a very hazy idea about inflation in year 2, but in a year's time it expects to be able to make a much better prediction.

Because future inflation rates are never known with certainty, neither Ms. Long nor Mr. Short can make a completely risk-free investment. But since they expect to learn a good deal about the inflation rate in year 2 from experience in year 1, next year they will be in a much better position to judge the appropriate interest rate in year 2. It is therefore more risky for either of them to make a forward commitment to lend in year 2. Even Ms. Long, who wants to invest for two years, would be incurring unnecessary risk by buying a two-year bond. Her least risky strategy is to invest in successive one-year bonds. She does not know what her reinvestment rate will be, but at least she knows that it will incorporate the latest information about inflation in year 2.

Of course this means that borrowers must offer some incentive if they want investors to lend long. Therefore the forward rate of interest f_2 must be greater than the expected spot rate $_1r_2$ by an amount that compensates investors for the extra inflation risk.

Example Suppose that the real interest rate is always 2%. Nominal interest rates therefore equal 2% plus the expected rate of inflation. Suppose that the *expected* inflation rate is 8% for both year 1 and year 2. However, inflation may accelerate to 10% in year 1, or it may decrease to 6%. To keep things simple, assume that the actual inflation rate for year 1 continues for year 2:

	Actual Inflation in Year 1	Actual Inflation in Year 2
Expected	0.10	0.10
inflation	0.08	0.08
rate = 0.08	0.06	0.06

Each outcome has a probability of one-third.

Now reconsider Ms. Long's problem. Suppose that she can lend for either one or two years at 10% (the 2% real rate plus the 8% expected inflation rate). If she invests in a one-year bond, she will get $1,000(1.1) = \$1,100$ in year 1. This amount is reinvested, but at what rate? The answer is that the future spot rate $_1r_2$ will be 2% plus the inflation rate experienced in year 1 and projected for year 2:

Actual Inflation Rate	Spot Interest Rate in Year 1
0.10	0.12
0.08	0.10
0.06	0.08

Thus the final payoffs to lending short are:

---

[20]The following is based on R.A. Brealey and S. Schaefer, "Term Structure and Uncertain Inflation," *Journal of Finance,* **32**:277–290 (May 1977).

	Year 1	Reinvest at	Final Payoff in Year 2
Invest for	$1,100	$_1r_2 = 0.12$	$1,232
first year	1,100	$_1r_2 = 0.10$	1,210
at $r_1 = 0.10$	1,100	$_1r_2 = 0.08$	1,188

Note that this strategy gives high payoffs when inflation turns out high.

Now, Ms. Long could lock in a $1,210 payoff in year 2 by purchasing a two-year bond at 10% [$1,000(1 + r_2)^2 = 1,000(1.1)^2 = \$1,210$]. But this would not lock in her *real* return. In fact, lending short is the *safer* strategy when the final payoffs are converted back to current dollars:

Strategy	Final Payoffs	Inflation Rate	Inflation-Adjusted Payoffs[21]
Buy two-year bond	$1,210	0.10	$1,000.00
	1,210	0.08	1,037.38
	1,210	0.06	1,076.90
Buy one-year bond and reinvest at year 1	1,232	0.10	1,018.18
	1,210	0.08	1,037.38
	1,188	0.06	1,057.32

A Comparison of Theories of Term Structure

We have described three views about why long and short interest rates differ. The first view, the expectations theory, is somewhat extreme, but over the past 55 years or so it appears to have done reasonably well. If we look back to Table 7-1, we find that the average annual return on an investment in long-term government bonds for the period 1926 to 1981 was 3.7% in Canada and 3.1% in the United States, while the average annual return on an investment in short-term Treasury bills was 3.6% and 3.1%, respectively. It appears that the long-term and short-term investment strategies yielded the same rate of return, but does this mean that the expectations theory is right?

Perhaps, but the expectations theory has few strict adherents. While it does serve to emphasize that long-term rates reflect, at least in part, investors' expectations about future short-term rates, both our other two theories suggest that long-term bonds ought to offer some additional return to compensate for additional risk. The liquidity-preference theory supposes that risk comes solely from the uncertainty about the underlying real rates, which may be a fair approximation in periods of price stability such as the early 1960s. The inflation-premium theory supposes that the risk comes solely from uncertainty about the inflation rate, which may be a fair approximation in periods of fluctuating inflation such as the 1970s.

If short-term rates of interest are significantly lower than long-term rates, it is often tempting to borrow short-term rather than long-term. Our discussion of term structure theories should serve to warn against such naive strategies. One reason for higher long rates could be that short rates are expected to rise in the future. Also, investors who buy long bonds may be accepting liquidity or inflation risks for which they correctly want compensation. The decision to "stay short" when the term structure is upward-sloping can be justified only if one feels that investors are *overestimating* future increases in interest rates or *overestimating* the risks of lending long.

---

[21] The inflation-adjusted payoffs are calculated by dividing by $(1 + i)^2$. In this case i is the *actual* inflation rate.

If the risk of bond investment comes primarily from uncertainty about the real rate, then the safest strategy for investors is to hold bonds that match their liabilities. For example, the firm's pension fund generally has long-term liabilities. The liquidity-preference theory, therefore, implies that the pension fund should favour long-term bonds. If the risk comes from uncertainty about the inflation rate, then the safest strategy is to hold short bonds. For example, most pension funds have real liabilities that depend on the level of wage inflation. The inflation-premium theory implies that, if a pension fund wants to minimize risk, it should favour short-term bonds.

21-4 ALLOWING FOR THE RISK OF DEFAULT

You should by now be familiar with some of the basic ideas about why interest rates change and why short rates may differ from long rates. It only remains to consider our third question: "Why do some borrowers have to pay a higher rate of interest than others?"

The answer is obvious: bond prices go down, and interest rates go up, when the probability of default increases. But when we say "interest rates go up," we mean *promised* interest rates. If the borrower defaults, the *actual* interest rate paid to the lender is less than the promised rate. The *expected* interest rate may go up with increasing probability of default, but this is not a logical necessity.

These points can be illustrated by a simple numerical example. Suppose that the interest rate on one-year *risk-free* bonds is 9%. Backwoods Chemical Company has issued 9% notes with face values of $1,000, maturing in one year. What will the Backwoods notes sell for?

The answer is easy—if the notes are risk-free: just discount principal ($1,000) and interest ($90) at 9%:

$$\text{PV of notes} = \frac{\$1,000 + 90}{1.09} = \$1,000$$

Suppose instead that there is a 20% chance that Backwoods will default. If default does occur, holders of its notes receive nothing. In this case, the possible payoffs to the note holder are:

	Payoff	Probability
Full payment	$1,090	0.8
No payment	0	0.2

The expected payment is 0.8($1,090) + 0.2($0) = $872.

We can value the Backwoods notes like any other risky asset, by discounting their expected payoff ($872) at the appropriate opportunity cost of capital. We might discount at the risk-free interest rate (9%) if Backwoods's possible default is totally unrelated to other events in the economy. In this case the default risk is wholly diversifiable, and the beta of the notes is zero. The notes would sell for

$$\text{PV of notes} = \frac{\$872}{1.09} = \$800$$

An investor who purchased these notes for $800 would receive a *promised* yield of about 36%:

$$\text{Promised yield} = \frac{\$1{,}090}{\$800} - 1 = 0.363$$

That is, an investor who purchased the notes for $800 would earn a 36.3% rate of return *if* Backwoods does not default. Bond traders therefore might say that the Backwoods notes "yield 36%." But the smart investor would realize that the bond's *expected* yield is only 9%, the same as on risk-free bonds.

This of course assumes that risk of default with these notes is wholly diversifiable, so that they have no market risk. In general, risky bonds do have market risk (that is, positive betas) because default is more likely to occur in recessions when all businesses are doing poorly. Suppose that investors demand a 2% risk premium and an 11% expected rate of return. Then the Backwoods notes will sell for 872/1.11 = $785.59 and offer a promised yield of (1,090/785.59) − 1 = 0.388, or about 39%.

You rarely see traded bonds offering 39% yields. But at one point in 1970, LTV Corporation, a diversified operating company whose operations include being a primary supplier of steel products to the automotive industry, had a bond issue (the 5s of 1988) which sold for 20% of face value and offered a promised yield of about 27%.[22] The bonds sold at such a low price because the odds of default seemed high. As it turned out, however, the bondholders were lucky: LTV did not default, and the bondholders received a substantial capital gain as the company recovered and the threat of default receded. In February 1985 the bonds sold at 80% of par, exactly four times their value in 1970.

Bond Ratings

The relative quality of most bonds traded in Canada can be judged from bond ratings given by Canadian Bond Rating Service (CBRS) and Dominion Bond Rating Service. Certain Canadian bond issues are also rated by United States financial service companies, Moody's and Standard and Poor's. These issues are usually ones sold in the United States as well as in Canada.

Table 21-6 provides the categories in which CBRS classifies bonds.[23] Bonds rated B+ + or above are generally considered to be *investment grade* bonds. Commercial banks and many pension funds and other financial institutions are not allowed to invest in bonds unless they are investment grade.

Bond ratings are judgements about firms' financial and business prospects. If there is insufficient information to permit a judgement, the bond will not be rated. There is no fixed formula by which ratings are calculated. Nevertheless, underwriters, bond portfolio managers, and others who follow the bond market closely can get a fairly good idea how a bond will be rated by looking at a few key numbers, such as the firm's debt-equity ratio, the variability of its income, and the size of the issue.

---

[22]That is, if

$$\text{Price (percent of par)} = 20 = \sum_{t=1}^{18} \frac{5}{(1 + y)^t} + \frac{100}{(1 + y)^{18}}$$

then y, the yield to maturity, equals about 0.27. This calculation assumes annual, instead of semiannual, coupon payments.

[23]About 10% of rated bonds are classified A+ +, 15% A+, 25% A, 25% B+ +, and 20% B+. The remainder are predominantly B or C.

Table 21-6   Key to CBRS bond ratings.

A + +   Highest Quality

This category encompasses bonds of outstanding quality. They possess the highest degree of protection of principal and interest. Companies rated A + + are generally large national and/or multi-national corporations whose products or services are essential to the Canadian economy.

These companies are the acknowledged leaders in their respective industries and have clearly demonstrated their ability to best withstand adverse economic or trade conditions either national or international in scope. Characteristically these companies have had a long and creditable history of superior debt protection, in which the quality of their assets and earnings has been constantly maintained or improved, with strong evidence that this will continue.

A +   Very Good Quality

Bonds rated A + are very similar in characteristics to those rated A + + and can also be considered superior in quality. These companies have demonstrated a long and satisfactory history of growth with above-average protection of principal and interest on their debt securities.

These bonds are generally rated lower in quality because the margin of assets or earnings protection may not be as large or as stable as those rated A + +. In both these categories the nature or quality of the asset and earning coverages are more important than the numerical values of the ratios.

A   Good Quality

Bonds rated A are considered to be good quality securities and to have favourable long-term investment characteristics. The main feature that distinguishes them from the higher rated securities is that these companies are more susceptible to adverse trade or economic conditions and the protection is consequently lower than for the categories A + + and A +.

In all cases the A rated companies have maintained a history of adequate assets and earnings protection. There may be certain elements that may impair this protection sometime in the future. Confidence that the current overall financial position will be maintained or improved is slightly lower than for the above rated securities.

B + +   Medium Grade

Issues rated B + + are classified as medium or average grade credits and are considered to be investment grade. These companies are generally more susceptible than any of the higher rated companies to swings in economic or trade conditions that would cause a deterioration in protection should the company enter a period of poor operating conditions.

There may be factors present either from within or from without the company that may adversely affect the long-term level of protection of the debt. These companies bear closer scrutiny but in all cases both interest and principal are adequately protected at the present time.

B +   Lower Medium Grade

Bonds which are rated B + are considered to be lower medium grade securities and have limited long-term protective investment characteristics. Assets and earnings coverage may be modest or unstable.

A significant deterioration in interest and principal protection may occur during periods of adverse economic or trade conditions. During periods of normal or improving economic conditions, assets and earnings protection are adequate; however, the company's ability to continually improve its financial position and the level of debt protection is at present limited.

B   Poor Quality

Securities rated B lack most qualities necessary for long-term fixed income investment. Companies in this category have a general history of volatile operating conditions, and the assurance has been in doubt that principal and interest protection will be maintained at an adequate level. Current

---

[24]The different kinds of debt are explained in Chapter 22.

Table 21-6   (*Continued*)

coverages may be below industry standards and there is little assurance that debt protection will significantly improve.

C   Speculative

Securities in this category are clearly speculative. The companies are generally junior in many respects and there is little assurance that the adequate coverage of principal and interest can be maintained uninterruptedly over a period of time.

D   Default

Bonds in this category are in default of some provisions in their trust deed and the companies may or may not be in the process of liquidation.

Rating Suspended

A company that has its rating suspended is experiencing severe financial or operating problems of which the outcome is uncertain. The company may or may not be in default but at present there is uncertainty as to the company's ability to pay off its debt.

Source: *An Introduction to Bond and Commercial Paper Ratings*, Canadian Bond Rating Service, 1985.

Examples of corporate bond issues in the various CBRS categories are provided in Table 21-7. It is interesting to note that the bond ratings reflect the perceived riskiness of the industry within which the company operates. AEC Power Ltd. is in the relatively stable utilities industry and has an A + + rating on its first mortgage bonds. Hudson's Bay Company is in the more volatile merchandising industry and has a B + rating on its debentures.[24] The "low" and "high" remarks beside the IPSCO and Scott Paper ratings are trend indicators and reflect the companies' relative strength within the rating category.

Since bond ratings reflect the probability of default, it is not surprising that there is also a close correspondence between a bond's rating and its promised yield. For example, at the end of 1978, the promised yield on long-term Canadian corporate bonds rated A by CBRS was 0.3% less than on bonds rated B + +, and the yield on bonds rated B + + was 0.6% less than on bonds rated B +. The spread between the promised yields on long-term Canadian government bonds and B + corporates was 1.4%.

Once a bond rating service such as CBRS or Moody's rates a bond, the rating is not changed unless there is a significant shift in the company's financing or prospects. But the rating agencies do change their minds when conditions warrant it.

Table 21-7   CBRS bond ratings for selected Canadian corporate bond issues.

Company	Bonds Rated	Rating
AEC Power Ltd.	First Mortgage Bonds	A + +
Gulf Canada Ltd.	Debentures	A + +
Northern Telecom Ltd.	Sinking Fund Debentures	A +
John Labatt Ltd.	Sinking Fund Debentures	A +
John Labatt Ltd.	Convertible Subordinate Debentures	A
Southam Inc.	Debentures	A
IPSCO	First Mortgage Sinking Fund Bonds	B + + (low)
Scott Paper	Sinking Fund Debentures	B + + (high)
Hudson's Bay Company	Debentures	B +
Rolland Inc.	Sinking Fund Debentures	B +

Source: *Master Index*, Canadian Bond Rating Service, December 1984.

In July 1965 the issue of an additional \$175 million of New York City bonds led Moody's to downrate the city's debt from A to Baa.[25] In subsequent testimony to the congressional Subcommittee on Economic Progress, a city official claimed that the rating services were "causing leading cities to be shortchanged out of hundreds of millions of dollars in unwarranted interest charges." Suggested remedies included the idea that a federal agency be established that could rate municipal bonds "more objectively." We leave it to the reader to judge whether Moody's is likely to have *caused* the increased interest charges, as New York City suggested, or whether the rating change just reflected a widespread disillusionment with the city's debt. Ten years later, after New York had nearly defaulted, Moody's was again the subject of criticism—this time for overoptimistic ratings. "Moody's," complained Senator Eagleton, "continued to signal 'All is well,'" even while the city "was floundering on the financial rocks and was being abandoned by its crew of bankers and money men." A bond rater's lot is not always a happy one.

*Option Pricing and Risky Debt

In Section 20-2 we showed that holding a corporate bond is equivalent to lending money with no chance of default *but* at the same time giving stockholders a put option on the firm's assets. When a firm defaults, its stockholders are in effect exercising their put. The put's value is the value of limited liability—of stockholders' right to walk away from their firm's debts in exchange for handing over the firm's assets to its creditors. To summarize,

Bond value = bond value assuming no chance of default − value of put

Thus valuing bonds should be a two-step process. The first step is easy: calculate the bond's value assuming no default risk. (Discount promised interest and principal payments at the yield on comparable Government of Canada issues.) Second, calculate the value of a put written on the firm's assets, where the maturity of the put equals the maturity of the bond, and the exercise price of the put equals the interest and principal payments promised to bondholders.

Owning a corporate bond is *also* equivalent to owning the firm's assets *but* giving a call option on these assets to the firm's stockholders.[26]

Bond value = asset value − value of call on assets

Thus you also can calculate a bond's value, given the value of the firm's assets, by valuing a call on these assets, and subtracting the call value from the asset value. (The call value is just the value of the firm's common stock.)

Therefore, if you can value puts and calls on a firm's assets, you can value its debt.[27]

In practice, this is a bit more difficult than it sounds. The put or call you have to value is usually not the simple option described in Chapter 20, but a much more complex one. Suppose, for example, that Backwoods Chemical issues a ten-year bond

---

[25] In descending order of probability of default, the Moody's bond ratings are Aaa, Aa, A, Baa, Ba, B, Caa, Ca and C. Like CBRS, the first four of these categories are considered to be investment quality.

[26] Again, see Section 20-2.

[27] However, option valuation procedures cannot value the *assets* of the firm. Puts and calls must be valued as a proportion of asset value. For example, note that the Black-Scholes formula (Section 20-5) requires stock price in order to compute the value of a call option.

---

that pays interest annually and is retired by ten sinking fund payments starting a year after issue. We can still think of Backwoods stock as a call option that can be exercised by making interest and sinking fund payments. But there is not one such payment but ten of them. To value Backwoods stock we would have to value ten sequential one-year call options. The first option can be exercised by making the first interest and sinking fund payment when it comes due. By exercise stockholders obtain a second call option, which can be exercised by making the second interest and sinking fund payment. The reward of exercising is a third call option, and so on. When the tenth option is finally exercised, the debt is fully repaid and stockholders regain unencumbered ownership of Backwoods's assets.

Of course if the firm does not make interest and sinking fund payments when due, bondholders take over and stockholders are left with nothing. In other words, by not exercising one call option, stockholders give up all subsequent call options.

Valuing Backwoods stock when the ten-year bond is issued is equivalent to valuing the first of the ten call options. But you cannot value the first option without prospectively valuing the nine following ones.[28] Even this example understates the practical difficulties, because large firms may have dozens of outstanding debt issues with different interest rates, sinking fund schedules, seniority, and maturities, and also convertible issues, preferred shares and so on. But do not lose heart. Computers can solve these problems, more or less by brute force, even in the absence of simple, exact evaluation formulas.

Differences between
interest rate on bond
and risk-free interest rate

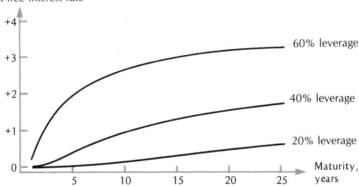

Figure 21-6 How the interest rate on risky corporate debt changes with leverage and maturity. These curves are calculated using option pricing theory under the following simplifying assumptions: (1) The risk-free interest rate is constant for all maturities. (2) The standard deviation of the return on the company's assets is 25% per annum. (3) No dividends are paid. (4) Debt is in the form of discount bonds (that is, only one payment is made, at maturity). (5) Leverage is the ratio of the *market* value of the debt to the *market* value of the debt plus equity.

Figure 21-6 shows a simple application. The figure is designed to give you some feel for the effect of default risk on (promised) bond yields. It takes a company with average operating risk and shows how the interest rate should increase with the amount of bonds that are issued and their maturity. You can see, for example, that, if the company raises 20% of its capital in the form of 20-year bonds, it should pay about one-half of

---

[28]The other approach to valuing Backwoods's (subtracting put value from risk-free bond value) is no easier. The analyst would be confronted by not one simple put, but by a package of ten sequential puts.

a percentage point above the government borrowing rate to compensate for the default risk. Companies with more leverage or with longer-maturity bonds ought to pay higher premia.[29]

In practice, interest rate differentials tend to be greater than those shown in Figure 21-6. High-grade corporate bonds typically offer promised yields about one percentage point greater than Government of Canada bonds. Does this mean that these companies are paying too much for their debt?

Probably not; there are a number of other possible explanations. For example, notice that Figure 21-6 makes several artificial assumptions. One assumption is that the company does not pay dividends. If it does regularly pay out part of its assets to stockholders, there may be substantially fewer assets to protect the bondholder in the event of trouble. In this case, the market may be quite justified in requiring a higher yield on the company's bonds. Also, most publicly issued corporate bonds are less marketable than federal government bonds, which trade every day in large quantities. Lawrence Fisher has conducted an important study of the corporate bond market in which he concluded that differences in marketability were a principal reason for differences in interest rates.[30]

*Valuing Government Loan Guarantees

In the summer of 1971 Lockheed Corporation was in trouble. It was nearly out of cash after absorbing heavy cost overruns on military contracts and, at the same time, committing more than $800 million[31] to the development of the L1011 TriStar airliner. Introduction of the TriStar had been delayed by unexpected problems with its Rolls-Royce engines, and it would be many years before the company could recoup its investment in the plane. Lockheed was on the brink of bankruptcy. (Rolls-Royce was itself driven to the brink by the costs of fixing the engine problems. It was taken over by the British government.)

After months of suspense and controversy, the United States government rescued Lockheed by agreeing to guarantee up to $250 million of new bank loans. If Lockheed had defaulted on these loans, the banks could have gotten their money back directly from the government.

From the banks' point of view, these loans were as safe as Treasury notes. Thus, Lockheed was assured of being able to borrow up to $250 million at a favourable rate.[32] This assurance in turn gave Lockheed's banks the confidence to advance the rest of the money the firm needed.

The loan guarantee was a helping hand—a subsidy—to bring Lockheed through a difficult period. What was it worth? What did it cost the government?

This loan guarantee did not turn out to cost the government anything, because Lockheed survived, recovered, and paid off the loans the government guaranteed. Does that mean that the value of the guarantee to Lockheed was also zero? Does it mean the government absorbed no risks when it gave the guarantee in 1971, when Lockheed's survival was still uncertain? Of course not. The government absorbed the risk of default.

---

[29]But beyond a certain point (not shown in Figure 21-6), the yield premia begin to decline with increasing maturity.

[30]L. Fisher, "Determinants of Risk Premiums on Corporate Bonds," *Journal of Political Economy,* **67**:212–237 (June 1959).

[31]See U. Reinhardt, "Break-Even Analysis for Lockheed's TriStar: An Application of Financial Theory," *Journal of Finance,* **28**:821–838 (September 1973).

[32]Lockheed paid the current Treasury bill rate plus a fee of roughly 2% to the government.

Obviously the banks' loans to Lockheed were worth more with the guarantee than they would have been without it.

The present value of a loan guarantee is the amount lenders would be willing to pay to relieve themselves of all risk of default on an otherwise equivalent unguaranteed loan. It is the difference between the present value of the loan with the guarantee and its present value without the guarantee. A guarantee can clearly have substantial value on a large loan when the chance of default by the firm is high.

It turns out that a loan guarantee can be valued as a put on the firm's assets, where the put's maturity equals the loan's maturity, and its exercise price equals the interest and principal payments promised to lenders. We can easily show this equivalence by starting with the definition of the value of the guarantee.

Value of guarantee = value of guaranteed loan − loan value without guarantee

Without a guarantee, the loan becomes an ordinary debt obligation of the firm. We know from Section 20-2 that

Value of ordinary loan = value assuming no chance of default − value of put

The loan's value, assuming no chance of default, is exactly its guaranteed value. Thus the put value equals the difference between the values of a guaranteed and an ordinary loan. This is exactly the value of the loan guarantee.

Thus option pricing theory should lead to a way of calculating the actual cost of the government's many loan guarantee programs. This will be a healthy thing. The government's possible liability under existing guarantee programs is enormous: for example, the Canadian Deposit Insurance Corporation (CDIC) insures certain bank and trust company customer deposits up to a maximum of $60,000. Should a particular financial institution fail, each of its customers is guaranteed to receive the amount of his or her deposit or $60,000, whichever is less. Whether a careful estimate of the cost of this program has ever been made is doubtful. But this may change as option pricing theory is applied to the valuation of risky debt, especially in light of the recent experiences with Pioneer Trust, Canadian Commercial Bank, and Northlands Bank.

21-5   SUMMARY

Efficient debt management presupposes that you understand how bonds are valued. That means you need to consider three problems:

1. What determines the general level of interest rates?
2. What determines the difference between long-term and short-term rates?
3. What determines the difference between the interest rates on company and government debt?

Here are some things to remember.

The rate of interest depends on the demand for savings and the supply. The *demand* comes from firms who wish to invest in new plant and equipment. The *supply* of savings comes from individuals who are willing to consume tomorrow rather than today. The equilibrium interest rate is the rate that produces a *balance* between the demand and supply.

In *real* terms, the intersection of these demand and supply curves appears to shift only gradually over time. Most of the variation in interest rates appears to be due to changes in the expected level of inflation. The best-known theory about the effect of inflation on interest rates is that suggested by Irving Fisher. He argued that the nominal, or money rate of interest, is equal to the expected real rate plus the expected inflation rate. If the expected inflation rate increases by 1%, so too will the money rate of interest. During the past 30 years Fisher's simple theory has not done a bad job of explaining changes in short-term interest rates in the United States and Canada.

The value of any bond is equal to the cash payments discounted at the spot rates of interest. For example the value of a ten-year bond with a 5% coupon equals

$$\text{PV (percent of face value)} = \frac{5}{1 + r_1} + \frac{5}{(1 + r_2)^2} + \cdots + \frac{105}{(1 + r_{10})^{10}}$$

Bond dealers generally look at the yield to maturity on a bond. This is simply the internal rate of return y, the discount rate at which

$$\text{Bond price} = \frac{5}{1 + y} + \frac{5}{(1 + y)^2} + \cdots + \frac{105}{(1 + y)^{10}}$$

The yield to maturity y is a complex average of the spot interest rates r_1, r_2, and so on. Like most averages it can be a useful summary measure but it can also hide a lot of interesting information. We would like you to use some of the new techniques that produce estimates of the spot rates of interest.

The one-period spot rate r_1 may be very different from the two-period spot rate r_2. In other words, investors often want a different annual rate of interest for lending for one year than for two years. Why is this? The *expectations theory* says that bonds are priced so that the expected rate of return from investing in bonds over any period is independent of the maturity of the bonds held by the investor. The expectations theory predicts that r_2 will exceed r_1 *only* if *next* year's one-period interest rate is expected to rise.

The *liquidity-preference* theory points out that you are not exposed to risks of changing interest rates and changing bond prices if you buy a bond that matures exactly when you need the money. However, if you buy a bond that matures *before* you need the money, you face the risk that you may have to reinvest your savings at a low rate of interest. And, if you buy a bond that matures *after* you need the money, you face the risk that the price will be low when you come to sell it. Investors don't like risk and they need some compensation for taking it. Therefore when we find that r_2 is generally higher than r_1, it may mean that investors have relatively short horizons and have to be offered an inducement to hold long bonds.

No bonds are risk-free in real terms. If inflation rates are uncertain, the safest strategy for an investor is to keep investing in short bonds and to trust that the rate of interest on these bonds will vary as inflation varies. Therefore another reason r_2 may be higher than r_1 is that investors have to be offered an inducement to accept additional inflation risk.

Finally, we come to our third question: "What determines the difference between interest rates on company and government debt?" Company debt sells at a lower price than government debt. This discount represents the value of the company's option to default. We showed you how the value of this option varies with the degree of leverage and time to maturity. In Canada, Canadian Bond Rating Service and Dominion Bond Rating Service and, in the United States, Moody's and Standard and Poor's rate company bonds according to their default risk, and the price of bonds is closely related to these ratings.

FURTHER READING

The classic work on interest rates is:

Irving Fisher, *The Theory of Interest: As Determined by Impatience to Spend Income and Opportunity to Invest It*, Augustus M. Kelley, Publishers, New York, 1965. Originally published in 1930.

Fisher's work also anticipated Lutz and Lutz's expectations hypothesis of the term structure of interest rates.

F.A. Lutz and V.C. Lutz, *The Theory of Investment of the Firm*, Princeton University Press, Princeton, N.J., 1951.

The liquidity-premium hypothesis is due to Hicks, and our description of the effect of inflation on term structure is taken from Brealey and Schaefer.

J.R. Hicks, *Value and Capital: An Inquiry into Some Fundamental Principles of Economic Theory*, 2d ed., Oxford University Press, Oxford, 1946.
R.A. Brealey and S. Schaefer, "Term Structure and Uncertain Inflation," *Journal of Finance*, **32**:277–290 (May 1977).

Good reviews of the term structure literature may be found in Nelson and Roll. Roll applies modern finance theory to the term structure problem. Dobson, Sutch, and Vanderford review empirical tests of term structure theories.

R. Roll, *The Behavior of Interest Rates: An Application of the Efficient Market Model to U.S. Treasury Bills*, Basic Books, Inc., Publishers, New York, 1970.
S. Dobson, R. Sutch, and D. Vanderford, "An Evaluation of Alternative Empirical Models of the Term Structure of Interest Rates," *Journal of Finance,* **31**:1035–1066 (September 1976).
C.R. Nelson, "The Term Structure of Interest Rates: Theories and Evidence," in J.L. Bicksler, ed., *Handbook of Financial Economics*, North-Holland Publishing Company, Amsterdam, 1980.

Here are three papers that discuss measurement of the term structure:

W. Carleton and I. Cooper, "Estimation and Uses of the Term Structure of Interest Rates," *Journal of Finance,* **31**:1067–1084 (September 1976).
J. McCulloch, "Measuring the Term Structure of Interest Rates," *Journal of Business,* **44**: 19–31 (January 1971).
S.M. Schaefer, "Measuring a Tax Specific Term Structure of Interest Rates in the Market for British Government Securities," *Economic Journal*, **91**:415–438 (June 1981).

The Brennan and Schwartz paper is a readable description of how the concept of immunization can be extended to derive consistent relationships between bond prices.

M.J. Brennan and E.S. Schwartz, "Bond Pricing and Market Efficiency," *Financial Analysts Journal,* **38**:49–56 (September–October 1982).

Fama's tests indicate that the expected real rate of interest was essentially constant between 1953 and 1971. However, if you read Fama's paper, you should also read the replies by Hess and Bicksler and by Nelson and Schwert.

E.F. Fama, "Short-Term Interest Rates as Predictors of Inflation," *American Economic Review,* **65**:269–282 (June 1975).
P. Hess and J. Bicksler, "Capital Asset Prices versus Time Series Models as Predictors of Inflation," *Journal of Financial Economics,* **2**:341–360 (December 1975).
C.R. Nelson and G. Schwert, "Short-Term Interest Rates as Predictors of Inflation: On Testing the Hypothesis That the Real Rate of Interest is Constant," *American Economic Review,* **67**:478–486 (June 1977).

Evidence on long-run average interest rates in Canada and the United States, respectively, may be found in:

P.P. Boyle, H.H. Panjer, and K.P. Sharp, "Report on Canadian Economic Statistics 1924–1983," Canadian Institute of Actuaries, Ottawa (July 1984).

R.G. Ibbotson and R.A. Sinquefield, *Stocks, Bonds, Bills and Inflation: The Past and the Future*, Financial Analysts Research Foundation, Charlottesville, Va., 1982.

The classic empirical study on valuing risky debt is by Lawrence Fisher. Robert Merton has shown how option pricing theory can be applied to risky debt.

L. Fisher, "Determinants of Risk Premiums on Corporate Bonds," *Journal of Political Economy*, **67**:212–237 (June 1959).

R. Merton, "On the Pricing of Corporate Debt: The Risk Structure of Interest Rates," *Journal of Finance*, **29**:449–470 (May 1974).

QUIZ

1. The real interest rate is determined by the demand and supply for capital. Refer again to Figure 21-2:
   (*a*) What will happen to the amount of investment and saving if firms' investment prospects improve? How will the equilibrium interest rate change? Assume the curve representing the supply of capital (saving) does not shift.
   (*b*) What will happen to the amount of investment and saving if individuals' willingness to save increases at each possible interest rate? How will the equilibrium interest rate change? Assume firms' investment opportunities do not change.

2. (*a*) What is the formula for the value of a two-year, 5% bond in terms of spot rates?
   (*b*) What is the formula for its value in terms of yield to maturity?
   (*c*) If the two-year spot rate is higher than the one-year rate, is the yield to maturity greater or less than the two-year spot rate?
   (*d*) In each of the following sentences choose the correct term from within the parentheses:
   "The (yield-to-maturity/spot-rate) formula discounts all cash flows from one bond at the same rate even though they occur at different points in time." "The (yield-to-maturity/spot-rate) formula discounts all cash flows received at the same point in time at the same rate even though the cash flows may come from different bonds."

3. Use Table 21-1 to check your answers to the following:
   (*a*) If interest rates rise, do bond prices rise or fall?
   (*b*) If the bond yield is greater than the coupon, is the price of the bond greater or less than 100?
   (*c*) If the price of a bond exceeds 100, is the yield greater or less than the coupon?
   (*d*) Do high coupon bonds sell at higher or lower prices than low coupon bonds?

4. Use Table 21-1 to answer the following questions:
   (*a*) What is the yield to maturity on a 7%, eight-year bond selling at $74\frac{3}{4}$?
   (*b*) What is the approximate price of a 5%, nine-year bond yielding 10%?
   (*c*) A 9%, 12-year bond yields 14%. If the yield remains unchanged, what will be its price six months hence? Calculate the investor's total return over the six months.

5. (*a*) Suppose that the one-year spot rate of interest at time 0 is 1% and the two-year spot rate is 3%. What is the forward rate of interest for year 2?
   (*b*) What does the expectations theory of term structure say about the relationship between this forward rate and the one-year spot rate at time 1?
   (*c*) Over a very long period of time, the term structure in Canada has been, on average, upward-sloping. Is this evidence for or against the expectations theory?

(*d*) What does the liquidity-preference theory say about the relationship between the forward rate and the one-year rate at time 1?

(*e*) If the liquidity-preference theory is a good approximation and you have to meet long-term liabilities (university tuition for your children, for example), is it safer to invest in long-term or short-term bonds? Assume inflation is predictable.

(*f*) If the inflation-premium theory is a good approximation and you have to meet long-term real liabilities, is it safer to invest in long-term or short-term bonds?

(*g*) What does the inflation-premium theory say about the relationship between the forward rate and the one-year spot rate at time 1?

6. (*a*) State the four CBRS ratings that are generally known as "investment grade" ratings.

(*b*) Other things equal, would you expect the yield to maturity on a corporate bond to increase or decrease with:
   (i) The company's business risk?
   (ii) The expected rate of inflation?
   (iii) The risk-free rate of interest?
   (iv) The degree of leverage?

*7. (*a*) How in principle would you calculate the value of a government loan guarantee?

(*b*) The difference between the price of a government bond and a simple corporate bond is equal to the value of an option. What is this option and what is its exercise price?

QUESTIONS AND PROBLEMS

1. Why might Fisher's theory about inflation and interest rates *not* be true?

2. You have estimated spot interest rates as follows:

Year	Spot Rate, %
1	$r_1 = 5.00$
2	$r_2 = 5.40$
3	$r_3 = 5.70$
4	$r_4 = 5.90$
5	$r_5 = 6.00$

(*a*) What are the discount factors for each date (that is, the present value of $1 paid in year *t*)?

(*b*) What are the forward rates for each period?

(*c*) Calculate the PV of each of the following:
   (i) 5%, two-year bond
   (ii) 5%, five-year bond
   (iii) 10%, five-year bond

(*d*) Use Table 21-1 to find the approximate yield to maturity on each of these bonds. (Note that bond tables assume semiannual interest payments: in our examples annual payments reduce yield by roughly 0.05%).

(*e*) Explain intuitively why the yield to maturity on the 10% bond is less than on the 5% bond.

3. Look at the spot interest rates shown in problem 2. Suppose that someone told you that the six-year spot interest rate was 4.80%. Why would you not believe him or her? How could you make money if he or she was right? What is the minimum sensible value for the six-year spot rate?

4. Look just one more time at the spot interest rates shown in problem 2. What can you deduce about the one-year spot interest rate in four years if:
   (*a*) The expectations theory of term structure is right?
   (*b*) The liquidity-preference theory of term structure is right?
   (*c*) The term structure contains an inflation uncertainty premium?

5. Assume the term structure of interest rates is upward-sloping, as in Figure 21-5. How would you respond to the following comment? "The present term structure of interest rates makes short-term debt more attractive to corporate treasurers. Firms should avoid new long-term debt issues."

6. Here is a harder one. It has been suggested that the Fisher theory is a tautology. If the real rate of interest is defined as the difference between the nominal rate and the expected inflation rate, then the nominal rate *must* equal the real rate plus the expected inflation rate. In what sense is Fisher's theory *not* a tautology?

7. Look up the prices of ten Government of Canada bonds with different coupons and different maturities. Use bond tables to calculate how their prices would change if the yield to maturity increased by one percentage point. Are long-term bonds or short-term bonds most affected by the change in yields? Are high-coupon bonds or low-coupon bonds most affected?

8. Look up prices of ten corporate bonds with different coupons and maturities. Be sure to include some low-rated bonds on your list. Now estimate what these bonds would sell for if the Canadian government had guaranteed them. Calculate the value of the guarantee for each bond. Can you explain the differences between the ten guaranteed values?

9. Look in a recent issue of *The Financial Post* at the Corporate Bonds price quotations.
   (*a*) Bid and ask prices are reported for each of the corporate bonds listed in *The Financial Post*. The bid price is the price at which the bond dealer is standing ready to buy the bond from you, and the ask price is the price at which the bond dealer is standing ready to sell the bond to you. Thus the difference between the bid and ask prices (that is, the spread) is the mark-up the dealer demands as compensation for market making services. If you buy the Bell Canada 9.40s of 2002, what is your promised yield to maturity? (Assume annual interest payments.)
   (*b*) How much higher is the yield on this Bell Canada issue than on a Government of Canada issue with similar maturity?
   (*c*) Glance quickly through the list of corporate bonds and find one with a very high yield to maturity. Why do you think the yield on this bond is so high?
   (*d*) Would the expected return be more or less than the yield to maturity?

10. Under what conditions can the expected real interest rate be negative?

11. Bond rating services usually charge corporations for rating their bonds.
    (*a*) Why do they do this, rather than charge those investors who use the information?
    (*b*) Why will a company pay to have its bonds rated even when it knows that the service is likely to assign a below-average rating?
    (*c*) A few companies are not willing to pay for their bonds to be rated. What can investors deduce about the quality of these bonds?

12. A 6%, six-year bond yields 12% and a 10%, six-year bond yields 8%. Calculate the six-year spot rate. (Assume semiannual coupon payments.)

13. In 1985, North West Trust "Nuggets" were priced as follows:

Maturity	Price
1990	54.345
1992	43.713
1994	35.161
1995	31.346
2000	18.951
2004	12.372
2006	9.996

(*a*) Estimate the spot rates of interest.

(*b*) If the expectations theory is correct, what is the expected one-year rate of interest (that is, the one-year forward rate) in 1994?

(*c*) Again, if the expectations theory is correct, what is the expected two-year interest rate in 2004?

14. Are high-coupon bonds more likely to yield more than low-coupon bonds when the term structure is upward-sloping or when it is downward-sloping?

*15. Look back to the first Backwoods Chemical example at the start of Section 21-4. Suppose that the firm's book balance sheet is:

Backwoods Chemical Company (Book Values)			
Net working capital	$ 400	$1,000	Debt
Net fixed assets	1,600	1,000	Equity (net worth)
Total assets	$2,000	$2,000	Total liabilities and net worth

The debt has a one-year maturity and a promised interest rate of 9%. Thus, the promised payment to Backwoods's creditors is $1,090. Use Appendix Tables 6 and 7 to value the Backwoods debt and equity.

*16. In Section 21-2, we stated that the duration of Potterton's lease equalled the duration of its new debt. Show that this is so.

*17. In Section 21-2, we stated that the duration of the 10s of '95 was 4.193 years. Construct a table like Table 21-3 to show that this is so.

*18. Fill in the blanks from the list of terms below.

Duration is _____ of the time to each cash payment. If two bonds have the same maturity, the one with the _____ will provide a greater proportion of its cash flows in the earlier years. It will, therefore, have a _____ duration.

A bond's volatility measures the percentage change in _____ for a 1% change in _____. Volatility is simply the _____ by (1 + yield). Bonds with long duration (that is, _____ maturities or _____ coupons) are _____ volatile than those with a short duration.

Pension funds with fixed liabilities often want to protect themselves against interest rate changes. If the portfolio is _____, the duration of the assets is _____ the duration of the liabilities.

If short-term and long-term interest rates do not move exactly together, it would not be sufficient to ensure that assets and liabilities have the same duration. You would need to ensure that they were both equally affected by a change in the short-term rate and equally affected by a change in the _____ rate.

Terms: Lower coupon, duration, multiplied by, greater than, divided by, more or less than, a weighted average, price, the sum, yield, short, high, longer, long-term, low, long, equal to, immunized, shorter, less, higher coupon

THE MANY DIFFERENT KINDS OF DEBT

In Chapter 14 we introduced you to some of the different kinds of debt. For example, we saw that debt may be short-term or long-term, may consist of straight bonds or may be convertible into common stock, may be issued domestically or may be sold overseas, and so on.

As a financial manager, you need to choose the type of debt that makes sense for your company. We begin our analysis of this problem by looking in this chapter at the different kinds of straight bonds. After describing the form of the debt contract, we will examine the differences between senior and junior bonds and between secured and unsecured bonds. Then we will describe how bonds are repaid by means of a sinking fund, and how firms and bondholders reserve the right to "call" bonds at an earlier date. Finally, we will look at some restrictive provisions in the bond agreement. These restrictive provisions seek to prevent the company from doing anything that would reduce the value of the bonds.

We will not only describe the different features of corporate debt: we will also try to say *why* sinking funds, call provisions, and the like exist. They are not simply matters of custom: there are generally good economic reasons for their use.

Debt may be sold to the public by means of a general cash offer or may be placed privately with a limited number of financial institutions. One important kind of private debt is the bank term loan. This may run from one to eight years, which is rather shorter than most bonds. We will discuss these term loans in more detail in Chapter 30 when we describe short-term bank lending.

Another form of private debt is the project financing. This is the glamorous part of the debt market. The words *project finance* always conjure up images of multimillion dollar loans to finance mining ventures in exotic parts of the world. We examine project finance in Appendix 22-1. You'll find there's something to the popular image, but it's not the whole story,

Finally, there is a large market for standard long-term private placement bonds. These private placements are closely related to the publicly issued bonds that we are going to look at in this chapter. Whether you decide to make a private placement or a public issue will depend partly on the relative issue costs, for a public issue involves higher fixed costs but a lower rate of interest.[1] But your choice should not depend solely on these costs. There are three other ways in which the private placement bond may differ from its public counterpart.

First, if you place an issue privately with one or two financial institutions, it may be necessary to sign only a simple promissory note. This is just an IOU that lays down certain conditions the borrowers must observe. However, when you make a public issue of debt, you must worry about who is to represent the bondholders in any subsequent negotiations and what procedures are needed for paying interest and principal. Therefore the contractual arrangement has to be that much more complicated.

The second characteristic of publicly issued bonds is that they are highly standardized products. They have to be—investors are constantly buying and selling them without

---

[1] See Section 15-5.

checking the fine print in the agreement. This is not so necessary in private placements. They are not regularly traded: they are bought and held by large institutions that are well equipped to evaluate any unusual features. Furthermore, because private placements involve lower fixed issue costs, they tend to be issued by small companies. These are just the companies that most need custom-tailored debt.

All bond agreements seek to protect the lender by imposing a number of conditions on the borrower. In the case of private placements, these restrictions may be very severe. For example, if the borrower wishes to issue any more bonds, the firm may have to get the permission of the existing bondholders. Because there are only one or two lenders involved, this permission is usually easily obtained. That would not be possible with publicly issued debt. Therefore the limitations are usually less stringent.

We are not going to discuss private placement bonds separately in this chapter because the greater part of what we shall have to say about public issues is also true of private placements. Just bear the following in mind:

1. That the private placement contract is simpler than the public issue contract

2. That the private placement contract is more likely to have nonstandard features

3. That it often imposes more stringent conditions on the borrower, but is more easily renegotiated.

22-1 THE BOND CONTRACT

Indenture or Trust Deed

As we have seen, a private issue of debt typically consists of a simple promissory note or IOU. The contract in any public issue of bonds usually takes the form of an **indenture** or **trust deed** between the borrower and a trust company. The trust company is the representative of the bondholders. It must see that the terms of indenture are observed, administer any sinking fund, and look after the bondholders' interests in the event of default.

A copy of the bond indenture is filed with the securities commission. It is a turgid legal document,[2] and its main provisions are summarized in the prospectus to the issue. To give you some feel for these provisions, Appendix 22-2 contains details of a debenture issue in October 1984 by Interprovincial Pipe Line (NW) Ltd.

We will use the prospectus to illustrate some features of the bond contract. As we do so, you might consider whether even these summary documents are not unduly obscure. In particular, like most legal documents, they review only the conditions and safeguards that exist and do nothing to draw your attention to any omissions or unusual features.

The Bond Terms

The first page of the prospectus contains a table showing the price and cost of the issue. Notice two things about the price. First, although the bonds have a face value of

---

[2]For example, Section 1.03 of the indenture for a bond issue by J.C. Penney, a large general merchandise retailer in the United States, says: "In any case where several matters are required to be certified by, or covered by an opinion of, any specified Person, it is not necessary that all such matters be certified by, or covered by the opinion of, only one such Person, or that they be so certified or covered by only one document, but one such Person may certify or give an opinion with respect to some matters and one or more other such Persons as to other matters, and any such Person may certify or give an opinion as to such matters in one or several documents." Try saying that three times very fast.

$1,000, their prices are always shown as a percentage of face value. Second, bond prices in Canada and the United States are usually quoted *net of accrued interest*. That means the bond buyer must pay out not only the quoted price, but also the amount of any interest that may have accrued. Interprovincial planned to issue the bonds on November 15, exactly the interest date, and so in this case the accrued interest is 0%. But suppose the bonds have been issued on December 15. In that case, one month of interest would have accumulated. One month of interest at 12.7% a year is $\frac{1}{2} \times 12.7 = 1.06\%$. Therefore, the buyer would have had to pay a price of 100% plus 1.06% accrued interest.

The bonds were offered to the public at a price of 100%[3] but Interprovincial sold the issue to the underwriters at 98.85%. The difference represented the underwriters' fee. The total amount of the issue was $75 million of which $900,000 went to the underwriters.

Turn now to the second page of the prospectus, entitled "Prospectus Summary." This section provides a summary of the salient features of the bond issue. Notice that interest is to be paid semiannually at a fixed rate of 12.7% a year. Some bonds don't pay interest at all, and in other cases interest has to be paid only if the company earns sufficient profits. Sometimes the interest payment varies with the Treasury bill rate, and in a number of foreign countries interest payments go up and down with the rate of inflation. Still in other cases, the bonds are linked to the price of a physical commodity, such as gold or oil. Appendix 22-3 tells you about these unusual animals.

The regular interest payment is like a hurdle the company must keep jumping. If the company ever fails to pay the interest on its debt, the lender can demand his or her money back immediately instead of waiting until matters have deteriorated further. Thus interest payments provide additional protection for the lender.[4]

Now look at the "Details of the Offering" on the eighth page of Interprovincial's prospectus. The principal and semiannual interest payments will be payable at any branch of the Canadian bank designated in the debentures. These bonds are said to be in *bearer* form. The bond certificate constitutes evidence of ownership, so the bondholder must detach each coupon and claim his or her interest as well as final principal at the designated bank.

Sometimes bonds are issued in *registered* form. This means that the company's registrar will record the ownership of each bond. If the bond is *fully registered*, the company will pay both the interest and the principal directly to each owner. Occasionally a bond issue is *registered as to principal*. This means that the bondholder will receive his or her final principal directly from the company and must claim the interest payments by redeeming the detachable coupons on the bond certificate.

22-2   SECURITY AND SENIORITY

The Interprovincial Pipe Line (NW) issue is a **debenture**. This means that it is an unsecured (or occasionally secured) obligation of the company.[5] The word also usually indicates that the debt has a maturity of 15 years or more—shorter unsecured loans are

---

[3]The issue price is not always 100%. Occasionally bonds are issued at a discount or a premium. An example of a discount bond is included in Appendix 22-3.

[4]See F. Black and J.C. Cox, "Valuing Corporate Securities: Some Effects of Bond Indenture Provisions," *Journal of Finance*, **31**:351–367 (May 1976). Black and Cox point out that the interest payment would be a trivial hurdle if the company could sell assets to make the payment. Such sales are, therefore, prohibited.

[5]There are international differences in terminology. In Great Britain, *debenture* usually signifies bonds that have a *prior* claim on the firm's assets.

usually termed **notes**. Both debentures and notes may be senior claims (like the Interprovincial issue, where the Series B Debenture ranks *pari passu* with the firm's other senior debentures), or they may be subordinated to the senior bonds or to *all* other creditors. Occasionally they may be guaranteed by another company (like the Interprovincial issue) or jointly guaranteed by several companies.[6] Private placements are sometimes guaranteed by the company's management. It does not necessarily matter that the manager is not personally wealthy—the threat of personal ruin always concentrates the mind wonderfully.

Since 1900, unsecured debentures and notes have become progressively more popular and almost all bond issues by industrial and financial companies are now unsecured. By contrast, the greater proportion of utility and railroad bonds continue to be secured on specific company assets.

When a company defaults on a secured obligation, the trustee or debtor may take possession of the relevant assets. If these are insufficient to satisfy the claim, the remaining debt will have a general claim alongside any unsecured debt against the other assets of the firm.[7]

The vast majority of secured debt consists of **mortgage bonds**. Some of these mortgages are "closed," so that no more bonds may be issued against the mortgage. However, usually there is no specific limit to the amount of bonds that may be secured (in which case the mortgage is said to be *open* or there is a specific limit that has not been reached (in which case the mortgage is said to be *limited open end*). Mortgage bonds sometimes provide a claim against a specific building but they are more often secured on substantially all of the company's property.[8] The issuer undertakes to insure this property and to keep it in good repair. Frequently the indenture will provide for a fixed annual contribution for such maintenance with any unspent balance being used to redeem bonds. Of course the value of any mortgage depends not only on how well the property is maintained but on whether it has value in alternative uses. A custom-built machine for producing buggy whips will not be worth much if the market for buggy whips dries up.

Collateral trust bonds closely resemble mortgage bonds except that in this case the claim is against securities held by the corporation. Generally these bonds are issued by railroad or industrial holding companies—that is, firms whose main assets consist of common stock in a number of subsidiaries. This stock can be pledged as collateral for borrowing by the parent company. The problem for the lender is that the stock is junior to *all* other claims on the assets of the subsidiaries, and so the collateral trust issue will usually include detailed restrictions on the freedom of the subsidiaries to issue debt or preferred stock.

The third principal form of secured debt is the **equipment trust certificate**. This is most frequently used to finance new railroad rolling stock. Under this arrangement a trustee obtains formal ownership of the equipment. The railroad makes a down payment of 10% to 25% of the cost and the balance is provided by a package of trust certificates with different maturities that might typically run from 1 to 15 years. Only when all these debts have finally been paid off does the railroad become the formal owner of

---

[6]The joint guarantee is a common feature of railroad terminal bonds.

[7]Sometimes a company will issue first and second mortgage bonds. The first mortgage bonds have the first claim against the assets, then come the second mortgage bonds, and finally the unsecured debt.

[8]Many mortgage bonds are secured not only by existing property but also by "after-acquired" property. However, if the company buys only property that is already mortgaged, the bondholder would have only a junior claim on the new property. Therefore, mortgage bonds with after-acquired property clauses also restrict the extent to which the company can purchase additional mortgaged property.

the equipment. Because the trustee holds the title to the pledged equipment and can immediately repossess it in the event of default, equipment trust certificates offer good security to their holders. Bond rating agencies such as CBRS and Moody's therefore, usually rate equipment trust certificates one grade higher than the railroad's regular debt. In the case of Canadian Pacific Ltd., CBRS rates the equipment trust certificates as A + +, while the collateral trust certificates are rated as A + .

22-3   REPAYMENT PROVISIONS

Information on the repayment of the Interprovincial's debt issue is provided on the ninth page of the prospectus. Although the issue does not mature for 20 years, part of the issue is repaid earlier by means of a *sinking fund*. From the end of third year, the company is obliged to pay $3 million to the trustee annually—that is, 4% of the total amount of the issue. This payment can be in the form of either cash or bonds that the company has bought back. If it is cash, then the trustee will use the money to repurchase bonds in the marketplace or it will select bonds by lottery and redeem them at par. This mandatory payment is sufficient to redeem 68% of the issue before maturity and to reduce the average life of the bond from 20 to 13.9 years.[9]

Most bonds have provisions for sinking funds. Generally these sinking funds contain a mandatory and an optional element (unlike the Interprovincial issue). The optional element allows the company to make additional payments each year, and these payments can be credited against future mandatory ones. Utility first mortgage bonds, on the other hand, often have a wholly optional fund, and a number of private placements (particularly those in extractive industries) require a payment only when net income exceeds some specified level.[10]

Most "sinkers" begin to operate after about ten years. For lower-quality issues the payments are usually sufficient to redeem the entire issue in equal instalments over the life of the bond. In contrast, high-quality bonds often have light sinking fund requirements with large "balloon" payments at maturity. Generally bonds may be redeemed for the sinking fund at par but some issues provide for a gently declining schedule of repayment prices. The company is also usually entitled to contribute bonds that it has called.

We saw earlier that interest payments provide a regular test of the company's solvency. Sinking funds are an additional check that the firm can keep servicing its debt. That is why long-dated, low-quality issues generally involve larger sinking funds.

This increased security tends to make sinking fund bonds *more* valuable. On the other hand, sinking funds also usually give the borrower an option. If the price of the bond is low, the firm can satisfy the sinking fund requirement by buying bonds in the market. If the price is high, it can call the bonds by lottery at par. This call feature tends to make sinking fund bonds *less* valuable.

We can't make any general statements about the effect of the typical mandatory sinking fund. But we can predict the effect of an optional fund. It offers the holders no extra protection and is in effect a limited option to call bonds at par. Therefore an optional sinking fund must decrease the value of the bond.

If the bonds are privately placed, the sinking fund cannot buy the bonds in the marketplace—it *must* call them at par. Therefore in this case the sinking fund does not

---

[9]4% of (3 + 4 + . . . + 19) plus 32% of 20 = 13.9 years. This is the conventional method of calculating average life, although it might be useful if each period were weighted by the *present value* of the amount retired (that is, if we measured the bond's *duration*: see Section 21-2).

[10]Strictly speaking, the private placement amortization provision does not involve establishment of a sinking fund.

give the borrower any option. Similarly, instead of having sinking funds, equipment trust certificates consist of a package of bonds that mature in successive years. Such bonds are usually called *serial bonds*.[11] A package of serial bonds is rather like a sinking fund bond. Both provide regular prepayments of the debt. But the serial bond does not give the borrower any option—the borrower must redeem the bonds at par. Therefore, other things equal, a package of serial bonds is more valuable than a sinking fund bond.

The Call Provision

Interprovincial also has an option to buy back or "call" the entire bond issue. If it does so, it is required to pay a premium that is equal in the first year to the annual coupon and that declines progressively to zero. Interprovincial is subject to a particular limitation on the use of the call option. During the first 15 years after issue, it is prohibited from calling the bond in order to replace it with another issue yielding less than the 12.7% offering yield on the original bond.

The repayment provisions of the Interprovincial bond are typical of Canadian industrial debentures. The majority of such issues mature in 20 years, are callable at a premium that is virtually equal to the coupon, and are "nonrefundable" (NR) for ten years or more "below interest cost."

Other kinds of bonds tend to provide more limited call options. For example, notes or medium-maturity mortgage bonds typically have a maturity of seven to ten years and are either wholly noncallable (NC) or nonrefundable for all except the last two years of this time. Short-maturity issues and equipment trust certificates cannot be called at any time.

*Valuing the Call Provision

The option to call a bond is obviously attractive to the issuer. If interest rates decline and bond prices rise, the issuer has the opportunity to repurchase the bonds below their true value. For example, suppose that by the year 2000, yields on investment-quality bonds have fallen to 6%. A 12.7% bond with four years to maturity would then be worth 123.2% or $1,232. The call provision allows Interprovincial to repurchase the bonds that are worth $1,232 for only $1,021. Or the company can, if it chooses, hold on and hope to do better by calling the bonds in the year 2001.

How can Interprovincial know when to call its bonds? The answer is simple. Other things being equal, if it wishes to maximize the value of its stock, it must minimize the value of its bond. Therefore, it should never call the bond if its market value is less than the call price, for that would just be giving a present to the bondholders. Equally, it *should* call the bond if it is worth *more* than the call price.

Of course, investors take the call option into account when they buy or sell the bond. They know that the company will call the bond as soon as it is worth more than the call price. Therefore no investor will be willing to pay more than the call price for the bond. The market price of the bond may, therefore, reach the call price but it will not rise above it. This gives the company the following rule for calling its bonds?[12] *Call*

---

[11]Do not confuse *serial bond* with *series bond*, which merely indicates that several issues of a bond are sold under the same indenture.

[12]See M.J. Brennan and E.S. Schwartz, "Savings Bonds, Retractable Bonds, and Callable Bonds," *Journal of Financial Economics*, **5**:67–88 (1977). Of course this assumes that the bond is correctly priced—that investors are acting rationally and that they expect *the firm* to act rationally. Also, note that a company may wish to call the bond in order to escape from a restrictive covenant in the indenture.

the bond when, and only when, the market price reaches the call price. If we know how bond prices behave over time, we can modify our basic option-valuation model of Chapter 20 to give us the value of the callable bond, *given* that investors know the company will call the issue if ever the market price reaches the call price. For example, look at Figure 22-1. It illustrates the relationship between the value of a straight bond and the value of a callable bond. Suppose that the value of the straight bond is very low. In this case there is little likelihood that the company will ever wish to call its bonds. (Remember that it will only call the bonds if they are worth more than the call price.) Therefore the value of the callable bond will be almost identical to the value of the straight bond. Now suppose that the straight bond is worth exactly 100. In this case there is a good chance that the company will wish at some time to call its bonds. Therefore the value of our callable bond will be slightly less than that of the straight bond. If interest rates decline further, the price of the straight bond will move above 100. But nobody will ever pay *more* than 100 for the callable bond.

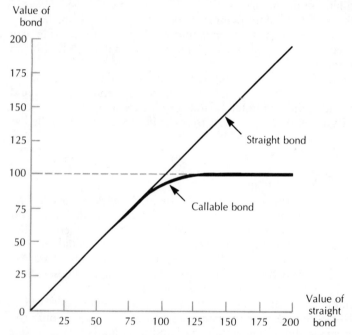

Figure 22-1 Relationship between the value of a callable bond and the value of a straight (noncallable) bond. The callable bond is assumed to be callable at par any time prior to the bond's maturity.

The Extendible/Retractable Provision

From time to time the Government of Canada and some Canadian corporations issue **extendible** or **retractable bonds**. Both of these types of bonds are like callables, in the sense that they provide an option to redeem the bond at a time other than the stated maturity. The difference between callable bonds and extendible/retractables is that the bondholder, not the issuer, owns the option.

An *extendible bond* allows its holder to extend the maturity of the bond for an additional specified period. For example, the Government of Canada currently has outstanding a 14.75% extendible bond with a maturity date of July 1986. At any time prior to April 1986, this bond may be exchanged at par value for another bond with the same coupon interest rate but with a maturity date of July 1993. In other words, this bond provides its owner with the right to buy (or with a call option on) a longer-term bond where the exercise price is equal to the par value of the existing bond. Such a bond provides investors with protection from decreases in the interest rate.

A *retractable bond* is just the reverse of an extendible bond. The bondholder holds an option to sell back or "put" the long-term bond to the issuer at a specified time before maturity. The exercise price of the option is again the par value of the original issue. Andrés Wines Ltd. has outstanding an 11% retractable debenture maturing in June 1997. This issue provides the bondholder with the right to redeem the bond at par on June 1, 1985. Should the bondholder choose not exercise the option at that point in time, the bond will revert to a straight debenture maturing in 1997. Retractable bonds protect the investor from increases in interest rates after the bond is issued.

*Valuing the Extendible/Retractable Provision

Extendible bonds and retractable bonds are essentially the same creature. Each is equivalent to a short-term bond plus a call option or to a long-term bond with a put option. For this reason we will focus on the retractable provision. The reader is left to develop a comparable analysis for the extendible provision.

The option to shorten the maturity of a bond protects the bondholder from increases in the interest rate. If interest rates rise and bond prices fall, the bondholder has the opportunity to put the bonds to the issuer at the par value, which may be well above the current market value. Suppose, for example, that the interest rate on nonretractable issues comparable to the Andrés retractable issue rises to 18% on June 1, 1984. An 11% bond with 13 years to maturity would then be worth about $656.50. The retractability feature allows the holder of an Andrés bond to redeem the bond for $1,000 when the current market value is $343.50 less.

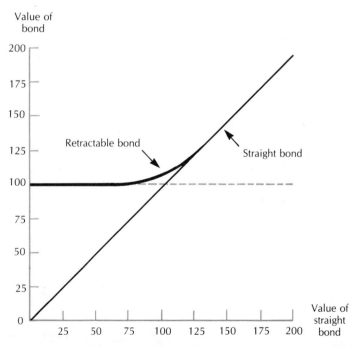

Figure 22-2   Relationship between the value of a retractable bond and the value of a straight (nonretractable) bond. The retractable bond is assumed to be retractable at par anytime prior to the bond's maturity.

Like callable bonds, investors take the value of the option into account when they buy or sell the bond. With retractables, however, it is the bondholder who receives the privilege, so prospective buyers are willing to pay more for a retractable bond than an otherwise comparable bond with no retractability feature. Thus, the price of a retractable bond is bounded from below by the price of a straight bond as well as the par value of the bond, as is demonstrated in Figure 22-2.

22-4 RESTRICTIVE COVENANTS

The difference between a corporate bond and a comparable Treasury bond is that the company has an option to default—the government supposedly doesn't. That is a valuable option.[13] If you don't believe us, think whether, other things being equal, you would prefer to be a shareholder in a company with limited liability or in a company with unlimited liability. Of course the answer is that you prefer to have the option to walk away from your debts. Unfortunately every silver lining has its cloud, and the drawback to having a default option is that corporate bondholders expect to be compensated for giving it to you. That is why corporate bonds sell at lower prices and therefore higher yields than government bonds.

Investors know that there is a risk of default when they buy a corporate bond. But they still want to make sure that the company plays fair. They don't want it to gamble with their money or to take any other unreasonable risks.[14] Therefore, the bond agreement includes a number of restrictive covenants to prevent the company from purposely increasing the value of its default option.

Suppose Nocturnal Aviation Ltd. has a market value of $100 million and total senior debt of $10 million. That means that the value of Nocturnal could fall by about 90% before the company would want to default. To put it another way, the point at which the company would want to exercise its option is about 10% of the value of the assets.

Now suppose that Nocturnal announces a further $10 million bond issue. The company now has a market value of $110 million and senior debt of $20 million. It would now be willing to default if the value of the assets falls by only 82%. The original debenture holders are slightly worse off. If they had known about the new issue, they would not have been willing to pay quite such a high price for their bonds.

The reason the new issue hurts the original debenture holders is that it alters the *ratio* of senior debt to company value. They would not object to the bond issue if the company kept the ratio the same by simultaneously issuing common stock.

Private placements of bonds often place very stringent limitations on the company's freedom to borrow. In fact many private loan agreements go so far as to prohibit *any* further issue of funded debt without the consent of the lender. These additional restrictions are only possible because it is so much simpler to modify a private agreement.

Why don't companies limit *subordinated* as well as senior debt? The answer is that the subordinated debtor does not get *any* money until the senior bondholders are paid in full. The senior bondholders, therefore, view subordinated debentures in almost the same way that they view equity: they would be happy to see an issue of either.[15] Of course, the converse is not true. A holder of subordinated debentures does care both about the total amount of debt and the proportion that is senior to their claim. As a

---

[13]In Chapters 20 and 21 we showed that this option to default is equivalent to a put option on the assets of the firm.

[14]We described in Chapter 18 some of the games that managers could play at the expense of the bondholders. See Section 18-3.

[15]In practice the courts do not always observe the strict rules of precedence. Therefore the subordinated debtholder may receive *some* payment even when the senior debtholder is not fully paid off.

result, the indenture for an issue of subordinated debt generally includes a restriction on both total debt and senior debt.

Another worry for any bondholders is that the company may issue more secured debt than they had anticipated. An issue of mortgage bonds usually imposes a limit on the amount of secured debt. This is not necessary when you are issuing debentures. As long as the debenture holders are given equal treatment, they do not care how much you mortgage your assets. Therefore the bond agreement for a debenture issue usually includes a so-called **negative pledge clause**, in which the debenture holders simply say, "Me too."[16]

During the 1950s and 1960s many companies found that they could circumvent some of these restrictions if, instead of borrowing money to buy an asset, they entered into a long-term agreement to rent or lease it. For the debtholder this arrangement was very similar to secured borrowing. Therefore indentures began to include limitations on leasing.

Leases are an example of a hidden debt. After their fingers had been burned, bondholders began to impose restrictions on leases. But you want to impose restrictions *before* your fingers are burned. Perhaps, therefore, lenders should be placing restrictions on other kinds of hidden debt such as those that we describe in Appendix 22-1, "Project Finance," or such as unfunded pension liabilities, which we describe in Chapter 33.

We have talked about how an unscrupulous company can try to increase the value of the default option by issuing more debt. But that is not the only way in which it can exploit its existing bondholders. For example, we know that the value of an option is affected by dividend payments. If the company pays out large dividends to its shareholders and doesn't replace the cash with an issue of stock, there are less assets available to cover the debt. Therefore, most bond issues restrict the amount of dividends that the company may pay. Usually these restrictions prohibit the company from paying dividends if their cumulative amount would exceed the sum of (1) cumulative consolidated net income, (2) the proceeds from the sale of stock or conversion of debt, and (3) a dollar amount equal to about one year's dividend.

Negative Covenants

The restrictions on new debt issues or dividend payments are sometimes known as *negative covenants*. They prevent the company from doing things that would benefit the shareholders at the expense of the bondholders but they don't make the bonds safe.

Lenders don't want to wait until the company is worthless—they want an opportunity to demand repayment at the first sign of trouble. That is why they impose a number of hurdles for the company to jump. The most obvious hurdles are the regular interest payments and sinking fund contributions. If these obligations are not met, the loan becomes repayable immediately. Therefore, a company will always try to make the payment if it possibly can.

Another, rather different hurdle is the repayment of other outstanding debt. Many issues contain a so-called *cross-default* clause. This says that the company is in default if it fails to meet its obligations on any of its other debt issues.

Positive Covenants

Most indentures also include "positive" or "affirmative" covenants, which impose certain duties on the borrower. In the case of public bond issues, these affirmative covenants are generally fairly innocuous. For example, a firm may be obliged to furnish its debenture

---

[16]If the company *does* issue secured debt, the negative pledge clause allows the debenture holders to demand repayment. But it does not invalidate the security given to the other debtholders.

holders with a copy of its annual accounts. If it doesn't do so, it is in default on the bonds.

Many privately placed issues of debt impose much more onerous affirmative covenants. The most common of these are covenants to maintain at all times some minimum level of working capital and to maintain a minimum level of net worth. If the amount of working capital or net worth is a good guide to the value of the company, the lender is putting a ceiling on the amount he or she can lose.

We do not want to give the impression that the lenders are constantly seeking an opportunity to cry "default" and then demand their money back. If the company does default, the lenders have the *right* to claim repayment but they will not generally do so. The more usual result is that the lenders or the trustee will seek a detailed explanation from the company and discuss possible changes in its operating policy. It is only as a last resort that lenders demand early repayment and force the company into bankruptcy.

22-5 SUMMARY

Now that you have read this chapter, you should have a fair idea of what you are letting yourself in for when you make a public issue of bonds. The detailed agreement is set out in the indenture between your company and a trustee, but the main provisions are summarized in the prospectus to the issue.

The indenture states whether the bonds are senior or subordinated and whether they are secured to unsecured. Most bonds are unsecured debentures or notes. This means that they are general claims on the corporation. The principal exceptions are utility mortgage bonds, collateral trust bonds, and equipment trust certificates. In the event of default the trustee to these issues can repossess the company's assets in order to pay off the debt.

Most long-term bond issues have a *sinking fund*. This means that the company must set aside enough money each year to retire a specified number of bonds. A sinking fund reduces the average life of the bond and it provides a yearly test of the company's ability to service its debt. It therefore protects the bondholders against the risk of default. But there is another side to sinking funds. If the company can choose whether it will redeem bonds for the sinking fund at par or whether it will repurchase them in the marketplace, it effectively has call option. Therefore sinking funds may make the issue more or less valuable.

Most long-dated bonds may be called at a premium, which is initially equal to the coupon and which declines progressively to zero. There is one common limitation to this right—companies are generally prohibited from calling the bond in the first few years if they intend to replace it with another bond at a lower rate of interest. The option to call the bond may be very valuable; if interest rates decline and bond values rise, you may be able to call a bond that would be worth substantially more than the call price. Of course, if investors know that you may call the bond, the call price will act as a ceiling on the market price. Your best strategy, therefore, is to call the bond as soon as the market price hits the call price. You are unlikely to do better than that.

The bond indentures also lays down certain conditions. Some of these conditions consist of things the company must *not* do: these are called *negative* covenants. Here are some examples:

1. Issues of senior bonds usually prohibit the company from issuing further senior debt if the ratio of net tangible assets to senior debt would fall short of some specified minimum.

2. Issues of subordinated bonds usually also prohibit the company from issuing further senior or junior debt if the ratio of net tangible assets to all debt would fall short of some specified minimum.

3. Unsecured bonds incorporate a *negative pledge* clause, which prohibits the company from securing additional debt without giving equal treatment to the existing unsecured bonds.

4. Most bonds place a limit on the company's dividend payments.

Conditions that require the company to take positive steps to protect the bondholders are known as *positive* covenants. In public bond issues these conditions are generally innocuous. The really important positive covenants are those that give the bondholder the chance to claim a default and get money out while the company still has a substantial value. For example, some bond issues require the company to maintain a minimum level of working capital or net worth. Since a deficiency in either is a good indication of financial weakness, this condition is tantamount to giving the bondholders the right to demand their money back as soon as life appears hazardous.

If you place a bond privately, there is no need to appoint a trustee and you will probably just sign a simple promissory note. Private placements are less standardized than public issues and they impose more stringent negative and affirmative covenants. Otherwise they are close counterparts of publicly issued bonds.

FURTHER READING

Ananthanarayanan and Schwartz and Brennan and Schwartz focus on valuing the options implicit in callable, extendible and retractable bonds. Kraus provides a general discussion of call provisions.

A.L. Ananthanarayanan and E.S. Schwartz, "Retractable and Extendible Bonds: The Canadian Experience," *Journal of Finance*, **35**:31–47 (May 1980).

M.J. Brennan and E.S. Schwartz, "Savings Bonds, Retractable Bonds and Callable Bonds," *Journal of Financial Economics*, **5**:67–88 (1977).

A. Kraus, "An Analysis of Call Provisions and the Corporate Refunding Decision," *Midland Corporate Finance Journal*, **1**:46–60 (Spring 1983).

For a general description of the use of sinking funds, see:

F.C. Thompson and R.L. Norgaard, *Sinking Funds*, Financial Executive Research Foundation, New York, 1967.

Smith and Warner provide an extensive survey and analysis of covenants:

C.W. Smith and J.B. Warner, "On Financial Contracting: An Analysis of Bond Covenants," *Journal of Financial Economics*, **7**:117–161 (June 1979).

APPENDIX 22-1 PROJECT FINANCE

The privately placed loans that we have referred to in this chapter are direct obligations of the parent or one of its principal subsidiaries. In recent years there has been considerable interest in a new type of private loan that is tied as far as possible to the fortunes of a particular project and that minimizes the exposure of the parent. Such a loan is usually referred to as *project financing* and is the specialty of large banks.[17]

An Example from the Oil Industry

Let us look at how British Petroleum (BP) used project financing to pay for development of its huge Forties Field in the North Sea. Since BP needed to finance very large capital

---

[17]Project financing is not exclusively made through private loans. The publicly issued International Pipe Line (NW) debentures discussed in this chapter were used to finance the costs of the construction of a pipeline from Norman Wells in the Northwest Territories to Zama, Alberta.

expenditures elsewhere in the world, management wanted to segregate the financing of the Forties Field project as far as possible from BP's other fund-raising activities. Ideally it would have liked to isolate its other business completely from the fate of the North Sea but no bank could be expected to take the risk of lending solely on the security of a field that was not yet producing.

BP's solution is illustrated in Figure 22-3. A syndicate of 66 major banks agreed in 1972 to lend a total of $945 million—the largest industrial bank loan in history. But instead of lending the money directly to BP, they lent it to a company called Norex, which was controlled by the banks. Norex in turn paid the money to BP Development, the subsidiary of BP that was responsible for developing the Forties Field. But Norex's payment to BP Development was not in the form of a loan: it was an advance payment for future deliveries of oil. In other words, in return for the money BP Development promised to deliver to Norex an agreed quantity of oil. Of course, the last thing that the banks wanted was a load of oil on their doorsteps. Therefore, they also arranged for another BP subsidiary, BP Trading, to repurchase the oil from Norex at a prescribed price.

Payments to Norex had to be completed by 1982. But, because a number of unpredictable factors affected the development of the Forties Field, the speed with which Norex was paid off was tied to the production rate of the field.

The banks consented to bear the ultimate risk that the oil reserves were insufficient to service their loan. However, they were protected against three other hazards. The first was the possible failure of BP Development to construct the necessary facilities. The agreement, therefore, specified in considerable detail the manner in which the field should be developed and BP guaranteed that its subsidiary would carry out this plan.

The second danger was that the field might be depleted more rapidly than was envisaged. To protect the banks against this possibility BP guaranteed that the difference between the market value of the oil produced and the amount needed to service the loan should be paid into a "reclaim account," which could be drawn upon by Norex if the oil flow was subsequently reduced.

The third risk was that of *force majeure*. If it proved impossible to produce any oil before the end of 1978 and if the assessed reserves would have been adequate on a 44% recovery factor to service the Norex loan, then Norex could claim repayment from a restitution account that was guaranteed by BP.

One effect of this complicated financing arrangement was that the banks accepted some of the risk associated with the Forties Field. For example, if the oil reserves were

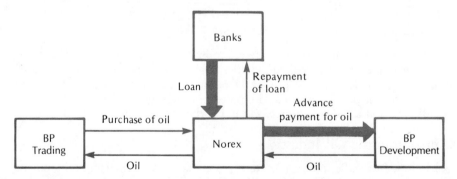

Figure 22-3   Financing for the Forties Field project. The banks made a loan to Norex, which then made an advance payment to BP Development for future deliveries of oil. This oil was resold to BP Trading at an agreed-on price. These payments by BP Trading allowed Norex to repay the banks. The heavy arrows show how the banks provided financing; the lighter arrows show how BP repaid the banks.

inadequate to service the banks' loan to Norex, the banks had no claim against BP's other assets. A second difference between the Forties project financing and a straight bank loan was that the project financing did not show up in BP's balance sheet as a debt. Instead, BP Trading's promise to repurchase the oil from Norex was recorded as a deferred liability against future oil delivery.

Project Finance—Some Common Features

The arrangement for the Forties Field project illustrates the most important features of project financing. The basic requirement of any project financing is that the project can be physically isolated from the parent and that it offers the lender tangible security. The additional research and legal costs also mean the project financing is only economic when the sums involved are very large. It is perhaps not surprising, therefore, that the projects have usually been major mineral extraction and processing developments, that they have been joint ventures, and that they have been located overseas.

Project finance is often provided in the form of a straight loan to the operating company. However, the BP Forties financing is an example of an alternative arrangement known as a *production payment*. In this case the banks do not lend to either the parent or the operating company. Instead they lend to a vehicle company (such as Norex), which is controlled by them. This vehicle company then uses the money to make an advance payment to the project's owner against future delivery of the product. Throughout the life of the production payment the project's owner is obliged to pay to the vehicle company a certain proportion of production. The vehicle company in turn sells the product and pays the money to the banks for application against its loan. When it originally sells the production payment, the project owner will usually promise to develop and operate the mineral deposit. However, the company that buys the payment generally has recourse only against the specific reserves and so bears the risk that they may be inadequate or uneconomic.

We can classify all project financings according to the contractual obligations of the project owners. The purest, but least common, method of financing offers the lender "no recourse" against the owners at any stage. This notion of "no recourse" is somewhat imprecise, for the lenders may well require a general assurance from the parent company that it will do its best to ensure the success of the project. Although these "keepwell agreements" or "comfort letters" are usually too general to be sued upon, they do represent a potentially embarrassing moral commitment on the part of the parent.

One of the most common threats to a successful project loan is a serious delay in completion. Occasionally the project may even turn out to be technically infeasible. Our second class of loans, therefore, consists of those that are supported by a completion guarantee. Such a guarantee may be provided by the project's stockholders or by an insurance company in the form of "completion bonding." It will generally specify a completion date and will require that the plant has been operated for a given period and at a given production quantity, quality, and cost.

The third and largest group of project loans provides the lender with limited recourse against the firms undertaking the project. Here are three examples of how this may be done:

1. *The throughput arrangement.* Many oil pipeline loans involve a "throughput arrangement." This states that, if other companies do not make sufficient use of the pipeline, the owners will themselves ship enough oil through it to provide the pipeline company with the cash that it needs to service the loan.

2. *The cost company arrangement.* Under a cost company arrangement the project's owners receive all of the project's output free of charge. In exchange they agree to pay all operating costs including loan service. Thus the project has no net income

and each parent firm simply includes in its income statement its share of the project's expenses.

3. *The cash deficiency arrangement.* Under this arrangement, the project's owners agree to provide the operating company with enough funds to maintain a certain level of net working capital or ratio of current assets to current liabilities.

Regardless of the precise arrangement, it is important in any project financing that the payments on the loan should correspond as closely as possible to the ability of the project to generate earnings. For example, if the project's completion date is uncertain, the first payment date on the loan may simply be set as so many months after completion. If the loan involves a large final payment, it is common to include an "earnings recapture" clause under which a proportion of any surplus earnings is applied to reduce the final payment. A lender who bears the risk of inadequate reserves will wish to ensure that the reserves are not depleted too rapidly. In these cases, therefore, it is common to assign a *proportion* of revenues to loan repayments rather than a fixed sum.

The Benefits of Project Finance

A number of motives have been suggested for the use of project finance rather than direct borrowing by the parent companies. On the surface it is tempting to believe that the value of a project to the parents is enhanced if it can be made to stand alone as a self-financing entity, so that the parents from its success and are isolated from its failure. Such a result is improbable. Present values, as we know, are additive, so that the sum of the values of the separate entities is equal to the value of the combined entity. The parent stockholders will, therefore, only benefit if the banks fail to charge appropriately for their added risk. When we look at actual project financings, we find that not only are the stockholders rarely isolated from the vicissitudes of the project but the rate of interest on the loan is directly related to the support that the stockholders are willing to provide. The interesting feature of project finance is the way in which it permits the stockholders to transfer certain risks. For example, if BP had borrowed on the general credit of the parent company, it would have remained exposed to the uncontrollable risk of inadequate North Sea reserves. By arranging the financing in the form of a project loan, it effectively purchased insurance against a risk that could have seriously affected the remainder of its business. Correspondingly, with many loans for projects in politically unstable countries the lenders effectively provide insurance against adverse government action. Indeed, although the host government might not hesitate to expropriate a venture that was wholly financed by the parent company, it is likely to be much more wary of its standing with a group of leading international banks.

A further motive that has been suggested for project financing is that it may not be shown as debt in the company's balance sheet. We have already seen how BP's financing of the Forties Field project showed up as a deferred liability against future oil deliveries. In some cases the owner's guarantees may not be shown in the balance sheet at all. In this case, the financing is said to be "off balance sheet." Of course this is an advantage only if capital markets are inefficient and lenders and stockholders cannot, or do not, recognize these hidden liabilities.

Project finance can often be costly to arrange. The fee charged by the managing bank for organizing the loan typically lies between $1/8$% and $1/2$% of the amount involved. Despite this, the arrangement may be simpler than a direct loan to the parent companies. This is partly because the projects are often jointly owned by several parents, but it is also because the security for the lenders commonly derives as much from the contractual arrangements as from the tangible assets. A bank's security for a pipeline loan depends critically on the existence of throughput arrangements, its security for a tonnage oxygen loan depends on sales contracts with the steel companies, and its security for a tanker loan depends on the charter agreements. In such instances it may be more straightforward to tie the loan directly to these arrangements. Moreover, by separating this project from the rest of the parent company's operations, there are savings in information costs. Thus, the banks involved in the financing of the Forties Field project were able to limit their attention to the prospects for that field; correspondingly, institutions that take up any other BP debt could largely ignore the prospects for Forties Field. Given the high costs of information on new mineral developments, such specialization makes good sense.

APPENDIX 22-2 EXCERPTS FROM A PROSPECTUS FOR A DEBENTURE ISSUE

Additional Issue   *Project Financing*

$75,000,000

Interprovincial Pipe Line (NW) Ltd.
(a wholly-owned subsidiary of Interprovincial Pipe Line Limited)
12.70% Debentures, Series B

To be dated November 15, 1984   To mature November 15, 2004

The 12.70% Debentures, Series B (the "Series B Debentures") will be secured by an assignment by the Company of the Norman Wells Pipeline Agreement among Imperial Oil Limited, Interprovincial Pipe Line (NW) Ltd. (the "Company") and Interprovincial Pipe Line Limited. The Series B Debentures will not be redeemable before November 15, 1999, for other than sinking fund purposes, from the proceeds of funds borrowed at a lower interest cost. Particulars of sinking fund, redemption and other material attributes are set forth under "Details of the Offering".

Financial support provided by

Imperial Oil Limited

Under the terms of the Norman Wells Pipeline Agreement, Imperial Oil Limited is required to pay to the Company amounts which will enable the Company to service the Series B Debentures. Reference is made to "The Norman Wells Pipeline Agreement".

In the opinion of counsel, the Series B Debentures will be eligible for investment under the Canadian and British Insurance Companies Act and other statutes as set forth under "Eligibility for Investment".

Price: 100 and accrued interest, if any

We, as principals, conditionally offer these Series B Debentures, subject to prior sale, if, as and when issued by the Company and accepted by us in accordance with the conditions contained in the underwriting agreement referred to under "Plan of Distribution" and the approval of certain legal matters on behalf of the Company by Osler, Hoskin & Harcourt, Toronto and on our behalf by Blake, Cassels & Graydon, Toronto.

	Price to the public (1)	Underwriters' fee	Net proceeds to the Company (2)
Per Debenture.................................	100.00%	1.15%	98.85%
Total..	$75,000,000	$862,500	$74,137,500

(1) Plus accrued interest, if any, to the date of delivery.

(2) Before deducting expenses of issue estimated at $175,000 which will be paid out of the general funds of the Company.

Subscriptions will be received subject to rejection or allotment in whole or in part and the right is reserved to close the subscription books at any time without notice. It is expected that the Series B Debentures will be available for delivery on or about November 15, 1984.

October 24, 1984

Source: International Pipe Line (NW) Ltd., 12.70% Debentures.

TABLE OF CONTENTS

ELIGIBILITY FOR INVESTMENT

In the opinion of Osler, Hoskin & Harcourt, counsel to the Company, and in the opinion of Blake, Cassels & Graydon, counsel to the underwriters, the Series B Debentures offered by this prospectus, on the date of issue, will be eligible investments, without resort to the so-called "basket" provisions, but subject to general investment provisions for:

(i) insurance companies registered or licensed under the Canadian and British Insurance Companies Act (Canada), the Foreign Insurance Companies Act (Canada) and the Insurance Act (Alberta) and insurance companies incorporated or organized under the Insurance Act (Ontario);

(ii) loan companies regulated under the Loan Companies Act (Canada) and loan corporations registered under the Loan and Trust Corporations Act (Ontario);

(iii) trust companies regulated or registered under the Trust Companies Act (Canada), the Loan and Trust Corporations Act (Ontario) and the Loan and Investment Societies Act (Quebec); and

(iv) pension funds regulated or registered under the Pension Benefits Standards Act (Canada), the Pension Benefits Act (Ontario), the Pension Benefits Act (Alberta) and An Act respecting supplemental pension plans (Quebec).

In the opinion of such counsel, the Series B Debentures will also be eligible investments for registered retirement savings plans and for registered home ownership savings plans under the Income Tax Act (Canada), and the provisions of An Act respecting Insurance (Quebec) would not preclude the investment by an insurance company in the Series B Debentures, subject to the general investment provisions of that act.

Metric Conversion Table

To Convert from	To	Multiply by
Cubic metres (m^3)	Barrels	6.3
Kilometres (km)	Miles	0.6
Metres (m)	Feet	3.3
Millimetres (mm)	Inches	0.04

Note: In this prospectus "cubic metres per day" has been abbreviated to "m^3/d".

2

INTERPROVINCIAL PIPE LINE (NW) LTD.

PROSPECTUS SUMMARY

Issue: . . . . $75,000,000 12.70% Debentures, Series B.

Price: . . . .   100% and accrued interest, if any.

Interest Payment Dates: . . . .   Payable semi-annually on May 15 and November 15, commencing May 15, 1985.

Sinking Fund: . . . .   An annual sinking fund commencing on November 15, 1987 to produce an average life of approximately 13.9 years.

Redemption: . . . .   Not redeemable for financial advantage prior to November 15, 1999. Otherwise redeemable at par plus a premium of 12.70% in the first year, declining to par after November 15, 2002, together with accrued interest.

Financial Support: . . . .   The Series B Debentures will be direct obligations of Interprovincial Pipe Line (NW) Ltd. and will be secured by an assignment of the benefits of the Norman Wells Pipeline Agreement including the right to receive moneys payable by Imperial Oil Limited.

Use of Proceeds:. . . . .   The net proceeds of this issue will be applied toward the costs of construction of the Norman Wells Pipeline System. The Company is financing the Pipeline System on the basis of a debt to equity ratio of 75% to 25%.

Norman Wells Pipeline System:. . . . .   The Company is engaged in the construction of an oil pipeline extending 866 km from the Norman Wells oil field being developed by a subsidiary of Imperial Oil Limited in the Northwest Territories to connect with the pipeline of Rainbow Pipe Line Company, Ltd. at Zama in northern Alberta. The initial design capacity of the Pipeline System is approximately 4 800 m^3/d of crude oil and other liquid hydrocarbons. The construction and operation of the Pipeline System are regulated by the National Energy Board.

3

THE COMPANY

Interprovincial Pipe Line (NW) Ltd. was incorporated on March 3, 1980 under the Canada Business Corporations Act. All of the Company's outstanding shares are owned by Interprovincial Pipe Line Limited ("Interprovincial"). The registered office of the Company is at 1202 Interprovincial Pipe Line Tower, 10201 Jasper Avenue, Edmonton, Alberta.

The Company is constructing a 324 mm diameter pipeline extending 866 km (the "Pipeline System") from the Norman Wells oil field being developed by Esso Resources Canada Limited, a wholly-owned subsidiary of Imperial Oil Limited ("Imperial"), in the Northwest Territories to connect with the pipeline of Rainbow Pipe Line Company, Ltd. (the "Rainbow Pipeline") at Zama in northern Alberta. Crude oil and other liquid hydrocarbons will be transported through the facilities of the Company and the Rainbow Pipeline to Edmonton, Alberta, for delivery to refineries in the Edmonton area, or to the pipelines of Interprovincial or other carriers for transportation to Canadian or U.S. refineries.

The Pipeline System is expected to be completed at a capital cost of $400 million, including a capitalized allowance for debt and equity funds used during construction of $62 million. Construction progress has exceeded targets and installation of two-thirds of the pipe for the total project has been completed. The Company expects to complete the Pipeline System in the spring of 1985 and it is anticipated that full operations will commence shortly thereafter. The initial design capacity of the Pipeline System is approximately 4 800 m^3/d of crude oil and other liquid hydrocarbons.

The portion of the Rainbow Pipeline to be used for shipment of oil to Edmonton has a capacity of approximately 39 200 m^3/d. The average throughput of the Rainbow Pipeline during 1983 was approximately 22 800 m^3/d. The Company is confident that there will be sufficient capacity in the Rainbow Pipeline to accommodate the throughput of the Pipeline System. Imperial is a one-third shareholder of Rainbow Pipe Line Company, Ltd.

All services required by the Company for the construction, operation, maintenance and management of the Pipeline System are provided by Interprovincial pursuant to a management agreement.

Imperial, the Company and Interprovincial are parties to the Norman Wells Pipeline Agreement dated as of January 1, 1980 as amended by an agreement made as of April 1, 1982 and clarified by a letter agreement dated August 29, 1983 (collectively the "Pipeline Agreement"). The Pipeline Agreement specifies the terms and conditions governing the financing, construction and operation of the Pipeline System.

The Company and Interprovincial are parties to an agreement with two Canadian chartered banks (the "Bank Loan Agreement") to provide financing for the Pipeline System, including a facility to finance cost overruns. A total of $275 million remains available to the Company under the Bank Loan Agreement.

The principal properties of the Company comprise rights of way, the partly constructed Pipeline System, materials and work in progress for the completion of construction and a portfolio of short term securities being maintained pending requirement of funds for construction.

NORMAN WELLS OIL FIELD

The Norman Wells oil field is located at Norman Wells, which is situated on the Mackenzie River in the Northwest Territories. The Norman Wells oil field was discovered by Imperial in 1920. Following reservoir studies and evaluation well drilling, Imperial has concluded that there are significant volumes of oil in place in the reservoir beneath the Mackenzie River. Esso Resources Canada Limited is undertaking a field-wide water flood of the Norman Wells oil field and Imperial expects that this will increase total field production of crude oil and natural gas liquids from 500 m^3/d to 4 600 m^3/d. The Government of Canada has a one-third carried interest in the Norman Wells oil field.

Imperial estimates probable reserves to be some 43 million m^3 of oil and natural gas liquids recoverable by primary recovery techniques and by a field-wide water flood project. Based on information supplied by Imperial,

4

the Company estimates that pipeline throughput in 1985 will be 4 100 m³/d. This level is expected to increase to 4 600 m³/d by 1990 at which time throughput will begin to decline, reaching 1 000 m³/d over 20 years.

The Pipeline System has the potential for transporting crude oil and other liquid hydrocarbons provided by other shippers. Several companies are engaged in exploration for oil in the vicinity of the route of the Pipeline System. In August 1984 the southernmost 29 km of the Pipeline System was placed in service to transport approximately 400 m³/d for another shipper.

IMPERIAL OIL LIMITED

Imperial is an integrated oil company and is active in all phases of the petroleum industry in Canada, including the exploration for and production of crude oil and natural gas. In Canada, it is a major producer of crude oil, a large refiner and marketer of petroleum products and a significant supplier of natural gas. Imperial is a major participant in Syncrude, a joint venture for the production of upgraded crude oil. It is also engaged in mineral exploration, development and production and in the manufacture and sale of chemicals, fertilizers and building materials. Exxon Corporation owns 69.6% of the outstanding shares of Imperial, with the remaining shares being publicly held.

Imperial's financial performance for the periods indicated is summarized below.

	Year ended December 31				
	1983	1982	1981	1980	1979
	(millions of dollars)				
Total revenues	$9,027	$8,618	$8,185	$6,349	$4,906
Net income	290	267	465	682	493
Internal funds from operations	708	830	839	893	702
Long term debt and other obligations	1,180	1,028	946	618	611
Shareholders' equity	4,231	4,103	4,042	3,789	2,440
Total assets	8,049	7,486	7,096	6,244	4,668

Source: Imperial

INTERPROVINCIAL PIPE LINE LIMITED

Interprovincial, directly and through its wholly-owned United States subsidiary, Lakehead Pipe Line Company, Inc. ("Lakehead"), owns and operates an oil pipeline system for the transportation of crude oil and other liquid hydrocarbons. The pipeline system constitutes the only crude oil pipeline connecting the oil fields of Alberta across the Canadian prairies through the Great Lakes region of the United States to Toronto, Ontario and Montreal, Quebec, with lateral lines to Nanticoke, Ontario and Buffalo, New York, and includes a line between Superior, Wisconsin and Sarnia, Ontario, via Chicago, Illinois. Deliveries are made en route in the Canadian prairies and the midwestern United States.

Interprovincial and Lakehead are primarily engaged in the business of transporting, at established tariffs, crude oil and other liquid hydrocarbons through their common carrier pipeline system. During 1983, 41 shippers tendered 49 types of products for shipment through the system. The five principal shippers were Gulf Canada Limited, Imperial, Petro-Canada, Shell Canada Limited and Texaco Canada Limited. Products shipped averaged 198 900 m³/d during 1983 and can be grouped into the following classifications:

(i) light, medium and heavy crude oil from conventional sources;

(ii) crude oils extracted from Alberta oil sands deposits;

(iii) natural gas liquids which include propane, butane and condensate; and

(iv) refined petroleum products such as gasoline, diesel fuel and heating fuel.

In Canada, interprovincial pipeline operations are regulated by the National Energy Board (the "NEB" or the "Board"). In the United States, the Federal Energy Regulatory Commission (the "FERC") has regulatory authority over the rates, regulations and accounting practices of Lakehead. In 1982, an industry-wide decision by the FERC concerning ratemaking for oil pipelines prescribed that companies will be allowed to set tariffs to recover

5

operating and interest costs and to provide a return on equity. The return is applied to a rate base which incorporates a weighted average of the reproduction cost and the original cost of the pipeline facility. This decision is currently under review by the FERC.

THE NORMAN WELLS PIPELINE AGREEMENT

The Company, Interprovincial and Imperial entered into the Pipeline Agreement to provide for the financing, construction and operation of the Pipeline System for the transportation of crude oil and other liquid hydrocarbons from the Norman Wells oil field to Zama, Alberta. The Pipeline Agreement has a term of 25 years from the date when "leave to open" the Pipeline System is granted by the NEB but will end earlier if and when the debt for financing the construction of the Pipeline System is retired.

The Pipeline Agreement provides that the Company will construct, maintain and operate the Pipeline System and that Interprovincial will enter into a management agreement with the Company to provide the services required for the construction, operation, maintenance and management of the Pipeline System. The Pipeline Agreement also contemplates that Imperial will tender for transportation in the Pipeline System all petroleum production from the Norman Wells oil field (except that needed for local requirements), and will pay transportation tolls based on the full cost of service with the requirement to pay a Minimum Bill in the circumstances described below. Both Imperial and the Company have a right to withdraw from the arrangements contemplated by the Pipeline Agreement in accordance with the terms of abandonment described below. Interprovincial has agreed to cause the Company to perform its obligations under the Pipeline Agreement and Imperial has agreed to cause its subsidiary, Esso Resources Canada Limited, to proceed with diligence to increase the production capacity of the Norman Wells oil field.

The Company is required to finance the Pipeline System on the basis of a debt to equity ratio of 75% to 25%. Pursuant to the Pipeline Agreement, Imperial has agreed to the Bank Loan Agreement and to the issue of the Series A and Series B Debentures; future consents of Imperial will be obtained as required for the debt financing of the Pipeline System.

Shippers which tender petroleum for transportation through the Pipeline System will pay the full cost of service for transportation based upon a tariff which includes an agreed rate of return of 16% on equity. The full cost of service tariff includes the following items:

(i) operating expenses including maintenance, transportation and general expenses;

(ii) depreciation and amortization expense;

(iii) normalized income taxes;

(iv) interest expense; and

(v) the return on equity mentioned above.

The Pipeline Agreement also provides for a Minimum Bill, which is payable by Imperial to the Company to the extent amounts collected by the Company from all shippers, including Imperial, in any operating month during the term of the Pipeline Agreement do not aggregate an amount equal to one-twelfth of the estimated annual Minimum Bill. The Minimum Bill includes the following items:

(i) operating expenses including maintenance, transportation and general expenses;

(ii) income taxes currently payable;

(iii) interest expense; and

(iv) depreciation, defined for purposes of the Minimum Bill as the amount required to retire the Company's debt in accordance with its terms.

The Pipeline Agreement provides that either the Company or Imperial may abandon the Pipeline System at any time for any reason. In the event that either party initiates the abandonment, the other party has the right to elect to continue the Pipeline System under certain conditions.

6

In the event of abandonment of the Pipeline System prior to commencement of operations:

(i) if notice is given by Imperial that it does not wish to proceed with the arrangement and the Company then elects to abandon, Imperial will assume the Company's debt obligations relating to the Pipeline System, pay to the Company that portion of the cost of the Pipeline System not included in the debt obligations so assumed, and pay those costs reasonably incurred to abandon the Pipeline System;

(ii) if notice of abandonment is given by the Company and Imperial does not then elect to continue the Pipeline System, Imperial will assume the Company's debt obligations relating to the Pipeline System; and

(iii) if notice of abandonment is given by the Company and Imperial elects to continue the Pipeline System, the Company will sell the Pipeline System to Imperial and Imperial will assume the Company's debt relating to the Pipeline System and pay to the Company that portion of the cost of the Pipeline System not included in the debt obligations so assumed.

In the event of abandonment of the Pipeline System after the commencement of operations and prior to the expiration of the Pipeline Agreement:

(i) if Imperial gives, or is deemed to have given, notice that it is unwilling or unable to tender petroleum for the remainder of the term, and the Company then elects to abandon, Imperial will pay to the Company the Minimum Bill for the remaining term of the Pipeline Agreement;

(ii) if the Company elects to abandon, or is deemed to have done so, and Imperial then elects not to continue the Pipeline System, Imperial will pay to the Company the Minimum Bill until the Pipeline Agreement expires; and

(iii) if the Company elects to abandon and Imperial elects to continue the Pipeline System, the Company will sell the Pipeline System to Imperial and Imperial will assume the Company's debt obligations relating to the Pipeline System.

If Imperial gives notice of abandonment either prior to or after commencement of operations, the Company may elect to continue the Pipeline System in which event the Pipeline Agreement terminates. However, the trust indenture securing the Series A and Series B Debentures provides that the Company cannot so elect unless it has provided the Trustee with a guarantee or letter of credit with respect to the payment of principal and interest on the Debentures from one or more of the existing five largest Schedule A chartered banks.

THE MANAGEMENT AGREEMENT

The Company and Interprovincial have entered into a management agreement dated as of January 1, 1982 (the "Management Agreement") under which the Company appointed Interprovincial to provide the services required for the construction, operation, maintenance and management of the Pipeline System. Interprovincial is being reimbursed by the Company for services provided and related overheads pursuant to this agreement. Amounts charged for services under the Management Agreement were as follows: in 1982, $733,542, in 1983, $1,158,518 and $1,300,833 to August 31, 1984.

THE BANK LOAN AGREEMENT

The Company, Interprovincial and two chartered banks entered into the Bank Loan Agreement to provide initial financing for the Pipeline System. The Bank Loan Agreement now provides that up to $275 million may be advanced prior to the completion of the Pipeline System or December 31, 1987, whichever is earlier. Funds available under the Bank Loan Agreement will be reduced by the amount of this issue and any further long-term fixed rate indebtedness incurred to finance the construction of the Pipeline System. Funds may be drawn in Canadian or U.S. dollars at floating rates of interest or at fixed rates of interest by way of LIBOR loans or bankers' acceptances. The Bank Loan Agreement also provides a backup line of credit for commercial paper issued by the Company.

The loans outstanding at the time "leave to open" the Pipeline System is obtained are repayable over a ten year term commencing on that date, and with minor exceptions may be prepaid at any time without penalty. Mandatory quarterly repayments of principal are required to be the greater of 1% of the loans outstanding at the

7

time of "leave to open" or an amount equal to a portion of the depreciation expense of the Pipeline System determined by rateably allocating the depreciation expense over all debt relating to the Pipeline System.

Advances pursuant to the Bank Loan Agreement are secured by the Bank Debentures. See "Details of the Offering".

GOVERNMENT REGULATION

Under the National Energy Board Act (the "NEB Act"), the NEB has regulatory power over the construction, operation and maintenance of pipelines within federal jurisdiction. The NEB Act provides that a company subject to the Board's jurisdiction shall not make any unjust discrimination in tolls, service or facilities against any person or locality. The Board has power to disallow any tariff or toll and to require a company to substitute a tariff satisfactory to the Board for a tariff originally determined by that company. A company's accounting records must be kept according to standards established by the Oil Pipeline Uniform Accounting Regulations and are subject to audit by the Board.

In its reasons for the decision which resulted in the granting of the Certificate of Public Convenience and Necessity No. OC-35 which authorizes construction of the Pipeline System, the Board set forth a number of conditions to be met by the Company. These included filing a variety of studies and other material data for Board approval prior to construction. These approvals have been obtained.

The NEB approved the form and content of the Company's "full cost of service" tariff, including the 16% return on equity, and the Rules and Regulations which will apply to the transportation of petroleum through the Pipeline System, all as contained in the Pipeline Agreement.

The Board in its order respecting tariffs declared that if additional shippers intend to use the Pipeline System the Board may review the structure of the full cost of service tariff. The order requires the Company to submit for review and approval its estimate of the full cost of service prior to the beginning of each operating year, and requires that any operating expenses in excess of the approved estimate not be included in the actual full cost of service until such amounts are approved by the Board. The Board is currently reviewing the allocation among shippers of the full cost of service tariff.

Following completion of the Pipeline System, a "leave to open" order is required from the Board before the Pipeline System may be operated. "Leave to open" the southernmost 29 km of the Pipeline System has been obtained.

CAPITALIZATION

	Authorized	Outstanding June 30, 1984	Outstanding August 31, 1984	Outstanding August 31, 1984 after giving effect to this issue
		(Unaudited)	(Unaudited)	(Unaudited)
Debt				
Debentures				
13.40% Series A due April 1, 2004 ...	$100,000,000	$100,000,000	$100,000,000	$100,000,000
12.70% Series B due November 15, 2004	$200,000,000	—	—	75,000,000
Project financing (1)		46,600,000	60,200,000	—
		$146,600,000	$160,200,000	$175,000,000
Shareholder's Equity				
Common Shares	unlimited	$ 81,025,000	$ 81,025,000	$ 81,025,000
		(81,026 shs)	(81,026 shs)	(81,026 shs)
Retained Earnings.		11,432,000	11,432,000 (2)	11,432,000 (2)
		$ 92,457,000	$ 92,457,000	$ 92,457,000

Notes:

1. All amounts owed by the Company under the Bank Loan Agreement are collaterally secured by the pledge of Bank Debentures which rank pari passu with the Series A and Series B Debentures (see "Details of the Offering"). The Bank Debentures are deemed to be outstanding at any time only to the extent of all amounts then owing by the Company under the Bank Loan Agreement. A total of $275 million remains available to the Company under the Bank Loan Agreement.

2. Amounts shown for retained earnings in the August 31, 1984 columns are as of June 30, 1984.

USE OF PROCEEDS

The net proceeds from this sale of the Series B Debentures will amount to approximately $73,962,500, and will be applied as required toward the costs of construction of the Pipeline System. These proceeds will initially be used to reduce borrowings under the Bank Loan Agreement and, on an interim basis, the balance will be invested in short term securities.

8

The total debt requirement of the Pipeline System is expected to be $300 million. The Company proposes to fund the remaining requirements by incurring further indebtedness pursuant to the Bank Loan Agreement and through the issue of additional debt securities. The Company's current intention is to replace bank borrowings on a timely basis as financial market conditions and other factors dictate. The equity requirement for the project, anticipated to be $100 million, will be satisfied by Interprovincial through its share investment in the Company and the accumulated retained earnings from the project.

PLAN OF DISTRIBUTION

Under an agreement dated October 24, 1984, between the Company and Wood Gundy Inc. and McLeod Young Weir Limited as underwriters, the Company has agreed to sell and the underwriters have agreed to purchase, on November 15, 1984, or such other date as the Company and the underwriters may agree upon but in any event not later than November 29, 1984, subject to the terms and conditions stated therein, all but not part of the $75,000,000 principal amount of Series B Debentures at an aggregate price of $75,000,000 plus accrued interest, if any, from November 15, 1984 to the date of delivery, payable to the Company against delivery of such Series B Debentures. This agreement provides for the Company to pay the underwriters out of its general funds a fee of $862,500 on account of the services rendered by the underwriters. The obligation of the underwriters to take up the Series B Debentures under such agreement may be terminated at their discretion on the basis of their assessment of the state of the financial markets and may also be terminated upon the occurrence of certain stated events. In connection with the offering, the underwriters may overallot or effect transactions which stabilize or maintain the market price of the Series B Debentures at a level above that which might otherwise prevail in the open market; such transactions, if commenced, may be discontinued at any time.

DETAILS OF THE OFFERING

The following is a summary of the material attributes and characteristics of the Series B Debentures which does not purport to be complete. For full particulars reference should be made to the Trust Indenture referred to below.

Trust Indenture

The Series B Debentures will be issued pursuant to the provisions of a trust indenture dated as of March 1, 1984, between the Company and Montreal Trust Company of Canada, as trustee (the "Trustee") providing for the creation and issue of debentures (the "Debentures") and a supplemental indenture to be made as of November 15, 1984, (together the "Trust Indenture"). The aggregate principal amount of the Debentures which may be issued by the Company is not limited by the Trust Indenture, but Debentures may only be issued to finance construction of the Pipeline System.

The Series B Debentures will be direct obligations of the Company and will rank pari passu with the Series A Debentures, the Bank Debentures and all other Debentures (except as to sinking funds pertaining exclusively to any particular series).

The Company issues Bank Debentures under the Trust Indenture, which are pledged to two chartered banks as security for loans from those banks to the Company under the Bank Loan Agreement. Notwithstanding the stated principal amount of Bank Debentures at any time issued, they are deemed to be outstanding only to the extent of all amounts owing by the Company to the said banks under the Bank Loan Agreement from time to time and are repayable only in accordance with the terms of the Bank Loan Agreement.

Interest

The Series B Debentures will bear interest at the rate of 12.70% per annum from November 15, 1984. The principal of and half-yearly interest on the Series B Debentures will be payable in lawful money of Canada on May 15 and November 15 in each year commencing May 15, 1985 at any branch in Canada of the bank designated in the Series B Debentures.

Denominations

Series B Debentures will be issued in coupon form registrable as to principal only in the denominations of $1,000, $25,000 and $100,000 and in fully registered form in denominations of $1,000 and integral multiples thereof.

Security

All outstanding Debentures are secured pursuant to the Trust Indenture by an assignment to the Trustee by the Company of substantially all its rights under any Shipping Agreement and under the Pipeline Agreement,

9

including a right to receive all moneys due thereunder and a right to give a notice of abandonment under the Pipeline Agreement following the occurrence of an Event of Default under the Trust Indenture.

The Trust Indenture also provides for a first and specific mortgage (subject to Permitted Encumbrances) upon the real estate, rights of way and other immovable properties that form part of the Pipeline System and are described in the Schedule to the Trust Indenture and fixed plant and fixed equipment situate thereon, together with cash balances and evidences of indebtedness deposited from time to time with the Trustee. The Trust Indenture contains provisions for the release of property from the said mortgage when the disposal of such property would not interfere with the operation of the Pipeline System. In some circumstances, certain of the Bank Debentures, for a limited period, may not have the benefit of the said mortgage.

Sinking Fund

The Company will covenant in the Trust Indenture to make payments to the Trustee, as and by way of a sinking fund, sufficient to retire 4% of the total of original issues of Series B Debentures on November 15 in each of the years 1987 to 2003 inclusive, so as to retire 68% of the issue prior to maturity. The sinking fund will produce an average life for the Series B Debentures of approximately 13.9 years.

Series B Debentures redeemed (other than for sinking fund purposes) or purchased will establish a sinking fund credit equal to the principal amount thereof which may be applied to the satisfaction in whole or in part of any subsequent sinking fund payment. Series B Debentures will be redeemable out of sinking fund moneys at the principal amount thereof plus accrued interest.

Redemption and Purchase

The Series B Debentures will not be redeemable prior to November 15, 1999, other than for sinking fund purposes, unless the Company shall have filed with the Trustee a certified copy of a resolution of its directors declaring that such Series B Debentures are being redeemed otherwise than as part of a refunding or anticipated refunding operation involving the application, directly or indirectly, of funds borrowed in connection with or in anticipation of such refunding operation having an interest rate or cost of less than 12.70% per annum. Subject to the foregoing, the Series B Debentures will be redeemable prior to maturity, other than for sinking fund purposes, in whole at any time or in part from time to time, at the option of the Company on not less than 30 days' notice, at prices equal to the following percentages of the principal amount thereof, together in every case with accrued and unpaid interest to the date fixed for redemption:

If redeemed in the 12 months ending November 15	Percentage	If redeemed in the 12 months ending November 15	Percentage
1985	112.70	1995	105.60
1986	111.95	1996	104.90
1987	111.20	1997	104.20
1988	110.50	1998	103.50
1989	109.80	1999	102.80
1990	109.10	2000	102.10
1991	108.40	2001	101.40
1992	107.70	2002	100.70
1993	107.00	2003	100.00
1994	106.30	2004	100.00

The Company will reserve the right to purchase Series B Debentures in the market or by tender to all Series B Debenture holders, at any price, or by private contract at prices not exceeding the foregoing percentages of the principal amount thereof plus accrued and unpaid interest and the costs of purchase.

10

Covenants

The following is a summary of certain covenants which will be applicable under the Trust Indenture so long as any Series B Debentures remain outstanding.

Additional Debentures

The Company will not issue additional Debentures except in accordance with the Pipeline Agreement.

Completion of Pipeline System

The Company will use its best endeavours to construct and complete the Pipeline System on or before December 31, 1987 subject to the terms of the Pipeline Agreement.

Maintenance of Agreements

The Company will use its best efforts (i) to keep the Pipeline Agreement in full force and effect and to collect all amounts from time to time payable to the Company under that agreement, (ii) to keep the Management Agreement in full force and effect and (iii) to collect all amounts from time to time payable to the Company under any Shipping Agreement. The Company will not assign or consent to the assignment of any rights or obligations under the Pipeline Agreement or the Management Agreement or terminate, amend or modify the terms thereof in any respect which, in the opinion of the Trustee, is adverse to the interests of the Debenture holders. The Company will not assign or consent to the assignment of any Shipping Agreement. Notwithstanding these covenants, the Company may assign or encumber the Pipeline Agreement or any Shipping Agreement to secure equally with the Debentures any issue of additional debt securities the proceeds of which are used exclusively to finance the Pipeline System. The Company shall not give a notice of its intention to continue the Pipeline System in response to a notice of abandonment given by Imperial (if to do so would cause the termination of the Pipeline Agreement), unless it has provided the Trustee with a guarantee or letter of credit with respect to the payment of principal and interest on the Debentures from one or more of the existing five largest Schedule A chartered banks.

Creation of Security

The Company will not:

(i) create or assume any encumbrance on property comprising the Pipeline System, other than Permitted Encumbrances and encumbrances to secure Debentures; or

(ii) create or assume any encumbrance on property not comprising part of the Pipeline System, other than Permitted Encumbrances, if the indebtedness of the Company to which the encumbrance relates has been created or assumed upon terms which, in the opinion of the Trustee, permit the lender to have any recourse to or interfere, in any way which is materially adverse to the interests of the Debenture holders, with the operation of the Pipeline System.

Modification

The rights of a Debenture holder under the Trust Indenture may be modified. For that purpose, among others, the Trust Indenture contains provisions for making binding upon all Debenture holders resolutions passed by the affirmative vote of holders of not less than 66⅔% of the principal amount of the Debentures voting at a meeting of Debenture holders or by instruments in writing signed by the holders of not less than 66⅔% of the principal amount of the outstanding Debentures, subject to the provisions of the Trust Indenture.

11

APPENDIX 22-3   SOME UNUSUAL BONDS

The bonds that we have looked at in this chapter all involve an unconditional fixed dollar obligation. In other words, interest is fixed from the outset at so many dollars a year: if you don't pay it, you are in default. In this appendix, we look at five unusual creatures—the original issue discount bond, the income bond, the floating-rate bond, the indexed bond, and the commodity-linked bond.

Original Issue Discount Bonds

A bond that pays a very low rate of interest must be sold at a substantial discount on its face value. Such a bond is termed a "deep discount" bond. A bond that pays no interest at all must be offered at an even lower price. Such a bond is called a "pure discount" bond.

Since 1981, a number of United States companies have issued discount bonds. These are generally known as "original issue discount" (OID) bonds. For example, in June 1981, General Motors Acceptance Corporation issued $750 million of ten-year OID notes. These notes did not pay any interest, but they were issued at a price of $252.50 for each note. Thus, they offered a prospective fourfold increase in value over ten years, which is equivalent to a compound return of 14.8% a year.

Table 22-1   GMAC's original issue discount bonds were expected to appreciate by an increasing percentage amount each year, but the IRS allowed GMAC to deduct the same *dollar* amount each year from taxable income.

Year	(1) PV at Start of Year	(2) Change in PV During Year	(3) Allowable Tax Write-off
1	$252.5	$ 37.3	$ 74.75
2	289.8	42.8	74.75
3	332.5	49.1	74.75
4	381.6	56.3	74.75
5	437.9	64.6	74.75
6	502.5	74.1	74.75
7	576.6	85.1	74.75
8	661.7	97.6	74.75
9	759.4	112.0	74.75
10	871.4	128.6	74.75
Total		$747.5	$747.50

Table 22-1 shows the expected yearly change in the value of the GMAC notes. In year 1, the prospective appreciation is $0.148 \times 252.5 = \$37.3$. At the start of year 2, the expected value of the notes is $252.5 + 37.3 = \$289.8$, and the appreciation in year 2 is $0.148 \times 289.8 = \$42.8$, and so on. Of course, the total appreciation over the ten years is $1,000 - 252.5 = \$747.5$.

The attractions of OID debt resulted largely from a temporary quirk in the tax rules. The IRS recognized that, even if debt does not pay interest, it is still costly to the issuer. Therefore, it allowed the company to deduct a portion of the original issue discount from taxable income. But, in calculating this deduction, the IRS employed simple, rather than compound, interest. Thus GMAC was permitted to deduct the same amount in each year, $747.5/10 = \$74.75$.

If you compare columns 2 and 3 of Table 22-1, you will see that in the early years of the loan's life, GMAC could deduct more than the cost of the loan from its taxable income. For example, in year 1, each note cost GMAC $37.3 or 14.8% of the amount of the loan. However, when calculating taxable profits, GMAC could deduct $74.75 or 29.6% of the amount of the loan. From year 7 onward, the deduction is less than the cost of the loan but, other things equal, GMAC benefitted from having the extra tax shield in the early years.

Of course, this is not the whole story. Just as the IRS pretended that GMAC paid interest of $74.75 a year, so it pretended that the noteholders received interest of $74.75 a year. Therefore, there was an advantage to OID debt only if the marginal investor had a lower tax rate than the borrower. This takes us back to the capital structure controversy of Chapter 18. As long as only a few companies issued OID debt, there were enough tax-exempt investors who were happy to hold them. But, as more OID debt was issued, those companies who came late on the scene could expect to face higher rates of interest.

By 1982, the IRS had become sufficiently concerned about the loss of tax revenue that it began to use compound interest to calculate the tax deduction. From that point on, the tax incentives to issue OID debt disappeared.[18]

Income Bonds

An income bond is like any other debt except that interest has to be paid only to the extent that it is covered by the year's earnings.[19]

On the surface, income bonds offer the best of both worlds. Because they pay interest only when the company can afford to do so, they have many of the advantages of preferred stock. A company that issues income bonds or preferred is unlikely to be driven into bankruptcy by a temporary decline in earnings and can, therefore, afford a more levered capital structure.

But income bonds don't share the disadvantages of preferred. The decision as to what the company can afford depends on a well-defined rule and not on the whim of the directors. In addition the income bond is a contractual obligation ranking ahead of preferred and common stock. So the tax authorities sometimes allow the company to deduct income bond interest when calculating taxable profits. (However, Canadian income bonds get a dividend tax treatment unless they are issued as part of a corporate reorganization arising from insolvency and have a term of less than five years.)

Therefore, if you believe there is a tax advantage to debt but you are hesitant to run the risks of bankruptcy, income bonds would seem to be the answer. You would think, therefore, that the world ought to be full of them. But it is not. Many income bonds were issued in connection with railroad reorganizations, and a number of fairly small industrial companies have used them to replace their preferred shares. But the only United States company to rely heavily on income bonds was Gamble-Skogmo, which had issued $237 million of them before its acquisition in 1980 by the Wickes Companies, Inc. (Wickes filed for bankruptcy in 1982.)

---

[18]For a further analysis of the initial tax incentives for OID debts, see D. Pyle, "Is Deep Discount Debt Financing a Bargain?" *Chase Financial Quarterly*, **1**:39–61 (1981).

[19]Earnings are usually defined as net of any other debt interest and sinking fund contributions. Sometimes the company may be allowed to deduct preceding years' deficits and to make a contribution to a capital improvement fund.

[20]A good discussion of the attractions of income bonds is provided in J.J. McConnell and G.G. Schlarbaum, "Returns, Risks, and Pricing of Income Bonds, 1956–1976 (Does Money Have an Odor?)," *Journal of Business*, **54**:33–64 (January 1981).

Floating-Rate Bonds

In July 1974, Citicorp, the holding company for Citibank, offered $850 million of notes maturing in 1989. The unusual feature of this huge issue was that the interest rate was set at 1% above the rate on 90-day Treasury bills and was, therefore, free to vary as bill yields varied. Since the bond was long-term debt of the bank holding company, the terms of the offer were not subject to the ceiling on the rate that banks could pay for savings or time deposits. The Citicorp issue was snapped up by investors, and a number of other companies followed suit with similar issues.

The concept of floating-rate debt was by no means new. For example, banks often make floating-rate term loans. In these cases the rate is usually tied to the prime rate—that is, the rate that banks charge their most favoured customers. The unusual feature about the Citicorp issue was the fact that it extended the floating-rate concept to long-term publicly issued bonds.

Is there a general case for issuing floating-rate bonds? One possible answer was suggested in Chapter 21 where we argued that it is riskier to buy a fixed-rate long-term bond than a succession of short-term bonds when inflation is very uncertain, because short interest rates reflect the latest inflation forecasts. Perhaps it makes sense for companies to issue floating-rate bonds in times of uncertain inflation.

Indexed Bonds

Payments on an indexed bond are linked to the rate of inflation. Therefore an indexed bond gives the investor a return that is fixed in real terms. Indexed debt is common in countries that have suffered from persistent inflation. For example, it has been used extensively in France, Israel, Finland, Sweden, the United Kingdom, and many South American countries. Whenever inflation rears its head in the United States, so do proponents of indexed bonds.

Instead of being tied to the general rate of inflation, payments are sometimes indexed to the price of a particular commodity—French Rail, for example, has issued a bond linked to the price of third-class rail travel and that therefore resembles a long-term transferable season ticket. A few United States companies have also sought to limit shareholders' risk by tying bond payments to the price of a particular commodity. For instance, Petro-Lewis has issued a bond whose payments are linked to the price of oil. If the oil price falls, Petro-Lewis's income falls, but this is partly mitigated by a reduction in the cost of its debt.

Should you issue an indexed bond? It could well be popular with pension funds that need protection against inflation, but a sudden increase in the inflation rate could land you in trouble if your earnings do not go up at the same time.[21] But perhaps there are other things you could do. For example, suppose that you issue a package of two bonds. Bond A pays a low rate of interest when inflation is below, say, 5% and a high rate of interest when inflation is above 5%. Bond B does just the opposite; it pays a low rate when inflation is *above* 5% and a high rate when inflation is *below* 5%. Your total interest bill is fixed whatever happens, but the investor who wants the extra protection against inflation can hold bond A and sell bond B to someone who is less worried about inflation or who doesn't mind taking the risk.[22] We have never come across such securities, but they might be popular with investors.

---

[21]The timing of payments on an indexed bond can be advantageous. Payments are likely to be low in the early years and high in the later years. Since the cash inflows on many projects are also low in the early years and high in the later years, the cash payments on an indexed bond may be more closely linked to the firm's income.

[22]For a more general version of this idea see N.H. Hakansson, "The Purchasing Power Fund: A New Kind of Financial Intermediary," *Financial Analysts Journal*, **32**:49–59 (November–December, 1976).

Commodity-Linked Bonds

Occasionally, firms will attempt to reduce the coupon interest rate by offering the bond buyer an opportunity to share in the potential price appreciation of a physical commodity. For example, in 1980, Sunshine Mining Company, the largest United States silver mining operator, issued 8.5% $1,000 par value bonds with 15 years to maturity. At maturity these bonds could be redeemed at the par value or at the price of 50 ounces of silver, whichever was greater.[23]

In this case the buyer of the bond is buying a straight bond plus a call option. Suppose the yield on an otherwise comparable straight bond was 18% at the time of the Sunshine issue. The value of an 8.5% straight bond was therefore about $516. If the Sunshine bonds were issued at par, the bond buyer paid $1,000 − 516 = $484 for the right to buy 50 ounces of silver for $1,000 at the end of 15 years. Was this a reasonable amount to pay for such an option?

The value of the silver option can be estimated using the Black-Scholes call option pricing formula. Suppose the yield on a 15-year government bond was 10% per year and that the standard deviation of silver returns is 20%. The price of silver at the time of issue was $16 an ounce. Thus, the price of the call is determined by the call option formula in Section 20-5:

$$\text{Present value of call} = 800 \, N(d_1) - 1000 e^{-0.1(15)} N(d_2)$$

where

$$d_1 = \{\ln(800/1{,}000) + [0.1 + 0.5(0.2)^2]15\} / 0.2\sqrt{15} \text{ and } d_2 = d_1 - 0.2\sqrt{15}$$

The values of d_1 and d_2 are 2.04 and 1.26, respectively. Using Table 8(b), the values of $N(d_1)$ and $N(d_2)$ are 0.9793 and 0.8962, respectively. The call value is

$$\text{Present value of call} = 800 \, (0.9793) - 1{,}000 \, (0.2231) \, (0.8962) = \$583.50$$

It would appear that the bondholders received a bargain in the sense that the option appears to be worth about $100 more than they paid for it.

QUIZ

1. Select the most appropriate term from within the parentheses:
   (a) (High-grade utility bonds/Low-grade industrial bonds) generally have only light sinking fund requirements.
   (b) (Short-dated notes/Long-dated debentures) are often noncallable.
   (c) Collateral trust bonds are often issued by (utilities/industrial holding companies).
   (d) (Utility bonds/Industrial bonds) are usually unsecured.
   (e) Equipment trust certificates are usually issued by (railroads/financial companies).

2. (a) If interest rates rise, will callable or noncallable bonds fall more in price?
   (b) The Belgian government has issued bonds that may be repaid after a specified date at the option of *either* the government or the bondholder. If each side acts rationally, what will happen on that date?

3. Indicate which of the following sinking funds increase the value of a bond at the time of issue:
   (a) An optional sinking fund operating by drawings at par

---

[23]This example was taken from E.S. Schwartz, "The Pricing of Commodity-Linked Bonds," *Journal of Finance*, **37**:525–539 (May 1982). You first saw it in Section 14-5.

(*b*) A mandatory sinking fund operating by drawings at par *or* by purchases in the market

(*c*) A mandatory sinking fund operating by drawings at par

4. (*a*) As a senior debtholder would you like the company to issue more junior debt, would you prefer it not to do so, or would you not care?

(*b*) You hold debt secured on the company's existing property. Would you like the company to issue more unsecured debt, would you prefer it not to do so, or would you not care?

5. Use the Interprovincial prospectus (but not the text) to answer the following questions:

(*a*) Who are the underwriters of the issue?

(*b*) Who is the trustee for the issue?

(*c*) How many dollars does the company receive for each debenture after the deduction of *all* expenses?

(*d*) Is the debenture "bearer" or "registered"?

(*e*) Does the investor have to collect payment of each coupon?

(*f*) What proportion of the issue is retired each year by the mandatory sinking fund?

(*g*) At what price is the issue callable in 1995?

(*h*) Can the company call the bond in 1995 and replace it with a debenture yielding 7%?

6. Look at the Interprovincial prospectus:

(*a*) How much would you have to pay to buy one bond on January 15, 1985? Don't forget accrued interest.

(*b*) When is the first interest payment on the bond and what is the amount of that payment?

(*c*) On what date do the bonds finally mature and what is the principal amount of the bonds that is due to be repaid that date?

(*d*) Suppose that the market price of the bonds rises to 102 and thereafter does not change. When should the company call the issue?

QUESTIONS AND PROBLEMS

1. After a sharp change in interest rates, newly issued bonds generally sell at yields different from outstanding bonds of the same quality. One suggested explanation is that there is a difference in the value of the call provision. Explain how this could arise.

2. Obtain a prospectus for a recent issue of debentures and compare the terms and conditions with the Interprovincial issue.

3. What restrictions are usually imposed on a company's freedom to issue further debt? Be as precise as possible. Explain carefully the reasons for such restrictions.

4. Explain carefully why senior and subordinated bond indentures place different restrictions on a company's freedom to issue additional debt.

5. An extendible bond is a bond whose maturity may be extended at the investor's option. Sketch a diagram similar to Figure 22-2 showing the relationship between the value of a straight bond and an extendible bond.

6. What determines the value of an indexed bond? Should the rate of interest on an indexed bond be higher or lower than the expected real rate on a nominal bond?

7. Explain carefully why bond indentures place limitations on the following actions:

(*a*) Sale of the company's assets

(*b*) Payment of dividends to shareholders

(*c*) Issue of additional senior debt

8. Look up the terms of a commodity-linked bond (for example, the Petro-Lewis oil bond *or* the International Refining gold bond). Find out what has happened to the payments on these bonds as the commodity price has changed. Have these bonds increased shareholders' risk or reduced it?

9. Suppose that instead of issuing the original issue discount bonds, GMAC had raised the same amount of money by an issue of 14.80% ten-year notes at a price of $100.

(*a*) What face amount of notes would GMAC have needed to issue?

(*b*) Value the gain to GMAC from the issue of OID debt rather than the 14.80% notes. (You may assume either the MM or Miller theory of debt and taxes.)

(*c*) Show that the gain to GMAC disappears if the annual tax deduction is calculated using compound interest rather than simple interest.

10. Does the issue of additional junior debt harm senior bondholders? Would your answer be the same if the junior debt matured *before* the senior debt? Explain.

11. "It does not make any sense to measure a single term structure of risky interest rates, because the structure of risky interest rates is likely to be different for each company." Explain why this is so. Illustrate your answer with examples of why two companies could have different term structures.

WARRANTS AND CONVERTIBLES

In Chapter 22 we looked at bonds, but many debt issues are either packages of bonds and warrants or convertible bonds. The warrant gives its owner the right to buy common stock for cash. A convertible bond gives its owner the right to exchange the bond for stock.

There is also convertible preferred stock—it is often used to finance mergers, for example. Convertible preferred gives its owner the right to exchange the preferred share for common stock.

What are these strange hybrids, and how should you value them? Why are they issued? We will answer each of these questions in its turn.

23-1 WHAT IS A WARRANT?

A significant proportion of private placement bonds (as much as 20% in some recent years)[1] and a smaller proportion of public issues are sold with warrants. In addition, warrants are sometimes attached to issues of common stock or preferred stock or are given to underwriters as compenstion for their services.

Here is an example of a typical issue of warrants. In November 1972, Alta Industries raised $15 million by selling packages of bonds and warrants. Each package consisted of one $7^3/_4$% subordinated debenture due 1992 plus 15 warrants. Each warrant gave the right to buy one share of common stock for $32.75 at any time before January 1978. Since the price of the common at the time of issue was $29, this exercise price was 13% above the initial share price. Each package or "unit" was issued at $1,000.

Occasionally bonds and warrants can be traded only as a package, but the Alta Industries warrants were detachable. This means that they could be traded separately as soon as the issue was distributed. Immediately after issue the bonds sold separately for about $980. Thus the 15 warrants sold for $20, or about $1.33 each.

The warrant holder was not entitled to vote or to receive dividends. But the exercise price of the warrant was adjusted for any stock dividends or splits. For example, if Alta Industries stock had split 2 for 1, the exercise price would automatically have been reduced to $32.75/2 = $16.375.

Most warrant issues resemble that of Alta Industries, but occasionally they are more exotic. In 1984, for example, Lac Minerals Ltd. issued $50 million of 8% $1,000 debentures with each debenture having attached four gold purchase warrants. This type of warrant is unusual because it is not written on the company's common stock. Rather, this warrant provides its holder with the right to buy a physical commodity, specifically 0.5 troy ounces of gold at a purchase price of $230 (U.S.).

But even stock purchase warrants are not without complication. In 1968 Loew's Theaters in the United States acquired Lorillard Corporation. For each share, Loew's offered a subordinated debenture with a face value of $62, plus one warrant. The warrant

---

[1] See E. Shapiro and C.R. Wolf, *The Role of Private Placements in Corporate Finance*, Division of Research, Graduate School of Business Administration, Harvard University, Boston, 1972, p. 61.

entitled its owner to buy one share of Loew's common stock at any time between 1968 and 1980. The exercise price was set at $35.00 for the first four years, $37.50 for the next four years, and $40.00 for the final four years. Also, as an alternative to paying cash, the warrant holder could simply send in an equivalent nominal amount of the debentures. If the debentures were worth less than their face value, this alternative would be more attractive than paying cash.

Valuing Warrants

As a trained option spotter (having read Chapter 20), you have probably already classified the Alta Industries warrant as a five-year American call option exercisable at $32.75. You can depict the relationship between the value of the warrant and the value of the common stock with our standard option shorthand, as in Figure 23-1. The lower limit on the value of the warrant is the heavy line in the figure. If the price of Alta Industries stock is less than $32.75, the lower limit on the warrant price is zero: if the price of the stock is greater than $32.75, the lower limit is equal to the stock price minus $32.75.[2] Investors in warrants sometimes refer to this lower limit as the *theoretical* value of the warrant. It is a misleading term because both theory and practice tell us that before the final exercise date the value of the warrant should lie *above* the lower limit, on a curve like the one shown in Figure 23-1.

The height of this curve depends on two things. As we explained in Section 20-4, it depends on the variance of the stock returns per period (σ^2) times the number of periods before the warrant expires ($\sigma^2 t$). It also depends on the rate of interest times the length of the option period ($r_f t$). If the warrant has no unusual features and the stock pays no dividends, then the value of the option can be estimated from the Black-Scholes formula described in Section 20-5.

Of course as time runs out on a warrant, its price snuggles closer and closer to the lower bound. On the final day of its life, its price hits the lower bound. For the Alta Industries warrant, the final price was zero. On January 16, 1978, the final day of the warrant's life, Alta Industries shares closed well below the exercise price, and so the warrants expired worthless.

Value of
warrant

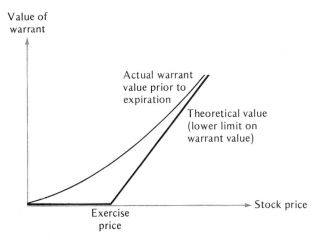

Figure 23-1 Relationship between warrant value and stock price. The heavy line is the lower limit for warrant value. Warrant value falls to the lower limit just before the option expires. Before expiration, warrant value lies on a curve like the one shown here.

---

[2]Do you remember why this is a lower limit? What would happen if, by some accident, the warrant price was *less* than the stock price minus $32.75? (See Section 20-4.)

Two Complications: Dividends and Dilution

Thus far our discussion of warrants has just repeated what was said about call options in Chapter 20, but special problems are often encountered in applying these principles to warrants. For example, we have seen that the exercise price may change over time. Another problem occurs when warrants are issued against dividend-paying stocks. The warrant holder is not entitled to dividends. In fact the warrant holder loses every time a cash dividend is paid, because paying the dividend reduces stock price and thus reduces the value of the warrant. It may pay to exercise the warrant before maturity in order to capture the extra income.[3]

Remember that the Black-Scholes option-valuation formula assumes that the stock pays no dividends. Thus it will not give the theoretically correct value for a warrant issued by a dividend-paying firm.[4]

Another complication is that exercising the warrants increases the number of shares. Therefore, exercise means that the firm's assets and profits are spread over a larger number of shares. For example, Alta Industries' earnings in 1973 were $2.24 per share on an "undiluted" basis (that is, ignoring warrants). If the warrants had been exercised in 1973 and if *total* earnings had been unaffected by the influx of cash from exercise, earnings *per share* would have been only $2.07. In other words, *diluted earnings* per share were $2.07.[5] Firms with significant amounts of warrants or convertible issues outstanding are now required to report earnings on a "fully diluted" basis.

---

[3]This may make sense if the dividend payment is larger than the interest that could be earned on the exercise price. By *not* exercising the warrant holder keeps the exercise price and can put this money to work.

[4]If the warrant holder does not want to lose the dividend, he or she should exercise the warrant just before the stock goes ex-dividend. This suggests a rough-and-ready way to estimate the value of a warrant on a dividend-paying stock. First, use the Black-Scholes formula to check what the warrant would be worth if the only possible exercise date were just before the stock next goes ex-dividend. Next, see whether you would be better off if the only possible exercise date were just before the second ex-dividend date. You can use the Black-Scholes formula to do this if the present value of the *first* dividend is subtracted from the stock price. Repeat this exercise for each ex-dividend date, remembering on each occasion to deduct from the stock price the present value of the dividends missed by not exercising earlier. Since you can in fact choose to exercise your warrant on the most favourable of these dates, the actual value of the warrant should be roughly equal to the highest of your calculated values.

R.E. Whaley, "Valuation of American Call Options on Dividend-Paying Stocks: Empirical Tests," *Journal of Financial Economics*, 10:29–58 (March 1982), p. 32, has shown that this approximation understates the theoretical value of the warrant, although he does so in the context of pricing an American call option on a dividend-paying stock. The degree of underpricing is particularly acute the larger the dividends and the further the warrant is in-the-money. The theoretically correct value of the warrant may be obtained by using a generalization of the American call option formula, which appears in R.E. Whaley, "On the Valuation of American Call Options on Stocks with Known Dividends," *Journal of Financial Economics*, 9:207–211 (June 1981).

[5]Alta Industries' undiluted earnings per share (EPS) for 1973 equal actual 1973 net income ($6.029 million) divided by the average number of shares outstanding in 1973 (2,689,000):

$$EPS = \frac{\$6,029,000}{2,689,000} = \$2.24$$

There were 225,000 warrants outstanding. If they had been converted in 1973, the number of outstanding shares would have increased to 2,689,000 + 225,000 = 2,914,000. EPS would have declined to $2.07:

$$EPS \text{ (diluted)} = \frac{\$6,029,00}{2,914,000} = \$2.07$$

The problem of dilution never arises with call options. If you buy or sell an option on the Toronto Stock Exchange, you have no effect on the assets of the company or the number of shares outstanding.

*Adjusting for Dilution in Valuing Warrants

How does dilution affect warrant price and stock price? We can answer this question by a simple numerical example. Suppose that a firm has 1 million shares outstanding selling at $50 per share. There are also 500,000 warrants about to expire with an exercise price of $40. The warrants are trading at $10 ($50 − $40).

Let us call the *total* market value of the common stock *and* warrants the company's *old equity*:

$$\text{Old equity} = \text{common stock} + \text{warrants}$$
$$= 50(1,000,000) + 10(500,000) = \$55,000,000$$

When the warrants are exercised, the value of equity will increase by the exercise money (500,000 warrants times $40 per warrant, or $20,000,000):

$$\text{New equity} = \text{old equity} + \text{exercise money}$$
$$= \$55,000,000 + \$20,000,000 = \$75,000,000$$

After exercise the former warrant holder will own one-third of the outstanding shares. Therefore their investment will be worth

$$\frac{1}{3}\,(\text{new equity}) = \frac{1}{3}\,(\text{old equity} + \text{exercise money})$$

$$= \frac{1}{3}\,(75,000,000) = \$25,000,000$$

Of course, it pays to exercise, because $25 million exceeds the exercise money ($20 million) that the warrant holders have to put up. They gain $5 million, or $10 per warrant, by exercising rather than letting the options expire. This is why the warrants are worth $10 just before the expiration date.

Note also that the price per share is unchanged by exercise. After exercise there will be 1,500,000 shares outstanding, and stock price is

$$\frac{\text{New equity}}{1,500,000} = \frac{\$75,000,000}{1,500,000} = \$50$$

The general rule for deciding whether to exercise is to exercise if

$$\frac{N_w}{N + N_w}(\text{old equity} + \text{exercise money}) \; exceeds \; \text{exercise money}$$

where N_w is the number of shares warrant holders can purchase and N is the number of shares if the warrants are not exercised. The expression $N_w/(N + N_w)$ is the proportion of outstanding shares held by (former) warrant holders if all of them exercise. In our example, $N_W/(N + N_W) = 500,000/1,500,000 = 1/3$.

We can rearrange this expression. Exercise if

$$\frac{N_W}{N + N_W}(\text{old equity}) \; \textit{exceeds} \; \frac{N}{N + N_W}(\text{exercise money})$$

In our example, it pays to exercise if

$$\frac{1}{3}(\text{old equity}) \; \textit{exceeds} \; \frac{2}{3}(\text{exercise money})$$

Thus, instead of thinking of these warrants as options to buy one-third of the *common stock*, it is more correct to think of them as options to buy one-third of the old *equity* (that is, stock and warrants). And, instead of thinking of the warrants' owners as having to pay over the whole of the exercise money, it is more correct to think of them as paying two-thirds of the exercise money. In the Black-Scholes option formula, the ratio of asset price to exercise price (P/EX) should not be[6]

$$\frac{\text{Value of common stock}}{\text{Warrant exercise money}}$$

but

$$\frac{P}{\text{EX}} = \frac{1/3 \; \text{old equity}}{2/3 \; \text{exercise money}}$$

In general, set

$$\frac{P}{\text{EX}} = \frac{[N_W/(N + N_W)] \times \text{old equity}}{[N/(N + N_W)] \times \text{exercise money}} = \frac{N_W \times \text{old equity}}{N \times \text{exercise money}}$$

The variance rate σ^2 used in the Black-Scholes formula should be the variance of old equity (common stock plus warrants), not the variance of common stock alone.

Note that the expression for P/EX for use in the Black-Scholes formula depends on old equity, which is defined as the value of a portfolio of all outstanding shares *and warrants*. It may seem as if you need to know what the warrants are worth in order to compute their value! But that is not quite right. The formula does not call for warrant value but for the value of *equity*. Given equity value, the formula calculates how the overall value of equity should be split up between stock and warrants. Thus, the formula could be used to check whether an observed warrant price matches its estimated value. Or, suppose that your underwriter advises you that $1 million extra could be raised by issuing a package of bonds and warrants rather than the bonds alone. Is this a fair price?

---

[6]See F. Black and M. Scholes, "The Pricing of Options and Corporate Liabilities," *Journal of Political Economy*, 81:637–654 (May–June 1973), pp. 648, 649. Note that these modifications are necessary to apply the Black-Scholes formula. They are not really needed by the warrant holder, who simply has to decide whether to exercise at maturity. If using the formula given in the text, P/EX is greater than one, then the price of the stock will exceed the exercise price of the warrant, and the warrant holder will of course exercise.

You could check using the Black-Scholes formula. The value of "old equity" used in the formula would be the market value of presently outstanding shares plus $1 million.

Warrants on Bonds

Most warrants are changeable into common stock, but some companies have issued warrants on bonds. For example, in 1982, Citicorp, a holding company for the second-largest bank in the United States sold 100,000 warrants that gave the option to buy 11% seven-year Citicorp notes at any time within the next three years.

The Black-Scholes option model will give a rough measure of the value of these Citicorp warrants. However, it doesn't make much sense to assume that the short-term interest rate is constant, while at the same time assuming that the price of the Citicorp notes can fluctuate. So, if you want an accurate estimate of the value of the warrants, you need to use a more elaborate version of the model that takes account of changes in the short-term interest rate.[7]

23-2 WHAT IS A CONVERTIBLE BOND?

The convertible bond is a close relative to the bond-warrant package. Also, many companies choose to issue convertible preferred as an alternative to issuing packages of preferred stock and warrants. We will concentrate on convertible bonds, but almost all our comments also apply to convertible preferred issues.

Here is an example of a convertible bond. In 1981 John Labatt Limited issued $47 million of 11% convertible subordinated debentures, due in the year 2001. The issue is in many respects similar to any other junior debenture. It has a sinking fund, and it is callable at a premium after three years. The special feature of the issue is that the debenture can be converted at any time up to and including June 1, 1991 into approximately 31.621 (that is $1,000 par value of bond/$31.625 stated share price) Class A common shares. In other words, the owner has at any time up until June 1991 the option to return the debenture to Labatt and receive 31.621 shares of Labatt stock in exchange. The number of shares received for each debenture is called the debenture's *conversion ratio*. The conversion ratio of this Labatt debenture is 31.621.

The conversion ratio for the Labatt debenture was computed on the basis of the face value of the bond and the *conversion price* for the shares, both terms stated in the bond's indenture. In order to receive the shares of Labatt stock, you had to surrender debentures with a face value of $1,000. This $1,000 could be applied to the purchase of common shares at a conversion price of $31.625 per share. Therefore the conversion ratio for this Labatt issue is $1,000/$31.625 or approximately 31.621.

At the time of issue the price of Labatt stock was about $28. Therefore the conversion price was about 13% greater than the stock price. This may be slightly lower than usual. A more typical spread between the conversion price and the stock price at issue would be 20% of the stock price.

Convertibles are usually protected against stock splits or dividends. For example, if Labatt paid a 10% stock dividend in June 1987, the conversion price would decrease from $31.625 to $28.75. Thus the conversion ratio would increase from 31.621 to approximately 34.782.

---

[7]The following authors have developed more elaborate versions of the Black-Scholes model that can be used for pricing warrants on bonds: G. Courtadon, "The Pricing of Options on Default-Free Bonds," *Journal of Financial and Quantitative Analysis*, **17**:75–100 (March 1982); and M.J. Brennan and E.S. Schwartz, "Alternative Methods for Valuing Debt Options," Working Paper 888, Faculty of Commerce and Business Administration, University of British Columbia, June 1982.

The Labatt convertible is a fairly typical issue, but you can come across more complicated cases. Often the conversion price is stepped up over time. Litton Industries in the United States, on the other hand, once issued a convertible in which the conversion price was stepped down. Occasionally the owner must surrender the bond and pay a cash conversion fee in order to receive the common stock.

Valuing Convertible Bonds

The owner of a convertible bond owns a bond and a call option on the firm's stock. So does the owner of a bond-warrant package. There are differences, of course, the most important being the requirement that a convertible owner give up the bond in order to exercise the call option. The owner of a bond-warrant package can exercise the warrant for cash and keep the bond. Nevertheless, understanding convertibles is easier if you analyze them first as bonds and then as call options.

The price of a convertible bond depends on its *bond value* and its *conversion value*. The bond value is what the bond would sell for if it could *not* be converted. The conversion is what the bond would sell for if it had to be converted immediately.

How would we compute the Labatt convertible's bond value? This clearly depends on the general level of interest rates and investor's perceptions of the risk of default. Suppose that we catch this convertible at a time when similar nonconvertible issues are yielding 12%. Also suppose that the Labatt convertible has a remaining maturity of 16 years. Then its bond value is found by discounting the $110 coupon and the final $1,000 principal repayment at 12%:

$$\text{Bond value} = \sum_{t=1}^{16} \frac{\$110}{(1.12)^t} + \frac{\$1,000}{(1.12)^{16}} = \$930.26 \text{ or about } \$930$$

Bond value establishes a "floor" or lower bound to the price of a convertible issue. But the height of the floor depends on how well the issuing firm is doing. If it falls on hard times the bonds may not be worth very much. Figure 23-2(*a*) illustrates this by plotting bond value against firm value. Note that low firm values and low bond prices go together; that "floor" can have a nasty slope. In the worst case, when the firm is worthless, its bonds are also worthless. On the other hand, bond value increases if the firm does well. The upper limit to the bond value is what it would be worth if the probability of default were zero.

Conversion value is the value of the bond if holders converted it immediately. Investors usually calculate conversion value by multiplying the stock price by the number of shares into which each bond can be converted. The Labatt bond can be converted into 31.621 shares. Thus, if the stock price is $35, conversion value is $31.621 \times \$35 = \$1,107$. Figure 23-2(*b*) shows that conversion value rises in line with the value of the firm.

A convertible can *never sell for less* than its conversion value. If it did, smart investors would buy the convertible, exchange it for stock, and sell the stock. Their profit would be equal to the difference between the conversion value and the price of the convertible.

Therefore there are *two* lower bounds to the price of any convertible: its bond value and its conversion value. The heavy line in Figure 23-2(*c*) shows their combined effect. When the firm does well, conversion value exceeds bond value; the investor would choose to convert if forced to make an immediate choice. Thus the convertible's value must at least equal its conversion value.

Bond value exceeds conversion value when the firm does poorly and firm value is low. The owners of the convertible issue would hold on to their bonds if forced to

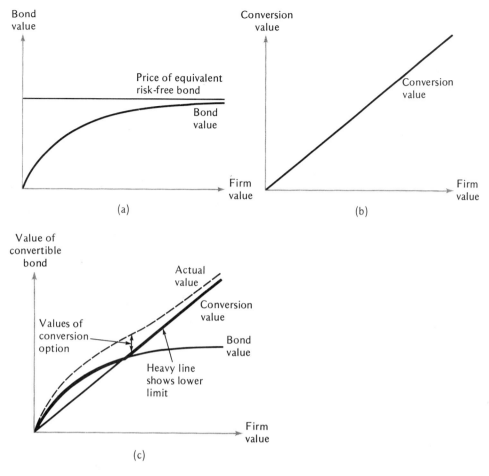

Figure 23-2 (*a*) As the market value of the firm increases, debt is better secured and bond prices rise. Thus if the firm does extremely well, the bond value of a convertible approaches the price of an equivalent nonconvertible bond with no risk of default. On the other hand, bond values fall sharply if the firm's value falls to a very low level. (*b*) Conversion value (the value of a convertible bond if converted immediately) rises in proportion to firm value. (*c*) Value of a convertible bond as a function of firm value. The heavy line shows the lower limit to the value of a convertible bond: either bond value or conversion value, whichever is larger. The actual value of the bond exceeds the lower limit (except at maturity). The difference between the dashed line and the heavy line is the value of the conversion option.

make an immediate decision for or against conversion. In this case bond value is the effective lower bound.

Of course convertible bondholders *do not have to make a now-or-never choice for or against conversion.* They can wait, and then, with the benefit of hindsight, take whatever course turns out to give them highest payoff. Thus a convertible is always worth *more* than its lower-bound value (except when time runs out at the bond's maturity). Its actual selling price will behave as shown by the dashed line in Figure 23-2(*c*). The difference between the dashed line and the lower bound is the value of a call option on the firm. Remember, however, that this option can only be exercised by giving up the bond. In other words, the option to convert is a call option with an exercise price equal to the bond value.

Dividends and Dilution Revisited

If you want to value a convertible, it is easiest to break the problem down into two parts. First estimate bond value, then add the value of the conversion option.

When you value the conversion option, you need to look out for the same things that make warrants more tricky to value than traded options. For example, you must remember that the convertible owner is missing out on the dividends on the common stock. If these dividends are higher than the interest on the bonds, it may pay to convert before the final exercise date in order to pick up the extra cash income.

Dilution may also be important. If the debentures are converted, the company saves on its interest payments and is relieved of having to eventually repay the loan; on the other hand, net profits have to be divided among a large number of shares.[8] Companies are obliged to show in their statements how conversion affects earnings per share if the savings on interest are not sufficient to offset the increase in the number of shares. That is, if fully diluted earnings per share are less than undiluted earnings, both numbers must appear in the financial statements.

Forcing Conversion

Most convertible bonds are callable at a premium. If the company calls the bond, the owner has a brief period, usually about 30 days, within which to either convert the bond or surrender it. If the bond is surrendered, the investor receives the call price in cash.

Calling the bond obviously does not affect the total size of the company pie, but it can affect the size of the individual slices. In other words, conversion has no effect on the total value of the firm's assets, but it does affect how asset value is *distributed* among the different classes of security holders. Therefore, if you want to maximize your shareholders' slice of the pie, you must minimize the convertible bondholders'. That means you must not call the bonds if they are worth *less* than the call price, for that would be giving the bondholders an unnecessary present. Similarly, you must not allow the bonds to remain uncalled if their value is *above* the call price, for that would not be minimizing the value of the bonds. Therefore the rule for calling a convertible debenture is exactly the same as the rule for calling any other bond: *Call the bond when, and only when, its value reaches the call price.*

Managers are fickle creatures. No sooner do they issue convertibles, than they seem to want to get rid of them. They often complain of "overhanging" convertibles—that is, ones that are not being converted. They feel that overhanging convertibles limit their freedom of action. In view of these complaints, you might expect that managers would be only too eager to call their convertibles. But Ingersoll has found that in practice it is just the reverse. Firms seldom call their convertibles until they are worth much *more* than the call price. For example, Ingersoll looked at 124 firms that called their convertible debentures between 1968 and 1975. All but six delayed the call too

---

[8]Thus investors are imprecise when they calculate conversion value as the share price times the number of shares into which each bond is converted. A convertible bond actually gives an option to acquire a fraction of the "new equity"—the equity *after* conversion. When conversion occurs the *total* value of equity (price per share times number of outstanding shares) is increased because one of the firm's debt liabilities is extinguished. On the other hand, the number of shares is increased. If conversion is worthwhile, price per share is less than it would be if the conversion option did not exist. Any formal valuation model for convertible bonds has to take this effect into account. The adjustments would be similar to those for warrants, presented earlier in this chapter. For example, the horizontal axis in Figure 23-2 really refers to the portion of the value of the common stock and convertible to which each convertible debenture is entitled.

Table 23-1 Convertible bonds outstanding at year-end 1978 with high conversion values relative to call price.

Issuing Firm	Coupon	Maturity	Call Price	Conversion Value
Allied Artists	8.75	1987	103.01	161
Allied Stores	4.50	1981	100.38	$161\frac{1}{4}$
Baxter-Travenol	4.00	1987	100.88	$231\frac{7}{8}$
Black & Decker	4.00	1992	101.80	$163\frac{1}{4}$
Circle K. Corp.	6.00	1981	101.00	$398\frac{5}{8}$
Hilton Hotels	5.50	1995	103.05	$317\frac{1}{8}$
Ramada Inns	8.00	1995	104.80	$129\frac{1}{8}$
Standex International	5.00	1987	102.25	$179\frac{3}{8}$
UAL, Inc.	8.00	2003	107.60	$138\frac{1}{4}$
Union Pacific	4.75	1999	101.59	$184\frac{5}{8}$

Notes:
1. Data as of December 1978, from Moody's *Bond Record.*
2. All issues except the Union Pacific are convertible subordinated debentures. The Union Pacific issue is not subordinated.
3. Coupons, call prices, and conversion values are given as percentages of par value.

long, and the typical company waited until conversion value was 44% above the call price.[9]

Table 23-1 shows several convertible issues outstanding in the United States at the end of 1978. Each of the issues has current conversion value well above the current call price. Therefore these companies could have called the bonds and forced conversion. Finance theory implies they should have done so. The reason for firms' reluctance to call convertibles is not known.

Of course Table 23-1 is not a random sample of convertible issues. We chose extreme cases to illustrate a point. We could have presented another table of convertible issues with conversion values well below call prices.

23-3 THE DIFFERENCE BETWEEN WARRANTS AND CONVERTIBLES

We have dwelt on the basic similarity between warrants and convertibles. Now let us look at some of the differences.

1. *Warrants are usually issued privately.* Packages of bonds with warrants or preferred stock with warrants tend to be more common in private placements. By contrast, most convertible bonds or preferreds are issued publicly.

2. *Warrants can be detached.* When you buy a convertible, the bond and the option are bundled up together. You cannot sell them separately. This may be inconvenient. If your tax position or attitude to risk inclines you to bonds, you may not want to hold options as well. Sometimes warrants are also "nondetachable." But usually you can keep the bond and sell off the warrant.

3. *Warrants may be issued on their own.* Warrants do not have to be issued in conjunction with other securities. Often they are used to compensate investment bankers for

---

[9]J.E. Ingersoll, "An Examination of Corporate Call Policies on Convertible Securities," *Journal of Finance*, **32**:463–478 (May 1977).

underwriting services. Many companies also give their executives long-term options to buy stock. These executive stock options are not usually called warrants but that is exactly what they are. Companies rarely sell warrants directly to investors for cash (except as part of a package), but there is no reason that they shouldn't and some people think it would be a good idea.

4. *Warrants are exercised for cash.* When you exercise warrants, you generally put up extra cash. When you convert a debenture, you simply exchange your bond for common stock. Therefore bond-warrant packages and convertible bonds have different effects on the company's cash flow and on its capital structure.

5. *Receipts from warrants may be taxable.* There is an important tax difference between warrants and convertibles. When a company issues a package of bonds and warrants, the value of each of the two instruments is written into the prospectus. If the warrants subsequently expire without being exercised, Revenue Canada will generally insist that the company treat the money that is received for the warrants as capital gain.[10] Therefore, if a company issues warrants, it may later have to pay tax on one-half of their value. This is an odd rule, completely inconsistent with the tax treatment of other securities. If your firm issues a convertible bond, but the conversion option subsequently proves worthless, is the firm taxed on the amount investors originally paid for the conversion option? No. If it issues *any* other kind of security, which later declines in value, is the investor's capital loss treated as taxable income to the firm? No.

6. *You cannot call warrants.* Suppose that a company issues a bond-warrant package and then several years later decides that it would like to tidy up its financial structure by getting rid of the warrants. It may be able to call the *bonds* but it cannot usually call the warrants.[11] It can raise the dividend on the stock and try to force exercise that way. Or it can tempt the warrant holders by a temporary reduction in the exercise price. The company that issues a convertible debenture has a much simpler way to extinguish the conversion option. It just calls the bond.

23-4 WHY DO COMPANIES ISSUE WARRANTS AND CONVERTIBLES?

You hear many arguments for issuing warrants and convertibles but most of them have a "Heads I win, tails you lose" flavour.[12] Several surveys have also been made of companies that issue convertibles.[13] They have revealed two main motives for the choice of financing. A large number of managers look on convertibles as "cheap debt." A somewhat higher proportion regard them as a deferred sale of stock at an attractive price.

We have seen that a convertible is like a package of a straight bond and an option. The difference between the market value of the convertible and that of the straight

---

[10]The Internal Revenue Service in the United States deems the money received from unexercised warrants to be ordinary income at the time the warrant expires.

[11]A small fraction of warrant issues is callable.

[12]For examples, refer back to our discussion in Section 20-3 of the alleged advantages of warrants.

[13]See, for example, E.F. Brigham, "An Analysis of Convertible Debentures: Theory and Some Empirical Evidence," *Journal of Finance* 23:35–54 (March 1966).

---

bond is therefore the price investors place on the call option. The convertible is "cheap" only if this price overvalues the option.

What then of the other managers—those who regard the issue as a deferred sale of common stock? A convertible bond gives you the right to buy stock by giving up a bond.[14] Bondholders may decide to do this, but then again they may not. Thus issue of a convertible bond *may* amount to a deferred stock issue. But if the firm *needs* equity capital, a convertible issue is an unreliable way of getting it.

Taken at their face value the motives of management are irrational. Convertibles are not just cheap debt nor are they a deferred sale of stock. But we suspect that these simple phrases encapsulate some more complex and rational motives.

Notice that convertibles tend to be issued by the smaller and more speculative firms. They are almost invariably unsecured and generally subordinated. Now put yourself in the position of a potential investor. You are approached by a small firm with an untried product line that wants to issue some junior unsecured debt. You know that, if things go well, you will get your money back but, if they do not, you could easily be left with nothing. Since the firm is in a new line of business, it is very difficult to assess the chances of trouble. Therefore you don't know what the fair rate of interest is. Also, you may be worried that once you have made the loan, management will be tempted to run extra risks. It may borrow additional senior debt or it may decide to expand its operations and go for broke on your money.[15] In fact, if you charge a very high rate of interest, you could be encouraging this to happen. What can management do to protect you against a misestimate of the risk and to assure you that its intentions are honourable? In crude terms, it can give you a piece of the action. You don't mind the company running unanticipated risks, as long as you share in the gains as well as the losses.

Convertible securities and warrants make sense whenever it is unusually costly to assess the risk of debt or whenever investors are worried that management may not act in the bondholders' interest.

The relatively low coupon rate on convertible bonds may also be a convenience for rapidly growing firms facing heavy capital expenditures. They may be willing to give up the conversion option to reduce immediate cash requirements for debt service. Without the conversion option, lenders might demand extremely high (promised) interest to compensate for the probability of default. This would not only force the firm to raise still more capital to pay for debt service, it would increase the risk of financial distress. Paradoxically, lenders' attempts to protect themselves against default may actually increase the probability of financial distress by increasing the burden of debt service on the firm.[16]

---

[14]That is much the same as already having the stock together with the right to sell it for the convertible's bond value. In other words, instead of thinking of a convertible as a bond plus a call option, you could think of it as the stock plus a put option. Now you see why it is wrong to think of a convertible as equivalent to the sale of stock: it is equivalent to the sale of both stock *and* a put option. If there is any possibility that investors will want to hold on to their bond, the put option will have some value.

[15]D. Galai and R.W. Masulis discuss the potential conflicts of interest between bondholders and stockholders. These conflicts are most serious when debt is risky (that is, when the probability of default is high). Some scholars believe this effect puts an absolute limit on the amount of ordinary (nonconvertible) debt the firm can issue. See their article, "The Option Pricing Model and the Risk Factor of Stock," *Journal of Financial Economics,* **3**:53–82 (1976).

[16]This fact led to an extensive literature on "credit rationing." A lender rations credit if it is irrational to lend more to a firm regardless of the interest rate the firm is willing to *promise* to pay. Whether this can happen in efficient, competitive capital markets is controversial. For a review of this literature see E. Baltensperger, "Credit Rationing: Issues and Questions," *Journal of Money, Credit and Banking,* **10**:170–183 (May 1978).

23-5   SUMMARY

Instead of issuing straight bonds, companies may sell either packages of bonds and warrants or convertible bonds.

A warrant is just a long-term call option issued by the company. You already know a good deal about valuing call options. You know from Chapter 20 that call options must be worth at least as much as the stock price less the exercise price. You know that their value is greatest when they have a long time to expiration, when the underlying stock is risky, and when the interest rate is high.

Warrants are somewhat trickier to evaluate than the call options that are traded on the options exchanges. First, because they are long-term options, it is important to take into account the fact that the warrant holder does not receive any dividends. Second, dilution must be allowed for.

A convertible bond gives its holder the right to swap the bond for common stock. The rate of exchange is usually measured by the *conversion ratio*—that is, the number of shares that the investor gets for each bond. Sometimes the rate of exchange is expressed in terms of the *conversion price*—that is the face value of the bond that must be given up in order to receive one share.

Convertibles are like a package of a bond and a call option. When you evaluate the conversion option you must again remember that the convertible holder does not receive dividends and that conversion results in dilution of the common stock. There are two other things to watch out for. One is the problem of default risk. If the company runs into trouble, you may not only have a worthless conversion option, you may also have a worthless bond. Second, the company may be able to force conversion by calling the bond. It should do this as soon as the market price of the convertible reaches the call price. Many companies do not call their bonds until well after this point. Nobody knows why.

You hear a variety of arguments for issuing warrants or convertibles. Convertible bonds and bonds with warrants are almost always junior bonds and are frequently issued by risky companies. We think this says something about the reasons for their issue. Suppose that you are lending subordinated debt to a untried company. You are worried that the company may turn out to be riskier than you thought or that it may issue additional senior bonds. You can try to protect yourself against such eventualities by imposing very restrictive conditions on the debt, but it is often simpler to say that you don't mind the company taking some extra risk as long as you get a piece of the action. The convertible and bond-warrant package give you a chance to participate in the firm's successes as well as its failures. They diminish the possible conflicts of interest between bondholder and stockholder.

FURTHER READING

The items listed in Chapter 20 under "Further Reading" are also relevant to this chapter, in particular Black and Scholes's discussion of warrant valuation and Roll, Geske, and Whaley's discussion of American call option valuation.

Ingersoll's work represents the "state of the art" in valuing convertibles:

J.E. Ingersoll, "A Contingent Claims Valuation of Convertible Securities." *Journal of Financial Economics*, **4**:289–322 (May 1977).

Ingersoll also examines corporate call policies on convertible bonds in:

J.E. Ingersoll, "An Examination of Corporate Call Policies on Convertible Securities," *Journal of Finance*, **32**:463–478 (May 1977).

Brennan and Schwartz's paper was written at about the same time as Ingersoll's and reaches essentially the same conclusions. They also present a general procedure for valuing convertibles.

M.J. Brennan and E.S. Schwartz, "Convertible Bonds: Valuation and Optimal Strategies for Call and Conversion," *Journal of Finance*, **32**:1699–1715 (December 1977).

Two useful articles on warrants are:

E.S. Schwartz, "The Valuation of Warrants: Implementing a New Approach," *Journal of Financial Economics*, **4**:79–93 (January 1977).
D. Galai and M.A. Schneller, "Pricing of Warrants and the Value of the Firm," *Journal of Finance*, **33**:1333–1342 (December 1978).

For a nontechnical discussion of the pricing of convertibles and the reasons for their use, see:

M.J. Brennan and E.S. Schwartz, "The Case for Convertibles," *Chase Financial Quarterly*, **1**:27–46 (Spring 1982).

QUIZ

1. Associated Elk warrants entitle the owner to buy one share at $40.
   (*a*) What is the theoretical value of the warrant if the stock price is
      (i) $20?
      (ii) $30?
      (iii) $40?
      (iv) $50?
      (v) $60?
   (*b*) Plot the theoretical value of the warrant against the stock price.
   (*c*) Suppose the stock price is $60 and the warrant price is five dollars. What would you do?

2. In 1984 BC Sugar Refinery issued one-half million warrants attached to a 1 million share common stock issue. Each warrant can be exercised before 1988 at a price of $25 per share. Suppose the current share price is $23.00.
   (*a*) Does the warrant holder have a vote?
   (*b*) Does the warrant holder receive dividends?
   (*c*) If the stock were to split 5-for-1, how would the exercise price be adjusted?
   (*d*) Suppose that, instead of reducing the exercise price after the 5-for-1 split, the company gave each warrant holder the right to buy *five* shares at $25 apiece. Would this have the same effect?
   (*e*) Is there any benefit to exercising the warrant today?
   (*f*) If there is no benefit to exercising the warrant today, does that mean the current warrant price should be equal to zero?
   (*g*) *Other things being equal,* would the warrant be more or less valuable if:
      (i) The company increased its dividend payout rate?
      (ii) The interest rate declined?
      (iii) The stock became riskier?
      (iv) The company extended the exercise period?
      (v) The company reduced the exercise price?
   (*h*) A few companies issued perpetual warrants (that is, warrants with no final exercise date). Suppose that the BC Sugar warrants are perpetual. In what circumstances might it make sense for investors to exercise their warrants?

3. Amalgamated Sludge has outstanding 10 million warrants, each of which may be converted into one share of common stock. Assume

Net income = $40 million
Number of shares outstanding = 20 million

(a) Calculate earnings per share.
(b) Calculate earnings per share on a fully diluted basis.

4. Suppose that Maple Aircraft has issued a $4^3/_4$% convertible subordinated debenture due 1993. The conversion price is $47.00 and the debenture is callable at 102.75. The market price of the convertible is 91% of face value and the price of the common is $41.50. Assume the value of the bond in the absence of a conversion feature is about 65% of face value.

(a) What is the conversion ratio of the debenture?
(b) If the conversion ratio were 50, what would be the conversion price?
(c) What is the conversion value?
(d) At what stock price is the conversion value equal to the bond value?
(e) Can the market price be less than the conversion value?
(f) How much is the convertible holder paying for the option to buy one share of common stock?
(g) By how much does the common have to rise by 1993 to justify conversion?
(h) When should Maple call the debenture?

QUESTIONS AND PROBLEMS

1. Refer again to the Alta Industries warrant discussed in Section 23-1. Alta Industries had approximately 2.7 million shares and 225,000 warrants outstanding. The warrant's exercise price was $32.75.

(a) Suppose that Alta Industries' stock price had been $40 per share just before expiration. What would the warrants have sold for? Is this the warrants' theoretical value?
(b) Suppose that stock price had been $40 per share a year *prior* to expiration. Would the warrants have sold for more or less than your answer to (a)? Would they have sold for their theoretical value? Explain.
(c) Suppose that Alta Industries' undiluted earnings had been $3 per share in 1973. Calculate its diluted earnings per share.

*2. Describe how you would use the Black-Scholes formula to compute the value of the Alta Industries warrant a year before its expiration, assuming a stock price of $40 and a warrant price of $15. What ratio of exercise price to stock price would you use in the formula? Is this significantly different from $32.75/40 = 0.82$?

3. Occasionally firms extend the life of warrants that would otherwise expire unexercised. What is the cost of doing this? Could such an extension be rational despite the cost? (*Hint*: See point 5, Section 23-3.)

*4. Here's a question on dilution. The Electric Bassoon Company has outstanding 2,000 shares with a total market value of $20,000 *plus* 1,000 warants with a total market value of $5,000. Each warrant gives its holders the option to buy one share at $20. We define the company's "old equity" as the shares plus warrants.

(a) What is the current market value of the old equity?
(b) What is the total amount of exercise money?
(c) If the warrants are exercised, what proportion of the market value of the old equity plus exercise money is held by the former warrant holders?

(d) Complete the following sentence: "The Electric Bassoon warrant holders will exercise if their proportion of the old equity *and of the exercise money is greater* than . . ."

(e) Another way to express the previous statement is that the Electric Bassoon warrant holders will exercise if their proportion (x) of the old equity is greater than a certain proportion (y) of the exercise money. In the case of the Electric Bassoon Company, what are x and y?

(f) How much will their share of the old equity have to be worth before they will exercise?

(g) What is their share of the old equity *currently* worth?

(h) By how much must the old equity increase before the warrant holders can exercise at a profit?

5. The Surplus Value Company had $10 million (face value) of convertible bonds outstanding in 1980. Each bond has the following features:

Conversion price	$25
Current call price	105 (percent of face value)
Current trading price	130 (percent of face value)
Maturity	1990
Current stock price	$30 (per share)
Interest rate	10 (coupon as percent of face value)

(a) What is the bond's conversion value?

(b) Can you explain why the bond is selling above conversion value?

6. Growth-Tech has issued $10 million of a 10% subordinated convertible debenture. Assume:

Net income = $50 million
Number of shares outstanding = 2.5 million
Conversion ratio = 50
Tax rate = 50%

(a) Calculate earnings per share.

(b) Calculate earnings per share on a fully diluted basis.

7. Associated Elk warrants have an exercise price of $40. The share price is $50. The dividend on the stock is $3 and the interest rate is 10%.

(a) Would you exercise your warrants now or later? State why.

(b) If the dividend increased to $5, it could pay to exercise now if the stock price had low variability and it could be better to exercise later if the stock price had high variability. Explain why.

8. "The company's decision to issue warrants should depend on the management's forecast of likely returns on the stock." Do you agree?

9. In each case, state which of the two securities is likely to provide the higher return:

(a) When the stock price rises (stock *or* convertible bond?).

(b) When interest rates fall (straight bond *or* convertible bond?).

(c) When the specific risk of the stock decreases (straight bond *or* convertible bond?).

(d) When the dividend on the stock increases (stock *or* convertible bond?).

10. Towncorp has issued three-year warrants to buy 12% perpetual debentures at a price of 120%. The current interest rate is 12% and the standard deviation of returns on the bond is 20%. Use the Black-Scholes model to obtain a rough estimate of the value of Towncorp warrants.

11. Moose Stores has outstanding 1 million shares of common stock with a total market value of $40 million. It now announces a rights issue of 1 million warrants at $5 each. Each warrant entitles the owner to buy one Moose share for a price of $30 at any time within the next five years. Moose Stores has stated that it will not pay a dividend within this period.

    The standard deviation of the returns on Moose's equity is 20% a year, and the interest rate is 8%.

    (*a*) What is the market value of each warrant?

    (*b*) What is the market value of each share after the warrant issue? (*Hint*: The value of the shares is equal to the total value of the equity less the value of the warrants.)

12. Look again at question 11. Suppose that Moose now forecasts the following dividend payments:

End Year	Dividend
1	$2.00
2	3.00
3	4.00
4	5.00
5	6.00

    Reestimate the market values of the warrant and stock.

13. Occasionally it is said that issuing convertible bonds is better than issuing stock when the firm's shares are undervalued. Suppose that the financial manager of the Butternut Furniture Company does in fact have inside information indicating that the Butternut stock price is too low. Butternut's future earnings will in fact be higher than investors expect. Suppose further that the inside information cannot be released without giving away a valuable competitive secret. Clearly selling shares at the present low price would harm Butternut's existing shareholders. Will they also lose if convertible bonds are issued? If they do lose in this case, is the loss more or less than if common stock is issued?

    Now suppose that investors forecast earnings accurately, but still undervalue the stock because they overestimate Butternut's actual business risk. Does this change your answers to the questions posed in the preceding paragraph? Explain.

14. Banks or insurance companies sometimes negotiate "equity kickers" when lending money. The firm pays interest and also gives warrants to the lender. Thus the lender has an equity interest in the firm (via the warrants) and shares in the rewards if the firm is successful. Of course, in negotiating the loan, the lender always has the alternative of forgoing the warrants and demanding a higher interest rate instead. What are the advantages of the "equity kicker" arrangement compared to this alternative? In what circumstances would use of the equity kicker be more sensible?

15. In April 1984 Lac Minerals attached gold purchase warrants to a debenture issue. The warrant provides the right to buy 0.5 ounces of gold at an exercise price of $230 at any time up to and including April 1989. If the riskless rate of interest was 10% at that time, the standard deviation of the rate of return on gold 30% and the market price of gold $300 per ounce (that is, $150 per 0.5 ounces), what was the approximate value of the gold purchase warrant? (*Hint*: An investment in gold is like an investment in a non-dividend-paying stock, so an American call option on gold may be priced using the European call option formula.)

LEASING

CHAPTER 24

Most of us occasionally rent a car, bicycle, or boat. Usually such personal rentals are short-lived—we may rent a car for a day or week. But in corporate finance longer-term rentals are common. A rental agreement that extends for a year or more and involves a series of fixed payments is called a **lease**.

Firms lease as an alternative to buying capital equipment. Computers are often leased; so are trucks, railroad cars, aircraft, and ships. Just about every kind of asset has been leased sometime by somebody, including electric power plants, nuclear fuel, handball courts, and zoo animals.

Every lease involves two parties. The *user* of the asset is called the *lessee*. The lessee makes periodic payments to the *owner* of the asset, who is called the *lessor*. For example, if you sign an agreement to rent an apartment for a year, you are the lessee and the owner is the lessor.

You often see references to the *leasing industry*. This refers to lessors. (Almost all firms are lessees to at least a minor extent). Who are the lessors?

The largest group of lessors is equipment manufacturers. For example, GATX is the largest lessor of railcars (it leased about 58,000 cars at the end of 1982); IBM is the largest lessor of computers, and Xerox is the largest lessor of copiers.

Banks are the second largest group. They account for roughly one-third of the dollar volume of leased assets, versus about one-half for equipment manufacturers. Most of the remaining volume is accounted for by independent leasing companies.

The independent leasing companies offer a variety of services. Some act as lease brokers (arranging lease deals) as well as lessors. Others specialize in leasing automobiles, trucks, and standardized industrial equipment; they succeed because they can buy equipment in quantity, service it efficiently, and if necessary resell it at a good price. Independent computer leasing companies got started because some people believed that IBM's leasing charges were too high. Computer leasing companies buy equipment, mainly from IBM, and lease it to computer users at rates below IBM's.

24-1 WHAT IS A LEASE?

Leases come in many forms, but in all cases the lessee (user) promises to make a series of payments to the lessor (owner). The lease contract specifies the monthly or semi-annual payments, with the first payment usually due as soon as the contract is signed. The payments are usually level, but their time pattern can be tailored to the user's needs. For example, suppose that a manufacturer leases a machine to produce a complex new product. There will a year's "shakedown" period before volume production is possible. In this case, it might be possible to arrange for lower payments during the first year of the lease.

When a lease is terminated, the leased equipment reverts to the lessor. However, the lease agreement often gives the user the option to repurchase the equipment or take out a new lease.

Some leases are short-term and cancellable during the contract period at the option of the lessee: these are generally known as *operating leases*. Others extend over most of the estimated economic life of the asset and cannot be cancelled or can be cancelled only if the lessor is reimbursed for any losses: these are called *capital, financial,* or *full-payout* leases.[1]

Financial leases are a *source of financing.* Signing a financial lease contract is like borrowing money. There is an immediate cash inflow because the lessee is relieved of having to pay for the asset. But the lessee also assumes a binding obligation to make the payments specified in the lease contract. The user could have borrowed the full purchase price of the asset by accepting a binding obligation to make interest and principal payments to the lender. Thus the cash flow consequences of leasing and borrowing are similar. In either case, the firm raises cash now and pays it back later. A large part of this chapter will be devoted to comparing leasing and borrowing as financing alternatives.

Leases also differ in the services provided by the lessor. Under a *full-service* or *rental* lease, the lessor promises to maintain and insure the equipment and to pay any property taxes due on it. In a *net* lease, the lessee agrees to maintain the asset, insure it, and pay any property taxes. Most financial leases are net leases.

Most financial leases are arranged for brand new assets. The lessee identifies the equipment he or she would like to use, arranges for the leasing company to buy it from the manufacturer, and signs a contract with the leasing company. This is called a *direct* lease. In other cases, the firm sells an asset it already owns and leases it back from the buyer. These *sale and lease-back* arrangements are common in real estate. For example, firm X may wish to raise cash by selling a factory, but still retain use of the factory. It could do this by selling the factory for cash to a leasing company and simultaneously signing a long-term lease contract for the factory. Legal ownership of the factory passes to the leasing company but the right to use it stays with firm X.

You may also encounter *leveraged* leases. These are financial leases in which the lessor borrows part of the purchase price of the leased asset, using the lease contract as security for the loan. Leveraged lease deals are complicated, and so we defer discussion of them to the end of this chapter.

Example of a Financial Lease

Imagine yourself in the position of Thomas Pierce, III, president of Widdicombe Transportation Company. Your firm was established by your grandfather, who was quick to capitalize on the growing demand for transportation between Widdicombe and nearby townships. The company has owned all its vehicles from the time it was formed; you are now reconsidering that policy. Your operating manager wants to buy a new bus costing $100,000. Widdicombe will own the bus for six years and then sell it for $10,000. The bus manufacturer is anxious to make a deal, so it is guaranteeing these prices with a sale and repurchase contract.

You are convinced that the investment in additional equipment is worthwhile. However, the representative of the bus manufacturer (ever anxious to make a deal) has pointed out that her firm would also be willing to lease the bus to you for six years for an annual payment of $18,000. Widdicombe would remain responsible for all maintenance, insurance, and operating expenses.

Table 24-1 shows the direct cash-flow consequences of signing the lease contract. (An important indirect effect is considered later.) The consequences are:

---

[1]In the shipping industry, a financial lease is often termed a *bareboat charter* or *demise hire.*

Table 24-1 Direct cash-flow consequences of the lease contract offered to Widdicombe Transportation Company (figures in thousands). The tax rate is 46%, the CCA rate is 30%, and there is a salvage value of $10,000 in year 6. Under the half-year rule, CCA is taken at 15% for the first year and at 30% thereafter.

	Year						
	0	1	2	3	4	5	6
1. Cost of new bus/salvage	100						−10
2. Investment tax credit lost	−10						
3. Lease payment	−18	−18	−18	−18	−18	−18	
4. Tax shield on lease payment	8.28	8.28	8.28	8.28	8.28	8.28	
5. Lost CCA tax shield and terminal loss benefit	−6.21	−10.56	−7.39	−5.17	−3.62	−2.53	−1.31
6. Total	74.07	−20.28	−17.11	−14.89	−13.34	−12.25	−11.31

1. Widdicombe does not have to pay for the bus. This is equivalent to a cash inflow of $100,000 in year 0. On the other hand, it loses the right to salvage the bus for $10,000 in year 6.

2. The investment tax credit (ITC) is lost because Widdicombe is no longer the bus's legal owner. We have assumed that the ITC rate is 10%.

3. Widdicombe must pay $18,000 per year for six years to the lessor. The first payment is due immediately.

4. However, these lease payments are fully tax-deductible. At a 46% marginal tax rate, the lease payments generate tax shields of $8,280 per year. You could say that the after-tax cost of the lease payment is $18,000 − $8,280 = $9,720.

5. Widdicombe no longer owns the bus, so it cannot claim capital cost allowance (CCA) on it. Therefore it gives up a valuable CCA tax shield in years 0 to 5. In Table 24-1, we have assumed the bus would be in Asset Class 10, with a 30% CCA rate. Moreover, Widdicombe loses the tax effects of salvaging the bus in year 6. We have assumed that the bus would have been the only asset in its class, so Widdicombe also gives up a terminal loss tax benefit.[2]

Analyzing leases usually requires a sharp pencil because the value of the benefits is often very close to that of the costs. We have taken care to incorporate the exact tax effects of the half-year rule, as discussed in Appendix 6-1. Thus, CCA is taken at half the normal rate in year 0, and at the full 30% rate for years 1 to 5. The undepreciated capital cost (UCC) at the end of year 5 is

$$(100 − 10) \times (1 − 0.15) \times (1 − 0.30)^5 = 12.86 \text{ or } \$12,860$$

If Widdicombe had owned the bus, it could have claimed a terminal loss in year 6 and achieved a tax saving of $(12,860 − 10,000) \times 0.46 = \$1,310$.

We must emphasize that Table 24-1 assumes that Widdicombe will pay taxes at the full 46% marginal rate. If the firm were sure to lose money, and therefore pay no taxes, lines 2, 4, and 5 would be left blank. The investment tax credit is worth nothing to a firm that pays no taxes, for example.

---

[2]As discussed in Chapter 6, the bus would often be grouped with the other assets in Class 10, but in this case, we'll suppose that the bus is to be used on a new route, which Revenue Canada deems to be a separate business for tax purposes. If the bus is grouped with other Class 10 assets, and the UCC of the class exceeds the salvage value, Widdicombe would be left with a perpetual CCA tax shield, instead of a terminal loss.

Who *Really* Owns the Leased Asset?

To a lawyer or a tax accountant, this would be a silly question: the lessor is clearly the *legal* owner of the leased asset. That is why the lessor is allowed to deduct depreciation from taxable income, and to claim the investment tax credit.

From an *economic* point of view, you might say that the *user* is the real owner, because in a *financial* lease the user faces the risks and receives the rewards of ownership. If the new bus turns out to be hopelessly costly and unsuited for Widdicombe's routes, that is Widdicombe's problem, not the lessor's. If it turns out to be a great success, the profit goes to Widdicombe, not the lessor. The success or failure of the firm's business operations does not depend on whether the buses are financed by leasing or some other financial instrument.

In many respects, a financial lease is equivalent to the secured loan. The lessee must make a series of fixed payments and, if the lessee fails to do so, the lessor can repossess the asset. Thus we can think of a balance sheet like this:

Widdicombe Transportation Company (figures in thousands of dollars)			
Bus	100	100	Loan secured by bus
All other assets	1,000	450	Other loans
		550	Net worth
Total assets	1,100	1,100	Total liabilities and net worth

as being economically equivalent to a balance sheet like this:

Widdicombe Transportation Company (figures in thousands of dollars)			
Bus	100	100	Financial lease
All other assets	1,000	450	Other loans
		550	Net worth
Total assets	1,100	1,100	Total liabilities and net worth

Having said this, we must immediately add two qualifications. First, legal ownership makes a big difference when a financial lease expires, because the lessor gets the salvage value of the asset. Once a secured loan is paid off the user owns the asset free and clear.

Legal ownership also makes a difference in bankruptcy or reorganization. When a lessee fails to make a lease payment, the lessor can of course recover the asset. But suppose that the asset is worth much less than the future payments the lessee had promised to make. Obviously the lessor loses. The lessor can try to recoup this loss from the firm, but the lessor is an unsecured creditor.

Contrast what happens when a firm defaults on payments to a secured lender. The lender has a prior claim on the asset that secured the loan, and if this asset's value is less than the loan principal plus unpaid interest, the lender can enter a claim for the *full* amount of the difference.

Of course neither the lessor nor the secured lender can be sure its claim will be paid. Each has to get in line with other creditors. Our point is that lessees and secured creditors have different rights when the asset user gets into trouble.

Leasing and Revenue Canada

We have already explained that the lessor, as legal owner, usually enjoys the CCA tax shields and any investment tax credit generated by the leased asset. Lease payments are then treated as rents, which are taxable income for the lessor and a tax-deductible expense for the lessee.

However, the tax authorities are suspicious by nature, and they will require a different tax treatment unless they are satisfied that the arrangement is a genuine lease rather than a disguised instalment purchase. Here are examples of "lease-option" contracts that maybe treated as a sale. In these cases, the lessee gets CCA, and is deemed to have received a loan where the lease payment is regarded as a combination of interest and principal repayment. The lessor is deemed to have made a sale and taken back a loan.

1. The lessee receives an option to acquire the asset for, say, $1 when the lease expires. Such a provision would effectively give the asset's salvage value to the lessee.

2. The lessee guarantees an "option" purchase price that will be paid to the lessor at the expiration of the lease.

Revenue Canada is also suspicious of "sale-leaseback" agreement where someone sells an asset but continues to use it under a lease. These are treated as secured loans if, for example, the asset is sold for less than market value and the lease contract has one of the features described above.

Lessors also face another type of tax problem: they cannot use tax losses generated by the capital cost allowances on their leasing assets to "shelter" or reduce their other taxable income.[3] This is a potential problem since the transfer of CCA tax shields from the lessee to the lessor is often the main reason a lease can be negotiated. However, the CCA tax shields can be pooled within the leasing business and applied against taxable income generated by leasing. CCA tax shields are largest in the early years of the life of an asset, while lease payments are usually constant over time. This means that any given lease will often generate a tax loss early in its life and taxable income later. Thus the lessor would be well-advised to have a whole portfolio of leases of different ages, in order to avoid having to carry forward the tax losses.

Leasing and the Accountants

Until the end of 1976 financial leases were *off-balance-sheet financing*. That is, a firm could buy an asset, finance it through a financial lease, and show neither the asset nor the lease contract on its balance sheet. The firm was required only to add a brief footnote to its accounts describing its lease obligation. Accounting standards now require that all *capital* (financial) leases be *capitalized*.[4] That is, the present value of the lease payments must be calculated and shown alongside debt on the right-hand side of the balance sheet. The same amount must be shown as an asset on the left-hand side of the balance sheet.[5]

In order to implement this new requirement, accountants had to come up with objective rules for distinguishing between operating and capital (financial) leases. They defined capital leases as leases that meet *any one* of the following requirements:

1. The lease agreement transfers ownership to the lessee before the lease expires.

---

[3] See Sections 1100(11)–(16), Part XI of the Canadian *Income Tax Regulations*.

[4] See "Accounting for Leases," *Statement of Financial Accounting Standards No. 13*, Financial Accounting Standards Board, Stamford, Conn., 1976; and "Leases," Section 3065, *CICA Handbook, Accounting Recommendations*, Canadian Institute of Chartered Accountants, Toronto, 1978.

[5] This "asset" is then amortized over the life of the lease. The amortization is deducted from book income, just as depreciation is deducted for a purchased asset.

2. The lessee can purchase the asset for a bargain price when the lease expires.

3. The lease lasts for at least 75% of the asset's estimated economic life.

4. The present value of the lease payments is at least 90% of the asset's value (less any investment tax credit taken by the lessor).

All other leases are operating leases as far as the accountants are concerned.

Some financial managers have tried to take advantage of this arbitrary boundary between operating and financial leases. Suppose that you wanted to finance a computer-controlled machine tool costing $1 million. The machine tool is expected to last for 12 years. You could sign a lease contract for 8 years, 11 months (just missing requirement 3) with lease payments having a present value of $899,000 (just missing requirement 4). You also make sure the lease contract avoids requirements 1 and 2. Result? You have off-balance-sheet financing. This lease would not have to be capitalized, although it is clearly a long-term, fixed obligation.

Now we come to the $64 question: "Why should anyone *care* whether financing is off balance sheet or on balance sheet?" Shouldn't the financial manager worry about substance rather than appearance?

When a firm obtains off-balance-sheet financing, the conventional measures of financial leverage, such as the debt-equity ratio, understate the true degree of financial leverage. Some believe that financial analysts do not always notice off-balance-sheet lease obligations (which are still referred to in footnotes) or the greater volatility of earnings that results from the fixed lease payments. They may be right, but we would not expect such an imperfection to be widespread.

We saw in Chapter 22 that, when a company borrows money, it must usually consent to certain restrictions on future borrowing. Early bond indentures did not include any restrictions on the extent to which the company could lease. Therefore leasing was seen as a way to circumvent restrictive covenants. Loopholes such as these are easily stopped and most bond indentures now include limits on leasing.

Long-term lease obligations ought to be regarded as debt whether or not they appear on the balance sheet. Financial analysts may overlook minor debts. But major lease obligations are generally recognized and taken into account.

In May 1979, *Business Week* described the financial problems facing San Diego Gas and Electric Company (SDG&E). A "cash squeeze" on the company led to the following sale and lease-back deal:

> In March [the company] sold a new generating unit for $132 million to a group of banks headed by Bank of America and then took a lease on the plant. . . . Its near-term profit picture has not been affected. But ultimately, the desperate measure will remove a huge asset from the utility's rate [i.e., asset] base, thus lowering potential profits and further weakening SDG&E's bond rating. "The rating agencies look at the $132 million obligation as if it were long-term debt," explains [Robert E. Morris, the company's president].[6]

24-2 WHY LEASE?

You hear many suggestions about why companies should lease equipment rather than buy it. Let us look at some sensible reasons and then at one or two that are more dubious.

---

[6]Reprinted from the May 28, 1979, issue of *Business Week* by special permission; © 1979 by McGraw-Hill, Inc., New York, N.Y. 10020. All rights reserved, P. 110.

Sensible Reasons for Leasing

Short-Term Leases are Convenient   Suppose you want the use of a car for a week. You could buy one and sell it seven days later, but that would be silly. Quite apart from the fact that registering ownership is a nuisance, you would spend some time selecting a car, negotiating purchase, and arranging insurance. Then at the end of the week you must negotiate resale, and cancel registration and insurance. When you need a car only for a short time, it clearly makes sense to rent it. You save the trouble of registering ownership and you know the effective cost. In the same way, it pays a company to lease equipment that it needs for only a short time. Of course this kind of lease is always an operating lease.

Cancellation Options are Valuable   Computers are frequently leased on a short-term cancellable basis. It is difficult to estimate how rapidly such equipment will become obsolete, because the technology of computers is advancing rapidly and somewhat unpredictably. Leasing with an option to cancel passes the risk of premature obsolescence from the user to the lessor. Usually the lessor is a computer manufacturer or a computer leasing specialist, and therefore knows more about the risk of obsolescence than the user. Thus the lessor is better equipped than the user to bear these risks. It makes sense for the user to pay the lessor for the option to cancel. The payment comes in the form of higher lease payments.

Maintenance is Provided   Under a full-service lease, the user receives maintenance and other services. Many lessors are well equipped to provide efficient maintenance. However, bear in mind that these benefits are likely to be reflected in higher lease payments.

Standardization Leads to Low Administrative and Transaction Costs   Suppose that you operate a leasing company that specializes in financial leases for trucks. You are effectively lending money to a large number of firms (the lessees), which may differ considerably in terms of size and risk. But, because the underlying asset is in each case the same saleable item (a truck), you can safely "lend" the money (lease the truck) without conducting a detailed analysis of each firm's business. You can also use a simple, standard lease contract. This standardization makes it possible to "lend" small sums of money without incurring large investigative, administrative, or legal costs. Therefore leasing is often a relatively cheap source of cash for the small company. It offers long-term financing on a flexible, piecemeal basis, with lower transaction costs than in a private placement or a public bond or stock issue.

Tax Shields Can be Used   Sometimes lessors can make better use of depreciation (CCA) tax shields or the investment tax credit generated by an asset than the asset's user. Therefore it may make sense for the leasing company to own the equipment and pass on some of the tax benefits to the lessee in the form of low lease payments. We will see exactly how this works in the next section of this chapter.

Some Dubious Reasons for Leasing

We have already mentioned one dubious reason for leasing, that is, leasing in order to obtain off-balance-sheet financing. Here are three more dubious reasons.

Leasing Affects Book Income   Leasing can make the firm's balance sheet and income statement *look* better by increasing book income or decreasing book asset value, or both.

A lease that qualifies as off-balance-sheet financing[7] affects book income in only one way: the lease payments are an expense. If the firm buys the asset instead, and borrows to finance it, both depreciation and interest expense are deducted. Leases are usually set up so that payments in the early years are less than depreciation plus interest under the buy-and-borrow alternative. Consequently, leasing increases book income in the early years of an asset's life. The book rate of return can increase even more dramatically, because the book value of assets (the denominator in the book-rate-of-return calculation) is understated if the leased asset never appears on the firm's balance sheet.

Leasing's impact on book income should in itself have no effect on firm value. In efficient capital markets investors will look through the firm's accounting results to the true values of the assets and the liability incurred to finance it.

Leasing Avoids Capital Expenditure Controls In many companies lease proposals are scrutinized as carefully as capital expenditure proposals, but in others leasing may enable an operating manager to avoid the elaborate approval procedures needed to buy an asset. Although this is a dubious reason for leasing, it may be influential, particularly in the public sector. For example, city hospitals have sometimes found it politically more convenient to lease their medical equipment than to ask the city government to provide funds for purchase. Another example is provided by the United States Navy, which at one point leased a fleet of new tankers instead of asking Congress for the money to buy them.

Leasing Preserves Capital Leasing companies provide "100% financing"; they advance the full cost of the leased asset. Consequently, they often claim that leasing preserves capital, allowing the firm to save its cash for other things.

But the firm can also "preserve capital" by borrowing money. If Widdicombe leases a $100,000 bus rather than buying it, it does conserve $100,000 cash. It could also (1) buy the bus for cash and (2) borrow $100,000 using the bus as security. Its bank balance ends up the same whether it leases or buys and borrows. It has the bus in either case, and it incurs a $100,000 liability in either case. What's so special about leasing?

24-3 VALUING FINANCIAL LEASES

Leasing does offer special advantages to some firms in some circumstances. However, there is no point in further discussion of these advantages until you know how to value financial lease contracts.

A First Pass at Valuing a Lease Contract

When we left Thomas Pierce, III, president of Widdicombe Transportation, he had just set down in Table 24-1 the *direct* cash-flow consequences of the financial lease contract proposed by the bus manufacturer.

The direct cash flows are typically assumed to be *safe* flows that investors would discount at approximately the same rate as the interest and principal payments on a secured bond issued by the lessee. This assumption is reasonable for the lease payments because the lessor is effectively making a loan to the lessee. But the various tax shields might carry enough risk to deserve a higher rate. For example, Widdicombe might be confident it could make the lease payments, but not confident that it could earn enough taxable income to use these tax shields. In that case the cash flows generated by the tax shields would probably deserve a higher discount rate than the borrowing rate used for the lease payments.

---

[7]It is difficult to generalize about the effects of leasing on book income when the leases are capitalized.

A lessee might, in principle, end up using a separate discount rate for each line of Table 24-1, each rate chosen to fit the risk of that line's cash flow. But established, profitable firms usually find it reasonable to simplify by discounting the types of flows shown in Table 24-1 at a single rate, the rate of interest the firm would pay if it borrowed rather than leased. We will assume Widdicombe's borrowing rate is 10%.

Once the discount rate is set, the present value of the cash flows stemming from the lease is easily calculated. We discount the sum of lines 1 through 5 from Table 24-1 at 10%:

$$NPV = 74.07 - \frac{20.28}{1.1} - \frac{17.11}{(1.1)^2} - \frac{14.89}{(1.1)^3} - \frac{13.34}{(1.1)^4} - \frac{12.25}{(1.1)^5} - \frac{11.31}{(1.1)^6}$$

$$= +7.20 \text{ or } \$7,200$$

If we were to stop here, we would conclude that the proposed lease contact is a good deal. But we would be wrong.

Financial Leases Displace Debt

Unless investors are fooled by off-balance-sheet financing, firms that lease more will end up borrowing less, other things being equal. Leasing displaces borrowing. This indirect effect of leasing must be taken into account if leases are to be properly evaluated.

Table 24-2 Comparison of capital structures under lease financing and normal financing for Widdicombe Transportation Company (figures in thousands of dollars).

Normal Financing				Lease Financing			
1. Starting balance sheet				1. Starting balance sheet			
NWC	100	500	D	NWC	100	500	D
FA	900	500	E	FA	900	500	E
	1,000	1,000			1,000	1,000	
Buy bus				Lease bus			
2. New balance sheet				2. New balance sheet			
NWC	100	550	D	NWC	100	500	D
Bus	100			Bus	100	100	LL
FA	900	550	E	FA	900	500	E
	1,100	1,100			1,100	1,100	
Compare new balance sheets: $100 lease liability displaces $100 of debt.				3. New balance sheet after adjustment to regain target debt ratio			
				NWC	100	450	D
				Bus	100	100	LL
				FA	900	550	E
					1,100	1,100	

Key:
NWC = Net working capital
FA = Fixed (long-term) assets
D   = Debt
LL = Lease liability
E   = Equity

In what sense does a lease displace debt? The answer is given by Table 24-2, which compares Widdicombe's overall financing policy with and without the lease contract.

Table 24-2 requires some explanation, however. It assumes Widdicombe starts with net working capital (NWC) of $100,000 and fixed assets (FA) of $900,000. Total asset value is $1 million. The firm has $500,000 debt (D) outstanding and $500,000 equity (E). We assume this 50-50 debt-equity split represents Widdicombe's target debt ratio—Mr. Pierce's best judgement about Widdicombe's optimal debt ratio.

Mr. Pierce has decided to acquire the bus. The only question is how to finance its cost of $100,000. Under normal financing the firm would borrow $50,000 and raise $50,000 equity by retaining earnings or perhaps issuing stock. That gives the new balance sheet shown on the left-hand side of Table 24-2. Note that fixed assets increase by $100,000, the cost of the bus, and debt and equity each increase by $50,000.

Now look at the right-hand side of the table. If Widdicombe leases, it acquires an asset. Thus we add $100,000 to fixed assets. It also assumes a lease liability. We assume for now that the present value of the lease liability is $100,000.[8] Thus we add a $100,000 lease liability (LL) to the second balance sheet under the lease alternative.

This balance sheet suggests that the lease provides "100% financing." Only $500,000 equity is required, $50,000 less than the amount required under normal financing. But this is accomplished only by moving Widdicombe away from its target debt ratio— remember that the lease liability is really a debt under another name. If Widdicombe stops at the second balance sheet, it will have a total debt of $600,000 including the lease liability, and an effective debt ratio of 55%.

In order to get back to its *target* debt ratio of 50%, Widdicombe will have to increase equity by $50,000 and reduce borrowing by the same amount. The result is the third balance sheet on the right-hand side of Table 24-2. Total debt, including the lease liability, is $550,000 (D + LL = $450,000 + $100,000 = $550,000).

Now compare the final balance sheets under normal and lease financing. Under the lease financing alternative, debt (D) ends up (in balance sheet 3) at $450,000, $100,000 less than under normal financing. Thus the $100,000 lease liability *displaces* the same amount of debt. *Leasing has no effect on the required amount of equity.* Thus any comparison of lease versus normal financing really forces us to choose between leasing and borrowing.

If Widdicombe wanted to *increase* its target debt ratio to 55%, we would still compare leasing with borrowing. The issue would be whether to increase the debt ratio by leasing or to increase it by issuing regular debt.

We do not mean to imply that firms immediately rebalance their capital structures every time they lease an asset, but only that they tend to return to their target capital structures over time. Widdicombe might regain the 50% debt ratio by financing its *next* bus with 100% equity, for example. Or it might reduce next year's dividends by $50,000, and repay $50,000 of debt with the cash that otherwise would have been paid out to stockholders.

Calculating the Equivalent Loan

We have now established that leasing displaces debt. The correct comparison is between leasing on the one hand and "buy and borrow" on the other. Most methods of evaluating leases recognize this, but the real problem is to work out exactly how much debt is displaced by leasing at each point in time. If we do not get the right answer to this

---

[8]Actually, this overstates the liability for two reasons. First, the lease doesn't really provide $100,000 of financing. As Table 24-1 shows, the immediate cash inflow is only $74,070. Second, the liability created does not necessarily equal the financing provided. If it did, then the lease would be a zero-NPV transaction, and all this analysis would hardly be necessary. These issues are considered in more detail later in this chapter.

question, we cannot evaluate leases properly. Therefore we must identify an *equivalent loan*—a loan that exactly matches the lease liability at each point in time, or, in other words, a loan that commits the firm to exactly the same cash outflows as the lease would.

Look once more at Table 24-1. The sums of the cash flows shown in this table are as follows:

	Year					
	0	1	2	3	4	5	6
Cash flow (in thousands of dollars)	+ 74.07	− 20.28	− 17.11	− 14.89	− 13.34	− 12.25	− 11.31

You can think of the cash flows in years 1 through 6 as the "debt service" of the lease. Table 24-3 shows a loan with *exactly* the same debt service. The initial amount of the loan is $75,840 but $20,280 is paid out in year 1, $17,110 in year 2, and so on (see line 5). The outstanding balance at the end of each year is shown in line 1.

How do we know the equivalent loan is really equivalent? Because it generates the same cash outflows as the lease. Compare line 5 of Table 24-3 with the lease cash flows shown in Table 24-1.

Table 24-3   Details of the equivalent loan for the lease contract offered to Widdicombe Transportation Company (figures in thousands of dollars; cash outflows shown with negative sign).

	Year					
	0	1	2	3	4	5	6
1. Amount borrowed at year's end	75.84	59.66	45.77	33.35	21.81	10.73	0.00
2. Interest paid at 10%		− 7.58	− 5.97	− 4.58	− 3.34	− 2.18	− 1.07
3. Interest paid after 46% tax shield		− 4.10	− 3.22	− 2.47	− 1.80	− 1.18	− 0.58
4. Principal repaid		− 16.18	− 13.89	− 12.42	− 11.54	− 11.08	− 10.73
5. Net cash flow of borrowing: line 1 in year 0, sum of lines 3 and 4 in years 1–6	75.84	− 20.28	− 17.11	− 14.89	− 13.34	− 12.25	− 11.31

Note:
Line 5 in this table equals the total cash flow shown in Table 24-1 for years 1 through 6.

Our example illustrates two general points about leases and equivalent loans. First, leasing a $100,000 bus does not generate $100,000 in financing. Look again at Table 24-1: the net immediate cash flow is only $74,070. This is the true financing provided. Second, initial borrowing under an equivalent loan does *not* in general equal the amount of financing provided by the lease. The equivalent loan depends on the lease liability—that is, it depends on the present value of the cash outflows to which the lessee is committed.

Calculating the Value of the Lease

Now we have all the information required to evaluate the proposed bus lease. All you have to do is:

Compare the financing provided by the lease with the financing provided by the equivalent loan.

Look at the *difference* between the cash flows from leasing and the cash flows from the equivalent loan:

	Year						
	0	1	2	3	4	5	6
Cash flows from leasing	74.07	−20.28	−17.11	−14.89	−13.34	−12.25	−11.31
Cash flows of equivalent loan	75.84	−20.28	−17.11	−14.89	−13.34	−12.25	−11.31
Difference (1)–(2)	−1.77	0	0	0	0	0	0

The *only* difference is that the equivalent loan would generate $1,770 more cash immediately. The cash flows afterwards are identical.[9]

If you can devise a borrowing plan that gives the same cash flow as the lease in every future period, but a higher immediate cash inflow, then the lease should be rejected. Mr. Pierce should not lease the bus, because the proposed lease provides less immediate financing than the equivalent loan.

Thus we have a simple, obvious decision rule. The only trick is to calculate the financing provided by the equivalent loan. The calculation can be done two ways:

1. *Hard way*: Construct a table like Table 24-3.

2. *Easy way*: Discount the lease cash flows at the *after-tax* interest rate the firm would pay on an equivalent loan.

Let's try the easy method on the bus lease. Widdicombe faces a 10% borrowing rate and a 46% marginal tax rate. If $r_D = 0.10$ and $T_c = 0.46$, it discounts at $r_D(1 - T_c)$ = 0.10(1 − 0.46) = 0.054.

$$\frac{\text{PV of lease}}{\text{cash flows}} = \frac{20.28}{1.054} + \frac{17.11}{(1.054)^2} + \frac{14.89}{(1.054)^3} + \frac{13.34}{(1.054)^4} + \frac{12.25}{(1.054)^5} + \frac{11.31}{(1.054)^6}$$

$$= 75.84 \text{ or } \$75,840$$

We get exactly the same equivalent loan as in Table 24-3.

The Story So Far

We concluded that the lease contract offered to Widdicombe Transportation was *not* attractive because the lease provided $1,770 less financing than the equivalent loan. The underlying principle is as follows: a financial lease is superior to buying and borrowing if the financing provided by the lease exceeds the present value of the liability created by the lease.

The principle implies this formula:

$$\frac{\text{Net value}}{\text{of lease}} = \frac{\text{initial financing}}{\text{provided}} = \sum_{t=1}^{N} \frac{\text{LCF}_t}{[1 + r(1 - T_c)]^t}$$

---

[9]In practice, Mr. Pierce might view $1,770 as a small change compared to the cost of the bus. The lease is very close to a break-even deal. But remember that the lease looked like a very good deal (NPV = +$7,200) when we took a first pass at valuing it.

---

where LCF$_t$ is the cash outflow attributable to the lease in period t and N is the duration of the lease. Initial financing provided equals the cost of the leased asset minus any immediate lease payment or other cash outflow attributable to the lease.

Notice that our formula applies to net financial leases. Any insurance, maintenance, and other operating costs picked up by the lessor have to be evaluated separately and added to the value of the lease. If any of the cash flows are riskier than debt, they will deserve a higher discount rate.

Suppose, for example, that the bus manufacturer offers to provide routine mainte-nance with the lease that would otherwise cost $3,000 per year after tax. Moreover, it is now refusing to guarantee the repurchase price in the sale-repurchase offer. Mr. Pierce feels that $10,000 is still the best estimate of the salvage value of the bus in year 6, but he recognizes that this is now a risky cash flow. Thus the value of the lease increases by the present value of the maintenance savings. Also, the reduction in the present value of the opportunity cost of salvage increases the value of the lease.

Mr. Pierce uses a 12% discount rate for the risky maintenance costs and risky salvage value.[10] We'll assume the maintenance savings occur in years 1 to 5. They are worth

$$\sum_{t=1}^{5} \frac{3,000}{(1.12)^t} = \$10,810$$

Determining the change in the value of the lease that results from the increase in the risk of the salvage value requires more care, since the salvage value *and* the terminal loss are affected. Denote the undepreciated capital cost of the bus just prior to salvage by UCC. We previously calculated it to be $12,860, but we'll just call it UCC, partly to remind us that it is riskless, unlike the salvage value. The expected salvage value plus terminal loss benefit is then

$$\$10,000 + 0.46 \, (\text{UCC} - 10,000) = \$5,400 + 0.46 \, \text{UCC}$$

Of this cash flow, $5,400 is risky and 0.46 UCC is riskless. Thus we only need to change the discount rate on the $5,400 from 5.4% to 12% to capture the impact of the increase in salvage value risk on the value of the lease.

Remember that we previously calculated the value of the lease as $-\$1,770$. The revised value of the lease is therefore

$$-\$1,770 + 10,810 - \frac{5,400}{(1.12)^6} + \frac{5,400}{(1.054)^6} = \$10,240$$

Now the lease looks like a good deal.

Remember also that the value of the lease is its incremental value relative to buying and borrowing. A positive lease value means that *if* you acquire the asset, lease financing is advantageous. It does not prove you should acquire the asset.

However, sometimes favourable lease terms rescue a capital investment project. Suppose that Widdicombe had decided *against* buying a new bus because the NPV of the $100,000 investment was $-\$5,000$ assuming normal financing. The bus manufac-turer could rescue the deal by offering a lease with a value of, say, $+\$8,000$. By offering

---

[10]These risky cash flows may affect the debt capacity of the firm, so we must either add in the PV of the change in the interest tax shields associated with the change in debt capacity or use an adjusted discount rate to account for interest tax shields. These issues will be discussed later in the chapter, but for simplicity, we'll assume that the 12% discount rate is adjusted for any interest tax shields.

such a lease, the manufacturer would in effect cut the price of the bus to $92,000, giving the bus-lease package a positive value to Widdicombe.

24-4 WHEN DOES LEASING PAY?

We have examined the value of a lease from the viewpoint of the lessee. However, the lessor's criterion is simply the reverse. As long as lessor and lessee are in the same tax bracket, every cash outflow to the lessee is an inflow to the lessor, and vice versa. In our numerical example, the bus manufacturer would project cash flows in a table like Table 24-1, but with the signs reversed. The value of the lease to the bus manufacturer would be

$$
\begin{aligned}
\text{Value of lease to lessor} &= -74.07 + \frac{20.28}{1.054} + \frac{17.11}{(1.054)^2} + \frac{14.89}{(1.054)^3} \\
&\quad + \frac{13.34}{(1.054)^4} + \frac{12.25}{(1.054)^5} + \frac{11.31}{(1.054)^6} \\
&= +\$1,770
\end{aligned}
$$

In this case, the values to lessee and lessor exactly offset ($-1,770 + 1,770 = 0$). The lessor can win only at the lessee's expense.

But both lessee and lessor can win if their tax rates differ. Suppose that Widdicombe paid no tax ($T_c = 0$). Then the only cash flows of the bus lease would be

	Year						
	0	1	2	3	4	5	6
Cost of new bus/salvage	+100						−10
Lease payment	−18	−18	−18	−18	−18	−18	

These flows would be discounted at 10%, because $r_D(1 - T_c) = r_D$ when $T_c = 0$. The value of the lease is

$$
\begin{aligned}
\text{Value of lease} &= +100 - \sum_{t=0}^{5} \frac{18}{(1.10)^t} - \frac{10}{(1.10)^6} \\
&= +26.12 \text{ or } \$26,120
\end{aligned}
$$

In this case there is a net gain of $1,770 to the lessor (who has the 46% tax rate) *and* a net gain of $26,120 to the lessee (who pays zero tax). This mutual gain is at the expense of the government. On the one hand, the government gains from the lease contract because it can tax the lease payments. On the other hand, the contract allows the lessor to take advantage of depreciation and interest tax shields, which are of no use to the lessee. However, because the depreciation is accelerated, and the interest rate is positive, the government suffers a net loss in the present value of its tax receipts as a result of the lease.

Now you should begin to understand the circumstances in which the government makes a loss on the lease and the other two parties gain. Other things being equal, there are potential gains to lessor and lessee when:

1. The lessor's tax rate is higher than the lessee's.

2. The depreciation tax shield is received early in the lease period.

3. The lease period is long and the lease payments are concentrated toward the end of the period.

4. The interest rate r_D is high—if it were zero there would be no advantage in present value terms to postponing tax.

24-5 EVALUATING A LARGE, LEVERAGED LEASE

Now let us try using our new-found knowledge to evaluate a large leasing deal. In 1971 Anaconda began to build a $138 million aluminum-reduction mill at Sebree, Kentucky. The company's original intention was to finance the project largely by a private placement of debt, but, before it could do so, two things happened. First, the Allende government expropriated Anaconda's Chilean copper mines and so provided the company with a $356 million tax-deductible loss. Second, the United States Congress reinstated the investment tax credit (then 7%).

Anaconda clearly was unlikely to pay taxes for a number of years. If it went ahead and bought the mill, it could not make immediate use of the investment tax credit or the depreciation tax shields. By leasing the mill, however, Anaconda could pass on

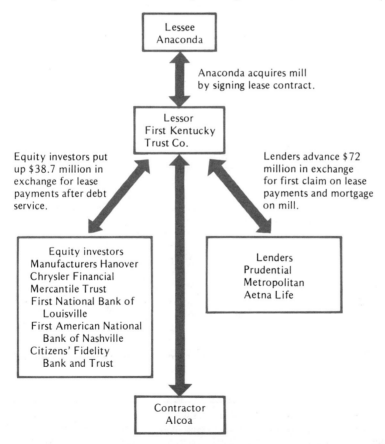

Figure 24-1 How Anaconda arranged a lease on its aluminum reduction mill. This is a leveraged lease because part of the cost of the plant was raised by borrowing.

these benefits to someone who could use them.[11] It therefore decided to purchase only the real estate at Sebree and to pay $1.1 million to a leasing broker, U.S. Leasing International, to put together a leveraged lease for the $110.7 million of plant and equipment. Figure 24-1 shows how this was arranged. First Kentucky Trust Company issued $39 million of equity to a group of banks and leasing companies and $72 million of debt to a group of insurance companies. It then used this money to purchase the mill and lease it to Anaconda. Anaconda agreed to make 40 lease payments, prepaid semiannually, over a 20-year period. The first 21 payments were set at $3.99 million each and the last 19 at $5.46 million each.

The $72 million loan was secured by a first claim on Anaconda's lease payments and by a mortgage on the plant. It was *not* secured by First Kentucky or the equity investors. It was a *nonrecourse* loan: if Anaconda had defaulted on the lease payments, the insurance companies' only protection would have been the value of the mill, and a general claim against Anaconda.

This is called a *leveraged* lease because part of the cost of the plant was raised by a loan secured by the asset and the lease payments. The lessor, First Kentucky Trust, really acted as an intermediary, receiving the lease payments from Anaconda, paying the debt service, and distributing what was left over to the equity investors. First Kentucky in effect financed the lease contract by selling off debt and equity claims against it.

But let's look at the lease contract itself from the lessor's viewpoint. The initial outlay was $110.7 million less the investment tax credit of $7.75 million and the initial

Table 24-4   Value of Anaconda lease to lessor (figures in millions of dollars).

Item	Present Value
1. Price	−110.7
2. Investment tax credit	+7.7
3. Depreciation tax shield	+44.3
4. After-tax lease payments	+60.8
5. Salvage value	+0.9
Total value to *lessor*	+3.0

Notes:
1. Assumed tax rate is $T_c = 0.5$.
2. The adjusted discount rate for items 3 and 4 is 4.5625%. (The present values were actually calculated assuming semiannual cash flows and an equivalent semiannual rate.)
3. The discount rate for item 5 is 15%, our guesstimate of the average cost of capital for Anaconda's assets.
4. The depreciation schedule was based on an 11-year depreciable life and a 5% book salvage value. The double-declining-balance method was used for the first two years and then a switch was made to sum-of-the-years' digits. This appears to be the fastest write-off available under 1973 regulations.
5. The lessor's estimate of the plant's after-tax salvage value appears to be $10.9 million. This is not from the horse's mouth; it is inferred from other information.
6. In principle, ownership of the salvage value also creates debt capacity. We have not included an estimate of the NPV of this capacity to the lessors. It is in any event a small number.

Source: S.C. Myers, D.A. Dill, and A.J. Bautista, "Valuation of Financial Lease Contracts," *Journal of Finance*, 31:799–819 (June 1976), table 1, p. 809.

---

[11]The Anaconda lease was described in P. Vanderwicken, "Powerful Logic of the Leasing Boom," *Fortune*, 87:132–161 (November 1973). Our analysis of its present value is taken from S.C. Myers, D.A. Dill and A.J. Bautista, "Valuation of Financial Lease Contracts," *Journal of Finance*, 31:799–819 (June 1976), and J.R. Franks and S.D. Hodges, "Valuation of Financial Lease Contracts: A Note," *Journal of Finance*, 33:647–669 (May 1978).

prepaid lease payment. The major subsequent cash inflows were the 39 semiannual lease payments, the depreciation tax shields, and the salvage value in 1993.

As frequently happens in financial analysis, the hardest problem is to choose the right discount rate. Here is one way to look at it. The interest rate on the insurance companies' loan was 9.125%. Because this debt is also protected by the lessor's equity, the lease payments must be *riskier* than the debt. On the other hand, the depreciation tax shield must be *safer* than the lease payments, for once the contract is signed, the size of the shields is independent of Anaconda's fortunes. Since our formula calls for a single rate of discount for both the after-tax lease payments and the depreciation tax shield, we will compromise on a discount rate of 9.125%. The adjusted discount rate is 4.5625%, assuming a marginal tax rate of 50%.

The present value calculations are set out in Table 24-4 along with a list of the other assumptions, we have made. You can see that for the lessor the lease was moderately profitable: its net value was roughly 3% of the plant's cost.

It is not so easy to evaluate the lease from Anaconda's side because we do not know when Anaconda expected to resume paying taxes. But we can work out how much the lease was worth to Anaconda under varying assumptions about its future tax position. The results are presented in Figure 24-2. Notice that if Anaconda paid taxes immediately, it would lose exactly the $3.0 million that the lessor gained. The break-even point comes after only three years, and thereafter the value of the lease arrangement to Anaconda rises rapidly to the maximum of about $35 million. It appears that the deal was a good one for Anaconda.

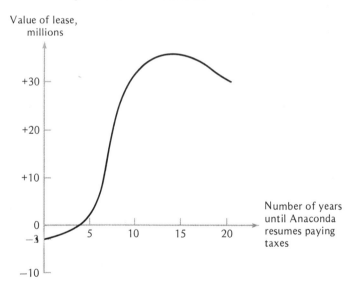

Figure 24-2   The value of the aluminum reduction mill to Anaconda increases rapidly as its "tax holiday" is extended. If the holiday extends for 15 years, the lease is worth about $36 million.
Source: J.R. Franks and S.D. Hodges, "Value of Financial Lease Contracts: A Note," *Journal of Finance*, **33**:667 (May 1978), Table 3.

24-6   A GENERAL RULE FOR VALUING DEBT-EQUIVALENT CASH FLOWS

Let's review. Before deciding whether to accept or reject a financial lease, the financial manager has to:

1. Understand the lease contract

2. Identify the lease cash flows
3. Calculate the lease's NPV

The third step is the easiest: just discount the lease cash flows at the after-tax borrowing rate, $r_D(1 - T_c)$. The resulting NPV is the difference between the immediate cash inflow provided by the lease and the cash that could be raised by issuing an equivalent loan.

The equivalent loan trick works because the lease generates *debt-equivalent cash flows.* Thus lease cash flows can be "zeroed out" by the principal and after-tax interest payments on the equivalent loan.

However, we can apply this trick to *any* debt-equivalent cash flow. Any safe,[12] nominal cash flow can be valued by discounting at an after-tax borrowing rate. Here is an example.

Valuing Subsidized Loans

Suppose you're considering purchase of a $100,000 machine. The manufacturer sweetens the deal by offering to finance the purchase by lending you $100,000 for five years, with annual interest payments of 5%. You would have to pay 13% to borrow from a bank. Your marginal tax rate is 30% ($T_c = 0.3$).

How much is this loan worth? If you take it, the cash flows are:

Period	0	1	2	3	4	5
Cash flow (in thousands)	$100	−5	−5	−5	−5	−105
Tax shield		+1.5	+1.5	+1.5	+1.5	+1.5
After-tax cash flow	$100	−3.5	−3.5	−3.5	−3.5	−103.5

The net present value of this subsidized loan equals its flows discounted at the after-tax borrowing rate on an *un*subsidized loan:[13] $r_D(1 - T_c) = 0.13(1 - 0.3) = 0.091$. Therefore:

$$\text{NPV} = +100 - \frac{3.5}{1.091} - \frac{3.5}{(1.091)^2} - \frac{3.5}{(1.091)^3} - \frac{3.5}{(1.091)^4} - \frac{103.5}{(1.091)^5}$$

$$= +21.73 \text{ or } \$21,730$$

The manufacturer has effectively cut the machine's purchase price from $100,000 to ($100,000 − $21,730) = $78,270. You can now go back and recalculate the machines' NPV using this fire-sale price.

Some Further Examples

Here are some further examples of debt-equivalent cash flows:

Payout Fixed by Contract   Suppose you sign a maintenance contract with a truck leasing firm, which agrees to keep your leased trucks in good working order for the next

---

[12]In theory, "safe" means literally risk-free, like the cash returns on a government bond. In practice, it means that the risk of not receiving the cash flow is small.

[13]In Section 19-1, we calculated the NPV of subsidized financing using the *pretax* borrowing rate. Now you can see that was a mistake. Using the pretax rate implicitly defines the equivalent loan in terms of pretax cash flows, violating a rule promulgated way back in Section 6-1: always estimate cash flows on an after-tax basis.

two years in exchange for 24 fixed monthly payments. These payments are debt-equiv-alent flows.[14]

Capital Cost Allowance Tax Shields Capital projects are normally valued by dis-counting the total after-tax cash flows they are expected to generate. Capital cost allowance (CCA) tax shields contribute to project cash flow, but they are not valued separately; they are just folded into project cash flows along with dozens, or hundreds, of other specific inflows and outflows. The project's opportunity cost of capital reflects the average risk of the resulting aggregate.

However, suppose we ask what CCA tax shields are worth *by themselves*. For a firm that's sure to pay taxes, CCA tax shields are a safe, nominal flow. Therefore, they should be discounted at the firm's after-tax borrowing rate.[15]

Suppose you buy a depreciable asset for $200,000, and it belongs in Asset Class 8, for which the CCA rate is 20%. Your marginal tax rate is still 30%, and your pretax borrowing rate is still 13%. The after-tax discount rate is $r = r_D (1 - T_c) = 0.13 (1 - 0.3) = 0.091$. Ignoring the half-year rule for CCA, Chapter 6 gives the following formula for the present value of the perpetual CCA tax shields on the asset:

$$\text{PV of CCA} = \frac{CdT_c}{r + d} = \frac{200,000 \, (0.20) \, (0.30)}{0.091 + 0.20} = \$41,237$$

*Adjusted Present Value and Adjusted Discount Rates for Debt-Equivalent Cash Flows

In Chapter 19, we introduced the concept of adjusted present value or APV. For a capital investment project APV is defined as:

Project APV = base-case NPV

+ sum of the present values of the side effects of accepting the project

Base-case NPV is the project NPV calculated at the opportunity cost of capital—in other words, the project's net value if it were a separate, all-equity-financed mini-firm. The side effects might include transaction costs on security issues required to finance the project, interest tax shields on debt supported by the project, or subsidized financing available only if the project is accepted. Because a project's APV represents its overall contribution to firm value, the decision rule is to accept the project if its APV is positive.

We can just as well apply the APV concept to debt-equivalent cash flows, for example, the lease cash flows shown in Table 24-1. In this case, the base-cash NPV is the NPV of the lease's *direct* cash-flow consequences, discounted at a rate (or rates) appropriate to the risk of those flows. We have already done this calculation for the bus lease. Using a 10% discount rate, the NPV of the total cash flows shown in Table 24-1 is +$7,200.

---

[14]We assume you are locked into the contract. If it can be cancelled without penalty, you may have a valuable option.

[15]The CCA tax shields are cash inflows, not outflows as for the lease and the subsidized loan. For safe, nominal inflows, the relevant question is, "How much could the firm borrow if it uses the inflow for debt service?" Answer: The after-tax inflow discounted at the after-tax borrowing rate.

The major side effect of the lease is that it displaces debt. The cost of the displaced debt is the NPV of the after-tax cash flows of the equivalent loan. The loan generates an immediate cash inflow of $75,840, but commits the firm to subsequent outflows, as shown in line 5 of Table 24-3. The NPV of these flows at Widdicombe's 10% borrowing rate is:

$$NPV = +75.84 - \frac{20.28}{(1.1)} - \frac{17.11}{(1.1)^2} - \frac{14.89}{(1.1)^3} - \frac{13.34}{(1.1)^4} - \frac{12.25}{(1.1)^5} - \frac{11.31}{(1.1)^6}$$

$$= +8.97 \text{ or } \$8,970$$

Since the lease *displaces* debt, we subtract the debt's NPV from the lease's base-case NPV:

$$APV \text{ of lease} = \text{base-case NPV} - \text{NPV of equivalent loan}$$

$$= +7.20 - 8.97 = -1.77 \text{ or } -\$1,770$$

This is *exactly* the result obtained by the equivalent loan method in Table 24-3.

You may have wondered why the equivalent loan has a positive NPV. Widdicombe would be borrowing at a 10% interest rate, and then discounting the resulting flows at 10%. Shouldn't $NPV = 0$? The answer is no, because the interest payments generate tax shields. The present value of the tax shields (the difference between lines 2 and 3 in Table 24-3) is the NPV of the equivalent loan:

$$\frac{\text{PV of tax shields}}{\text{on equivalent loan}} = \frac{3.49}{1.1} + \frac{2.74}{(1.1)^2} + \frac{2.11}{(1.1)^3} + \frac{1.53}{(1.1)^4} + \frac{1.00}{(1.1)^5} + \frac{0.49}{(1.1)^6}$$

$$= 8.97 \text{ or } \$8,970$$

In Chapter 19 we also introduced the idea of *adjusting* the opportunity cost of capital to take account of a project's financing side effects. For any project there is some adjusted discount rate for which

$$\text{NPV at adjusted discount rate} = APV$$

$$= \text{NPV at opportunity cost of capital}$$

$$+ \text{present value of financing side effects}$$

Unfortunately there is no general formula for calculating the adjusted discount rate, [16] but the formulas originally suggested by Modigliani and Miller (MM) and Miles and Ezzell are often useful approximations. The MM formula is

$$r^* = r(1 - T_c L)$$

where r = the opportunity cost of capital for the cash flows being discounted

---

[16] Of course you can always calculate the adjusted discount rate if you know APV. But in that case, what's the point? The only reason you need an adjusted discount rate is to calculate (an estimate of) APV.

T_c = the firm's marginal tax rate[17]

L = the project's proportional contribution to the firm's borrowing power

How would we apply this formula to the Widdicombe lease? Since the lease generates debt-equivalent flows, the opportunity cost of capital is the borrowing rate: $r = r_D = 0.10$.

Since the lease *displaces* debt, we interpret L as the amount of debt displaced per dollar of debt. The displacement is dollar for dollar, so $L = 1$. Finally, for Widdicombe, the marginal tax rate is $T_c = 0.46$.

Now substitute in the MM formula:

$$r^* = r(1 - T_c L) = r_D(1 - T_c \times 1)$$
$$= 0.10(1 - 0.46) = 0.054 \text{ or } 5.4\%$$

In other words, MM's adjusted discount rate for safe, nominal flows is just the after-tax cost of borrowing.

We get the same result from the Miles-Ezzell formula:

$$r^* = r - L r_D T_c \left(\frac{1 + r}{1 + r_D} \right)$$

For debt-equivalent cash flows, $r = r_D$ and $L = 1$. Thus:

$$r^* = r_D - 1 \times r_D T_c \left(\frac{1 - r_D}{1 + r_D} \right)$$
$$= r_D - r_D T_c = r_D(1 - T_c)$$

24-7 SUMMARY

A lease is just an extended rental agreement. The owner of the equipment (the *lessor*) allows the user (the *lessee*) to operate the equipment in exchange for regular lease payments.

There is a wide variety of possible arrangements. Short-term, cancellable leases are known as *operating leases*: in these cases the lessor bears the risk of obsolescence. Long-term, noncancellable leases are called *full payout, financial,* or *capital* leases: in these cases the lessee bears the risk of obsolescence. Operating leases make sense when you want to use the equipment for only a short time or where the lessor has some control over the obsolescence rate. Financial leases are *sources of financing* for assets the firm wishes to acquire and use for an extended period.

Many vehicle or office equipment leases include insurance and maintenance. They are *full-service* leases. If the lessee is responsible for insurance and maintenance, the lease is a *net* lease.

---

[17]We actually wrote MM's formula as $r^* = r(1 - T^* L)$, where T^* is the net realizable tax shield per dollar of interest. We are simplifying here by just assuming that $T^* = T_c$, the corporate tax rate. If T^* is less than T_c, as it may well be in practice, the link between the equivalent loan method and the adjusted discount rate formulas in Chapter 19 is much more difficult to show. Nevertheless, it's reassuring that the formulas in Chapter 19 work for debt-equivalent cash flows as long as you *assume* $T^* = T_c$.

Frequently the lessor acquires the asset directly from the manufacturer. This is a *direct lease*. Sometimes the lessor acquires the asset from the user and then leases it back to the user. This is a *sale and lease-back*.

Most leases involve only the lessee and the lessor. But, if the asset is very costly, it may be convenient to arrange a *leveraged lease*, in which the cost of the leased asset is financed by issuing debt and equity claims against the asset and the future lease payments.

There are a number of reasons that companies sometimes prefer to lease equipment rather than buying it. For example, there may be good tax reasons. If the operator cannot use the capital cost allowance tax shield, it makes sense to sell the equipment to someone who can. Also, the lessor may be better able to bear the risk of obsolescence, or be in a better position to resell second-hand assets. The lessor may be able to offer a very good deal on maintenance. Finally, it may be much less costly in time and effort to arrange a simple lease contract on a standard item of equipment than to arrange a normal loan.

A financial lease is like a debt. Therefore if you want to evaluate a lease, you must compare the effect of leasing the equipment with that of buying and borrowing. The trick is to set up the comparison properly, so that the lease competes with an *equivalent loan*. The equivalent loan commits the firm to exactly the same after-tax cash payments as the lease would.

A financial lease is superior to buying and borrowing if the financing provided by the lease exceeds the value (that is, principal amount) of the equivalent loan. Thus, the net value of a lease contract is:

Value of lease = financing provided by lease − value of equivalent loan

The value of the equivalent loan equals the lease cash flows discounted at the *after-tax* rate of interest the firm would pay on the equivalent loan:

$$\text{Value of equivalent loan} = \sum_{t=1}^{N} \frac{\text{LCF}_t}{(1 + r_D(1 - T_c))^t}$$

Here LCF_t is the cash outflow attributable to the lease in period t, and N is the last period in which the lease affects cash flow.

Actually, this formula works for any safe, nominal—that is, *debt-equivalent*—cash flow. You just discount the after-tax flow at the after-tax borrowing rate.

We can also analyze leases from the lessor's side of the transaction using the same approaches we developed for the lessee. If lessee and lessor are in the same tax bracket, they will receive exactly the same cash flows, but with signs reversed. Thus, the lessee can gain only at the lessor's expense, or vice versa. However, if the lessee's tax rate is lower than the lessor's, then both can gain at the government's expense.

Although this chapter was mostly devoted to financial leases, we included a few hints on analyzing operating leases. Remember that many operating leases have valuable options attached to them—for example, the right to renew the lease at a prespecified rate or to purchase the asset at a prespecified price.

FURTHER READING

The approach to lease valuation presented in this chapter is based on:

S.C. Myers, D.A. Dill, and A.J. Bautista, "Valuation of Financial Lease Contracts," *Journal of Finance*, 31:799–819 (June 1976).

J.R. Franks and S.D. Hodges, "Valuation of Financial Lease Contracts: A Note," *Journal of Finance*, 3:647–669 (May 1978).

Other useful works include Fabozzi's book and the theoretical discussions of Miller and Upton, and Lewellen, Long, and McConnell:

F.J. Fabozzi, *Equipment Leasing: A Comprehensive Guide for Executives*, Dow Jones-Irwin, Inc., New York, 1982.

M.H. Miller and C.W. Upton, "Leasing Buying and the Cost of Capital Services," *Journal of Finance*, **31**:761–786 (June 1976).

W.G. Lewellen, M.S. Long, and J.J. McConnell, "Asset Leasing in Competitive Capital Markets," *Journal of Finance*, **31**:787–798 (June 1976).

The options embedded in some lease contracts are discussed in:

T.E. Copeland and J.F. Weston, "A Note on the Evaluation of Cancellable Operating Leases," *Financial Management*, **11**:68–72 (Summer 1982).

J.J. McConnell and J.S. Schallheim, "Valuation of Asset Leasing Contracts," *Journal of Financial Economics*, **12**:237–261 (August 1983).

The valuation of debt-equivalent cash flows is discussed in:

R.S. Ruback, "Calculating the Present Value of Riskless Cash Flows," Working Paper, Sloan School of Management, MIT, June 1983.

QUIZ

1. The following terms are often used to describe leases:
   (A) Direct
   (B) Full-service
   (C) Operating
   (D) Financial
   (E) Rental
   (F) Net
   (G) Leveraged
   (H) Sale and lease-back
   (I) Full-payout
   Match each of these terms with one of the following statements:

   (A) The initial lease period is shorter than the economic life of the asset.
   (B) The initial lease period is long enough for the lessor to recover the cost of the asset.
   (C) The lessor provides maintenance and insurance.
   (D) The lessee provides maintenance and insurance.
   (E) The lessor buys the equipment from the manufacturer.
   (F) The lessor buys the equipment from the prospective lessee.
   (G) The lessor finances the lease contract by issuing debt and equity claims against it.

2. Some of the following reasons for leasing are rational. Others are irrational, or assume imperfect or inefficient capital markets. Which of the following reasons are the rational ones?
   (*a*) The lessee's need for the leased asset is only temporary.
   (*b*) Specialized lessors are better able to bear the risk of obsolescence.
   (*c*) Leasing provides 100% financing and thus preserves capital.
   (*d*) Leasing allows firms with low marginal tax rates to "sell" investment tax credits and CCA tax shields.
   (*e*) Leasing increases earnings per share.
   (*f*) Leasing reduces the transaction cost of obtaining external financing.
   (*g*) Leasing avoids restrictions on capital expenditures.

3. True or false?
   (a) Leasing payments are usually made at the start of each period. Thus the first payment is usually made as soon as the lease contract is signed.
   (b) Financial leases can still provide off-balance-sheet financing.
   (c) The trade-off faced by a prospective lessee is not "lease versus buy," but "lease versus borrow."
   (d) An equivalent loan's principal plus after-tax interest payments exactly match the after-tax cash flows of the lease.
   (e) A financial lease should not be undertaken unless it provides more financing than the equivalent loan.
   (f) It makes sense for firms that pay no taxes to lease from firms that do.
   (g) Other things equal, the net tax advantage to leasing increases as nominal interest rates increase.

4. Suppose that National Waferonics has before it a four-year lease proposal for a machine it may invest in. The firm constructs a table like Table 24-1. The bottom line of its table shows the lease cash flows:

	Year			
	0	1	2	3
Lease cash flow	+62,000	−26,800	−22,200	−17,600

   These flows reflect the cost of the machine, lost investment tax credits, CCA tax shields and the after-tax payments. Ignore salvage value. Assume the firm could borrow at 10% and faces a 46% marginal tax rate.
   (a) What is the value of the equivalent loan?
   (b) What is the value of the lease?
   (c) Suppose the machine's NPV under normal financing is −$5000. Should National Waferonics invest? Should it sign the lease?

5. Your firm is sued for patent infringement and loses the case. The judge orders it to pay damages of $1 million in four annual instalments, with the first $250,000 payment due immediately. The payments are not tax deductible. Your firm's normal borrowing rate is 15% and its marginal tax rate is 40%. What is the present value of the liability created by the judge's award?

QUESTIONS AND PROBLEMS

1. Look again at the bus lease as discussed in Sections 24-1 and 24-4.
   (a) What is the value of the lease if Widdicombe's marginal tax rate is $T_c = 0.30$?
   (b) What would the lease value be if Widdicombe had to use straight-line depreciation as CCA, for tax purposes? Assume the bus is to be depreciated to a value of $10,000 over six years, and that the half-year rule does not apply.

2. Recalculate the value of the lease to Widdicombe Transportation if the company pays no taxes until year 3. Calculate the lease cash flows by modifying Table 24-1. Remember that the after-tax borrowing rate for periods 1 and 2 differs from the rate for periods 3 through 6.

3. Refer to Table 24-2, which assumes the present value of the liability created by the bus lease is $100,000. Later in the chapter we showed that this liability is really only $75,840, the value of the equivalent loan. Reconstruct Table 24-2 using the correct value for the lease liability. Show that leasing still should displace debt on a dollar-for-dollar basis.

4. NNW Airlines proposes to lease a $1 million aircraft. The terms require five annual lease payments of $150,000 prepaid. NNW pays tax at 46%. If it purchases the aircraft, it would receive a 10% investment tax credit and would put the remainder of the aircraft cost in a 25% CCA class, separate from its other Class 9 assets. The half-year rule applies, and the aircraft will be worthless after five years. The interest rate is 10%. Draw up a schedule like Table 24-1 showing the incremental cash flows from leasing.
   (a) How much debt has been displaced by the lease? Show how the debt displaced by the lease declines over time.
   (b) By how much would the NPV of the lease change if the salvage value of the aircraft after five years is expected to be $200,000? Assume that a 12% discount rate is appropriate for such risky salvage flows.

5. Nodhead College needs a new computer. It can either buy it for $250,000 or lease it from Compulease. The lease terms require Nodhead to make six annual payments (prepaid) of $40,000. Nodhead pays no tax. Compulease pays tax at 46%. Compulease would place the computer in Class 10 (30%) with all its other computers. It runs a multimillion dollar leasing business and always has a substantial UCC in Class 10. The half-year rule for CCA applies. The computer will have no residual value at the end of year 5. The interest rate is 8%.
   (a) What is the NPV of the lease for Nodhead College?
   (b) What is the NPV for Compulease?
   (c) What is the overall gain to the two parties if the lease is undertaken?

6. Many companies calculate the internal rate of return of the incremental after-tax cash flows from leasing. What problems do you think this may give rise to? To what rate should the IRR be compared?

7. A Prince Edward Island potato farmer pays $400,000 for a custom-built machine for digging potatoes and transporting them to a French-fry factory 12 kilometres away. He is unsure whether the machine falls in Class 10 (30%) or Class 22 (50%). How much difference does this asset class question make to the machine's NPV? Assume the farmer can borrow at 16% and is in a 50% tax bracket. Suppose the machine will never be salvaged.

8. The overall gain to leasing is the sum of the lease's value to the lessee and its value to the lessor. Construct simple numerical examples showing how this gain is affected by:
   (a) The rate of interest
   (b) The choice of CCA rate
   (c) The difference between the tax rates of the lessor and lessee
   (d) The duration of the lease.

9. Discuss the following two opposite statements. What do you think makes the most sense?
   (a) "Leasing is tax avoidance and should be legislated against."
   (b) "Leasing ensures that the government's investment incentives work. It does so by allowing companies in non-taxpaying positions to take advantage of CCA and the investment tax credit."

10. The Safety Razor Company has a large tax loss carry-forward and does not expect the pay taxes for another 15 years. The company is therefore proposing to lease $100,000 of new machinery. The lease terms consist of six equal lease payments prepaid annually. The lessor would group the machinery with its other Class 8 (20%) assets, and this class always has a large UCC. There is no salvage value at the end of the lease. The tax rate is 46% and the interest rate is 10%. Wilbur Occam, the president of Safety Razor, wants to know the maximum lease payment

that his company should be willing to make and the minimum payment that the lessor is likely to accept. Can they negotiate a deal? How would your answer differ if the lessor is allowed a 50% CCA rate on the machinery?

11. Here is a very hard question. Merton Miller argues that companies that pay corporate income tax should be indifferent between issuing debt and equity (see Section 18-2). Suppose that he is right. Then companies that do not pay income tax should prefer to issue equity rather than debt. They should also prefer to lease rather than issue debt. Does this mean that they should be indifferent between leasing and issuing equity?

FINANCIAL PLANNING

ANALYZING FINANCIAL PERFORMANCE

"Divide and conquer" is the only practical strategy for presenting an extensive, complex field like financial management. We have broken the financial manager's job down into a series of clearly but narrowly defined topics, including capital budgeting, dividend policy, stock issue procedures, debt policy, and leasing. But in the end the financial manager has to consider the combined effects of these decisions on the firm as a whole.

In this chapter we look at how you can use financial data to analyze a firm's past performance and assess its current financial standing. For example, you may need to check whether your own firm's financial performance is in the ballpark of standard practice. Or you may wish to understand the policies of a competitor or to check on the financial health of a customer.

Understanding the past is a necessary prelude to contemplating the future. Therefore, the other chapters in Part 8 are devoted to financial planning. Chapter 26 shows how managers use long-term financial plans to establish concrete goals and to anticipate surprises. Chapter 27 then discusses short-term planning, where the focus is on ensuring that the firm has enough cash to pay its bills and puts any spare cash to good use. Chapter 27 also serves as an introduction to Part 9, which covers the management of the firm's short-term assets and liabilities.

But all that comes later. The business at hand is to analyze financial performance. We start with the time-honoured method of financial ratio analysis. We discuss how ratios are used, and we note the limitations of the accounting data, which most of the ratios are based on.

25-1 FINANCIAL RATIOS

We have all heard stories of financial whizzes who in minutes can take a company's accounts apart and find its innermost secrets in financial ratios. The truth, however, is that financial ratios are no substitute for a crystal ball. They are just a convenient way to summarize large quantities of financial data and to compare firms' performance. Ratios help you to ask the right questions but they don't answer them.

Financial ratios fall into four groups: leverage ratios, liquidity ratios, profitability or efficiency ratios, and market value ratios. We will illustrate the most common measures in each group with the aid of the 1983 income statement and balance sheets of Dofasco, Inc., one of the largest steel producers in Canada. Selected information from Dofasco's financial statements is provided in Table 25-1.

Leverage Ratios

Suppose that you are considering whether you should extend credit to a would-be customer. One of the first things that you will wish to know is what other debts the firm has. Our first set of ratios, therefore, summarize the firm's financial leverage.

Debt Ratio Financial leverage is usually measured by the ratio of long-term debt to total long-term capital. Since long-term lease agreements also commit the firm to a series of fixed payments, it makes sense to include the value of lease obligations with the long-term debt.[1] Thus for Dofasco:

$$\text{Debt ratio} = \frac{\text{long-term debt} + \text{value of leases}}{\text{long-term debt} + \text{value of leases} + \text{shareholders' equity}}$$

$$= \frac{404}{404 + 74 + 940} = 0.28$$

Another way to measure this is in terms of the company's debt-equity ratio:

Table 25-1 Summary of financial statements for Dofasco, Inc. (figures in millions of dollars).

	1983	1982
Balance Sheet:[1]		
Cash and short-term securities	324	180
Receivables	209	137
Inventories	442	453
Total current assets	975	770
Plant and equipment	1,173	1,237
Other long-term assets	27	16
Total assets	2,175	2,023
Current liabilities	388	177
Long-term debt and capital leases	404	430
Other long-term liabilities	369	332
Shareholders' equity:		
Preferred shares	74	226
Common shares	940	858
Total liabilities	2,175	2,022
Income statement:		
Sales	1,606	
Cost of goods sold	1,285	
Selling, administrative, and general expenses	99	
Other income	23	
Earnings before interest and tax (EBIT)	245	
Interest	43	
Tax	81	
Net income	120	
Preferred dividends	17	
Available to common shareholders	103	
Other financial information:[2]		
Depreciation	78	
Number of shares (in millions)	49.762	
Earnings per share (dollars)	$ 2.10	
Dividends per share (dollars)	$ 0.69	
Share price (dollars)	$19.67	

[1]Columns may not add because of rounding.
[2]Number of shares and per share value have been adjusted for January 24, 1984, 3-for-1 split.

---

[1]Preferred dividends also involve a series of fixed payments and are sometimes included with debt in the numerator of the debt ratio. In the context of the leverage ratios considered here, however, preferred shares are regarded as equity and are combined with common shares to compute total shareholders' equity.

$$\text{Debt-equity ratio} = \frac{\text{long-term debt} + \text{value of leases}}{\text{equity}} = \frac{404}{74 + 940} = 0.40$$

Notice that both these measures make use of book (that is, accounting) values rather than market values. The market value of the company finally determines whether debtholders get their money back, so you would expect analysts to look at the face amount of the debt as a proportion of the total market value of debt and equity. The main reason that they don't do this is that market values are often not readily available. Does it matter much? Perhaps not; after all, the market value includes the value of intangible assets generated by research and development, advertising, staff training, and so on. These assets are not readily saleable and, if the company falls on hard times, the value of these assets may disappear altogether. For some purposes, it may be just as well to follow the accountant and to ignore these intangible assets entirely.

Also, this measure of leverage takes account only of long-term debt obligations. Managers sometimes also define debt to include all liabilities other than equity:

$$\frac{\text{Total liabilities} - \text{equity}}{\text{Total liabilities}} = \frac{2,175 - 1,014}{2,175} = 0.53$$

Some fixed obligations are not shown on the balance sheet at all but are simply recorded in the notes to the accounts. For example, companies promise pension benefits to their employees. If the firm's pension fund is insufficient to cover these obligations, the company will one day have to provide the money. This deficiency is recorded in the notes to the accounts and in some cases it is larger than all the other debt put together. Managers usually ignore it when calculating a firm's leverage but they shouldn't.

Times Interest Earned   Another measure of financial leverage is the extent to which interest is covered by earnings before interest and taxes (EBIT) plus depreciation. In the case of Dofasco:[2]

$$\text{Times interest earned} = \frac{\text{EBIT} + \text{depreciation}}{\text{interest}} = \frac{245 + 78}{43} = 7.5$$

Often analysts use an average of earnings over several years. The idea here is to smooth out temporary peaks and troughs. However, we will see later that there is no general tendency for earnings to bounce back after a fall or to sink back after a rise. The current level of earnings is likely to be a better guide to the future than some past average.

The regular interest payment is a hurdle that companies must keep jumping if they are to avoid default. The "times interest earned" ratio measures how much clear air there is between hurdle and hurdler. Always bear in mind that such summary measures tell only a part of the story. For example, it would make sense to include other fixed charges such as regular repayments of existing debt or long-term lease payments.

Earnings Variability   A large debt burden is a problem only if there is uncertainty about future earnings. You may, therefore, want to look at the variability of the company's earnings over time.

---

[2]The numerator of "times interest earned" can be defined in several ways. Sometimes depreciation is excluded. Sometimes it is just net earnings plus interest—that is, earnings before interest but after tax. This last definition seems nutty to us, because the point of "times interest earned" is to assess the risk that the firm won't have enough money to pay interest. If EBIT falls below interest obligations, the firm won't have to worry about taxes. Interest is paid before the firm pays income taxes.

There is no generally accepted measure of variability. Since earnings may vary from positive to negative, you cannot simply calculate the variability of percentage changes. An alternative is to look at the standard deviation of year-to-year earnings changes relative to the average level of earnings.[3] Thus

$$\text{Earnings variability} = \frac{\text{standard deviation } (\text{EBIT}_{t+1} - \text{EBIT}_t)}{\text{average EBIT}}$$

Liquidity Ratios

If you are extending credit or lending to a company for a short period, you are not just interested in the total asset coverage of the debt. You want to know whether the company will be able to lay its hands on the cash to repay you. That is why credit analysts and bankers look at several measures of liquidity.

Another reason that managers focus on liquid assets is that the figures are more reliable. The book value of a catalytic cracker may be a fairly poor guide to its true value, but at least you know what cash in the bank is worth.

Liquidity ratios also have some less desirable characteristics. Because short-term assets and liabilities are easily changed, measures of liquidity can rapidly become out of date. You might not know what that catalytic cracker is worth but you can be fairly sure that it won't disappear overnight. Also, companies generally choose a slack period for the end of their financial year. At these times the companies are likely to have more cash and less short-term debt than during busier seasons.

Net Working Capital to Total Assets   Current assets are those assets that the company expects to turn into cash in the near future; current liabilities are liabilities that it expects to meet in the near future. The difference between the current assets and the current liabilities is known as net working capital. It roughly measures the company's potential reservoir of cash. Managers often express net working capital as a proportion of total assets:

$$\frac{\text{Net working capital}}{\text{Total assets}} = \frac{975 - 388}{2,175} = 0.27$$

Current Ratio   Another measure that serves a similar purpose is the current ratio:

$$\text{Current ratio} = \frac{\text{current assets}}{\text{current liabilities}} = \frac{975}{388} = 2.5$$

Changes in the current ratio can mislead. For example, suppose that a company borrows a large sum from the bank and invests it in marketable securities. If nothing else alters, net working capital is unaffected but the current ratio changes.

Quick (or Acid-Test) Ratio   Some assets are closer to cash than others. If trouble comes, inventories may not sell at anything above fire-sale prices. (Trouble typically comes *because* the firm can't sell its finished product inventory for more than production cost.) Thus, inventories are often excluded when measuring liquidity:

---

[3]You might also want to divide the standard deviation of changes in EBIT by current EBIT minus interest. The higher this ratio, the greater the odds that EBIT will fall below interest charges.

$$\text{Quick ratio} = \frac{\text{current assets} - \text{inventories}}{\text{current liabilities}} = \frac{975 - 442}{388} = 1.4$$

Cash Ratio A company's most liquid assets are its holdings of cash and marketable securities. That is why financial analysts also look at the cash ratio:

$$\text{Cash ratio} = \frac{\text{cash} + \text{marketable securities}}{\text{current liabilities}} = \frac{324}{388} = 0.84$$

Of course, lack of cash may not matter if the firm can borrow on short notice. Who cares whether a firm has actually borrowed from the bank or whether it has a guaranteed line of credit that enables it to borrow if it chooses? None of the standard liquidity measures takes the firm's "reserve borrowing power" into account.

Interval Measure Instead of looking at a firm's liquid assets relative to its current liabilities, it may be useful to measure whether they are large relative to the firm's regular cash outgoings. One suggestion is the so-called interval measure:

$$\text{Interval measure} = \frac{\text{current assets} - \text{inventories}}{\text{average daily expenditures from operations}}$$

$$= \frac{975 - 442}{(1,384 \div 365)} = 141 \text{ days}$$

Thus Dofasco has sufficient liquid assets to finance operations for 141 days, even if it receives no further cash.

Profitability or Efficiency Ratios

Financial analysts employ another set of ratios to judge how efficiently companies are using their assets. As we will see, there is a much greater degree of ambiguity in these ratios. For example, we can be fairly sure that it is safer to lend to a company that has relatively little leverage and a predominance of liquid assets. But how should the lender interpret the fact that a firm has a high profit margin? Perhaps it is in a low-volume, high-markup business. (Jewellers operate on higher profit margins than food wholesalers but they are not necessarily safer.) Or perhaps it is more vertically integrated than its rivals. Again, that is not necessarily safer. Perhaps it charges higher prices, which is a bad sign. Or perhaps it has lower costs, which is a good sign. We think that you should use these profitability ratios to help you *ask* the important questions rather than to help answer them.

Sales to Total Assets The sales-to-assets ratio shows how hard the firm's assets are being put to use.

$$\frac{\text{Sales}}{\text{Average total assets}} = \frac{1,606}{(2,175 + 2,023) \div 2} = 0.76$$

A high ratio could indicate that the firm is working close to capacity. It may prove difficult to generate further business without an increase in invested capital.

Sales to Net Working Capital Net working capital can be measured more accurately than other assets. Also the level of net working capital can be adjusted more rapidly to reflect temporary fluctuations in sales. Thus managers sometimes focus on how hard working capital has been put to use.

$$\frac{\text{Sales}}{\text{Average net working capital}} = \frac{1,606}{(587 + 593) \div 2} = 2.7$$

Net Profit Margin   If you want to know what proportion of sales finds its way into profits, you look at the profit margin. Thus

$$\text{Net profit margin} = \frac{\text{EBIT} - \text{tax}}{\text{sales}} = \frac{245 - 81}{1,606} = 0.102 \text{ or } 10.2\%$$

Inventory Turnover   Managers sometimes look at the rate at which companies turn over their inventories. In Dofasco's case,

$$\text{Inventory turnover} = \frac{\text{cost of goods sold}}{\text{average inventory}} = \frac{1,285}{(442 + 453) \div 2} = 2.9$$

A high inventory turnover is often regarded as a sign of efficiency. But don't jump to conclusions—it may simply indicate that the firm is living from hand to mouth.

Average Collection Period   The average collection period measures the speed with which customers pay their bills:

$$\text{Average collection period} = \frac{\text{average receivables}}{\text{average daily sales}}$$

$$= \frac{(209 + 137) \div 2}{1,606 \div 365} = 39 \text{ days}$$

A low ratio is again believed to indicate an efficient collection department, but it sometimes results from an unduly restrictive credit policy.

Return on Total Assets   Managers often measure the performance of a firm by the ratio of income to total assets. Income is usually defined as earnings before interest but after taxes. Also, since the assets are likely to change over the year, it is common to measure return on the average of the assets at the beginning and end of the year:[4]

---

[4]This measure is sometimes misleading if it is used to compare firms with different capital structures. The reason is that firms that pay more interest pay less taxes. Thus this ratio reflects differences in financial leverage as well as in operating performance. If you want a measure of operating performance alone, we suggest adjusting taxes by adding back interest tax shields (interest payments × marginal tax rate). This gives the taxes the firm would pay if all-equity financed. Thus

$$\text{Return on total assets} = \frac{\text{EBIT} - (\text{taxes} + \text{interest tax shields})}{\text{average total assets}}$$

$$= \frac{245 - (81 + 0.46 \times 43)}{(2,175 + 2,073) \div 2} = 6.9\%$$

We could use this measure to compare the operating performance of two firms even if they had radically different debt ratios.

Sometimes net income after interest and taxes is used in the numerator. This is an odd measure: equity income ought to be compared with equity investment, not with total assets.

$$\text{Return on total assets} = \frac{\text{EBIT} - \text{taxes}}{\text{average total assets}}$$

$$= \frac{245 - 81}{(2,175 + 2,023) \div 2} = 0.078 \text{ or } 7.8\%$$

Another measure focuses on the return on the firm's equity:

$$\text{Return on equity} = \frac{\text{earnings available for common}}{\text{average common equity}}$$

$$= \frac{103}{(940 + 858) \div 2} = 0.115 \text{ or } 11.5\%$$

The assets in a company's books are valued on the basis of their original cost (less any depreciation). A high return on assets does not mean that you could buy the same assets today and get a high return. Nor does a low return on assets imply that the assets could be better employed elsewhere. Thus return on assets does not tell you whether the firm's assets are being used efficiently.

Some profitability or efficiency ratios can be linked together in useful ways. For example, the return on assets depends on the firm's sales-to-assets ratio and profit margin:

$$\frac{\text{Income}}{\text{Assets}} = \frac{\text{sales}}{\text{assets}} \times \frac{\text{income}}{\text{sales}}$$

All firms would like to earn a higher return on assets, but their ability to do so is limited by competition. If the expected return on assets is fixed by competition, firms face a trade-off between the sales-to-assets ratio and the profit margin. Thus we find that fast-food chains, which turn over their capital frequently, also tend to operate on low profit margins. Hotels have relatively low sales-to-assets ratios but tend to compensate for this with higher margins.

Firms often seek to increase their profit margin by becoming more vertically integrated—for example, they may acquire a supplier or one of their sales outlets. Unfortunately, unless they have some special skill in running these new businesses, they are likely to find that any gain in profit margin is offset by a decline in the sales-to-assets ratio.

Payout Ratio The payout ratio measures the proportion of earnings that is paid out as dividends. For Dofasco:

$$\text{Payout ratio} = \frac{\text{dividend}}{\text{earnings per share}} = \frac{0.69}{2.10} = 0.33$$

We saw in Section 16-2 that managers don't like cutting dividends because of a temporary shortfall in earnings. Therefore, if a company's earnings are particularly variable, management is likely to play safe by setting a low average payout ratio.

When earnings fall unexpectedly, the payout ratio is likely to rise temporarily. Likewise, if earnings are expected to rise next year, management may feel that it can pay slightly more generous dividends than it would otherwise have done.

Earnings not paid out as dividends are plowed back into the business.

Proportion of earnings plowed back $= 1 -$ payout ratio

$$= \frac{\text{earnings} - \text{dividend}}{\text{earnings}}$$

If you multiply this figure by the return on equity, you can see how rapidly the shareholders' investment is growing as a result of plowback. Thus for Dofasco:

$$\text{Growth in equity from plowback} = \frac{\text{earnings} - \text{dividend}}{\text{earnings}} \times \frac{\text{earnings}}{\text{equity}}$$

$$= 0.33 \times 0.115 = 0.038 \text{ or } 3.8\%$$

If Dofasco can continue to earn 11.5% on its book equity, both earnings and equity will grow at 3.8% a year.

Market Value Ratio

There is no law that prohibits the financial manager from introducing data that are not in the company accounts. For example, if you were analyzing a steel company, you might want to look at the cost per tonne of steel produced or the sales per employee. Frequently managers find it helpful to look at ratios that combine accounting and stock market data. Here are four of these market-based ratios.

Price-Earnings Ratio   The price-earnings, or *P/E*, ratio is a common measure of the esteem in which the company is held by investors. In the case of Dofasco:[5]

$$P/E \text{ ratio } = \frac{\text{stock price}}{\text{earnings per share}} = \frac{19.67}{2.10} = 9.4$$

What does it mean when a company's stock sells on a high or low *P/E*? To answer this question you may find it helpful to look back to a formula that we introduced in Chapter 4. If a company's dividends are expected to grow at a steady rate, then the current stock price is

$$P_0 = \frac{\text{DIV}_1}{r - g}$$

In this formula DIV_1 measures the expected dividend next year, r is the return that investors require from similar investments, and g is the expected rate of dividend growth. In order to find the *P/E* ratio, simply divide through by expected earnings per share

$$\frac{P_0}{\text{EPS}_1} = \frac{\text{DIV}_1}{\text{EPS}_1} \times \frac{1}{r - g}$$

Thus a high *P/E* ratio may indicate that (1) investors expect high dividend growth (g); or (2) that the stock has low risk and, therefore, that investors are content with

---

[5]We use 1983 earnings per share and the price per share at the end of 1983. Since stockholders always look forward, not back, it would be better to use earnings that were forecasted for 1984. See Section 4-4.

a low prospective return (r); or (3) the company is expected to achieve average growth while paying out a high proportion of earnings (DIV_1/EPS_1).

Dividend Yield The stock's dividend yield is simply the expected dividend as a proportion of the stock price. Thus for Dofasco:

$$\text{Dividend yield} = \frac{\text{dividend per share}}{\text{stock price}} = \frac{0.69}{19.67} = 0.035 \text{ or } 3.5\%$$

Again it is helpful to consider a company with a steady expected growth in dividends. In this case:

$$\text{Dividend yield} = \frac{DIV_1}{P_0} = r - g$$

Thus a high yield may indicate that investors expect low dividend growth or that the stock's risk merits a high expected return.

Market-to-Book Ratio The market-to-book ratio is the ratio of stock price to book value per share. For Dofasco:

$$\text{Market-to-book ratio} = \frac{\text{stock price}}{\text{book value per share}} = \frac{19.67}{940 \div 49.762} = 1.04$$

Book value per share is just stockholders' book equity (net worth) divided by the number of shares outstanding. Book equity equals common stock plus retained earnings—the net amount that the firm has received from stockholders or reinvested on their behalf. Thus Dofasco's market-to-book ratio of 1.04 means that the firm is worth only 4% more than past and present stockholders have put into it.

Tobin's q The ratio of the market value of a company's debt and equity to the replacement cost of its assets is often referred to as Tobin's q, after the economist James Tobin.[6] This ratio is like the market-to-book ratio, but there are several important differences. The numerator q includes all the firm's debt and equity securities, not just its common stock. The denominator includes all assets, not just the firm's net worth. Moreover, these assets are not entered at original cost, as shown in the company's books, but at what it would cost to replace them. Inflation has driven many assets' replacement cost well above original cost. In Canada, companies of a certain minimum inventory and asset size are required to report the estimated replacement cost as a supplement to their regular financial statements.[7]

Tobin argued that firms have an incentive to invest when q is greater than one (that is when capital equipment is worth more than it costs to replace), and that they will

---

[6]J. Tobin, "A General Equilibrium Approach to Monetary Theory," *Journal of Money, Credit, and Banking*, 1:15–29 (February 1969).

For estimates of q see R.H. Gordon and D.F. Bradford, "Taxation and the Stock Market Valuation of Capital Gains and Dividends: Theory and Empirical Results," *Journal of Public Economics*, 14 (October 1980); G. Von Furstenberg, "Corporate Investment: Does Market Valuation Really Matter?" *Brookings Papers on Economic Activity*, 2:347–397 (1977); and E.B. Lindberg and S.A. Ross, "Tobin's q Ratio and Industrial Organization," *Journal of Business*, 54:1–33 (January 1981).

[7]The conditions under which a publicly traded firm must report replacement cost information are given in the *CICA Handbook*, Section 4510.

stop investing only when q falls to one. Conversely, there may be occasions when q is less than one (that is, when equipment is worth less than it would cost to replace), and at these times firms have no incentive to invest.

Of course it is possible to think of cases when the existing assets are worth much more than they cost but there is no scope for further profitable investment. Nevertheless, a high market value is usually a sign that investors believe there are good opportunities in your business.

We should also expect that q would be higher for firms with a strong competitive advantage. Table 25-2 seems to bear this out. The companies with the highest values of q tend to be those that have had very strong brand images or patent protection. Those with the lowest values have generally been in highly competitive and shrinking industries.

Table 25-2   Average values of Tobin's q, 1960–1977.

	High q's		Low q's
Avon Products	8.53	Cone Mills	0.45
Polaroid	6.42	Holly Sugar	0.50
Xerox	5.52	Federal Paper Bond	0.52
Searle	5.27	National Steel	0.53
MMM	4.87	Graniteville	0.55
Schering-Plough	4.30	Publicker Industries	0.59
IBM	4.21	Medusa Corp.	0.60
Coca-Cola	4.21	Lowenstein	0.61
Smithkline	4.19	U.S. Steel	0.62
Eli Lilly	4.02	Dan River	0.67

Source: E.B. Lindberg and S.A. Ross, "Tobin's q Ratio and Industrial Organization," Journal of Business, 54:1–33 (January 1981).

Choosing a Benchmark

We have shown you how to calculate the principal financial ratios for Dofasco. But you still need some way of judging whether a ratio is high or low.

A good starting point is to compare the 1983 ratios with equivalent figures for Dofasco in earlier years. For example, you can see from the first two columns of Table 25-3 that Dofasco appears to be a stronger company in 1983 than it had been during the previous five years. It was considerably more profitable, although it was more highly levered, and it was more illiquid. Investors also seemed to be more optimistic about Dofasco's products, for they placed a higher value on its earnings and assets than in earlier years.[8] But you should now dig behind these figures. For example, check that Dofasco has not cut back its research and development expenditures, for that would be maintaining current earnings at the expense of future earnings. Find out what was happening to inventories. In 1983, the fall in the quantity of inventories reduced the cost of goods sold by $11 million. This also can't recur indefinitely. Also, examine the 42% increase in the debt ratio and the 21% decrease in the current ratio. Are they a source of concern? In sum, don't just measure whether Dofasco's financial ratios have changed: try to understand *why* they have changed.

---

[8]Averages of ratios are somewhat odd animals. For example, you wouldn't want to take an average of *P/E* ratios if one company had negligible earnings. In Table 25-3 we have scaled all the industry data by dividing by the year's total assets. Then we have calculated the ratio of the average of one item to the average of the other item.

Table 25-3   Financial ratios for Dofasco, Inc. and other steel companies.

	1983	1978–1982	Other Companies in the Steel Industry, 1983*
Leverage ratios:			
Debt ratio	0.40	0.28	0.33
Total liabilities—equity / Total liabilities	0.53	0.49	0.51
Times interest earned	7.5	8.8	1.2
Liquidity ratios:			
Net working capital to total assets	0.27	0.31	0.26
Current ratio	2.5	3.4	2.8
Quick ratio	1.4	1.6	1.1
Cash ratio	0.84	0.72	0.22
Interval measure (in days)	141	107	86
Profitability (or efficiency) ratios:			
Sales to total assets	0.76	0.81	0.67
Sales to net working capital	2.7	2.7	2.5
Net profit margin (%)	10.2	10.8	− 16.3
Inventory turnover	2.9	3.0	2.5
Average collection period (days)	39	44	55
Return on total assets (%)	7.8	9.1	− 11.2
Return on equity (%)	11.5	16.0	− 2.4
Market value ratios:			
Price-earnings ratio	9.4	8.5	**
Dividend yield (%)	3.5	5.8	2.8
Market-to-book ratio	1.04	0.78	0.85

*Algoma Steel, Stelco, IPSCO, and Ivaco.
**Three of the four other steel companies had negative earnings in 1983.

It is also helpful to compare Dofasco's financial position with that of other firms. However, you would not expect companies in different industries to have similar financial ratios. For example, a steel producer is unlikely to have the same profit margin as a jeweller or the same leverage as a finance company. It makes sense, therefore, to limit the comparison to other firms in the same industry. The third column of Table 25-3 sets out the average financial ratios for the other steel producers. Dofasco appears to be more profitable and financially stronger than the other steel companies. But once again you should not stop there. For example, notice that Dofasco's new leverage and liquidity ratios are now in line with industry averages. This tends to mitigate the concern raised when Dofasco's current and past values were compared. Note also that the difference in the return on assets stems largely from the difference in profit margins. Was this due to greater efficiency or to a difference in the type of business? You can obtain some clues by comparing segment counts, which break profitability down according to product and area of operation. Are there any indications that the difference in margins may be temporary? A closer examination of the cost of goods sold may help you decide.

Financial ratios for industries are published by Dun and Bradstreet Canada, Statistics Canada, and others. Table 25-4 gives selected leverage, liquidity, and profitability ratios for major industry groups. This should give you a feel for some differences between industries.

Table 25-4   Selected financial ratios for major industry groups, 1983.

Industry[1]	Debt-Equity Ratio	Current Ratio	Net Profit Margin	Collection Period[2]	Return on Equity[3]
All manufacturers	0.56	1.7	0.048	42	0.149
Food	0.66	1.3	0.011	23	0.145
Tobacco	0.77	1.4	0.006	20	0.197
Paper products	0.36	1.9	0.042	49	0.090
Publishing and printing	0.67	1.0	0.071	57	0.281
Iron and steel mills	0.54	2.8	0.045	50	0.086
Electrical equipment, industrial	0.49	1.7	0.047	65	0.140
Retail trade	0.68	1.4	0.035	12	0.289

[1]The industry classifications and ratios are from *Key Business Ratios, 1983 Edition*, Dun and Bradstreet Canada.
[2]Collection period is average daily sales divided by end-of-year receivables.
[3]Return on equity includes preferred dividends in numerator and the value of the preferred shares in the denominator.

Which Financial Ratios?

Be selective in your choice of financial ratios, because many ratios tell you similar things. For illustration, Table 25-5 shows the correlation between the nine financial ratios.[9] Notice that the correlation between the debt-equity ratio and the long-term debt-equity ratio is 0.8. This suggests that you may not need to calculate both these ratios. Conversely, there is almost no relationship between a firm's current ratio and the return on equity. You can get additional information by looking at both figures.

Table 25-5   Correlations between different financial ratios; all industries 1975 (rank correlations).

	Long-term debt-equity ratio	Debt-equity ratio	Times interest earned	Current ratio	Quick ratio	Interval measure	Return on assets	Return on equity	Inventory turnover
Long-term debt-equity ratio	1.0								
Debt-equity ratio	0.8	1.0							
Times interest earned	−0.6	−0.6	1.0						
Current ratio	−0.4	−0.6	0.3	1.0					
Quick ratio	−0.3	−0.5	0.3	0.7	1.0				
Interval measure	−0.1	−0.2	0.1	0.2	0.5	1.0			
Return on assets	−0.3	−0.4	0.9	0.2	0.3	0.1	1.0		
Return on equity	−0.1	−0.1	0.6	0.0	0.1	0.1	0.8	1.0	
Inventory turnover	0.1	0.1	0.2	−0.4	0.0	−0.2	0.2	0.3	1.0

Source: G. Foster, *Financial Statement Analysis*, Prentice-Hall, Inc., Englewood Cliffs, N.J., 1978.

[9]The correlations are rank correlations. In other words, they measure whether a company's ranking in terms of one ratio corresponds to its ranking in terms of the second ratio.

25-2   THE EARNINGS RECORD

Figure 25-1 summarizes Dofasco's earnings record over the past six years.

To interpret this record you need to take into account what was happening to other companies. The reason for this is that Dofasco is affected by the state of the economy as a whole and by the prosperity of its particular industry. The importance of these external influences on a company's income is shown in Table 25-6 for United States companies. On average an estimated 27% of the yearly variation in income is due to changes in the aggregate income of all corporations. A further 18% is explained by changes in the industry's income.

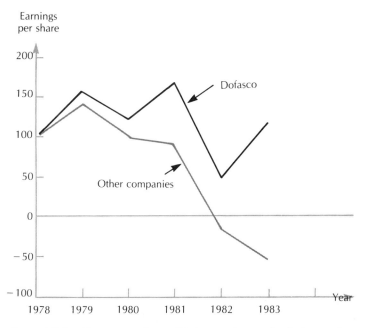

Figure 25-1   Earnings per share of Dofasco and a sample of other steel companies, 1978–83, expressed as a percent of 1978 earnings per share. Note that the other steel companies' earnings were negative in 1982 and 1983.

Figure 25-1 shows the average earnings performance of other Canadian companies doing business in the steel industry. We can now start to ask sensible questions about Dofasco's record. For example, why were the earnings of steel companies so weak in 1982 and 1983? Was it because of depressed business conditions and an influx of imports competing for whatever business was available in Canada? If so, we know two danger signals to look out for in the future. Why did Dofasco buck the industry trend to a small extent in 1982 and to a great extent in 1983? During this period, car and appliance sales accelerated. Since Dofasco is the dominant supplier of flat-rolled steel in Canada, it managed to weather some difficult times within the steel industry.

Throughout the sample period, Dofasco's earnings seemed to have performed better both in absolute terms and relative to the other companies. Is this a sign that Dofasco has entered a period of more rapid growth? Not necessarily. Statisticians who have studied the time path of earnings' reported earnings conclude that earnings behave much like stock prices—that is, they seem to follow a random walk.[10] There is almost

---

[10]See, for example, R. Ball and R. Watts, "Some Time Series Properties of Accounting Income," *Journal of Finance*, **27**:663–682 (June 1972).

no relationship between a company's earnings growth in one period and that in the next. Therefore, do not extrapolate growth mechanically. A firm with above-average earnings growth may sustain it, but it is equally likely to be followed by below-average growth.

Table 25-6 Percentage of changes in net income due to economywide influences and industry influences (measured for 457 firms, 1957–1975).

	Economywide Influence	Industry Influence
Textile products	45%	10%
Paper	37	42
Electric utilities	35	52
Retail—department stores	34	26
Textile apparel manufacturing	33	28
Oil—integrated domestic	31	49
Chemicals—major	29	27
Air transport	27	5
Retail—food chains	23	12
Tire & rubber goods	22	29
Natural gas	22	9
Steel—minor	20	16
Office & business equipment	16	20
Aerospace	15	1
Auto parts & accessories	13	31
Building materials	12	15
Drugs—ethical	5	51
Average	27%	18%

Source: G. Foster, *Financial Statement Analysis*, Prentice-Hall, Inc., Englewood Cliffs, N.J., 1978.

Since earnings changes are unrelated from one year to the next, your best measure of past growth is the simple average of past annual percentage growth rates. There is little point in fitting a trend line to past earnings, and such a trend line tells you little about likely future earnings.

Of course there are many other sources of information that may help you forecast earnings. For example, when a firm enjoys a high *P/E* ratio despite disappointing earnings, it suggests investors expect an earnings rebound. Or suppose a firm announces a significant technological jump ahead of its competitors: you don't need a Ph.D. to figure out the likely impact on earnings.

*The Meaning of Accounting Earnings

Economists often define earnings as cash flow plus the change in value of the company's assets. But we know from looking at the behaviour of stock prices that asset values fluctuate widely and unpredictably from year to year. So it looks as if the company's published earnings follow a much smoother path than economic earnings. Accountants don't really try to track year-to-year economic income. They seem more interested in showing the long-run average profitability of the firm's assets.[11] However, they often don't achieve that objective either.

---

[11]Fischer Black has made this point in an extreme but very interesting way. See F. Black, "The Magic in Earnings: Economic Earnings versus Accounting Earnings," *Financial Analysts Journal*, **36**:3–8 (November–December 1980).

We described the biases in accounting profitability measures in Chapter 12. A few more words are needed here because accountants provide most of the input for financial ratios.

How Accounting Earnings are Calculated   We emphasized in Chapter 6 that accounting earnings differ from cash flow. Accountants start with cash flow, but they allocate cash outflows to two categories—current and capital expenditures. Current expenditures are deducted from earnings right away.[12] Capital expenditures are capitalized and then depreciated over the following years.

A tricky problem for the accountant is to decide which outflows are to be capitalized. When a company builds a new factory, there is an outflow of cash but shareholders also acquire an asset that is likely to bring higher cash flows in the future. Therefore, accountants are prepared to treat such expenditures as capital investments. But what about the cost of research and development, or staff training, or a new advertising campaign? These expenditures are also investments in the future but accountants are reluctant to recognize investments in intangible assets. Therefore, they deduct such expenditures from current earnings.[13]

If a high-tech company makes a large investment in research and development (R&D), financial statements are likely to understate true earnings. But investors recognize that some of the expenses are really an investment in the future. Therefore, the stock sells at a high price relative to published earnings. Subsequently, when the investment in R&D begins to pay off, published earnings are likely to rise rapidly. But investors are aware that the company is now running down its capital; so the stock price will not keep pace with earnings.[14]

A company's income statement shows the actual operating cash flows but it does not show the actual change in asset value. Instead, accountants set up a depreciation schedule ahead of time and, except in abnormal circumstances, they stick to it. Thus the company's income statement reflects partly what actually happened (the operating cash flow) and partly what was forecast to happen (the depreciation in asset value).

When accountants set up the depreciation schedule in advance, they do not make detailed forecasts of how the value of each asset is likely to vary over time. Instead they rely on a few standard rules of thumb such as straight-line depreciation. If an investment takes several years to reach full profitability, then in the early years straight-line depreciation will overstate the likely fall in the investment's value and in the later years it will understate it. For example, suppose that a paper manufacturer opens a new mill. Large paper mills take a notoriously long time to reach maximum efficiency. Therefore, if the company depreciates its assets straight-line, the financial statements will initially understate true earnings and the stock will sell at a high price relative to the published figure.

Of course decisions on which items to capitalize and how to depreciate them are not the only potential sources of distortion in earnings. Our message, however, is a general one. If you wish to use a company's earnings as a guide to its value, you need to "normalize" those earnings for temporary distortions that stem from particular accounting techniques.

---

[12]This is obviously an oversimplification. Accountants also try to record income and expenditure in the year in which it accrues rather than when the bills are paid.

[13]Accountants prefer assets you can kick. Since you can't see or touch intangible assets, how can you be *sure* they are there?

[14]When the stock price does not respond to the increased earnings, managers sometimes feel that investors are irrational or ungrateful. They forget that the *real* increase in earnings occurred several years earlier.

---

*How Inflation Affects Book Returns

We will steer clear of "inflation accounting" because the subject is so complex when one gets down to practical proposals. We will just remind you how inflation bears on standard book earnings.

First, inflation increases the nominal value of work-in-process and finished inventory. Suppose you are a clothing manufacturer. In January you make up 1,000 men's suits worth $300 apiece, but you do not sell the suits until June. During this time your competitors have raised their prices by 6% and you have quite literally followed suit. Thus the goods are finally sold for $300 \times 1.06 = \$318$.

Part of your profit on this batch of suits can be attributed to inflation while the suits sat in inventory. You receive an inventory profit of $18 per suit.

Inventory profits are profits. You are better off with them than without. They are properly included in nominal income. However, they are not a part of real income, except to the extent that inventories appreciate faster than the general price level.

There is a second problem. As inflation progresses, the net book value of fixed assets get more and more out of date—that is, book value understates current value or replacement cost. Thus book depreciation is too low.[15]

Inflation has a third effect on book profits of firms that borrow. Lenders are paid back in inflated future dollars, so they demand a higher interest rate to compensate for the declining real value of their loan. The part of the interest rate that compensates for expected inflation is called the *inflation premium.*

The full interest payment, including the inflation premium, is deducted from the firm's net book income. But book income does not recognize the compensating gain that the stockholders make at the expense of lenders. Remember, lenders gain from the inflation premium but lose as inflation drives down the real value of their asset. Stockholders lose by paying the inflation premium but gain because inflation drives down the real value of their obligation. Book income recognizes stockholders' loss but not the offsetting gain.[16]

25-3 APPLICATIONS OF FINANCIAL ANALYSIS

We have discussed how to calculate and interpret summary measures of a company's financial position. We conclude this chapter with a brief glimpse at some of the ways that these measures can help the financial manager.

Using Financial Ratios in Credit Analysis

Suppose that you are a credit analyst or bank lending officer with the job of deciding whether a particular company is likely to repay its debts. What can you learn from the company's financial statements?

To answer this question William Beaver compared the financial ratios of 79 firms that subsequently failed with the ratios of 79 that remained solvent.[17] Beaver's sample of failed firms behaved much as you would expect. They had more debt than the

---

[15]At the same time the money value of the assets is rising, but that appreciation is also not shown in the income statement.

[16]For a good, provocative discussion of inflationary biases in book income see F. Modigliani and R.A. Cohn, "Inflation, Rational Valuation and the Market," *Financial Analysts Journal*, 35:24–44 (March–April 1979).

[17]See W.H. Beaver, "Financial Ratios and Predictors of Failure," *Empirical Research in Accounting: Selected Studies. Supplement to Journal of Accounting Research*, 1966, 77–111.

surviving firms and they had a lower return on sales and assets. They had less cash but more receivables. As a result they had somewhat lower current ratios and dramatically lower cash ratios. Contrary to popular belief, the failed firms had less, rather than more, inventory.

Figure 25-2 provides some idea of the predictive power of these financial ratios. You can see that five years before failure the group of failed firms appeared to be consistently less healthy. As we move progressively closer to the date of collapse, the difference between the two groups becomes even more marked.

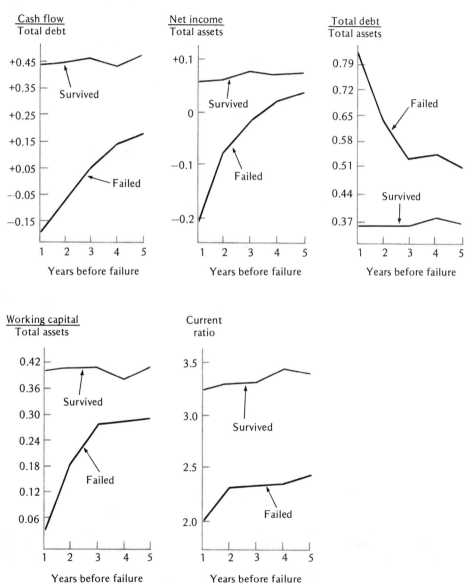

Figure 25-2 Beaver's study showed that the financial ratios of firms which subsequently fail are different from those of firms which survive. Note that the horizontal axis measures the number of years *before* failure: thus moving from right to left brings the failed firms *closer* to failure.

Source: W.H. Beaver, "Financial Ratios and Predictors of Failure," *Empirical Research in Accounting: Selected Studies. Supplement to Journal of Accounting Research*, 1966, pp. 77–111, fig. 1, p. 82.

Instead of looking at a number of separate clues, it may be more useful to combine the different bits of information into a single measure of the likelihood of bankruptcy. We will describe in Chapter 28 how companies construct such a measure.

Using Financial Ratios to Estimate Market Risk

Chapter 9 described how the return that investors require from a company's stock depends on its market risk or beta. If you have a sufficient history of stock price data, you can estimate beta by looking at the extent to which the price was affected by fluctuations in the market.

Because such stock price data are not always available, financial economists have examined whether accounting data can be used to estimate beta. The pioneering study is by Beaver, Kettler, and Scholes.[18] In addition to calculating the usual financial ratios, Beaver, Kettler, and Scholes calculated an "accounting beta." In other words, they estimated the sensitivity of each company's earnings changes to changes in the aggregate earnings of all companies. An accounting beta of less than 1.0 means that on average the company's earnings changed by less than 1% for each 1% change in aggregate earnings. Conversely an accounting beta of more than 1.0 implies that the firm's earnings changed by more than 1% for each 1% change in aggregate earnings.

Table 25-7 summarizes the findings of this study. Not only the accounting beta but also the firm's leverage and payout ratio appear to provide useful clues to market risk.

Instead of looking at financial ratios one by one, Rosenberg and Marathe looked at a combination of ratios and obtained a single estimate of beta that was about as accurate as you could get from stock price data.[19] They suggested that you can get even better estimates of risk by taking both accounting measures and stock price data into account.

Table 25-7 Correlations between stock market betas and financial ratios.

	1947–1956	1957–1965
Accounting beta	0.44	0.23
Leverage	0.23	0.22
Average payout ratio	−0.49	−0.29
Asset size	−0.06	−0.16
Asset growth	0.27	0.01
Liquidity	−0.13	0.05

Source: W.H. Beaver, P. Kettler, and M. Scholes, "The Association Between Market-Determined and Accounting-Determined Measures of Risk Measures," *The Accounting Review*, **45**:654–682 (October 1970).

Using Financial Ratios to Predict Bond Ratings

Moody's bond ratings are widely used as a yardstick of bond quality. Therefore, they are a pointer as to which investors are likely to buy your company's bonds and what interest rate they will require. Financial managers pay considerable attention to their company's bond ratings and would like to know in advance how a new issue of bonds

---

[18]W.H. Beaver, P. Kettler, and M. Scholes, "The Association Between Market-Determined and Accounting-Determined Risk Measures," *The Accounting Review*, **45**:654–682 (October 1970).

[19]See B. Rosenberg and V. Marathe, "The Prediction of Systematic and Residual Risk," *Proceedings of the Seminar on the Analysis of Security Prices*. Center for Research in Security Prices, Graduate School of Business, University of Chicago, November 1975.

would be rated and how a change in circumstances would affect the ratings on existing debt.

James Horrigan examined the relationship between the bond ratings and financial ratios of 254 companies.[20] The companies with the highest bond rating tended to be large, with little debt outstanding, a high return on assets, and a high profit margin. Surprisingly, they had low liquidity ratios. Horrigan also combined several ratios into a single measure of bond quality. In subsequent years this composite measure correctly predicted Moody's rating for 58% of new bond issues.

25-4 SUMMARY

If you are analyzing a company's financial statement, there is a danger of being overwhelmed by the sheer volume of data. That is why managers use a few salient ratios to summarize the firm's leverage, liquidity, profitability, and market valuation. We have described some of the more popular financial ratios.

We offer the following general advice to users of financial ratios.

1. Financial ratios seldom provide answers but they do help you ask the right questions.
2. There is no international standard for financial ratios. A little thought and common sense is worth far more than blind application of formulas.
3. Be selective in your choice of ratios. Different ratios often tell you similar things.
4. You need a benchmark for assessing a company's financial position. It is usual to compare financial ratios with the company's ratios in earlier years and with the ratios of other firms in the same business.

You can learn something about why a company's earnings change by comparing its earnings record with that of other firms. But be careful not to extrapolate past rates of earnings growth—earnings follow approximately a random walk.

Accounting earnings don't incorporate the year-by-year fluctuations in the value of the company's assets. Instead, accountants try to provide a picture of long-run sustainable earnings. Therefore, you can often get some idea of a company's value by multiplying its earnings by a standard price-earnings multiple. Sometimes the procedures used by accountants may temporarily depress earnings. For example, accountants generally deduct expenditure on intangible assets from current earnings. Also, if an investment takes a while to reach maximum profitability, straight-line depreciation will lead to an understatement of earnings in the early years. In these cases the earnings should be capitalized at a higher multiple.

Financial statement analysis helps you understand what makes the firm tick. We looked briefly at three particular applications. First, healthy firms have different financial ratios than firms that are heading for insolvency. Second, financial ratios provide valuable clues about a firm's market risk. Finally, we saw that a company's financial ratios can be used to predict the rating on a new issue of bonds.

FURTHER READING

There are some good general texts on financial statement analysis. See, for example:

G. Foster, *Financial Statement Analysis*, Prentice-Hall, Inc., Englewood Cliffs, N.J., 1978.
B. Lev, *Financial Statement Analysis: A New Approach*, Prentice-Hall, Inc., Englewood Cliffs, N.J., 1978.

[20]J.O. Horrigan, "The Determination of Long Term Credit Standing with Financial Ratios," *Empirical Research in Accounting: Selected Studies*, 1966. *Supplement to Journal of Accounting Research*, 1966, 44–62.

Fischer Black's provocative paper argues that the object of accounting rules is to produce an earnings figure that moves as nearly as possible in line with company values:

F. Black, "The Magic in Earnings: Economic Earnings versus Accounting Earnings," *Financial Analysts Journal*, **36**:3–8 (November–December 1980).

Three classic articles on the application of financial ratios to specific problems are:

W.H. Beaver, "Financial Ratios and Predictors of Failure," *Empirical Research in Accounting: Selected Studies. Supplement to Journal of Accounting Research*, 1966, 77–111.
W.H. Beaver, P. Kettler, and M. Scholes, "The Association Between Market-Determined and Accounting-Determined Risk Measures," *The Accounting Review*, **45**:654–682 (October 1970).
J.O. Horrigan, "The Determination of Long Term Credit Standing with Financial Ratios," *Empirical Research in Accounting: Selected Studies. Supplement to Journal of Accounting Research*, 1966, 44–62.

QUIZ

1. Table 25-8 gives abbreviated balance sheets and income statements for Tuktoyaktuk Manufacturing Inc. Calculate the following financial ratios:

Table 25-8   Income statement and balance sheets for Tuktoyaktuk Manufacturing, Inc. for fiscal year ending December 31, 1985.

Income statement		
Sales		$2,979
Cost of goods sold		2,053
Selling, general and administrative expenses		598
Operating income		328
Interest expense		64
Income before taxes		264
Taxes		128
Net earnings		136
Dividends		31
	Start of Year	End of Year
Balance sheet		
Assets:		
Cash and marketable securities	$ 43	$ 74
Inventory	437	502
Accounts receivable	74	84
Other current assets	16	19
Total current assets	570	679
Net property, plant, and equipment	726	740
Other assets	181	200
Total assets	1,477	1,619
Liabilities:		
Accounts payable	317	330
Other current liabilities	133	157
Total current liabilities	450	487
Long-term debt, including capitalized leases	232	221
Other long-term liabilities	98	110
Stockholders' equity	697	801
Total liabilities and stockholders' equity	$1,477	$1,619

(a) Debt ratio
(b) Times interst earned
(c) Current ratio
(d) Quick ratio
(e) Net profit margin
(f) Inventory turnover
(g) Return on net worth
(h) Payout ratio

2. There are no universally accepted definitions of financial ratios, but five of the following ratios make no sense at all. Substitute the correct definitions.

(a) Debt-equity ratio $= \dfrac{\text{long-term debt} + \text{value of leases}}{\text{long-term debt} + \text{value of leases} + \text{equity}}$

(b) Return on equity $= \dfrac{\text{EBIT} - \text{tax}}{\text{average equity}}$

(c) Payout ratio $= \dfrac{\text{dividend}}{\text{stock price}}$

(d) Profit margin $= \dfrac{\text{EBIT} - \text{tax}}{\text{sales}}$

(e) Inventory turnover $= \dfrac{\text{sales}}{\text{average inventory}}$

(f) Current ratio $= \dfrac{\text{current liabilities}}{\text{current assets}}$

(g) Sales to net working capital $= \dfrac{\text{average sales}}{\text{net working capital}}$

(h) Interval measure $= \dfrac{\text{current assets} - \text{inventories}}{\text{average daily expenditure from operations}}$

(i) Average collection period $= \dfrac{\text{sales}}{\text{average receivables} \div 365}$

(j) Quick ratio $= \dfrac{\text{current assets} - \text{inventories}}{\text{current liabilities}}$

(k) Tobin's $q = \dfrac{\text{market value of assets}}{\text{replacement cost of assets}}$

3. True or false?
   (a) A company's debt-equity ratio is always less than one.
   (b) The quick ratio is always less than the current ratio.
   (c) The return on equity is always less than the return on assets.
   (d) Successive earnings levels are unrelated to each other.
   (e) Successive earnings changes are unrelated to each other.

(*f*) Earnings follow roughly a random walk. This means that if earnings turn out to be higher than expected, you should revise upward your forecast of future earnings by a similar proportion.

(*g*) Accounting earnings follow a less smooth path than economic earnings.

(*h*) If a project is slow to reach full profitability, straight-line depreciation is likely to produce an overstatement of profits in the early years.

(*i*) A substantial new advertising campaign by a cosmetics company will tend to depress earnings and cause the stock to sell at a low price-earnings multiple.

4. In each of the following cases, explain briefly which of the two companies is likely to be characterized by the higher ratio:

(*a*) Debt-equity ratio: a shipping company or a computer software company

(*b*) Payout ratio: United Foods Inc. or Computer Graphics Inc.

(*c*) Ratio of sales to assets: an integrated pulp and paper manufacturer or a paper mill

(*d*) Average collection period: A supermarket chain or a mail order company

(*e*) Price-earnings multiple: Basic Sludge Company or Fledgling Electronics

(*f*) Tobin's *q*: an iron foundry or a pharmaceutical company with strong patent protection

QUESTIONS AND PROBLEMS

1. Discuss alternative measures of financial leverage. Should the market value of equity be used or the book value? Is it better to use the market value of debt, the book value, or the book value discounted at the risk-free interest rate? How should you

Table 25-9   Balance sheet and income statement of Transylvania Railroad.

	Millions of Dollars	
	December 1985	December 1984
Balance sheet		
Fixed assets, net	▪ ▪ ▪	25
Cash	▪ ▪ ▪	20
Accounts receivable	▪ ▪ ▪	34
Inventory	▪ ▪ ▪	26
Total current assets	▪ ▪ ▪	80
Total	▪ ▪ ▪	105
Equity	▪ ▪ ▪	30
Long-term debt	▪ ▪ ▪	20
Notes payable	30	35
Accounts payable	25	20
Total current liabilities	▪ ▪ ▪	55
Total	115	105
Income statement		
Sales	▪ ▪ ▪	
Cost of goods sold	▪ ▪ ▪	
Selling, general and administrative expenses	10	
Depreciation	20	
EBIT	▪ ▪ ▪	
Interest	▪ ▪ ▪	
Earnings before tax	▪ ▪ ▪	
Tax	▪ ▪ ▪	
Available for common	▪ ▪ ▪	

treat off-balance-sheet obligations such as pension liabilities? How would you treat preferred stock, deferred tax reserves, and minority interest?

2. As you can see, someone has spilt ink over some of the entries in the balance sheet and income statement of Transylvania Railroad (Table 25-9). Can you use the following information to work out the missing entries?

- Financial leverage   =   0.4
- Times interest earned   =   8
- Current ratio   =   1.4
- Quick ratio   =   1.0
- Cash ratio   =   0.2
- Return on total assets   =   0.18
- Return on equity   =   0.41
- Inventory turnover   =   5.0
- Receivables' collection period   =   71.2 days

3. Use financial ratio analysis to compare two companies chosen from the same industry.

4. Read and discuss Fischer Black's paper "The Magic in Earnings."

5. Describe some of the ways that the choice of accounting technique can temporarily depress or inflate earnings.

APPROACHES TO FINANCIAL PLANNING

A camel looks like an animal designed by a committee. If the firm made all its financial decisions piecemeal, it would end up with a financial camel. Therefore smart financial managers consider the overall effect of financing and investment decisions. This process is called *financial planning*, and the end result is a *financial plan*.

Financial planning is necessary because investment and financing decisions interact and should not be made independently. In other words, the whole may be more or less than the sum of the parts.

It is also necessary to help financial managers avoid surprises and think ahead about how they should react to unavoidable surprises. In Chapter 10 we stressed that financial managers are unwilling to treat capital investment proposals as "black boxes." They insist on understanding what makes projects work and what could go wrong with them. They attempt to trace out the possible impact of today's decisions on tomorrow's opportunities. The same approach is, or should be, taken when financing and investment decisions are considered in the aggregate. Without financial planning, the firm itself becomes a black box.

Finally, financial planning helps establish concrete goals to motivate managers and provide standards for measuring performance.

Financial planning is not easy to write about—it is the sort of topic that attracts empty generalities or ponderous detail. A full, formal treatment is beyond the scope of this book and probably beyond the capability of its authors. But there are a few specific, helpful points we can make. We will first summarize what financial planning is and what it is not. Second, we will describe the contents of a typical completed financial plan, and we will describe what the firm has to be able to do in order to plan successfully. Finally, we will discuss the use of *financial models* in the planning process.

26-1 WHAT FINANCIAL PLANNING IS AND IS NOT

What Financial Planning is Not: Burmah's Crisis

In December 1974 Burmah Oil Company had a narrow brush with financial disaster. We will not tell the full story, but only recount the immediate causes of Burmah's crisis. We use this crisis as a basis for asking what financial planning is and what it is not.

The Situation In the early 1960s Burmah was a holding company whose major asset was a substantial block of British Petroleum (BP) stock. But in 1966 it embarked on an aggressive diversification program. By 1974 Burmah's major assets were oil in the ground, largely under the North Sea; a fleet of oil tankers, mostly chartered to shippers on a voyage-by-voyage or "spot" basis; refineries; a portfolio of smaller companies in a variety of businesses; and the BP shares.

Burmah's expansion had been largely debt-financed. The firm found it easy to borrow using its BP shares as security. In early 1974 it borrowed $420 million from a group of banks headed by Chase Manhattan Bank. The immediate use for these funds was Burmah's purchase of the oil assets of Signal Corporation, an American conglomerate. At the same time Burmah's tanker operations were rapidly expanded. Many of the tankers were financed by long-term financial leases, which we saw in Chapter 24 to be essentially equivalent to secured debt.

Now, 1974 was not a happy year for the world's stock markets. The Arab oil embargo exacerbated both inflation and recession. In London, stock prices experienced their sharpest decline since the Great Crash of 1929. By the beginning of October, the price of BP shares had fallen 49% from levels at the end of 1973. Thus, the huge borrowing power derived from Burmah's investment in BP suddenly disappeared. As a result Burmah could no longer meet the terms of the bank loan, which required that Burmah's debt not exceed a stated proportion of its total capital.

The banks were willing to renegotiate, however. In exchange for a higher rate of interest, they agree to value the BP shares at prices higher than actual market value, thereby satisfying the original covenant. At the same time a new covenant was introduced, which required interest charges to be covered $1\frac{1}{2}$ times by profits.

The renegotiation therefore shifted the focus from the value of the BP shares to Burmah's profitability. Since 30% of Burmah's operating profits were generated by the tanker subsidiary, the progress of that business was obviously crucial. But Burmah felt safe, since projections made in May 1974 indicated that total profits from tankers in 1974 would be similar to profits in 1973.

Spot tanker rates had risen sharply in 1973, reflecting high demand for Middle Eastern crude oil. However, the rise was rapidly reversed by the Arab oil embargo at the end of the year. Spot tanker rates declined by 75% within 12 months.[1]

The first public hint of difficulties was in December 1974, when *Business Week* revealed the renegotiation of the loan and asserted that Burmah had run into a "serious cash squeeze." Burmah was quick to deny the charge. Its cash position, it announced, was "certainly no worse than anyone else's. We are well aware of our future cash needs and facilities are available to meet them." The statement was not sufficient to stem the series of rumours that now began to flood the London Stock Exchange. Finally, on a rainy Christmas Eve the chairman of Burmah called on the Bank of England to reveal that the tanker operations were now likely to show a large loss and that the group was forecasting only a small total profit for the year. In consequence the company expected to be in default on its recently renegotiated loan. Furthermore, the prolonged decline in the value of Burmah's BP holdings had also put Burmah in default on an earlier issue of long-term bonds.

The Bank of England did agree to save Burmah. It purchased 78 million BP shares for the then prevailing price of £2.30 per share, guaranteed $650 million of Burmah debt, and provided a £75 million line of credit, secured by Burmah's American assets. Burmah also began negotiating the sale of its American assets to raise cash to repay its debts. It was not a happy ending, but it could have been worse.

The Lessons for Financial Planning   Could Burmah's financial misfortunes have been avoided by better financial planning?

---

[1] Later, in 1975, spot rates fell so low that half of Burma's fleet was idle.

They may have reflected only bad luck. The oil embargo was an "act of God" that hardly anyone anticipated. But did Burmah comprehend the risks it was taking on when it secured the $420 million loan first with BP shares and later with the profits of its tanker business? The volatility of the stock market should have been obvious—as should the volatility of spot tanker rates: there had been dramatic increases in spot rates, and anyone with a sense of history should have realized that prices can fall as fast as they rise. Did Burmah's financial planners ever ask, "What will we do if BP's stock price falls out of bed?" or "What will we do if there is a sudden drop in demand in the spot tanker market?" These are questions they *should* have asked. If they did not ask them, it was poor financial planning. If they did, but decided to press on anyway, then we cannot fault their planning, although we may, with hindsight, fault their judgement.

Our discussion of the role of financial planning in Burmah's close call suggests two generalizations:

1. Financial planning does *not* attempt to minimize risks. It is a process of deciding which risks to take and which risks are unnecessary or not worth taking.

2. Financial planning is *not* just forecasting. Forecasting concentrates on the most likely future outcome. But Burmah's problems show us that financial planners have to worry about unlikely events as well as likely ones. No one could have forecasted the oil embargo and its consequences, but the possible effects of unlikely, but extremely unpleasant, surprises should be considered in financial planning.

What is Financial Planning?

We have used Burmah's story to illustrate what financial planning is not. But what *is* it?

Financial Planning is a Process   Financial planning is a *process* of:

1. Analyzing the interactions of the financing and investment choices open to the firm

2. Projecting the future consequences of present decisions, in order to avoid surprises and understand the links between present and future decisions

3. Deciding which alternatives to undertake (these decisions are embodied in the final financial plan)

4. Measuring subsequent performance against the goals set in the financial plan

Of course, there are different kinds of planning. Short-term financial planning is discussed in the next chapter. In short-term planning the *planning horizon* is rarely longer than the next 12 months. The firm wants to make sure it has enough cash to pay its bills and that short-term borrowing and lending are arranged to the firm's advantage.

Here we are more concerned with long-term planning, where a typical horizon is five years, although some firms look out ten years or more. For example, it can take ten years or more for an electric utility to design, obtain approval for, build, and test a major generating plant.

Financial Planning Focuses on Aggregate Investment by Division or Line of Business   Financial planners try to look at the big picture, and to avoid getting bogged down in detail. Thus the long-term planning process usually looks only at the *total* capital investment outlays of divisions or business units. A large number of small investment proposals are aggregated and, in effect, treated as a single project.

For example, at the beginning of the planning process the corporate staff might ask each division to submit three alternative business plans covering the next five years:

1. An *aggressive growth* plan calling for heavy capital investment and new products, increased share of existing markets, or entry of new markets

2. A *normal growth* plan in which the division grows with its markets but not significantly at the expense of its competitors

3. A plan of *retrenchment* and specialization designed to minimize required capital outlays—this may amount to gradual liquidation of the division

The planners might add a fourth option:

4. *Divestiture*—Sale or liquidation of the division

Each alternative has a stream of forecasted cash flows associated with it. Therefore the alternatives can be analyzed as four mutually exclusive capital projects.

Financial planners normally abstain from capital budgeting analysis on a project-by-project basis. Planners address capital investment on a grander scale. Of course, some projects are large enough to have significant individual impact. When in 1978 Boeing committed $3 *billion* to two new planes (the 757 and 767 models), you can safely bet that these two capital projects were explicitly analyzed in the context of Boeing's long-range financial plan.

26-2 CONTENTS OF A COMPLETED FINANCIAL PLAN

A completed financial plan for a large corporation is a substantial document. A smaller corporation's plan would have the same elements but less detail and documentation. For the smallest, youngest businesses, the financial plan may be entirely in the financial manager's head. The basic elements of the plans will be similar, however, for firms of any size.

Pro Forma Statements

The plan will present *pro forma* (that is, forecasted) balance sheets, income statements, and statements describing sources and uses of cash. Because these statements embody the firm's financial goals, they may not be strictly unbiased forecasts. The earnings target in the plan may be somewhere between an honest forecast and the earnings management *hopes* to achieve.

Capital Expenditure and Business Strategy

The plan will also describe planned capital expenditure, usually broken down by category (investment for replacement, for expansion, for new products, for mandated expenditures like pollution control equipment, and so on) and by division or line of business. There will be a narrative description of why these amounts are needed for investment, and also of the business strategies to be used to reach the financial goals. The descriptions might cover areas such as research and development efforts, steps to improve productivity, design and marketing of new products, pricing strategy, and so on.

These written descriptions, record the end result of discussions and negotiation between operating managers, corporate staff, and top management. They ensure that everyone involved in implementing the plan understands what is to be done.[2]

---

[2]Also, managers come up with better strategies when they are forced to present them formally and expose them to criticism. Haven't you often found that you didn't *really* understand an issue until you were forced to explain it to someone else?

Planned Financing

Most plans contain a summary of planned financing together with narrative backup as necessary. This part of the plan should logically include a discussion of dividend policy, because the more the firm pays out, the more capital it will have to find from sources other than retained earnings.

The complexity and importance of financing plans varies tremendously from firm to firm. A firm with limited investment opportunities, ample operating cash flow, and a moderate dividend payout accumulates considerable "financial slack" in the form of liquid assets and unused borrowing power. Life is relatively easy for the managers of such firms, and their financing plans are routine. Whether that easy life is in the interest of their stockholders is another matter.

Other firms have to raise capital in large amounts by selling securities. Naturally, they give careful attention to planning what kinds of securities are to be sold, and when. Such firms may also find their financing plans complicated by covenants on their existing debt. For example, electric utility bonds usually prohibit the firm from issuing more bonds if interest coverage drops below a certain level. Typically, the minimum level is two times earnings.

Utilities have enormous appetites for capital and relatively generous dividend payouts. In normal times they may issue a new series of bonds every year, almost like clockwork. But when earnings are depressed, as they were in the mid-1970s, alternative financing plans have to be developed. A common response was much heavier reliance on short-term loans from banks, coupled with more frequent stock issues than the utilities liked. But whatever the response, considerable midnight oil was burned by utility financial managers during this period.

Two Requirements for Effective Planning

The requirements for effective planning follow from the purposes of planning and the desired end result. Two points deserve emphasis.

Forecasting   First is the ability to forecast accurately and consistently. Perfect or even good accuracy may not be obtainable—if it were, the need for planning would be much less. Still the firm must do the best it can.

Effective planning requires administrative procedures to ensure that relevant information and expertise are not passed by, even if they are inconveniently scattered through the firm. Also, many planners reach outside the firm. Many organizations such as Data Resources, Inc. (DRI) and the Conference Board of Canada specialize in preparing macroeconomic and industry forecasts for use by corporations.

Inconsistency of forecasts is a potential problem because planners draw on information from many sources. Forecasted sales may be the sum of separate forecasts made by managers of several business units. Left to their own devices, these managers may make different assumptions about inflation, growth of the national economy, availability of raw materials, and so on. Achieving consistency is particularly hard for vertically integrated firms, where the raw material for one business unit is the output of another. For example, an oil company's refining division might plan to produce more gasoline than the marketing division plans to sell. The oil company's planners would be expected to uncover this inconsistency and align the plans of the two divisions.

Corporations often find that working out a consistent aggregate forecast of sales, cash flow, income, and so on, is complex and time-consuming. However, many of the calculations can be automated by using a corporate model. We will comment on corporate models in a moment.

Finding the Optimal Financial Plan In the end the financial manager has to be able to judge which plan is best. We would like to present a model or theory that tells the manager exactly how to make that judgement, but we cannot. There is no model or procedure that comprehends all the complexity and intangibles encountered in financial planning.

As a matter of fact there never will be one. This bold statement is based on BMSW's third law.[3]

- *Axiom.* The supply of unsolved problems is infinite.

- *Axiom.* The number of unsolved problems that humans can hold in their minds is at any time limited to ten.

- *The law.* Therefore, in any field there will always be ten problems that can be addressed but that have no formal solution.

You will note that the last chapter of this book discusses ten unsolved problems in finance.

Financial planners have to face the unsolved issues, and cope as best they can by judgement. Take dividend policy, for example. At the end of Chapter 16 we were unable to say for sure whether a generous dividend policy was a good or bad thing. Nevertheless, financial planners have to *decide* on the dividend policy.

Financial Planning as Managing a Portfolio of Options

Another problem that is often crucial in financial planning is the dependency of future investment opportunities on today's capital investment decisions. You often find firms investing to enter a market for "strategic" reasons: that is, not because the immediate investment has positive net present value, but because it establishes the firm in the market and creates *options* for possibly valuable follow-up investments.

In other words, there is a two-stage decision. At the second stage (the follow-up project) the financial manager faces a standard capital budgeting problem. But at the first stage projects may be valuable primarily for the options they bring with them. In principle the financial manager could value a first-stage project's "strategic value" using the option pricing theory introduced in Chapter 20, but so far this approach is unexplored territory.

Sometimes there are three or more stages. Think of the progress of a technological innovation from its inception in basic research, to product development, to pilot production and market testing, and finally to full-scale commercial production. The decision to produce at commercial scale is a standard capital budgeting problem. The decision to proceed with pilot production and test marketing is like purchasing an option to produce at commercial scale. The commitment of funds to development is like purchasing an option for pilot production and test marketing: the firm acquires an option to purchase an option. The investment in research at the very first stage is like acquiring an option to purchase an option to purchase an option.

Here we will stick our necks out by predicting that option pricing theory will eventually allow formal analysis of sequential investment decisions like the ones just discussed, and that financial planning eventually will be thought of not as a search for a single investment plan, but rather as the management of the portfolio of options held by the firm. This portfolio consists not of traded puts and calls, but of *real options*

---

[3]The second law is presented in Section 12-2.

(options to purchase real assets on possibly favourable terms) or options to purchase other real options.[4]

26-3 FINANCIAL PLANNING MODELS

Most corporate financial models are simulation models designed to project the financial consequences of alternative financial strategies under specified assumptions about the future. The models range from general-purpose ones, not much more complicated than the illustration presented later in this section, to models containing literally hundreds of equations and interacting variables. Naturally the most complex models are used by the largest firms.

Most large firms have a financial model, or have access to one.[5] Sometimes they may use more than one, perhaps a detailed model integrating capital budgeting and operational planning, a simpler model focusing on the aggregate impacts of financing strategy, and a special model for evaluating mergers.

The reason for the popularity of such models is a simple and practical one. They support the financial planning process by making it easier and cheaper to construct pro forma financial statements. The models automate an important part of planning that used to be boring, time-consuming, and labour-intensive.

Executive Fruit's Financial Model

Table 26-1 shows current (year-end 1985) financial statements for Executive Fruit Company. Judging by these figures, the company is ordinary in almost all respects. Its earnings before interest and taxes were 10% of sales revenue. Net earnings were $90,000 after paying of taxes and 9% interest on $400,000 outstanding debt. The company paid out 60% of its earnings as dividends.

Executive Fruit's operating cash flow was not sufficient to pay the dividend and also to provide the cash needed for investment and to expand net working capital. Therefore $64,000 of common stock was issued. The firm ended the year with debt equal to 40% of total capitalization.

Now suppose that you are asked to prepare pro forma statements for Executive Fruit Company for 1986. You are told to assume business as usual *except* that (1) sales and operating costs are expected to be up 30% over 1985, and (2) common stock is not to be issued again. You interpret "business as usual" to mean that (3) interest rates will remain at 9%, (4) the firm will stick to its traditional 60% dividend payout, and (5) net working capital and fixed assets will increase by 30% to support the larger sales volume.

These assumptions lead to the pro forma statements shown in Table 26-2. Note that projected net income is up by 23%, to $111,000, which is heartening. But a glance at the "sources and uses of funds" statement shows that $404,000 has to be raised for additional working capital and for replacement and expansion of fixed capital.[6] Executive

---

[4]The concept of real options was introduced in S.C. Myers, "Determinants of Corporate Borrowing," *Journal of Financial Economics*, 5:147–175 (November 1977).

[5]Some firms use general-purpose models developed by banks, management consultants, or commercial computer time-sharing firms.

[6]Executive Fruit's existing fixed capital is assumed to depreciate by $104,000 in 1985. Thus it has to invest $104,000 simply to maintain the net book value of its fixed assets. Total investment is $104,000 plus the growth in net fixed assets required by the increased sales volume. Incidentally, we realize that requiring the net book value of fixed assets to grow in lockstep with sales volume is an arbitrary and probably unrealistic assumption. We adopt it only to keep things simple.

Fruit's generous dividend payout and its decision against another stock issue mean that $255,600 has to be raised by additional borrowing. The result is an increase in the book debt ratio to more than 50% and a reduction in pretax interest coverage ratio to 4.8. (Earnings before interest and taxes divided by interest is $231/59 = 4.8$.)

We have spared you the trouble of actually calculating the figures necessary for Table 26-2. The calculations do not take more than a few minutes for this simple example, *provided* you set up the calculations correctly and make no arithmetic mistakes.

Table 26-1 1985 financial statements for Executive Fruit Company (all figures in thousands of dollars).

Income Statement			
Revenue (REV)	2,160		
Cost of goods sold (CGS)	1,944		
Earnings before interest and taxes	216		
Interest (INT)[a]	36		
Earnings before taxes	180		
Tax at 50% (TAX)	90		
Net income (NET)	90		

Sources and Uses of Funds			
Sources			
Net income (NET)	90		
Depreciation (DEP)[b]	80		
Operating cash flow	170		
Borrowing (ΔD)	0		
Stock issues (SI)	64		
Total sources	234		
Uses			
Increase in net working capital (ΔNWC)	40		
Investment (INV)	140		
Dividends (DIV)	54		
Total uses	234		

Balance Sheets			
	1984	1983	Change
Assets			
Net working capital (NWC)[c]	200	160	+40
Fixed assets (FA)	800	740	+60[d]
Total assets	1,000	900	+100
Liabilities			
Debt (D)	400	400	0
Book equity(E)	600	500	+100[e]
Total liabilities	1,000	900	+100

[a] Interest is 9% of the $400 in outstanding debt.
[b] Depreciation or capital cost allowance is a non-cash expense. Therefore we add it back to net income to find operating cash flow.
[c] Net working capital is defined as current assets less current liabilities.
[d] The increase in the book value of fixed assets equals investment less depreciation. Change in FA is ΔFA $=$ INV $-$ DEP $= 140 - 80 = 60$.
[e] Book equity increases by retained earnings less dividends plus stock issues. Change in E is $\Delta E =$ NET $-$ DIV $+$ SI $= 90 - 54 + 64 = 100$.

Table 26-2 1986 pro forma financial statements for Executive Fruit Company (all figures in thousands of dollars).

Income Statement		
Revenue (REV)	2,808 }	(+30%)
Cost of goods sold (CGS)	2,527 }	
Earnings before interest and taxes	281	
Interest (INT)	59	
Earnings before tax	222	
Tax (TAX)	111	
Net income (NET)	111	(+23%)

Sources and Uses of Funds		
Sources		
Net income (NET)	111	
Depreciation (DEP)	104	
Operating cash flow	215	
Borrowing (ΔD)	255.6	
Stock issues (SI)	0	
Total sources	470.6	
Uses		
Increase in net working capital (ΔNWC)	60	(+30%)
Investment (INV)	344	
Dividends (DIV)	66.6	
Total uses	470.6	

Balance Sheets			
	1985	1984	Change
Assets			
Net working capital (NWC)	260	200	+ 60
Fixed assets (FA)	1,040	800	+240
Total assets	1,300	1,000	+300
Liabilities			
Debt (D)	655.6	400	+255.6
Book equity (E)	644.4	600	+ 44.4
Total liabilities	1,300.0	1,000	+300.0

Assumptions:

CGS	Assumed to remain at 90% of REV.
INT	Nine percent of debt (D). This assumes all new debt is taken out early in 1985 so that a full year's interest must be paid.
TAX	Tax rate remains at 50%.
DEP	Capital cost allowance or depreciation remains at 10% of fixed assets. This assumes that a full year's depreciation is taken on all new investment made in 1985.
ΔD	Balancing item. Executive Fruit must borrow $255.6 to cover planned expenditures.
SI	Executive Fruit's management has decided not to issue stock in 1985, therefore SI = 0.
ΔNWC, NWC	Net working capital expands in proportion to the increase in REV.
INV, FA	Required fixed assets FA are assumed to expand in proportion to the growth in sales. Investment must therefore cover depreciation plus the increase in FA.
DIV	Payout stays at 60% of NET.
E	The increase in equity equals retained earnings (NET − DIV) plus stock issues (SI). NET − DIV + SI = 111 − 66.6 + 0 = 44.4

If that time requirement seems trivial, remember that in reality you probably would be asked for four similar sets of statements covering each year from 1986 to 1989. Probably you would be asked for alternative projections under different assumptions (for example a 25% instead of 30% growth rate of revenue) or different financial strategies (for example freezing dividends at their 1984 level of $54,000). This would be lots of work. Building a model and letting the computer toil in your place has obvious attractions.

Table 26-3 shows a 15-equation model for Executive Fruit. There is one equation for each variable needed to construct pro forma statements like Tables 26-1 and 26-2. Of the equations, six are accounting identities ensuring that the income statement adds up, the balance sheet balances, and sources of funds match uses. The functions of the equations are as follows: (1) and (8) set revenues and stock issues equal to values specified by the model user. Equations (2), (12), and (13) specify cost of goods sold, net working capital, and fixed assets as constant proportions of sales. The remaining equations relate interest to debt outstanding (3), taxes to income (4), depreciation to fixed assets (6), and dividends to net income (11).

Table 26-3   Financial model for Executive Fruit Company.

Income Statement Equations

(1) REV = forecast by model user	
(2) CGS = a_1REV	
(3) INT = $a_2 D$	(a_2 = interest rate)
(4) TAX = a_3(REV − CGS − INT)	(a_3 = tax rate)
(5) NET = REV − CGS − INT − TAX	(accounting identity)

Sources and Uses Statement Equations

(6) DEP = a_4FA	
(7) ΔD = ΔNWC + INV + DIV − NET − DEP − SI	(accounting identity)
(8) SI = value specified by model user	
(9) ΔNWC = NWC − NWC(−1)	(accounting identity)
(10) INV = DEP + FA − FA(−1)	(accounting identity)
(11) DIV = a_5NET	(a_5 = dividend payout ratio)

Balance Sheet Equations

(12) NWC = a_6REV	
(13) FA = a_7REV	
(14) $D = \Delta D + D(-1)$	(accounting identity)
(15) $E = E(-1)$ + NET − DIV + SI	(accounting identity)

Note:
(−1) means a number taken from the previous year's balance sheet. These numbers are constants, not variables.

The *input* for our model comprises nine items: a sales forecast (REV), a decision on the amount of stock to be issued (SI), and seven coefficients, a_1, through a_7, tying cost of goods sold to revenue, interest payments to borrowing, and so on. Take the coefficient a_5, for example. In developing Table 26-2 we assumed dividends to be 60% of net income. In the model this would be expressed as $a_5 = 0.6$.

Table 26-4 shows that our model works. In the table we insert the value for REV, SI, and a_1 through a_7 that correspond to the assumptions underlying Table 26-2. And we get the right answers, confirming that the model can be used to forecast Executive Fruit's financial results. All we would have to do is to give the computer the 9 input items, tell it to solve the 15 simultaneous equations, and instruct it to print out the results in the format of Table 26-2.

Table 26-4 Model forecast for Table 26-2.

Income Statement

(1) REV = forecast = 2,808

(2) CGS = 0.9 REV $(a_1 = 0.9)$
    =0.9(2,808) = 2,527

(3) INT = 0.09 D $(a_2 = 0.09)$
    = 0.09(655.6) = 59

(4) TAX = 0.5(REV − CGS − INT) $(a_3 = 0.5)$
    =0.5(2,808 − 2,527 − 59) = 111

(5) NET = REV − CGS − INT − TAX
    = 2,808 − 2,527 − 59 − 111 = 111

Sources and Uses of Funds Statement

(6) DEP = 0.1 FA $(a_4 = 0.1)$
    = 0.1(1,040) = 104

(7) ΔD = ΔNWC + INV + DIV − NET − DEP − SI
    = 60 + 344 + 66.6 − 111 − 104 − 0 = 255.6

(8) SI = specified as 0

(9) ΔNWC = NWC − NWC(−1)
    = 260 − 200 = 60

(10) INV = DEP + FA − FA(−1)
    = 104 + 1,040 − 800 = 344

(11) DIV = 0.6 NET $(a_5 = 0.6)$
     = 0.6(111) = 66.6

Balance Sheet

(12) NWC = 0.093 REV $(a_6 = 0.093)$
     = 0.093(2,808) = 260

(13) FA = 0.37 REV $(a_7 = 0.37)$
     = 0.37(2,808) = 1,040

(14) D = ΔD + D(−1)
     = 255.6 + 400 = 655.6

(15) E = E(−1) + NET − DIV + SI
     = 600 + 111 − 66.6 + 0 = 644.4

Pitfalls in Model Design

The Executive Fruit model is too simple for practical application. You probably have already thought of several ways to improve it—by keeping track of the number of outstanding shares, for example, and printing out earnings and dividends per share. Or you might want to distinguish short-term lending and borrowing opportunities, now buried in net working capital.

But beware: there is always the temptation to make a model bigger and more detailed. You may end up with an exhaustive model that is too cumbersome for routine use.

Excessive detail gets in the way of the intended use of corporate planning models, namely, to project the financial consequences of a variety of strategies and assumptions. The fascination of detail, if you give in to it, distracts attention from crucial decisions like stock issues and dividend policy, debt policy, and allocation of capital by business area. Sometimes decisions like these end up being made not by the financial manager, but by rules of thumb "wired into" the model, just as the Executive Fruit model arbitrarily sets dividends equal to a constant proportion of net income.

There is No Finance in Corporate Financial Models

Why do we say that there is no finance in corporate financial models? The first reason is that most such models incorporate an accountant's view of the world. They are designed to forecast accounting statements, and their equations naturally embody the accounting conventions employed by the firm. Consequently the models do not emphasize the tools of financial analysis: incremental cash flow, present value, market risk, and so on.

Second, corporate financial models produce no signposts pointing toward optimal financial decisions. They do not even tell which alternatives are worth examining. All this is left up to their users.

BMSW's third law implies that no model can find the best of all financial strategies. However, it is possible to build linear programming models that help search for the best financial strategy subject to specified assumptions and constraints. These "intelligent" financial planning models should prove more flexible tools for sensitivity analysis and more effective in screening alternative financial strategies. Ideally they will suggest strategies that would never occur to the unaided financial manager.

The appendix to this chapter sketches a linear programming model based on the modern finance theory presented in this book.

26-4 SUMMARY

Most firms take financial planning seriously and devote considerable resources to it. What do they get for this effort?

The tangible product of the planning process is a financial plan describing the firm's financial strategy and projecting its future consequences by means of pro forma balance sheets, income statements, and statements of sources and uses of funds. The plan establishes financial goals and is a benchmark for evaluating subsequent performance. Usually it also describes why that strategy was chosen and how the plan's financial goals are to be achieved.

The plan is the end result. The process that produces the plan is valuable in its own right. First, planning forces the financial manager to consider the combined effects of all the firm's investment and financing decisions. This is important because these decisions interact and should not be made independently.

Second, planning, if it is done right, forces the financial manager to think about events that could upset the firm's financial progress and to devise strategies to be held in reserve for counterattack when unhappy surprises occur. Planning is more than forecasting, because forecasting deals with the most likely future. Planners also have to think about events that may occur even though they are unlikely.

To repeat: financial planning is a *process* of:

1. Analyzing the interactions of the financing and investment choices open to the firm

2. Projecting the future consequences of present decisions, in order to avoid surprises and understand the links between present and future decisions

3. Deciding which alternatives to undertake (these decisions are embodied in the final financial plan)

4. Measuring subsequent performance against the goals set in the financial plan.

In this chapter we discussed "long-range" or "strategic" planning, in which the *planning horizon* is usually five years or more in the future. This kind of planning deals with aggregate decisions: for example, the planner would worry about whether the broadaxe division should invest in heavy capital investment and rapid growth but not whether the division should choose machine tool A versus tool B. In fact, planners must be constantly on guard against the fascination of detail, because giving in to it means slighting crucial issues like investment strategy, debt policy, and the choice of a target dividend payout ratio.

There is no theory or model that leads straight to *the* optimal financial strategy. Consequently financial planning proceeds by trial and error. Many different strategies may be projected under a range of assumptions about the future before one strategy is finally chosen.

The dozens of separate projections that may be made during this trial and error process generate a heavy load of arithmetic and paperwork. Firms have responded by developing corporate planning models to forecast the financial consequences of specified strategies and assumptions about the future. These models are efficient and widely used. But remember that there is not much finance in them. Their primary purpose is to produce accounting statements. It is often difficult to calculate a strategy's present value from model output. The models do not search for the best financial strategy, but only trace out the consequences of a strategy specified by the model user.

One of the most difficult aspects of deciding what strategies to examine closely is that the best strategy may not be an obvious one. In the appendix to this chapter we describe a linear programming model that is based on the concepts of finance rather than accounting, and that does help the financial manager search for the best financial plan.

FURTHER READING

Corporate planning has an extensive literature of its own. Good books include:

R.N. Anthony, *Planning and Control Systems: A Framework for Analysis*, Division of Research, Graduate School of Business Administration, Harvard University, Boston, 1965.
P. Lorange, and R.F. Vancil, *Strategic Planning Systems*, Prentice Hall, Inc., Englewood Cliffs, N.J., 1977.

Our description of what planning is and is not was influenced by:

P. Drucker, "Long-Range Planning: Challenge to Management Science," *Management Science*, 5:238–249 (April 1959).

Here are four references on corporate models:

W.T. Carleton, C.L. Dick, Jr., and D.H. Downes, "Financial Policy Models: Theory and Practice," *Journal of Financial and Quantitative Analysis*, 8:691–709 (December 1973).
W.T. Carlton and J.M. McInnes, "Theory, Models and Implementation in Financial Management," *Management Science*, 28:957–978 (September 1982).
D. Chambers, "Programming the Allocation of Funds Subject to Restrictions on Reported Results," *Operational Research Quarterly*, 18:407–432 (December 1967).
E. Lerner and A. Rappaport, "Limit DCF in Capital Budgeting," *Harvard Business Review*, 46:133–139 (September–October 1968).

LONGER is presented in:

S.C. Myers and G.A. Pogue, "A Programming Approach to Corporate Financial Management," *Journal of Finance*, 29:579–599 (May 1974).

APPENDIX 26-1 LONGER

This appendix is a brief introduction to LONGER, a linear programming model devised by Myers and Pogue to support financial planners.[7] Other applications of linear programming to financial planning are described in "Further Reading" for this chapter.

LONGER differs from the typical corporate financial model described in this chapter in two important respects. First, it *optimizes*: it calculates the *best* financial plan, given specified assumptions, and constraints. The typical planning model merely *projects* the consequences of a financial strategy chosen by the model user. Second, the model is based on finance theory rather than accounting. It assumes well-functioning capital markets. Consequently its objective is to maximize the firm's net present value. It relies on value additivity and the Modigliani-Miller theory that the chief advantage of debt is the tax shields created by debt interest payments.

LONGER will be introduced by a simple numerical example. Then extensions of the model are briefly described. The final part of this appendix shows how the shadow prices generated as part of LONGER's solution are interpreted. The shadow prices are an easy way to understand *adjusted present value* or APV, which measures the value of capital projects which have important financing side effects. APV and its practical implications were covered more fully in Chapter 19. This appendix should give a deeper appreciation of the APV method and the assumptions underlying it.

Example[8]

Consider a firm that has to decide how much to invest or borrow in the coming year. Let:

x = New investment, in millions of dollars. (We assume for simplicity that the firm has only one project.)

y = New borrowing, in millions of dollars.

Also, assume that:

1. Available investment opportunities can absorb $1 million at most. The investments generate a perpetual stream of after-tax cash flows. Let the expected average value of these flows be C. In this case $C = 0.09x$; thus the project offers a 9% internal rate of return.

2. Assume that the market will capitalize the returns at the rate $r = 0.10$. Thus, if all-equity financing is used, these assets generate a net present value of $-\$0.10$ per dollar invested $(-x + 0.09x/0.10 = -0.1x)$.

3. The firm's policy is to limit new debt to 40% of new investment.

4. The firm has $800,000 in cash available.

5. Any excess cash is paid out in dividends.

6. The additions to debt and equity are expected to be permanent.

---

[7]S.C. Myers and G.A. Pogue, "A Programming Approach to Corporate Financial Management," *Journal of Finance*, **29**:579–599 (May 1974).

[8]This example is based on one presented by Myers and Pogue, op. cit.

For simplicity we begin with the Modigliani-Miller valuation formula for the firm.[9] If the firm does nothing (x and $y = 0$) then V will be given by

$$V = V_0 + T_c D$$

where V_0 = market value of firm's *existing* assets if they were all-equity financed

T_c = marginal corporate income tax rate (0.5 in this example)

D = amount of debt *already* outstanding, excluding any borrowing for new project

The amount $T_c D$ is the present value of the tax shields generated by the outstanding debt, assuming the debt is permanent.

For our example,

$$V = V_0 + 0.5D - 0.1x + 0.5y$$

Now V_0 and D are fixed and therefore not relevant to the choice of x and y. Therefore we can just maximize the quantity $-0.1x + 0.5y$, subject to constraints on the amount invested ($x \leq 1$), the amount of debt issued ($y \leq 0.4x$), and the balance of sources and uses of funds ($x \leq y + 0.8$).

The Solution This is the linear programming problem depicted in Figure 26-1. First look at the shaded area representing the set of feasible solutions. The feasible region is below the line $x = 1$ because the firm's investment opportunity will absorb $1 million at most. It is below the line $x = 0.8 + y$ because the amount invested is limited to cash on hand ($0.8 million) plus additional borrowing. It is above and to the left of the line $y = 0.4x$ because new debt is limited to 40% of new investment.

The firm does not want to invest (because NPV = $-$0.10 per dollar invested) but it does want to borrow, and in order to borrow it has to invest. Thus, firm value is maximized when $x = 1$, $y = 0.4$. The firm invests and borrows as much as it can.

However, note that the constraint $x \leq 0.8 + y$ is not binding at the optimal solution. The firm borrows $200,000 more than it needs for investment. Thus it has $200,000 available for dividends.

Why does the optimal solution call for investing in a project with a negative net present value? The reason is that the project allows the firm to issue more debt, and the value of tax savings generated by the debt more than offsets the investment's inadequate return. (In fact, the optimal solution remains $x = 1.0$, $y = 0.4$ so long as the investment generates more than $-$0.20 per dollar invested. If it generates less than that, $-$0.30, for example, the solution becomes $x = y = 0$.) The debt capacity constraint thus makes financing and investment decisions interdependent.

Effects of Dividend Policy The sources-uses constraint is not binding in the example, and therefore does not create an interaction of financing and investment decisions. However, what if it is binding? What if the firm has, say, only $500,000 cash on hand?

At first glance the effect is to change the sources-uses constraint to $x \leq 0.5 + y$, which changes the optimal solution to $x = 5/6$, $y = 1/3$. However, if we consider dividend policy, then we should also allow new issues of equity. The constraint should really be

---

[9]See Section 18-1.

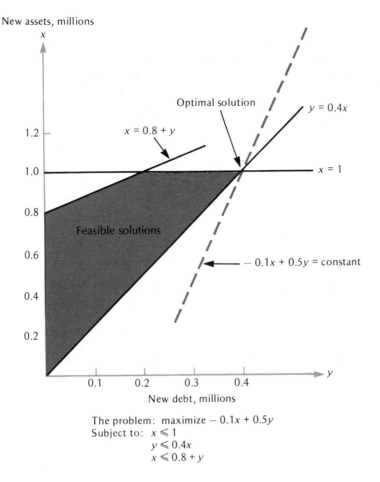

New assets, millions

The problem: maximize $-0.1x + 0.5y$
Subject to: $x \le 1$
$y \le 0.4x$
$x \le 0.8 + y$

Figure 26-1 In this example, the firm can invest at most $1 million and borrow 40% of new investment. Funds for the new investment must come from existing cash ($0.8 million) or new borrowing. The investment is not attractive in its own right (NPV = $-\$0.1x$), but the firm is willing to invest in order to borrow because the tax shields created by borrowing outweigh the net loss in value attributable to the new investment.

$$x + \text{DIV} \le 0.5 + y + \text{SI}$$

where DIV and SI are dividends paid and equity issued in millions. If dividend policy is irrelevant, then DIV and SI have no effect in the objective function, and the constraint itself is irrelevant. Thus, the optimal solution remains at $x = 1$, $y = 0.4$. The firm must make a $100,000 stock issue, but this is a mere detail once the investment and borrowing decisions are made.

However, in practice there would be transaction costs associated with the stock issue. These costs would have to be subtracted from the objective function, and the sources-uses constraint would become relevant and binding. The solution values for x and y will clearly be affected, if the transaction cost is large enough.

Thus, the sources-uses constraint becomes important only if there are transaction costs to security issues or dividend policy matters for other reasons.

Extending the Model

The example we have just examined was limited to two variables by our goal of presenting it graphically on the two dimensions of the printed page. But the computer does not need a picture like Figure 26-1 to solve a linear program. We can extend LONGER to a practical level of detail by adding variables and constraints.

We have already referred to one extension. Suppose that the firm can pay dividends or issue common stock, but that cash available is cut to $0.5 million. The linear program becomes

Maximize: $-0.1x + 0.5y + a\,\text{DIV} + b\,\text{SI}$

Subject to: $x \le 1$

$y \le 0.4x$

$x + \text{DIV} \le 0.5 + y + \text{SI}$

If dividend policy is irrelevant, then both a and b are set at zero. But in practice b would have to be negative to reflect the transaction costs of a stock issue. and a might be positive, negative, or zero depending on your position on the dividend controversy (see Chapter 16).

Now suppose that there is a second investment opportunity to invest up to $2 million in a project offering $0.12 of NPV per dollar invested. However, the performance of project 2 is less predictable than project 1's performance, and so the firm is willing to borrow only 20% of the amount invested in project 2. Our model now becomes

Maximize: $-0.1x_1 + 0.12x_2 + 0.5y + a\,\text{DIV} + b\,\text{SI}$

Subject to: $x_1 \le 1$

$x_2 \le 2$

$y \le 0.4x_1 + 0.2x_2$

$x_1 + x_2 + \text{DIV} \le 0.5 + y + \text{SI}$

Because present values add, we can include as many projects as we like without upsetting the linear form of the objective. Moreover, there is no need for included projects to have the same risk or time pattern of cash flows. There is nothing wrong with setting an office building alongside a wildcat oil well, so long as you can come up with a net present value for each.

If we introduce projects with irregular patterns of cash flow over time, we would naturally want to allow borrowing to vary period by period. Suppose that the firm has a five-year planning horizon. Then we could replace the debt variable y with five new variables $y_1, y_2, \ldots, y_5$, where y_t is planned total borrowing for year t. This naturally suggests that dividends and stock issues should be allowed to vary over time also. Our objective function becomes

Maximize: $-0.1x_1 + 0.12x_2$

$+ c_1 y_1 + c_2 y_2 + \cdots + c_5 y_5$

$+ a_1 \text{DIV}_1 + a_2 \text{DIV}_2 + \cdots + a_5 \text{DIV}_5$

$+ b_1 \text{SI}_1 + b_2 \text{SI}_2 + \cdots + b_5 \text{SI}_5$

Also, we will now need 12 constraints: two limiting the amount that can be invested in each project, five limiting the amount that can be borrowed in each of the five years covered by the financial plan, and five constraints ensuring that planned uses of funds do not exceed planned sources in any year.

Still more constraints might be added. The financial manager might wish to try to avoid any planned cut in dividends, for example. This would call for five more constraints:

$$DIV \geq \text{dividends in period 0}$$
$$DIV_2 \geq DIV_1$$
$$DIV_3 \geq DIV_2$$
$$DIV_4 \geq DIV_3$$
$$DIV_5 \geq DIV_4$$

Some firms might require that their financial plan generate a steady growth in reported (book) earnings. Suppose that the target growth rate is g. Then we would need five more constraints of the form $Z_t \geq (1 + g)Z_{t-1}$, where Z_t represents forecasted earnings in year t. The variable Z_t would be determined by the other decision variables in the programming model.

But we must immediately add a caveat: any constraint on acceptable *book* earnings, as opposed to economic earnings, raises difficult issues. Should the firm be willing to sacrifice present value just to achieve regular growth in reported earnings? If capital markets are efficient, investors ought to be able to look through any fluctuations of short-run earnings to the true, underlying value of the firm. If so, any constraint on earnings is superfluous at best.

Constraints on the growth of book earnings might perhaps be useful for keeping track of how pursuit of present value affects reported earnings. It may be that the financial plan can be changed to generate a pretty earnings pattern. If there is a real conflict between value and book earnings, comparing solutions with and without this constraint will at least awaken financial managers to the cost of that pretty pattern.[10]

There are several other items of optional equipment that most might wish to add to LONGER, but we will stop at this point. You may wish to refer to Myers and Pogue's paper and the other suggested readings for the full story.

Comparison of LONGER with the Typical Corporate Planning Model

A full-scale linear programming model for financial planning would become formidably complex, but no more so than a typical simulation model.[11] The two models applied to the same firm would have approximately the same number of variables, and the number of constraints included in LONGER would about match the number of equations in the simulation model. But the input requirements for LONGER would be greater because an objective function must be specified. In return, LONGER allows the planner to screen all feasible financial strategies, to reject the inferior ones automatically, and to identify the best strategy consistent with the assumptions and constraints embodied in the model.

However, linear programming models do not automate the *decisions* required by the financial plan. No model can capture all the issues that the financial manager must face. Nor would access to an optimization model change the trial and error process of

---

[10]Eugene Lerner and Arnold Rappaport demonstrate the conflicts between pursuit of value and short-run earnings in "Limit DCF in Capital Budgeting," *Harvard Business Review*, **46**:133–139 (September–October 1968).

[11]Note our warning on the temptation to excessive detail. See Section 26-3.

developing a financial plan; it only promises to make that process somewhat more efficient. The optimum plan generated by any run of LONGER does no more than reflect the assumptions and constraints specified by the model user, who will naturally explore a variety of assumptions and constraints before reaching a final decision.[12]

Shadow Prices or Marginal Costs

The solution to any linear program includes a shadow price or marginal cost for each constraint. There are three constraints in the simple numerical example introduced at the start of this appendix, and therefore three shadow prices:

Constraint	Shadow Price	Explanation
Limit on investment $(x \leq 1)$	0.1	Project NPV is $-0.1x$. But investment supports $0.4x$ in debt worth \$0.50 per dollar borrowed. $-0.1x + 0.4(0.5x) = +0.1x$
Limit on debt $(y \leq 0.4x)$	0.5	\$1 of additional debt generates tax shields worth \$0.50
Limit on available cash $(x \leq 0.8 + y)$	0	Firm has surplus cash at optimal solution. Additional cash has NPV of zero.

A shadow price is defined as the change in the objective per unit change in the constraint.[13] In our example the objective is to increase net present value. Therefore the shadow price of 0.1 on the investment limit means that, if the firm were allowed to invest \$1,000,001 instead of \$1 million, net present value would increase by 10 cents. The shadow price of 0.5 on the debt limit means that if the firm were allowed to borrow \$400,001 instead of \$400,000, holding investment fixed at \$1 million, value would increase by 50 cents.

The limit on available cash is not binding at the optimal solution. The firm borrows \$200,000 more than it needs, and so the shadow price on that constraint is zero. That is, extra cash would have a *net* present value of zero.

Consider a slightly more complex example. Cash on hand is reduced to \$500,000. Equity issues and dividend payments are allowed, but transactions cost absorb 10% of the net proceeds of any issue. The linear programming problem changes to:

Maximize: $-0.1x + 0.5y + (0)\text{DIV} - 0.1\text{SI}$

Subject to: $x \leq 1$

$$y \leq 0.4x$$

$$x + \text{DIV} \leq 0.5 + y + \text{SI}$$

The solution is $x = 1$, $y = 0.4$, DIV = 0, and SI = 0.1. The firm invests and borrows as before, but has to issue \$100,000 of equity to raise the necessary cash for investment.

The shadow prices for this problem are as follows:

---

[12] Williard T. Carleton, Charles L. Dick, Jr., and David H. Downes give a comprehensive and insightful discussion of the differences in design and use of the two model types, and argue that optimization models are potentially more useful, in "Financial Policy Models: Theory and Practice," *Journal of Financial and Quantitative Analysis*, 8:691–709 (December 1973).

[13] Shadow prices are valued only for marginal shifts in the constraints. The range over which shifts qualify as marginal varies from problem to problem.

Constraint	Shadow Price	Explanation
Limit on investment ($x \leq 1$)	0.04	(See below.)
Limit on debt ($y \leq 0.4x$)	0.6	$1 of additional debt generates tax shields worth $0.50 *and* reduces equity issued by $1, saving $0.01 in issue costs.
Limit on available cash ($x + \text{DIV} \leq 0.5 + y + \text{SI}$)	0.1	Extra cash reduces equity issued and saves $0.10 per $1.

The shadow price on project investment goes down by 0.06, from $0.10 to $0.04 per dollar invested. This occurs because additional investment can be only 40% debt-financed. The remainder must come from issuing new equity. Therefore, the value of the opportunity to invest an additional dollar decreases by $0.6 \times 0.1 = 0.06$.

The shadow prices on the investment limits are particularly interesting because they show the project's net marginal contribution to firm value, when all of the project's financing side effects are accounted for. In this example the project's marginal contribution is 4 cents per dollar invested. Remember that the project has negative NPV separately considered. But it has one favourable side effect (investment allows the firm to borrow) and one unfavourable side effect (investment requires equity issues and generates issue costs).

The shadow price for the project can be calculated by starting with its base-case NPV of -0.1, adding the value of its marginal contribution to corporate borrowing, and subtracting the marginal cost of the equity issue needed to finance it:

$$\begin{array}{c} \text{Net contribution} \\ \text{to firm value} \end{array} = \begin{array}{c} \text{base-case} \\ \text{NPV} \end{array} + \begin{array}{c} \text{value of project's} \\ \text{marginal contribution} \\ \text{to borrowing power} \end{array} - \begin{array}{c} \text{marginal cost} \\ \text{of equity issue} \\ \text{needed to finance} \\ \text{project} \end{array}$$

Investing $1 more effectively loosens the debt constraint by $0.40 and tightens the cash constraint by $1. Therefore we can "price out" the project's financing side effects by noting the shadow prices on these two constraints. Extra borrowing power is worth 60 cents per dollar and cash used up costs 10 cents per dollar. Therefore

Net contribution to firm value $= -0.1 + 0.4(0.6) - (1.00)(0.1) = 0.04$

"Net contribution to firm value" is no more or less than *adjusted present value*, or APV. APV is calculated automatically as a by-product of LONGER. But, as you saw in Chapter 19, for simple problems you an calculate APV by hand. You need APV because it is the only generally reliable approach to capital budgeting when investment decisions have important financing side effects.

QUIZ

1. True or false?
   (*a*) Financial planning should attempt to minimize risk.
   (*b*) The primary aim of financial planning is to obtain better forecasts of future cash flows and earnings.
   (*c*) Financial planning is necessary because financing and investment decisions interact and should not be made independently.
   (*d*) Firms' planning horizons rarely exceed three years.
   (*e*) Individual capital investment projects are not considered in a financial plan unless they are very large.

(*f*) Financial planning requires accurate and consistent forecasting.

(*g*) Financial planning models should include as much detail as possible.

2. List the major elements of a completed financial plan.

3. "There is no finance in financial planning models." Explain.

QUESTIONS AND PROBLEMS

1. What are the dangers and disadvantages of using a financial model? Discuss.

2. Should a financial plan be considered an unbiased forecast of future cash flows, earnings, and other financial variables? Why or why not?

3. How would Executive Fruit's financial model change if dividends were cut to zero in 1985? Use the revised model to generate a new financial plan for 1985. Show how the financial statements given in Table 26-2 would change. Do you think the new plan is an improvement on the old one? Discuss.

4. The balancing item in the Executive Fruit model is borrowing. What is meant by *balancing item*? How would the model change if dividends were made the balancing item instead? In that case how would you suggest that planned borrowing be determined?

5. Construct a new model for Executive Fruit based on your answer to question 4. Does your model generate a feasible financial plan for 1985? (*Hint*: If it doesn't, you may have to allow the firm to issue stock.)

6. Executive Fruit's financial manager believes that revenues in 1985 could rise by as much as 50% or by as little as 10%. Recalculate the pro forma financial statements under these two assumptions. How does the rate of growth in revenues affect the firm's borrowing requirement?

7. (*a*) Use the Executive Fruit model (Table 26-3) to produce pro forma income statements, balance sheets, and sources and uses of funds statements for 1986 and 1987. Assume "business as usual" except that sales and costs expand by 30% per year, as do fixed assets and net working capital. The interest rate is forecasted to remain at 9%, and stock issues are ruled out. Executive Fruit also plans to stick to its 60% dividend payout ratio. (*Hint*: Interest expense depends on additional borrowing, which in turn depends on profit after interest and taxes. You may find it helpful to rearrange the equations so that you can calculate interest first.)

(*b*) What are the firm's debt ratio and interest coverage under this plan?

(*c*) Can the company continue to finance expansion by borrowing?

8. Discuss the relative merits of descriptive financial models, such as the Executive Fruit model, and optimizing models such as LONGER. Descriptive models are much more commonly used in practice. Why do you think this is so?

9. Table 26-5 shows the 1987 financial statements for the Executive Cheese Company. Annual depreciation is 10% of fixed assets at the beginning of this year, plus 10% of new investment. The company plans to invest a further $200 per year in fixed assets for the next five years, and forecasts that the ratio of revenues to total assets at the start of each year will remain at 1.75. Fixed costs are expected to remain at $53 and variable costs at 80% of revenue. The company's policy is to pay out two-thirds of net income as dividends and to maintain a book debt ratio of 20%.

(*a*) Construct a model like the one in Table 26-3 for Executive Cheese.

(*b*) Use your model to produce a set of financial statements for 1988.

Table 26-5 Financial statements for Executive Cheese Company (figures in thousands of dollars).

Income Statement for 1987	
Revenue	$1,785
Fixed costs	53
Variable costs (80% of revenue)	1,428
Depreciation	80
Interest (at 8%)	24
Taxes (at 40%)	80
Net income	$ 120

Sources and Uses of Funds for 1987	
Sources	
Operating cash flow	$ 200
Borrowing	36
Stock issues	104
Total sources	$ 340
Uses	
Increase in net working capital	60
Investment	200
Dividends	80
Total uses	$ 340

Balance Sheet, Year-End		
	1987	1986
Assets		
Net working capital	$ 400	$ 340
Fixed assets	800	680
Total assets	$1,200	$1,020
	1987	1986
Liabilities		
Debt	$ 240	$ 204
Book equity	960	816
Total liabilities	$1,200	$1,020

10. Our model for Executive Fruit is an example of a "top down" planning model. Some firms use a "bottom up" financial planning model, which incorporates forecasts of revenues and costs for particular products, advertising plans, major investment projects, and so on. What are the advantages and disadvantages of the two model types? What sort of firms would you expect to use each type and what would they use them for?

SHORT-TERM FINANCIAL PLANNING

Most of this book is devoted to long-term financial decisions such as capital budgeting and the choice of capital structure. Such decisions are called *long-term* for two reasons. First, they usually involve long-lived assets or liabilities. Second, they are not easily reversed, and therefore may commit the firm to a particular course of action for several years.

Short-term financial decisions generally involve short-lived assets and liabilities, and usually they *are* easily reversed. Compare, for example, a 60-day bank loan for $50 million with a $50 million issue of 20-year bonds. The bank loan is clearly a short-term decision. The firm can repay it two months later and be right back where it started. A firm might conceivably issue a 20-year bond in January and retire it in March, but it would be extremely inconvenient and expensive to do so. In practice, such a bond issue is a long-term decision, not only because of the bond's 20-year maturity, but because the decision to issue it cannot be reversed on short notice.

A financial manager responsible for short-term financial decisions does not have to look far into the future. The decision to take the 60-day bank loan could properly be based on cash-flow forecasts for the next few months only. The bond issue decision will normally reflect forecasted cash requirements five, ten, or more years into the future.

Managers concerned with short-term financial decisions can avoid many of the difficult conceptual issues encountered elsewhere in this book. In a sense, short-term decisions are easier than long-term decisions—but they are not less important. A firm can identify extremely valuable capital investment opportunities, find the precise optimal debt ratio, follow the perfect dividend policy, and yet founder because no one bothers to raise the cash to pay this year's bills. Hence the need for short-term planning.

In this chapter, we will review the major classes of short-term assets and liabilities, show how long-term financing decisions affect the firm's short-term financial planning problem, and describe how financial managers trace changes in cash and working capital. We will also describe how managers forecast month-by-month cash requirements or surpluses and how they develop short-term investment and financing strategies.

Part 9 of the book takes a more detailed look at working capital management. Chapter 28 examines the decision to extend credit to the firm's customers. Chapter 29 describes the decisions to hold cash (instead of investing cash to earn interest) and the relationship between firms and commercial banks. Chapter 30 describes the many channels firms can use to invest or raise funds for short periods.

27-1 THE COMPONENTS OF WORKING CAPITAL

Short-term or *current* assets and liabilities are collectively known as **working capital**. Table 27-1 gives a breakdown of current assets and current liabilities for all Canadian manufacturing firms with more than $10 million in assets in the third quarter of 1984. Note that total current assets were $70.4 billion and current liabilities were $41.5 billion. **Net working capital** (current assets less current liabilities) was $28.8 billion.

Table 27-1 Current assets and liabilities for manufacturing corporations in Canada, third quarter, 1984 (figures in millions of dollars).

Current Assets[a]		Current Liabilities[a]	
Cash	1,856	Short-term loans	11,064
Short-term loans to affiliates	1,658	Accounts payable	25,969
Marketable securities	7,747	Corporate income taxes payable	1,427
Accounts receivable	28,016	Portion of long-term debt payable	
		within one year	1,321
Inventories	31,262		
Other current assets	1,469	Other current liabilities	1,715
Total	70,350	Total	41,496

[a]Net working capital (current assets − current liabilities) is $70,350 − $41,496 = $28,854.

Source: Statistics Canada, *Industrial Corporations*, Financial Statistics, Catalogue 61–003, Third Quarter, 1984, pp. 22–25. Reproduced by permission of the Minister of Supply and Services Canada.

One important current asset is *accounts receivable*. When one company sells goods to another company or a government agency, it does not usually expect to be paid immediately. These unpaid bills or *trade credit* make up the bulk of accounts receivable. Companies also sell some goods on credit to the final consumer. This *consumer credit* makes up the remainder of accounts receivable.[1] We will discuss the management of receivables in Chapter 28. You will learn how companies decide which customers are good or bad credit risks and when it makes sense to offer credit.

Another important current asset is *inventory*. Inventories may consist of raw materials, work in process, or finished goods awaiting sale and shipment.

Firms *invest* in inventory. The cost of holding inventory includes not only storage cost and the risk of spoilage or obsolescence, but also the opportunity cost of capital— that is, the rate of return offered by other, equivalent-risk investment opportunities.[2] The benefits to holding inventory are often indirect. For example, a large inventory of finished goods (large relative to expected sales) reduces the chance of a "stockout" if demand is unexpectedly high. A producer holding a small finished goods inventory is more likely to be caught short, unable to fill orders promptly. Similarly, large raw materials inventories reduce the chance that an unexpected shortage would force the firm to shut down production or use a more costly substitute material.

Bulk orders for raw materials, although they lead to large average inventories, may be worthwhile if the firm can obtain lower prices from suppliers. (That is, bulk orders may yield quantity discounts.) Firms will often hold large inventories of finished goods, for similar reasons. A large inventory of finished goods allows longer, more economical production runs. In effect, the production manager gives the firm a quantity discount.

The task of inventory management is to assess these benefits and costs and to strike a sensible balance. In manufacturing companies the production manager is best placed

---

[1]Sales of all manufacturing corporations were $49,735 million in the third quarter of 1984. Table 27-1 shows that accounts receivable were $28,016 million, about 56% of the quarter's sales. Since the accounts receivable are measured at the quarter's end, they must represent the last 56% of the quarter's sales. This amounts to $0.56 \times 13 = 7.3$ weeks. If this ratio of accounts receivable to annual sales is maintained, accounts receivable will always reflect the 7.3 weeks' sales.

[2]How risky are inventories? It is hard to generalize. Many firms just assume inventories have the same risk as typical capital investments and therefore calculate the cost of holding inventories using the firm's average opportunity cost of capital. You can think of many exceptions to this rule of thumb, however. For example, some electronics components are made with gold connections. Should an electronics firm apply its average cost of capital to its inventory of gold? (See Section 9-3.)

to make this judgement. Since the financial manager is not usually directly involved in inventory management, we will not discuss the inventory problem in detail.

The remaining current assets are cash and marketable securities. The cash consists of currency, demand deposits (funds in chequing accounts), and time deposits (funds in savings accounts). The principal marketable security is commercial paper (short-term unsecured notes sold by other firms) and bankers' acceptances (short-term promissory notes sold by other firms and backed by chartered banks). Other securities include Treasury bills and sales finance paper (secured or unsecured notes sold by finance companies or firms with finance subsidiaries).

In choosing between cash and marketable securities, the financial manager faces a task like that of the production manager. There are always advantages to holding large "inventories" of cash—they reduce the risk of running out of cash and having to raise more on short notice. On the other hand, there is a cost to holding idle cash balances rather than putting the money to work in marketable securities. In Chapter 29 we will tell you how the financial manager collects and pays out cash and decides on an optimal cash balance.

We have seen that a company's principal current asset consists of unpaid bills from other companies. One firm's credit must be another's debit. Therefore it is not surprising that a company's principal current liability consists of *accounts payable*—that is, outstanding payments to other companies.

To finance its investment in current assets, a company may rely on a variety of short-term loans. Commercial banks are by far the largest source of such loans, but an industrial firm may also borrow from other sources. Other ways of borrowing include issuing bankers' acceptances and selling commercial paper.

Many short-term loans are unsecured, but sometimes the company may offer its inventory or receivables as security. For example, a firm may decide to borrow short-term money secured by its accounts receivable. When its customers have paid their bills, it can use the cash to repay the loan. An alternative procedure is to *sell* the receivables to a financial institution and let it collect the money. In other words, some companies solve their financing problem by borrowing on the strength of their current assets; others solve it by selling their current assets. In Chapter 30 we will look at the varied and ingenious methods of financing current assets.

27-2 LINKS BETWEEN LONG-TERM AND SHORT-TERM FINANCING DECISIONS

All businesses require capital—that is, money invested in plant, machinery, inventories, accounts receivable, and all the other assets it takes to run a business efficiently. Typically, these assets are not purchased all at once but obtained gradually over time. Let us call the total cost of these assets the firm's *cumulative capital requirement*.

Most firms' cumulative capital requirement grows irregularly, like the wavy line in Figure 27-1. This line shows a clear upward trend, as the firm's business grows. But there is also seasonal variation around the trend: in the figure the capital-requirements line peaks late in each year. Finally, there would be unpredictable week-to-week and month-to-month fluctuations, but we have not attempted to show these in Figure 27-1.

The cumulative capital requirement can be met from either long-term or short-term financing. When long-term financing does not cover the cumulative capital requirement, the firm must raise short-term capital to make up the difference. When long-term financing *more* than covers the cumulative capital requirement, the firm has surplus cash available for short-term investment. Thus the amount of long-term financing raised, given the cumulative capital requirement, determines whether the firm is a short-term borrower or lender.

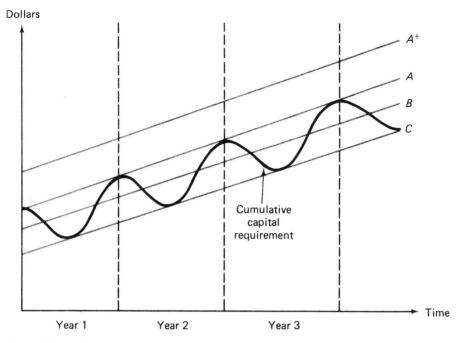

Dollars

A^+

A

B

C

Cumulative
capital
requirement

Time

Year 1   Year 2   Year 3

Figure 27-1   The firm's cumulative capital requirement (heavy line) is the cumulative investment in plant, equipment, inventory and all other assets needed for the business. In this case the requirement grows year by year, but there is seasonal fluctuation within each year. The requirement for short-term financing is the difference between long-term financing (lines A^+, A, B, and C) and the cumulative capital requirement. If long-term financing follows line C, the firm *always* needs short-term financing. At line B, the need is seasonal. At lines A and A^+, the firm never needs short-term financing. There is always extra cash to invest.

Lines A, B, and C in Figure 27-1 illustrate this. Each depicts a different long-term financing strategy. Strategy A always implies a short-term cash surplus. Strategy C implies a permanent need for short-term borrowing. Under B, which is probably the most common strategy, the firm is a short-term lender during part of the year and a borrower during the rest.

What is the *best* level of long-term financing relative to the cumulative capital requirement? It is hard to say. There is no convincing theoretical analysis of this question. We can make several practical observations, however.

Matching Maturities

Most financial managers attempt to "match maturities" of assets and liabilities. That is, they finance long-lived assets like plant and machinery with long-term borrowing and equity.

Permanent Working-Capital Requirements

Most firms make a permanent investment in net working capital (current assets less current liabilities). They finance this investment from long-term sources.[3]

---

[3]In a sense this statement is true by definition. If net working capital (current assets less current liabilities) is positive, it must be financed by long-term debt or equity. Our point is that firms *plan* it that way.

The Comforts of Surplus Cash

Many financial managers would feel more comfortable under strategy A than strategy C. Strategy A^+ (the highest line) would be still more relaxing. A firm with a surplus of long-term financing never has to worry about borrowing to pay next month's bills. But is the financial manager paid to be comfortable? Firms usually put surplus cash to work in Treasury bills or other marketable securities. This is at best a zero-NPV investment for a tax-paying firm.[4] Thus we think that firms with a *permanent* cash surplus ought to go on a diet, retiring long-term securities to reduce long-term financing to a level at or below the firm's cumulative capital requirement. That is, if the firm is on line A^+, it ought to move down to line A, or perhaps even lower.

27-3 TRACING CHANGES IN CASH AND WORKING CAPITAL

Table 27-2 compares 1984 and 1985 year-end balance sheets for Cimarron Mattress Company. Table 27-3 shows the firm's income statement for 1985. Note that Cimarron's cash balance increased by $1 million during 1985. What caused this increase? Did the extra cash come from Cimarron Mattress Company's additional long-term borrowing, from reinvested earnings, from cash released by reducing inventory, or from extra credit extended by Cimarron's suppliers? (Note the increase in accounts payable.)

Table 27-2   Year-end balance sheets for 1984 and 1985 for Cimarron Mattress Company (figures in millions of dollars).

	1984	1985
Current assets		
Cash	4	5
Marketable securities	0	5
Inventory	26	25
Accounts receivable	25	30
Total current assets	55	65
Fixed assets		
Gross investment	56	70
Less depreciation	−16	−20
Net fixed assets	40	50
Total assets	95	115
Current liabilities		
Bank loans	5	0
Accounts payable	20	27
Total current liabilities	25	27
Long-term debt	5	12
Net worth (equity and retained earnings)	65	76
Total liabilities and net worth	95	115

[4]But what is the NPV of an investment in Treasury bills? The answer depends on your position on the "debt and taxes" controversy discussed in Section 18-2. If there is a tax advantage to borrowing, as most people believe, there must be a corresponding tax *dis*advantage to lending, and investment in Treasury bills has a negative NPV. On the other hand, if Merton Miller is right, and there is no tax advantage to borrowing, then Treasury bills are a zero-NPV investment.

Table 27-3 Income statement for 1985 for Cimarron Mattress Company (figures in millions of dollars).

Sales	350
Operating costs	−321
	29
Depreciation	−4
	25
Interest	−1
Pretax income	24
Tax at 50%	−12
Net income	−12

Note:
Dividend = $1 million
Retained earnings = $11 million

Table 27-4 Sources and uses of cash for 1985 for Cimarron Mattress Company (figures in millions of dollars).

Sources	
Issued long-term debt	7
Reduced inventories	1
Increased accounts payable	7
Cash from operations:	
Net income	12
Depreciation	4
Total sources	31
Uses	
Repaid short-term bank loan	5
Invested in fixed assets	14
Purchased marketable securities	5
Increased accounts receivable	5
Dividend	1
	30
Increase in cash balance	1

The correct answer is "all the above," as well as many other activities and actions taken by the firm during the year. All we can say is that *sources* of cash exceeded *uses* by $1 million.

Financial analysts often summarize sources and uses of cash in a statement like the one shown in Table 27-4. The statement shows that Cimarron *generated* cash from the following sources:

1. It issued $7 million of long-term debt.
2. In reduced inventory, releasing $1 million.
3. It increased its accounts payable, in effect borrowing an additional $7 million from its suppliers.
4. By far the largest source of cash was Cimarron's operations, which generated $16 million. See Table 27-3, and note: income ($12 million) understates cash flow because depreciation is deducted in calculating income. Depreciation is *not* a cash outlay. Thus, it must be added back in order to obtain operating cash flow.

Cimarron *used* cash for the following purposes:

1. It paid a $1 million dividend. (*Note:* The $11 million increase in Cimarron's equity is due to retained earnings: $12 million of equity income, less the $1 million dividend.)

2. It repaid a $5 million short-term bank loan.[5]

3. It invested $14 million. This shows up as the increase in gross fixed assets in Table 27-2.

4. It purchased $5 million of marketable securities.

5. It allowed accounts receivable to expand by $5 million. In effect, it lent this additional amount to its customers.

Tracing Changes in Net Working Capital

Financial analysts often find it useful to collapse all current assets and liabilities into a single figure for net working capital. Cimarron's net working capital balances were (in millions):

	Current Assets	Less	Current Liabilities	Equals	Net Working Capital
Year-end 1984	$55	–	$25	=	$30
Year-end 1985	$65	–	$27	=	$38

Table 27-5 gives balance sheets that report only net working capital, not individual current asset or liability items.

Table 27-5   Condensed year-end balance sheets for 1984 and 1985 for Cimarron Mattress Company (figures in millions of dollars).

	1984	1985
Net working capital	30	38
Fixed assets		
Gross investment	56	70
Less depreciation	– 16	– 20
Net fixed assets	40	50
Total assets	70	88
Long-term debt	5	12
Net worth	65	76
Long-term liabilities and net worth[a]	70	88

[a]When only *net* working capital appears on a firm's balance sheet, this figure (the sum of long-term liabilities and net worth) is often referred to as *total capitalization.*

"Sources and uses" statements can likewise be simplified by defining "sources" as actions or activities that contribute to net working capital, and "uses" as actions or activities that use up working capital. In this context working capital is usually referred to as *funds*, and a *"sources and uses of funds" statement* is presented.

---

[5]This is principal repayment, not interest. Sometimes interest payments are explicitly recognized as a use of funds. If so, operating cash flow would be defined *before* interest, that is, as net income plus interest plus depreciation.

In 1984 Cimarron contributed to net working capital by:

1. Issuing $7 million of long-term debt
2. Generating $16 million from operations

It used up net working capital by:

1. Investing $14 million
2. Paying a $1 million dividend

The year's changes in net working capital are thus summarized by Cimarron Mattress Company's "sources and uses of funds" statement, given in Table 27-6.

Table 27-6 Sources and uses of funds (net working capital) for 1985 for Cimarron Mattress Company (figures in millions of dollars).

Sources	
Issued long-term debt	7
Cash from operations	
Net income	12
Depreciation	4
	23
Uses	
Invested in fixed assets	14
Dividend	1
	15
Increase in net working capital	8

Profits and Cash Flow

Now look back to Table 27-4, which shows sources and uses of *cash*. We want to register two warnings about the entry called *cash from operations*. It may not actually represent real dollars—dollars you can buy beer with.

First, depreciation may not be the only noncash expense deducted in calculating income. For example, most firms use different accounting procedures in their tax books than in their reports to shareholders. The point of special tax accounts is to minimize current taxable income. The effect is that the shareholder books overstate the firm's current asset tax liability,[6] and after-tax cash flow from operations is therefore understated.

Second, income statements record sales when made, not when the customer's payment is received. Think of what happens when Cimarron sells goods on credit. The company records a profit at the time of sale but there is no cash inflow until the bills are paid. Since there is no cash inflow, there is no change in the company's cash balance, although there is an increase in working capital in the form of an increase in accounts receivable. No net addition to cash would be shown in a "sources and uses"

---

[6]The difference between taxes reported and paid to Revenue Canada shows up on the balance sheet as an increased deferred tax liability. The reason a liability is recognized is that accelerated depreciation and other devices used to reduce current taxable income do not eliminate taxes, they only delay them. Of course this reduces the present value of the firm's tax liability, but still the ultimate liability has to be recognized. In the "sources and uses" statements an increase in deferred taxes would be treated as a source of funds. In the Cimarron Mattress example we ignore deferred taxes.

statement like Table 27-4. The increase in cash from operations would be offset by an increase in accounts receivable.

Later, when the bills are paid, there is an increase in the cash balance. However, there is no further profit at this point and no increase in working capital. The increase in the cash balance is exactly matched by a decrease in accounts receivable.

That brings up interesting characteristics of working capital. Imagine a company that conducts a very simple business. It buys raw materials for cash, processes them into finished goods, and then sells these goods on credit. The whole cycle of operations looks like this:

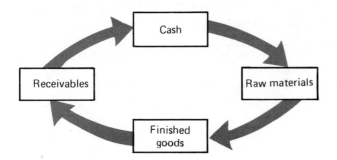

If you draw up a balance sheet at the beginning of the process, you see cash. If you delay a little, you find the cash replaced by inventories of raw materials and, still later, by inventories of finished goods. When the goods are sold, the inventories give way to accounts receivable and finally, when the customers pay their bills, the firm draws out its profit and replenishes the cash balance.

There is only one constant in this process—namely, working capital. The components of working capital are constantly changing. That is one reason that (net) working capital is a useful summary measure of current assets or liabilities.

The strength of the working capital measure is that it is unaffected by seasonal or other temporary movements between different current assets or liabilities. But the strength is also its weakness, for the working capital figure hides a lot of interesting information. In our example cash was transformed into inventory, then into receivables, and back into cash again. But these assets have different degrees of risk and liquidity. You can't pay bills with inventory or with receivables—you must pay with cash.

27-4 CASH BUDGETING

The past is interesting only for what one can learn from it. The financial manager's problem is to forecast *future* sources and uses of cash. These forecasts serve two purposes. First, they alert the financial manager to future cash needs. Second, the cash-flow forecasts provide a standard, or budget, against which subsequent performance can be judged.

Preparing the Cash Budget: Inflow

There are at least as many ways to produce a quarterly cash budget as there are to skin a cat. Many large firms have developed elaborate "corporate models," which allow their computer to do much of the work. The procedures of smaller firms are less formal. But there are common issues that all firms must face when they forecast. We will illustrate these issues by continuing the example of Cimarron Mattress.

Most of Cimarron's cash inflow comes from the sale of mattresses. We therefore start with a sales forecast by quarter[7] for 1986:

	Quarter			
	First	Second	Third	Fourth
Sales (millions of dollars)	87.5	78.5	116	131

But sales become accounts receivable before they become cash. Cash flow comes from *collections* on accounts receivable.

Most firms keep track of the average time it takes customers to pay their bills. From this they can forecast what proportion of a quarter's sales are likely to be converted into cash in that quarter, and what proportion is likely to be carried over to the next quarter as accounts receivable. Suppose that 80% of sales are "cashed in" in the immediate quarter and 20% in the next. Table 27-7 shows forecasted collections under this assumption.

Table 27-7 To forecast Cimarron Mattress's collections on accounts receivably you have to forecast sales and collection rates (figures in millions of dollars).

	First Quarter	Second Quarter	Third Quarter	Fourth Quarter
1. Receivables at start of period	30	32.5	30.7	38.2
2. Sales	87.5	78.5	116	131
3. Collections				
Sales in current period (80%)	70	62.8	92.8	104.8
Sales in last period (20%)	15[a]	17.5	15.7	23.2
Total collections	85	80.3	108.5	128.0
4. Receivables at end of period	32.5	30.7	38.2	41.2
4 = 1 + 2 − 3				

[a]Sales in the fourth quarter of the previous year were $75 million.

In the first quarter, for example, collections from current sales are 80% of $87.5, or $70 million. But the firm also collects 20% of the previous quarter's sales, or 0.2(75) = $15 million. Therefore total collections are $70 + $15 = $85 million.

Cimarron started the first quarter with $30 million of accounts receivable. The quarter's sales of $87.5 million were *added* to accounts receivable, but $85 million of collections were *subtracted*. Therefore, as Table 27-7 shows, Cimarron ended the quarter with accounts receivable of $30 + 87.5 − 85 = $32.5 million. The general formula is

Ending accounts receivable = beginning accounts receivable

+ sales − collections

The top section of Table 27-8 shows forecasted sources of cash for Cimarron Mattress. Collection of receivables is the main source but it is not the only one. Perhaps the firm plans to dispose of some land, or expects a tax refund or payment of an insurance

[7]Most firms would forecast by month instead of by quarter. Sometimes weekly or even daily forecasts are made. But presenting a monthly forecast would triple the number of entries in Table 27-7 and subsequent tables. We wanted to keep the examples as simple as possible.

claim. All such items are included as "other" sources. It is also possible that you may raise additional capital by borrowing or selling stock, but we don't want to prejudge that question. Therefore for the moment, we just assume that Cimarron will not raise further long-term finance.

Table 27-8   Cimarron Mattress's cash budget for 1986 (figures in millions of dollars).

	First Quarter	Second Quarter	Third Quarter	Fourth Quarter
Sources of cash				
Collections on accounts receivable	85	80.3	108.5	128
Other	0	0	12.5	0
Total sources	85	80.3	121	128
Uses of cash				
Payments on accounts payable	65	60	55	50
Labour, administrative, and other expenses	30	30	30	30
Capital expenditures	32.5	1.3	5.5	8
Taxes, interest, and dividends	4	4	4.5	5
Total uses	131.5	95.3	95	93
Sources minus uses	−46.5	−15.0	+26	+35
Calculation of short-term financing requirement				
1. Cash at start of period	5	−41.5	−56.5	−30.5
2. Change in cash balance (sources less uses)	−46.5	−15.0	+26	+35
3. Cash at end of period[a] 1 + 2 = 3	−41.5	−56.5	−30.5	+ 4.5
4. Minimum operating cash balance	5	5	5	5
5. Cumulative short-term financing required[b] 5 = 4 − 3	46.5	61.5	35.5	0.5

[a] Of course firms cannot literally hold a negative amount of cash. This is the amount the firm will have to raise to pay its bills.
[b] A negative sign would indicate a cash *surplus*. But in this example the firm must raise cash for all quarters.

Preparing the Cash Budget: Outflow

So much for the incoming cash. Now for the outgoing cash. It is a universal fact that there seem to be many more uses for cash than there are sources. For simplicity, we have condensed the uses into four categories in Table 27-8:

1. *Payments on accounts payable.* You have to pay your bills for raw materials, parts, electricity, and so on. The cash-flow forecast assumes all these bills are paid on time, although Cimarron could probably delay payment to some extent. Delayed payment is sometimes called *stretching your payables.* Stretching is one source of short-term financing, but for most firms it is an expensive source, because by stretching they lose discounts given to firms that pay promptly. This is discussed in more detail in Section 28-1.

2. *Labour, administrative, and other expenses.* This category includes all other regular business expenses.

3. *Capital expenditures.* Note that Cimarron Mattress plans a major capital outlay in the first quarter.

4. *Taxes, interest, and dividend payments.* This includes interest on presently outstanding long-term debt, but does not include interest on any additional borrowing to meet cash requirements in 1986. At this stage in the analysis, Cimarron does not know how much it will have to borrow, or whether it will have to borrow at all.

The forecasted net inflow of cash (sources minus uses) is shown in the box in Table 27-8. Note the large negative figure for the first quarter: a $46.5 million forecasted *outflow*. There is a smaller forecasted outlay in the second quarter, and then substantial cash inflows in the second half of the year.

The bottom part of Table 27-8 (below the box) calculates how much financing Cimarron will have to raise if its cash-flow forecasts are right. It starts the year with $5 million in cash. There is a $46.5 million cash outflow in the first quarter, and so Cimarron will have to obtain at least $46.5 − 5 = $41.5 million of additional financing. This would leave the firm with a forecasted cash balance of exactly zero at the start of the second quarter.

Most financial managers regard a planned cash balance of zero as driving too close to the edge of the cliff. They establish a *minimum operating cash balance* to absorb unexpected cash inflows and outflows. Also, banks usually require firms to maintain a minimum average cash balance as partial compensation for services the bank provides to the firm—this is described in more detail in Chapter 29. We will assume that Cimarron's minimum operating cash balance is $5 million. That means it will have to raise the full $46.5 million cash outflow in the first quarter, and $15 million more in the second quarter. Thus its cumulative financing requirement is $61.5 million in the second quarter. This is the peak, fortunately: the cumulative requirement declines in the third quarter by $26 million to $35.5 million. In the final quarter, Cimarron is almost out of the woods: its cash balance is $4.5 million, just $0.5 million shy of its minimum operating balance.

The next step is to develop a *short-term financing plan* that covers the forecasted requirements in the most economical way possible. We will move on to that topic after two general observations.

1. The large cash outflows in the first two quarters do not necessarily spell trouble for Cimarron Mattress. In part, they reflect the capital investment made in the first quarter: Cimarron is spending $32.5 million, but it should be acquiring an asset worth that much or more. In part, the cash outflows reflect low sales in the first half of the year; sales recover in the second half.[8] If this is a predictable seasonal pattern, the firm should have no trouble borrowing to tide it over the slow months.

2. Table 27-8 is only a best guess about future cash flows. It is a good idea to think about the *uncertainty* in your estimates. For example, you could undertake a sensitivity analysis, in which you inspect how Cimarron's cash requirements would be affected by a shortfall in sales or by a delay in collections. The trouble with such sensitivity analyses is that you are only changing one item at a time, whereas in practice a downturn in the economy might affect, say, sales levels *and* collection rates. An alternative but more complicated solution is to build a model of the cash budget, and then to simulate to determine the probability of cash requirements significantly above or below the forecasts shown in Table 27-8.[9] If cash requirements

---

[8]Maybe people buy more mattresses late in the year when the nights are longer.

[9]In other words, you could use Monte Carlo simulation. See Section 10-2.

are difficult to predict, you may wish to hold additional cash or marketable securities to cover a possible unexpected cash outflow.

27-5   THE SHORT-TERM FINANCING PLAN

Cimarron's cash budget defines its problem: its financial manager must find short-term financing to cover the firm's forecasted cash requirements. There are dozens of sources of short-term financing, but for simplicity we start by assuming that there are just two options.

Options for Short-Term Financing

1. Unsecured Bank Borrowing   Cimarron has an existing arrangement with its bank allowing it to borrow up to $41 million at an interest cost of 11.5% per year or 2.875% per quarter. The firm can borrow and repay whenever it wants so long as it does not exceed the credit limit. Cimarron does not have to pledge any specific assets as security for the loan. This kind of arrangement is called a **line of credit**.[10]

When a company borrows on an unsecured line of credit, it is generally obliged to maintain a **compensating balance** on deposit at the bank. In our example, Cimarron has to maintain a balance of 20% of the amount of the loan. In other words, if the firm wants to raise $100, it must actually borrow $125, because $25 (20% of $125) must be left on deposit in the bank.

2. Stretching Payables   Cimarron can also raise capital by putting off paying its bills. The financial manager believes that Cimarron can defer the following amounts in each quarter:

Quarter	1	2	3	4
Amount deferrable (millions of dollars)	52	48	44	40

That is, $52 million can be saved in the first quarter by *not* paying bills in that quarter. (Table 27-8 assumes these bills *are* paid in the first quarter.) If deferred, these payments *must* be made in the second quarter. Similarly, $48 million of quarter 2's bills can be deferred to quarter 3 and so on.

Stretching payables is often costly, however, even if no ill will is incurred. The reason is that suppliers often offer discounts for prompt payment. Cimarron loses this discount if it pays late. In this example we assume the lost discount is 5% of the amount deferred. In other words, if a $100 payment is delayed, the firm must pay $105 in the next quarter.

The First Financing Plan

With these two options, the short-term financing strategy is obvious: use the line of credit first, if necessary up to the $41 million credit limit. If cash requirements exceed the credit limit, stretch payables.

Table 27-9 shows the resulting financing plan. In the first quarter the plan calls for borrowing the full amount available under the line of credit ($41 million) and stretching

---

[10]Lines of credit are discussed in more detail in Chapter 30.

Table 27-9   Cimarron Mattress's first financing plan (figures in millions of dollars).

	First Quarter	Second Quarter	Third Quarter	Fourth Quarter
New borrowing				
1. Line of credit	41	0	0	0
2. Stretching payables	3.6	20	0	0
3. Total	44.6	20	0	0
Repayments				
4. Line of credit	0	0	4.8	36.2
5. Stretched payables	0	3.6	20	0
6. Total	0	3.6	24.8	36.2
7. Net new borrowing	44.6	16.4	−24.8	−36.2
8. Plus securities sold	5[a]	0	0	0
9. Less securities bought	0	0	0	0
10. Total cash raised	49.6	16.4	−24.8	−36.2
Interest payments				
11. Line of credit	0	1.2	1.2	1.0
12. Stretching	0	0.2	1.0	0
13. Less interest on marketable securities	−0.1[a]	0	0	0
14. Net interest paid	−0.1	1.4	2.2	1.0
15. Additional funds for compensating balance[b]	3.2	0	−1.0	−2.2
16. Cash required for operations[c]	46.5	15	−26	−35
17. Total cash required	49.6	16.4	−24.8	−36.2

[a]Cimarron held $5 million in marketable securities at the end of 1985. The yield is assumed to be 2.4% per quarter.

[b]Twenty percent of the amount borrowed on the line of credit in excess of $25 million. Cimarron's $5 million minimum operating cash balance serves as compensating balance for loans up to $25 million.

[c]From Table 27-8.

$3.6 million of payables (see lines 1 and 2 in the table). In addition, the firm sells the $5 million of marketable securities it held at the end of 1985 (line 8). Thus, under this plan it raises $49.6 million in the first quarter (line 10).

Why raise $49.6 million when Table 27-8 shows a cash requirement of only $46.5 million? The major reason is that the $41 million borrowed under the line of credit requires a compensating balance of 20% of $41 million, or $8.2 million. Cimarron can cover part of this with its $5 million minimum balance, but $3.2 million still has to be raised (line 15).

In the second quarter, the plan calls for Cimarron to maintain line of credit borrowing at the upper limit and stretch $20 million in payables. This raises $16.4 million after the $3.6 million of payables stretched in the first quarter are paid.

Again, the amount of cash raised exceeds the amount required for operations ($16.4 versus $15 million). In this case, the difference is the interest cost of the first quarter's borrowing: $1.2 million for the line of credit and $0.2 million for the stretched payables (lines 11 and 12).[11]

In the third and fourth quarters the plan calls for Cimarron to pay off its debt. In turn, this releases cash tied up by the compensating balance requirement of the line of credit.

Evaluating the First Plan   Does the plan shown in Table 27-9 solve Cimarron's short-term financing problem? No: the plan is feasible, but Cimarron can probably do better. The most glaring weakness of this first plan is its reliance on stretching payables, an extremely expensive financing device. Remember that it costs Cimarron 5% *per quarter* to delay paying bills—20% per year at simple interest. The first plan would merely stimulate the financial manager to search for cheaper sources of short-term borrowing. Perhaps the $41 million limit on the line of credit could be increased, for example.

The financial manager would ask several other questions as well. For example:

1. Does Cimarron need a larger reserve of cash or marketable securities to guard against, say, its customers stretching their payables (thus slowing down collections on accounts receivable?)

2. Does the plan yield satisfactory current and quick ratios?[12] Its bankers may be worried if these ratios deteriorate.[13]

3. Are there intangible costs of stretching payables? Will suppliers begin to doubt Cimarron's creditworthiness?

4. Does the plan for 1986 leave Cimarron in good financial shape for 1987? (Here the answer is yes, since Cimarron will have paid off all short-term borrowing by the end of the year.)

5. Should Cimarron try to arrange long-term financing for the major capital expenditure in the first quarter? This seems sensible, following the rule of thumb that long-term assets deserve long-term financing. It would also reduce the need for short-term borrowing dramatically. A counter argument is that Cimarron is financing the capital investment *only temporarily* by short-term borrowing. By year-end, the investment is paid for by cash from operations. Thus Cimarron's initial decision not to seek immediate long-term financing may reflect a preference for ultimately financing the investment with retained earnings.

6. Perhaps the firm's operating and investment plans can be adjusted to make the short-term financing problem easier. Is there any easy way of deferring the first quarter's large cash outflow? For example, suppose that the large capital investment in the first quarter is for new mattress-stuffing machines to be delivered and installed in the first half of the year. The new machines are not scheduled to be ready for full-scale use until August. Perhaps the machine manufacturer could be persuaded to accept 60% of the purchase price on delivery and 40% when the machines are installed and operating satisfactorily.

Short-term financing plans are developed by trial and error. You lay out one plan, think about it, then try again with different assumptions on financing and investment alternatives. You continue until you can think of no further improvements.

---

[11]The interest rate on the line of credit is 11.5% per year or 11.5/4 = 2.875% per quarter. Thus the interest due is 0.02875(41) = 1.2, or $1.2 million. The "interest" cost of the stretched payables is actually the 5% discount lost by delaying payment. Five percent of $3.6 million is $180,000, or about $0.2 million.

[12]These ratios are discussed in Chapter 25.

[13]We have not worked out these ratios explicitly, but you can infer from Table 27-9 that they would be fine at the end of the year but relatively low in midyear, when Cimarron's borrowing is high.

Trial and error is important because it helps you understand the real nature of the problem the firm faces. Here we can draw a useful analogy between the *process* of planning and Chapter 10, "A Project is Not a Black Box." In Chapter 10 we described sensitivity analysis and other tools used by firms to find out what makes capital investment projects tick and what can go wrong with them. Cimarron's financial manager faces the same kind of task: not just to choose a plan, but to understand what can go wrong with it, and what will be done if conditions change unexpectedly.[14]

We cannot trace through each trial and error in Cimarron Mattress's search for the best short-term financing plan. The reader may be buried in numbers already. Instead we will wrap up this chapter by looking at Cimarron's second try.

The Second Financing Plan

The second financing plan, shown in Table 27-10, reflects two significant new assumptions.

Table 27-10   Cimarron Mattress's second financing plan (figures in millions of dollars).

	First Quarter	Second Quarter	Third Quarter	Fourth Quarter
New borrowing				
1. Line of credit	41	0	0	0
2. Secured borrowing (receivables pledged)	6.1	16.4	0	0
3. Total	47.1	16.4	0	0
Repayments				
4. Line of credit	0	0	2.0	36.7
5. Secured borrowing	0	0	22.4	0
6. Total	0	0	24.4	36.7
7. Net new borrowing	47.1	16.4	−24.4	−36.7
8. Plus securities sold	2.5[a]	0	0	0
9. Less securities bought	0	0	0	0
10. Total cash raised	49.6	16.4	−24.4	−36.7
Interest payments				
11. Line of credit	0	1.2	1.2	1.1
12. Secured borrowing	0	0.2	0.8	0
13. Less interest on marketable securities	−0.1[a]	−0.1	−0.1	−0.1
14. Net interest paid	−0.1	1.3	2.0	1.0
15. Additional funds for compensating balance[b]	3.2	0	−0.4	−2.8
16. Cash required for operations[c]	46.5	15	−26	−35
17. Total cash required	49.6	16.4	−24.4	−36.7

[a]Cimarron held $5 million in marketable securities at the end of 1985.

[b]Twenty percent of the amount borrowed on the line of credit in excess of $25 million. Cimarron's $5 million minimum operating cash balance serves as compensating balance for loans up to $25 million.

[c]From Table 27-8.

Note: There are minor inconsistencies in this table because of rounding.

---

[14]This point is even more important in *long-term* financial planning. See Chapter 26.

1. A commercial financial company[15] has offered to lend Cimarron up to 80% of its accounts receivable at an interest rate of 15% per year or 3.75% per quarter. In return, Cimarron is to pledge accounts receivable as security for the loan. This is clearly cheaper than stretching payables. It appears much more expensive than the bank line of credit—but remember that the line of credit requires a 20% compensating balance, whereas every dollar borrowed against receivables can be spent.

2. The financial manager is uncomfortable with the first plan, which includes no cushion of marketable securities. The second plan calls for a $2.5 million marketable securities portfolio held throughout the year.

A comparison of Table 27-9 and Table 27-10 shows that the second plan is broadly similar to the first, except that borrowing against receivables replaces stretching payables, and the firm holds $2.5 million of marketable securities. The second plan is also cheaper than the first. This can be seen by comparing net interest paid (line 14) under the two plans.

	Quarter				Total
	1	2	3	4	
First plan	−0.1	1.4	2.2	1.0	4.5
Second plan	−0.1	1.3	2.0	1.0	4.2

Over the year the second plan saves $4.5 − $4.2 = $0.3 million, or about $300,000 of interest.[16]

A Note on Short-Term Financial Planning Models

Working out a consistent short-term plan requires burdensome calculations.[17] Fortunately much of the arithmetic can be delegated to a computer. Many large firms have built *short-term financial planning models* to do this. The financial manager specifies forecasted cash requirements or surpluses, interest rates, credit limits, and so on, and the model grinds out a plan like those shown in Tables 27-9 and 27-10. The computer also produces balance sheets, income statements, and whatever special reports the financial manager may require.

Smaller firms that do not want custom-built models can rent general-purpose models offered by banks, accounting firms, management consultants, or specialized computer "software" firms.

Most of these models are *simulation* programs.[18] They simply work out the consequences of the assumptions and policies specified by the financial manager. *Optimization*

---

[15]Commercial finance companies are nonbank financial institutions that specialize in lending to businesses.

[16]These are pretax figures. We simplified this example by forgetting that each dollar of interest paid is a tax-deductible expense.

[17]If you doubt that, look again at Table 27-9 or 27-10. Notice that the cash requirements in each quarter depend on borrowing in the previous quarter, because borrowing creates an obligation to pay interest. Also, borrowing under a line of credit may require additional cash to meet compensating balance requirements; if so that means still more borrowing and still higher interest charges in the next quarter. Moreover, the problem's complexity would have been tripled had we not simplified by forecasting per quarter rather than by month.

[18]Like the simulation models described in Section 10-2, except that the short-term planning models rarely include uncertainty explicitly. The models referred to here are built and used in the same way as the long-term financial planning models described in Section 26-3.

models for short-term financial planning are also available. These models are usually linear programming models. They search for the *best* plan from a range of alternative policies identified by the financial manager.

As a matter of fact, we used a linear programming model developed by Pogue and Bussard[19] to generate Cimarron Mattress's financial plans. Of course in that simple example we hardly needed a linear programming model to identify the best strategy: it was obvious that Cimarron should always use the line of credit first, turning to the second-best alternative (stretching payables or borrowing against receivables) only when the limit on the line of credit was reached. The Pogue-Bussard model nevertheless did the arithmetic quickly and easily.

Optimization helps when the firm faces complex problems with many interdependent alternatives and restrictions for which trial and error might never identify the *best* combination of alternatives.

Of course the best plan for one set of assumptions may prove disastrous if the assumptions are wrong. Thus the financial manager has to explore the implications of alternative assumptions about future cash flows, interest rates, and so on. Linear programming can help identify good strategies, but even with an optimization model the financial plan is still sought by trial and error.

27-6 SUMMARY

Short-term financial planning is concerned with the management of the firm's short-term, or *current* assets and liabilities. The most important current assets are cash, marketable securities, inventory, and accounts receivable. The most important current liabilities are bank loans and accounts payable. The difference between current assets and current liabilities is called *(net) working capital*.

Current assets and liabilities are turned over much more rapidly than the other items on the balance sheet. Short-term financing and investment decisions are more quickly and easily reversed than long-term decisions. Consequently, the financial manager does not need to look so far into the future when making them.

The nature of the firm's short-term financial planning problem is determined by the amount of long-term capital it raises. A firm that issues large amounts of long-term debt or common stock, or which retains a large part of its earnings, may find that it has permanent excess cash. In such cases there is never any problem paying bills, and short-term financial planning consists of managing the firm's portfolio of marketable securities. We think that firms with permanent cash surpluses ought to return the excess cash to their stockholders.

Other firms raise relatively little long-term capital and end up as permanent short-term debtors. Most firms attempt to find a golden mean by financing all fixed assets and part of current assets with equity and long-term debt. Such firms may invest cash surpluses during part of the year and borrow during the rest of the year.

The starting point for short-term financial planning is an understanding of sources and uses of cash.[20] Firms forecast their net cash requirements by forecasting collections on accounts receivable, adding other cash inflows, and subtracting all forecasted cash outlays.

---

[19]G.A. Pogue and R.N. Bussard, "A Linear Programming Model for Short-Term Financial Planning under Uncertainty," *Sloan Management Review*, 13:69–99 (Spring 1972).

[20]We pointed out in Section 27-3 that sources and uses of *funds* are often analyzed rather than sources and uses of cash: anything that contributes to working capital is called *source of funds*; anything that diminishes working capital is called a *use of funds*. "Sources and uses of funds" statements are relatively simple because many sources and uses of cash are buried in changes in working capital. However, in forecasting, the emphasis is on cash flow: you pay bills with cash, not working capital.

If the forecasted cash balance is insufficient to cover day-to-day operations and to provide a buffer against contingencies, you will need to find additional finance. It may make sense to raise long-term finance if the deficiency is permanent and large. Otherwise you may choose from a variety of sources of short-term finance. For example, you may be able to borrow from a bank on an unsecured line of credit, you may borrow offering receivables or inventory as security, or you may be able to finance the deficit by not paying your bills for a while. In addition to the explicit interest costs of short-term financing, there are often implicit costs. For example, the firm may be required to maintain a compensating balance at the bank, or it may lose its reputation as a prompt payer if it raises cash by delaying payment on its bills. The financial manager must choose the financing package that has lowest total cost (explicit and implicit costs combined) and yet leaves the firm with sufficient flexibility to cover contingencies.

The search for the best short-term financial plan inevitably proceeds by trial and error. The financial manager must explore the consequences of different assumptions about cash requirements, interest rates, limits on financing from particular sources, and so on. Firms are increasingly using computerized financial models to help in this process. The models range from simple programs that merely help with the arithmetic to linear programming models that help find the best financial plan, given the financial manager's assumptions about cash requirements, interest rates, and so on.

FURTHER READING

Here are two general textbooks on working capital management.

K.V. Smith, *Guide to Working Capital Management*, McGraw-Hill Book Company, New York, 1979.
D.R Mehta, *Working Capital Management*, Englewood Cliffs, N.J., Prentice-Hall, Inc., 1974.

Pogue and Bussard present a linear programming model for short-term financial planning:

G.A. Pogue and R.N. Bussard, "A Linear Programming Model for Short-Term Financial Planning under Uncertainty," *Sloan Management Review*, **13**:69–99 (Spring 1972).

The following two references survey how firms use corporate models in financial planning:

P.H. Grinyer and J. Wooller, *Corporate Models Today—A New Tool for Financial Management*, 2d ed., Institute of Chartered Accountants, London, 1978.
J.W. Traenkle, E.B. Cox, J.A. Bullard, *The Use of Financial Models in Business*, Financial Executive's Research Foundation, New York, 1975.

QUIZ

1. Listed below are six different transactions that Cimarron Mattress might make. Indicate how each transaction would affect each of the following:
    (*a*) Cash
    (*b*) Working capital

    The transactions are:

    1. Pay out $2 million cash dividend
    2. A customer pays a $2,500 bill resulting from a previous sale
    3. Cimarron pays $5,000 previously owed to one of its suppliers
    4. Borrow $1 million long-term and invest the proceeds in inventory
    5. Borrow $1 million short-term and invest the proceeds in inventory
    6. Sell $5 million of marketable securities for cash

2. Here is a forecast of sales by National Bromide for the first four months of 1983 (figures in thousands of dollars):

Month	1	2	3	4
Cash sales	15	24	18	14
Sales on credit	100	120	90	70

On the average 50% of credit sales are paid for in the current month, 30% in the next month, and the remainder in the month after that. What is the expected cash inflow from operations in months 3 and 4?

3. Fill in the blanks in the following statements:
   (a) A firm has a cash surplus when its _____ capital exceeds its _____. The surplus is normally invested in _____.
   (b) In developing the short-term financial plan, the financial manager starts with a _____ budget for the next year. This budget shows the _____ generated or absorbed by the firm's operations, and also the minimum _____ needed to support these operations. The financial manager may also wish to invest in _____ as a reserve for unexpected cash requirements.
   (c) Short-term financing plans are developed by _____ and _____, often aided by computerized _____.

4. State how each of the following events would affect the firm's balance sheet. State whether each change is a source or use of cash and whether it is a source or use of funds.
   (a) An automobile manufacturer increases production in response to a forecasted increase in demand. Unfortunately, the demand does not increase.
   (b) Competition forces the firm to give customers more time to pay for their purchases.
   (c) Inflation increases the value of raw material inventories by 20%.
   (d) The firm sells a parcel of land for $100,000. The land was purchased five years earlier for $200,000.
   (e) The firm repurchases its own common stock.
   (f) The firm doubles its quarterly dividend.
   (g) The firm issues $1 million of long-term debt and uses the proceeds to repay a short-term bank loan.

QUESTIONS AND PROBLEMS

1. Table 27-11 shows Cimarron Mattress's year-end 1983 balance sheet, and Table 27-12 shows its income statement for 1984. Work out statements of sources and uses of cash and sources and uses of funds for 1984.

2. Work out a short-term financing plan for Cimarron Mattress Company assuming the limit on the line of credit is raised from $41 to $50 million. Otherwise adhere to the assumptions used in developing Table 27-10.

3. Look again at Cimarron Mattress's second plan in Table 27-10. Note that the line of credit is cheaper than borrowing against accounts receivable. Would you expect this to be true in practice? Why or why not?

4. Suppose that Cimarron's bank offers to forget about the compensating balance requirement if the firm pays interest at a rate of 3.375% per quarter. Should the firm accept this offer? Why or why not? (Except for this change, follow the assumptions underlying Table 27-10.) Would your answer change if Cimarron's cash requirements in quarters 1 and 2 were much smaller—say, only $20 million and $10 million, respectively?

Table 27-11   Year-end balance sheet for 1983 (figures in millions of dollars).

Current assets		Current liabilities	
Cash	4	Bank loans	4
Marketable securities	2	Accounts payable	15
Inventory	20	Total current liabilities	19
Accounts receivable	22		
Total current assets	48	Long-term debt	5
		Net worth (equity and	
Fixed assets		retained earnings)	60
Gross investment	50	Total liabilities	
Less depreciation	−14	and net worth	84
Net fixed assets	36		
Total assets	84		

Table 27-12   Income statement for 1984 (figures in millions of dollars).

Sales	300
Operating costs	−285
	15
Depreciation	−2
	13
Interest	−1
Pretax income	12
Tax at 50%	−6
Net income	6

Note:
Dividend   = $1 million
Retained earnings = $5 million

5. In some countries the market for long-term corporate debt is limited, and firms turn to short-term bank loans to finance long-term investments in plant and machinery. When a short-term loan comes due, it is replaced by another one, so that the firm is always a short-term debtor. What are the disadvantages of such an arrangement? Does it have any advantages? (*Hint*: See Section 21-3, especially "Introducing Inflation.")

6. Suppose a firm has surplus cash, but is *not* paying taxes. Would you advise it to invest in Treasury bills or other safe, marketable securities? How about investment in the preferred or common stock of other companies? (*Hint*: Your answer will reflect your stand on the "debt and taxes" controversy. See Section 18-1).

SHORT-TERM
FINANCIAL DECISIONS

CREDIT MANAGEMENT

CHAPTER

·28·

Chapter 27 provided an overall idea of what is involved in short-term financial management. It is time to get down to detail.

When companies sell their products, they sometimes demand cash on or before delivery, but in most cases they allow some delay in payment. If you turn back to the balance sheet in Table 27-1, you can see that these accounts receivable constitute on the average about one-third of a firm's current assets. These receivables include both trade credit and consumer credit. The former is by far the larger and will, therefore, be the main focus of this chapter.

Credit management involves five main steps:

1. First, you must determine the terms on which you propose to sell your goods. How long are you going to give customers to pay their bills? Are you prepared to offer a cash discount for prompt payment?

2. Second, you must decide what evidence you need of indebtedness. Do you just ask the buyer to sign a receipt, or do you insist on some more formal IOU?

3. Third, you must consider which customers are likely to pay their bills. Do you judge this from the customers' past records or past financial statements? Or do you rely on a bank reference?

4. Fourth, you must decide how much credit you are prepared to extend to each customer. Do you play safe by turning down any doubtful prospects? Or do you accept the risk of a few bad debts as part of the cost of building up a large regular clientele?

5. Finally, after you have granted credit, you have the problem of collecting the money when it becomes due. How do you keep track of payments? What do you do about reluctant payers?

We will discuss each step in turn.

28-1 TERMS OF SALE

Not all business transactions involve credit. For example, if you are producing goods to the customer's specification or incurring substantial delivery costs, then it may be sensible to ask for cash before delivery (CBD). If you are supplying goods to a wide variety of irregular customers, you may require cash on delivery (COD).

If your product is expensive and custom-designed and built for each customer, a formal sales contract will be signed. Often such contracts provide for **progress payments** as work is carried out. For example, a large, extended consulting contract might call for 30% payment after completion of field research, 30% more on submission of a draft report, and the remaining 40% when the project is finally completed.

When we look at transactions that do involve credit, we encounter a wide variety of arrangements and considerable jargon. In fact each industry seems to have its own particular usage with regard to payment terms. These norms have a rough logic. The seller will naturally demand earlier payment if its customers are in a high-risk business, if their accounts are small, or if the goods are perishable or quickly resold.

In order to induce customers to pay before the final date, it is common to offer a cash discount for prompt settlement.[1] For example, a manufacturer may require payment within 30 days but offer a 5% discount to customers who pay within 10 days. These terms are referred to as *5/10, net 30*. If a firm sells goods on terms of 2/30, net 60, customers receive a 2% discount for payment within 30 days and must pay in full within 60 days.

Cash discounts are often very large. For example, a customer who buys on terms of 5/10, net 30 may decide to forgo the cash discount and pay on the 30th day. This means that the customer obtains an extra 20 days' credit but pays about 5% more for the goods. This is equivalent to borrowing money at a rate of 155% per annum.[2] Of course any firm that delays payment beyond the due date gains a cheaper loan but damages its reputation for creditworthiness.

You can think of the terms of sale as fixing both the price for the cash buyer and the rate of interest charged for credit. For example, suppose that a firm reduces the cash discount from 5% to 4%. That would represent an *increase* in the price for the cash buyer of 1% but a *reduction* in the implicit rate of interest charged the credit buyer from just over 5% per 20 days to just over 4% per 20 days.

For many items that are bought on a recurrent basis, it is inconvenient to require separate payment for each delivery. A common solution is to pretend that all sales during the month in fact occur at the end of the month. Thus goods may be sold on terms of 8/10, EOM, net 60. This allows the customer a cash discount of 8% if the bill is paid within ten days of the end of month (EOM); otherwise the full payment is due within 60 days of the invoice date.[3] When purchases are subject to seasonal fluctuations, manufacturers often encourage customers to take early delivery by allowing them to delay payment until the usual order season. This practice is known as "season dating."

28-2 COMMERCIAL CREDIT INSTRUMENTS

The terms of sale define the amount of any credit but not the nature of the contract. Repetitive sales to domestic customers are almost always made on **open account** and involve only an implicit contract. There is simply a record in the seller's books and a receipt signed by the buyer.

If an order is very large and there is no complicating cash discount, the customer may be asked to sign a **promissory note**. This is just a straightforward IOU, worded along the following lines:

---

[1] In addition, many companies allow an "anticipation rate"—that is, a discount calculated to give a normal rate of interest to those customers who miss the cash discount but pay before the final date. Some firms also add a service charge for late payment.

[2] The cash discount allows you to pay $95 rather than $100. If you do not take the discount, you get a 20-day loan but you pay $5/95 = 5.26\%$ more for your goods. There are $365/20 = 18.25$ 20-day periods in a year. A dollar invested for 18.25 periods at 5.26% per period grows to $(1.0526)^{18.25} = \$2.55$, a 155% return on the original investment.

[3] Terms of 8/10, prox., net 60 would entitle the customer to a discount if the bill was paid within ten days of the end of the following (or "proximo") month.

Sixty days after date I promise to pay to the order of the XYZ Company one thousand dollars ($1,000.00) for value received.

Signature

Such an arrangement is not common, but it has two advantages. First, as long as it is payable to "order" or to "bearer," the holder may sell this note or use it as security for a loan. Second, the note eliminates the possibility of any subsequent disputes about the existence of the debt; the customer knows that he or she may be sued immediately for failure to pay on the due date.

If you want a clear commitment from the buyer, it is more useful to have it *before* you deliver the goods. In this case the simplest procedure is to arrange a **commercial draft**.[4] It works as follows. The seller draws a draft ordering payment by the customer and sends this draft to the customer's bank together with the shipping documents. If immediate payment is required, the draft is termed a **sight draft**; otherwise, it is known as a **time draft**. Depending on whether it is a sight or a time draft, the customer either pays up or acknowledges the debt by adding the word *accepted* and his or her signature. The bank then hands the shipping documents to the customer and forwards the money or the **trade acceptance** to the seller.[5] The latter may hold the trade acceptance to maturity or may use it as security for a loan.

If the customer's credit is for any reason suspect, the seller may ask the customer to arrange for his or her bank to accept the time draft. In this case, the bank guarantees the customer's debt. These **bank acceptances** are often used in overseas trade; they have a higher standing and greater negotiability than a trade acceptance.

The exporter who requires greater certainty of payment can ask the customer to arrange for an **irrevocable letter of credit**. In this case the customer's bank sends the exporter a letter stating that it has established a credit in his or her favour at a bank in Canada. The exporter then draws a draft on the customer's bank and presents it to the bank in Canada together with the letter of credit and the shipping documents. The bank in Canada arranges for this draft to be accepted or paid and forwards the documents to the customer's bank.

In some cases, the exporter will accept a letter of credit from a **confirming house** that is not a bank, but a finance house in the business of providing letters of credit. Their collateral is less secure than a bank would get, so they charge more for their service.

If you sell goods to a customer who proves unable to pay, you cannot get your goods back. You simply become a general unsecured creditor of the company, in common with other unfortunates. You can avoid this situation by making a **conditional sale**, so that title to the goods remains with the seller until full payment is made. It is used for goods that are bought on an instalment basis. In this case, if the customer defaults on the payments, the goods can be immediately repossessed by the seller.

28-3   CREDIT ANALYSIS

Firms are not allowed to discriminate between customers by charging them different prices. Neither may they discriminate by offering the same prices but different credit terms.[6] You *can* offer different terms of sale to different *classes* of buyer. You can offer

---

[4] Commercial drafts are sometimes known by the more general term *bills of exchange.*

[5] You often see the terms of sale defined as SD-BL. This means that the bank will hand over the bill of lading in return for payment on a sight draft.

[6] Price discrimination, and by implication credit discrimination, is prohibited by law.

volume discounts, for example, or discounts to customers willing to accept long-term purchase contracts. But as a rule, if you have a customer of doubtful standing, you keep to your regular terms of sale for that customer class. You protect yourself by restricting the volume of goods that the customer may buy on credit.

There are a number of ways in which you can find out whether customers are likely to pay their debts. The most obvious indication is whether they have paid promptly in the past. Prompt payment is generally a good omen; but beware of the customer who establishes a high credit limit on the basis of a series of small payments and then disappears, leaving you with a large unpaid bill.

If you are dealing with a new customer, you will probably check with a credit agency. Dun and Bradstreet is by far the largest of these agencies: its regular *Reference Book*

Key to Ratings

ESTIMATED FINANCIAL STRENGTH			COMPOSITE CREDIT APPRAISAL			
			HIGH	GOOD	FAIR	LIMITED
5A	$50,000,000	and over	1	2	3	4
4A	$10,000,000 to	49,999,999	1	2	3	4
3A	1,000,000 to	9,999,999	1	2	3	4
2A	750,000 to	999,999	1	2	3	4
1A	500,000 to	749,999	1	2	3	4
BA	300,000 to	499,999	1	2	3	4
BB	200,000 to	299,999	1	2	3	4
CB	125,000 to	199,999	1	2	3	4
CC	75,000 to	124,999	1	2	3	4
DC	50,000 to	74,999	1	2	3	4
DD	35,000 to	49,999	1	2	3	4
EE	20,000 to	34,999	1	2	3	4
FF	10,000 to	19,999	1	2	3	4
GG	5,000 to	9,999	1	2	3	4
HH	Up to	4,999	1	2	3	4

GENERAL CLASSIFICATION

ESTIMATED FINANCIAL STRENGTH			COMPOSITE CREDIT APPRAISAL		
			GOOD	FAIR	LIMITED
1R	$125,000	and over	2	3	4
2R	$50,000 to	$124,999	2	3	4

EXPLANATION

When the designation "1R" or "2R" appears, followed by a 2, 3 or 4, it is an indication that the Estimated Financial Strength, while not definitely classified, is presumed to be in the range of the ($) figures in the corresponding bracket, and while the Composite Credit Appraisal cannot be judged precisely, it is believed to fall in the general category indicated.

"INV." shown in place of a rating indicates that the report was under investigation at the time of going to press. It has no other significance.

"FB" (Foreign Branch). Indicates that the headquarters of this company is located in a foreign country (including Canada). The written report contains the location of the headquarters.

ABSENCE OF RATING, expressed by two hyphens (--), is not to be construed as unfavorable but signifies circumstances difficult to classify within condensed rating symbols. It suggests the advisability of obtaining a report for additional information.

EMPLOYEE RANGE DESIGNATIONS IN REPORTS ON NAMES NOT LISTED IN THE REFERENCE BOOK

KEY TO EMPLOYEE RANGE DESIGNATIONS

Certain businesses do not lend themselves to a Dun & Bradstreet rating and are not listed in the Reference Book. Information on these names, however, continues to be stored and updated in the D&B Business Information File. Reports are available on such businesses and instead of a rating they carry an Employee Range Designation (ER) which is indicative of size in terms of number of employees. No other significance should be attached.

ER 1	1000 or more	Employees
ER 2	500-999	Employees
ER 3	100-499	Employees
ER 4	50- 99	Employees
ER 5	20- 49	Employees
ER 6	10- 19	Employees
ER 7	5- 9	Employees
ER 8	1- 4	Employees
ER N		Not Available

Figure 28-1   Key to Dun and Bradstreet ratings.

Source: Used by permission of Dun and Bradstreet Canada Limited.

provides credit ratings on nearly 3 million domestic and foreign firms. Figure 28-1 tells you how to interpret these ratings. In addition to its rating service, Dun and Bradstreet provides on request a full credit report on a potential customer.

Credit agencies usually report the experience that other firms have had with your customer. You can also get this information by contacting the firms directly or through a credit bureau or through a better business bureau.

Your bank can also make a credit check. It will contact the customer's bank and ask for information on the customer's average bank balance, access to bank credit, and general reputation.

In addition to checking with your customer's bank, it might make sense to check what everybody else in the financial community thinks about your customer's credit standing. Does that sound expensive? Not if your customer is a public company. You just look at the Canadian Bond Rating Service rating for the customer's outstanding bonds.[7] You can also compare prices of these bonds to prices of other firms' bonds. (Of course the comparisons should be between bonds of similar maturity, coupon, and so on.) Finally, you can look at how the customer's stock price has been behaving recently. A sharp fall in price doesn't mean that the company is in trouble, but it does suggest that prospects are less bright than formerly.

Financial Ratio Analysis

We have suggested a number of ways to check whether your customer is a good risk. You can ask your collection manager, a specialized credit agency, a credit bureau, a banker, or the financial community at large. But, if you don't like relying on the judgement of others, you can do your own homework. Ideally this would involve a detailed analysis of the company's business prospects and financing, but this is usually too expensive. Therefore credit analysts concentrate on the company's financial statements, using rough rules of thumb to judge whether the firm is a good credit risk. The rules of thumb are based on *financial ratios*. Chapter 25 described how these ratios are calculated and interpreted.

Numerical Credit Scoring

Analyzing credit risks is like police detective work. You have a lot of clues—some important, some minor, some fitting into a neat pattern, others contradictory. You must weigh these clues to come up with an overall judgement.

In a small village the local police officer can generally rely on experience and knowledge of the locality. Personal judgement is everything. In a large city the police force cannot operate like this. It needs a systematic way to gather and sort all the information that comes into police headquarters. Likewise, when the firm has a small, regular clientele, the credit manager can easily handle the investigation process informally. But when the company is dealing directly with consumers or with a large number of small trade accounts, some streamlining is essential. In these cases it may make sense to use a mechanical scoring system to prescreen credit applications.

During the years 1952 to 1958 one typical medium-sized bank granted over 100,000 personal loans.[8] Each loan applicant was required to answer a standard questionnaire, of which a condensed version is shown in Table 28-1. In total only 1.2% of these loans subsequently defaulted. Some categories of borrower, however, proved to be much

---

[7]See Section 21-4.

[8]See P.F. Smith, "Measuring Risk on Consumer Installment Credit," *Management Science*, 11:327–340 (November 1964).

worse credit risks than others. We have added the actual default rates for each category in the right-hand margin of Table 28-1. For example, you can see that 7.0% of the borrowers who had no telephone subsequently defaulted. Similarly, borrowers who lived in rented rooms, had no bank account, needed the loan to pay medical bills, and so on, were much worse credit risks than the average.

Table 28-1 A condensed version of a questionnaire used by a bank for personal loan applicants. We have added in parentheses the percentage of borrowers in each category who subsequently defaulted.

1.	Do you have:	
	1 or more telephones?	(0.7)
	No telephone?	(7.0)
2.	Do you:	
	Own your home?	(0.7)
	Rent a house?	(2.2)
	Rent an apartment	(3.3)
	Rent a room?	(7.3)
3.	Do you:	
	Have one or more bank accounts?	(0.8)
	No bank account?	(2.6)
4.	Is the purpose of the loan:	
	To buy an automobile?	(0.8)
	To buy household goods?	(0.6)
	To pay medical expenses?	(2.5)
	Other?	(1.3)
5.	How long did you spend in your last residence?	
	6 months or less?	(3.1)
	7 to 60 months?	(1.4)
	More than 60 months?	(0.8)
6.	How long did you spend in your last job?	
	6 months?	(3.2)
	7 to 60 months?	(1.5)
	More than 60 months?	(0.9)
7.	What is your marital status:	
	Single?	(1.6)
	Married?	(1.0)
	Divorced?	(2.9)
8.	What is your postal zone?	(0.1 to 11.4)
9.	For how long do you require the loan:	
	12 months or less?	(1.6)
	More than 12 months?	(1.0)
10.	What is your occupation?	(0.4 to 3.5)
11.	What is your monthly income:	
	$200 or less?	(2.3)
	$200 to $1,000?	(1.1)
	More than $1,000?	(0.7)
12.	What is your age:	
	25 or under?	(1.5)
	26 to 30?	(1.8)
	More than 30?	(1.0)
13.	How many are there in your family:	
	One?	(1.6)
	Two to seven?	(1.1)
	Eight or more?	(2.6)

Source: Reprinted by permission from P.F. Smith, "Measuring Risk on Consumer Installment Credit," *Management Science*, 11:327–340 (November 1964), Copyright 1964 The Institute of Management Science.

Given this experience, it might make sense for the bank to calculate an overall risk index for each applicant.[9] For example, it could construct a rough-and-ready index simply by adding up all the probabilities in Table 28-1. The wretch who gave the most unfavourable response to each question would have a risk index of

$$7.0 + 7.3 + 2.6 + \cdots + 2.6 = 51.8$$

As if he (or she) didn't have enough troubles!

Constructing Better Risk Indexes

Many lenders that use credit scoring systems employ ad hoc formulas. You should be able to do better than this.

Just adding up the separate probabilities, as in our bank example, isn't the answer, for it ignores the interactions between the different factors. It may be much more alarming when single applicants have a family of eight than when married ones do. On the other hand, you may not be so concerned when single applicants live in a rented room (unless, of course, they also have a family of eight).

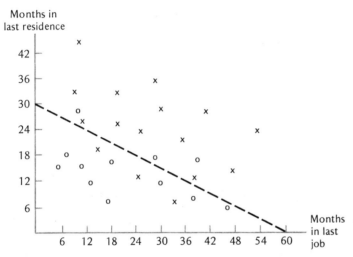

Figure 28-2 The x's represent a hypothetical group of bank borrowers that subsequently repaid their loans; the o's represent those that defaulted. The sloping line discriminates between the two groups on the basis of time spent in last home and time spent in last job. The line represents the equation $Z = 2$ (months in last residence) $+ 1$ (months in last job) $= 60$. Borrowers who plot above the line have "Z-scores" greater than 60.

Suppose that you take just two factors—time spent in last residence and time spent in last job. You then plot a scatter diagram like Figure 28-2. The x's represent customers that subsequently paid their debts: the o's represent customers that defaulted. Now try to draw a straight dividing line between the two groups. You can't wholly separate them but the line in our diagram keeps the two groups as far apart as possible. (Note that there are only three x's below the line and three o's above it.) This line tells us that, if we wish to *discriminate* between the good and bad risks, we should give only

---

[9]There are some measures you *cannot* use in calculating this risk index or in any other credit evaluation: the applicant's sex or race, for example.

half as much weight to job stability as we give to home stability. The index of credit-worthiness is

$$\text{Index of creditworthiness} = Z = 2 \text{ (months in last residence)}$$
$$+ 1 \text{ (months in last job)}$$

You minimize the degree of misclassification if you predict that applicants with Z scores over 60 will pay their bills and that those with Z scores below 60 will not pay.[10]

In practice we do not need to confine our attention to just two variables nor do we need to estimate the equation by eye. Multiple discriminant analysis (MDA) is a straightforward statistical technique for calculating how much weight to put on each variable in order to separate the sheep from the goats.[11]

Edward Altman has used MDA to predict bad business risks. Altman's object was to see how well financial ratios could be used to distinguish which firms would go bankrupt during the period 1946–1965. MDA gave him the following index of creditworthiness:[12]

$$Z = 3.3 \frac{\text{EBIT}}{\text{total assets}} + 1.0 \frac{\text{sales}}{\text{total assets}} + 0.6 \frac{\text{market value equity}}{\text{book value of debt}}$$
$$+ 1.4 \frac{\text{retained earnings}}{\text{total assets}} + 1.2 \frac{\text{working capital}}{\text{total assets}}$$

This equation did a good job at distinguishing the bankrupt and nonbankrupt firms. Of the former, 94% had Z scores of *less* than 2.7 the year before they went bankrupt. In contrast 97% of the nonbankrupt firms had Z scores *above* this level.[13]

28-4 THE CREDIT DECISION

Let us suppose that you have taken the first three steps toward an effective credit operation. In other words, you have fixed your terms of sale; you have decided whether to sell on open account or to ask your customers to sign an IOU; and you have established a procedure for estimating the probability that each customer will pay up. Your next step is to work out which of those customers should be offered credit.

If there is no possibility of repeat orders, the decision is relatively simple. Figure 28-3 summarizes your choice. On the one hand, you can refuse credit. In this case you make neither a profit nor a loss. The alternative is to offer credit. Suppose that the probability that the customer will pay up is p. If the customer does pay, you receive additional revenues (REV) and you incur additional costs; your net gain is the present value of REV − COST. Unfortunately, you can't be certain that the customer will pay; there is a probability $(1 - p)$ of default. Default means you receive nothing and

---

[10]The quantity 60 is an arbitrary constant. We could just as well have used 6. In that case the Z score is

$Z = 0.2 \text{ (months in last residence)} + 0.1 \text{ (months in last job)}$

[11]MDA is not the only statistical technique that you can use for this purpose. Probit and logit are two other potentially very useful techniques.

[12]EBIT is earnings before interest and taxes. E.I. Altman, "Financial Ratios, Discriminant Analysis and the Prediction of Corporate Bankruptcy," *Journal of Finance*, 23:589–609 (September 1968).

[13]This equation was fitted with hindsight. The equation did slightly less well when used to predict bankruptcies after 1965.

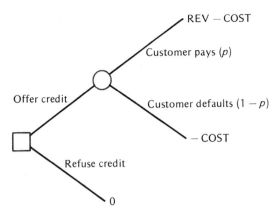

Figure 28-3 If you refuse credit, you make neither profit nor loss. If you offer credit, there is a probability p that the customer will pay and you will make REV − COST; there is a probability $(1 - p)$ that the customer will default and you will lost COST.

incur the additional costs. The *expected* profit from the two courses of action is therefore as follows:

	Expected Profit
Refuse credit	0
Grant credit	p PV(REV − COST) − $(1 - p)$ PV(COST)

You should grant credit if the expected profit from doing so is greater than the expected profit from refusing.

Consider for example the case of the Cast Iron Company. On each nondelinquent sale Cast Iron receives revenues with a present value of $1,200 and incurs costs with a value of $1,000. Therefore the company's expected profit if it offers credit is

$$p \text{ PV(REV − COST)} - (1 - p) \text{ PV(COST)} = p \times 200 - (1 - p) \times 1,000$$

If the probability of collection is $\frac{5}{6}$, Cast Iron can expect to break even:

$$\text{Expected profit} = \frac{5}{6} \times 200 - \left(1 - \frac{5}{6}\right) \times 1,000 = 0$$

Therefore Cast Iron's policy should be to grant credit whenever the chances of collection are better than five out of six.

*When to Stop Looking for Clues

We told you earlier where to *start* looking for clues about a customer's creditworthiness, but we never said anything about when to *stop*. Now we can work out how your profits would be affected by more detailed credit analysis.

Suppose that Cast Iron Company's credit department undertakes a study to determine which customers are most likely to default. It appears that 95% of its customers have been prompt payers and 5% have been slow payers. On the other hand, customers with a record of slow payment are much more likely to default on the next order than those with a record of prompt payment. On the average 20% of the slow payers subsequently default but only 2% of the prompt payers do so.

In other words, consider a sample of 1,000 customers, none of which has defaulted yet. Of these 950 have a record of prompt payment and 50 have a record of slow payment. On the basis of past experience Cast Iron should expect 19 of the prompt payers to default in the future and 10 of the slow payers to do so:

Category	Number of Customers	Probability of Default	Expected Number of Defaults
Prompt payers	950	0.02	19
Slow payers	50	0.20	10
All customers	1,000	0.029	29

Now the credit manager faces the following decision: Should the company refuse to give any more credit to customers that have been slow payers in the past?

If you are aware that a customer has been a slow payer, the answer is clearly "yes". Every sale to slow payers has only an 80% chance of payment ($p = 0.8$). Selling to a *slow* payer, therefore, gives an expected *loss* of $40:

$$\text{Expected profit} = p\text{PV(REV} - \text{COST)} - (1 - p)\text{PV(COST)}$$
$$= 0.8(200) - 0.2(1,000) = -\$40$$

But suppose that it costs $10 to search through Cast Iron's records to determine whether a customer has been a prompt or slow payer. Is it worth doing so? The expected payoff to such a check is

$$\text{Expected payoff to credit check} = \text{probability of identifying a slow payer}$$
$$\times \text{ gain from not extending credit}$$
$$- \text{ cost of credit check}$$
$$= (0.05 \times 40) - 10 = -\$8$$

In this case checking isn't worth it. You are paying $10 to avoid a $40 loss 5% of the time. But suppose that a customer orders ten units at once. Then checking is worthwhile because you are paying $10 to avoid a *$400* loss 5% of the time:

$$\text{Expected payoff to credit check} = (0.05 \times 400) - 10 = \$10$$

The credit manager therefore decides to check customers' past payment records only on orders of more than five units. You can verify that a credit check on a five-unit order just pays for itself.

Our illustration is simplistic, but you have probably grasped the message. You don't want to subject each order to the same credit analysis. You want to concentrate your efforts on the large and doubtful orders.

Credit Decisions with Repeat Orders

So far we have ignored the possibility of repeat orders. But one of the reasons for offering credit today is that you may get yourself a good, regular customer.

Figure 28-4 illustrates the problem.[14] Cast Iron has been asked to extend credit to a new customer. You can find little information on the firm and you believe that the probability of payment is no better than 0.8. If you grant credit, the expected profit on this order is

Expected profit on initial order $= p_1 \times \text{PV(REV)} - \text{COST})$

$$- (1 - p_1) \times \text{PV(COST)}$$

$$= (0.8 \times 200) - (0.2 \times 1{,}000) = -\$40$$

You decide to refuse credit.

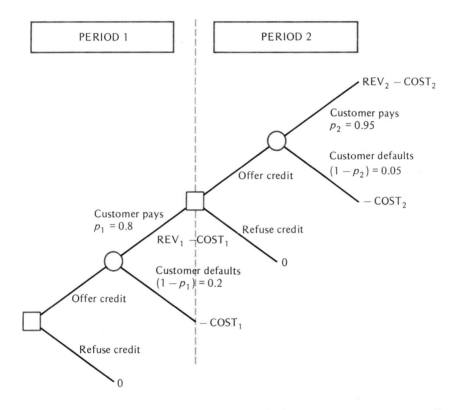

Figure 28-4   In this example there is only a 0.8 probability that your customer will pay in period 1; but if payment is made, there will be another order in period 2. The probability that the customer will pay for the second order is 0.95. The possibility of this good repeat order more than compensates for the expected loss in period 1.

This is the correct decision if there is no chance of a repeat order. But look again at the example shown in the decision tree, Figure 28-4. If the customer does pay up, there will be a reorder next year. Because the customer has paid once, you can be 95% sure that he or she will pay again. For this reason any repeat order is very profitable:

[14]Our example is adapted from H. Bierman, Jr. and W.H. Hausman, "The Credit Granting Decision," *Management Science*, **16**:B519–B532 (April 1970).

Next year's expected profit on repeat order $= p_2 \text{PV}(\text{REV}_2 - \text{COST}_2)$

$$- (1 - p_2)\text{PV}(\text{COST}_2)$$
$$= (0.95 \times 200) - (0.05 \times 1{,}000)$$
$$= \$140$$

Now you can re-examine today's credit decision. If you grant credit today, you receive the expected profit on the initial order *plus* the possible opportunity to extend credit next year:

Total expected profit $=$ expected profit on initial order

+ probability of payment and repeat order

$\times$ PV(next year's expected profit on repeat order)

$= -40 + 0.80 \times \text{PV}(140)$

At any reasonable discount rate you ought to extend credit. For example, if the discount rate is 20%,

$$\text{Total expected profit (present value)} = -40 + \frac{0.8(140)}{1.2} = \$53.33$$

In this example you should grant credit even though you expect to make a loss on the order. The expected loss is more than outweighed by the possibility that you will secure a reliable and regular customer.

Some General Principles

Sometimes the credit manager faces clear-cut choices. In these circumstances it may be possible to estimate fairly precisely the consequences of a more liberal or a more stringent credit policy. But real-life situations are generally far more complex than our simple examples. Customers are not all good or bad. Many of them pay consistently late: you get your money, but it costs more to collect and you lose a few months' interest. Then there is the question of risk. You may be able to measure the revenues and costs, but at what rate do you discount them?

Like almost all financial decisions, credit allocation involves a strong dose of judgement. Our examples are intended as reminders of the issues involved rather than as cookbook formulas. Here are the basic things to remember.

1. Maximize Profit   As credit manager your job is not to minimize the number of bad accounts; it is to maximize expected profit. You must, therefore, recognize that you are concerned with a trade-off. The best that can happen is that the customer pays promptly; the worst is default. In the one case the firm receives the full additional revenues from the sale less the additional costs; in the other it receives nothing and loses the costs. You must weigh the chances of these alternative outcomes. If the margin of profit is high, you are justified in a liberal credit policy; if it is low, you cannot afford many bad debts.

2. Concentrate on the Dangerous Accounts   You should not expend the same effort on analyzing all credit applications. If an application is small or clear-cut, your decision should be largely routine; if it is large or doubtful, you may do better to move straight to a detailed credit appraisal. Most credit managers don't make credit decisions on an order-by-order basis. Instead they set a credit limit for each customer. The sales representative is required to refer the order for approval only if the customer exceeds this limit.

3. Look beyond the Immediate Order The credit decision is a dynamic problem. You cannot look only at the immediate future. Sometimes it may be worth accepting a relatively poor risk as long as there is a likelihood that the customer will grow into a regular and reliable buyer. New businesses must, therefore, be prepared to incur more bad debts than established businesses. This is part of the cost of building up a good customer list.

28-5 COLLECTION POLICY

It would be nice if all customers paid their bills by the due date. But they don't, and, since you may also occasionally "stretch" your payables, you can't altogether blame them.

The credit manager keeps a record of payment experiences with each customer. The manager knows that company A always takes the discount and that company Z is generally slow 90 days. In addition the manager monitors overdue payments by drawing up a schedule of the aging of receivables. This may look roughly like Table 28-2.

When a customer is in arrears, the usual procedure is to send a statement of account and to follow this at intervals with increasingly insistent letters, telephone calls, or cables. If none of these has any effect, most companies turn the debt over to a collection agency or an attorney. The fee for such services is usually between 15% and 40% of the amount collected. An insolvent customer may become bankrupt. In Appendix 28-1 we describe what happens when an individual or firm files for bankruptcy.

There is always a potential conflict of interest between the collection department and the sales department. Sales representatives commonly complain that they no sooner win new customers than the collection department frightens them off with threatening letters. The collection manager, on the other hand, bemoans the fact that the sales force is concerned only with winning orders and does not care whether the goods are subsequently paid for.

Table 28-2   An aging schedule of receivables (figures in dollars).

Customer's Name	Amount Not Yet due	1 Month Overdue	2 Months Overdue	More Than 2 Months Overdue	Total Owed
A	10,000	—	—	—	10,000
.	.	.	.	.	.
.	.	.	.	.	.
.	.	.	.	.	.
Z	5,000	4,000	6,000	15,000	30,000
Total	200,000	40,000	15,000	43,000	265,000

Factoring and Credit Insurance

The large firm has some advantages in managing its accounts receivable. First, it may be possible for divisions to pool information on the creditworthiness of their customers. Second, there are potential economies of scale in record keeping, billing, and so on, especially if the process can be computerized. Third, debt collection is a specialized business that calls for experience and judgement. The small firm may not be able to hire or train a specialized credit manager. However, it may be able to obtain some of these economies by farming part of the job out to a **factor**.

Factoring works as follows. The factor and the client agree on credit limits for each customer and on the average collection period. The client then notifies each customer that the factor has purchased the debt. Thereafter, for any sale the client sends a copy of the invoice to the factor, the customer makes payment directly to the factor, and the factor pays the client on the basis of the agreed average collection period regardless of whether the customer has paid. There are, of course, costs to such an operation, and the factor typically charges a fee of 1% to 2% of the value of the invoice.[15]

This factoring arrangement provides assistance with collection and insurance against bad debts. It is known as *maturity factoring*. In addition to these services, the factor is generally also willing to advance 70% to 80% of the value of the accounts at an interest cost of 2% or 3% above the prime rate. Factoring that provides collection, insurance, and finance is generally termed *old-line factoring*.[16]

If you don't want help with collection but do want protection against bad debts, you can obtain credit insurance. The credit insurance company obviously wants to be certain that you do not throw caution to the winds by extending boundless credit to the most speculative accounts. It therefore generally imposes a maximum amount that it will cover for accounts with a particular credit rating. Thus it may agree to insure up to a total of $100,000 of sales to customers with the highest Dun and Bradstreet rating, up to $50,000 to those with the next highest rating, and so on. You may claim not only if the customer actually becomes insolvent but also if an account is overdue. Such a delinquent account is then turned over to the insurance company, which makes vigorous efforts to collect.

The Export Development Corporation (EDC), a federal Crown corporation, has several credit-related programs for Canadian exporters. It provides insurance for up to 90% of a short-term credit transaction (totalling $1.8 billion in 1984). Banks are more willing to lend against such insured receivables. The EDC itself also provides financing, particularly for large transactions, for which bank financing may be hard to obtain. This amounted to a total of $1.56 billion in 1984.

28-6 SUMMARY

Credit management involves five steps. The first task is to establish normal terms of sale. This means that you must decide the length of the payment period and the size of any cash discounts. In most industries these conditions are standardized.

Your second step is to decide the form of the contract with your customer. Most domestic sales are made on open account. In this case the only evidence that the customer owes you money is the entry in your ledger and a receipt signed by the customer. Particularly if the customer is foreign, you may require a more formal contract. We looked at three such devices—the promissory note, the trade acceptance, and the letter of credit.

The third task is to assess each customer's creditworthiness. There is a variety of sources of information—your own experience with the customer, the experience of other creditors, the assessment of a credit agency, a check with the customer's bank,

---

[15]Many factors are subsidiaries of banks. Their typical client is a relatively small manufacturing company selling on a repetitive basis to a large number of industrial or retail customers. Factoring is particularly common in the clothing industry.

[16]Under an arrangement known as *with-recourse factoring*, the company is liable for any delinquent accounts. In this case the factor provides collection, but not insurance.

---

the market value of the customer's securities, and an analysis of the customer's financial statements. Firms that handle a large volume of credit information often use a formal system for combining the various sources into an overall credit score. These numerical scoring systems help to separate the borderline cases from the obvious sheep or goats. We showed how you can use statistical techniques such as multiple discriminant analysis to give an efficient measure of default risk.

When you have made an assessment of the customer's credit standing, you can establish sensible credit limits. The job of the credit manager is not to minimize the number of bad debts; it is to maximize profits. This means that you should increase the customer's credit limit as long as the probability of payment times the expected profit is greater than the probability of default times the cost of the goods. Remember not to be too shortsighted in reckoning the expected profit. It is often worth accepting the marginal applicant if there is a chance the applicant may grow into a regular and reliable customer.

Finally, you must *collect*. This requires tact and judgement. You want to be firm with the truly delinquent customer, but you don't want to offend the good one by writing demanding letters just because a cheque has been delayed in the mail. You will find it easier to spot troublesome accounts if you keep a careful record of the aging of receivables.

These five steps are interrelated. For example, you can afford more liberal terms of sale if you are very careful about to whom you grant credit. You can accept higher-risk customers if you are very active in pursuing any late payers. A good credit policy is one that adds up to a sensible whole.

FURTHER READING

Two of the standard texts on the practice and institutional background of credit management are:

T.N. Beckman and R.S. Foster, *Credits and Collections: Management and Theory*, 8th ed., McGraw-Hill Book Company, New York, 1969.

R.H. Cole, *Consumer and Commercial Credit Management*, 4th ed., Richard D. Irwin, Inc., Homewood, Ill., 1972.

Much more analytical discussions of the credit granting decision are contained in:

H. Bierman, Jr., and W.H. Hausman, "The Credit Granting Decision," *Management Science*, **16**:B519–B532 (April 1970).

D.R. Mehta, *Working Capital Management*, Prentice-Hall, Inc., Englewood Cliffs, N.J., 1974.

Smith's and Altman's papers are both concerned with the problem of numerical credit scoring. Smith's interest, however, is with predicting default on personal loans, whereas Altman is interested in corporate failure.

P.F. Smith, "Measuring Risk on Consumer Installment Credit," *Management Science*, **11**:327–340 (November 1964).

E.I. Altman, "Financial Ratios, Discriminant Analysis and the Prediction of Corporate Bankruptcy," *Journal of Finance*, **23**:589–609 (September 1968).

Altman's book provides a general survey of the bankruptcy decision. The other three studies listed below are principally concerned with an analysis of the conflicting interests of different security holders.

E.I. Altman, *Corporate Bankruptcy in America*, Heath, Lexington Books, Lexington, Mass., 1971.

J.I. Bulow and J.B. Shoven, "The Bankruptcy Decision," *Bell Journal of Economics and Management Science*, **9**:437–457 (Autumn 1978).

M. White, "Bankruptcy and Reorganization: Economic and Public Policy Considerations," *Summer Institute Paper No.* 80–14, National Bureau of Economic Research, December 1980.

J.B. Warner, "Bankruptcy, Absolute Priority, and the Pricing of Risky Debt Claims," *Journal of Financial Economics,* **4**:239–276 (May 1977).

APPENDIX 28-1   BANKRUPTCY PROCEDURES

We are sure that nobody who reads this book is likely to go bankrupt. But you may still have occasion to deal with individuals or companies that are bankrupt or insolvent. In this appendix, we outline the procedures involved in bankruptcy. We will first discuss things that are common to personal and business bankruptcy, and then discuss some issues that are important only for personal (consumer) bankruptcy. Business bankruptcies in Canada account for about 25% of all bankruptcies, but they account for over 60% of the dollar value of liabilities in bankruptcies.

Bankruptcy law in Canada is largely a federal matter, and the main body of law regarding bankruptcy is the *Bankruptcy Act* of 1950, although the *Winding-up Act* and the *Companies Creditors' Arrangement Act* also deal with insolvency. Several replacement acts have been drafted since then, but none have been passed into law. It is reasonable to expect a new act regarding bankruptcy and insolvency in the near future.

Security and the Priority of Creditors

Creditors can be **secured** by instruments such as the trust indenture of a bond, a charge on specific assets (as in a mortgage), a conditional sale, or a floating charge on inventories or accounts receivable.

The secured creditors do not need to force the debtor into bankruptcy to "realize their security" (that is, to be paid). They seize the secured assets by means of a **receivership**. In this case, a **receiver** (typically someone who is also a licensed **trustee** in bankruptcy), seizes, forecloses, or repossesses the secured assets for disposition and often operates the debtor's business. Any value realized by the sale over and above the amount of secured debt reverts to the **estate** of the debtor. If the liquidation of the assets providing the security does not extinguish the debt, federal law allows the creditor an unsecured claim on the remaining amount of unpaid debt in any bankruptcy proceeding involving the debtor. However, provincial law may prevent the secured creditor from realizing any value beyond the sale of the underlying asset. A notorious example of this occurred in Alberta during the recession of the early 1980s. Many householders, finding the value of their house to be less than the amount of their mortgage, defaulted on their mortgages. The lenders found they had no recourse to the borrower beyond the foreclosure and sale of the house. Some bold householders even engaged in a "dollar-deal": they sold their houses to third parties for $1, yet were able to continue living in the houses for several months as the lengthy foreclosure proceedings went on. Neither party would make mortgage payments during that period, because they had little, if any, incentive to do so.

The claims of **unsecured** creditors are satisfied under the *Bankruptcy Act* according to the following **priority** scheme:

1. Funeral expenses of a deceased bankrupt.

2. Administrative costs, in the following order (a) expenses and fees of a bankruptcy trustee[17]; (b) legal costs of bankruptcy.

---

[17]The trustee's fee structure is voted upon by the creditors and typically depends on the amount of money distributed to the creditors.

3. A levy paid to the federal government to defray the costs of supervising the bankruptcy.[18]

4. Wages, salaries, and commissions earned within the three months prior to the bankruptcy (up to $500), by employees of the bankrupt.

5. Municipal taxes.

6. Up to three months arrears of rent for any property in which the bankrupt is a tenant.

7. The legal costs of the creditor who petitions the debtor into bankruptcy.

8. Debts owed to the government under a Workers' Compensation Act, the *Unemployment Insurance Act* and the *Income Tax Act*.

9. Liabilities to employees for injuries sustained that are not covered by Workers' Compensation, but only to the extent that they are insured by a third party.

10. Any other debts owed to federal or provincial governments.

11. All other unsecured creditors.

The creditors listed in the first ten categories above are called **preferred creditors**. Creditors who are in the same category rank equally in their claim on the debtor's estate (assets), and prior to creditors in subsequent categories. That is, the creditors in one category must be fully paid before those in the next category receive anything.

Who is Involved in a Bankruptcy?

Besides the creditors and debtor, bankruptcy law entails appointment of a trustee who acts on behalf of the unsecured creditors to liquidate the debtor's estate and distribute the funds to the creditors. The creditors also appoint one to five **inspectors**, who essentially act as corporate directors overseeing the work of the trustee.

The **official receiver** is an officer of the court in bankruptcy who ensures that the trustee follows the law. If the creditors are concerned that assets of the debtor will be lost to them between the time of the filing of a petition for bankruptcy with the courts and the time of granting a receiving order allowing the trustee to liquidate and distribute the assets, the creditors can apply for the appointment of an **interim receiver**. This person is usually also the trustee and can take possession of the debtor's property and conserve the value of assets (this may include selling perishable property), but otherwise is not supposed to interfere with the debtor's business.[19]

How a Bankruptcy Occurs

A debtor is **insolvent** if it has liabilities exceeding $1,000 and is unable to meet its debt obligations as they come due. An insolvent debtor or business may voluntarily go into bankruptcy by making an **assignment** of its property for the benefit of its creditors. Alternatively, the creditors may **petition** the courts for a **receiving order**, which will involuntarily force the insolvent debtor into bankruptcy. In either event, the debtor loses most of its assets, which the trustee distributes to the creditors in the form of

---

[18]This levy is paid out of the total disbursement made to the unsecured creditors. It is 2% of the first $1,000,000, plus $1/2$% of the next $1,000,000 and $1/10$% of any larger amounts.

[19]The person (typically a bankruptcy trustee) appointed to seize and dispose of the assets providing security for a debt is also called a receiver. We pointed out earlier that the seizure of secured assets does not involve bankruptcy law, so there is no relation between the official receiver in bankruptcy and the receiver who seizes a secured asset. The former is an officer of the court, while the latter is typically a licensed bankruptcy trustee.

dividends. The advantage of an assignment is timeliness: the insolvent may be able to extinguish its debt obligations before the value of the assets in the estate drops substantially, and perhaps may be even able to work its way out of bankruptcy.

Within 3 to 12 months of the date of the assignment or receiving order, the estate has been liquidated and the trustee applies to the court to obtain a **discharge** for the debtor from its debts. The court may refuse the discharge if the bankrupt person has displayed reprehensible conduct, but more likely it will give an absolute, conditional, or suspended discharge.

An Alternative to Bankruptcy: The Proposal

An insolvent debtor may propose an alternative to bankruptcy called a **proposal** or a **proposal for arrangement.** This can provide an extension of time for the repayment of some or all of the debt. This procedure (like many legal procedures) does not recognize the time value of money, so the economic value of the repayment is less than the true economic value of the liability. Alternatively the proposal may provide for a **composition**, in which case the creditors agree to forgive some of the debt.

Creditors will often accept a proposal, if they believe the debtor can generate a higher present value of payments as a "going concern" that stays in business than would be realized by an immediate liquidation of the debtor's assets in a bankruptcy. As soon as the debtor files a proposal, all creditor actions are **stayed**, or suspended, until the proposal (or a modification of it) is accepted. Thus, both the proposal and the filing of the proposal "buy time" for the debtor. The debtor will often offer a proposal to avoid impairment of its credit rating and to keep alive the call option on the firm's future cash flows (where the exercise price is the proposed scheme of repayments).

Clearly, a proposal is more workable if the debtor is not too insolvent. Indeed, the proposal can be struck down by the courts if it does not provide reasonable security for the payment of "50 cents on the dollar" for the debts owing to the unsecured creditors. The total assets of all insolvent debtors that filed proposals in 1981 was 65% of the total liabilities, whereas the total assets of all debtors that went bankrupt in 1981 was only 34% of the total liabilities. Proposals are used in fewer than 5% of insolvencies. The payment scheme set out in the proposal must be consistent with the priority scheme we discussed earlier for the creditors in a bankruptcy.

The creditors must meet and vote on a **special resolution** to decide whether to accept the proposal. Acceptance requires the approval of creditors representing 75% of the value of the claims against the debtor, as well as 50% of the number of creditors. (These percentages are taken as a proportion of the creditors present or represented by proxy at the meeting.) If the creditors reject the proposal, the debtor becomes bankrupt.

Attacking Fraudulent Conveyances and Fraudulent Preferences

If a debtor knows it is likely to become bankrupt in the near future, it may be tempted to voluntarily convey or give property to friends, relatives, or associated corporations, or to pay off debts to certain creditors without regard to the preference rules or priority rules set for payment to unsecured creditors in a bankruptcy. These transfers are called **fraudulent conveyance** and **fraudulent preference**, respectively. These can be **attacked** by the trustee, who asks the courts to **set aside** or **void** such transfers. To be attacked, they must have occurred within 3 months of the bankruptcy, or if the transfer was to a related person or corporation, within 12 months of the bankruptcy. A fraudulent conveyance can be an indictable or criminal offence.

Special Issues for Personal Bankruptcies

The bankrupt person is exempted from losing certain basic items, such as some furniture, clothing, personal effects, and some tools of a trade. Provincial laws may enhance this exemption. Part of the person's salary (typically 50% of the salary in excess of the poverty line) may be **garnisheed** or paid over to the trustee in bankruptcy for the benefit of the creditors, but this ceases once the bankrupt receives a discharge from the bankruptcy. So-called **after-acquired property**—that is, property acquired between the date of bankruptcy (when the receiving order or assignment was made) and the date of discharge (the date the court relieves the bankrupt of further obligations)—goes to the benefit of the creditors. This makes little difference to a bankrupt corporation, since it generally acquires property only in exchange for assets that would have gone to the estate for the benefit of the creditors anyway. However, it does mean that a consumer bankrupt who receives a large bequest on the death of a relative between the date of bankruptcy and the date of discharge will lose that bequest to the creditors.

Bankruptcy does not relieve the bankrupt of certain liabilities, such as matrimonial debts (alimony and maintenance), liabilities arising out of fraud or embezzlement, and debts owing to suppliers of "necessaries of life." The rationale for not relieving a bankrupt person from liabilities associated with obtaining the necessaries of life is to avoid inducing the suppliers to withhold such items from people in financial distress.

The administration costs of a proposal are too high for it to be a viable alternative to bankruptcy for many consumer debtors. As a result, Part X of the *Bankruptcy Act* was added to allow a **consolidation order** to provide for the orderly payment of consumer debt as an alternative to bankruptcy. Like a proposal, it only provides for the deferral of the repayment of debt, rather than a reduction in its amount. If the amount of the debt exceeds $1,000 or if it is an arrears of wages that would normally come under a mechanics' lien act, the consolidation order can only proceed with the consent of the creditor. Moreover, only six provinces allow consolidation orders. In particular, Ontario and Québec do not allow consolidation orders.

The Choice between Liquidation and Reorganization

Here is a simple view of the bankruptcy decision. Whenever a payment is due to creditors, management checks the value of the equity. If the value is positive, the firm pays the creditors (if necessary raising the cash by an issue of shares). If the equity is valueless, the firm defaults on its debt and petitions for bankruptcy. If the assets of the bankrupt firm can be put to better use elsewhere, the firm is liquidated and the proceeds are used to pay off the creditors. Otherwise, the creditors simply become the new owners and the firm continues to operate.[20]

In practice, matters are rarely so simple. For example, we observe that firms often petition for bankruptcy even when the equity has a positive value. And firms are often reorganized even when the assets could be used more efficiently elsewhere. Here are some reasons.

1. Although the reorganized firm is legally a new entity, it is entitled to any tax-loss carry-forwards belonging to the old firm. If the firm is liquidated rather than re-organized, any tax-loss carry-forwards disappear.[21] Thus there is an incentive to continue in operation.

---

[20]If there are several classes of creditor, the junior creditors initially become the owners of the company and are responsible for paying off the senior debt. They now face exactly the same decision as the original owners. If their equity is valueless, they will also default and turn over ownership of the company to the next class of creditors.

[21]However, the dollar amount of debt that is forgiven in a consolidation proposal is applied to reduce the dollar amount of the tax-loss carry-forward.

2. If the firm's assets are sold off, it is easy to determine what is available to pay the creditors. However, when the company is reorganized, it needs to conserve cash as far as possible. Therefore, claimants are generally paid in a mixture of cash and securities. This makes it less easy to judge whether they receive their entitlement. For example, each bondholder may be offered $300 in cash and $700 in a new bond that pays no interest for the first two years and a low rate of interest thereafter. A bond of this kind in a company that is struggling to survive may not be worth much, but the bankruptcy court usually looks at the face value of the new bonds and may therefore regard the bondholders as paid off in full.

   Senior creditors who know they are likely to get a raw deal in a reorganization are likely to press for a liquidation. Shareholders and junior creditors prefer a reorganization. They hope that the court will not interpret the pecking order too strictly and that they will receive some crumbs.

3. Although shareholders and junior creditors are at the bottom of the pecking order, they have a secret weapon—they can play for time. Bankruptcies often take several years before a plan is presented to the court and agreed to by each class of creditor. (The bankruptcy proceedings of the Missouri Pacific Railroad took a total of 22 years.) When they use delaying tactics, the junior claimants are betting on a stroke of luck that will rescue their investment. On the other hand, the senior claimants know that time is working against them, so they may be prepared to accept a smaller payoff as part of the price for getting a plan accepted.

4. While a reorganization plan is being drawn up, the company is likely to need additional working capital. It is therefore allowed to buy goods on credit and borrow money.[22] Postpetition creditors have priority over the old creditors and their debt may even be secured by assets that are already mortgaged to existing debtholders. This also gives the prepetition creditors an incentive to settle quickly, before their claim on assets is diluted by the new debt.

QUIZ

1. Company X sells on a 1/30, net 60, basis. Customer Y buys goods with an invoice of $1,000.
   (a) How much can Y deduct from the bill if he or she pays on day 30?
   (b) What is the effective annual rate of interest if Y pays on the due date rather than day 30?
   (c) Indicate if you would expect X to require shorter or longer payment if each of the following were true:
   (i)   The goods are perishable.
   (ii) The goods are not rapidly resold.
   (iii) The goods are sold to high-risk firms.

2. The lag between purchase date and the date at which payment is due is known as the "terms lag." The lag between the due date and the initial payment date is termed the "due lag," and the lag between the purchase and payment dates is the "pay lag." Thus,

   pay lag = terms lag + due lag

---

[22]Of course, the debtor must inform any new creditors that it is a bankrupt.

State how you would expect the following events to affect each type of lag.
(*a*) The company imposes a service charge on late payers.
(*b*) A recession causes customers to be short of cash.
(*c*) The company changes its terms from net 10 to net 20.

3. Complete the following passage by selecting the appropriate terms from the following list (some terms may be used more than once): *acceptance, open, commercial, trade, Canada, his or her own, note, draft, account, promissory, bank, the customer's, letter of credit, shipping documents, irrevocable, Canadian.*

Most goods are sold on _____ _____. In this case the only evidence of the debt is a record in the seller's books and a signed receipt. When the order is very large, the customer may be asked to sign a _____ _____, which is just a simply IOU. An alternative is for the seller to arrange a _____ _____ ordering payment by the customer. In order to obtain the _____ _____, the customer must acknowledge this order and sign the document. This signed acknowledgement is known as a _____ _____. Sometimes the seller may also ask _____ bank to sign the document. In this case it is known as a _____ _____. The fourth form of contract is used principally in overseas trade. The customer's bank sends the exporter a _____ stating that it has established a credit in his or her favour at a bank in Canada. The exporter then draws a draft on _____ bank and presents it to _____ bank together with the _____ and _____. The bank then arranges for this draft to be accepted and forwards the _____ to the customer's bank.

4. The Branding Iron Company sells its irons for $50 a piece wholesale. Production cost if $40 per iron. There is a 25% chance that wholesaler Q will go bankrupt within the next year. Q orders 1,000 irons and asks for six months' credit. Should you accept the order? Assume a 10% per year discount rate, no chance of a repeat order, and that Q will pay either in full or not at all.

*5. Look back at Section 28-4. Cast Iron's costs have increased from $1,000 to $1,050. Assuming there is no possibility of repeat orders, answer the following:
(*a*) When should Cast Iron grant or refuse credit?
(*b*) If it costs $12 to determine whether a customer has been a prompt or slow payer in the past, when should Cast Iron undertake such a check?

*6. Look back at the discussion in Section 28-4 of credit decisions with repeat orders. If $p_1 = 0.8$, what is the minimum level of p_2 at which Cast Iron is justified in extending credit?

7. True or false?
(*a*) Exporters who require greater certainty of payment arrange for the customers to sign a bill of lading in exchange for a sight draft.
(*b*) Multiple discriminant analysis is often used to construct an index of credit-worthiness. This index is generally called a "Z score."
(*c*) It makes sense to monitor the credit manager's performance by looking at the proportion of bad debts.
(*d*) If a customer refuses to pay despite repeated reminders, the company will usually turn the debt over to a factor or an attorney.
(*e*) The Export Development Corporation insures export credits.

8. (This question refers to Appendix 28-1.) True or false?
(*a*) Individuals may file for bankruptcy or opt for an arrangement. In the latter case, a repayment plan is drawn up and approved by the creditors.
(*b*) When a company becomes bankrupt, it is usually in the interests of the equity-holders to seek a liquidation rather than a reorganization.

(c) The Department of National Revenue has first claim on the company's assets in the event of bankruptcy.

(d) In a reorganization, creditors may be paid off with a mixture of cash and securities.

(e) When a company is liquidated, one of the most valuable assets to be sold is often the tax-loss carry-forward.

QUESTIONS AND PROBLEMS

1. Here are some common terms of sale. Can you explain what they mean?
   (a) 2/30, net 60
   (b) net 10
   (c) 2/5, net 30, EOM
   (d) 2/10 prox, net 60

2. Some of the items in question 1 involve a cash discount. Calculate the rates of interest paid by customers who pay on the due date instead of taking the cash discount.

3. As treasurer of the Universal Bed Corporation, Aristotle Procrustes is worried about his bad-debt ratio, which is currently running at 6%. He believes that imposing a more stringent credit policy might reduce sales by 5% and reduce the bad-debt ratio to 4%. If the cost of goods sold is 80% of the selling price, should Mr. Procrustes adopt the more stringent policy?

4. Jim Khana, the credit manager of Velcro Saddles, is reappraising the company's credit policy. Velcro sells on terms of net 30. Cost of goods sold is 85% of sales and fixed costs are a further 5% of sales. Velcro classifies customers on a scale of 1 to 4. During the past five years, the collection experience was as follows:

Classification	Defaults as % of Sales	Average Collection Period in Days for Nondefaulting Accounts
1	0.0	45
2	2.0	42
3	10.0	50
4	20.0	80

The average interest rate was 15%.

What conclusions (if any) can you draw about Velcro's credit policy? What other factors should be taken into account before changing this policy?

5. Look again at question 4. Suppose (a) that it costs $95 to classify each new credit applicant and (b) that an almost equal proportion of new applicants falls into each of the four categories. In what circumstances should Mr. Khana not bother to undertake a credit check?

6. Until recently, Augean Cleaning Products sold its products on terms of net 60, with an average collection period of 75 days. In an attempt to induce customers to pay more promptly, it has changed its terms to 2/10, EOM, net 60. The initial effect of the changed terms is as follows:

Percent of Sales With Cash Discount	Average Collection Periods (days)	
	Cash Discount	Net
60	30[a]	80

[a] Some customers deduct the cash discount even though they pay after the specified date.

Calculate the effect of the changed terms assuming that the change does not affect sales volume. Assume:

(a) The interest rate is 12%.

(b) There are no defaults.

(c) Cost of goods sold is 80% of sales.

7. Look back at question 6. Assume that the change in credit terms results in a 2% increase in sales. Recalculate the effect of the changed credit terms.

8. Financial ratios were described in Chapter 25. If you were the credit manager, to which financial ratios would you pay most attention? Which do you think would be the least informative?

9. Discuss in which ways real-life decisions are more complex than the decision illustrated in Figure 28-4. How do you think these differences ought to affect the credit decision?

10. Discuss the problems with developing a numerical credit scoring system for evaluating personal loans.

11. If a company experiences a sudden decrease in sales, the aging schedule in Figure 28-2 will suggest that an abnormally high proportion of payments is overdue. Show why this happens. Can you suggest an alternative form of presentation that would make it easier to recognize a change in customer payment patterns?

12. Why do firms grant "free" credit? Would it be more efficient if all sales were for cash and late payers were charged interest?

13. Sometimes a firm sells its receivables at a discount to a wholly owned "captive finance company." This captive finance company is financed partly by the parent, but it also issues substantial amounts of debt. What are the possible advantages to such an arrangement?

14. Explain why equity can sometimes have a positive value even when companies petition for bankruptcy.

15. Reliant Umbrellas has been approached by Plumpton Variety Stores of Manitoba. Plumpton has expressed interest in an initial purchase of 5,000 umbrellas at $10 each on Reliant's standard terms of 2/30, net 60. Plumpton estimates that if the umbrellas prove popular with customers, its purchases could be in the region of

Table 28-3   Plumpton Variety Stores: Summary Financial Statements (figures in millions).

	1983	1982		1983	1982
Cash	$ 1.0	$ 1.2	Payables	$ 2.3	$ 2.5
Receivables	1.5	1.6	Short-term loans	3.9	1.9
Inventory	10.9	11.6	Long-term debt	1.8	2.6
Fixed assets	5.1	4.3	Equity	10.5	11.7
Total assets	$18.5	$18.7	Total liabilities	$18.5	$18.7

	1983	1982
Sales	$55.0	$59.0
Cost of goods, sold	32.6	35.9
Selling, general and administrative expenses	20.8	20.2
Interest	0.5	0.3
Tax	0.5	1.3
Net income	0.6	1.3

30,000 umbrellas a year. After deducting variable costs, this would provide an addition of $47,000 to Reliant's profits.

Reliant has been anxious for some time to break into the lucrative Manitoba market, but its credit manager has some doubts about Plumpton. In the past five years, Plumpton had embarked on an aggressive program of store openings. In 1983, however, it went into reverse. The recession combined with aggressive price competition caused a cash shortage. Plumpton laid off employees, closed one store, and deferred store openings. The company's Dun and Bradstreet rating is only fair and a check with Plumpton's other suppliers reveals that, although Plumpton has traditionally taken cash discounts, it has recently been paying 30 days slow. A check through Reliant's bank indicates that Plumpton has unused credit lines of $350,000 but has entered into discussions with the banks for a renewal of a $1,500,000 term loan due at the end of the year.

Table 28-3 summarizes Plumpton's latest financial statements.

As credit manager of Reliant, what is your attitude to extending credit to Plumpton?

CASH MANAGEMENT

At the end of 1984, citizens and corporations in Canada held approximately $30 billion in cash. This included $13 billion of currency and $17 billion of demand deposits with banks. Cash pays no interest. Why, then, do sensible people hold it? Why, for example, don't you take all your cash and invest it in interest-bearing securities? The answer of course is that cash gives you more *liquidity* than securities. You can use it to buy things. It is hard enough getting cab drivers to give you change for a $10 bill, but try asking them to split a Treasury bill!

In equilibrium all assets in the same risk class are priced to give the same expected marginal benefit. The benefit from holding Treasury bills is the interest that you receive; the benefit from holding cash is that it gives you a convenient store of liquidity. In equilibrium the marginal value of this liquidity is equal to the marginal value of the interest on an equivalent investment in Treasury bills. This is just another way of saying that Treasury bills are investments with zero net present value—they are fair value relative to cash.

Does this mean that it does not matter how much cash you hold? Of course not. The marginal value of liquidity declines as you hold increasing amounts of cash. When you have only a small proportion of your assets in cash, a little extra can be extremely useful; when you have a substantial holding, any additional liquidity is not worth much. Therefore, as financial manager you want to hold cash balances up to the point where the marginal value of the liquidity is equal to the value of the interest forgone.

If that seems more easily said than done, you may be comforted to know that production managers must make a similar trade-off. Ask yourself why they carry inventories of raw materials. They are not obliged to do so; they could simply buy materials day by day, as needed. But then they would pay higher prices for ordering in small lots, and they would risk production delays if the materials were not delivered on time. That is why they order more than the firm's immediate needs.

But there is a cost to holding inventories. Interest is lost on the money that is tied up in inventories, storage must be paid for, and often there is spoilage and deterioration. Therefore production managers try to strike a sensible balance between the costs of holding too little inventory and those of holding too much.

That is all we are saying you need to do with cash. Cash is just another raw material that you require to carry on production. If you keep too small a proportion of your funds in the bank, you will need to make repeated small sales of securities every time you want to pay your bills. On the other hand, if you keep excessive cash in the bank, you are losing interest. The trick is to hit a sensible balance.

The trade-off between the benefits and costs of liquidity is one essential part of cash management. The other part is making sure that the collection and disbursement of cash is as efficient as possible. To understand this we will have to look closely at the relationships between firms and their banks. Most of the latter part of this chapter is devoted to the mechanics of cash collection and disbursement and the services offered by banks to assist firms in cash management.

29-1 INVENTORIES AND CASH BALANCES

Let us take a look at what economists have had to say about managing inventories and then see whether some of these ideas may help us to manage cash balances. Here is a simple inventory problem.

Everyman's Bookstore experiences a steady demand for *Principles of Corporate Finance* from customers who find that it makes a serviceable bookend. Suppose that the bookstore sells 100 copies of the book a year and that it orders Q books at a time from the publishers. Then it will need to place $100/Q$ orders per year:

$$\text{Number of orders per year} = \frac{\text{sales}}{Q} = \frac{100}{Q}$$

Just before each delivery, the bookstore has effectively no inventory of *Principles of Corporate Finance*. Just *after* each delivery it has an inventory of Q books. Therefore its *average* inventory is midway between 0 books and Q books:

$$\text{Average inventory} = \frac{Q}{2} \text{ books}$$

For example, if the store increases its regular order by one book, the average inventory increases by $\frac{1}{2}$ book.

There are two costs to holding this inventory. First, there is the carrying cost. This includes the cost of the capital that is tied up in inventory, the cost of shelf space, and so on. Let us suppose that these costs work out to a dollar per book per year. The effect of adding one more book to each order is therefore to increase the average inventory by $\frac{1}{2}$ book and the carrying cost by $\frac{1}{2} \times \$1.00 = \$0.50$. Thus the marginal carrying cost is a constant $\$0.50$:

$$\text{Marginal carrying cost} = \frac{\text{carrying cost per book}}{2} = \$0.50$$

The second type of cost is the order cost. Imagine that each order placed with the publisher involves a fixed clerical and handling expense of $2. Table 29-1 illustrates what happens to order costs as you increase the size of each order. You can see that the bookstore gets a large reduction in costs when it orders two books at a time rather than one, but thereafter the savings from increases in order size steadily diminish. In fact, the *marginal* reduction in order cost depends on the *square* of the order size:[1]

$$\text{Marginal reduction in order cost} = \frac{\text{sales} \times \text{cost per order}}{Q^2} = \frac{\$200}{Q^2}$$

---

[1] Let T = total order cost, S = sales per year, and C = cost per order. Then

$$T = \frac{SC}{Q}$$

Differentiate with respect to Q:

$$\frac{dT}{dQ} = -\frac{SC}{Q^2}$$

Thus, an *increase* of dQ reduces T by SC/Q^2.

Table 29-1 How order cost varies with order size.

Order Size, Number of Books	Number of Orders Per Year	Total Order Costs, Dollars
1	100	200
2	50	100
3	33	66
4	25	50
10	10	20
100	1	2

Here, then, is the kernel of the inventory problem. As the bookstore increases its order size, the number of orders falls but the average inventory rises. Costs that are related to the number of orders decline; those that are related to inventory size increase. It is worth increasing order size as long as the decline in order cost outweighs the increase in carrying cost. The optimal size is the point at which these two effects exactly offset each other. In our example this occurs when $Q = 20$:

$$\text{Marginal reduction in order cost} = \frac{\text{sales} \times \text{cost per order}}{Q^2} = \frac{\$200}{20^2} = \$0.50$$

$$\text{Marginal carrying cost} = \frac{\text{carrying cost per book}}{2} = \$0.50$$

The optimal order size is 20 books. Five times a year the bookstore should place an order for 20 books, and it should work off this inventory over the following ten weeks. Its inventory of *Principles of Corporate Finance* will therefore follow the sawtoothed pattern in Figure 29-1.

The general formula for optimum order size is found by setting marginal reduction in order cost equal to the marginal carrying cost and solving for Q:

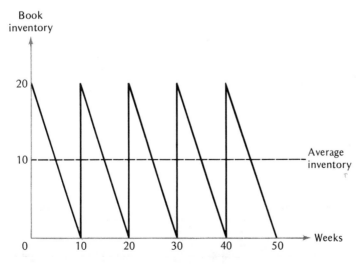

Figure 29-1 Everyman's bookstore minimizes inventory costs by placing 5 orders per year for 20 books per order. That is, it places orders at about ten week intervals.

Marginal reduction in order cost = marginal carrying cost

$$\frac{\text{Sales} \times \text{cost per order}}{Q^2} = \frac{\text{carrying cost}}{2}$$

$$Q^2 = \frac{2 \times \text{sales} \times \text{cost per order}}{\text{carrying cost}}$$

$$Q = \sqrt{\frac{2 \times \text{sales} \times \text{cost per order}}{\text{carrying cost}}}$$

In our example,

$$Q = \sqrt{\frac{2 \times 100 \times 2}{1}} = \sqrt{400} = 20$$

The Extension to Cash Balances

William Baumol was the first to notice that this simple inventory model can tell us something about the management of cash balances.[2] Suppose that you keep a reservoir of cash that is steadily drawn down to pay bills. When it runs out you replenish the cash balance by selling Treasury bills. The main carrying cost of holding this cash is the interest that you are losing. The order cost is the fixed administrative expense of each sale of Treasury bills. In these circumstances your inventory of cash also follows a sawtoothed pattern like Figure 29-1.

In other words, your cash management problem is exactly analogous to the problem of optimum order size faced by Everyman's Bookstore. You just have to redefine variables. Instead of books per order, Q becomes the amount of Treasury bills sold each time the cash balance is replenished. Cost per order becomes cost per sale of Treasury bills. Carrying cost is just the interest rate. Total cash disbursements take the place of books sold. The optimum Q is

$$Q = \sqrt{\frac{2 \times \text{annual cash disbursements} \times \text{cost per sale of Treasury bills}}{\text{interest rate}}}$$

Suppose that the interest rate on Treasury bills is 8%, but every sale of bills costs you $20. Your firm pays out cash at a rate of $105,000 per month or $1,260,000 per year. Therefore the optimum Q is

$$Q = \sqrt{\frac{2 \times 1,260,000 \times 20}{0.08}}$$

$$= \$25,100 \text{ or about } \$25,000$$

Thus your firm would sell approximately $25,000 of Treasury bills four times a month—about once a week. Its average cash balance will be $25,000/2 or $12,500.

---

[2]W.J. Baumol, "The Transactions Demand for Cash: An Inventory Theoretic Approach," *Quarterly Journal of Economics,* **66**:545–556 (November 1952).

In Baumol's model a higher interest rate implies a lower Q.[3] In general, when interest rates are high, you want to hold small average cash balances. On the other hand, if you use up cash at a high rate or if there are high costs to selling securities, you want to hold large average cash balances. Think about that for a moment. *You can hold too little cash.* Many financial managers point with pride to the tight control that they exercise over cash and to the extra interest that they have earned. These benefits are highly visible. The costs are less visible but they can be very large. When you allow for the time that the manager spends in monitoring her cash balance, it may make sense to forgo some of that extra interest.

The Miller-Orr Model

Baumol's model works well as long as the firm is steadily using up its cash inventory. But that is not what usually happens. In some weeks the firm may collect some large unpaid bills and therefore receive a net *inflow* of cash. In other weeks it may pay its suppliers and so incur a net *outflow* of cash.

Economists and management scientists have developed a variety of more elaborate and realistic models that allow for the possibility of both cash inflows and outflows. Let us look briefly at a model developed by Miller and Orr.[4] It represents a nice compromise between simplicity and realism.

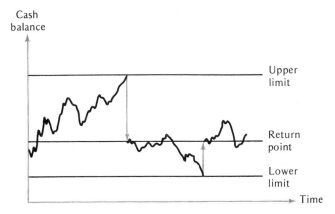

Figure 29-2   In Miller and Orr's model the cash balance is allowed to meander until it hits an upper or lower limit. At this point the firm buys or sells securities to restore the balance to the return point, which is the lower limit plus one-third of the spread between the upper and lower limits.

Miller and Orr consider how the firm should manage its cash balance if it cannot predict day-to-day cash inflows and outflows. Their answer is shown in Figure 29-2. You can see that the cash balance meanders unpredictably until it reaches an upper limit. At this point the firm buys enough securities to return the cash balance to a more normal level. Once again the cash balance is allowed to meander until this time it hits a lower limit. When it does, the firm *sells* enough securities to restore the balance to its normal level. Thus the rule is to allow the cash holding to wander freely until

---

[3]Note that the interest rate is in the denominator of the expression for optimal Q. Thus, increasing the interest rate reduces the optimal Q.

[4]M.H. Miller and D. Orr, "A Model of the Demand for Money by Firms," *Quarterly Journal of Economics,* **80**:413–435 (August 1966).

it hits an upper or lower limit. When this happens, the firm buys or sells securities to regain the desired balance.

How far should the firm allow its cash balance to wander? Miller and Orr show that the answer depends on three factors. If the day-to-day variability in cash flows is large or if the fixed cost of buying and selling securities is high, then the firm should set the control limits far apart. Conversely, if the rate of interest is high, it should set the limits close together. The formula for the distance between barriers is[5]

$$\begin{matrix} \text{Spread between} \\ \text{upper and lower} \\ \text{cash balance limits} \end{matrix} = 3 \left(\frac{3}{4} \times \frac{\text{transaction cost} \times \text{variance of cash flows}}{\text{interest rate}} \right)^{1/3}$$

Have you noticed one odd feature about Figure 29-2? The firm does not return to a point halfway between the lower and upper limits. The firm always returns to a point one-third of the distance from the lower to the upper limit. In other words, the return point is

$$\text{Return point} = \text{lower limit} + \frac{\text{spread}}{3}$$

Always starting at this return point means the firm hits the lower limit more often than the upper limit. This does not minimize the number of transactions—that would require always starting exactly in the middle of the spread. However, always starting in the middle would mean a larger average cash balance and larger interest costs. The Miller-Orr return point minimizes the sum of transaction costs and interest costs.

Using the Miller-Orr Model

The Miller-Orr model is easy to use. The first step is to set the lower limit for the cash balance. This may be zero, some minimum safety margin above zero, or a balance necessary to keep the bank happy—more on bank requirements later in the chapter. The second step is to estimate the variance of cash flows. For example, you might record net cash inflows or outflows for each of the last 100 days and compute the variance of those 100 sample observations. More sophisticated measurement techniques could be applied if there were, say, seasonal fluctuations in the volatility of cash flows. The third step is to observe the interest rate and the transaction cost of each purchase or sale of securities. The final step is to compute the upper limit and the return point and to give this information to a clerk with instructions to follow the "control limit" strategy built into the Miller-Orr model. Table 29-2 gives a numerical example.

This model's practical usefulness is limited by the assumptions it rests on. For example, few managers would agree that cash inflows and outflows are entirely unpredictable, as Miller and Orr assume. The manager of a toy store knows that there will be substantial cash inflows around Christmas time. Financial managers know when dividends will be paid and when income taxes will be due. In Chapter 27 we described how firms forecast cash inflows and outflows and how they arrange short-term investment and financing decisions to supply cash when needed and put cash to work earning interest when it is not needed.

---

[5]This formula assumes the expected daily change in the cash balance is zero. Thus it assumes that there are no systematic upward or downward trends in the cash balance. If the Miller-Orr model is applicable you need only know the variance of the daily cash flows, that is the variance of the daily *changes* in the cash balance.

Table 29-2   Numerical example of the Miller-Orr model.

A. Assumptions:
    1. Minimum cash balance = $10,000
    2. Variance of daily cash flows = 6,250,000 (equivalent to a standard deviation of $2,500 per day.)
    3. Interest rate = 0.025% per day
    4. Transaction cost for each sale or purchase of securities = $20
B. Calculation of spread between upper and lower cash balance limits:

$$\text{Spread} = 3\left(\frac{^3/_4 \times \text{transaction cost} \times \text{variance of cash flows}}{\text{interest rate}}\right)^{1/3}$$

$$= 3\left(\frac{^3/_4 \times 20 \times 6{,}250{,}000}{0.00025}\right)^{1/3}$$

$$= 21{,}634 \text{ or about } \$21{,}600$$

C. Calculate upper limit and return point:

$$\text{Upper limit} = \text{lower limit} + 21{,}600 = \$31{,}600$$

$$\text{Return point} = \text{lower limit} + \frac{\text{spread}}{3} = 10{,}000 + \frac{21{,}600}{3} = \$17{,}200$$

D. Decision rule:
    If cash balance rises to $31,600, invest $31,600 − 17,200 = $14,400 in marketable securities; if cash balance falls to $10,000, sell $7,200 of marketable securities and replenish cash.

This kind of short-term financial plan is usually designed to produce a cash balance that is stable at some lower limit. But there are always fluctuations that financial managers cannot plan for, certainly not on a day-to-day basis. You can think of the Miller-Orr policies as responding to the cash inflows and outflows that cannot be predicted, or that are not *worth* predicting. Trying to predict *all* cash flows would chew up enormous amounts of management time.

The Miller-Orr model has been tested on daily cash-flow data for several firms. It performed as well as or better than the intuitive policies followed by these firms' cash managers. However, the model was not an unqualified success; in particular, simple rules of thumb seem to perform just as well.[6] The Miller-Orr model may improve our *understanding* of the problem of cash management, but it probably will not yield substantial savings compared with policies based on a manager's judgement, providing of course that the manager understands the trade-offs we have discussed.

Raising Cash by Borrowing

So far we have assumed that surplus cash is invested in securities such as Treasury bills and that cash is replenished when necessary by selling these securities. The alternative may be to replenish cash by borrowing—for example, by drawing on a bank line of credit.

Borrowing raises another problem. The interest rate that you pay to the bank is likely to be higher than the rate that you receive on securities. As financial manager, you

---

[6]For a review of tests of the Miller-Orr model, see D. Mullins and R. Homonoff, "Applications of Inventory Cash Management Models," in S.C. Myers, ed., *Modern Developments in Financial Management*, Frederick A. Praeger, Inc., New York, 1976.

therefore face a trade-off. To earn the maximum interest on your funds, you want to hold low cash balances, but this means that you are more likely to have to borrow to cover an unexpected cash outflow. For example, suppose you can either hold cash that pays no interest or you can invest in securities that pay interest at 10%. The cost of keeping cash balances is the interest forgone by not investing the money in securities.

Cost of cash balances $= 10\%$

If you need more cash at short notice, it may be difficult or costly to sell securities, but you can borrow from the bank at 12%. In this case, there is a simple rule for maximizing expected return. You should adjust the cash balances until the probability that you will need to borrow from the bank equals[7]

$$\frac{\text{Cost of cash balances}}{\text{Cost of borrowing}} = \frac{10}{12} = 0.83$$

When we look at the problem this way, the best cash balance depends on the cost of borrowing and the extent of uncertainty about future cash flow. If the cost of borrowing is high relative to the interest rate on securities, you should make sure that there is only a low probability that you will be obliged to borrow. If you are very uncertain about the future cash flow, you may need to keep a large cash balance in order to be confident that you will not have to borrow. If you are fairly sure about cash flow, you can keep a lower cash balance.

Cash Management in the Largest Corporations

For very large firms, the transaction costs of buying and selling securities become trivial compared with the opportunity cost of holding idle cash balances. Suppose that the interest rate is 8% per year or roughly $^8/_{365} = 0.022\%$ per day. Then the daily interest earned by $1 million is $0.00022 \times 1,000,000 = \$220$. Even at a cost of $50 per transaction, which is generous, it pays to buy Treasury bills today and sell them tomorrow rather than to leave $1 million idle overnight.

A corporation with $1 billion of annual sales has an average daily cash flow of $1,000,000,000/365, about $2.7 million. Firms of this size end up buying or selling

---

[7]See, for example, J.H.W. Gosling, "One-Period Optimal Cash Balances," unpublished paper presented to the European Finance Association, Scheviningen, Holland, 1981. Instead of keeping the money in cash you may be able to keep it in very liquid securities that are therefore easily sold, but pay only a low rate of interest. The model works in this case also. For example, suppose that the interest rate on these liquid balances is 4%. Then the cost of investing in liquid balances is the interest that you forgo by not investing in the less marketable securities:

Cost of liquid balances $= 10 - 4 = 6\%$

The cost of borrowing is the difference between the interest that you pay on the borrowing and the rate that you earn on liquid balances:

Cost of borrowing $= 12 - 4 = 8\%$

Our rule states that you should adjust the liquid balances until the probability that you will need to borrow equals

$$\frac{\text{Cost of liquid balances}}{\text{Cost of borrowing}} = \frac{6}{8} = 0.75$$

securities once a day, every day, unless by chance they have only a small positive cash balance at the end of the day.

Why do such firms hold any significant amounts of cash? There are basically two reasons. First, cash may be left in non-interest-bearing accounts to compensate banks for the services they provide. Second, large corporations may have literally hundreds of accounts with many different banks and bank branches. It is often better to leave idle cash in some of these accounts than to monitor each account daily and make daily transfers between them.

One major reason for the proliferation of bank accounts is decentralized management. You cannot give a subsidiary operating autonomy without giving its managers the right to spend and receive cash.

Good cash management nevertheless implies some degree of centralization. You cannot maintain your desired inventory of cash if all the subsidiaries in the group are responsible for their own private pools of cash. And you certainly want to avoid situations in which one subsidiary is investing its spare cash at 7% while another is borrowing at 8%. It is not surprising, therefore, that even in highly decentralized companies there is generally central control over cash balances and bank relations.

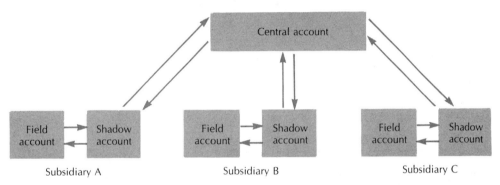

Figure 29-3   Firms often centralize cash management by setting up field accounts and mirror accounts for each subsidiary. Money is periodically transferred between the shadow accounts and the central account.

Figure 29-3 illustrates one way in which companies control their total cash balances using a "zero balance account" system. Each operating subsidiary maintains a field account in a local bank branch, and the branch also sets up a "shadow" or "mirror" account. The subsidiary writes cheques from and deposits cheques to the field account, and the branch periodically (often daily) sets the balance in the shadow account so that the two accounts sum to zero. The bank accommodates this transaction with an offsetting transaction in a central master account for the whole firm. The central account serves as the general reservoir of cash for the entire firm, and allows the treasurer to efficiently manage one balance, while the subsidiaries have daily autonomy over their cash receipts and disbursements.

29-2   CASH COLLECTION SYSTEMS

We have talked loosely about a firm's cash balance; it is now time to be more precise. Suppose that the United Carbon Company has $1 million on demand deposit with its bank. It now pays one of its suppliers by writing a cheque for $200,000. The company's ledgers are immediately adjusted to show a cash balance of $800,000. But the company's bank won't learn anything about this cheque until it has been deposited at the supplier's bank and presented to United Carbon's bank for payment.[8] During this time United Carbon's bank continues to show in its ledger that the company has a balance of $1 million. The company obtains the benefit of an extra $200,000 in the bank while the cheque is clearing. This sum is often called *payment float*.

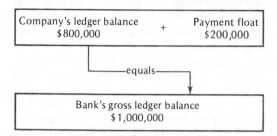

This "float" sounds like a marvellous invention, but unfortunately it can also work in reverse. Suppose that in addition to paying its supplier, United Carbon *receives* a cheque for $100,000 from a customer. It deposits the cheque, and both the company and the bank increase the ledger balance by $100,000:

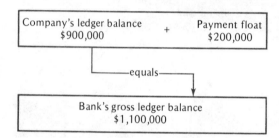

But this money isn't available to the company until the bank has presented the cheque and received the funds from the customer's bank. In the meantime, the bank will show that United Carbon has a *net collected balance* of $1 million and a *collection float* of $100,000:

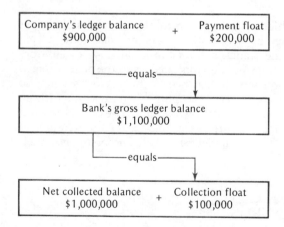

---

[8]Cheques deposited with a bank are cleared internally if the cheque is drawn on the same bank in which it is deposited, and otherwise through the Canadian Payments Association clearing system. These systems are fast and only take one or two days. However, the time taken in the mail system and the time taken by the supplier to process the cheque can be substantial. Bills are generally regarded as being paid on the date stamped on the payment envelope.

Notice that the company gains as a result of the payment float and loses as a result of the collection float. The difference is often termed the *net float*. In our example, the net float is $100,000. The company's net collected balance is therefore $100,000 greater than the balance shown in its ledger.

Managing Float

As financial manager your concern is with the net collected balance, not with the company's ledger balance. If you know that it is going to be a week or two before some of your cheques are presented for payment, you may be able to get by on a smaller cash balance. This game is often called *playing the float*.

You can increase your net collected cash balance by increasing your net float. This means that you want to ensure that cheques paid in by customers are cleared rapidly and those paid to suppliers are cleared slowly. Perhaps this may sound like rather small beer, but think what it can mean to a company like GM. GM's daily sales average over $100 million. Therefore if it can speed up the collection process by one day, it frees more than $100 million, which is available for investment or payment to GM stockholders.

Speeding Up Collections

One way to speed up collections is by a method known as **concentration banking**. In this case, customers in a particular area make payment to a local branch office rather than to company headquarters. The local branch office then deposits the cheques into a local branch bank account. Surplus funds are periodically transferred to the company's principal branch, which is known as the *concentration branch*. Sometimes the company's branch office does not even have its own bank account, and instead makes a deposit at a local bank branch directly into the head office account. Sometimes the company's branch office deals with a different bank from the head office, in which case the funds are transferred to the bank of the head office by a *depository transfer cheque*. The main advantage of concentration banking is the reduction in mailing time that arises because the branch office is nearer to the customer.[9]

Often concentration banking is combined with a **lock-box system**. It works as follows: The company rents a locked post office box in each principal region. All customers within a region are instructed to send their payments to the post office box. The local bank branch, as agent for the company, empties the box at regular intervals and deposits the cheques in the company's account.

How many collection points do you need if you use a lock-box system or concentration banking? The answer depends on where your customers are and on the speed of Canada Post. For example, suppose that you are thinking of opening a lock box. The bank shows you a map of mail delivery times. From that and knowledge of your customers' locations, you come up with the following data:

- Average number of daily payments to lock box = 150
- Average size of payment = $1,200
- Rate of interest *per day* = 0.02%
- Saving in mailing time = 1.2 days
- Saving in clearing time = 0.8 days

[9] If the company is in the United States, another advantage to concentration banking arises because banks are not allowed to branch across state lines. Thus it is often faster to clear the customer's cheque in the same locality as the bank on which it is written. The company's head office and branch will usually have to deal with different banks, so the branch office will transfer the funds to the head office with a wire transfer or a depository transfer cheque.

On this basis, the lock box would increase your collected balance by:

150 items per day $\times$ \$1,200 per item $\times$ (1.2 + 0.8) days saved = \$360,000

Invested at 0.02% per day, that gives a daily return of:

0.0002 $\times$ \$360,000 = \$72.00

The bank's charge for operating the lock-box system depends on the number of cheques processed. Suppose that the bank charges \$0.20 per cheque. That works out at 150 $\times$ 0.20 = \$30.00 per day. You are ahead by \$72.00 − 30.00 = \$42.00 per day, plus whatever your firm saves from not having to process the cheques itself.

Our example assumes that the company has only two choices. It can do nothing or it can operate the lock box. But maybe there is some other lock-box location, or some mixture of locations, that would be still more effective. Of course, you can always find this out by working through all possible combinations, but it may be simpler to solve the problem by linear programming. Many banks offer linear programming models to solve the problem of locating lock-boxes.[10]

Canadian firms can also arrange for lock boxes to receive payments from United States customers. For example, the 1984 takeover of the Harris Bank of Chicago by the Bank of Montreal gave the latter bank access to a lock-box network of six banks in key American cities. Other Canadian banks provide lock boxes in United States cities near the border and transfer the material by courier to a nearby Canadian city for processing.

Controlling Disbursements

Speeding up collections is not the only way to increase the net float. You can also do so by slowing down disbursements. For example, suppose that United Carbon pays one of its Toronto suppliers with a cheque mailed from Toronto. The cheque might spend one or two days in the mail, one day being processed by the supplier, and one day in the cheque clearing system before the funds are drawn from its bank account. But if United Carbon mails the cheque from Vancouver or Halifax, it will spend more time in the mail, thereby increasing its float.

In the United States, this scheme is often extended to take advantage of the slow United States cheque clearing system by also making the cheque payable from a bank in a remote location.[11] The United States Federal Reserve guarantees a maximum clearing time of two days on all cheques cleared through its system, so the supplier can use the funds within two days of presenting the cheque at its bank. However, because United States banks cannot branch across state lines, because the United States Federal Reserve is itself an amalgamation of distinct Federal Reserve Districts, and because the Federal Reserve System does not even have a monopoly on the clearing business, the actual clearing time is typically longer than this. The resulting float that is created is at the expense of the United States Federal Reserve system and is called "Fed float." The Federal Reserve does object and has been trying to prevent remote disbursement.

The Canadian Payments Association clearing system is much more efficient, because it is unified. All banks in Canada must join the system and near-banks (such as trust

---

[10]See, for example, A. Kraus, C. Janssen, and A. McAdams, "The Lock-Box Location Problem," *Journal of Bank Research*, 1:50–58 (Autumn 1970).

[11]Remote disbursement accounts are described in I. Ross, "The Race is to the Slow Payer," *Fortune*, 75–80, (April 1983).

---

companies, credit unions, and caisses populaires) are allowed to join the system. The system has ten clearing centres located in major Canadian cities to facilitate the exchange of cheques and magnetic tapes. Items presented before 15:00 Eastern Time are settled on the same day. With same-day settlement, there is very little float created by the clearing system.

29-3 BANK RELATIONS

General Considerations

Banks like demand deposits. After setting aside a portion of the deposit in a reserve account with the Bank of Canada, they can relend these deposits and earn interest on them. Banks would, therefore, be prepared to pay interest to attract demand deposits, but the government prohibits them from doing so.

One thing that governments never learn is that it is very difficult to legislate prices. Although they stop banks from offering money in payment for demand deposits, they do not stop them from offering services to attract deposits. Therefore, if a firm keeps a sufficiently large balance with the bank, the bank will process the firm's cheques without charge, it will operate a lock-box system—it will provide all kinds of advice and services.[12] This system of **balances** is a mechanism by which the banks pay for demand deposits.[13]

Thus firms can pay for bank services by maintaining interest-free demand deposits. Notice that this system of indirect rewards makes it much more difficult to determine how far you should be prepared to run down your cash balance before selling securities. If it is going to provide you with services, the bank will insist that you maintain a specified average level of balances over the month. Therefore you don't want to allow your cash inventory to run down to zero before replenishing it.

What Happens if Money Pays Interest?

The prohibition on paying interest on demand deposits is breaking down gradually. Individuals have access to savings accounts with cheque-writing privileges. Of course, banks are less likely to offer "free" services, such as cheque processing, on interest-bearing accounts.

Even if interest-bearing chequing accounts become the norm, firms and individuals will still face a trade-off between liquidity and forgone interest, because chequing accounts will normally offer lower interest rates than direct investment in securities. (Otherwise banks will lose money; and in the long run they cannot offer a money-losing service.) Thus, the less money kept in the chequing account, the more interest earned. Yet low balances in chequing accounts means frequent sales or purchases of securities, and thus frequent transaction costs. This is the same problem we started the chapter with.

---

[12]Often the bank will allow your balance to do double duty—that is, it can both pay for cheque handling and similar services, and also serve as compensating balance for a loan. This means that it is worth borrowing from those banks that provide you with tangible services. See G.A. Pogue, R.B. Faucett, and R.N. Bussard, "Cash Management: A Systems Approach," *Industrial Management Review,* **11**:55–76 (Winter 1970).

[13]For a discussion of the role of compensating balances, see D.W. Mullins, "Restriction on the Rate of Interest on Demand Deposits and a Theory of Compensating Balances," *Journal of Finance,* **31**:233–251 (May 1976).

29-4 SUMMARY

Cash provides liquidity, but it doesn't pay interest. Securities pay interest, but you can't use them to buy things. As financial manager you want to hold cash up to the point where the marginal value of liquidity is equal to the interest that you could earn on securities.

Cash is just one of the raw materials that you need to do business. It is expensive keeping your capital tied up in large inventories of raw materials when it could be earning interest. Why do you hold inventories at all? Why not order materials as and when you need them? The answer is that it is also expensive to keep placing many small orders. You need, therefore, to strike a balance between holding too large an inventory of cash (and losing interest on the money) and making too many small adjustments to your inventory (and incurring additional administrative costs). If interest rates are high, you want to hold relatively small inventories of cash. If your cash needs are variable and your administrative costs are high, you want to hold relatively large inventories.

If the securities are not easily sold, you have the alternative of borrowing to cover a cash deficiency. Again, you face a trade-off. Since banks charge a high interest rate on borrowing, you want to keep sufficiently large liquid funds that you don't need to keep borrowing. On the other hand, by having large liquid balances, you are also not earning the maximum return on your cash.

The cash shown in the company ledger is not the same as the net collected balance in your bank account. The difference is the net float. When you have written a large number of cheques awaiting clearance, the net collected balance will be larger than the ledger balance. When you have just deposited a large number of cheques that have not yet been collected by the bank, the net collected balance will be smaller. If you can predict how long it will take cheques to clear, you may be able to "play the float" and get by on a smaller cash balance.

You can also *manage* the float by speeding up collections and slowing down payments. One way to speed collections is by *concentration banking*. Customers make payment to a regional office that then pays the cheques into a local bank branch account. Surplus funds are transferred from the local account to a concentration bank. An alternative technique is *lock-box banking*. In this case customers send their payments to a local post office box. A local bank branch empties the box at regular intervals and clears the cheques. Concentration banking and lock-box banking reduce mailing time and the time required to clear cheques.

Banks provide many services. They handle cheques, manage lock boxes, provide advice, obtain references, and so on. Sometimes firms pay cash for these services, but more often they pay for them by maintaining sufficient cash balances with the bank.

In many cases you will want to keep larger balances than are needed to pay for the tangible services. One reason is that the bank may be a valuable source of ideas and business connections. Another reason is that you may use the bank as a source of short-term funds. Leaving idle cash at your bank may be implicit compensation for the willingness of the bank to stand ready to advance credit when needed. A large cash balance may, therefore, be good insurance against a rainy day.

FURTHER READING

Baumol and Miller and Orr were the pioneers in applying inventory models to cash management.

W.J. Baumol, "The Transactions Demand for Cash: An Inventory Theoretic Approach," *Quarterly Journal of Economics,* **66**:545–556 (November 1952).

M.H. Miller and D. Orr, "A Model of the Demand for Money by Firms," *Quarterly Journal of Economics,* **80**:413–435 (August 1966).

Models of the Miller-Orr type have been developed to cover a variety of more complicated situations. Two examples are:

W.H. Hausman and A. Sanchez-Bell, "The Stochastic Cash Balance Problem with Average Compensating Balance Requirements," *Management Science,* **21**:849–857 (April 1975).

B.H. Stone, "The Use of Forecasts and Smoothing in Control Limit Models for Cash Management," *Financial Management,* **1**:72–84 (Spring 1972).

Mullins and Homonoff review tests of inventory models for cash management.

D. Mullins and R. Homonoff, "Applications of Inventory Cash Management Models," in S.C. Myers, ed., *Modern Developments in Financial Management,* Frederick A. Praeger, Inc., 1976.

Other useful readings include Mullins's discussion of reserve requirements and the pricing of bank services; Pogue, Faucett, and Bussard's model for taking float into account in the design of a banking system; and Kraus, Janssen, and McAdam's analysis of the lock-box location problem. The last two articles give an up-to-date view of banking systems.

D.W. Mullins, "Restriction on the Rate of Interest on Demand Deposits and a Theory of Compensating Balances," *Journal of Finance,* **31**:233–251 (May 1976).

G.A. Pogue, R.B. Faucett, and R.N. Bussard, "Cash Management: A Systems Approach," *Industrial Management Review,* **11**:55–76 (Winter 1970).

A. Kraus, C. Janssen, and A. McAdams, "The Lock-Box Location Problem," *Journal of Bank Research,* **1**:50–58 (Autumn 1970).

S.F. Maier and J.H. Vander Weide, "What Lock-Box and Disbursement Models Really Do," *Journal of Finance,* **37**:361–371 (May 1983).

B.K. Stone, "The Design of a Company's Banking System," *Journal of Finance,* **37**:373–385 (May 1983).

QUIZ

1. Everyman's Bookstore has experienced an increase in demand for *Principles of Corporate Finance.* It now expects to sell 200 books a year. Unfortunately inventory carrying costs have increased to $2 per book per year whereas order costs have remained steady at $2 per order.
   (*a*) What is the marginal carrying cost (for a unit increase in order size)?
   (*b*) At what point does the marginal carrying cost equal the marginal reduction in order cost?
   (*c*) How many orders should the store place per year?
   (*d*) What is its average inventory?

2. Now assume that Everyman's Bookstore uses up cash at a steady rate of $20,000 a year. The interest rate is 2% and each sale of securities costs $2.
   (*a*) What is the marginal carrying cost of the cash (for a $1 increase in order size)?
   (*b*) At what point does the marginal carrying cost equal the marginal reduction in order costs?
   (*c*) How many times a year should the store sell securities?
   (*d*) What is its average cash balance?

3. In the Miller and Orr cash balance model the firm should allow the cash balance to move within limits.
   (*a*) What three factors determine how far apart these limits are?
   (*b*) How far should the firm adjust its cash balance when it reaches the upper or lower limit?
   (*c*) Why does it not restore the cash balance to the halfway point?

4. Suppose that you can hold cash that pays no interest or invest in securities paying interest of 8%. The securities are not easily sold on short notice and, therefore, you must make up any cash deficiency by drawing on a bank line of credit, that charges interest at 10%. Should you invest more or less in securities if
   (a) You are unusually uncertain about future cash flows?
   (b) The interest rate on bank loans rises to 11%?
   (c) The interest rate on securities and on bank loans both rise by the same proportion?
   (d) You revise downward your forecast of future cash needs?

5. A company has the following cash balances:

   Company's ledger balance = $600,000

   Bank's gross ledger balance = $625,000

   Net collected balance = $550,000

   (a) Calculate the payment float and collection float.
   (b) Why does the company gain from the payment float?
   (c) Suppose the company adopts a policy of writing cheques on a remote bank branch. How is this likely to affect the three measures of cash balance?

6. Anne Teak, the financial manager of a furniture manufacturer, is considering operating a lock-box system. She forecasts that 300 payments a day will be made to lock boxes with an average payment size of $1,500. The bank's charge for operating the lock boxes is *either* $0.40 a cheque *or* compensating balances of $800,000.
   (a) If the interest rate is 9%, which method of payment is cheaper?
   (b) What reduction in the time to collect and process each cheque is needed to justify use of the lock-box system?

7. Complete the following passage by choosing the appropriate term from the following list: *lock-box banking, payment float, concentration banking, collection float, net float.*

   The firm's net collected balance is equal to its ledger balance plus the _____ and minus the _____. The difference between the collected balance and the ledger balance is often called the _____. Firms can increase their cash resources by speeding up collections. One way to do this is to arrange for payments to be made to regional offices, which pay the cheques into local bank branches. This is known as _____. Surplus funds are then transferred from the local branch to one of the company's main bank branches. Another technique is to arrange for a local bank branch to collect the cheques directly from a post office box. This is known as _____.

QUESTIONS AND PROBLEMS

1. Indicate how you would expect a firm's cash balance to respond to the following changes:
   (a) Interest rates increase.
   (b) The volatility of daily cash flow decreases.
   (c) The transaction cost of buying or selling marketable securities goes up.

2. A firm maintains a separate account for cash disbursements. Total disbursements are $100,000 per month spread evenly over the month. Administrative and trans-

action costs of transferring cash to the disbursement account are $10 per transfer. Marketable securities yield 1% per month. Determine the size and number of transfers that will minimize the cost of maintaining the special account.

3. Refer again to Table 29-2. Calculate the optimal strategy under the following alternative assumptions:
   (a) Minimum cash balance = $20,000.
   (b) Standard deviation of daily cash flows = $5,000.
   (c) Interest rate = 0.03% per day.
   (d) Transaction cost of each purchase or sale of securities = $25.

4. Suppose that the rate of inflation accelerates from 5% to 10% per year. Would firms' cash balances go up or down relative to sales? Explain.

5. A United States company settles the collection fund balances of its subsidiaries once a week. (That is, each week it transfers any balances in their accounts to a central account.) The cost of a wire transfer is $2. A depository transfer cheque costs $0.20. Cash transferred by wire is available the same day, but the parent must wait three days for depository transfer cheques to clear. Cash can be invested at 12% per year. How much money must be in a collection account before it pays to use a wire transfer?

6. The financial manager of JAC Cosmetics is considering opening a lock box in Calgary. Cheques cleared through the lock box will amount to $300,000 per month. The lock box will make cash available to the company three days earlier.
   (a) Suppose that the bank offers to run the lock box for a $20,000 compensating balance. Is the lock box worthwhile?
   (b) Suppose that the bank offers to run the lock box for a fee of $0.10 per cheque cleared instead of a compensating balance. What must the average cheque size be for the fee alternative to be less costly? Assume an interest rate of 6% per year.
   (c) Why did you need to know the interest rate to answer (b) but not to answer (a)?

7. On January 25, Coot Company has $250,000 deposited with a bank. On January 27, the company writes and mails cheques of $20,000 and $60,000 to suppliers. At the end of the month, Coot's financial manager deposits a $45,000 cheque received from a customer in the morning mail and picks up the end-of-month account summary from the bank. The manager notes that only the $20,000 payment of the 27th has cleared the bank. What are the company's ledger balance and payment float? What is the company's net float?

8. Knob, Inc., is a nationwide distributor of furniture hardware. The company now uses a central billing system for credit sales of $180 million annually. First Commercial, Knob's principal bank, offers to establish a new concentration banking system for a flat fee of $100,000 per year. The bank estimates that mailing and collection time can be reduced by three days. By how much will Knob's collection float be reduced under the new system? How much extra interest income will the new system generate if the extra funds are used to reduce borrowing under Knob's line of credit with First Commercial? Assume the borrowing rate is 12%. Finally, should Knob accept First Commercial's offer if collection costs under the old system are $40,000 per year?

9. A few years ago, the United States brokerage firm of Merrill Lynch increased its float by mailing cheques drawn on west coast banks to customers in the east and cheques drawn on east coast banks to customers in the west. A subsequent class action suit against Merrill Lynch revealed that in 28 months from September 1976

Merrill Lynch disbursed $1.25 billion in 365,000 cheques to New York State customers alone. The plaintiff's lawyer calculated that by using a remote bank branch Merrill Lynch had increased its average float by $1\frac{1}{2}$ days.[14]

(a) How much did Merrill Lynch disburse per day to New York State customers?

(b) What was the total gain to Merrill Lynch over the 28 months, assuming an interest rate of 8%?

(c) What was the present value of the increase in float if the benefits were expected to be permanent?

(d) Suppose that the use of remote bank branches had involved Merrill Lynch in extra expenses. What was the maximum extra cost per cheque that Merrill Lynch would have been prepared to pay?

---

[14]See, for example, I. Ross, "The Race is to the Slow Payer," op. cit.

CHAPTER

SHORT-TERM LENDING AND BORROWING

30

If a company has a temporary cash surplus, it can invest in short-term securities. If it has a temporary deficiency, it can replenish cash by selling securities or by borrowing on a short-term basis. In Chapter 29 you learned something about when to make such changes. But you need to know more than that. There is an elaborate menu of short-term securities; you should be familiar with the most popular entrées. Similarly there are many kinds of short-term debts and you should know their distinguishing characteristics. That is why we have included the present chapter on short-term lending and borrowing. You will encounter little in the way of new theory, but there is a good deal of interesting institutional material.

30-1 SHORT-TERM LENDING

The market for short-term investments is generally known as the **money market**. The money market has no physical marketplace. It consists of a loose agglomeration of banks and dealers linked together by telex, telephones, and computers. But a huge volume of securities is regularly traded on the money market, and competition is vigorous.

Most large corporations manage their own money-market investments, buying and selling securities denominated in multiples of $50,000 or $100,000 through banks or dealers. Smaller corporations find that these investments are too large or "chunky," so they put their cash into interest-bearing deposits at banks. This latter option is generally not available to small American corporations, since the American interest rate ceilings under Regulation Q (which is now being phased out) make small bank deposits unattractive. Instead, many of them use "money market mutual funds," which hold a diversified portfolio of high quality, short-term securities, and sell shares to private individuals and small corporations. There is no such need for money market funds in Canada, because Canada no longer sets interest ceilings on bank deposits.

Valuing Money-Market Investments

When we value long-term debt, it is important to take default risk into account. Almost anything may happen in 20 years; even today's most respectable company may get into trouble eventually. This is the basic reason corporate bonds offer higher yields than Treasury bonds.

Short-term debt is not risk-free either. When Penn Central failed in the United States, it had $82 million of short-term commercial paper outstanding. After that shock, investors became much more discriminating in their purchases of commercial paper and the spread between interest rates on high- and low-quality paper widened dramatically.

Our examples of failure are exceptions that prove the rule; in general the danger of default is less for money-market securities issued by corporations than for corporate bonds in general. There are two reasons for this. First, the range of possible outcomes is less for short-term investments. Even though the distant future may be clouded, you can usually be confident that a particular company will survive for at least the next month. Second, only well-established companies can borrow in the money market. If you are only going to lend money for one day, you can't afford to spend too much time or resources in evaluating the loan. Thus you will consider only blue-chip borrowers.

Despite the high quality of money-market investments, there are often substantial differences in yield between corporate and Canadian government securities. For example, in May 1985 the rate of interest on three-month commercial paper was about one-half a percentage point higher than on Treasury bills. Why is this? One answer is the risk of default on commercial paper. Another is that the investments have different degrees of liquidity or "moneyness." Investors prefer Treasury bills because they are a little easier to turn into cash on short notice. Securities that can be converted quickly and cheaply into cash offer relatively low yields.

Calculating the Yield on Money-Market Investments

Many money-market investments are pure discount securities. This means that they don't pay interest: the return consists of the difference between the amount you pay and the amount you receive at maturity. Unfortunately, it is no good trying to persuade Revenue Canada that this difference represents a capital gain. It is wise to that one and will tax your return as ordinary income.

Yields in Canada are quoted in two different ways: the **true yield basis** and the **commercial discount basis**. The true yield is an annualized rate of interest, to be compounded at a frequency corresponding to the term of the security. For example, on Thursday, May 23, 1985, 91-day Treasury bills were issued at a true yield of 9.34%. Since 91 days is approximately one quarter, this was 9.34% compounded quarterly. The yield earned over 91 days was $9.34 \times (91/365) = 2.33\%$, or 9.67% compounded annually.[1] The issue price was simply the present value of $100 discounted one period at 2.33%:

$$\frac{100}{1 + 0.0233} = \$97.72$$

For each $97.72 that you invested on May 23, the government agreed to pay $100 to you 91 days later.

At the same time, commercial and finance company 90-day paper (which we will discuss below) was quoted on a commercial discount basis at 9.50%. That is, the price of 90-day paper was $100 - 9.50 \times 90/365 = \$97.66$. For each $97.66 you invested, the borrower would pay $100 to you 90 days later. The yield over 90 days was $(100 - 97.66)/97.66 = 2.40\%$, equivalent to 9.73% compounded quarterly, or 10.09% compounded annually.[2]

---

[1]Since these yields are compounded at various frequencies, depending on the term to maturity of the investment, different yields are not directly comparable to each other, unless they are for the same term to maturity. Thus, it is better to use the equivalent annually compounded rate as discussed in Chapter 3:

$(1.0233)^{365/91} - 1 = 0.0967$ or 9.67%

[2]By way of comparison, we should note that United States money market securities are quoted on a *360-day discount basis*. That is, in the United States, the paper is said to be discounted at

$$\frac{(100 - 97.66)}{100} \times \frac{360}{90} = 0.0937 \text{ or } 9.37\%$$

Notice that the quoted American discount is less than both the equivalent Canadian true yield and the equivalent Canadian commercial discount.

Government of Canada Treasury Bills

Table 30-1 summarizes the characteristics of the principal money-market investments. The first item on our list is Government of Canada Treasury bills. These mature in 91 days, 182 days, or 1 year.[3] The 91- and 182-day bills are issued every week, and the 1 year bills are issued every two weeks, in multiples of $1,000. Sales are by auction on Thursdays. You enter a bid through a bank or an investment dealer and take your chance of receiving an allotment at your bid price.[4] You don't have to submit a bid in the auction in order to invest in Treasury bills. There is an excellent secondary market in which millions of dollars of bills are bought and sold every day.

Part of the "depth" of this market arises because banks can use T-bills as part of their secondary reserves,[5] and they buy and sell T-bills to adjust their overall liquidity. Another source of depth is that T-bills can be used by **jobbers** as security for a loan from the Bank of Canada. Jobbers are investment dealers who maintain an inventory in and make a market in Government of Canada securities. In return for this service, they (like the banks) are given the privilege of using the Bank of Canada as a lender of last resort. (They use the privilege much more frequently than the banks.) They borrow from the Bank of Canada by means of a **purchase and resale agreement** (PRA). To accomplish this, they sell Government of Canada securities, like Treasury bills, to the Bank of Canada and repurchase them at a later pre-specified date and price. The security acts as a form of collateral for the loan.

Treasury bills are quoted on a true yield basis.

Provincial and Municipal Securities

The provinces, municipalities, and their Crown corporations and agencies issue various short-term securities, such as treasury bills and short-term **paper**. Sometimes they also issue **tax-anticipation notes**, which are short-term notes that will be paid off by the receipt of tax payments. The provinces and municipalities have reduced their reliance on bank loans by going directly into the money market for short-term financing in recent years. There is a good secondary market for their securities. While each situation must be dealt with on an individual basis, these securities are regarded as secure and generally pay only a small interest premium over federal T-bills.

Bank Time Deposits and Certificates of Deposit[6]

If a firm puts its money in a **demand deposit**, it can withdraw it whenever it chooses. On the other hand, the bank does not pay interest on the deposit. An alternative is

---

[3]They are often cited more simply as being 90-, 180-, or 360-day bills, respectively.

[4]In the United States Treasury bill auction, such bids are called *competitive* bids. Individuals are also allowed to place *noncompetitive* bids, which are filled at the average price of the successful competitive bids. The advantage of these bids is that you can be sure of getting your bills with a noncompetitive bid.

[5]Banks are required to maintain primary reserves in the form of cash and non-interest-bearing deposits with the Bank of Canada. They also must maintain secondary reserves in the form of certain securities like T-bills.

[6]There are "near-banks" that accept interest-bearing deposits, including trust companies, credit unions, caisses populaires, and provincial treasury branches. They cater mainly to individuals rather than corporations, and they offer deposit instruments that are similar to those offered by banks. For simplicity, we will simply refer to banks in the following material, even though it would be more accurate to continually use the phrase "banks, trust companies and many other near-banks."

Table 30-1 Money-market instruments.

Investment	Borrower	Maturities When Issued	Marketability	Basis for Calculating Interest	Notes
Treasury bills	Government of Canada	91, 182 days and 1 year	Excellent secondary market	Discounted	91- and 182-day bills auctioned weekly, 1-year bills auctioned bi-weekly
Treasury bills and paper	Provinces, municipalities, and their agencies	Various maturities	Good secondary market	Discounted	Tax-anticipation notes also issued
Bank savings deposits and certificates of deposit (CDs)	Banks and trust companies	Overnight to 7 years	No secondary market	Yield basis, interest at maturity	Deposits in Canadian or United States dollars; CDs sometimes can be cashed early
Negotiable certificates of deposit (CDs)	Banks and trust companies	30 days to 1 year	Good secondary market	Discounted	Cannot be cashed before maturity
Swapped deposits	Banks	30 days to 1 year	No secondary market	All-in yield, interest at maturity	Deposit in United States dollars or pounds sterling is hedged against exchange risk
Eurodollar deposits	Foreign (branches of) banks	Overnight to 1 year; also on demand basis	No secondary market	Yield basis, interest at maturity	Dollar time deposits at overseas banks
Negotiable London dollar certificates of deposit	London branches of American, Canadian, Japanese, and British banks	30 days to 1 year	Good secondary market	Yield basis, interest at maturity	Receipts for dollar time deposits at overseas banks
Finance company paper	Sales and finance companies	Typically 30 to 365 days	Good secondary market in prime paper	Usually discounted	Placed directly with investors, or through dealers
Corporate paper	Leading industrial firms	Typically 30 to 90 days	Modest secondary market; see buy-backs	Can be discounted or interest bearing	Placed through dealers; sometimes can be cashed early
Bankers' acceptances	Corporations	A few days to 1 year; typically 30 to 90 days	Good secondary market	Discounted	Repayment guaranteed by borrower and bank
Buy-back agreements and call loans	Dealers in Government of Canada securities	Overnight to about 3 months	No secondary market	Yield basis, interest at maturity	Collateral provided by money-market securities; terms set to suit lender (perhaps including daily call privilege)

to place the money in a **time** or **notice deposit**, but there may be a wait before the money can be withdrawn.

The risk of default on a bank time deposit is small. Until the 1985 failures of the Canadian Commercial Bank and the Northlands Bank, Canada had gone for over half a century without a bank failure. Moreover, bank and trust company deposits that mature within five years are insured for up to $60,000 with the Canada Deposit Insurance Corporation (CDIC), a federal Crown corporation. Therefore, you can be sure of getting at least that much of your money back. The government may also choose to bail out uninsured depositors when a bank fails. Since this is a political decision, it is not something a corporate treasurer can count on.

There are several kinds of time deposits. One of the most popular is the regular **savings account**. You may invest almost any sum you choose in a savings account. The bank can insist that you give 15 days' notice before withdrawing funds, but in practice it is always prepared to pay out on demand. Savings accounts are, therefore, very liquid; and although they offer fairly low rates of interest, they are widely used by individuals and small companies.

Investment in a savings account is for an undefined period. In other words, you can withdraw funds as you need them. An alternative form of time deposit is the **fixed-term deposit**, sometimes just called a **term deposit**. In this case you lend your money for a fixed period. If you find that you need the money before maturity, the bank will often allow you to withdraw, but you suffer a penalty in the form of a reduced rate of interest.

Term deposits are rather like short-term bonds. The company "lends" the bank so many dollars; in return, the bank promises to repay the money with interest at the end of the period agreed on. As evidence of the debt, the borrower may give the company a **certificate of deposit** (CD), **term note**, or **term deposit receipt**. (The terminology varies amongst the banks and trust companies.) The certificate is just the bank's promise to repay the loan. These term deposits are typically for a period of 30 days to 5 years, however, they have been issued for terms as short as 1 day and as long as 7 years. They are not transferrable or negotiable: the only way the company can get cash is to sell the certificate back to the bank, usually facing a penalty in the form of a lower interest rate.

However, there are bank deposits of $100,000 or more that are negotiable securities. They are called **bearer notes** or **negotiable certificates of deposit**. Therefore, if you decide that you need the money before maturity, you don't have to ask the bank: you just sell your bearer note to another investor. When the loan matures, the new owner of the note presents it to the bank and receives payment. There is an active market in these notes, so they are quite "liquid." They are typically sold at a discount.

Swapped Deposits

Another type of time deposit that you can get in Canada is the **swapped deposit**. It is an American dollar deposit combined with a spot exchange of Canadian dollars to American dollars and a forward exchange of American dollars to Canadian dollars at the maturity date of the deposit. (The forward transaction guarantees the rate of exchange that will apply at the termination of the deposit, and we will discuss this more in Chapter 32.)

At first, this seems like an overly complicated combination of three different transactions for a short-term investment, but fortunately the banks are in the business of providing each of the three types of transaction separately. With a swap deposit, they put the whole package together and quote you a single "all-in yield" or Canadian-dollar interest rate. You are "hedged" and not exposed to foreign-exchange risk. The all-in yield can be compared directly with the interest rates quoted on interest-bearing Canadian dollar deposits. They are not negotiable or transferable, and it is difficult, if not impossible, to withdraw the funds early.[7]

Swap deposits are also available with exchange into other currencies, such as the pound sterling, but most use the United States dollar.

Eurodollar Investments

Eurodollars are deposits of dollars with foreign banks or foreign branches of domestic banks. Because they are located offshore, they are not subject to the same degree of regulation that domestic deposits are. This is particularly important for American depositors, whose domestic banks have otherwise been restricted by interest rate ceilings and requirements that the deposits must be for at least 30 days. The interest rate on eurodollar deposits tends to be slightly higher than on domestic deposits and somewhat less affected by domestic monetary policy.[8]

The London branches of large American, Canadian, and Japanese banks and the principal British banks issue London dollar CDs. These are simply receipts for dollars deposited in London. There is an active secondary market allowing a depositor to sell or transfer one of these deposits prior to maturity, but there are no early withdrawal privileges.

The main difference between a swapped deposit and a eurodollar deposit is the currency the lender uses. A swapped deposit uses the lender's currency, but a eurodollar deposit uses the borrower's (or some third) currency. Thus, the eurodollar deposit exposes the lender to foreign exchange risk. Both are "offshore" sources of funds in the sense that the loan is made in a country that is foreign to the borrower.

In addition to eurodollar CDs you can hold eurodollar commercial paper and bankers' acceptances (described below).

Commercial Paper

A bank is a kind of intermediary. It borrows short-term funds from one group of firms or individuals[9] and relends the money to another group. It makes its profit by charging the borrower a higher rate of interest than it offers the lender.

Sometimes it is very convenient to have a bank in the middle. It saves lenders the trouble of looking for borrowers and assessing their creditworthiness, and it saves borrowers the trouble of looking for lenders. Depositors do not care whom the bank lends to: they only need to satisfy themselves that the bank as a whole is safe.

There are also occasions on which it is *not* worth paying an intermediary to perform these functions. Large, safe, and well-known companies can bypass the banking system by issuing their own short-term notes. These notes are known as **commercial paper**. If the company is a finance company, the paper is sometimes called **acceptance paper** or **finance paper**; otherwise, it is often called **corporate paper**.[10] While many finance

---

[7]To allow you to withdraw your money, the bank has to negotiate the early withdrawal of the United States dollar deposit, engage in a spot exchange of United States dollars to Canadian dollars, and close out the forward contract for the exchange of United States dollars to Canadian dollars. The terms of these transactions cannot be determined in advance.

[8]We discuss eurodollars in more detail in Chapter 32.

[9]Remember that any bank deposit can be thought of as a loan from the depositor to the bank.

[10]Commercial paper is also issued by United States bank holding companies. A bank holding company is a firm that owns a bank and some other subsidiaries, such as a leasing subsidiary. The holding company is often used to get around some of the United States restrictions on widespread branch banking by selling commercial paper outside of the state in which the bank is located.

---

companies, such as General Motors Acceptance Corporation, provide financing for consumer and industrial goods, many also engage in other types of lending, including term loans and mortgages.

Often these firms set up their own marketing department and sell their issues directly to investors. Others issue their paper through dealers (who maintain an inventory in these securities) or agents, who find a suitable investor and are paid a commission for their services. The commission is typically about $\frac{1}{8}$% per annum—that is, 180-day paper would generate a commission of about $\frac{1}{2} \times \frac{1}{8} = \frac{1}{16}$%. This is a specific example of underwriting as discussed in Chapter 15.

Maturities of commercial paper may range from a few days to a year[11] or more, but corporate paper typically matures in 30 to 90 days. There is a good secondary market for "prime" paper, and some paper can be repaid early, at the option of the lender. Sometimes commercial paper is interest-bearing, and sometimes it is issued at a discount. In the latter case, the yield is generally quoted on a commercial discount basis.

Only nationally known companies can find a market for their commercial paper, and even then dealers are reluctant to handle a company's paper if there is any uncertainty about its financial position.[12] Companies generally back their issue of commercial paper by arranging a special backup line of credit with a bank. This guarantees that they can find the money to repay the paper.

Sometimes, commercial paper is secured. The security can consist of a pledge of accounts receivable or a floating charge on all assets of the company. If the paper is issued by a "captive" finance company—one that provides financing to purchasers of goods produced by its parent—it is usually guaranteed by the parent. The risk of default is small for commercial paper. The most notable default in Canada arose from the 1965 failure of Atlantic Acceptance, a finance company.

By cutting out the intermediary, major companies are able to borrow at rates that may be 1% to $1\frac{1}{2}$% below the prime rate charged by banks. Even after allowing for a dealer's commission and the cost of compensating balances on any backup line of credit, this is still a substantial saving. Firms have generally been reluctant to imperil good relations with banks by reducing their borrowing too far. Nevertheless, there is no doubt that banks have felt the competition from commercial paper and have been prepared to reduce their rates to blue-chip customers. Banks also have had to make their prime rates more sensitive to the changing money market conditions that affect the yields on commercial paper and other money market instruments. Otherwise, if interest rates rise, for example, and banks are slow to increase their prime rates, corporate borrowers will switch from commercial paper to bank loans just at a time when the cost of borrowing to the bank rises. Previously, banks tried to "administer" their prime rates with gradual adjustments.

Bankers' Acceptances

A banker's acceptance begins life as a **draft** (which is effectively a post-dated cheque) for the bank to pay a given sum at a future date. The bank then guarantees this draft by writing "accepted" on it, although there is a clear agreement that the writer of the draft (the borrower) will deposit enough funds with the bank in time to cover the future

---

[11]To avoid having to file a prospectus, the borrower often has the issue mature within one year and sells the debt in multiples of $50,000 or more.

[12]Bond rating firms such as Canadian Bond Rating Service and Moody's publish quality ratings for commercial paper. Investors rely on these ratings, along with other information, when they compare the quality of different firms' paper.

payment. Once accepted, the draft becomes the bank's *and* the borrower's IOU. It is a negotiable security.

This security can then be bought or sold at a discount and is quoted on a true yield basis. The yield is slightly greater than that on Treasury bills of the same maturity. However, the borrower must compensate the bank for taking on some risk. Typically, there is a **stamping fee** of about $1/2$% per annum, and there may be requirements associated with maintaining a line of credit with the bank. The creditworthiness of the bank is an important factor in determining the value of the guarantee. Thus, a banker's acceptance may have to yield as much as $1/4$% more if it is accepted by a small Schedule B bank rather than a large Schedule A bank.

A banker's acceptance may arise in one of two ways. We saw in Chapter 28 that an acceptance may be arranged when a company is buying goods on credit. In this case the draft is originally made payable to the supplier of the goods. Another important way of creating a banker's acceptance in Canada arose in 1962. A corporate borrower can make a draft payable to itself, get it accepted by a bank, and then endorse it, without making it payable to any particular party. In this way, it becomes payable to the bearer and is very marketable. Money market dealers[13] and banks maintain inventories and make markets in these securities, and there is an active secondary market.

Buy-backs

We have seen that the money market dealers can borrow from the Bank of Canada against the collateral of Government of Canada securities by means of a purchase and resale agreement. They also borrow from corporations and institutional investors under similar terms by means of a **repurchase agreement** or **buy-back**,[14] in which case the lenders are known colloquially as **country banks** or **offstreet** lenders.[15] The country bank is protected by the collateral of the security involved as well as the backing of the investment dealer doing the borrowing. Other types of collateral used in country banking include corporate, provincial, and municipal securities.

The terms of a buy-back are usually customized to the needs of the lender. Thus, if a lender is accumulating cash in preparation for a dividend, interest, or other known payment at a specific date, the buy-back is arranged to be liquidated on that date. On other occasions, buy-backs are set to mature on a daily basis, or are for an indefinite period, but with a daily call or renegotiation privilege accorded to both the borrower and the lender. Such loans are called **call loans**.

30-2 FLOATING-RATE PREFERRED STOCK—AN ALTERNATIVE TO MONEY-MARKET SECURITIES

There is no law preventing firms from making short-term investments in long-term securities. If your firm has $1 million set aside for an income tax payment, it could buy

---

[13]From 1962 to 1981, investment dealers could use a banker's acceptance in a purchase and resale agreement (PRA) with the Bank of Canada, when using the central bank as a lender of last resort. The intent was to improve the marketability of bankers' acceptances. Parliament decided that the bankers' acceptance market was sufficiently well-established, so it stopped this with the 1980 revision of the *Bank of Canada Act*. Now, only Government of Canada securities are eligible for PRA. See Daryl Merrett, "The Evolution of Bankers' Acceptances in Canada," *Bank of Canada Review*, 3–12, October 1981.

[14]In the United States, such agreements are also called "RPs" or "repos."

[15]Buy-backs can use a broad range of collateral, including commercial paper and bankers' acceptances. Banks provide day loans, call loans, and special call loans to investment dealers, and these are similar to buy-backs.

---

a long-term bond on April 1 and sell it on April 30, when the tax instalment is due. However, the danger in this strategy is obvious: what happens if bond prices fall by 10% in April? There you are, with a $1 million liability to the Receiver General of Canada and bonds worth only $900,000. Of course bond prices could also go up, but why take the chance? Corporate treasurers entrusted with excess funds for short-term investment are naturally averse to the price volatility of long-term bonds.

You might think that common and preferred stocks would be equally unattractive short-term investments for excess cash, but that is not quite right, because these securities have an important tax advantage for corporations and individuals. Canadian corporations do not have to pay any tax on dividend income received from other Canadian corporations, and individuals can take advantage of the dividend tax credit. We discussed this in Chapter 16.

If you invest the firm's surplus cash in a short- or long-term debt, the firm must pay tax on the interest it receives. Thus, for $1 of interest, a firm in a 46% marginal tax bracket ends up with only $0.54. However, if you invest the surplus cash in stock and receive $1 of dividends, you get to keep it all. The tax rate on dividends received is zero.

Suppose you consider putting that $1 million in some other corporation's preferred shares.[16] The zero tax rate is very tempting. On the other hand, since preferred dividends are fixed, the prices of preferred shares change when long-term interest rates change. A $1 million investment in preferred shares could be worth only $900,000 on April 30, when the tax instalment is due. Wouldn't it be nice if someone invented a preferred share that was insulated from fluctuating interest rates?

Well, there are such securities—the so-called floating-rate preferreds, which pay dividends that go up and down with the general level of interest rates.[17] The prices of these securities are less volatile than fixed-dividend preferreds, and they are a safer haven for firms' excess cash. Indeed, some of these preferreds have their dividend adjusted *exactly* when their market price moves away from the initial issue price.

However, why would any firm want to *issue* floating-rate preferreds? Dividends must be paid out of *after-tax* income, interest from before-tax income. Thus if a taxpaying firm wants to issue a floating-rate security, it would normally prefer to issue debt rather than equity in order to generate interest tax shields.

But there are plenty of firms that either are not paying taxes or are facing a low marginal tax rate because they have other ways of shielding taxable income. These firms cannot make full use of an interest tax shield. Moreover, they have been able to issue floating-rate preferreds at yields *lower* than the yields they would have to pay on a floating-rate debt issue. The corporations and individuals buying the preferreds are happy with this lower yield because they either pay no tax on the dividends or receive a dividend tax credit.

Floating-rate preferreds were invented in Canada in the mid-1970s, and they were bought mainly by banks, often in a private placement. However, Parliament noticed that heavy use of these non-taxable investments allowed many banks to pay little or no tax, so it changed the law to make banks pay tax on so-called **term preferred**

---

[16]Preferred shares are usually better short-term investments for a corporation than common shares. The preferred shares' expected return is virtually all dividends; most common shares are expected to generate capital gains, too. The corporate tax on capital gains is usually $\frac{1}{2} \times 46 = 23\%$, as discussed in Chapter 16. Corporations therefore have a strong incentive to like dividends and dislike capital gains.

[17]Often there are limits on the maximum and minimum dividends that can be paid. Thus if interest rates leap to 100%, the preferred dividend rate would hit a ceiling of, say, 15%. If interest rates fall to 1%, the preferred dividend rate would hit a floor at, say, 5%.

dividends—that is, dividends on preferred shares that could be redeemed within ten years of their initial issue. This cooled off the market for awhile.

Then they were reinvented in the United States in May 1982, when Chemical New York Corporation, the holding company for Chemical Bank, raised $200 million. The securities proved so popular that over $4 billion of floating-rate preferreds were issued by spring 1983, including $1.5 billion in one four-day period in February 1983. Then the novelty wore off and the frequency of new issues slowed down.

Meanwhile, the Canadian banks decided to try another angle with floating-rate preferreds. In addition to *buying* floating-rate preferreds, they decided to *sell* them. Many industrial corporations have done the same. There is another item in the menu of investment opportunities open to corporate money managers. There is also another item on the menu of the short-term floating-rate sources of financing for corporations, a topic we will turn to now.

30-3   SHORT-TERM BORROWING

You now know where to invest your surplus cash. But suppose that you have the opposite problem and face a temporary cash deficit. Where can you find the short-term funds?

Unsecured Loans

The simplest and most common solution is to arrange an unsecured loan from your bank. For example, many companies rely on unsecured bank loans to finance a temporary increase in inventories. Such loans are described as *self-liquidating*—in other words, the sale of the goods provides the cash to repay the loan. Another popular use of bank loans is for construction or "bridging" finance. In this case the loan serves as interim financing until a project is completed and long-term financing is arranged.

Companies that frequently require short-term bank loans often ask their bank for a line of credit. This allows them to borrow at any time up to an established limit.[18] A line of credit usually extends for a year and is then subject to review by the bank's loan committee. Banks are often anxious that companies not use a line of credit to cover their need for long-term finance. Thus, they often require the company to "clean up" its short-term bank loans for at least one month during the year.

The interest rate on a line of credit is usually tied to the bank's prime rate of interest. In addition to the interest charge, banks usually insist that in return for a line of credit the firm must maintain an interest-free demand deposit at the bank. A typical requirement is that the firm maintain a minimum average compensating balance equal to 10% of funds potentially available under the line of credit plus 10% of the amount actually borrowed. If as a result the firm maintains a higher cash balance than it otherwise would, the interest forgone on the additional deposit represents an extra cost to the loan.[19]

Earlier in the chapter we noted that large companies sometimes bypass the banking system and issue their own short-term unsecured debt, that is, commercial paper. Even

---

[18]Most lines of credit are not formal commitments. The bank reserves the right to refuse additional credit if there is a significant deterioration in the borrower's financial position. If the borrower requires an unconditional guarantee that money will be available, the bank commonly charges an additional standby fee.

[19]Thus bank deposits often do double duty: they serve as transaction balances and they also serve as compensating balance for a loan. But sometimes, particularly in periods of "tight money," banks insist that borrowers maintain compensating balances *in addition* to normal transaction balances.

after allowing for the issue expenses and the cost of backup lines of credit, commercial paper is generally substantially cheaper than a bank loan. Remember, however, that when times are hard and money is tight, the bank will give priority to its regular customers. Thus few firms bypass the banking system entirely, even in good times when commercial paper is cheap and easy to sell.

Loans Secured by Receivables

Banks often ask firms to provide security for loans. Since the bank is lending on a short-term basis, the security generally consists of liquid assets such as receivables, inventories, or securities. Sometimes the bank will accept a "floating lien" or "floating charge" against receivables and inventory. This gives it a general claim against these assets, but it does not specify them in detail, and it sets few restrictions on what the company can do with the assets. More commonly, banks will require specific collateral.

If the bank is satisfied with the credit standing of your customers and the soundness of your product, it may be willing to lend you as much as 80% of the value of accounts receivable. In return, you pledge your receivables or "assign your book debts" as collateral for the loan. If you fail to pay your debt, the bank can collect the receivables and apply the proceeds to repaying the debt. If the proceeds are insufficient, you are liable for any deficiency. The loan is therefore said to be *with recourse*.

When you pledge receivables, you must keep the bank up to date on credit sales and collections. When you deliver goods to your customers, you send the bank a copy of the invoice, together with a form of assignment, which gives the bank the right to the money your customers owe you. Then the firm can borrow up to the agreed proportion of this collateral.[20]

Each day, as you make new sales, your collateral increases and you can borrow more money. Each day customers pay their bills. This money is placed in a special collateral account under the bank's control and is periodically used to reduce the size of the loan. Therefore, as the firm's business fluctuates, so does the amount of collateral and the size of the loan.

A few receivables loans are on a notification basis. In this case the bank informs your customer of the lending arrangement and asks for the money to be paid directly to the bank. Firms generally do not like their customers to know they are in debt, and therefore such loans are made more frequently without notification.

Receivables loans can be obtained not only from banks but also from finance companies that specialize in lending to businesses.

Loans against receivables are flexible, and they provide a continuous source of funds. Also, banks are willing to lend the firm more with collateral than without it. However, it can be costly for borrower and lender alike to supervise and record changes in the collateral. Therefore the rate of interest on receivables financing is usually high, and there may be an additional service charge on the loan.

We discussed factoring in Chapter 28. Don't confuse factoring with lending against receivables. Factors *buy* your receivables and, if you wish, advance a proportion of the money. They are, therefore, responsible for collecting the debt and suffer any losses if the customers don't pay up. When you pledge your receivables as collateral for a loan, *you* remain responsible for collecting the debt and *you* suffer if a customer is delinquent.

---

[20]Thus there are three main pieces of documentation: (1) the collateral agreement (or security agreement), which defines the terms under which the collateral is given; (2) the form of assignment under which specific assets are pledged; and (3) a promissory note against which money is borrowed.

Loans Secured by Inventory

Banks and finance companies also lend on the security of inventory, but they are choosy about the collateral they will accept. They want to make sure that they can identify and sell the inventory if you default. Automobiles and other standardized, nonperishable commodities are good collateral for a loan; work in process and ripe Camemberts are poor collateral.

The procedure for lending against inventories depends on where the goods are stored. If you place goods in a public warehouse,[21] the warehouse company gives you a **warehouse receipt** and will then release the goods only on the instructions of the holder of the receipt.[22] Because the holder of the receipt controls the inventory, the receipt can be used as collateral for a loan.[23] Notice, however, that the warehouse receipt only identifies the goods and where they are stored. It doesn't guarantee the grade of the goods, nor does it guarantee your claim to the goods, nor does it provide insurance against fire, theft, and other hazards. Therefore the lender will also need to be satisfied on all these matters.

Lenders want to make sure that goods are not released without their permission. Therefore the law states that a warehouse receipt can be issued only by a bona fide warehouse company independent of the company that owns the goods. That is fine if you want to store your goods in a large public warehouse—but what do you do if you want to keep them on your own premises? The answer is that you establish a **field warehouse**. In other words, you arrange for a warehouse company to lease your warehouse or storage area. The warehouse company puts up signs stating that a field warehouse is being operated. It then remains responsible for storing your pledged goods and releases them only on the instructions of the holder of the warehouse receipt.

The important feature of warehouse loans is that goods are physically segregated and under the control of an independent warehouse company. Suppose, however, that you are an automobile dealer who needs to finance an inventory of new cars. You can't put the cars in a warehouse; you need to keep them in the showroom under your control. The common solution is to enter into a **floor planning** arrangement. Under this arrangement the finance company buys the cars from the manufacturer and you hold them in trust for the finance company. As evidence of this, you sign a *trust receipt* that identifies the cars involved. You are free to sell the cars, but when you do so, the proceeds are used to redeem the trust receipt. To make sure that the collateral is properly maintained, the finance company will make periodic inspections of the inventory.

The fact that liquid assets are easily saleable does not always make them good collateral. It also means the lender has to make sure that the borrower doesn't suddenly sell the assets and run off with the money. If you want to make your hair stand on end, read the story of the great salad oil swindle.[24] Fifty-one banks and companies made loans of nearly $200 million to the Allied Crude Vegetable Oil Refining Corporation. Warehouse receipts issued by a field warehousing company were taken as security. Unfortunately, the cursory inspections by the employees of the field warehousing company failed to uncover the fact that, instead of containing salad oil, Allied's storage

---

[21] Also called a *terminal warehouse*.

[22] Most warehouse receipts are nonnegotiable. In this case the warehouse company merely requires written instructions from the holder. If they are negotiable, the company will release goods only on presentation of the receipt itself.

[23] A similar procedure may be followed when goods are in transit. In this case the bank exercises control over the goods by holding the bill of lading.

[24] For an excellent account see N. Miller, *The Great Salad Oil Swindle*, Victor Gollancz, Ltd. London, 1966.

tanks were mainly filled with soap stock, seawater, and unidentifiable sludge. When the fraud was discovered, the president of Allied went to jail, the field warehousing company went into bankruptcy, and the 51 lenders were left out in the cold, looking for their $200 million. Lenders have been more careful since then.

30-4 TERM LOANS

The principal form of medium-term debt financing is the **term loan**. Most such loans are made by banks and have maturities of one to eight years. Insurance companies often make longer-maturity term loans, and a number of term loans are split between banks and insurance companies.

Term loans are usually repaid in level amounts over the period of the loan, although sometimes there may be no payment for the first couple of years or there may be a large final "balloon" or "bullet" payment.

Banks can accommodate repayment patterns to the anticipated cash flows of the borrowing firm. For example, the first principal repayment might be delayed for a year pending completion of a new factory. Often term loans are renegotiated in midstream— that is, before maturity. Banks are usually willing to do this if the borrowing firm is an established customer, remains creditworthy, and has a sound business reason for making the change.

The rate of interest on the term loan is sometimes fixed for the life of the loan. But usually it is linked to the prime rate. Thus, if the rate is set at "1% over prime," the borrower may pay 5% in the first year when prime is 4%, $5\frac{1}{2}$% in the second year when prime is $4\frac{1}{2}$%, and so on. Occasionally these variable-rate term loans include a "collar," which sets upper and lower limits on the interest that can be charged.

In addition to the interest cost the borrower is usually obliged to maintain a minimum interest-free demand deposit with the bank. This compensating balance is commonly set at 10% to 20% of the amount of the loan, so that the true interest rate, calculated on the money the firm can actually use, may be significantly higher than the quoted interest rate.

Term loans are for the most part unsecured debt. The conditions of a term loan are like those of the most unsecured bonds. They generally do not include the very restrictive negative conditions of private placement bonds, but they do impose affirmative conditions on net worth and working capital. Because many term loans are made to small companies, they often impose conditions on senior management. For example, the bank may require the company to insure the lives of senior managers, may place limits on management's remuneration, and may require personal guarantees for the loan.

A variant on the straight loan is the *revolving line of credit*. This is a legally assured line of credit that is reviewed annually. The company pays interest on any borrowings plus an "insurance premium" of about $\frac{1}{2}$% on the unused amount, as well as maintains a compensating balance with the bank.

Revolving credit agreements are relatively expensive compared to straight lines of credit or short-term bank loans. But in exchange for the extra cost, the firm receives a valuable option: it has guaranteed[25] access to the bank's money at a fixed spread above the prime rate. This amounts to a put option, because the firm can sell its debt to the bank on fixed terms even if its own creditworthiness deteriorates.[26]

---

[25]This guarantee is not absolute. Most revolving credit agreements contain a clause allowing the bank to refuse to lend additional funds if there is a "materially adverse change" in the firm's creditworthiness. However, this clause is rarely invoked by banks, except in extreme circumstances (for example, if a borrower is discovered to be lying or concealing important adverse developments).

[26]Gregory Hawkins has analyzed revolving credit agreements using option pricing theory. See "An Analysis of Revolving Credit Agreements," *Journal of Financial Economics,* 10:59–81 (March 1982).

30-5 SUMMARY

If you have more cash than you currently need, you can invest the surplus in the money market. The principal money-market investments are:

- Treasury bills
- Certificates of deposit
- Swapped deposits
- London dollar certificates of deposit
- Commercial paper
- Bankers' acceptances
- Buy-back agreements

No two of these securities are exactly the same. If you want to make effective use of your cash, you need to be aware of the differences in their liquidity, risk, and yield. Table 30-1 summarizes the main features of money-market instruments. Figure 30-1 shows money-market rates as reported in *The Globe and Mail* for April 6, 1985.

Most corporations making short-term investments of excess cash buy one or more of the instruments described in Table 30-1. But there are many alternatives, including floating-rate preferreds. These securities are attractive for two reasons. First, corporations

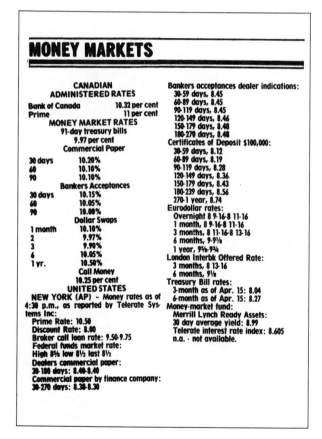

Figure 30-1   Short-term interest rates in April 1985.
Source: *The Globe and Mail*, Report on Business.

pay no tax on the dividends received. Second, the dividend paid moves up and down with changes in interest rates, so the preferred shares' prices are more or less stabilized. For many companies surplus cash is not a worry: their problem is to finance a temporary cash deficiency. One of the main sources of short-term funds is the unsecured bank loan. This is often taken out under a bank line of credit, which entitles the firm to borrow up to an agreed limit. The interest rate that banks charge on unsecured loans must be sufficient to cover not only the opportunity cost of capital for the loans but also the costs of running a loan department. As a result large, regular borrowers have found it cheaper to bypass the banking system and issue their own short-term unsecured debt. This debt is known as *commercial paper.*

If you ask to borrow more and more, you will eventually be asked to provide security for the loan. Sometimes this security consists of a floating lien on receivables and inventories, but more frequently you will be asked to pledge specific assets. The bank or finance company will take precautions to make sure that the collateral is properly identified and within its control. For example, when you borrow against receivables the bank must be informed of all sales of goods and the resulting accounts receivable must be pledged to the bank. As customers pay their bills, the money is paid into a special collateral account under the bank's control. Similarly, when you borrow against stocks of raw materials, the bank will insist that the goods are held by an independent warehouse company. As long as the bank holds the warehouse receipt for these goods, they cannot be released without the bank's permission. Loans secured on finished goods are usually made under a floor planning arrangement. In this case you will be required to sign a trust receipt that you are merely holding the specified goods in trust for the lender, and the lender will make periodic inspections to see that you are keeping your promise.

Bank loans with maturities exceeding one year are called *term loans.* The firm agrees to pay interest based on the bank's prime rate and to repay principal in regular instalments. Special patterns of principal payments over time can often be negotiated to meet the firm's special needs, however. Usually compensating balances are required.

Banks also provide medium-term financing through revolving credits, which guarantee the firm access to a line of credit. Revolving credits can often be converted into regular term loans.

FURTHER READING

For a detailed description of the money market and short-term lending opportunities in Canada and the United States, respectively, see:

S. Sarpkaya, *The Money Market in Canada*, 3rd ed., CCH Canadian Ltd., Don Mills, Ont., 1984.

M. Stigum, *The Money Market: Myth, Reality and Practice*, 2d ed., Richard D. Irwin, Inc., Homewood, Illinois, 1983.

A good book discussing the borrowing and lending practices of Canadian banks is:

J.A. Galbraith, *Canadian Banking*, Ryerson Press, Toronto, 1970.

QUIZ

1. Choose the investment that best fits the accompanying description.
    (*a*) Maturity often overnight: repurchase agreements or bankers' acceptances?
    (*b*) No secondary market: bankers' acceptances or swapped deposits?
    (*c*) Issued by banks: Treasury bills or certificates of deposit?
    (*d*) Can be deposited with the Bank of Canada by a money-market jobber: bankers' acceptances or Treasury bills?

(*e*) Used in country banking: savings deposits or Treasury bills?
(*f*) Discounted: bankers' acceptances or swapped deposits.
(*g*) Sold by auction: bearer notes or Treasury bills?

2. In late May 1984, 91-day Treasury bills were quoted at a yield of 11.35%.
   (*a*) What was the price of a 91-day T-bill?
   (*b*) What was the equivalent annually compounded yield?
   (*c*) If these T-bills were offered for sale in the United States, at what discount would they be quoted?

3. Complete the following passage by selecting the most appropriate terms from the following list: *floating lien, field warehouse, clean-up provision, commercial paper, floor planning, line of credit, prime rate, public warehouse, compensating balance, trust receipt, warehouse receipt, collateral, with recourse.*

   Companies with fluctuating capital needs often arrange a _____with their bank. To make sure that this facility is not used to provide permanent funds, the bank sometimes incorporates a _____. The interest on any borrowing is tied to the bank's _____. In addition the bank generally requires that the company keep a _____ on deposit at the bank. Some large companies bypass the banking system and issue their own short-term unsecured debt. This is called _____.
      Secured short-term loans are sometimes covered by a _____ on all receivables and inventory. Generally, however, the borrower pledges specific assets as _____. If these assets are insufficient to repay the debt, the borrower is liable for the deficiency. Therefore such loans are said to be _____. Warehouse loans are examples of secured short-term loans. The goods may be stored in a _____ or in a _____ that is established by the warehouse company on the borrower's premises. The warehouse company issues a _____ to the lender and releases the goods only on his or her instructions. Loans to automobile dealers are usually made on a different basis. The dealer holds the inventory on behalf of the lender and issues a _____. This arrangement is known as _____.

4. Consider three securities:
   (*a*) A floating-rate bond
   (*b*) A preferred share paying a fixed dividend
   (*c*) A floating-rate preferred
      A financial manager responsible for short-term investment of excess cash would probably choose the floating-rate preferred over *either* of the other two securities. Why? Explain briefly.

5. Here are six questions about term loans:
   (*a*) Who makes term loans?
   (*b*) Are compensating balances usually required?
   (*c*) Are term loans usually secured loans? That is, are they usually backed up by specific collateral?
   (*d*) How is the interest rate usually determined?
   (*e*) What is a balloon payment?
   (*f*) What is a revolving line of credit?

QUESTIONS AND PROBLEMS

1. Look up current interest rates offered by short-term investment alternatives. Suppose that your firm has $1 million excess cash to invest for the next two months. How would you invest this excess cash? How would your answer change if the excess cash is $5,000, $20,000, $100,000, or $100 million?

2. At one point in 1984, Government of Canada 90-day Treasury bills were quoted at 11.35%, 90-day bankers' acceptances were quoted at 11.6%, finance paper was quoted at 11.6%, and United States 90-day Treasury bills were quoted at 10.6%.
   (a) What was the effective yield of each of these investments, compounded annually?
   (b) Why were bankers' acceptances quoted at the same rate as finance paper, even though bankers' acceptances are guaranteed by the borrower *and* a bank?
   (c) Would you infer that Canadian or United States T-bills were a better investment? Why?

3. Interest rates on bank loans exceed rates on commercial paper. Why don't all firms issue commercial paper rather than borrowing from banks?

4. Do you think you could make money by setting up a firm that would (a) issue commercial paper and (b) relend money to businesses at a rate slightly higher than the commercial paper rate, but still less than the rate charged by banks?

5. Roy's Toys needs an extra $1 million in October to build up inventory for the Christmas season. First Commercial has offered to lend at 9% subject to a 20% compensating balance. The Bank of Anyprovince will lend at 11% with no strings attached. Which bank is offering the better deal? Why? Would your answer change if Roy's Toys already had a $100,000 normal working balance at First Commercial? (Assume in this case that the working balance can be used to cover part of the compensating balance.)

6. Axle Chemical Corporation's treasurer has forecast a $1 million cash deficit for the next quarter. However, there is only a 50% chance this deficit will actually occur. The treasurer estimates that there is a 20% probability the company will have no deficit at all, and a 30% probability that it will actually need $2 million in short-term financing. The company can either take out a 90-day unsecured loan at 1% per month or establish a line of credit costing 1% per month on the amount borrowed plus a commitment fee of $20,000. Both alternatives also require a 20% compensating balance for outstanding loans. If excess cash can be reinvested at 9%, which source of financing gives the lower expected cost?

7. Suppose that you are a banker responsible for approving corporate loans. Nine firms are seeking secured loans. They offer the following assets as collateral:
   (a) Firm A, a heating oil distributor, offers a tanker load of fuel oil in transit from the Middle East.
   (b) Firm B, a wine wholesaler, offers 1,000 cases of Beaujolais Nouveau, located in a field warehouse.
   (c) Firm C, a stationer, offers an account receivable for office supplies sold to the city of Regina.
   (d) Firm D, a bookstore, offers its entire inventory of 15,000 used books.
   (e) Firm E, a wholesale grocer, offers a boxcar full of bananas.
   (f) Firm F, an appliance dealer, offers his inventory of electric typewriters.
   (g) Firm G offers 100 ounces of gold.
   (h) Firm H, a government securities dealer, offers its portfolio of Treasury bills.
   (i) Firm I, a boat builder, offers a half-completed luxury yacht. The yacht will take four months more to complete.
   Which of these assets are most likely to be good collateral? Which are likely to be poor collateral? Explain.

8. Any one of the assets mentioned in the preceding question *could* be acceptable collateral under certain circumstances if appropriate safeguards were taken. What circumstances? What safeguards? Explain.

9. The first floating-rate preferreds were successfully issued at initial dividend yields *below* yields on Treasury bills. How was this possible? The preferreds were clearly

riskier than the bonds. What would you predict for the *long-run* relationship between yields on bills and floating-rate preferreds? (We say "long-run" to give time for all firms who will want to issue floating-rate preferreds to get around to doing so.)

10. Most floating-rate preferreds have both a "floor" and a "ceiling" on their dividend rate. (See Section 30-2, fn. 17.) How do these limits affect the behaviour of the *prices* of these securities as interest rates change? Why do you think the issuing companies included the limits in the first place?

11. Term loans usually require firms to pay a fluctuating interest rate. For example, the interest rate may be set at "1% above prime." The prime rate sometimes varies by several percentage points within a single year.

Suppose that your firm has decided to borrow $40 million for five years. It has three alternatives:

(a) Borrow from a bank at the prime rate, currently 10%. The proposed loan agreement requires no principal repayments until the loan matures in five years.

(b) Issue 26-week commercial paper, currently having a true yield of 9%. Since funds are required for five years, the commercial paper will have to be "rolled over" semiannually. That is, financing the $40 million requirement for five years will require ten successive commercial paper sales.

(c) Borrow from an insurance company at a fixed rate of 11%. As in the bank loan, no principal has to be repaid until the end of the five-year period.

What factors would you consider in analyzing these alternatives? Under what circumstances would you choose (a)? Under what circumstances would you choose (b) or (c)? (*Hint*: Don't forget Chapter 21.)

MERGERS, INTERNATIONAL FINANCE, AND PENSIONS

MERGERS

The extent of merger activity in Canada is remarkable. For example, Table 31-1 lists just a few of the more important mergers that occurred during the years 1979 through 1981. You can see that they involve big money. During periods of intense merger activity financial managers spend significant amounts of time either searching for firms to acquire or worrying whether some other firm will acquire them.

Table 31-1 Some important mergers, 1979–1981.

Acquiring Company	Selling Company	Payment (millions of dollars)
Dome Petroleum	Hudson's Bay Oil and Gas	$1,700 (U.S.)
Petro-Canada	Petrofina Canada, Inc.	1,460
Woodbridge Co.	The Bay	641
Dome Petroleum	Mesa Petroleum (Canada) Ltd.	640
Noranda Mines Ltd.	MacMillan Bloedel Ltd.	626
Olympia and York Investments Ltd.	Abitibi-Price Inc.	618
Sulpetro Ltd.	CanDel Oil Ltd.	546

Source: W.T. Stanbury and G.B. Reschenthaler, "Reforming Canadian Competition Policy: Once More unto the Breach," *The Canadian Business Law Journal,* **5**:381–437 (September 1981).

When you buy another company, you are making an investment, and the basic principles of capital investment decisions apply. You should go ahead with the purchase if it makes a net contribution to shareholders' wealth. But mergers are often awkward things to evaluate. First, you have to be careful to define benefits and costs properly. Second, buying a company is more complicated than buying a new machine; in particular, special tax, legal, and accounting issues must often be addressed. Third, integrating an entire company into your operations is much more complex than installing a single new machine; you need to be aware of some of the things that may go wrong. Finally, you need to have a general understanding of why mergers occur and who typically gains or loses as a result of them.

We will start by defining the benefits and costs of a merger. The following sections consider possible motives for mergers—some sensible and some dubious—and look at how the cost of a merger should be estimated. We will also comment on the legal, tax, and accounting problems encountered in putting two firms together.

We would have liked to close by presenting a general theory explaining mergers, but unfortunately no satisfactory theory exists. In our opinion, no one has a rational economic explanation for the wide fluctuations in aggregate merger activity. On the other hand, a good deal is known about the profitability of mergers. We will summarize this evidence.

In earlier chapters we have asserted that present values add. If this is so, a merger between two firms would not *in itself* make shareholders better or worse off. Unless there is some change in the firms' operations, the value of the combined firm would be equal to the sum of the values of the separate parts. In the appendix to this chapter we show you that present values *do* add as long as capital markets are perfect and investors' diversification opportunities are unrestricted.

31-1 DEFINING THE ECONOMIC GAINS AND COSTS OF MERGERS[1]

Suppose that you are the financial manager of firm A and that you wish to analyze the possible purchase of firm B. The first thing to think about is whether there is an *economic gain* from the merger. There is an economic gain *only if the two firms are worth more together than apart.* For example, if you think that the combined firm would be worth PV_{AB}, and that the separate firms are wort PV_A and PV_B, then[2]

$$GAIN = PV_{AB} - (PV_A + PV_B)$$

If this gain is positive, there is an economic justification for merger. But you also have to think about the *cost* of acquiring firm B. As we will show later, this can depend on the way the merger is financed. Let us begin, however, with the easy case in which payment is made in the form of cash. Then the cost of acquiring B is equal to the cash payment minus B's value as a separate entity. Thus

$$COST = CASH - PV_B$$

The net present value to A of a merger with B is measured by the difference between the gain and the cost. Therefore, you should go ahead with the merger if its net present value, defined as

$$NPV = GAIN - COST = PV_{AB} - (PV_A + PV_B) - (CASH - PV_B)$$

is positive.

We like to write the merger criterion in this way because it focuses attention on two distinct questions. When you estimate the benefit, you concentrate on whether there are any gains to be had from the merger. When you estimate cost, you are concerned with the division of these gains between the two companies.

An example may help make this clear. Firm A has a value of $2 million, B a value of $200,000. Merging the two would allow cost savings with a present value of $120,000. This is the gain to be had from the merger. Thus

$$PV_A = \$2,000,000$$

$$PV_B = \$200,000$$

$$GAIN = +\$120,000$$

$$PV_{AB} = \$2,320,000$$

---

[1]This chapter's definitions and interpretations of the gains and costs of merger generally follow those set out in S.C. Myers, "A Framework for Evaluating Mergers," in S.C. Myers (ed.), *Modern Developments in Financial Management*, Frederick A. Praeger, Inc., New York, 1976.

[2]We use PV here to refer to the value of the whole firm—that is, its assets, not just its common equity.

Suppose that B is bought for cash, say for $250,000. The cost of the merger is

$$COST = CASH - PV_B$$
$$= \$250,000 - \$200,000 = \$50,000$$

Note that the stockholders of firm B—the people on the other side of the transaction—are ahead by $50,000. *Their* gain is *your* cost. They have captured $50,000 of the $120,000 merger gain. Thus when we write down the NPV of the merger from A's viewpoint, we are really calculating that part of the gain that A's stockholders get to keep. The NPV of this merger therefore is

$$NPV = PV_{AB} - (PV_A + PV_B) - (CASH - PV_B)$$

Net gain to A's stockholders $\ =\ $ overall gain to merger

$$- \text{ part of gain captured by B's stockholders}$$

$$\$70,000 \ =\ \$120,000 - \$50,000$$

Just as a check, let's confirm that A's stockholders really come out $70,000 ahead. They start with a firm worth $PV_A = \$2$ million. They pay out $250,000 cash to B's stockholders and end up with a firm worth $2,320,000. Thus their net gain is

$$NPV = \text{wealth with merger} - \text{wealth without merger}$$
$$= (PV_{AB} - CASH) - PV_A$$
$$= (\$2,320,000 - \$250,000) - \$2,000,000$$
$$= +\$70,000$$

Note: Right and Wrong Ways to Estimate Benefits of Mergers

Some companies estimate the benefits of a merger by discounting detailed forecasts of the cash flows of the combined firm to give a figure for PV_{AB}. Then they deduct the current market values of the separate entities to give an estimate of the gain from the merger. There are two dangers in this procedure. First, current stock prices may already anticipate the gain. Second, and more important, you are likely to make large errors in your forecasts of the cash flows. Many mergers will, therefore, *appear* to offer gains just because you are overoptimistic in your forecasts of the cash flows. The important thing is to concentrate your attention on the *changes* in cash flow that would result from the merger. *Ask yourself why the two firms should be worth more together than apart.*[3]

31-2 SENSIBLE MOTIVES FOR MERGERS

Mergers are often categorized as *horizontal, vertical,* or *conglomerate.* A horizontal merger is one that takes place between two firms in the same line of business; most of the mergers around the turn of the century were of this type. A vertical merger is one in

---

[3]The same advice holds when you are contemplating the *sale* of part of your business. There is no point saying to yourself "This is an unprofitable business and should be sold." Unless the buyer can run the business better than you can, the price you receive will reflect the poor prospects.

which the buyer expands forward in the direction of the ultimate consumer or back toward the source of raw materials. A conglomerate merger involves companies in unrelated lines of business. The distribution of types of mergers in Canada during 1974 was 68% horizontal, 9% vertical, and 23% conglomerate.[4]

With these distinctions in mind, let us consider motives for mergers—that is, reasons two firms may be worth more together than apart.

Economies of Scale

Just as most of us believe that we would be happier if only we were a little richer, so every manager seems to believe that his or her firm would be more competitive if only it were just a little bigger. The quest for these *economies of scale*[5] is probably one of the most prevalent motives for mergers. For example, in postwar Europe governments and companies were alarmed at the challenge from rival American corporations. They rushed to put together larger groups of firms. New steel and chemical groups were created that could handle very large scale investments; electronics and computer firms were combined to spread research and development costs over larger sales and assets bases; automobile groups were formed to achieve the production and marketing economies enjoyed by large American automobile manufacturers, and so on.

Economies of scale are the natural goal of horizontal mergers. But such economies have been claimed in conglomerate mergers too. The architects of these mergers have pointed to the economies that come from sharing central services such as office management and accounting, financial control, executive development, and top-level management.

There are innumerable examples of possible economies of scale. But merging isn't always the best way of achieving them. It is always easier to buy another business than it is to integrate it with yours afterwards. Some of those European combinations still operate as a collection of separate and sometimes competing operations with different production facilities, research efforts, and marketing forces. Even economies in central services may be elusive. The complicated structure of conglomerate companies may actually increase the administrative staff. And top-level managers of conglomerates often find that their general skills are not easily applied to the specialized problems of individual subsidiaries.

Economies of Vertical Integration

Vertical mergers seek economies in vertical integration. Large industrial companies commonly like to gain as much control as possible over the production process by expanding back toward the output of the raw material and forward to the ultimate consumer. One way to achieve this is to merge with a supplier or a customer.

One reason for vertical integration is that it makes coordination and administration easier. We can illustrate by a somewhat extreme example. Think of an airline that does not own any planes. If it schedules a flight from Toronto to Vancouver, it sells tickets and then rents a plane for that flight from a separate company. This strategy might work on a small scale, but it would be an administrative nightmare for a major carrier. There would be hundreds of flights and rental agreements daily. Moreover, the

---

[4]Minister of Supply and Services Canada, *Report of the Royal Commission on Corporate Concentration*, March 1978, p. 147, Table 6.4.

[5]Economies of scale are enjoyed when the average unit cost of production goes down as production increases. One way of achieving economies of scale is by spreading fixed costs over a larger volume of production.

---

agreements could not be independently negotiated. For example, the airline might have to make sure that the plane from Toronto shows up in Vancouver in time to be rented for a subsequent flight from Vancouver to Calgary. In view of these difficulties, it is not surprising that all major airlines have integrated backwards, away from the consumer, by buying and flying airplanes rather than patronizing rent-a-plane companies.

Sometimes technology or expertise picked up at one stage of production may be useful at another stage. For example, a producer of exotic metal alloys might merge with a fabricator if the producer's special knowledge improves the fabricator's efficiency.

This is far from a complete discussion of the advantages of vertical integration—we have merely given examples of why it may make sense. If there are economies of vertical integration, a merger is one way to achieving them.

Eliminating Inefficiencies

There are always firms whose earnings could be increased by better operating or financial management. Such firms are natural targets for acquisition by other firms with better management.

If this motive is important, one would expect that *poorly* performing firms would tend to be targets for acquisition. This seems to be the case. Ellert, for example, found that investors in firms that were subsequently acquired earned relatively low rates of return over several years before the merger.[6] Apparently many of these firms fell on bad times and were subsequently rescued by a merger.

Of course a merger is not the only way to improve management. But it may be the only simple and practical way. Managers are naturally reluctant to fire or demote themselves, and stockholders of large public firms do not usually have much *direct* influence on how their firm is run or who runs it.[7]

Unused Tax Shields

Sometimes a firm may have potential tax shields but not have the profits to take advantage of them. For example, after the expropriation of its Cuban sugar plantations, Bangor Punta had substantial tax-loss carry-overs, which it could not use. It therefore combined with other firms that were generating taxable profits so that the tax-loss carry-over could be used.[8]

---

[6]J.C. Ellert, "Mergers, Antitrust Law Enforcement and Stockholder Returns," *Journal of Finance*, 31:715–732 (May 1976), p. 728. These firms' fortunes began to improve about seven months, on the average, before the merger announcement. The higher returns over this period anticipated the premium paid to selling firms. See Section 31-7.

[7]It is difficult to assemble a large enough block of stockholders to effectively challenge management and the incumbent board of directors at the firm's annual meeting. Stockholders can have enormous indirect influence, however. Their displeasure shows up in the firm's stock price. A low stock price may, for example, encourage a takeover bid by another firm.

[8]Mergers undertaken *just* to use tax-loss carry-forwards may be challenged by Revenue Canada, and the use of the carry-forwards may be denied. Suppose that you own a profitable firm. You find another company on the ropes, with large cumulative losses. If you bought up that company and then liquidated its assets, Revenue Canada would probably regard the tax-loss carry-forwards as liquidated also and not allow you to use them to reduce your taxable income. But the tax rules are funny: if the company on the rocks bought *you*, then gradually and discreetly closed down its own business and continued with yours, Revenue Canada may accept the deal and let it use the tax-loss carry-forwards.

Mergers as a Use for Surplus Funds

Here's another tax argument for mergers. Suppose that your firm is in a mature industry. It is generating a substantial amount of cash, but it has few profitable investment opportunities. It could invest the surplus cash in marketable securities, but that is at best a zero-NPV investment. It could pay an extra dividend, but that would increase the amount of income tax paid by its shareholders. Or it could return the funds to its shareholders by repurchasing its own stock, but that's not a good solution if Revenue Canada says that the repurchase is a disguised dividend payment.

If for some reason the firm decides not to purchase its own shares, it can instead purchase someone else's. Thus, there is a rationale for acquisitions *financed by cash* if internal investments yield less than the opportunity cost of capital. That is why firms with a surplus of cash and a shortage of good investment opportunities often turn to mergers as a way of redeploying capital. If they do not do so, someone else may take them over and redeploy the capital for them. Firms with excess cash are widely regarded as natural targets for acquisition.

Combining Complementary Resources

Many small firms are acquired by large ones that can provide missing ingredients necessary for the overall firm's success. The small firm may have a unique product, for example, but lack the engineering and sales organizations necessary to produce and market it on a large scale. It may be quicker and cheaper to merge with a firm that already has ample engineering and sales talent than for the small firm to develop that talent from scratch. The two firms have *complementary resources*—each has what the other needs—and so it can make sense for them to merge. The two firms are worth more together than apart because each acquires something it does not have and gets it cheaper than it would acting on its own. Also, the merger may open up opportunities that neither firm would pursue otherwise.

Of course two large firms may also merge because they have complementary resources. But we think that real gains of this nature occur more often when small firms are acquired by large ones.

31-3   SOME DUBIOUS REASONS FOR MERGERS

The benefits that we have described so far all make economic sense. Other arguments that are sometimes given for mergers are more dubious. Let us look at some of the dubious ones.

Diversification

We have suggested that the shareholders of a cash-rich company may prefer to see it use that cash for acquisitions rather than distribute it as extra dividends. That is why we often see cash-rich firms in stagnant industries merging their way into fresh woods and pastures new.

But what about diversification as an end in itself? It is obvious that diversification reduces risk. Isn't that a gain from merging?

The trouble with that argument is that diversification is easier and cheaper for the stockholder than for the corporation. No one has shown that investors pay premiums for diversified firms—in fact, discounts are common. For example, Kaiser Industries was dissolved as a United States holding company in 1977 because its diversification apparently *subtracted* from its value. Kaiser Industries' main assets were shares of Kaiser Steel, Kaiser Aluminium, and Kaiser Cement. These were independent companies, and the stock of each was publicly traded. Thus you could value Kaiser Industries by looking at the stock prices of Kaiser Steel, Kaiser Aluminium, and Kaiser Cement. But Kaiser Industries' stock was selling at a price reflecting a significant *discount* from the value of its investment in these companies. The discount vanished when Kaiser Industries revealed its plan to sell its holdings and distribute the proceeds to its stockholders.

Why the discount existed in the first place is a puzzle. But the example at least shows that diversification does not increase value.[9]

There are exceptional cases in which personal diversification may be more expensive than corporate diversification. For example, perhaps you were lucky enough to invest in IBM in 1955. Since then the price of the stock has appreciated dramatically. If you just held on to your investment, you may now have a very undiversified portfolio. You know that is not a good idea. On the other hand, if you sell any of your IBM stock, you will be liable for a substantial capital gains tax. IBM would help you if it bought, say, a copper mining firm or other firms in areas unrelated to IBM's main business. Then by holding IBM stock you would hold a somewhat diversified portfolio.

If you are the president and majority owner of a closely held corporation, you are likely to have exactly the same problem. You may be wealthy, but you have all your eggs in that one corporate basket. You could sell off a substantial part of your shares but this could result in a large liability for capital gains tax. It may be better to merge with a firm in another line of business, and hold on to the shares of that firm. By so doing you will have your eggs in two baskets rather than one.

The Bootstrap Game: Mergers and Earnings per Share[10]

During the 1960s some conglomerate companies made acquisitions that offered no evident economic gains. Nevertheless the conglomerates' aggressive acquisition strategy produced several years of rising earnings per share and stock prices. To see how this can happen, let us look at the acquisition of Muck and Slurry by the well-known conglomerate World Enterprises.

The position before the merger is set out in the first two columns of Table 31-2. Notice that because Muck and Slurry has relatively poor growth prospects, its stock

Table 31-2   Impact of merger on market value and earnings per share of World Enterprises.

	World Enterprises (before merger)	Muck and Slurry	World Enterprises (after acquiring Muck and Slurry)
1. Earnings per share	$2.00	$2.00	$2.67
2. Price per share	$40.00	$20.00	$40.00
3. Price-earnings ratio	20	10	15
4. Number of shares	100,000	100,000	150,000
5. Total earnings	$200,000	$200,000	$400,000
6. Total market value	$4,000,000	$2,000,000	$6,000,000
7. Current earnings per dollar invested in stock (line 1 divided by line 2)	$0.05	$0.10	$0.067

Note: When World Enterprises purchases Muck and Slurry, there are no gains. Therefore, total earnings and total market value should be unaffected by the merger. But earnings *per share* increase. World Enterprises only issues 50,000 of its shares (priced at $40) to acquire the 100,000 Muck and Slurry shares (priced at $20).

[9]Appendix 31-1 provides a simple proof that corporate diversification does not affect value in perfect capital markets as long as investors' diversification opportunities are unrestricted.

[10]The discussion of the bootstrap game follows S.C. Myers, "A Framework for Evaluating Mergers," op. cit.

sells at a lower price-earnings ratio than World Enterprises (line 3). The merger, we assume, produces no economic benefits, and so the firms should be worth exactly the same together as apart. The market value of World Enterprises after the merger should be equal to the sum of the separate values of the two firms (line 6).

Since World Enterprises stock is selling for double the price of Muck and Slurry stock (line 2), World Enterprises can acquire the 100,000 Muck and Slurry shares for 50,000 of its own shares. Thus World will have 150,000 shares outstanding after the merger.

Total earnings double as a result of the merger (line 5), but the number of shares increases by only 50%. Earnings *per share* rise from $2.00 to $2.67. We call this a *bootstrap effect* because there is no real gain created by the merger and no increase in the two firms' combined value. Since stock price is unchanged, the price-earnings ratio falls (line 3).

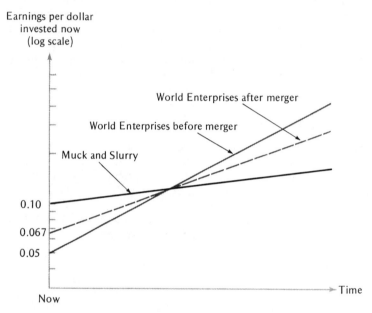

Figure 31-1 Effects of merger on earnings growth. By merging with Muck and Slurry, World Enterprises increases current earnings but accepts a slower rate of future growth. Its stockholders should be no better or worse off unless investors are fooled by the bootstrap effect.
Source: S.C. Myers, "A Framework for Evaluating Mergers," in S.C. Myers (ed.), *Modern Developments in Financial Management*, Frederick A. Praeger, Inc., New York, 1976, fig. 1, p. 639.

Figure 31-1 illustrates what is going on here. Before the merger $1 invested in World Enterprises bought 5 cents of current earnings and rapid growth prospects. On the other hand, $1 invested in Muck and Slurry bought 10 cents of current earnings but slower growth prospects. If the *total* market value is not altered by the merger, then $1 invested in the merged firm gives 6.7 cents of immediate earnings. Thus, World Enterprises' shareholders see a jump in immediate earnings but slower growth, and the Muck and Slurry shareholders get lower immediate earnings but faster growth. Neither side gains or loses provided everybody understands the deal.

The art of the financial manipulator is to ensure that the market does *not* understand the deal. Suppose that investors are fooled by the exuberant confidence of the president of World Enterprises and by plans to introduce modern management techniques into the Earth Sciences Division (formerly known as Muck and Slurry). They could easily mistake the 33% increase in earnings per share for real growth. If they do, the price of World Enterprises' stock rises and the shareholders of both companies receive something for nothing.

You should now see how to play the bootstrap, or "chain letter," game. Suppose that you manage a company enjoying a high price-earnings ratio. The reason it is high is that investors anticipate rapid growth in future earnings. You achieve this growth not by capital investment, product improvement, or increased operating efficiency, but by purchasing slow-growing firms with low price-earnings ratios. The long-run result will be slower growth and a depressed price-earnings ratio, but in the short run earnings per share can increase dramatically. If this fools investors, you may be able to achieve the higher earnings per share without suffering a decline in your price-earnings ratio. But in order to *keep* fooling investors, you must continue to expand by merger *at the same compound rate*. Obviously you cannot do this forever; one day expansion must slow down or stop. Then earnings growth will cease, and your house of cards will fall.

This kind of game is not played much now, after investors' bitter experience with it in the 1960s. But there is still a widespread belief that you should not acquire companies with higher price-earnings ratios (*P/E*s) than your own. Here's an example from the journal *Long Range Planning*:

> ITT's low PE ratio made the acquisition of typical growth companies, such as electronics manufacturers, too costly. ITT therefore decided to move into the service industry where PE ratios were lower, so that acquisitions by an exchange of stock could be accomplished without watering down its own EPS. . . . [ITT] constantly surveys the market for new acquisition prospects which could provide an opportunity for entry into a growth market at interesting PE ratios.[11]

But you know better than to believe that low-*P/E* stocks are cheap and high-*P/E* stocks are dear. If life were as simple as that, we should all be wealthy by now. Beware of false prophets who suggest that you can appraise mergers on the basis of their immediate impact on earnings per share.

Lower Financing Costs

You often hear it said that merged firms are able to borrow more cheaply than the separate units. In part this is true. We have already seen (in Section 15-4) that there are significant economies of scale in making new issues. Therefore, if firms can make fewer, larger security issues by merging, there is a genuine saving.

But when people say that borrowing costs are lower for the merged firm, they usually mean something more than lower issue costs. They mean that when two firms merge, they can borrow at lower interest rates than they could separately. This of course is exactly what we should expect in a well-functioning bond market. While the two firms are separate, they do not guarantee each other's debt; if one fails, the bondholder in that company cannot ask the other for money. But after the merger each enterprise effectively does guarantee the other's debt—if one part of the business fails, the bondholders can still take their money out of the other part. Because these mutual guarantees make the debt less risky, lenders demand a lower interest rate.

Does the lower interest rate mean a net gain to the merger? Not necessarily. Compare the following two situations:

1. *Separate issues*: Firm A and firm B each make a $50 million bond issue.

2. *Single issue*: Firms A and B merge and the new firm AB makes a single $100 million issue.

---

[11]B. Hako, "Strategies for Diversification," *Long Range Planning*, 5:65–69 (June 1972).

Of course AB would pay a lower interest rate, other things being equal. But it does not make sense for A and B to merge just to get that lower rate. The firms' shareholders do gain from the lower rate but they lose by having to guarantee each other's debt. In other words, they get the lower interest rate only by giving bondholders better protection. There is no *net* gain.

In Sections 20-2 and 21-4 we showed that

Bond value = bond value (assuming no chance of default)

  − value of shareholders' (put) option to default

Merger increases bond value (or reduces the interest payments necessary to support a *given* bond value) only by reducing the value of stockholders' options to default. In other words, the value of the default option for AB's $100 million issue is less than the combined values of the two default options on A and B's separate $50 million issues.

Now suppose that A and B each borrow $50 million and *then* merge. If the merger is a surprise, it will be a happy surprise for the bondholders. The bonds they thought were guaranteed by one of the two firms end up guaranteed by both. The stockholders lose, other things being equal, because they have given bondholders better protection but have received nothing for it.

There is one situation in which mergers can create value by making debt safer. In Section 18-3 we described the choice of an optimal debt ratio as a trade-off of the value of tax shields on interest payments made by the firm against the present value of possible costs of financial distress due to borrowing too much. Merging decreases the probability of financial distress, other things being equal. If it allows increased borrowing, and increased value from the interest tax shields, there will be a net gain to the merger.[12]

31-4 ESTIMATING THE COST OF A MERGER

Estimating Cost When the Merger is Financed by Cash

The cost of a merger is the premium that the buyer pays for the selling firm over its value as a separate entity. It is a straightforward problem to estimate cost as long as the merger is financed by cash. However, it is important to bear in mind that if investors *expect* A to acquire B, the market value of B may be a poor measure of its value as a separate entity. Thus it may help to rewrite our formula for cost as

$$\text{COST} = (\text{CASH} - MV_B) + (MV_B - PV_B)$$

  = premium paid over market value of B

  + difference between market value of B and its value as a separate entity

---

[12]This merger rationale was first suggested by W.G. Lewellen, "A Pure Financial Rationale for the Conglomerate Merger," *Journal of Finance*, **26**:521–537 (May 1971). If you want to see some of the controversy and discussion this idea led to, look at R.C. Higgins and L.D. Schall, "Corporate Bankruptcy and Conglomerate Merger," *Journal of Finance*, **30**:93–114 (March 1975), and D. Galai and R.W. Masulis, "The Option Pricing Model and the Risk Factor of Stock," *Journal of Financial Economics*, **3**:53–81, esp. pp. 66–69 (January–March 1976).

This is one of the few places in this book where we have drawn an important distinction between market value (MV) and the true or "intrinsic" value (PV) of the firm as a separate entity. The problem here is not that the market value of B is wrong, but that it may not be the value of firm B as a separate entity. Potential investors in B's stock will see two possible outcomes and two possible values:

Outcome	Value of B's Stock
1. No merger	PV_B: Value per share of B as a separate firm
2. Merger occurs	PV_B *plus* some part of the benefits of the merger

If the second outcome is possible, the stock price we observe for B will overstate PV_B. This is exactly what *should* happen in a competitive capital market. Unfortunately it complicates the task of a financial manager evaluating a merger.

Here is an example. Suppose that just before the merger announcement we observe the following:

	Firm A	Firm B
Market price per share	$75	$15
Number of shares	100,000	60,000
Market value of firm	$7,500,000	$900,000

Firm A intends to pay $1,200,000 cash for B. If B's market price reflects only its value as a separate entity, then

$$COST = (CASH - MV_B) + (MV_B - PV_B)$$
$$= \$300,000 + 0 = \$300,000$$

However, suppose that B's share price has already risen $2 because of rumours of a favourable merger offer. Then

$$COST = (CASH - MV_B) + (MV_B - PV_B)$$
$$= \$300,000 + \$120,000 = \$420,000$$

Notice that if the market made a mistake and the market value of B were *less* than its true value as a separate entity, the cost would be negative. In other words, B would be a *bargain* and the merger would be worthwhile from A's point of view, even if the two firms are worth no more together than apart.[13] Of course A's stockholders' gain would be B's stockholders' loss, because B is being sold for less than its true value.

Firms have made acquisitions just because their managers believed they had spotted a company whose intrinsic value was not fully appreciated by the stock market. However, we know from the evidence on market efficiency that as often as not cheap stocks turn out to be expensive. It is not easy for outsiders, whether investors or managers, to find firms that are truly undervalued by the market.

---

[13]Of course, if the shares are bargain-priced, A doesn't need a merger to profit by its special knowledge. It can just buy up B's shares on the open market and hold them passively, waiting for other investors to wake up to B's true value.

If firm A is wise, it will not go ahead with a merger if the cost exceeds the gain. Conversely, firm B will not consent to a merger if it thinks the cost is negative, for a negative cost to A means a negative gain to B. This gives us a range of possible cash payments that would allow the merger to take place. Whether the payment is at the top or the bottom of this range depends on the relative bargaining power of the two participants. For example, if A makes an acquisition solely in order to use a tax-loss carry-over, then it could equally well merge with B, C, D, or X; firm B has nothing special to offer, and its management is in no position to demand a large fraction of the gains. In this case, the cost of the merger to A is likely to be relatively low.

Estimating Cost When the Acquisition is Financed by Stock

Estimating cost is more complicated when a merger is financed by an exchange of shares. Suppose that firm A offers 16,000 shares instead of $1,200,000 cash. Since A's share price before the announcement is $75 and B's market values is $900,000, the cost *appears* to be

$$\text{APPARENT COST} = 16,000 \times \$75 - \$900,000 = \$300,000$$

However, the apparent cost may not equal the true cost. There are three reasons for this. First, B's value as a separate entity may not be $900,000. Second, A's value as a separate entity may not be $7,500,000. Third, because B's shareholders are partners in the merged firm, they will receive some part of the merger gains. In other words, the value of the shares paid over to B's shareholders depends on the value of the combined firms. If B's shareholders end up owning the fraction x of the combined firms, the true cost is

$$\text{COST} = x\text{PV}_{AB} - \text{PV}_B$$

That is, $x\text{PV}_{AB}$ is the value of what B's stockholders get, and PV_B is the value of what they give up. Their net gain is their share of the merger benefits and also the cost of the merger from the viewpoint of A's stockholders.

In our example, B's shareholders will receive 16,000 shares. Thus their share of the merged firms will be

$$x = \frac{16,000}{100,000 + 16,000} = 0.138$$

Suppose that the market values just before the announcement of the merger accurately reflect the firm's separate values ($\text{MV}_A = \text{PV}_A$ and $\text{MV}_B = \text{PV}_B$). Assume that the merger produces gains with a present value of $400,000. Then

$$\text{PV}_{AB} = \text{PV}_A + \text{PV}_B + \text{GAIN} = \$7,500,000 + \$900,000 + \$400,000$$
$$= \$8,800,000$$

and

$$\text{TRUE COST} = x\text{PV}_{AB} - \text{PV}_B = 0.138(\$8,800,000) - \$900,000$$
$$= \$314,000$$

The reason the true cost exceeds the apparent cost is that stock prices observed *before* the merger is announced do not reflect the merger gains or their division between A's stockholders and B's stockholders. Suppose that we calculate share prices and market values *after* the merger is negotiated and announced.

	Firm A	Firm B
1. Proportions of ownership in merged firms	0.862	0.138
2. Market value (line 1 times PV_{AB}, PV_{AB} = $8,800,000)	$7,586,000	$1,214,000
3. Number of shares	100,000	60,000
4. Price per share	$75.86	$20.23

With this information we can easily calculate the true cost, either as the difference between the value of firm A shares offered and the value of B as a separate entity,

$$COST = 16,000(\$75.86) - \$900,000 = \$314,000$$

or as the gain in the market value of firm B following the merger announcement:

$$COST = MV_B \text{ (after announcement)} - MV_B \text{ (before announcement)}$$
$$= 60,000(\$20.23) - \$900,000$$
$$= \$314,000$$

Unfortunately you cannot do these calculations until *after* the announcement of the merger. In negotiating the merger, you have to estimate its cost *before* it is announced. That is why you need the formula

$$COST = xPV_{AB} - PV_B$$

We can now understand the key distinction between cash and stock as financing instruments. If cash is offered, the cost of the merger is unaffected by the merger gains. If stock is offered, cost depends on the gains, because they must be shared with B's owners.

Stock financing also mitigates the effect of overvaluation or undervaluation of either firm. Suppose, for example, that A overestimates B's value as a separate entity, perhaps because rumours of a merger have already driven up B's stock price. Thus A makes too generous an offer. Other things being equal, A's stockholders are better off if it is a stock offer rather than a cash offer. With a stock offer, the inevitable bad news about B's true value will fall partly on the shoulders of B's stockholders.

31-5   THE MECHANICS OF A MERGER

Anti-combines Law and the Foreign Investment Review Act

One subject on which you may need early advice is federal anti-combines law. In Canada, the Combines Investigation Act safeguards public interest by making it an indictable offense to merge (combine) two or more companies in a way that reduces or potentially reduces competition within an industry. While the purpose of the Act is well-intended, the enforcement of the anti-combines provisions has not been effective. In fact, the *Proposals for a New Competition for Canada, Second Stage* (1977) notes that there ". . . has never been [in Canada] a conviction after a full trial which was not reversed on appeal." For example, in the early 1970s K.C. Irving Limited went about acquiring all five of the English-language daily newspapers in New Brunswick. Naturally such an action did not go without notice, and Irving was convicted on a merger charge in 1974. On appeal, however, the Supreme Court of Canada said that the law had not been violated, and it reversed the decision.

In the United States the enforcement of the federal legislation governing the reduction of competition (that is, antitrust law) has been more effective. The principal weapon in the American crusade against the ogre of monopoly is the Clayton Act. It forbids the acquisition of assets or stock where the effect *"may be* substantially to lessen competition, or to *tend* to create monopoly." The Federal Trade Commission (FTC) is also empowered to prohibit "unfair methods of competition" and "unfair or deceptive practices." Thus, antitrust law can be forced in one of two ways: by a civil suit by the United States Justice Department, or in a proceeding by the FTC. Both the Justice Department and the FTC have the right to seek injunctions delaying a merger, and in many cases this has been sufficient to ensure its failure.

Aside from the public's concern about reduced competition, Canadians are also sensitive to foreign takeovers of Canadian businesses. The Foreign Investment Review Act prohibits a foreign takeover if it is not of significant benefit to Canadians, and Investment Canada, formerly called the Foreign Investment Review Agency (FIRA), is assigned to review and approve or disapprove each proposal. Occasionally, it may give conditional approval of a takeover as was the case in the Chevron takeover with Gulf Oil. In early 1984 Chevron Corp. of the United States acquired Gulf Canada Ltd. by virtue of its $13.2 billion (U.S.) takeover of Gulf Oil Corp. The transfer of Gulf Canada control was allowed with the condition that Chevron sell Gulf Canada to a Canadian buyer at a fair price by the end of April 1985. In March of 1985 Olympia and York Development Limited made its first offer for Gulf Canada, and by the end of May the final details were arranged: Olympia and York acquired Gulf Canada from Chevron for $3 billion.

The Form of Acquisition

Let us suppose that you have been advised that the purchase of company B would not be challenged on anti-combines grounds. The next thing you will want to consider is the best way to effect the acquisition. You have the following choices.

Statutory Amalgamation or Merger We have been using the term *merger* to indicate *any* combination of two companies, but this convention is too broad in the legal sense. In Canada, a merger or, more precisely, a *statutory amalgamation* refers to the case where all of the assets and all of the liabilities of the selling company are transferred to, and absorbed by, the buying corporation, and where the selling company disappears as a separate entity. It also applies to the case where an entirely new corporation is formed and both selling entities disappear.[14]

In a merger the buyer automatically assumes *all* the assets and *all* the liabilities of the seller, and so the mechanics of a merger are comparatively simple. This is an advantage. For example, it is not necessary to transfer separate title to each individual asset.

However, there are drawbacks to merger. The automatic assumption of liabilities places a greater onus on the buyer to ensure that no liabilities have been overlooked; after the two firms have merged, there is no one to whom the buyer can complain if a mistake has been made. The complete absorption of the seller also requires broad agreement among shareholders. Under the various provincial Business Corporations

---

[14]In the United States, the term *merger* refers to the case where one of the firms continues to exist and the term *amalgamation* or consolidation is reserved for the case where an entirely new entity is formed.

Acts, a merger must have the approval of a required majority (usually two-thirds or three-quarters) of the stockholders. Even with majority approval, however, the acts also provide dissenting shareholders with the right to challenge the merger agreement in court if they feel the price per share is below "fair value."

Acquisition of Stock The essential feature of a merger is that the buyer acquires all the seller's assets and all its liabilities. An alternative procedure is for the buyer to purchase the seller's stock in exchange for cash, shares, or other securities issued by the buyer.[15] Generally speaking, the mechanics of such an exchange are simple. However, since the buyer's post-purchase holdings of the selling company's shares are expected to exceed 20% of the voting shares, the purchase is labelled a "take-over bid" and must comply with provincial Securities Act rules that are designed to ensure equitable treatment of the selling firm's shareholders.[16] In Ontario, for example, the take-over bid rules require, among other things, that the buying company send the details of the take-over bid to all shareholders of the selling company.

There is one major disadvantage in acquiring a firm by buying up its stock. As long as Aunt Agatha holds out and refuses to sell her ten shares, the two businesses cannot be completely integrated. Complete integration requires a further step—for example, a formal amalgamation.

Acquisition of Assets A third approach is to buy the seller's assets. Payment is made to the selling *firm* (not directly to its stockholders). The payment can be in the form of cash, the buyer's shares, or other securities issued by the buyer. The selling company can then, if it chooses, dissolve itself. If it does so, the receipts from the sale of its assets are paid out to its stockholders.

In this approach the buyer acquires individual, specific assets. (The buyer may also assume specific liabilities.) Thus the buyer can acquire only part of the seller's business, and can be more confident of *not* acquiring a hidden liability. Also, since the buyer is acquiring property rather than a share interest in property, the buyer does not have to worry about having minority shareholders. Although federal and provincial business corporation acts go some way in protecting shareholders who are unhappy about the sale of assets, they do not require the same degree of acquiescence by shareholders as they do in mergers. For example, there is usually no need for specific approval from the buyer's shareholders, and typically it is necessary to obtain only a 50% vote of the seller's shareholders. Neither group of shareholders can force an independent valuation of the acquired assets.

But the acquisition of assets also has disadvantages. First, the courts may hold that a particular exchange is effectively a merger and, therefore, require additional attention to the rights of the selling shareholders. A second problem is that transferring assets individually is likely to create additional legal and administrative costs.

Some Tax Considerations

An acquisition may be either taxable or tax-free. In a taxable acquisition, the selling stockholders are treated, for tax purposes, as having *sold* their shares, and they must report any capital gains or losses on their income tax forms. In a tax-free acquisition, the selling shareholders are viewed as *exchanging* their old shares for essentially similar new ones; no capital gains or losses are recognized.

---

[15]S. Martin, "Business Combinations in Canada: 1960–1968," in D. Morin and W. Chippindale, (eds.), *Acquisitions and Mergers in Canada*, Methuen, Toronto, 1970 reported that 80% of acquisitions in Canada were through acquisition of shares.

[16]All of the rules regarding take-over bids in Ontario are presented in sections 88 through 100 of the Securities Act, 1978 in *Ontario Securities Legislation*, CCH Clearinghouse Limited, 1980.

The tax status of the acquisition also affects the taxes paid by the firm afterwards. After a tax-free acquisition, the firm is taxed as if the two firms had always been together. In a taxable acquisition, the assets of the selling firm are revalued and the depreciation deductible for tax purposes is recalculated.

A very simple example will illustrate these distinctions. In 1985 Captain B forms Seacorp, which purchases a fishing boat for $300,000. The boat is depreciated for tax purposes over 20 years on a straight-line basis (no salvage value). Thus annual depreciation is $300,000/20 = $15,000, and in 1995 the boat has a net book value of $150,000.

But in 1995 Captain B finds that, owing to inflation, careful maintenance, and good times in the fishing industry, the boat is really worth $280,000. In addition, Seacorp holds $50,000 of marketable securities.

Now suppose that Captain B sells the firm to Baycorp for $330,000. The possible tax consequences of the acquisition are as shown in the accompanying table.

	Taxable	Tax-Free
1. Impact on Captain B	Captain B must recognize a $30,000 capital gain	Capital gain can be deferred until Captain B sells the Baycorp shares
2. Impact on Baycorp	Boat is revalued at $280,000; annual depreciation increases to $280,000/10 = $28,000 (assuming ten years of remaining life)	Boat's value remains at $150,000, and depreciation at $15,000 per year

Captain B is better off with a tax-free deal, because capital gains taxes can be deferred. Baycorp, on the other hand, should prefer a taxable deal because depreciation tax shields are higher.

It should be clear from these remarks that tax-free status is not an unmitigated blessing and that there can often be a divergence of interests between the buying corporation and the selling stockholders. The latter will generally prefer a tax-free arrangement if they are showing a profit on their original investment; they will prefer a taxable arrangement if they are showing a loss. Correspondingly, the buying corporation will prefer a taxable arrangement if the current values of depreciable assets are substantially larger than their depreciable values in the hands of the seller.

Requirements for Tax-Free Status

We have not yet told you what determines whether an acquisition is tax-free. The basic requirement is that the selling stockholders receive common or preferred shares in the surviving corporation. The detailed rules for each form of acquisition are somewhat more complex, but they are sketched below:[17]

- **Amalgamation or merger**   To establish tax-free status for a merger, all of the property of the selling corporation must become the property of the buying corporation; all of the liabilities of the selling corporation must become the liabilities of the buying corporation; and, all of the shareholders of the selling corporation must become shareholders in the buying corporation.
- **Acquisition of stock**   When the shares of the selling firm are acquired, it will be treated as tax-free only if payment is *entirely* in the form of the buying corporation's

---

[17]For a readable discussion of the roll-over tax treatment of amalgamations and share-for-share exchanges, see Chapter 15 of I.G. Riehl and G.W. Riehl, *Incorporation and Income Tax in Canada*, CCH Canadian Limited, 1984.

shares and only if, immediately after the acquisition, the buyer has 10% of the voting shares of the selling corporation. Also, prior to the exchange, the buying and selling companies must be dealing with each other "at arm's length," and the selling company must not control or own more than 50% of the shares of the buying company.

- **Acquisition of assets** A tax-free exchange of assets for shares is a trickier proposition, but, under certain conditions,[18] it may be possible. Again, the payment must be entirely in the form of the buying corporation's shares.

The discussion above is the last point in this chapter where we will need to distinguish the three ways of arranging a combination of two firms. Henceforth we will relapse into using the word *merger* in its everyday sense, to refer to any combination of two firms into one.

The Tender Offer

The arrangement of a merger usually takes place by amicable negotiations between the managements of the buyer and seller. However, if the seller's management objects to a merger, the would-be buyer (firm A) can go over the heads of firm B's recalcitrant officers and appeal directly to its stockholders. There are two ways of doing this. First, A can ask for the right to vote the shares of B's stockholders at B's next annual meeting. This is called a *proxy fight*, because the right to vote someone else's shares is called a *proxy*.

Proxy fights are expensive and difficult to win. The alternative strategy is to make a *tender offer* directly to B's shareholders, who will normally tender (agree to sell) their shares to A if the tender offer is generous enough. If A can accumulate 50% of the voting stock of B, then A has control of B and the ability to force a merger.

But managers threatened by tender offers do not always take them lying down. In fact, managers often display enormous ingenuity in their efforts to repel unwanted bidders.[19] For example, in 1969 Northwest Industries made a $1 billion tender offer for B.F. Goodrich. In reply the latter took out a $250 million bank loan, promised the lender that the loan would be repaid in the event of a takeover, and used the money to prepay income taxes and accounts payable. This meant that Northwest would have been faced with a $250 million immediate cash outflow in the event of a successful merger. Next Goodrich acquired another firm in the same line of business as Northwest Industries, and so created an antitrust barrier to a merger. (The Justice Department sought an injunction against the tender offer.) Third, Goodrich managed to place stock in friendly hands when it acquired Gulf Oil's interest in a joint venture in exchange for 700,000 shares. (Gulf did not support the proposed merger.) Finally, the company looked about for another, more congenial company that would be willing to acquire it. In the face of such defenses the tender offer by Northwest Industries failed.[20]

Merger Negotiations and Battles

Takeover battles often resemble a many-sided game of poker. For example, consider the acquisition of Cities Service in 1982.[21] Cities is a leading United States oil producer

---

[18]The technical rules for such exchanges are provided in subsection 85(1) of the *Income Tax Act*.

[19]Sometimes friendly tender offers are made with the acquiescence of the selling firm's management.

[20]For a good description of the Northwest—B.F. Goodrich tender fight, see T. O'Hanlon, "Goodrich's Four-Ply Defense," *Fortune*, **80**:110–113 (July 1969).

[21]The Cities Service takeover is described in R.S. Ruback, "The Cities Service Takeover: A Case Study," *Journal of Finance*, **38**:319–330 (May 1983).

that holds a 13.2% interest in the Syncrude oil sands project in northern Alberta. The battle for Cities began in May, when Mesa Petroleum made a merger bid. Cities' directors opposed the merger and in a defensive move made a counterbid for Mesa. Over the following month Mesa's bid was revised once and Cities' bid was revised twice before both companies agreed to drop their bids for one another. Cities repurchased the stock that had been bought by Mesa and in exchange Mesa agreed not to attempt a hostile takeover of Cities for five years.

The principal reason for the cessation of hostilities between Mesa and Cities was the announcement that Gulf Oil had agreed to acquire Cities' stock at a price that was substantially above Mesa's offer. Unfortunately, this proposal fell foul of the United States Federal Trade Commission (FTC), which issued a temporary restraining order. Shortly thereafter Gulf withdrew its offer.

In response Cities charged Gulf with not attempting to resolve the FTC's objections and it filed a $3 billion lawsuit against Gulf. At the same time it began to solicit other takeover bids. The only interested suitor to emerge was Occidental Petroleum. Occidental's initial offer for Cities was revised twice and finally accepted. The battle for Cities Service had last three months and involved a total of nine bids from four separate companies.

Many of these bids consisted of a two-tier offer. For example, Occidental's final offer for Cities consisted of a tender offer of $55 a share for 45% of the stock and a package of fixed income securities worth about $40 a share for the remaining stock. In effect, Occidental was saying, "Last one through the door does the washing up." The plan worked, for almost all Cities' stockholders rushed to take advantage of the cash offer.[22]

In several instances the bidders employed both carrot and stick; for example, Occidental followed up its initial friendly offer for Cities with a hostile tender before finally reaching a friendly agreement.

The generous Gulf offer provided Cities' shareholders with a cumulative profit of almost 80%, but the collapse of that offer and the shortage of other possible suitors caused Cities' stock price to lose all its earlier gains. From then on Cities was in a relatively weak bargaining position and the Occidental offer resulted in a profit of only 12% for Cities' stockholders. The merger scarcely affected Occidental's stock price, which suggests that investors believed the merger to be a zero-NPV investment. Gulf's stockholders fared the worst. It's high-priced offer led to a 14% fall in the price of Gulf stock. Even though this offer was subsequently withdrawn, the prospect of a costly lawsuit left Gulf's stock price depressed.

Takeover battles are undoubtedly exciting for the individuals involved, but many onlookers are concerned that the wheeling and dealing is not in the public interest. The result is pressure for more legislation to protect those who are most affected by mergers.

A Note on Merger Accounting

Mergers sometimes raise complex accounting issues. One such issue is whether a merger should be treated as a *purchase of assets* or as a *pooling of interests*.[23] In efficient capital

---

[22]To protect themselves against these two-tier offers, some United States companies have modified their charters, requiring that the price paid to the later sellers should be at least as high as the price paid to earlier ones. In Canada, provincial securities acts dictate that only a single offer price may be tendered in a take-over bid and, if the tender offer is oversubscribed, the shares are allocated on a pro rata basis.

[23]When two or more companies join through an exchange of voting shares in which none of the companies can be identified as the acquirer, a *new entity* has been created. Under the new entity method, the assets and liabilities are combined in the new entity's financial statements at fair value. See Section 1580.10 of the *CICA Handbook*.

Table 31-3 Purchasing versus pooling in the merger of A Corporation and B Corporation (figures in millions of dollars).

Initial Balance Sheets							
A Corporation				B Corporation			
NWC	2.0	3.0	D	NWC	0.1	0	D
FA	8.0	7.0	E	FA	0.9	1.0	E
	10.0	10.0			1.0	1.0	

Balance Sheets of AB Corporation

	AB Corporation		
Under pooling of interests:	NWC	2.1	3.0	D
	FA	8.9	8.0	E
		11.0	11.0	

	AB Corporation		
Under purchase accounting, assuming that	NWC	2.1	3.0	D
A Corporation pays $1.8 million for	FA	8.9	8.8	E
B Corporation:	Goodwill	0.8		
		11.8	11.8	

Key:
NWC = Net working capital
FA = Net book value of fixed assets
D = Debt
E = Book value of equity

markets, the choice between these two methods should make no difference whatsoever, but the *CICA Handbook*, Section 1580.18, recommends that the ". . . purchase method should be used to account for all business combinations, except for those rare transactions where an acquirer cannot be identified."

The essential differences between the two methods are illustrated in Table 31-3. The table shows what happens when A Corporation buys B Corporation, leading to a new AB Corporation. The two firms' initial (book) balance sheets are shown at the top of the table. The next balance sheet shown is AB Corporation's under *pooling of interest*. Note that this is nothing more than the two firms' separate balance sheets added together.

The final balance sheet shows what happens when purchase accounting is used. We assume that B Corporation has been purchased for $1.8 million, 180% of book value.

Why did A Corporation pay an $800,000 premium over book value? There are two possible reasons. First, the true values of A's *tangible* assets—its working capital, plant, and equipment—may be greater than $1 million. We will assume this is *not* the reason; that is, we assume the assets listed on its balance sheet are valued there correctly.[24] Second, A Corporation may be paying for *intangible* assets that are not listed on B Corporation's balance sheet. The intangible asset may be a promising product or technology developed by B Corporation, for example. Or it may be no more than B Corporation's share of the economic gains of the merger.

Under the purchase method of accounting, A Corporation is viewed as buying an asset worth $1.8 million—as indeed it is. The problem is how to show that asset on the left-hand side of AB Corporation's balance sheet. B Corporation's tangible assets

[24]If the assets were worth more than their previous book values, they would be reappraised and their current values entered on AB Corporation's balance sheet. Goodwill (see below) would be decreased by an amount equal to the write-up of tangible assets.

are worth only $1 million. This leaves $0.8 million. The accountant takes care of this by creating a new asset category called *goodwill* and assigning $0.8 million to it.

All this is somewhat arbitrary, but reasonable enough. Intangible assets do have value, and so there's no reason such assets shouldn't be shown on the balance sheet when a firm buys them.

Nevertheless, most managers prefer to pool when they can. The reason is that goodwill has to be amortized over a period not exceeding 40 years, and the periodic amortization charges have to be deducted from reported income. Thus AB Corporation's reported income will be reduced by at least $800,000/40 = $20,000 each year. Under pooling, goodwill never appears, and so reported income is at least $20,000 higher.

Now all this has absolutely no cash consequences. The amortization charges are *not* cash outflows and they are not tax-deductible expenses. Thus the choice between purchase and pooling should have no effect on the value of the merged firms.

Hong, Mandelker, and Kaplan tested this proposition by looking at a sample of 159 acquisitions made between 1954 and 1964, a period in which there were fewer restrictions on pooling than there are now.[25] They found no evidence that acquiring firms did better under pooling than under purchase accounting.

31-6 POSTMERGER INTEGRATION

Many merger problems arise simply because the buyer overestimates the value of particular assets. For example, some of the inventory may be unsaleable or some of the receivables uncollectible. Other difficulties arise when the buyer overlooks such hidden liabilities as an inadequately funded pension plan, an outstanding obligation to install antipollution equipment, a warranty issued on a defective product, or an outstanding fixed-price contract.

Yet the most serious problems are often the administrative ones encountered after the merger. Integrating two independent firms is a complex task. Whether the merger succeeds depends as much on the care with which it is planned as on the size of the potential economic gain. Differences in administrative procedures, accounting methods, and production processes and standards are all common sources of difficulty.

Perhaps the most serious potential problems stem from the reactions of the people involved. For example, small, closely held corporations are sometimes sold because the founders are aging and eager to diversify, relax a little, and enjoy the fruits of many years' work and worry. In this case the sellers' managers may see the sale as a golden opportunity to reduce their golf handicaps. Unless this is tacitly agreed before the merger, the scope for acrimony and failure is obvious. In other cases problems may stem from the fact that the entrepreneurial qualities needed to build a small company are not necessarily identical to the qualities needed to direct a small part of a major concern. And, lest we seem to be implying that management disagreements are only a problem where the acquired company is small, consider the following passage from *The Wall Street Journal* on the Colonial-Seaboard merger.

> Samuel Kosman, Seaboard chairman, said Seaboard actually is "buying back" Colonial, which was a Seaboard subsidiary until sold about a year ago to a group headed by Irwin Solomon, President of Colonial.

---

[25]H. Hong, G. Mandelker, and R.S. Kaplan, "Pooling vs. Purchase: The Effects of Accounting for Mergers on Stock Prices," *Accounting Review*, **53**:31–47 (January 1978). The requirements for pooling were tightened in 1970 by the Accounting Principles Board of the American Institute of Certified Public Accountants. The requirements are set out in Opinions No. 16 and No. 17 of the board (New York, 1970). The opinions state, among other requirements for pooling, that the seller's stockholders must remain stockholders of the merged firm, and that the buyer must finance the merger by exchanging its common stock for at least 90% of the seller's shares.

But Colonial said the fact Seaboard would be the surviving company is only "technically correct." In fact, said a Colonial spokesman, Colonial will have a controlling 9 seats on the new board to Seaboard's 8. Mr. Kosman of Seaboard agreed that this is correct, but maintained, "They are merging into us and it is an acquisition by us no matter how you slice it."

A spokesman for Colonial said Mr. Kosman would be chairman of the new company, but only "on a part-time basis," putting in no more than "3 to 5 hours a week" at that job.

Countered Mr. Kosman, "They don't know what they are talking about and you can quote me on that. There's no question about it—I'll be a full-time chairman and chief executive officer."

Later a Colonial official could only gulp and say, "I'll defer to Mr. Kosman's statement. He'll be a full-time chairman."[26]

Other common postmerger problems arise in the wider area of personnel management. News of a pending merger inevitably creates considerable unease among employees. The chances of labour unrest are obviously magnified if the firms have hitherto been represented by different unions and if the merger is expected to lead to layoffs. Problems are also likely to stem from differences in remuneration levels. For example, if the two firms hope to achieve scale economies by integrating their sales forces, they are likely to encounter considerable resistance if the sales staffs are used to working under different incentive compensation schemes. The potential economic gains from a merger can rapidly disappear if management solves these problems by standardizing on the most generous aspects of each firm's pay scales and fringe benefits.

31-7 MERGER WAVES AND PROFITABILITY

The vast literature on mergers contains a great deal of speculation but only a few general facts. The following three are the most important ones:

1. Mergers come in waves. The crests of the waves seem to coincide with buoyant stock prices.

2. Selling companies gain from mergers.

3. It is *not* clear whether acquiring companies gain, on the average, in mergers, or whether mergers on the average generate positive economic gains overall.

Mergers Come in Waves

The first episode of intense merger activity occurred at the turn of the century and the second in the 1920s. There was a further boom from 1967 to 1969 and then again in 1981 to 1982. Each episode coincided with a period of buoyant stock prices. However, the two postwar booms were distinguished by a high proportion of diversifying mergers and by the emergence of dozens of pure conglomerate firms.

Nobody really knows why merger activity is so volatile. If mergers are prompted by economic motives, at least one of these motives must be "here today and gone tomorrow," and it must be somehow associated with high stock prices. But none of the economic motives for merger that we looked at in this chapter has anything to do with the general level of the stock market. None burst on the scene in 1967, departed in 1970, and reappeared in 1981. For example, potential economies of scale or of vertical integration are worth having in both bull and bear stock markets.

---

[26] *The Wall Street Journal*, January 31, 1967, p. 8. Cited in A.R. Wyatt and D.E. Kieso, *Business Combinations: Planning and Action*, International Textbook Company, Scranton, Pa., 1969.

It is true that mergers may result from mistakes of valuation on the part of the stock market. In other words, the buyer may believe that investors have underestimated the value of the seller or may hope that they *will* overestimate the value of the combined firm. But we see (with hindsight) that mistakes are made in bear markets as well as bull markets. Why don't we see just as many firms hunting for bargain acquisitions when the stock market is low? It is possible that "suckers are born every minute," but it is difficult to believe that they can be harvested only in bull markets.

Companies are not the only active buyers and sellers in bull markets. Investors also trade much more heavily after a rise in share prices. Again nobody has a good economic explanation of why this should be the case. Perhaps the answer has nothing to do with economics. Perhaps merger booms and stock market trading are behavioural phenomena—human beings, like some animals, seem to be more active when the weather is sunny.

Selling Companies Gain by Merger

In most mergers there is a clear "buyer"—usually the larger firm—and a clear "seller." The selling stockholders almost always receive a premium over the pre-merger value of their shares. The average premium is about 20% in the case of mergers and 30% in the case of tender offers.[27]

Sometimes premiums are much higher, however. When Dupont acquired Conoco in 1981, it paid a premium of 81% or $3 billion for Conoco's stock.[28]

Do Mergers Generate Net Benefits?

Figure 31-2 summarizes the results of a study by Asquith of about 200 mergers in the United States during the period 1962–1976. You can see that the sellers received a healthy gain.

Asquith's analysis of the stock market performance of the acquiring firms shows you how investors *expected* the mergers to work out. It would be difficult to argue with the view that on average investors thought that the acquirers would just about break even on the deal.

Over the longer term Asquith's study shows a slight tailing off in the performance of the acquirers. Does that mean the mergers worked out slightly less well than investors expected? It's possible, but there may be so many other things happening to these firms that it is hard to be sure.

If buyers roughly break even and sellers make substantial gains, shouldn't there be an overall gain? Once again, we can't be certain. In most mergers the buyer is so much larger than the seller that even quite large percentage gains or losses on acquisition would not show up very clearly in the buyer's share price. Therefore there may be or may not be overall benefits to mergers. If there are, it is possible that the buyer gets some of those benefits. But it seems fairly clear that the buyer gets proportionally less than the seller out of a merger.

---

[27]See M.C. Jensen and R.S. Ruback, "The Market for Corporate Control: The Scientific Evidence," *Journal of Financial Economics*, **11**:5–50 (April 1983).

[28]Presumably Dupont foresaw gains worth more than $3 billion, but it is not easy to spot where they were likely to come from. The two companies were in different industries, and Dupont did not plan to change Conoco's management or to merge any part of its operations. The merger led to a fall of $800 million in the value of Dupont stock. So presumably investors thought that the merger created more than $2 billion of additional value. For an interesting account of the Dupont–Conoco merger, see R.S. Ruback, "The Conoco Takeover and Stockholder Returns," *Sloan Management Review*, **23**: 13–33 (Winter 1982).

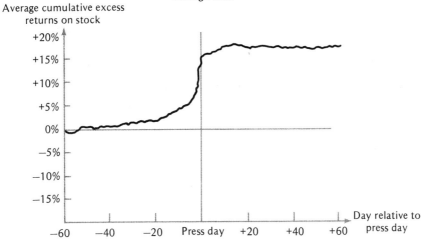

Selling Firms

Average cumulative excess returns on stock

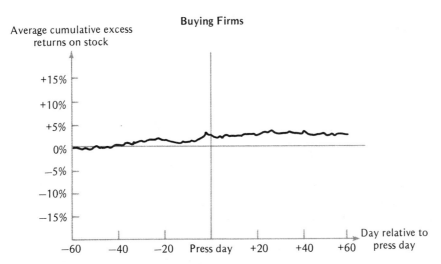

Buying Firms

Average cumulative excess returns on stock

Figure 31-2 Asquith's study confirms that selling firms receive substantial premiums. Stockholders of buying firms roughly break even.

Note: The cumulative returns are adjusted to remove price fluctuations attributable to movements of the overall stock market.

Source: P. Asquith, "Merger Bids, Uncertainty, and Stockholder Returns," *Journal of Financial Economics*, **11**:51–83 (April 1983), Figures 1 and 2, pp. 62–63.

31-8 SUMMARY

A merger generates an economic gain if the two firms are worth more together than apart. Suppose that firms A and B merge to form a new entity AB. Then the gain from the merger is

$$GAIN = PV_{AB} - (PV_A + PV_B)$$

Gains from mergers may reflect economies of scale, economies of vertical integration, improved efficiency, fuller use of tax shields, the combination of complementary resources, or redeployment of surplus funds. We don't know how common these benefits are, but they do make economic sense. Sometimes mergers are undertaken to reduce the costs of borrowing, diversify risks, or play the bootstrap game. These motives are dubious.

You should go ahead with the merger if the gain exceeds the cost. Cost is the premium that the buyer pays for the selling firm over its values as a separate entity. It is easy to estimate when the merger is financed by cash. In that case,

$$COST = CASH - PV_B$$

When payment is in the form of shares, the cost depends on the value of the combined firm. For example, if B's shareholders end up owning the fraction x of the combined firm

$$COST = xPV_{AB} - PV_B$$

The mechanics of buying a firm are much more complex than those of buying a machine. First, you have to make sure that the purchase is unlikely to fall foul of combines and foreign investment laws. Second, you have a choice of procedures. In a merger[29] all the assets and liabilities of the buyer are absorbed into those of the seller. In an acquisition of stock the buyer acquires the stock of the seller rather than the company itself. In an acquisition of assets the buyer purchases the individual assets of the seller. Third, you have to worry about the tax status of the merger. In a tax-free merger the tax position of the corporation and the stockholders is not changed. In a taxable merger the buyer can depreciate the full cost of the tangible assets acquired, but the stockholders in the selling corporation may be taxed on any capital gains. Finally, remember that most mergers are amicably negotiated between the directors of the two companies; but if the seller is reluctant, the would-be buyer can decide to make a tender offer or engage in a proxy fight.

Buying another firm is relatively easy. Integrating it successfully with your own is difficult. We gave as an example of the difficulties encountered some of the personnel problems that arise when there is no clear understanding of the future role of the seller's management or when employees of the two firms are not compensated equally. You need to think about these problems *before* you merge.

Finally, we listed three empirical facts about mergers. Mergers occur in waves and are associated with buoyant stock prices. Nobody knows why. Sellers gain from mergers— a typical premium is about 20%. Buyers on the average seem to break even. Overall, it is not clear that the typical merger generates significant economic gains.

FURTHER READING

The approach to analyzing mergers presented in this chapter is based on:

S.C. Myers, "A Framework for Evaluating Mergers," in S.C. Myers (ed.), *Modern Developments in Financial Management*, Frederick A. Praeger, Inc., New York, 1976.

The first chapters of Reid's book provide a useful history of merger "waves." Morin and Chippindale and the Royal Commission Report provide some general background of mergers and their effects in Canada, and Steiner provides a general treatment of mergers and their impact on the economy of the United States.

---

[29]In this sentence the word *merger* is used in its technical, legal sense.

D. Morin and W. Chippindale, eds., *Acquisitions and Mergers in Canada*, Methuen, Toronto, 1970.

Report of the Royal Commission on Corporate Concentration, Minister of Supply and Services Canada, 1978.

S.R. Reid, *Mergers, Managers and the Economy*, McGraw-Hill Book Company, New York, 1968.

P.O. Steiner, *Mergers: Motives, Effects, Policies*, The University of Michigan Press, Ann Arbor, 1975.

Jensen and Ruback have recently reviewed the extensive empirical work on mergers. The same issue of the *Journal of Financial Economics* also contains a collection of some of the more important empirical studies.

M.C. Jensen and R.S. Ruback, "The Market for Corporate Control: The Scientific Evidence," *Journal of Financial Economics*, **11**:5–50 (April 1983).

Hong, Mandelker, and Kaplan investigate the impact of different accounting treatments of mergers on the performance of merging firms' common stocks.

H. Hong, G. Mandelker, and R.S. Kaplan, "Pooling vs. Purchase: The Effects of Accounting for Mergers on Stock Prices," *Accounting Review*, **53**:31–47 (January 1978).

Finally, we note Shad's article, which estimates merger premiums and discusses some practical issues arising in merger negotiations.

S.R. Shad, "The Financial Realities of Mergers," *Harvard Business Review*, **47**:133–146 (November–December 1969).

APPENDIX 31-1 CONGLOMERATE MERGERS AND VALUE ADDITIVITY

A pure conglomerate merger is one that has no effect on the operations or profitability of either firm. If corporate diversification is in stockholders' interests, a conglomerate merger would give a clear demonstration of its benefits. But, if present values add up, the conglomerate merger would not make stockholders better or worse off.

In this appendix we examine more carefully our assertion that present values add. It turns out that values *do* add as long as capital markets are perfect and investors' diversification opportunities are unrestricted.

Call the merging firms A and B. Value additivity implies

$$PV_{AB} = PV_A + PV_B$$

where

PV_{AB} = the market value of the combined firms just after the merger

and

PV_A, PV_B = the separate market values of A and B just before the merger

For example, we might have

PV_A = $100 million ($200 per share times 500,000 shares outstanding)

and

PV_B = $200 million ($200 per share times 1,000,000 shares outstanding)

Suppose A and B are merged into a new firm AB, with one share in AB exchanged for each share of A or B. Thus there are 1,500,000 AB shares issued. *If* value additivity holds, then PV_{AB} must equal the sum of the separate values of A and B just before the merger, that is $300 million. That would imply a price of $200 per share of AB stock.

But note that the AB shares represent a portfolio of the assets of A and B. Before the merger investors could have bought one share of A and two of B for $600. Afterwards they can obtain a claim on *exactly* the same real assets by buying three shares of AB.

Suppose that the opening price of AB shares just after the merger is $200, so that $PV_{AB} = PV_A + PV_B$. Our problem is to determine if this is an equilibrium price; that is, whether we can rule out excess demand or supply at this price.

In order for there to be excess demand, there must be some investors who are willing to increase their holdings of A and B as a consequence of the merger. Who could they be? The only thing new created by the merger is diversification, but those investors who want to hold assets of A *and* B will have purchased A's and B's stock before the merger. The diversification is redundant and consequently won't attract new investment demand.

Is there a possibility of excess supply? The answer is yes. For example, there will be some shareholders in A who did not invest in B. After the merger they cannot invest solely in A, but only in a fixed combination of A and B. Their AB shares will be less attractive to them than the pure A shares, so they will sell part or all their AB stock. In fact, the only AB shareholders who will *not* wish to sell are those who happened to hold A and B in exactly a 1:2 ratio in their premerger portfolios!

Since there is no possibility of excess demand, but a definite possibility of excess supply, we seem to have

$$PV_{AB} \leq PV_A + PV_B$$

That is, corporate diversification can't help, but it may hurt investors by restricting the types of portfolios they can hold. This is not the whole story, however, since investment demand for AB shares might be attracted from other sources if PV_{AB} drops below $PV_A + PV_B$. To illustrate, suppose there are two other firms, A^* and B^*, which are judged by investors to have the same risk characteristics as A and B, respectively. Then before the merger,

$$r_A = r_{A^*} \text{ and } r_B = r_{B^*}$$

where r is the rate of return expected by investors. We'll assume $r_A = r_{A^*} = 0.08$ and $r_B = r_{B^*} = 0.20$.

Consider a portfolio one-third invested in A^* and two-thirds in B^*. This portfolio offers an expected return of 16%.

$$r = x_A \cdot r_{A^*} + x_B \cdot r_{B^*}$$
$$= \frac{1}{3}(0.08) + \frac{2}{3}(0.20) = 0.16$$

A comparable portfolio of A and B before their merger also offered a 16% return.

As we have noted a new firm AB is really a portfolio of firms A and B, with portfolio weights of $\frac{1}{3}$ and $\frac{2}{3}$. Thus it is equivalent in risk to the portfolio of A^* and B^*. Thus the price of AB shares must adjust so that it likewise offers a 16% return.

What if AB shares dropped below $200, so that PV_{AB} is less than $PV_A + PV_B$? Since the assets and earnings of firms A and B are the same, the price drop means that the expected rate of return on AB shares has risen above the return offered by the A^*B^* portfolio. That is, if r_{AB} exceeds $\frac{1}{3}r_A + \frac{2}{3}r_B$, then r_{AB} must also exceed $\frac{1}{3}r_{A^*} + \frac{2}{3}r_{B^*}$.

But this is untenable: investors A^* and B^* could sell part of their holdings (in a 1:2 ratio), buy AB, and obtain a higher expected rate of return with no increase in risk.

On the other hand, if PV_{AB} rises above $PV_A + PV_B$, the AB shares will offer an expected return less than that offered by the A^*B^* portfolio. Investors will unload the AB shares, forcing their price down.

The only stable result is for AB shares to stick at $200. Thus, value additivity will hold exactly in a perfect-market equilibrium if there are ample substitutes for the assets A and B. If A and B have unique risk characteristics, however, then PV_{AB} can fall below $PV_A + PV_B$. The reason is that the merger curtails investors' opportunity to custom-tailor their portfolios to their own needs and preferences. This makes investors worse off, reducing the attractiveness of holding the shares of firm AB.

In general, the condition for value additivity is that investors' opportunity set—that is, the range of risk characteristics attainable by investors through their portfolio choices—is independent of the particular portfolio of real assets held by the firm. Diversification per se can never expand the opportunity set given perfect security markets. Corporate diversification may reduce the investors' opportunity set, but only if the real assets the corporations hold lack substitutes among traded securities or portfolios.

In a few cases the firm may be able to expand the opportunity set. It can do so if it finds an investment opportunity that is unique—a real asset with risk characteristics shared by few or no other financial assets. In this lucky event the firm should not diversify, however. It should set up the unique asset as a separate firm so as to expand investors' opportunity set to the maximum extent. If Gallo by chance discovered that a small piece of its vineyards produced wine comparable to Chateau Margaux, it would not throw that wine into the Hearty Burgundy vat.

QUIZ

1. Indicate which of the following hypothetical mergers is horizontal, vertical, or conglomerate:
   (a) IBM acquires Control Data.
   (b) Control Data acquires Safeway.
   (c) Safeway acquires General Foods.
   (d) General Foods acquires IBM.

2. Velcro Saddles is contemplating the acquisition of Pogo Ski Sticks, Inc. The values of the two companies as separate entities are $20 million and $10 millions respectively. Velcro Saddles estimates that by combining the two companies, it will reduce marketing and administrative costs by $500,000 per year in perpetuity. Velcro Saddles can either pay $14 million cash for Pogo or offer Pogo a 50% holding in Velcro Saddles. If the opportunity cost of capital is 10%,
   (a) What is the gain from merger?
   (b) What is the cost of the cash offer?
   (c) What is the cost of the stock alternative?
   (d) What is the NPV of the acquisition under the cash offer?
   (e) What is its NPV under the stock offer?

3. Indicate which of the following mergers are *not* likely to be classed as tax-free:
   (a) A merger undertaken solely for the purpose of taking advantage of tax-loss carry-forwards.
   (b) An acquisition of assets, which are immediately resold.
   (c) Payment is entirely in the form of voting stock.
   (d) Firm A acquires firm B for cash.

4. Indicate whether each of the following is true or false:
   (a) Sellers almost always gain in mergers.
   (b) Buyers almost always gain in mergers.
   (c) Firms that do unusually well tend to be acquisition targets.
   (d) Merger activity in Canada varies dramatically from year to year.
   (e) On the average, mergers produce substantial economic gains.
   (f) Tender offers require the approval of the selling firm's management.
   (g) If a merger can be treated as a pooling of interest rather than a purchase, reported earnings are usually increased.
   (h) The cost of a merger is always independent of the economic gain produced by the merger.
   (i) The cost of a merger to the buyer equals the gain realized by the seller.

5. Indicate which of the following motives for mergers make economic sense:
   (a) Merging to achieve economies of scale
   (b) Merging to reduce risk by diversification
   (c) Merging to redeploy cash generated by a firm with ample profits but limited growth opportunities
   (d) Merging to make fuller use of tax-loss carry-forwards
   (e) Merging just to increase earnings per share

QUESTIONS AND PROBLEMS

1. Examine several recent mergers and suggest the principal motives for merging in each case.

2. Examine a recent merger in which at least part of the payment made to the seller was in the form of stock. Use stock market prices to obtain an estimate of the gain from the merger and the cost of the merger.

3. The Muck and Slurry merger has fallen through (see Section 31-3). But World Enterprises is determined to report earnings per share of $2.67. It therefore acquires the Wheelrim and Axle Company. You are given the following facts:

	World Enterprises	Wheelrim and Axle	Merged Firm
Earnings per share	$2.00	$2.50	$2.67
Price per share	$40.00	$25.00	?
Price-earnings ratio	20	10	?
Number of shares	100,000	200,000	?
Total earnings	$200,000.00	$500,000.00	?
Total market value	$4,000,000.00	$5,000,000.00	?

Once again there are no gains from merging. In exchange for Wheelrim and Axle shares, World Enterprises issues just enough of its own shares to ensure its $2.67 earnings per share objective.
   (a) Complete the above table for the merged firm.
   (b) How many shares of World Enterprises are exchanged for each share of Wheelrim and Axle?
   (c) What is the cost of the merger to World Enterprises?
   (d) What is the change in the total market value of those World Enterprises shares that were outstanding before the merger?

4. Explain the distinction between a tax-free and a taxable merger. State the circumstances in which you would expect buyer and seller to agree to a taxable merger.

5. As treasurer of Leisure Products, Inc., you are investigating the possible acquisition of Plastitoys. You have the following basic data:

	Leisure Products	Plastitoys
Earnings per share	$5.00	$1.50
Dividend per share	$3.00	$0.80
Number of shares	1,000,000	600,000
Stock price	$90.00	$20.00

You estimate that investors currently expect a steady growth of about 6% in Plastitoys' earnings and dividends. Under new management this growth rate would be increased to 8% per year, without any additional capital investment required.

(a) What is the gain from the acquisition?

(b) What is the cost of the acquisition if Leisure Products pays $25 in cash for each share of Plastitoys?

(c) What is the cost of the acquisition if Leisure Products offers one share of Leisure Products for every three shares of Plastitoys?

(d) How would the cost of the cash offer and the share offer alter if the expected growth rate of Plastitoys were not changed by the merger?

6. Look again at Table 31-3. Suppose that B Corporation's fixed assets are re-examined and found to be worth $1.2 million instead of $0.9 million. How would this affect the AB Corporation's balance sheet under purchase accounting? How would the value of AB Corporation change? Would your answer depend on whether the merger is taxable?

7. Do *you* have any rational explanation for the great fluctuations in aggregate merger activity and the apparent relationship between merger activity and stock prices?

8. "Legislation is needed to ensure that shareholders of target companies are fairly treated."

"Acquiring companies need some inducement to act. Legislation to protect the target shareholders is likely to remove this inducement."

What do you think? For example, do you think that there should be a ban on two-tier bids, such as the Occidental bid for Cities Service?

CHAPTER

INTERNATIONAL FINANCIAL MANAGEMENT

•32•

So far we have talked principally about doing business at home. But many Canadian companies have substantial interests in other countries. Of course your objectives in international finance are still the same. You want to buy assets that are worth *more* than they cost, and you want to pay for them by issuing liabilities that are worth *less* than the money raised. It is when you come to apply these criteria to your international business that you come up against some additional problems.

The unique feature of international management is that you need to deal with more than one currency. We are, therefore, going to look at how foreign exchange markets operate, why exchange rates change, and what you can do to protect yourself against exchange risks.

The financial manager must also remember that interest rates differ from country to country. For example, in the fall of 1982, the rate of interest was about 4% in Switzerland, $10\frac{1}{2}$% in the United States, $12\frac{1}{2}$% in Canada, and 150% in Brazil. We are going to discuss the reasons for these differences in interest rates. We will also talk about some of the implications for financing overseas operations. Should the parent company provide the money? Should it try to finance the operation locally? Or should it treat the world as its oyster and borrow wherever interest rates are lowest?

Finally we will discuss how international companies decide on capital investments. How do they choose the discount rate? And how does the financing method affect the choice of project? You'll find that the basic principles of capital budgeting are the same but there are a few pitfalls to look out for.

32-1 THE FOREIGN EXCHANGE MARKET

A Canadian company that imports goods from Germany buys Deutschemarks in order to pay for the purchase. A Canadian company exporting to Germany receives Deutschemarks, which it sells in exchange for dollars. Both firms make use of the foreign exchange market.[1]

Except in a few European centres, the foreign exchange market has no central marketplace. All business is conducted by telephone or telex. The principal dealers are the largest commercial banks and the central banks. Any corporation that wants to buy or sell currency usually does so through a commercial bank.

Exchange rates in Canada are quoted in terms of the number of dollars needed to buy one unit of foreign currency. Therefore, a rate of $0.4069/DM means that each Deutschemark costs you $0.4069. Or, to put it another way, you get 1/0.4069 = 2.4576 DM for your dollar.

---

[1] Alternatively, trade may take place in dollars. In this case the Canadian importer pays for goods in dollars and the German exporter sells those dollars to buy Deutschemarks. Similarly, the Canadian exporter may demand payment in dollars: in this case the German importer must sell Deutschemarks to buy those dollars.

FOREIGN EXCHANGE

MID MARKET RATES IN CANADIAN FUNDS, Feb. 18, 1985. Prepared by the Bank of Nova Scotia.

Country	Currency	Noon	Previous Noon
United States	Dollar	$1.3405	$1.3399
1 month forward		1.3419	1.3413
2 months forward		1.3431	1.3427
3 months forward		1.3447	1.3443
6 months forward		1.3493	1.3487
12 months forward		1.3540	1.3537
Britain	Pound	1.4645	1.4779
1 month forward		1.4599	1.4736
2 months forward		1.4550	1.4692
3 months forward		1.4527	1.4669
6 months forward		1.4509	1.4655
12 months forward		1.4512	1.4661
*Algeria	Dinar	.2576	.2593
*Argentina	Peso	.00570	.00591
Australia	Dollar	.9866	.9915
Austria	Shilling	.05779	.05846
Bahamas	Dollar	1.3405	1.3399
*Barbados	Dollar	.6743	.6746
Belgium	Franc	.02025	.02042
Bermuda	Dollar	1.3405	1.3399
*Brazil	Cruzeiro	.00036	.00038
*Bulgaria	Lev	1.2853	1.2847
*Chile	Peso	.01024	.01037
*China	Renminbi	.4787	.4785
*Cyprus	Pound	1.9980	2.0241
*Czechoslovakia	Koruna	.1901	.1900
Denmark	Krone	.1136	.1144
East Germany	Mark	.4069	.4103
*Egypt	Pound	1.6150	1.6616
Finland	Markka	.1961	.1979
France	Franc	.1331	.1340
Greece	Drachma	.01014	.01015
Hong Kong	Dollar	.1719	.1718
*Hungary	Forint	.02597	.02595
*Iceland	Krona	.03198	.03240
India	Rupee	.1056	.1051
Ireland	Punt	1.2695	1.2756
*Israel	Shekel	.00190	.00193
Italy	Lira	.000658	.000663
*Jamaica	Dollar	.2580	.2579
Japan	Yen	.005157	.005218
*Jordan	Dinar	3.3214	3.3464

Country	Currency	Noon	Previous Noon
Lebanon	Pound	.1072	.1005
Luxembourg	Franc	.02025	.02042
Malaysia	Ringgit	.5268	.5286
Mexico	Peso	.00585	.00583
Netherlands	Guilder	.3595	.3623
New Zealand	Dollar	.6113	.6123
Norway	Krone	.1420	.1427
*Pakistan	Rupee	.08485	.08640
*Poland	Zloty	.00964	.00963
Portugal	Escudo	.00754	.00751
*Romania	Leu	.2926	.2925
*Saudi Arabia	Riyal	.3755	.3753
Singapore	Dollar	.5945	.5988
South Africa	Rand	.7032	.7018
Spain	Peseta	.00740	.00744
*Sudan	Pound	1.0311	1.0307
Sweden	Krona	.1440	.1447
Switzerland	Franc	.4784	.4822
*Taiwan	Dollar	.03424	.03418
*Trinidad,Tobago	Dollar	.5630	.5628
*USSR	Rouble	1.5241	1.5235
*Venezuela	Bolivar	.1094	.1094
West Germany	Mark	.4069	.4103
1 month forward		.4082	.4116
3 month forward		.4112	.4146
Antigua, Grenada St. Lucia	E.C.Dollar	.5007	.5005
*Yugoslavia	Dinar	.00582	.00591
*Zambia	Kwacha	.5736	.5794

Prepared by the Royal Bank of Canada

The U.S. dollar was up $0.0009 at $1.3407 in terms of Canadian dollars in Toronto Thursday. Pound sterling closed at $1.4677, down $0.0177.

In New York, the Canadian dollar was down $0.0005 at $0.7459 in terms of U.S. funds. The pound was down $0.0139 at $1.0948.

The ECU exchange rate for the Canadian dollar was unavailable.

(*Indicates rates changed monthly)

Figure 32-1 An example of the foreign currency table in *The Globe and Mail* (February 19, 1985). *Source*: *The Globe and Mail*, Report on Business, and The Bank of Nova Scotia.

Figure 32-1 reproduces a table of exchange rates from *The Globe and Mail*. Except where otherwise stated, the table gives the price of the currency for immediate delivery. This is known as the **spot rate of exchange**. You can see that the spot rate for the Deutschemark is 0.4069/DM.

The term *immediate delivery* is a relative one, for spot currency is usually purchased for two-day delivery. For example, suppose that you need 100,000 DM to pay for imports from Germany. On Monday you telephone your bank in Toronto and agree to purchase 100,000 DM at $0.4069/DM. The bank does not hand you a wad of banknotes over the counter. Instead it instructs its German correspondent bank to transfer 100,000 DM to the account of the German supplier on Wednesday. The bank debits your account by $40,690 on Monday.

In addition to the spot exchange market, there is also a **forward market**. In the forward market you buy and sell currency for future delivery—usually 1, 3, 6 or 12 months' time. If you know that you are going to pay out or receive foreign currency at some future date, you can insure yourself against loss by buying or selling forward.[2]

---

[2]Recently currency options and currency futures options have been introduced in the United States. These contracts are more directly analogous to foreign exchange insurance than forward contracts in the sense that you pay an option premium today to gain the right, but not the obligation, to buy or sell the foreign currency at a specified price at some future date.

Thus, if you need 100,000 DM three months hence, you can enter into a three-month *forward contract*. The *forward rate* on this contract is the price you agree to pay in three months when the 100,000 Deutschemarks are delivered.

If you look again at Table 32-1, you see that the three-month forward rate for the Deutschemark is quoted at $0.4112/DM. If you buy Deutschemarks for three months' delivery, you pay more dollars than if you buy the spot. In this case, the Deutschemark is said to trade at a forward *premium* relative to the dollar, because forward Deutschemarks are more expensive than spot ones. Expressed as an annual rate, the forward premium is:

$$4 \times \frac{(0.4112 - 0.4069)}{0.4069} \times 100 = 4.227$$

You could say that the dollar was selling at a 4.2% *forward discount*.

32-2   SOME BASIC RELATIONSHIPS

You can't develop a consistent international financial policy until you understand the reasons for differences in exchange rates and interest rates. Therefore let us consider the following four problems:

- **Problem 1**   Why is the dollar rate of interest ($r_\$$) different from the sterling rate ($r_\pounds$)?
- **Problem 2**   Why is the forward rate of exchange ($f_{\$/\pounds}$) different from the spot rate ($S_{\$/\pounds}$)?
- **Problem 3**   What determines next year's expected spot rate of exchange between dollars and pounds [$E(S_{\$/\pounds})$]?
- **Problem 4**   What is the relationship between the inflation rate in Canada ($i_\$$) and the British inflation rate ($i_\pounds$)?

Suppose that individuals were not worried about risk and that there were no barriers or costs to international trade. Then the rates of spot exchange, forward exchange, interest, and inflation would stand in the following simple relationship to one another.

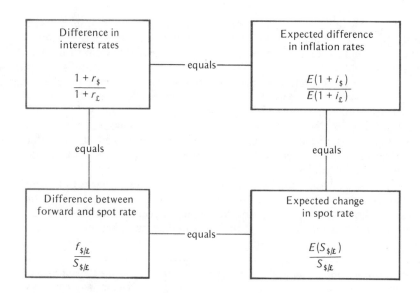

Why should this be so?

Interest Rates and Exchange Rates

You have $1 million to invest for one year. Is it better to make a dollar loan or a sterling loan? Let's work out a numerical example.

Dollar Loan   The rate of interest on a one-year dollar deposit is 11%. Therefore, at the end of the year, you get $1,000,000 \times 1.11 = \$1,110,000$.

Sterling Loan   The current spot rate of exchange is $1.4645/£. For $1 million, you can buy $1,000,000/1.4645 = £682,827$. The rate of interest on a one-year sterling deposit is 12%. Therefore, at the end of the year, you get $682,827 \times 1.12 = £764,766$. Of course you don't know what the exchange rate is going to be in one year's time. But that doesn't matter. You can fix today the price at which you will sell your pounds. The one-year forward rate is $1.4512/£. Therefore, by selling forward, you can make sure that you will get $764,766 \times 1.4512 = \$1,109,828$ at the end of the year.

Thus, the two investments offer almost exactly the same rate of return. They have to—they are both risk-free. If the domestic interest rate were different from the "covered" foreign rate, you would have a money machine.

When you make the sterling loan you lose because you get a lower interest rate. But you gain because you sell sterling forward at a higher price than you have to pay for it today.

The interest rate differential is

$$\frac{1 + r_\$}{1 + r_£}$$

And the differential between the forward spot exchange rates is

$$\frac{f_{\$/£}}{S_{\$/£}}$$

Interest rate parity theory says that the interest rate differential must equal the differential between the forward and spot exchange rates.

The Forward Discount and Changes in Spot Rates

Now let us think how the forward discount is related to changes in spot rates of exchange. If people didn't care about risk the forward rate of exchange would depend solely on what people expect the spot rate to be. For example, if the one-year foward rate on sterling is $1.4512/£, that can only be because traders expect the spot rate in one year's time to be $1.4512/£. If they expected it to be higher than this, nobody would be willing to sell pounds at the forward rate; if they expected it to be lower, nobody would be willing to buy at the forward rate.

Therefore the *expectations theory* of exchange rates tells us that the percentage difference between the forward rate and today's spot rate is equal to the expected change in the spot rate:

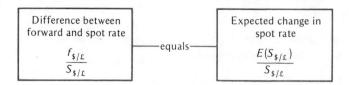

| Difference between forward and spot rate $\dfrac{f_{\$/\pounds}}{S_{\$/\pounds}}$ | —equals— | Expected change in spot rate $\dfrac{E(S_{\$/\pounds})}{S_{\$/\pounds}}$ |

In deriving the expectations theory we assumed that traders don't care about risk. If they do care, the forward rate can be either higher or lower than the expected spot rate. For example, suppose that you have contracted to receive £100,000 sterling in three months. You can wait until you receive the money before you change it into dollars, but this leaves you open to the risk that the price of sterling may fall over the next three months. Your alternative is to *sell* the sterling forward. In this case, you are fixing today the price at which you will sell the sterling. Since you avoid risk by selling sterling forward, you may be willing to do so even if the forward price of sterling is a little *lower* than the expected spot price.

Other companies may be in the opposite position. They may have contracted to pay out sterling in three months. They can wait until the end of the three months and then buy sterling, but this leaves them open to the risk that the price of sterling may rise. It is safer for these companies to fix the price today by *buying* sterling forward. These companies may, therefore, be willing to buy forward even if the forward price of sterling is a little *higher* than the expected spot price.

Thus some companies find it safer to *sell* sterling forward, while others find it safer to *buy* sterling forward. If the first group predominates, the forward price of sterling is likely to be less than the expected spot price. If the second group predominates, the forward price is likely to be greater than the expected spot price.

Changes in the Exchange Rate and Inflation Rates

Now we come to the third side of our quadrilateral—the relationship between changes in the spot exchange rate and inflation rates. Suppose that you notice that silver can be bought in Toronto for $8.50 a troy ounce and sold in London for £6. You think you may be on to a good thing. You decide to buy silver for $8.50 and put it on the first plane to London, where you sell it for £6. Then you exchange your £6 into $6 \times 1.4645 = \$8.79$. You have a gross profit of $0.29 an ounce. Of course you have to pay transportation and insurance costs out of this, but there should still be something left over for you.

Money machines don't exist—not for long. As others notice the disparity between the price of silver in London and the price in Toronto, the price will be forced down in London and up in Toronto until the profit opportunity disappears. Arbitrage ensures that the dollar price of silver is about the same in the two countries.

Of course silver is a standard and easily transportable commodity, but to some degree you might expect that the same forces would be acting to equalize the domestic and foreign prices of other goods. Those goods that can be bought more cheaply abroad will be imported, and that will force down the price of the domestic product. Similarly, those goods that can be bought more cheaply in Canada will be exported, and that will force down the price of the foreign product.

This is often called the *law of one price*.[3] Just as the price of goods in Safeway must be roughly the same as the price of goods in Dominion, so the price of goods in England

---

[3]Economists tend to use the phrase *law of one price* when they are talking about the price of a single good. The notion that the price level of goods in general must be the same in two countries is often called the *purchasing power parity theory*.

when converted into dollars must be roughly the same as the price in Canada. Therefore we have

£ price of good × price of £ = $ price of good

or equivalently,

$$\text{Price of £} = \frac{\text{\$ price of good}}{\text{£ price of good}}$$

If the price of sterling is always equal to the ratio of domestic prices, then any *change* in the ratio of domestic prices must be matched by a *change* in the price of sterling. For example, if inflation is 5% in Canada and 10% in Britain, then in order to equalize the dollar price of goods in the two countries, the price of sterling must fall by (0.05 − 0.10)/(1.10) or about 5%. Therefore the law of one price suggests that in order to estimate changes in the spot rate of exchange, you need to estimate differences in relative inflation rates:[4]

<table>
<tr>
<td>Expected difference
in inflation rates

$\dfrac{E(1 + i_\$)}{E(1 + i_£)}$</td>
<td>——— equals ———</td>
<td>Expected change in spot rate

$\dfrac{E(S_{\$/£})}{S_{\$/£}}$</td>
</tr>
</table>

Interest Rates and Inflation Rates

Now for the fourth leg! Just as water flows downhill, so capital always flows where the returns are greatest. In equilibrium the expected *real* return on capital is the same in different countries.

But bonds don't promise you a fixed *real* return: they promise a fixed *money* payment. Therefore we have to think about how the money rate of interest in each country is related to the real rate of interest. One answer to this has been provided by Irving Fisher, who argued that the money rate of interest will reflect the amount of expected inflation.[5] In this case Canada and Britain will both offer the same expected *real* rate of interest and the difference in money rates will be equal to the expected difference in inflation rates:

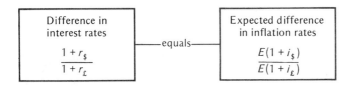

<table>
<tr>
<td>Difference in
interest rates

$\dfrac{1 + r_\$}{1 + r_£}$</td>
<td>—equals—</td>
<td>Expected difference
in inflation rates

$\dfrac{E(1 + i_\$)}{E(1 + i_£)}$</td>
</tr>
</table>

---

[4]We are suggesting here that the *expected* difference in the inflation rate equals the *expected* change in the exchange rate. Notice, however, that the law of one price also implies that the *actual* difference in the inflation rate always equals the *actual* change in the exchange rate.

[5]We discussed the Fisher effect in Section 21-1.

Is Life Really that Simple?

We have described above four simple theories that link together interest rates, forward exchange rates, spot exchange rates, and inflation rates. Notice that the four theories are mutually consistent. This means that, if any three are correct, the fourth must also be correct. Conversely, if any one is wrong, at least one other is wrong.[6]

You now have a simple model against which to compare actual economic behaviour. Therefore let us look briefly at how well it can predict prices.

1. Interest Rate Parity Theory Interest rate parity theory says that the sterling rate of interest covered for exchange risk should be the same as the dollar rate. In the example we gave you earlier we use the rates of interest on eurodollar and eurosterling loans. We'll tell you more about eurocurrencies later in the chapter. Just remember for now that the eurocurrency market is an international market for short-term loans that is very free of government regulation. It was not good luck that in our example the eurodollar rate was almost identical to the covered eurosterling rate. In the eurocurrency market, interest rate parity almost always holds.[7] In fact dealers *set* the forward price of sterling by looking at the difference between the interest rates on eurosterling and eurodollars. But the domestic money markets are more subject to government influence and the rates of interest may be slightly different from eurocurrency rates. For example, there has frequently been a significant covered interest differential between the Canadian domestic Treasury bill rate and the British domestic Treasury bill rate. Taxes and government regulations prevented the citizens of one country from switching out of their own country's bills and covering their exchange risk in the forward market.

2. The Expectations Theory of Forward Rates The expectations theory of forward rates does not imply that managers are perfect forecasters. Sometimes the *actual* future spot rate will jump above previous forward rates. Sometimes it will fall below. But if the theory is correct, we should find that *on the average* the forward rate is equal to the future spot rate. The theory passes this simple test with flying colours.[8] That is important news for the financial manager; it means that the company that always covers its foreign exchange commitments does not have to pay any extra for this insurance.[9]

---

[6]Notice also that two of these theories—interest rate parity and the law of one price—rely on arbitrage arguments. If transaction costs are small and traders are on their toes, these theories must hold. The other two theories involve some views about risk—they do *not* have to hold if everyone agrees that one currency is riskier than the other.

[7]See, for example, T. Agmon and S. Bronfield, "The International Mobility of Short-Term Covered Arbitrage Capital," *Journal of Business Finance and Accounting*, **2**:269–278 (Summer 1975), and J.A. Frenkel and R.M. Levich, "Covered Interest Arbitrage: Unexploited Profits?" *Journal of Political Economy*, **83**:325–338 (April 1975).

[8]See, for example, R.Z. Aliber, "Attributes of National Monies and the Interdependence of National Monetary Policies" in *National Monetary Policies and the International Financial System*, R.Z. Aliber (ed.), University of Chicago Press, 1974, pp. 111–126; B. Cornell, "Spot Rates, Forward Rates and Exchange Market Efficiency," *Journal of Financial Economics*, **5**:55–65 (1977); R.M. Levich, "Tests of Forecasting Models and Market Efficiency in the International Money Market," in *The Economics of Exchange Rates: Selected Studies*, A. Frenkel and H.G. Johnson (eds.), Addison-Wesley Publishing Company, Inc., Reading, Mass., 1978.

[9]You sometimes hear financial managers talk about the *cost* of forward cover in terms of the forward discount. But the relevant measure of the cost of forward cover is the difference between the forward rate and the *expected* spot rate.

Although *on the average* the forward rate is equal to the future spot rate, it does seem to provide an exaggerated estimate of the likely change in the spot rate.[10] Therefore, when the forward rate appears to predict a sharp rise in the spot rate, the actual rise generally turns out to be less. And when the forward rate appears to predict a sharp decline in the spot rate, the actual decline is also likely to be less. This result is *not* consistent with the expectations hypothesis. It suggests that, although you are unlikely to lose in the *long run* by covering forward, you *are* likely to lose by buying forward currency when the dollar is at a large discount or by selling it when the dollar is at a high premium.

We should also warn you that the forward rate does not tell you very much about the future spot rate. For example, if the forward rate is higher than today's spot rate, the chances are only a little better than even that the spot rate will rise in the future.[11] This does not indicate that the forward rate is a poor measure of managers' expectations: it just means that it is extremely difficult to predict future exchange rates. Therefore beware of any economist who claims to predict exchange rates with confidence.

3. The Law of One Price   What about the third side of our quadrilateral—the law of one price? No one who has compared prices in foreign stores with prices at home really believes that the law of one price holds exactly. On the other hand, there is clearly some relationship between inflation and changes in exchange rates. For example, between 1970 and 1980, the inflation rate in Turkey was 17.7% per year higher than in other countries. If exchange rates had not adjusted, Turkish exporters would have found it increasingly hard to sell their goods. But of course, exchange rates did adjust. In fact, on average one unit of foreign currency bought 17% more Turkish pounds each year than before. Thus in terms of foreign currency, the price of Turkish goods scarcely changed. Turkey is a somewhat extreme case,[12] but in Figure 32-2 we have plotted the relative inflation rate of 101 countries against the annual change in the exchange rate. You can see that, although the relationship is far from exact, large differences in inflation rates are generally accompanied by a shift in the exchange rate.

Strictly speaking, the law of one price implies that the differential inflation rate is always identical to the change in the exchange rate. But we don't have to go as far as that. We should be content if the *expected* difference in the inflation rate equals the *expected* change in the spot rate. That's all we wrote on the third side of our quadrilateral. In order to test this, Richard Roll looked at exchange rates of 23 countries between 1957 and 1976.[13] He found that on the average today's exchange rate provided the best estimate of the inflation-adjusted exchange rate. In other words, your estimate of the inflation differential is also your best estimate of the change in the exchange rate.

4. Capital Market Equilibrium   Finally, we come to the relationship between interest rates in different countries. Do we have a single world capital market with the same *real* rate of interest in all countries? Can we even extend the notion and think of a single world market for risk capital, so that the real opportunity cost of capital for risky

---

[10]See, for example, K. Alamouti, "Spot Rates, Forward Rates, and the Expectations Hypothesis in the Foreign Exchange Market," Working Paper, London Business School, 1980.

[11]See, for example, R.M. Levich, "Tests of Forecasting Models and Market Efficiency in the International Money Market," in A. Frenkel and H.G. Johnson (eds.), op. cit.

[12]There are *more* extreme cases. Between 1970 and 1980, inflation in Chile was 99% a year higher than in other countries and on average one unit of foreign currency bought 115% more pesos each year than before. There wasn't room to include Chile in Figure 32-2.

[13]R. Roll, "Violations of the 'Law of One Price' and Their Implications for Differentially Denominated Assets," in M. Sarnat and G. Szego (eds.), *International Finance and Trade*, Ballinger Press, Cambridge, Mass., 1979.

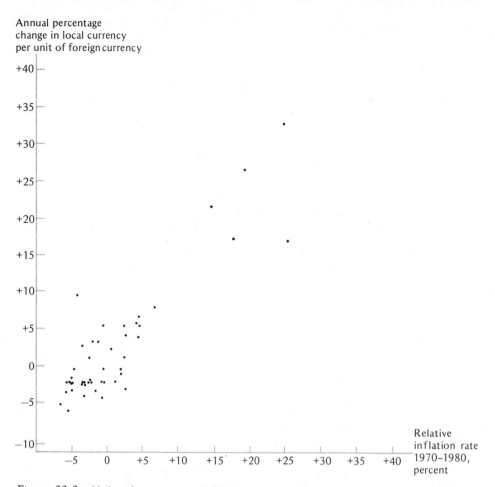

Annual percentage
change in local currency
per unit of foreign currency

Relative
inflation rate
1970–1980,
percent

Figure 32-2 High inflation rates and declining exchange rates usually go hand in hand. In this diagram, each point represents the experience of a different country between 1970 and 1980. The vertical axis shows the depreciation of a foreign currency relative to the average. The horizontal axis shows the inflation rate relative to the average.

investments is the same in all countries? It is an attractive idea. Unfortunately, the evidence is scanty.

Since governments cannot control interest rates in the international eurocurrency markets, we might expect that in these markets, differences between the expected real rates of interest would be small. Governments have more control over their domestic rates of interest, at least in the short run. Therefore, it's possible for a country to have a real rate of interest in the domestic market that is below the real rate in other countries. But it is not easy to maintain this position indefinitely. Individuals and companies are capable of great ingenuity in transferring their cash from countries with low real rates of interest to those with high real rates of interest.

We cannot show you the relationship between interest rates and expected inflation, but in Figure 32-3 we have plotted the average interest rate in each of 24 countries, against the inflation that subsequently occurred. You can see that in general, the countries with the highest interest rates, also had the highest inflation rates. But there are some signs that the difference in interest rates exaggerates the likely difference in inflation rates. In other words, countries with high *nominal* rates of interest also tended to have relatively high *real* rates of interest.

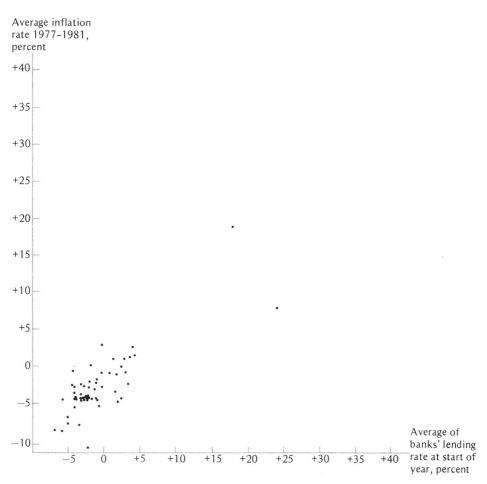

Figure 32-3 Countries with the highest interest rates generally have the highest subsequent inflation rates. In this diagram, each point represents the experience of a different country between 1977 and 1981.

Source: Morgan Guaranty BankWorld Financial Markets.

32-3 INSURING AGAINST CURRENCY RISKS

Here is a common problem in international financial management. The Outland Steel Company has a small but profitable export business. Contracts involve substantial delays in payment, but since the company has had a policy of always invoicing in dollars, it is fully protected against changes in exchange rates. More recently the export department has become unhappy with this practice and believes that it is causing the company to lose valuable orders to Japanese and German firms that are willing to quote in the customer's own currency.

You sympathize with these arguments, but you are worried about how the firm should price long-term export contracts when payment is to be made in foreign currency. If the value of the currency declines before payment is made, the company may take a large loss. You want to take currency risk into account when you price these contracts, but you also want to give the sales force as much freedom of action as possible.

Notice that you can insure yourself against this currency risk by selling the foreign currency forward.[14] This means that you can separate the problem of negotiating individual contracts from that of managing the company's foreign exchange exposure. The sales force can allow for currency risk by pricing on the basis of the forward exchange rate.[15] And you, as financial manager, can decide whether the company *ought* to insure.

Insure or speculate? We generally vote for insurance. First, it makes life simpler for the firm.[16] Second, it does not cost much. (In fact, the cost is zero if the forward rate equals the expected spot rate, as the expectations theory of forward rates implies.) Third, the foreign exchange market seems reasonably efficient, at least for major currencies. Speculation should be a zero-NPV game unless financial managers have information superior to that of the pros who make the market.

Is there any other way that Outland Steel can protect itself against exchange loss? Of course. It can borrow foreign currency against its receivables, sell the foreign currency spot, and invest the proceeds in Canada. Interest rate parity theory tells us that in free markets the difference between selling forward and selling spot should be exactly equal to the difference between the interest that you have to pay overseas and the interest that you can earn at home. But as we have seen, when capital markets are highly regulated, it may sometimes be cheaper to arrange foreign borrowing rather than forward cover.[17]

Therefore there are three lessons that you can learn from our simple theories about forward rates. First, you can use forward rates to tell you how to allow for exchange risk in contract pricing. Second, the expectations theory suggests that insurance against exchange risk is usually worth having. Third, interest parity theory is a reminder that you can insure either by selling forward or by borrowing foreign currency and selling spot.

32-4 INTERNATIONAL INVESTMENT DECISIONS

Outland Steel's export business has risen to the point at which it is worth establishing a subsidiary in Holland to hold inventories of steel. Outland's decision to invest overseas should be based on the same criteria as the decision to invest in Canada—that is, the company must identify the incremental cash flows, discount them at a rate that reflects the opportunity cost of capital, and accept all projets with a positive NPV.

Here are two ways that Outland could calculate the net present value of its Dutch venture:

Method 1 Outland could follow the practice of many international companies and do all its capital budgeting calculations in dollars. In this case it must first estimate the guilder cash flows from its Dutch operation and convert these into dollars at the projected exchange rate. These dollar cash flows can then be discounted at the dollar cost of capital to give the investment's net present value in dollars.

---

[14]Of course, if you do not know the exact payment date, you cannot be sure of the appropriate delivery date for the forward contract.

[15]If differences in tax treatment affect the profitability of overseas sales, you may want to adjust the forward rates for tax.

[16]It also relieves shareholders of worrying about the foreign exchange exposure they may have acquired by purchase of the firm's shares.

[17]Sometimes also governments attempt to prevent currency speculation by limiting the amount that companies can sell forward.

Method 2 In order to avoid making forecasts of the exchange rate, Outland could simply discount the estimated guilder cash flows at a guilder cost of capital. Having calculated the project's net present value in terms of guilders, Outland could then convert this figure into dollars at the current exchange rate.

Each method has three steps, but the steps are in different orders:

	Method 1	Method 2
Step 1	Estimate future cash flow in guilders	Estimate future cash flow in guilders
Step 2	Convert to dollars (at forecasted exchange rates)	Calculate present value (use guilder discount rate)
Step 3	Calculate present value (use dollar discount rate)	Convert to dollars (use spot rate)

Suppose it uses method 1. Where do the exchange rate forecasts come from? It would be foolish for Outland to accept a poor project just because management is particularly optimistic about the guilder—if Outland wishes to speculate in this way, it can simply buy guilders forward. Equally, it would be foolish for Outland to reject a good project just because it is pessimistic about the prospects for the guilder. The company would do much better to go ahead with the project and sell guilders forward. In that way, it would get the best of both worlds.

Thus, as long as a company can alter its exchange exposure, its international capital expenditure decisions should not depend on whether the manager feels that a currency is wrongly valued. Instead of using its own exchange rate forecasts, Outland should base its capital investment decision on the foreign exchange market's consensus forecasts. To measure this consensus forecast, Outland can make use of the simple relationships described earlier in the chapter. If investors are on their toes, the expected movement in the exchange rate is equal to the difference between the interest rate in the two countries.

If Outland uses either of our two methods, its investment decision is also going to be heavily influenced by its assumption about the Dutch inflation rate. Although Outland's financial manager may well have his own views about Dutch inflation, it would again be foolish to let these views influence the investment decision. After all there are more efficient ways to speculate on the inflation rate than by building (or not building) a steel distribution depot.[18] So the financial manager of Outland would do much better to assume that in efficient capital markets, the difference between the Dutch and Canadian interest rates reflects the likely difference in the inflation rates.

Does it matter which of our two methods Outland uses to appraise its investment? It does if Outland employs its own forecasts of the exchange rate and inflation rate. However, as long as Outland assumes our simple parity relationships between interest rates, exchange rates, and inflation, the two methods will give the same answer.

Example We will illustrate the general point with a very simple example. Suppose Outland's Dutch facility is expected to generate a net cash flow of 200,000 *guilders* one year hence. How much is this cash flow worth today if Outland wants a 20% *dollar* return from its Dutch investment?

Outland's financial manager looks in the newspaper and finds that the current spot exchange rate is 0.50 dollars per guilder ($S_{\$/G} = 0.50$). The one-year risk-free interest rate is 11% in Canada ($r_\$ = 0.11$) and 15% in Holland ($r_G = 0.15$).

---

[18]For example, if the manager believes that investors have underestimated the Dutch inflation rate, he should issue long-term guilder bonds and invest in short-term guilder bonds.

The financial manager sees right away that the consensus forecast of the Dutch inflation rate (i_G) must be approximately four percentage points higher than the domestic rate ($i_\$$). For example, if $i_\$ = 0.08$,

$$\frac{1 + r_\$}{1 + r_G} = \frac{E(1 + i_\$)}{E(1 + i_G)}$$

$$\frac{1.11}{1.15} = \frac{1.08}{1 + i_G}$$

implies $i_G = 0.119$. The financial manager therefore checks that the 200,000 guilder cash-flow forecast is consistent with this inflation rate. Then she extracts the market's forecast of the expected spot rate one year hence.

$$\frac{1 + r_\$}{1 + r_G} = \frac{E(1 + i_\$)}{E(1 + i_G)} = \frac{E(S_{\$/G})}{S_{\$/G}}$$

$$\frac{1.11}{1.15} = \frac{1.08}{1.119} = \frac{E(S_{\$/G})}{0.50}$$

which implies $E(S_{\$/G}) = 0.483$.

Now she computes present value by method 1.

$$PV = \frac{C_1 \text{ (in guilders)} \times E(S_{\$/G})}{1 + r_G}$$

$$= \frac{200{,}000 \times 0.483}{1.2} = \$80{,}500$$

Notice that she discounted at 20%, not the domestic interest rate of 11%. The cash flow is risky, so a risk-adjusted rate is appropriate.

Just as a check, the financial manager tries method 2. Now she needs a risk-adjusted rate in guilders. Fortunately our formula relating interest rates and inflation rates also works for risky rates of return.

$$\frac{1 + r_\$}{1 + r_G} = \frac{E(1 + i_\$)}{E(1 + i_G)} = \frac{E(S_{\$/G})}{S_{\$/G}}$$

$$\frac{1.2}{1 + r_G} = \frac{1.08}{1.119} = \frac{0.483}{0.50}$$

implies $r_G = 0.243$ or 24.3%.

Thus, by method 2:

$$PV = \frac{C_1 \text{ (in guilders)} \times S_{\$/G}}{1 + r_G}$$

$$= \frac{200{,}000 \times 0.50}{1.243} = \$80{,}500$$

There is one further technical point. Suppose the financial manager were valuing a cash flow t periods out. She would use the same relationships between interest rates, inflation rates, and forecasted spot rates. However, the interest and inflation rates would have to be compounded over t periods. In general:

$$\frac{(1 + r_\$)^t}{(1 + r_G)^t} = \frac{[E(1 + i_\$)]^t}{[E(1 + i_G)]^t} = \frac{E_t(S_{\$/G})}{S_{\$/G}}$$

*32-5 THE COST OF CAPITAL FOR FOREIGN INVESTMENT

Now we need to think more carefully about the risk of overseas investment and the reward that investors require for taking this risk. Unfortunately, these are issues on which few economists can agree.[19]

Remember that the risk of an investment cannot be considered in isolation, but depends on the securities that the investor holds in his or her portfolio. For example, at one financial extreme, we can imagine a single world capital market in which investors from each country hold well-diversified international portfolios. In that case, Outland would incur exactly the same risk on its Dutch project as a local steel company and it would need to earn exactly the same return. At the other extreme, we can imagine a world in which capital markets are completely segmented so that Canadian investors hold only Canadian stocks and Dutch investors hold only Dutch stocks. In these circumstances, Outland and the Dutch company do not face the same risk. An investment in the Dutch steel industry might appear to be a relatively low-risk project to Outland's shareholders who hold only Canadian shares, whereas it might seem a relatively high-risk project to a Dutch company whose shareholders hold only Dutch shares. So Outland would be satisfied with a lower return on the project than the Dutch company would demand.

The truth seems to lie between these two extremes. Canadians are free to hold foreign shares. But even though international diversification would substantially reduce risk, most investors are reluctant to invest a large part of their money overseas. Nobody knows quite why this is so—maybe it is simply that there are extra costs in figuring out which foreign shares to purchase. Or perhaps investors are worried that a foreign government will expropriate their shares, restrict dividend payments, or catch them by a change in tax law.

Corporations have the same worries when they consider foreign direct investment. Their costs must be generally smaller than individual investors', however, for we know that corporate investment overseas is very large. In 1984, for example, more than 88% of Massey-Ferguson's sales were outside Canada. Canadian investors diversify mainly through their holdings of multinational companies.

What is the right opportunity cost of capital for foreign investment? We can't give a precise answer. But we disagree with the frequent practice of automatically marking up the domestic cost of capital when foreign investment is considered.

---

[19]Why not? One fundamental reason is that economists have never been able to agree on what makes one country different from another. Is it just that they have different currencies? Or is it that their citizens have different tastes? Or is it that they are subject to different regulations and taxes? The answer affects the relationship between security prices in different countries. See, for example, F.L.A. Grauer, R.H. Litzenberger, and R.E. Stehle, "Sharing Rules and Equilibrium in an International Capital Market Under Uncertainty," *Journal of Financial Economics*, 3:233–256 (June 1976), B.H. Solnik, "An Equilibrium Model of the International Capital Market," *Journal of Economic Theory*, 8:500–524 (1974), and F. Black, "International Capital Market Equilibrium with Investment Barriers," *Journal of Financial Economics*, 1:337–352 (December 1974).

There seem to be two motives for the markup. First, managers see extra uncertainty in returns on foreign investment. However, remember that much of this risk is uncorrelated with the risks stockholders face at home. Apparently there are still unexploited opportunities for overseas investment to reduce risk through diversification. If so, investors may be willing to accept a somewhat *lower* return from international than from domestic investment.[20] In other words, corporate international diversification may have value *if* the firm can invest abroad more cheaply and conveniently than investors can on their own accounts.

Managers may also mark up the required return for foreign investment to cover the risk of expropriation, foreign exchange restrictions, or unfavourable tax changes. A fudge factor is added to the discount rate to cover these costs. We think managers should leave the discount rate alone and reduce expected cash flows instead. Adjusting cash flows brings management's assumptions about "political risks" out in the open for scrutiny and sensitivity analysis.

32-6 FINANCING FOREIGN OPERATIONS

Outland can pay for its Dutch venture in three ways. It can export capital from Canada, it can borrow Dutch guilders, or it can borrow wherever interest rates are lowest.

Notice that if Outland exports funds to its Dutch subsidiary and the guilder is later devalued, the parent may suffer an exchange loss. Other things equal, the Dutch assets will be worth fewer dollars than before. In this case, Outland could protect itself against exchange risk by borrowing guilders. It would then have both a Dutch asset and an offsetting Dutch liability.

Unfortunately, other things are rarely equal, for the devaluation may be accompanied by changes in the guilder value of Outland's assets. Remember that the law of one price states that any change in the guilder exchange rate will be exactly offset by a relative change in the price of Dutch goods. Of course you know better than to take that theory literally, but it may not be too bad an approximation in the case of readily exportable goods such as steel inventory. In other words, even if the guilder is devalued, Outland's steel inventory may largely hold its value in terms of dollars. Therefore, rather than finance the entire venture by guilder debt, it may be safer to finance it by a mixture of guilders and dollars.

Some overseas investments may have almost no exchange risk. For example, since oil prices are fixed in U.S. dollars, Exxon's investment in the British North Sea is largely immune to the devaluation of sterling. Exxon's least-risky strategy is therefore to finance its North Sea investment with U.S. dollars rather than pounds. Conversely, other firms may be exposed to exchange risk even though all their business is conducted in Canada. For example, since a devaluation of the yen is likely to reduce the dollar price of Japanese cars, a Ford dealer may be exposed to changes in the Japanese exchange rate and could protect himself or herself against exchange risk by financing partly with yen.

Many companies do look at the nature of their foreign assets before deciding how much finance should be provided by the parent and how much should be borrowed locally. For example, they may believe that fixed assets are likely to keep their dollar

---

[20]American investors behave as if they expect foreign shares to give them a 4% to 5% lower return than United States shares. These apparently modest expectations suggest a standard for American companies who are expanding abroad. Their opportunity cost of capital on overseas investment is the return that shareholders expect from investing abroad on their own account, which seems to be about 4% to 5% lower than the cost of capital for domestic investment in the United States. See I.A. Cooper and E. Kaplanis, "Costs to Cross-Border Investment and International Equity Market Equilibrium," Working Paper, London Business School, 1983.

value in the event of exchange rate changes. In this case, they would finance fixed assets mainly by the export of dollars and finance receivables mainly by local borrowing.[21]

What about Outland's third financing alternative? Instead of borrowing in Holland, where the interest rate is about 10%, perhaps Outland should borrow in Switzerland, where the rate is about $2^1/_2$%. However, you must ask yourself *why* the Swiss rate is so low. Unless you know that the Swiss government is deliberately holding the rate down by restrictions on the export of capital, you should suspect that the real cost of capital is roughly the same in Switzerland as it is anywhere else. The nominal interest rate is low only because investors expect a low domestic rate of inflation and a strong currency. The advantage of the low rate of interest is, therefore, likely to be offset by the fact that when you come to repay the loan, each franc will cost you more dollars than currently.

The International Capital Markets

We have discussed in general terms whether Outland should finance its Dutch subsidiary with a loan denominated in dollars or guilders or Swiss francs. Now we must look more closely at what is involved when a company issues a loan to finance its overseas operations. We will find that there is often a basic choice between raising a local loan or raising a loan on the international capital markets. For example, Outland can borrow dollars from the domestic branch of a Canadian bank at the local rate of interest, or it can borrow **eurodollars** in the **eurocurrency** market, which is an international market for short-term capital.

A eurodollar is not some strange banknote—it is simply a Canadian dollar deposit in a bank outside Canada or an American dollar deposit in a bank outside the United States.[22] For example, suppose that a Canadian oil company buys crude oil from an Arab sheik and pays for it with a $1 million cheque drawn on the Royal Bank of Canada. The sheik then deposits the cheque with his account at Barclays Bank in London. As a result Barclays has an asset in the form of a $1 million credit in its account with the Royal Bank. It also has an offsetting liability in the form of a dollar deposit. The dollar deposit is placed outside Canada: it is, therefore, a eurodollar deposit. Barclays can use its new deposit base to make a eurodollar loan—perhaps to Outland Steel.

You have probably gathered from our description that eurocurrency banking is a wholesale rather than a retail business. The customers are corporations and governments—not individuals. They don't want chequing accounts; they want to earn interest on their money. Therefore they make short-term time deposits or they buy somewhat longer-term certificates of deposit. They borrow anything from overnight call money to eight-year term loans. Interest rates in the eurocurrency market may be fixed, but generally are floating. Floating rates are usually tied to the rate at which the banks lend to one another.

If we lived in a world without regulations and taxes, the interest rate on a eurodollar loan would have to be the same as the rate on a domestic dollar loan, the interest rate on a eurosterling loan would have to be the same as the rate on a domestic sterling loan, and so on. However, the eurocurrency markets exist only because individual governments attempt to regulate domestic bank lending as part of monetary policy. For example, between 1963 and 1974 the United States government controlled the export

---

[21]For an example, see N.F. Hoyt, Jr., "The Management of Currency Exchange Risk by the Singer Company," *Financial Management*, 1:13–20 (Spring 1972).

[22]Thus, technically speaking, Canadian dollar deposits in United States banks and United States dollar deposits in Canadian banks are eurodollar deposits. The prefix "euro" has been adopted because most of the eurodollar deposit activity is conducted in Europe, principally in London.

of funds for corporate investment. Therefore companies that wished to expand abroad were forced to turn to the eurodollar market. This additional demand for eurodollar loans tended to push the eurodollar interest rate above the domestic rate. At the same time Regulation Q limited the rate of interest that banks in the United States could pay on domestic deposits; this also tended to keep the eurodollar rate of interest above the domestic rate. By early 1974 the restrictions on the export of funds had been removed and the Regulation Q ceiling on large deposits had been erased. In consequence, the differential between the interest rate on eurodollars and the rate on domestic deposits narrowed.

So far we have talked about sources of short- and medium-term capital. But suppose that Outland Steel wished to raise long-term debt for its foreign expansion. The simplest way to do this is to make a so-called **foreign bond** issue. In this case it issues bonds on a foreign capital market just like any local firm. The bond must of course be denominated in the local currency and the terms must conform to local custom. For Canadian borrowers the most important markets for foreign bonds have been the United States and England; for American borrowers, Switzerland and, to a lesser extent, Germany.[23]

Foreign bonds are issued nationally and are subject to local regulations. But there is also an international market for long-term debt known as the **eurobond** market. A eurobond is a bond that is sold simultaneously in a number of countries by an international syndicate.

Eurobonds have been issued in many currencies, but generally you want to choose a currency that is actively traded, fully convertible, and relatively stable. The United States dollar has been the most popular choice, followed by the Deutschemark and the Dutch guilder.[24] Occasionally, when a eurobond has been denominated in a weak currency the holder has been given an option to ask for payment to be made in another currency. Sometimes also eurobond issues make each payment in a mixture of currencies—"currency cocktails." The most common of these have been the European Unit of Account (or EUA) and the European Composite Unit (or Eurco).

Eurobonds show almost as much variety as domestic issues. Most are straight bonds, but many companies have issued convertible eurobonds or eurobonds with warrants. Most are fixed-rate but there have been a number of issues of floating-rate bonds. The most common maturity is 10 or 12 years, but there is again a considerable spread around this figure.

The issue procedure for a eurobond is much like that of any Canadian or American domestic issue. The offering is preceded by a prospectus and then is marketed by a large international underwriting syndicate.[25]

As in the case of the eurocurrency market, government regulation and taxes are responsible for any difference between the domestic rate of interest and the rate on eurobonds. The eurobond market grew up during the 1960s because the United States government imposed an interest equalization tax on the purchase of foreign securities and because it discouraged American corporations from exporting capital. Therefore both European firms and American multinationals were forced to tap the relatively small European markets. With the removal of the interest equalization tax in 1974 and

---

[23]The largest market for foreign bonds is in New York. In recent years about 20% of long-term bond issues in New York have consisted of "Yankee bonds," that is, bonds issued by foreign companies and governments.

[24]Switzerland has strongly discouraged eurobonds denominated in Swiss francs.

[25]The principal differences are (a) the large size of the underwriting syndicate and (b) the fact that the terms of the issue are not finally settled until after the selling group has assessed the degree of interest in the bonds. Euroguilder issues are unusual in that they are managed by the Dutch banks on a "best-efforts" basis.

---

the relaxation of the controls on capital exports, the eurobond rates on American issues have come closer to the American domestic rates. But the eurobond market remains less susceptible to the effects of government regulation of domestic markets.

Now you see why we said that for many currencies there are two capital markets. Outland Steel can either borrow a currency in its domestic market or it can borrow it in the international market. The international market for short- and medium-term loans is the eurocurrency market and the international market for long-term loans is the eurobond market. Rates of interest in the international market track rates in the corresponding domestic markets fairly closely, but the correspondence is far from exact. Sometimes it is cheaper to borrow in one than in another.

Repatriating Funds

Outland's choice of initial financing should also depend on how it plans to use the profits of its Dutch subsidiary. In the early years the venture may well run a continuing financial deficit, but Outland hopes that it will generate a cash surplus eventually. You need to think about how you can repatriate this surplus.

Broadly speaking, international affiliates make the following payments to the parent company:
• Dividends
• Interest and repayment of parent company loans
• Royalties for use of trade names and patents
• Management fees for central services
• Payments for goods supplied by the parent.
There are two reasons you should be concerned with the form of the payment.

First there is a political consideration. Multinational corporations are always exposed to the criticism that they siphon funds out of countries in which they do business. Governments are, therefore, liable to limit the company's freedom to repatriate any of its profits. They are most likely to do this when there is considerable uncertainty about the rate of exchange, which is when you would most like to get your money out.

You may find that there are more onerous restrictions on the payment of dividends to the parent than on the payment of interest or principal on an intercompany loan. Therefore it may be better for the parent to put up part of the funds in the form of a loan. Royalty payments and management fees are also somewhat less politically sensitive than dividends, particularly if they are levied equally on all foreign operations. A company can also, within limits, alter the price of goods that are bought or sold within the group, and it can require more or less prompt payment for such sales.

The second factor that you need to consider is taxes. Companies are generally subject to local taxes on their local earnings. Therefore Outland's Dutch subsidiary will pay corporate tax in Holland on all profits that it earns there and also a Dutch withholding tax on any dividends that are remitted to Canada. In Canada, the Dutch subsidiary's earnings are again taxable. However, many countries (including Holland) have a double taxation agreement with Canada whereby the company can offset the payment of any local taxes against the Canadian tax liability on the foreign business income (that is, the Canadian corporation is allowed a foreign business income tax credit in the amount of the Dutch taxes paid).[26]

---

[26]The use of the foreign business income tax credit regime is one of two systems available for eliminating double taxation on income received from a foreign affiliate. A deductions from dividends system is described under paragraphs 113(1)(b) and (c) of the *Income Tax Act*, but this second approach is more complex and generally leads to the same Canadian tax bill. A numerical example of both approaches is provided on pages 31–33 of K.J. Dancey, R.A. Friesen, and D.Y. Timbrell, *Canadian Tax of Foreign Affiliates*, 3rd ed., CCH Canadian Limited, Don Mills, Ontario.

In our Outland Steel example, the Dutch subsidiary pays corporate income tax in Holland at a rate of 48% on its profits and a withholding tax of 15%[27] on any dividends remitted to Canada. Thus, as shown in the left-hand portion of Table 32-1, if the profits before tax in Holland are $100, the dividends received by the parent in Canada are $44.20. In Canada, the dividends received ($44.20) are grossed-up by the foreign income taxes paid ($48.00), making $92.20, which is taxable, so the Canadian tax liability is 46% of $92.20, or $42.21. However, before paying the Canadian taxes, the parent may take a foreign business income tax credit in the amount of the total foreign taxes paid, $55.80 (that is, $48.00 foreign income tax plus $7.80 withholding tax), or the Canadian tax liability, whichever is less. Since the Canadian tax bill is only $42.21, the tax credit for the year is $42.21, and $13.59 (that is, 55.80 − 42.21) is carried into the next tax year. As a result, the $44.20 in dividends received from the Dutch subsidiary is available for distribution in Canada.

Table 32-1 How to calculate Canadian tax on income earned by Outland Steel's Dutch subsidiary (figures in dollars).

	Dutch Corporate Tax = 48%		Dutch Corporate Tax = 24%	
Profits before tax		100.00		100.00
Dutch corporate income tax		48.00		24.00
Net profits in Holland		52.00		76.00
Withholding tax in Holland	$(0.15 \times 52 =)$	7.80	$(0.15 \times 76 =)$	11.40
Received in Canada		44.20		64.60
Canadian corporate income tax	$(0.46 \times 92.20 =)$ 42.21		$(0.46 \times 88.60 =)$ 40.76	
Less Canadian foreign business income tax credit		42.21		35.40
Canadian tax payable		0.00		5.36
Available for dividend		44.20		59.24

The right-hand portion of Table 32-3 demonstrates the mechanics of our example if the Dutch corporate income tax rate fell to 24%. Notice that, because the total foreign tax obligation is less than the Canadian tax liability, additional corporate income taxes of $5.36 are payable in Canada. But, on an after-tax basis, there appears to be incentive to invest in low-tax countries, since $59.24 is now available for distribution in Canada.

If the subsidiary is operating in a high-tax country with a double-tax agreement, however, you may do better to arrange a loan from the parent to the subsidiary. The parent company must pay Canadian tax on the interest received, but the foreign subsidiary can deduct the interest before paying the local tax. (A withholding tax on the interest payments is still collected by the foreign government, however.) Another way to transfer income from high-tax areas to low-tax areas is to levy royalties or management fees on the subsidiary. Or it may be possible to change the transfer prices on sales of goods within groups. The tax and customs authorities are well aware of these incentives to minimize taxes and they will insist that all such intergroup payments are reasonable.

---

[27]In general, the withholding tax rate between Canada and other countries is 15% of the gross dividends. One notable exception: if a Canadian parent owns more than 10% of a United States subsidiary, or vice versa, the withholding tax rate is 10%.

The Game of International Finance

In some ways, the game of international finance is more complex and more fun than the game at home. The financial manager can work with dozens of currencies, tax systems and local capital markets, plus a variety of purely international markets. We couldn't close this chapter without giving some examples of the ingenuity international financial managers bring to their work.

Offshore Finance Subsidiaries

Large firms often set up wholly owned subsidiaries incorporated "offshore," for example, in Luxembourg or the Netherlands Antilles. These subsidiaries issue debt to the euro-bond market and hand over the proceeds to the parent or its overseas *operating* subsidiaries. Debt service goes back to bondholders through the finance subsidiary.

Why doesn't the parent issue the eurobonds directly? If it did, the Canadian government would extract a withholding tax on interest payments. It may also try to impose an estate tax if the bondholder kicks the bucket. There are no such tax worries on a bond issued by a finance subsidiary incorporated in a tax haven such as the Netherlands Antilles. Thus the subsidiary can borrow more cheaply than the parent can.

Export Financing

Most governments find some way to subsidize exports. The most common device is a subsidized interest rate loan. This creates special opportunities for firms with production facilities in several countries. Here is a deal worked out by Massey-Ferguson, as described in a paper by Donald Lessard and Alan Shapiro.[28]

> The key to Massey's strategy is to view the many foreign countries in which it has plants not only as markets, but also as potential sources of financing for exports to third countries. For example, in early 1978, Massey-Ferguson had the opportunity to ship 7,200 tractors worth $53 million to Turkey, but was unwilling to assume the risk of currency inconvertibility. Turkey, at that time, already owed $2 billion to various foreign creditors and it was uncertain whether it would be able to come up with dollars to pay off its debts (especially since its reserves were at about zero).
>
> Massey solved this problem by manufacturing these tractors at its Brazilian subsidiary, "Massey-Ferguson do Brasil," and selling them to Brazil's Interbras, the trading company arm of Petrobras, the Brazilian national oil corporation. Interbras in turn arranged to sell the tractors to Turkey and pay Massey in cruzeiros. The cruzeiro financing for Interbras came from Cacex, the Banco do Brasil department that is in charge of foreign trade. Cacex underwrote all the political, commercial and exchange risks as part of the Brazilian government's intense export promotion drive. Prior to choosing Brazil as a supply point, Massey made a point of shopping around to get the best export credit deal available.

Financing Deals to Reduce Political Risk

Think about what political risk of a foreign investment really is. It is the threat that a foreign government will change the rules of the game—that is, break a promise or understanding—*after* the investment is made. Multinational corporations have devised financing arrangements to help keep foreign governments honest.

---

[28]"A Framework for Global Financing Choices," Working Paper, Sloan School of Management, MIT, October 1982, p. 17.

Suppose your firm is contemplating investing $500 million to reopen the San Tomé silver mine in Costaguana, with modern machinery, smelting equipment, and shipping facilities.[29] The Costaguanan government agrees to invest in roads and other infra-structures and to take 20% of the silver produced by the mine in lieu of taxes. The agreement is to run for 25 years.

The project's NPV on these assumptions is quite attractive. But what happens if a new government comes to power five years from now and imposes a 50% tax on "any precious metals exported from the Republic of Costaguana?" Or changes the govern-ment's share of output from 20% to 50%? Or simply takes over the mine, "with fair compensation to be determined in due course by the Minister of Natural Resources of the Republic of Costaguana?"

No contract can absolutely restrain a sovereign power. But you can arrange project financing to make these acts as painful as possible for the foreign government.[30] For example, you might set up the mine as a subsidiary corporation, which then borrows a large fraction of the required investment from a consortium of major international banks. If your firm guarantees the loan, make sure the guarantee stands only if the Costaguanan government honours its contract. The government will be reluctant to break the contract if that causes a default on the loans and undercuts the country's credit standing with the international banking system.

If possible, you should finance part of the project with a loan from the World Bank (or one of its affiliates). Include a *cross-default* clause, so that a default to any creditor automatically triggers default on the World Bank loan. Few governments have the guts to take on the World Bank.

Here is another variation on the same theme. Arrange to borrow, say, $450 million through the Costaguanan Development Agency. In other words, the development agency borrows in international capital markets and relends to the San Tomé mine. Your firm agrees to stand behind the loan providing the government keeps *its* promises. If it does keep them, the loan is your liability. If not, the loan is *its* liability.

These arrangements do work. In the late 1960s, Kennecott Copper, an integrated producer of metals and minerals (subsequently acquired in 1981 by Standard Oil of Ohio), financed a major expansion of a copper mine in Chile using the arrangements like those we have just described. In 1970 a new government came to power, headed by Salvador Allende, who vowed to take over all foreign holdings in Chile giving "ni un centavo" in exchange. Kennecott's mine was spared.

32-7 INTERACTIONS OF INVESTMENT AND FINANCING DECISIONS

You cannot entirely divorce the value of an international project from the way that it is financed. For example, the taxes paid on Outland Steel's Dutch venture depend on the form in which it remits profits to Canada. If it lends funds to the subsidiary rather than providing equity, the group will pay more tax in Canada and less in Holland.

Major international investments often have so many possible financing side effects that it's foolhardy to try to reduce the project analysis to one stream of cash flows and one adjusted discount rate. You need the adjusted present value (APV) rule, which we introduced in Chapter 19. Remember that APV is defined as (1) "base-case" project NPV plus (2) the sum of the present values of the project's financing side effects.

---

[29]The early history of the San Tomé mine is described in Joseph Conrad's *Nostromo*.

[30]We discussed project financing in Appendix 22-1.

The base-case NPV of an international project is calculated assuming all-equity financing from the parent firm, and that all income is paid out as dividends at the first opportunity.

The next step is to value the financing side effects. If you finance the project in part by a loan from the parent rather than equity, you should calculate the value of any tax savings that result. And if the project also allows the firm *as a whole*[31] to borrow more on its account, you should also calculate separately the value of any tax shields on this debt.

When you calculated your base-case net present value, you assumed that all funds for the project were exported from Canada and all income was remitted as soon as possible. But you may do better to raise some of the money locally. Or you may already have surplus funds abroad that you are not allowed to repatriate or that you do not wish to repatriate for tax reasons. Instead of remitting all income by the normal channels, you may be able to remit some income more profitably in the form of royalties or management fees, or you may prefer to retain the funds overseas for further expansion. Such benefits should also be valued separately.[32]

There are many other financing side effects. The subsidized financing provided to Massey-Ferguson by Brazil is one example. So make a complete list, value each side effect separately, and add up all the values to get APV.

32-8 SUMMARY

The international financial manager has to cope with different currencies, interest rates, and inflation rates and must be familiar with a variety of different capital markets and tax systems. The most we can hope to do in these pages is to whet your appetite.

To produce order out of chaos, the international financial manager needs some model of the relationship between exchange rates, interest rates, and inflation rates. We described four very simple but useful theories.

Interest rate parity theory states that the interest differential between two countries must be equal to the difference between the forward and spot exchange rates. In the international markets arbitrage ensures that parity almost always holds. There are two ways to hedge against exchange risk—one is to take out forward cover, the other is to borrow or lend abroad. Interest rate parity tells us that the cost of the two methods should be similar.

The expectations theory of exchange rates tells us that the forward rate equals the expected spot rate. If you believe the expectations theory, you will generally insure against exchange risks.

In its strict form the law of one price states that $1 must have the same purchasing power in every country. That doesn't square very well with the facts, for differences in inflation rates are not perfectly related to changes in exchange rates. This means that there may be genuine exchange risks in doing business overseas. On the other hand the differential inflation rate is just as likely to be above as below the change in the exchange rate.

---

[31]Don't confuse a foreign subsidiary's debt with its contribution to the firm's *overall* debt capacity. For example, we spoke of borrowing 80% to 90% of the $500 million cost of the San Tomé mine, but we did not assume the mine would support that debt. Instead we assumed the firm could use relatively more of its overall borrowing capacity in Costaguana and less in Canada. It could finance the project by committing its debt capacity instead of its cash.

[32]See, for example, D.R. Lessard, "Evaluating Foreign Projects—An Adjusted Present Value Approach," in D. Lessard (ed.), *International Financial Management: Theory and Application*, Warren, Gorham & Lamont, Boston, 1979.

Finally, we saw that in an integrated world capital market, real rates of interest would have to be the same. In practice government regulation and taxes can cause differences in real interest rates. But do not simply borrow where interest rates are lowest. Those countries are also likely to have the lowest inflation rates and the strongest currencies.

With these precepts in mind we looked at three common problems in international finance. First, we showed how you can use the forward markets or the loan markets to price and insure long-term export contracts.

Second, we considered the problem of international capital budgeting. It makes no difference which currency you use for your calculations as long as you assume that prices, interest rates, and exchange rates are linked together by the simple theories that we described above. The main difficulty is to select the right discount rate. If there is a free market for capital, the discount rate for your project is the return that your shareholders expect from investing in foreign securities. This rate is difficult to measure, but we argued against just adding a premium for the "extra risks" of overseas investment.

Finally, we looked at the problem of financing overseas subsidiaries. We saw that you can sometimes best protect yourself against exchange risk by borrowing in the local currency. You may be able to finance your overseas investment by borrowing in the local capital market or by borrowing in the eurocurrency or eurobond market. The latter are truly international capital markets, which are largely free of government regulation. The interest rates in the euromarkets may, therefore, differ from the rates in the local market. When you draw up a financing plan for your foreign subsidiary, you must also think about how you will remit any surplus cash to Canada. You may attract less tax and fewer restrictions if the subsidiary pays off a loan from the parent rather than paying dividends. As a result, you can't separate financing and investment decisions, and an adjusted present value analysis is required.

FURTHER READING

There are a number of useful textbooks in international finance. Here is a small selection:

R.Z. Aliber, *Exchange Risk and Corporate International Finance*, Halsted Press, New York, 1978.

D.K. Eiteman and A.I. Stonehill, *Multinational Business Finance*, 2nd ed., Addison-Wesley Publishing Company, Inc., Reading, Mass., 1979.

R. Rodriguez and E. Carter, *International Financial Management*, Prentice-Hall, Inc., Englewood Cliffs, N.J., 1976.

M. Levi, *International Finance: Financial Management and the International Economy*, McGraw-Hill, New York, 1983.

G. Feiger and B. Jacquillat, *International Finance: Text and Cases*, Allyn and Bacon, Inc., Boston, 1982.

And here is a sample of articles on some of the relationships between interest rates, exchange rates, and inflation rates:

1 Forward rates and spot rates

R.Z. Aliber, "Attributes of National Monies and the Interdependence of National Monetary Policies" in *National Monetary Policies and the International Financial System*, R.Z. Aliber (ed.), University of Chicago Press, 1974, pp. 111–126.

B. Cornell, "Spot Rates, Forward Rates and Exchange Market Efficiency," *Journal of Financial Economics*, 5:55–65 (1977).

R.M. Levich, "Tests of Forecasting Models and Market Efficiency in the International Money Market," in *The Economics of Exchange Rates; Selected Studies*, A Frenkel and H.G. Johnson (eds.) Addison-Wesley Publishing Company, Inc., Reading, Mass., 1978.

2 Interest rate parity

T. Agmon and S. Bronfield, "The International Mobility of Short-Term Covered Arbitrage Capital," *Journal of Business Finance and Accounting*, 2:269–278 (Summer 1975).

J.A. Frenkel and R.M. Levich, "Covered Interest Arbitrage: Unexploited Profits?" *Journal of Political Economy*, **83**:325–338 (April 1975).

3 Law of one price

L.H. Officer, "The Purchasing Power Theory of Exchange Rates: A Review Article," *IMF Staff Paper*, March 1976.

R. Roll, "Violations of the 'Law of One Price' and Their Implications for Differentially Denominated Assets," in M. Sarnat and G. Szego (eds.), *International Finance and Trade*, Ballinger Press, Cambridge, Mass., 1979.

4 International capital market Equilibrium

F. Black, "International Capital Market Equilibrium with Investment Barriers," *Journal of Financial Economics*, **1**:337–352 (December 1974).

F.L.A. Grauer, R.H. Litzenberger, and R.E. Stehle, "Sharing Rules and Equilibrium in an International Capital Market Under Uncertainty," *Journal of Financial Economics*, **3**:233–256 (June 1976).

B.H. Solnik, "An Equilibrium Model of the International Capital Market," *Journal of Economic Theory*, **8**:500–524 (1974).

R.M. Stultz, "A Model of International Asset Pricing," *Journal of Financial Economics*, **9**:383–406 (December 1981).

QUIZ

1. Look at Table 32-2.
   - (*a*) How many U.S. dollars do you get for your dollar?
   - (*b*) What is the six-month forward rate for the U.S. dollar?
   - (*c*) Is the Canadian dollar at a forward discount or premium on the U.S. dollar?
   - (*d*) Calculate the annual percentage discount or premium on the U.S. dollar.
   - (*e*) If the six-month interest rate on eurodollars is $10^7/_8\%$, what do you think is the six-month eurodollar interest rate on U.S. dollars?
   - (*f*) According to the expectations theory, what is the expected spot rate for U.S. dollars in six-months?
   - (*g*) According to the law of one price, what then is the expected difference in the rate of price inflation in Canada and the United States?

2. An importer is due to take delivery of silk scarves from Italy in three months' time. If the price is fixed in lira, would the importer protect against foreign exchange risk by buying lire forward or by selling them forward?

3. (*a*) Which of the following items do you need if you do all your capital budgeting calculations in your own currency?
     - (i) Forecasts of future exchange rates
     - (ii) Forecasts of the foreign inflation rate
     - (iii) Forecasts of the domestic inflation rate
     - (iv) Foreign interest rates
     - (v) Domestic interest rates
   - (*b*) Which of the above items do you need if you do all of your capital budgeting calculations in the foreign currency?

4. Choose the appropriate term from within each pair of parentheses:
   - (*a*) The principal lenders in the eurobond market are (the major international banks, private individuals).

(b) A bond that is issued on another country's capital market and in accordance with local regulations is known as (a foreign bond, a eurobond).

(c) If an overseas subsidiary is operating in a high-tax country with a double-tax agreement, it is usually desirable for the parent company to receive (interest payments, dividend payments) from the subsidiary.

(d) Most eurobonds are placed with investors in (the United Kingdom, Switzerland).

(e) For Canadian borrowers, the most important market for foreign bonds has been (the United States, Switzerland).

(f) The most popular currency for eurobonds has been (the United States dollar, sterling).

5. A firm in Canada is due to receive payment of 1 million DM in eight years' time. It would like to protect itself against a decline in the value of the Deutschemark but it finds it difficult to get forward cover for such a long period. Is there another way it can protect itself?

6. Company A has two overseas subsidiaries in countries X and Y. Canada has a 50% rate of corporate tax, X has a 60% rate, and Y has a 40% rate. Both X and Y have a 15% withholding tax on interest and dividends and have a double taxation agreement with Canada. Suppose that the company earns $100 pretax in both countries.

(a) What taxes would be paid in Canada and overseas if it remitted all net income in the form of dividends?

(b) What taxes would be paid if the foreign subsidiaries remitted $40 in the form of interest and the residual in the form of dividends?

7. The following table shows interest rates and exchange rates for the Canadian dollar and the French franc. Complete the missing entries:

	3 Months	6 Months	1 Year
Eurodollar interest rate	$11\frac{1}{2}$%	$12\frac{1}{4}$	?
Eurofranc interest rate	$19\frac{1}{2}$%	?	20%
Spot francs per dollar	7.0500	7.0500	7.0500
Spot dollars per franc	?	?	?
Forward francs per dollar	?	?	7.5200
Forward discount on franc, % per year	?	−6.3%	?

QUESTIONS AND PROBLEMS

1. Look at the Foreign Exchange column in a recent issue of *The Globe and Mail.*

(a) How many Canadian dollars are worth one American dollar today?

(b) How many U.S. dollars are worth one Canadian dollar?

(c) Suppose that you arrange today to buy U.S. dollars in 180 days. How many U.S. dollars could you buy for each Canadian dollar?

(d) If forward rates reflect market expectations, what is the likely spot exchange rate for the West German Deutschemarks in 90 days' time?

2. Figure 32-1 shows the 180-day forward rate on the British sterling.

(a) Is the dollar at a forward discount or premium on sterling?

(b) What is the annual *percentage* discount or premium?

(c) If you have no other information about the two currencies, what is your best guess about the spot rate on sterling six months hence?

(d) Suppose that you expect to receive 100,000 pounds sterling in six months. How many dollars is this likely to be worth?

3. Look at Figure 32-1. If the three-month interest rate on eurodollars is 14.375%, what do you think is the three-month eurocurrency interest rate on British sterling? Explain what would happen if the rate was substantially above your figure.

4. Look in *The Globe and Mail*. How many French francs can you buy for one dollar? How many Deutschemarks can you buy? What rate do you think a German bank would quote for buying or selling French francs? Explain what would happen if it quoted a rate that was substantially above your figure.

5. What do our four basic relationships imply about the relationship between two countries' interest rates and the expected change in the exchange rate? Explain why you would or would not expect them to be related.

6. Ms. Rosetta Stone, the treasurer of International Reprints, Inc., has noticed that the interest rate in Switzerland is about $2^{1}/_{4}$%, substantially below the rates in most other countries. She is, therefore, suggesting that the company should make an issue of Swiss franc bonds. What considerations ought she first to take into account?

7. What considerations should a Canadian company take into account when deciding how to finance its overseas subsidiaries?

8. Explain briefly each of the following terms:
   (*a*) The European Composite Unit
   (*b*) Interest equalization tax
   (*c*) Double-tax agreements
   (*d*) A eurodollar

9. A Canadian firm is evaluating an investment in Switzerland. The project costs 20 million Swiss francs and it is expected to produce an income of 3 million francs a year in real terms for each of the next ten years. The expected inflation rate in Switzerland is 5% per year and the firm estimates that an appropriate discount rate for the project would be about 8% above the risk-free rate of interest. Calculate the net present value of the project in dollars using each of the two methods described in this chapter. Currently, $.4654 buys one Swiss franc in the spot market. The interest rate was about 4% in Switzerland and $10^{1}/_{2}$% in Canada.

10. Suppose that a Canadian firm does all its capital budgeting calculations both in dollars *and* in a foreign currency. Which method will give a higher NPV if the firm assumes that:
   (*a*) The real interest rate in Canada is lower than in the foreign country and the real exchange rate is constant;
   (*b*) The real value of the foreign currency will appreciate against the dollar and the real interest rates are equal?

11. A diversified Canadian company has 20 operating subsidiaries. About 80% of the firm's output is exported, largely to the United States, the United Kingdom, Mexico, Brazil, and Italy. In addition the firm imports components from Hong Kong and Italy. All exports are billed in the local currency and all imports in dollars. The average delay before payment is about two months. The operating subsidiaries are largely autonomous units and hitherto they have been free to cover foreign exchange exposure as they see fit. You have been asked to discuss whether this makes sense. Can you suggest a more efficient procedure without interfering unduly with the autonomy of the individual units? How would you cope with exports to overseas subsidiaries of the company? Suppose that the company's principal raw material is purchased from a Canadian merchant who in turn purchases it from the United States. Should the company take this fact into account when looking at its foreign exchange exposure?

12. When investing overseas it is often worth entering into a joint venture with a local company that is familiar with the market. However, joint ventures can often lead to disagreements about financial policy. Why?

13. Here is a fairly hard question.

    Company X operates in the United States and is expecting a cash inflow of £100,000 in six months. It therefore decides to sell six months' sugar futures in London and to buy six months' sugar futures in New York. Has the company hedged itself against a decline in the value of sterling? What does this imply about the relationship between the forward price of sterling, the futures price of sugar in London, and the futures price in New York?

PENSION PLANS

At the end of 1982, current and past employees of General Motors (GM) had earned the right to pensions that were valued by the actuary at $16.3 billion.[1] To help cover this liability, the company had put aside in its pension fund $14.4 billion leaving an "unfunded" liability of $1.9 billion.

Although it is not shown on the company's balance sheet, this pension liability is a debt that one day the company will be obliged to honour. If you do add it into the balance sheet, GM's 1982 book assets and liabilities look like this:

Assets	Amount in Billions	Liabilities	Amount in Billions
Pension fund	$14.4	Pension liability	$16.3
Plant & equipment	21.5	Long-term debt	4.5
Other long-term assets	5.8	Equity	15.4
Current assets	14.0	Other long-term liabilities	6.3
		Current liabilities	12.4
	$55.8		$55.8

The "augmented" balance sheet shows that the value of the assets in the GM pension fund is nearly as large as the book value of all the company's plant and equipment. And the value of the pension liability is nearly four times the book value of all GM's long-term debt.

The point that we are making is that the company's pension plan is a major responsibility for you as financial manager. You can always call on the specialist advice of the actuary, pension consultant, and investment manager, but you are the one in the middle. You must understand the arguments behind the advice you receive, and you must be able to grasp its implications for company policy. That is why we have included a chapter on pensions.

Our purpose in this chapter is threefold. First, we consider briefly the pension benefits companies offer. Second, we look at how the actuary calculates the cost of these benefits by drawing up a pension plan balance sheet. This balance sheet affects the amount of money that the company must put aside each year in its pension fund. Finally, we see how the financial manager helps to set the objectives of the pension fund and to monitor its performance.

In our discussion of pensions we shall make occasional reference to the federal and provincial regulations governing Canadian pension plans. These acts lay down a set of standards for the pension plan and for the way in which a company should pay for it.

---

[1]These are vested liabilities. In other words, they are the liabilities GM would incur if all its employees had left the firm at the end of 1982.

No financial manager can now ignore the pension plan—these regulations have made sure of that.

33-1 TYPES OF PENSION PLANS

When they retire, most employees draw three pensions. One is the Old Age Security (OAS) benefit that is provided by the federal government. Every Canadian citizen is allowed to draw this benefit once he or she has reached age of 65. The second is a Canada Pension Plan (CPP) benefit, which is paid from the Canada Pension Plan premiums the employee has contributed during his or her lifetime. The third is the private company pension. For lower-paid workers, the federally administered OAS and CPP benefits are likely to be larger than the company pension: for higher-paid workers it is the other way around.

It is often said that there are at least as many company pension schemes in Canada as there are companies. That may be true, but we can notice some general patterns.

The majority of company pension schemes are known as *defined-benefit plans*—that is, they offer an employee a promise such as so many dollars a month from age 65 or a specified proportion of his or her final salary.

Defined-benefit schemes fall into two groups. One group consists of schemes that are negotiated directly between a company and a labour union as part of regular bargaining. Typically, such negotiated schemes provide for a flat annual benefit of, say, $250 for each year of service, but some schemes relate the benefit to both the length of service and the employee's wage classification.

The scale of benefits in union-negotiated plans is regularly *renegotiated* to take account of changes in wage levels. However, plans covering salaried or nonunion employees are not continuously revised in this way. Therefore, instead of promising a flat annual benefit, they almost always link the benefit directly to the employee's pay. This is done in one of two ways. "Career-average" formulas are based on the employee's average compensation during the years of membership. For example, a company might pay a pension equal to 2% of the employee's compensation in each year that he or she was a member of the scheme. Career-average plans offer relatively poor protection in periods of rapid inflation; therefore companies have tended to move increasingly to "final-average" plans. These usually base the pension on the employee's average compensation in his or her final five years of service.

Traditionally, pension plans make no promises to increase pensions after retirement, but some companies have in fact given voluntary increases in times of high inflation. More recently a few schemes have linked the pension to the Consumer Price Index.

An employee who leaves the company before the normal retirement age is usually entitled to some portion of the pension benefits that have been earned. This entitlement to a part of one's pension is known as *vesting*. Before federal and provincial legislation, pension plans contained a wide variety of vesting provisions. Some plans offered 100% vesting—that is, an employee did not lose any pension by leaving the company. In these cases the rate of employee turnover made no difference to the cost of the pension scheme. In other companies employees received nothing if they quit before the age of 65. In these cases the company's financial manager hoped for a high rate of employee turnover.

Currently the minimum standard for vesting in most provinces of Canada is "age 45 plus ten years of service." This means that an employee's pension plan becomes fully vested after he or she has worked for the company for ten years and has reached the age of 45. If employees quit before both of these conditions are met, they lose their pension.

In addition to the basic employee's pension, pension plans usually provide a number of other benefits. For example, they include death benefits before and after retirement and they offer special arrangements for employees who retire as a result of disability. Sometimes pension plans also offer inducements to employees who retire early.

33-2 THE PENSION PLAN BALANCE SHEET

In order to judge the cost of the pension plan, the actuary usually draws up a regular balance sheet that looks something like Table 33-1.

Table 33-1 Pension plan balance sheet.

Assets	Liabilities
PV pension fund	PV expected benefits from past service
PV contributions for future service	PV expected future service costs
Deficit (surplus)	
Total assets	PV expected benefits = total liabilities

You can see that there are two principal liabilities. First, there are the pensions that have *already* been earned by current employees and retired employees. Second, there are the pensions that you expect employees to earn by their *future* service for you. The sum of these two numbers measures the present value of all the pension commitments.

The pension plan also has two main assets. First, there is the amount that the firm has already put aside in the pension fund. Second, there is the value of the regular contributions to the fund that the firm plans to make in the future for its current employees. If all goes well, the value of the fund and the planned contributions should be sufficient to cover the liabilities. But suppose that the investments in the pension fund perform badly or that the company increases the pension benefits. In that case, the assets will be less than the liabilities and there will be a deficit. The deficit is simply the balancing item. It represents an additional unplanned payment that you will have to make sometime.

So much for the bare bones of the pension plan balance sheet. Now we need to flesh them out.

Valuing the Liabilities

The actuary who values pension liabilities is asking how much the company needs to earmark if it is going to honour its promises to each member of the plan. The problem is that there are many things that could happen to the firm's employees. Some may leave the company and so receive only vested benefits. Some may die in harness, in which case their beneficiaries receive the preretirement death benefit. Many will continue with the company until retirement and subsequently draw their pension to a ripe old age. And so on. The actuary needs to estimate how many employees are likely to fall into each category and what benefits they are likely to receive.[2] These benefits can then be discounted to arrive at the present value of expected benefits. This is the amount of money that the company needs to earmark—it is the total liability of the pension plan.

---

[2] Often it is fairly easy to estimate the odds. For example, the actuary uses mortality tables to estimate the probability of death. It is far less easy to estimate whether an employee will leave the company or what his or her final salary will be.

Employees have already earned part of these expected benefits by their service to date. They are expected to earn the remainder by their future service. The actuary divides the plan's liabilities into these two parts:

Pension Liabilities
PV expected benefits for past service
+ PV expected future service costs
= PV expected benefits

There are two common definitions of what is due to past and, therefore, what is due to future. Some actuaries like to think of the proportion of payments that have accrued as a result of past service. In that case, we have:

Definition 1 PV expected benefits for past service = PV *accrued* benefits.

Others say that all employees have so far earned is the pension that they would receive if they left the firm today. Thus we have:

Definition 2 PV expected benefits for past service = PV *vested accrued* benefits.

For employees who are fully vested, the two definitions are the same. For employees who are only partially vested, their past service earns them less if they leave the firm today than if they stay on. Therefore PV vested accrued benefits *is less* than PV accrued benefits.

Valuing the Pension Fund

Now let us look at the asset side of the pension plan balance sheet. The first asset is the **pension fund**. This results from past contributions by the company. These contributions are generally paid into a trust and invested in a diversified portfolio of securities.

Many actuaries just enter into their balance sheet the total market value of these securities. But the majority of actuaries are unhappy with this figure. They do not believe that markets are efficient and they feel that market prices fluctuate too much. Therefore they use historical cost or a smoothed combination of past market values.

If the assets in the fund do not cover the benefits that have accrued, the company has an *unfunded* liability. Thus for GM:

Unfunded liability = PV accrued benefits − PV fund assets

$$= 16.2 - 13.8 = \$2.4 \text{ million}$$

This liability must be reported in a footnote to the company's balance sheet.[3]

Valuing Future Contributions

The second asset in the pension plan is the stream of contributions to cover future service. These are generally referred to as *normal costs*. The pension fund should be

---

[3]There may be a difference between the method used to calculate the measure of unfunded liability shown in the accounts and the method used by the firm to determine whether the contribution rate is adequate. For example, the unfunded liability in the accounts is always based on the market value of the pension fund.

large enough to cover any benefits resulting from past service, and future normal costs should cover benefits resulting from future service.

Actuaries use several methods to estimate normal cost. If the plan offers a simple dollar payment based on years of service, the actuary generally bases the estimate on what is known as the *accrued-benefit cost method*. The basic idea behind this method is that the company should contribute each year the present value of any benefits that have accrued in that year.

The other methods of estimating normal cost are usually termed *projected-benefit cost methods or level cost methods*. Their object is to even out contributions so that the company provides each year an equal dollar amount per employee or an equal proportion of its wage bill.

Estimating the Deficit

We have mentioned that, if everything goes according to plan, the pension fund should cover benefits arising from past service and the stream of normal costs should cover benefits from future service.

But things do not always go according to plan. Here are some of the things that can go wrong:

- There may be a decline in the value of securities in the pension fund.
- Employee turnover may be lower than predicted.
- The union may negotiate increased pension benefits.

The first two changes are examples of what are called *experience losses*—that is, they are losses that result from the difference between expectations and experience. The third misfortune represents a new cost and gives rise to a *supplemental liability*.[4]

Suppose that things do go wrong. It is possible that the actuary's method of calculating normal cost makes an automatic adjustment for the deficiency. In other words, the actuary may increase the estimate of normal costs to bring the balance sheet back into balance.

If normal costs are *not* increased in this way, the present value of expected benefits will exceed the present value of the assets in the pension fund plus the future normal costs. The plan will be in deficit.

The company is not obliged to make good this deficit immediately. Indeed, before regulation many companies did not make any contribution toward the large supplemental liabilities created by improvements in pension benefits. Uniroyal, which did not begin to amortize such liabilities until 1966, found that by 1978 these liabilities had grown to $520 million, or 82% of stockholders' equity. Experience losses (or losses resulting from a change in actuarial assumptions) are generally amortized over 15 years. Supplemental liabilities and deficits resulting from changes in actuarial assumptions are generally amortized over 30 years.

Another Look at the Pension Plan Balance Sheet

You now know how to interpret the pension plan balance sheet. But don't forget that it is no better than the judgement of the plan's actuary. One of the actuary's most difficult decisions is the choice of discount rate. Historically, actuaries have not allowed in their calculations for any general wage inflation. They have counterbalanced this by choosing a relatively low discount rate. But you encounter some funds that assume

---

[4]When a plan is first established, a supplemental liability may arise if employees receive any credit for earlier service.

a discount rate that is *less* than the projected rate of salary increase and others that assume a discount rate that is 5% *higher* than the rate of salary increase. Such differences in assumptions can cause huge differences in the pension plan balance sheet.[5] Many companies find that a change in actuarial assumptions can do wonders to improve the earnings picture. For example, GM's 1981 profits benefitted from a reduction of $411 million in its pension costs. How did GM reduce the costs? Simply by increasing the rate used to discount the pension liabilities from 8.2% to 10%.

Fund Contributions and Pension Insurance

You can easily envisage a system in which pension plans are not funded. The company does not put anything aside. It just waits until the pensions become due and then pays them out of current income. That system is all very well as long as the company continues to grow and prosper; but if it runs into difficulties, there may be no money to pay the pensioners. In Canada, provincial laws try to prevent such problems by requiring the company to make regular contributions to the pension fund. In the United States, regulation is carried one step further and also provides a guarantee that the pensions will be paid.

Since the various provincial laws are not uniform with respect to fund contributions[6] and since no province has initiated comprehensive pension benefit guarantee program, our discussion will focus on the more complete federal pension regulation in the United States—the 1974 Employee Retirement Security Act (ERISA) and its attendent Pension Benefit Guarantee Corporation (PBGC).

Before the introduction of ERISA in 1974, U.S. companies were obliged to fund only normal costs (and the interest on supplemental liabilities). We have already seen that some companies such as Uniroyal offered substantial increases in pension benefits but did not make any contributions to cover the supplemental liabilities. As a result the value of the Uniroyal pension fund fell far short of its accrued liabilities. ERISA imposes more stringent funding rules. Basically, companies are now obliged to cover normal costs and to amortize any supplemental liabilities or other deficiency.

In 1964 Studebaker closed its plant at South Bend, Indiana, and terminated the pension plan. Employees at South Bend became entitled to all accrued benefits. But there was not enough money in the pension fund to cover these benefits and most employees were left without a pension. To guard against such misfortunes, ERISA set up a new agency, the Pension Benefit Guarantee Corporation (PBGC).[7] If any plan is terminated and there is not enough money in the fund to pay pensions, the PBGC will make up most of the deficiency. But Congress did not want companies to be able to walk away from their pension promises. Therefore it also legislated that the PBGC could recover this money from the company itself. Its claim ranks alongside the tax collector's claim and ahead of all unsecured creditors.

Notice the importance of this change. Before ERISA, pension plans were essentially paper promises. A company could terminate a plan whenever it chose. If the fund was insufficient to cover benefits, the employees suffered. Since ERISA the employee's

---

[5]It is sometimes said that, as long as the actuary correctly estimates the difference between the discount rate and the growth in salaries, the absolute numbers don't matter. But if some of the benefits are not completely tied to the growth in salaries, the absolute numbers *do* matter.

[6]There is considerable public interest in providing uniform pension policy across Canada. Unfortunately such reform is still in its planning stage.

[7]The PBGC is financed by a levy on companies with qualified pension plans. In 1982, this levy was $2.60 per employee per year.

pension is effectively guaranteed. On the other hand, any unfunded liabilities are now a very senior debt of the corporation. When the bank is deciding whether to lend your company money or when a bond analyst is rating your company's bonds, it should be looking not just at the debt shown on the balance sheet but at the potentially very large debt to the PBGC.[8]

What ERISA gave with one hand, it partly took away with the other, for it limited the PBGC's claim on the company's assets to 30% of net worth.[9] If the company's net worth is small, the PBGC can be left with a hefty bill to pay. For example, in 1981 Chrysler's unfunded liabilities were substantially larger than its net worth. If Chrysler had gone under, the PBGC would have been obliged to pay out over $500 million to make up the deficiency. This alone gave the government a strong incentive to rescue Chrysler; bankruptcy for Chrysler would probably have meant bankruptcy for the PBGC.

Because the PBGC's claim is limited, there is an incentive for companies in financial distress to terminate their pension plans voluntarily. For example, in 1979 AlloyTek was a small company with large debts and a large unfunded pension liability—at least until it took advantage of a loophole in ERISA. By voluntarily terminating its pension plan, AlloyTek obliged the PBGC to take over the unfunded pension liability in exchange for 30% of the value of its nearly worthless equity. So far only one company has followed AlloyTek's example, but the PBGC worries that one day some ailing industrial giant may decide that 30% of net worth is a small price to pay for unloading its unfunded pension liability onto the PBGC.[10]

33-3 MANAGING THE PENSION FUND

There are two methods of funding a pension plan. The employer can enter into a contract with an insurance company by which the employer agrees to pay the pension contributions over to the insurance company, which guarantees to provide a certain level of retirement benefits. The more common procedure (accounting for about 70% of contributions) is to pay the contributions into a trust fund.

Some plans use a split-funded system. Under such a system one portion is placed with the insurance company and the remainder is put in the trust fund.

Some companies appoint their own investment manager to run the trust fund but in the majority of cases management of the fund is given to one or more banks or investment management companies. The financial manager does not, therefore, need to be an expert on investment matters but is likely to have some responsibility for coordinating with the investment manager. The financial manager needs to be able to form a view on fund objectives and to check whether the investment manager is earning his or her keep.

---

[8]For an account of how Moody's bond ratings reflect the company's pension liabilities, see "ERISA—A Bond Rater's View," *Moody's Bond Survey*, February 1978. Of course lenders are not the only ones affected by large unfunded pension liabilities. Feldstein and Seligman have produced evidence that share prices also fully reflect such liabilities: see M. Feldstein and S. Seligman, "Pension Funding, Share Prices and National Savings," *Journal of Finance*, **36**:801–824 (September 1981).

[9]Unfortunately ERISA never defined "net worth." It seems probable that it refers to the market value of the firm's equity, but nobody knows for sure.

[10]The PBGC also has the right to terminate a plan if its liability is likely to increase to an "unreasonable" extent. If the PBGC took this provision literally, it would always terminate a plan before the unfunded liability exceeded 30% of net worth. In practice, however, the PBGC has not been willing to terminate a plan as long as it continues to meet the minimum funding requirement.

Risk

Some managers believe that they can reduce the cost of a pension scheme by investing in securities with greater risk and greater expected return. But if the securities are properly priced, you cannot increase the present value of the pension fund by changing its composition. Therefore, you cannot change the size of the total pie that is to be shared between the employees and shareholders.

Although the fund's composition cannot alter the size of the total pie, there are circumstances in which it can affect the size of the individual slices. For example, before ERISA pensions were not guaranteed. So, if the fund performed badly, employees could lose their pensions. On the other hand, if the fund performed better than expected, employees were not entitled to any of the extra return and the company could reap the reward in the form of reduced contributions. Thus employees bore part of the risk of the pension fund's investments but received none of the extra rewards that risk-bearing may bring.[11]

Since the establishment of the Pension Benefit Guarantee Corporation, the employee is protected against the consequences of a risky investment policy, and so to some extent is the PBGC itself. Therefore, the present value of the pension promise and the present value of the company's shares are now largely unaffected by the composition of the pension fund. This means that the shareholders ultimately bear all the risk of the pension fund's investments, so that any change in the value of these investments comes straight out of the shareholders' pockets.

Simulating the Pension Plan

Even if the composition of the fund does not make the employee or shareholder better off, it still makes sense to be aware of the possible consequences of alternative investment strategies. In Chapter 10 we saw how firms use Monte Carlo simulation to probe more deeply into their capital budgeting decisions.[12] In just the same way, many financial managers are also using simulation to analyze their pension plans. It doesn't tell them what is an optimal investment or funding policy, but it does illustrate the rewards and risks involved.

You start with the current pension plan balance sheet. The liabilities consist of the present value of the pensions you expect to pay; the assets consist of the pension fund plus the present value of expected future contributions. Now you construct a model of how this balance sheet might change. To do this you must think about what proportion of your work force may leave, how much salaries may increase, what could happen to the value of your investments in stocks and bonds, and so on. Your model must recognize that these different events may be related. For example, a high level of inflation will usually result in both an increase in salaries and a rise in interest rates. A change in the price of long-term bonds is usually associated with a parallel but smaller change in the price of short-term bonds. And so on.

The second step is to assign odds to the different things that could happen. Then you ask your computer to play the role of fate by picking an outcome for each of these

---

[11]The difference between the value of a safe pension and that of a risky pension is equal to the value of the company's option to default on its promise. By increasing the riskiness of the fund, management increases the value of this default option. As we explained in Chapter 20, the option to default is like a put option. The pension put was first discussed in W. Bagehot (pseud.), "Risk and Reward in Corporate Pension Funds," *Financial Analysts Journal*, **28**:80–84 (January–February 1982). See also J.L. Treynor, W. Priest, and P. Regan, *The Financial Reality of Pension Funding Under ERISA*, Dow Jones-Irwin, Inc., Homewood, Ill., 1976.

[12]See Section 10-2.

---

events and working out what your balance sheet would look like at the end of the year. Having calculated the balance sheet for one year ahead, you repeat the process. The computer simulates what happens in year 2 and calculates the balance sheet at the end of year 2.

When you have reached year 20, you go back to the beginning and get the computer to simulate an alternative sequence of events. After a few hundred iterations you should get a good idea of the best and the worst that could happen.

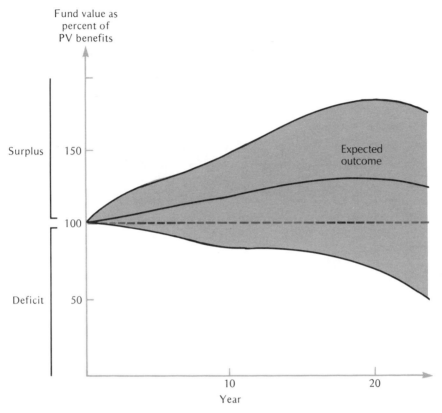

Figure 33-1 Simulating the value of the pension fund.

For example, you might find that the picture looks like Figure 33-1. In this case, the fund starts from a position of balance—in other words, the value of the pension fund in year 0 is equal to the value of the benefits. But given your current investment policy, the expectation is that the pension plan will move into surplus. Of course the outcome is by no means certain, but there is a 90% probability that it will lie within the shaded area in Figure 33-1.

Are you willing to accept the odds? Before you decide, you should look at what could happen if you change your investment policy. For example, Figure 33-2 provides a snapshot of how a change in the investment mix would affect the plan's surplus or deficit in year 10. As you increase the investment in common stocks, the expected surplus also increases. But there is also a greater spread of outcomes.

Sometimes you may find that a portfolio that is very risky for one fund may be safe for another. For example, suppose that most of the participants in the plan have retired on fixed pensions. It may be possible to choose a mixture of medium-term Canadian government bonds that will provide this money without any risk.[13] On the other hand, if most of the participants are young and entitled to a pension based on final salary, the least risky portfolio is one that gives the best protection against inflation. In Chapter 21 we discussed Irving Fisher's theory that short-term interest rates fully reflect the market's latest inflation forecasts. If you believe Fisher, then the portfolio that gives the best protection against inflation is likely to consist largely of short-term government bonds.

Many investment firms and pension consultants now offer clients a simulation service. Remember—these services don't tell you what you should do. They just describe what you are letting yourself in for.

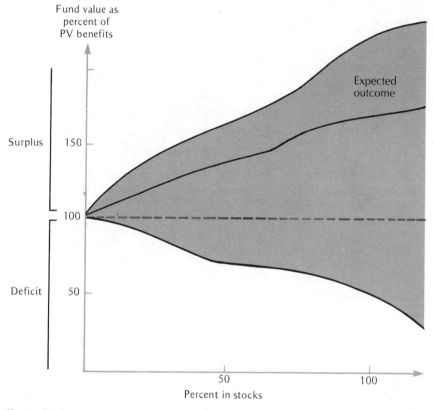

Figure 33-2 Simulating the effect of investment policy on fund value in year 10 assuming increased investment in common stocks.

Taxes and Investment Policy

We have seen that if the company can default on its pension promise, both the size of the pension fund and its investment policy may be important to shareholders and employees. But suppose that pension benefit guarantees make it impossible for the company to default. Does it then matter whether it makes more than the minimum

---

[13]In recent years, some firms have earmarked the portion of the fund that is needed to pay their fixed pensions, and they have invested the money in a "dedicated portfolio." This is a portfolio of bonds that generates future cash flows that exactly cover the fixed obligations. The investment manager tries to find the least expensive portfolio that meets this requirement.

contribution to the pension fund or whether the fund is invested in stocks or bonds? Fisher Black and Irwin Tepper have suggested an interesting reason that these decisions may matter very much.[14]

Imagine that a firm needs to pay pensions of P a year in perpetuity and that it does not set up a pension fund—it just makes each pension payment as it comes due. Since the pension payment is a tax-deductible expense, the net annual cost to the firm is $(1 - T_c)P$.

Table 33-2 Two strategies for paying pension of P a year in perpetuity.

	Current Cash Flows	Future Cash Flows
Strategy 1:		
Pay pensions when due	—	$-(1 - T_c)P$
Strategy 2:		
1. Borrow P/r	$+ P/r$	$-(1 - T_c)r \times (P/r) = -(1 - T_c)P$
2. Place P/r in pension fund	$-(1 - T_c)P/r$	—
3. Invest fund in corporate bonds	—	$r \times (P/r) = +P$
4. Pay pensions from pension fund income	—	$-P$
Total cash flows, strategy 2:	$+ T_c P/r$	$-(1 - T_c)P$
Cash-flow advantage of strategy 2 over strategy 1	$+ T_c P/r$	—

Table 33-2 outlines an alternative strategy. Rather than waiting until the pension becomes due, the firm can borrow P/r and put it in the pension fund. Since this pension fund contribution is tax-deductible, the firm receives an immediate tax saving of $T_c P/r$. If the pension fund invests in corporate bonds, it earns an annual income of $r \times (P/r) = P$, which is just sufficient to pay the future pensions. In addition, the firm has to pay interest on its borrowing, which after tax is equal to

$$(1 - T_c) \, r \times \frac{P}{r} = (1 - T_c)P$$

Both strategies involve future cash payments of $(1 - T_c)P$, but the second strategy provides an immediate cash benefit of $T_c P/r$. So it is best to borrow and give the proceeds to the pension fund to invest in bonds.

It is tempting to think that this benefit comes from the decision to fund the pension scheme, but this is not so. Funding the pension scheme offers no advantage in itself. The benefit arises only when the pension fund is invested in corporate bonds. In this case, the firm can borrow at the after-tax rate of interest and earn the pretax rate of interest on corporate bonds held in the pension fund.[15]

---

[14]See F. Black, "The Tax Consequences of Long-Run Pension Policy," *Financial Analysts Journal*, 1–28 (July–August 1980), and I. Tepper, "Taxation and Corporate Pension Policy," *Journal of Finance*, **36**:1–14 (March 1981).

[15]Suppose the earnings of the pension fund were taxed at the corporate rate T_c. Then under strategy 2 the firm would have to contribute $P/r(1 - T_c)$ to the pension fund. The after-tax cost would be $(1 - T_c)[P/r(1 - T_c)] = P/r$, which exactly offsets the amount borrowed. Thus strategy 2 would have no current cash-flow advantage over strategy 1. Try reworking Table 33-3 under this assumption.

Example We will put some numbers on this. Suppose that your company plans to set aside $10 million a year in perpetuity for the payment of pensions. Since this is a tax-deductible expense, the after-tax cash outlay is $(1 - 0.46) 10 = \$5.4$ million per year. This is set out in the first line of Table 33-3.

Table 33-3   Two strategies for paying pensions of $10 per year in perpetuity (figures in millions).

	Current Cash Flows	Future Cash Flows
Strategy 1:		
Pay pensions when due	—	$-(1 - 0.46)10 = -\$5.4$
Strategy 2:		
1. Borrow 10/0.10 = $100	+ 100	$-(1 - 0.46)10 = -\$5.4$
2. Place $100 in pension fund	$-(1 - 0.46)100 = -54$	—
3. Invest fund in corporate bonds	—	$(+ 0.10 \times 100) = +10$
4. Pay pensions from pension fund income	—	-10
Total cash flows, strategy 2:	+$46	−$5.4
Cash-flow advantage of strategy 2 over strategy 1	+$46	—

The second section of Table 33-3 shows what happens if you follow Black and Tepper's advice. You arrange for your firm to borrow $100 million at 10%. The annual tax-rate interest payment on this debt is $(1 - 0.46) 10 = \$5.4$ million—exactly the same as the after-tax pension expense. The $100 million is placed in the pension fund and invested in bonds earning 10%. Thus each year the fund generates income of $0.10 \times 100 = \$10$ million, which is just enough to pay the annual pensions. You have now substituted one fixed expense of $5.4 million a year (interest on the debt) for another (the cost of the pension). So all future cash flows are unchanged. But by contributing $100 million to the pension fund today, you also earn an immediate tax shield of $0.46 \times 100 = \$46$ million. Thus Black and Tepper's strategy has made your shareholders $46 million better off.

Notice that your firm issues an additional $100 million of bonds, but through the pension fund, it also *owns* an additional $100 million of bonds. So the firm's *aggregate* leverage is unchanged. If the pension fund invests in equities rather than bonds, the aggregate leverage would increase. Therefore, if your firm was at its optimal debt-equity ratio before the bond issue, it would no longer be so afterwards.

Black and Tepper's plan is new and revolutionary. Some people may raise practical objections to the plan. However, most of these objections are likely to assume inefficient capital markets. As one pension consultant commented, "It's hard to believe. But its harder not to believe. Since corporate pension funds hold more than $100 billion in stocks, the . . . strategy is potentially worth $50 billion."[16]

33-4   MEASURING FUND PERFORMANCE

If you pay an investment company a substantial fee for managing your pension fund, it makes sense to monitor how well it is doing its job. The need to measure pension fund performance has spawned an industry of consultants and analysts.

---

[16]J. W. O'Brien, "New Bond Strategy: What Can It Do for Pension Sponsors?" *Pensions and Investments*, July 1980.

The first step in performance measurement is to calculate the fund's rate of return. Your concern is with *total* return. Therefore you must include in your calculations both dividends and capital appreciation. You are also interested only in market values. Therefore you must look at market prices and ignore the prices at which securities may be recorded in the fund's books.

One way to calculate the fund's rate of return is to list all cash flows in and out of the fund together with the final value of the fund; then you find the rate of discount that equates these benefits to the initial fund value:

$$\text{Initial fund value} = \frac{\text{year 1 cash flow}}{1 + y} + \frac{\text{year 2 cash flow}}{(1 + y)^2} + \cdots$$

$$+ \frac{\text{year } N \text{ fund value}}{(1 + y)^N}$$

The quantity y in this formula is our old friend the internal rate of return.

Unfortunately the internal rate of return is inappropriate for measurement of performance, because it is affected by the timing of cash flows that may be beyond the manager's control. For example, suppose that you have two managers, each of whom follows a strategy of investing an entire fund in the market index. Each manager starts with $10 million. Over the first year the index falls by 50% leaving each manager with an investment of $5 million. At that point company A puts $1 million more *into* its pension fund and company B takes $1 million *out* of its fund. Therefore A has $6 million invested in the market and B has $4 million. Over the second year the market recovers to its initial level giving A a fund worth $12 million and B a fund worth $8 million. To find the internal rate of return we set out the cash flows and final value and solve for the return y:

Fund A: $10 = \dfrac{-1}{1 + y} + \dfrac{12}{(1 + y)^2} \qquad y = 4.7\%$

Fund B: $10 = \dfrac{+1}{1 + y} + \dfrac{8}{(1 + y)^2} \qquad y = -5.4\%$

Notice that the manager of fund A was fortunate to receive a cash *inflow* at the bottom of the market and so has a positive rate of return. The manager of fund B was unfortunate to have a cash *outflow* at the bottom of the market and so has a negative rate of return. But you wouldn't want to conclude from this that the manager of A was more skilled at picking stocks than the manager of B.

The internal rate of return is sometimes called the **dollar-weighted rate of return**—it gives equal weight to each dollar invested. In performance measurement you need a measure of the return that gives equal weight to each unit of time. A familiar example of a **time-weighted rate of return** is the return on a share in a mutual fund. The value of *your* investment in a mutual fund is not directly affected by whether other people are putting money into the fund or taking it out.

When you measure the performance of a pension fund, you need to pretend that it is a mutual fund and then look at the performance of one share in the fund. In our example that is easy. Regardless of whether you bought a share in fund A or fund B, the value of your investment would have halved in the first year and doubled in the second year. Therefore by the end of the two years you would have been back where you started. The time-weighted return is the same for both fund A and fund B.

To calculate the time-weighted rate of return you need to identify how much of the gain in the value of the fund was attributable to new cash. You can do that precisely only if you know the date of each cash flow *and* the market value of the fund at that date. Mutual funds value their portfolios every day, but some pension funds leave as much as a year between valuations. The Bank Administration Institute in the United States in cooperation with the University of Chicago sponsored a study of performance measurement which, among other things, devised two possible ways to *estimate* time-weighted rates of return when you don't have frequent fund valuations. It was an extremely careful study, and its recommendations have become a standard for performance measures throughout the world.

Choosing the Performance Yardstick

Suppose that you now have an estimate of the time-weighted returns on your pension fund. That in itself won't tell you whether the investment manager has done a good job. Maybe the average return was high because interest rates were high or because the stock market rose or because the manager held particularly volatile stocks. This may sound obvious, but it certainly was not so on Wall Street in 1967 and 1968. These were the heydays of the "high-growth" mutual funds. As the Dow Jones average rose 20%, many of these funds appreciated by more than 60%, and their youthful managers were widely acclaimed. Subsequently, when the Dow Jones declined by 10%, many of these funds depreciated by more than 40%, and their managers were managers no more. The truth, of course, was that most of the managers of these funds were neither prodigies nor charlatans: they simply held high-beta portfolios, which behaved accordingly.[17]

The object of performance measurement is to work out how far the fund's return was due to general market movements and how much was due to the skill of the manager.

Step 1 If a fund invests in Treasury bills, it can be sure of earning the risk-free rate of interest. If it invests in risky securities, the return may turn out to be higher or lower than the risk-free rate of interest. The premium that the fund receives for taking on risk is equal to the difference between the return on the fund and the risk-free rate of interest:[18]

Fund risk premium = average fund return − average rate of interest

$$= r - r_f$$

Step 2 The fund may obtain a positive risk premium because markets in general have been buoyant or because the manager has been successful at picking stocks. It may obtain a negative risk premium because markets have been depressed or because the manager has picked the wrong stocks. You can break down the premium into two further components—the premium *anyone* could have achieved and the additional premium that your manager achieved.

Suppose that the manager has invested in a portfolio with a beta (β) of 0.8. Anyone could have constructed a portfolio with a beta of 0.8 just by putting 80% of the portfolio in the market index and the remainder in Treasury bills. The risk premium on this benchmark portfolio would have been:

---

[17]For an entertaining account of these years, read Adam Smith, *The Money Game*, Random House, Inc., New York, 1967.

[18]Notice that in judging performance you are concerned with the *arithmetic* average of the returns.

Benchmark portfolio's risk premium $= 0.8 \times$ risk premium on market

$$= \beta(r_m - r_f)$$

The quantity $\beta(r_m - r_f)$ measures the risk premium on an unmanaged portfolio with the same market risk as your fund. This is the premium anyone could have achieved. The difference between the risk premium on the actual fund and the risk premium on the benchmark portfolio must be due to the manager's success in picking stocks. This gain from picking stocks is often called alpha (α).[19]

$\alpha =$ gain from picking stocks

$\quad =$ fund risk premium $-$ benchmark portfolio's risk premium

$\quad = (r - r_f) - \beta(r_m - r_f)$

Step 3 Unfortunately, a manager who tries to pick stocks cannot simultaneously hold the entire market. In other words, to some extent all the manager's eggs must be put into a limited number of baskets. Some of the gains from picking stocks are, therefore, needed just to compensate for this unnecessary unique risk that has been taken on.

In step 2 we measured the gains from picking stocks by comparing the reward on the actual fund with the reward on an unmanaged benchmark portfolio. The actual fund had the same market risk as the benchmark portfolio but it also had unique risk. Therefore it had more *total* risk.

You can imagine a second benchmark portfolio that is constructed to have the same *total* risk as the fund. If we call the total risk of the fund σ and the total risk of the market σ_m, then this second benchmark portfolio would consist of the fraction σ/σ_m invested in the market index and the remainder invested in Treasury bills. The risk premium on the portfolio would be

$$\frac{\sigma}{\sigma_m}(r_m - r_f)$$

You can now measure the net gain from your manager's stock selection:
Net gain from picking stocks $=$ fund risk premium

$\quad\quad\quad\quad\quad -$ risk premium on second benchmark portfolio

$$= (r - r_f) - \frac{\sigma}{\sigma_m}(r_m - r_f)$$

The difference between the gain and the *net* gain from picking stocks is the extra return that the manager needed just in order to compensate for the avoidable unique risk.[20]

---

[19]Step 2 is equivalent to measuring the difference between the actual return and the return predicted by the capital asset pricing model. Thus the case for step 2 is strongest if we are sure that the capital asset pricing model is right and that we have measured the true market portfolio. Since we cannot be sure, we do not know that the benchmark portfolio is the *best possible* naive strategy. Nevertheless, the benchmark is plausible and provides a useful way to adjust for market fluctuations.

[20]Our measures for gain from picking stocks and net gain from picking stocks were originally suggested by M.C. Jensen in "The Performance of Mutual Funds in the Period 1945–64," *Journal of Finance*, **23**:389–416 (May 1968), and in a slightly different form by W.F. Sharpe in "Mutual Fund Performance," *Journal of Business*, **39**:119–138 (January 1966). Our description of these measures follows E.F. Fama, "Components of Investment Performance," *Journal of Finance*, **27**:551–568 (June 1972).

Measuring Performance—An Example

Here is an added bonus for you. You can use these techniques to measure the performance of your own common stock portfolio. Let us work through an example.

Table 33-4 sets out all the necessary data. It shows the risk-free interest rate and the yearly returns on your portfolio and the market index. At the bottom of the table we have calculated three numbers—the average return, the market risk (β), and the total risk (σ).

Table 33-4   To measure the performance of your portfolio, you need the following data.

Year	Return on Your Portfolio	Return on TSE 300 Total Return Composite Index
1975	27	20
1976	21	11
1977	−4	10
1978	40	29
1979	25	44
1980	35	30
1981	−1	−10
1982	−4	6
1983	30	35
1984	2	−2
Average return, %	$r = 17.1$	$r_m = 17.3$
Beta	$\beta = 0.79$	$\beta_m = 1.00$
Standard deviation, %	$\sigma = 17.1$	$\sigma_m = 17.2$

Note: The average Treasury bill rate from 1975 to 1984 was 9.7%.

Now we can start to analyze the average return on your portfolio.

Step 1   By investing in Treasury bills, you could have gotten an average return of $r_f = 9.7\%$. Instead of investing in Treasury bills, you took a risk in your portfolio: you got an average return of $r = 17.1\%$. Taking risk has resulted in a premium of 7.4%:

$$r - r_f = 17.1 - 9.7 = 7.4\%$$

Step 2   Your portfolio had a beta of 0.79. Anyone could have constructed a portfolio with a beta of 0.79, just by putting 79% of his or her money in the market portfolio and the remainder in Treasury bills. The risk premium on this easy-to-pick portfolio would have been

$$\beta(r_m - r_f) = 0.79 \times (17.3 - 9.7) = 6.0\%$$

By trying to pick stocks, you got an average-risk premium of 7.4%; if you hadn't tried to pick stocks, you could have gotten a risk premium of 6.0%. Therefore your gain from picking stocks was

$$(r - r_f) - \beta(r_m - r_f) = 7.4 - 6.0 = 1.4\%$$

Step 3   If you tried to pick stocks, you must have been less than fully diversified. Therefore you took on some unique risk. Your total risk was $\sigma = 17.1\%$. Anyone could have constructed a portfolio with a total risk of 17.1% just by putting $\sigma/\sigma_m = 17.1/17.2 = 0.99$ or 99% of the money in the market portfolio and the remainder in Treasury bills. The risk premium on this second easy-to-pick portfolio would have been

$$\frac{\sigma}{\sigma_m}(r_m - r_f) = 0.99(17.3 - 9.7) = 7.5\%$$

The *net* gain from your efforts was, therefore,

$$(r - r_f) - \frac{\sigma}{\sigma_m}(r_m - r_f) = 7.4 - 7.5 = 0.1\%$$

It appears that you are about on par with most professional managers.

Some Cautions about Performance Measurement

We should issue three warnings about performance measurement. First, investment management is a highly competitive business, so that it is extremely rare to find managers that consistently outperform naive strategies by any dramatic amount. Occasionally you find portfolios that are very inferior to the unmanaged benchmark portfolio, and for this reason the principal value of performance measurement may well lie in alerting trustees to instances of gross incompetence. It is equally important to remember that there are many aspects of the manager's job that are not being measured, such as choosing an appropriate level of risk and undertaking various administrative functions.

Second, since you are looking for relatively minor differences in performance, it is all the more important to be careful in your comparisons.

Third, unusual performance in any one year will more often than not be due to chance rather than skill. To be certain that the result is not due to chance, you need to examine performance over a very long period. Since you cannot usually afford to wait for such confirmation, it is important to calculate confidence limits on your performance measures.

The biggest problem in measuring performance arises when the fund has substantial holdings in real estate or overseas investments. In such cases, it does not make much sense to compare the fund with a package of Canadian common stocks and Treasury bills. Many performance measures, therefore, do not even try to adjust to fund return for the effect of market fluctuations. They simply report the return and leave the client to judge whether the risk was acceptable.

33-5 SUMMARY

By tradition, corporate finance texts ignore the company's pension plan. But the financial manager is spending more and more time worrying about it. On the average the annual pension contribution amounted to almost 30% of companies' pretax profits. The obligation not covered by the pension fund is often substantially greater than the long-term debt shown in the balance sheet. That is why we have included this brief discussion of how the financial manager assesses the cost of the plan and oversees the management of the fund.

Most private pension plans are of two kinds. Some are regularly negotiated with the labour union: they typically offer their employees a flat benefit related solely to years of service. Others are provided for nonunion or salaried employees: they generally offer a pension that is related to both years of service and final salary. Pension schemes differ in the benefit they give to employees who quit *before* retirement age. But the recent federal and provincial pension laws now lay down certain minimum standards for vesting.

The plan's actuary draws up a regular balance sheet of the plan. The liabilities consist of the value of all the benefits that the company expects to pay to current participants. They include those that have already accrued to them as a result of past service and those that are expected to accrue as a result of future service. To meet these liabilities the pension plan has two principal assets. One is the value of the pension fund; the other is the present value of the planned contributions or "normal costs." If these assets fall short of the liabilities, there is a deficiency and the company must generally make additional contributions to eliminate this deficiency over 25 or 30 years.

Even with provincial regulation governing fund contributions, however, employees can be sure that they will get their pensions only if there are sufficient assets in the pension fund. In the United States the Pension Benefit Guarantee Corporation (PBGC) insures employees' pensions. And the PBGC can recover from the company whatever is needed to pay the pensions. That makes the pension promise a very important and senior debt.

Company contributions may be paid to an insurance company, which will in exchange contract to provide future benefits. More commonly the contributions are paid into a trust fund, which is run by a bank or investment management company. The financial executive generally has the responsibility for coordination with the manager of the fund and thus has at least two things to worry about—first, deciding on the appropriate objectives for the fund, and, second, monitoring the performance of the fund manager.

It is pointless looking for *the* optimal risk strategy for a pension fund. In an efficient market all securities are zero-NPV investments. Therefore you are unlikely to find a balance between bonds and stocks that makes *everyone* better off. If the pension obligation is really risk-free, your choice of investments may not even make one group better off at the expense of another. Nevertheless it makes sense to know what you are letting yourself in for. Many companies try to judge this by simulating the performance of the pension plan over different future periods.

Because the income of the pension fund is not taxed, it makes sense for the company to borrow money at the after-tax interest rate and give it to the pension fund, which can earn the pretax interest rate by investing in corporate bonds.

To measure the performance of the pension fund you first need to calculate its rate of return. It is no good looking at the internal rate of return, because that depends on when the company decides to put more money into the fund. You need to pretend that the fund is a mutual fund and that the new contributions are used to buy additional shares in the mutual fund.

In order to judge whether the manager is doing a good job, you need some benchmark against which to compare the fund's performance. The trick here is to look at a benchmark portfolio that has the same risk as the fund but that anyone could have picked.

FURTHER READING

Some interesting views on the status of pension funds in Canada are provided in

D.D. Ezra and K.P. Ambachtsheer, *The Struggle for Pension Fund Wealth*, Pagurian Press, Toronto, 1983.

A useful general review of pension funding policy and the impact of ERISA is given in

J. Bulow, "Analysis of Pension Funding Under ERISA," National Bureau of Economic Research, Working Paper No. 402, November 1979.

Bagehot's article (which was written before ERISA) shows that the company's pension obligation resembles a risky debt. The value of this debt is reduced if the pension plan is unfunded or if the pension fund invests in risky securities. The studies by Sharpe and Treynor, Priest and Regan discuss how funding policy is affected by ERISA.

W. Bagehot (pseud.), "Risk and Reward in Corporate Pension Funds," *Financial Analysts Journal,* **28**:80–84 (January–February 1972).

W.F. Sharpe, "Corporate Pension Funding Policy," *Journal of Financial Economics*, 3:183–193 (June 1976).

J.L. Treynor, W. Priest, and P. Regan, *The Financial Reality of Pension Funding Under ERISA*, Dow Jones-Irwin, Inc., Homewood, Ill., 1976.

Irwin Tepper provides a very useful discussion of pension plan simulation in:

I. Tepper, "Risk vs. Return in Pension Fund Investment," *Harvard Business Review*, **55**:100–107 (March–April 1977).

The following articles discuss the implications of the pension fund's tax-free status for funding and investment policy:

F. Black, "The Tax Consequences of Long-Run Pension Policy," *Financial Analysts Journal*, 1–28 (July–August 1980).

J. Bulow, "Tax Aspects of Corporate Pension Funding Policy," National Bureau of Economic Research, Working Paper No. 724, July 1981.

A.F. Ehrbar, "How to Slash Your Company's Tax Bill," *Fortune*, 122–124 (February 23, 1981).

I. Tepper, "Taxation and Corporate Pension Policy," *Journal of Finance,* **36**:1–14 (March 1981).

The Bank Administration Institute provides a standard reference on the measurement of pension fund performance. The articles by Jensen, Sharpe, and Fama are concerned with the problem of adjusting for risk in performance measurement. Roll's article offers a contrary view and criticizes the modern theory of performance measurement.

Measuring the Investment Performance of Pension Funds, Bank Administration Institute, Park Ridge, Ill., 1968.

M.C. Jensen, "The Performance of Mutual Funds in the Period 1945–64," *Journal of Finance*, **23**:389–416 (May 1968).

W.F. Sharpe, "Mutual Fund Performance," *Journal of Business*, **39**:119–138 (January 1966).

E.F. Fama, "Components of Investment Performance," *Journal of Finance*, **27**:551–568 (June 1972).

R. Roll, "Ambiguity When Performance is Measured by the Securities Market Line," *Journal of Finance*, **33**:1051–1069 (September 1978).

QUIZ

1. Which of the following statements are true?
   (*a*) The time-weighted return is unaffected by the timing of cash flows into or out of the fund.
   (b) Vested benefits are those that are invested on behalf of the employee or pensioner.
   (c) If a pension plan defaults on its promise, the Pension Benefit Guarantee Corporation will make up the major part of any deficiency.
   (d) The PBGC's claim on the company's assets is limited to 30% of net worth.
   (e) Most pensions are linked to the employee's final salary.
   (f) Black and Tepper recommend that companies should increase their own borrowing and invest the money in the pension fund in bonds.

2. By the end of the year 1981, Ford's balance sheet was as follows (figures in millions):

Current assets	$10,177	Current liabilities	$ 9,940
Plant, equipment,		Debt and other liabilities	5,719
and other assets	12,844	Equity	7,362
Total assets	$23,021	Total liabilities	$23,021

The company's pension plan for its United States employees had vested accrued liabilities of $6,830 million, and the pension fund had total assets of $6,170 million.

(a) Construct an augmented balance sheet for Ford that includes both the pension plan's assets and liabilities.
(b) Show how the published balance sheet and the augmented balance sheet would change if Ford contributed $1,000 million cash to the pension fund.
(c) Show how both balance sheets would change if the value of the securities in the pension fund fell by $2,000 million.

Table 33-5   See Quiz, question 3.

Assets	Liabilities
PV pension fund	PV expected benefits for past service
PV future normal costs	PV expected future service costs
Deficit (surplus)	
Total assets	PV expected benefits

---

3. Table 33-5 shows a pension plan balance sheet. Indicate where in the balance sheet you would enter the value of each of the following items:
(a) 5,000 shares of IBM, which are held in trust for members of the pension scheme
(b) A pension of $10,000 a year, which is currently being paid to Ms. Smith
(c) A pension worth $20,000 a year, which you expect to have to pay to Mr. Brown (age 25), who has just joined the firm
(d) An amount equal to 5% of Mr. Brown's salary, which the company plans to put aside each month in order to pay his pension
(e) The total amount of $600 million that the company needs to earmark for pensions
(f) Additional benefits worth $50 million that have just been negotiated by the union

---

Table 33-6   See Quiz, question 4.

Assets (millions of dollars)		Liabilities (millions of dollars)	
Pension fund	720	Vested accrued benefits	540
Future normal costs	600	Unvested accrued benefits	220
Unamortized experience losses	90	Expected future service costs	900
Unamortized supplemental		Expected benefits	1,660
liabilities	100		
Losses from changes in			
actuarial assumptions	150		
Total assets	1,660		

---

4. Table 33-6 is the balance sheet for the pension plan of Mealy and Briars, Inc.
(a) Explain the meaning of each of the terms in the table.

(b) Calculate:
   (i) The unfunded vested accrued benefits
   (ii) The unfunded accrued benefits
(c) Assuming that normal costs are not altered, show how the balance sheet would change if each of the following were true:
   (i) The value of securities in the pension fund falls by $50 million
   (ii) The union negotiates increased pensions worth $80 million

5. If a pension fund is obliged to make a large cash disbursement near the bottom of the market, will the time-weighted rate of return be (a) the same as (b) greater than, or (c) less than the internal rate of return?

6. The financial manager of Olde's Rope company has observed that the average return was 10% on common stocks, 5% on Treasury bills, and 11% on the firm's pension fund. The market return had an annual standard deviation of 20% and the fund return had an annual standard deviation of 16% and a beta of 0.6.
(a) What was the risk premium on the pension fund?
(b) What was the total gain from picking stocks?
(c) After allowing for the unique risk—what was the net gain from picking stocks?

7. A pension fund starts the year with $50 million. By midyear it has appreciated to $60 million, at which point it pays out pensions of $20 million. In the second half of the year, the fund appreciates by a further 50%.
(a) What is the annually compounded time-weighted rate of return?
(b) Is the annually compounded dollar-weighted rate of return
   (i) 21.7%
   (ii) 72.5%
   (iii) 8%
(c) Suppose that the fund had a midyear cash inflow of $20 million rather than an outflow. Would this increase or reduce the time-weighted rate of return?
(d) Would it increase or reduce the dollar-weighted rate of return?

QUESTIONS AND PROBLEMS

1. Look at the annual report and accounts of any Canadian company and calculate an augmented balance sheet that includes the assets and liabilities of the pension plan.

2. You have been asked to evaluate the performance of your firm's pension fund over the last five years. You fit the following equation to 60 *monthly* returns:

$$r = \alpha + \beta(r_m - r_f),$$

where r = portfolio return
   r_m = market return
   r_f = risk-free interest rate

You estimate that α = 5.8% per month and β = 0.63.

Other facts:

1. The average of the r's was 0.23%
2. The average of the r_m's was 0.14%
3. The average of the r_f's was 0.38%

4. The ratio of the standard deviation of the r's to the standard deviation of the r_m's was 0.90.

What can you infer from these statistics?

Can you say whether the fund management did a good job?

3. (a) Show how an increase in the inflation rate is likely to affect the pension plan's surplus or deficit when most members of the plan:
   (i) Are still employed
   (ii) Are retired

   (b) It is sometimes said that, as long as the actuary makes a good forecast of the *difference* between the rate of return and the inflation rate, the precise levels don't matter. Is this true?

4. The PBGC's ability to recover money from the company depends on the definition of "30% of net worth." What definition do you think would make most sense?

*5. Suppose that a company must pay pensions of $10 million a year in perpetuity. The rate of interest is 10% and the corporate tax rate is 46%.
   (a) If the company does not fund the pension liability, what is the net annual cost to the company of these pensions?

   (b) If it does fund the pension liability, it eliminates this fixed future outflow. It can, therefore, increase its borrowings. How much more can the company afford to borrow if it funds the pension?

   (c) How much must the pension fund invest today in bonds to ensure that it can pay each year's pensions?

   (d) What is the net cost to the company of placing this money in the pension fund?

   (e) If the company borrows and funds the pension scheme in this way, what is the increase in stockholder wealth?

*6. To illustrate Black and Tepper's strategy, we analyzed a company that has a fixed pension obligation in perpetuity. But their strategy does not assume perpetuities. Can you rework Table 33-2 for a company that must pay pensions of $P in year t only?

*7. In Section 33-2, we illustrated the Black and Tepper strategy with an example of a company paying pensions of $10 million a year. Assume that this company has assets of $200 million and no outstanding debt. Construct balance sheets for the company both before and after it follows the Black and Tepper strategy. Then construct the augmented balance sheets that include the assets and liabilities of the pension plan.

*8. Does Black and Tepper's strategy increase the risk for (a) the bondholders, (b) the shareholders, or (c) the PBGC? Would the risk be any different if the company made an issue of new equity, which was then placed in the pension fund and invested in common stocks?

*9. "Black and Tepper's strategy assumed that there is a tax shield to debt. If Miller's 'Debt and Taxes' article is right, the strategy no longer works." Is this true?

10. "Funded pension plans impose an excessive cost on the economy. We will be forced to change to a 'pay-as-you-go' system." What does the speaker mean? Is the statement right?

11. During the past decade, two pension funds had exactly the same cash inflows and outflows and provided the same internal rate of return over the period. However, they provided different time-weighted rates of return. How is this possible?

12. Here is a hard one. Should the pension fund's *current* investment policy be affected by the company's plans for future recruiting?

13. Here is another hard one. "If the pension fund performs badly, the company will have to make extra contributions. If the fund performs well, the company may be able to reduce its level of contributions. Since contributions to the fund are a charge before tax, the pension fund should behave *as if* its returns are taxed at the corporate income tax rate." Does the speaker have a point?

14. Why do we have company pension schemes? Would it be better to let individuals make their own savings arrangements for their old age?

CONCLUSIONS

CONCLUSION: WHAT WE DO AND DO NOT KNOW ABOUT FINANCE

CHAPTER
·34·

We have had our say and it is now time to sign off. Let us finish by thinking about some of the things that we do and do not know about finance.

34-1 WHAT WE DO KNOW: THE FIVE MOST IMPORTANT IDEAS IN FINANCE

What would you say if you were asked to name the five most important ideas in finance? Here is our list.

1 Net Present Value

When you wish to know the value of a used car, you look at prices in the second-hand car market. Similarly, when you wish to know the value of a future cash flow, you look at prices being quoted in capital markets, where claims to future cash flows are traded. If you can buy cash flows for your shareholders at a cheaper price than they would have to pay in the capital market, you have increased the value of their investment.

This is the simple idea behind *net present value* (NPV). When we calculate a project's NPV, we are asking whether the project is worth more than it costs. We are estimating its worth by calculating what its cash flows would be worth if a claim on them were offered separately to investors and traded in the capital markets.

That is why we calculate NPV by discounting future cash flows at the opportunity cost of capital—that is, at the expected rate of return offered by securities having the same degree of risk as the project. In well-functioning capital markets, all equivalent-risk assets are priced to offer the same expected rate of return. By discounting at the opportunity cost of capital, we calculate the price at which investors in the project could expect to earn that rate of return.

Like most good ideas, the net present value rule is "obvious when you think about it." But notice what an important idea it is. The NPV rule allows thousands of share-holders, who may have vastly different levels of wealth and attitudes toward risk, to participate in the same enterprise and to delegate its operation to a professional financial manager. They give the manager one simple instruction: "Maximize present value."

2 The Capital Asset Pricing Model

Some people say that modern finance is all about the capital asset pricing model. That's nonsense. If the capital asset pricing model had never been invented, our advice to financial managers would be essentially the same. The attraction of the model is that it gives us a manageable way of thinking about the required return on a risky investment.

Again it is an attractively simple idea. There are two kinds of risk—those that you can diversify away and those you can't. You can measure the *nondiversifiable*, or *market*, risk of an investment by the extent to which the value of the investment is affected by a change in the *aggregate* value of all the assets in the economy. This is called the *beta* of the investment. The only risks that people care about are the ones they can't get rid of—the nondiversifiable ones. This is why the required return on an asset increases in line with its beta.

Many people are worried by some of the rather strong assumptions behind the capital asset pricing model, or they are concerned about the difficulties of estimating a project's beta. They are right to be worried about these things. In 10 or 20 years' time we will probably have much better theories than we do now. But we will be extremely surprised if those future theories do not still insist on the crucial distinction between diversifiable and nondiversifiable risk—and that, after all, is the main idea underlying the capital asset pricing model.

3 Efficient Capital Markets

The third fundamental idea is that security prices accurately reflect available information and respond rapidly to new information as soon as it becomes available. This *efficient-market theory* comes in three versions, corresponding to different definitions of "available information." The weak form (or random-walk theory) says that prices reflect only the information in past prices. The semistrong form says that prices reflect all publicly available information, and the strong form holds that prices reflect all acquirable information.

Don't misunderstand the efficient-market idea. It doesn't say that there are no taxes or costs; it doesn't say that there aren't some clever people and some stupid ones. It merely implies that competition in capital markets is very tough—there are no money machines, and security prices reflect the true underlying values of assets.

Statistical tests have uncovered a few apparent inefficiencies in capital markets, but most tests support the theory. We recommend that financial managers assume that capital markets are efficient unless they have a strong, specific reason to believe otherwise. That means trusting market prices and trusting investors to recognize true economic value.

4 Value Additivity and the Law of Conservation of Value

The principle of *value additivity* states that the value of the whole is equal to the sum of the values of the parts. It is sometimes called the *law of conservation of value*.

When we appraise a project that produces a succession of cash flows, we always assume that values are additive. In other words we assume

$$PV(project) = PV(C_1) + PV(C_2) + \cdots + PV(C_t) + \cdots$$

$$= \frac{C_1}{1 + r} + \frac{C_2}{(1 + r)^2} + \cdots + \frac{C_t}{(1 + r)^t} + \cdots$$

We similarly assume that the sum of the present value of projects A and B equals the present value of a composite project AB.[1] But value additivity also means that you

---

[1]That is, if

$$PV(A) = PV[C_1(A)] + PV[C_2(A)] + \cdots + PV[C_t(A)] + \cdots$$

$$PV(B) = PV[C_1(B)] + PV[C_2(B)] + \cdots + PV[C_t(B)] + \cdots$$

and if for each period t, $C_t(AB) = C_t(A) + C_t(B)$, then

$$PV(AB) = PV(A) + PV(B)$$

can't increase value by putting two whole companies together unless you thereby increase the total cash flow. In other words, there are no benefits to mergers solely for diversification. And if the rule works for addition, it also works for subtraction. Therefore, financing decisions that simply subdivide the same cash flows in a different way just change the packaging: they don't increase overall firm value. This is the basic idea behind Modigliani and Miller's famous article. Other things being equal, changes in capital structure do not affect firm value. As long as the *total* cash flow generated by the firm's assets and operations is unchanged by capital structure, total value is independent of capital structure. The value of the whole pie does not depend on how it is sliced.[2]

5 Option Theory

In everyday conversation we often use the word *option* as synonymous with *choice* or *alternative*; thus we speak of someone as *having a number of options*. In finance an option refers specifically to the opportunity to trade in the future on terms that are fixed today. Smart managers know that it is often worth paying today for the option to buy or sell an asset tomorrow. However, it is only recently that we have become aware that options are ubiquitous in finance. For example, *limited liability* simply refers to the shareholders' option to default. Instead of paying its debts, the company has the option to hand over all its assets to its creditors.

If options are so important, the financial manager needs to know how to value them. Finance experts have known for some time the relevant variables—the exercise price and the exercise date of the option, the risk of the underlying asset, and the rate of interest. But it was Black and Scholes who first showed how these can be put together in a usable formula.

The Black-Scholes formula was developed for simple call options. It does not directly apply to the more complicated options often encountered in corporate finance. That is why one of the most exciting areas of research is extending the basic principles of option valuation to cover the more complicated cases.

Are these five ideas exciting theories or plain common sense? Call them what you will, they are basic to the financial manager's job. If by reading this book you really understand these ideas and know how to apply them, you have learned a great deal.

34-2 WHAT WE DO NOT KNOW: TEN UNSOLVED PROBLEMS IN FINANCE

Since the unknown is never exhausted, the list of what we do not know about finance could go on forever. But, following BMSW's third law (see Section 26-2), we will list and briefly discuss ten unsolved problems that seem ripe for productive research.

1 How are Major Financial Decisions Made?

Arnold Sametz commented in 1964 that "we know very little about how the great non-routine financial decisions are made."[3] That is no less true today. We know quite a bit

---

[2]If you *start* with the cash flow $C_t(AB)$ and split it into two pieces, $C_t(A)$ and $C_t(B)$, then total value is unchanged. That is, $PV[C_t(A)] + PV[C_t(B)] = PV[C_t(AB)]$. See footnote 1.

[3]A.W. Sametz, "Trends in the Volume and Composition of Equity Finance," *Journal of Finance*, **19**:450–469 (September 1964). See p. 469.

about asset values, but we do not know very much about the decisions that give rise to these values. What is the process that causes one company to make a major investment and another to reject it? Why does one company decide to issue debt and another to issue equity? If we knew why companies make particular decisions, we would be better able to help improve those decisions.

Our ignorance is largest when it comes to major *strategic* decisions. In Section 12-1 we described strategic planning as "capital budgeting on a grand scale." Strategic planning attempts to identify the lines of businesses where the firm has the greatest long-run opportunities and to develop a plan for achieving success in those businesses. But it is hard to calculate the NPV of major strategic decisions. Think, for example, of a firm that makes a major commitment to the design and manufacture of computer memories. It is really embarking on a long-term effort that will require capital outlays over many years. It cannot identify all of those future projects, much less evaluate their NPVs. Instead, it decides to go ahead because the computer memory business is growing rapidly, because firms already in that business are doing well, and because it has intangible assets—special technology, perhaps—which it thinks will give it a leg up on the competition.

Strategic planning is a "top-down" approach to capital budgeting: you choose the businesses you want to be in and make the capital outlays necessary for success. It's perfectly sensible and natural for firms to look at capital investments that way *in addition to* looking at them "bottom-up." The trouble is that we understand the bottom-up part of the capital budgeting process better than the top-down part.

Top-down and bottom-up should not be competing approaches to capital budgeting. They should be two aspects of a single integrated procedure. Not all firms integrate the two approaches successfully. No doubt some firms do so, but we don't really know how.

In Section 26-2 we suggested that option pricing theory might help unravel some of the mysteries of strategic planning. We will have to wait and see whether it does.

2 What Determines Project Risk and Present Value?

A good capital investment is one that has a positive NPV. We have talked at some length about how to calculate NPV, but we have given you very little guidance about how to find positive-NPV projects, except to say in Section 11-4 that projects have positive NPVs when the firm can earn economic rents. But why do some companies earn economic rents while others in the same industry do not? Are the rents merely windfall gains, or can they be anticipated and planned for? What is their source, and how long do they persist before competition destroys them? Very little is known about any of these important questions.

Here is a related question: Why are some real assets risky and others relatively safe? In Section 9-4 we suggested a few reasons for differences in project betas—differences in operating leverage, for example, or in the extent to which a project's cash flows respond to the performance of the national economy. These are useful clues, but we have as yet no general procedure for estimating project betas. Assessing project risk is therefore still largely a seat-of-the-pants matter.

3 Risk and Return—Have We Missed Something?

The capital asset pricing model is an enormous step toward understanding the relationship between risk and expected return, but there are many puzzles left, some statistical and some theoretical.

The statistical problems arise because the capital asset pricing model is hard to prove or disprove conclusively. It appears that average returns from low-beta stocks are too high (that is, higher than the capital asset pricing model predicts) and those from high-beta stocks are too low; but this could be a problem with the way the tests are conducted and not with the model itself.[4] In addition, some tests indicate that average return has been related to diversifiable risk as well as to beta.[5] That is, of course, inconsistent with the capital asset pricing model, which states that diversifiable risk does not bother investors and therefore does not affect expected or average return. Of course, these statistical results could be spurious—an accidental result of inadequate testing procedures. But if they are true, they pose a puzzle: if investors are concerned with diversifiable risk, then corporations ought to be able to increase value just by diversifying. Yet there is evidence that investors do *not* pay extra for firms that diversify.[6] It is hard to see why they would pay extra, because investors can usually diversify more cheaply and effectively than firms can. Maybe diversifiable risk only *appears* to matter because it happens to be correlated with some other variable X that, along with beta, truly determines the expected rates of return demanded by investors. That would resolve the puzzle; but we cannot yet identify variable X and prove that it matters.[7]

Meanwhile work is proceeding on the theoretical front to relax the simple assumptions underlying the capital asset pricing model. Here is an example: Suppose that you love fine wine. It may make sense for you to buy shares in a grand cru chateau, even if that soaks up a large fraction of your personal wealth and leaves you with a relatively undiversified portfolio. However, you are *hedged* against a rise in the price of fine wine: your hobby will cost more in a bull market for wine, but your stake in the chateau will make you correspondingly richer. Thus you are holding a relatively undiversified portfolio *for a good reason*. We would not expect you to demand a premium for bearing that portfolio's diversifiable risk.

In general, if two people have different tastes, it may make sense for them to hold different portfolios. You may hedge your consumption needs with an investment in winemaking, whereas somebody else may do better to invest in Dairy Queen. The capital asset pricing model isn't rich enough to deal with such a world. It assumes that all investors have similar tastes: the "hedging motive" does not enter, and therefore they hold the same portfolio of risky assets.

Merton and Ross have extended the capital asset pricing model to accommodate the hedging motive. (Ross's approach is called arbitrage pricing theory.) If enough investors are attempting to hedge against the same thing, their models imply a more complicated risk-return relationship. However, it is not yet clear who is hedging against what, and so their models remain difficult to test. Breeden has shown that the Merton model can be simplified to a single risk factor—changes in the "marginal utility of consumption"—but it is difficult to get good empirical data to take advantage of his theoretically well-defined factor.[8]

---

[4]See R. Roll, "A Critique of the Asset Pricing Theory's Tests; Part 1: On Past and Potential Testability of the Theory," *Journal of Financial Economics*, **4**:129–176 (March 1977); and for a critique of the critique, D. Mayers and E.M. Rice, "Measuring Portfolio Performance and the Empirical Content of Asset Pricing Models," *Journal of Financial Economics*, **7**:3–28 (March 1979).

[5]For example, see I. Friend, R. Westerfeld, and M. Granito, "New Evidence on the Capital Asset Pricing Model," *Journal of Finance*, **33**:903–916 (June 1978).

[6]Remember how Kaiser Industries' value was *reduced* by diversification? See Section 31-3.

[7]For example, A. Kraus and R. Litzenberger have suggested that variable X is skewness of portfolio returns. See "Skewness Preference and the Valuation of Risk Assets," *Journal of Finance*, **31**:1085–1100 (September 1976).

[8]See R. Merton, "An Intertemporal Capital Asset Pricing Model," *Econometrica,* **4**:867–887 (1973); D. Breeden, "An Intertemporal Asset Pricing Model with Stochastic Comsumption and Investment Opportunities," *Journal of Financial Economics*, **7**:265–296 (1979); and S. Ross, "The Arbitrage Theory of Capital Asset Pricing," *Journal of Economic Theory*, **13**:341–360 (1976).

4 Are There Important Exceptions to the Efficient-Markets Theory?

The efficient-markets theory is strong, but how strong is it? We know no theory is perfect—there must be exceptions. What are the exceptions and how important are they?

We noted some apparent exceptions in Section 13-2. No doubt others will be uncovered.[9] Understanding what is really going on in these cases will take further work and thought.

Let us take one case as an example. Canistraro and Basu found that stocks with low price-earnings ratios (P/Es) have yielded, on the average, higher returns than stocks with higher P/Es but the same betas.[10] Thus, whatever your target portfolio beta is, you can apparently generate superior returns, on the average, by investing in low-P/E stocks.

Now this could mean one of two things:

1. The stock market is inefficient and consistently underprices stocks with low P/Es.

2. The price-earnings ratio happens to be correlated with variable X, that mysterious second risk variable that investors may rationally take into account in pricing shares.

Until we know what variable X is, or can prove that it does not exist, we will not know whether the superior past performance of low-P/E stocks really is an exception to the efficient-market theory.

5 How are Complex Options Valued?

We have made great strides in valuing options, but there is plenty left to do. The options encountered in corporate finance are usually too complex for simple valuation procedures like the Black-Scholes model. In Section 21-4, for example, we described how the federal government gave Lockheed a helping hand by agreeing to stand behind $250 million of borrowing. It would take an elaborate computer program to value this guarantee, and such programs are not now generally available. They will be, however, and when they are we will be able to tell the government what its loan guarantees really cost.

We will also be able to answer a variety of other questions. For example, a corporation planning a debt issue will be able to estimate how a change in the terms of the issue affects how much investors should be willing to pay for it. This will be particularly useful when the terms are complicated and unusual; if similar securities are not traded, then value has to be estimated from first principles.

Of course, the buyer of a security is just as much interested in its true value as the issuer. Maybe investors will have their own computer programs. For that matter, we will not be surprised if firms such as Canadian Bond Rating Service in Canada and Moody's in the United States end up using option pricing theory to help them assign bond ratings.

6 How Can We Explain Issue Procedures for Common Stocks?

Chapter 15 described how corporations issue common stocks. In that chapter we came across several things that just do not make sense. Here are two examples.

---

[9] For recent work on possible exceptions to the efficient-markets theory see the "Symposium on Some Anomalous Evidence on Capital Market Efficiency," a special issue of the *Journal of Financial Economics,* **6** (June–September 1978).

[10] R. Canistraro, "The Predictive Ability of Price-Earnings Ratios for Determining Risk-Adjusted Performance of Common Stocks," unpublished M.S. thesis, M.I.T., 1973, and A. Basu, "The Investment Performance of Common Stocks in Relation to Their Price-Earnings Ratios: A Test of the Efficient-Market Hypothesis," *Journal of Finance,* **32**:663–682 (June 1977).

Example 1: Why do Firms Avoid Rights Issues? The cheapest way to issue stock is by making a rights issue *without* paying an underwriter for a standby agreement guaranteeing the issue's success. (The need for the standby agreement can be eliminated by reducing the issue price.) Yet many corporations avoid rights issues. Why?

Example 2: Why are Unseasoned Issues Underpriced? Unseasoned issues—that is, firms' first offerings to the general public—are significantly underpriced by underwriters. On the average, investors who buy at the issue price do very well over the few weeks after the issue. It is not clear why underwriters want to hand this windfall gain to investors, but the *real* puzzle is why issuing firms let the underwriters get away with it. Any time a firm issues shares for less than they are worth, the new stockholders win and the original stockholders lose.

Is there some hidden reason for avoiding rights issues that firms appreciate but cannot articulate? Is there some hidden reason for underpricing new issues? We hope so, because if no such reasons are found, we may have to conclude that many financial managers are acting irrationally.

7 How Can We Explain Capital Structure?

If firms are free to choose the level of borrowing that they think best, the total supply of debt in the economy will approximate the amount that investors demand. No manager can expect to increase (or reduce) the value of his or her firm just by changing the firm's capital structure. That is the idea behind Merton Miller's theory of capital structure (see Section 18-2). It is a cogent argument. But why then do firms have different capital structures? Merton Miller's reply to that question is that arbitrary but harmless differences in capital structure can persist indefinitely.

Is Miller right? Does it really not matter how much your firm borrows? We have come across several reasons it *may* matter. Perhaps managers are concerned with potential bankruptcy costs. Perhaps managers use capital structure to signal information to their shareholders.[11] Perhaps differences in capital structure reflect differences in the relative importance of growth opportunities. So far, none of these possibilities has been either proved relevant or definitely excluded.

The upshot of the matter is that we still don't have an accepted, coherent theory of capital structure. It is not for want of argument on the subject.

8 How Can We Resolve the Dividend Controversy?

We spent all of Chapter 16 on dividend policy without being able to resolve the dividend controversy. Many people believe dividends are good, others believe they are bad, and still others believe they are irrelevant. If pressed, we recommend low dividends in the United States and higher dividends in Canada, other things being equal, but we can't be dogmatic about it, for two reasons. First, conclusive statistical proof is hard to come by. Second, it is hard to say that so many firms are wrong. Many managers speak with pride about the "generosity" of their dividend policy and faithfully increase dividends in line with earnings, yet we cannot come up with a fully convincing theory to say that they are either right or wrong.

We don't mean to disparage existing research but only to say that more is in order. Whether future research will change anybody's mind is another matter. In 1979 Joel Stern wrote an article for the editorial page of *The Wall Street Journal*[12] arguing for low

---

[11]See S. Ross, "The Determination of Financial Structure: The Incentive-Signalling Approach," *Bell Journal of Economics*, **8**:23–40 (Spring 1977).

[12]Joel Stern, "The Dividend Question," *The Wall Street Journal*, July 16, 1979, p. 13.

American dividends and citing statistical tests in support of his position. The article attracted several strongly worded responses, including one from a manager who wrote,

> . . . While Mr. Stern is gamboling from pinnacle to pinnacle in the upper realms of the theoretical, those of us in financial management are down below slogging through the foothills of reality.[13]

9 What is the Value of Liquidity?

Unlike Treasury bills, cash pays no interest. On the other hand, cash provides more liquidity than Treasury bills. People who hold cash must believe that this additional liquidity offsets the loss of interest. In equilibrium, the marginal value of the additional liquidity must equal the interest rate on bills.

Now what can we say about corporate holdings of cash? It is wrong to ignore the liquidity gain and to say that the cost of holding cash is the lost interest. This would imply that cash always has a *negative* NPV. Equally it is foolish to say that, because the marginal value of the liquidity is equal to the loss of interest, it doesn't matter how much cash a firm holds. This would imply that cash always has a *zero* NPV.

We know that the marginal value of cash to a holder declines with the size of the cash holding, but we don't really understand how to value the liquidity service of cash. In our chapters on working-capital management we largely finessed the problem by presenting models that are really too simple,[14] or by speaking vaguely of the need to ensure an "adequate" liquidity reserve. We cannot successfully tackle the problem of working-capital management until we have a theory of liquidity.

The problem is that liquidity is a matter of degree. A Treasury bill is less liquid than cash, but it is still a highly liquid security because it can be sold and turned into cash easily and almost instantaneously.[15] Corporate bonds are less liquid than Treasury bills; trucks are less liquid than corporate bonds; specialized machinery is less liquid than trucks; and so on. But even specialized machinery can be turned into cash if you are willing to accept some delay and cost of sale. The broad question is therefore not "How much cash should the firm hold?" but "How should it divide its total investment between relatively liquid and relatively illiquid assets?"—holding other things constant, of course. That question is hard to answer. Obviously, every firm must be able to raise cash on short notice, but we have no good theory of how much potential cash is enough or how quickly the firm should be able to get it. To complicate matters further, we note that cash can be raised on short notice by borrowing or selling other securities, as well as by selling assets. The financial manager with a $1 million unused line of credit may sleep just as soundly as the manager of a firm holding $1 million in marketable securities.

10 How Can We Explain Merger Waves?

In 1968, at the peak of the postwar merger movement, Joel Segall noted:

> There is no single hypothesis which is both plausible and general and which shows promise of explaining the current merger movement. If so, it is correct to say that there is nothing known about mergers; there are no useful generalizations.[16]

---

[13] *The Wall Street Journal*, August 20, 1979, p. 16. The letter was from A.J. Sandblute, senior vice-president of Minnesota Light and Power Company.

[14] For example, models based only on the transaction costs of switching between cash and interest-bearing assets. See Section 27-1.

[15] That is, you can realize the asset's true economic value in a quick sale. Liquidity means that you don't have to accept a discount from true value if you want to sell the asset quickly.

[16] J. Segall, "Merging for Fun and Profit," *Industrial Management Review*, **9**:17–30 (Winter 1968).

Of course there are many plausible reasons two firms might wish to merge. If you single out a *particular* merger, it is usually possible to think up a reason that merger could make sense. But that leaves us with a special hypothesis for each merger. What we need is a *general* hypothesis explaining merger waves—for example, why everybody seemed to be merging in 1968 and nobody five years later. On that score we are not much advanced from the level of ignorance Segall noted in 1968.[17]

34-3   A FINAL WORD

That concludes our list of unsolved problems. We have given you the ten uppermost in our minds. If there are others that you find more interesting and challenging, by all means construct your own list and start thinking about it.

It will take years for our ten problems to be finally solved and replaced with a fresh list. In the meantime, we invite you to go on to further study of what we *already* know about finance. We also invite you to apply what you have learned from reading this book.

Now that the book is done, we sympathize with Huckleberry Finn. At the end of his book, he says,

> . . . So there ain't nothing more to write, and I am rotten glad of it, because if I'd'a'knowed what a trouble it was to make a book I wouldn't'a' tackled it, and I ain't a'going to no more.

---

[17]Some recent empirical work on merger activity is contained in "Symposium on the Market for Corporate Control: The Scientific Evidence," a special volume of the *Journal of Financial Economics*, **11**(April 1983).

APPENDIX: FINANCIAL TABLES

Appendix Table 1   Discount factors: Present value of $1 to be received after t years $= 1/(1+r)^t$

Number of years	1%	2%	3%	4%	5%	6%	7%	8%	9%	10%	11%	12%	13%	14%	15%
1	.990	.980	.971	.962	.952	.943	.935	.926	.917	.909	.901	.893	.885	.877	.870
2	.980	.961	.943	.925	.907	.890	.873	.857	.842	.826	.812	.797	.783	.769	.756
3	.971	.942	.915	.889	.864	.840	.816	.794	.772	.751	.731	.712	.693	.675	.658
4	.961	.924	.888	.855	.823	.792	.763	.735	.708	.683	.659	.636	.613	.592	.572
5	.951	.906	.863	.822	.784	.747	.713	.681	.650	.621	.593	.567	.543	.519	.497
6	.942	.888	.837	.790	.746	.705	.666	.630	.596	.564	.535	.507	.480	.456	.432
7	.933	.871	.813	.760	.711	.665	.623	.583	.547	.513	.482	.452	.425	.400	.376
8	.923	.853	.789	.731	.677	.627	.582	.540	.502	.467	.434	.404	.376	.351	.327
9	.914	.837	.766	.703	.645	.592	.544	.500	.460	.424	.391	.361	.333	.308	.284
10	.905	.820	.744	.676	.614	.558	.508	.463	.422	.386	.352	.322	.295	.270	.247
11	.896	.804	.722	.650	.585	.527	.475	.429	.388	.350	.317	.287	.261	.237	.215
12	.887	.788	.701	.625	.557	.497	.444	.397	.356	.319	.286	.257	.231	.208	.187
13	.879	.773	.681	.601	.530	.469	.415	.368	.326	.290	.258	.229	.204	.182	.163
14	.870	.758	.661	.577	.505	.442	.388	.340	.299	.263	.232	.205	.181	.160	.141
15	.861	.743	.642	.555	.481	.417	.362	.315	.275	.239	.209	.183	.160	.140	.123
16	.853	.728	.623	.534	.458	.394	.339	.292	.252	.218	.188	.163	.141	.123	.107
17	.844	.714	.605	.513	.436	.371	.317	.270	.231	.198	.170	.146	.125	.108	.093
18	.836	.700	.587	.494	.416	.350	.296	.250	.212	.180	.153	.130	.111	.095	.081
19	.828	.686	.570	.475	.396	.331	.277	.232	.194	.164	.138	.116	.098	.083	.070
20	.820	.673	.554	.456	.377	.312	.258	.215	.178	.149	.124	.104	.087	.073	.061
21	.811	.660	.538	.439	.359	.294	.242	.199	.164	.135	.112	.093	.077	.064	.053
22	.803	.647	.522	.422	.342	.278	.226	.184	.150	.123	.101	.083	.068	.056	.046
23	.795	.634	.507	.406	.326	.262	.211	.170	.138	.112	.091	.074	.060	.049	.040
24	.788	.622	.492	.390	.310	.247	.197	.158	.126	.102	.082	.066	.053	.043	.035
25	.780	.610	.478	.375	.295	.233	.184	.146	.116	.092	.074	.059	.047	.038	.030
26	.772	.598	.464	.361	.281	.220	.172	.135	.106	.084	.066	.053	.042	.033	.026
27	.764	.586	.450	.347	.268	.207	.161	.125	.098	.076	.060	.047	.037	.029	.023
28	.757	.574	.437	.333	.255	.196	.150	.116	.090	.069	.054	.042	.033	.026	.020
29	.749	.563	.424	.321	.243	.185	.141	.107	.082	.063	.048	.037	.029	.022	.017
30	.742	.552	.412	.308	.231	.174	.131	.099	.075	.057	.044	.033	.026	.020	.015

E.g.: If the interest rate is 10% per year, the present value of $1 to be received at the end of year 5 is $0.621.

						Interest rate per year									Number
16%	17%	18%	19%	20%	21%	22%	23%	24%	25%	26%	27%	28%	29%	30%	of years
.862	.855	.847	.840	.833	.826	.820	.813	.806	.800	.794	.787	.781	.775	.769	1
.743	.731	.718	.706	.694	.683	.672	.661	.650	.640	.630	.620	.610	.601	.592	2
.641	.624	.609	.593	.579	.564	.551	.537	.524	.512	.500	.488	.477	.466	.455	3
.552	.534	.516	.499	.482	.467	.451	.437	.423	.410	.397	.384	.373	.361	.350	4
.476	.456	.437	.419	.402	.386	.370	.355	.341	.328	.315	.303	.291	.280	.269	5
.410	.390	.370	.352	.335	.319	.303	.289	.275	.262	.250	.238	.227	.217	.207	6
.354	.333	.314	.296	.279	.263	.249	.235	.222	.210	.198	.188	.178	.168	.159	7
.305	.285	.266	.249	.233	.218	.204	.191	.179	.168	.157	.148	.139	.130	.123	8
.263	.243	.225	.209	.194	.180	.167	.155	.144	.134	.125	.116	.108	.101	.094	9
.227	.208	.191	.176	.162	.149	.137	.126	.116	.107	.099	.092	.085	.078	.073	10
.195	.178	.162	.148	.135	.123	.112	.103	.094	.086	.079	.072	.066	.061	.056	11
.168	.152	.137	.124	.112	.102	.092	.083	.076	.069	.062	.057	.052	.047	.043	12
.145	.130	.116	.104	.093	.084	.075	.068	.061	.055	.050	.045	.040	.037	.033	13
.125	.111	.099	.088	.078	.069	.062	.055	.049	.044	.039	.035	.032	.028	.025	14
.108	.095	.084	.074	.065	.057	.051	.045	.040	.035	.031	.028	.025	.022	.020	15
.093	.081	.071	.062	.054	.047	.042	.036	.032	.028	.025	.022	.019	.017	.015	16
.080	.069	.060	.052	.045	.039	.034	.030	.026	.023	.020	.017	.015	.013	.012	17
.069	.059	.051	.044	.038	.032	.028	.024	.021	.018	.016	.014	.012	.010	.009	18
.060	.051	.043	.037	.031	.027	.023	.020	.017	.014	.012	.011	.009	.008	.007	19
.051	.043	.037	.031	.026	.022	.019	.016	.014	.012	.010	.008	.007	.006	.005	20
.044	.037	.031	.026	.022	.018	.015	.013	.011	.009	.008	.007	.006	.005	.004	21
.038	.032	.026	.022	.018	.015	.013	.011	.009	.007	.006	.005	.004	.004	.003	22
.033	.027	.022	.018	.015	.012	.010	.009	.007	.006	.005	.004	.003	.003	.002	23
.028	.023	.019	.015	.013	.010	.008	.007	.006	.005	.004	.003	.003	.002	.002	24
.024	.020	.016	.013	.010	.009	.007	.006	.005	.004	.003	.003	.002	.002	.001	25
.021	.017	.014	.011	.009	.007	.006	.005	.004	.003	.002	.002	.002	.001	.001	26
.018	.014	.011	.009	.007	.006	.005	.004	.003	.002	.002	.002	.001	.001	.001	27
.016	.012	.010	.008	.006	.005	.004	.003	.002	.002	.002	.001	.001	.001	.001	28
.014	.011	.008	.006	.005	.004	.003	.002	.002	.002	.001	.001	.001	.001	.000	29
.012	.009	.007	.005	.004	.003	.003	.002	.002	.001	.001	.001	.001	.000	.000	30

Appendix Table 2   Accumulation factors: Future value of $1 by the end of t years $= (1+r)^t$

Number of years	Interest rate per year														
	1%	2%	3%	4%	5%	6%	7%	8%	9%	10%	11%	12%	13%	14%	15%
1	1.010	1.020	1.030	1.040	1.050	1.060	1.070	1.080	1.090	1.100	1.110	1.120	1.130	1.140	1.150
2	1.020	1.040	1.061	1.082	1.102	1.124	1.145	1.166	1.188	1.210	1.232	1.254	1.277	1.300	1.322
3	1.030	1.061	1.093	1.125	1.158	1.191	1.225	1.260	1.295	1.331	1.368	1.405	1.443	1.482	1.521
4	1.041	1.082	1.126	1.170	1.216	1.262	1.311	1.360	1.412	1.464	1.518	1.574	1.630	1.689	1.749
5	1.051	1.104	1.159	1.217	1.276	1.338	1.403	1.469	1.539	1.611	1.685	1.762	1.842	1.925	2.011
6	1.062	1.126	1.194	1.265	1.340	1.419	1.501	1.587	1.677	1.772	1.870	1.974	2.082	2.195	2.313
7	1.072	1.149	1.230	1.316	1.407	1.504	1.606	1.714	1.828	1.949	2.076	2.211	2.353	2.502	2.660
8	1.083	1.172	1.267	1.369	1.477	1.594	1.718	1.851	1.993	2.144	2.305	2.476	2.658	2.853	3.059
9	1.094	1.195	1.305	1.423	1.551	1.689	1.838	1.999	2.172	2.358	2.558	2.773	3.004	3.252	3.518
10	1.105	1.219	1.344	1.480	1.629	1.791	1.967	2.159	2.367	2.594	2.839	3.106	3.395	3.707	4.046
11	1.116	1.243	1.384	1.539	1.710	1.898	2.105	2.332	2.580	2.853	3.152	3.479	3.836	4.226	4.652
12	1.127	1.268	1.426	1.601	1.796	2.012	2.252	2.518	2.813	3.138	3.498	3.896	4.335	4.818	5.350
13	1.138	1.294	1.469	1.665	1.886	2.133	2.410	2.720	3.066	3.452	3.883	4.363	4.898	5.492	6.153
14	1.149	1.319	1.513	1.732	1.980	2.261	2.579	2.937	3.342	3.797	4.310	4.887	5.535	6.261	7.076
15	1.161	1.346	1.558	1.801	2.079	2.397	2.759	3.172	3.642	4.177	4.785	5.474	6.254	7.138	8.137
16	1.173	1.373	1.605	1.873	2.183	2.540	2.952	3.426	3.970	4.595	5.311	6.130	7.067	8.137	9.358
17	1.184	1.400	1.653	1.948	2.292	2.693	3.159	3.700	4.328	5.054	5.895	6.866	7.986	9.276	10.76
18	1.196	1.428	1.702	2.026	2.407	2.854	3.380	3.996	4.717	5.560	6.544	7.690	9.024	10.58	12.38
19	1.208	1.457	1.754	2.107	2.527	3.026	3.617	4.316	5.142	6.116	7.263	8.613	10.20	12.06	14.23
20	1.220	1.486	1.806	2.191	2.653	3.207	3.870	4.661	5.604	6.727	8.062	9.646	11.52	13.74	16.37
21	1.232	1.516	1.860	2.279	2.786	3.400	4.141	5.034	6.109	7.400	8.949	10.80	13.02	15.67	18.82
22	1.245	1.546	1.916	2.370	2.925	3.604	4.430	5.437	6.659	8.140	9.934	12.10	14.71	17.86	21.64
23	1.257	1.577	1.974	2.465	3.072	3.820	4.741	5.871	7.258	8.954	11.03	13.55	16.63	20.36	24.89
24	1.270	1.608	2.033	2.563	3.225	4.049	5.072	6.341	7.911	9.850	12.24	15.18	18.79	23.21	28.63
25	1.282	1.641	2.094	2.666	3.386	4.292	5.427	6.848	8.623	10.83	13.59	17.00	21.23	26.46	32.92
26	1.295	1.673	2.157	2.772	3.556	4.549	5.807	7.396	9.399	11.92	15.08	19.04	23.99	30.17	37.86
27	1.308	1.707	2.221	2.883	3.733	4.822	6.214	7.988	10.25	13.11	16.74	21.32	27.11	34.39	43.54
28	1.321	1.741	2.288	2.999	3.920	5.112	6.649	8.627	11.17	14.42	18.58	23.88	30.63	39.20	50.07
29	1.335	1.776	2.357	3.119	4.116	5.418	7.114	9.317	12.17	15.86	20.62	26.75	34.62	44.69	57.58
30	1.348	1.811	2.427	3.243	4.322	5.743	7.612	10.06	13.27	17.45	22.89	29.96	39.12	50.95	66.21

E.g.: If the interest rate is 10% per year, an investment of $1 today will be worth $1.611 at the end of year 5.

16%	17%	18%	19%	20%	21%	22%	23%	24%	25%	26%	27%	28%	29%	30%	Number of years
1.160	1.170	1.180	1.190	1.200	1.210	1.220	1.230	1.240	1.250	1.260	1.270	1.280	1.290	1.300	1
1.346	1.369	1.392	1.416	1.440	1.464	1.488	1.513	1.538	1.562	1.588	1.613	1.638	1.664	1.690	2
1.561	1.602	1.643	1.685	1.728	1.772	1.816	1.861	1.907	1.953	2.000	2.048	2.097	2.147	2.197	3
1.811	1.874	1.939	2.005	2.074	2.144	2.215	2.289	2.364	2.441	2.520	2.601	2.684	2.769	2.856	4
2.100	2.192	2.288	2.386	2.488	2.594	2.703	2.815	2.932	3.052	3.176	3.304	3.436	3.572	3.713	5
2.436	2.565	2.700	2.840	2.986	3.138	3.297	3.463	3.635	3.815	4.002	4.196	4.398	4.608	4.827	6
2.826	3.001	3.185	3.379	3.583	3.797	4.023	4.259	4.508	4.768	5.042	5.329	5.629	5.945	6.275	7
3.278	3.511	3.759	4.021	4.300	4.595	4.908	5.239	5.590	5.960	6.353	6.768	7.206	7.669	8.157	8
3.803	4.108	4.435	4.785	5.160	5.560	5.987	6.444	6.931	7.451	8.005	8.595	9.223	9.893	10.60	9
4.411	4.807	5.234	5.695	6.192	6.727	7.305	7.926	8.594	9.313	10.09	10.92	11.81	12.76	13.79	10
5.117	5.624	6.176	6.777	7.430	8.140	8.912	9.749	10.66	11.64	12.71	13.86	15.11	16.46	17.92	11
5.936	6.580	7.288	8.064	8.916	9.850	10.87	11.99	13.21	14.55	16.01	17.61	19.34	21.24	23.30	12
6.886	7.699	8.599	9.596	10.70	11.92	13.26	14.75	16.39	18.19	20.18	22.36	24.76	27.39	30.29	13
7.988	9.007	10.15	11.42	12.84	14.42	16.18	18.14	20.32	22.74	25.42	28.40	31.69	35.34	39.37	14
9.266	10.54	11.97	13.59	15.41	17.45	19.74	22.31	25.20	28.42	32.03	36.06	40.56	45.59	51.19	15
10.75	12.33	14.13	16.17	18.49	21.11	24.09	27.45	31.24	35.53	40.36	45.80	51.92	58.81	66.54	16
12.47	14.43	16.67	19.24	22.19	25.55	29.38	33.76	38.74	44.41	50.85	58.17	66.46	75.86	86.50	17
14.46	16.88	19.67	22.90	26.62	30.91	35.85	41.52	48.04	55.51	64.07	73.87	85.07	97.86	112.5	18
16.78	19.75	23.21	27.25	31.95	37.40	43.74	51.07	59.57	69.39	80.73	93.81	108.9	126.2	146.2	19
19.46	23.11	27.39	32.43	38.34	45.26	53.36	62.82	73.86	86.74	101.7	119.1	139.4	162.9	190.0	20
22.57	27.03	32.32	38.59	46.01	54.76	65.10	77.27	91.59	108.4	128.2	151.3	178.4	210.1	247.1	21
26.19	31.63	38.14	45.92	55.21	66.26	79.42	95.04	113.6	135.5	161.5	192.2	228.4	271.0	321.2	22
30.38	37.01	45.01	54.65	66.25	80.18	96.89	116.9	140.8	169.4	203.5	244.1	292.3	349.6	417.5	23
35.24	43.30	53.11	65.03	79.50	97.02	118.2	143.8	174.6	211.8	256.4	309.9	374.1	451.0	542.8	24
40.87	50.66	62.67	77.39	95.40	117.4	144.2	176.9	216.5	264.7	323.0	393.6	478.9	581.8	705.6	25
47.41	59.27	73.95	92.09	114.5	142.0	175.9	217.5	268.5	330.9	407.0	499.9	613.0	750.5	917.3	26
55.00	69.35	87.26	109.6	137.4	171.9	214.6	267.6	333.0	413.6	512.9	634.9	784.6	968.1	1193	27
63.80	81.13	103.0	130.4	164.8	208.0	261.9	329.1	412.9	517.0	646.2	806.3	1004	1249	1550	28
74.01	94.93	121.5	155.2	197.8	251.6	319.5	404.8	512.0	646.2	814.2	1024	1286	1611	2015	29
85.85	111.1	143.4	184.7	237.4	304.5	389.8	497.9	634.8	807.8	1026	1301	1646	2078	2620	30

Appendix Table 3 Annuity table: Present of $1 *per year* for each of t years $= 1/r - 1/[r(1+r)^t]$

Number of years							Interest rate per year								
	1%	2%	3%	4%	5%	6%	7%	8%	9%	10%	11%	12%	13%	14%	15%
1	.990	.980	.971	.962	.952	.943	.935	.926	.917	.909	.901	.893	.885	.877	.870
2	1.970	1.942	1.913	1.886	1.859	1.833	1.808	1.783	1.759	1.736	1.713	1.690	1.668	1.647	1.626
3	2.941	2.884	2.829	2.775	2.723	2.673	2.624	2.577	2.531	2.487	2.444	2.402	2.361	2.322	2.283
4	3.902	3.808	3.717	3.630	3.546	3.465	3.387	3.312	3.240	3.170	3.102	3.037	2.974	2.914	2.855
5	4.853	4.713	4.580	4.452	4.329	4.212	4.100	3.993	3.890	3.791	3.696	3.605	3.517	3.433	3.352
6	5.795	5.601	5.417	5.242	5.076	4.917	4.767	4.623	4.486	4.355	4.231	4.111	3.998	3.889	3.784
7	6.728	6.472	6.230	6.002	5.786	5.582	5.389	5.206	5.033	4.868	4.712	4.564	4.423	4.288	4.160
8	7.652	7.325	7.020	6.733	6.463	6.210	5.971	5.747	5.535	5.335	5.146	4.968	4.799	4.639	4.487
9	8.566	8.162	7.786	7.435	7.108	6.802	6.515	6.247	5.995	5.759	5.537	5.328	5.132	4.946	4.772
10	9.471	8.983	8.530	8.111	7.722	7.360	7.024	6.710	6.418	6.145	5.889	5.650	5.426	5.216	5.019
11	10.37	9.787	9.253	8.760	8.306	7.887	7.499	7.139	6.805	6.495	6.207	5.938	5.687	5.453	5.234
12	11.26	10.58	9.954	9.385	8.863	8.384	7.943	7.536	7.161	6.814	6.492	6.194	5.918	5.660	5.421
13	12.13	11.35	10.63	9.986	9.394	8.853	8.358	7.904	7.487	7.103	6.750	6.424	6.122	5.842	5.583
14	13.00	12.11	11.30	10.56	9.899	9.295	8.745	8.244	7.786	7.367	6.982	6.628	6.302	6.002	5.724
15	13.87	12.85	11.94	11.12	10.38	9.712	9.108	8.559	8.061	7.606	7.191	6.811	6.462	6.142	5.847
16	14.72	13.58	12.56	11.65	10.84	10.11	9.447	8.851	8.313	7.824	7.379	6.974	6.604	6.265	5.954
17	15.56	14.29	13.17	12.17	11.27	10.48	9.763	9.122	8.544	8.022	7.549	7.120	6.729	6.373	6.047
18	16.40	14.99	13.75	12.66	11.69	10.83	10.06	9.372	8.756	8.201	7.702	7.250	6.840	6.467	6.128
19	17.23	15.68	14.32	13.13	12.09	11.16	10.34	9.604	8.950	8.365	7.839	7.366	6.938	6.550	6.198
20	18.05	16.35	14.88	13.59	12.46	11.47	10.59	9.818	9.129	8.514	7.963	7.469	7.025	6.623	6.259
21	18.86	17.01	15.42	14.03	12.82	11.76	10.84	10.02	9.292	8.649	8.075	7.562	7.102	6.687	6.312
22	19.66	17.66	15.94	14.45	13.16	12.04	11.06	10.20	9.442	8.772	8.176	7.645	7.170	6.743	6.359
23	20.46	18.29	16.44	14.86	13.49	12.30	11.27	10.37	9.580	8.883	8.266	7.718	7.230	6.792	6.399
24	21.24	18.91	16.94	15.25	13.80	12.55	11.47	10.53	9.707	8.985	8.348	7.784	7.283	6.835	6.434
25	22.02	19.52	17.41	15.62	14.09	12.78	11.65	10.67	9.823	9.077	8.422	7.843	7.330	6.873	6.464
26	22.80	20.12	17.88	15.98	14.38	13.00	11.83	10.81	9.929	9.161	8.488	7.896	7.372	6.906	6.491
27	23.56	20.71	18.33	16.33	14.64	13.21	11.99	10.94	10.03	9.237	8.548	7.943	7.409	6.935	6.514
28	24.32	21.28	18.76	16.66	14.90	13.41	12.14	11.05	10.12	9.307	8.602	7.984	7.441	6.961	6.534
29	25.07	21.84	19.19	16.98	15.14	13.59	12.28	11.16	10.20	9.370	8.650	8.022	7.470	6.983	6.551
30	25.81	22.40	19.60	17.29	15.37	13.76	12.41	11.26	10.27	9.427	8.694	8.055	7.496	7.003	6.566

E.g.: If the interest rate is 10% per year, the present value of $1 to be received at the end of each of the next 5 years is $3.791.

						Interest rate per year									Number
16%	17%	18%	19%	20%	21%	22%	23%	24%	25%	26%	27%	28%	29%	30%	of years
.862	.855	.847	.840	.833	.826	.820	.813	.806	.800	.794	.787	.781	.775	.769	1
1.605	1.585	1.566	1.547	1.528	1.509	1.492	1.474	1.457	1.440	1.424	1.407	1.392	1.376	1.361	2
2.246	2.210	2.174	2.140	2.106	2.074	2.042	2.011	1.981	1.952	1.923	1.896	1.868	1.842	1.816	3
2.798	2.743	2.690	2.639	2.589	2.540	2.494	2.448	2.404	2.362	2.320	2.280	2.241	2.203	2.166	4
3.274	3.199	3.127	3.058	2.991	2.926	2.864	2.803	2.745	2.689	2.635	2.583	2.532	2.483	2.436	5
3.685	3.589	3.498	3.410	3.326	3.245	3.167	3.092	3.020	2.951	2.885	2.821	2.759	2.700	2.643	6
4.039	3.922	3.812	3.706	3.605	3.508	3.416	3.327	3.242	3.161	3.083	3.009	2.937	2.868	2.802	7
4.344	4.207	4.078	3.954	3.837	3.726	3.619	3.518	3.421	3.329	3.241	3.156	3.076	2.999	2.925	8
4.607	4.451	4.303	4.163	4.031	3.905	3.786	3.673	3.566	3.463	3.366	3.273	3.184	3.100	3.019	9
4.833	4.659	4.494	4.339	4.192	4.054	3.923	3.799	3.682	3.571	3.465	3.364	3.269	3.178	3.092	10
5.029	4.836	4.656	4.486	4.327	4.177	4.035	3.902	3.776	3.656	3.543	3.437	3.335	3.239	3.147	11
5.197	4.988	4.793	4.611	4.439	4.278	4.127	3.985	3.851	3.725	3.606	3.493	3.387	3.286	3.190	12
5.342	5.118	4.910	4.715	4.533	4.362	4.203	4.053	3.912	3.780	3.656	3.538	3.427	3.322	3.223	13
5.468	5.229	5.008	4.802	4.611	4.432	4.265	4.108	3.962	3.824	3.695	3.573	3.459	3.351	3.249	14
5.575	5.324	5.092	4.876	4.675	4.489	4.315	4.153	4.001	3.859	3.726	3.601	3.483	3.373	3.268	15
5.668	5.405	5.162	4.938	4.730	4.536	4.357	4.189	4.033	3.887	3.751	3.623	3.503	3.390	3.283	16
5.749	5.475	5.222	4.990	4.775	4.576	4.391	4.219	4.059	3.910	3.771	3.640	3.518	3.403	3.295	17
5.818	5.534	5.273	5.033	4.812	4.608	4.419	4.243	4.080	3.928	3.786	3.654	3.529	3.413	3.304	18
5.877	5.584	5.316	5.070	4.843	4.635	4.442	4.263	4.097	3.942	3.799	3.664	3.539	3.421	3.311	19
5.929	5.628	5.353	5.101	4.870	4.657	4.460	4.279	4.110	3.954	3.808	3.673	3.546	3.427	3.316	20
5.973	5.665	5.384	5.127	4.891	4.675	4.476	4.292	4.121	3.963	3.816	3.679	3.551	3.432	3.320	21
6.011	5.696	5.410	5.149	4.909	4.690	4.488	4.302	4.130	3.970	3.822	3.684	3.556	3.436	3.323	22
6.044	5.723	5.432	5.167	4.925	4.703	4.499	4.311	4.137	3.976	3.827	3.689	3.559	3.438	3.325	23
6.073	5.746	5.451	5.182	4.937	4.713	4.507	4.318	4.143	3.981	3.831	3.692	3.562	3.441	3.327	24
6.097	5.766	5.467	5.195	4.948	4.721	4.514	4.323	4.147	3.985	3.834	3.694	3.564	3.442	3.329	25
6.118	5.783	5.480	5.206	4.956	4.728	4.520	4.328	4.151	3.988	3.837	3.696	3.566	3.444	3.330	26
6.136	5.798	5.492	5.215	4.964	4.734	4.524	4.332	4.154	3.990	3.839	3.698	3.567	3.445	3.331	27
6.152	5.810	5.502	5.223	4.970	4.739	4.528	4.335	4.157	3.992	3.840	3.699	3.568	3.446	3.331	28
6.166	5.820	5.510	5.229	4.975	4.743	4.531	4.337	4.159	3.994	3.841	3.700	3.569	3.446	3.332	29
6.177	5.829	5.517	5.235	4.979	4.746	4.534	4.339	4.160	3.995	3.842	3.701	3.569	3.447	3.332	30

Appendix Table 4   Value of e^{rt}: Future value of $1 invested at a *continuously compounded* rate r for t years

rt	.00	.01	.02	.03	.04	.05	.06	.07	.08	.09
0.00	1.000	1.010	1.020	1.030	1.041	1.051	1.062	1.073	1.083	1.094
0.10	1.105	1.116	1.127	1.139	1.150	1.162	1.174	1.185	1.197	1.209
0.20	1.221	1.234	1.246	1.259	1.271	1.284	1.297	1.310	1.323	1.336
0.30	1.350	1.363	1.377	1.391	1.405	1.419	1.433	1.448	1.462	1.477
0.40	1.492	1.507	1.522	1.537	1.553	1.568	1.584	1.600	1.616	1.632
0.50	1.649	1.665	1.682	1.699	1.716	1.733	1.751	1.768	1.786	1.804
0.60	1.822	1.840	1.859	1.878	1.896	1.916	1.935	1.954	1.974	1.994
0.70	2.014	2.034	2.054	2.075	2.096	2.117	2.138	2.160	2.181	2.203
0.80	2.226	2.248	2.270	2.293	2.316	2.340	2.363	2.387	2.411	2.435
0.90	2.460	2.484	2.509	2.535	2.560	2.586	2.612	2.638	2.664	2.691
1.00	2.718	2.746	2.773	2.801	2.829	2.858	2.886	2.915	2.945	2.974
1.10	3.004	3.034	3.065	3.096	3.127	3.158	3.190	3.222	3.254	3.287
1.20	3.320	3.353	3.387	3.421	3.456	3.490	3.525	3.561	3.597	3.633
1.30	3.669	3.706	3.743	3.781	3.819	3.857	3.896	3.935	3.975	4.015
1.40	4.055	4.096	4.137	4.179	4.221	4.263	4.306	4.349	4.393	4.437
1.50	4.482	4.527	4.572	4.618	4.665	4.711	4.759	4.807	4.855	4.904
1.60	4.953	5.003	5.053	5.104	5.155	5.207	5.259	5.312	5.366	5.419
1.70	5.474	5.529	5.585	5.641	5.697	5.755	5.812	5.871	5.930	5.989
1.80	6.050	6.110	6.172	6.234	6.297	6.360	6.424	6.488	6.554	6.619
1.90	6.686	6.753	6.821	6.890	6.959	7.029	7.099	7.171	7.243	7.316
2.00	7.389	7.463	7.538	7.614	7.691	7.768	7.846	7.925	8.004	8.085
2.10	8.166	8.248	8.331	8.415	8.499	8.585	8.671	8.758	8.846	8.935
2.20	9.025	9.116	9.207	9.300	9.393	9.488	9.583	9.679	9.777	9.875
2.30	9.974	10.07	10.18	10.28	10.38	10.49	10.59	10.70	10.80	10.91
2.40	11.02	11.13	11.25	11.36	11.47	11.59	11.70	11.82	11.94	12.06
2.50	12.18	12.30	12.43	12.55	12.68	12.81	12.94	13.07	13.20	13.33
2.60	13.46	13.60	13.74	13.87	14.01	14.15	14.30	14.44	14.59	14.73
2.70	14.88	15.03	15.18	15.33	15.49	15.64	15.80	15.96	16.12	16.28
2.80	16.44	16.61	16.78	16.95	17.12	17.29	17.46	17.64	17.81	17.99
2.90	18.17	18.36	18.54	18.73	18.92	19.11	19.30	19.49	19.69	19.89

Appendix Table 4   (continued)

rt	.00	.01	.02	.03	.04	.05	.06	.07	.08	.09
3.00	20.09	20.29	20.49	20.70	20.91	21.12	21.33	21.54	21.76	21.98
3.10	22.20	22.42	22.65	22.87	23.10	23.34	23.57	23.81	24.05	24.29
3.20	24.53	24.78	25.03	25.28	25.53	25.79	26.05	26.31	26.58	26.84
3.30	27.11	27.39	27.66	27.94	28.22	28.50	28.79	29.08	29.37	29.67
3.40	29.96	30.27	30.57	30.88	31.19	31.50	31.82	32.14	32.46	32.79
3.50	33.12	33.45	33.78	34.12	34.47	34.81	35.16	35.52	35.87	36.23
3.60	36.60	36.97	37.34	37.71	38.09	38.47	38.86	39.25	39.65	40.04
3.70	40.45	40.85	41.26	41.68	42.10	42.52	42.95	43.38	43.82	44.26
3.80	44.70	45.15	45.60	46.06	46.53	46.99	47.47	47.94	48.42	48.91
3.90	49.40	49.90	50.40	50.91	51.42	51.94	52.46	52.98	53.52	54.05
4.00	54.60	55.15	55.70	56.26	56.83	57.40	57.97	58.56	59.15	59.74
4.10	60.34	60.95	61.56	62.18	62.80	63.43	64.07	64.72	65.37	66.02
4.20	66.69	67.36	68.03	68.72	69.41	70.11	70.81	71.52	72.24	72.97
4.30	73.70	74.44	75.19	75.94	76.71	77.48	78.26	79.04	79.84	80.64
4.40	81.45	82.27	83.10	83.93	84.77	85.63	86.49	87.36	88.23	89.12
4.50	90.02	90.92	91.84	92.76	93.69	94.63	95.58	96.54	97.51	98.49
4.60	99.48	100.5	101.5	102.5	103.5	104.6	105.6	106.7	107.8	108.9
4.70	109.9	111.1	112.2	113.3	114.4	115.6	116.7	117.9	119.1	120.3
4.80	121.5	122.7	124.0	125.2	126.5	127.7	129.0	130.3	131.6	133.0
4.90	134.3	135.6	137.0	138.4	139.8	141.2	142.6	144.0	145.5	146.9
5.00	148.4	149.9	151.4	152.9	154.5	156.0	157.6	159.2	160.8	162.4
5.10	164.0	165.7	167.3	169.0	170.7	172.4	174.2	175.9	177.7	179.5
5.20	181.3	183.1	184.9	186.8	188.7	190.6	192.5	194.4	196.4	198.3
5.30	200.3	202.4	204.4	206.4	208.5	210.6	212.7	214.9	217.0	219.2
5.40	221.4	223.6	225.9	228.1	230.4	232.8	235.1	237.5	239.8	242.3
5.50	244.7	247.2	249.6	252.1	254.7	257.2	259.8	262.4	265.1	267.7
5.60	270.4	273.1	275.9	278.7	281.5	284.3	287.1	290.0	292.9	295.9
5.70	298.9	301.9	304.9	308.0	311.1	314.2	317.3	320.5	323.8	327.0
5.80	330.3	333.6	337.0	340.4	343.8	347.2	350.7	354.2	357.8	361.4
5.90	365.0	368.7	372.4	376.2	379.9	383.8	387.6	391.5	395.4	399.4

E.g.: If the continuously compounded interest rate is 10% per year, an investment of $1 today will be worth $1.105 by the end of year 1, $1.162 by the end of year 1.5 and $1.221 by the end of year 2.

Appendix Table 5
Continuous annuity table: Present value of $1 per year received in a continuous stream for each of t years discounted at an *annually compounded* rate r is $[1 - 1/(1+r)^t]/[\ln(1+r)]$

Number of years	1%	2%	3%	4%	5%	6%	7%	8%	9%	10%	11%	12%	13%	14%	15%
1	.995	.990	.985	.981	.976	.971	.967	.962	.958	.954	.950	.945	.941	.937	.933
2	1.980	1.961	1.942	1.924	1.906	1.888	1.871	1.854	1.837	1.821	1.805	1.790	1.774	1.759	1.745
3	2.956	2.913	2.871	2.830	2.791	2.752	2.715	2.679	2.644	2.609	2.576	2.543	2.512	2.481	2.450
4	3.921	3.846	3.773	3.702	3.634	3.568	3.504	3.443	3.383	3.326	3.270	3.216	3.164	3.113	3.064
5	4.878	4.760	4.648	4.540	4.437	4.338	4.242	4.150	4.062	3.977	3.896	3.817	3.741	3.668	3.598
6	5.824	5.657	5.498	5.346	5.202	5.063	4.931	4.805	4.685	4.570	4.459	4.353	4.252	4.155	4.062
7	6.762	6.536	6.323	6.121	5.930	5.748	5.576	5.412	5.256	5.108	4.967	4.832	4.704	4.582	4.465
8	7.690	7.398	7.124	6.867	6.623	6.394	6.178	5.974	5.780	5.597	5.424	5.260	5.104	4.956	4.816
9	8.609	8.244	7.902	7.583	7.284	7.004	6.741	6.494	6.261	6.042	5.836	5.642	5.458	5.285	5.121
10	9.519	9.072	8.658	8.272	7.913	7.579	7.267	6.975	6.702	6.447	6.208	5.983	5.772	5.573	5.386
11	10.42	9.884	9.391	8.935	8.512	8.121	7.758	7.421	7.107	6.815	6.542	6.287	6.049	5.826	5.617
12	11.31	10.68	10.10	9.572	9.083	8.633	8.218	7.834	7.478	7.149	6.843	6.559	6.294	6.048	5.818
13	12.19	11.46	10.79	10.18	9.627	9.116	8.647	8.216	7.819	7.453	7.115	6.802	6.512	6.242	5.992
14	13.07	12.23	11.46	10.77	10.14	9.571	9.048	8.570	8.131	7.729	7.359	7.018	6.704	6.413	6.144
15	13.93	12.98	12.12	11.34	10.64	10.00	9.423	8.897	8.418	7.980	7.579	7.212	6.874	6.563	6.276
16	14.79	13.71	12.75	11.88	11.11	10.41	9.774	9.201	8.681	8.209	7.778	7.385	7.024	6.694	6.390
17	15.64	14.43	13.36	12.41	11.55	10.79	10.10	9.482	8.923	8.416	7.957	7.539	7.158	6.809	6.490
18	16.48	15.14	13.96	12.91	11.98	11.15	10.41	9.742	9.144	8.605	8.118	7.676	7.275	6.910	6.577
19	17.31	15.83	14.54	13.39	12.38	11.49	10.69	9.983	9.347	8.777	8.263	7.799	7.380	6.999	6.652
20	18.14	16.51	15.10	13.86	12.77	11.81	10.96	10.21	9.533	8.932	8.394	7.909	7.472	7.077	6.718
21	18.95	17.18	15.65	14.31	13.14	12.11	11.21	10.41	9.704	9.074	8.511	8.007	7.554	7.145	6.775
22	19.76	17.83	16.17	14.74	13.49	12.40	11.44	10.60	9.861	9.203	8.618	8.095	7.626	7.205	6.824
23	20.56	18.47	16.69	15.15	13.82	12.67	11.66	10.78	10.01	9.320	8.713	8.173	7.690	7.257	6.868
24	21.35	19.10	17.19	15.55	14.14	12.92	11.87	10.94	10.14	9.427	8.799	8.243	7.747	7.303	6.905
25	22.13	19.72	17.67	15.93	14.44	13.16	12.06	11.10	10.26	9.524	8.877	8.305	7.797	7.344	6.938
26	22.91	20.32	18.14	16.30	14.73	13.39	12.24	11.24	10.37	9.612	8.947	8.360	7.841	7.379	6.966
27	23.68	20.91	18.60	16.65	15.01	13.60	12.40	11.37	10.47	9.692	9.010	8.410	7.880	7.410	6.991
28	24.44	21.49	19.04	16.99	15.27	13.80	12.56	11.49	10.56	9.765	9.066	8.454	7.915	7.437	7.012
29	25.19	22.06	19.47	17.32	15.52	13.99	12.70	11.60	10.65	9.831	9.118	8.494	7.946	7.461	7.031
30	25.94	22.62	19.89	17.64	15.75	14.17	12.84	11.70	10.73	9.891	9.164	8.529	7.973	7.482	7.047

E.g.: If the interest rate is 10% per year, a continuous cash flow of $1 per year for each of 5 years is worth $3.977. A continuous flow of $1 in year 5 only is worth $3.977 – $3.326 = $0.651.

						Interest rate per year									Number
16%	17%	18%	19%	20%	21%	22%	23%	24%	25%	26%	27%	28%	29%	30%	of years
.929	.925	.922	.918	.914	.910	.907	.903	.900	.896	.893	.889	.886	.883	.880	1
1.730	1.716	1.703	1.689	1.676	1.663	1.650	1.638	1.625	1.613	1.601	1.590	1.578	1.567	1.556	2
2.421	2.392	2.365	2.337	2.311	2.285	2.259	2.235	2.211	2.187	2.164	2.141	2.119	2.098	2.077	3
3.016	2.970	2.925	2.882	2.840	2.799	2.759	2.720	2.682	2.646	2.610	2.576	2.542	2.509	2.477	4
3.530	3.464	3.401	3.340	3.281	3.223	3.168	3.115	3.063	3.013	2.964	2.917	2.872	2.828	2.785	5
3.972	3.886	3.804	3.724	3.648	3.574	3.504	3.436	3.370	3.307	3.246	3.187	3.130	3.075	3.022	6
4.354	4.247	4.145	4.048	3.954	3.865	3.779	3.696	3.617	3.542	3.469	3.399	3.331	3.266	3.204	7
4.682	4.555	4.434	4.319	4.209	4.104	4.004	3.909	3.817	3.730	3.646	3.566	3.489	3.415	3.344	8
4.966	4.819	4.680	4.547	4.422	4.302	4.189	4.081	3.978	3.880	3.786	3.697	3.612	3.530	3.452	9
5.210	5.044	4.887	4.739	4.599	4.466	4.340	4.221	4.108	4.000	3.898	3.801	3.708	3.619	3.535	10
5.421	5.237	5.063	4.900	4.747	4.602	4.465	4.335	4.213	4.096	3.986	3.882	3.783	3.689	3.599	11
5.603	5.401	5.213	5.036	4.870	4.713	4.566	4.428	4.297	4.173	4.057	3.946	3.841	3.742	3.648	12
5.759	5.542	5.339	5.150	4.972	4.806	4.650	4.503	4.365	4.235	4.112	3.997	3.887	3.784	3.686	13
5.894	5.662	5.446	5.245	5.058	4.882	4.718	4.564	4.420	4.284	4.157	4.036	3.923	3.816	3.715	14
6.010	5.765	5.537	5.326	5.129	4.945	4.774	4.614	4.464	4.324	4.192	4.068	3.951	3.841	3.737	15
6.111	5.853	5.614	5.393	5.188	4.998	4.820	4.655	4.500	4.355	4.220	4.092	3.973	3.860	3.754	16
6.197	5.928	5.679	5.450	5.238	5.041	4.858	4.687	4.529	4.381	4.242	4.112	3.990	3.875	3.767	17
6.272	5.992	5.735	5.498	5.279	5.076	4.889	4.714	4.552	4.401	4.259	4.127	4.003	3.887	3.778	18
6.336	6.047	5.782	5.538	5.313	5.106	4.914	4.736	4.571	4.417	4.273	4.139	4.014	3.896	3.785	19
6.391	6.094	5.821	5.571	5.342	5.130	4.935	4.754	4.586	4.430	4.284	4.149	4.022	3.903	3.791	20
6.439	6.134	5.855	5.600	5.366	5.150	4.952	4.768	4.598	4.440	4.293	4.156	4.028	3.908	3.796	21
6.480	6.168	5.883	5.623	5.385	5.167	4.966	4.780	4.608	4.448	4.300	4.162	4.033	3.913	3.800	22
6.516	6.197	5.908	5.643	5.402	5.181	4.977	4.789	4.616	4.455	4.306	4.167	4.037	3.916	3.802	23
6.546	6.222	5.928	5.660	5.416	5.192	4.986	4.797	4.622	4.460	4.310	4.170	4.040	3.918	3.804	24
6.573	6.244	5.945	5.674	5.427	5.201	4.994	4.803	4.627	4.464	4.314	4.173	4.042	3.920	3.806	25
6.596	6.262	5.960	5.686	5.437	5.209	5.000	4.808	4.631	4.468	4.316	4.175	4.044	3.922	3.807	26
6.615	6.277	5.973	5.696	5.445	5.216	5.005	4.813	4.635	4.471	4.318	4.177	4.046	3.923	3.808	27
6.632	6.291	5.983	5.705	5.452	5.221	5.010	4.816	4.637	4.473	4.320	4.179	4.047	3.924	3.809	28
6.647	6.302	5.992	5.712	5.457	5.225	5.013	4.819	4.640	4.474	4.322	4.180	4.048	3.925	3.810	29
6.659	6.312	6.000	5.718	5.462	5.229	5.016	4.821	4.641	4.476	4.323	4.181	4.048	3.925	3.810	30

Appendix Table 6

Call option prices (Black-Scholes model): Call option value as a *percent* of share price when the time to expiration of the option is t, the exercise price is EX, the stock price is P, the continuously compounded risk-free interest rate is r_f, and the stock returns have a variance of σ^2 per period.

Share price divided by PV of exercise price = $P/[EX\ e^{-r_f t}]$

$\sigma\sqrt{t}$	0.50	0.55	0.60	0.65	0.70	0.75	0.80	0.85	0.90	0.92	0.94	0.96	0.98	1.00
0.05	.00	.00	.00	.00	.00	.00	.00	.00	.03	.10	.27	.60	1.16	1.99
0.10	.00	.00	.00	.00	.00	.01	.05	.24	.79	1.18	1.69	2.32	3.09	3.99
0.15	.00	.00	.00	.01	.05	.18	.50	1.15	2.25	2.83	3.49	4.24	5.07	5.98
0.20	.00	.01	.04	.14	.35	.77	1.48	2.54	3.99	4.67	5.42	6.22	7.07	7.97
0.25	.03	.09	.24	.53	1.03	1.78	2.83	4.19	5.86	6.60	7.38	8.21	9.06	9.95
0.30	.15	.35	.70	1.25	2.04	3.10	4.42	5.99	7.79	8.57	9.37	10.20	11.05	11.92
0.35	.44	.84	1.44	2.26	3.33	4.63	6.15	7.87	9.76	10.55	11.36	12.19	13.04	13.89
0.40	.94	1.58	2.43	3.52	4.82	6.32	7.99	9.81	11.75	12.55	13.36	14.18	15.01	15.85
0.45	1.67	2.55	3.66	4.96	6.45	8.10	9.89	11.77	13.74	14.54	15.35	16.16	16.98	17.80
0.50	2.61	3.74	5.06	6.55	8.20	9.97	11.83	13.76	15.73	16.53	17.33	18.13	18.94	19.74
0.55	3.75	5.09	6.61	8.26	10.03	11.88	13.80	15.75	17.72	18.52	19.31	20.10	20.88	21.67
0.60	5.06	6.60	8.27	10.05	11.91	13.83	15.78	17.75	19.71	20.49	21.27	22.04	22.82	23.58
0.65	6.51	8.22	10.03	11.91	13.84	15.80	17.77	19.74	21.68	22.45	23.22	23.98	24.73	25.48
0.70	8.08	9.93	11.85	13.82	15.80	17.79	19.77	21.72	23.64	24.40	25.15	25.90	26.64	27.37
0.75	9.76	11.72	13.73	15.76	17.78	19.78	21.76	23.70	25.59	26.34	27.07	27.80	28.52	29.23
0.80	11.51	13.58	15.65	17.72	19.77	21.78	23.74	25.66	27.52	28.25	28.98	29.69	30.39	31.08
0.85	13.33	15.48	17.61	19.71	21.76	23.77	25.72	27.61	29.44	30.15	30.86	31.56	32.24	32.92
0.90	15.20	17.41	19.58	21.70	23.76	25.75	27.68	29.54	31.34	32.04	32.72	33.40	34.07	34.73
0.95	17.12	19.37	21.57	23.69	25.75	27.72	29.63	31.46	33.21	33.90	34.57	35.23	35.88	36.52
1.00	19.06	21.35	23.56	25.68	27.73	29.68	31.56	33.35	35.07	35.74	36.39	37.04	37.67	38.29
1.05	21.03	23.34	25.55	27.67	29.69	31.62	33.47	35.22	36.90	37.55	38.19	38.82	39.44	40.04
1.10	23.01	25.33	27.54	29.65	31.65	33.55	35.35	37.08	38.72	39.35	39.97	40.58	41.18	41.77
1.15	25.00	27.33	29.53	31.61	33.58	35.45	37.22	38.90	40.50	41.12	41.72	42.32	42.90	43.47
1.20	27.00	29.32	31.50	33.56	35.50	37.33	39.06	40.71	42.26	42.87	43.45	44.03	44.60	45.15
1.25	28.99	31.30	33.46	35.48	37.39	39.19	40.88	42.48	44.00	44.59	45.16	45.72	46.27	46.80
1.50	38.78	40.94	42.93	44.78	46.49	48.08	49.57	50.96	52.27	52.78	53.27	53.75	54.22	54.67
2.00	56.51	58.20	59.73	61.12	62.39	63.56	64.64	65.64	66.58	66.93	67.28	67.62	67.95	68.27
2.50	70.80	71.99	73.06	74.02	74.90	75.70	76.43	77.11	77.74	77.98	78.21	78.44	78.66	78.87
3.00	81.43	82.22	82.91	83.54	84.10	84.62	85.09	85.52	85.92	86.07	86.22	86.36	86.50	86.64
3.50	88.83	89.31	89.73	90.12	90.46	90.77	91.06	91.32	91.56	91.65	91.74	91.82	91.91	91.99
4.00	93.64	93.92	94.16	94.38	94.58	94.76	94.92	95.07	95.21	95.26	95.31	95.36	95.40	95.45
4.50	96.57	96.73	96.86	96.98	97.08	97.18	97.27	97.35	97.42	97.45	97.48	97.50	97.53	97.56
5.00	98.26	98.34	98.40	98.46	98.52	98.57	98.61	98.65	98.69	98.71	98.72	98.73	98.75	98.76

E.g.: If the share price is $0.90, the present value of the exercise price is $1.00, the variance of stock returns is $(0.5)^2$ per year, and the time to expiration of the option is one year, the call option value is 15.73% of the share price.

				Share price divided by PV of exercise price = $P/[EX\,e^{-rt}]$										
1.00	1.02	1.04	1.06	1.08	1.10	1.15	1.20	1.25	1.30	1.35	1.40	1.45	1.50	$\sigma\sqrt{t}$
1.99	3.11	4.45	5.95	7.54	9.14	13.05	16.67	20.00	23.08	25.93	28.57	31.03	33.33	0.05
3.99	5.01	6.13	7.34	8.63	9.96	13.39	16.79	20.04	23.09	25.93	28.57	31.03	33.33	0.10
5.98	6.95	7.99	9.07	10.20	11.36	14.37	17.41	20.40	23.29	26.04	28.63	31.06	33.35	0.15
7.97	8.91	9.88	10.90	11.93	12.99	15.71	18.46	21.19	23.85	26.43	28.89	31.24	33.46	0.20
9.95	10.86	11.80	12.76	13.73	14.72	17.23	19.75	22.27	24.73	27.13	29.44	31.66	33.78	0.25
11.92	12.81	13.72	14.63	15.56	16.49	18.84	21.20	23.53	25.83	28.06	30.23	32.32	34.32	0.30
13.89	14.76	15.63	16.51	17.40	18.29	20.52	22.73	24.92	27.07	29.16	31.20	33.16	35.06	0.35
15.85	16.70	17.54	18.39	19.25	20.10	22.22	24.32	26.39	28.42	30.39	32.30	34.16	35.95	0.40
17.80	18.62	19.45	20.27	21.09	21.91	23.94	25.95	27.91	29.83	31.69	33.51	35.26	36.96	0.45
19.74	20.54	21.34	22.14	22.93	23.72	25.68	27.59	29.46	31.29	33.06	34.78	36.45	38.06	0.50
21.67	22.45	23.23	24.00	24.77	25.53	27.41	29.25	31.04	32.78	34.47	36.11	37.69	39.23	0.55
23.58	24.34	25.10	25.85	26.59	27.33	29.14	30.91	32.62	34.29	35.91	37.47	38.98	40.44	0.60
25.48	26.22	26.96	27.69	28.41	29.12	30.87	32.57	34.22	35.82	37.36	38.86	40.30	41.70	0.65
27.37	28.09	28.80	29.51	30.21	30.90	32.59	34.23	35.81	37.35	38.83	40.26	41.65	42.98	0.70
29.23	29.94	30.63	31.32	32.00	32.67	34.30	35.88	37.41	38.88	40.31	41.68	43.01	44.29	0.75
31.08	31.77	32.44	33.11	33.77	34.42	36.00	37.52	39.00	40.42	41.78	43.11	44.38	45.61	0.80
32.92	33.58	34.24	34.89	35.52	36.15	37.68	39.16	40.58	41.94	43.26	44.53	45.75	46.93	0.85
34.73	35.38	36.01	36.64	37.26	37.87	39.35	40.77	42.14	43.46	44.73	45.95	47.13	48.26	0.90
36.52	37.15	37.77	38.38	38.98	39.57	41.00	42.38	43.70	44.97	46.19	47.37	48.50	49.59	0.95
38.29	38.90	39.51	40.10	40.68	41.25	42.64	43.97	45.24	46.47	47.65	48.78	49.87	50.92	1.00
40.04	40.64	41.22	41.79	42.36	42.91	44.25	45.54	46.77	47.96	49.09	50.18	51.23	52.24	1.05
41.77	42.35	42.91	43.47	44.01	44.55	45.85	47.09	48.28	49.43	50.52	51.57	52.58	53.55	1.10
43.47	44.03	44.58	45.12	45.65	46.17	47.43	48.63	49.78	50.88	51.93	52.95	53.92	54.85	1.15
45.15	45.69	46.23	46.75	47.26	47.76	48.98	50.14	51.25	52.31	53.33	54.31	55.24	56.14	1.20
46.80	47.33	47.85	48.35	48.85	49.33	50.51	51.63	52.71	53.73	54.71	55.65	56.56	57.42	1.25
54.67	55.12	55.56	55.99	56.41	56.82	57.81	58.76	59.65	60.51	61.33	62.11	62.86	63.57	1.50
68.27	68.58	68.89	69.19	69.48	69.76	70.45	71.10	71.71	72.30	72.85	73.38	73.89	74.37	2.00
78.87	79.08	79.28	79.48	79.67	79.86	80.31	80.74	81.15	81.53	81.89	82.24	82.57	82.88	2.50
86.64	86.77	86.90	87.02	87.15	87.26	87.55	87.82	88.07	88.31	88.54	88.75	88.96	89.16	3.00
91.99	92.07	92.14	92.22	92.29	92.36	92.53	92.69	92.84	92.99	93.12	93.25	93.37	93.49	3.50
95.45	95.49	95.54	95.58	95.62	95.66	95.76	95.85	95.94	96.02	96.09	96.16	96.23	96.30	4.00
97.56	97.58	97.60	97.63	97.65	97.67	97.72	97.77	97.82	97.86	97.90	97.94	97.98	98.01	4.50
98.76	98.77	98.78	98.79	98.81	98.82	98.84	98.87	98.89	98.91	98.93	98.95	98.97	98.99	5.00

Appendix Table 7 Put option prices (Black-Scholes model): Put option value as a *percent* of share price when the time to expiration of the option is t, the exercise price is EX, the stock price is P, the continuously compounded risk-free interest rate is r_f, and the stock returns have a variance of σ^2 per period.

Share price divided by PV of exercise price = $P/[EX\ e^{-r_f t}]$

$\sigma\sqrt{t}$	0.50	0.55	0.60	0.65	0.70	0.75	0.80	0.85	0.90	0.92	0.94	0.96	0.98	1.00
0.05	100.0	81.82	66.67	53.85	42.86	33.33	25.00	17.65	11.14	8.80	6.65	4.76	3.20	1.99
0.10	100.0	81.82	66.67	53.85	42.86	33.34	25.05	17.88	11.90	9.88	8.07	6.49	5.13	3.99
0.15	100.0	81.82	66.67	53.86	42.91	33.52	25.50	18.80	13.36	11.52	9.88	8.41	7.11	5.98
0.20	100.0	81.83	66.71	53.98	43.21	34.11	26.48	20.19	15.10	13.37	11.80	10.38	9.11	7.97
0.25	100.0	81.91	66.91	54.38	43.88	35.11	27.83	21.84	16.97	15.30	13.77	12.37	11.10	9.95
0.30	100.1	82.17	67.36	55.10	44.90	36.43	29.42	23.64	18.90	17.26	15.75	14.37	13.09	11.92
0.35	100.4	82.65	68.10	56.11	46.19	37.96	31.15	25.52	20.87	19.25	17.75	16.36	15.08	13.89
0.40	100.9	83.40	69.10	57.36	47.67	39.65	32.99	27.46	22.86	21.24	19.74	18.35	17.05	15.85
0.45	101.7	84.37	70.32	58.81	49.31	41.44	34.89	29.42	24.85	23.24	21.73	20.33	19.02	17.80
0.50	102.6	85.55	71.72	60.40	51.06	43.30	36.83	31.41	26.84	25.23	23.72	22.30	20.98	19.74
0.55	103.8	86.91	73.27	62.11	52.89	45.22	38.80	33.40	28.84	27.21	25.69	24.26	22.92	21.67
0.60	105.1	88.41	74.94	63.90	54.77	47.16	40.78	35.39	30.82	29.19	27.65	26.21	24.86	23.58
0.65	106.5	90.03	76.69	65.76	56.70	49.14	42.77	37.38	32.79	31.15	29.60	28.15	26.77	25.48
0.70	108.1	91.75	78.52	67.66	58.66	51.12	44.77	39.37	34.76	33.10	31.54	30.07	28.68	27.37
0.75	109.8	93.54	80.40	69.60	60.64	53.12	46.76	41.34	36.70	35.03	33.46	31.97	30.56	29.23
0.80	111.5	95.39	82.32	71.57	62.63	55.11	48.74	43.31	38.64	36.95	35.36	33.85	32.43	31.08
0.85	113.3	97.29	84.27	73.55	64.62	57.10	50.72	45.26	40.55	38.85	37.24	35.72	34.28	32.92
0.90	115.2	99.23	86.25	75.54	66.61	59.09	52.68	47.19	42.45	40.73	39.11	37.57	36.11	34.73
0.95	117.1	101.2	88.23	77.54	68.60	61.06	54.63	49.10	44.33	42.59	40.95	39.40	37.92	36.52
1.00	119.1	103.2	90.23	79.53	70.58	63.01	56.56	51.00	46.18	44.43	42.78	41.20	39.71	38.29
1.05	121.0	105.2	92.22	81.52	72.55	64.96	58.47	52.87	48.02	46.25	44.58	42.99	41.48	40.04
1.10	123.0	107.2	94.21	83.49	74.50	66.88	60.35	54.72	49.83	48.04	46.35	44.75	43.22	41.77
1.15	125.0	109.1	96.19	85.46	76.44	68.78	62.22	56.55	51.61	49.82	48.11	46.48	44.94	43.47
1.20	127.0	111.1	98.17	87.40	78.35	70.66	64.06	58.35	53.38	51.56	49.84	48.20	46.64	45.15
1.25	129.0	113.1	100.1	89.33	80.25	72.52	65.88	60.13	55.11	53.28	51.54	49.88	48.31	46.80
1.50	138.8	122.8	109.6	98.62	89.34	81.41	74.57	68.61	63.39	61.47	59.65	57.91	56.26	54.67
2.00	156.5	140.0	126.4	115.0	105.2	96.89	89.64	83.29	77.69	75.63	73.66	71.78	69.99	68.27
2.50	170.8	153.8	139.7	127.9	117.8	109.0	101.4	94.76	88.85	86.67	84.59	82.60	80.70	78.87
3.00	181.4	164.0	149.6	137.4	127.0	118.0	110.1	103.2	97.03	94.77	92.60	90.53	88.54	86.64
3.50	188.8	171.1	156.4	144.0	133.3	124.1	116.1	109.0	102.7	100.3	98.12	95.99	93.95	91.99
4.00	193.6	175.7	160.8	148.2	137.4	128.1	119.9	112.7	106.3	104.0	101.7	99.52	97.44	95.45
4.50	196.6	178.5	163.5	150.8	139.9	130.5	122.3	115.0	108.5	106.1	103.9	101.7	99.57	97.56
5.00	198.3	180.2	165.1	152.3	141.4	131.9	123.6	116.3	109.8	107.4	105.1	102.9	100.8	98.76

E.g.: If the share price is $0.90, the present value of the exercise price is $1.00, the variance of stock returns is $(0.5)^2$ per year, and the time to expiration of the option is one year, the put option value is 26.84% of the share price.

1.02	1.04	1.06	1.08	1.10	1.15	1.20	1.25	1.30	1.35	1.40	1.45	1.50	$\sigma\sqrt{t}$
1.15	.61	.29	.13	.05	.00	.00	.00	.00	.00	.00	.00	.00	0.05
3.05	2.28	1.68	1.22	.87	.34	.12	.04	.01	.00	.00	.00	.00	0.10
4.99	4.14	3.41	2.79	2.27	1.32	.74	.40	.21	.11	.05	.03	.01	0.15
6.95	6.04	5.23	4.53	3.90	2.66	1.79	1.19	.78	.50	.32	.20	.13	0.20
8.90	7.95	7.10	6.32	5.63	4.18	3.09	2.27	1.65	1.20	.87	.62	.45	0.25
10.85	9.87	8.97	8.15	7.40	5.80	4.53	3.53	2.75	2.13	1.65	1.28	.99	0.30
12.80	11.79	10.85	9.99	9.20	7.47	6.07	4.92	3.99	3.24	2.63	2.13	1.73	0.35
14.74	13.70	12.73	11.84	11.01	9.18	7.66	6.39	5.34	4.46	3.73	3.12	2.62	0.40
16.66	15.60	14.61	13.68	12.82	10.90	9.28	7.91	6.75	5.77	4.94	4.23	3.63	0.45
18.58	17.50	16.48	15.53	14.63	12.63	10.92	9.46	8.21	7.14	6.21	5.41	4.73	0.50
20.49	19.38	18.34	17.36	16.44	14.37	12.58	11.04	9.70	8.54	7.54	6.66	5.89	0.55
22.38	21.25	20.19	19.19	18.24	16.10	14.24	12.62	11.21	9.98	8.90	7.95	7.11	0.60
24.26	23.11	22.03	21.00	20.03	17.83	15.90	14.22	12.74	11.44	10.29	9.27	8.37	0.65
26.13	24.96	23.85	22.80	21.81	19.55	17.56	15.81	14.27	12.91	11.69	10.61	9.65	0.70
27.98	26.79	25.66	24.59	23.57	21.26	19.21	17.41	15.81	14.38	13.11	11.97	10.96	0.75
29.81	28.60	27.45	26.36	25.33	22.95	20.86	19.00	17.34	15.86	14.53	13.34	12.27	0.80
31.62	30.39	29.23	28.12	27.06	24.64	22.49	20.58	18.87	17.33	15.96	14.72	13.60	0.85
33.42	32.17	30.98	29.85	28.78	26.31	24.11	22.14	20.39	18.81	17.38	16.09	14.93	0.90
35.19	33.92	32.72	31.57	30.48	27.96	25.71	23.70	21.90	20.27	18.80	17.47	16.26	0.95
36.94	35.66	34.44	33.27	32.16	29.59	27.30	25.24	23.39	21.72	20.21	18.83	17.58	1.00
38.68	37.37	36.13	34.95	33.82	31.21	28.87	26.77	24.88	23.16	21.61	20.19	18.90	1.05
40.38	39.07	37.81	36.61	35.46	32.81	30.43	28.28	26.35	24.59	23.00	21.55	20.22	1.10
42.07	40.73	39.46	38.24	37.08	34.38	31.96	29.78	27.80	26.01	24.38	22.88	21.52	1.15
43.73	42.38	41.09	39.85	38.67	35.94	33.47	31.25	29.24	27.41	25.74	24.21	22.81	1.20
45.37	44.00	42.69	41.44	40.24	37.47	34.97	32.71	30.65	28.79	27.08	25.52	24.09	1.25
53.16	51.72	50.33	49.00	47.73	44.77	42.09	39.65	37.43	35.40	33.54	31.82	30.24	1.50
66.62	65.04	63.53	62.07	60.67	57.41	54.43	51.71	49.22	46.93	44.81	42.85	41.04	2.00
77.12	75.44	73.82	72.27	70.77	67.27	64.08	61.15	58.45	55.97	53.67	51.53	49.55	2.50
84.81	83.05	81.36	79.74	78.17	74.51	71.15	68.07	65.23	62.61	60.18	57.93	55.82	3.00
90.11	88.30	86.56	84.88	83.27	79.49	76.03	72.84	69.91	67.20	64.68	62.34	60.16	3.50
93.53	91.69	89.92	88.21	86.57	82.72	79.18	75.94	72.94	70.17	67.59	65.20	62.97	4.00
95.62	93.76	91.97	90.24	88.58	84.68	81.10	77.82	74.78	71.97	69.37	66.94	64.68	4.50
96.81	94.94	93.13	91.40	89.73	85.80	82.20	78.89	75.84	73.01	70.38	67.94	65.66	5.00

Share price divided by PV of exercise price = $P/[\text{EX}\,e^{-r_f t}]$

Appendix Table 8   Cumulative normal probability: $N(d)$ = the probability that a unit normally distributed random variable will be less than d.

d	-.00	-.01	-.02	-.03	-.04	-.05	-.06	-.07	-.08	-.09
-3.40	.0003	.0003	.0003	.0003	.0003	.0003	.0003	.0003	.0003	.0002
-3.30	.0005	.0005	.0005	.0004	.0004	.0004	.0004	.0004	.0004	.0003
-3.20	.0007	.0007	.0006	.0006	.0006	.0006	.0006	.0005	.0005	.0005
-3.10	.0010	.0009	.0009	.0009	.0008	.0008	.0008	.0008	.0007	.0007
-3.00	.0013	.0013	.0013	.0012	.0012	.0011	.0011	.0011	.0010	.0010
-2.90	.0019	.0018	.0018	.0017	.0016	.0016	.0015	.0015	.0014	.0014
-2.80	.0026	.0025	.0024	.0023	.0023	.0022	.0021	.0021	.0020	.0019
-2.70	.0035	.0034	.0033	.0032	.0031	.0030	.0029	.0028	.0027	.0026
-2.60	.0047	.0045	.0044	.0043	.0041	.0040	.0039	.0038	.0037	.0036
-2.50	.0062	.0060	.0059	.0057	.0055	.0054	.0052	.0051	.0049	.0048
-2.40	.0082	.0080	.0078	.0075	.0073	.0071	.0069	.0068	.0066	.0064
-2.30	.0107	.0104	.0102	.0099	.0096	.0094	.0091	.0089	.0087	.0084
-2.20	.0139	.0136	.0132	.0129	.0125	.0122	.0119	.0116	.0113	.0110
-2.10	.0179	.0174	.0170	.0166	.0162	.0158	.0154	.0150	.0146	.0143
-2.00	.0228	.0222	.0217	.0212	.0207	.0202	.0197	.0192	.0188	.0183
-1.90	.0287	.0281	.0274	.0268	.0262	.0256	.0250	.0244	.0239	.0233
-1.80	.0359	.0351	.0344	.0336	.0329	.0322	.0314	.0307	.0301	.0294
-1.70	.0446	.0436	.0427	.0418	.0409	.0401	.0392	.0384	.0375	.0367
-1.60	.0548	.0537	.0526	.0516	.0505	.0495	.0485	.0475	.0465	.0455
-1.50	.0668	.0655	.0643	.0630	.0618	.0606	.0594	.0582	.0571	.0559
-1.40	.0808	.0793	.0778	.0764	.0749	.0735	.0721	.0708	.0694	.0681
-1.30	.0968	.0951	.0934	.0918	.0901	.0885	.0869	.0853	.0838	.0823
-1.20	.1151	.1131	.1112	.1093	.1075	.1056	.1038	.1020	.1003	.0985
-1.10	.1357	.1335	.1314	.1292	.1271	.1251	.1230	.1210	.1190	.1170
-1.00	.1587	.1562	.1539	.1515	.1492	.1469	.1446	.1423	.1401	.1379
-0.90	.1841	.1814	.1788	.1762	.1736	.1711	.1685	.1660	.1635	.1611
-0.80	.2119	.2090	.2061	.2033	.2005	.1977	.1949	.1922	.1894	.1867
-0.70	.2420	.2389	.2358	.2327	.2296	.2266	.2236	.2206	.2177	.2148
-0.60	.2743	.2709	.2676	.2643	.2611	.2578	.2546	.2514	.2483	.2451
-0.50	.3085	.3050	.3015	.2981	.2946	.2912	.2877	.2843	.2810	.2776
-0.40	.3446	.3409	.3372	.3336	.3300	.3264	.3228	.3192	.3156	.3121
-0.30	.3821	.3783	.3745	.3707	.3669	.3632	.3594	.3557	.3520	.3483
-0.20	.4207	.4168	.4129	.4090	.4052	.4013	.3974	.3936	.3897	.3859
-0.10	.4602	.4562	.4522	.4483	.4443	.4404	.4364	.4325	.4286	.4247
0.00	.5000	.4960	.4920	.4880	.4840	.4801	.4761	.4721	.4681	.4641

E.g.: The probability that a unit normally distributed random variable will be less than -1.96 is 0.025 and the probability that a unit normally distributed random variable will be less than 2.00 is 0.9772.

d	.00	.01	.02	.03	.04	.05	.06	.07·	.08	.09
0.00	.5000	.5040	.5080	.5120	.5160	.5199	.5239	.5279	.5319	.5359
0.10	.5398	.5438	.5478	.5517	.5557	.5596	.5636	.5675	.5714	.5753
0.20	.5793	.5832	.5871	.5910	.5948	.5987	.6026	.6064	.6103	.6141
0.30	.6179	.6217	.6255	.6293	.6331	.6368	.6406	.6443	.6480	.6517
0.40	.6554	.6591	.6628	.6664	.6700	.6736	.6772	.6808	.6844	.6879
0.50	.6915	.6950	.6985	.7019	.7054	.7088	.7123	.7157	.7190	.7224
0.60	.7257	.7291	.7324	.7357	.7389	.7422	.7454	.7486	.7517	.7549
0.70	.7580	.7611	.7642	.7673	.7704	.7734	.7764	.7794	.7823	.7852
0.80	.7881	.7910	.7939	.7967	.7995	.8023	.8051	.8078	.8106	.8133
0.90	.8159	.8186	.8212	.8238	.8264	.8289	.8315	.8340	.8365	.8389
1.00	.8413	.8438	.8461	.8485	.8508	.8531	.8554	.8577	.8599	.8621
1.10	.8643	.8665	.8686	.8708	.8729	.8749	.8770	.8790	.8810	.8830
1.20	.8849	.8869	.8888	.8907	.8925	.8944	.8962	.8980	.8997	.9015
1.30	.9032	.9049	.9066	.9082	.9099	.9115	.9131	.9147	.9162	.9177
1.40	.9192	.9207	.9222	.9236	.9251	.9265	.9279	.9292	.9306	.9319
1.50	.9332	.9345	.9357	.9370	.9382	.9394	.9406	.9418	.9429	.9441
1.60	.9452	.9463	.9474	.9484	.9495	.9505	.9515	.9525	.9535	.9545
1.70	.9554	.9564	.9573	.9582	.9591	.9599	.9608	.9616	.9625	.9633
1.80	.9641	.9649	.9656	.9664	.9671	.9678	.9686	.9693	.9699	.9706
1.90	.9713	.9719	.9726	.9732	.9738	.9744	.9750	.9756	.9761	.9767
2.00	.9772	.9778	.9783	.9788	.9793	.9798	.9803	.9808	.9812	.9817
2.10	.9821	.9826	.9830	.9834	.9838	.9842	.9846	.9850	.9854	.9857
2.20	.9861	.9864	.9868	.9871	.9875	.9878	.9881	.9884	.9887	.9890
2.30	.9893	.9896	.9898	.9901	.9904	.9906	.9909	.9911	.9913	.9916
2.40	.9918	.9920	.9922	.9925	.9927	.9929	.9931	.9932	.9934	.9936
2.50	.9938	.9940	.9941	.9943	.9945	.9946	.9948	.9949	.9951	.9952
2.60	.9953	.9955	.9956	.9957	.9959	.9960	.9961	.9962	.9963	.9964
2.70	.9965	.9966	.9967	.9968	.9969	.9970	.9971	.9972	.9973	.9974
2.80	.9974	.9975	.9976	.9977	.9977	.9978	.9979	.9979	.9980	.9981
2.90	.9981	.9982	.9982	.9983	.9984	.9984	.9985	.9985	.9986	.9986
3.00	.9987	.9987	.9987	.9988	.9988	.9989	.9989	.9989	.9990	.9990
3.10	.9990	.9991	.9991	.9991	.9992	.9992	.9992	.9992	.9993	.9993
3.20	.9993	.9993	.9994	.9994	.9994	.9994	.9994	.9995	.9995	.9995
3.30	.9995	.9995	.9995	.9996	.9996	.9996	.9996	.9996	.9996	.9997
3.40	.9997	.9997	.9997	.9997	.9997	.9997	.9997	.9997	.9997	.9998

GLOSSARY

Accelerated depreciation Any depreciation method that produces larger deductions for depreciation in the early years of a project's life; e.g., *double-declining-balance depreciation, sum-of-the-years' digits depreciation.*[1]

Accounts payable (payables, trade debt) Money owed to suppliers.

Accounts receivable (receivables, trade credit) Money owed by customers.

Accrued-benefit cost method Method for estimating the *normal costs* of a pension plan. Its principle is that the company should contribute each year the present value of any benefits that have accrued (cf. *level cost method*).

Accrued interest Interest that has been earned but not yet paid.

Acid-test ratio *Quick ratio.*

AcSC Accounting Standards Committee of the Canadian Institute of Chartered Accountants.

Adjusted present value *Net present value* of an asset if financed solely by equity plus the present value of financing side effects.

Aging schedule Record of the length of time that *accounts receivable* have been outstanding.

All-or-none underwriting Underwriting whereby the issue is cancelled if the *underwriter* is unable to resell the entire issue.

American option Option that can be exercised any time before the final exercise date (cf. *European option*).

AMEX American Stock Exchange.

Amortization Repayment of a loan by instalments.

Annuity Investment that produces a level stream of cash flows for a limited number of periods.

Anticipation Plan whereby customers who pay before the final due date may be entitled to deduct a normal rate of interest.

Appropriation request Formal request for funds for a capital investment project.

Arbitrage Purchase of one security and simultaneous sale of another to give a riskfree profit.

ASE Alberta Stock Exchange.

Authorized share capital Maximum number of shares that a company can issue, as specified in the firm's articles of incorporation.

Balloon payment Large final payment (e.g., when a loan is repaid in instalments).

Bank acceptance Written demand that has been accepted by a bank to pay a given sum at a future date (cf. *trade acceptance*).

Basis point 0.01 %.

Bear market Decline in security prices (cf. *bull market*).

Bearer security Security for which primary evidence of ownership is possession of the certificate (cf. *registered security*).

Benefit-cost ratio *Profitability index.*

Best-efforts underwriting Underwriting whereby *underwriters* do not commit themselves to selling an issue but promise only to use their best efforts.

Beta Measure of *market risk.*

Bill of exchange General term for a document demanding payment.

Bill of lading Document establishing ownership of goods in transit.

---

[1] Italicized words are defined elsewhere in the glossary.

Blue-chip company Large and respected company.

Blue-sky laws State laws covering the issue and trading of securities.

Bond Long-term debt.

Break-even analysis Analysis of the level of sales at which a project would just break even.

Bridging loan Short-term loan to provide temporary financing until more permanent financing is arranged.

Bull market Rise in security prices (cf. *bear market*).

Buy-back *Repurchase agreement; purchase and resale agreement.*

Call option Option to buy an asset at a specified exercise price on or before a specified exercise date (cf. *put option*).

Call premium Difference between the price at which a company can call its *bonds* and their *par value*.

Capital budget List of planned investment projects, usually prepared annually.

Capital lease *Financial lease.*

Capital market Financial market (particularly the market for long-term securities).

Capital rationing Shortage of capital that forces a company to choose between projects.

Capital structure Mix of different securities issued by a firm.

Capitalization Long-term debt, *preferred stock*, and *net worth*.

Career-average plan Pension plan offering a pension that depends on the employee's average compensation during his or her years of membership (cf. *final average plan*).

Cash budget Forecast of sources and uses of cash.

Cash-deficiency arrangement Plan whereby a project's shareholders agree to provide the operating company with sufficient *net working capital*.

CBOE Chicago Board Options Exchange.

CBRS Canadian Bond Rating Service.

CCA Capital cost allowance: the tax depreciation system in Canada.

CD *Certificate of Deposit.*

CDIC Canadian Deposit Insurance Corporation.

Certainty-equivalent cash flow Certain cash flow that would have the same value as a particular risky cash flow.

Certificate of deposit (CD) Certificate issued by a bank as evidence of a time deposit.

Characteristic line Line representing the relationship between *expected returns* on an asset and returns on the market.

CICA The Canadian Institute of Chartered Accountants.

Clean-up provision Requirement by banks that companies "clean up" their short-term bank loans for at least one month during the year.

Closed-end mortgage Mortgage against which no more debt may be issued (cf. *open-end mortgage*).

Collar Upper and lower limits on the interest rate charged on a *floating rate bond*.

Collateral Assets that are given as security for a loan.

Collateral trust bonds *Bonds* secured by common stocks that are owned by the borrower.

Collection float Cheques deposited by a company that have not yet been cleared (cf. *payment float*).

Commercial draft (Bill of exchange) Demand for payment.

Commercial paper Unsecured notes issued by companies and maturing within nine months.

Commodity-linked bond Bond with an opportunity to share in the potential price appreciation of a physical commodity—e.g., the price of silver.

Compensating balance Non-interest-bearing demand deposit to compensate banks for bank loans or services.

Competitive bidding Means by which public utility *holding companies* are required to choose their *underwriter* (cf. *negotiated underwriting*).

Completion bonding Insurance that a construction contract will be successfully completed.

Compound interest Reinvestment of each interest payment on money invested, to earn more interest (cf. *simple interest*).

Concentration banking System whereby customers make payments to a regional collection centre. The collection centre pays the funds into a regional bank branch account and surplus money is transferred to the company's principal branch.

Conditional sales Sales in which ownership does not pass to the buyer until payment is completed.

Conglomerate merger *Merger* between two companies in unrelated businesses (cf. *horizontal merger, vertical merger*).

Contingent project Project that cannot be undertaken unless another project is also undertaken.

Continuous compounding Assumption that interest is compounded continuously rather than at fixed intervals.

Controller Officer responsible for budgeting, accounting, and auditing in a firm (cf. *treasurer*).

Conversion price *Par value* of a *convertible security* divided by the number of shares into which it may be exchanged.

Conversion ratio Number of shares for which a *convertible security* may be exchanged.

Convertible security *Bond* or *preferred stock* that may be converted at the holder's option into the company's common stock.

Correlation coefficient Measure of the closeness of the relationship between two or more variables.

Cost company arrangement Arrangement whereby the shareholders of a project receive output free of charge but agree to pay all operating and financing charges of the project.

Cost of capital *Opportunity cost of capital.*

Coupon Interest payment on debt.

Covariance Measure of the co-movement between two variables.

Covenant Clause in a loan agreement.

CPP Canada Pension Plan.

Cross-default clause Clause in a loan agreement stating that the company is in default if it fails to meet its obligation on any other debt issue.

Cum dividend *With dividend.*

Cum rights *With rights.*

Cumulative preferred stock Stock which takes priority over common stock as regards dividend payments. Dividends may not be paid on common stock until all past *dividends* on *preferred* have been paid.

Cumulative voting System whereby a stockholder may cast all his or her votes for one candidate (cf. *majority voting*).

Current asset Asset that will normally be turned into cash within a year.

Current liability Liability that will normally be repaid within a year.

Current ratio *Current assets* divided by *current liabilities*—a measure of liquidity.

DBRS Dominion Bond Rating Service.

DCF Discounted cash flow.

Debenture Unsecured *bond*, usually with maturity of 15 years or more.

Decision tree Method of representing alternative sequential decisions and the possible outcomes from those decisions.

Depository transfer cheque Cheque made out directly by a local bank branch to a particular company.

Depreciation (1) Reduction in the book or market value of an asset. (2) Portion of an investment that can be deducted from taxable income.

Dilution Diminution in the proportion of income and assets to which each share is entitled.

Direct lease *Lease* in which the *lessor* purchases new equipment from the manufacturer and leases it to the *lessee* (cf. *sale and leaseback*).

Discount bond Debt sold for less than its *principal value*. If a discount bond pays no interest, it is called a "pure" discount bond.

Discount factor *Present value* of $1 received at a stated future date.

Discount rate Rate used to calculate the *present value* of future cash flows.

Disintermediation Withdrawal of funds from a financial institution in order to invest them directly (cf. *intermediation*).

Dividend Payment by a company to its stockholders.

Dividend tax credit Personal tax credit that reduces double taxation of dividends from Canadian firms.

Dividend yield Annual *dividend* divided by share price.

Dollar-weighted rate of return *Internal rate of return* (cf. *time-weighted rate of return*).

Double tax agreement Agreement between two countries that taxes paid abroad can be offset against domestic taxes levied on foreign *dividends*.

Duration The (weighted) average time to an asset's cash flows.

EBIT Earnings before interest and taxes.

Economic income Cash flow plus change in *present value*.

Economic rents Profits in excess of the competitive level.

EDC Export Development Corporation.

Efficient market Market in which security prices reflect information instantaneously.

Efficient portfolio Portfolio that offers the lowest risk (*standard deviation*) for its *expected return* and the highest expected return for its level of risk.

EPS Earnings per share.

Equipment trust certificate Form of *secured debt* generally used to finance railroad equipment. The trustee retains ownership of the equipment until the debt is repaid.

Equity (1) Common stock and *preferred stock.* Often used to refer to common stock only. (2) *Net worth.*

Equivalent annual cash flow *Annuity* with the same *net present value* as the company's proposed investment.

ERISA Employee Retirement Income Security Act in the United States.

ESOP Employee stock-ownership plan.

Eurobond *Bond* that is marketed internationally.

Eurodollar deposit Dollar deposit with a bank outside Canada.

European option Option that can be exercised only on final exercise date (cf. *American option*).

Evergreen credit *Revolving credit* without maturity.

Exchange of assets Acquisition of another company by purchase of its assets in exchange for cash or shares.

Exchange of stock Acquisition of another company by the purchase of its stock in exchange for cash or shares.

Ex dividend Term describing a purchase of shares by which the buyer is not entitled to the *dividend* (cf. *with dividend, cum dividend*).

Ex rights Purchase of shares in which the buyer is not entitled to the rights to buy shares in the company's *rights issue* (cf. *with rights, cum rights, rights on*).

Exercise price (Striking price) Price at which a *call option* or *put option* may be exercised.

Expected return Average of possible returns weighted by their probability.

Experience losses In a pension plan, losses resulting from any difference between expectations and experience (e.g., a decline in the value of the pension fund's securities).

Extendible bond Bond which allows its holder to extend the maturity for an additional prespecified period.

External finance Finance that is not generated by the firm: new borrowing or an issue of stock (cf. *internal finance*).

Extra dividend *Dividend* that may or may not be repeated.

Face value *Par value.*

Factoring Arrangement under which a financial institution buys a company's *accounts receivable* and collects the debt.

FASB Financial Accounting Standards Board in the United States.

FCIA Foreign Credit Insurance Association in the United States.

FDIC Federal Deposit Insurance Corporation in the United States.

Field warehouse Warehouse rented by a warehouse company on another firm's premises (cf. *public warehouse*).

Final-average plan Pension plan offering a pension that depends on the employee's average compensation in his or her final years of service (cf. *career-average plan*).

Financial assets Pieces of paper that represent claims on *real assets.*

Financial lease (capital lease, full-payout lease) Long-term, non-cancellable *lease* (cf. *operating lease*).

Financial leverage (gearing) Use of debt to increase the *expected return* on *equity*. Financial leverage is measured by the ratio of long-term debt to long-term debt plus equity (cf. *operating leverage*).

Float See *collection float, payment float*.

Floating lien General *lien* against a company's assets or against a particular class of assets.

Floating-rate bond *Bond* whose interest payment varies with the short-term interest rate.

Floor planning Arrangement used to finance inventory. A finance company buys the inventory, which is then held in trust by the user.

Foreign bond A *bond* issued on the domestic *capital market* of another country.

Forward cover Purchase or sale of forward foreign currency in order to offset a known future cash flow.

Forward exchange rate Exchange rate fixed today for exchanging currency at some future date (cf. *spot exchange rate*).

Forward interest rate Interest rate fixed today on a loan to be made at some future date (cf. *spot interest rate*).

Free cash flow Cash not retained and reinvested in the business.

Full-payout lease *Financial lease*.

Full-service lease (rental lease) *Lease* in which the *lessor* promises to maintain and insure the equipment (cf. *net lease*).

Funded debt Debt maturing after more than one year (cf. *unfunded debt*).

Future service costs Value of the pensions that are expected to accrue from employees' future service.

Garnishment A procedure for a debt to be settled by deduction from the debtor's wages.

Gearing *Financial leverage*.

General cash offer Issue of securities offered to all investors (cf. *rights issue*).

Growth stocks Stocks of companies that have an opportunity to invest money to earn more than the *opportunity cost of capital* (cf. *income stocks*).

Hedging Buying one security and selling another in such a way as to produce a riskless portfolio.

Hell-or-high-water clause Clause in a *lease* agreement that obliges the *lessee* to make payments regardless of what subsequently happens to the *lessor* or the equipment.

Holding company Company whose sole function is to hold stock in a number of operating subsidiaries.

Horizontal merger *Merger* between two companies manufacturing similar products (cf. *vertical merger, conglomerate merger*).

Hurdle rate Minimum acceptable rate of return on a project.

Immunization Construction of a portfolio of investments whose value is unaffected by interest rate changes.

Income bonds *Bonds* on which interest is payable only if earned.

Income stocks Stocks of companies that earn only the *opportunity cost of capital* on their new investments (cf. *growth stocks*).

In-the-money option A call option whose exercise price is below the current underlying stock price or a put option whose exercise price is above the current stock price.

Indenture Formal agreement—e.g., establishing the terms of a *bond* issue.

Indexed bonds *Bonds* on which payments are linked to an index—e.g., a retail price index.

Intangible assets Nonmaterial assets such as technical expertise, trademarks, and patents (cf. *tangible assets*).

Integer programming Variant of *linear programming* where the solution values must be integers.

Interest cover *Times interest earned*.

Interest rate parity theory Theory that the differential between the *forward exchange rates* and *spot exchange rates* is equal to the differential between the foreign and domestic interest rates.

Intermediation Investment through a financial institution (cf. *disintermediation*).

Internal finance Finance generated within a firm by retained earnings and *depreciation* (cf. *external finance*).

Internal rate of return (dollar-weighted rate of return, IRR) Discount rate at which investment has zero *net present value*.

Interval measure The number of days that a firm can finance operations without additional cash income.

Investment banker *Underwriter*.

Investment-grade bonds *Bonds* rated Baa or above.

Investment tax credit Proportion of new capital investment that can be used to reduce a company's tax bill.

IRR *Internal rate of return*.

IRS Internal Revenue Service in the United States.

Junior debt *Subordinated debt*.

Lease Long-term rental agreement.

Legal capital Value at which a company's shares are recorded in its books.

Lessee User of a leased asset (cf. *lessor*).

Lessor Owner of a leased asset (cf. *lessee*).

Letter of credit Letter from a bank stating that it has established a credit in a company's favour.

Letter stock Privately placed common stock, so called because the securities commissions require a letter from the purchaser that the stock is not intended for resale.

Level cost method (projected-benefit cost method) Method for estimating the *normal costs* of a pension plan. Its principle is that the company should contribute each year an equal amount per employee or an equal proportion of its wage bill (cf. *accrued-benefit cost method*).

Leverage See *financial leverage, operating leverage*.

Leveraged lease *Lease* in which the *lessor* finances part of the cost of the asset by an issue of debt secured by the asset.

Liabilities, total liabilities Total value of financial claims on a firm's assets. Equals (1) total assets *or* (2) total assets minus *net worth*.

Lien Lender's claim on specified assets.

Limited liability Limitation of shareholders' losses to the amount invested.

Linear programming (LP) Technique for finding the maximum value of some equation subject to stated linear constraints.

Line of credit Agreement by a bank that a company may borrow at any time up to an established limit.

Liquid assets Assets that are easily and cheaply turned into cash—notably cash itself and short-term securities.

Liquidating dividend *Dividend* that represents a return of capital.

Liquidity premium (1) Additional return for investing in a security that cannot easily be turned into cash. (2) Difference between the *forward interest rate* and the expected *spot interest rate*.

Load-to-load Arrangement whereby the customer pays for the last delivery when the next one is received.

Lock-box system Form of *concentration banking*. Customers send payments to a post office box. A local bank branch collects from the post office box, processes the cheques and transfers surplus money to the company's principal bank branch.

LP *Linear programming*.

Majority voting Voting system under which each director is voted upon separately (cf. *cumulative voting*).

Market capitalization rate *Expected return* on a security.

Market risk (systematic risk) Risk that cannot be diversified away.

Maturity factoring *Factoring* arrangement that provides collection and insurance of *accounts receivable*.

MDA *Multiple discriminant analysis*.

ME Montreal Exchange.

Merger Acquisition in which all assets and liabilities of the selling company are absorbed by the buyer (cf. *exchange of assets, exchange of stock*). More generally, any combination of two companies.

Money market Market for short-term safe investments.

Money-market fund *Mutual fund* which invests solely in short-term safe securities.

Monte Carlo simulation Method for calculating the probability distribution of possible outcomes from a project.

Mortgage bond *Bond* secured against plant and equipment.

Multiple discriminant analysis (MDA) Statistical technique for distinguishing between two series on the basis of their observed characteristics.

Mutual fund Managed investment fund whose shares are sold to investors.

Mutually exclusive projects Two projects that cannot both be undertaken.

NASD National Association of Security Dealers in the United States.

Negative pledge clause Clause under which the borrower agrees not to permit an exclusive *lien* on any of its assets.

Negotiated underwriting Method of choosing underwriters. Most firms may choose their *underwriter* by negotiation (cf. *competitive bidding*).

Net lease *Lease* in which the *lessee* promises to maintain and insure the equipment (cf. *full-service lease*).

Net present value A project's net contribution to wealth—*present value* minus initial investment.

Net working capital *Current assets* minus *current liabilities*.

Net worth Book value of a company's common stock, surplus, and retained earnings.

Nominal interest rate Interest rate expressed in money terms (cf. *real interest rate*).

Nonrefundable debt Debt that may not be called in order to replace it with another issue.

Normal costs Stream of contributions to a pension plan that is required to cover future employee service.

Normal distribution Symmetric bell-shaped probability distribution that can be completely defined by its mean and *standard deviation*.

Note Unsecured debt, usually with maturity of less than 15 years.

NYSE New York Stock Exchange.

Off-balance-sheet financing Financing that is not shown as a liability in a company's balance sheet.

Old-line factoring *Factoring* arrangement that provides collection, insurance, and finance for *accounts receivable*.

Open account Arrangement whereby sales are made with no formal debt contract. The buyer signs a receipt, and the seller records the sale in the sales ledger.

Open-end mortgage Mortgage against which additional debt may be issued (cf. *closed-end mortgage*).

Operating lease Short-term cancellable lease (cf. *financial lease*).

Operating leverage Fixed operating costs, so called because they accentuate variations in profits (cf. *financial leverage*).

Opportunity cost of capital (hurdle rate, cost of capital) *Expected return* that is forgone by investing in a project rather than in comparable financial securities.

Option See *call option, put option*.

Original issue discount (OID) debt Debt that is initially offered at a price below *face value*.

OSC Ontario Securities Commission.

Out-of-the-money option A call option whose exercise price is above the current underlying stock price, or a put option whose exercise price is below the current stock price.

Par value (face value) Value of security shown on certificate.

Payables *Accounts payable*.

Payback period Time taken for a project to recover the initial investment.

Payment float Cheques written by a company that have not yet cleared (cf. *collection float*).

Payout ratio *Dividend* as a proportion of earnings per share.

PBGC Pension Benefit Guarantee Corporation.

P/E ratio Share price divided by earnings per share.

Perpetuity Investment offering a level stream of cash flows in perpetuity.

Pooling of interest Method of accounting for *mergers*. The consolidated balance sheet of the merged firm is obtained by combining the balance sheets of the separate firms.

Postaudit Evaluation of an investment project after it is undertaken.

Preemptive right Common stockholder's right to anything of value distributed by the company.

Preferred stock Stock which takes priority over common stock as regards dividends. *Dividends* may not be paid on common stock unless the dividend is paid on all preferred stock. The dividend rate on preferred is usually fixed at time of issue.

Present value Discounted value of future cash flows.

Prime rate Rate at which banks lend to their most favoured customers.

Principal Amount of debt that must be repaid.

Privileged subscription issue *Rights issue.*

Production payment Loan in the form of advance payment for future delivery of a product.

Profitability index (Benefit-cost ratio) Ratio of a project's *present value* to the initial investment.

Pro forma Projected.

Project finance Debt that is largely a claim against the cash flows from a particular project rather than against a firm's entire assets.

Project note (PN) *Note* issued by public housing agencies or urban renewal agencies.

Projected-benefit cost method *Level cost method.*

Promissory note Promise to pay.

Prospectus Summary of the *registration* statement providing information on an issue of securities.

Proxy vote Vote cast by one person on behalf of another.

Public warehouse (Terminal warehouse) Warehouse operated by an independent warehouse company on its own premises (cf. *field warehouse*).

Purchase and resale agreement (PRA) *Repurchase agreement.*

Put option Option to sell an asset at a specified exercise price on or before a specified exercise date (cf. *call option*).

q The ratio of the market value of an asset to its replacement cost.

Quadratic programming Variant of *linear programming* where the equations are quadratic rather than linear.

Quick ratio (acid-test ratio) Measure of liquidity: (Current assets − inventory) divided by current liabilities.

Real assets *Tangible assets* and *intangible assets* used to carry on business (cf. *financial assets*).

Real interest rate Interest rate expressed in terms of real goods; i.e., *nominal interest rate* adjusted for inflation.

Receivables *Accounts receivable.*

Record date Date set by directors when making dividend payment. *Dividends* are sent to stockholders who are registered on the record date.

Recourse Term describing a type of loan. If a loan is with recourse, the lender has a general claim against the parent company if the *collateral* is insufficient to repay the debt.

Red herring Preliminary *prospectus.*

Refunding Replacement of existing debt with a new issue of debt.

Registered security Security whose ownership is recorded by the company's *registrar* (cf. *bearer security*).

Registrar Financial institution appointed to record issue and ownership of company securities.

Registration The process of obtaining United States *SEC* approval for a public issue of securities.

Regression analysis In statistics, a technique for finding the line of best fit.

Regular dividend *Dividend* that the company expects to maintain in the future.

Regulation A issue Security issues of under $400,000. Regulation A issues are partially exempt from United States SEC *registration* requirements.

Regulation Q Limit on the rate of interest that United States banks may pay on (small) deposits.

Rental lease *Full-service lease.*

Repo *Repurchase agreement.*

Repurchase agreement (RP, repo, buy-back, purchase and resale agreement) Purchase of government securities from a securities dealer with an agreement that the dealer will repurchase them at a specified price.

Residual risk *Unique risk.*

Retained earnings Earnings not paid out as *dividends*.

Retractable bond Bond which allows its holder to sell back the bond at a prespecified date before maturity.

Return on equity Usually, equity earnings as a proportion of the book value of equity.

Revenue Canada Reviews and assesses tax returns.

Revolving credit Legally assured *line of credit* with a bank.

Rights issue (privileged subscription issue) Issue of securities that is offered to current stockholders (cf. *general cash offer*).

Rights on *With rights.*

Risk premium (Expected) additional return for making a risky investment rather than a safe one.

ROI Return on investment. Generally, book income as a proportion of net book value.

Roll-over CD A package of successive *certificates of deposit*.

RP *Repurchase agreement.*

R squared Square of the *correlation coefficient*—the proportion of the variability in one series that can be explained by the variability of one or more other series.

Sale and lease-back Sale of an existing asset to a financial institution that then *leases* it back to the user (cf. *direct lease*).

Salvage value Scrap value of plant and equipment.

Season datings Extended credit for customers who order goods out of the peak season.

Seasoned issue Issue of a security for which there is an existing market (cf. *unseasoned issue*).

SEC Securities and Exchange Commission in the United States.

Secondary market Market in whch one can buy or sell *seasoned issues* of securities.

Secondary offering Procedure for selling large blocks of seasoned issues of stock on a stock exchange.

Secured debt Debt which, in the event of default, has first claim on specified assets.

Security market line Line representing the relationship between *expected return* and *market risk*.

Self-liquidating loan Loan to finance *current assets*. The sale of the current assets provides the cash to repay the loan.

Semistrong-form efficient market Market in which security prices instantaneously reflect all publicly available information (cf. *weak-form efficient market* and *strong-form efficient market*).

Senior debt Debt which, in the event of default, must be repaid before *subordinated debt* receives any payment.

Sensitivity analysis Analysis of the effect on project profitability of possible changes in sales, costs, and so on.

Serial bonds Package of *bonds* that mature in successive years.

Series bond *Bond* which may be issued in several series under the same *indenture*.

Shelf registration A procedure that allows companies to file one *registration* statement covering several issues of the same security in the United States.

Short sale Sale of a security that the investor does not own.

Sight draft Demand for immediate payment (cf. *time draft*).

Simple interest Interest calculated only on the initial investment (cf. *compound interest*).

Simulation See *Monte Carlo simulation.*

Sinking fund Fund that is established by a company to retire debt before maturity.

Skewed distribution Probability distribution in which an unequal number of observations lie below and above the mean.

Special dividend *Dividend* that is unlikely to be repeated.

Specific risk *Unique risk*.

Spot exchange rate Exchange rate on currency for immediately delivery (cf. *forward exchange rate*).

Spot interest rate Interest rate fixed today on a loan that is made today (cf. *forward interest rate*).

Spread (underwriter's spread) Difference between the price at which an *underwriter* buys an issue from a company and the price at which the underwriter sells it to the public.

Standard deviation Square root of the *variance*—a measure of variability.

Standard error In statistics, a measure of the possible error in an estimate.

Standby agreement In a *rights issue*, agreement that the *underwriter* will purchase any stock that is not purchased by the stockholders.

Statutory amalgamation Merger where all of the assets and all of the liabilities of the selling company are absorbed by the buying company and where the selling company disappears.

Stock dividend *Dividend* in the form of stock rather than cash.

Stock split "Free" issue of shares to existing shareholders.

Straight-line depreciation Method of depreciation whereby each year the company depreciates a constant proportion of the initial investment less *salvage value*.

Striking price *Exercise price* of a *call option* or *put option*.

Strip bonds A bond that is *stripped* of its coupons.

Strong-form efficient market Market in which security prices reflect instantaneously *all* information available to investors (cf. *weak-form efficient market and semistrong-form efficient market*).

Subordinated debt (junior debt) Debt over which senior debt takes priority. In the event of bankruptcy, subordinated debt-holders receive payment only after *senior debt* is paid off in full.

Sum-of-the-years' digits depreciation Method of *accelerated depreciation*.

Sunk costs Costs which have been incurred and cannot be reversed.

Supplemental liability Additional liability to a pension plan that results from an increase in promised benefits.

Systematic risk *Market risk*.

Take-up fee Fee paid to *underwriters* of a *rights issue* on any stock that they are obliged to purchase.

Tangible assets Physical assets such as plant, machinery, factories, and offices (cf. *intangible assets*).

Tax-anticipation bill Short-term bill issued by various governments that can be surrendered at face value in payment of taxes.

Tax-free merger Generally, merger that does not change the tax position of the corporation or its stockholders.

Tender offer General offer made directly to a firm's shareholders to buy their stock.

Terminal warehouse *Public warehouse*.

Term loans Medium-term privately placed loans, usually made by banks.

Term structure of interest rates Relationship between interest rates on loans of different maturities.

Throughput arrangement Arrangement by which shareholders of a pipeline company agree to make sufficient use of the pipeline to enable the pipeline company to service its debt.

Time draft Demand for payment at a stated future date (cf. *sight draft*).

Times interest earned (interest cover) Earnings before interest and tax, divided by interest payments.

Time-weighted rate of return Rate of return that gives equal weight to each time period; used in investment performance measurement (cf. *dollar-weighted rate of return*).

Tombstone Advertisement listing the *underwriters* to a security issue.

Trade acceptance Written demand that has been accepted by an industrial company to pay a given sum at a future date (cf. *bank acceptance*).

Trade credit   *Accounts receivable.*

Trade debt   *Accounts payable.*

Transfer agent   Individual or institution appointed by a company to look after the transfer of newly issued securities.

Treasurer   Principal financial manager (cf. *controller*).

Treasury bill   Short-term discount debt maturing in less than one year, issued regularly by the federal government.

Treasury stock   Common stock that has been repurchased by the company and held in the company's treasury.

Trust receipt   Receipt for goods that are to be held in trust for the lender.

TSE   Toronto Stock Exchange.

TSE 300 Index   Value-weighted stock index comprised of 300 TSE stocks.

Underpricing   Issue of securities below their market value.

Underwriter (investment banker)   Firm which buys an issue of securities from a company and resells it to investors.

Unfunded debt   Debt maturing within one year (cf. *funded debt*).

Unique risk (residual risk, specific risk, unsystematic risk)   Risk that can be reduced by diversification.

Unseasoned issue   Issue of a security for which there is no existing market (cf. *seasoned issue*).

Value additivity   Rule that the value of the whole equals the sum of the values of the parts.

Variance   Mean squared deviation from the expected value—a measure of variability.

Venture capital   Capital to finance a new firm.

Vertical merger   *Merger* between a supplier and its customer (cf. *horizontal merger, conglomerate merger*).

Vesting   Employee's entitlement to a part of his or her pension if he or she leaves before retirement.

VSE   Vancouver Stock Exchange.

Warehouse receipt   Evidence that a firm owns goods stored in a warehouse.

Warrant   Long-term *call option* issued by a company.

Weak-form efficient market   Market in which security prices instantaneously reflect the information contained in the past history of security prices. In such a market security prices follow a random walk (cf. *semistrong-form efficient market* and *strong-form efficient market*).

Weighted average cost of capital   *Expected return* on a portfolio of all the firm's securities.

With dividend (cum dividend)   Term describing a purchase of shares by which the buyer is entitled to the *dividend* (cf. *ex dividend*).

With rights (cum rights, rights on)   Term describing a purchase of shares by which the buyer is entitled to the rights to buy shares in the company's *rights issue* (cf. *ex rights*).

Withholding tax   Tax levied on *dividends* and interest paid abroad.

Working capital   *Current assets* and *current liabilities*. The term is commonly used as synonymous with *net working capital*.

Writer   Option seller.

Yield to maturity   *Internal rate of return* on a bond.

ANSWERS TO QUIZ QUESTIONS

CHAPTER 1

1. (a) Real
   (b) Executive airplanes
   (c) Brand names
   (d) Financial
   (e) Bonds
   (f) Investment
   (g) Capital budgeting
   (h) Financing.

2. a, c, and d.

3. c, d, e, and g are real assets. Others are financial.

CHAPTER 2

1. (a) Negative
   (b) $NPV = \dfrac{C_1}{1 + r}$
   (c) $NPV = C_0 + \dfrac{C_1}{1 + r}$
   (d) It is the return forgone by investing in the project rather than the capital market.
   (e) The return offered by default-free government bonds.

2. $DF_1 = 0.867$; discount rate $= 0.154$, or 15.4%.

3. (a) 0.090
   (b) 0.833
   (c) 0.769

4. (a) $\text{Return} = \dfrac{\text{profit}}{\text{investment}}$
      $= \dfrac{132 - 100}{100}$
      $= 0.32$, or 32%.
   (b) Negative (if the rate of interest r *equals* 32%, NPV = 0).

(c) $PV = \dfrac{132}{1.10} = 120$, or \$120,000
(d) $NPV = -100 + 120 = 20$, or \$20,000

5. Net present value rule: Invest if NPV is positive. Rate-of-return rule: Invest if the rate of return exceeds the opportunity cost of capital. They give the same answer.

6. (a) $1 + r = 5/4$. Therefore $r = 0.25$, or 25%
   (b) $2.6 - 1.6 = \$1$ million
   (c) \$3 million
   (d) $\text{Return} = (3 - 1)/1 = 2.0$, or 200%
   (e) Marginal return $=$ rate of interest $= 25\%$
   (f) $PV = 4 - 1.6 = \$2.4$ million
   (g) $NPV = -1.0 + 2.4 = \$1.4$ million
   (h) \$4 million (\$2.6 million cash + NPV)
   (i) \$1 million
   (j) \$3.75 million

7. They will vote for (a) only. The other tasks can be carried out just as efficiently by stockholders.

CHAPTER 3

1. \$1.00

2. $125/139 = 0.899$

3. $596 \times 0.285 = 170$

4. $\dfrac{374}{(1.09)^9} = 172$

5. $PV = \dfrac{432}{1.15} + \dfrac{137}{(1.15)^2} + \dfrac{797}{(1.15)^3}$
   $= 375.84 + 103.57 + 524.42$
   $= 1,003.83$

6. $100 \times (1.15)^8 = 305.90$

7. $232 \times (1 + r)^2 = 312.18$ implies $r = 0.16$, or 16%.

8. $\text{NPV} = -1{,}548 + \dfrac{138}{0.09} = -14.67$

9. Find g so that $\text{NPV} = 0$.
$$\text{NPV} = -2{,}590 + \frac{220}{0.12 - g} = 0$$
implies $g = 0.035$, or 3.5%.

10. PV of $502 at $t = 1, 2, \ldots, 9$ at 13% $= 502 \times 5.132 = 2{,}576.26$. Future value $= 2{,}576 \times (1.13)^9 = 7{,}739.19$.

11. (a) Let S_t = salary in year t
$$\text{PV} = \sum_{t=1}^{30} \frac{S_t}{(1.08)^t}$$
$$= \sum_{t=1}^{30} \frac{20{,}000\,(1.05)^{t-1}}{(1.08)^t}$$
$$= \sum_{t=1}^{30} \frac{20{,}000/1.05}{(1.08/1.05)^t}$$
$$= \sum_{t=1}^{30} \frac{19{,}048}{(1.029)^t}$$
$$= 19{,}048 \left[\frac{1}{0.029} - \frac{1}{0.029\,(1.029)^{30}} \right]$$
$$= 378{,}222$$

(b) PV (salary $\times$ 0.05) $= 18{,}911$. Future value $= 18{,}911 \times (1.08)^{30} = 190{,}295$.

(c) Annual payment = initial value $\div$ annuity factor; 20-year annuity factor at 8% = 9.818; annual payment = $190{,}295/9.818 = 19{,}382$.

12.

Period	Discount Factor	Cash Flow	Present Value
0	1.0	−40,000	−40,000
1	0.893	+10,000	+ 8,930
2	0.797	+20,000	+15,940
3	0.712	+30,000	+21,360
		Total = NPV =	$6,230

13. (a) PV $= 1/0.10 = \$10$

(b) $\text{PV} = \dfrac{1}{0.10\,(1.10)^7} = \dfrac{10}{2} = \$5$ (approx.)

(c) PV $= 10 - 5 = \$5$ (approx.)

(d) $\text{PV} = \dfrac{C}{r - g} = \dfrac{10{,}000}{0.10 - 0.05} = \$200{,}000$

14. (a) From Appendix Table 1, $1/(1.05)^5 = 0.784$. You therefore need to set aside $10{,}000 \times 0.784 = \$7{,}840$.

(b) From Appendix Table 3, the present value of $1 a year for six years at 8% is $4.623. Therefore you need to set aside $12{,}000 \times 4.623 = \$55{,}476$.

(c) From Appendix Table 2, $1.08^6 = 1.587$. Therefore, at the end of six years you would have $1.587 \times (60{,}476 - 55{,}476) = \$7{,}935$.

(d) From Appendix Table 2, $1 grows to $1.762 by year 5 at an annually compounded rate of 12%. From Appendix Table 4, $1 grows to $1.762 by year 5 at a continuously compounded rate of about 11.4%.

CHAPTER 4

1. $P_0 = \dfrac{10 + 210}{1.10} = \$200$

2. $r = \dfrac{5}{40} = 0.125$

3. $P_0 = \dfrac{10}{0.10 - 0.05} = \$200$

4. $\dfrac{15}{1.10} + \text{PVGO} = 200$; therefore PVGO $= \$50$

5. b and c (a ignores the cost of the investments needed to produce the earnings).

6. (a) $\text{PV} = \dfrac{1{,}050}{1.08} = 972.22$

(b) $\text{PV} = \dfrac{50}{1.08} + \dfrac{1{,}050}{(1.08)^2} = 946.50$

(c) $PV = \sum_{t=1}^{5} \dfrac{50}{(1.08)^t} + \dfrac{1,050}{(1.08)^6}$

$= 861.33$

7. The increased return has larger impact on the longer term bonds.

(a) $PV = \dfrac{1,050}{(1.1)^2} = 954.55$

(b) $PV = \dfrac{50}{1.1} + \dfrac{1,050}{(1.1)^2} = 913.22$

(c) $PV = \sum_{t=1}^{5} \dfrac{50}{(1.1)^t} + \dfrac{1,050}{(1.1)^6}$

$= 782.25$

CHAPTER 5

1. The opportunity cost of capital is the expected rate of return investors could earn at any given level of risk.

2. (a) A = three years, B = two years, C = three years
   (b) B
   (c) A, B, and C
   (d) B and C (NPV_B = \$3.378; NPV_C = \$2,405)
   (e) False
   (f) True

3. (a) $\dfrac{1,000}{4,000} = 0.25$, or 25%

4. (a) True
   (b) False

5. (a) \$15,750; \$4,250; \$0
   (b) 100%

6. (a) (i) Both (IRR is greater than the cost of capital). (ii) The *incremental* cash flows on B are: −2,000, +1,100, +1,210. The IRR on these incremental flows is 10%. Since this is greater than the cost of capital, the incremental investment in A is worthwhile.
   (b) NPV of incremental investment = 690 − 657 = \$33

7. (a) A = 2,000/1,600 = 1.25; B = 2,400/2,100 = 1.14
   (b) (i) Both. (ii) The incremental flows on B are −500, +240, +288. The

profitability index on the incremental investment is 400/500 = 0.8. Therefore, accept A.

8. (a) C (if both projects have NPV = 0 at the same discount rate, the project with the later cash flows must have the higher NPV if we use a lower discount rate).
   (b) No (you are effectively "borrowing" at a higher rate of interest).

CHAPTER 6

1. a, b, d, g, h.

2. Real cash flow = 100,000/1.1 = 90,909; real discount rate = (1.15/1.1) − 1 = 0.0455

   $PV = \dfrac{90,909}{1.0455} = 86,953$, four francs short because of rounding error.

3. (a) NPV_A = \$100,000; NPV_B = \$180,000
   (b) Equivalent cash flow of A = 100,000/1.736 = \$57,604; equivalent cash flow of B = 180,000/2.487 = \$72,376
   (c) NPV perpetual chain of machine A = 57,604/0.10 = \$576,040; NPV perpetual chain of machine B = 72,376/0.10 = \$723,760
   (d) Machine B.

4. Replace at end of five years (\$80,000 > 72,376).

5. 1, 2, 4 and 6.

6. Soft rationing means provisional capital constraints imposed by management as an aid to financial control. This doesn't rule out raising more money if necessary. Firms facing hard rationing can't raise money from capital markets.

7. Purchase cost and PV of after-tax net revenue stream
   = −150,000 + 89,418 = −60,582.
   PV of perpetual CCA tax shield on \$150,000
   $= \dfrac{150,000 \times 0.2 \times 0.4}{0.12 + 0.2} = 37,500$

(a) (i) NPV $= -60,582 + 37,500$
$$+ \frac{20,000}{(1.12)^9}$$
$$- \frac{20,000 \times 0.2 \times 0.4}{0.12 + 0.2}$$
$$\times \frac{1}{(1.12)^9}$$
$$= -17,673$$

(ii) NPV $= -60,582 + 37,500$
$$+ \left(200,000 - 0.4 \right.$$
$$\left. \times \frac{(200,000 - 150,000)}{2} \right)$$
$$\times \frac{1}{(1.12)^9}$$
$$- \frac{150,000 \times 0.2 \times 0.4}{0.12 + 0.2}$$
$$\times \frac{1}{(1.12)^9}$$
$$= 31,911$$

(b) UCC in year 9 $= 150,000 \times$
$(1 - 0.2)^9 = 20,133$

(i) NPV $= -60,582 + 37,500$
$+ (20,000 + 0.4$
$\times (20,133$
$$- 20,000)) \frac{1}{(1.12)^9}$$
$$- \frac{20,133 \times 0.2 \times 0.4}{0.12 + 0.2}$$
$$\times \frac{1}{(1.12)^9}$$
$$= -17,666$$

(ii) NPV $= -60,582 + 37,500$
$+ (30,000 + 0.4$
$\times (20,133$
$$- 30,000)) \times \frac{1}{(1.12)^9}$$
$$- \frac{20,133 \times 0.2 \times 0.4}{0.12 + 0.2}$$
$$\times \frac{1}{(1.12)^9}$$
$$= -15,502$$

(iii) NPV $= -60,582 + 37,500$
$+ (200,000 + 0.4$
$\times (20,133$
$- 150,000))$
$$\times \frac{1}{(1.12)^9}$$
$$- 0.4 \times \frac{1}{2}$$
$\times (200,000$
$- 150,000)$
$$\times \frac{1}{(1.12)^9}$$
$$- \frac{20,133 \times 0.2 \times 0.4}{0.12 + 0.2}$$
$$\times \frac{1}{(1.12)^9}$$
$$= 24,886$$

(c) UCC in year 0 $= 150,000 -$
$100,000 = 50,000$
UCC in year 9 $= 50,000 \times$
$(1 - 0.2)^9 = 6,711$
NPV $= -60,582 + 0.4$
$\times 100,000$
$$+ \frac{50,000 \times 0.2 \times 0.4}{0.12 + 0.2}$$
$+ (20,000 + 0.4 \times (6,711$
$$- 20,000)) \times \frac{1}{(1.12)^9}$$
$$- \frac{6,711 \times 0.2 \times 0.4}{0.12 + 0.2}$$
$$\times \frac{1}{(1.12)^9}$$
$$= -3,392.$$

8. The only reason you may want to take CCA at a reduced rate would be that you are going to have a higher tax rate in the future so that a CCA tax shield in more valuable then, but suppose this is not the case here. Recaptured depreciation merely forces you to take into income "excess" CCA that you took earlier and received a tax shield for. That is, at recapture time, you merely pay for the same dollar benefit you already received earlier. Under the time value of money, facing a recapture like this is the best thing to do, so you should claim CCA at the maximum rate.

CHAPTER 7

1. (a) 12%
   (b) 8%
   (c) 0%
   (d) 20%
   (e) Less, because the market portfolio is diversified.

2. Standard deviation of returns, correlated, less, unique risk, market risk, capital asset pricing, security market line, zero, riskfree rate, one, market portfolio.

3. (a) False
   (b) True
   (c) False—its *risk premium* would be twice as high.
   (d) True
   (e) True
   (f) False
   (g) True—if "risk" means standard deviation.
   (h) False

4. A: 1.0; B: 2.0; C: 1.5; D: 0; E: −1.0

5. 1.3 (Diversification does not affect market risk.)

6. (a) $\sigma^2 = 330$; $\sigma = 18.2$
   (b) slightly lower.

7. (a) $r_f + \beta(r_m - r_f) = 4 + 0.75(10 - 4) = 8.5\%$
   (b) Teck Corporation has the highest beta and hence the highest expected return, which is $4 + 1.69(10 - 4) = 14.1\%$
   (c) Bell Canada has an expected return of $4 + 0.32(10 - 4) = 5.9\%$
   (d) Lower
   (e) Higher
   In (d) and (e), note that the expected return on the market portfolio is unchanged. Thus, in Figure 7-8, the security market line still goes through the market, but the riskfree intercept is now higher (6% rather than 4%). This decreases the expected returns of high beta securities and increases the expected returns of low beta securities.

8. *b*

9. $r_A = r_f + 0.5 (r_m - r_f) = 7$
   $r_B = r_f + 1.5 (r_m - r_f) = 15$
   $r_B - r_A = r_m - r_f = 8 = $ market risk premium
   $r_A = r_f + 0.5 \times 8 = 7$ implies $r_f = 3$
   $r_m - 3 = 8$ implies $r_m = 11$ = expected return on market

CHAPTER 8

1. (a) Figure 8-16: diversification reduces risk (for example, a mixture of portfolios A and B would have less risk than the average of A and B).
   (b) Those along line *AB* in Figure 8-15.
   (c) See Figure 1, below.

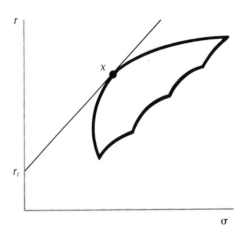

Figure 1 Chapter 8, quiz question 1(c).

2. (a) Portfolio A (higher expected return, same risk)
   (b) Cannot say (depends on investor's attitude to risk)
   (c) Portfolio F (lower risk, same expected return)

3.

$x_1^2\sigma_1^2$	$x_2x_3\sigma_{12}$	$x_1x_3\sigma_{13}$
$x_1x_2\sigma_{12}$	$x_2^2\sigma_2^2$	$x_1x_3\sigma_{23}$
$x_1x_3\sigma_{13}$	$x_2x_3\sigma_{23}$	$x_3^2\sigma_3^2$

4. *a, b*

5. *d*

6. (a) See Figure 2.
(b) A, D, G
(c) F
(d) 15% in C
(e) Put 25/32 of your money in F and lend 7/32 at 12%.

Expected return = 7/32 × 12 + 25/32 × 18 = 16.7%
Standard deviation = 7/32 × 0 + 25/32 × 32 = 25%

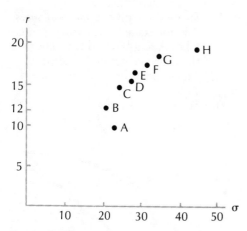

Figure 2 Chapter 8, question 6.

If you could borrow without limit, you would achieve as high an expected return as you'd like, with correspondingly high risk of course.

7. (a) 30%
(b) zero
(c) 0.75
(d) Less than 1.0 (the portfolio's risk is the same as the market, but some of this risk is unique risk).

CHAPTER 9

1. It will tend to overinvest in risky projects, and pass valuable safe projects by.

2. Suppose $r_f = 7\%$.
$r = r_f + \beta(r_m - r_f) = 7 + 2.0(8)$
$= 23\%$

$$NPV = -100,000 + \frac{150,000}{1.23}$$
$$= +21,950$$

3. BETA = market risk measure. Average risk would imply beta = 1.0
ALPHA = average price change on stock when market return was zero
R-SQR = ratio of market risk to total risk of stock—that is, proportion of variance of stock return attributable to market risk
RESID STD DEV-N = stock's unique risk, measured as a standard deviation
STD ERR OF BETA = measure of extent of possible error in beta estimate
ADJUSTED BETA = beta estimate adjusted for fact that high estimated betas tend to be overestimates of true betas, and low estimated betas tend to be underestimates
NUMBER OF OBSERV = number of monthly returns used to estimate betas and alpha

4. $\beta_{ASSETS} = 0 \times 0.40 + 0.5 \times 0.60$
$= 0.30$
$r = 10 + 0.30(20 - 10) = 13\%$

5. (a) $r_f + \beta(r_m - r_f) = 8 + 1.5 \times 10$
$= 23\%$

(b) $\beta_{ASSETS} = \beta_{DEBT} \left(\dfrac{debt}{debt + equity} \right)$
$+ \beta_{EQUITY}$
$\times \left(\dfrac{equity}{debt + equity} \right)$
$= 0 \times \dfrac{4}{4 + 6} + 1.5$
$\times \dfrac{6}{4 + 6}$
$= 0.9$

(c) $r_f + \beta_{ASSETS} (r_m - r_f) = 8 + 0.9$
$\times 10 = 17\%$
(d) $r = 17\%$
(e) $r_f + \beta(r_m - r_f) = 8 + 1.2 \times 10$
$= 20\%$

6. (a) A (higher fixed cost).
(b) E (more cyclical revenues).

7. $CEQ_t/[(1 + r_f)^t]$; less than one; $r_f + \beta(r_m - r_f)$; decrease

8. (a) $\text{PV} = \dfrac{110}{1 + r_f + \beta(r_m - r_f)}$

$\qquad\qquad + \dfrac{121}{[1 + r_f + \beta(r_m - r_f)]^2}$

$\qquad = \dfrac{110}{1.10} + \dfrac{121}{1.10^2}$

$\qquad = \$200$

(b) $\dfrac{\text{CEQ}_1}{1.05} = \dfrac{110}{1.10}$, $\text{CEQ}_1 = \$105$

$\quad\ \dfrac{\text{CEQ}_2}{1.05^2} = \dfrac{121}{1.10^2}$, $\text{CEQ}_2 = \$110.25$

(c) $a_1 = \dfrac{105}{110} = 0.95$

$\quad\ a_2 = \dfrac{110.25}{121} = 0.91$

CHAPTER 10

1. (a) Detailed analysis of capital investment projects, to identify what cash
flows depend on, what can go wrong,
whether the project could be abandoned if performance is disappointing, and so on.

(b) Analysis of how project profitability
and NPV changes if different assumptions are made about sales, cost,
and other key variables.

(c) Determines the level of future sales
at which project profitability or NPV
equals zero.

(d) An extension of sensitivity analysis
which explores all possible outcomes and weighs each by its
probability.

(e) A graphical technique for displaying possible future events and decisions taken in response to those
events.

(f) The additional present value created by the option to bail out of a
project, and recover part of the initial investment, if the project performs poorly.

(g) The additional present value created by the option to invest more
and expand output, if a project performs well.

2. $-\$30$ million.

3. (a) NPV = old NPV

$\qquad -$ additional
investment

$\qquad -$ reduction in
$\quad +$ net variable
costs

$\qquad$ increase in
$\quad +$ depreciation tax
shield

$\qquad = 34.3 - 150$

$\qquad + \displaystyle\sum_{t=1}^{10} \dfrac{(0.5 \times 40)}{(1.10)^t}$

$\qquad + \displaystyle\sum_{t=1}^{10} \dfrac{(0.5 \times 15)}{(1.10)^t}$

$\qquad = \$53$ million

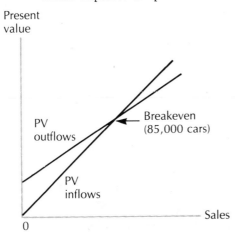

Present
value

PV
outflows

Breakeven
(85,000 cars)

PV
inflows

Sales

0

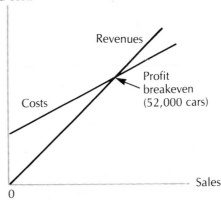

Revenues
and costs

Revenues

Costs

Profit
breakeven
(52,000 cars)

Sales

0

Figure 3 Chapter 10, quiz question 3(c).

(b) Variable costs = $260 million on 100,000 cars.

(c) The left-hand chart in Figure 3 shows that expected sales have to be at least 85,000 for the project to have a positive NPV. The right-hand graph shows that the firm can report an *accounting* profit if sales exceed 52,000.

4. (a) "Optimistic" and "pessimistic" rarely show the full probability distribution of outcomes.

(b) Sensitivity analysis changes variables one at a time; in practice, all variables change, and the changes are often interrelated. Sensitivity analysis using scenarios can help in this regard.

5. (a) False
(b) True
(c) True
(d) True
(e) True
(f) False
(g) True
(h) True

6. (a) Describe how project cash flow depends on the underlying variables.

(b) Specify probability distributions for forecast errors for these cash flows.

(c) Draw from the probability distributions to simulate the cash flows.

7. NPV (pretest) = 34.3 − 0.1 = $34.2 million

NPV (don't pretest) = 0.9 × 34.3
+ 0.1
× (−27.1)
= $28.2 million

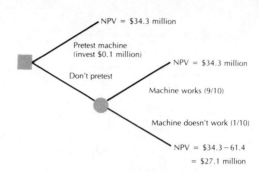

8. See Table 1. The decision tree shows the probability of finding oil earlier. At 15,000 feet, the expected payoff to further drilling is $(0.25 \times 1) + (0.75 \times -3) = -\$2$ million. This is greater than the payoff to stopping. Therefore Big should drill to 20,000 feet. At 10,000 feet the expected payoff to drilling to 15,000 feet is $0.8 \times [(0.25 \times 1) + (0.75 \times -3)] + (0.2 \times 2) = -\$1.2$ million. This is greater than the payoff to stopping. Therefore Big should drill to 15,000 feet. The expected payoff to drilling to 10,000 feet is $(0.5 \times 3) + (0.5 \times -1.2) = \$0.9$ million. As long as the certainty equivalent value of this payoff is positive, Big should drill to 10,000 feet initially, but be prepared to go all the way to 20,000 feet.

CHAPTER 11

1. Your best estimate is $2,000 per hectare, the actual market value. Why do

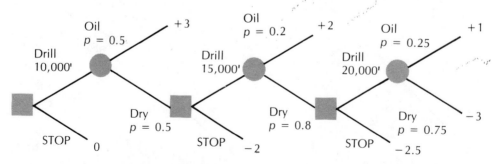

TABLE 1 See quiz question 8, Chapter 10.

---

a discounted-cash-flow analysis to estimate market value when you can observe it directly?

2. (*a*) False
   (*b*) True
   (*c*) True
   (*d*) False

3. $15

4. DC-8s should have been valued at market prices for used airplanes. The *low book* depreciation charge was irrelevant. Alitalia should have compared the total costs of operating 747s and DC-8s, in which the DC-8s' cost includes the opportunity cost of capital on, and depreciation of, their actual secondhand value. *Note*: If 747s and DC-8s were perfect substitutes in terms of range, passenger comfort, and so on, we would expect the DC-8s' secondhand value to adjust until their total operating costs per seat mile were the same as the 747s'.

5. It depends first on competition among capital equipment producers. If other producers can quickly match the new machine, its advantages are passed on to its buyers. But then the buyers will compete to pass on the machine's advantages to their customers. In the end, producers will realize positive NPVs from buying the machine only if they are in a position to make better use of it than their competitors.

CHAPTER 12

1. (*a*) False
   (*b*) False—top management usually makes the final decision on major projects.
   (*c*) True
   (*d*) True
   (*e*) False
   (*f*) True

2. Cash flow, economic, less, greater.

3.

	Year 1	Year 2	Year 3
Cash flow	0	78.55	78.55
PV at start of year	120.00	144.00	65.46
PV at end of year	144.00	65.46	0
Change in value during year	+24.00	−78.55	−65.46
Expected economic income	+24.00	+28.80	+13.09

4. (*a*) False
   (*b*) False—firms have a considerable range of choice.
   (*c*) True
   (*d*) True

CHAPTER 13

1. *c*

2. Weak, semistrong, strong, fundamental, strong, technical, weak

3. *c* and *f*

4. (*a*) Decline to $200
   (*b*) Remain at 2%
   (*c*) Less
   (*d*) A slight abnormal fall (the split is likely to have led investors to expect an above-average rise in dividends)

5. (*a*) False
   (*b*) True
   (*c*) False
   (*d*) True
   (*e*) False
   (*f*) True (a small change in price *in the absence of new information* causes a large increase in demand)

CHAPTER 14

1. (*a*) 40,000/0.50 = 80,000 shares
   (*b*) 78,000 shares

(c) 2,000 shares are held as Treasury stock

(d) 20,000 shares

(e)
Common stock	$ 45,000
Additional paid-in capital	25,000
Retained earnings	30,000
Common equity	100,000
Treasury stock	5,000
Net common equity	$ 95,000

2. (a) 80 votes

(b) 10 × 80 = 800 votes

3. (a) Funded

(b) Eurobond

(c) Subordinated

(d) Debentures

(e) Sinking fund

(f) Call

(g) Prime rate

(h) Floating rate

(i) Lease

4. Internally generated cash, 64; Financial deficit, 34; New share issues, 10; Long-term debt issues, 31; Short-term debt issues, 1.

CHAPTER 15

1. (a) Treasury bills

(b) Unseasoned stock

(c) Seasoned stock

(d) Bond issue by utility holding company

(e) Bond issue by industrial company

(f) Bond issue by a large industrial company

2. (a) E

(b) F

(c) D

(d) A

(e) G

(f) C

(g) B

3. A = a, c (n.b. underpricing is *not* a cost in a rights issue)

B = a, b, d

C = e.

4. (a) A large issue

(b) A bond issue

(c) A large competitive bond issue

(d) A rights issue

(e) A small private placement of bonds

5. (a) Number of rights needed to purchase one share: 2

(b) Number of new shares: 50

(c) Amount of new investment: $500

(d) Total value of company after issue: $4,500

(e) Total number of shares after issue: 150

(f) Cum-rights price: $40

(g) Ex-rights price: $30

(h) Price of a right: $10

Neither [buying a share ex rights costs $30; buying and exercising the rights costs (2 × 10) + 10 = $30].

6. Value of right
$$= \frac{\text{ex-rights price} - \text{issue price}}{N}$$

CHAPTER 16

1. (a) A, e; B, d; C, c; D, a; E, b

(b) The stock price should fall on the ex-dividend date to reflect the fact that the shares have lost the dividend.

(c) (4 × 0.35)/30 = 4.67%

(d) 1.40/3.00 = 47%

(e) Let p_0 = price before stock dividend and p_1 = price after stock dividend. Then $(1 + 0.10)p_1 = p_0$ so that $p_1 = p_0/1.10$ and the price drop is $p_0 - p_1 = p_0(1 - 1/1.1)$ which is a 9.1% drop.

2. c, d, and e are false.

3. (a) 35%

(b) 77% per year

4. See Tables 2 and 3.

5. (a) (i) Lo, (ii) Lo

(b) (i) Lo, (ii) Hi

(c) Indifferent

(d) Hi (dividends are untaxed, but capital gains are taxed as regular income)

6. (a) $10

(b) $9

Table 2 Company Does Not Pay Dividend

Cash	0	0	Debt
Existing fixed assets	4,500	5,500 + NPV	Equity
New project	1,000 + NPV		
	$5,500 + NPV	$5,500 + NPV	

Table 3 Company Pays $1,000 Dividend

Cash	0	0	Debt
Existing fixed assets	4,500	1,000	Value of new stock
New project	1,000 + NPV	4,500 + NPV	Value of original stock
	$5,500 + NPV	$5,500 + NPV	

Note: Because the new stockholders continue to receive stock worth $1,000, the value of the original stock declines by $1,000 which exactly offsets the dividend.

(c) $9/0.85 = $10.59. (An investor who buys with-dividend and sells immediately ex-dividend receives the ex-price + $9 after-tax income + a tax loss worth 0.15 × (with-dividend price − ex-dividend price.) Therefore, in equilibrium, the with-dividend price = ex-dividend price + $9 + 0.15 × (with-dividend

7. The implicit corporate tax rate T_c solves

$$\frac{1}{1 - T_c} = 1 + 1/3 \text{ so that } T_c = 25\%.$$

The provincial tax rate T_{prov} solves T_c = (0.2) (1 + T_{prov}) so that T_{prov} = 25%.

CHAPTER 17

1. (a) $0.10P$
   (b) Buy 10% of B's debt + 10% of B's equity
   (c) $0.10(P − 100)$
   (d) Borrow an amount equal to 10% of B's debt and buy 10% of A's equity

2. Note the market value of Copperhead is far in excess of its book value:

	Market Value
Common stock	
(8 million shares at $2)	$16,000,000
Short-term loans	$2,000,000

Ms. Kraft owns 0.625% of the firm, which proposes to increase common stock to $17 million and cut short-term debt. Ms. Kraft can offset this by (a) borrowing 0.00625 × 1,000,000 = $6,250, and (b) buying that much more Copperhead stock.

3. Expected return on assets is
$$r_A = 0.08 \times 30/80 + 0.16 \times 50/80$$
$$= 0.13$$
The new return on equity will be
$$r_E = 0.13 \times 20/60 \ (0.13 - 0.08)$$
$$= 0.147$$

4. (a) (i) $\beta_A = \left(\dfrac{D}{D + E} \times \beta_D\right)$
$$+ \left(\frac{E}{D + E} \times \beta_E\right)$$
$$1.0 = (0.5 \times 0) + (0.5 \times \beta_E)$$
$$\therefore \beta_E = 2.0$$

(ii) $\beta_D = 0$

(iii) $\beta_A = 1.0$

(b) (i) 0.10

(ii) $r_A = \left(\dfrac{D}{D + E} \times r_D\right)$
$$+ \left(\frac{E}{D + E} \times r_E\right)$$
$$0.10 = (0.5 \times 0.05) + (0.5 \times r_E)$$
$$r_E = 0.15$$

(iii) $r_D = 0.05$
(iv) $r_A = 0.10$
(c) (i) 50%
(ii) 6.7 (that is, the *P/E* ratio falls to offset the increase in EPS).

5. (a)

Operating income, dollars	500	1,000	1,500	2,000
Interest, dollars	250	250	250	250
Equity earnings, dollars	250	750	1,250	1,750
Earnings per share	0.33	1.00	1.67	2.33
Return on shares, %	3.3	10	16.7	23.3
Return on debt, %	10	10	10	10

(b) $\beta_A = \left(\dfrac{D}{D + E} \times \beta_D \right)$

$\qquad + \left(\dfrac{E}{D + E} \times \beta_E \right)$

$0.8 = (0.25 \times 0) + (0.75 + \beta_E)$

$\beta_E = 1.07$

6. (a) True, so long as the market value of "old" debt does not change.
(b) False. MM's Proposition I says only that overall firm value ($V = D + E$) does not depend on capital structure.
(c) False. Borrowing increases equity risk even if debt is default-risk free.
(d) False. Limited liability affects the relative values of debt and equity, not their sum.
(e) True. Limited liability protects shareholders if the firm defaults.
(f) True—but the required rate of return on equity and the firm's assets are the same if the firm borrows against risk-free assets. In this case r_A, r_D and r_E all equal the risk-free rate of interest.
(g) False. The shareholders could make the same debt issue on their own account.

(h) True. To put it more precisely, it assumes that the expected rate of return to equity goes up, but stockholders' required rate of return goes up proportionately. Therefore, stock price is unchanged.
(i) False. The formula $r_E = r_A + D/E$ $(r_A - r_D)$ does not require $r_D = $ a constant.
(j) False. The clientele has to be willing to pay extra for the debt, which they will not do if plenty of corporate debt issues are already available.

7. See Figure 17-5.

CHAPTER 18

1. (a) PV tax shield
$= \dfrac{T_c(r_D D)}{1 + r_D}$
$= \dfrac{0.46(0.08 \times 1,000)}{1.08}$
$= \$34.07$
(b) PV tax shield
$= \sum\limits_{t=1}^{5} \dfrac{T_c(r_D D)}{(1 + r_D)^t}$
$= \sum\limits_{t=1}^{5} \dfrac{0.46(0.08 \times 1,000)}{(1.08)^t}$
$= \$146.93$
(c) PV tax shield $= T_c D = \$460$

2. (a) PV tax shield $= T_c D = \$16$
(b) $T_c \times 20 = \$8$
(c) New PV tax shield
$= \sum\limits_{t=1}^{5} \dfrac{0.40(0.08 \times 60)}{(1.08)^t} = \$7.67$
Therefore, company value $= 168 - 24 + 7.67 = \$151.67$

3. Aggregate amount of debt should decline until no debtholder has a marginal tax rate greater than 40%.

4. See Table 4. Consider $1,000 of pretax income.

5. A firm with no taxable income saves no taxes by borrowing and paying interest.

Table 4

Case	(1) Corporate Tax	(2) Cash Flow to Investor	(3) Federal Personal Tax	(4) Provincial Personal Tax	(5) Net Cash Flow (2 − 3 − 4)
a (bond)	0	1,000	0	0	1,000
a (equity)	400	600	− 225	− 113	938
b, c (bond)	0	1,000	250	125	625
b (equity)	400	600	0	0	600
c, d (equity)	400	600	0	0	600
d, e (bond)	0	1,000	350	175	475
e (equity)	400	600	90	45	465
f (bond)	400	600	180	90	330

Bond income is preferred in cases a, b, c, and e, and equity income is preferred in cases d, f.

The interest payments would simply add to its tax-loss carry-forwards. Such a firm would have little tax incentive to borrow.

6. (a) Stockholders win. Bond value falls, since the value of assets securing the bond has fallen.

(b) Bondholder wins if we assume the cash is left invested in Treasury bills. The bondholder is sure to get $26 plus interest. Stock value is zero, because there is no chance that firm value can rise above $50.

(c) The bondholders lose. The firm adds assets worth $10 and debt worth $10. This would increase Circular's debt ratio, leaving the old bondholders more exposed. The old bondholders' loss is the stockholders' gain.

(d) Both bondholders and stockholders win. They share the (net) increase in firm value. The bondholders' position is not eroded by the issue of a junior security. (We assume that the preferred does not lead to still more game playing, and that the new investment does not make the firm's *assets* safer or riskier.)

(e) Bondholders lose because they are at risk for longer. Stockholders win.

7. Specialized, intangible assets such as growth opportunities are most likely to lose value in financial distress. Safe, tangible assets with good second-hand markets are least likely to lose value. Costs of financial distress are thus likely to be less for, say, real estate firms or trucking companies than for advertising firms or high-tech growth companies.

CHAPTER 19

1. APV = base − case NPV ± PV financing side effects
   (a) APV = 0 − 0.15(500,000)
      = − 75,000
   (b) APV = 0 + 175,000 = +175,000
   (c) APV = 0 + 76,000 = +76,000
   (d) APV = 0 − 0.15(500,000)
      + 76,000
      = + 1,000

2. APV = base case NPV + PV tax shield. If we use $T^* = 0.40$ instead of $T_c = 0.46$, PV tax shield = (0.40/0.46)747,000 = 650,000. APV = +170,000 + 650,000 = 820,000. With $T^* = 0.10$, PV tax shield = (0.10/0.46)747,000 = 162,000. APV = +170,000 + 162,000 = 332,000.

3. APV = base case NPV + PV tax

   shield $= \dfrac{C_1}{1 + r} - I +$

   $\dfrac{r_D L T^* (\text{APV} + I)}{1 + r_D},$

   where I = investment

   $= \dfrac{1,200}{1.20} - 1,000$

   $+ \dfrac{0.10 \times 0.30 \times 0.20(\text{APV} + 1,000)}{1.1}$

   APV = +5.48

4. (a) $r^* = r(1 - T^* L) = 0.20(1 - 0.20$
      $\times 0.30)$
      $= 0.188$

   (b) $r^* = r - L r_D T^* \left(\dfrac{1 + r}{1 + r_D} \right)$
      $= 0.20 - 0.30 \times 0.10$
      $\times 0.20 \left(\dfrac{1.2}{1.1} \right)$
      $= 0.1935$

   (c) NPV($@ \ r^* = 0.188$) $= \dfrac{1,200}{1.188}$
      $- 1,000 = +10.10$

   NPV($@ \ r^* = 0.1935$) $= \dfrac{1,200}{1.1935}$
      $- 1,000 = +5.48$

   The Miles-Ezzell formula gives the right answer.

5. $D = 75 \times 0.9 = \$67.5$ million
   $E = 42 \times 2.5 = \$105$ million
   $V = D + E = \$172.5$ million
   $r^* = (1 - T_c)r_D \ D/V + r_E \ E/V$
      $= (1 - 0.23)0.16(67.5/172.5)$
      $+ 0.25(105/172.5)$
      $= 0.20$ or 20%

6. Miles Ezzell formula.

   $r^* = r - L r_D T^* \left(\dfrac{1 + r}{1 + r_D} \right)$

   If $r^* = 0.20$
      $L = 67.5/172.5$
      $T^* = T_c = 0.23$
      $r_D = 0.16$
   then
      $r^* = 0.20$
      $= r - (67.5/172.5)0.16(0.23)$
      $\left(\dfrac{1 + r}{1.16} \right)$

7. No. The more debt you use, the higher rate of return equity investors will require. (Lenders may demand more also.) Thus there is a hidden cost of the "cheap" debt: it makes equity more expensive.

CHAPTER 20

1. Call; exercise; put; exercise; European; American; call; assets; bondholders (lenders); assets; promised payment to bondholders.

2. (a) Call
   (b) Put
   (c) Call
   (d) Call
   (e) Put
   (f) Call
   (g) Call
   (h) Put

3. Figure 20-8(a) represents a call seller; Figure 20-8(b) represents a call buyer.

4. (a) The exercise price of the put option (that is, you'd sell stock for the exercise price).
   (b) The value of the stock (that is, you would throw away the put and keep the stock).

5. Buy a call and lend the present value of the exercise price.

6. The lower bound is the option's value if it expired immediately; either zero or the stock price less the exercise price, whichever is larger. The upper bound is the stock price.

7. (a) Zero
   (b) Stock price less the present value of the exercise price.

8. The call price
   (a) Increases
   (b) Decreases
   (c) Increases
   (d) Increases
   (e) Decreases
   (f) Decreases

9. True. The beta and standard deviation of an option always exceeds its stock's.

The risk of an option decreases as the stock price increases.

10. With an exercise price of 60,
$$\sigma \times \sqrt{t} = 0.06 \times \sqrt{3} = 0.10$$
$$P/(EXe^{-r_f t}) = 60/(60e^{-0.01 \times 3}) = 1.03$$
(a) Call price = approximately 0.056 × 60 = 3.36
(b) Put price = approximately 0.0267 × 60 = 1.60

11. According to the Black-Scholes formula, the values of d_1 and d_2 are
$$d_1 = [\ln(P/EX) + r_f t + \sigma^2 t/2]/\sigma \sqrt{t}$$
$$= [\ln(60/60) + 0.01(3)$$
$$+ 0.06^2(3)/2] / 0.06\sqrt{3}$$
$$= 0.0354 / 0.1039 = 0.34$$
$$d_2 = d_1 - \sigma\sqrt{t}$$
$$= 0.34 - 0.10 = 0.24$$
Using Appendix Table 8(b) to find the values of $N(d_1)$ and $N(d_2)$,
$$N(d_1) = N(0.34) = 0.6331$$
$$N(d_2) = N(0.24) = 0.5948$$
$$\text{Call price} = PN(d_1) - EXe^{-r_f t}N(d_2)$$
$$= 60(0.6331)$$
$$- 60(0.9704)(0.5948)$$
$$= 37.99 - 34.63 = 3.36$$
The probability that the call option will be in-the-money at expiration is 0.5948; the present value of the expected terminal stock price conditional upon the call option being in-the-money at expiration times the probability that the call will be in-the-money at expiration is $37.99; and, the present value of the cost of exercising the option at expiration times the probability that the call will be in-the-money at expiration is $34.63.

12. From Quiz question 11, the values of d_1 and d_2 are 0.34 and 0.24, respectively. Using Appendix Table 8(a) to find the values of $N(-d_1)$ and $N(-d_2)$,
$$N(-d_1) = N(-0.34) = 0.3669$$
$$N(-d_2) = N(-0.24) = 0.4052$$
$$\text{Put price} = EXe^{-r_f t}N(-d_2)$$
$$- PN(-d_1)$$
$$= 60(0.9704)(0.4052)$$
$$- 60(0.3669)$$
$$= 23.59 - 22.01 = 1.58$$
In a risk-neutral world, the put option formula may be thought of as:

Present value of put option $= e^{-r_f t}$ $[EX - E(P_t \mid P_t > EX)]\text{Prob}(P_t > EX)$. Thus, the probability that the put option will be in-the-money at expiration is 0.4052; the present value of the benefit of exercising the put conditional upon the put option being in-the-money at expiration times the probability that the put will be in-the-money at expiration is $23.59; and, the present value of the expected cost of exercising the option at expiration times the probability that the put will be in-the-money at expiration is $22.01.

CHAPTER 21

1. (a) Investment and savings increase. So does the interest rate.
   (b) Investment and savings increase. The interest rate falls.

2. (a) $PV = \dfrac{50}{1 + r_1} + \dfrac{1,050}{(1 + r_2)^2}$

   (b) $PV = \dfrac{50}{1 + y} + \dfrac{1,050}{(1 + y)^2}$

   (c) Less (it is between the one-year and two-year spot rates)
   (d) Yield to maturity; spot rate

3. (a) Fall
   (b) Less than 100
   (c) Less than the coupon
   (d) Higher prices, other things equal

4. (a) 12%
   (b) 70.88
   (c) We know the bond is worth 71.33 now, and will be worth 73.51 after two years, when the bond will have ten years to maturity. Interpolating, the price six months from now should be approximately 71.88. Total return is
   $$\frac{71.88 - 71.33 + 4.5}{71} = 0.071 \text{ or}$$
   $$7.1\%$$

5. (a) $(1 + r_2)^2 = (1 + r_1)(1 + f_2)$
   $$1.03^2 = 1.01 \times (1 + f_2)$$
   $$f_2 = 0.05, \text{ or } 5\%$$

(b) The expected one-year spot rate at time 1, $E(_1r_2)$, equals the forward rate f_2.

(c) Against (unless one believes that investors have generally expected interest rates to rise).

(d) The forward rate equals the expected spot rate *plus* a liquidity premium.

(e) Long-term bonds.

(f) Short-term bonds.

(g) The forward rate equals the expected spot rate plus a premium for the inflation risk.

6. (a) A++, A+, A, and B++
   (b) (i) Increase
       (ii) Increase
      (iii) Increase (that is, value of default-free bond decreases; also, value of default option decreases)
       (iv) Increase

7. (a) Value of guarantee = value of put (that is, shareholders' option to put the company to the bondholders for the face value of the bond)
   (b) Put option; exercise price is face value of bond.

CHAPTER 22

1. (a) High-grade utility bonds
   (b) Short-dated notes
   (c) Industrial holding companies
   (d) Industrial bonds
   (e) Railroads

2. (a) Noncallable bonds (callable bonds neither rise nor fall as much in price).
   (b) They will disappear (each side should exercise its option at 100).

3. Sinking fund c (an optional sinking fund reduces bond value; a sinking fund that gives the firm the option to purchase in the market may increase or decrease bond value).

4. (a) You would like an issue of junior debt.
   (b) You prefer it not to do so (unless it is also junior debt). The existing property may not be sufficient to pay off your debt.

5. (a) Wood Gundy Inc.
   (b) Montreal Trust Company of Canada
   (c) 98.85% of face value
   (d) Bearer
   (e) Yes
   (f) 4%
   (g) 105.60 on or before November 15th; 104.90 after
   (h) No

6. (a) 100 plus 2/6 of 6.35 = 102.12
   (b) May 1985; 6.35%
   (c) November 15, 2004; 32% of the initial issue
   (d) It should call all bonds in just after November 15, 2000

CHAPTER 23

1. (a) (i) 0
       (ii) 0
      (iii) 0
       (iv) $10
        (v) $20
   (b)

Theoretical value of warrant (heavy line)

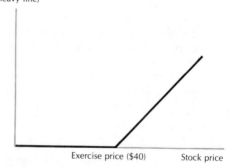

Exercise price ($40)   Stock price

(c) Buy the warrant and exercise, then sell the stock.
   Net gain = −5 − 40 + 60
            = +$15.

2. (a) No
   (b) No
   (c) 1/5 × $25 = $5
   (d) No

(e) No

(f) No

(g) (i) less; (ii) less; (iii) more; (iv) more; (v) more

(h) When the share price is no longer less than the warrant price plus the exercise price. This will occur when the dividends on the stock outweigh the interest on the exercise price.

3. (a) EPS = $2.00
   (b) Diluted EPS = $1.33

4. (a) 1,000/47 = 21.28
   (b) 1,000/50 = $20.00
   (c) 21.28 × 41.50 = $883.12, or 88.31%
   (d) 650/21.28 = $30.55
   (e) No (not if the investor is free to convert immediately)
   (f) $12.22, that is, (910 − 650)/21.28
   (g) (47/41.50) − 1 = 0.13, or 13%
   (h) When the price reaches 102.75

CHAPTER 24

1. A, c; B, d or i; C, b or e; D, f; E, a; F, h; G, g

2. a, b, d, and f

3. (a) True
   (b) True
   (c) True
   (d) True
   (e) True
   (f) True
   (g) True

4. (a) $60,442, the present value of the lease cash flows from $t = 1$ to $t = 3$, discounted at $r(1 − T_c) = 0.10(1 − 0.46) = 0.054$.
   (b) $62,000 − 60,442 = 1,558$.
   (c) It should not invest. The lease's value of $+1,558$ does not offset the machine's negative NPV. It would be happy to sign the same lease on a more attractive asset.

5. $PV = \sum_{t=1}^{3} \dfrac{250,000}{(1.09)^t} = 883,000$

Note: This is a safe nominal flow. Therefore, discount at the after-tax borrowing rate, $r(1 − T_c) = 0.15(1 − 0.4) = 0.09$.

CHAPTER 25

1. (a) 0.22
   (b) 4.49. *Note*: This is just operating income divided by interest. Table 25-8 does not give a figure for depreciation.
   (c) 1.39
   (d) 0.36
   (e) 0.07
   (f) 4.37
   (g) 0.18
   (h) 0.23

2. The illogical ratios are a, b, c, f, and i. The correct definitions are:

Debt-equity ratio $= \dfrac{\text{long-term debt} + \text{value of leases}}{\text{equity}}$

Return on equity $= \dfrac{\text{earnings available for common}}{\text{average equity}}$

Payout ratio $= \dfrac{\text{dividend}}{\text{earnings per share}}$

Current ratio $= \dfrac{\text{current assets}}{\text{current liabilities}}$

Average collection period $= \dfrac{\text{sales}}{\text{average receivables} \div 365}$

3. (a) False
   (b) True
   (c) False
   (d) False
   (e) True (as a general rule)
   (f) True
   (g) False
   (h) False
   (i) False—it will tend to increase the price-earnings multiple.

4. (a) Shipping company
   (b) United Foods
   (c) Paper mill
   (d) Mail order company

(e) Fledgling Electronics

(f) Pharmaceutical company

CHAPTER 26

1. (a) False (it is a process of deciding which risks to take).

    (b) False (financial planning is concerned with possible surprises as well as expected outcomes).

    (c) True (financial planning considers both the investment and financing decisions).

    (d) False (a typical horizon for long-term planning is five years).

    (e) True (investments are usually broken down by category).

    (f) True (perfect accuracy is unlikely to be obtainable, but the firm needs to produce the best possible consistent forecasts).

    (g) False (excessive detail distracts attention from the crucial decisions).

2. *Pro forma* financial statements (balance sheets, income statements, and sources and uses of cash); description of planned capital expenditure, and a summary of planned financing.

3. Most financial models are designed to forecast accounting statements. They do not focus on the factors that directly determine firm value, such as incremental cash flow or risk.

CHAPTER 27

1.

Cash	Working Capital
1. $2 million decline	$2 million decline
2. $2,500 increase	Unchanged
3. $5,000 decline	Unchanged
4. Unchanged	$1 million increase
5. Unchanged	Unchanged
6. $5 million increase	Unchanged

2. Month 3: $18 + (0.5 \times 90) + (0.3 \times 120) + (0.2 \times 100) = \$119,000$

Month 4: $14 + (0.5 \times 70) + (0.3 \times 90) + (0.2 \times 120) = \$100,000$

3. (a) Long-term financing, cumulative capital requirement, marketable securities

    (b) Cash, cash, cash, marketable securities

    (c) Trial, error, financial models

4. (a) Inventories go up (use).

    (b) Accounts receivable go up (use).

    (c) No change shown on the firm's books.

    (d) Decrease in assets (source).

    (e) Net worth declines (use).

    (f) Retained earnings fall (use).

    (g) Long-term debt increases (source), short-term debt falls (use).

CHAPTER 28

1. (a) 1% of $1,000 = $10

    (b) 1% for 30 days = 12% per annum simple interest or 12.7% compound interest.

    (c) (i) Shorter
        (ii) Longer
        (iii) Shorter

2. (a) Due lag decreases, therefore pay lag decreases.

    (b) Due lag increases, therefore pay lag increases.

    (c) Terms lag increases, therefore pay lag increases.

3. Open account, promissory note, commercial draft, shipping documents, trade acceptance, the customer's, bank acceptance, letter of credit, the customer's, his or her own, letter of credit, shipping documents, shipping documents

4. PV of Q's order
$$= \frac{0.75 \times 50}{1.10^{1/2}} - 40$$
$$= -\$4.25 \text{ per iron or } -\$4,250 \text{ in total}$$

5. (a) Expected profit $= p(1,200 - 1,050) - 1,050 (1 - p) = 0$
$p = 0.875$

Therefore, grant credit if probability of payment exceeds 87.5%.
(b) Expected profit from selling to slow payer: $0.8(150) - 0.2(1,050) = -90$. Break-even point for credit check: $(0.05 \times 90 \times \text{units}) - 12 = 0$. Units $= 2.67$.

6. Total expected profit on initial order
$$= -40$$
$$+ \frac{0.8[(p_2 \times 200) - 1,000 (1 - p_2)]}{1.2}$$
$$= 0$$
$$p_2 = 0.88, \text{ or } 88\%$$

7. (a) False
   (b) True
   (c) False
   (d) False—should be collection agency or lawyer
   (e) True

8. (a) True
   (b) False
   (c) False
   (d) True
   (e) False. Tax loss carry-forwards are extinguished by liquidation.

CHAPTER 29

1. (a) Carrying cost per book/2 = $1
   (b) $(200 \times 2)/Q^2 = 1$
       $Q = \sqrt{400} = 20$ books
   (c) 200/20 = 10 orders
   (d) $Q/2 = 10$ books

2. (a) Carrying cost/2 = $0.01
   (b) $(20,000 \times 2)/Q^2 = \$0.01$
       $Q = \sqrt{4,000,000} = \$2,000$
   (c) 20,000/2,000 = 10 orders
   (d) $Q/2 = \$1,000$

3. (a) Interest rate, cost of each transaction, and variability of cash balance.
   (b) It should restore it to one-third of the distance between the lower and upper limits.
   (c) By holding a lower cash balance, the firm increases the transaction frequency but earns more interest.

4. (a) Less
   (b) Less
   (c) Invest the same amount
   (d) More

5. (a) Payment float = $25,000. Collection float = $75,000
   (b) It can earn interest on these funds.
   (c) Payment float increases slightly. The bank's gross ledger balance and net collected balance increase by the same amount.

6. (a) The $0.40 per cheque fee is cheaper at $300 \times 0.40 = \$120$ per day. The cost of putting up $800,000 of compensating balances is $0.09 \times 800,000 = \$72,000$ per year, or $72,000/365 = \$197$ per day.
   (b) The lock-box system costs $120 per day, or $43,800 per year. You would need $487,000 additional cash to generate this much interest. Thus, the lock-box system must generate at least this much cash. The cash flow is $300 \times 1,500 = \$450,000$ per day. Thus the lock box must speed up average collection time by $487,000/450,000 = 1.08$ days.

7. Payment float; collection float; net float; concentration banking; lock-box banking.

CHAPTER 30

1. (a) Repurchase agreements
   (b) Swapped deposits
   (c) Certificates of deposit
   (d) Treasury bills
   (e) Treasury bills
   (f) Banker's acceptances
   (g) Treasury bills

2. (a) $97.25
   (b) 11.84%
   (c) 11.01%

3. Line of credit; clean-up provision; prime rate; compensating balance; commercial paper; floating lien; collateral; with recourse; public warehouse; field ware-

house; warehouse receipt; trust receipt; floor planning

4. None of the floating-rate preferred dividend is taxed versus 100% of bond interest. The fixed-dividend preferred shares this tax advantage but its price fluctuates more than the floating rate preferred's.

CHAPTER 31

1. (a) Horizontal
   (b) Conglomerate
   (c) Vertical
   (d) Conglomerate

2. (a) $5 million (We assume that the $500,000 saving is an after-tax figure.)
   (b) $4 million
   (c) $7.5 million
   (d) +$1 million
   (e) −$2.5 million

3. a, b, and d

4. (a) True
   (b) False
   (c) True
   (d) True
   (e) False (They may produce gains, but "substantial" is stretching it.)
   (f) False
   (g) True (assuming that the purchase price exceeds the value of the tangible assets acquired)
   (h) False
   (i) True

5. a and d; c can also make sense, although merging is not the only way to redeploy excess cash.

CHAPTER 32

1. (a) $1/1.3405 = 0.7460$
   (b) 1.3493

(c) discount (that is, you give up less in Canadian dollars for one U.S. dollar in the spot market)

(d) $4 \times \dfrac{1.3493 - 1.3405}{1.3405} \times 100$
   $= 2.626\%$

(e) $\dfrac{0.10875 - r_{US}}{1.10875} = 0.02626$ or r_{US}
   $= 0.0796$ or 7.96%

(f) 1.3493

(g) 7.96%

2. Selling forward.

3. (a) Once it has forecasted cash flows in the foreign currency, it needs (i) to convert to dollars and (v) to discount.
   (b) It needs (iv) to discount and spot interest rates to convert NPV into dollars.

4. (a) Private individuals
   (b) A foreign bond
   (c) Interest payments
   (d) Switzerland
   (e) The United States
   (f) The U.S. dollar

5. It can borrow the present value of 1 million DM, sell the Deutschemarks in the spot market, and invest the proceeds in a two-year dollar loan.

6. (a)

	Overseas X	Overseas Y
Foreign corporate tax	60.00	40.00
Withholding tax	6.00	9.00
Canadian corporate tax	0.00	0.00

(b)

	Overseas X	Overseas Y
Foreign corporate tax*	36.00	24.00
Withholding tax	9.60	11.40
Canadian corporate tax	0.00	9.90

* Interest in most countries is deductible for corporate tax.

7.

	3 Months	6 Months	1 Year
Eurodollar interest rate (%)	$11\frac{1}{2}$	$12\frac{1}{4}$	12.5
Eurofranc interest rate (%)	$^f19\frac{1}{2}$	19.7	20
Forward francs per dollar	7.17	7.28	7.5
Forward discount on franc, % per year	−6.7	−6.3	−6.3

Note: Spot dollars per franc = 1/7.0500 = 0.1418.

CHAPTER 33

1. (*a*) True
   (*b*) False
   (*c*) True
   (*d*) True
   (*e*) True, although "final salary" may mean an average over the last few years before retirement.
   (*f*) True

2. (*a*) See Table 5.

Table 5

Current assets		Current liabilities	$ 9,940
	$10,770		
Pension fund	6,830	Debt and other liabilities	5,719
Plant, equipment and other assets	12,844	Pension liabilities	6,830
Total assets	$29,851	Equity	7,362
		Total liabilities	$29,851

(*b*) The published balance sheet would show $1,000 million less cash. The augmented balance sheet would show this fall in cash, but an offsetting increase in the pension fund.

(*c*) The published balance sheet would not change. In the augmented balance sheet, the pension fund and equity would both fall by $2,000 million.

3. (*a*) Pension fund
   (*b*) Expected benefits for past service
   (*c*) Expected future service costs
   (*d*) Future normal costs
   (*e*) Expected benefits (that is, total liabilities)
   (*f*) Deficit

4. (*a*) Pension fund = investments held in trust for plan members
   Future normal costs = contributions to cover future service
   Unamortized experience losses = losses that result from difference between expectations and experience
   Unamortized supplemental liabilities = liability from improved pension benefits
   Losses from changes in actuarial assumptions = for example, effect of change in assumed discount rate
   Vested accrued benefits = benefits that would need to be paid if employees left firm immediately
   Unvested accrued benefits = benefits that have accrued but will be paid only if employment continues
   Expected future service costs = expected benefits to be paid for future service
   (i) 540 − 720 = −$180 million (that is, vested benefits are fully funded)
   (ii) 760 − 720 = $40 million
   (iii) 720/760 = 0.95
   (iv) 720/540 = 1.33
   (*c*) (i) Pension fund = 670
   Experience losses = 140
   (ii) Supplemental liabilities = 180
   Total assets = 1,740

5. Greater

6. (*a*) $r - r_f = 6\%$
   (*b*) $(r - r_f) - \beta(r_m - r_f) = 3\%$
   (*c*) $(r - r_f) - (\sigma/\sigma_m)(r_m - r_f) = 2\%$

7. (*a*) 80%
   (*b*) 72.5%
   (*c*) The time-weighted rate of return would not change.
   (*d*) The dollar-weighted rate of return would decrease.

INDEX

Canada Business Corporations Act, 299n., 300, 350
Canada Deposit Insurance Corporation (CDIC), 715
Canada Pension Plan (CPP), 788
Canada Savings Bonds, 399n.
Canadian Bond Rating Service (CBRS), 511, 512-13, 528, 673, 717n.
Cancellation options, 579
Canistraro, R., 818
Capital:
  cost of, see Cost of capital.
  equity, 428. See also Equity.
  investment-opportunity schedule and demand for, 491
  leasing to preserve, 580. See also Leasing.
  (See also Net working capital; Working capital; entries beginning with the term: Cash)
Capital asset pricing model, 139-42, 143-45, 175-205, 813-14, 816-17
  asset betas determination in, 191-93
  to calculate certainty equivalents, 201-202
  to calculate expected returns, 141-42
  and discounted cash flow, 193-99
  measuring betas in, 177-91
    asset betas and equity betas, 188
    business and financial risk, 189-91
    Canadian beta estimates, 185-86
    example, 186-91
    industry betas and divisional cost of capital, 183-84
    infrequent trading, 184-86
    stability of betas over time, 178-81
    using a beta book, 181-82
  and Proposition I, 402-403
  validity and role of, 165-68
  value additivity and, 143-45
Capital budgeting, 125-205
  and capital asset pricing model, see Capital asset pricing model.
  and evaluating performance of investments, 261-69
    accounting rate of return as performance measure, 263-64
    controlling projects in progress, 261
    dealing with biases in accounting profitability measures, 268-69
    evaluating operating performance, 262
    example of measuring profitability, 264-68
    measuring incremental cash flows after the fact, 262
    postaudits, 261-62
  financing decisions separated from, 277
  problems and solutions in, 258-61
  and project authorizations, see Project authorizations.
  risk and, see Risk.
Capital cost allowance (CCA), 59, 90, 91
  CCA tax shields, 90-96, 576-77, 579, 591
  "half-year rule," 113-15
  and leasing, 575, 576-77, 579, 591
Capital expenditures:
  in cash budget, 657
  in financial plan, 627

leasing avoiding controls on, 580
program of, with limited resources, 106-110
Capital gains, 91, 92
  taxation of, 360-62
Capital investment: and return on book value, 69. See also entries beginning with the term: Investment.
Capitalization rate:
  defined, 46
  estimating, 49-54
Capital leases, see Financial leases.
Capital market equilibrium, 767-68
Capital markets:
  dividend policy irrelevant to, 354-57. See also Dividends, controversy over policy on.
  history of, 125-33
  imperfect, 21
  importance of, 3-4
  international, 775-77
  lesson on, in efficient-market theory, 286
  perfectly competitive, 20
  and smoothing consumption patterns, 16
Capital rationing, 106-110
  more elaborate models of, 108-109
  profitability index under, 107-108
  use of models involving, 109-110
Capital requirements, cumulative, 648-50
Capital structure:
  changes in, 309-311, see also Financing decisions.
  defined, 384, see also Debt policy.
  Miller's theory of, 414-16, 819
  tax integration and, 413-14
Career-average plans, 788
Carleton, W. T., 642n.
Carrington, T., 335n.
Carry-back and carry-forward of capital losses, 112-13
Cash:
  acquisition financed with, 736
  borrowing to raise, 699-700
  estimating cost of merger with financing with, 740-42
  (See also entries beginning with the term:Liquidity)
Cash balances, 696-97. See also Cash management, inventories and cash balances in.
Cash before delivery (CBD), 669
Cash budgeting, 654-58
Cash carry-forward, 116
Cash collection system, 701-705
Cash deficiency arrangement, 538
Cash discount, 670
Cash flow:
  accounting profits distinguished from, 85-86
  adjusted discount rates for debt-equivalent, 591-93
  and average return on book, 69-70
  discounted, see Discounted cash flow.
  estimating, 100
    on incremental basis, 86-88
  incremental, 86-88, 262
  in Monte Carlo simulation, 220-21
  net present values as dependent on, 66

Trustee in bankruptcy, 684
Turnbull, S. M., 194*n.*

Undepreciated capital cost (UCC), 91, 92, 93, 575, *see also* Capital cost allowance.
Underpricing, 320
Underwriters in general cash offer, 321-22
  role of underwriter, 319
Unique risk, 135-36
Unseasoned issue, 320
Unsecured bank borrowing, 658, 720-21
Unsecured creditor, 684-85
Unsecured loans, 658, 720-21
Urquhart, M. C., 126*n.*

Value:
  law of conservation of, 387-88, 814-15
  true, 282-83
  understanding, 5
Value additivity, 143-45, 387, 814-15
  concept of, as basis for analysis, 438
  conglomerate mergers and, 755-57
  diversification and, 143-45
Vanderwicken, P., 588*n.*
Variance in measuring portfolio risk, 129-33
Vermaelen, T., 376
Vertical mergers:
  defined, 733-34
  economies of, 734-35
  (*See also* Mergers)
Vesting, pension plan, 788, 790
Volatility, duration and, 501-503
von Furstenberg, G., 609*n.*
Voting system, corporate, 300-301

Wagner, W. H., 134, 135-36
Walter, J. E., 288*n.*
Warehouse receipt, 722
Warrants, 556-61
  on bonds, 556, 561
  defined, 556-57, 568
  differences between convertible bonds and, 565-66
  and dilution, 558-61

issuing, 469-70
as option, 304
reasons for issuing, 566-67, 568
rights certificates, 326*n.*
valuing, 557, 568
Watts, R., 353*n.*, 613*n.*
Weighted average cost of capital:
  formula for, 446-50
  minimizing, 394-95
Westerfield, R., 817*n.*
Whaley, R. E., 259, 446, 479, 558*n.*
Williams, J., 185, 186
Williams, J. B., 50*n.*, 354*n.*, 384*n.*
Williamson, S., 430*n.*
Willis, I., 295
Winter, E. L., 323*n.*
With-dividend shares, 350
Withholding tax, 363, 778
With-recourse factoring, 682*n.*
Wolf, C. R., 556*n.*
Working, H., 281*n.*
Working capital:
  components of, 646-48
  in estimating cash flow, 87
  merger and, 749
  net, *see* Net working capital.
  permanent requirements for, 649
  profits and, 653-54
  statement of, 652-53
  tracing changes in cash and, 650-54. *See also entries beginning with the term:* Cash.
  (*See also* Financial planning, short-term)
Wyatt, A.R., 751*n.*

Yield on dividends:
  market capitalization rate as equal to, 50
  market value ratio and, 609
Yield to maturity, 45, 495-503
  measuring, 496-99
  problems with, 499

Zero balance account, 701
Zero-one programming, 109

SOME USEFUL FORMULAS

(The section number indicates the principal reference in the text.)

PERPETUITY *(3-2)*

The value of a perpetuity of $1 per year is:

$$PV = \frac{1}{r}$$

ANNUITY *(3-2)*

The value of an annuity of $1 per year for t years (t year annuity factor) is:

$$PV = \frac{1}{r} - \frac{1}{r(1 + r)^t}$$

$$= \frac{1}{r}\left(1 - \frac{1}{(1 + r)^t}\right)$$

A GROWING PERPETUITY

(the "Gordon" model) *(3-2)*

If the initial cash flow is $1 at the end of year 1 and if cash flows thereafter grow at a constant rate of g in perpetuity,

$$PV = \frac{1}{r - g}$$

CONTINUOUS COMPOUNDING *(3-3)*

If r is the continuously compounded rate of interest, the present value of $1 received in year t is:

$$PV = \frac{1}{e^{rt}} = e^{-rt}$$

CAPITAL COST ALLOWANCE *(6-2)*

The undepreciated capital cost left at the end of year t for an asset with CCA rate d and capital cost C is:

$$UCC_t = C(1 - d)^t$$

The CCA tax shield for year t is:

$$CCA = CdT_c(1 - d)^{t-1}$$

The present value of the perpetual CCA tax shield is:

$$PV = \frac{CdT_c}{r + d}$$

EQUIVALENT ANNUAL COST *(6-4)*

If an asset has a life of t years, the equivalent annual cost is:

$$\frac{PV(costs)}{t \text{ year annuity factor}}$$

MEASURES OF RISK *(7-2 to 7-4 and 8-1)*

Variance of returns $= \sigma^2$
$= $ expected value of $(\tilde{r} - r)^2$

Standard deviation of returns
$= \sqrt{variance} = \sigma$

Covariance between returns of stocks 1 and 2 $= \sigma_{12} = $ expected value of $[(\tilde{r}_1 - r_1)(\tilde{r}_2 - r_2)]$

Correlation between returns of stocks 1 and 2 $= \rho_{12}$

$$= \frac{\sigma_{12}}{\sigma_1\sigma_2}$$

Beta of stock i is $\beta_i = \dfrac{\sigma_{im}}{\sigma_m^2}$

VARIANCE OF PORTFOLIO RETURNS *(8-1)*

The variance of returns on a portfolio with proportion x_i invested in stock i is:

$$\sum_{i=1}^{N} \sum_{j=1}^{N} x_i x_j \sigma_{ij}$$

CAPITAL ASSET PRICING MODEL *(8-2)*

The expected risk premium on a risky investment is:

$$r - r_f = \beta(r_m - r_f)$$